The Blue Ribbon
Country Cookbook

The Blue Ribbon Country Cookbook

The New Standard of American Cooking

By Diane Roupe

ILLUSTRATIONS BY SHARON K. SODER

CLARKSON POTTER/PUBLISHERS
NEW YORK

Copyright © 1998 by Diane Roupe

Published by Clarkson N. Potter, Inc., New York, New York.
Member of the Crown Publishing Group.

Random House, Inc. New York, Toronto, London, Sydney, Auckland
www.randomhouse.com

CLARKSON N. POTTER is a trademark and POTTER and colophon are registered trademarks of Random House, Inc.

Printed in the United States of America

Design by Julie Baker Schroeder

Library of Congress Cataloging-in-Publication Data
Roupe, Diane.
    The blue ribbon country cookbook: the new standard of American cooking /
by Diane Roupe; illustrations by Sharon K. Soder.
    Includes index.
1. Cooker, American—Midwestern style. 2. Cookery—Middle West. I. Title.
TX715.2.M53R68   1998
641.5977—dc21   97-43569

ISBN 0-676-80687-2

Contents

Preface

Over its 200-year history, America has conceived and nurtured to maturity a distinct culture. While a progeny of the Western world, American culture has its own set of fingerprints, identifiable and unlike any other.

The amalgamation of multi-cultured peoples into a newly organized, free society has yielded a rich, hybrid culture—a microcosm of the world. This cross-fertilization of foreign cultures continues to nourish America's own culture, as enclaves of foreign peoples across the land receive constant, fresh cultural infusions from new immigrants.

To buttress the American utopia, Providence provided a vast expanse of diverse land, lavish with natural resources.

The food of the Midwest United States is a reflection of the American culture and the underlying foreign subcultures. It is a litany of imaginative dishes which combine the bounteous produce of America's greatest expanse of fertile land with Old-World recipes and cooking styles first brought by European settlers in covered wagons and now by peoples from the four corners of the globe via jet airplanes. The offspring of this union is a signature American cuisine.

Ethnic food prepared by people new to our shores as well as third- and fourth-generation Americans who cling to their cultural roots remains an important part of Midwest food. The preciously guarded traditional recipes are passed down from generation to generation and are served especially at holiday time or on other festive family occasions.

Midwest food reflects the American culture in another way: it is, at once, the old and the ever-changing new. It is Roast Stuffed Turkey with Sage Dressing, served with Mashed Potatoes and Gravy and Corn Relish on Thanksgiving Day. And it is boneless, skinless Rosemary Chicken Breasts with Red Raspberry Sauce. It is Grace Montognese's Braciole (steak rolls) handed down from her Italian-born mother, and it is her with-it-generation Gumdrop-Oatmeal Cookies adored by her grandchildren. It is authentic Norwegian Kringla served at the McDonald's in Story City, Iowa.

It is not surprising that from the Midwest's beautiful land, diverse ethnic heritage, and devotion to good cooking and wonderful food has come a culinary style marked by supreme savoriness, infinite variety, and endless plenitude. *The Blue Ribbon Country Cookbook* is a comprehensive collection of more than 1,000 recipes and 100 cooking techniques at the heart of present-day Midwest food—one of America's most popular fares and one of the blue ribbon cuisines of the world.

Recipes Tagged with Winning Ribbons

Recipes for my winning entries at the Iowa State Fair are tagged as follows:

 Recipe for a **BLUE RIBBON WINNER** (first place) at the Iowa State Fair.

 Recipe for a **RED RIBBON WINNER** (second place) at the Iowa State Fair.

In addition, three recipes for other people's winning entries are included and tagged. Those recipes are:

Pat Berry's JULEKAKE (Norwegian Christmas Bread) (page 422).

Joy McFarland's MILE-HIGH TORTE (page 568).

Louise Piper's MULBERRY JAM (page 756).

Introduction

The Midwest's Blue Ribbon Bounty

Mornings on my grandparents' Iowa farm began with the sun peeking over the horizon of cornfields. My brother and I looked forward to the farm-style breakfast of eggs we had gathered the afternoon before, thick strips of side meat (bacon) cut from the savory slabs smoke-cured in the small smokehouse out back, and pancakes slathered with home-churned butter (kept cool in a bucket hung in the cistern) and made even more luscious with a generous amount of warm maple syrup poured over top. As we watched Grandfather leave for the morning's farm work, row after row of glinting, green corn leaves in the field near the house rustled in the hot, summer breeze.

If chicken was planned for our noon dinner, soon after breakfast we would help Grandmother catch the plumpest birds to fry for the big meal. Often we would accompany Grandmother to the cave—a cool, dark place beneath the farmhouse where home-canned goods, potatoes, and apples were stored. Grandmother would pick whatever she needed from that musty-smelling cellar to prepare the next meal.

Food was important on the farm. Even though I understood more esoteric concepts of nutrition, I knew that food was essential in providing enough energy to face the strenuous chores of tilling the soil. But to us, as city kids visiting the family farm, food, more importantly, was one of the purest pleasures in a simpler way of life.

For generations of farm women throughout the Midwest—even for those who have left the farm and moved to the cities—the preparation of food has been more than a necessary event; it has been a source of personal satisfaction and a fundamental form of identity. Before women generally had the opportunity or desire to prove themselves in the business world, many competed in the domestic arena through state fair cooking competitions, which were their testing grounds; the esteemed blue ribbon was their goal. Today, women, men, and people of all ages and from all walks of Midwest life are measuring their culinary prowess in elaborate state fair food shows, where a blue ribbon is still the venerated prize.

A HISTORY OF BLUE RIBBON COOKING

Blue ribbon cooking is a rich and vital part of Midwestern cuisine, representing the very best of the foods we serve our family and friends. Rooted in heritage and characterized by unsurpassed quality, these award-winning recipes are part of a tradition that goes back for generations, forming an unbroken link to our past—and a tradition that still continues today, with constant innovations and, hopefully, improvements.

Like our American culture, blue ribbon competition has undergone changes over the years. State fair entries no longer are the exclusive domain of women. And as our palates become increasingly educated through an explosion of interest in gourmet fare, health, and more recently, a returned emphasis on the family and "cocooning," blue ribbon winners reflect a new, inevitable sophistication.

But through all the cultural and social changes reflected in blue ribbon cooking, the basic activity and its meaning are much the same—as resilient and down-to-earth as the row after row of contiguous cornstalks streaming over the Iowa landscape. Blue ribbon cooking is the definitive text on Midwest cooking. It is refreshingly real— an authentic expression of the individual Heartland cook at her or his best. It's a preeminent culinary legacy.

Blue ribbon cooking can be learned; but also, in a sense, it can be inherited. The latter, I believe, is what happened to me. Long before I began working full-time in the food profession, the Iowa State Fair had helped develop my confidence in an ability to understand good food.

Competition at the fair (though not necessarily in the food division) was a birthright in my family. Although my father was an attorney and our family lived in Des Moines, competing at the Iowa State Fair each year was a given. Our family never severed its roots in the land (my father owned several farms and taught my brother and me, long before we knew how to drive a car, how to drive a tractor and cultivate corn). The fair was the place we revealed and revitalized our rural ties.

Our family's heritage of state fair competitions began at the turn of the century with my great-grandfather's family taking blue ribbons for their Belgian and Percheron draft horses. By the late 1940's and early '50's, the entries were Shorthorn cattle and Duroc hogs shown by my father and brother. In recent years, my niece and nephew carried on the tradition by taking numerous blue ribbons showing quarter horses. In fact, my niece went on to become a world champion.

During my childhood excursions to the fair, Mother and I would gravitate to the food exhibits then housed under the grandstand, while the men were off showing livestock. Mother and I had a natural interest in these displays, as we had always grown and canned our own tomatoes, green beans, corn, apples for Apple Butter, and other vegetables and fruits. We could relate to the tantalizing foods on display— and to the nervous excitement among the contestants. I was especially drawn to the canned fruit classes, with jar after jar of spectacularly colored fruit which had been meticulously packed. But as a child and then adult, I, for some reason, remained on the outside looking in—until 1987, when I returned to Iowa to work on this book.

It was fair time when I arrived back in the Midwest. As I took my perennial tour of the food exhibits, I vowed that the following year, I would be among the contestants.

That first year, I entered seventeen classes. My

dream was to win one blue ribbon. Instead, I won four. The blue ribbon I took for best piecrust always will be my most cherished, for my entry was chosen over piecrusts baked by the likes of Armetta Keeney and Louise Piper, world-class pie bakers. In addition to the blues, that year I also won three red ribbons (second place) and four white ribbons (third place)—enough to hook me on entering state fair food competitions. Each year thereafter, through 1992, I competed, garnering fifty additional blues and forty-six more red ribbons. (Recipes for these winning entries are included in this cookbook and are tagged with a ribbon illustration.) Since 1993, I have served as a judge at the fair, so, of course, have not been a competitor.

THE RIGORS OF SHOWING FOOD

Preparing food for the fair is an involved, time-consuming ritual that hasn't changed much from the days of the first Iowa State Fair in 1854. I joined the majority of blue ribbon winners in growing many of my own vegetables, fruits, and herbs. It's no surprise that ingredients fresh from the garden have the best chance of winning. In 1990, the cherries I picked from a tree in our backyard and immediately canned as Cherry Sauce with Kirschwasser took first place in the Fruit Topping class. Cherries from that same wonderful tree went into a jar of Cherry Jam which was selected by esteemed judge Colleen Shaw as blue ribbon winner in the Cherry Jam class at the 1992 fair, and then was awarded first overall among twenty classes of jam by the judging panel.

When my brother and I picked wild black raspberries early one morning in July of 1990, I made sure they were in the jars within three hours after returning home. That speed in preparation preserved the freshness, color, and texture of the fruit and resulted in a blue ribbon in the class Wild Fruits of Iowa—Jam. All the time-consuming effort was made worthwhile by the judge's comment: "perfect consistency."

It is a requirement that food exhibitors at the Iowa State Fair be residents of the state. Entries must be made in the home kitchen, and the culinary arts cannot be a means of livelihood for the exhibitor (except the special decorated cakes classes for professionals and for commercial cake shops and bakeries). Catalogs listing classes and rules for food entries are issued in June and registration must be completed by July 1. (The fair is held mid-August.) But for a veteran exhibitor, the work begins long before arrival of the catalog. Because many of the classes are the same year in and year out, seasoned competitors begin planning their entries months in advance. As soon as one year's fair draws to a close, some contestants begin working toward the next. Because of seasonal foods, too, it's necessary to work about a year in advance to enter certain classes. Peaches, pears, plums, and apples are at their height in the late summer and early fall, not long after most state fairs have ended.

Deciding which classes to enter can pose a real dilemma. In 1997, there were 881 food classes judged over 14 days at the Iowa fair (135 of these classes were in the junior and intermediate divisions for young people). It is impossible to register for all the classes you would like to enter. Some judicious selecting has to occur up front, and it's never easy. Perhaps because it's food at stake, the analogy that comes to mind is attending a sumptuous buffet and knowing you just can't eat it all. You have to pick and choose.

The night before cake and cookie entries are due isn't restful for contestants who enter numerous classes, since all entries must be frosted as near the hour of judging as possible to ensure freshness and quality. And the night before the pie contest, most of the winning pie bakers never turn down the sheets because pies must be baked as close to judging time as possible to retain their best attributes and compete well. All-nighters are in order, too, when food entries involve intricate garnish and decoration—especially if the class is scheduled for the morning or early afternoon.

Getting your entries to the fairgrounds is an

ordeal in itself. For folks living in rural areas, driving in with food entries aboard can be a production. Some people outfit their vehicles with special shelving just for the once-a-year occasion. It's especially tedious work transporting ornately decorated foods. Bumpy roads and hot summer days do not help. Large, thick plastic foam packing boxes are a godsend, keeping the food either hot or cold while in transit. Fortunately for me, transportation logistics were a family affair. My brother willingly pitched in, arriving at my house early in the morning to pack the first load in his Suburban, haul it to the fairgrounds, and then make at least two more shuttles before the 5:30 P.M. deadline on the day before judging commenced, when many of the food entries to be judged during the first two days of the show had to be delivered. I will never forget that day in 1991. I was putting the finishing touches on my Marble Cake decoration right up to the last possible minute—5:10 P.M. We got to the fairgrounds with only three minutes to spare. But when the cake won a blue ribbon, the mad rush to get it there was immediately forgotten. Food entries in classes to be judged on subsequent days of the show could be delivered up to fifteen minutes before the judging commenced.

SOME BLUE RIBBONS ARE SPECIAL

While the thrill of hearing your name declared the winner of a blue ribbon never becomes banal, some wins stand out over time. At the 1990 fair when my jar of Plums in Port Wine won first place overall among the nineteen classes of canned fruits, my thoughts flashed back forty years ago, to the time I stood before those glassed-in food display cases with my mother. I don't mind saying it was a source of pride to face the new glass cases and see my own entry draped in blue. Friends add to the joy, too, when they make special visits to the exhibit room to see your winning entries.

Anyone familiar with Rodgers and Hammerstein's musical *State Fair*, based on the Iowa State Fair, will appreciate my delight in winning the blue ribbon for canned Mincemeat—now a historic class at the fair. In the story, the farmwife's generous dose of brandy in her mincemeat not only titillated the palate of one of the judges, but made him a little tipsy—all resulting in her winning the blue ribbon. Caution: My recipe for Brandied Mincemeat also calls for a liberal lacing of good brandy.

Another standout blue ribbon was the one I received for Quail in Nests—a wild game entry which, again, was a family affair. It seemed I finally could share a ribbon with my brother, who had shot the quail the previous fall in southern Iowa and carefully dressed and frozen them for use in this entry. The dish even received media coverage, making it a memorable win.

There is a special kind of satisfaction when a traditional family favorite wins the blue. In some cases, blue ribbons are the result of generations of refinement of a particular food product. The blue ribbon I won in 1989 for Chili Sauce is a prime example. My entry evolved from an original recipe of my grandmother's. My mother, who is known for her marvelous Chili Sauce, had altered the recipe over the years. She had taught me to make her version which I, in turn, had adapted further, modifying the spices slightly to conform with today's taste trends.

When planning recipes to include in this cookbook, one of the first things I did was to comb through my grandmother's old cookbook. In her own handwriting, I found a scrumptious recipe for an old favorite, Date Pudding, which she had specified was to be served warm with a rich Amber Sauce. Testing proved the dessert even better than I had imagined. It took a blue ribbon in the Fruit Pudding class in the popular Recipes of Yesteryear division, and then was awarded first place overall among all twenty-nine classes in the division. My grandmother finally had been appropriately honored for her fine cooking and the indelible inspiration she handed down to later generations.

The importance blue ribbons can hold in winners' hearts is most dramatically illustrated in a letter mailed to the Iowa State Fair Food Department in 1986 from the daughter of Mary Florence Ponder, an annual food exhibitor for twenty-five years at the Iowa State Fair until her death in 1949. The letter related that in recognition of the many ribbons Mrs. Ponder had won and, in particular, a special award she had received in 1946, the year of Iowa's centennial, her tombstone had been engraved with the epitaph: "Centennial Winner 1946 Iowa State Fair."

Of course, no matter how hard the effort, contestants do not always win. The slightest flaw—a speck of stem found floating in a jar of fruit, or raisins that have not been properly plumped in certain cookies—may throw an entry out of the running. Also, it can't be overlooked that the judging of food is subjective. While one judge may think pumpkin pie should be moderately spiced and decorated with whipped cream, another may prefer more spice and a simpler appearance.

Every regular contestant has her or his share of bloopers. In 1991, one of mine occurred in preparing a decorated ham for entry in the Culinary Artists of the Year division. I planned to decorate my ham with a piped replica of that year's Iowa State Fair logo—a large blue ribbon surrounded by intricate caricatures of a horse, hog, ear of corn, and other state fair icons. Wally Hawxby, manager of the meat department at Dahl's, one of the fine Midwest supermarkets, placed a special order for a twenty-five-pound ham from Chicago.

I worked two days and the intervening night on the project, which involved garlands of flowers elaborately carved out of vegetables to surround the ham, bundles of miniature steamed vegetables tied with bows of chives, and other time-consuming garnishes to bedeck the platter. I covered the entire ham with a white, chicken stock–based gelatin (Chaud-Froid Sauce) and then glazed it. The results were quite good. The last undertaking on my masterpiece was to pipe the logo using the many colors I had mixed. I had nearly completed the task and everything seemed to be going well, when the colors started running down the sides of the ham. No amount of wiping with cotton-covered toothpicks, or re-refrigeration could save the day. Even though it was a hopeless case, I decided to take the entry, but of course, came home with no ribbon.

Then there was the Peanut Butter Fudge fiasco. The second year I showed, I made two batches, trying to achieve just the right consistency and gloss. My second attempt was good and I was entertaining visions of the blue. But this was the first time I had entered a candy class, and I hadn't read the rules thoroughly enough; I had no idea *six* pieces of candy were required on each entry plate. I had only *four,* as required for cookie entries with which I was familiar. Veteran candy judge Ester Mae Cox, of course, disqualified my entry, making it even more disheartening by her remark, "Too bad, this is really creamy fudge." After that, I read the fine print twice. Ester Mae (now a judging colleague and good friend of mine) awarded a red ribbon for my Peanut Butter Fudge in 1992, when I entered it again.

BIG CLASSES AND TOUGH COMPETITION

The competition in all divisions becomes keener each year. With 7,457 entries by 508 exhibitors at the 1997 Iowa State Fair, a second-place red ribbon has nearly as much clout as a blue. There are few mediocre entries these days. In general, only the serious, talented cooks compete—and in the Midwest, where good home cooking still is a valued custom, there are many of these folks.

Winners must have a talent for understanding and executing foods that reflect current taste trends and standards of excellence. Decoration, garnish, and presentation have become increasingly important. But even the most beautifully applied frosting never will compensate for any deficiencies in the basic quality or flavor of the cake.

State fair judging is professional and unbiased. In Iowa, home economists with the Cooperative

Extension Service at Iowa State University, together with faculty members from the university's Department of Food Science and Human Nutrition, play a vital role in maintaining the standards of excellence as judges and consultants. Many other judges are home economists and food industry professionals affiliated with national food companies, such as Kraft Foods, Inc., Tone Brothers, Inc. (spices), and The Quaker Oats Company. Food editors and specialists from *Better Homes and Gardens* magazine (published in Des Moines) also lend their expertise in calling the winners.

For this cookbook, I have selected more than 1,000 recipes I believe to be among the most representative of contemporary Midwest cooking —a difficult task, given the region's immense food repertoire. The book is intended to define today's Midwest cuisine—the result of a long tradition of superlative cooking. It is presented as a legacy of the Midwest state fair blue ribbon winners who, over decades of hard, loving work, have been instrumental in establishing a cuisine to be enjoyed around the world.

Breadbasket of the Nation

Tucked in the central part of the United States between the more venerable East and experimental West, the twelve states that comprise the Midwest are sometimes unjustly overlooked as not having any regional identity and character all their own. Although the Midwest will never boast the historic edge of the earlier-settled Eastern Seaboard, and probably won't choose to compete with the West Coast in trend-setting, there's one key factor about the region that

marks its importance: the Midwest is the breadbasket of the nation.

Thanks to glacial retreat at the end of the Ice Age, some of the best soil in the world blankets the Midwestern states—Ohio, Michigan, Indiana, Wisconsin, Illinois, Minnesota, Iowa, Missouri, North Dakota, South Dakota, Nebraska, and Kansas. This expanse of naturally fertile land, cultivated with sophisticated agricultural technology, has made the Midwest one of the most agriculturally productive regions on the earth. Forty percent of the 1996 cash receipts from all agricultural commodities produced in the United States came from here—an impressive fact, considering that it wasn't until the early 1800's that the region was settled. Ohio, the most easterly of the Midwest states, was the first to gain statehood in 1803. It was close to a century later, in 1889, before North and South Dakota, on the western border of the region, joined the union.

In agricultural commodity statistics, the Midwest takes the lead over other regions of the country. Five of the top seven agricultural states are located here. In 1996, the region accounted for 84 percent of the nation's corn, 82 percent of the soybeans, 71 percent of the hogs, 78 percent of the oil crops, 73 percent of the feed crops, and 49 percent of the wheat. For fiscal year 1996, 48 percent of the total United States agricultural exports came from the Midwest.

The rich, fertile soil and hot, humid summers, which provide ideal weather for farming, attracted early European immigrants from Germany, England, Norway, Denmark, Sweden, Holland, Czechoslovakia, and other countries to the Midwest prairie. The abundance of wild deer, elk, antelope, ducks, prairie chickens, turkeys, partridge, and quail was vital in providing the necessary food for survival. Welcome additions to the daily fare were the plentiful raspberries, strawberries, blueberries, gooseberries, and plums found growing in the wild. In the northern reaches of the area, pioneers discovered a profusion of lakes and rivers teeming

The Twelve Midwest States

with pike, bass, perch, and catfish amid the lush forests of pine and birch.

This treasury of natural resources sustained the Midwest's settlers through the overwhelming hardships and backbreaking labor required to turn over the virgin soil, build shelter out of sod and logs, and support families over the bitter-cold winter months.

Carving out an existence from the virgin prairie wasn't approached haphazardly. The land survey system adopted by Congress in 1785 provided an organized plan for the settlement of farmland all over America and resulted in the patchwork-quilt appearance of the Midwest today—a sight familiar to air travelers.

Before being sold by the federal government, land was laid out in rectangular townships of six square miles. Each township was divided into 36 sections of 640 acres which, in turn, could be subdivided into halves, quarters, or smaller pieces.

Under the Homestead Act passed by Congress in 1862, up to a quarter section—160 acres—could be granted to a settler for only ten dollars and five years of continuous residency. Until comparatively recent time, the typical Midwest family farm consisted of approximately 160 acres—not only as the natural outcome of the Homestead Act, but also because that was about the maximum number of arable acres an average single family could farm without the benefit of present-day mechanization.

For years it was easy to distinguish the 160-acre farms from the air—one after another in all directions—in their neat checkerboard pattern. Each 640-acre section, or square mile, is bordered by roads, and resting within them there were commonly four distinct farms with houses and outbuildings.

But the 160-acre family farm is quickly becoming obsolete. Today, large self-propelled combines and gigantic tractors pulling huge planters and tilling equipment make it possible for a single family to crop-farm 1,000 or more acres of land. Fences around former 160-acre farms have been removed and the farm buildings have been razed to provide more land for cultivation. The 1987 United States census revealed that among farms of 180 acres or more, close to 20 percent of Iowa farmland was in farms of 1,000 acres or more.

MODERN-DAY FARMING

The past fifty years have witnessed a revolutionary change in the style of farm life. As late as 1940, less than one third of America's farms had electricity. Almost all do now. Traveling down rural roads in the Midwest today, you see modern farmhouses much like their urban counterparts. Sophistication is everywhere. Grain farms have elaborate clusters of round storage bins; dairy farms are outfitted with state-of-the-art barns in which herds of cows are milked with electric milkers. The milk goes directly from the cows through stainless steel, sanitized pipes into refrigerated bulk storage tanks, from which it is picked up daily for delivery to the processors. Many dairy-farm families complain (or brag) that their barns cost more than their homes.

Mammoth equipment stored in machine sheds is expensive—and essential for large-scale farming. Tractors can cost as much as $170,000 and the largest combines, fully equipped, cost over $200,000. Successful farming is now a science as well as a big business, and it takes a hefty financial commitment.

But despite the changes, the land continues to be at the heart of life in the Midwest. Generation after generation, families pursue farming because they love the lifestyle. Their primary focus is not on money even though the land they own and farm may be worth $2,000 an acre, and their livestock and equipment may be valued at several hundred thousand dollars. They choose to spend their years in the open spaces with their hands in the soil; and they prefer a more simple way of life. They are not lured by the fast track.

Midwest farm women are fabulous cooks. They enjoy the reputation of being consummate bakers of pies, breads, and cakes. Indeed, one of America's finest cooking styles has evolved out of the prodigious, fertile land of the Midwest, and an industrious people of rich ethnic diversity who attach paramount importance to the preparation and consumption of good food.

It is startling to reflect on how young this nation really is, as exemplified by the comparatively recent settlement of the Midwest. It was only one hundred years ago that my grandfather came to Iowa in a horse-drawn wagon. In a brief 150- to175-year span, steadfast, hardworking people have converted the unsettled Midwest grass prairie into a virtual breadbasket, supplying much of this nation's food and a significant amount of food for the world's people.

Heartland State Fairs

The modern state fair . . . has for its object the placing of a state on exhibition and the teaching of the people through object lessons. . . . The greatest benefit that can be derived from a fair is derived from the exhibitor who makes up his mind early in the season to become such and who spends that season in preparation.

—KANSAS FARMER
(quoted in *Greater Iowa,* July 1, 1910)

Showcasing the best. That has been the keystone of state fairs throughout their vibrant history, since the nation's first state fair was held in September 1841, in Syracuse, New York. The competitive spirit—our American heritage—thrives at these colorful events, which remain the primary arenas for judging the nation's finest

The Kansas State Fair

Wisconsin State Fair Park

State INDIANA Fair

IOWA STATE FAIR

Illinois STATE FAIR

South Dakota STATE FAIR

North Dakota State Fair

MICHIGAN STATE FAIR

Minnesota State Fair

the Missouri State Fairgrounds

NEBRASKA STATE FAIR

agricultural and food products. State fairs have been central, in fact, to the development of the United States as one of the greatest agricultural and food-producing nations of the world.

Having moved west with the pioneers, state fairs continue to flourish to this day. The Midwest's first state fair was held in 1849 in Michigan. By the end of the 1850's, most of the other Midwest states had followed suit, hosting their own fairs. Missouri and Kansas launched state fairs shortly after the turn of the century, and North Dakota joined the parade later, with its first official state fair held in 1965.

INCEPTION DATES OF OFFICIAL MIDWEST STATE FAIRS

INCEPTION DATE	STATE
1849	Michigan
1850	Ohio
1851	Indiana
1851	Wisconsin
1853	Illinois
1854	Iowa
1854	Minnesota
1857	Nebraska
1885	South Dakota
1901	Missouri
1913	Kansas
1965	North Dakota

The history and essence of all the great Midwest state fairs are similar. Originally, they were sponsored by state agricultural societies as vehicles for education. When the fertile land of the Midwest was settled in the 1800's, county and state fairs provided the setting for the exchange of agricultural know-how and for updating on scientific advancements.

The Iowa State Fair, one of the oldest and largest agricultural expositions in the country, stands as a model of the twelve remarkable Heartland state fairs. And, of course, the Iowa fair holds a special place in my life.

The first Iowa State Fair was held in Fairfield, Iowa, in 1854, just eight years following statehood. Families traveled to the fair in covered wagons, camping along the way and in the campgrounds after arriving at the fair. Frontiersmen with long pistols in their belts arrived on horseback. The *Fairfield Ledger* estimated that 7,000 or 8,000 people attended the fair, the largest assemblage in the state's history.

Since that first gathering, the Iowa State Fair has continued to be the state's single largest event, with more than 946,000 people in attendance during the 1997 eleven-day run, breaking all previous fairgoing records. People still love to camp at the fair. An estimated 30,000 fair visitors utilized the fair's 160-acre modern campground—most in motor homes and other recreational vehicles.

In 1878, the Iowa State Fair moved to Des Moines. This site, along with most of the original buildings, remains the location of the fair today. Of course, new, modern structures have been added to the fairgrounds, including an air-conditioned facility which houses the Food Department, where entries in the food show are judged and exhibited, and educational food demonstrations are conducted.

In concert with the educational purpose of state fairs, demonstrations of the latest technological phenomena often have been featured. For example, a demonstration of the telegraph was the star attraction at the 1909 Iowa State Fair. Pre-fair publicity tantalized fairgoers with the promise that wireless messages would be flashed back and forth through space, between the fairgrounds and downtown Des Moines.

Attendees witnessed an even greater marvel in 1911, when the Wright Brothers gave air flight exhibitions four times daily. And the 1927 fair was highlighted with guest appearances by

Charles Lindbergh and Clarence Chamberlain, fresh from their conquests of the Atlantic.

STATE FAIRS REMAIN VITALLY IMPORTANT

Farmers and others in the food-producing industries continue to gather at Heartland state fairs for the purpose of education. They go to see the newest machinery and equipment, and to acquire up-to-the-minute information concerning major livestock and farming priorities. Present topics of paramount interest include the breeding and feeding of livestock for lowfat meat, protection of the environment in the use of herbicides and pesticides, and consumer food safety as affected by the use of drugs in livestock production.

Through the years, standards for the ideal in agricultural commodities, livestock, and food have been established through showing and judging at Midwest state fairs. Standards undergo constant evaluation and change. For instance, in the Food Department, all canned goods now entered in competition must be in compliance with the new United States Department of Agriculture canning guidelines adopted in 1989. Among other things, these guidelines set forth safety requirements regarding methods of canning, jar headspace, and processing times. Any canned goods that do not meet the new USDA standards in all respects are automatically disqualified by the judges. This rule is strictly enforced.

Professionals with the Cooperative Extension Service (see page 14) and faculty members of the Department of Food Science and Human Nutrition at Iowa State University are available, year-round, for assistance in complying with these mandates. I utilize their services, often, in helping to determine processing times for products not specifically listed in the guidelines, and to solve problems that arise in the course of canning.

Besides fulfilling an acute function, Midwest state fairs are a wonderful, poignant romance in the classical American saga. They mirror life in the Heartland—quarter horses, dairy cattle, cherry pie, quilts, apple butter, corn and soy-beans, baton twirling, lemonade, cinnamon rolls, horseshoe pitching, and country-western music.

Although agriculture, livestock, and food remain the central theme of Midwest state fairs, the scope of activities has broadened considerably over the years to include the showing and judging of many diverse items such as art, photography, weaving, pottery, homemade wine and beer, wood carvings, and all types of needlework. People from the city as well as the farm are involved in the fair these days.

Fairs have always been family oriented. From the beginning, women, children, and teens were included in planned activities and educational programs, and were encouraged to attend. Prior to the 1863 Iowa State Fair, the fair secretary advertised, "Do not be afraid to bring your wives and daughters. Parties having ladies in company will receive special consideration from the superintendent of the camp." In earlier days, state fairs presented one of the only opportunities young people had to meet eligibles who lived beyond their own counties. It was "boy meets girl" in the most proper and acceptable surroundings.

Entertainment and fun are a big part of the fair. Most seasoned fairgoers consider it a "must" to see the full-size, sculptured butter cow (about 1,500 pounds of butter) in the agriculture building. Sculpted each year by Norma Duffield (Duffy) Lyons, the butter cow has become the unofficial Iowa State Fair mascot. (Duffy is the niece of Phil Stong, author of the novel *State Fair* on which the musical was based.) Long lines also form in the swine barn to see the newly farrowed baby pigs—they tug at everyone's heartstrings.

Among the myriad of interesting events to watch is the popular and highly acclaimed Weed Identification Contest, conducted with the cooperation of Iowa State University and three leading agribusiness chemical companies.

If you like country music—and most Midwesterners do—a long list of the top names in country music presents shows to sold-out audiences in the grandstand every year. In addition, an impressive roster of well-known stars performs free of charge at several locations around the fairgrounds.

Most fairgoers scour the daily schedule of activities before heading for the fairgrounds. Otherwise, favorite contests might be missed— events such as Sheep Shearing, Fiddlers, Yodeling and Whistling, Accordion Playing, and Bucksawing and Woodchopping. Other popular attractions include the Taffy Pull, Old-Fashioned Hymn Sings, Speed Chess and Backgammon Tournaments, Duck and Turkey Calling, and Clogging and Square Dancing. For an old-fashioned good time, there's the Ladies' Rolling Pin Throw, Cow Chip Throwing Championship, Mother/Daughter Look-a-Like Contest, Hog-Calling Contest, and Rooster Crowing Contest. My all-time pick in this category of just-for-fun contests is the Ladies' Husband Calling Contest.

At nighttime, a stroll through the sprawling Midway, with all its frivolity of scary rides, bright lights, and barkers, offers competitive fair entrants welcome relief from the work and tension of showing their livestock, food, or other products.

FAIRGOING INVOLVES AWESOME EATING

Forget dieting during fair time. "Fair fare" may not be the world's healthiest, but it's out-of-this-world terrific and definitely worthy of a once-a-year calorie splurge. I arrive at the fair hungry, with the first order of business to track down a mouthwatering corn dog. In case you haven't savored one of these incredible goodies, it's a hot dog on a stick which has been dipped in corn bread-type batter and fried. Most people squirt mustard over top. Then, it's on to one of the lemonade stands. At the Iowa State Fair, my favorites are run by the Braffords, where your order is made from real lemons as you wait thirsting for a swig of that ambrosial, sour-sweet nectar splashing around the frosty ice cubes.

For the first dessert of the day, it's a Wonder Bar—an ice cream bar dipped in chocolate and rolled in oodles of nuts right before your eyes.

As the day rolls on, it will be punctuated by rest stops for funnel cakes, a bratwurst, fudge, perhaps a turkey leg (yes—the *whole* leg) if you're really starving, and more of that revitalizing lemonade. For dinner, it's get-in-line-early at the Iowa Pork Producers tent for an Iowa Pork Chop dinner prepared by volunteer pork producers on gigantic grills as you enter. A whopping 17,556 of these chops were devoured by devotees of this succulent dish at the 1996 fair (see recipe on page 251). Or, you may want to partake of a juicy steak served in the Cattlemen's Beef Quarters.

The judging of food was a featured activity of state fairs from their inception. The premium list from the 1864 Iowa State Fair, held at Burlington, Iowa, included a division entitled "Dairy, Pantry, and Kitchen," which was comprised of two "classes." Among the seventeen items to be judged in the first class were firkins of butter, boxes of honey, barrels of flour, yeast bread, water crackers, fruitcake, and pound cake. An amazingly comprehensive list of twenty-nine preserves, jellies, butters, and pickles was included in the second class. Premium lists of the early Midwest state fair food shows disclose the nature and makeup of Midwest food in its formative years. To read 125 years of Midwest state fair food show premium lists is to chronicle the evolution of Midwest cooking.

By 1992, the Iowa State Fair food competition had ballooned to the largest of all the state fairs nationally. In 1997, $36,930 prize money was awarded in 881 classes with 7,457 separate food entries at the Iowa event. Organizational wizard Arlette Hollister, Superintendent of the Iowa State Fair Food Department, expertly plans and manages the annual show.

Among the items judged at the 1997 Iowa fair were 98 classes of cakes; 142 classes of cookies; and 92 classes of jams, jellies, preserves, butters, conserves, and marmalades. A myriad of foods was judged in specialized divisions including classes for pasta, chili, bratwurst, turkey, ostrich, ethnic dishes, soybeans, rice, tofu, casseroles, cranberries, fresh herb cooking, and many others. In step with current trends in eating, divisions for low-sodium cooking, foods made with honey, and heart-healthy cooking were included.

Food exhibited at the Iowa State Fair today is the paragon of Midwest cooking. The long tables of gorgeous rolls, pies, cakes, and canned goods rolled in for judging are beautiful to see and exquisite to taste. Indeed, some of the best food from America's kitchens is exhibited and judged at Heartland state fairs.

Because it is considered important to encourage young people to learn how to cook and to take an interest in diet and nutrition, seventy classes in the 1997 Iowa State Fair food show were for young people eight to eleven years of age (junior division), and sixty-five classes were for twelve- to seventeen-year-olds (intermediate division).

Historic records of the 1916 Iowa State Fair include a report on culinary activities carried on in the boys' and girls' building. The report trumpeted the food-related events by observing that "probably the most interesting feature of the program was the canning demonstration given each day. Sanitary and scientific methods of preserving fruit[s] and vegetables were demonstrated. There was also a fine collection of canned goods on exhibition, the work of the . . . club members."

In the early 1920's, the Boys' and Girls' Club adopted the name "4-H Club." Under the 4-H banner, food demonstrations and an extensive food contest have continued to be held each year at the fair, and are now conducted in the large 4-H exhibits building that has supplanted the old boys' and girls' building. (The 4-H food contest is in addition to the classes for youth exhibitors in the state fair Food Department.)

It is interesting to note that development of the 4-H concept, a program of "learning by doing" for youth, is attributed to several people, including a Midwesterner—O. H. Benson, who was Wright County, Iowa, superintendent of schools from 1905 to 1911. In 1909, he originated the 4-H emblem—a four-leaf clover with the letter *H* on each leaf standing for "head," "heart," "hands," and "health." In 1996, there were over 70,000 4-H Clubs in the United States, with about 1.5 million members, plus more than 4 million additional young people participating in other 4-H programs. Beyond our shores, there are 4-H and 4-H-type organizations in over 50 foreign countries. 4-H Clubs are part of 4-H Youth Development, a division of the Cooperative Extension Service (see page 14).

Midwest state fairs, the land-grant colleges, and The Cooperative Extension Service form a close-knit, interrelated system which has been greatly responsible for the high development of agricultural expertise in the United States. Research, education, standard-setting, and practical application in the areas of agriculture, livestock, and food are linked through this tripartite system which has functioned so efficiently and effectively. The immense contributions by private agribusiness interests, which have worked cooperatively with this system, also must be given recognition.

Land-grant colleges were established under the Morrill Act of 1862. This Act provided federal assistance to the states for the organization and support of agriculture and mechanic arts colleges. The fundamental purpose of the Morrill Act was to establish programs of study on practical subjects at the college level. The Iowa State College of Agriculture and Mechanic Arts (renamed Iowa State University of Science and Technology in 1959) was one of the first land-grant colleges established under the act. The close liaison between Iowa State University and the Iowa State Fair has contributed to the eminent success of both institutions. Since 1923, the President of Iowa State University has been an ex-officio member of the Fair Board.

The impetus for home economics curricula resulted from the Morrill Act. Midwest land-grand colleges, being less tied to the rigors of traditionalism, led the way in the previously unorthodox concept of educating women for the domestic arts. Iowa State College, Kansas Agricultural College, and Illinois Industrial University were pioneers.

Mary B. Welch, wife of the President of Iowa State College, was one of the originators of home economics education, which she began to develop—from scratch—at the college in 1870. Through her efforts, a model kitchen was demonstrated at the 1880 Iowa State Fair. During the 1882–83 school year, Mrs. Welch gave a series of lectures to a group of women in Des Moines, which is credited as being the first well-organized home economics extension activity in the United States.

The Cooperative Extension System, created by the Smith-Lever Cooperative Extension Act of 1914, is the educational agency of the United States Department of Agriculture, and is jointly funded and conducted by the Department of Agriculture, the land-grant universities, and local governments. This network links research, science, and technology to the needs of people where they live and work. The Cooperative Extension Services at the land-grant universities have state, county, and area staff members who develop educational programs to assist farmers, families, individuals, and communities. The concept had its genesis in Sioux City, Iowa, in 1903, when a representative of Iowa State College and a group of Iowa farmers organized a farm experimental plan.

The close ties that have always existed among the Home Economics Department of Iowa State University, the Cooperative Extension Service, and the Food Department of the Iowa State Fair are exemplary of the interrelationship between these institutions. Home economists with the Cooperative Extension Service and Home Economics Department faculty members at Iowa State University have been guiding lights in the development and maintenance of the Iowa State Fair's prestigious Food Department. They have perennially served as consultants and judges.

The Midwest has been blessed with some of the richest soil found anywhere in the world. This prized natural resource is the foundation upon which an energetic people has developed one of the most productive agricultural and food-producing regions on the globe. Through the years, Heartland state fairs have been the standard-setters and showcases for these achievements.

Midwest Food: America's Own

Midwest cooking derives from three Midwestern attributes: our country's greatest expanse of fertile land, a rich ethnic diversity, and a lifestyle in which good food is a valued priority.

The fruits, vegetables, and grains which thrive in the bountiful Midwest soil; the domestic livestock and poultry bred and fed on the beautiful land; and the indigenous wild game and fish have blended with traditional recipes and cultural eating patterns of the European immigrants who settled the region, and their descendants, to create a food and cooking style unique to America. Midwest cooking is from the land and people in our nation's agricultural Heartland.

Until relatively recent times, the Midwest cooking repertoire consisted principally of the dishes created and prepared by farmwives using the meats, poultry, eggs, milk, vegetables, and fruits produced on their own 160-acre farms, supplemented by wild game and, in the northern tier of Midwest states, fish caught in the copious lakes and rivers. These farm women, steeped in the work ethic, were innovative cooks. They brought with them the ethnic cooking of their native lands—Norway, Holland, Germany, Finland, Sweden, Denmark, England, and other countries—which they combined with new dishes created from the prolific issue of the land. Food was important. It was necessary in order to sustain the ardent physical labor involved in farming, and it was one of the major pleasures in a simple way of life. Baking pies, cakes, breads, and rolls was a ritual.

To this exemplary cooking tradition, a further dimension has been added: a more sophisticated and sometimes more complex cooking style enjoyed by a citizenry which is well-educated and better-traveled, and takes pleasure in the continued pursuit of fine food. Concentration on food and cooking is still a characteristic of Midwest people.

Because expert home cooking remains the cultural norm, the Midwest is characterized more aptly by huge, magnificent food stores than by countless superb restaurants.

Almost without exception, all women, regardless of economic strata, know how to cook, and in harmony with the prevailing trend, more and more men are becoming enthusiastic, capable cooks who take pride in their newfound culinary expertise. The exchange of recipes is universal across the Midwest states; in fact, many of the recipes in this cookbook are based on recipes gathered from friends over the years. Throughout the Midwest, there are church and organizational cookbooks galore in which members have pooled their favorite recipes. Church dinners, potlucks, family holiday gatherings, and home-cooked dinners for friends abound.

Whether a fancy dinner party or an informal barbecue, most people entertain their friends and family with meals prepared themselves and served in their homes. The talent for cooking and serving attractive, elegant food is highly admired by both men and women in the Midwest, and is an accomplishment sure to win generous praise. Cooking for others is considered a gift of self. Especially at holiday time, there is much gift giving of homemade culinary specialties such as sweet breads; home-canned jams, jellies, and pickles; and platters of luscious cookies and candies.

A COMPLETE CUISINE

Because of the vast spectrum of foods raised in and on Midwest land, and the plurality of ethnic backgrounds, Midwest cooking is extremely wide-ranging. Unlike some other regional cooking, it cannot be labeled with a handful of easily identifiable characteristics. It is a complete cuisine—never monotonous—and too important to be a passing trend. It has virtually no unfilled gaps.

I have concluded that the best way to describe Midwest cooking is to list some of the Midwest's most pervasive foods and dominant eating traditions. The following list is not all-encompassing by any means, but I hope it is representative enough to help answer the question so often asked, "What is Midwest food?" A short narrative describing specific Midwest foods and the Heartland cooking style in greater detail introduces each chapter of this book.

Cinnamon rolls

Quick breads

Baking powder biscuits

Doughnuts

Big breakfasts

Pancakes and waffles

American fries for breakfast

Homemade yeast breads

Soft dinner rolls

Deviled eggs

Lemonade

Salad as the appetizer course

Salad with all dinners

Lettuce-based tossed vegetable salads

Fancy molded salads

Thousand Island salad dressing

Scalloped vegetables

A vegetable with all dinners

Tomatoes

Green bell peppers

Onions

Cucumbers

Morel mushrooms

Corn (on-the-cob, chowder, cream-style, scalloped, and more)

Home-grown herbs

Baked beans

Bean soup

Chili

Cheese soup

Potato salad in the summer

Mashed potatoes and gravy

Wild rice

French-fried onion rings

Egg salad sandwiches

Spaghetti

Beef (steaks, steaks, and more steaks; pot roast; meat loaf)

Pork (Iowa pork chops, ham, and roast pork loin)

Chicken

Fried chicken on the 4th of July

Walleyes, crappies, and bass

Shrimp cocktail as an appetizer with special dinners

Wild game (pheasant, quail, ducks, geese, and venison)

Stews

Casseroles (all kinds)

Turkey for Thanksgiving and Christmas

Ham for Easter

Sage dressing (stuffing)

Pies (all kinds)

Homemade ice cream

Cakes (all kinds, double- and single-layer)

Strawberry shortcake made with angel food cake

Brownies

Cookies (all kinds)

Skim milk for drinking

Strawberries, raspberries, and blueberries

Fruit for dessert

Fudge and divinity (at holiday time)

Popcorn

Cheddar, Swiss, and blue cheese

Cheese and crackers

Pickles and relishes with meals

Chili sauce

Home-canned jams, jellies, butters, and fruits

Even though a distinctive Midwest cooking style has developed over the years, this continuity is satisfyingly punctuated with a degree of piquant variation in fare from area to area due to enclaves of particular ethnic groups, and foods uniquely indigenous to certain localities.

For example, Old-World favorites like Sauerbraten with Potato Dumplings, Cucumber Salad, and Red Cabbage with Red Wine take their place with regularity at tables in households of German heritage in Wisconsin and Nebraska. At Christmastime, the aroma of spicy cookies waft from these Germanic kitchens when Lebkuchen, Pfeffernüsse, Zimtsterne, and Springerle are whisked from the oven. Norwegian heritage is preserved in North Dakota and Minnesota when fond, old family recipes for Kringla are repeated generation after generation.

Melt-in-your-mouth Dutch Letters, Apple Bread, and Janhagel Koekjes (cookies), available in bakeries in the Holland Dutch communities of Grand Rapids and Holland, Michigan, and Pella and Orange City, Iowa, are known far and wide to Midwesterners, who often travel miles for these goodies.

Wonderful foods which flourish in the special climate and soil of particular locales also affect local eating customs. Michigan blueberries, Minnesota wild rice, and Missouri hickory nuts are staples in all kinds of creative recipes logged in local cookbooks from these states.

While game birds are pervasive throughout the Midwest, the kinds of birds hunters bag in the fall vary somewhat with the region. For instance, succulent ducks and geese are proudly brought home by sports people along the Missouri, Mississippi, and Illinois river migratory flyways, while the delicacy of quail is the privilege of family diners in eastern Kansas, northern Missouri, and southern Iowa, where coveys of these tiny morsels abound. Pheasants—perhaps the most savored of all Midwest game birds— are abundant in South Dakota and are plentiful bounty in several other Midwest states as well.

Midwest food can stand alongside the fine cuisines of the world. It belongs to all America because it is of the nation's agricultural Heartland. It is a product of our culture and is uniquely American. It is America's own.

Special Information

Notes About Recipe Ingredients

HIGH-QUALITY PRODUCTS. Prepared foods are only as good as the products which go into them. The whole equals the sum of its parts. Select fresh, high-quality foods to bring into your kitchen. Neither the combining of inferior products with other foods nor the cooking process will disguise poor-quality products.

EGGS. Recipes are based on the use of extra-large eggs unless otherwise specified. For best results with the recipes herein, extra-large eggs should be used unless otherwise specified; however, if extra-large eggs are not available, large eggs may be substituted in most recipes. A few recipes, in which the volume of eggs is critical, specify the number of large eggs which may be used in substitution for extra-large eggs.

BUTTER. Use lightly salted butter unless otherwise specified.

SUBSTITUTION OF MARGARINE FOR BUTTER. Margarine may be substituted for butter in most recipes; however, in my opinion, the flavor of the end product will be adversely affected in most cases. For example, cakes and cookies made with butter have a deep, rich taste which is missing when margarine is substituted in the same recipes. (See page 795 for more on this subject.)

MILK. In general, when whole milk is specified in a recipe, fat-free (skim) milk or lowfat (1% or 2%) milk should not be substituted. While fat-free (skim) milk is a good-tasting, nonfat, healthful product for drinking, the use of whole milk in baked goods and for most cooking results in finer end products. Try to select ways other than eliminating whole milk from cooking to reduce fat in the family diet.

PURE VANILLA EXTRACT. Use of *pure* vanilla extract is specified in the recipes. Imitation vanilla results in inferior flavor.

BAKING POWDER. Remember to watch the expiration date on the container and discard after that date.

WINE AND ALCOHOLIC LIQUOR. Use *good* wine and alcoholic liquor for cooking. Poor-quality wine and spirits produce second-class flavor in finished dishes.

GROUND BEEF. Lean ground beef is called for in these recipes. The ground beef should be 97% lean, pure ground beef containing no fillers, such as carrageenin or oat bran, and no additives, such as salt or hydrolyzed vegetable protein.

HAZELNUTS. Hazelnuts are also known as filberts.

COMMERCIAL CAN SIZES. The sizes of commercial cans of food often change (generally becoming smaller). In many cases, using a can of food which varies slightly in size from that specified in a recipe will not affect the outcome of the prepared food. The cook will have to make this determination. If there is a significant variation in can size from the recipe specification, it may necessitate using a portion of food from a second can or reducing the amount of food used from a single, larger can.

FLOUR STORAGE. For convenient use, all-purpose flour may be stored in an airtight canister placed in a dry, cool place on the kitchen counter. Surplus all-purpose flour may be stored in a dry place at cool, room temperature. For storage, place the paper package of remaining flour in a zipper-seal plastic bag. Flour stored at room temperature should be used within 6 months.

Wheat germ and flour containing part germ, such as whole wheat flour, should be stored in the refrigerator or freezer to prevent rancidity caused by oil in the germ. For refrigeration or freezing, wheat germ and small quantities of flour may be placed in glass jars with tight lids; larger quantities of flour may be left in their original paper packages and sealed tightly in zipper-seal plastic bags.

Refrigerated or frozen wheat germ and flour should be brought to room temperature before being used in a baked product.

Glossary

n. = *noun,* v. = *verb,* adj. = *adjective*

Almond Paste: *n.* Blanched almonds blended to an oily consistency, then mixed with a sugar and water syrup which has been cooked to 240° F., and then kneaded.

Amandine: *adj.* Prepared or garnished with almonds.

Amaretto: *n.* An almond-flavored liqueur, although apricot pits are often used to flavor it rather than almonds. Amaretto di Saronno, the original Amaretto, comes from Saronno, Italy.

Applejack: *n.* Apple brandy.

Arrowroot: *n.* The starch from the root of a tropical plant used to thicken glazes and sauces. Flavorless and colorless, it produces exceptionally clear, smooth glazes and sauces. Ideal for use in mixtures which should not boil because, unlike cornstarch and flour, it requires no cooking and reaches its maximum capability as a thickener at a temperature below the boiling point (see Thickener Equivalencies, page 29).

Aspic: *n.* Jellied meat, poultry, fish, or vegetable broth used to mold or coat foods—usually meat, poultry, fish, or vegetables.

Bake: *v.* To cook a food product, covered or uncovered, in an oven.

Barbecue: *v.* (1) To cook meats, poultry, fish, shellfish, or wild game outdoors on a grate or rotisserie over hot coals, or in a smoker, applying barbecue sauce (see definition below). (2) To cook meats, poultry, fish, shellfish, or wild game indoors, using barbecue sauce.

Barbecue Sauce: *n.* A highly seasoned and tomato-based sauce containing vinegar and/or wine and a sweetener; generally used on foods grilled or smoked outdoors, but may also be used on foods prepared indoors.

Baste: *v.* To spoon or brush a liquid or sauce over a food while it is cooking for one or more of the following purposes: (1) to keep the food moist, (2) to help cook the top surface of the food, or (3) to add flavor. The liquid or sauce may or may not be from the pan or other container in which the food is cooking. A bulb baster is an efficient utensil for drawing liquid from around a cooking food and expelling it over the food to baste.

Batter: *n.* A thick but pourable raw mixture of ingredients, usually including flour.

Beat: *v.* To rapidly move a single food or a mixture of foods for the purpose of smoothing, blending or combining, and/or incorporating air, using (1) an electric mixer, (2) a hand-operated rotary beater (sometimes referred to as an eggbeater), or (3) a spoon, fork, or whisk by repeatedly lifting the food(s) in a circular motion from the bottom to the top of the bowl or sauce dish.

Blanch: *v.* To dip briefly in boiling water, generally for the purpose of loosening the skin of a food for peeling or for the purpose of cooking briefly (see To Blanch, page 44).

Blend: *v.* To mix two or more ingredients together until the separate ingredients are indistinguishable.

Boil: *v.* (1) To heat a liquid until it reaches a temperature at which large vapor bubbles form rapidly, rise and burst below the surface of the liquid, and leave the liquid, agitating the surface. At sea level, water boils at 212°F. Due to less atmospheric pressure in higher altitudes, the boiling point of water decreases as the altitude above sea level increases. To a lesser extent, weather conditions are another factor which causes fluctuations in the temperature at which water boils (see Boiling Point of Water at Various Altitudes, page 712). (2) To cook food in a boiling liquid.

Bouquet Garni: *n.* A small bunch of flavorful herbs—usually assorted and preferably fresh—tied together, added to foods (such as soups, stews, and sauces) during cooking, and removed before serving. A bouquet garni traditionally consists of parsley, thyme, and a bay leaf; however, any single herb or combination of herbs may be used. The herbs may be tied in a cheesecloth bag, if desired. Dried herbs may also be placed in a cheesecloth bag, and used in substitution for fresh herbs. (See To Make a Fresh Bouquet Garni, page 38.)

Braise: *v.* To cook a food in a small amount of liquid at a low simmer in a covered skillet or pan.

Brandy: *n.* An alcoholic liquor distilled from wine.

Bread: *v.* To coat food with ground, dry bread or a ground, dry, breadlike product such as cracker crumbs, cornmeal, or cornflake crumbs, in preparation for cooking. Often, the food to be breaded is first dipped in beaten egg and/or milk, or some other liquid, to help achieve adherence of the crumbs.

Brine: *n.* A strong salt and water solution used in pickling, curing, and fermenting food for the purpose of preserving it and/or imparting flavor.

Broil: *v.* To cook food by direct exposure beneath a dry heat source.

Broth: *n.* The strained liquid produced by the long, slow simmering of meat, poultry, fish, bones, and vegetables—alone or in combination. Used in making sauces, soups, and other dishes. Usually clarified when served as a thin soup. Also known as stock.

Brown: *v.* As a first step in cooking a food (often meat), to cook it quickly on all sides in a small amount of fat over medium to high heat until a golden to deep-brown color for the purpose of sealing in the juices and enhancing the flavor and color of the finished, cooked food.

Bun: *n.* A round and rather flat plain or sweet yeast roll.

Butterfly: *v.* To split—usually meat or shrimp—nearly in two and lay open, making the product resemble a butterfly. The butterflied product may be cooked open or may be stuffed, with the butterfly "wings" encasing the stuffing.

Canapé: *n.* A small, attractively cut piece of bread (untoasted or toasted) or a small cracker topped with a tasty spread or other food and often an eye-appealing decoration or garnish; served as an hors d'oeuvre. "Canapé" is a French word meaning "couch."

Candied: *adj.* (1) Fruit—especially the peel—or ginger which has been cooked in a syrup until tender and translucent and then drained. Candied foods are used in cooking, or some are eaten alone as a candylike product, such as candied orange peel. (2) Sweet potatoes or other foods cooked in a syrup or with a sweet glaze.

Capers: *n.* Flower buds of the caper plant, a Mediterranean shrub, which are pickled and used in cooking for flavoring or garnish.

Casserole: *n.* (1) A container, usually glass, in which food is baked and served. It generally has built-in handles and a lid. (2) The dish baked and served in a casserole.

Caviar: *n.* The roe (eggs) of large fish. True caviar—and the finest—is the black roe of the beluga sturgeon, which is imported from Russia and Iran. Red caviar is the roe of salmon. Yellow caviar is also marketed.

Celery Hearts: *n.* The small, tender, pale green to nearly white celery stalks (and leaves) at the very center of a bunch of celery.

Chop: *v.* To cut into small, usually irregular, pieces, using a knife or other sharp implement.

Chutney: *n.* A highly spiced, thick relish of Indian origin, containing fruits, spices (usually including ginger), vinegar, sugar (often brown sugar), often raisins, and often onions and/or garlic; used primarily as a condiment (see definition), especially with curry dishes, but also used as an ingredient in other dishes.

Clarified Butter: *n.* The clear, yellow liquid which rises to the top of slowly melted butter, separated from the milk solids which settle on the bottom of the pan. The fat floating on top of the clarified butter is skimmed off, and, using a baster, the clarified butter is drawn off, leaving the milk solids on the pan bottom.

Cobbler: *n.* A baked fruit dessert covered with a biscuitlike crust.

Coddle: *v.* To cook food (usually unshelled eggs) in liquid at just below the boiling point.

Cognac: *n.* A brandy (see definition) produced in the Cognac region of France.

Combine: *v.* To mix two or more ingredients or combination of ingredients together until the separate and/or combination ingredients are evenly distributed but still distinguishable, as in adding nuts to cake batter.

Condiment: *n.* A sauce, relish, or seasoning placed on or beside food, usually at the table, to enhance flavor.

Core: *v.* To remove the central, often inedible, part of some fruits such as apples.

Court Bouillon: *n.* A well-seasoned liquid, usually consisting of water, wine and/or vinegar, vegetables, and seasoning, in which fish or shellfish is poached.

Cream: *v.* To beat, usually using an electric mixer on high speed, a fat (generally butter, margarine, or shortening) until smooth, fluffy, and completely blended if creamed with another product such as sugar.

Crème de Cassis: *n.* A black currant–flavored liqueur.

Croquette: *n.* A mixture of ground or minced foods, usually meat, fish, and/or vegetables, molded into a cone shape, coated with beaten egg and crumbs, and deep-fat fried or baked.

Croutons: *n.* Small cubes of toasted bread, seasoned or unseasoned, used as an ingredient or garnish in salads and other dishes.

Crudités: *n.* Raw vegetables cut into small strips or pieces and served, usually with a dip, as an hors d'oeuvre or first-course appetizer.

Cube: *v.* To cut food into chunks with 6 equal square sides greater than ¼ inch square.

Currants: *n.* (1) Any of several varieties of a tiny, acid berry which grows on shrubs of the genus *Ribes*. There are red, black, and white currants, red currants being the most common. Gooseberries are related to currants. (2) Dried Black Corinth grapes, called Zante currants (unrelated to the fruit in the first definition).

Curry Powders: *n.* Various blends of several ground, pungent spices and herbs. Originated in India.

Cut In: *v.* To cut solid fat, such as butter or lard, into particles and/or small pieces while simultaneously mixing it with a dry ingredient, usually flour or a flour mixture, using a wire pastry blender or two knives.

Dash: *n.* Less than ⅛ teaspoon.

Deep-Fat Fry: *v.* To cook a food by immersing in hot fat. Also known as French fry.

Deglaze: *v.* To release food particles stuck to the bottom of a pan in which food has been cooked by adding liquid to the pan, placing it over low heat, and scraping the bottom with a spoon or spatula.

Deviled: *adj.* Seasoned highly with spices and/ or condiments such as mustard.

Dice: *v.* To cut food into small pieces with 6 equal sides ¼ inch square or less.

Dollop: *n.* A spoonful of soft food, such as whipped cream, usually informally placed on the top of another food.

Dough: *n.* A very thick, unpourable raw mixture of ingredients, usually including flour, which is stiff enough to be kneaded or shaped.

Dredge: *v.* To coat a solid food with a fine, dry ingredient, such as flour, or a mixture of dry ingredients, by pulling the food across the ingredient or mixture or by sprinkling the ingredient or mixture over the food.

Dress: *v.* To eviscerate and otherwise prepare an animal, fowl, or fish for cooking after killing.

Drippings: *n.* Juices and fat which run off meats and fowl during cooking.

Dumpling: *n.* (1) A bread product that is a portion of batter dropped (dumped) onto boiling liquid, such as soup, stew, or water, to cook, covered, by low-boiling/steaming (see Dumplings, page 448). (2) A formed ball of dough that may include various foods, such as chopped, riced, or ground vegetables and/or meats, dropped into boiling liquid, such as broth or water, to cook; for example, Potato Dumplings (page 334), matzoh balls,

and liver dumplings. (3) A vegetable, fruit, meat, fish, or shellfish dipped in batter and deep-fat fried; for example, tempura and some fritters (not the Corn Fritters or Apple Fritters on page 457 of this cookbook, which are fried in a small amount of oil in a skillet). (4) A whole fruit or large pieces of fruit wrapped in pastry and baked usually in a syrup; for example, Apple Dumplings (page 650). (5) Food encased in pasta or other dough and cooked in boiling liquid or deep-fat fried; for example, ravioli and egg rolls.

Dutch Oven: *n.* A heavy—often aluminum— round pot with small side handles and a tight-fitting, domed lid, both usually made of the same metal as the pot; sometimes equipped with a rack. Commonly 4- or 6- quart capacity. Generally used for browning, braising, and roasting.

Fillet: *n.* A strip, piece, or slice of boneless meat or fish, especially the tenderloin of beef, and the strip or piece of flesh from either side of a fish.

Fillet: *v.* To cut fillets.

Filet Mignon: *n.* A thick steak cut from the small end of a tenderloin of beef.

Fluted: *adj.* In the shape of a continuous series of scallops or rounded grooves.

Fold: *v.* To move a utensil, usually a spoon, briefly and carefully through a mixture in a vertical circular motion (down the back of the bowl, across the bottom, up, and over) to blend or combine an ingredient(s) with the mixture while (1) retaining the air in both the new ingredient(s) and the mixture and (2) incorporating new air.

Fowl: *n.* Any bird, domestic or wild.

Fritter: *n.* A small amount of batter, usually containing a vegetable, fruit, or meat, which is deep-fat fried or sautéed.

Fry: *v.* To cook a food in fat in a skillet, pan, or griddle over heat. (See definitions for Deep-Fat Fry and Sauté.)

Giblets: *n.* The liver, heart, and gizzard of poultry.

Glaze: *n.* (1) A thin, translucent, sweet, soft-gel coating usually brushed on or drizzled over fruit fillings in pies, tarts, and desserts to give a smooth sheen and add flavor. (2) A thin, translucent mixture used to coat foods before serving to give a glossy appearance and add flavor. (3) A very thin frosting (usually powdered sugar frosting) used to coat certain doughnuts and ice certain cakes and breads. (4) Concentrated meat stock.

Glaze: *v.* To apply glaze.

Gluten: *n.* The viscous (or thick) and elastic proteins, particularly in wheat flour, which, when mixed with liquid and manipulated (stirred/kneaded), develop into strands. These help retain, in doughs and batters, gas bubbles created by leavening agents such as yeast, baking powder, and steam. This allows doughs and batters to rise, resulting in light baked products.

Grand Marnier: *n.* A French orange-flavored liqueur with a cognac brandy base (see definition for Cognac).

Grate: *v.* To break down a semi-hard product to a texture resembling finely rolled cracker crumbs, usually by rubbing the product against a sharp, densely pronged, metal kitchen tool made for this purpose, or by processing it in a food processor or blender.

Gravy Skimmer: *n.* A spouted liquid measuring cup designed for separating and pouring off the drippings from the fat in meat pan juices.

Green Onion: *n.* A young onion pulled before the bulb has enlarged. Also known as scallion.

Grill: *v.* To cook food by direct exposure over direct heat, as in cooking food on a grate directly over charcoal in an outdoor grill.

Grind: *v.* To reduce food to small fragments or powder with the use of a grinder or other kitchen implement or tool.

Herbs: *n.* The fresh or dried green leaves of certain plants used for flavoring foods.

Hors d'Oeuvres: *n.* Small, attractive savories served as appetizers, usually with cocktails, before a meal and before proceeding to the table.

Hull: *v.* (1) To remove the green, leafy sepals at the stem end of a fruit, plus the pith (the central strand of tissue) of strawberries. (2) To remove the outer covering of a fruit or seed.

Intermezzo: *n.* A minor course in a meal, usually consisting of a small serving of sorbet or sherbet, served between principal courses for the purpose of cleansing the palate.

Julienne: *v.* To cut into very narrow, square or rectangular matchstick-like strips, usually not exceeding ¼ inch wide by 2 to 2½ inches long.

Kahlúa: *n.* A brand of coffee-flavored liqueur (see definition) produced in Mexico.

Kirschwasser: *n.* Cherry brandy. A German word meaning "cherry water." It is pronounced "keersh-vahser."

Knead: *v.* To manipulate dough—for the purposes of gaining cohesiveness and developing the gluten—by placing it on a lightly floured surface, folding the dough in half toward you, pushing the dough with the heels of your hands, turning it one-quarter, and repeating this procedure for a specific time or until the dough is smooth and elastic. (See Kneading Dough, page 414.)

Lard: *n.* A soft, solid fat rendered from the fatty tissue of pork. Leaf lard, from leaf fat around the kidneys, is the finest lard.

Leavening Agent: *n.* A gas—air, steam, or carbon dioxide—which is incorporated into, or forms in, a batter or dough, causing it to rise, increase in volume, and become light and porous during preparation and cooking. Baking soda (sodium bicarbonate), baking powder, and yeast are products used in cooking which, when activated, produce carbon dioxide by a chemical or biological reaction. (See Leavening, page 34.)

Liqueur: *n.* A sweetened, alcoholic liquor, such as brandy, flavored with fruit, nuts, spices, herbs, or seeds. The best liqueurs usually are made with a cognac (see definition) base.

Liquor: *n.* (1) A distilled alcoholic beverage, usually whiskey, vodka, gin, rum, and brandy. (2) A natural (as in oysters) or other concentrated liquid surrounding food.

Lukewarm: *adj.* Approximately 97 to 100°F. (body temperature); tepid.

Lyonnaise: *adj.* Prepared with onions, as in lyonnaise potatoes.

Macaroon: *n.* A cookie made principally of egg whites, sugar, coconut or almond paste, and flavoring.

Marinade: *n.* A liquid consisting of one or more ingredients, usually with seasonings, in which a food, usually meat, fowl, or fish, is immersed for a period of time prior to cooking for the purpose of imparting flavor and/or tenderizing.

Marinate: *v.* To let food stand in a marinade.

Marzipan: *n.* A candy made with sweetened almond paste which is often colored and molded into miniature fruits and vegetables, animals, flowers, and other forms.

Meringue: *n.* A mixture of stiffly beaten egg whites and sugar which is (1) piled high on top of pies or other desserts and baked until golden (a soft product), or (2) used to make pie or other dessert shells (a hard product).

Mince: *v.* To chop into tiny pieces.

Mocha: *adj.* Flavored with coffee, often in combination with chocolate.

Mousse: *n.* A light, airy, molded dish, usually a dessert or an appetizer, made with gelatin and/or egg whites, and often whipped cream. Dessert mousses are usually smooth in texture; solid ingredients in appetizer mousses are usually ground, minced, or chopped.

Nonpareils: *n.* Tiny sugar pellets, in various colors, used to decorate cookies, cakes, doughnuts, candies, and other sweet foods.

Parboil: *v.* To partially cook in boiling water, preliminary to additional cooking by a different method.

Pare: *v.* To cut the skin or outer layer off a tight-skinned product, such as a potato. (In contrast to "peel"—see definition.)

Parfait: *n.* A dessert made by layering variously flavored ice creams and/or sherbets, fruit sauces, syrups, and whipped cream in a special, tall, narrow, short-stemmed parfait glass. Eaten with an iced-tea spoon.

Pâté: *n.* (1) Ground or diced meat, fish, or fowl, usually highly seasoned and sometimes with added ingredients, which is packed into a loaf pan and baked. May have an aspic and/or pastry covering. Served cold, thinly sliced, and usually as a first course. (2) A spread made of seasoned, finely ground or pureed meat, fish, or fowl.

Pectin: *n.* Water-soluble substances found in the cell walls and intercellular layers of fruits. Combined with sugar and acid in correct proportions, pectin forms a gel which is the basis for jellied sweet spreads such as jelly and jam. Commercially packaged powdered or liquid fruit pectin is often used in making these jellied products.

Peel: *n.* The skin or outer layer of a loose-skinned product such as a banana or a blanched tomato (see definition for Blanch), which can be stripped off with little or no cutting.

Peel: *v.* To strip the skin or outer layer off a loose-skinned product, such as a banana, with little or no cutting. (In contrast to "pare"—see definition.)

Petit Four: *n.* A fancy, dainty sweet consisting of a very small, usually square, piece of cake covered with icing glaze and usually decorated with a piped flower or other piped decoration. The cake may be layered with a filling(s).

Phyllo: *n.* Also known as "filo." A paper-thin pastry dough which is usually layered when used in making desserts and other dishes, producing a flaky pastry when baked. Usually available, frozen, in supermarkets. "Phyllo" is from the Greek word meaning "leaf."

Pickle: *n.* A food prepared in a seasoned vinegar mixture or a brine solution to preserve it and/or impart flavor.

Pilaf: *n.* Seasoned rice, often browned, with added meat, poultry, shellfish, and/or vegetables.

Pinfeather: *n.* An undeveloped, new feather just coming through the skin of a fowl.

Pit: *n.* The centralized seed of certain one-seeded fruits. Also known as a stone.

Pit: *v.* To remove the pit (also known as the stone) from certain one-seeded fruits.

Poach: *v.* To cook in liquid at a simmer. A cooking method used especially when care is to be taken to retain the shape of the food product.

Poultry: *n.* Domestic birds raised for eggs and/or meat.

Puff Pastry: *n.* A light, flaky, high–rising pastry made of many thin, alternating layers of flour dough and butter. Usually available, frozen, in supermarkets.

Puree: *v.* To whip, press, or mash a solid or semisolid food to a smooth, thick consistency, but not liquefied. A blender, food processor, food mill, or sieve is often used to puree a food.

Reduce: *v.* To boil or simmer a liquid or thin mixture, uncovered, for the purpose of condensing it by evaporation.

Relish: *n.* (1) A chopped vegetable(s) and/or fruit(s) cooked in vinegar and seasonings; eaten as a complement to other food. (2) Raw vegetables, olives, and other such food, commonly finger-type, served as an hors d'oeuvre or an appetizer at the table.

Rind: *n.* A usually tough outer layer; for example, the peel of a fruit.

Roast: *v.* To cook, uncovered, by dry heat in an oven or on an outdoor grill using indirect heat. Also, to cook food products in hot coals or ashes.

Roaster: *n.* Similar to a Dutch oven (see definition) except oval shaped and usually larger; 8-quart capacity is common for a large roaster.

Rolling Boil: *n.* A full, rapid boil, when water-vapor bubbles continuously and rapidly burst below the surface of the liquid, causing extreme agitation over the entire surface as they leave the liquid. A full rolling boil cannot be stirred down.

Roulade: *n.* A thin piece of meat or other food that is rolled around vegetables or another filling; usually browned and then baked or braised.

Salt Pork: *n.* Exceptionally fat pork which has been cured in salt; generally used in foods to add flavor.

Sauté: *v.* To cook in a small amount of fat in a skillet over heat.

Scald: *v.* (1) To heat liquid to just under the boiling point. Milk reaches the scalding point when tiny bubbles appear at the edge of the pan. (2) To dip a food briefly in boiling water. Also known as blanch (see definition).

Scallion: *n.* Same as green onion (see definition).

Scallop: *n.* Any of a number of bivalve mollusks of the family *Pectinidae*. In the United States, the large adductor muscle which closes the valves is the part eaten. The most commonly eaten species are the large sea scallop (*Placopecten magellanicus*) and the tiny bay scallop (*Aequipecten irradians*), although other species are available in various regions of the United States.

Scallop: *v.* To bake a food or a combination of foods in a sauce or liquid, usually with a crumb topping.

Score: *v.* To cut shallow slits, often in a diamond pattern, in the surface of meats or other foods, to prevent surface fat from curling during cooking, to tenderize, to mark for later cutting, or for decorative purposes.

Sherbet: *n.* Sorbet (see definition) that contains milk or cream.

Shred: *v.* To cut a semi-hard food into tiny or small strips, usually by rubbing it against a sharp, perforated metal kitchen tool made for this purpose, or by cutting it very thinly with a knife.

Shuck: *v.* (1) To remove the husks from some foods such as corn. (2) To remove the shells from mollusks, such as oysters.

Sift: *v.* To put one or more dry ingredients, such as flour, baking powder, and baking soda, through a wire-mesh sifter or sieve for the purpose of removing any lumps and/or mixing the ingredients and/or incorporating air.

Simmer: *n.* When liquid reaches a temperature just below the boiling point at which time small water-vapor bubbles, which form principally on the bottom of the pan, slowly rise to the surface and break.

Sorbet: *n.* An ice usually made with fruit juice and/or pureed or very finely chopped fruit pulp, and a sugar and water syrup. Egg white or gelatin may also be ingredients.

Soufflé: *n.* A very light, airy, high-rising, baked dessert or savory usually made with a sauce or mixture containing egg yolks, beaten egg whites, and sometimes pureed or ground food. Special round, straight-sided dishes are generally used for baking soufflés. Soufflés must be served immediately after removal from the oven, before they lose their height and puffiness due to the escape of air.

Spices: *n.* The pungently flavored roots, stems, bark, seeds, buds, or fruit of certain plants and trees used for seasoning foods.

Steam: *v.* (1) To cook food in steam by placing it in a perforated, metal container suspended over boiling or simmering water in a covered pan. (2) To cook food in an airtight container lowered into low-simmering water, as in steamed puddings.

Stir: *v.* To move a utensil, usually a spoon, through a liquid or a pliable mixture, principally in a circular motion around a bowl or pan, for the purpose of mixing ingredients or preventing a mixture from sticking to the bottom of a pan during cooking.

Stir-Fry: *v.* To cook, in a wok (see definition) or skillet, bite-sized slices or pieces of meat and/or vegetables in a small amount of oil over medium-high to high heat, stirring and turning constantly. The vegetables are cooked until just tender but still crisp.

Stock: *n.* Same as broth (see definition).

Tapioca: *n.* A starch from the root of the tropical cassava plant. Available in granular form (quick-cooking tapioca) and two sizes of small, round pellets (small pearl and large pearl tapioca). Most commonly used to make tapioca pudding and as a thickener in fruit pies and other fruit desserts. Also available in flour form.

Tepid: *adj.* Moderately warm; lukewarm (see definition).

Toast: *v.* To brown a food by exposure to dry heat.

Triple Sec: *n.* An orange-flavored liqueur (see definition).

Truss: *v.* To bind the legs and wings of a fowl close to the carcass, and to bind the carcass cavities, usually with poultry skewers and/or cotton string, in preparation for cooking.

Vinaigrette: *n.* A salad dressing (or sauce) made of oil and vinegar. Seasonings and other additions may be used. Variations on vinaigrette substitute lemon juice or wine for the vinegar. (See headnotes for Vinaigrette Dressings and Basic Vinaigrette Dressing, page 152.)

Vinegar: *n.* An acetic and other acid solution produced by fermentation. Four common types of vinegar are cider, distilled white, wine, and malt. Herb, fruit, nut, and other flavored vinegars usually are made by flavoring wine vinegars.

Whip: *v.* To beat (see definition) very rapidly and vigorously for the purpose of incorporating air and increasing volume, as in whipped cream.

Wine: *n.* The fermented juice of grapes. Also, the fermented juice of other fruits or other plant products.

Wok: *n.* A bowl-shaped, Asian cooking utensil used like a skillet; especially good for stir-frying (see definition for Stir-Fry).

Zest: *n.* Very small, thin curls or pieces of the colored, outer part of the peel of citrus fruits; used for flavoring or decoration.

Food Safety

There is greater prevalence of foodborne illness than most people realize. It is estimated that 33 million cases of food poisoning occur in the United States each year. It is further estimated that 85 percent of these cases could have been avoided if consumers had followed safe food storage, handling, and cooking practices.

Food poisoning, caused by harmful bacteria, parasites, and viruses, normally produces intestinal flu–like symptoms which last a few hours to several days. However, in the case of botulism, or when foodborne illness strikes infants and young people, pregnant women, elderly people, ill persons, or people with weakened immune systems, it can be serious or sometimes fatal.

You are usually unaware that harmful bacteria are present. They are microscopic in size, and you normally can't taste, smell, or see them. Of course, when food has an unusual odor or appearance, it should be discarded immediately, untasted. Most moldy food should be discarded. The poisons that molds can form are found *under* the surface of food. Hard cheeses, salamis, and firm fruits and vegetables can sometimes be safely saved if a large section of the food around and under the mold is cut away.

Safe storage, sanitation, and proper cooking are critical factors in food safety. Below are general food safety guidelines, as well as particular food safety procedures for packed lunches, picnics, and microwave ovens. Food safety guidelines for several specific foods are found in other sections of *The Blue Ribbon Country Cookbook,* as follows:

Meat Safety, page 157
Meat Safety for Outdoor Cooking,
    page 249
Poultry and Stuffings (Dressings) Safety,
    page 203
Fish and Shellfish Safety, page 220
Egg Safety, page 262

• When you are doing errands, do your grocery shopping last—just before you return home. At the grocery store, select perishable foods requiring refrigeration after you have selected the nonperishable items on your list. Transport perishable foods home and get them under refrigeration as soon as possible.

• Do not purchase any food you will not use by the expiration date given on the packaging.

• Refrigerate perishable foods at 40° F. or below. Keep your refrigerator as cold as possible without freezing stored milk and fresh vegetables. Keep your freezer and the freezing compartment of your refrigerator at 0° F. or below. At 0° F. bacterial growth is stopped. Use an appliance thermometer to check the temperatures of your refrigerator and freezer.

EQUIVALENCIES

Food	Quantity	Approximate Equivalency
Apples	1 lb.	3 c. sliced
Beans, navy, dried	½ lb. (1 c.)	2½ c. cooked
Bran flakes crumbs	2 c. unrolled flakes	1 c. rolled crumbs
Bread crumbs		
dry bread	1 slice	¼ c. processed or rolled crumbs
fresh bread	1 slice	½ c. crumbs
Butter	¼ lb. (1 stick)	½ c. or 8 tbsp.
Carrots, fresh	1 lb.	3 c. shredded
Cheese,		
cheddar	4 oz.	1 c. shredded
cottage cheese	8 oz.	1 c.
cream cheese	3 oz.	¼ c. plus 2 tbsp.
Parmesan	4 oz.	1 c. grated
Romano	4 oz.	1 c. grated
Swiss	4 oz.	1 c. shredded
Chocolate		
baking squares	1 oz.	1 square
chips	6 oz.	1 c.
Coconut		
flaked	7 oz.	2⅔ c.
shredded	7 oz.	2⅓ c.
Cookie crumbs		
chocolate wafers	15 2¼-inch wafers	1 c. rolled crumbs
vanilla wafers	22 wafers	1 c. rolled crumbs
Cracker crumbs		
graham crackers	20 squares	1½ c. finely rolled crumbs
Ritz crackers	12 crackers	½ c. rolled crumbs
saltines	10 crackers	½ c. rolled crumbs

Food	Quantity	Approximate Equivalency
Cream		
sour cream (commercial)	8.5 oz.	1 c.
sour cream (homemade)	8 oz.	1 c.
whipping cream	1 c. (½ pint)	2 c. whipped
Gelatin, unflavored	¼-oz. envelope	2 tsp.
Honey	16 oz.	1⅓ c.
Mandarin orange segments, canned	11-oz. can, drained	1 c.
	11-oz. can, drained; segments cut in half widthwise	¾+ c.
	15-oz. can, drained	1½ c.
	15-oz. can, drained; segments cut in half widthwise	1¼ c.
Milk		
evaporated	5-oz. can	½ c. plus 2 tbsp.
	12-oz. can	1½ c.
sweetened condensed	14-oz. can	1¼ c.
Mushrooms, fresh	8 oz.	3 c. sliced
Nuts		
almonds	1 lb. in shells	1 c. shelled
Brazil nuts	1 lb. in shells	1½ c. shelled
cashews	1 lb. shelled	3¼ c.
hazelnuts	1 lb. in shells	1½ c. shelled
hickory nuts	1 lb. in shells	⅔ c. shelled
peanuts	1 lb. in shells	2 c. shelled
pecans	1 lb. in shells	2 c. halves, shelled

Food	Quantity	Approximate Equivalency
Nuts *(cont.)*		
walnuts, black	1 lb. in shells	½ c. shelled
walnuts, English	1 lb. in shells	1¾ c. halves, shelled
Pasta		
macaroni, elbow	7 oz. (2 c.)	4 c. cooked
noodles, egg	8 oz.	6 c. cooked
spaghetti	8 oz.	4 c. cooked
Popcorn	¼ c.	8 c. popped
Rice, white, long-grain	1 c.	3½ c. cooked
Rice, wild	1¼ c.	4 c. cooked
Shortening, vegetable	1 lb.	2⅓ c.
Soup, condensed, canned	10¾-oz. can	1½ c.

Food	Quantity	Approximate Equivalency
Sugar		
brown, light or dark	1 lb.	2¼ c. packed
granulated	1 lb.	2¼ c.
powdered	1 lb. unsifted	4 c.
Syrup, corn, light or dark	16 oz. (1 pint)	2 c.
Water chestnuts, chopped, canned	6.8-oz. jar, drained	⅔ c.

THICKENER EQUIVALENCIES

2 tablespoons flour =
2 tablespoons quick-cooking tapioca =
1 tablespoon cornstarch =
1 tablespoon arrowroot

- Thaw food in the refrigerator or in the microwave oven (see Microwave Ovens [page 31] for procedural information), not on the kitchen counter or in the sink. Thawing proceeds from the outside in, so surface bacteria can multiply to illness-causing levels before food is thawed all the way through.

- Before storing packages of raw meat, poultry, fish, and shellfish in the refrigerator, place the packages on plates to prevent raw juices from dripping onto other foods.

- The danger temperature zone for the growth of foodborne bacteria is between 40 and 140° F. In this temperature range, foodborne bacteria can double in number every 20 minutes. The rule is: never leave either raw or cooked perishable foods unrefrigerated for more than 2 hours. Normally, bacteria do not multiply to dangerous levels in less than 2 hours.

- Promptly refrigerate leftovers. When refrigerating a large quantity of food, divide it among small, shallow containers for quick cooling. Avoid packing the refrigerator. To keep food at a safe temperature, it is necessary for the cool refrigerator air to circulate.

- Hot cooking temperatures kill most bacteria found in raw foods. For information on safe cooking temperatures for meats, poultry and stuffings (dressings), fish, shellfish, and eggs, refer to the other food safety sections listed above.

- Use a meat thermometer or instant thermometer (page 44) to gauge the internal temperature of meats, poultry, and other foods.

- Properly refrigerated, leftover cooked foods may safely be served cold. When reheating leftover cooked foods, bring gravies, sauces, and soups to a boil. Thoroughly heat other leftover foods to at least 165° F. (steaming hot).

- An astonishing number of bacteria are carried by hands. Wash your hands with soap and hot water immediately before commencing to prepare food. Wash your hands again with soap and hot water after handling raw or cooked meat, poultry, fish, shellfish, and eggs, before you handle other food. Use a utensil, rather than your hands, to mix meat, salads, and other foods.

• Wash kitchen tools and equipment, cutting boards and other work surfaces, sink, and faucet handles with hot, soapy water after they come in contact with raw or cooked meat, poultry, fish, shellfish, and eggs, and before they come in contact with other food.

• Use clean utensils and a clean platter or bowl to serve cooked meat, poultry, fish, shellfish, and eggs. Do not reuse utensils, platters, or bowls that came in contact with these foods before they were cooked unless they are first washed in hot, soapy water.

• Do not use food from damaged containers. Check cans for dents and bulging lids, and glass jars for cracks. Check paper packages for leaks and stains.

• Do not purchase refrigerated foods that are not cold to the touch. Frozen foods should be completely solid.

• Wash fresh fruits and vegetables well to remove soil as well as bacteria, viruses, and insecticide sprays.

• Wash kitchen towels, dishcloths, and sponges often. When washing the cloth items, use the hottest water setting on the washer.

• When entertaining, keep perishable foods which will be served cold, refrigerated until serving time. Remove perishable foods from serving tables when they have been unrefrigerated more than 2 hours, or serve cold perishable foods on ice. Hot foods left on serving tables for consumption by guests over a period of time should be kept heated to 145° F. or above, by use of chafing dishes or other suitable methods.

• Keep pets and insects away from food, kitchen counters and sinks, and dining tables.

• For additional information on the safe storage, handling, and preparation of meat and poultry products, as well as information on the labeling of these foods, call the Meat and Poultry Hotline, a service of the U.S. Department of Agriculture's Food Safety and Inspection Service, Monday through Friday, 10:00 A.M.–4:00 P.M. Eastern time. The national toll-free number is 800-535-4555. In Washington, D.C., call 202-720-3333.

PACKED LUNCHES

• Keep perishable foods cold. If a refrigerator is not available for storage of your packed lunch, pack it in a small, lunch-sized, insulated cooler or bag. Place a zipper-seal plastic bag filled with ice cubes or a frozen packet of ice or ice substitute in the cooler or bag to keep the contents cold. A thermos may be used to keep milk or juice cold.

• If you prepare your lunch the night before, refrigerate the perishables, such as meat, poultry, fish, and shellfish, and sandwiches and foods containing perishables such as eggs and mayonnaise. Pack your lunch the next morning just before leaving.

• Good food choices for packed lunches are:

  ~ Canned meats, poultry, and fish which can be opened and eaten immediately. If the can does not have a self-opener, make sure that the can opener you use has been washed.

  ~ Commercially precooked and ready-to-eat meats such as bologna, salami, and corned beef.

  ~ Fresh fruits and vegetables.

• Keep perishable foods that will be microwaved at lunchtime in a refrigerator or in an insulated cooler or bag.

• Do not leave lunch containers in the sun or near a warm radiator or other heat source.

- Wash your hands with soap and hot water before eating lunch, or use disposable wet wipes.

- Wash the lunch container after each use to prevent bacteria from growing. An occasional washing with baking soda will help eliminate odors.

PICNICS

- Pack all perishable foods in an insulated cooler kept cool with sufficient ice cubes or frozen packets of ice or ice substitute.

- Thoroughly chill perishable foods before placing them in the cooler. Cans or bottles of beverages should be cold before placing them in the same cooler with perishable foods.

- If you are packing a large quantity of cold beverages for a number of people, pack the beverages in one insulated container and the perishable foods in another. This will help avert the danger of perishable foods being exposed to warm air by frequent opening of the cooler lid.

- Salads with commercial mayonnaise are safe if kept cold. Avoid cream and custard pies, cream puffs, cream-filled rolls, and other pudding- and custard-like foods.

- When driving to and from the picnic site, try to avoid transporting the coolers in the hot trunk of the car. If possible, carry the coolers in the passenger area.

- At the picnic site, keep the coolers in the shade. Avoid opening the lid of the cooler holding perishable foods too often. If possible, replenish melting ice in the cooler.

- If running water is not available for picnickers responsible for the final preparation and serving of the food to wash their hands, take along disposable wet wipes.

- In hot weather of 85° F. or above, do not leave food out more than 1 hour (not includ-

ing cooking time for items grilled at the picnic site).

- Put leftover, perishable foods back in the cooler as soon as you finish eating. The leftovers should be safe to save if you are gone from home no longer than 4 to 5 hours, and the perishable foods are kept cold in the cooler except when cooked and/or served.

MICROWAVE OVENS

Unique characteristics of microwave cooking present problems in achieving the uniform cooking or reheating of food. Uneven cooking in microwave ovens can leave cool or cold spots in food where foodborne pathogens can survive and cause illness.

When food is cooked or reheated in a microwave oven, cold spots in the food can occur because of the irregular way in which the microwaves enter the oven and are absorbed by the food. Further, microwaves cook food from the outside to the inside; therefore, outer portions of food may become fully cooked or reheated while inner portions remain cool. Additionally, microwaves heat fats, sugars, and liquids more quickly than other food elements. These factors and others create food safety hazards, which can be alleviated with the application of special microwaving procedures.

- Use only containers approved for microwave use. Glass and glass ceramic dishes are safe for use in a microwave oven. Do not reuse containers and trays provided with microwavable foods. They have been designed for one-time use with a particular food product.

  Avoid using metal-trimmed dishes and containers, and metal twist ties. TV dinners in aluminum foil trays no deeper than ¾ inch may be microwaved. Large pieces of aluminum foil should not be used; however, small pieces of foil may be used to cover poultry legs and other small areas over food, provided the foil ends are wrapped smoothly over the food or area being covered. Any aluminum foil should be kept at least 1 inch from the sides of the oven.

Do not use dairy cartons, margarine tubs, and other such containers designed for cold storage. The high heat of a microwave oven could cause chemicals from these containers to invade cooking food.

Carefully follow the instructions in the manufacturer's manual that accompanies your microwave.

- Cover the food container used for microwaving food with a glass lid or plastic wrap. Vent the plastic wrap and make certain it does not touch the food. (Unless plastic wrap is heavy duty, it could melt when coming in contact with hot food.) Covering food in this manner helps retain steam, which aids in obtaining thorough and even cooking, and in destroying bacteria and other pathogens. A small amount of water added to the food assists to create additional steam.

  Waxed paper is also safe for covering food in the microwave. Plain white paper towels and napkins may be used to cover food provided they have not been made from recycled material.

- Rotate the food container during cooking to achieve even cooking. If your microwave does not have a turntable, rotate the food container by hand once or twice during cooking. Move food inside the container several times during cooking; stir soups, stews, and sauces.

- Adhere to the standing time called for in the recipe or package instructions. Food continues to cook during the standing time. Specified standing times are usually about ⅓ the length of cooking times.

- Use the microwave oven temperature probe, a meat thermometer, or an instant thermometer to make certain that food has reached a safe temperature. Check the internal temperature of the food at several places.

- Debone large pieces of meat before cooking. Bone can prevent meat around it from cooking thoroughly.

- Cook large pieces of meat at 50 percent power for longer time periods. This will help achieve proper cooking of inner areas of the meat without overcooking the outer portions. Commercial oven bags are safe for use in the microwave and are useful in helping to secure even cooking and a tender final product.

- Do not use the microwave oven for cooking whole, stuffed poultry. Poultry bones and density of the stuffing (dressing) prevent even and thorough cooking.

- Before commencing to thaw food in the microwave oven, remove the food from its store wrap. Plastic trays, paper wrapping, and other packaging material not designed for microwaving may contain chemicals which could transfer to the food under the high heat of a microwave oven.

- Do not defrost or hold food at room temperature in the microwave for longer than 2 hours.

- After thawing food in the microwave, immediately proceed to finish cooking it. The heat of the microwave may cause outer portions of the food to commence cooking, raising the outer temperature of the food to a level conducive to quick bacteria multiplication.

- If the microwave oven is used to partially cook food, immediately transfer the partially cooked food to a conventional oven, broiler, or grill for completion of the cooking. Do not partially cook food and then complete the cooking at a later time (even if the partially cooked food will be stored in the refrigerator).

- Heat leftovers and other cooked foods to at least 165° F. (steaming hot).

The Functions of Ingredients in Batters and Doughs

Flour, liquid, fat, sugar, eggs, leavening, and salt are the basic ingredients used in batters and doughs. The quality of home-baked products depends on the proportions of ingredients, how they are mixed, and the cooking temperatures and times. These relationships affect the color, flavor, texture, shape, and volume of the final product.

FLOUR

Flour contains proteins that combine with liquid to form gluten. This sticky, elastic material gets stronger and more elastic as the batter is stirred or the dough is kneaded. These strands of gluten form a network of cells that expand when heated. Baking "sets" this framework.

Flour also contains starch, which absorbs liquid and swells. When heated, this adds body to the framework of baked foods.

Three common types of flour are:

All-purpose flour. A blend of hard and soft wheat flours, which makes it versatile for many products. It is usually enriched, and may be bleached or unbleached.

Bread flour. Made from hard wheat and is rich in protein, which forms strong gluten. It is desirable for yeast breads.

Cake flour. Made from soft wheat. Since it is lower in protein, less gluten is developed. Thus, it produces more tender cakes.

When the same amount of liquid is used, both all-purpose flour and bread flour produce a stiffer dough than cake flour.

Whole wheat, buckwheat, rye, barley, and soy are among other types of flours used in batters and doughs.

LIQUID

Some type of liquid is needed to develop the gluten, gelatinize the starch, activate the leavening agent, and dissolve the sugar and salt to distribute them through the batter or dough.

The proportion of water and flour helps determine the amount of gluten formed.

Milk is the most commonly used liquid, although fruit juice and water also can be used. Whole milk is 87.69 percent water and also contains protein. Milk tends to give baked products a finer texture, better color, and somewhat different flavor than water.

FAT

Shortening, cooking oil, butter, and margarine make baked products tender and rich. They also help retain freshness and serve to blend and distribute flavorings. When butter is used, it gives a special flavor to the final product.

Since fat is insoluble in any of the other ingredients, it separates the particles of dough. During baking, the fat melts while other ingredients are setting up. It is easy for the leavening gas to expand into the tiny areas of melted fat. However, excess fat weakens the gluten structure and can cause the product to decrease in volume or fall.

Vegetable shortenings and oils are 100 percent fat. By contrast, butter and margarine combine 80 percent fat with 20 percent water and milk solids.

SUGAR

Although primarily added for sweetening, sugar has additional functions. Because it caramelizes with heat, sugar helps the product brown during baking. It also increases the tenderness of the product.

Honey, corn syrup, and molasses are sugars and can be substituted for granulated sugar. However, the amount of liquid used also must be adjusted.

Noncaloric sweetening agents require special recipes. They contribute a sweet flavor but do not tenderize or increase browning. Sometimes they lose their sweetening power and become bitter with heat.

EGGS

By their emulsifying action, egg yolks bring about even distribution of fat in batters and doughs. They promote tenderness and a fine texture. The egg proteins, along with gluten, form the structure of the product.

Beaten eggs, particularly beaten egg whites, aid in leavening because of the formation of tiny air cells. The air expands on heating and steam is formed from the moisture of the egg. As the egg proteins coagulate with heating, the cell walls become set.

LEAVENING

Leavening is produced by the release and/or expansion of gas within a batter or dough. A variety of substances contribute to lighten the batter or dough.

Air is incorporated in baking mixtures in several ways. The most common is folding beaten egg whites into the batter. Other ways include beating whole eggs, creaming sugar and fat, and beating the batter itself.

Heating the batter or dough causes the air bubbles to expand, making the batter light. Angel food cakes depend on the incorporation of air for one-half to two-thirds of their leavening.

Baking powder releases gas during mixing and/or baking and is used in most cakes and quick breads. Baking powder contains baking soda (sodium bicarbonate) and acid-reacting ingredients. In the presence of moisture and heat, these components react to form carbon dioxide gas, which expands and leavens.

Baking powder contains cornstarch to keep the mixture dry by absorbing moisture, and to standardize measuring.

Baking soda is required to neutralize an acid ingredient such as buttermilk, sour cream, sour milk, or molasses. The combination releases carbon dioxide gas, which leavens the batter or dough.

Steam provides the leavening in batters containing large proportions of liquid, such as popovers and cream puffs. When water is heated, it produces more than 1,600 times its volume in steam.

Yeast is a microscopic plant that grows rapidly in a warm, moist medium. It ferments sugar and/or starch to form carbon dioxide gas and alcohol. The gas is the principal leavener, but the alcohol vaporizes during baking and also helps in leavening. During baking, the heat expands the gas, stops the yeast action in the raised dough, evaporates the alcohol, and sets the gluten.

SALT

The major function of salt in baked products is to add and enhance flavor. In yeast breads, it helps to control the action of the yeast, thus improving texture.

This section consists of edited extractions from Publication N-2857: What's in a Recipe? *published by Iowa State University, Cooperative Extension Service, Ames, Iowa, in March 1986, and prepared by Phyllis Olson and Diane Nelson.*

For additional information on the function of ingredients in yeast dough, see Yeast Breads and Rolls, page 412.

Techniques

TO COOK AND BAKE AT HIGH ALTITUDES

Atmospheric pressure decreases as altitude increases. This fact has several ramifications which affect cooking and baking. As altitude increases:

- water and other liquids boil at lower temperatures;

- water and other liquids evaporate faster at a given temperature;

- leavening gases expand more.

These principles necessitate adjustments in ingredients, temperature, time, and procedures in the cooking and baking of many foods at high altitudes. Most cookbook recipes, including those herein, are written for use at sea level. (see Note, page 37). This section gives some guidelines for adjusting sea-level recipes for use at higher altitudes. While adjustments for altitude are definitive in the preparation of some food products such as the processing of home-canned foods, exact formulas cannot be given for modifications of sea-level recipes for many items, such as cakes, quick and yeast breads, and cookies. Cooks and bakers will need to experiment with adjustments to specific recipes for these products in order to fine-tune modifications—if modifications are needed at all.

At sea level, the temperature of boiling water is 212° F. For each 500 feet above sea level, the boiling point of water decreases approximately 1° F. See Boiling Point of Water at Various Altitudes (page 712) for a chart and a more complete explanation.

GENERAL COOKING: Because water boils at lower temperatures at higher altitudes, it often takes longer to cook foods at high elevations. In addition, it may be necessary to increase liquid due to greater vaporization before foods are fully cooked.

BOILED CANDIES AND FROSTINGS: When making boiled candies and frostings, the temperature of the boiling sugar mixture (syrup) exceeds the temperature of boiling water as the water in the syrup evaporates. The less water in the syrup, the higher the temperature rises above the boiling point of water. The temperature of the boiling syrup, gauged by a candy thermometer, is the most accurate way of determining when sufficient water has evaporated.

In principle, for each 500 feet above sea level, the temperature to which candies and frostings are boiled should be decreased 1° F. from the temperature called for in sea-level recipes. However, another factor should be taken into account: at any given altitude, the atmospheric pressure frequently varies somewhat due to changing weather conditions. Thus, atmospheric conditions also affect the boiling point of water (see page 712). Therefore, it is a good practice to test the temperature of boiling water immediately before commencing to make boiled candy or frosting.

To test for the boiling point of water, attach the candy thermometer to a saucepan of water. Bring the water to a boil and let it boil for a few minutes, or until the thermometer indicator stops rising. The thermometer reading will give the current boiling point of water from which any necessary adjustments in the recipe can be calculated. For example, if the thermometer registers 210° F. (2° F. below 212° F., the boiling point of water at sea level) and the sea-level candy recipe to be followed calls for the syrup to be brought to 234° F., the temperature to which the syrup should be boiled will be decreased 2° F., or to 232° F.

It should be noted that candy thermometers are not always precisely accurate. Testing for the boiling point of water will accommodate any inaccuracy in the thermometer.

SHORTENED CAKES: Most sea-level cake recipes do not require adjustment when used at altitudes of less than 3,000 feet above sea level. At altitudes of 3,000 feet and above, adjustments may be necessary.

GUIDELINE ADJUSTMENTS TO SEA-LEVEL RECIPES
FOR SHORTENED CAKES BAKED AT HIGH ALTITUDES

| | Altitude of Baking Location | | |
Adjustment	3,000 feet	5,000 feet	7,000 feet
Baking Powder For each teaspoon, decrease	⅛ teaspoon	⅛ to ¼ teaspoon	¼ teaspoon
Sugar For each cup, decrease	0 to 1 tablespoon	0 to 2 tablespoons	1 to 3 tablespoons
Liquid For each cup, increase	1 to 2 tablespoons	2 to 4 tablespoons	3 to 4 tablespoons

At high altitudes, cakes made using sea-level recipes may rise excessively due to less atmospheric pressure. This overexpansion stretches the cell structure of the cake, causing coarse texture or causing the cake to fall if the cells break. A decrease in the leavening agent usually will correct this problem. Also, an increase in baking temperature by 15° F. to 25° F. will help set the cake structure before it collapses.

Faster and excessive evaporation of liquid in cakes baked at high altitudes causes dryness and a higher concentration of sugar, resulting in a weakened cell structure. (One of the functions of sugar in cake batter is to increase tenderness; see The Functions of Ingredients in Batters and Doughs, page 33.) This problem may be alleviated by a reduction in sugar and/or an increase in liquid. Because eggs help strengthen cell structure, the addition of an egg or an egg yolk may be warranted.

Fat, like sugar, weakens cell structure. Therefore, in a very rich cake, a reduction of fat by 1 to 2 tablespoons per cup may be part of the solution.

The chart, above, gives ranges for adjustments in baking powder, sugar, and liquid for shortened cakes baked at designated high altitudes. It is suggested that the smaller adjustments be used when first modifying a recipe.

ANGEL FOOD AND SPONGE CAKES: Air is one of the primary leavening agents in angel food and sponge cakes (see page 517). Much of the air in these cakes is incorporated by the inclusion of numerous beaten egg whites. At high altitudes, air incorporation can be reduced in these cakes by beating the egg whites only until soft peaks fall over, and not until they are stiff. An increase in flour by 1 or 2 tablespoons, a reduction in sugar by 1 or 2 tablespoons, and an increase in baking temperature are other suggested modifications.

QUICK BREADS: To adjust sea-level recipes for baking cake-type quick breads at high altitudes, follow the recommendations for Shortened Cakes, above.

Biscuit and muffin-type quick bread recipes generally need no alteration for use in high altitudes due to the resilience of their cell structure, which deters overexpansion. However, due to inadequate neutralization, baking powder and baking soda can sometimes produce a bitter or alkaline taste in these products baked at high altitudes. If this occurs, flavor generally can be enhanced by a slight decrease in these leavening agents.

YEAST BREADS: Yeast breads rise more rapidly at high altitudes. Since a shorter rising period reduces the desired time for development of flavor, it is particularly advisable to let the dough rise twice before shaping. Be careful to allow the dough to rise only until doubled in bulk (see Raising Dough, page 415).

Flour is generally drier in high, dry locations, making the flour capable of greater liquid absorption. As a result, less flour may be required at higher elevations.

COOKIES: While many sea-level cookie recipes may be used without adjustment at high altitudes, slight adjustments often improve the quality of the end results. Possible adjustments include slight increases in baking temperature, liquid, and flour; and slight decreases in baking powder or baking soda, sugar, and fat.

PIECRUST: Sea-level piecrust recipes usually do not require modification for use at high altitudes. However, slightly more liquid may be needed due to the general occurrence of drier flour in higher elevations.

PUDDINGS AND CREAM PIE FILLINGS: At altitudes above 5,000 feet, puddings and cream pie fillings made in a double boiler do not reach a high enough temperature to achieve maximum gelatinization of cornstarch or flour ingredients used as thickeners. Therefore, in locations above 5,000 feet, these products should be made in a saucepan over direct heat.

HOME-CANNED PRODUCTS: Altitude is a critical factor in the safe canning of foods at every altitude. Length of processing time in boiling-water bath canning and pounds of pressure in pressure canning are determined, in part, by the altitude of the canning location. The Canning chapter (pages 700–783) contains detailed information on this subject.

NOTE: Recipes specifically written for use at high altitudes are available. Contact the local Cooperative Extension Service office serving your county for assistance in securing such recipes.

Several excellent high-altitude recipe booklets have been published by Colorado State University Cooperative Extension. Copies may be secured at reasonable prices. For information, write:

Cooperative Extension Resource Center
115 General Services Building
Colorado State University
Fort Collins, Colorado 80523

TO USE HERBS

WHAT ARE HERBS? There is not a clear-cut consensus as to the definition of an herb (pronounced "erb" in the United States, and "herb" in England). Herbalists, lexicographers, botanists, and culinarians vary in their opinions as to what makes an herb an herb—particularly when contrasting herbs with spices.

As applied to culinary use, I define herbs and spices, as follows:

> **Herbs:** The fresh or dried green leaves of certain plants used for flavoring foods.
>
> **Spices:** The pungently flavored roots, stems, bark, seeds, buds, or fruit of certain plants and trees used for seasoning foods.

Strictly speaking, by these definitions dillweed and fennel weed are herbs, while dill seed and fennel seed are spices. However, dill seed and fennel seed often are categorized as herbs along with the leaves of these plants. I plead "culinary license" in siding with these exceptions in my own definitions.

Herbalists frequently label certain flowers as herbs based upon their aromatic, cosmetic, or medicinal utility. However, for culinary purposes, I prefer to exclude edible flowers from designation as herbs (see Edible Flowers, page 381).

Since ancient times, both herbs and spices have been highly valued for their medicinal, aromatic, cosmetic, and culinary uses as well as for their beauty. In early history, they also were employed in religious rites and were steeped in symbolism. Herbs, an essential part of Roman gardens, were cultivated, studied, and widely used in monasteries for many centuries.

By the 1400's, herb gardens had become quite widespread.

Herbs and spices continue to play a central role in modern-day life, primarily as flavor-enhancers for food. While spices have been consistently prized and heavily used, especially in sweet, baked goods and desserts, herbs are enjoying a groundswell of new popularity in everyday cooking in the Middle West and across the nation.

In the agricultural Heartland, the pleasure of herb gardening is undergoing a renaissance, buoyed by herb study clubs which focus on both the cultivation of herbs and their use in cooking. The nutritional benefits derived from the substitution of herbs for food flavorings high in fat and cholesterol have given further impetus to the resurgent interest in herb cookery.

COOKING WITH HERBS: In cooking, herbs may be used fresh or dried. Fresh herbs are definitely preferable because a measure of characteristic flavor and aroma, as well as potency, is lost when herbs are dried. This is particularly apparent when subtle, delicately flavored herbs, such as chervil and summer savory, are dried. Another hazard in using dried herbs is their relatively short shelf life of approximately 9 to 12 months. When kept too long, herbs lose much of their individualistic flavor and aroma, deteriorating to a grasslike state. To best retard this deterioration, freshly dried and crushed herbs should be placed in tightly covered jars or bottles and stored in a dark, dry, cool place.

In general, fresh and dried herbs may be used interchangeably if the proportions are altered. Use 3 portions of fresh herbs to 1 portion of dried herbs; in other words:

3 teaspoons (1 tablespoon) fresh herbs =
  1 teaspoon dried herbs.

Be prudent and cautious about using multiple herbs to flavor the same dish. While many herbs such as parsley, chives, and chervil, are successfully used in combination with other herbs, be careful when it comes to using more than one predominant herb in a single dish. And avoid overwhelming the flavor of a dish with too great a quantity of herbs. Properly used, herbs should complement, not overtake.

To use dried, crushed (not ground) herbs that can be removed from a dish after cooking, place them in a cheesecloth bag (page 44).

The Herb Chart on pages 40–43 suggests some of the foods which popularly used herbs complement.

TO SNIP FRESH HERBS: Fresh herbs are commonly snipped into tiny pieces for use in cooking. First, wash the sprigs of herbs in cold water and place them in a colander to drain. Bounce the herbs in the colander to expel as much water as possible. Place the herbs, single layer, between layers of paper towels to dry.

Using your fingers or kitchen scissors, remove the leaves from the stems of the herbs; discard the stems. Place the leaves on a cutting board, the top of which is at least 1¼ inches higher than the counter surface (to allow space for the scissoring procedure, to follow). Holding the kitchen scissors parallel with the top of the cutting board, while containing the herb leaves with your free hand, snip the leaves to the desired fineness, cutting through the entire little pile of herbs with each cut of the scissors.

An exception to this procedure is the method used to snip chives. The structure of chive leaves allows them to be cut into uniform pieces using standard scissor-cutting procedure.

Snipped fresh herbs may be stored in the refrigerator in small, airtight containers for 2 to 4 days.

TO MAKE A FRESH BOUQUET GARNI: A fresh bouquet garni is an assortment of selected fresh herb sprigs, tied together and added during cooking to dishes, such as soups and stews, for flavor enhancement. It is removed from the dish and discarded after the cooking period.

While the traditional bouquet garni usually consists of parsley, thyme, and a bay leaf, any single herb or combination of herbs may be used, and any number of sprigs may be included. Commonly, bouquets garnis are made of 2 to 10 sprigs. Among the herbs often included in bouquets garnis are:

Parsley	Marjoram
Thyme	Savory
Bay leaves	Chervil
Chives	Tarragon
Basil	Celery leaves

(Note: Celery leaves are usually classified nowadays as a vegetable.)

To make a bouquet garni, gather the herb sprigs in your hand as you would a bouquet of flowers. Using white cotton string, securely tie the bouquet together at the stem end of the herb sprigs. When preparing herb sprigs for inclusion in a bouquet garni, leave sufficiently long stems for tying so the leafy ends of the sprigs can fan out, allowing the cooking liquids to flow more freely through the herbs.

Alternatively, the fresh herbs may be tied loosely in a cheesecloth bag (page 44).

TO DRY HERBS: While it is preferable to use fresh herbs, the relatively short Midwest growing season permits fresh herbs from the garden only during a few summer months. Even though a greater variety of fresh herbs is available nowadays in good supermarkets, the quality is often disappointing and the price quite high. Midwest herb gardeners rely heavily upon their supply of dried summer herbs for use in cold-weather dishes. Anyway, preparing dried herbs is fun and the extra supply makes much-appreciated holiday gifts.

While herbs may be dried in an electric dehydrator, the instructions that follow are for drying herbs by hanging. In addition to the fact that most households are not equipped with an electric dehydrator, the hanging procedure results in equally fine herbs for cooking and is a more satisfactory method of handling large quantities of harvested herbs. Most herbs, except chives, may be successfully dried by hanging.

Herbs are at their height of flavor when the plants are mature, but just *before* they bloom.

The flower buds should be pruned. Despite vigilance, if herb plants are allowed to bloom, the blooms should be snipped off (unless being reserved for use as edible flowers (see page 382).

To prepare herbs for drying, cut off branches of the plants and use extra-long pieces of twine to tie them in small bundles. Tie the bundles near the bottom of the branches in order to allow as much air as possible to circulate around the leaves while drying. The diameter of the branch bundles, where tied, should not exceed approximately 2 ½ inches after tying. Leave the long ends of twine uncut, and use them to tie each bundle *upside down* on a clothesline located preferably in the basement, or, alternatively, in the garage. The bundles should not be in direct sunlight which might cause fading, and should be protected from dust which would cause the final product to be dirty.

Allow the bundles to hang until the leaves are dry and brittle—approximately one month, depending upon the dryness of the basement (or other hanging location). Keep the basement well ventilated and as free as possible from dampness. Let the bundles hang only as long as it takes the leaves to thoroughly dry. A measure of flavor, color, and aroma will be lost each week they are allowed to hang thereafter.

Process one bundle at a time on a large table covered with waxed paper. Use kitchen scissors or your fingers to carefully remove the leaves, discarding the stems. Place a small quantity of leaves in a large bowl and crush them in your hands repeatedly until crumbled to tiny pieces. Transfer the processed herbs to another bowl.

Repeat the procedure until all the dried leaves are processed. Place a small quantity of the processed herbs in a small airtight bottle to keep in the kitchen for immediate use. Place the remainder in airtight, glass jars or bottles and store them in a dark, dry, cool place such as a metal cabinet in the basement. A large plateful of charcoal placed in the cabinet will help to retain dryness. After 9 to 12 months, stored dried herbs lose their original potency and flavor.

HERB CHART

	SOUPS STEWS	SALADS	MEATS	POULTRY
BASIL	Tomato, Vegetable, Chicken, and Minestrone Soups; Beef, Pork, Veal and Bratwurst Stews	Greens; Vegetable; Tomato and Onion; Chicken; Shellfish; Italian and Vinaigrette Salad Dressings	Beef, Pork, Veal, and Lamb; Meat Casseroles; Swiss Steak; Italian Meat and Sauce Dishes	Baked Chicken; Sautéed Chicken Breasts; Turkey Dishes
BAY LEAVES	Vegetable Beef Soup; Beef and Chicken Broth; Corn Chowder; Bratwurst, Beef, and Fish Stews	Seldom Used	Beef; Beef and Noodles; Sauerbraten; Italian Meat Sauces; Lamb	Certain Chicken Dishes such as Chicken Cacciatore
CHERVIL	Vegetable and Cream Soups; Broths; Decoration for Most Soups; Fish Soups and Stews; Meat and Vegetable Stews	Vegetable; Chicken; Turkey; Greens; Sliced Tomatoes; Cottage Cheese; Egg; Potato	Beef; Veal; Béarnaise Sauce	Baked Chicken; Chicken Casseroles; Cornish Game Hens; Turkey Dishes; Stuffings
CHIVES	Vegetable and Chicken Noodle Soups; Soup Topping; Decoration for Many Soups and Stews	Greens; Vegetable; Cucumber; Potato; Cottage Cheese; Avocado; Vinaigrette Salad Dressing	Ground Beef and Pork Dishes; Ham Salad; Veal	Chicken Breasts; Turkey Casseroles
CORIANDER (Cilantro; Chinese Parsley)	Tomato Soup; Garnish for Chicken and Pea Soups	Greens; Vegetable; Bell Pepper; Tomato	Garnish for Beef and Pork; Lamb; Smoked Meats	Cornish Game Hens; Chicken
DILLWEED	Cucumber, Vegetable, Tomato, Split Pea, and Chicken Soups; Chowders	Cucumber; Shrimp; Cottage Cheese; Cabbage; Potato; Vegetable; Fish; Salad Dressings	Cold Sliced Beef; Veal; Lamb	Chicken Casseroles; Turkey Dishes
FENNEL WEED	Tomato, Cucumber, and Lentil Soups; Meat and Fish Stews	Shrimp; Other Shellfish; Fish; Green Bean; Pasta; Greens; Salad Dressings	Beef; Pork; Lamb	Chicken; Goose; Duck
MARJORAM	Chicken, Onion, Fish, Tomato, and Potato Soups; Meat and Vegetable Stews	Greens; Vegetable; Cottage Cheese; Cabbage; Fish; Shellfish; Chicken; Salad Dressings	Veal; Ground Beef Dishes; Braised Beef Dishes; Lamb; Meat Sauces	Baked Chicken; Turkey; Chicken and Turkey Casseroles; Duck; Stuffings

FISH SHELLFISH	WILD GAME	VEGETABLES	EGGS CHEESE	BREADS
Halibut; Baked and Poached Fish; Salmon; Tuna; All Shellfish	Quail; Venison; Rabbit; Duck; Moose	Tomatoes; Zucchini; Potatoes; Lima Beans; Peas; Corn; Carrots; Asparagus; Broccoli	Scrambled Eggs; Omelets; Pasta and Cheese Dishes; Cheese Spreads; Combined with Grated Parmesan or Romano Cheese; Cottage Cheese; Cream Cheese; Cheese Sauces	Yeast Breads; Muffins; Toasted Herb Bread; Sautéed Toast Points
Poached Salmon; Poached Shellfish; Shrimp Dishes	Braised Pheasant; Venison; Rabbit; Antelope; Grouse; Partridge; Quail	Potatoes; Tomatoes; Beets; Sauerkraut	Rarely Used	Not Used
Mild Fish Fillets; Baked Fish Dishes; Fish Sauces	Partridge; Quail; Pheasant; Woodcock; Wild Turkey; Stuffings	Carrots; Spinach; Potatoes; Peas; Zucchini; Tomatoes; Cabbage; Squash	Omelets; Scrambled Eggs; Baked Egg Dishes; Cottage Cheese; Cream Cheese; Cheese Dips and Spreads; Cheese Sauces	Toasted Herb Bread
Salmon; Most Baked and Broiled Fish; Shellfish Dishes; Green Sauce	Quail; Rabbit; Partridge; Wild Turkey	Potatoes; Creamed Peas; Tomatoes; Lima Beans; Corn; Onions; Artichokes	Omelets; All Egg Dishes; Cheese Sauces; Cottage Cheese; Cream Cheese	Toasted Herb Bread
All Shellfish	Quail; Grouse	Corn; Tomatoes; Onions; Beets; Potatoes; Salsa	Cream Cheese Spreads; Cottage Cheese	Quick Breads
Salmon; Tuna; All Fish and Shellfish; Green Sauce	Prairie Chicken; Wild Turkey Breast	Potatoes; Parsnips; Carrots; Cucumbers; Peas; Green Beans; Brussels Sprouts; Cauliflower	Baked Egg Dishes; Creamed Eggs; Cottage Cheese; Casseroles with Cheese Sauces; Swiss and Cheddar Cheese Spreads; Cheese Sauces	Yeast Breads; Bagels; Croutons; Toasted Herb Bread; Sautéed Toast Points
Broiled Fish Fillets; Salmon; Mackerel; Shellfish; Fish Sauces	Duck; Goose; Moose	Tomatoes; Cucumbers; Green Beans; Cabbage; Onions; Zucchini; Potatoes	Vegetable Omelets; Baked Egg Dishes; Cottage Cheese; Cheese Spreads	Yeast Breads; Toasted Herb Bread
Tuna, Swordfish, and Halibut Steaks; Salmon; Lobster; Crab Dishes; Fish Sauces	Duck; Goose; Wild Turkey; Venison; Rabbit; Elk; Stuffings	Green Beans; Broccoli; Asparagus; Brussels Sprouts; Eggplant; Sauerkraut; Corn; Carrots	Egg Dishes; Scrambled Eggs; Omelets; Cheese Dishes; Cheese Spreads	Bagels; Toasted Herb Bread

HERB CHART (continued)

	SOUPS STEWS	SALADS	MEATS	POULTRY
MINT	Split Pea, Cold Cucumber, Lentil, Black Bean, and Cream of Vegetable Soups	Decoration for Fruit Salads; Melon; Cucumber; Fish; Mint-flavored Mayonnaise for Fruit Salads	Lamb and Lamb Sauces; Veal Sauces; Mint Jelly for Lamb Garnish	Cold Sliced Chicken and Turkey
OREGANO	Cream of Broccoli, Tomato, Vegetable Beef, and Minestrone Soups; Chowders; Gumbos; Meat Stews	Vegetable; Fish; Shellfish	Meat Loaf; Spanish Rice; Italian Meatballs and Sauces; Veal; Pork; Meat Stuffings	Chicken
PARSLEY	Potato, Vegetable, Wild Rice, and Tomato Soups; Beef and Chicken Broth; Corn Chowder; Chili; Beef, Pork, and Veal Stews	Greens; Vegetable; Wild Rice; Chicken; Turkey; Fish; Egg; Italian and Vinaigrette Salad Dressings	All Meats; Meat Roulades; Ground Beef, Veal, Pork, and Ham Dishes; Swiss Steak; Italian Meat and Sauce Dishes; Béarnaise Sauce	Baked Chicken; Chicken and Turkey Dishes; Duck; Goose; Plate Decoration for All Poultry
ROSEMARY	Pea, Chicken, and Potato Soups; Fish Chowder; Bratwurst Stews; Meat and Vegetable Stews	Beef, Pork, and Lamb; Vegetable; Greens; Fish; Shellfish; Salad Dressings	Beef; Roast Pork; Lamb; Ham; Meat Sauces and Gravies	Chicken; Turkey; Duck; Cornish Game Hens; Stuffings
SAGE	Chicken, Turkey; Tomato, and Fish Soups; Chowders; Pork Stews	Cottage Cheese; Chicken; Turkey; Duck; Goose; Pork; Asparagus; Artichoke; Salad Dressings	Pork Sausage; Roast Pork; Ground Pork Dishes; Lamb; Sauces and Gravies	Stuffings for Chicken and Turkey; Chicken and Turkey Casseroles; Duck; Goose; Sauces and Gravies
SUMMER SAVORY	Vegetable, Onion, Pea, Lentil, and Chicken Noodle Soups; Broths; Meat and Vegetable Stews	Vegetable; Greens; Cabbage; Potato; Tomato; Cucumber; Poultry	Pork Sausage; Beef; Pork; Veal; Lamb; Calf's Liver; Sauces and Gravies	Baked Chicken; Turkey Casseroles; Cornish Game Hens; Stuffings
TARRAGON	Tomato, Vegetable, Chicken, Dried Bean, Pea, and Cream Soups; Chowders; Meat Stews	Zucchini; Green Bean; Lettuce and Vegetable; Tomato; Fish; Shellfish; Salad Dressings	Beef; Pork; Veal; Lamb; Béarnaise Sauce	Baked and Creamed Chicken; Turkey Dishes; Duck; Goose; Sauces and Gravies
THYME	Vegetable, Pea, Chicken, Beef, and Tomato Soups; Fish Chowders; Gumbos	Greens; Fish; Shellfish; Green Bean; Tomato; Chicken; Turkey; Vegetable; Salad Dressing	Beef; Stuffed Cabbage Leaves and Stuffed Onions using Ground Beef; Lamb; Veal; Barbecue Sauce; Sauces and Gravies	Scalloped Chicken; Turkey Casseroles; Baked Chicken; Corn Bread Dressing; Wild Rice Dressing

FISH SHELLFISH	WILD GAME	VEGETABLES	EGGS CHEESE	BREADS
Baked and Broiled Fish; Fish Sauces; Salmon	Cold Sliced Wild Turkey Breast	Peas; Celery; Carrots; Potatoes; Green Beans; Spinach; Eggplant	Cottage Cheese; Cream Cheese	Seldom Used
All Fish; Fish Sauces; Scalloped Oysters	Venison; Pheasant; Dove; Antelope	Tomatoes; Mushrooms; Eggplant; Onions; Asparagus; Broccoli; Potatoes; Squash; Bell Peppers	Scrambled Eggs; Omelets; Pizza; Cheese Sauces; Cheese Spreads	Yeast Breads
Baked Fish; Tuna; Salmon; Swordfish and Halibut Steaks; Escargots; Scalloped Oysters; Most Shellfish; Green Sauce; Caper Sauce	Goose, Duck, and Venison Pâtés; Woodcock; Quail; Pheasant; Baked Duck; Goose; Grouse; Stuffings	Carrots; Potatoes; Tomatoes; Beets; Cauliflower; Sautéed Onions and Mushrooms; Most Vegetables	Garnish for Deviled Eggs and Egg Dishes; All Egg Dishes; Cottage Cheese; Cheese Dips and Spreads; All Cheese Dishes; Combined with Grated Parmesan or Romano Cheese	Yeast Breads; Dumplings; Toasted Sesame Bread; Toasted Parmesan-Parsley Bread; Toasted Herb Bread; Sautéed Toast Points
Full-flavored Fish; Halibut; Tuna; Salmon; All Shellfish	Venison; Elk; Moose; Goose; Antelope; Duck; Rabbit; Dove	Cauliflower; Kohlrabi; Carrots; Onions; Zucchini; Red Bell Peppers; Turnips	Baked Egg Dishes; Selected Cheese Dishes; Cheese Sauces	Yeast Breads; Corn Bread; Biscuits; Dumplings; Toasted Herb Bread
All Fish; Stuffings for Fish; Special Flavoring for Shellfish	Partridge; Prairie Chicken; Grouse; Pheasant; Quail; Duck; Goose; Stuffings	Brussels Sprouts; Tomatoes; Green Beans; Artichokes; Eggplant; Zucchini; Carrots; Celery	Creamed Eggs; Egg Casseroles; Cheese Spreads; Baked Dishes with Cheese; Swiss Cheese Sauces	Yeast Breads; Buns; Dumplings; Corn Bread; Corn Fritters
All Baked and Broiled Fish; All Shellfish; Fish Sauces	Partridge; Quail; Grouse; Prairie Chicken; Pheasant	Carrots; Peas; Green Beans; Zucchini; Cauliflower; Rutabagas; Asparagus; Lima Beans; Artichokes	Scrambled Eggs; Omelets; Soufflés; Cream Cheese; Cheese Dips; Casseroles with Cheese	Dumplings; Biscuits; Toasted Herb Bread
Baked and Broiled Fish; Poached Fish; Lobster; Fish Sauces	Elk; Moose; Duck; Goose; Pheasant; Partridge	Green Beans; Tomatoes; Asparagus; Kohlrabi; Sautéed Onions and Mushrooms; Spinach; Beets	Egg Dishes; Soufflés; Cheese Casseroles; Cottage Cheese; Cheese Spreads	Croutons; Toasted Herb Bread
Poached Salmon; Baked and Broiled Fish; Shellfish Dishes; Fish Sauces; Fish and Shellfish Spreads	Venison; Duck; Quail; Goose; Rabbit; Pheasant; Partridge; Wild Turkey; Stuffings	Onions; Potatoes; Carrots; Tomatoes; Asparagus; Eggplant; Sauerkraut; Spinach; Cauliflower	Egg Dishes; Scrambled Eggs; Cottage Cheese; Casseroles with Cheese; Cheese Dips and Spreads	Yeast Breads; Muffins; Dumplings; Rolls; Corn Bread; Biscuits; Toasted Herb Bread

TO MAKE A CHEESECLOTH BAG FOR HERBS OR SPICES

To make a cheesecloth bag to hold herbs or spices that are to be removed from the dish after cooking and then discarded, cut 4 layers of plain, untreated cheesecloth into a square large enough to hold the herbs or spices to be used (usually about 7 inches square). Draw the corners of the cheesecloth together and tie the bag very securely with white, cotton sewing thread. Do not pull the bag too tightly, leaving space for the liquid to flow freely through the herbs or spices.

TO USE A MEAT THERMOMETER

Meat thermometers are used to gauge the internal temperature of meats and fowl during roasting or baking to determine degree of doneness.

MEATS: Insert the meat thermometer into the meat—preferably before commencing to cook—positioning the pointed tip of the thermometer at the center of the thickest part of the meat, not touching bone or fat.

To help in determining how deep to insert the thermometer, hold the thermometer against the side of the meat with the pointed tip at the depth which will reach the center of the thickest part of the meat; then, place your thumb on the thermometer stem at the top surface of the meat. While continuing to hold your thumb on the thermometer stem, insert the thermometer into the thickest part of the meat to the depth of your thumb.

WHOLE FOWL: Insert the meat thermometer into one of the inner thigh areas near the breast—preferably before commencing to cook—making certain that the tip of the thermometer is not touching bone.

POSITION ADJUSTMENT: During cooking, meat thermometers often work away from their original position. Therefore, when the thermometer reaches the temperature for desired doneness, push it deeper into the meat or fowl and watch the gauge to see whether or not the temperature drops. If it does, additional cooking time will be required.

INSTANT THERMOMETERS: Small, instant thermometers are convenient and helpful for certain applications. They register the temperature of meats, fowl, and other foods in just a few seconds and are used toward the end of cooking. They are not left in food in the oven.

The best and most common type of instant thermometer has a 1-inch dial head and a very thin probe, allowing a minimum loss of juices when the flesh of meats or fowl is pierced. Instant thermometers make it easy to quickly find the temperature at two or more locations in a piece of meat or a fowl.

In general, a regular meat thermometer is the most practical for use with many meats and with whole fowl because it allows the internal temperature to be monitored throughout the cooking period with only one invasion of the flesh.

TO BLANCH

"Blanch" means to dip briefly in boiling water, generally for the purpose of loosening the skin of a food for peeling or for the purpose of cooking briefly. To blanch a food, bring water to a rapid boil in the bottom of a blancher or in a saucepan or kettle. If using a blancher, place the food in the top of the blancher and lower it into the boiling water. If using a saucepan or kettle, drop the food directly into the boiling water. Leave the boiling water over heat, and use a timer to accurately time the blanching process. Follow the recipe for suggested blanching time.

To blanch for peeling, tomatoes require approximately 45 seconds and peaches require approximately 1 minute in boiling water. Blanching times will vary somewhat, depending upon the ripeness and variety of the produce. During the blanching process, use a wooden mixing spoon to turn over foods that float in order that the boiling water reaches all surfaces.

When the blanching time is completed, immediately remove the food from the boiling water and immerse it in cold water to stop the cooking.

TO SEED AND CORE TOMATOES

In general, when seeded and cored tomatoes are used in food preparation, the tomatoes should be blanched (page 44) and peeled prior to seeding and coring.

To seed and core tomatoes, first quarter the tomatoes lengthwise. Then, using your thumb, remove and discard the seeds and the pouches containing them. Using a small paring knife, cut away and discard all white and greenish core and membrane. Only red tomato flesh should remain.

TO PARE CARROTS

The quickest and best way to remove the thin outer skin of carrots is to use a vegetable parer. When carrots are pared with a vegetable parer, their round shape is retained, the pared surface of the carrots is smooth, and very little of the flesh is pared away. When a vegetable parer is not available, carrots may also be pared by scraping them with the blade of a sharp paring knife.

TO PARE AND CORE CUCUMBERS

TO PARE CUCUMBERS: Cut a slice off both ends of the cucumbers to trim. Then, use a vegetable parer to pare.

TO CORE CUCUMBERS: Cut the cucumbers in half lengthwise. Using a serrated-type apple corer, scoop out the seeds and cores, leaving only the cucumber flesh.

TO PEEL PEARL ONIONS

Place pearl onions in a saucepan; cover with boiling water and let stand 2 minutes. Drain the onions and immediately immerse them in cold water to halt the cooking process. Drain the onions in a colander. With the aid of a small paring knife, peel the onions.

TO EXTRACT ONION JUICE

Over waxed paper, rub a peeled onion back and forth over a metal grater. Pour off and save the onion juice that accumulates on the waxed paper. Reserve the remaining grated onion pulp for other uses.

TO CHOP RAISINS AND OTHER DRIED AND CANDIED FRUITS

Use a wet knife or wet kitchen scissors to chop raisins and other dried and candied fruits. A wet cutting tool will minimize the problem of stickiness.

TO DUST NUTS, RAISINS, AND FRUITS WITH FLOUR

To help prevent nuts, raisins, and chopped fruits from sinking to the bottom of cakes and breads, dust them with flour before adding them to the batter. For dusting, use flour from the *measured* flour in the recipe before any other ingredients, such as baking soda or baking powder, are added. Measure 1 tablespoon flour to dust 2 cups nuts and/or raisins. To dust damp, chopped fruit, measure 2 tablespoons flour for each 2 cups chopped fruit. Place nuts and/or raisins and/or chopped fruit in a mixing bowl; sprinkle with flour and stir until evenly coated.

TO PLUMP RAISINS AND OTHER DRIED FRUITS

Place measured raisins or other dried fruit in a saucepan; add hot water to cover. Cover the pan. Bring to a boil over high heat. Immediately remove from the heat. Let stand, covered, until cool. Drain in a colander or sieve. The juice may be retained for serving over fresh fruit, braising pork, or other uses.

TO GRATE PARMESAN AND ROMANO CHEESES

Use a food processor to grate Parmesan and Romano cheeses. Cut the cheese into 1-inch-square chunks; using the steel blade, grate 1 cup at a time, using on/off turns until the cheese is of desired fineness.

A hand-operated, drum-style grater (see illustration, page 50) is sometimes used to "grate" Parmesan and Romano cheeses. While this kitchen tool reduces the cheese to a consistency generally compatible with its intended use, the tool actually finely shreds the cheese rather than grating it.

TO SHRED FRESH HORSERADISH

Purchase firm horseradish root which is not sprouting and does not have greenish tinges. Pare only as much of the root as you plan to use. Shred the pared root medium-finely to finely. Freshly shredded horseradish quickly loses some of its pungency and browns in color; therefore, it should be shredded shortly before serving unless it is to be prepared with vinegar (see To Make Prepared Horseradish, right column) or added to a sauce. To store unpared horseradish root, dampen it very slightly, wrap it tightly in plastic wrap, and refrigerate.

TO MAKE PREPARED HORSERADISH

Cut horseradish root into 1-inch pieces. In a food processor, mince the horseradish root (see Note). Uncover the processor bowl away from your face to avoid the pungent aroma. Place the minced horseradish root in a small glass mixing bowl. Add enough white wine vinegar to moisten the horseradish. Add a dash of sugar and a dash of salt; stir to combine.

Place the Prepared Horseradish in a glass jar; cover and refrigerate. Best when eaten within 1 to 2 weeks.

NOTE: If a food processor is not available, the horseradish root may be grated or shredded finely by hand, using a simple grater/shredder kitchen tool.

CREAMED PREPARED HORSERADISH: Follow Prepared Horseradish recipe, above, adding unwhipped whipping cream to the other ingredients to moisten the horseradish.

TO USE FRESH GINGER

To use fresh ginger, pare the ginger root and then grate or slice it. Fresh ginger may be stored in the refrigerator in a zipper-seal plastic bag up to approximately 1 month.

TO CUT CITRUS ZEST

Zest (see definition, page 27) is cut from the thin, colored, outer part of the peel of citrus fruits. To cut citrus zest, first wash the fruit well, removing any brand names or other markings which may be stamped on the surface. Pull a citrus zesting tool (see illustration) firmly across the unpeeled fruit to cut tiny curls of zest. If a citrus zester is not available, a small, handheld, metal shredder may be used. When cutting zest, try to exclude any of the white membrane which lies underneath the colored, outer portion of the peel. Not only does the white membrane have a bitter taste, but also, inclusion of any of it will generally make the zest too thick.

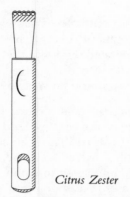
Citrus Zester

To cut pieces of zest rather than tiny curls, use a vegetable parer or a sharp paring knife.

If not using zest immediately, place it in a very small sauce dish, cover securely with plastic wrap, and refrigerate to retain its moisture, pliability, and color. Zest may be satisfactorily stored in this manner only for a brief period of time—no longer than 1 day.

TO GRATE CITRUS RIND

Select unblemished fruit to use for grating citrus rind (see definition, page 25). Wash the fruit well, removing any brand names or other markings which may be stamped on the surface. Leave the fruit whole, and use a small, handheld, metal, prong-type grater—not a shredder—to grate (see definition, page 23) the rind. Grate only the thin, colored, outer part of the fruit's peel. Try not to include any of the white membrane beneath the outer, colored portion of the peel. The white membrane has a bitter taste and is not the flavor desired when grated citrus rind is called for in a recipe.

When finely grated rind is specified, as is often the case, use a very finely pronged grater (see illustration). Grate over waxed paper and use a paring knife or a tiny kitchen brush (such as a toothbrush reserved only for use as a kitchen tool) to help remove grated rind that

does not fall onto the waxed paper and builds up between the tiny prongs. One medium-sized lemon or 1 very small orange will yield about 1 teaspoon of finely grated rind.

*Finely
Pronged Grater*

If grated citrus rind will not be used immediately, place it in a very small sauce dish, cover securely with plastic wrap, and refrigerate to retain its moisture and color. Grated citrus rind may be satisfactorily stored in this manner up to 1 day.

TO SECTION ORANGES
AND GRAPEFRUIT

Using a small, sharp, thin-bladed knife, cut a small slice off both the stem and blossom ends of the fruit. Then, cut away the peel, including all white membrane on the outer surface of the fruit meat, cutting circularly around the fruit to preserve its round shape.

To cut away sections, make lengthwise cuts along both sides of the membranes which divide the sections, cutting to the core of the fruit. Carefully remove each released section as it is cut away; remove any seeds. Properly sectioned fruit should be free of all membrane.

Cut away the sections over a bowl in order to retain any juice which may be released from the fruit during the cutting process. With your hands, squeeze the fruit which remains after the sections have been removed to extract additional juice.

TO MAKE DRIED BREAD CUBES

To make dried bread cubes, use a type of sliced, fresh bread which is rather firm. Do not use the very soft-style bread. Lay the bread slices single layer on waxed paper to dry slightly before cutting into cubes. This will help prevent crushing the bread when slicing and will aid in cutting more uniform cubes. Using a very sharp, thin-bladed knife, cut each slice into ½-inch-square cubes. The bread crusts may or may not be cut away before cutting the cubes. (Generally, the crusts are not removed when preparing bread cubes for stuffings.) Place the bread cubes single layer on waxed paper. Let stand (uncovered) to dry at least 24 hours, turning the cubes with a spatula at least 3 times. When completely dry, use immediately or store in an airtight container for up to 3 days at room temperature.

TO MAKE CROUTONS

PLAIN CROUTONS
1 cup ½-inch-square fresh, white bread cubes with crusts removed (about 2 slices bread)
2 tablespoons butter, melted

Spread the fresh bread cubes single layer on waxed paper; let stand to dry at least 24 hours, turning occasionally with a spatula.

Preheat the broiler.

In a small saucepan, melt the butter over low heat. Remove from the heat. Add the dried bread cubes; using a spoon, toss lightly. Place the croutons single layer in a small, shallow baking pan; toast under the broiler until golden brown, turning several times to toast all sides of the cubes. Remove from the broiler and place pan on a wire rack; cool croutons, uncovered. Store in a covered jar up to 1 week in the refrigerator or up to 3 months in the freezer.

GARLIC CROUTONS: Follow the Plain Croutons recipe, above, except: simmer, briefly, ½ pressed garlic clove in the butter prior to tossing with the dried bread cubes. Or, add ⅛ teaspoon garlic powder to the melted butter.

ONION CROUTONS: Follow the Plain Croutons recipe, above, except: simmer, briefly, 1 teaspoon grated onions in the butter prior to tossing with the dried bread cubes. Or, add ⅛ teaspoon onion powder to the melted butter.

HERB CROUTONS: Follow the Plain Croutons recipe, above, except: add ¼ teaspoon dried parsley, leaf basil, leaf thyme, leaf tarragon, leaf chervil, dillweed, or other dried herb to the melted butter; stir to combine. If fresh herbs are used, add ¾ teaspoon fresh herbs to the melted butter. More than 1 herb may be used. Herbs may also be added to the melted butter just prior to tossing Garlic Croutons and Onion Croutons (recipes, above).

TO MAKE BREAD CRUMBS

DRIED BREAD CRUMBS
Cut fresh bread, including the crust, into small cubes. Spread single layer on waxed paper; let stand (uncovered) to dry at least 24 hours. Using a spatula, turn the bread cubes 2 or 3 times during the drying period. When the cubes are very dry, crumb them in a food processor or blender, or roll them with a rolling pin. One slice of bread makes approximately ¼ cup dried crumbs. Store in a covered jar up to 3 days at room temperature, up to 1 week in the refrigerator, or up to 3 months in the freezer.

FRESH BREAD CRUMBS
Tear slices of fresh bread into pieces approximately 1 inch square. Place up to 3 slices torn bread at a time in a food processor and process until crumbled finely. If a food processor is not available, pull small pieces of bread from the slices or from an unsliced loaf and crumble them between your fingers.

Use of the crust is optional, depending upon

its softness. One slice of bread makes approximately ½ cup fresh crumbs. Use immediately or store in a covered jar up to 1 week in the refrigerator or up to 3 months in the freezer.

TO MAKE, STORE, AND USE BUTTERED CRUMBS

BUTTERED CRACKER CRUMBS
¼ cup rolled cracker crumbs
   (6 Ritz crackers or 5 saltines)
1 tablespoon butter, melted

Using a rolling pin, roll the crackers medium-finely; set aside. In a small saucepan, melt the butter over low heat. Remove from the heat; add the crumbs and stir until the crumbs are evenly coated with butter.

BUTTERED BREAD CRUMBS: Follow the Buttered Cracker Crumbs recipe, substituting ¼ cup Dried Bread Crumbs (page 48) for rolled cracker crumbs.

STORING BUTTERED CRUMBS: For use within 3 days, buttered crumbs may be stored in a covered jar in the refrigerator. Otherwise, buttered crumbs store well in the freezer. Store in a tightly covered, labeled jar up to 3 months.

USING BUTTERED CRUMBS TO TOP CASSEROLE DISHES: When preparing casserole dishes topped with buttered crumbs, add the buttered-crumb topping just before baking to prevent the crumbs from becoming soggy. Approximately ¼ cup buttered crumbs will top a dish to be baked in a 2-quart round baking dish or a 7 × 11-inch baking dish.

TO CRUMB CORNFLAKES

Measure the cornflakes; transfer to a food processor or blender. Process a few seconds until the cornflakes are of desired texture. If using a blender, it may be necessary to stop the blender once or twice and shake the covered beaker to redistribute the unprocessed flakes. Approximately 2½ cups cornflakes makes ½ cup crumbs.

TO GRIND MOST FOODS OTHER THAN NUTS AND COFFEE BEANS

To grind (see definition, page 23) most foods other than nuts and coffee beans, use a hand-cranked food grinder, generally called a "meat grinder" although it is used to grind many foods in addition to meats (see illustration). Meat grinders come with coarse- and fine-blade fittings for adaptation to specific uses. Some meat grinders come with additional fittings such as a sausage stuffer.

Meat grinders reduce foods to small, fairly uniform fragments. Meat grinders do not shred or splinter food during grinding, and the ground food retains its original consistency quite well. For uniform size, shape, and texture, and for an attractive finished food, a meat grinder is a requisite tool in the preparation of many foods.

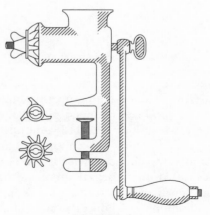

Meat Grinder

Although food processors often are used to chop foods, they generally are not well suited for grinding foods because often they do not cut foods into a uniform size and shape, and some foods may become paste-like or partially liquefy during processing.

TO PREPARE BROKEN, CHOPPED, GROUND, AND GRATED NUTS

BROKEN NUTS: Break nuts into pieces with your fingers. Broken nuts are more coarse in size than chopped nuts.

CHOPPED NUTS: Most nuts can be chopped in a hand-operated, rotary nut chopper with metal (not plastic) blades (see illustration). If you desire more finely chopped nuts, run the nuts through the chopper two or more times.

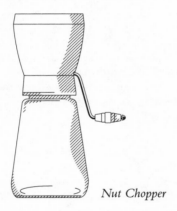

Nut Chopper

Almonds are very firm; therefore the use of slivered almonds for chopping simplifies the process and produces chopped pieces of more consistent size. Chop slivered almonds in a hand-operated rotary nut chopper. Run the nuts through the chopper twice if necessary.

Whole almonds, **Brazil nuts**, and **hazelnuts** are too firm to chop in a hand-operated rotary nut chopper. Chop these nuts in a food processor.

GROUND NUTS: Grind nuts in a food processor until very fine. Do not overprocess or nuts will form a butter. Nuts may also be ground in a

blender, although it is more difficult to achieve a consistent coarseness (some large pieces of nuts may remain unground while, simultaneously, other very small pieces turn to butter).

GRATED NUTS: Grate nuts in a hand-operated, drum-style grater (see illustration). Use a grater made of heavy-duty metal or plastic. Flimsy metal graters are not sturdy enough to grate nuts successfully. Ground nuts (see above) often may be substituted for grated nuts if they are ground carefully to prevent their becoming too oily and butterlike. Very firm nuts, such as almonds, Brazil nuts, and hazelnuts—especially when they are whole—are difficult to grate in a hand-operated grater, and it is recommended that they be ground in a food processor.

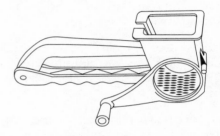

Drum-Style Grater

TO TOAST NUTS AND SEEDS

To toast shelled almonds, pine nuts, sesame seeds, or other nuts and seeds, spread the nuts or seeds in a shallow baking pan. Bake 6 minutes, or until lightly browned, at 350° F., turning once or twice with a spatula during the baking period. Watch closely during baking to prevent overbrowning.

TO TOAST HAZELNUTS AND REMOVE SKINS: Shell hazelnuts and place them in a shallow baking pan. Bake 20 minutes at 350° F., turning once or twice with a spatula during the baking period. When cool enough to handle, remove the skins by rubbing the warm hazelnuts between your fingers or in a tea towel. It is extremely difficult (and for most uses, unnecessary) to remove every bit of skin covering the hazelnuts; however, perfectionists may use a small paring knife to help remove little pieces of skin that do not rub off easily.

TO SHELL, SKIN, AND BOIL CHESTNUTS

To shell and skin chestnuts, use a small, sharp knife to cut a cross on the flat side of the chestnuts. Place, single layer, in a baking pan. Bake 15 minutes at 450° F. Remove the shells and inner skin while the chestnuts are still warm.

To boil chestnuts, place shelled and skinned chestnuts in a saucepan; add water to cover. Boil, covered, about 20 minutes until tender; drain.

TO BLANCH ALMONDS

Shelled almonds may be blanched for the purpose of removing the skin that tightly covers the nutmeats.

To blanch shelled almonds, place the nuts in a mixing bowl or saucepan. Pour boiling water over the nuts until covered; let stand 1 minute. Then, immediately drain the nuts in a sieve. Briefly run cold water over the nuts to halt the heating. Pinch each almond between your thumb and index finger to slip off the skin. Place the skinned almonds between two layers of paper towels to partially dry. When the excess water covering the nuts has been absorbed by the paper towels, place the almonds single layer on two layers of clean, dry paper towels; let stand, uncovered, until thoroughly dry.

TO STORE NUTS

Stale nuts have spoiled many a batch of cookies and brownies, as well as other dishes. Even in state fair food competitions, a surprising number of entries containing less-than-fresh nuts are encountered in a day of cookie judging.

Light, air, warmth, and moisture all cause nuts to become rancid quite quickly. Unless used immediately upon purchase, nuts should be stored in the freezer either in their unopened bag, or if opened, in a tightly covered glass jar or plastic container or in a zipper-seal plastic bag.

Nuts defrost rapidly and may be broken, chopped, ground, or grated just a few minutes after removal from the freezer. After preparing and measuring partially thawed nuts, it is best to leave them in an *uncovered* bowl as they continue to warm at room temperature. If covered, condensation can cause the nuts to become slightly damp and lose some of their snap. Hurry unused nuts back to the freezer.

Broken and chopped nuts may be stored in the freezer satisfactorily. If more than one kind of chopped nuts is stored, use freezer tape to label the containers because it is sometimes difficult to distinguish types of nuts after they have been chopped.

Nuts may be stored in the freezer for approximately 6 to 8 months. After that, they begin to lose their flavor. The freezer life of nuts depends, to a degree, upon how fresh they were when purchased. In many cases, the consumer has no way of knowing how long nuts have been sitting on the grocery shelf or stored in a warehouse. Expiration dates, which are given on some packages, are an indication of age; however, some observed expiration dates allow for nuts to remain on unrefrigerated, bright grocery shelves for many months. It is not unusual to purchase nuts found to be past their prime when tasted at home.

Before using nuts which have been frozen for 6 or more months, it is best to taste them before using to determine if they still have their characteristic and full flavor.

TO MEASURE INGREDIENTS

The accurate measurement of ingredients is critical to the successful production of many prepared foods such as breads, pastry, cakes, cookies, and sauces. In fact, consistent, reliable cookery leans heavily on the dependability of measuring. The rigid overtones of this statement are not meant to throw cold water on the important and satisfying works of culinary art created by inventive cooks who assemble a little of this, some of that, and a wee bit of the other to culminate in one-of-a-kind *chefs d'oeuvre*. However, soon after the creative high begins to fade, best that the *artiste de cuisine* take pencil and paper in hand and translate the inspired dish into measurable portions or, alas, it may be lost to ephemeral memory. All of the traditional foods we love were born of inspired minds, but they were also reduced to notations (recipes) so they could be enjoyed more than once.

MEASURING UTENSILS: There are three fundamental sets of measuring utensils that are standard in a well-equipped kitchen:

- Measuring spoons (¼ teaspoon, ½ teaspoon, 1 teaspoon, and 1 tablespoon).

- Fractional measuring cups (¼ cup, ⅓ cup, ½ cup, and 1 cup).

- Glass measuring cups with pouring spouts (1 cup, 2 cups, and 4 cups).

PREPARATION FOR MEASURING: Before commencing to measure and prepare a food, assemble all the measuring utensils and other kitchen tools and cooking equipment which will be needed.

Place a piece of waxed paper on the counter before beginning the measuring process. Measuring over waxed paper expedites kitchen cleanup.

TO MEASURE DRY INGREDIENTS: For correct measurement, dry ingredients must be measured in fractional measuring cups or measuring spoons which are overfilled and then leveled. Accurate measurement of dry ingredients cannot be achieved by filling fractional measuring cups or measuring spoons less than overfull before leveling, or by using glass measuring cups with pouring spouts due to the fact

that their capacity is greater than the amount of dry ingredients to be measured.

Stir dry ingredients, such as flour, cornmeal, baking powder, baking soda, and spices, before they are measured for the purpose of aerating.

Use a scoop or spoon to lightly place flour, cornmeal, and other such prestirred dry ingredients in a fractional measuring cup or a measuring spoon, filling it to slightly overflowing. Do not cause the dry ingredient to settle or pack in the measuring utensil by touching the top surface of the mounded ingredient with the scoop or spoon, or by shaking the measuring utensil, tapping the side of the utensil, or rapping the bottom of the utensil on the counter. To level the dry ingredient with the top of the measuring utensil, draw the flat side of a table knife blade across the top of the measuring cup or measuring spoon, letting the excess drop onto the waxed paper. Use the table knife or a spoon to gather the excess and return it to the storage package or canister.

Many recipes call for flour to be sifted *before* it is measured. See To Sift Flour (page 56) for sifting and measuring procedures.

Prestirred baking powder, baking soda, and spices may be measured by lightly dipping a measuring spoon directly into their containers. Slightly overfill the measuring spoon; then, draw the flat side of a table knife blade across the spoon, letting the excess drop back into the container or onto the waxed paper. Most baking powder containers are designed with a strip of thin metal across one side of the top for use in leveling measuring spoons dipped into the container. This is a completely satisfactory method of leveling.

To measure ⅛ teaspoon of a dry ingredient, measure ¼ teaspoon of the ingredient and then use a knife to divide the measured portion in half.

TO MEASURE BROWN SUGAR: Contrary to the procedure used to measure most other dry ingredients, brown sugar is packed into a fractional measuring cup or a measuring spoon before it is measured. Use a spoon to place brown sugar in a fractional measuring cup, intermittently packing it firmly into the cup with your thumbs. Measuring spoons may be dipped directly into the brown sugar and then packed into the spoon with your thumbs. To level the cup or measuring spoon, draw the flat side of a table knife blade across the top, letting the excess brown sugar drop onto the waxed paper.

After a package of brown sugar has been opened, transfer the sugar to a quart-sized glass jar with a tight-fitting lid for storage at room temperature in the cupboard. Improperly stored brown sugar quickly dries out, making it difficult, if not impossible, to measure and evenly combine with other ingredients.

TO MEASURE LIQUID INGREDIENTS: All three types of measuring utensils—measuring spoons, fractional measuring cups, and glass measuring cups with pouring spouts—may be used to measure liquid ingredients. I prefer using measuring spoons or fractional measuring cups in most cases. To measure liquids in a glass measuring cup with a pouring spout, the measuring cup must be placed on a level counter—not held in the hand. Then, while measuring the liquid, the measuring line of the cup must be viewed at *eye level,* which requires the cook to do a deep knee bend in front of the counter.

The top surface of contained liquid, called the "meniscus," is not level. It is crescent-shaped. The liquid at the center of a filled measuring utensil is higher than at the edges of the utensil. Liquid is measured at the outside edge, or brim, of the top surface. Therefore, to measure liquid in a measuring spoon or fractional measuring cup, *completely* fill the utensil to the outside brim. When measuring liquid in a glass measuring cup with a pouring spout, the liquid should be even with the line on the measuring cup which designates the amount to be measured.

Some liquid is retained on the inside surface of measuring utensils after the liquid is poured from them. For this reason, when a glass measuring cup with a pouring spout is used to measure liquid, a measuring cup as close as possible in size to the amount of liquid to be measured should be used. An inaccurate mea-

surement will occur if measured liquid is poured from a proportionately oversized glass measuring cup.

For accurate measurement, it is necessary to use a small, rubber spatula to empty measured viscous liquids such as honey, corn syrup, and molasses from the measuring utensil. (See To Measure and Store Honey, page 54.)

TO MEASURE PLASTIC FATS (butter, margarine, vegetable shortening, and lard): The measurement lines printed on most wrappings covering ¼-pound sticks of butter and margarine may be relied upon for measuring tablespoons and teaspoons (1 stick = ½ cup = 8 tablespoons = 24 teaspoons). Use a small, sharp knife to cut through the wrapping and butter or margarine at the desired measurement line.

Similar to measured sticks of butter and margarine but twice the size, 1-cup sticks of vegetable shortening with fractional measurement lines on the foil wrappers are now available on supermarket shelves. This packaging provides a reliable, convenient way of measuring vegetable shortening. To my knowledge, premeasured lard is unavailable.

To measure vegetable shortening or lard not purchased in premeasured packaging, it must be packed into a fractional measuring cup or a measuring spoon and then leveled. Cold, hardened vegetable shortening or lard is somewhat difficult to pack in measuring utensils because air spaces between the pieces of hard fat must be eliminated if an accurate measurement is to be achieved. To measure cold vegetable shortening or lard, use a table knife to cut medium chunks of the fat for placement in a fractional measuring cup, or small pieces for placement in a measuring spoon. Very firmly press the fat into the measuring utensil, a portion at a time, with your thumbs. When the utensil is packed slightly more than full, draw the flat side of a table knife blade across the top of the utensil to remove the excess. In the process of packing, the warmth of your thumbs will slightly soften the fat. When it is important to use very cold fat in the preparation of a food such as pastry piecrust, it is advisable to measure the lard (or vegetable shortening) a little in advance of use, and then to refrigerate it until just ready for incorporation in the product being prepared.

When recipes do not call for the use of cold vegetable shortening or lard, the fat may be softened at room temperature, making it easier to measure. Lard or vegetable shortening to be used in pastry piecrust and other foods in which very cold fat is to be cut into other ingredients, may also be softened prior to measuring if, after measurement, it is refrigerated for a lengthy period of time until it cools to refrigerator temperature throughout, and rehardens.

TO MEASURE AND STORE HONEY: When measuring honey, use a wet measuring spoon or cup to avoid sticking. Also use a wet, small rubber spatula to empty the measuring utensil. Store honey at room temperature, not in the refrigerator.

TO MEASURE OTHER FOODS: Other foods—whole, grated, shredded, chopped, cubed, or prepared in any other designated fashion—may be measured using any of the three types of measuring utensils (see Measuring Utensils, above). Selection of the measuring utensil is dependent upon the quantity and makeup of the food to be measured and the preference of the cook.

TO USE A PASTRY CLOTH AND A STOCKINET-COVERED ROLLING PIN

The purpose of using a pastry cloth and a stockinet-covered rolling pin is to provide surfaces which help prevent pastry and dough from sticking when they are rolled, kneaded, or otherwise handled. While some good pie and cookie bakers roll their pastry and dough on wooden boards, I have always achieved better results, with less effort, using a pastry cloth and stockinet-covered rolling pin, and I recommend their use.

Pastry cloths and stockinet covers for rolling

pins are usually sold together. The best pastry cloths are made of preshrunk canvas and come equipped with a frame to keep the cloth from shifting. The frame consists of two narrow, wooden slats which slide into the hemmed top and bottom of the pastry cloth, and two metal rods which run along the sides of the pastry cloth and loop over the ends of the wooden slats to hold the cloth tightly. The front of each metal rod hangs over the edge of the kitchen counter or other work surface to prevent the frame and pastry cloth from slipping. A taut, secure pastry cloth greatly assists in the production of evenly rolled pastry and dough. Stockinet rolling pin covers are fairly standard. They are made of knit material and fit any regular rolling pin (see illustration).

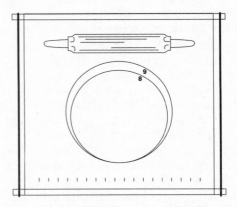

Pastry Cloth and Stockinet-Covered Rolling Pin

If a pastry cloth with a frame is not available at a local cookware store, one may be ordered from Sweet Celebrations Inc. (see Product Sources, page 850).

Pastry cloths without frames are more commonly available. They also usually come with a knit stockinet rolling pin cover. When using a pastry cloth without a frame, the pastry cloth can be held more securely by placing a flour canister (or other heavy object) on one of the upper corners of the pastry cloth, and a sugar canister (or other heavy object) on the other upper corner of the pastry cloth.

Pastry cloths and stockinet-covered rolling

pins nearly always are floured immediately before use. Often they are floured lightly, but sometimes more heavily, depending upon the consistency of the pastry or dough in a particular recipe and the task to be performed (rolling, kneading, etc.).

To flour a pastry cloth, use a flour scoop to sprinkle flour over the area of the pastry cloth to be used (generally, most of the cloth). Then, with your hand, spread the flour evenly over the cloth, exerting slight downward pressure to press a little of the flour into the fabric. This helps produce an evenly floured, nonstick surface. When rolling pastry and cookie dough, it is desirable to have only as much loose flour on the pastry cloth as required to prevent sticking. When pastry and dough are rolled over loose flour, a portion of the flour assimilates into the pastry or dough, thereby causing the rolled product to become more dry. The same general technique used in flouring a pastry cloth is used to flour a stockinet-covered rolling pin.

It is usually necessary to lightly reflour the pastry cloth and/or stockinet covering on the rolling pin before rolling, kneading, or handling each portion of pastry or dough. If little pieces of moistened flour are left on the surface of the pastry cloth after rolling a portion of pastry or dough, before proceeding to roll the next portion, lightly flour the pastry cloth and use the back of a spatula to clear the pastry cloth surface, pushing the flour to the extreme top of the pastry cloth in the same manner that you would use to clean a griddle surface. Then, lightly reflour the pastry cloth. Sometimes, bits of pastry or dough cling to the stockinet covering the rolling pin. When this happens, lightly reflour the spot of pastry or dough and then use your fingernail or a knife to remove it. It will be necessary to reflour the cleared spot on the stockinet.

When rolling pastry or dough of proper consistency on a properly floured pastry cloth using a stockinet-covered, then properly floured rolling pin, the pastry or dough will virtually glide over the pastry cloth as it spreads. A few well-executed rolls outward from the center of the pastry or dough to the edges, and the job is done. Especially in the case of pastry, where minimum handling is critical, use of a pastry cloth and stockinet-covered rolling pin can significantly improve the finished baked product.

I also use a pastry cloth for kneading and handling yeast-bread and -roll dough, although I call for use of either a pastry cloth or a wooden board in the yeast-bread and -roll recipes in this book. Some bread bakers prefer to work on a wooden board; however, I get better results using a pastry cloth.

Recipes in this book specify when the use of a pastry cloth and/or stockinet-covered rolling pin is recommended. Sometimes, when a perfectly flat finish is desired on rolled dough (unmarked by the thread pattern of a knit stockinet), such as in Springerle cookies (page 636), a pastry cloth and an uncovered rolling pin are used.

Pastry cloths and stockinets should be washed after use. I do not put pastry cloths in the dryer, but hang them over a clothesline or rod until thoroughly dry.

Rolling pins should not be washed by immersing them in water because water will seep inside around the handles and cause damage. After use, simply wipe the rolling pin with a warm, damp sponge, and wipe it dry with a clean tea towel.

TO GREASE AND FLOUR BAKING PANS

To grease and flour a baking pan, use a pastry brush to spread a thin application of room-temperature vegetable shortening over the entire inside of the pan, including the bottom and sides. Then, sprinkle about 2 tablespoons of all-purpose flour over the bottom of the pan. Over the kitchen sink, tilt the pan back and forth until all the greased surfaces are coated with flour. Turn the pan upside down and tap it on the rim of the sink to expel excess flour.

SPECIAL GREASE FOR BAKING PANS

½ cup vegetable shortening, softened
½ cup vegetable oil
½ cup all-purpose flour

Place the ingredients in a medium mixing bowl. Using an electric mixer, beat on high speed until perfectly smooth. Place in an airtight plastic container; store in the refrigerator. Special Grease will keep in the refrigerator for several months.

Special Grease replaces both the grease and flour when used to prepare a pan. (Do not flour the pan after applying Special Grease.)

WHEN TO USE SPECIAL GREASE: Special Grease helps prevent many cakes and certain other baked products from sticking to the pans in which they are baked. Many cake recipes in this cookbook specify the recommended use of Special Grease on the pans. It is also excellent for use in baking muffins and casserole dishes.

Most cookies which require baking on greased cookie sheets are best when baked on cookie sheets which have been lightly greased with vegetable shortening or vegetable oil. The flour in Special Grease can cause a slight residue on the bottoms of baked cookies; however, this cookbook specifies the use of Special Grease in certain cookie recipes because of its unique nonstick quality.

When recipes in this cookbook call for the pans to be *greased and floured,* Special Grease should not be used either in total substitution or in substitution for the grease. Rather, the procedure given in the first paragraph of this section, above, should be used.

TO SIFT FLOUR

There are three purposes for sifting flour:

- To pulverize any lumps in the flour or other ingredients with which the flour is sifted.

- To help evenly combine the flour with other dry ingredients with which it is sifted; most commonly, these include leavens (baking powder and baking soda); seasonings, such as salt and spices; and flavorings, such as powdered cocoa.

- To incorporate air, helping to make the end product lighter.

Recipe ingredient lists give instructions about flour sifting in one of three ways:

- 1 cup sifted flour (flour is to be sifted *before* measuring).

- 1 cup flour, sifted (flour is to be sifted *after* measuring).

- 1 cup flour (if flour is to be sifted at all, instructions are given in the recipe procedures).

If the flour is to be sifted *before* measuring, a simple, small 1-cup sifter is a very convenient and workable means of accomplishing the task. On a large piece of waxed paper, hold the small sifter over the properly sized fractional measuring cup (1 cup in the above examples), scoop flour lightly into the sifter, and sift it into the measuring cup until the cup is slightly more than full. Without shaking the cupful of sifted flour, causing it to settle or pack, draw the flat side of a table knife blade across the top of the measuring cup, letting the excess flour drop onto the waxed paper (see To Measure Dry Ingredients, page 52). Generally, recipes call for sifted and measured flour to be subsequently sifted with other ingredients, in which case, the sifted, measured flour can be placed immediately in the top of a regular-sized sifter, ready for sifting with other ingredients. For convenience and conservation of counter space, one large piece of waxed paper may be used for all the flour-sifting procedures involved in most recipes, using the left side of the paper for the initial sifting and measuring, and situating the large sifter on the right side of the paper for the final sifting. After placing sifted and measured flour in the large sifter, use the table knife to remove all flour which has spilled onto the waxed paper during the measuring process. The waxed paper will then be free of any unmeasured flour and may be used for the final sifting procedure.

When recipes call for the flour to be sifted *after* it is measured, measure the flour and place it directly in the large sifter for sifting.

Recipe procedures for baked goods often call for unsifted, measured flour to be sifted with other ingredients. In general cooking (in contrast to baking), flour usually is measured and used directly in the dish, with no sifting involved.

There are two common types of regular-sized (5-cup is preferable) kitchen sifters. One type looks like a wire mesh, basket-type sieve and operates with a rotary crank. The other type is cylindrical in shape, with three tiers of wire mesh which serve to sift the ingredients three times in a single operation. This latter type sifter is operated by repeatedly gripping and releasing the handle, and is my preference. Triple sifting better achieves all three purposes for sifting stated above. Particularly in cake baking, when evenly combined ingredients and optimal air incorporation are important factors, triple sifting is a must. It saves time and energy to triple sift in one operation.

Whichever type sifter is used, during the sifting process the bottom of the sifter should be held about 6 inches above the waxed paper or top of the sifted pile of ingredients. This will help incorporate air into the flour and other sifted ingredients.

When a large quantity of ingredients is placed in a triple sifter, the gripping handle is more difficult to operate and the ingredients are somewhat slow in working through the three screens of wire mesh. To overcome this sluggishness, continue holding the sifter by the handle with one hand, and beat against the side of the sifter with the other hand until some of the ingredients have sifted, at which time the gripping-releasing procedure may be resumed. Sifting quality is not diminished by using the beating methodology.

Because the incorporation of air is one of the purposes of sifting, the final sifting of flour and other ingredients should be delayed until these ingredients are about to be added to the batter or dough.

Use a scoop to transfer sifted ingredients from the waxed paper to the mixing bowl. Scoop beneath the pyramid of sifted ingredients in order not to crush the light, airy flour or flour mixture.

Do not wash flour sifters because it is difficult to expel wet flour from the fine, wire mesh. After using, firmly tap both ends of the sifter against the kitchen sink rim to remove excess flour. Then, wipe the inside and outside of the sifter with a clean, barely damp towel. Store in a dry kitchen cabinet. Sifters made of stainless steel are preferable because they will not rust and are usually constructed more sturdily.

If food requiring the sifting of whole-wheat flour is prepared often, it is a good practice to equip the kitchen with two sifters—one for white flour and one for whole-wheat and dark rye flours as well as other fibrous and/or darker-colored flours and food products. This will preclude small particles of coarse grain, which may become trapped in the sifter, from infusing sifted white flour, and will prevent any discoloration of sifted white flour due to previously sifted darker flours or food products.

Commercial flours labeled "presifted" should be sifted anyway, if sifting is called for in the recipe. While presifted flour may virtually be void of lumps, thus fulfilling the first purpose for sifting, sifting is still necessary to accomplish the second and third purposes—to thoroughly combine the flour with other dry ingredients, and to incorporate air. Proper sifting of flour and other ingredients is one of the elements that makes the difference between "okay baking" and "exceptional baking."

TO SIFT POWDERED SUGAR

Over a piece of waxed paper, place powdered sugar in a medium (about 6 inches in diameter) sieve. Hold the sieve by the handle and use short, quick, back and forth, and up and down motions of the hand and arm to sift the powdered sugar onto the waxed paper. To sift powdered sugar directly onto the top of cakes, cookies, and other desserts, use a very small, handheld strainer. Powdered sugar does not sift satisfactorily through most flour sifters.

TO MAKE SOUR MILK AND SOUR CREAM

1 CUP SOUR MILK

Pour 1 tablespoon freshly squeezed, strained lemon juice into a 1-cup glass measuring cup with pouring spout. Add whole milk to fill the measuring cup to the 1-cup measuring line. Let stand 5 minutes. Stir briefly to blend. Use immediately.

½ CUP SOUR MILK

Pour 1½ teaspoons freshly squeezed, strained lemon juice into a 1-cup glass measuring cup with pouring spout. Add whole milk to fill the measuring cup to the ½-cup measuring line. Let stand 5 minutes. Stir briefly to blend. Use immediately.

SOUR CREAM

Follow either Sour Milk recipe, above, substituting unwhipped whipping cream for whole milk.

TO MAKE SEASONED SALT

Some commercially purchased seasoned salt contains MSG (monosodium glutamate), which many people prefer to avoid eating. The following is a recipe for seasoned salt which may be used in lieu of the commercial product.

SEASONED SALT

¾ teaspoon salt
½ teaspoon garlic powder
¼ teaspoon pepper
¼ teaspoon ground thyme
¼ teaspoon ground sage
¼ teaspoon ground cardamom
¼ teaspoon sugar
⅛ teaspoon paprika
⅛ teaspoon cayenne pepper
⅛ teaspoon ground cumin
⅛ teaspoon ground turmeric

Place all ingredients in a small mixing bowl; stir to combine.

MAKES 1 TABLESPOON

Hors d'Oeuvres, First-Course Appetizers, and Snacks

Home entertaining—the main kind in the central states—gets off to a flying start with something cool to drink (with or without spirits) followed promptly by tempting, lush hors d'oeuvres, creations of the hostess/host. At least one or two cold selections await eager guests upon arrival, with a hot savory usually following a bit later.

Frequently, a spread or dip surrounded by an interesting assortment of wafers is included in the coffee-table offerings. These snappy-tasting concoctions are popular with party planners not only because they can be prepared in advance, but also because they are not labor-intensive—an important consideration, since the entire dinner to follow is usually the lone responsibility of the hostess/host.

In addition to the principal hors d'oeuvre fare, little dishes of tantalizing snacks, such as fancy nuts or Oyster Cracker Snacks (page 83), are usually judiciously placed near customary conversation hubs before the doorbell begins to ring.

Since Midwest cooks are always on the prowl for new hors d'oeuvre ideas, there is sure to be an exchange of recipes at such gatherings if an exceptionally delicious tidbit is served and the hostess/host is willing to divulge the ingredients—and most are. This is the route by which several recipes in this chapter found their way into my recipe box.

Amid warm socialization with friends, and tempting morsels constantly being passed under their noses, guests at these Midwest soirees soon learn to pace themselves. The little goodies that are intended to whet everyone's appetite can easily become the meal if one throws caution to the wind. For this reason, the Midwest hors d'oeuvre ritual usually supplants an appetizer course served at the table, and the meal begins with salad—far and away the most frequent and favored first course in the Heartland.

Even when dining in restaurants and private clubs, the more common practice is to skip the traditional appetizer course, even though a few appetizers are offered on most menus, and go directly to the ubiquitous salad course. Sometimes, there is a choice between salad and soup.

Exceptions to this generality are formal banquets or special celebratory dinners when shrimp cocktail—considered by many to be the most choice first course—or a well-seasoned broth such as Consommé Madrilène (page 91) or Sherried Beef Broth (page 88) are favorite selections. First-course broths are often served with Cheese Straws (page 450).

Some dishes that are standard first-course fare in other parts of the country are served as hors d'oeuvres in the Midwest; for example, mousses. When a mousse is served as a pre-dinner appetizer, it is made in an attractive, large mold and served on a beautiful platter supplied with a small knife and appropriate wafers. Similarly, pâtés made in very small loaf pans may be sliced, arranged on a tray with accompanying thin, cocktail-sized bread slices, and served in the living room or on the porch before guests proceed to the dining room for dinner.

On the more informal side, Midwest grills and steak houses often specialize in superb French-Fried Onion Rings (page 326) which are ordered with drinks as a type of first course after diners are seated at the table. They are served in a large, often napkin-lined bowl, and passed informally. Most good eating establishments which serve French-Fried Onion Rings prepare them to perfection—very thinly sliced with the rings completely separated and drained well after frying. They arrive at the table light and airy, not greasy. Even though French-Fried Onion Rings come under the heading of a health no-no, a few bites, occasionally, as a prelude to a fabulous Midwest steak dinner, should not be bypassed.

For spur-of-the-moment entertaining or everyday home dining, cheese and crackers, served while dinner is being readied, are always a hit. Cheddar, Colby, Swiss, and blue cheeses are among the favorites. Midwesterners' affinity for cheese is probably due, in part, to the fact that so much of it is produced here. In fact, in 1996, 53% of all the cheese produced in the United States came from the Midwest States. Wisconsin, known as America's Dairyland, is the nation's largest cheese-producing state.

Cold Hors d'Oeuvres

CHUTNEY DIP

3 ounces cream cheese, softened
8 ounces commercial sour cream
1 tablespoon finely grated onions
¾ teaspoon curry powder
⅛ teaspoon chili powder
⅛ teaspoon salt
½ cup chutney, large pieces chopped, home canned (page 776) or commercially canned
Paprika for decoration
Ridged potato chips or crackers

In a medium mixing bowl, place the cream cheese, sour cream, onions, curry powder, chili powder, and salt; using an electric mixer, beat on high speed until no lumps of cream cheese remain. Add the chutney; using a spoon, fold in to combine. Turn into a serving bowl and sprinkle sparingly with paprika. Serve with potato chips or crackers.

MAKES ABOUT 2 CUPS
(4 DOZEN HORS D'OEUVRES)

RAW VEGETABLE PLATTER WITH VEGETABLE DIP

On a platter, attractively arrange a selection of raw vegetables around a bowl of Vegetable Dip (recipe follows). The following vegetables, as well as others of choice, may be used:

Beet strips*
Broccoli flowerets*
Carrot strips
Cauliflower flowerets*
Celery strips
Cherry tomatoes
Cucumber slices
Green and yellow zucchini slices or strips
Green onions
Green, red, yellow, orange, and purple bell
  pepper strips
Radish roses (page 404)
Turnip strips

May be steamed (page 302) 1 minute to bring out color and enhance flavor. Immediately after steaming, place the steamer basket containing the vegetables under cold, running water to stop the cooking. Drain well. Place carefully in a zipper-seal plastic bag; refrigerate until completely cold. Vegetables should be steamed and prepared separately to preserve their individual colors and tastes.

VEGETABLE DIP
1 cup mayonnaise
1 tablespoon finely grated onions
1 tablespoon cider vinegar
1 tablespoon prepared horseradish,
  homemade (page 46) or commercially
  canned
1/2 teaspoon curry powder
Finely snipped, fresh chives for garnish

In a small mixing bowl, place the mayonnaise, onions, vinegar, horseradish, and curry powder; stir well. Transfer the dip to a serving bowl and garnish with chives.

MAKES ABOUT 1 CUP

VARIATION: Hot Swiss Cheese Sauce (page 368) makes a tasty and different dip for raw vegetables.

KALE DIP

1 10-ounce package frozen chopped kale
16 ounces commercial sour cream
1 1.4-ounce package vegetable soup mix
1 8-ounce can (1 cup) sliced bamboo
  shoots, chopped
1 teaspoon white wine vinegar
1 teaspoon soy sauce
Assorted crackers

AT LEAST 6 HOURS BEFORE SERVING: In the sink, place the kale in a colander and defrost, allowing the liquid to drain off.

When defrosted, press the kale to extract any remaining liquid. Chop the kale into somewhat smaller pieces to make the dip easier to spread and eat. In a medium mixing bowl, place the kale, sour cream, vegetable soup mix, bamboo shoots, vinegar, and soy sauce; using a spoon, stir until combined well. Cover and refrigerate at least 6 hours to allow the soup mix to soften and the flavors to blend. Serve in a bowl and surround with crackers; supply a small knife for spreading.

MAKES ABOUT 3 1/2 CUPS
(7 DOZEN HORS D'OEUVRES)

ABC DIP

1/3 cup sliced almonds, chopped coarsely
3 strips bacon, fried crisply, drained
    between paper towels, and crumbled
1 1/2 cups shredded sharp cheddar cheese
1 tablespoon plus 1 teaspoon finely grated
    onions
3/4 cup Miracle Whip salad dressing
Paprika for decoration
Assorted crackers

In a small mixing bowl, place the almonds, bacon, cheese, onions, and salad dressing; stir lightly to combine. Turn into a serving bowl; sprinkle with paprika to decorate. Place bowl on a doily-lined plate. Arrange crackers on plate around the bowl of dip.

**MAKES ABOUT 2 CUPS
(4 DOZEN HORS D'OEUVRES)**

SUMMER SAUSAGE-HORSERADISH DIP

8 ounces soft-style cream cheese
1/2 cup mayonnaise
3 tablespoons honey
1/4 teaspoon salt
1/8 teaspoon dry mustard
1 cup finely ground (page 49), fully cooked
    cervelat summer sausage*
2 tablespoons undrained, prepared
    horseradish, homemade (page 46) or
    commercially canned
3/4 cup finely chopped green bell peppers
2 tablespoons finely grated onions
Low-sodium whole-wheat crackers

Cervelat is the name given to a classification of semi-dry, mildly seasoned, smoked summer sausages. Most cervelats are made with both pork and beef. Thuringer is probably the most popular. Other cervelats include Farmer, Goettinger, Goteborg, Gothaer (made with pork

only), Holsteiner, and Landjaeger. Any of these cervelats may be used in this recipe.*

In a medium mixing bowl, place the cream cheese, mayonnaise, honey, salt, and dry mustard; using a spoon, stir vigorously until completely smooth and blended. Add the summer sausage, horseradish, green peppers, and onions; stir to combine. Serve with crackers.

**MAKES ABOUT 3 CUPS
(6 DOZEN HORS D'OEUVRES)**

SHRIMP WITH DIPS

Boil fresh shrimp (page 229); shell, leaving the tails on, and devein (page 229). Refrigerate in a covered container until cold. Arrange attractively on a platter and serve with one or more of the following sauces for dipping:

Cocktail Sauce (page 361)
Louis Dressing (page 151)
Hot Swiss Cheese Sauce (page 368)

GUACAMOLE

The salad dressing in this version of guacamole not only adds a zingy flavor, but also allows advance preparation of the hors d'oeuvre by using the dressing to spread over the avocado mixture, thus sealing it and preventing it from darkening. You stir the guacamole just before serving. Bacon also adds a new, delicious twist to this ever-popular savory.

2 large ripe avocados
1 tablespoon minced onions
1 garlic clove, pressed
1/4 teaspoon chili powder
1/2 cup Miracle Whip salad dressing
4 slices bacon
1 medium tomato
Tortilla chips

Peel, pit, and cut the avocados into small chunks; place the chunks in a blender. Add the onions, garlic, and chili powder; process the mixture in the blender until pureed. Place the mixture in a glass mixing bowl. Using a small, narrow spatula, spread evenly and smoothly in bowl. Spoon the salad dressing over the avocado mixture; using a clean, small, narrow spatula, carefully spread until smooth, sealing in the avocado mixture to prevent it from discoloring. Cover the bowl tightly and refrigerate.

Fry the bacon until crisp; drain well between paper towels. Using your fingers, crumble the bacon into small pieces. Place the pieces in a covered container and refrigerate. Blanch the tomato for 45 seconds (page 44); stem, peel, quarter, seed, and core it (page 45). Then chop it finely. Measure ½ cup chopped tomato; place it in a covered container and refrigerate. Reserve the remaining chopped tomato for other uses.

At serving time, add the bacon and chopped tomato to the bowl containing the avocado mixture and salad dressing. Using a tablespoon, stir together the avocado mixture, salad dressing, bacon, and tomatoes until evenly combined. Transfer the guacamole to a medium-shallow serving bowl. Serve it with tortilla chips for dipping.

MAKES ABOUT 2 CUPS
(4 DOZEN HORS D'OEUVRES)

TACO SPREAD

11 ounces cream cheese, softened
½ cup commercial sour cream
2 tablespoons plus 1 teaspoon commercial taco seasoning mix
1 tablespoon vegetable oil
1 pound lean, pure ground beef
½ cup finely chopped onions
1 garlic clove, pressed
12 ounces (1½ cups) commercially canned mild picante salsa

8 ounces (2 cups) shredded cheese for tacos
½ cup sliced, pitted ripe olives
1¾ cups coarsely chopped iceberg lettuce, well dried
2 cups blanched (page 44), peeled, stemmed, quartered, seeded and cored (page 45), and diced (about ¼-inch square) tomatoes
1 10-ounce bag tortilla chips

In a small mixing bowl, place the cream cheese, sour cream, and taco seasoning mix; using an electric mixer, beat on high speed until smooth and blended. Using a tablespoon and a small, narrow spatula, press the cream cheese mixture evenly onto the bottom of a 9 × 13-inch baking dish; cover and refrigerate.

Place the vegetable oil in an electric skillet or a skillet on the range over medium heat (350° F. in an electric skillet); using a spatula, distribute the oil over the bottom of the skillet. Add the ground beef; using a large spoon, break up the chunks of meat as it begins to brown. Add the onions and garlic; sauté until the contents are lightly browned, stirring often. Cool to room temperature; spread evenly over the cream cheese mixture in the baking dish; press *very lightly*. Spread evenly in layers over the beef mixture in the following order: salsa, shredded cheese, olives, lettuce, and tomatoes. Cover and refrigerate.

To serve, place tortilla chips in an attractive basket or bowl next to the Taco Spread. Provide 1 or 2 small knives for spreading.

MAKES ABOUT 9 CUPS
(11 DOZEN HORS D'OEUVRES)

LAST-MINUTE CHEESE SPREAD

A good-tasting hors d'oeuvre you can prepare in a jiffy after a quick trip to the grocery store. A simple sprig of parsley will doll up the top of the spread.

12 ounces soft-style cream cheese
2 tablespoons whole milk*
1 cup shredded sharp cheddar cheese
4 ounces blue cheese, crumbled
Assorted crackers

Lowfat or skim milk may be substituted.

In a medium mixing bowl, place the cream cheese and milk; using a spoon, stir until blended. Add the cheddar cheese and blue cheese; stir until evenly combined. Serve the spread in an attractive bowl surrounded by assorted crackers. Supply a small knife for spreading.

**MAKES ABOUT 2½ CUPS
(5 DOZEN HORS D'OEUVRES)**

BLUE CHEESE SPREAD

12 ounces small-curd cottage cheese
4 ounces Maytag blue cheese, crumbled
8 ounces commercial sour cream
2 tablespoons chopped green tops of
    green onions
1 tablespoon finely grated yellow onions
Additional chopped green tops of green
    onions for decoration
Assorted crackers

Place the cottage cheese in a sieve. Using the back of a tablespoon, press the cottage cheese against the mesh to drain it.

In a medium mixing bowl, place the drained cottage cheese, blue cheese, sour cream, 2 tablespoons green onion tops, and grated yellow onions; using a spoon, stir to combine. Turn into a serving bowl; sprinkle with green onion tops

to decorate. Serve with crackers. Supply a small knife for spreading.

**MAKES ABOUT 2½ CUPS
(5 DOZEN HORS D'OEUVRES)**

BLUE CHEESE-WHISKEY SPREAD

4 ounces Maytag blue cheese, room
    temperature
3 ounces cream cheese, softened
¼ cup (4 tablespoons) butter, softened
2 tablespoons Canadian whiskey
1 tablespoon honey
2 tablespoons finely grated onions
1 small garlic clove, pressed
1 tablespoon finely snipped fresh parsley
Additional finely snipped, fresh parsley for
    decoration
Crackers, such as onion-flavored melba
    rounds

THE DAY BEFORE SERVING: Blue Cheese-Whiskey Spread should be made at least 24 hours in advance of serving to allow the ingredient flavors to blend.

In a small mixing bowl, place the blue cheese, cream cheese, and butter; using an electric mixer, beat on high speed until blended and creamy. Add the whiskey, honey, onions, and garlic; beat on high speed until blended. Add 1 tablespoon parsley; using a tablespoon, stir until evenly distributed. Turn into a serving bowl; sprinkle sparingly with parsley to decorate. Place the bowl of spread in a larger, plastic storage bowl; cover the storage bowl tightly; refrigerate. (Refrigerating the bowl of spread in a larger storage bowl eliminates the need to directly cover the surface of the spread and spoil its appearance).

ONE HOUR BEFORE SERVING: Remove the spread from refrigerator. Lift the serving bowl containing the spread from the storage bowl; let it stand at room temperature, allowing the spread to soften slightly. Place the bowl of spread on a doily-lined plate and surround with crackers; provide a small knife for spreading.

**MAKES ABOUT 1½ CUPS
(3 DOZEN HORS D'OEUVRES)**

SYMPHONY SPREAD

1 8-ounce can commercial crushed
    pineapple in juice
16 ounces cream cheese, softened
1 tablespoon homemade Seasoned Salt
    (page 58)*
½ cup finely chopped green bell peppers
2 tablespoons finely chopped onions
1 cup chopped pecans
Yellow, orange, and red bell pepper strips
Broccoflower (green cauliflower) flowerets,
    or broccoli or cauliflower flowerets
Bok choy stalk strips
Assorted crackers

  *Commercial seasoned salt may be substituted;
  however, try to select a seasoned salt that does
  not have monosodium glutamate as an
  ingredient.*

Drain the pineapple, reserving the juice. Pour the juice into a small mixing bowl; set the fruit aside. Add the cream cheese and seasoned salt to the pineapple juice; using an electric mixer, beat on high speed until smooth and blended. Add the drained crushed pineapple, green peppers, onions, and pecans; using a spoon, stir to combine. Turn the spread into a serving bowl and surround with pepper strips, broccoflower (or broccoli or cauliflower) flowerets, bok choy strips, and assorted crackers.

**MAKES ABOUT 3½ CUPS
(7 DOZEN HORS D'OEUVRES)**

BRAUNSCHWEIGER SPREAD

Braunschweiger is a soft, smooth, smoked pork liver sausage. Its name derives from the German town of Braunschweig.

8 ounces braunschweiger
16 ounces commercial sour cream
1 1-ounce package onion soup mix
Cocktail-sized pumpernickel bread

AT LEAST 6 HOURS BEFORE SERVING: Place the braunschweiger in a medium mixing bowl; let it stand at room temperature until slightly softened.

Using a tablespoon, mash the braunschweiger. Add the sour cream; using an electric mixer, beat on medium speed until blended. Add the onion soup mix; using a spoon, stir to combine. Cover and refrigerate at least 6 hours to allow the soup mix to soften and flavors to blend.

Spoon the Braunschweiger Spread into a serving bowl; place it on a doily-lined plate and surround it with slices of pumpernickel bread. Provide a small knife for spreading.

**MAKES ABOUT 3 CUPS
(6 DOZEN HORS D'OEUVRES)**

ALTERNATIVE SERVING SUGGESTION: Spread Braunschweiger Spread on cocktail-sized pumpernickel bread slices prior to serving; garnish each canapé with a small, fresh parsley leaf or a thin slice of tiny, sweet gherkin pickle.

DRIED BEEF AND GREEN PEPPER SPREAD

This is one of my sister-in-law's standbys served at family gatherings for years. We love it! Hope you do too. The recipe has been in Dee's files for so long, she can't remember the source. This is often the case with many Midwest recipes handed down and exchanged over the years (and generations).

16 ounces cream cheese, softened
3 tablespoons finely grated onions
2 garlic cloves, pressed
1 tablespoon white wine Worcestershire sauce
5 ounces sliced dried beef, chopped finely (about 1⅓ cups)
1½ cups finely chopped green bell peppers (about 1½ medium green peppers)
Low-sodium whole-wheat crackers

Preheat the oven to 300° F.

In a medium mixing bowl, place the cream cheese, onions, garlic, and Worcestershire sauce; using an electric mixer, beat on high speed until creamy. Add the dried beef and green peppers; using a spoon, stir until evenly combined. Turn the mixture into a 1-quart round baking dish. Cover the dish and heat the mixture in the oven until *warm,* not hot, stirring twice during the warming period (about 30 minutes). The purpose of warming the mixture is to blend the flavors while retaining the crispness of the green peppers. Do not allow the mixture to become hot and begin to bubble. Transfer the warm mixture to a serving bowl; cover and refrigerate it until cold. Serve with crackers; provide a knife for spreading.

**MAKES ABOUT 3½ CUPS
(7 DOZEN HORS D'OEUVRES)**

TRIPLE-LAYER CAVIAR SPREAD

½ cup (¼ pound) butter, softened
3 extra-large eggs, hard-cooked (page 264) and chopped
8 ounces commercial sour cream
¾ cup finely chopped onions
3½ ounces caviar
Small, plain water crackers

AT LEAST 6 HOURS BEFORE SERVING: In a blender, place the butter and chopped eggs; process until the mixture is a smooth, buttery consistency. Using a small, narrow spatula, spread the mixture evenly over the bottom of a 7- or 8-inch flat-bottomed crystal serving plate with short sides (or an 8-inch glass pie plate). In a small mixing bowl, place the sour cream and onions; stir to combine. Spoon the sour cream mixture over the egg-butter layer in the serving plate; using a small, narrow spatula, spread evenly and smoothly. Cover well with plastic wrap and then aluminum foil; refrigerate at least 6 hours.

Shortly before serving, carefully spoon the caviar over the sour cream layer in the serving dish and spread evenly. Place the serving dish on a round, silver or crystal plate; surround the caviar serving dish with crackers. Provide a small serving knife.

**MAKES ABOUT 3 CUPS
(6 DOZEN HORS D'OEUVRES)**

BOK CHOY STUFFED WITH RED CAVIAR

1 bunch bok choy* (page 307)
8 ounces soft-style cream cheese
1 tablespoon finely grated onions
2 ounces red salmon caviar
3 hard-cooked, extra-large egg yolks, finely grated

If bok choy is not available, celery may be substituted.

Clean the bok choy thoroughly. Split the white stalks in half lengthwise. Cut the split stalks into 2-inch-long pieces; dry with paper towels; set aside. In a small mixing bowl, place the cream cheese and onions; stir to blend. Add ⅔ of the caviar; stir carefully to combine. Using a knife, stuff the bok choy pieces with the cream cheese mixture. Sprinkle the stuffed bok choy with the grated egg yolks; garnish the tops with the remaining caviar. Cover carefully; refrigerate until ready to serve.

MAKES ABOUT 4 DOZEN

CUCUMBER WHEELS

2 seedless cucumbers, about 1 foot long each
1 5-ounce jar prepared horseradish
½ teaspoon finely snipped, fresh dillweed
2 teaspoons sugar
¼ teaspoon salt
⅛ teaspoon white pepper
½ cup whipping cream, whipped
Tiny sprigs of fresh dillweed for decoration

Pare 1 cucumber (page 45). Cut evenly into ⅜-inch slices (about 30 slices). Using a tiny, ⅜-inch melon baller, carefully scoop out a well in the center seed section of each cucumber slice, leaving the bottom of each slice intact and uncut. Place the slices, well side down, on 3 layers of paper towels; let stand.

Pare the remaining cucumber. Cut into ½-inch slices; cut each slice into quarters. Measure 4 cups quartered cucumber slices; reserve any remaining slices for other uses. Place the 4 cups quartered cucumber slices in a food processor, ⅓ at a time, and process, using on/off turns, until they reach the consistency of pulp. Be careful not to completely liquefy them. Secure 2 layers of damp cheesecloth in a medium-sized sieve and place over a deep pan. Pour the cucumber pulp into the cheesecloth to strain. When strained, lift the cheesecloth containing the strained pulp off the sieve; pull the 4 corners

of the cheesecloth together and twist to make a cheesecloth bag of pulp. Wring and squeeze the bag to extract nearly all liquid until there remains ½ cup measured pulp; set aside.

Place the horseradish in a medium-sized sieve to drain. With your hand, firmly press the horseradish in the sieve to extract as much liquid as possible until there remains ¼ cup measured, drained, packed horseradish. In a medium mixing bowl, place the drained cucumber pulp, drained horseradish, ½ teaspoon dillweed, sugar, salt, and white pepper; stir to combine. Add the whipped cream; fold in.

Using a decorating bag fit with large round tip number 1A (page 383), pipe a mound of horseradish mixture into the well in each cucumber slice. Gently tuck a tiny sprig of fresh dillweed (using a pair of kitchen tweezers, if you have them) into the top of each mound of horseradish mixture for decoration. Place the Cucumber Wheels in a dome-covered container and refrigerate them until serving time.

MAKES 30

CUCUMBER AND CHEESE CANAPÉS

3 ounces cream cheese, softened
2 teaspoons chili sauce, home canned (page 783) or commercially canned
2 teaspoons light rum
3 slices thinly sliced white bread
12 thin, seedless cucumber slices

In a small mixing bowl, place the cream cheese, chili sauce, and light rum; using an electric mixer, beat on high speed until smooth and blended; set aside. Toast the bread. Using a sharp knife, cut off the crusts. Cut each piece of toast into 4 squares. Spread the cream cheese mixture on the toast squares. Place a slice of cucumber on top of each square. Cover and refrigerate them until serving time.

MAKES 12

CHERRY TOMATOES STUFFED WITH CURRIED CHICKEN SALAD

3 dozen uniformly sized cherry tomatoes
4 cups finely ground (page 49), cooked
   chicken breasts (page 204)
1½ cups minced celery
2 teaspoons finely grated onions
¾ cup mayonnaise
½ cup Miracle Whip salad dressing
1 tablespoon curry powder
½ teaspoon salt
½ teaspoon white pepper
3 ounces cream cheese, softened
Yellow paste food coloring (optional)

Using a very sharp, thin-bladed paring knife, cut a generous slice off the stem end of the tomatoes; discard the slices. Using the knife, carefully remove the seeds and cores from the tomatoes; as they are prepared, place them upside down on paper towels to drain. After preparing all the tomatoes, turn them right side up and place them in an airtight container; refrigerate until ready to stuff.

In a medium mixing bowl, place the chicken, celery, and onions; stir to combine and set aside. In a small mixing bowl, place the mayonnaise, salad dressing, curry powder, salt, and white pepper; stir until well combined. Add the mayonnaise mixture to the chicken mixture; stir to combine.

Using a demitasse spoon, mound the chicken salad in the tomatoes and pack it with your thumb. Set the filled tomatoes aside. Place the cream cheese in a small mixing bowl; using an electric mixer, beat on high speed until smooth. Add a tiny amount of food coloring to tint yellow; beat the mixture until evenly blended. Using a decorating bag fit with small open-star tip number 15 (page 383), pipe a small star (page 389) on top of each stuffed tomato.

MAKES 6 DOZEN

PETITE POTATOES

2½ dozen tiny, unpared, new red potatoes,
   steamed (page 328)
Vegetable oil
16 ounces commercial sour cream
¼ cup very finely grated onions
Black caviar
Red caviar

Place the steamed potatoes on 2 layers of paper towels to drain and cool. When cool, dampen a paper towel with vegetable oil and rub the potatoes to lightly oil the skins. Using a sharp, thin-bladed knife, cut the potatoes in half lengthwise. Using a ⅞-inch melon baller, scoop a ⅞-inch-diameter and ¼-inch-deep round section of potato flesh out of the center of each potato half to form a cup. Place the potatoes on plastic wrap in a flat-bottomed dish; cover and refrigerate them until cold.

In a small mixing bowl, place the sour cream and onions; stir to combine. Using a decorating bag fit with medium round tip number 8 (page 383), pipe a mound of the sour cream mixture into the cup in each potato half (or use 2 demitasse spoons to mound the mixture in the potatoes). Refrigerate the filled potatoes on plastic wrap in a dome-covered container until shortly before serving.

Close to the time of serving, place the black caviar and red caviar separately on 4 layers of paper towels to drain. Using a tiny ⅜-inch melon baller or 2 demitasse spoons, place a small amount of caviar on top of each mound of sour cream mixture in the potatoes. Place the black caviar on half of the potatoes and the red caviar on the remaining half. Placing the caviar on the sour cream mixture too far in advance of serving may result in the caviar running slightly.

MAKES 5 DOZEN

STUFFED FENNEL STICKS

3 dozen small (about ½ inch in diameter) fresh fennel stalks from 1 fennel bulb
1½ ounces (3 tablespoons) Montrachet or other type chèvre cheese*
Snipped, fresh fennel weed
3 dozen very small, pimiento-stuffed green olives, sliced thinly

*A soft, goat's milk cheese.

Wash and dry the fennel stalks. Using a small paring knife, remove all outside strings around the stalks. (The strings on fennel stalks are very tough and must be removed to make this piquant hors d'oeuvre palatable.) When the outside strings are removed, the stalks will have a green and white striped appearance. (Or, using a vegetable parer, pare the stalks thinly.) Using a small, sharp knife, cut the stalks in half lengthwise. Then cut the halves widthwise into 1¾-inch (bite-sized) sticks. Using a small table knife, stuff each stick with ¼ teaspoon cheese. Sprinkle a scant amount of fennel weed over the cheese. Garnish each stick with 3 overlapping olive slices.

MAKES 3 DOZEN

RED AND GREEN VEGETABLE TRAY

Red bell peppers, cut into ¼-inch strips
Radish Roses (page 404)
Cherry tomatoes
Pimiento-stuffed green olives
Fresh snow peas, steamed 30 seconds (page 327)
Fresh green asparagus spears, blanched (page 44) 1 minute
Bite-sized, fresh broccoli flowerets, steamed (page 302) 1 minute
Small, fresh Brussels sprouts, steamed (page 302) 2 minutes

Fresh green beans, steamed (page 302) 2 minutes
Fresh, frozen, or canned (in water) artichoke hearts, cooked (if fresh or frozen) and cut in half lengthwise
1 recipe Vegetable Dip (page 61)

Steam, blanch, or cook the vegetables separately (to preserve their individual colors and flavors), as specified above. Then, immediately place each vegetable in a colander and rinse under cold, running water to stop the cooking. Drain well. Place the vegetables carefully in separate zipper-seal plastic bags and refrigerate until completely cold.

To serve, spoon Vegetable Dip into a bowl and place it in the center of a round tray. Arrange the vegetables in pinwheel fashion around the bowl of dip.

VARIATIONS: Any other red or green vegetables may be added or substituted.

MINI BAGELS WITH SMOKED SALMON

20 presliced mini bagels, about 2½ inches in diameter (available at most supermarkets)
10 ounces cream cheese, softened
8 ounces thinly sliced smoked salmon
About 5 ounces alfalfa sprouts

Separate the halves of the bagels (each half is to be an individual hors d'oeuvre). Spread each bagel half with approximately 1½ teaspoons cream cheese. Cut slices of the smoked salmon to fit on the bagel halves; place 1 slice on each half. Sprinkle alfalfa sprouts atop the smoked salmon on each hors d'oeuvre. Keep refrigerated in an airtight container until ready to serve.

MAKES 40

TARTLETS WITH CRABMEAT FILLING

1 cup boiled, fresh or frozen Alaskan king crabmeat (page 230),* chilled and finely chopped
¼ cup finely diced, pimiento-stuffed green olives
¼ cup chopped pecans
2 tablespoons minced celery
2 teaspoons finely minced onions
1½ teaspoons freshly squeezed, strained lemon juice
¼ cup Miracle Whip salad dressing
1 recipe Tartlet Shells (page 469)
36 thin slices of small, pimiento-stuffed green olives for decoration

Canned and drained crabmeat may be substituted.

In a medium mixing bowl, place the crabmeat, ¼ cup diced olives, pecans, celery, onions, and lemon juice; stir to combine. Add the salad dressing; stir to combine. Using a demitasse spoon, mound the crabmeat mixture in the Tartlet Shells. Decorate the top of each filled tartlet with an olive slice.

MAKES ABOUT 3 DOZEN

VARIATIONS: The Tartlet Shells may also be filled with finely chopped Lobster Salad (page 146), Ham Salad (page 352), Egg Salad (page 352), or other fillings of your choice and invention.

DILL PICKLE ROLL-UPS

4 2.5-ounce packages lean beef (3¾-inch squares of thin, pressed beef found in the cold-cut section of the grocery store)
8 ounces cream cheese, softened
2 16-ounce jars kosher dill gherkins (small dill pickles)

THE DAY BEFORE SERVING: On a cutting board, place 2 pieces of the lean beef on top of each other symmetrically. Place a dill pickle lengthwise along the bottom edge of the stacked beef, lining up one end of the pickle evenly with the left side of the beef. Cut the right side of the beef, from top to bottom, evenly with the right end of the pickle. Reserve the cutaway portion of the meat to make small roll-ups or for other uses. Remove the pickle from the top of the beef. Spread a moderately thin layer of cream cheese over the beef. Replace the pickle on the beef. Roll the beef, jelly-roll fashion, around the pickle; place, seam down, in a flat-bottomed glass dish; cover lightly and refrigerate.

SHORTLY BEFORE SERVING: Using a small, sharp knife, cut the rolls into ¼- to ½-inch slices. Arrange in a single layer on a serving plate.

MAKES ABOUT 13 DOZEN

CHRISTMAS CHEESE BALL

8 ounces cream cheese, softened
1 tablespoon minced onions
1 teaspoon Worcestershire sauce
2 ounces blue cheese, finely crumbled
4 ounces medium cheddar cheese, finely shredded
2 tablespoons finely chopped green bell peppers
1 tablespoon finely chopped pimientos
¾ cup broken English walnuts
Assorted crackers

In a small mixing bowl, place the cream cheese, onions, and Worcestershire sauce; using an electric mixer, beat on high speed until creamy and smooth. Add the blue cheese; resume beating on high speed until creamed. Add the cheddar cheese; beat on medium speed until mixed, leaving some visible pieces of yellow cheddar cheese; set aside. In a small bowl, place the green peppers and pimientos; stir to combine. Add the peppers and pimientos to the cheese mixture; using a spoon, stir until evenly distributed. Cover and refrigerate 1 hour.

Scatter the walnuts on waxed paper. Remove the cheese mixture from the refrigerator; form it into a ball and roll it in the walnuts until evenly covered. Wrap the cheese ball in plastic wrap; refrigerate. Serve with assorted crackers of choice.

**MAKES ABOUT 2½ CUPS
(5 DOZEN HORS D'OEUVRES)**

CHRISTMAS CRACKERS

2½ dozen small, plain water crackers
8 ounces soft-style cream cheese
Mint jelly
Commercially canned wild lingonberries in
   sugar

Spread the crackers generously with cream cheese, forming a slight mound in the center of each cracker. Using the back of a melon baller, make a cup in the center of the cream cheese. Fill each cream cheese cup in half of the crackers with ½ teaspoon mint jelly. Fill each cream cheese cup in the remaining half of the crackers with ½ teaspoon lingonberries. Arrange on a white doily-lined plate.

MAKES 2½ DOZEN

VARIATIONS: Cherry Jelly (page 740) and Blush Wine Jelly (page 746) may also be used as fillings.

SHRIMP-CHEESE LOG

8 ounces cream cheese, softened
½ cup (¼ pound) butter, softened
2 tablespoons chili sauce, home canned
   (page 783) or commercially canned
1 teaspoon white wine (optional)
4 dashes Tabasco pepper sauce
1 drop liquid red food coloring (optional)
1 cup coarsely chopped boiled, fresh
   shrimp (page 229)
2 ounces blue cheese, crumbled
⅓ cup pitted, small green olives cut into
   fourths
1 tablespoon plus 1 teaspoon well-drained,
   packed, prepared horseradish, homemade
   (page 46) or commercially canned
⅔ cup toasted pine nuts (page 50),
   chopped
Assorted crackers

In a medium mixing bowl, place the cream cheese, butter, chili sauce, white wine, pepper sauce, and food coloring; using an electric mixer, beat on high speed until blended. Add the shrimp, blue cheese, olives, and horseradish; using a spoon, stir to combine. Cover and refrigerate about 1½ hours until the mixture is sufficiently set to handle and mold.

Divide the mixture in half; form into two 6-inch-long logs. Scatter the pine nuts on waxed paper; roll each log in the nuts. Roll firmly enough to secure the nuts on each log. Refrigerate to set firmly. Serve with crackers. Furnish a cheese knife on the serving plate.

**MAKES ABOUT 3 CUPS
(3 DOZEN HORS D'OEUVRES PER LOG)**

CHUTNEY CHEESE BALL

8 ounces cream cheese, softened
2 ounces blue cheese, softened
⅓ cup chopped chutney, home canned
   (page 776) or commercially canned
½ cup chopped, toasted unblanched
   almonds (chop, page 50; then toast,
   page 50)
Assorted crackers

THE DAY BEFORE SERVING: In a small mixing bowl, place the cream cheese and blue cheese; using an electric mixer, beat on high speed until well blended. Add the chutney; using a spoon, stir to combine. Cover and refrigerate at least 3 hours until firm enough to form into a ball.

Scatter the almonds on waxed paper. Remove the cheese mixture from the refrigerator; form into a ball and roll in the almonds until evenly covered. Wrap the cheese ball in plastic wrap; refrigerate overnight.

TO SERVE: Reshape the ball, flatten slightly, and place on a small plate. Serve with crackers.

MAKES ABOUT 2 CUPS
(4 DOZEN HORS D'OEUVRES)

Other Cold Hors d'Oeuvre Recipes

Deviled Eggs (page 267)
Hickory-Smoked Ham Mousse (page 82)
Shrimp Mousse with Dill (page 80)

Hot Hors d'Oeuvres

HOT BOURBON-CHEESE DIP

8 ounces cream cheese, softened
½ cup Miracle Whip salad dressing
1 tablespoon bourbon
1 teaspoon lemon pepper
1 cup (4 ounces) shredded brick cheese
1 cup (4 ounces) shredded Swiss cheese
3 tablespoons minced onions
6 slices bacon, fried crisply, drained well
   between paper towels, and crumbled
¼ cup chopped pecans
¼ cup rolled Ritz crackers
Onion-flavored melba rounds

Preheat the oven to 350°F.

Place the cream cheese in a medium mixing bowl; using an electric mixer, beat on high speed to smooth slightly. Add the salad dressing, bourbon, and lemon pepper; resume beating on high speed until very smooth. Add the brick cheese, Swiss cheese, and onions; using a spoon, stir to combine. Place the mixture in a 9-inch glass pie plate; using a small, narrow spatula, spread evenly. Distribute the bacon evenly over the surface of the mixture. Sprinkle the pecans evenly over the bacon. Just before baking, sprinkle the cracker crumbs over the top. Bake, uncovered, 20 minutes. Remove from the oven and place on a wire rack; let stand 5 minutes to cool slightly before serving. Serve with onion-flavored melba rounds. Provide a small knife.

MAKES ABOUT 2¾ CUPS
(5 DOZEN HORS D'OEUVRES)

ARTICHOKE DIP

1 9-ounce package frozen artichoke hearts
  cooked well, drained, and chopped (about
  1 1/2 cups chopped artichoke hearts)*
1 cup mayonnaise
1 cup freshly grated Parmesan cheese
  (page 46)
1 very small garlic clove, pressed
1 tablespoon very finely chopped onions
Assorted crackers

  *Fresh or canned (in water) artichoke hearts
  may be substituted. Canned artichoke hearts
  are precooked and do not require additional
  cooking for this recipe.*

Preheat the oven to 350°F. Grease a 1-quart
round baking dish.

  In a medium mixing bowl, place the artichoke hearts, mayonnaise, Parmesan cheese, garlic, and onions; stir well to combine. Place the
mixture in the prepared baking dish; bake 20
minutes or until bubbly. Serve warm with
crackers.

**MAKES ABOUT 3 CUPS
(6 DOZEN HORS D'OEUVRES)**

ASPARAGUS ROLLS

*I receive more recipe requests from friends for this sim-
ple hors d'oeuvre than for any other hors d'oeuvre
I serve.*

36 medium-small fresh asparagus spears*
1 pound sliced bacon
36 slices of thinly sliced, soft-style, very
  fresh, white sandwich bread (the least
  expensive kind of bread works best with
  this recipe)
1 1/2 cups Miracle Whip salad dressing
1/2 cup plus 2 tablespoons butter, softened

  *One 10 1/2-ounce can of small green asparagus
  tips, drained, may be substituted. Canned
  asparagus tips are precooked and do not
  require additional cooking for this recipe.*

Wash the asparagus spears and cut them exactly
4 inches long; discard the cutaway stalks or
reserve for other use. Boil the asparagus spears
(page 303) 3 minutes; rinse them in cold water
to stop the cooking. Drain the spears well. Place
the spears on a plate; cover and refrigerate. Fry
the bacon until crisp; drain well between paper
towels. With your fingers, crumble the bacon.
Place the bacon in a small storage container;
cover and refrigerate.

  Assemble the Asparagus Rolls no longer than
2 hours before serving. To assemble, cut the
crusts off the bread slices. Keep the bread slices
covered to retain softness. Using a small, narrow
spatula, spread salad dressing liberally on one
side of each slice of bread (about 2 teaspoons
per slice) to within about 1/4 inch of the edges.
Sprinkle about 1 tablespoon crumbled bacon
over the salad dressing on each bread slice. Place
1 asparagus spear diagonally across the center of
each slice. Roll each slice diagonally around the
asparagus spear and place in a shallow, ungreased
baking pan, with the unsealed corner of bread
down. Place the Asparagus Rolls side by side,
touching each other, in the pan. Using a table
knife, spread about 1/2 teaspoon butter over the
top of each roll. Cover the pan tightly with aluminum foil until ready to serve.

  When ready to serve, preheat the broiler.
Uncover the pan of Asparagus Rolls and place
under the broiler, 6 inches from the heat. Leave
under the broiler just a few minutes until the
tops of the rolls are golden brown. Watch constantly as they can overbrown very quickly. Using a spatula, transfer the Asparagus Rolls to a
doily-lined tray and serve immediately.

MAKES 3 DOZEN

CRABMEAT SUPREME WITH SAUTÉED TOAST POINTS

1 pound cooked lump crabmeat, frozen or canned and drained
11 ounces cream cheese, softened
2 tablespoons butter
1/2 cup finely chopped green bell peppers
1/4 cup drained, minced capers
1/2 cup mayonnaise
1 tablespoon finely snipped, fresh parsley
1 tablespoon drained, prepared horseradish, homemade (page 46) or commercially canned
1/4 teaspoon salt
Dash cayenne pepper
2 teaspoons Worcestershire sauce
1/4 cup dry white wine
1/4 cup Buttered Bread Crumbs (page 49)
Paprika
2 recipes Sautéed Toast Points (page 430)

Preheat the oven to 375°F. Lightly butter a 1-quart round baking dish.

Place the crabmeat in a small mixing bowl. With your fingers, carefully remove any bits of cartilage or shell and discard; set aside. Place the softened cream cheese in a medium mixing bowl; set aside. In a skillet, over medium-low heat, melt the butter; add the green peppers and sauté until soft but not browned (about 3 minutes). Add the green peppers, capers, mayonnaise, parsley, horseradish, salt, cayenne pepper, Worcestershire sauce, and white wine to the cream cheese; using an electric mixer, beat on medium-high speed until the ingredients are well blended. Add the crabmeat; using a spoon, fold in. Pour into the prepared baking dish. Sprinkle the bread crumbs on top. Bake uncovered for 30 minutes.

To serve, sprinkle sparingly with paprika. Place the casserole in the center of a serving dish and surround with Sautéed Toast Points. Supply 1 or 2 small knives for serving.

MAKES 4 DOZEN HORS D'OEUVRES

DEVILED HAM DELECTABLES

1 4¼-ounce can deviled ham
1 finely grated, hard-cooked, extra-large egg yolk (page 264)
2 teaspoons finely grated onions
2 teaspoons prepared mustard
1/4 teaspoon dry mustard
1/8 teaspoon salt
Dash white pepper
1/4 cup Miracle Whip salad dressing
3 extra-large egg whites, room temperature
2½ dozen plain melba rounds
1 tablespoon finely shredded, sharp cheddar cheese

In a medium mixing bowl, place the deviled ham, grated egg yolk, onions, prepared mustard, dry mustard, salt, white pepper, and salad dressing; stir until thoroughly combined. Cover and refrigerate if hors d'oeuvres are to be served later.

Just before ready to serve, preheat the broiler. Remove the deviled ham mixture from the refrigerator; uncover and set aside.

Place the egg whites in a medium mixing bowl; using an electric mixer, beat on high speed until stiff but still moist and glossy. Add the egg whites to the deviled ham mixture; quickly fold in. Spread the mixture on melba rounds. Sprinkle a scant amount of cheese over the deviled ham mixture on each melba round. Place the rounds in a shallow baking pan; broil 4 inches from the heat until bubbly. Watch carefully. Serve immediately.

MAKES ABOUT 2½ DOZEN

GOUDA IN PUFF PASTRY

1 7-ounce round of Gouda cheese
1 sheet frozen puff pastry (½ of a
  17¼-ounce package)
1 extra-large egg
1 teaspoon whole milk
¼ teaspoon garlic powder
1 tablespoon freshly grated Parmesan
  cheese (page 46)
Plain butter crackers

3 HOURS BEFORE SERVING: Remove the red wax
covering from the Gouda cheese. Place the
cheese on a small plate; cover with plastic wrap
and let stand at room temperature.

1½ HOURS BEFORE SERVING: Remove 1 sheet of
frozen puff pastry from the package; place it
folded on a floured pastry cloth; let stand 20
minutes to thaw. Unfold the puff pastry carefully on the pastry cloth; let stand an additional
15 minutes to continue thawing.

Meanwhile, in a small mixing bowl, place the
egg and milk; using an electric mixer, beat
briefly until blended; set aside.

Preheat the oven to 400° F.

Cover a rolling pin with a stockinet (page 54);
flour the stockinet lightly. Roll the pastry sheet
to a 10½-inch square. Place an inverted 9-inch
pie pan on the pastry; using a small, sharp knife,
cut the pastry around the periphery of the
inverted pie pan to form a circle of pastry. Lift
the pie pan from pastry. Lift the excess pastry
from the edges of the circle and reserve for
optional cutout decoration (see Note). Place the
Gouda cheese, more-rounded side down, in the
center of the pastry circle. Sprinkle the garlic
powder on the cheese round; using your fingers,
rub the powder evenly over the exposed surface
of the cheese. Sprinkle the Parmesan cheese
over the cheese round. Using the back of a teaspoon, press the Parmesan cheese onto the
exposed top of the cheese round.

Using a soft, small pastry brush, brush the egg
mixture around the edges of the pastry circle to
help seal the pastry in the next step. Pull 2 opposite sides of the pastry circle snugly over the
cheese round; using your fingers, pinch the pastry edges together to seal (stretch pastry slightly
if necessary). Pull the remaining edges of the
pastry snugly over the cheese round, wrapping it
like a package. Use your hands to *lightly*—and
with minimum handling—press the pastry
against the Gouda to retain the circular shape of
the round. Using kitchen scissors, cut away ½-
to ¾-inch excess pastry from the last edges of
pastry pulled over the cheese round; brush the
cut pastry edges with the egg mixture and pinch
to seal.

Turn over the pastry-wrapped cheese round
and place, seam side down, on the pastry cloth.
Brush all exposed pastry surfaces with the egg
mixture. (Do not brush the underneath seam
side.) Decorate the pastry, if desired, using the
excess pastry (see Note). Using a spatula, place
the pastry-wrapped cheese round on a
parchment-paper-lined cookie sheet. (If parchment paper is not available, place it on an
ungreased cookie sheet.) Bake 20 minutes.

Remove from the oven; using a spatula, transfer the baked Gouda to a serving plate. Let stand
15 minutes before serving; then serve immediately. Supply a very sharp knife with which
guests may cut small wedges of the pastry-
wrapped cheese. Arrange crackers in a dish next
to the cheese. Because warm Gouda runs
slightly, it is better to eat this hors d'oeuvre atop
a light, buttery cracker.

NOTE: To decorate the top of the pastry-wrapped
Gouda, use tiny, flour-dipped cutters in designs
or an X-Acto knife to cut a design, such as a
flower, out of the rolled, excess puff pastry.
Brush the back of each pastry cutout with the
egg mixture and very lightly press it onto the
unbaked, pastry-wrapped Gouda round which
has been brushed with the egg mixture. When
all parts of the decoration have been arranged,
brush the top of the decoration with the egg
mixture. Follow the baking procedure in the
recipe.

MAKES ABOUT 16 HORS D'OEUVRES

SAUSAGE PUFFS

12 ounces sage-seasoned bulk pork sausage
¼ cup fine Dried Bread Crumbs (page 48)
1 tablespoon snipped, fresh parsley
¼ cup minced onions
1 extra-large egg, beaten
1 sheet frozen puff pastry (½ of a
  17¼-ounce package)
Sprigs of fresh sage for decoration
  (optional)
Sprigs of fresh parsley for decoration
  (optional)

Preheat the oven to 400°F.

In a medium bowl, place the sausage, crumbs, parsley, onions, and egg; stir to combine. Divide the mixture into thirds and shape into 3 rolls, each 7½ inches long. Place the rolls in a shallow, ungreased baking pan; bake 20 minutes. Remove from the oven and transfer the rolls onto 3 layers of paper towels to drain and cool. Meanwhile, place 1 sheet of frozen puff pastry, folded, on a floured pastry cloth; let stand 20 minutes to thaw.

Preheat the oven to 425°F.

Unfold the puff pastry carefully on the pastry cloth; let stand an additional 15 minutes to continue thawing. Using a sharp knife, cut the pastry into quarters (approximately square). Cover a rolling pin with a stockinet (page 54); flour the stockinet lightly. Roll 3 of the pastry quarters into rectangles approximately 6 × 9 inches; reserve the fourth pastry quarter for other uses. Place 1 roll of sausage along the 9-inch side of 1 of the pastry rectangles; roll the sausage, jelly-roll fashion, in the pastry. With your fingers, seal the side seam and ends of the pastry roll well. Repeat the procedure with the other 2 sausage rolls. Place the pastry rolls in an ungreased 10½ × 15½-inch cookie pan; bake 12 to 15 minutes. Using a sharp, thin-bladed knife, cut each roll widthwise into ½-inch slices. Serve immediately. The serving plate may be decorated with sprigs of fresh sage and parsley.

MAKES 42

PIGS IN A BLANKET
Saucijzebroodjes

A popular, traditional Holland Dutch pastry, Pigs in a Blanket are most often enjoyed at Dutch coffee tijd *(time) in the mid-morning or mid-afternoon, when fairly substantial fare may be served. Pigs in a Blanket are most commonly made in approximately 3-inch lengths; however, in this recipe I have shortened them to about 2 inches for serving as hors d'oeuvres.*

FILLING
¾ pound seasoned, lean bulk sausage
¾ pound lean, pure ground beef
¾ teaspoon salt
¼ teaspoon pepper
2 teaspoons finely crushed, dried leaf sage
½ cup Dutch rusk crumbs*
1 tablespoon half-and-half or whole milk

  *Dried Bread Crumbs (page 48) may be substituted.

In a medium mixing bowl, place the sausage, ground beef, salt, pepper, sage, rusk crumbs, and half-and-half; stir until thoroughly combined. Using a 1-inch trigger scoop and your hands, form the mixture into 1-inch-diameter balls. With the palms of your hands, roll each ball into a 1¾-inch-long by ½-inch-diameter roll; cover and refrigerate.

DOUGH
2 cups all-purpose flour
1 tablespoon baking powder
2 teaspoons sugar
¾ teaspoon salt
½ cup lard, refrigerated
1 extra-large egg, beaten
½ cup whole milk
About ¾ teaspoon lard to top pastries

Preheat the oven to 350°F.

Onto waxed paper, sift together the flour, baking powder, sugar, and salt; place in a large mixing bowl. Using a pastry blender, cut ½ cup lard into the flour mixture until it is the texture of cornmeal, with a few pieces the size of small peas; set aside. Place the egg in a small bowl; using an electric mixer, beat on medium speed. Add the milk; beat briefly to blend. Add the egg mixture to the flour mixture all at once; using a fork, mix *quickly*. Lightly flour your hands; form the dough into a ball and knead 30 seconds on a floured pastry cloth.

Divide the dough in half; wrap one half in plastic wrap and place in the refrigerator while working with the other half. Cover a rolling pin with a stockinet (page 54); flour the stockinet lightly. Roll half of the dough to ⅛-inch thickness. With a sharp, thin-bladed knife, cut the dough into 2 × 2½-inch rectangles. Place one roll of filling on each rectangle; roll the dough around the filling; pinch the side seam and ends to close. Place, side seam down, in an ungreased 10½ × 15½-inch cookie pan. Repeat the procedure with the remaining half of dough. Place a tiny dot of lard (about half the size of a chocolate chip) on top of each pastry. Bake 30 minutes. Serve hot.

MAKES ABOUT 4 DOZEN

VARIATION: Pigs in a Blanket may be made in lengths up to 3 inches.

PIZZA MUSHROOMS

1 pound (about 4 dozen) medium-small
    (bite-sized), fresh mushrooms
⅓ cup white wine vinegar
⅔ cup water
¼ teaspoon dry mustard
¼ teaspoon salt
⅛ teaspoon white pepper
⅔ cup commercially canned pizza sauce
⅓ cup finely chopped pepperoni
⅓ cup finely chopped green bell peppers
2 tablespoons finely chopped onions
⅔ cup finely shredded mozzarella cheese

THE DAY BEFORE SERVING: Wash the mushrooms and remove the stems by snapping them out of the caps. Set the mushroom caps aside, stem side down, on 3 layers of paper towels; reserve the stems for other uses or discard. In a pint glass jar, place the vinegar, water, dry mustard, salt, and white pepper. Cover and shake vigorously until blended; set aside. Place the mushroom caps in a ½-gallon zipper-seal plastic bag; add the vinegar mixture (marinade) and seal the bag securely. Turn the bag until all the mushrooms are coated with the marinade. Place the bag in a shallow, glass dish (in case of leakage); refrigerate. Turn the bag several times during the 24-hour marinating period.

THE DAY OF SERVING: In a small mixing bowl, place the pizza sauce, pepperoni, green peppers, and onions; stir until combined. Cover and refrigerate.

3 HOURS OR LESS BEFORE SERVING: Drain the mushrooms in a sieve or colander; discard the marinade or reserve for other uses. Place the mushrooms, stem side down, on 3 layers of paper towels to continue draining. Lay another paper towel over the mushrooms and pat dry. Using a teaspoon and your thumb, fill the stem cavities of the mushrooms with the pizza sauce mixture, mounding the mixture generously and patting it until smooth and symmetrical. Place the stuffed mushrooms in a very shallow baking pan. If not ready to serve, cover with plastic wrap and refrigerate.

SERVING TIME: Preheat the oven to 350° F.

Heat the stuffed mushrooms, uncovered, for 8 minutes. Remove from the oven.

Preheat the broiler.

Sprinkle a generous amount of mozzarella cheese over the stuffing in each mushroom. Place the pan of mushrooms under the broiler, 6 inches from the heat; watch carefully and remove from the broiler as soon as the cheese melts. Be careful not to overbroil, causing the cheese to overheat and become less attractive. Immediately remove the stuffed mushrooms from the pan and place them briefly on 3 layers of paper towels to dry the round bottoms of the mushrooms. Arrange the Pizza Mushrooms on a doily-lined serving tray or plate, and serve while hot.

MAKES ABOUT 4 DOZEN

SWEDISH MEATBALLS

1 cup whole milk
1 extra-large egg
2 slices white bread, crusts cut away
1 pound lean, pure ground beef
1 pound lean ground pork
1 pound ground ham
2 tablespoons vegetable shortening
1 cup packed dark brown sugar
1 tablespoon cornstarch
½ cup red wine vinegar
½ cup beef broth, homemade (page 87) or
   commercially canned
1 tablespoon tomato catsup, home canned
   (page 781) or commercially canned
1 teaspoon dry mustard

Grease a 2-quart round baking dish; set aside.

In a large mixing bowl, place the milk and egg; using an electric mixer, beat on medium speed until blended. Place the bread in the egg mixture and let soak thoroughly; then, using the electric mixer, beat the bread mixture on medium-low speed until the bread is broken into tiny pieces. Add the beef, pork, and ham; using a mixing spoon, mix until completely and evenly combined. Using a 1-inch trigger scoop or melon baller, measure the meat mixture and roll in the palms of your hands to form small, uniform meatballs. In an electric skillet or skillet on the range, melt the shortening over medium heat (350° F. in an electric skillet). Distribute the melted shortening over the bottom of the skillet. Add the meatballs and brown well, rolling often to maintain their round shape. Cook in batches if necessary. Drain the meatballs on 3 layers of paper towels. Place the drained meatballs in the prepared baking dish; set aside.

Preheat the oven to 300° F.

In a small saucepan, place the brown sugar, cornstarch, vinegar, beef broth, catsup, and dry mustard; stir to combine. Over medium heat, bring the mixture to a boil, stirring constantly; pour over the meatballs. Bake, uncovered, 2 hours. Serve in the baking dish or transfer to a chafing dish. Provide fancy toothpicks in an attractive container next to the meatballs and a small plate on which used toothpicks may be discarded.

MAKES ABOUT 9 DOZEN

WATER CHESTNUT ROLL-UPS

1 8-ounce can whole water chestnuts
¼ cup packed dark brown sugar
½ teaspoon dry mustard
¼ cup tomato catsup, home canned
   (page 781) or commercially canned
8 slices bacon

Preheat the broiler.

Drain the water chestnuts in a small sieve; place on 2 layers of paper towels to dry; set aside. In a small sauce dish, place the brown sugar and dry mustard; stir to combine; set aside. Place the catsup in a small sauce dish; set aside. Cut each bacon slice into thirds widthwise; set aside. Dip each water chestnut in the catsup, roll in the brown sugar mixture to coat, and wrap in a piece of bacon. Place, seam up, in a shallow baking pan. Broil, 6 inches from the heat, about 6 minutes. Remove from the broiler. Place a cellophane-frilled toothpick in each roll-up. Lift each roll-up from the baking pan, lightly blot it on 2 layers of paper towels, and place it on a doily-lined serving dish. Serve immediately.

MAKES ABOUT 2 DOZEN

BOURBON BANGERS

1¼ cups tomato catsup, home canned
    (page 781) or commercially canned
½ cup packed dark brown sugar
1 tablespoon finely grated onions
2 teaspoons prepared mustard
½ cup bourbon
1 pound fully cooked, smoked, cocktail-
    sized sausages

In a medium saucepan, place the catsup, brown sugar, onions, mustard, and bourbon; stir to combine. Bring the mixture to a simmer over medium-high heat. Reduce the heat to low and slowly simmer, uncovered, 5 minutes, stirring occasionally. Add the sausages and heat through. Serve in a chafing dish with an attractive holder full of cellophane-frilled toothpicks on the side.

MAKES ABOUT 4 DOZEN

WINGLETS ORIENTAL

1½ pounds (about 16) drumstick sections
    of chicken wings
¼ cup packed light brown sugar
½ teaspoon dry mustard
2 tablespoons butter
¼ cup soy sauce

Preheat the oven to 350° F. Butter an 8 × 8-inch baking dish.

Place the drumsticks in the prepared baking dish; set aside. In a small bowl, place the brown sugar and dry mustard; stir to combine; set aside. Place the butter in a small saucepan; melt over low heat. Add the soy sauce and brown sugar mixture. Bring to a boil over medium heat, stirring constantly; pour over drumsticks. Bake 45 minutes, turning once after 25 minutes baking time. Drain briefly on paper towels.

MAKES ABOUT 16

SPINACH BARS

1 cup all-purpose flour
1 teaspoon baking powder
1 teaspoon salt
2 extra-large eggs
6 tablespoons butter, melted
2 pounds fresh spinach, cooked, well
    drained, and finely chopped (not
    buttered; page 339) (about 1 cup)
¼ cup finely grated onions
1 pound Monterey Jack cheese, shredded

Preheat the oven to 350° F. Using a pastry brush, grease a 10½ × 15½ × 1-inch cookie pan with vegetable oil. Using paper towels, remove the excess oil; set aside.

Onto waxed paper, sift together the flour, baking powder, and salt; set aside. Place the eggs in a medium mixing bowl; using an electric mixer, beat lightly on medium speed. Add the butter; beat on medium speed until blended. Add the flour mixture; beat on low speed only until blended. Add the spinach, onions, and cheese; using a mixing spoon, fold in until evenly combined. Spoon the mixture into the prepared cookie pan; using a large, narrow spatula, spread lightly and evenly. Bake 40 minutes.

Remove from the oven and place on a wire rack; let cool 5 minutes. Then, using a sharp, thin-bladed knife, cut into 64 bars. Using a small spatula, remove the bars from the pan and place momentarily on 3 layers of paper towels to dry the bottom surfaces before transferring to a serving plate. Serve immediately.

MAKES 64

First-Course Appetizers

SHRIMP MOUSSE WITH DILL

¾ pound raw, unshelled shrimp, boiled
    (page 229), shelled and deveined (page
    229), and chilled
½ cup tomato juice
1 tablespoon plus 1 teaspoon (2 envelopes)
    unflavored gelatin
1 cup tomato juice
2 teaspoons sugar
¼ teaspoon salt
16 ounces commercial sour cream
1 tablespoon freshly squeezed, strained
    lemon juice
1 tablespoon cider vinegar
2 teaspoons onion juice (page 45)
½ teaspoon Worcestershire sauce
2 dashes Tabasco pepper sauce
1 tablespoon packed, snipped, fresh
    dillweed
2 recipes Dill Sauce (page 363)
Sprigs of fresh dillweed for decoration

Lightly oil (see To Lightly Oil a Salad Mold,
page 109) a 4½ × 8½-inch loaf pan; set aside.

Using a food processor, process the shrimp, in
2 batches, pulsing until finely flaked (about 1½
cups finely flaked shrimp). Place the processed
shrimp in a bowl; cover and refrigerate. Pour
½ cup tomato juice into a small sauce dish.
Sprinkle the gelatin over the juice; stir in; let
stand 15 minutes.

Pour 1 cup tomato juice into a small saucepan; bring to a boil over high heat. Turn off the
heat; add the gelatin mixture, sugar, and salt; stir

until completely dissolved. Remove the saucepan from the range; set aside. In a blender or
food processor, place the sour cream, lemon
juice, vinegar, onion juice, Worcestershire sauce,
and pepper sauce. Add the tomato juice mixture; process in the blender or food processor
until completely blended. Add 1 tablespoon dillweed; process very briefly only until evenly distributed. Add the shrimp; process very briefly
only until combined. Turn the mixture into the
prepared loaf pan. Using a small, narrow spatula,
spread smoothly. Refrigerate until cold; then
cover with plastic wrap and aluminum foil (over
the plastic wrap). Return to the refrigerator;
wait until completely set (at least 8 hours) before
serving.

To serve, unmold (page 109) on a flat cutting
surface. Cut widthwise into 18 ⅜-inch slices
(page 109). Spoon about 1½ tablespoons Dill
Sauce into the center of small, individual serving plates; using the back of the spoon, spread
the sauce over the center section of each plate.
Lay 1 slice of Shrimp Mousse over the sauce on
each plate (some of the sauce should be visible
beyond the edges of the mousse slice). Decorate
the top of each Shrimp Mousse slice with a
small, feathery sprig of fresh dillweed.

SERVES 18

VARIATION ~ **TO SERVE AS AN HORS D'OEUVRE:**
Mold the Shrimp Mousse with Dill in a lightly
oiled 4-cup curved fish mold (mold the remaining Shrimp Mousse in a small 1-cup mold for
later use). Unmold the mousse (page 109) on an
appropriate serving plate; decorate the plate
with fresh dill sprigs. Supply a small, wide-
bladed knife. Arrange small, plain water crackers
on a dish or in a napkin-lined basket and place
beside the mousse serving plate. (Eliminate the
Dill Sauce.)

SHRIMP COCKTAIL

Leaf lettuce
¼ cup plus 2 tablespoons chopped celery
½ cup boiled, fresh or frozen Alaskan king
    crabmeat (page 230)* chopped
30 to 36 medium-sized, raw, unshelled
    shrimp, boiled (page 229), shelled with
    the tails removed, and deveined
    (page 229)
½ recipe Cocktail Sauce (page 361)

*Canned and drained crabmeat may be
substituted.*

All ingredients should be cold before assembling
the Shrimp Cocktail. Line crystal sherbet glasses
with leaf lettuce. Sprinkle 1 tablespoon chopped
celery in the bottom of each glass over the lettuce. Distribute 1 tablespoon plus 1 teaspoon
chopped crabmeat over the chopped celery in
each glass. Arrange 5 or 6 shrimp, depending
upon their size and the size of the sherbet
glasses, on top of the crabmeat. Spoon Cocktail
Sauce over the shrimp.

Place each sherbet glass of Shrimp Cocktail
on a small, doily-lined plate. Cocktail forks
should be provided with each diner's table
service.

SERVES 6

SCALLOPED LOBSTER

¼ cup plus 2 tablespoons all-purpose flour
½ teaspoon salt
Dash of cayenne pepper
¾ cup (¼ pound plus 4 tablespoons) butter
¼ cup plus 2 tablespoons dry sherry
1 quart half-and-half
6 extra-large egg yolks, slightly beaten
2½ cups boiled lobster meat (page 230)
    cut into small, bite-sized pieces (about
    2 pounds uncooked lobster tails)
1 cup Buttered Bread Crumbs (page 49)
Sprigs of fresh lemon thyme (optional)

Preheat the oven to 350° F. Butter twelve 5-
inch-diameter by 1-inch-deep round baking
dishes appropriate for serving; set aside.

In a small bowl, place the flour, salt, and
cayenne pepper; stir to combine; set aside. In the
top of a double boiler, over low boiling water,
melt the butter. Remove the top of the double
boiler from the bottom pan. Add the flour mixture to the melted butter; stir until perfectly
smooth. Add the sherry and half-and-half; stir
in. Return the top of the double boiler to the
bottom pan. Over low boiling water, cook the
mixture until heated through. In a small bowl,
spoon some of the hot mixture into the egg
yolks and stir in. Add the egg yolk mixture to
the mixture in the double boiler; stir vigorously
to blend. Continue cooking and stirring until
the mixture begins to thicken. Add the lobster
and cook *just until the mixture thickens,* stirring
constantly. Remove the top of the double
boiler.

Using a slotted spoon, distribute the hot lobster meat among the 12 prepared baking dishes,
spreading the meat evenly on the bottom of
each dish. Then, fill each dish with sauce. Top
with buttered crumbs. Bake 5 minutes or until
hot.

Preheat the broiler.

Place the baking dishes of Scalloped Lobster
under the broiler; brown lightly. Garnish the top
of each serving with a small sprig of lemon
thyme, if desired. Place each baking dish on a
doily-lined, salad-sized plate.

SERVES 12

SCALLOPED KING CRAB: Follow the Scalloped
Lobster recipe, above, substituting boiled Alaskan
king crabmeat (page 230) for the lobster meat.

HICKORY-SMOKED HAM MOUSSE

¼ cup cold water
1 tablespoon plus 1 teaspoon (2 envelopes)
    unflavored gelatin
⅔ cup boiling water
3 tablespoons Miracle Whip salad dressing
2 tablespoons beer mustard*
2 tablespoons cream-style, prepared
    horseradish, homemade (page 46) or
    commercially canned
¼ teaspoon paprika
2 tablespoons snipped, fresh parsley
3 cups (about 13½ ounces) fully cooked,
    finely ground, hickory-smoked ham
1 cup (½ pint) whipping cream
2 tablespoons powdered sugar
Sprigs of fresh parsley for decoration
1 recipe Horseradish Sauce (page 361)

*If beer mustard is not available, Düsseldorf
mustard or a brown mustard with smooth
consistency may be substituted.*

Lightly oil (see To Lightly Oil a Salad Mold,
page 109) a 4½ × 8½-inch loaf pan; set aside.

Pour ¼ cup cold water into a small mixing
bowl. Sprinkle the gelatin over the cold water;
let stand 15 minutes. Add ⅔ cup boiling water
to the gelatin mixture; stir until completely dissolved. Pour the gelatin mixture into a blender
or food processor. Add the salad dressing, beer
mustard, horseradish, and paprika; process until
fully blended. Add parsley; process briefly to
combine. Add ham; process briefly until combined. Set aside.

Pour the whipping cream into a medium
mixing bowl; using an electric mixer, beat on
high speed until the cream begins to thicken.
Add the powdered sugar; beat on medium speed
until stiff; set aside. Turn the blender or food
processor on, briefly, to recombine the ham
mixture. Transfer the ham mixture to a large
mixing bowl. Add the whipped cream; using a
large mixing spoon, fold in. Turn the mixture
into the prepared loaf pan; using a small, narrow
spatula, spread smoothly. Refrigerate until cold;
then, cover with plastic wrap and aluminum foil
(over the plastic wrap). Return to the refrigerator; wait until completely set (at least 8 hours)
before serving.

To serve, unmold (page 109) on a flat cutting
surface. Cut widthwise into 18 ⅜-inch slices
(page 109). Place 1 slice of Ham Mousse on each
individual serving plate; decorate with parsley
sprigs. Pass the Horseradish Sauce in an attractive
crystal or silver serving bowl at the table.

SERVES 18

VARIATION ~ **TO SERVE AS AN HORS D'OEUVRE:**
Mold Hickory-Smoked Ham Mousse in a decorative, lightly oiled 4-cup mold. Line a serving
plate with red-tip Boston lettuce leaves. Unmold the mousse (page 109) on the lettuce
leaves. Serve with stoned rye crackers; provide a
small, wide-bladed knife. (Eliminate the Horseradish Sauce.)

Other First-Course Appetizers

Broiled Grapefruit (page 347)
Chicken-Macaroni Loaf (page 286)
Creamed Mushrooms in tiny rice ring molds
    (page 324, see Serving Suggestions)
Fettucine Alfredo (page 283)
French-Fried Onion Rings (page 326)
Venison Pâté (page 243)
Wild Duck Pâté (page 243)
Wild Goose Pâté (page 242)

Snacks

MUNCHIES

1 12-ounce package Corn Chex cereal
7 ounces (about 1½ cups) dry-roasted
   mixed nuts
¾ cup (¼ pound plus 4 tablespoons) butter
1½ cups packed light brown sugar
⅓ cup light corn syrup
¼ teaspoon baking soda

Preheat the oven to 300°F.

In a very large mixing bowl, place the cereal
and nuts; stir to combine, being careful not to
crumble the cereal; set aside. Place the butter in
a medium, heavy saucepan; melt the butter over
medium heat. Remove from the heat. Add the
brown sugar and corn syrup; stir together. Bring
to a full boil over medium-high heat, stirring
constantly. Remove from the heat. Add the baking soda; stir until well blended. Pour over the
cereal mixture; using a large mixing spoon, stir
until evenly coated. Transfer the mixture to an
ungreased 9 × 13-inch baking pan; distribute
evenly. Place in the oven for 15 minutes.

Remove from the oven; invert the pan of hot
mixture onto a large area of waxed paper. Using
a large mixing spoon, distribute the mixture
over the waxed paper; let stand 1 hour to cool
and dry. Then, using your hands, break into
small clumps; store in an airtight container.
Keeps up to 1 week at room temperature.

MAKES ABOUT 12 CUPS

BEER NUTS

1 cup sugar
½ cup water
12 ounces raw peanuts
Salt

Preheat the oven to 300°F. Butter a 9 × 13-inch
baking pan; set aside.

In a medium skillet, place the sugar and
water; stir together. Over medium-high heat,
bring the mixture to a boil; add the peanuts and
boil 7 minutes (no more). Using a slotted mixing spoon, place the peanuts in the prepared
baking pan; sprinkle with salt. Discard the syrup.
Bake the peanuts 30 minutes, turning 3 times
with a spatula. Remove from the oven and place
on a wire rack to cool. Store in a covered quart
jar. Keeps up to 1 month.

MAKES 2¼ CUPS

OYSTER CRACKER SNACKS

1 10-ounce package oyster crackers
¾ cup vegetable oil
1 1-ounce package ranch salad dressing
   mix
2 tablespoons dried dillweed

Place the crackers in a large mixing bowl; set
aside. In a small mixing bowl, place the vegetable oil and salad dressing mix; using a spoon,
beat until blended. Drizzle over the crackers and
toss. Sprinkle the dillweed over the crackers and
toss again. Let stand several hours at room temperature, stirring lightly several times. Store in
an airtight container in the refrigerator up to 1
month.

MAKES ABOUT 6 CUPS

GRANOLA

1 18-ounce box (about 6 cups) quick-cooking rolled oats, uncooked
¾ cup untoasted (raw) wheat germ
⅓ cup sesame seeds
1 cup coarsely chopped hazelnuts
¾ cup flaked coconut
½ cup packed light brown sugar
½ cup (¼ pound) margarine, melted
½ cup honey
1½ teaspoons pure vanilla extract
1½ cups raisins
1 8-ounce package dried mixed fruit, coarsely diced (2 cups) (optional)

Preheat the oven to 350° F.

Pour the oats into an ungreased 9 × 13-inch baking pan. Bake 10 minutes, turning once with a spatula after 5 minutes of baking. Meanwhile, in a medium mixing bowl, place the wheat germ, sesame seeds, hazelnuts, coconut, and brown sugar; stir to combine; set aside. Place the margarine in a small saucepan; over very low heat, melt the margarine. Remove from the heat. Add the honey and vanilla; stir vigorously until completely blended; set aside. Remove the oats from the oven and transfer to a very large mixing bowl. Leave the oven on at 350° F.

Add the wheat germ mixture to the oats; stir until evenly combined. Add the honey mixture; stir until the mixture is evenly dampened. Spoon the mixture equally into two 9 × 13-inch ungreased baking pans. Bake 20 minutes, turning the mixture every 5 minutes to achieve even browning. Remove from the oven and place the pans on wire racks; cool 5 minutes. Add the raisins and mixed fruit (if included), dividing equally between the 2 pans; stir to combine. Keep the pans on the wire racks and stir the Granola occasionally as it cools, breaking up any clumps of mixture sticking together.

When completely cool, store in zipper-seal plastic bags. Keeps up to 2 weeks at room temperature and up to 1 month in the refrigerator.

MAKES ABOUT 10 CUPS

SERVING SUGGESTIONS: Serve dry as a nutritious snack or serve with milk as a breakfast cereal.

Other Snack Recipes

Caramel Corn (page 690)
Spiced Pecans (page 688)

Soups and Stews

Soups

It's the stick-to-your-ribs kind of soups, brewed when snowdrifts bank against the house, that predominates in Heartland kitchens. More often than not, when soup is on the home menu, it is the main course for dinner, with leftovers zapped in the microwave at lunchtime the next day. This soup-as-the-main-course practice results, in part, from the fact that first-course appetizers (including soup) are uncommonly served in Midwest households (see pages 59–60 for more about this).

After Bean Soup (page 89), I would venture to say that Vegetable Soup (page 93) and Chili (page 97) are the soups most often prepared in many Mid-American homes. Corn Chowder (page 96) might be a close runner-up, with Potato Soup (page 94) enjoying its cadre of devotees.

Other kinds of soups more commonly are eaten when dining out at lunch, or are sometimes selected when dinner menus offer the option of soup or salad for the first course. Wisconsin Beer Cheese Soup (page 95), currently enjoying a wave of popularity, is such an example—often eaten in restaurants, but prepared somewhat infrequently in most Midwest home kitchens.

But keep in mind that the Midwest is a big place. When you enter Ohio coming from the east on Interstate 80, you will put about 1,250 miles on your car before you leave Nebraska, driving west, and there is bound to be some variation in soup-preparation and -eating customs along this route.

Any cuisine, no matter how wonderful, has some weak spots, and a book on Midwest cooking would be less than credible if the few vulnerable points in this otherwise superlative fare were not mentioned. One foible is overuse of canned soups in cooking, particularly creams of mushroom, celery, and chicken, which are often called for in recipes. While I would be the last cook in the world to say these palatable commercial soups do not have their place in occasional, day-to-day family dishes because of their quick-and-easy-to-use attributes, too much of a good thing is just that.

I have tried to present a collection of recipes, with attendant cooking-style descriptions, which represent the best of Midwest cooking today. Therefore, with few exceptions, the recipes do not include commercially canned cream soups. One of those exceptions is Green Bean Casserole (page 305). This traditional recipe, which calls for a can of cream of mushroom soup, is so ingrained in family eating habits (and faithfully prepared by memory), I wouldn't dream of tampering with it. Besides, it's great-tasting as is—a four-star, palate-pleasing comfort food! On the other hand, I replaced the can of cream of mushroom soup with other ingredients in the recipe for Broccoli-Rice Casserole (page 273), also a very popular dish in many Midwestern locales.

To assist readers who would like to enhance the flavor and quality of some Midwest dishes whose recipes call for commercially canned cream soups, made-from-scratch versions of cream of mushroom and cream of celery soups are given on page 89. Soups made with these recipes may be used in direct substitution for their canned counterparts.

Felicitous use of a canned commercial soup (other than cream-style) is exemplified in the Midwest oldie, Tomato Soup Salad Dressing (page 154), an excellent French-type dressing which counts among its ingredients one can of tomato soup.

Many recipes throughout this cookbook specify the alternative of using homemade or commercially canned chicken or beef broth. Of course, for exquisite flavor, homemade broth should be used; however, with the busyness of modern-day life, compromises are sometimes necessary.

Stews

When most Midwesterners think of stew, they think of beef stew, with potatoes, carrots, and onions. In fact, to many old-timers, that *is* stew. (Is there any other kind?) As much as Midwest families venerate this long-established—yet still great—dish (Farm-Style Beef Stew, page 100), it is surprising that the general Heartland-stew bill of fare does not offer greater variety.

Stews present a perfect opportunity for creative cooks to express their culinary prowess in unique, innovative food combinations, using all kinds of surprising ingredients—not to mention the secondary advantage of putting all the good food left in the refrigerator to happy use. Three new stew recipes for which I had the good fortune of winning blue ribbons (Brandied Pork Stew with Thyme Dumplings, page 98; Heartland Stew, page 102; and Soybean-Bratwurst Stew, page 104) are among the recipes in this chapter.

An exception to the Midwest's monolithic allegiance to beef stew is its annual bow to Oyster Stew (page 103), a Christmas eve tradition in many families across Middle America since settlement days. Amazingly, in the midst of sparse provisions, barrels and cans of oysters were frequently included in food supplies reaching the frontier in the mid-19th century. Oysters were extremely popular with pioneers who, in addition to making stew, pickled them or used them in oyster sauce to serve with turkey and fish, in dressing for wildfowl and poultry, and to prepare scalloped oysters.

The night-before-Christmas oyster stew tradition has held fast through the decades for some very good reasons: oyster stew is a delicacy of gourmet proportions, it is light dining before the following day's lavish feast, and it is easily prepared at the last minute—a boon to over-taxed holiday cooks. Of course, freshly shucked oysters are far superior, if available. Cook them only until slightly curled, and have the diners seated at the table—red candles flickering—ready with soup spoon at hand. Pass the heaping bowl of oyster crackers, and the excitement of Santa's imminent arrival will set in.

Soups

BEEF BROTH

Homemade broth discernibly improves the taste of foods in which it is used, and yet the mere idea of tak-ing the time to make homemade broth could be easily dismissed. But broth is so simple to make and can be left to simmer while you carry on other activities around the house or just relax. It is made in large quantities and freezes well, providing a superlative ingredient at your fingertips for weeks to come. Broth may be kept in the freezer (at 0° F. or below) up to 6 months.

2 pounds beef shank and 2 pounds beef knuckle, together containing a total of about ⅓ bone plus some fat
2 tablespoons vegetable shortening
2 cups water
14 cups water
1 large onion, coarsely chopped
½ cup coarsely chopped celery
½ cup pared and sliced carrots
4 large sprigs of fresh parsley
1 small bay leaf
4 whole cloves
5 whole black peppercorns
2 teaspoons salt

Cut the meat into 1-inch cubes, reserving the bones and fat. In a medium, heavy-bottomed skillet, melt the shortening over medium-high heat. Tilt the skillet back and forth to com-pletely cover the bottom with melted shorten-ing. Place ⅓ (only) of the meat in the skillet; brown well on all sides. Reduce the heat to low. Remove the browned meat from the skillet and place it in a kettle at least 8 quart in size; set aside. When the skillet cools, add 2 cups of water and deglaze. Pour the skillet liquid into the kettle with the meat. Add to the kettle the remaining ⅔ meat, bones, fat, 14 cups water, onion, celery, carrots, parsley, bay leaf, cloves, and peppercorns. Cover the kettle and bring the mixture to a boil over high heat. Reduce the heat and simmer the mixture *very slowly* 3½ hours, stirring occasionally. Add the salt; cover and simmer an additional ½ hour.

Using a slotted spoon, remove the beef and vegetables from the broth and reserve for other uses (see Note). Strain the broth through a sieve into a large bowl or plastic container; cover and refrigerate. When cold, spoon off and discard the congealed fat on top of the broth. Wipe the edges of the bowl (or container) with a clean, hot, damp cloth to remove all fat. The broth may be frozen in pint or quart plastic freezer containers.

NOTE: The reserved beef and vegetables may be used in making Cream of Vegetable-Beef Soup (page 93).

MAKES ABOUT 12 CUPS

CHICKEN BROTH

1 4-pound chicken, cut up
12 cups water
3 stalks celery (including 1 leafy top), cut
  into ½-inch pieces
3 carrots, pared and cut into ½-inch pieces
1 large onion, cut into large pieces
4 large sprigs of fresh parsley
1 small bay leaf
2 teaspoons salt
5 whole black peppercorns
½ teaspoon pepper

Wash the chicken under cold, running water. In a kettle at least 8 quart in size, place the chicken, water, celery, carrots, onion, parsley, bay leaf, salt, peppercorns, and pepper. Cover the kettle and bring the mixture to a boil over high heat. Reduce the heat and simmer the mixture *very slowly* 2 hours, stirring occasionally.

Using a slotted spoon, remove the chicken and vegetables from the broth and reserve for other uses (see Note). Strain the broth through a sieve into a large bowl or plastic container; cover and refrigerate. When cold, spoon off and discard the congealed fat on top of the broth. Wipe the edges of the bowl (or container) with a clean, hot, damp cloth to remove all fat. The broth may be frozen in pint or quart plastic freezer containers.

NOTE: The reserved vegetables may be (1) used in making Cream of Vegetable Soup (page 93), or (2) pressed through a food mill, then pureed in a blender and added to Beef Gravy (page 376) for a wonderful flavor-enhancer. Makes about 1¼ cups pureed vegetables.

MAKES ABOUT 10 CUPS

CLARIFIED BEEF OR CHICKEN BROTH

Cooks who have never clarified their homemade beef or chicken broths need not feel the least bit intimidated by this easy task. If the simple instructions are carefully followed, success is almost guaranteed.

4 cups Beef Broth (page 87) or Chicken
  Broth (left column)
1 extra-large egg, slightly beaten
1 eggshell, crushed

In a kettle or saucepan over medium heat, heat the broth until *just* warm. Add the egg and crushed egg shell; stir in. Increase heat to high and bring the mixture to the boiling point, stirring constantly. Reduce the heat, cover and simmer (do not boil) 15 minutes. Remove from the heat and let stand to settle. When the broth has settled, strain it through 4 layers of cheesecloth. This recipe may be doubled or tripled.

MAKES ABOUT 4 CUPS

SHERRIED BEEF BROTH

4 cups Clarified Beef Broth (recipe above)
¼ cup dry sherry, or to taste
¼ teaspoon salt, or to taste

Heat the Clarified Beef Broth. Add the sherry and salt. Serve with Rice Crackers (page 450).

MAKES ABOUT 4 CUPS

NOTE: Both recipes, above, may be doubled or tripled.

HOMEMADE EQUIVALENCIES OF COMMERCIALLY CANNED SOUPS

While very few recipes in this cookbook include the use of commercially canned soups, many Midwest casserole recipes call for canned cream soups, especially cream of mushroom and cream of celery. The following recipes may be substituted for one 10¾-ounce commercial can of condensed cream of mushroom soup (undiluted) and one 10¾-ounce commercial can of condensed cream of celery soup (undiluted), respectively, when these commercial soups are called for in recipes.

CREAM OF MUSHROOM SOUP

1 recipe Thick White Sauce (page 366)
1 tablespoon butter
½ cup coarsely chopped mushrooms

Make the Thick White Sauce; set aside. In a small, heavy-bottomed skillet, melt the butter over medium heat, being careful not to let it brown. Place the mushrooms in the skillet; sauté until the mushrooms give up their juices (about 3 minutes). Do not allow the mushrooms to brown. Add the mushrooms and pan juices to the white sauce; stir well.

MAKES 1½ CUPS

CREAM OF CELERY SOUP

1 recipe Thick White Sauce (page 366), substituting ½ teaspoon celery salt for ½ teaspoon salt
1 tablespoon butter
¼ cup minced celery
3 tablespoons minced leeks (whites only)

Make the Thick White Sauce; set aside. In a small, heavy-bottomed skillet, melt the butter over medium heat, being careful not to let it brown. Place the celery in the skillet; sauté 4 minutes. Do not allow the celery to brown. Remove from the heat. Using a slotted spoon, remove the celery (not the pan juices) from the skillet and add to the white sauce. Place the leeks in the same skillet; sauté 3 minutes over medium heat. Do not allow the leeks to brown. Add the leeks and pan juices to the white sauce; stir well.

MAKES 1½ CUPS

BEAN SOUP

Both smoked pork shank and smoked pork hock are used in this recipe. The shank supplies sufficient meat, and the hock gives additional flavor. Salt causes uncooked beans to become tough, so take care not to add the salt until the very end, after the beans have cooked. Little added salt is required in this recipe because the smoked pork imparts a salty flavor.

1 pound dried Great Northern beans
1½ pounds smoked pork shank
1 (about ½ pound) smoked pork hock
1 large onion
¼ cup packed light brown sugar
¼ teaspoon salt
¼ teaspoon plus ⅛ teaspoon pepper

Wash and sort the beans. Place the beans (unsoaked), pork shank, pork hock, and onion in an 8-quart kettle; add water to cover (about 10 cups). Cover the kettle and bring the mixture to a simmer over high heat. Reduce the heat and simmer for 1½ hours or until the beans are tender, stirring occasionally. Do not overcook, causing the beans to become mushy.

Remove from the heat. Remove and discard all the skin, bones, and fat from the meat. Tear the meat into bite-sized pieces and return to the soup. Using a spoon, break the onion into bite-sized pieces against the side of the kettle. Add the brown sugar, salt, and pepper; stir to combine. Cover the kettle; place it over the heat and simmer the mixture 5 minutes.

SERVES 10 AS A MAIN COURSE

ACCOMPANIMENT SUGGESTION: Hot Corn Bread (page 441) is traditionally served with Bean Soup.

TEN-BEAN SOUP

The Bean Mix portion of this recipe calls for mixing a total of 10 pounds of various beans, even though the soup uses only 2 cups of the mix. If your prefer not to have a quantity of leftover Bean Mix, just purchase fewer of the specified beans in equal quantities. My mother and several of her friends who liked and made this soup (I got the recipe from Mom) would bag their extra Bean Mix in 2-cup quantities and share it with each other. This bean-team approach kept everyone's cupboard stocked with ready Bean Mix, resulting in more frequent preparation of this hearty soup with less effort.

BEAN MIX
1 pound dried yellow split peas
1 pound dried green split peas
1 pound barley pearls
1 pound dried black beans
1 pound dried red beans
1 pound dried pinto beans
1 pound dried navy beans
1 pound dried Great Northern beans
1 pound dried lentils
1 pound dried black-eyed peas

Place all beans in a large bowl; stir until evenly distributed. Divide the bean mixture into ten 2-cup portions; place 9 of the 2-cup portions in individual zipper-seal plastic bags and reserve for future use or gift giving.

2 cups Bean Mix
8 cups water
2½ pounds smoked pork shanks
1 large onion, very coarsely chopped
1 garlic clove, pressed
1 16-ounce can commercial whole, peeled tomatoes, undrained, or 1 pint home-canned tomatoes (page 736), undrained
1 10-ounce can tomatoes and green chilies*

3 tablespoons packed dark brown sugar
1¼ teaspoons salt
¼ teaspoon pepper

*Found in the Mexican food section at the supermarket.

Wash and sort the 2 cups Bean Mix. Place the beans in a large, heavy-bottomed kettle; add cold water to 2 inches above the beans. Cover the kettle and soak the beans overnight.

Drain the beans in a sieve. Return the beans to the kettle; add 8 cups water; set aside. Rinse the pork shanks under cold, running water; add to the bean mixture. Add the onion and garlic. Cover the kettle; bring the mixture to a boil over high heat. Reduce the heat and simmer the mixture 1½ hours, stirring occasionally.

Then, place the tomatoes, with their liquid, in a medium mixing bowl; using the edge of a metal mixing spoon, chop the tomatoes coarsely. Add the cut-up tomatoes, tomatoes and green chilies, brown sugar, salt, and pepper to the bean mixture. Cover and simmer an additional 30 minutes, stirring occasionally. Remove from the heat. Remove the meat from the pork shanks; discard the bone and fat. Cut or tear the meat into bite-sized pieces and return to the soup. Cover the kettle and return the soup to a simmer; remove from the heat and serve.

SERVES 10

CONSOMMÉ MADRILÈNE

This truly sublime consommé is an impeccable first course for a grand, elegant dinner. Tomatoes combine with clarified beef and/or chicken broth and other flavorings in this timeless dish. I have chosen to use beef broth and have added a faint hint of sherry. Literally translated from the French, Consommé Madrilène means Madrid consommé. Tomatoes are associated with the cuisine of Madrid, thus explaining the name origin of this continental fare served across the Midwest.

2 cups drained, whole, peeled tomatoes, home canned (page 736) or commercially canned
2 cups Clarified Beef Broth (page 88)
1 tablespoon finely chopped celery
1 teaspoon grated onions
1 teaspoon freshly squeezed, strained lemon juice
5 whole black peppercorns
2 whole cloves
½ teaspoon salt
¼ teaspoon sugar
2 teaspoons dry sherry
2 drops liquid red food coloring*
Very thin slices of lemon for garnish

A few drops of beet juice may be substituted to produce an attractive red color.

Place the tomatoes in a blender or food processor and puree. Place the pureed tomatoes in a medium–large stainless steel saucepan. Add the beef broth, celery, onions, lemon juice, peppercorns, cloves, salt, and sugar; stir to combine. Cover the saucepan and bring the mixture to a simmer over medium heat, stirring occasionally. Reduce the heat and simmer, covered, 45 minutes, stirring occasionally.

Secure a piece of damp cotton flannel, napped side up, in a sieve over a deep pan. Pour the hot consommé over the cotton flannel and allow it to strain undisturbed; *do not* stir or squeeze, as this may cause the consommé to cloud.

Pour the strained consommé into a clean, stainless-steel saucepan. Add the sherry and food coloring; heat through. Ladle into bouillon cups. Float a thin slice of lemon on the top of each serving.

SERVES 6

COLD SHERRIED CUCUMBER SOUP

3 cups pared and cored (page 45) and coarsely cubed cucumbers
3 tablespoons finely chopped onions
2 tablespoons snipped, fresh dillweed
3 tablespoons cream sherry
2 teaspoons sugar
½ teaspoon salt
¼ teaspoon white pepper
16 ounces commercial sour cream
8 ounces plain lowfat yogurt
Small sprigs of fresh dillweed for garnish

Place the cucumbers, onions, snipped dillweed, sherry, sugar, salt, white pepper, sour cream, and yogurt in a blender or food processor. Process to liquefy the ingredients. Place the soup in a bowl or storage container; cover and refrigerate up to 1 day.

When ready to serve, stir the cucumber soup before ladling into soup cups; float a small sprig of dillweed on each serving.

MAKES ABOUT 5½ CUPS

CREAM OF TOMATO SOUP

2 16-ounce cans commercial whole, peeled
   tomatoes, undrained, or 1 quart home-
   canned Tomatoes (page 736), undrained*
3 tablespoons minced onions
1 teaspoon dried leaf basil
1 teaspoon sugar
¼ teaspoon celery seed
⅛ teaspoon white pepper
¼ teaspoon baking soda
¼ cup all-purpose flour
1 teaspoon salt
¼ teaspoon white pepper
¼ cup (4 tablespoons) butter
2 cups whole milk
2 cups (1 pint) half-and-half
6 sprigs of fresh coriander or 1 teaspoon
   snipped, fresh parsley for garnish

*6 cups blanched (page 44), stemmed, peeled,
cut-up, and cooked fresh tomatoes may be substituted. To cook, place the tomatoes in a
saucepan; do not add water. Cover the
saucepan. Bring the tomatoes to a simmer over
medium heat; reduce heat and simmer 8
minutes.*

In a medium-large saucepan, place the tomatoes, onions, basil, sugar, celery seed, and ⅛ teaspoon white pepper; stir to combine. Over
medium heat, simmer the mixture, uncovered,
30 minutes, until moderately thickened. Press
the mixture through a food mill to yield approximately 2½ cups. Add the baking soda; stir until
blended; cover and refrigerate.

In small bowl, place the flour, salt, and ¼ teaspoon white pepper; stir to combine; set aside.
In a large saucepan, melt the butter over low
heat. Remove from the heat; add the flour mixture and stir until completely smooth. Add the
milk and half-and-half; stir to mix. Place over
medium-low heat; cook until the milk mixture
thickens and is just under boiling, stirring constantly. Do not allow the mixture to boil.
Remove from the heat. If not ready to serve the
soup immediately, cover the saucepan and

refrigerate (separately from the tomato mixture).
The milk mixture and tomato mixture may be
refrigerated up to 24 hours before completing
and serving the soup.

When ready to serve, heat the milk mixture
over medium-low heat, stirring constantly (do
not allow to boil). Just before serving, add the
tomato mixture; heat through, stirring continuously (do not allow to boil). Ladle into soup
cups; garnish with the coriander or parsley.

SERVES 6

CREAM OF BROCCOLI SOUP

¼ cup all-purpose flour
1 teaspoon salt
¼ teaspoon white pepper
¾ teaspoon dried leaf oregano
¼ teaspoon curry powder
¼ cup (4 tablespoons) butter
⅔ cup finely chopped onions
3 cups whole milk
2 cups (1 pint) half-and-half
8 cups broccoli flowerets, steamed (page
   302) until tender

In a small bowl, place the flour, salt, white pepper, oregano, and curry powder; stir to combine;
set aside. In a large, heavy-bottomed skillet, melt
the butter over medium heat. Place the onions
in the skillet; sauté until tender, but not brown
(about 5 minutes). Remove from the heat and
add the flour mixture; stir until the flour mixture is completely smooth. Add the milk and
half-and-half; stir to mix. Place over medium-
low heat and cook until thick, stirring constantly. Do not allow to boil.

In a blender or food processor, place the
cooked cream mixture and broccoli; process
until smooth. Serve immediately or refrigerate
and heat through (do not allow to boil) before
serving. Best if served the day it is made.

SERVES 6

CREAM OF VEGETABLE SOUP

2 cups cooked mixed vegetables (such as carrots, celery, and onions) which have been pressed through a food mill when hot (measure after pressing)
¼ cup all-purpose flour
1 teaspoon dried leaf chervil
1 teaspoon celery salt
¼ teaspoon dried dillweed
⅛ teaspoon pepper
¼ cup (4 tablespoons) butter
1 cup whole milk
1 cup half-and-half
1 cup chicken broth, homemade (page 88) or commercially canned

Prepare the vegetables; set aside. In a small mixing bowl, place the flour, chervil, celery salt, dillweed, and pepper; set aside. In a medium saucepan, melt the butter over low heat. Remove from the heat; add the flour mixture and stir until the mixture is perfectly smooth. Add the milk, half-and-half, and chicken broth; stir to mix. Place over medium-low heat; cook until the mixture thickens and is just under boiling, stirring constantly. Do not allow the mixture to boil. Remove from the heat; add the pressed vegetables. Return to the heat and stir until the soup is hot (do not allow to boil).

SERVES 4

CREAM OF VEGETABLE-BEEF SOUP: Follow the Cream of Vegetable Soup recipe, above, including very tender, cooked beef with the vegetables pressed through a food mill (2 cups total pressed vegetables and beef).

SERVES 4

VEGETABLE SOUP

2 tablespoons butter
1½ cups coarsely chopped onions
6 cups homemade Chicken Broth (page 88) or 3 14½-ounce cans commercial chicken broth
1 14½-ounce can commercial, Italian-style stewed tomatoes
1 14½-ounce can commercial, regular stewed tomatoes
1½ cups pared and sliced carrots
1½ cups pared turnips cut into bite-sized cubes
1½ cups fresh green beans cut into 1¼-inch lengths
1 cup sliced celery
2 teaspoons drained, green peppercorns
1 teaspoon sugar
⅛ teaspoon ground allspice
1 large sprig of fresh parsley
2 sprigs of fresh savory
2 leafy celery tops
1 sprig of fresh basil
1 small bunch of fresh chives
1½ cups pared red potatoes cut into bite-sized cubes
1 cup fresh corn
1½ cups sliced zucchini

In a large, heavy-bottomed kettle, melt the butter over medium heat. Place the onions in the kettle. Sauté the onions until lightly golden (about 7 minutes), stirring often. Remove the kettle from the heat; let stand until the onions cool slightly. Then, add the chicken broth, Italian-style stewed tomatoes, regular stewed tomatoes, carrots, turnips, green beans, celery, green peppercorns, sugar, and allspice; stir to combine; set aside.

Make a bouquet garni (page 38) with the parsley, savory, celery tops, basil, and chives. Immerse the bouquet garni in the vegetable mixture in the kettle. Cover the kettle and place it over high heat. Bring the mixture to a boil;

(Recipe continues on next page)

reduce the heat and simmer, slowly, 10 minutes, stirring occasionally. Add the potatoes; stir to combine. Cover the kettle; simmer the mixture an additional 10 minutes. Add the corn and zucchini; stir to combine. Cover the kettle; simmer the mixture an additional 5 minutes. Remove from the heat. Remove and discard the bouquet garni.

SERVES 8 AS A MAIN COURSE

POTATO-LEEK SOUP

2 pounds russet potatoes (enough for
　　4 cups mashed potatoes; about 4 large
　　potatoes)
¼ cup whole milk
1 tablespoon butter
1½ cups thinly sliced leeks (about 6 leeks)
2 tablespoons butter
2 cups chicken broth, homemade
　　(page 88) or commercially canned
1 tablespoon snipped, fresh parsley
2 cups (1 pint) half-and-half
1 tablespoon instant chicken bouillon
　　granules
2 teaspoons salt
¼ teaspoon white pepper
Small, single, fresh parsley leaves for
　　decoration

Pare the potatoes, retaining them in a large saucepan of cold water to prevent discoloration. Drain the potatoes. Cut each potato into 3 pieces and return to the saucepan; add hot water to cover. Cover the pan and bring the potatoes to a boil over high heat; reduce the heat to medium and boil the potatoes moderately until they are tender (about 25 minutes). Drain well. Add the milk and 1 tablespoon butter; using an electric mixer, beat on high speed until the potatoes are fluffy with no lumps remaining. Measure 4 cups mashed potatoes; set aside.

Trim away and discard the root ends and leaves of the leeks, leaving only the white and greenish-white parts. Slice the leeks in half lengthwise and wash well, making certain all sand has been washed away. Thinly slice the leek halves widthwise; set aside. In a large saucepan, melt 2 tablespoons butter over low heat; add the leeks and sauté lightly about 3 minutes. Do not allow the leeks to brown. Remove from the heat; add the chicken broth and 1 tablespoon parsley. Cover and bring the leek mixture to a boil over medium heat; reduce the heat and simmer 1 hour.

Press the leek mixture through a food mill; then, return it to the saucepan. Add the mashed potatoes, half-and-half, bouillon granules, salt, and white pepper; using a handheld electric mixer, beat on medium-high speed until blended. Over medium heat, heat the soup through, stirring often. Ladle into soup cups or bowls; float parsley leaves on top of each serving.

SERVES 6

POTATO SOUP

6 slices bacon
2 pounds red potatoes, diced (about
　　6 medium potatoes)
1½ cups chopped onions
1½ cups chopped celery
5 cups water
1½ cups half-and-half
1 cup whole milk
½ cup cooking liquid (from cooking
　　bacon-vegetable mixture)
2 tablespoons snipped, fresh parsley
2 teaspoons salt
¼ teaspoon plus a dash of white pepper
1 tablespoon snipped, fresh parsley for
　　decoration

Cut each bacon slice widthwise into 6 pieces; place in a small, heavy-bottomed skillet. Over medium heat, fry the bacon pieces until medium done, but not crisp; drain between paper towels. In a large, heavy-bottomed kettle, place the bacon, potatoes, onions, celery, and water; stir to combine. Cover the kettle and bring the potato mixture to a boil over high heat; reduce the heat and cook the mixture at a brisk simmer for 30 minutes. Drain the potato mixture well in a sieve, reserving the cooking liquid; set aside.

Press the potato mixture through a food mill. Place the pressed mixture in the kettle. Add the half-and-half, milk, ½ cup reserved cooking liquid, 2 tablespoons parsley, salt, and white pepper; stir to combine. Cover the kettle and place over medium-low heat. Heat the soup only until hot; do not allow it to boil. Ladle into soup cups or bowls; sprinkle sparingly with snipped, fresh parsley.

SERVES 6

WILD RICE SOUP

¾ cup (¼ pound plus 4 tablespoons) butter
3 tablespoons minced onions
1 cup all-purpose flour
6 cups homemade Chicken Broth (page 88) or 3 14½-ounce cans commercial chicken broth
4 cups cooked wild rice (use 1¼ cups raw wild rice; page 276)
2 cups finely ground, fully cooked ham
2 cups pared and very finely shredded carrots (about 5 medium carrots)
½ cup plus 1 tablespoon ground, blanched almonds (page 50) (use one 2¼-ounce package whole, blanched almonds)
1 teaspoon salt
¼ teaspoon pepper
2 cups (1 pint) half-and-half
¼ cup dry white wine
2 tablespoons minced, fresh parsley for garnish

In a large kettle, melt the butter over low heat. Place the onions in the kettle; sauté 4 minutes, keeping the heat low to avoid burning the butter. Remove from the heat. Add the flour and stir until completely smooth. Return to low heat; cook the mixture for 1 minute, but do not

allow it to brown. Gradually add the broth, stirring constantly and combining thoroughly. Increase the heat to medium; bring the mixture to a boil and boil 1 minute. Add the rice, ham, carrots, almonds, salt, and pepper; stir to combine. Cover and simmer 5 minutes. Add the half-and-half and wine; heat through but do not allow to boil.

To serve, ladle the soup into soup bowls or cups and garnish each serving with minced parsley.

SERVES 8

SERVING SUGGESTIONS: This soup may be served as either a main course or an appetizer. When served as an appetizer, you may wish to thin it down with 2 additional cups of chicken broth.

WISCONSIN BEER CHEESE SOUP

½ cup all-purpose flour
¼ teaspoon salt
¼ teaspoon white pepper
Dash of cayenne pepper
1¾ cups homemade Chicken Broth (page 88) or 1 14½-ounce can commercial chicken broth
½ cup pared and very finely shredded carrots
½ cup very finely chopped celery
¼ cup (4 tablespoons) butter
½ cup minced onions
2 cups whole milk
1 teaspoon packed light brown sugar
1 pound shredded, sharp cheddar cheese
1 12-ounce can or bottle of beer
Popped popcorn for garnish

In a small mixing bowl, place the flour, salt, white pepper, and cayenne pepper; stir to combine; set aside. In a medium saucepan, place the chicken broth, carrots, and celery; stir to combine. Cover the saucepan. Bring the mixture to a boil over high heat; reduce the heat and sim-

(Recipe continues on next page)

mer 10 minutes until the vegetables are tender. Remove from the heat; set aside.

In a 3½-quart heavy-bottomed saucepan, heat the butter over medium heat. Place the onions in the saucepan; sauté 5 minutes until translucent but not brown. Remove from the heat. Add the flour mixture; stir until blended, with no lumps remaining. Add the chicken broth mixture and milk; stir to combine. Place over medium heat; cook the mixture until thickened and just under boiling, stirring constantly. Do not allow the mixture to boil. Add the brown sugar, cheese, and beer; stir constantly until the cheese melts. Continue cooking to just under boiling, stirring continuously. Do not allow the soup to boil. Remove from the heat.

To serve, ladle the soup into soup cups or bowls. Float a few kernels of popped corn on each serving.

MAKES ABOUT SIX 1-CUP SERVINGS

FISH CHOWDER

4 slices thickly sliced bacon, cut into 1-inch pieces
2½ pounds northern pike fillets,* carefully boned and cut into ¾-inch cubes
3 pounds red potatoes, pared and cut into 1-inch cubes
3 cups very coarsely chopped onions
About 5 cups hot water
2 tablespoons butter
1 teaspoon celery salt
¾ teaspoon salt
½ teaspoon pepper
½ teaspoon ground mace
½ cup all-purpose flour
2 12-ounce cans (3 cups) evaporated milk, divided
Paprika for decoration
Oyster crackers

Fillets of perch, walleye, or any other firm, mild fish may be substituted.

Place the bacon in an 8-quart heavy-bottomed kettle; fry over medium-low heat until done but not crisp. Remove the kettle from the heat; let stand until the bacon cools slightly. Add the fish, potatoes, onions, and enough hot water to cover. Cover the kettle; place it over high heat and bring the mixture to a boil. Reduce the heat and simmer the mixture about 10 minutes until the potatoes are just tender. Remove from the heat. Add the butter, celery salt, salt, pepper, and mace; stir to blend and combine; set aside.

In a glass jar or plastic container with a secure lid, place the flour and *1 cup* evaporated milk; cover and shake vigorously until blended. Add the flour mixture and remaining evaporated milk to the fish mixture in the kettle; stir well to blend. Place the kettle over medium heat; cook the chowder until it thickens and is just under boiling, stirring constantly. Do not allow the chowder to boil.

To serve, ladle the chowder into soup bowls and sprinkle lightly with paprika. Pass a big bowl of oyster crackers at the table.

SERVES 8

CORN CHOWDER

8 slices bacon
2 tablespoons all-purpose flour
½ teaspoon salt
½ teaspoon pepper
1 teaspoon dried parsley
¼ teaspoon poultry seasoning
¼ cup plus 2 tablespoons (6 tablespoons) butter
½ cup chopped onions
¼ cup chopped green bell peppers
½ bay leaf
4 cups (1 quart) milk
2 17-ounce cans commercial cream-style corn or 1 pint home-canned Cream-style Corn (page 733)
1 pound red potatoes, boiled (page 328), peeled, and cut into ⅜-inch cubes (about 2 cups potatoes)

In a large, heavy-bottomed skillet, fry the bacon over medium heat until crisp; drain between paper towels. Using your fingers, break the bacon into small pieces; place in a small container; cover, and refrigerate. In a small bowl, place the flour, salt, pepper, parsley, and poultry seasoning; stir to combine; set aside.

In a large, heavy-bottomed saucepan, melt the butter over medium heat. Place the onions and green peppers in the saucepan; sauté until tender, but not brown (about 5 minutes). Remove from the heat. Place the flour mixture in the saucepan; stir until the flour mixture is smooth. Add ½ bay leaf and milk; stir to mix. Return to medium heat. While stirring constantly, cook until smooth and slightly thickened, bringing the mixture nearly to a boil, but not allowing it to boil. Add the corn and potatoes; stir to combine. Heat through.

Just before serving, add the bacon, reserving a small amount to sprinkle over each serving of chowder for decoration.

SERVES 8

SERVING SUGGESTIONS: May be served as a first course or a main course.

DEE'S CHILI

This original recipe of Dee Staples, my sister-in-law, calls for just the right ingredients in just the right amounts to culminate in an incredibly good chili—a menu-must during Midwest winters.

2 tablespoons butter
1½ pounds lean, pure ground beef
¾ cup chopped onions
½ cup chopped green bell peppers
1 large garlic clove, pressed
2 14½-ounce cans commercial stewed tomatoes
1 15½-ounce can commercial tomato sauce
1 tablespoon chili powder*
1 teaspoon ground cumin
1 tablespoon dried parsley
2 teaspoons salt
1 teaspoon pepper
1 15-ounce can commercial chili beans, undrained
1 15½-ounce can commercial dark red kidney beans
8 ounces commercial sour cream (optional)
2 ounces finely shredded, sharp cheddar cheese (optional)

*For less spicy chili, reduce the amount of chili powder to 2 teaspoons.

In a large, heavy-bottomed skillet, melt the butter over medium heat. Tilt the skillet back and forth to completely cover the bottom with the melted butter. Place the ground beef in the skillet; brown until medium-browned, using a large, metal mixing spoon to break up the meat during the browning. Add the onions, green peppers, and garlic; continue cooking until the meat is well-browned (the onions and green peppers should be barely browned). Remove the skillet from the heat.

When the skillet cools, slightly, add the stewed tomatoes and tomato sauce; stir until the skillet is deglazed. Add the chili powder, cumin, parsley, salt, and pepper; stir to combine. Cover and simmer the mixture slowly for 1 hour. Add the chili beans and kidney beans; simmer, uncovered, an additional ½ hour.

To serve, ladle the chili into soup bowls. If desired, spoon a small dollop of sour cream over the center of the chili in each bowl, and sprinkle shredded cheese over the sour cream.

SERVES 8

Stews

BRANDIED PORK STEW WITH THYME DUMPLINGS

Blue Ribbon winner in the Stews of Iowa class, sponsored by the Iowa Farm Bureau, at the 1992 Iowa State Fair.

Ted Yanacek, accomplished gourmet cook, judged the class in which I entered this stew at the fair. He praised the ample amount of pork tenderloin, and inclusion of apples, golden raisins, and spices—rare ingredients in Midwest stews. (Although he didn't mention the brandy ingredient, I think it might have helped make this stew a winner.)

1 pound red potatoes
2 cups fresh green beans cut diagonally into 1-inch lengths
½ cup red bell peppers cut into ½-inch cubes
¾ cup water
1 tablespoon sugar
¼ teaspoon ground cinnamon
1½ cups Golden Delicious apples pared, cored, and cut into ¾-inch cubes
¼ cup all-purpose flour
1 teaspoon salt
½ teaspoon pepper
1¾ pounds pork tenderloin (2 whole tenderloins) cut into 1-inch cubes
3 tablespoons butter
2 tablespoons butter
⅓ cup finely chopped onions
½ cup water
4 cups clarified beef broth, homemade (page 88) or commercially canned
1½ cups sliced, fresh mushrooms
2 tablespoons snipped, fresh parsley
1 small bay leaf
1 teaspoon salt
½ teaspoon pepper
10 ounces (about 2 cups) pearl onions, peeled (page 45)
¼ cup golden raisins
1 recipe Thyme Dumplings (page 449)
½ teaspoon ground nutmeg
3 tablespoons good brandy

Pare the potatoes; drop into cold water as they are pared to prevent darkening. Cut the large potatoes in half. Place the potatoes in a large saucepan; add hot water to cover. Cover the pan. Bring the potatoes to a boil over high heat; reduce the heat and boil the potatoes moderately, for 15 minutes. Drain the potatoes; immerse in cold water to stop the cooking. Drain and cut the potatoes into ½-inch cubes. Place in a zipper-seal plastic bag; refrigerate.

Place the green beans in a medium saucepan; add water to cover. Cover the pan. Bring the green beans to a boil over high heat; reduce the heat and simmer the beans about 10 minutes until they are just tender. Drain; immerse the beans in cold water to stop the cooking. Drain the beans well in a colander; place in a zipper-seal plastic bag and refrigerate.

Steam the red peppers (page 302) 4 minutes. Immediately remove the steamer basket containing the peppers from the pan. Leave the peppers in the steamer basket and rinse them under cold, running water to stop the cooking. Drain the peppers well; place in a zipper-seal plastic bag and refrigerate.

In a small saucepan, place ¾ cup water, sugar, and cinnamon; stir to combine. Bring the mixture to a boil over high heat, stirring constantly. Add the apples. Return to a simmer; reduce the heat and simmer 3 minutes. Drain the apples well in a colander. (Do not immerse them in cold water.) Place in a bowl or container; cover and refrigerate.

In a small mixing bowl, place the flour, 1 teaspoon salt, and ½ teaspoon pepper; stir to combine. Sprinkle the flour mixture over a piece of waxed paper. Dredge the tenderloin cubes in the flour mixture and then place them on a clean piece of waxed paper; set aside. In an electric skillet or a large, heavy-bottomed skillet on the range, melt 3 tablespoons butter over medium-low heat (320° F. in an electric skillet). Tilt the skillet back and forth to completely cover the bottom with the melted butter. Place the tenderloin cubes in the skillet and brown well on all sides. Place the browned meat in a heavy-bottomed kettle; set aside.

Leave the skillet (in which the pork was cooked) over medium-low heat and add 2 additional tablespoons butter. When the butter melts, add ⅓ cup chopped onions. Brown the onions lightly; add to the meat in the kettle. Reduce the skillet heat to very low (220° F. in an electric skillet). When the skillet cools to the reduced temperature, add ½ cup water and deglaze.

Pour the skillet liquid into the kettle containing the meat. Add the beef broth, mushrooms, parsley, bay leaf, 1 teaspoon salt, and ½ teaspoon pepper; stir to combine. Cover the kettle and place it over medium heat. Bring the mixture to a low boil; reduce the heat and simmer 15 minutes, stirring occasionally. Add the pearl onions and raisins; stir to combine. Remove from the heat; set aside.

Prepare the Thyme Dumplings batter. Place the kettle of stew mixture over high heat; cover and bring the mixture to a boil. Drop the dumpling batter by the tablespoonful onto the top of the boiling stew. Cover the kettle; reduce the heat slightly, but keep the stew bubbling. Cook 15 minutes. *Do not lift the cover while the dumplings are cooking—not even to peek.* Remove from the heat. Uncover the kettle. Using a small spatula, remove the dumplings and place, single layer, in a pan; cover to keep warm.

Remove the bay leaf from the stew mixture and discard it. Add the nutmeg and brandy; stir to combine. Add the potatoes, green beans, red peppers, and apples; stir carefully to evenly distribute. Place the kettle of stew over medium-high heat. Bring the stew to a simmer; reduce the heat and simmer until heated through. Ladle the stew into a tureen. Using a small spatula, arrange the dumplings on top of the stew around the edge of the tureen.

SERVES 6

OVEN STEW

One would be hard-pressed to find a more simple stew to make than this one from the recipe box of Des Moines friend Gayle Hamilton. Quick-cooking tapioca is the thickener.

2¾ pounds round steak, ¾ inch thick
2 large onions, cut into eighths
3 large red potatoes, pared and cut into 1-inch cubes
4 stalks celery, sliced ½ inch thick
Leafy tops of 2 celery stalks, coarsely chopped
6 carrots, pared and cut, diagonally, into bite-sized pieces
3 cups fresh green beans snapped into 1½-inch lengths
4 cups tomato juice, home canned (page 737) or commercially canned
1 teaspoon salt
½ teaspoon pepper
1 tablespoon sugar
2 tablespoons quick-cooking tapioca
2 teaspoons dried leaf basil

Preheat the oven to 325° F.

Trim the fat and gristle from the round steak; cut it into ¾-inch cubes and spread them over the bottom of a heavy 8-quart roaster. Do not brown the meat. In layers, add the vegetables to the roaster in the following order: onions, potatoes, celery, leafy celery tops, carrots, and green beans; set aside.

In a medium mixing bowl, place the tomato juice, salt, pepper, sugar, tapioca, and basil; stir to combine. Pour evenly over the vegetables and meat; do not stir the stew contents. Cover and bake for 3 hours. Do not baste or stir the stew during the baking period. To serve, stir briefly and ladle into soup bowls.

SERVES 10 TO 12

FARM-STYLE BEEF STEW

½ cup all-purpose flour
¾ teaspoon salt
½ teaspoon pepper
2 pounds boned chuck, cut into 1¼-inch
  cubes
2 tablespoons butter
1 tablespoon butter
1 cup water
2 cups homemade Beef Broth (page 87) or
  1 14½-ounce can commercial beef broth
1 cup water
½ cup dry red wine
2 cups very coarsely chopped onions
¾ cup celery sliced ⅜ inch thick
Green leafy top of 1 celery stalk, chopped
1 garlic clove, pressed
½ bay leaf
¾ teaspoon Worcestershire sauce
1 pound carrots, pared and sliced ½ inch
  thick
2 pounds red potatoes, pared and cut into
  bite-sized cubes
1⅓ cups frozen peas (about ⅔ of a
  10-ounce package)
½ cup water

In a small mixing bowl, place the flour, salt, and pepper; stir to combine. Sprinkle the flour mixture over a piece of waxed paper. Lightly dredge the meat cubes in the flour mixture and then place them on a clean piece of waxed paper. Reserve the remaining flour mixture in a glass jar or plastic container with a secure lid.

In an electric skillet or a large, heavy-bottomed skillet on the range, melt 2 tablespoons butter over medium heat (350° F. in an electric skillet). Tilt the skillet back and forth to completely cover the bottom with the melted butter. Place the meat cubes, single layer, in the skillet; brown well on all sides. Add 1 additional tablespoon butter during browning when the skillet becomes dry. Place the browned meat cubes in a heavy-bottomed, 8-quart kettle; set

aside. Reduce the skillet heat to very low (220° F. in an electric skillet). When the skillet cools to the reduced temperature, add 1 cup water and deglaze.

Pour the skillet liquid into the kettle containing the browned meat. Add the beef broth, 1 cup water, wine, onions, sliced celery, chopped celery top, garlic, ½ bay leaf, and Worcestershire sauce; stir to combine. Cover the kettle and bring the mixture to a boil over high heat. Reduce the heat and simmer, moderately to slowly, 2 hours, until the meat is very tender, stirring occasionally. Stir more frequently during the last 45 minutes of simmering when the mixture thickens and becomes increasingly prone to stick to the bottom of the kettle.

Meanwhile, place the carrots in a medium saucepan; cover with water. Cover the saucepan and place it over high heat. Bring the carrots to a boil; reduce the heat and boil the carrots about 12 minutes, until they are just tender. Drain the carrots and let stand until cool; then, cover and refrigerate. Using the same procedure, boil the potatoes in a large saucepan for about 10 minutes, until just tender. Drain and let stand until cool; then, cover and refrigerate. Do not overcook the carrots and potatoes, or they will lose their shape in the stew.

When the meat mixture has simmered 2 hours and the meat is tender, remove the kettle from the heat. Add the carrots, potatoes, and frozen peas to the kettle mixture. Cover the kettle; set aside. Add ½ cup water to the reserved flour mixture; cover the jar or container and shake vigorously until blended. Add to the stew mixture in the kettle. Using a wooden mixing spoon, stir the stew contents to combine, being careful not to cut or break up the carrots and potatoes.

Place the kettle over medium heat; bring the stew to a low simmer, stirring often. Simmer 1 to 2 minutes until the stew thickens, stirring constantly. Ladle into soup bowls.

SERVES 8

VEAL STEW WITH
HERB DUMPLINGS

¼ cup all-purpose flour
½ teaspoon salt
¼ teaspoon pepper
1¼ pounds boned veal shoulder, cut into
  1-inch cubes
2 tablespoons butter
2 tablespoons butter
¼ cup minced onions
1 cup water
1 cup chicken broth, homemade (page 88)
  or commercially canned
1¼ teaspoons salt
¼ teaspoon pepper
1 teaspoon Worcestershire sauce
1 bay leaf
½ cup dry white wine
2½ cups water
1 pound red potatoes, pared and cut into
  small, bite-sized cubes (about 3 cups)
2 cups carrots pared and sliced ¼ inch
  thick
½ cup chopped celery
1 recipe Herb Dumplings (page 449)
1 16-ounce can commercial tomatoes,
  undrained, or 1 pint home-canned
  Tomatoes (page 736), undrained
1 16-ounce can commercial wax beans,
  drained, or 1 pint home-canned Wax
  Beans (page 733), drained
¾ cup cooked and drained frozen peas

In a small bowl, place the flour, ½ teaspoon salt, and ¼ teaspoon pepper; stir to combine. Sprinkle the flour mixture over a piece of waxed paper. Dredge the veal cubes in the flour mixture and then place them on a clean piece of waxed paper; set aside.

In an electric skillet or a large, heavy-bottomed skillet on the range, melt 2 tablespoons butter over medium heat (350° F. in an electric skillet). Tilt the skillet back and forth to completely cover the bottom with the melted butter. Place the veal cubes in the skillet; brown well on all sides. Remove the veal cubes from the skillet and place them in a bowl; set aside. Place an additional 2 tablespoons butter in the skillet; add the onions and brown. Reduce the skillet heat to very low (220° F. in an electric skillet). When the skillet cools to the reduced temperature, add 1 cup water and the chicken broth. Deglaze the skillet.

Pour the skillet mixture into a heavy-bottomed kettle. Add 1¼ teaspoons salt, ¼ teaspoon pepper, Worcestershire sauce, bay leaf, wine, and 2½ cups water; stir to combine. Add the veal cubes. Cover the kettle. Bring the mixture to a boil over high heat; reduce the heat and simmer the mixture 1 hour or until the veal is nearly tender. Add the potatoes, carrots, and celery; cover and continue simmering for 10 minutes. Meanwhile, prepare the Herb Dumplings batter; set aside.

Add the tomatoes, wax beans, and peas to the stew; cover and bring to a boil over high heat. Drop the dumpling batter by the tablespoonful onto the top of the boiling stew. Cover the kettle; reduce the heat slightly, but keep the stew bubbling. Cook 15 minutes. *Do not lift the cover while the dumplings are cooking—not even to peek.* Remove from the heat. Uncover the kettle; using a spatula, remove the dumplings and place them on a plate. Remove the bay leaf from the stew and discard it. Ladle the stew into individual soup bowls and place a dumpling on top of the stew in the center of each bowl.

SERVES 6

HEARTLAND STEW

Blue Ribbon winner in the Stews of Iowa class, sponsored by the Iowa Farm Bureau, at the 1988 Iowa State Fair.

½ pound beef tenderloin, ¾ inch thick
½ pound pork tenderloin, ½ inch thick
½ pound veal tenderloin, ¼ inch thick
½ cup all-purpose flour
1½ teaspoons salt
½ teaspoon pepper
¼ cup (4 tablespoons) butter
¼ cup (4 tablespoons) butter
½ cup minced onions
1 garlic clove, pressed
¼ cup water
3½ cups chicken broth, homemade
    (page 88) or commercially canned
½ teaspoon Worcestershire sauce
1 teaspoon salt
⅛ teaspoon pepper
½ teaspoon celery salt
2 tablespoons snipped, fresh parsley
1 tablespoon snipped, fresh basil
4 ounces (about 1½ cups) sliced, fresh
    mushrooms
¾ cup pearl onions, peeled (page 45)
1 cup fresh snow peas with ends trimmed
    off and strings removed
¾ cup carrots pared and sliced, diagonally,
    ¼ inch thick
¾ cup asparagus trimmed and cut,
    diagonally, into 2-inch lengths
½ cup miniature corn on the cob, frozen or
    commercially canned
2½ pounds russet potatoes (about
    5 medium potatoes)
1 cup half-and-half
¼ cup dry sherry
2 tablespoons butter
¼ teaspoon salt
1 extra-large egg, beaten
½ cup whole milk

Cut the beef into 1½-inch cubes, the pork into 1-inch cubes, and the veal into 1 × 1½-inch strips; set aside. In a small mixing bowl, place the flour, 1½ teaspoons salt, and ½ teaspoon pepper; stir to combine. Sprinkle the flour mixture over a piece of waxed paper. Dredge the meat in the flour mixture and place it on a clean piece of waxed paper; set aside. Reserve the remaining flour mixture in a glass jar or plastic container with a secure lid.

In a deep electric skillet or a Dutch oven, melt 4 tablespoons butter over medium heat (350° F. in an electric skillet). Place all the meat in the skillet and brown *very* well on all sides, adding more of the butter as needed. Remove the browned meat from the skillet and place it in a bowl; set aside. Add 4 more tablespoons butter to the skillet. Place the minced onions and garlic in skillet; sauté until golden brown. Reduce the skillet heat to very low (220° F. in an electric skillet).

When the skillet cools to the reduced temperature, add ¼ cup water and deglaze. Return the meat to the skillet. Add the chicken broth, Worcestershire sauce, 1 teaspoon salt, ⅛ teaspoon pepper, celery salt, parsley, and basil; stir to combine. Cover the skillet and increase the heat to medium low (320° F. in an electric skillet). Simmer the meat mixture for 15 minutes. Add the mushrooms; cover and simmer an additional 15 minutes or until all the meat is tender.

Meanwhile, briefly steam (page 302) separately the pearl onions until just tender and the snow peas 3 minutes. In a colander, rinse the onions and peas separately under cold running water to stop the cooking. Drain well and place in separate bowls; cover and set aside. Briefly boil (page 302) separately the carrots until just tender and the asparagus about 3 minutes. In a colander, rinse the carrots and asparagus separately under cold running water to stop the cooking. Drain well and place in separate bowls; cover and set aside. Do not cook the miniature corn. If the corn is frozen, thaw; if canned, drain. Place the corn in a bowl; cover and set aside. Pare, boil (page 328) and drain the potatoes; cover and keep warm on the back of the range. (Prepare the vegetables separately to preserve their individual colors and flavors.)

Add the pearl onions, snow peas, carrots, asparagus, and miniature corn to the cooked meat mixture in the skillet. Add the half-and-half to the reserved flour mixture; cover and shake vigorously until well blended. Place the stew over medium heat (350° F. in an electric skillet). While stirring the stew constantly, add the half-and-half mixture; bring to a boil, stirring continuously. Add the sherry; stir well to blend. Turn the stew into a 2½-quart round, ovenproof casserole; cover and keep warm.

Preheat the broiler.

Using an electric mixer, mash the potatoes on high speed, adding 2 tablespoons butter, ¼ teaspoon salt, beaten egg, and enough milk (approximately ½ cup) to make the potatoes fluffy. Using a decorating bag fit with large open-star tip number 8B (page 383), pipe a wide zigzag border (page 389) of mashed potatoes on top of the stew around the edge of the casserole (see Note). Brown the mashed-potato border under the broiler.

NOTE: If a decorating bag and tip are not available, spoon small mounds of mashed potatoes over the stew around the perimeter of the casserole. (Brown under the broiler.)

SERVES 6

OYSTER STEW

Oyster Stew is quickly and easily prepared. Plan to cook it just before serving, and once you begin the cooking, do not leave the stove unattended because Oyster Stew demands a watchful eye to prevent the butter from browning or burning, to allow the oysters to curl only slightly, and to prevent the stew from boiling after adding the milk and half-and-half.

1½ teaspoons celery salt
1 teaspoon salt
⅛ teaspoon pepper
¼ cup plus 2 tablespoons (6 tablespoons) butter
3 dozen (about 1¾ pounds) shucked, raw oysters with liquor
1 tablespoon plus 2 teaspoons Worcestershire sauce
Dash of Tabasco pepper sauce
2 cups whole milk
2 cups (1 pint) half-and-half
Paprika for decoration
Oyster crackers

In a small sauce dish, place the celery salt, salt, and pepper; stir to combine; set aside. In a heavy-bottomed kettle over medium-low heat, heat the butter until it sizzles, but do not allow the butter to brown. Add the oysters with all their liquor, celery salt mixture, Worcestershire sauce, and pepper sauce; stir to combine. Increase the heat to medium-high and cook until the oysters curl *slightly* (about 5 minutes). Do not allow the butter to burn. Add the milk and half-and-half. Heat the stew, but do not allow it to boil; stir often. Serve immediately. Ladle into soup bowls; sprinkle paprika over each serving. Place oyster crackers in a large serving bowl and pass at the table.

SERVES 4 OR 5

SOYBEAN-BRATWURST STEW

Most people eat soybeans frequently, if not daily, in the form of soybean oil. It is the major oil used in cooking oils called "vegetable oil," and it is also used in many margarines, shortenings, and salad dressings. Another soybean product, soy flour, is sometimes used in combination with wheat flour to make breads, cookies, and other baked goods (see the recipe for Soy Whole-Wheat Muffins, page 444). Despite our significant consumption of soybeans, mainly in the oil form, they are eaten in the whole bean form rather infrequently. Soybeans can be a nutritious and welcome addition to the more traditional varieties of beans we enjoy serving.

Soybeans are very firm, and, due to their high protein content, require lengthy cooking. I have found that dried soybeans are best when cooked in a pressure cooker because this manner of cooking results in softer beans than when they are boiled conventionally. Both methods of cooking are given in the procedures for this recipe.

8 ounces (about 1 cup) dried soybeans
4 cups cooking liquid from soybeans
2 cups commercial, 100% vegetable juice
1½ cups tomato juice, home-canned (page 737) or commercially canned
1 large onion, cut into eighths
1 garlic clove, pressed
5 slices bacon, cut into 1-inch pieces
½ cup chili sauce, home canned (page 783) or commercially canned
¾ teaspoon dried leaf rosemary
1 tablespoon snipped, fresh basil or
    1 teaspoon dried leaf basil
1 bay leaf
¾ teaspoon pepper
1 12-ounce can or bottle of beer
1 8-ounce package frozen miniature corn on the cob (about 1½ cups corn)*
2 cups carrots pared and sliced diagonally ½ inch thick
1 pound smoked bratwurst, sliced ¾ inch thick

½ cup all-purpose flour
1 cup water
2 teaspoons salt

*If frozen miniature corn on the cob is not available, about 1½ cups drained commercially canned miniature corn on the cob may be substituted. Make sure that the canned miniature corn is not pickled. Do not cook commercially canned miniature corn on the cob before adding it to the stew.

Wash the soybeans well and carefully sort them. Place the soybeans in a mixing bowl and add water to cover. Soak the beans for 12 hours.

In a sieve, drain and rinse the beans well. Cook the beans in a pressure cooker for 30 minutes at 15 pounds, following pressure cooker instructions and adding 1 tablespoon of vegetable oil to prevent frothing (see Note). Drain the soybeans, reserving the cooking liquid. Place the drained soybeans in a bowl or storage container; cover and refrigerate. In a heavy-bottomed kettle, place 4 cups reserved cooking liquid from the soybeans, vegetable juice, tomato juice, onion, garlic, bacon, chili sauce, rosemary, basil, bay leaf, pepper, and beer. Cover the kettle; bring the mixture to a boil over high heat. Reduce the heat and simmer the mixture, covered, 1½ hours.

Meanwhile, pour ½ inch water into a small saucepan. Cover the saucepan and bring the water to a boil over high heat. Add the corn; cover and return to a simmer. Reduce the heat and cook the corn briefly until just tender. Drain and set aside. Place the carrots in a medium saucepan; add water to cover. Cover the saucepan and bring the carrots to a boil over high heat. Reduce the heat to medium and cook the carrots until just tender (about 6 minutes). Drain and set aside.

After the stew mixture has simmered 1½ hours, add the drained soybeans and bratwurst; simmer, covered, for an additional 10 minutes.

In a glass jar or plastic container with a secure

lid, place the flour and 1 cup water; cover and shake vigorously until blended. Slowly add the flour mixture to the stew, stirring constantly. Add the salt; stir to blend. Add the corn and carrots; stir to evenly distribute. Cover and simmer 2 minutes. Ladle the stew into soup bowls.

NOTE: After soaking, draining, and rinsing the soybeans, they may be cooked by the traditional method rather than in a pressure cooker. To cook the beans by the traditional method, place them in a heavy-bottomed kettle. Add 4 cups of fresh water for each cup of soaked and drained beans. Cover the kettle and bring the mixture to a boil over high heat. Reduce the heat and skim off the excess foam. Simmer the beans about 3 hours until tender (the beans will remain somewhat firm). Add additional water during the cooking period if needed. Drain the cooked soybeans, reserving the cooking liquid, and continue to follow the recipe.

SERVES 8

SERVING SUGGESTION: Serve with Soy Whole-Wheat Muffins (page 444), butter, and Strawberry Jam, home canned (page 750) or commercially canned.

Salads and Salad Dressings

D inner without salad would not be dinner in the Midwest. When dining out, salad is nearly always the first course; when dining in, it's customarily served with the meal. And with new, lighter eating modes, it sometimes *is* the meal.

Every imaginable kind of salad graces the tables of salad-smitten Heartlanders, incorporating vegetables, fruits, eggs, cheese, meats, poultry, fish, shellfish, nuts, and most any other ingredient one can think of. But I suspect that the first thing that pops into a Midwest mind when the word "salad" is mentioned is lettuce with a variety of mixed vegetables—particularly, tomatoes, green peppers, celery, carrots, radishes, onions, and cucumbers, which are likely to be straight from the garden in the backyard if it's summertime.

While this Pavlovian lettuce-salad response may not be unique to Middle America, its molded salads are. And we're not talking about a can of fruit cocktail and a package of strawberry gelatin. This is the land of gelatin genius, where the art of making complex-tasting, gorgeous-looking molded fruit and vegetable salads has been mastered! Refrigerators from Minot, North Dakota, to Wichita, Kansas, and from Scottsbluff, Nebraska, to Youngstown, Ohio, harbor elegant gelatin-based salads that would be sure hits in four-star New York and Los Angeles restaurants.

In case you haven't experienced one of these top-echelon molded salads and want to try one, I might suggest that you launch your expedition into this delectable, shimmering wonderland with Apricot Salad (page 116). This recipe comes from my sister-in-law's family in Grinnell, Iowa, and the salad never fails to elicit instant praise whenever and wherever it is served.

On a hot summer day, there are few salads as cooling and calming (or as pretty) to serve luncheon guests as Cucumber-Dill Ring (page 135) unmolded on a beautiful platter decorated with Cucumber Roses (page 399) and sprigs of fresh dillweed. Serve it with Cold Poached Salmon Steaks (page 225) and thin slices of Lemon Bread (page 435), gather white and yellow zinnias from the garden for the center of the table, pour chilled Chardonnay into your best wineglasses, and "enjoy" until the heat of the day passes.

MAIN-COURSE SALADS

In concert with most Americans, people in the twelve middle states are opting more and more for main-course salads. They're the ticket for the health-conscious, and many of them can be whipped up in a flash. Salad-meal buffs can be detected at supermarket checkout counters by the things they unload from their carts: boneless, skinless chicken breasts; lean pieces of beef tenderloin; packages of interesting pastas; all kinds of chic, fresh vegetables like orange bell peppers, yellow and green zucchini, broccoflower, and sugar snap peas; carefully selected cheeses; fresh herbs; a big bottle of good-quality extra-virgin olive oil; and at least two kinds of enticing greens.

Of course, time-honored main-course luncheon salads, such as Hot Chicken Salad (page 141), Crabmeat Salad (page 145), and Lobster-Avocado Salad (page 147), have been, are, and will be ever-popular. Falling under the heading, "Everything old is new again," I recommend Tuna-Almond Luncheon Salad (page 143), an old, old recipe of my aunt's, which I lightened by substituting lemon-flavored lowfat yogurt for whipped cream, an ingredient called for in the original recipe.

A word about potato salad: There are just about as many versions of this Midland summer mainstay as there are cooks. Potato salad is a Midwest standard, but there is definitely no standard set of ingredients . . . beyond the potatoes. My version (page 133) is based on the way my mother made it, but with more sweet pickles. Mother never included enough pickles to satisfy Dad's and my taste buds, despite our perennial complaints. However, you will find just as many Midwesterners who will argue with equal vehemence that sweet pickles have no role whatsoever in potato salad. Vive la différence!

While Mom skimped on the pickles, she made up for it with the eggs. As I tested the recipe (neither of us had ever actually measured ingredients and written a recipe), Mother was looking over my shoulder and advised, "Call for plenty of eggs. That is what makes good potato salad."

A recipe for an authentic German potato salad, a classic in German communities in Wisconsin, Nebraska, Iowa, and other Midwest states, is found on page 134. I savored this particular potato salad at Gertrud Acksen's house in Stuttgart, Germany, on several occasions, and thought it was the most scrumptious version of this quintessential Deutschland dish I had ever eaten. Gertrud, who speaks little English (and I, little German), didn't have a written recipe, so she made the salad and dictated her ingredients and instructions to a mutual German friend who translated them for me for inclusion in this book. When you sit down to eat it, accompanied by a succulent wurst and a stein of German beer, close your eyes and you can almost see and hear an oompah band in lederhosen playing a polka.

It is hard to fault Midwest salad making, but its Achilles' heel continues to be overuse of iceberg lettuce. This dietary habit stems from the fact that until the last approximately twenty-five years, iceberg was often the only kind of lettuce readily available in this region, with the exception of leaf lettuce, which has been religiously grown in local summer gardens for years. But Midlanders are expanding their lettuce horizons to include a greater variety of greens, now readily available.

All types of salad dressings make their way into the myriad of current Midwest salads, but particular fondness for Thousand Island, Italian, and blue cheese remains constant.

Salad as a Separate Course in Home Dining

Serving most salads as a separate, first course could add to the pleasure of Midwest home dining. (It requires very little extra effort on the part of the cook.)

Food tastes best when the palate is not overtaxed with too many simultaneous flavors. Eating by courses allows the diner to experience in full measure the taste and texture of each food prepared for the meal. When more than one food is placed on a plate—as normally occurs with the main course—care should be exercised to plan foods and garnishes which complement each other in taste, color, smell, and texture, in order to achieve a combination which provides harmonious sensory satisfaction.

Another benefit of first-course salads at home is that the practice promotes the eating of more fresh vegetables and fruits and less fatty, high-calorie, and sweet foods which may follow in the meal. When a diner brings a healthy appetite to the table, a generous, fresh, appealing salad can go a long way toward assuaging hunger—a real assist in holding down portions of subsequently served, higher-calorie foods.

TO WASH AND PREPARE GREENS FOR SALADS

Greens should be washed and prepared on the day they are to be served. If processed too far in advance, they will tend to wilt and develop brown spots. To wash and prepare greens, other than heads of iceberg lettuce and cabbage (instructions for these greens follow), cut out the core (if the variety you are serving has one), trim back and discard long, tough stems on varieties such as watercress and spinach, separate the leaves or sprigs, and cut away any wilted leaves or brown spots.

Wash individual leaves or sprigs under cold, running water; then, place them in a sink filled with cold water for a second washing. Swish the greens gently in the water. Then, let them stand a few minutes to allow any sand or soil particles to gravitate to the bottom of the sink and away from the greens.

Lift the greens out of the water, lowering your hands into the water only as deeply as necessary to grasp them. Place the greens in a colander to drain. After allowing a few minutes for the greens to drain, rap the colander a few times on the bottom of the sink to expel additional water.

Fold a clean tea towel in half lengthwise, and lay it on the kitchen counter. Distribute the greens, front side up, over the tea towel; roll the towel loosely, starting from one of the short ends. Loosely fold the toweling under the ends of the roll and place it, seam down, in the vegetable storage drawer of the refrigerator. The tea towel will continue to absorb water from the surface of the greens.

As near serving time as possible, unroll the tea towel of greens. If the greens are still somewhat wet, wipe them lightly with a dry tea towel or with paper towels. Greens for salads should be crisp and nearly dry. Tear, cut, or leave greens whole, as called for in the salad recipe being prepared, and depending upon the size of the leaves.

When washing and preparing heads of iceberg lettuce and cabbage, the leaves are usually not separated. Wash and prepare these greens, as follows:

ICEBERG LETTUCE: Core the head and remove any wilted outer leaves. Hold the head upside down, under cold, running water, letting the water run into the head. Invert the head and place it in a colander to drain. Rap the colander a few times on the bottom of the sink to expel additional water. Wrap the head of lettuce in a dry tea towel and refrigerate in the vegetable storage drawer.

CABBAGE HEADS: Trim the stem and remove any wilted or discolored outer leaves. Wash the head under cold, running water; dry with a clean towel or with paper towels. Cut the head into quarters lengthwise through the stem end. Cut away the core from each quarter. No further washing is necessary. Place the cabbage quarters in zipper-seal plastic bags and refrigerate.

MOLDED SALADS

PREPARE MOLDED SALADS ONE DAY IN ADVANCE: To assure that molded salads are completely set, it is best to make them the day before they are to be served. When molded salads have gelled sufficiently to become stationary, cover them, in the refrigerator, with plastic wrap or aluminum foil to retain their fresh appearance and surface texture.

TO LIGHTLY OIL A SALAD MOLD: Brush the inside of the salad mold with a light coat of vegetable oil. Then, wipe nearly dry with paper towels.

TO REMOVE SALADS FROM SMALL, INDIVIDUAL MOLDS: Run a sharp, thin-bladed paring knife around the outer edge (and inner edge, if there is one) of the molded salad, penetrating the salad only ⅛ inch. Then, hold one mold at a time in a bowl of warm water for about 3 seconds, taking care not to get water on the gelatin salad. After removing each mold from the warm water, quickly turn it upside down on an individual salad plate. If the salad does not unmold, dip it again in warm water; or, with the mold upside down and in place slightly above the salad plate, slide a paring knife ½ inch into the outer edge

of the mold at a single place. This will sometimes help release the salad.

TO REMOVE SALADS FROM LARGE MOLDS: Run a sharp, thin-bladed paring knife around the outer edge (and inner edge, if there is one) of the molded salad, penetrating the salad only ⅛ inch. Place a serving plate upside down on top of the molded salad; then, holding the serving plate and mold securely, invert. The unmolded salad should now be in place above the serving plate. Place a clean tea towel under hot running water; wring out the towel. Cover the mold with the hot, moist towel and press, with your hands, against the entire surface of the mold. When the towel feels cool, place it under hot water again, and repeat the process. After 2 or 3 applications of the hot towel, the salad should drop from the mold onto the plate. If the salad continues not to release, *very carefully* lift the edge of the mold and slide a paring knife ½ inch into the outer edge of the mold, at a single place, to help release the salad. This is a hazardous procedure with very large molds, as it can cause the gelatin to split.

TO CUT MOLDED SALADS INTO INDIVIDUAL SERVINGS: Use a small, sharp, thin-bladed knife, about the size of a steak knife. Dip the knife blade into a tall glass of very hot water to warm the blade. Quickly wipe the blade dry; then, firmly make the desired cut. Redip the knife into hot water and dry it before making each cut.

To remove cut servings from the dish, use a small spatula as close to the size of the individual servings as possible.

Fruit Salads

CHAMPAGNE FRUIT SALAD

This is an enticing, impressive salad to serve at dinners, especially when the menu will be printed or hand-lettered.

2 cups poached, sliced, fresh peaches
   (see To Poach Fresh Peaches, below)
   (in off-seasons, substitute home-canned
   [page 720] or commercially canned
   peaches, drained)
2 cups fresh red or black raspberries, or
   1 cup of each
2 cups fresh blueberries
2 cups honeydew melon balls
1 cup halved or quartered (depending upon
   size) fresh strawberries
1 cup Black Corinth ("champagne")
   grapes*
1 recipe Champagne Salad Dressing
   (page 150)
Red-tip Boston lettuce
Additional red raspberries (or strawberries,
   if black raspberries are used) and Black
   Corinth grapes for garnish

   *Black Corinth is the variety of grapes from
   which dried currants (page 21) are made. They
   are tiny, seedless, red grapes and are nicknamed
   "champagne" grapes because in bunches they
   resemble champagne bubbles.*

In a very large mixing bowl, place the peaches, raspberries, blueberries, melon balls, strawberries, grapes, and Champagne Salad Dressing; toss to combine evenly. Spoon the fruit mixture onto 10 individual salad plates lined with red-tip Boston lettuce. Garnish each salad plate with red raspberries (or strawberries) and a small cluster of stemmed Black Corinth grapes.

SERVES 10

TO POACH FRESH PEACHES: Blanch the peaches (page 44) 1 minute; peel, pit, and cut in half. Drop the peach halves into a saucepan of boiling water; return to a simmer. Lower the heat and simmer 4 minutes. Immerse the poached peach halves in cold water to stop the cooking. Slice the peaches for use in the salad.

SERVING ALTERNATIVE: Serve Champagne Fruit Salad in a large serving bowl. Arrange red raspberries (or strawberries) and clusters of stemmed Black Corinth grapes around the edge of the bowl for garnish. Omit the red-tip Boston lettuce.

APPLE SALAD

2 cups unpared, quartered, cored, and
   sliced (see recipe procedures, below) firm
   red apples, such as Delicious or Jonathan
   (about 1 large apple or 2 medium-small
   apples)
½ cup sliced celery
¼ cup broken pecans
1 cup miniature marshmallows
1 recipe Special Mayonnaise Dressing
   (page 154)
Shredded iceberg lettuce

Wash the apples. Quarter and core them, leaving the skin on. Cut each quarter in half lengthwise, and slice ⅜ inch thick. Measure 2 cups apple slices; reserve any remaining slices for other uses. Place 2 cups apple slices in a medium mixing bowl. Add the celery, pecans, marshmallows, and Special Mayonnaise Dressing; stir to combine. Serve on a bed of shredded lettuce arranged on individual salad plates.

SERVES 4

FRESH PEAR SALAD WITH GINGER DRESSING

6 ounces cream cheese, softened
⅓ cup well-drained, commercial crushed pineapple in pineapple juice, reserving juice
3 tablespoons finely broken English walnuts
2 tablespoons ginger preserves
3 ripe Bartlett or Comice pears
2 tablespoons freshly squeezed, strained lemon juice
Leaf lettuce
Ginger Dressing (recipe follows)
¼ cup plus 2 tablespoons shredded, mild cheddar cheese

Place the cream cheese in a small mixing bowl; using an electric mixer, beat on high speed until creamy. Add the drained pineapple, walnuts, and ginger preserves; stir to combine; cover and refrigerate.

Shortly before serving, halve, core, and pare the pears. Brush the pears lightly with lemon juice to prevent discoloration. Line 6 individual salad plates with leaf lettuce and place one pear half on each plate. Using a 1½-inch trigger scoop, place a ball of the cream cheese mixture in the core cavity of each pear half. Spoon Ginger Dressing over each entire pear half (including the cream cheese filling). Sprinkle 1 tablespoon cheddar cheese over the dressing on each pear half.

SERVES 6

Ginger Dressing

½ cup mayonnaise
1 tablespoon reserved pineapple juice (from crushed pineapple, above)
¾ teaspoon very finely grated fresh ginger (page 46)
½ cup whipped cream (whip ½ cup whipping cream; then measure ½ cup)

In a small mixing bowl, place the mayonnaise, pineapple juice, and ginger; using an electric mixer, beat on medium speed until smooth and blended. Add the whipped cream; using a spoon, fold in.

PEACH AND COTTAGE CHEESE SALAD

Leaf lettuce
4 chilled peach halves, home canned (page 720) or commercially canned
1 cup small-curd cottage cheese
⅔ cup Poppy Seed Dressing (page 150)
3 red maraschino cherries, cut into eighths, for decoration

Line 4 small, individual salad plates with leaf lettuce. Tear additional leaf lettuce into bite-sized pieces; arrange in the center part of each plate to provide a low platform for the peach and cottage cheese and to make the salad plate look more lush.

Place 1 peach half, pit side up, in the center of each plate. Using a 2-inch trigger scoop, place a full scoop (about ¼ cup) of cottage cheese on top of each peach half. If the cottage cheese is especially creamy, drain off some of the liquid before scooping. Spoon about 1 tablespoon plus 1 teaspoon Poppy Seed Dressing over the cottage cheese and peach half on each plate. Sprinkle 5 pieces of maraschino cherry over the cottage cheese in each salad.

SERVES 4

VARIATION ~ **HOLIDAY DECORATION:** Substitute 2 red and 2 green maraschino cherries for 3 red maraschino cherries. Cut the cherries into eighths; arrange 3 red pieces and 3 green pieces on top of the cottage cheese on each plate.

TWENTY-FOUR-HOUR SALAD

2 extra-large eggs, beaten
¼ cup freshly squeezed, strained lemon
   juice
¼ cup sugar
2 tablespoons butter
1 cup (½ pint) whipping cream, whipped
1 15¼-ounce can commercial pineapple
   tidbits, well drained
1 17-ounce can commercial pitted white
   cherries, well drained
1½ cups orange sections (page 47) (about
   3 medium oranges)
1 cup seedless white grapes
1¼ cups fresh apricots cut into twelfths
   (about 4 apricots)*
2 cups miniature marshmallows
¼ cup slivered almonds, toasted (page 50)

*Or, 1 17-ounce can commercial apricot
halves, well drained. Cut each apricot half
into 6 pieces.*

Place the eggs in the top of a double boiler;
using a handheld electric mixer, beat slightly.
Add the lemon juice, sugar, and butter; stir. Place
the top of the double boiler over boiling water
in the bottom pan. Cook the mixture until
thick, stirring constantly. Remove the top of the
double boiler from the bottom pan and refrigerate until the mixture cools to room temperature, stirring occasionally. Add the whipped
cream; using a spoon, fold in; refrigerate.

   In a large mixing bowl, place the pineapple,
cherries, orange sections, grapes, apricots,
marshmallows, and whipped cream mixture;
fold carefully to combine. Place the salad in a
crystal serving bowl; cover and refrigerate for 24
hours. At serving time, sprinkle the top of the
salad with almonds.

SERVES 12

FROSTY CHRISTMAS SALAD

8 ounces cream cheese, softened
1 cup Miracle Whip salad dressing
1 cup (½ pint) whipping cream, whipped
2 cups fresh red raspberries
1 cup pared, sliced, then quartered kiwis
Thinly sliced, then halved kiwis for garnish
Additional red raspberries for garnish
Green leaf lettuce

In a small mixing bowl, place the cream cheese
and salad dressing; using an electric mixer, beat
on high speed until smooth and blended. Place
the cream cheese mixture in a large mixing
bowl. Add the whipped cream; using a spoon,
fold in. Add 2 cups raspberries and 1 cup kiwis;
carefully fold in until evenly distributed. Spoon
into a 7 × 11-inch baking dish; using a small,
narrow spatula, spread evenly. Cover tightly and
freeze.

   To serve, cut into 15 pieces using a sharp,
thin-bladed knife dipped intermittently into a
glass of warm water. Serve on individual salad
plates over pieces of green leaf lettuce. Garnish
the top of each serving with 2 small fans of kiwis
and a red raspberry.

SERVES 15

FROSTY FRUIT SALAD: Follow the Frosty Christmas Salad recipe, above, substituting 3 cups of
any combination of fresh and/or canned fruits
for the raspberries and kiwis. Garnish with
small, attractive pieces of the fruits used in the
salad.

SERVES 15

Molded Fruit Salads

STRAWBERRY-AVOCADO HOLIDAY SALAD

Strawberries and avocados would seem an unlikely combination, but they come together beautifully in this striking red and green holiday salad with a subtle, understated flavor.

1½ cups fresh strawberries quartered
  lengthwise
¼ cup cold water
2 teaspoons (1 envelope) unflavored gelatin
1 3-ounce package lime-flavored gelatin
1 cup boiling water
¼ cup cold water
½ cup mayonnaise
¼ cup freshly squeezed, strained lime juice
2 medium-sized ripe avocados
1 cup (½ pint) whipping cream
Leaf lettuce

Place the strawberries, single layer, randomly but evenly over the bottom of a 6 × 10-inch baking dish, with the outside surface of the berries against the bottom of the dish. Cover the dish with plastic wrap; refrigerate. Place ¼ cup cold water in a small sauce dish; sprinkle the unflavored gelatin over the water; let stand 10 minutes.

Meanwhile, place the lime-flavored gelatin in a medium mixing bowl. Add the boiling water; stir until the gelatin is completely dissolved. Add ¼ cup cold water; stir to blend. Remove the dish containing the strawberries from the refrigerator; uncover. Measure ½ cup lime gelatin mixture; pour over the strawberries; cover and refrigerate.

Add the unflavored gelatin mixture to the remaining lime gelatin mixture; stir, briskly, until the unflavored gelatin is completely dissolved and blended. Add the mayonnaise; using an electric mixer, beat on medium-high speed until fully blended. Refrigerate until the gelatin mixture is set about 1 inch around the edge of the bowl.

Meanwhile, pour the lime juice into a small bowl. Pit and peel the avocados (see Note); cut into chunks and immediately drop into lime juice and toss to coat to prevent discoloration. Place the avocado chunks and lime juice in a blender or food processor; process until pureed. Using a rubber spatula, scrape the avocado puree into a measuring cup. There should be approximately 1½ cups avocado puree. Cover and refrigerate.

Pour the whipping cream into a medium bowl; using an electric mixer, beat on high speed until softly whipped. Cover and refrigerate.

When the gelatin is set 1 inch around the edge of the bowl, remove it from the refrigerator. Using the electric mixer, beat the gelatin on high speed until fluffy. Add the avocado puree; beat until completely blended. Add the whipped cream; using a mixing spoon, fold in only until the color of the mixture is uniform. Spoon the mixture over the strawberry-gelatin layer in the dish; using a small, narrow spatula, spread evenly. Refrigerate until set; then, cover with plastic wrap.

To serve, use a small, sharp, thin-bladed knife to cut individual servings. Using a small spatula, carefully remove the servings from the dish and invert onto individual salad plates atop a small piece of leaf lettuce. The colorful, red strawberries in clear, green gelatin thus become the attractive top layer of the served salad.

NOTE: Cut the unpeeled avocados in half lengthwise. To separate from the pits, gently twist the avocado halves in opposite directions. Then peel.

SERVES 8 TO 10

ALTERNATIVE SERVING METHOD: To serve buffet style, the entire uncut salad may be unmolded onto a serving platter (page 109). Decorate the platter with leaf lettuce, sprigs of watercress, and unstemmed fresh strawberries.

CHRISTMAS GOOSEBERRY SALAD

2 pints home-canned Gooseberries in Syrup
  (page 717) or 2 16½-ounce cans
  commercial gooseberries in light syrup
1 6-ounce package lime-flavored gelatin
2 cups miniature marshmallows
2 cups finely chopped celery
1 cup broken English walnuts
1 cup fresh strawberries cut into ½-inch
  cubes
Leaf lettuce
1 recipe Thick Special Mayonnaise Dressing
  (page 154)
Fresh strawberries for decoration

Drain the gooseberries in a sieve, reserving the syrup (about 2 cups drained gooseberries). Place the gooseberries in a bowl; cover with plastic wrap and refrigerate. Add enough water to the reserved gooseberry syrup to make 4 cups liquid; pour into a medium saucepan and set aside. Place the gelatin in a large mixing bowl; set aside.

Over high heat, bring the gooseberry syrup mixture to a boil; pour over the gelatin; stir until the gelatin is completely dissolved. Add the marshmallows; stir until the marshmallows have completely melted. Refrigerate until the mixture begins to set and is the consistency of unbeaten egg whites, intermittently stirring vigorously to reblend. (The mixture may be placed in the freezer to hasten cooling if watched closely.)

When the mixture cools to egg-white consistency, stir to reblend. Add the celery, walnuts, and 1 cup strawberries; stir until evenly combined. Pour the mixture into a 9 × 13-inch baking dish; refrigerate. When firm, cover tightly with plastic wrap; refrigerate until completely set (at least 4 hours).

Cut into 18 individual servings (page 109). Place each serving on a lettuce-lined individual salad plate. Spoon 2 teaspoons Thick Special Mayonnaise Dressing over the center of each gelatin serving. For decoration, press ¼ or ½

(depending upon size) of a fresh strawberry into the dollop of dressing on each serving.

SERVES 18

MANDARIN ORANGE-GOOSEBERRY SALAD: To serve Gooseberry Salad at times other than Christmas, substitute one 15-ounce can commercial mandarin orange segments in light syrup for the fresh strawberries.

Drain the orange segments in a sieve, reserving the syrup. Cut the orange segments in half widthwise; reserve 18 segment halves to decorate the top of individual salad servings; set aside. Follow the salad recipe, adding the reserved orange segment syrup to the gooseberry syrup; then, adding enough water to make 4 cups liquid. Continue following the recipe, adding the unreserved segment halves (about 1 cup) to the salad in substitution for 1 cup cubed strawberries.

SERVES 18

RASPBERRY SHIMMER

1 10-ounce package frozen red raspberries
1 3-ounce package red raspberry-flavored
  gelatin
½ cup boiling water
8 ounces red raspberry-flavored, lowfat
  yogurt
Red-tip leaf lettuce
Fresh red raspberries for garnish (optional)

Remove the frozen raspberries from the freezer 1 hour before making the salad.

Place the gelatin in a medium mixing bowl. Add the boiling water; stir until completely thawed. Add the raspberries; stir until completely thawed. Add the yogurt; stir until blended. Ladle into 4 lightly oiled (page 109) individual molds; refrigerate until set. Unmold (page 109) on red-tip leaf lettuce arranged on small, individual salad plates. The salad plates may be garnished with fresh red raspberries.

SERVES 4

STRAWBERRY SHIMMER: Follow the Raspberry Shimmer recipe, above, substituting frozen strawberries, strawberry-flavored gelatin, and strawberry-flavored yogurt for the raspberry ingredients. Garnish with fresh strawberries.

CITRUS FRUIT THREE-LAYER PARTY SALAD

BOTTOM LAYER
1 3-ounce package orange-flavored gelatin
¾ cup boiling water
1 cup cold water
2 cups orange sections (page 47)
Orange zest (page 46) for decoration

Place the gelatin in a medium mixing bowl. Add the boiling water; stir until the gelatin is completely dissolved. Add the cold water; stir to blend. Refrigerate until the gelatin mixture begins to set and is the consistency of unbeaten egg whites (watch closely).

Meanwhile, distribute the orange sections, single layer, randomly over the bottom of a 7 × 11-inch baking dish. Pour the partially set gelatin over the orange sections; refrigerate until set (at least 4 hours). Using a citrus zester (page 47) cut orange zest and place in a small sauce dish; cover and refrigerate, reserving for decoration on the individual salad servings.

CENTER LAYER
12 ounces soft-style cream cheese, softened
½ cup chopped, slivered blanched almonds
  (page 50)

Prepare the center layer after the bottom layer is fully set.

Place the cream cheese in a small mixing bowl; using an electric mixer, beat on high speed until smooth and creamy. Add the almonds; stir until evenly distributed. Spoon the cream cheese mixture evenly and carefully over the surface of the bottom layer. Using a small, narrow spatula, spread evenly and smoothly. Refrigerate until cold and set (at least 4 hours).

TOP LAYER
1 3-ounce package lemon-flavored gelatin
¾ cup boiling water
1 cup cold water
2 cups white grapefruit sections (page 47)
Boston lettuce leaves

When the center layer is set, prepare the top layer. Follow the same procedure for preparing the gelatin as in the bottom layer, above. Distribute the grapefruit sections, single layer, randomly over the center layer. Pour the partially set gelatin over the grapefruit sections; refrigerate until set (at least 4 hours).

To serve, cut the salad into individual servings (page 109). Using a small spatula, place the servings on individual salad plates atop a small leaf of Boston lettuce (the grapefruit layer will be on top). Sprinkle a few curls of orange zest over the center of each salad serving.

SERVES 8 TO 10

VARIATION ~ **HOLIDAY DECORATION**
8 ounces soft-style cream cheese, softened
Bright green and red paste food coloring

For an attractive salad decoration for the Christmas holidays, pipe green and red holly near one corner or in the center of each salad serving. Eliminate the orange zest decoration.

To make piped holly, place the cream cheese in a small mixing bowl; using an electric mixer, beat briefly on high speed until smooth and fluffy. Spoon about ⅔ of the cream cheese into a small container or bowl. Using a toothpick, add a tiny amount of green paste food coloring; stir vigorously until completely blended. Spoon the remaining ⅓ cream cheese into another small container or bowl; tint red, using the same procedure. Using a decorating bag fit with medium leaf tip number 68 (page 383), pipe 2 green holly leaves (page 391). Using another decorating bag fit with small round tip number 3, add 3 small red berries (see Dots, page 389) where the stem ends of the holly leaves meet.

APRICOT SALAD

1 29-ounce can peeled or unpeeled commercial apricots in light or heavy syrup
1 8-ounce can commercial pineapple tidbits in pineapple juice
Additional pineapple juice, if necessary
1 6-ounce package orange-flavored gelatin
2 cups boiling water
2 cups miniature marshmallows
½ cup sugar
3 tablespoons plus 2 teaspoons all-purpose flour
1 extra-large egg
2 tablespoons butter
1 cup (½ pint) whipping cream, whipped
1¼ cups shredded Colby cheese
Lettuce leaves

In a sieve, drain the apricots and pineapple together, reserving the syrup and juice. Measure 2 cups reserved syrup and juice, adding additional pineapple juice, if necessary, to make 2 cups liquid; set aside. Place the drained apricots and pineapple tidbits in a blender or food processor. Chop the fruit finely in the blender or food processor, but do not puree; set aside.

Place the gelatin in a large mixing bowl. Add the boiling water; stir until the gelatin completely dissolves. Add 1 cup of the mixed apricot syrup and pineapple juice; stir to blend. Add the chopped fruit and marshmallows; stir until evenly combined. Pour into a 9 × 13-inch baking dish; refrigerate until firm.

Then, in a small mixing bowl, place the sugar and flour; stir to combine; set aside. Place the egg in the top of a double boiler; using a handheld electric mixer, beat slightly. Add the sugar mixture; stir well. Add the remaining 1 cup of mixed apricot syrup and pineapple juice, and butter; stir. Place the top of the double boiler over simmering water in the bottom pan. Cook the mixture until thick, stirring constantly. Remove the top of the double boiler from the

bottom pan; refrigerate until the mixture cools to room temperature, stirring occasionally.

After the mixture cools to room temperature, add the whipped cream; using a spoon, fold in. Spoon the whipped cream mixture over the set gelatin mixture; using a large, narrow spatula, spread evenly and smoothly. Sprinkle the top evenly with shredded cheese. Refrigerate until the whipped cream topping is set (at least 6 hours). Cut into 15 individual serving pieces (page 109). Serve on small salad plates lined with lettuce leaves.

SERVES 15

MANDARIN ORANGE SALAD

Orange frozen yogurt is a refreshing ingredient in this salad, which can also double as a dessert (omit the lettuce and decorate the plate with a sprig of fresh mint). This salad should be made a day in advance to allow sufficient time for it to set solidly.

2 11-ounce cans commercial mandarin orange segments in light syrup
1 3-ounce package lemon-flavored gelatin
1 pint orange frozen yogurt
1 banana
Bibb lettuce leaves

Drain the mandarin orange segments in a sieve, reserving the syrup. Reserve 8 orange segments for garnish; cover and refrigerate. Place the remaining orange segments in a bowl; cover and set aside. Measure 1 cup reserved syrup and place in a small saucepan; set aside.

Place the gelatin in a medium mixing bowl; set aside. Place the saucepan containing the syrup over medium-high heat; bring the syrup to a boil. Pour the syrup over the gelatin; stir until the gelatin is completely dissolved. Add the frozen yogurt while the gelatin mixture is still hot; stir until the yogurt completely melts and the mixture is smooth. Refrigerate the mixture exactly 10 minutes (no longer because the melted frozen yogurt has already made the mixture quite cold before you refrigerate it; over-refrigeration at this point will allow the mixture to set too firmly before adding the fruit).

Peel the banana; split in half lengthwise; slice. Add the sliced banana and orange segments to the gelatin mixture; carefully fold in. Ladle into 8 lightly oiled (page 109) individual molds; refrigerate until set (at least 8 hours, but preferably overnight). After the mixture is set, cover each mold with a small piece of aluminum foil.

It is not necessary to dip the molds containing this salad in warm water to unmold. To unmold, run a paring knife around the outer edge of each mold, penetrating the salad about ⅛ inch. Invert each mold over an individual salad plate lined with Bibb lettuce and slide the paring knife about ½ inch into the outer edge of the mold, at a single place, to release the salad. Garnish each salad with one of the reserved orange segments.

SERVES 8

CRANBERRY-ORANGE SALAD

2 cups raw cranberries
1 medium orange, unpeeled, quartered, and seeded
1 8-ounce can commercial crushed pineapple in pineapple juice
1 3-ounce package orange-flavored gelatin
½ cup sugar
1 cup finely diced celery
¾ cup quartered, seedless red grapes
½ cup broken English walnuts
Leaf lettuce
1 recipe Special Mayonnaise Dressing (page 154)
Small sprigs of celery leaves for garnish
Orange zest (page 46) for decoration

Wash and drain the cranberries. Using a food grinder (page 49), grind the cranberries and orange quarters (including peel) finely; place in a covered container and refrigerate. Drain the crushed pineapple in a sieve, reserving the juice. Cover the drained crushed pineapple; set aside. Add enough water to the pineapple juice to make 2 cups liquid; set aside. In a medium saucepan, place the gelatin and sugar; stir to combine. Add the pineapple juice mixture; stir to combine. Place over medium heat and stir until the gelatin and sugar are completely dissolved; refrigerate until the mixture begins to set and is the consistency of unbeaten egg whites.

Then, add the ground cranberries and oranges, crushed pineapple, celery, grapes, and walnuts; fold in until evenly combined. Ladle into 8 lightly oiled (page 109) individual molds; refrigerate until firm (at least 3 hours).

It is not necessary to dip the molds containing this salad in warm water to unmold if the molds were lightly oiled before filling. To unmold, run a paring knife around the outer edge of each mold, penetrating the salad about ⅛ inch. Invert each mold over an individual salad plate lined with leaf lettuce and slide the paring knife about ½ inch into the outer edge of the mold, at a single place, to release the salad. Top each molded salad with a dollop of Special Mayonnaise Dressing. Arrange a small sprig of celery leaves beside the molded salad on each plate and sprinkle a few curls of orange zest over the dressing.

SERVES 8

VARIATION: Substitute ¾ cup ground (page 49), unpeeled, firm red apples for the grapes.

CINNAMON-APPLE SALAD

2 tablespoons cinnamon imperials (candy
   red hots)
¼ cup boiling water
1 3-ounce package lemon-flavored gelatin
Dash of salt
¾ cup boiling water
2 cups cinnamon applesauce, homemade
   and pressed through a food mill (page
   344) or commercially canned
Dash of nutmeg
8 ounces cream cheese, softened
3 tablespoons Miracle Whip salad dressing
Ground cinnamon for decoration
Lettuce leaves

In a small bowl, dissolve the cinnamon imperials in ¼ cup boiling water; set aside. In a
medium bowl, place the lemon gelatin and salt;
add ¾ cup boiling water; stir until the gelatin
and salt are completely dissolved. Add the cinnamon imperial mixture; stir to blend. Add the
applesauce and nutmeg; stir until combined.
Pour into an 8 × 8-inch baking dish; refrigerate
until set (at least 3 hours).

   In a small mixing bowl, place the cream
cheese and salad dressing; using an electric
mixer, beat on high speed until blended. Spoon
the salad dressing mixture over the set gelatin
mixture; using a small, narrow spatula, spread
evenly. Sprinkle lightly with cinnamon. Refrigerate until the topping is set (at least 3 hours).
Cut into 9 squares (page 109); place individual
servings on lettuce-lined salad plates.

SERVES 9

*VARIATION ~ **VALENTINE'S DAY GARNISH:** To serve
Cinnamon-Apple Salad on Valentine's Day, add
a few drops of red liquid food coloring to the
cinnamon imperial and boiling water mixture.
Omit the ground cinnamon decoration and
decorate the top of each salad serving with additional cinnamon imperials or small, red gumdrop hearts.

GRAPE-BLUEBERRY GALAXY WITH PORT WINE DRESSING

¼ cup cold water
2 teaspoons (1 envelope) unflavored gelatin
¼ cup sugar
¾ cup boiling water
1 6-ounce can frozen, concentrated grape
   juice, thawed
¼ cup port wine
1 cup small, seedless white grapes
1 cup small, seedless red grapes
1 cup fresh blueberries
¼ cup broken pecans
Boston lettuce leaves
Sprigs of fresh mint for decoration
Port Wine Dressing (recipe follows)

Pour ¼ cup cold water into a small sauce dish;
sprinkle the gelatin over the water and let stand
10 minutes. Then, in a medium bowl, place the
sugar, ¾ cup boiling water, and gelatin mixture;
stir until the sugar and gelatin are completely
dissolved. Add the grape juice and wine; stir to
blend. Refrigerate until the mixture begins to
set and is the consistency of unbeaten egg
whites. Add the white grapes, red grapes, blueberries, and pecans; carefully fold in to evenly
combine. Ladle into 8 lightly oiled (page 109)
individual molds. Refrigerate until completely
set (at least 5 hours).

   To serve, place a crisp leaf of Boston lettuce
on each of 8 individual plates. Unmold the salads (page 109) onto the lettuce leaves. Decorate
each plate with a sprig of mint. Pass Port Wine
Dressing at the table.

SERVES 8

Port Wine Dressing

¾ cup whipping cream
⅓ cup mayonnaise
3 tablespoons port wine

Place the whipping cream in a medium bowl; using an electric mixer, beat on high speed until the cream holds soft peaks. Add the mayonnaise and wine; beat on medium speed until the consistency of thick salad dressing. Refrigerate. Stir well immediately before serving.

MOLDED PEAR SALAD

1 16-ounce can commercial pear halves in light syrup or 1 pint home-canned Plain Pears (page 723)
1 3-ounce package lemon-flavored gelatin
6 ounces cream cheese, softened
1 teaspoon freshly squeezed, strained lemon juice
½ cup finely broken pecans
⅓ cup maraschino cherries cut into eighths
1 cup (½ pint) whipping cream, whipped
Boston lettuce
2 ounces mild cheddar cheese, shredded (½ cup shredded cheese)

Drain the pears in a sieve, reserving the syrup. Cut the pears into ½-inch cubes; place in a bowl; cover and refrigerate. Measure 1 cup reserved syrup. (If necessary, add water to make 1 cup liquid.) Pour into a small saucepan; set aside. Place the gelatin in a medium mixing bowl; set aside. Place the saucepan containing the syrup over medium-high heat; bring the syrup to a boil. Pour over the gelatin; stir until the gelatin is completely dissolved.

Pour the gelatin mixture into a blender or food processor. Add the cream cheese and lemon juice; process until completely blended. Pour the processed mixture into a large mixing bowl; refrigerate until the mixture begins to set. Add the pears, pecans, maraschino cherries, and whipped cream; fold until evenly combined. Turn the mixture into a 7 × 11-inch baking dish; refrigerate until set (at least 5 hours).

To serve, cut into 15 servings (page 109). Using a spatula, place the servings on individual salad plates lined with Boston lettuce. Sprinkle the shredded cheese over the molded salad in each serving.

SERVES 15

MOLDED FRUIT SALAD

1 15-ounce can commercial mandarin orange segments in light syrup
1 16½-ounce can commercial pitted Royal Anne white cherries in heavy syrup
1 20-ounce can commercial pineapple tidbits in pineapple juice
1 6-ounce package cherry-flavored gelatin
2 cups boiling water
1 cup (½ pint) whipping cream
Shredded iceberg lettuce
15 additional mandarin orange segments for decoration (optional)

In a sieve, drain the orange segments, cherries, and pineapple, reserving the syrup/juice. Place the drained fruit in a bowl; cover and set aside. Measure 2 cups reserved syrup/juice; set aside. Place the gelatin in a large mixing bowl. Add the boiling water; stir until the gelatin is completely dissolved. Add the syrup/juice; stir to blend. Add the drained fruit; stir until evenly combined. Refrigerate until the gelatin begins to set and is the consistency of unbeaten egg whites.

Meanwhile, place the whipping cream in a medium bowl; using an electric mixer, beat until softly whipped; cover and refrigerate. When the gelatin reaches the consistency of unbeaten egg whites, add the whipped cream. Stir and fold until the whipped cream is combined and the fruits are evenly distributed. Pour into a 9 × 13-inch baking dish; refrigerate until completely set (at least 6 hours).

To serve, cut into 15 servings (page 109). Using a spatula, place the servings on individual salad plates lined with shredded lettuce. The top of each salad serving may be decorated with a mandarin orange segment.

SERVES 15

PINEAPPLE-CREAM CHEESE SALAD

This is a real old-timer we were always happy to find at our places when we took our chairs at my grandmother's table. In those days, it was called "30 Minute Salad" because—as it was made then—you let the recipe mixture stand 30 minutes after three of the additions. Clever names and unconventional procedures were characteristic of old Midwest recipes. They provided relief from the day in, day out routine of cooking, and engendered much conversation, recipe exchanging, and fun in the kitchen. Wacky Cake (page 544) is another example of this playful cooking humor.

1 20-ounce can commercial crushed
   pineapple in pineapple juice
1 6-ounce package lemon-flavored gelatin
1 cup boiling water
8 ounces cream cheese, softened
1 4-ounce jar pimientos, drained and
   chopped (4 tablespoons)
1 cup chopped pecans
2 cups (1 pint) whipping cream, whipped
Shredded iceberg lettuce
½ cup Cooked Salad Dressing (page 151)
Paprika for decoration

Drain the pineapple in a sieve, reserving the juice. Place the drained pineapple in a bowl; cover and refrigerate. Measure 1 cup reserved juice. (If necessary, add water to make 1 cup liquid.) Set aside. Place the gelatin in a large mixing bowl. Add the boiling water; stir until the gelatin is completely dissolved. Add the pineapple juice; stir to blend. Refrigerate until the mixture begins to set and is the consistency of unbeaten egg whites.

Meanwhile, place the cream cheese in a medium mixing bowl; using an electric mixer, beat on high speed until smooth and creamy. Add the crushed pineapple; stir to combine. Add the pimientos and pecans; stir until evenly distributed; set aside.

When the gelatin mixture reaches the consistency of unbeaten egg whites, add the pineapple

mixture; stir until combined. Add the whipped cream; fold in. Turn the mixture into a 9 × 13-inch baking dish; using a small, narrow spatula, spread evenly. Refrigerate until set (at least 6 hours). When set, cover with plastic wrap.

At serving time, cut into 16 pieces (page 109). Using a spatula, place the servings on a platform of shredded lettuce on individual salad plates. Place a dollop (about 1 teaspoon) of Cooked Salad Dressing atop each molded salad serving. Sprinkle paprika sparingly over the salad dressing.

SERVES 16

FROSTED LIME-WALNUT SALAD

1 cup chopped celery
1 tablespoon drained, chopped pimientos
½ cup broken English walnuts
1 20-ounce can (2½ cups) commercial
   crushed pineapple in pineapple juice
1 3-ounce package lime-flavored gelatin
¾ cup boiling water
1 cup small-curd cottage cheese, drained
Frosting (recipe follows)
8 Pineapple Tulips tinted yellow (page 403)
   for decoration (optional; see Alternative
   Decorations, below)
Sprigs of watercress or other greens for
   garnish

Place the celery, pimientos, and walnuts in separate bowls; cover and set aside. Drain the pineapple in a sieve, reserving the juice. Place the drained pineapple in a bowl; cover and refrigerate. Set aside the reserved juice. Place the gelatin in a medium mixing bowl; add the boiling water; stir until the gelatin is completely dissolved. Add the pineapple juice to the gelatin mixture; stir to blend. Refrigerate until the mixture begins to set and is the consistency of unbeaten egg whites.

Then, add the celery, pimientos, walnuts, pineapple, and cottage cheese; stir until evenly combined. Turn into a 6 × 10-inch baking dish; using

Then, add the celery, pimientos, walnuts, pineapple, and pineapple, and cottage cheese; stir until evenly combined. Turn into a 6 × 10-inch baking dish; using a small, narrow spatula, spread evenly. Refrigerate until set (at least 5 hours).

Spoon the Frosting over the set gelatin mixture; using a small, narrow spatula, spread evenly over the entire surface. Refrigerate. If desired, after the frosting sets, score the salad into 8 servings using a sharp, thin-bladed knife, and arrange a Pineapple Tulip on top of each serving.

At serving time, cut into 8 servings (page 109). Using a spatula, place the servings on individual salad plates. Garnish the plates with sprigs of watercress or other greens.

SERVES 8

Frosting

8 ounces cream cheese, softened
2 tablespoons commercial sour cream
2 tablespoons freshly squeezed, strained
    lemon juice

In a small mixing bowl, place the cream cheese, sour cream, and lemon juice; using an electric mixer, beat on high speed until very smooth.

ALTERNATIVE DECORATIONS
• For simpler decoration, sprinkle each salad serving with finely chopped English walnuts.

• For a holiday salad, decorate the top of each salad serving with finely diced pimientos and celery (use greenest outer stalks).

DOUBLE RECIPE: To double the recipe, double all the salad ingredients, including the Frosting. Place in a 9 × 13-inch baking dish.

GINGER ALE FRUIT SALAD

½ cup freshly squeezed, strained orange
    juice
1 tablespoon plus 1 teaspoon (2 envelopes)
    unflavored gelatin
1 15-ounce can commercial fruit cocktail in
    light syrup or 1 pint home-canned Fruit
    Cocktail (page 724)
¾ cup freshly squeezed, strained orange
    juice
¼ cup sugar
¼ cup freshly squeezed, strained lemon juice
1 10-ounce bottle (1¼ cups) ginger ale
½ cup broken pecans
Leaf lettuce

Pour ½ cup orange juice into the top of a double boiler. Sprinkle the gelatin over the orange juice; let stand 15 minutes.

Meanwhile, drain the fruit cocktail in a sieve, reserving the syrup. Place the drained fruit cocktail in a bowl; cover and refrigerate. Pour the reserved fruit cocktail syrup into a 1-cup glass measuring cup with pouring spout; add enough of the ¾ cup orange juice to make ¾ cup combined liquid. Pour into a medium mixing bowl; set aside. Reserve the remaining orange juice for other uses.

Add the sugar to the gelatin mixture in the top of the double boiler; stir to combine. Place the top of the double boiler over hot water in the bottom pan; stir the gelatin mixture just until dissolved. Add the gelatin mixture and lemon juice to the combined liquid in the mixing bowl; stir until blended. Add the ginger ale; stir to blend. Refrigerate until the mixture begins to set and is the consistency of unbeaten egg whites.

Then, add the fruit cocktail and pecans; stir to combine. Ladle into 8 lightly oiled (page 109) individual molds; refrigerate until fully set (at least 3 hours).

To serve, unmold (page 109) on leaf lettuce arranged an individual salad plates.

SERVES 8

Vegetable Salads

CAESAR SALAD

½ cup extra-virgin olive oil
2 tablespoons freshly squeezed, strained
  lemon juice
2 tablespoons balsamic vinegar
2 garlic cloves, pressed
2 ounces anchovy fillets
12 cups romaine lettuce cut into generous
  bite-sized pieces
½ cup freshly grated Parmesan cheese
  (page 46)
1¼ cups Garlic Croutons (page 48)

In a glass jar or plastic container with a secure
lid, place the olive oil, lemon juice, vinegar, and
garlic; cover and shake vigorously until the
dressing ingredients are blended; set aside.

Place the anchovy fillets in a small mixing
bowl; using the back of a spoon, mash until paste
consistency. Add about ¼ cup of the dressing to
the anchovy paste; stir until well combined;
cover and refrigerate. Cover and refrigerate the
remaining dressing.

Just before serving, place the lettuce in a large
crystal or wooden salad bowl. Add the remaining dressing; toss until the lettuce is well coated.
Add, in the following order, the anchovy mixture, Parmesan cheese, and Garlic Croutons; toss
until combined.

SERVES 6

BIBB LETTUCE, WATERCRESS, AND ARTICHOKE HEARTS SALAD

6 cups Bibb lettuce torn into bite-sized
  pieces
2 cups watercress sprigs with most of stems
  removed
1 14-ounce can artichoke hearts (not
  pickled) (about 8 large artichoke hearts),
  drained and quartered lengthwise
1½ cups sliced fresh mushrooms
⅔ cup Basic Vinaigrette Dressing
  (page 152)

In a large mixing bowl, place the lettuce, watercress, artichoke hearts, mushrooms, and Basic
Vinaigrette Dressing; toss to combine. Serve on
glass salad plates.

SERVES 4

VARIATION: 2 tablespoons pine nuts may be tossed
with the other ingredients.

SLICED TOMATOES AND LETTUCE SALAD

4 medium to large ripe tomatoes
Mixed greens of choice, torn into bite-sized
  pieces
Special Mayonnaise Dressing (page 154)
Paprika for decoration
Sprigs of watercress for garnish

Blanch (page 44), stem, peel, and slice the tomatoes; set aside. Arrange generous beds of greens
on individual, chilled salad plates. Over the
greens on each plate, place 2 or 3 overlapping
slices of tomatoes. Spoon 1 heaping tablespoon
of dressing over the tomatoes in each salad.
Sprinkle a sparing amount of paprika on the
center portion of the dressing. Garnish each
plate with a sprig of watercress.

SERVES 6

DUTCH LETTUCE SALAD

4 cups iceberg lettuce torn into bite-sized
  pieces
6 slices bacon, cut into 1-inch pieces, fried
  crisply, and drained between paper towels
2 extra-large eggs, hard-cooked (page 264)
  and chopped
1 cup pared and shredded carrots
1 tablespoon minced onions
¾ cup Cooked Salad Dressing made with
  ¼ cup plus 1 tablespoon sugar (page
  151)

In a large mixing bowl, place the lettuce, bacon,
eggs, carrots, onions, and Cooked Salad Dressing; toss to combine.

SERVES 4

BOSTON LETTUCE, HEARTS OF PALM, AND MUSHROOM SALAD

1 cup commercially canned hearts of palm
  drained and sliced ⅝ inch thick
8 cups Boston lettuce torn into bite-sized
  pieces
⅔ cup sliced, fresh mushrooms
2 extra-large eggs, hard-cooked (page 264)
  and coarsely chopped
½ cup Creamy Vinaigrette Dressing
  (page 152)

Test each heart of palm for tenderness before
slicing. Especially if the heart of palm is large in
diameter, it may be necessary to remove and discard the tough outer layer before slicing.

In a large mixing bowl, place the hearts of
palm, lettuce, mushrooms, eggs, and Creamy
Vinaigrette Dressing; toss to combine.

SERVES 4

HEARTS OF PALM–PERSIMMON SALAD

*This salad features two delicacies worthy of "company
fare" designation, but appropriately flavored for informal dining. Hearts of palm are just that: the center of
palmetto (cabbage) palm tree stems. Unless you live in
Florida, where they can be purchased fresh, hearts of
palm come to us canned from Florida, Brazil, and
Costa Rica. They've been one of my favorite salad
ingredients ever since I first ate them at the former
Well-of-the-Sea restaurant in Chicago when I was in
high school.*

*Persimmons are a shiny, bright orange, Asian fruit,
which is also grown in the United States. Persimmons
grown in this country are available September through
November, but imported persimmons may be found in
some produce markets through May. Wild American
persimmons, a different species from domestic persimmons, are smaller than domestic persimmons and are
extremely sour until fully ripe. The name "persimmon" is derived from the Native American Indian
word for this wild fruit.*

¾ cup commercially canned hearts of palm
  drained and sliced ¼ inch thick
¾ cup coarsely diced persimmons
¾ cup coarsely chopped celery
¾ cup thinly sliced radishes
1 recipe Sour Cream Salad Dressing
  (page 153)
Spinach leaves

Test each heart of palm for tenderness before
slicing. Especially if the heart of palm is large in
diameter, it may be necessary to remove and discard the tough outer layer before slicing.

In a medium mixing bowl, place the hearts of
palm, persimmons, celery, radishes, and Sour
Cream Salad Dressing; stir to combine. Arrange
the spinach leaves on 4 individual salad plates.
Spoon the salad in the center of each plate over
the spinach leaves.

SERVES 4

TOSSED SALADS

The following are suggested ingredients to include in tossed salads of your own invention. Toss the salad ingredients with a compatible dressing of your choice (pages 147–154).

GREENS
Arugula
Bibb lettuce
Bok choy
Boston lettuce
Red-tip Boston lettuce
Chinese cabbage
Green cabbage
Red cabbage
Belgian endive
Curly endive
Escarole
Iceberg lettuce
Leaf lettuce
Red-tip leaf lettuce
Radicchio
Romaine
Spinach
Watercress

VEGETABLES
Artichoke hearts (not pickled)
Green and white asparagus, boiled
Garbanzo beans (chickpeas)
Green and wax beans, boiled
Kidney beans, canned, drained, and rinsed
Lima beans, boiled
Beets, boiled
Green, red, yellow, orange, and purple bell peppers
Pimientos
Broccoli flowerets
Brussels sprouts, steamed
Carrots
Cauliflower flowerets
Celery
Corn, boiled
Cucumbers
Fennel bulbs
Hearts of palm

Mushrooms
Green onions
Red onions
Sweet onions
Green peas, boiled
Snow peas, blanched
Potatoes, pared or unpared, boiled
Radishes
Sauerkraut
Alfalfa sprouts
Bean sprouts
Daikon radish sprouts
Red and yellow cherry tomatoes
Red and yellow tomatoes
Water chestnuts
Green and yellow zucchini

FRUITS
Apples
Avocados
Dates
Figs
Grapes
Mandarin orange segments
Pineapple tidbits, canned
Prunes
Dark and golden raisins

MEATS, POULTRY, FISH, AND SHELLFISH
Beef tenderloin
Veal
Pork tenderloin
Bacon
Ham
Lamb
Ring bologna
Summer sausage
Chicken
Duck
Turkey
Anchovy fillets
Mild fish fillets
Salmon
Albacore tuna, solid white packed in water
Crabmeat
Lobster
Shrimp

OTHER INGREDIENTS

Capers

Cheeses, such as cheddar, Swiss, blue, feta, chèvre, Monterey Jack, Colby, provolone, Edam, Gouda, grated Parmesan, and grated Romano

Croutons

Hard-cooked eggs

Herbs, such as parsley, chives, basil, dill, chervil, marjoram, cilantro, savory, tarragon, and rosemary

Nuts, such as almonds, English walnuts, pecans, pine nuts, hickory nuts, and chestnuts

Ripe and green olives, pitted; also, pimiento-stuffed

Pasta

Rice

Sesame Seeds

ALL-YELLOW VEGETABLE SALAD

1½ cups whole, yellow teardrop tomatoes
1¼ cups cooked, cooled, and drained, fresh wax beans (page 305) cut into 1¼-inch lengths
1 cup yellow zucchini sliced ⅛ inch thick, then cut in half
½ cup coarsely chopped yellow bell peppers
⅔ cup Honey-Mustard Dressing (page 149)
Belgian endive

In a large mixing bowl, place the tomatoes, wax beans, yellow zucchini, yellow peppers, and Honey-Mustard Dressing; using a wooden mixing spoon, toss until evenly distributed. On each of 6 individual salad plates, arrange leaves of Belgian endive in flower-petal fashion (like spokes of a wheel). Spoon the salad in the center of each plate.

SERVES 6

SOPHISTICATED SALAD

3 cups arugula sprigs
3 cups radicchio torn into generous, bite-sized pieces
3 cups Belgian endive cut widthwise into generous, bite-sized pieces
1 14-ounce can artichoke hearts (not pickled) (about 8 large artichoke hearts), drained and quartered lengthwise
⅓ cup pine nuts
¾ cup Basic Vinaigrette Dressing (page 152)

In a large mixing bowl, place the arugula, radicchio, Belgian endive, artichoke hearts, pine nuts, and Basic Vinaigrette Dressing; toss to coat and evenly distribute. Serve on individual salad plates (clear glass salad plates are especially nice).

SERVES 6

SORORITY HOUSE SALAD

After a morning of classes, this was one of my favorite items to find on the lunch menu at my sorority house at Northwestern University in Evanston, Illinois. I have served it ever since.

6 cups romaine lettuce cut into generous, bite-sized pieces
6 cups iceberg lettuce cut into bite-sized pieces
4 extra-large eggs, hard-cooked (page 264) and coarsely chopped
1 cup sliced celery
1½ recipes Special Mayonnaise Dressing (page 154)
Paprika for decoration

In a large bowl, place the romaine lettuce, iceberg lettuce, eggs, celery, and Special Mayonnaise Dressing; toss until combined. Distribute among 8 individual salad plates. Sprinkle paprika sparingly over each salad.

SERVES 8

BEET AND WATERCRESS SALAD

2 cups cooked, fresh beets (page 306) cut julienne (page 23) or 1 16-ounce can commercial julienne beets, drained
2 cups watercress with large stems removed
1 cup sliced, fresh mushrooms
½ cup diced purple bell peppers*
2 tablespoons thinly sliced green onions (scallions)
½ cup Mild Creamy Vinaigrette Dressing (page 152)
6 medium-sized leaves of red-tip leaf lettuce
6 sprigs of watercress

Yellow bell peppers may be substituted if purple bell peppers are not available.

In a large mixing bowl, place the beets, 2 cups watercress, mushrooms, purple peppers, onions, and Mild Creamy Vinaigrette Dressing; toss and set aside. Line each of 6 individual salad plates with a leaf of red-tip leaf lettuce. Spoon the Beet and Watercress Salad over the lettuce leaves. Garnish each plate with a sprig of watercress.

SERVES 6

BROCCOLI-CAULIFLOWER SALAD

4 cups fresh broccoli flowerets
4 cups fresh cauliflower flowerets
1½ cups sliced radishes
½ cup sliced green onions (scallions)
1 6-ounce can pitted, medium, ripe olives, drained (1½ cups olives), cut in half widthwise
½ recipe Mild Creamy Vinaigrette Dressing (page 152)

Steam the broccoli flowerets (page 302) for 3 minutes. Immediately remove the steamer basket containing the broccoli from the pan. Leave the broccoli in the steamer basket and rinse under cold running water to stop the cooking. Drain well. Place the broccoli in a zipper-seal plastic bag; refrigerate until completely cold. Steam and store the cauliflower flowerets, following the same procedure as for the broccoli flowerets. Steam and prepare the broccoli and cauliflower separately to preserve their individual colors and flavors.

In a medium mixing bowl, place the broccoli, cauliflower, radishes, green onions, olives, and Mild Creamy Vinaigrette Dressing; using a wooden mixing spoon, toss lightly until the vegetables are coated with dressing and evenly distributed.

SERVES 8

COPPER PENNIES

2 pounds uniformly sized carrots, pared and sliced ¼ inch thick
½ cup sugar
1 teaspoon dry mustard
¾ teaspoon salt
½ teaspoon pepper
1 10¾-ounce can condensed tomato soup (undiluted)
1 teaspoon Worcestershire sauce
½ cup vegetable oil
1 medium to small onion, sliced as thinly as possible, separated into rings
1 medium green bell pepper, sliced into rings ⅛ inch thick, seeds removed, white core cut away, and rings cut into fourths

Place the carrots in a large saucepan; add water to cover. Cover and bring to a boil over high heat; reduce the heat and simmer the carrots gently about 12 minutes, until just tender. Drain in a colander; set aside to cool slightly.

In a large saucepan, place the sugar, dry mustard, salt, and pepper; stir to combine. Add the tomato soup, Worcestershire sauce, and vegetable oil; using a handheld electric mixer, beat on high speed until blended; set aside. In a large glass or pottery bowl, place the carrots, onions, and green peppers; toss lightly until evenly distributed; set aside.

Over medium heat, bring the tomato soup mixture to a simmer; pour evenly over the vegetables. Cool slightly; cover and refrigerate. Let stand 24 hours before serving.

MAKES ABOUT 2 QUARTS

COLORFUL MARINATED VEGETABLES WITH SWEET BASIL DRESSING

2 cups fresh broccoli flowerets
2 cups fresh cauliflower flowerets
1/4 pound (about 1 3/4 cups) fresh snow peas
1 cup carrots pared and sliced diagonally 1/8 inch thick
1 cup small cherry tomatoes
3/4 cup yellow bell peppers cut julienne (page 23) 1/4 inch wide by 1 1/2 inches long
3/4 cup Sweet Basil Dressing (page 150)

Steam the broccoli flowerets (page 302) for 2 minutes. Immediately remove the steamer basket containing the broccoli from the pan. Leave the broccoli in the steamer basket and rinse under cold running water to stop the cooking. Drain well. Place the broccoli in a zipper-seal plastic bag; refrigerate until completely cold. Steam and store the cauliflower flowerets, following the same procedure as for broccoli flowerets.

Remove the strings and ends from the snow peas (page 327). Steam the snow peas 1 minute and follow the same procedure as for preparing the broccoli flowerets. Steam and prepare the vegetables separately to preserve their individual colors and flavors.

In a large mixing bowl, place the broccoli, cauliflower, snow peas, carrots, cherry tomatoes, yellow peppers, and Sweet Basil Dressing; using a wooden mixing spoon, toss until combined. Cover and let stand in the refrigerator at least 1 hour. Toss again and serve.

SERVES 6

FIELD OF DREAMS SALAD

3 large ears yellow corn
1 10-ounce package frozen baby lima beans
3/4 cup pared and cored cucumbers (page 45) cut into 3/8-inch cubes
1/2 cup carrots pared and cut julienne (page 23) 1 inch long
1/2 cup diced celery
1/4 cup diced red bell peppers
1 cup blanched (page 44), stemmed, peeled, seeded, and cored (page 45) tomatoes cut into bite-sized chunks
1 tablespoon snipped, fresh chives
1/2 cup Honey-Mustard Dressing (page 149)
Boston lettuce

Prepare and boil the corn on the cob (page 315); place the hot ears of corn on a clean towel to cool. When cool enough to handle, cut the kernels off the cobs. Measure 1 1/2 cups corn; cover and refrigerate. Reserve the remaining corn for other uses. Cook the lima beans. Measure 1/2 cup drained beans; cover and refrigerate. Reserve the remaining lima beans for other uses. Wait until the corn and lima beans are cold to compose the salad.

Then, in a mixing bowl, place 1 1/2 cups corn, 1/2 cup lima beans, cucumbers, carrots, celery, and peppers; toss to combine. Add the tomatoes, chives, and Honey-Mustard Dressing; toss lightly until evenly distributed. Spoon the salad over leaves of Boston lettuce on individual salad plates.

SERVES 6

ALTERNATIVE SERVING SUGGESTION: Serve the salad in an attractive bowl lined with green leaf lettuce. On top and in the center of the salad, artistically arrange 3 ears of miniature corn on the cob (steamed and cooled if frozen, or without further cooking if commercially canned) with husks fashioned from softened green tops of leeks (page 401).

GARDEN SALAD

1/3 pound fresh snow peas
2 carrots, pared and sliced 3/8 inch thick
1 1/4 pounds tomatoes (3 medium-large tomatoes), blanched (page 44), stemmed, peeled, seeded and cored (page 45), and cut into bite-sized chunks
1 1/2 cups cucumber slices cut 3/16 inch thick
1/2 cup Basil Vinaigrette Dressing (page 153)
Leaf lettuce

Steam the snow peas 1 minute (page 327). Immediately remove the steamer basket containing the peas from the pan. Leave the peas in the steamer basket and rinse under cold running water to stop the cooking. Drain well. Place the snow peas in a zipper-seal plastic bag; refrigerate until completely cold.

Place the carrots in a small saucepan; add water to cover. Cover and bring to a boil over high heat; reduce the heat and simmer 3 minutes. Immediately place the carrots in a colander and rinse under cold running water to stop the cooking. Drain well. Place the carrots in a zipper-seal plastic bag; refrigerate until completely cold.

In a large mixing bowl, place the snow peas, carrots, tomatoes, cucumbers, and Basil Vinaigrette Dressing; toss gently to combine. Line individual salad plates with leaf lettuce; spoon the salad atop the lettuce. Or, serve family style in a lettuce-lined serving bowl.

SERVES 6

OPTIONAL DECORATIVE PRESENTATION: For a more decorative salad, use a fluted garnishing cutter (see illustration) to slice the carrots, and groove the cucumbers (page 399) before slicing them.

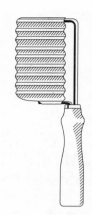

Fluted Garnishing Cutter

VEGETABLE COLLAGE WITH CHEVRE

1 1/2 cups tomatoes blanched (page 44), stemmed, peeled, quartered, seeded and cored (page 45), and cut into uniform, bite-sized pieces
1 cup fresh green beans snapped in half or into thirds, cooked (page 305), and cooled
2/3 cup coarsely chopped yellow bell peppers
3/4 cup celery sliced 1/4 inch thick
1/2 cup chèvre cheese* cut into small, bite-sized pieces
2 teaspoons fresh, snipped basil
White Wine Vinaigrette Dressing (page 153)
Boston lettuce

A soft goat's milk cheese.

In a medium bowl, place the tomatoes, green beans, peppers, celery, cheese, basil, and White Wine Vinaigrette Dressing; toss to evenly combine. Serve on individual salad plates atop Boston lettuce leaves or in a serving bowl lined with lettuce leaves.

SERVES 4

RHAPSODY SALAD
For Buffets

16 fresh asparagus spears, cut 5½ inches long
24 whole, fresh green beans
2 cups fresh broccoli flowerets
3 very large carrots, pared and sliced ¼ inch thick*
8 Roma tomatoes**
1 cup sliced celery
¼ cup uniformly chopped green bell peppers
1 tablespoon packed, snipped, fresh basil
8 ounces medium-sized, fresh mushrooms, sliced
1½ recipes (1½ cups) Basic Vinaigrette Dressing (page 152)
1 8-ounce package frozen miniature corn on the cob, thawed***
12 green onions (scallions), cut 6 inches long

For more flair, use a fluted garnishing cutter (see illustration, page 128) to slice the carrots.

**Also known as plum tomatoes and Italian tomatoes.*

***If frozen miniature corn on the cob is not available, about 1½ cups drained commercially canned miniature corn on the cob (not pickled) may be substituted.*

EARLY IN THE DAY: Boil the asparagus spears (page 303) 1 to 2 minutes. Remove from the heat, drain, and immediately cover with cold water to stop the cooking. Drain well. Carefully place the asparagus spears in a zipper-seal plastic bag and refrigerate. Place the green beans in a medium saucepan; add water to cover. Cover and bring to a boil over high heat. Reduce the heat to medium and simmer the beans about 3 minutes until very slightly tender. Remove from the heat and follow the same procedure as for the asparagus.

Steam the broccoli flowerets (page 302) for 2 minutes. Immediately remove the steamer basket containing the broccoli from the pan. Leave the broccoli in the steamer basket and rinse under cold running water to stop the cooking. Drain well. Place in a deep dish (to avoid crushing the flowerets); cover and refrigerate. Place the carrots in a small saucepan; add water to cover. Cover and bring to a boil over high heat. Reduce the heat to medium and cook the carrots about 2 minutes until very slightly tender. Then, follow the same procedure as for the asparagus.

LATER IN THE DAY: Slice the unpeeled tomatoes widthwise ¼ inch thick. Cut each slice in half; cut out the seeds and pulp. In a large bowl, place the tomatoes, carrots, celery, green peppers, and basil; do not stir. Refrigerate.

AT SERVING TIME: Slice the mushrooms and add to the bowl containing the tomatoes and other vegetables; set aside. Pour ½ cup Basic Vinaigrette Dressing into a flat-bottomed, deep dish, such as an 8 × 8-inch baking dish; place the asparagus in the dish and roll to cover with dressing. Arrange the asparagus in an upright bunch on the back side of a 3- to 4-inch-deep serving dish. Follow the same marinating procedure with the green beans, broccoli, and miniature corn on the cob, arranging each vegetable group attractively around the back sides of the dish.

Pour the dressing used for marinating and the remaining salad dressing over the vegetables in the bowl containing the tomatoes and other vegetables; toss carefully to combine. Turn the tomato mixture into the front of the serving dish to fill the dish. Arrange the green onions (unmarinated) among the vegetables at the back of the serving dish. Set serving tongs and a serving spoon next to the salad dish.

SERVES 10

CARROT, RAISIN, AND PINEAPPLE SALAD

1 pound carrots, pared and shredded (about 3 cups)
½ cup raisins, plumped (page 46) and drained
½ cup golden raisins, plumped (page 46) and drained
1 8-ounce can commercial pineapple tidbits in pineapple juice, drained
¾ cup Cooked Salad Dressing made with ¼ cup plus 1 tablespoon sugar (page 151)
Red-tip leaf lettuce
8 sprigs of fresh parsley for garnish

In a medium mixing bowl, place the carrots, raisins, golden raisins, pineapple, and Cooked Salad Dressing; stir to combine and evenly distribute the ingredients. Spoon onto 8 individual salad plates lined with lettuce. Garnish each plate with a sprig of parsley.

SERVES 8

PEA SALAD

This is one of the easiest to make and best-tasting Midwest salads. Keep a can of peas in the refrigerator for making it on the spur of the moment when you have cheese (it can be any cheddar) and celery on hand.

1 15¼-ounce can commercial peas, drained
1 cup shredded Colby cheese
½ cup coarsely chopped celery
1 recipe Special Mayonnaise Dressing (page 154)
¼ teaspoon salt
⅛ teaspoon pepper

In a medium mixing bowl, place the peas, cheese, and celery; set aside. In a small mixing bowl, place the Special Mayonnaise Dressing,

salt, and pepper; stir together. Pour the dressing mixture over the pea mixture; stir to combine.

SERVES 6

MARINATED CUCUMBERS AND ONIONS

4 cups (1½ pounds) seedless cucumbers sliced ⅛ inch thick* (paring is optional)
2 cups (¾ pound) medium-sized white onions sliced ⅛ inch thick, separated into rings
½ cup sugar
1 teaspoon salt
½ teaspoon white pepper
1 cup white vinegar
½ cup extra-virgin olive oil or vegetable oil
1 cup water

If seedless cucumbers are not available, substitute 1½ pounds cucumbers with seeds, pared (optional), cored (page 45), and sliced ⅛ inch thick.

In a large bowl, place the sliced cucumbers and onions; set aside. In a medium mixing bowl, place the sugar, salt, white pepper, vinegar, oil, and water; using an electric mixer, beat on high speed until blended. Pour over the cucumbers and onions; stir to combine and evenly distribute the vegetables. Refrigerate; let stand 24 hours before serving.

To serve, stir the ingredients; then, remove the cucumbers and onions from the marinade with a slotted spoon. Keep leftover cucumbers and onions refrigerated in the marinade. The marinade may be reused to make this dish a second time.

SERVES 4 TO 6

VARIATION: Tomatoes may be added to this recipe. Blanch (page 44), stem, peel, quarter, and seed and core (page 45) the tomatoes.

CUCUMBER SALAD

1½ pounds seedless cucumbers (about
    1½ large cucumbers), pared (page 45)
    and sliced ⅛ inch thick (about 4 cups
    sliced cucumbers)*
¼ cup commercial sour cream
2 tablespoons white vinegar
¼ teaspoon salt
⅛ teaspoon white pepper
1 tablespoon snipped, fresh chives
1 tablespoon snipped, fresh dillweed**

*Or 1½ pounds cucumbers with seeds (about
2 large cucumbers), pared and cored (page 45)
and sliced ⅛ inch thick.*

**If fresh dillweed is not available, substitute
1 teaspoon dried dillweed.*

Place the cucumbers in a medium mixing bowl;
set aside. In a separate medium mixing bowl,
place the sour cream, vinegar, salt, white pepper,
chives, and dillweed; stir well to combine. Pour
over the cucumbers; toss lightly to coat. Turn the
salad into a serving bowl.

SERVES 8

SERVING SUGGESTIONS
- Decorate the salad with a Cucumber Rose
  (page 399) and sprigs of fresh dillweed.

- Serve the salad in small, individual sauce
  dishes and decorate each serving with a sprig
  of fresh dillweed.

VARIATION: Substitute 1 tablespoon snipped, fresh
fennel weed for 1 tablespoon snipped, fresh dillweed. Decorate the salad with sprigs of fresh
fennel weed.

FRESH ASPARAGUS SALAD

Boston lettuce
12 or 16 (depending upon size) fresh
    asparagus spears, boiled (page 303) and
    chilled
2 extra-large eggs, hard-cooked (page 264)
    and sliced
1 tablespoon chopped pimientos
½ cup Honey-Mustard Dressing (page 149)

Line 4 individual salad plates with Boston lettuce leaves. Place additional torn pieces of lettuce evenly over the lettuce lining to form a
platform. Place 3 or 4 asparagus spears, side by
side, diagonally across each plate. Overlap ¼ of
the egg slices in a row on top of the asparagus
spears on each plate. Sprinkle the pimientos over
the egg slices and center portions of the asparagus spears. Spoon the Honey-Mustard Dressing
over all.

SERVES 4

ZUCCHINI AND GREEN BEAN
SALAD

2 cups yellow zucchini sliced ⅛ inch thick,
    then cut in half
2 cups fresh green beans cut into 1½-inch
    lengths, cooked (page 305) and cooled
¾ cup coarsely chopped radishes
⅔ cup Tarragon Vinaigrette Dressing
    (page 153)
6 medium-sized leaves of Boston lettuce

In a large mixing bowl, place the yellow zucchini, green beans, radishes, and Tarragon Vinaigrette Dressing; toss until evenly distributed.
Line 6 individual salad plates with the lettuce
leaves; spoon the salad over the lettuce.

SERVES 6

FANTASIA

¾ pound Roma tomatoes* (about
  4 tomatoes)
1 large cucumber
1 cup chopped celery hearts and leaves
  (page 21)
⅓ cup Basil Vinaigrette Dressing (page 153)

*Also known as plum tomatoes and Italian
tomatoes.*

Blanch the tomatoes (page 44); immediately
immerse in cold water. Stem, peel, quarter, and
seed and core (page 45) the tomatoes; cut each
quarter in half widthwise. Makes about 2 cups.
Place the tomatoes in a mixing bowl; set aside.
    Pare and core the cucumber (page 45); cut
into bite-sized chunks. Measure 2 cups cucumber chunks; add to the tomatoes in the bowl.
(Reserve any remaining cucumber chunks for
other uses.) Add the celery hearts and leaves, and
Basil Vinaigrette Dressing; toss to combine.
Serve cold on 6 small, chilled salad plates.

SERVES 6

NASTURTIUM SALAD

*Nasturtium blossoms and leaves are both beautiful
and edible. Plant them in your garden to use in marvelous, tony luncheon and dinner salads (see Edible
Flowers, page 381).*

3 cups Bibb lettuce torn into bite-sized
  pieces
3 cups leaf lettuce torn into bite-sized
  pieces
½ cup White Wine Vinaigrette Dressing
  (page 153)
12 or 20 (optional) freshly picked
  nasturtium blossoms plus leaves

In a large mixing bowl, place the Bibb lettuce
and leaf lettuce. Add the White Wine Vinaigrette

Dressing; toss. Place on 4 individual salad plates.
Arrange 3 or 5 freshly picked nasturtium blos-
soms plus leaves decoratively over each salad.
Serve immediately.

SERVES 4

KIDNEY BEAN SALAD

1 15½-ounce can commercial dark red
  kidney beans, drained and rinsed
2 extra-large eggs, hard-cooked (page 264)
  and coarsely chopped
1 cup chopped celery
½ cup chopped sweet gherkin pickles
⅛ teaspoon pepper
1 recipe Special Mayonnaise Dressing
  (page 154)
1 extra-large egg, hard-cooked (page 264)
  and sliced, for garnish

In a medium mixing bowl, place the kidney
beans, 2 chopped eggs, celery, pickles, pepper,
and Special Mayonnaise Dressing; toss until
evenly distributed. Place the salad in a serving
bowl; garnish with the sliced egg.

SERVES 5

THREE-BEAN SALAD

⅓ cup sugar
⅔ cup white vinegar
⅓ cup vegetable oil
1 teaspoon salt
½ teaspoon freshly ground pepper
2 cups fresh green beans cut or snapped
  into 1½-inch lengths, cooked (page 305)
  and cooled, or 1 16-ounce can
  commercial cut green beans, drained
2 cups fresh wax beans cut or snapped into
  1½-inch lengths, cooked (page 305) and
  cooled, or 1 16-ounce can commercial
  cut wax beans, drained

1 15½-ounce can commercial dark red
kidney beans, drained and rinsed
½ cup coarsely chopped green bell peppers

In a small mixing bowl, place the sugar, vinegar, vegetable oil, salt, and pepper; using an electric mixer, beat on high speed until blended; set aside. In a medium bowl, place the green beans, wax beans, kidney beans, and green peppers. Add the vinegar marinade; toss lightly. Refrigerate for 24 hours.

To serve, toss again and drain. If serving less than the entire salad, use a slotted spoon to remove the quantity of salad needed from the bowl, leaving the remainder in the marinade for serving at a later time.

SERVES 6 TO 8

COLESLAW

¾ pound cabbage (1 small head)
¾ cup Miracle Whip salad dressing
2 tablespoons half-and-half or whole milk
¼ teaspoon salt
¼ teaspoon pepper
Paprika for decoration

Wash, dry, and core the cabbage (page 109); chop finely in a food processor or by hand using a sharp knife. Measure 3 cups chopped cabbage and place in a medium mixing bowl; set aside. (Reserve any remaining cabbage for another use.) In a small mixing bowl, place the salad dressing, half-and-half, salt, and pepper; stir vigorously until blended. Add the dressing to the cabbage; stir to combine. Turn the salad into a serving bowl; sprinkle with paprika. Refrigerate until ready to serve.

SERVES 4

PINEAPPLE COLESLAW: In a sieve, drain one 8-ounce can commercial pineapple chunks in juice, reserving the juice. Cut the pineapple chunks into quarters; place in a bowl; cover and refrigerate. Cover the reserved juice and set aside.

Follow the Coleslaw recipe, above, substituting 2 tablespoons reserved pineapple juice for 2 tablespoons half-and-half. (Reserve remaining pineapple juice for other uses.) Add the pineapple pieces to the prepared coleslaw and stir to combine before transferring to a serving bowl. Decorate with paprika.

POTATO SALAD

3 pounds red potatoes, boiled (page 328); then peeled, quartered lengthwise, and sliced ¼ inch thick (about 5 cups sliced potatoes)
½ cup chopped onions
1 cup coarsely chopped celery
4 extra-large eggs, hard-cooked (page 264) and chopped
½ cup diced sweet gherkin pickles
2 teaspoons celery seed
1½ cups Miracle Whip salad dressing
1 teaspoon salt
¼ teaspoon white pepper
2 teaspoons sugar
1 tablespoon plus 1 teaspoon prepared mustard
1 extra-large egg, hard-cooked (page 264) and sliced, for garnish
Sprigs of parsley for decoration
Paprika for decoration

In a large mixing bowl, place the potatoes, onions, celery, eggs, and pickles; sprinkle the celery seed over the ingredients; set aside. In a small mixing bowl, place the salad dressing, salt, white pepper, sugar, and mustard; stir to combine. Pour the salad dressing mixture over the potato salad ingredients in the bowl; using a wooden mixing spoon, stir carefully to combine.

Turn the Potato Salad into a serving bowl. Arrange the egg slices and parsley sprigs over the salad around the perimeter of the serving bowl. Sprinkle the center lightly with paprika. Cover and refrigerate until serving time.

SERVES 14

GERTRUD'S GERMAN POTATO SALAD

2½ pounds medium, uniform red potatoes
¼ cup extra-virgin olive oil
2 tablespoons red wine vinegar
1 tablespoon Dijon mustard
1 teaspoon salt
1 teaspoon sugar
½ teaspoon pepper
¾ cup finely chopped onions
½ cup beef broth, homemade (page 87) or commercially canned
2 tablespoons snipped, fresh chives

Boil the potatoes, unpared (page 328), about 20 minutes, until just tender (the potatoes will continue cooking as they cool). Immediately drain the potatoes and immerse them briefly in cold water to help stop the cooking; drain. Let the potatoes stand until cooled to medium hot.

Meanwhile, in a covered, *heat-resistant* container or glass jar (such as a canning jar), place the olive oil, vinegar, mustard, salt, sugar, and pepper; cover and shake vigorously until blended; set aside.

When the potatoes have cooled to medium hot, peel and slice them widthwise 3/16 to ¼ inch thick. Separate the slices and place them in a large mixing bowl. Sprinkle the onions over the potatoes; cover to keep warm; set aside.

Pour the beef broth into a small saucepan; heat to boiling. Add the hot beef broth to the vinegar mixture; cover the container or jar and shake until blended. Pour back and forth over the potatoes and onions. Using a wooden spoon to help prevent breakage of the potato slices, toss, briefly and carefully, until the onions are combined and the potato slices are coated with the vinegar mixture. Turn the potato salad into a warmed serving bowl. Sprinkle the chives over the top of the salad to garnish; serve immediately. The salad should be served lukewarm.

SERVES 8

WILD RICE SALAD

1¼ cups raw wild rice, cooked (page 276)
⅓ cup green bell peppers cut into ¼-inch cubes
⅓ cup yellow bell peppers cut into ¼-inch cubes
⅓ cup red bell peppers cut into ¼-inch cubes
⅓ cup carrots pared and cut into ¼-inch cubes
⅔ cup sliced green onions (scallions) including some of the green tops
¼ cup chopped water chestnuts
2 tablespoons small, fresh parsley leaves (snip the single leaves from the stems)
½ cup extra-virgin olive oil
½ cup orange sherry wine vinegar*
½ teaspoon salt
¼ teaspoon coarsely ground pepper
⅔ cup commercially canned mandarin orange segments drained and cut in half widthwise (less than 1 11-ounce can commercial mandarin orange segments)

If orange sherry wine vinegar is not available, plain sherry wine vinegar or white wine vinegar may be substituted.

Let the cooked wild rice stand in the covered saucepan until cooled to room temperature. Then, place the rice in a large mixing bowl. Add the green peppers, yellow peppers, red peppers, carrots, onions, water chestnuts, and parsley; set aside.

In a pint jar, place the olive oil, vinegar, salt, and pepper; cover and shake vigorously to blend. Pour over the wild rice and vegetables in the mixing bowl. Using a wooden mixing spoon, toss until the vegetables are evenly distributed. Add the orange segments; toss carefully to evenly distribute.

To serve, spoon into a large serving bowl, preferably clear glass. Serve at room temperature.

SERVES 6 TO 8

OPTIONAL DECORATION: Use the remaining whole mandarin orange segments and sprigs of fresh parsley to decorate the top of the salad. Decoratively place the orange segments and parsley sprigs around the edge of the salad bowl. Or, fashion a flower blossom, using the orange segments as petals and parsley leaves as the center of the blossom.

Molded Vegetable Salads

CUCUMBER-DILL RING

1½ large seedless cucumbers*
½ cup cold water
1 tablespoon plus 1 teaspoon (2 envelopes) unflavored gelatin
1½ cups water
2 tablespoons sugar
¼ teaspoon salt
¼ cup plus 2 tablespoons freshly squeezed, strained lemon juice
16 ounces cream cheese, softened
16 ounces commercial sour cream
1 cup Miracle Whip salad dressing
¼ cup finely grated onions
2 tablespoons finely snipped, fresh dillweed**

Leaf lettuce
Cucumber Roses (page 399) for decoration (optional)
Sprigs of fresh dillweed for decoration

*If seedless cucumbers are not available, substitute cucumbers with seeds (about 2 large cucumbers)

**If fresh dillweed is not available, substitute 2 teaspoons dried dillweed.*

Pare the cucumbers (page 45); slice them widthwise into pieces approximately 1 inch wide. Using a food grinder (page 49), finely grind the cucumber pieces. Place the ground cucumbers in a sieve to drain. With your hand, press the ground cucumbers into the sieve to extract as much liquid as possible. Then, measure 1½ cups well-drained cucumbers. (Reserve any remaining drained cucumbers for other purposes.)

Pour ½ cup cold water into a small sauce dish; sprinkle the gelatin over the water; let stand 15 minutes. Pour 1½ cups water into a small saucepan. Bring the water to a boil over high heat; remove from the heat. Add the sugar and salt; stir until dissolved. Add the gelatin mixture; stir until completely dissolved. Add the lemon juice; stir to blend; set aside.

In a large mixing bowl, place the cream cheese and sour cream; using an electric mixer, beat on high speed until completely smooth. Add the salad dressing; beat until blended and fluffy. Add the onions; beat to combine. Add the ground cucumbers and 2 tablespoons dillweed; using a large mixing spoon, fold in. Turn into a lightly oiled (page 109) 10½-inch ring mold. Cover and refrigerate overnight.

To serve, unmold (page 109) on a large, round platter. Decorate the platter around the molded salad with leaf lettuce, Cucumber Roses, and sprigs of dillweed. If a fresh dill head is available, place it in the center of the mold.

SERVES 18

FLUFFY EGG CONFETTI SALAD

1 3-ounce package lemon-flavored gelatin
1 cup boiling water
½ teaspoon salt
½ cup cold water
½ cup Miracle Whip salad dressing
1 tablespoon plus 1 teaspoon prepared
  mustard
4 extra-large eggs, hard-cooked (page 264)
  and sliced
⅓ cup chopped green bell peppers
½ cup chopped celery
1 2-ounce jar pimientos, drained and
  chopped (2 tablespoons)
2 tablespoons thinly sliced green onions
  (scallions)
1 cup shredded Colby cheese
Leaf lettuce
2 extra-large eggs, hard-cooked (page 264)
  and sliced, for decoration
Extra chopped pimientos for decoration

Place the gelatin in a large mixing bowl. Add
the boiling water and salt; stir until the gelatin is
completely dissolved. Add the cold water, salad
dressing, and mustard; using an electric mixer,
beat on high speed until completely blended.
Refrigerate until the mixture is set about 1 inch
around the edge of the bowl.

Then, using the electric mixer, beat the gelatin mixture on high speed until light and fluffy.
Add the eggs, green peppers, celery, pimientos,
onions, and cheese. Using a mixing spoon, fold
in until the ingredients are evenly distributed.
Pour into a lightly oiled (page 109) 8-inch ring
mold. Refrigerate until completely set (at least
6 hours).

At serving time, unmold (page 109) on a serving plate lined with leaf lettuce. Decorate the
plate with slices of hard-cooked eggs and pieces
of well-drained pimientos fashioned like flower
blossoms.

SERVES 8

PERFECTION SALAD

½ cup cold water
1 tablespoon plus 1 teaspoon (2 envelopes)
  unflavored gelatin
½ cup sugar
½ teaspoon salt
2 cups boiling water
½ cup cider vinegar
2 tablespoons freshly squeezed, strained
  lemon juice
1 cup finely shredded cabbage
1 cup finely chopped celery
⅓ cup finely chopped green bell peppers
1 4-ounce jar sliced pimientos, drained
  (¼ cup)
Bibb lettuce leaves
Special Mayonnaise Dressing (page 154)

Pour ½ cup cold water into a small sauce dish;
sprinkle the gelatin over the water; let stand 15
minutes.

In a medium mixing bowl, place the sugar,
salt, boiling water, and gelatin mixture; stir until
the sugar is completely dissolved. Add the vinegar and lemon juice; stir to blend. Refrigerate
the mixture until it begins to set and is the consistency of unbeaten egg whites.

Add the cabbage, celery, green peppers, and
pimientos; stir until the vegetables are evenly
distributed. Ladle into 8 lightly oiled (page 109)
individual molds or 1 lightly oiled 1-quart mold.
Refrigerate until set (at least 3 hours for individual molds; at least 5 hours for a 1-quart mold).

To serve, unmold (page 109) individual salads
on plates lined with Bibb lettuce. If made in a 1-
quart mold, unmold (page 109) on a serving
platter and arrange lettuce leaves handsomely
around the salad. Pass Special Mayonnaise Dressing at the table.

SERVES 8

ZIPPY VEGETABLE SALAD MOLD

1 3-ounce package lemon-flavored gelatin
1 cup boiling water
½ cup Miracle Whip salad dressing
⅛ teaspoon salt
3 tablespoons cider vinegar
½ cup cold water
1 cup finely chopped cabbage
½ cup pared and grated carrots
½ cup sliced radishes
½ cup chopped celery
¼ cup diced green bell peppers
1 tablespoon finely grated onions
Leaf lettuce
8 Radish Gyroscopes (page 403) for garnish
   (optional)
8 tiny sprigs of celery leaves for garnish

Place the gelatin in a large mixing bowl. Add the boiling water; stir until the gelatin is completely dissolved. Add the salad dressing, salt, vinegar, and cold water; using an electric mixer, beat lightly until blended. Refrigerate until the mixture is set about 1 inch around the edge of the bowl.

Using an electric mixer, beat the gelatin mixture on high speed until light and fluffy. Add the cabbage, carrots, radishes, celery, green peppers, and onions; using a mixing spoon, fold in until the vegetables are evenly distributed. Ladle into 8 lightly oiled (page 109) individual molds. Refrigerate until set (at least 3 hours).

To serve, unmold (page 109) on individual salad plates lined with leaf lettuce. Garnish the top of each molded salad with a Radish Gyroscope and a tiny sprig of celery leaves.

SERVES 8

Main-Course Salads

SPINACH SALAD

1 pound fresh spinach
½ pound sliced bacon, cut into 1-inch pieces, fried crisply, and drained between paper towels
6 ounces sliced, fresh mushrooms
3 extra-large eggs, hard-cooked (page 264) and chopped
⅔ cup extra-virgin olive oil
¼ cup red wine vinegar
2 tablespoons dry red wine
2 teaspoons soy sauce
1 teaspoon dry mustard
1 teaspoon sugar
¼ teaspoon curry powder
½ teaspoon garlic salt
½ teaspoon freshly ground pepper

Wash the spinach twice, remove stems, and pat dry using a clean tea towel. In a large bowl, place the spinach leaves, bacon, mushrooms, and eggs; set aside. In a pint jar, place the olive oil, vinegar, wine, soy sauce, dry mustard, sugar, curry powder, garlic salt, and pepper; cover and shake vigorously until blended. Pour over the salad; toss until the ingredients are evenly combined.

**SERVES 4 AS A MAIN COURSE OR
8 AS A SALAD COURSE**

AVOCADO AND BANANA SALAD WITH CURRIED DRESSING

2 ripe avocados
2 teaspoons freshly squeezed, strained
  lemon juice
2 ripe bananas
2 tablespoons raisins, plumped (page 46)
  and drained
¼ cup very coarsely broken English
  walnuts
Leaf lettuce
Bibb lettuce
1 recipe Curried Mayonnaise Dressing
  (page 154)

Cut the avocados in half lengthwise and gently twist the halves apart; remove the pits. Peel the avocado halves and cut each half into thirds lengthwise. Using a soft brush, immediately brush all the surfaces of the avocado slices with lemon juice to prevent discoloration; set aside. Peel the bananas; cut in half widthwise. Then, slice each half in two lengthwise; set aside.

Line 4 luncheon plates with leaf lettuce. Using bite-sized pieces of Bibb lettuce, build a low platform over the central part of each plate. Arrange 3 avocado slices and 2 banana pieces in the center of each plate. Sprinkle the raisins and then walnuts over the fruit. Using a spoon, generously drizzle Curried Mayonnaise Dressing diagonally across the fruit, raisins, and nuts, leaving portions of the salad contents uncovered for a more attractive presentation.

SERVES 4

SERVING SUGGESTIONS: Arrange slices of Apricot Bread (page 432) and a small bunch of assorted seedless grapes (on their stems) on each plate. Place a small plate of Butter Roses (page 394) on the table.

CARNIVAL SALAD

¾ pound rotini pasta
1 cup yellow teardrop tomatoes
1 cup commercially canned artichoke
  hearts (not pickled) cut in half
  lengthwise
1 cup cooked and drained frozen miniature
  corn on the cob*
1 cup fresh snow peas, blanched (page 44)
1 cup pared and diagonally sliced carrots
1 cup avocados cut in half, lengthwise,
  pitted,** peeled, and sliced, widthwise
¾ cup yellow zucchini cut julienne
  (page 23)
¾ cup whole, giant pitted olives
½ cup sliced, fresh mushrooms
½ cup chopped green bell peppers
½ cup chopped yellow bell peppers
½ cup fresh asparagus diagonally cut into
  4-inch lengths, blanched (page 44)
Dressing (recipe follows)

*If frozen corn on the cob is not available,
1 cup drained commercially canned miniature
corn on the cob (not pickled) may be substituted. Do not cook commercially canned
miniature corn on the cob.*

**To pit the avocados, gently twist the cut halves
in opposite directions; then peel.*

Cook the rotini 12 minutes, until tender, in boiling water to which 1 tablespoon salt has been added; drain in a colander. Rinse the rotini under cold running water; drain well. Place in a large mixing bowl; refrigerate, uncovered, until chilled.

To the chilled rotini, add the tomatoes, artichoke hearts, corn, snow peas, carrots, avocados, yellow zucchini, olives, mushrooms, green peppers, yellow peppers, asparagus, and Dressing; using a wooden mixing spoon, toss until evenly combined. Serve in a large salad bowl (preferably a clear glass bowl because this salad looks so pretty).

**SERVES 10 AS A MAIN COURSE OR
20 AS A SIDE DISH**

Dressing

¾ cup extra-virgin olive oil
¼ cup white wine vinegar
2 tablespoons balsamic vinegar
1 tablespoon snipped, fresh basil
1 tablespoon snipped, fresh parsley
1 teaspoon dry mustard

In a pint jar, place the olive oil, white wine vinegar, balsamic vinegar, basil, parsley, and dry mustard; cover and shake vigorously until blended.

DECORATION SUGGESTION: For a splashy, colorful presentation, place a large Cucumber Rose (page 399) atop the center of the salad. Cut an inverted V at one end of briefly blanched snow peas to simulate ribbons. Place the cut snow peas around the Cucumber Rose in the fashion of spokes. Cut large flower petals from softened and peeled red and yellow bell peppers (page 402). Then, arrange the petals on top of the snow peas in a spoke-like fashion around the Cucumber Rose, alternating petal colors.

MACARONI SALAD

7 ounces (about 1¾ cups) small, elbow
  macaroni
1½ cups mild cheddar cheese cut into
  ⅜-inch cubes
¾ cup chopped green bell peppers
¾ cup chopped celery
⅓ cup sliced, small, pimiento-stuffed green
  olives (1 2-ounce jar unsliced olives)
¼ cup chopped onions
¾ cup Miracle Whip salad dressing
1 tablespoon prepared mustard
2 teaspoons sugar
½ teaspoon salt
¼ teaspoon white pepper
2 extra-large eggs, hard-cooked (page 264)
  and sliced, for garnish

Pour 2 quarts water into a kettle; cover and bring to a boil over high heat; uncover and add the macaroni. Boil the macaroni 8 to 10 minutes until tender; drain in a colander; rinse in cold water and *drain well.* Turn the macaroni into a large mixing bowl. Add the cheese, green peppers, celery, olives, and onions; set aside. In a small mixing bowl, place the salad dressing, mustard, sugar, salt, and white pepper; stir until blended. Add the salad dressing mixture to the bowl containing the macaroni; fold and stir until the ingredients are evenly combined.

Turn the salad into a large serving bowl. Arrange the egg slices on top of the salad in a circle around the edge of the bowl. Cover with plastic wrap and refrigerate until chilled (about 4 hours). Keeps up to 1 week in the refrigerator.

**SERVES 8 AS A MAIN COURSE OR
12 AS A SIDE DISH**

ALTERNATIVE INGREDIENTS: While the above recipe calls for ingredients considered by many people generally to be used in traditional Macaroni Salad, many other ingredients may be successfully added or substituted and are favored by some cooks and families. Among these other ingredients are:

Cubed, fully cooked ham
Cooked, drained peas
Steamed broccoli flowerets (page 302)
Chopped pimientos
Chopped red bell peppers
Pared, sliced carrots
Sliced radishes
Sliced green onions (scallions), including
  green tops
Diced sweet pickles

SEVEN-LAYER SALAD

This versatile salad works equally well as a main-course or side salad.

1 medium head or ½ extra-large head
    iceberg lettuce, cut into bite-sized pieces
3 cups sliced celery (about 7 stalks)
1 sweet onion (Vidalia or purple Bermuda),
    sliced, then quartered and separated into
    partial rings
2 10-ounce packages frozen peas, cooked
    briefly, drained well, and cooled
12 ounces sharp cheddar cheese, coarsely
    shredded
1 cup freshly grated Parmesan cheese
    (page 46)
1 pound sliced bacon, fried, drained
    between paper towels, and coarsely
    crumbled
1 quart mayonnaise
1 green bell pepper, cored and cut
    lengthwise into ¼-inch-wide strips, for
    garnish
Cucumber slices for garnish*

  *For more pizzazz, groove the cucumber slices
  (page 399).*

In a 6-quart glass bowl with straight sides, place in layers in the order listed: lettuce, celery, onion rings, peas, cheddar cheese, Parmesan cheese, and bacon. If the bowl becomes too full, the ingredients may be gently pressed down as the layers are added. Spoon the mayonnaise over the salad; using a small, narrow spatula, spread as evenly and smoothly as possible.

Arrange the green pepper slices over the mayonnaise in scallop fashion around the edge of the bowl. Place a cucumber slice in the center of each scallop. Cover the salad tightly with plastic wrap and refrigerate at least 6 hours before serving. May be successfully refrigerated up to 1½ days before serving (the lettuce will not wilt or become soggy).

**SERVES 10 AS A MAIN COURSE OR
20 AS A SIDE DISH**

ALTERNATIVE SERVING SUGGESTIONS
- The layers may be arranged in individual glass salad bowls with straight sides.

- For a smaller salad, cut the ingredient amounts in half. Arrange the salad in a smaller (3-quart) glass bowl with straight sides.

CHICKEN SALAD

4 cups cold, cooked, skinless chicken-breast
    meat cut into large, bite-sized pieces
    (cook and prepare about 4 pounds split
    chicken breasts *with* skin, page 204)
1 cup chopped celery
2 cups pared, quartered, and cored apples
    cut into bite-sized cubes
2 teaspoons freshly squeezed, strained
    lemon juice
1 cup mayonnaise
Boston lettuce
Fresh pineapple slices, Strawberry Fans
    (page 404), coarsely broken English
    walnuts, and fresh orange sections
    (page 47) for garnish

In a large mixing bowl, place the chicken and celery; set aside. Place the apple cubes in a medium mixing bowl. Add the lemon juice; toss until the apple cubes are evenly coated to prevent discoloration. Add the apple cubes and mayonnaise to the bowl containing the chicken and celery; toss until the ingredients are evenly combined; set aside.

Line 6 individual luncheon plates with Boston lettuce leaves. Place torn Boston lettuce leaves in the center of each plate to provide a platform for the chicken salad. Spoon the salad over the torn lettuce. Garnish the plates with pineapple slices, Strawberry Fans, English walnuts, and orange sections.

SERVES 6

MESQUITE-GRILLED CHICKEN SALAD

A wonderful recipe from The Diner in Des Moines, Iowa.

1⅓ pounds cold Mesquite-Grilled Chicken Breasts (page 254), cut into ¼-inch strips
2 cups green bell peppers cut julienne ¼ inch wide (page 23) (about 1 large green bell pepper)
1¼ cups chopped celery
⅓ cup chopped green onions (scallions), including some of the green tops
1 2-ounce jar pimientos, drained and chopped (2 tablespoons)
Dressing (recipe follows)
Iceberg lettuce
Romaine lettuce
4 ⅜-inch-wide, uniform slices honeydew melon for garnish
4 ⅜-inch-wide, uniform slices cantaloupe for garnish
Whole strawberries for garnish

In a large mixing bowl, place the chicken, green peppers, celery, onions, pimientos, and Dressing; toss until evenly combined; set aside. Line 4 dinner plates with leaves of iceberg and romaine lettuce. Using torn pieces of mixed iceberg and romaine lettuce, build a low platform over the center portion of each plate. Spoon the chicken salad over the lettuce platforms, dividing the salad evenly among the 4 plates. Garnish each plate with a slice of honeydew melon, a slice of cantaloupe, and strawberries.

SERVES 4

Dressing

1 8-ounce bottle (¾ cup) commercial Catalina salad dressing
½ small garlic clove, pressed
1 tablespoon chili powder
⅛ teaspoon ground cumin

In a pint jar, place the salad dressing, garlic, chili powder, and cumin; cover and shake vigorously until combined.

HOT CHICKEN SALAD

3 cups cooked, skinless chicken-breast meat cut into bite-sized pieces (cook and prepare about 3 pounds split chicken breasts *with* skin, page 204)
1½ cups chopped celery
⅓ cup chopped green bell peppers
¼ cup chopped green onions (scallions)
1 2-ounce jar pimientos, drained and chopped (2 tablespoons)
½ cup sliced almonds
⅔ cup Miracle Whip salad dressing
1 tablespoon freshly squeezed, strained lemon juice
⅛ teaspoon white pepper
¾ cup shredded cheddar cheese
1 cup coarsely crushed potato chips

Butter a 6 × 10-inch (1½ quart) baking dish; set aside.

Place the chicken in a large mixing bowl. Add the celery, green peppers, green onions, pimientos, and almonds; set aside. In a small bowl, place the salad dressing, lemon juice, and white pepper; stir vigorously until blended. Add the salad dressing mixture to the chicken mixture; toss until evenly combined. Turn the mixture into the prepared baking dish; sprinkle the cheese evenly over top. Cover and refrigerate until ready to heat.

Preheat the oven to 350° F.

Remove the baking dish from the refrigerator; uncover. Just before placing it in the oven, distribute the potato chips evenly over the top of the cheese in the baking dish. Bake, uncovered, 25 to 30 minutes, just until heated through and the cheese has melted. Serve with a spatula or spoon.

MAKES 6 GENEROUS SERVINGS

WARM CHICKEN-VEGETABLE SALAD WITH PISTACHIO NUTS AND RASPBERRY VINAIGRETTE DRESSING

5 cups spinach leaves torn into generous, bite-sized pieces
5 cups romaine cut into bite-sized pieces
½ cup pared and finely shredded carrots
½ cup finely chopped celery
⅔ cup red bell peppers diced ¼-inch square
⅔ cup yellow bell peppers diced ¼-inch square
½ pound Plain Grilled Chicken Breasts (page 255),* cut into ¼-inch strips
⅔ cup extra-virgin olive oil
1¼ cups sliced, fresh mushrooms
¼ cup plus 1 tablespoon minced shallots
1 teaspoon sugar
¼ teaspoon salt
¼ teaspoon pepper
⅓ cup red raspberry vinegar
¼ cup pistachio nuts
Whole spinach leaves

If a grill is not available, the chicken breasts may be sautéed in a heavy-bottomed skillet over medium-high heat on the range. Sauté the breasts 3 minutes on each side in half vegetable oil and half butter.

Preheat the oven to 350°F.

In a large mixing bowl, place the spinach, romaine, carrots, celery, red peppers, and yellow peppers; toss to combine; set aside. Wrap the chicken strips in airtight aluminum foil; place in the oven to heat.

Meanwhile, pour the olive oil into a small, heavy-bottomed skillet; place over medium heat. When the oil has heated, add the mushrooms and shallots; sauté 3 minutes, turning often. Remove the skillet from the heat; add the sugar, salt, and pepper; stir to combine. Let the skillet stand to cool slightly; then, add the vinegar. Return the skillet to medium heat; heat the mixture through, but do not bring it to a simmer. Add the pistachio nuts; stir to combine. Remove the skillet from medium heat; keep warm over very low heat.

Line 4 large, individual salad bowls (see Note) with whole spinach leaves; set aside. Add the heated chicken to the vegetable mixture in the bowl. Add the warm vinegar mixture; toss until evenly combined. Distribute the salad evenly among the 4 spinach-lined bowls. Place the salad bowls on serving plates. Serve immediately.

SERVES 4

NOTE: 8 × 2-inch-high clear glass salad bowls are nice to use for this salad.

ARABESQUE TURKEY SALAD

2 cups cold, cooked, white turkey meat cut into ½-inch cubes*
2 cups cold, cooked, dark turkey meat cut into ½-inch cubes*
¾ cup medium-finely chopped celery
¾ cup quartered, seedless red grapes
½ cup broken English walnuts
1 cup Cooked Salad Dressing (page 151)
Coarsely shredded iceberg lettuce
6 cold, thin, large slices turkey breast
Extra Cooked Salad Dressing
Capers for decoration

4 cups white turkey meat or 4 cups dark turkey meat may be substituted for 2 cups white turkey meat and 2 cups dark turkey meat.

In a large mixing bowl, place the white turkey meat cubes, dark turkey meat cubes, celery, grapes, walnuts, and 1 cup Cooked Salad Dressing; toss to combine; set aside.

Arrange a platform of shredded lettuce on 6 dinner plates. Pack ¾ cup of the turkey salad into a cone-shaped funnel; invert the funnel on the lettuce in the center of 1 of the plates; lift the funnel off the turkey salad. Wrap the cone-shaped turkey salad with 1 of the slices of turkey breast. Place a tiny dollop of dressing on top of the cone and decorate with 3 capers. Prepare the remaining 5 plates, repeating the preparation procedure. Extra Cooked Salad Dressing may be served on the side.

SERVES 6

ACCOMPANIMENT SUGGESTIONS: Place a Spiced Peach (page 774), fresh strawberries and blueberries, and a slice of Cranberry Nut Bread (page 434) on each plate. Place a small, crystal dish of Ribbed Butter Balls (page 396) on the table.

TUNA-ALMOND LUNCHEON SALAD

1 3-ounce package lemon-flavored gelatin
½ cup boiling water
1 10½-ounce can condensed chicken with rice soup (undiluted)
2 6-ounce cans solid, white albacore tuna, packed in water
½ cup chopped celery
½ cup chopped, slivered blanched almonds (about 2 ounces almonds)
1 2-ounce jar pimientos, drained and chopped (2 tablespoons)
8 ounces lemon-flavored, lowfat yogurt
½ cup Miracle Whip salad dressing
Bibb lettuce leaves
Additional Miracle Whip salad dressing for decoration
Pale yellow paste food coloring

Place the gelatin in a medium mixing bowl. Add ½ cup boiling water; stir until the gelatin is completely dissolved. Add the soup; stir to combine. Refrigerate until the mixture begins to set and is the consistency of unbeaten egg whites. Drain the tuna and break into small, bite-sized chunks. Add the tuna, celery, almonds, and pimientos to the gelatin mixture; stir until evenly combined. Add the yogurt and salad dressing; fold in. Turn into a 6 × 10-inch baking dish; refrigerate until set.

To serve, cut into 8 servings (page 109). Using a spatula, place the servings on individual plates lined with Bibb lettuce. Place additional salad dressing in a small bowl. Using a toothpick, add a tiny amount of paste food coloring; stir until evenly blended. Using a decorator bag fit with medium open-star tip number 18 (page 383), pipe a decoration on the top of each molded salad serving.

SERVES 8

SHRIMP LUNCHEON SALAD WITH FRESH GREEN BEANS AND SHERRIED DRESSING

Boston lettuce
20 large, raw, unshelled shrimp (about 1 pound), boiled (page 229), shelled with the tails removed and deveined (page 229), and chilled
½ pound fresh green beans, cut into 2-inch lengths, cooked (page 305), chilled, and drained
1 dozen yellow cherry tomatoes, cut in half lengthwise
12 small sprigs of fresh fennel weed for decoration
1 recipe Sherried Dressing with Fennel and Thyme (page 149)

Line four 9-inch plates with large, whole, Boston lettuce leaves. Then, generously mound torn Boston lettuce leaves over the entire center portion of the plates. Artistically arrange 5 shrimp, ¼ of the green beans, and 6 tomato halves over the lettuce on each plate. Decorate each plate with 3 sprigs of fresh fennel weed. Serve the Sherried Dressing with Fennel and Thyme on the side in 4 small, individual sauceboats placed on doily-lined plates, or pass the dressing in a large sauceboat at the table.

SERVES 4

MOLDED SHRIMP AND CUCUMBER RING

1½ pounds medium to small, raw,
    unshelled shrimp
¼ cup cold water
½ teaspoon unflavored gelatin
1 or 2 cucumbers, depending upon size
½ cup cold water
1 tablespoon plus 1 teaspoon (2 envelopes)
    unflavored gelatin
1 extra-large vegetable bouillon cube (or
    enough cubes for 2 cups bouillon)
¾ cup Miracle Whip salad dressing
2 tablespoons plus 1½ teaspoons freshly
    squeezed, strained lemon juice
1 tablespoon well drained, prepared
    horseradish, homemade (page 46) or
    commercially canned
1 cup (½ pint) whipping cream
5 drops green liquid food coloring
3 tablespoons finely sliced green onions
    (scallions) including green tops
Sprigs of watercress and fresh parsley for
    decoration
Additional boiled, shelled, and deveined
    shrimp for garnish
Grooved Cucumber Slices (page 399)* for
    garnish

Plain cucumber slices may be substituted.

Boil the shrimp (page 229); cover and refrigerate. When cold, shell and devein (page 229); cover and refrigerate. Lightly oil (page 109) an 8-inch ring mold; set aside.

Pour ¼ cup cold water into a very small saucepan; sprinkle ½ teaspoon gelatin over the water; let stand 15 minutes. Then, place over medium-low heat and stir until the gelatin is completely dissolved; pour into the prepared ring mold. Place 8 whole shrimp at even intervals on the bottom of the ring mold in the gelatin. The shrimp may not be entirely covered with the gelatin. Refrigerate until completely set (at least 3 hours).

Meanwhile, cut the remaining shrimp into fourths; cover and refrigerate. Pare the cucumber(s) (page 45) and finely shred them down to the seeds and core. (Discard the seeds and core.) Place the shredded cucumbers (and juice) in a small mixing bowl; let stand for at least 1 hour.

Place the shredded cucumbers and accumulated juice in a sieve over a bowl to drain. Press the shredded cucumbers with your hand to extract juice, reserving the strained juice in the bowl. Measure 1 cup shredded, drained cucumbers; cover and refrigerate. Add enough water to the reserved cucumber juice to make 2 cups liquid. Pour into a small saucepan; set aside. Pour ½ cup cold water into a small bowl; sprinkle 1 tablespoon plus 1 teaspoon unflavored gelatin over the water; let stand 15 minutes. Then, bring the cucumber juice mixture to a boil over high heat. Add the bouillon cube and gelatin mixture; remove from the heat and stir until dissolved. Pour the gelatin mixture into a medium mixing bowl. Add the salad dressing, lemon juice, and horseradish; using an electric mixer, beat lightly until blended. Refrigerate until the mixture is set about 1 inch around the edge of the bowl.

Meanwhile, pour the whipping cream into a medium mixing bowl; using the electric mixer with clean blades, beat on high speed until softly whipped; cover and refrigerate. When the gelatin mixture is set about 1 inch around the edge of the bowl, add the food coloring; using the electric mixer, beat on high speed until the mixture is fluffy and the food coloring is evenly blended. Add the shrimp, shredded cucumbers, onions, and whipped cream; using a mixing spoon, fold together until evenly combined and blended. Pour into the ring mold over the set shrimp-gelatin layer; refrigerate until set.

To serve, unmold (page 109 on a serving plate. Arrange sprigs of watercress and parsley around the molded salad. In an eye-appealing fashion, tuck the shrimp and Grooved Cucumber Slices into the greens to garnish.

SERVES 8

CRABMEAT SALAD

3 cups boiled, fresh or frozen Alaskan king
  crabmeat (page 230)* chilled and cut into
  bite-sized chunks
⅔ cup pared and cored cucumbers
  (page 45) diced ¼-inch square
⅔ cups chopped celery
1 tablespoon plus 1 teaspoon freshly
  squeezed, strained lemon juice
¼ teaspoon white pepper
½ cup whipping cream
½ cup mayonnaise
Watercress
Capers for decoration

*If fresh or frozen Alaskan king crabmeat is not
available, canned and drained crabmeat may be
substituted.*

In a medium mixing bowl, place the crabmeat,
cucumbers, celery, lemon juice, and white pepper; toss to combine; set aside.

Place the whipping cream in a small mixing
bowl; using an electric mixer, beat on high speed
until softly whipped. Add the mayonnaise; using
a large spoon, fold in. Add the mayonnaise mixture to the crabmeat mixture; stir lightly until
the crabmeat and vegetables are coated. Arrange
beds of watercress on 4 individual plates. Spoon
the salad over the watercress. Decorate the top of
the salads with a few capers.

SERVES 4

CRAB LOUIS

Boston lettuce leaves
Shredded iceberg lettuce
5 cups boiled, fresh or frozen Alaskan king
  crabmeat (page 230)* chilled and cut into
  bite-sized chunks
1 recipe Louis Dressing (page 151)
5 extra-large eggs, hard-cooked (page 264)
  and sliced (includes 1 sliced egg for
  garnish)
Thin slices of pared (page 45), seedless
  cucumbers for garnish
Ripe olives for garnish

*If fresh or frozen Alaskan king crabmeat is not
available, canned and drained crabmeat may be
substituted.*

Line 4 dinner or luncheon plates with Boston
lettuce leaves. Arrange a bed of shredded iceberg
lettuce in the center of each plate over the
Boston lettuce leaves. Heap the crabmeat over
the beds of shredded lettuce, evenly dividing the
crabmeat among the 4 plates. Spoon the Louis
Dressing liberally over the crabmeat. Artistically
arrange slices of 1 hard-cooked egg on top of
the crabmeat and dressing on each plate. Garnish
the plates with the remaining egg slices, and the
cucumber slices and olives.

SERVES 4

LOBSTER LOUIS: Follow the Crab Louis recipe,
above, substituting boiled, fresh or frozen lobster
meat (page 230) for the crabmeat. If fresh or
frozen lobster meat is not available, canned and
drained lobster meat may be substituted.

SEAFOOD MOSAIC

Whole leaf lettuce leaves
2 cups leaf lettuce torn into bite-sized
    pieces
2 cups Bibb lettuce torn into bite-sized
    pieces
2 cups romaine cut into bite-sized pieces
2 cups tomatoes blanched (page 44),
    stemmed, peeled, quartered, seeded and
    cored (page 45), and cut into bite-sized
    pieces
½ cup chopped celery
1½ recipes Sherried Dressing with Fennel
    and Thyme (page 149), divided
4 extra-large eggs, hard-cooked (page 264),
    chilled, and sliced*
½ pound raw, unshelled shrimp, boiled
    (page 229), shelled and deveined (page
    229), and chilled
1½ cups boiled, fresh or frozen lobster
    meat (page 230) chilled and cut into
    generous, bite-sized chunks
1½ cups boiled, fresh or frozen Alaskan
    king crabmeat (page 230) chilled and cut
    into generous, bite-sized chunks
1½ cups broiled fillet of walleye or sole
    (page 222) chilled and cut into generous,
    bite-sized pieces
1 cup boiled carrots (page 302) chilled
    and sliced
Sprigs of watercress for garnish

*For a fancier appearance, use a fluted egg slicer
(page 770) to slice the eggs.*

Line 4 large, shallow individual salad bowls (glass salad bowls are the nicest) with leaf lettuce leaves; set aside. In a large mixing bowl, place 2 cups torn leaf lettuce, Bibb lettuce, romaine, tomatoes, and celery. Add ½ cup Sherried Dressing with Fennel and Thyme; toss to combine. Spoon equally into the 4 salad bowls. Arrange separately over the top of each salad, 1 sliced egg and ¼ of each of the following: shrimp, lobster meat, crabmeat, fillet pieces, and carrots. Garnish each salad with sprigs of water-cress. Divide the remaining dressing among 4 small, individual sauceboats; place on small, doily-lined plates and serve, on the side, to each diner. Or pass the remaining dressing in a sauce-boat at the table.

SERVES 4

ACCOMPANIMENT SUGGESTION: Serve Toasted Herb Bread (page 428) as an accompaniment.

LOBSTER SALAD

4 cups boiled, fresh or frozen lobster meat
    (page 230)* chilled and cut into bite-
    sized chunks
¼ cup medium-finely chopped celery
½ cup mayonnaise
2 teaspoons freshly squeezed, strained
    lemon juice
Boston lettuce leaves
Tomato wedges for garnish
4 extra-large eggs, hard-cooked (page 264)
    and sliced, for garnish
Thin slices of pared (page 45), seedless
    cucumbers for garnish

*If fresh or frozen lobster meat is not available,
canned and drained lobster meat may be
substituted.*

In a medium mixing bowl, place the lobster meat and celery; set aside. In a small mixing bowl, place the mayonnaise and lemon juice; stir vigorously until blended. Pour the mayonnaise mixture over the lobster meat and celery; stir until evenly combined.

Line 4 dinner plates with Boston lettuce leaves. Place a few torn pieces of lettuce in the center of each plate to make a slightly elevated bed for the lobster salad. Spoon the lobster salad on the lettuce beds, evenly dividing the salad among the 4 plates. Garnish each plate with tomato wedges, 1 sliced hard-cooked egg, and cucumber slices.

SERVES 4

LOBSTER-AVOCADO SALAD

2 ripe avocados
¼ cup freshly squeezed, strained lemon
  juice
Boston lettuce leaves
3 cups boiled, fresh or frozen lobster meat
  (page 230)* chilled and cut into bite-
  sized chunks
8 Deviled Eggs (egg halves) (page 267) for
  garnish
Tomato wedges, julienne strips (page 23) of
  carrots and celery, lemon wedges, and
  sprigs of watercress for garnish
1 recipe Creamy Vinaigrette Dressing
  (page 152)

  *If fresh or frozen lobster meat is not available,
  canned and drained lobster meat may be
  substituted.*

Cut the avocados in half lengthwise and gently
twist the halves apart; remove the pits. Peel the
avocado halves. Using a soft brush, immediately
brush all the surfaces of the avocados with
lemon juice to help prevent discoloration; set
aside.

Line 4 dinner plates with Boston lettuce
leaves. Place an avocado half, pit side up, on each
plate. Pile the lobster meat on top of each avocado half, evenly dividing the lobster meat
among the 4 plates. Garnish each plate with 2
Deviled Eggs (halves), tomato wedges, carrot
and celery strips, lemon wedges, and sprigs of
watercress. Serve a small sauceboat of Creamy
Vinaigrette Dressing on the side to each diner,
or pass a large sauceboat of dressing.

SERVES 4

Salad Dressings

THOUSAND ISLAND DRESSING

*This is one of the all-time best salad dressings. When
it is made from scratch, with plenty of hard-cooked
eggs and other fresh ingredients, it's a winner! Because
such a great quantity of eggs and vegetables is included
in Thousand Island Dressing, it really qualifies as
more than a "dressing" and becomes a major part of
the salad. For this reason, it is often served with lettuce alone—traditionally, over a wedge of iceberg lettuce. Due to the fact that the dressing is heavy and
bulky, a strong, rigid green, such as iceberg lettuce, is
necessary to support the weight of the dressing. If you
wish to use an additional vegetable in the salad, quartered tomatoes may be placed on the salad plate or, if
the salad is served in bowls, on top of the salad near
the edge of the bowls.*

1 cup Miracle Whip salad dressing
½ cup chili sauce, home canned (page 783)
  or commercially canned
1¼ cups medium-finely chopped green bell
  peppers (about 1 medium pepper)
½ cup medium-finely chopped celery
½ cup minced onions
3 extra-large eggs, hard-cooked (page 264)
  and chopped

In a medium mixing bowl, place the salad dressing and chili sauce; stir until combined. Add the
green peppers, celery, onions, and eggs; stir until
evenly distributed. Place in a container or jar;
cover tightly and refrigerate up to 1 week.

MAKES ABOUT 3 CUPS

FRENCH DRESSING

¾ cup vegetable oil
¼ cup cider vinegar
⅔ cup tomato catsup, home canned (page 781) or commercially canned
⅓ cup sugar
1 tablespoon grated onions
1 teaspoon Worcestershire sauce
1 teaspoon prepared mustard
½ teaspoon salt
¼ teaspoon pepper
1 teaspoon paprika

In a pint jar, place the vegetable oil, vinegar, catsup, sugar, onions, Worcestershire sauce, mustard, salt, pepper, and paprika; cover and shake vigorously until blended. Refrigerate up to 3 weeks.

MAKES ABOUT 1¾ CUPS

ITALIAN SALAD DRESSING

1¼ cups extra-virgin olive oil
¼ cup white wine vinegar
2 tablespoons balsamic vinegar
1 large, firm cherry tomato, finely chopped (about 1 tablespoon)
1 tablespoon minced onions
1 tablespoon snipped, fresh parsley
1 garlic clove, sliced in half lengthwise
1½ teaspoons snipped, fresh basil (or ½ teaspoon dried leaf basil)
⅛ teaspoon pepper

In a pint jar, place the olive oil, white wine vinegar, balsamic vinegar, tomato, onions, parsley, garlic, basil, and pepper; cover and shake vigorously to combine. Refrigerate and let stand at least 24 hours to allow flavors to blend. The garlic slices may be removed after 2 days, depending upon desired intensity of garlic flavor. Keep refrigerated up to 1 week.

MAKES ABOUT 1¾ CUPS

LEMON PEPPER DRESSING

Recently, lemon pepper has come into vogue, perhaps on the wave of the chicken-breast trend. Not only is it a splendid seasoning for chicken, but lemon pepper is also a grand addition to dressings used on tossed salads. In this recipe, I softened the tartness, slightly, with a dab of honey.

¾ cup extra-virgin olive oil
¼ cup freshly squeezed, strained lemon juice
2 tablespoons dry white wine
2 tablespoons honey
1 tablespoon lemon pepper
1 teaspoon finely grated onions
¼ teaspoon garlic powder

In a pint jar, place the olive oil, lemon juice, wine, honey, lemon pepper, onions, and garlic powder; cover and shake vigorously until blended. Refrigerate up to 2 weeks.

MAKES ABOUT 1¼ CUPS

BLUE CHEESE DRESSING

4 ounces Maytag blue cheese, crumbled
½ cup commercial sour cream
½ cup mayonnaise
2 teaspoons minced shallots
3 tablespoons half-and-half
1 tablespoon cognac

In a blender or food processor, place the blue cheese, sour cream, mayonnaise, shallots, half-and-half, and cognac; process until smooth. Place in a glass jar; cover and refrigerate up to 1 week.

MAKES ABOUT 1½ CUPS

HONEY-MUSTARD DRESSING

Popular in recent years, this salad dressing pleases a cross section of palates with its tangy, yet slightly sweet flavor. It complements mixed vegetable salads, such as Field of Dreams Salad (page 127), and is a natural with tossed lettuce and vegetable combinations.

⅔ cup extra-virgin olive oil
⅓ cup white wine vinegar
2 tablespoons honey
1 tablespoon prepared mustard

In a pint jar, place the olive oil, vinegar, honey, and mustard; cover and shake vigorously until blended. Refrigerate up to 1 month.

MAKES ABOUT 1 CUP

MUSTARD DRESSING

¾ cup extra-virgin olive oil
¼ cup white wine vinegar
1 tablespoon Dijon mustard

In a pint jar, place the olive oil, vinegar, and mustard; cover and shake vigorously until blended. Refrigerate up to 1 month.

MAKES ABOUT 1 CUP

PARSLEY DRESSING

¾ cup extra-virgin olive oil
3 tablespoons white wine vinegar
2 tablespoons dry white wine
¼ cup fresh parsley leaves (snip single leaves from the stems)
1 tablespoon minced shallots
½ garlic clove, pressed
¼ teaspoon salt
⅛ teaspoon freshly ground pepper

In a pint jar, place the olive oil, vinegar, wine, parsley, shallots, garlic, salt, and pepper; cover and shake vigorously until blended. Refrigerate up to 1 week.

MAKES ABOUT 1 CUP

SHERRIED DRESSING WITH FENNEL AND THYME

The herbs fennel and thyme both complement shellfish, fish, greens, and tomatoes (see Herb Chart, pages 40–43). Accordingly, I created this dressing for the salad Seafood Mosaic (page 146), and also used it on Shrimp Luncheon Salad with Fresh Green Beans and Sherried Dressing (page 143). You may have your own favorite shellfish or fish salads on which you might find this dressing nice to use.

⅓ cup extra-virgin olive oil
⅓ cup orange sherry wine vinegar*
⅓ cup mayonnaise
2 tablespoons cream sherry
1 teaspoon sugar
½ teaspoon coarsely ground pepper
1½ teaspoons snipped, fresh fennel weed
1½ teaspoons snipped, fresh thyme

If orange sherry wine vinegar is not available, plain sherry wine vinegar or white wine vinegar may be substituted.

In a medium mixing bowl, place the olive oil, vinegar, mayonnaise, sherry, sugar, and pepper; using an electric mixer, beat on high speed until blended. Add the fennel weed and thyme; beat briefly on low speed to combine. Pour into a glass jar; cover and refrigerate up to 1 week.

MAKES ABOUT 1 CUP

POPPY SEED DRESSING

One of the most widely used and esteemed dressings for fruit salads, Poppy Seed Dressing is also excellent with lettuce and fruit combination salads.

⅔ cup sugar
1½ teaspoons paprika
1 teaspoon dry mustard
1 teaspoon salt
⅛ teaspoon garlic salt
½ cup red wine vinegar
1½ cups vegetable oil
2 tablespoons poppy seeds
2 teaspoons finely grated onions

In a medium mixing bowl, place the sugar, paprika, dry mustard, salt, and garlic salt; stir to combine. Add the vinegar; stir in. Using an electric mixer, beat the vinegar mixture on medium speed while slowly adding the vegetable oil; beat until well blended. Add the poppy seeds and onions; beat until combined. Pour into a glass jar; cover and refrigerate up to 3 weeks.

MAKES ABOUT 2⅓ CUPS

CHAMPAGNE SALAD DRESSING

The last-minute addition of bubbling champagne and a touch of brandy transforms this dressing into the near exotic. Sweetened with honey, it is appropriately used on fancy fruit salads such as Champagne Fruit Salad on page 110.

1¼ cups mayonnaise
¼ cup honey
1 tablespoon freshly squeezed, strained
    lemon juice
¼ cup champagne
1 teaspoon brandy

In a medium mixing bowl, place the mayonnaise, honey, and lemon juice; using an electric mixer, beat on medium-high speed until blended. Cover and refrigerate. Just before serving, add the champagne and brandy; stir to blend. Keeps up to 3 days in the refrigerator before adding the champagne and brandy.

MAKES ABOUT 1¾ CUPS

SWEET BASIL DRESSING

If you prefer a lightly sweetened dressing for vegetable salads, this one may be just the ticket. It features a generous amount of fresh basil—one of the more versatile herbs because it harmonizes well with so many different vegetables, meats, and other foods. When it comes to salads, basil is often unduly confined to use with tomatoes. A marinated vegetable salad recipe which combines Sweet Basil Dressing with 5 vegetables in addition to tomatoes may be found on page 127. (To assist in planning salads using various herbs, consult the Herb Chart, pages 40–43).

⅓ cup extra-virgin olive oil
⅓ cup vegetable oil
½ cup cider vinegar
3 tablespoons snipped, fresh basil
3 tablespoons sugar
¼ teaspoon white pepper

In a pint jar, place the olive oil, vegetable oil, vinegar, basil, sugar, and white pepper; cover and shake vigorously until blended. Refrigerate up to 1 week.

MAKES ABOUT 1¼ CUPS

COOKED SALAD DRESSING

While this timeless, ever-good salad dressing is traditionally made with whole milk (or cream), this version is made with evaporated milk, which I think you'll like.

3 tablespoons sugar*
2 tablespoons all-purpose flour
¾ teaspoon dry mustard
½ teaspoon salt
2 extra-large eggs
½ cup cider vinegar
2 tablespoons butter
1 5-ounce can (½ cup plus 2 tablespoons) evaporated milk
Dash of cayenne pepper

> *When using this dressing in fruit-intensive salads, the sugar may be increased to ¼ cup plus 1 tablespoon (5 tablespoons).*

In a small bowl, place the sugar, flour, dry mustard, and salt; stir to combine; set aside. Place the eggs in the top of a double boiler; using an electric mixer, beat well on high speed. Add the flour mixture; beat until blended. Add the vinegar; beat to blend. Place the top of the double boiler over (not in) boiling water in the bottom pan. Cook the mixture until very thick (about 2 minutes), beating continuously with a handheld electric mixer on low speed.

Remove the top of the double boiler from the bottom pan and place on a wire rack. Add the butter; stir until melted and blended. Add the evaporated milk and cayenne pepper; stir until completely blended. Then, using the electric mixer, beat very briefly on low speed to assure complete smoothness of the dressing. Pour into a jar; cover and refrigerate up to 2 weeks.

MAKES 1½ CUPS

LOUIS DRESSING

This dressing is most often associated with the dish Crab Louis (page 145), which is generally believed to have been created on the West Coast, probably in San Francisco, around the turn of the twentieth century. For decades, Crab Louis has been faithfully served in elegant hotel dining rooms and restaurants across the country. The dressing is equally fitting and wonderful with lobster in the adapted, traditional dish, Lobster Louis (page 145). Also, I like to serve Louis Dressing as a "new" dip for cold shrimp served as an hors d'oeuvre (page 62).

½ cup whipping cream
1 cup mayonnaise
⅓ cup chili sauce, home canned (page 783) or commercially canned
2 tablespoons finely grated onions
2 teaspoons freshly squeezed, strained lemon juice
2 dashes of Tabasco pepper sauce

Pour the whipping cream into a small mixing bowl; using an electric mixer, beat on high speed until moderately stiff; cover and refrigerate.

In a medium mixing bowl, place the mayonnaise, chili sauce, onions, lemon juice, and pepper sauce; using an electric mixer, beat on high speed just until blended. Add the whipped cream; using a small mixing spoon, fold in. Cover and refrigerate up to 5 hours.

MAKES ABOUT 2⅓ CUPS

VINAIGRETTE DRESSINGS

Most people agree that the most fundamental of all salad dressings is vinaigrette in all its forms and flavors (challenged only by ubiquitous mayonnaise). Vinaigrette has 2 basic ingredients: oil and vinegar. But the variations on this theme are nearly endless. The types of oil, vinegar, seasonings, and other ingredients used in vinaigrettes produce a range of flavors as diverse as the plumage on songbirds. Seven variations are given in the vinaigrette recipes that follow.

In all seven recipes, the oil called for is extra-virgin olive oil. It is the finest grade of olive oil, made from the first pressing of olives and containing no more than 1 percent oleic acid. Extra-virgin olive oils vary in flavor, depending upon the regions from which they come and the varieties of olives used in the making. Try various available extra-virgin olive oils and decide which one(s) you prefer.

Wine vinegars are generally considered the best for use in vinaigrettes. As with wine, wine vinegars differ greatly in taste and color. Herb wine vinegars are widely used in vinaigrettes to infuse herb flavorings.

Selecting the best-quality oils and vinegars is of paramount importance in making good vinaigrettes. Although top-flight oils and vinegars may be deemed expensive, they are usually more economical when purchased in larger quantities, and they keep for a long time when properly stored. (Store olive oil up to 6 months in a cool, dark place; store opened vinegar up to 6 months in the refrigerator or in a cool, dark place.)

Basic Vinaigrette Dressing

This basic vinaigrette is great for any occasion, from family meals at the kitchen table to formal dinner parties. It calls for balsamic vinegar, an exquisite Italian wine vinegar with an incomparable sweet-pungent flavor. Although made from the juice of the white grape Trebbiano, balsamic vinegar is very dark in color because it is aged in wooden barrels.

The basic formula for making vinaigrettes is 3 parts oil to 1 part vinegar, as in this recipe; however, this ratio is dependent upon the pungency of the vinegar used and the flavor desired. When using softer wine vinegars, I sometimes use ⅔ oil to ⅓ vinegar. If you

prefer less stringent vinaigrettes, adjust the oil-vinegar ratio in particular recipes to suit your own taste.

¾ cup extra-virgin olive oil
¼ cup balsamic vinegar
½ teaspoon dry mustard

In a pint jar, place the olive oil, vinegar, and mustard; cover and shake vigorously until blended. Refrigerate up to 1 month.

MAKES 1 CUP

Creamy Vinaigrette Dressing

1 cup Basic Vinaigrette Dressing (recipe, above)
1 cup Miracle Whip salad dressing

In a small mixing bowl, place the Basic Vinaigrette Dressing and the Miracle Whip salad dressing; using a handheld electric mixer, beat on medium speed until blended. Place in a glass jar; cover and refrigerate up to 2 weeks.

MAKES 2 CUPS

Mild Creamy Vinaigrette Dressing

1 cup Basic Vinaigrette Dressing (recipe, above)
1 cup mayonnaise

In a small mixing bowl, place the Basic Vinaigrette Dressing and the mayonnaise; using a handheld electric mixer, beat on medium speed until blended. Place in a glass jar; cover and refrigerate up to 2 weeks.

MAKES 2 CUPS

Mustard-Horseradish Vinaigrette Dressing

¾ cup extra-virgin olive oil
¼ cup balsamic vinegar
1 tablespoon Dijon mustard

1½ teaspoons prepared horseradish, homemade (page 46) or commercially canned

In a pint jar, place the olive oil, vinegar, mustard, and horseradish; cover and shake vigorously until blended. Refrigerate up to 2 weeks.

MAKES ABOUT 1 CUP

Basil Vinaigrette Dressing

¾ cup extra-virgin olive oil
2 tablespoons cider vinegar
3 tablespoons white wine vinegar
1 tablespoon snipped, fresh basil

In a pint jar, place the olive oil, cider vinegar, white wine vinegar, and basil; cover and shake vigorously until blended. Refrigerate up to 1 week.

MAKES ABOUT 1 CUP

Tarragon Vinaigrette Dressing

¾ cup extra-virgin olive oil
¼ cup tarragon white wine vinegar
1 tablespoon freshly squeezed, strained lemon juice
1 tablespoon snipped, fresh tarragon
1 tablespoon minced onions
⅛ teaspoon white pepper

In a pint jar, place the olive oil, vinegar, lemon juice, tarragon, onions, and white pepper; cover and shake vigorously until blended. Refrigerate up to 1 week.

MAKES ABOUT 1 CUP

White Wine Vinaigrette Dressing

⅔ cup extra-virgin olive oil
⅓ cup white wine vinegar
¼ teaspoon dry mustard
¼ teaspoon salt
⅛ teaspoon white pepper

In a pint jar, place the olive oil, vinegar, dry mustard, salt, and white pepper; cover and shake vigorously until blended. Refrigerate up to 1 month.

MAKES 1 CUP

SOUR CREAM SALAD DRESSING

This is a refined dressing for subtly flavored salads, such as Hearts of Palm–Persimmon Salad (page 123).

8 ounces commercial sour cream
3 tablespoons dry white wine
1 tablespoon finely grated onions
⅛ teaspoon salt

In a small mixing bowl, place the sour cream, wine, onions, and salt; stir until well combined. Cover and refrigerate up to 1 week.

MAKES ABOUT 1 CUP

YOGURT-TARRAGON SALAD DRESSING

This dressing goes well with a variety of salad ingredients, including lettuce, cabbage, tomatoes, green beans, asparagus, fish, and shellfish. For other salad vegetables and meats compatible with tarragon, consult the Herb Chart on pages 40–43.

8 ounces plain, lowfat yogurt
2 tablespoons tarragon white wine vinegar
1 tablespoon minced onions (optional)
¼ teaspoon dried leaf tarragon
⅛ teaspoon pepper
Dash of cayenne pepper

In a small mixing bowl, place the yogurt, vinegar, onions (if using), tarragon, pepper, and cayenne pepper; stir to combine. Cover and refrigerate up to 1 week.

MAKES ABOUT 1 CUP

SPECIAL MAYONNAISE DRESSING

A standard in our family since I can remember, this dressing is great for molded salads, Sliced Tomatoes and Lettuce Salad (page 122), Kidney Bean Salad (page 132), and lettuce and fruit combination salads.

½ cup Miracle Whip salad dressing
2 teaspoons sugar
2 teaspoons whole milk

In a small mixing bowl, place the salad dressing, sugar, and milk; stir vigorously until completely blended. Cover and refrigerate up to 3 days.

THIN SPECIAL MAYONNAISE DRESSING: Follow the Special Mayonnaise Dressing recipe, above, adding 1 additional teaspoon whole milk.

THICK SPECIAL MAYONNAISE DRESSING

¾ cup Miracle Whip salad dressing
1½ teaspoons sugar
1 teaspoon half-and-half

Follow the mixing procedure for Special Mayonnaise Dressing, above.

CURRIED MAYONNAISE DRESSING

This curried salad dressing pairs lusciously with both bananas and avocados. All three combine deliciously in the main-course salad, Avocado and Banana Salad with Curried Dressing, on page 138.

1/2 cup Miracle Whip salad dressing
3 teaspoons whole milk
2 teaspoons sugar
1 teaspoon curry powder

In a small mixing bowl, place the salad dressing, milk, sugar, and curry powder; stir vigorously until completely blended. Cover and refrigerate up to 3 days.

TOMATO SOUP SALAD DRESSING

This is an excellent French dressing made with a surprise ingredient—a can of tomato soup.

1 10¾-ounce can condensed tomato soup (undiluted)
1½ cups vegetable oil
¾ cup red wine vinegar
½ cup sugar
½ teaspoon paprika
2 teaspoons finely grated onions
1 garlic clove, pressed
1 teaspoon dry mustard
½ teaspoon salt
2 teaspoons Worcestershire sauce

In a large mixing bowl, place the tomato soup, vegetable oil, vinegar, sugar, paprika, onions, garlic, dry mustard, salt, and Worcestershire sauce; using an electric mixer, beat on medium-high speed until blended. Pour into a quart jar; cover and refrigerate up to 1 week.

MAKES 1 QUART

Meats

Fifty-three percent of all the meat animals produced in the United States in 1996, including 71 percent of the hogs and 45 percent of the cattle and calves, came from the 12 Midwest states. Is it any wonder that meat, par excellence, is synonymous with Midwest cooking?

Midwesterners are definitely spoiled when it comes to meat—they are accustomed to the very best. Overflowing meat market display cases feature thick, juicy steaks; rolled roasts perfectly tied and ready for the oven; mammoth, rosy hams; lean, red, freshly ground beef; thickly sliced, hickory-smoked bacon; and picture-perfect legs of lamb. And Heartland cooks know how to turn these utopian raw materials into showstopping meals.

While a vast amount of veal and lamb is raised in the central states, U.S. Department of Agriculture statistics verify that beef and pork predominate at Heartland tables. Less veal and lamb are consumed in Midwestern households than in households located in most other regions of the country.

Until very recent times, most farmers selected choice, young cattle and hogs from their feedlots and nurtured them with special rations and attention for their own family's ultimate consumption. We did. Our locker at the locker plant in Adel, Iowa, and later, our big deep freeze in the basement, were always brimming with select pork chops, sirloin steaks, cured side meat (bacon), and chuck roasts straight from the farms. Like most Midwesterners, we were brought up eating high-on-the-hog!

In the Midwest, the undisputed superstar of meats is beef steak, distinctly considered by Midlanders to be the most choice entrée. Most any special occasion customarily calls for steak—

from backyard birthday celebrations, where cooked-to-order T-bones are whisked off the grill and placed on the waiting plates of jeans-clad guests, to black-tie affairs where filet mignon takes center stage.

But keep your eyes on the up-and-coming starlet, the 1½-inch thick, tender, Iowa pork chop (center-cut loin pork chop), which sometimes steals the show nowadays, particularly on more informal occasions.

Midwest cooks' meat preparations perpetually draw rave reviews. Their pot roasts with vegetables are sensational, and their ground meat casseroles—both classic and inventive—draw top billing. Roast loin of pork, Swiss steak, and home-seasoned sausage receive family standing ovations, and other long-running hits include baked ham, roast leg of lamb, and breaded veal cutlets. But the Tony goes for their meat loaves, appearing regularly on dining tables everywhere.

Midwest meals are staged with a minimum of sauces served on the best cuts of meat—particularly choice steaks and chops. Few embellishments are warranted when the flavor of the meat itself is so supreme. Of course, less tender meat cuts are often enhanced by the addition of a savory sauce produced from the rich drippings in the braising pan. When sauce is called for, conventionally it is served over the meat, rarely under it. Gravy is most often cast over potatoes, and less commonly over meats.

Today's Leaner Meats

The meat we consume today is vastly leaner and thus more healthful than only fifteen years ago. This advancement is attributable to improved animal genetics, feeding methods, and management practices, as well as the trimming of substantially more fat from meat by both packers and retailers.

The U.S. Department of Agriculture's 1991 data on pork are particularly startling. The eight most commonly consumed cuts of fresh pork had, on average, 31 percent less total fat, 29 percent less saturated fat, 14 percent fewer calories, and 10 percent less cholesterol, after cooking and trimming, than reported in the USDA's 1983 data.

The National Beef Market Basket Survey,

BASED ON 3-OUNCE SERVINGS

	Calories	Total Fat (grams)	Saturated Fatty Acids (grams)	Cholesterol (milligrams)
Beef Eye of Round (roasted)[1]	141	3.99	1.45	59
Pork Tenderloin (roasted)[2]	139	4.09	1.41	67
Skinless Chicken Breast (roasted)	140	3.04	0.86	72
Beef Top Sirloin (broiled)[1]	162	5.78	2.25	76
Pork Boneless Top Loin Chop (broiled)[3]	173	6.60	2.31	68
Skinless Chicken Thigh (roasted)	178	9.25	2.58	81

[1]Separable lean only, trimmed to 0 inch fat.
[2]Separable lean only, trimmed to 0.02 inch fat before cooking.
[3]Separable lean only, trimmed to 0.11 inch fat before cooking.
Sources: USDA Agriculture Handbooks 8-5, 1979; 8-10, 1992; and 8-13, 1990, based on all grades.

conducted in 1987–1988 and supported by the U.S. Department of Agriculture and the beef industry, revealed that since the late 1970s and early 1980s, the overall average thickness of external fat for all retail beef cuts had been reduced from ½ inch to less than ⅛ inch, with 42.5 percent of the cuts having no external fat at all. The survey showed an overall 27.4 percent decrease in trimmable fat from beef steaks and roasts at the retail level over the same period. A follow-up survey in 1990 showed continued reductions.

The table of USDA statistics on page 156 shows that various cuts of beef and pork are now very comparable to skinless chicken with regard to calories, total fat, saturated fat, and cholesterol.

Complete bibliographical references for statistics contained in this section may be found on page 845.

Meat Safety

The Food Safety and Inspection Service of the U.S. Department of Agriculture exerts every effort to assure a safe meat supply for the nation. However, it is virtually impossible to produce completely bacteria-free, sterile, raw meat. Therefore, the proper storage, handling, and cooking of meat by consumers is of utmost importance to avoid foodborne illnesses.

Consumer adherence to the following basic practices will help ensure the consumption of safe meat:

- Generally, cook fresh beef, veal, and lamb to an internal temperature of 160° F. (medium) or 170° F. (well done). Larger cuts may be cooked to as low as 145° F. (150° F. is medium rare) provided they have not been scored or tenderized before cooking, thereby forcing surface bacteria into the center of the meat. When fresh beef, veal, and lamb are consumed rare (140° F.), there is some bacterial risk.

    Always cook ground beef, veal, and lamb to

an internal temperature of at least 160° F. with no pink meat or juices remaining, because bacteria can spread throughout ground meat during processing.

- Cook fresh pork (including fresh ham and ground pork) to an internal temperature of 160° F. (medium) or 170° F. (well done).

    Until recent years, a widespread belief prevailed that pork must be cooked until well done, with no pink remaining, to guard against trichinosis infection. Today, the microscopic parasite *Trichinella spiralis* (trichina) is a clinical rarity in hogs due to improved feeding practices by pork producers. Further, it is a scientific fact that trichina is destroyed when pork is cooked to an internal temperature of 137° F. This is well below 160° F., the current recommended temperature for cooking pork. At 160° F., pork is at its maximum tenderness, juiciness, and flavor, and many cuts are pink at the center. Federal regulations require that ready-to-eat pork products be heat-processed above 137° F. prior to sale. Freezing raw pork at 5° F. or below for 20 days or more also destroys trichina.

    Precooked ham may be reheated to 140° F.

- Use a meat thermometer or instant thermometer (see page 44) to assure internal meat temperatures.

- Refrigerate meat as soon as possible after purchase. This is particularly important in hot weather. Do your grocery shopping just before you plan to return home.

- Store both raw and cooked meat in the refrigerator at 40° F. or below. A temperature of 40° F. or below prevents most bacteria that cause foodborne illnesses from multiplying. Place packages of raw meat on plates before refrigeration to prevent raw meat juices from dripping onto other foods. Raw meat juices often contain bacteria.

- If raw meat will not be cooked within a few days after purchase, freeze it at 0° F. or below. Temperatures of 0° F. or below stop the growth of bacteria.

- Defrost meat in the refrigerator or in the microwave oven (see Food Safety: Microwave Ovens, page 31, for procedural information), not on the kitchen counter or in the sink. When defrosted at room temperature, the outer portions of meat can warm to a temperature which allows bacteria to multiply before the inside of the meat has thawed.

- Do not leave raw or cooked meat unrefrigerated for more than 2 hours (not including cooking time). The danger temperature zone is between 40 and 140° F. At these temperatures, foodborne bacteria can double in number every 20 minutes. Normally, bacteria will not reach dangerous levels in 2 hours, and most healthy people will not be affected.

- Throw away meat packaging material.

- Do not cook meat at an oven temperature lower than 325° F.

- Refrigerate or freeze leftover meat promptly. For rapid cooling, cut large pieces of meat into smaller portions and divide large quantities of food containing meat among several small containers.

- Cooked meat which has been properly refrigerated may safely be eaten unheated. To reheat leftover cooked meat, heat it to at least 165° F. (steaming hot).

- Wash your hands with soap and hot water before and after handling raw or cooked meat. Wash kitchen tools and equipment, cutting boards and other work surfaces, sink, and faucet handles with hot, soapy water after they come in contact with raw or cooked meat, and before they come in contact with other food.

For safety guidelines on the preparation of meat on outdoor grills, see Meat Safety for Outdoor Cooking, page 249.

For further information and answers to specific questions regarding meat safety, call the U.S. Department of Agriculture's Meat and Poultry Hotline at 800-535-4555 (in Washington, D.C., call 202-720-3333), Monday through Friday, 10:00 A.M.–4:00 P.M. Eastern time.

Beef

BEEF AND NOODLES

2 pounds boneless beef chuck, cut into 1-inch cubes
1 medium (about 1½ pounds) beef soup bone
1 carrot, pared and quartered
1 stalk celery with green leaves, cut in half or thirds, depending upon size
1 medium onion, quartered
1 bay leaf
1 teaspoon salt
½ teaspoon freshly ground pepper
About 8 cups water
2 cups homemade beef broth (page 87) or 1 14½-ounce can commercial beef broth
12 ounces medium-wide egg noodles
2 tablespoons all-purpose flour
¼ teaspoon salt
¼ teaspoon freshly ground pepper
½ cup water

EARLY IN THE DAY: In a large, heavy-bottomed kettle, place the beef cubes, soup bone, carrot, celery, onion, bay leaf, 1 teaspoon salt, and ½ teaspoon pepper. Add water to cover (about 8 cups). Cover the kettle. Over high heat, bring to a boil; reduce the heat and simmer until the beef cubes are fork-tender (about 1 hour and 15 minutes).

Remove from the heat. Using a slotted spoon, remove the beef cubes from the kettle and place in a bowl. Remove the soup bone from the kettle. Trim any lean meat from the bone; cut into bite-sized pieces and add to the beef cubes. Discard the bone. Cover the meat and refrigerate. Strain the kettle broth in a sieve; discard the vegetables and bay leaf. Measure the broth and keep

(Recipe continues on page 160)

Beef

· RETAIL CUTS ·
WHERE THEY COME FROM
HOW TO COOK THEM

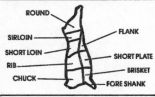

ROUND

SIRLOIN

SHORT LOIN

RIB

CHUCK

FLANK

SHORT PLATE

BRISKET

FORE SHANK

ROUND

Round Steak
Braise, Panfry

Top Round Roast
Roast

Top Round Steak
Broil, Panbroil, Panfry

Boneless Rump Roast
Roast, Braise

Bottom Round Roast
Braise, Roast

Tip Roast, Cap Off
Roast, Braise

Eye Round Roast
Braise, Roast

Tip Steak
Broil, Panbroil, Panfry

SIRLOIN

Sirloin Steak, Flat Bone
Broil, Panbroil, Panfry

Sirloin Steak, Round Bone
Broil, Panbroil, Panfry

Top Sirloin Steak
Broil, Panbroil, Panfry

FORE SHANK & BRISKET

Shank Cross Cut
Braise, Cook in Liquid

Brisket, Whole
Braise, Cook in Liquid

Corned Brisket, Point Half
Braise, Cook in Liquid

Brisket, Flat Half
Braise

CHUCK

Chuck Eye Roast
Braise, Roast

Boneless Top Blade Steak
Braise, Panfry

Arm Pot Roast
Braise

Boneless Shoulder Pot Roast
Braise

Cross Rib Pot Roast
Braise

Mock Tender
Braise

Under Blade Pot Roast
Braise, Roast

Blade Roast
Braise

7-Bone Pot Roast
Braise

Short Ribs
Braise, Cook in Liquid

Flanken-Style Ribs
Braise, Cook in Liquid

THIS CHART APPROVED BY
NATIONAL LIVE STOCK & MEAT BOARD

NATIONAL LIVE STOCK
MB
AND MEAT BOARD

SHORT LOIN

T-Bone Steak
Broil, Panbroil, Panfry

Boneless Top Loin Steak
Broil, Panbroil, Panfry

Tenderloin Roast
Roast, Broil

Porterhouse Steak
Broil, Panbroil, Panfry

Tenderloin Steak
Broil, Panbroil, Panfry

RIB

Rib Roast, Large End
Roast

Rib Roast, Small End
Roast

Rib Steak, Small End
Broil, Panbroil, Panfry

Rib Eye Roast
Roast

Rib Eye Steak
Broil, Panbroil, Panfry

Back Ribs
Braise, Cook in Liquid, Roast

FLANK & SHORT PLATE

Flank Steak
Broil, Braise, Panfry

Flank Steak Rolls
Braise, Broil, Panbroil, Panfry

Skirt Steak
Braise, Broil, Panbroil, Panfry

OTHER CUTS

Ground Beef
Broil, Panfry, Panbroil Roast (Bake)

Cubed Steak
Panfry, Braise

Beef for Stew
Braise, Cook in Liquid

Cubes for Kabobs
Broil, Braise

a note regarding quantity. Pour the measured broth into a large mixing bowl; refrigerate.

When cold, use a tablespoon or spatula to skim the congealed fat off the top of the broth; discard. Cover the skimmed broth and refrigerate.

30 MINUTES BEFORE SERVING: In a large kettle, place the refrigerated kettle broth. Add the beef broth; stir to blend. (The broth should total about 10 cups. If necessary, add additional beef broth.) Cover and bring to a boil over high heat. Add the noodles; boil, uncovered, until nearly tender (about 8 minutes), stirring often to keep the noodles separated. Add the beef cubes; stir to combine. Continue boiling briefly until heated through.

Meanwhile, in a small glass jar or plastic container with a secure lid, place the flour, ¼ teaspoon salt, ¼ teaspoon pepper, and ½ cup water; cover and shake vigorously until completely blended with no lumps remaining. (Use a spoon to break up lumps against the side of the container, if necessary.) Add the flour mixture to the beef and noodles; stir until blended. Simmer briskly until the broth thickens (about 2 minutes). Serve soon, before the noodles begin to stick together.

SERVES 8

SERVING SUGGESTION: Beef and Noodles are often served over Mashed Potatoes (page 332); however, they are also delicious served separately.

SWISS STEAK

If Swiss Steak isn't already in your cooking repertoire, I urge you to consider adding it. It's delectable!

¼ cup all-purpose flour
1 teaspoon salt
½ teaspoon pepper
5 pounds top round steak, butterflied, each half cut 1¾ inches thick
2 to 3 tablespoons vegetable shortening
¾ cup water

2 medium-large onions, sliced ¼ inch thick (about 3½ cups sliced onions)
1 16-ounce can commercial whole, peeled tomatoes or 1 pint home-canned Tomatoes (page 736), undrained
1 garlic clove, pressed
⅓ cup golden raisins
3 tablespoons snipped, fresh parsley
1 teaspoon dried leaf basil
1 large carrot, pared and cut julienne (page 23) ¼ inch wide by 2 inches long
¾ cup celery sliced ¼ inch thick

In a small bowl, place the flour, salt, and pepper; stir to combine; set aside. Place the round steak on a piece of waxed paper. Sprinkle ½ of the flour mixture over the steak. Using your hand, rub the flour mixture over the entire top surface of the steak. Using a metal-pronged meat tenderizer, lightly pound the flour mixture into the meat. Turn the steak over and repeat procedure, using the remaining ½ flour mixture; set aside.

In an electric skillet or a large, heavy skillet on the range, melt 2 tablespoons vegetable shortening over high heat (400° F. in an electric skillet). Tilt the skillet back and forth to completely cover the bottom with the melted shortening. Place the steak in the skillet; brown *very well* on both sides, turning once (about 7 to 8 minutes on each side). If needed, add 1 additional tablespoon shortening to the skillet after turning the meat. Using tongs, transfer the steak to a heavy roaster; set aside. Reduce the skillet heat to low (250° F. in an electric skillet).

Preheat the oven to 350° F.

When the skillet cools to the reduced temperature, add ¾ cup water and deglaze. Pour the skillet liquid *around* (not over) the steak in the roaster. Arrange the onions on top of the steak; set aside. Place the tomatoes (undrained) in a medium mixing bowl. Using a metal mixing spoon, break the tomatoes into large chunks. Add the garlic, raisins, parsley, and basil; stir to combine. Pour the tomato mixture over the onions on the steak. Cover the roaster. Bake for 3 hours. Remove from the oven. Baste; then, distribute the carrots and celery evenly over the steak. Cover; return to the oven and bake for an additional 30 minutes.

When done, place the Swiss Steak on a serving platter; cover lightly with aluminum foil to keep warm. Strain the roaster drippings through a sieve; serve in a sauceboat at the table.

SERVES 12

ACCOMPANIMENT SUGGESTIONS: Serve Swiss Steak with Mashed Potatoes (page 332) or buttered egg noodles (page 283).

TO CUT THE RECIPE IN HALF: Use one 2½ pound top round steak, 1¾ inches thick (not butterflied). Halve the remaining ingredients in the recipe. Bake for a total of 2½ hours, adding the carrots and celery for the last 30 minutes of baking.

BEEF STROGANOFF

2 pounds beef tenderloin, cut ½ inch thick
1 tablespoon vegetable shortening
2 tablespoons butter, divided
½ teaspoon salt, divided
¼ teaspoon pepper, divided
3 tablespoons butter
¼ cup minced shallots
1 pound fresh mushrooms, sliced
1 recipe Medium White Sauce (page 366), substituting ½ cup beef broth (home-made [page 87] or commercially canned) and ½ cup half-and-half for 1 cup whole milk
¼ cup dry sherry
12 cups water
12 ounces wide (not extra-wide) egg noodles
16 ounces commercial sour cream
2 tablespoons butter, melted.

Cut the beef tenderloin widthwise into ½-inch-wide strips. (Each strip will be approximately 2 inches long.) Set aside. In an electric skillet or a heavy skillet on the range, melt the vegetable shortening over medium-high heat (380° F. in an electric skillet). Tilt the skillet back and forth to completely cover the bottom with the melted shortening. Add 1 tablespoon butter; melt and spread to blend with the shortening. Place ½ of the tenderloin strips, single layer, in the skillet; sprinkle with ½ of the salt and pepper. Sauté quickly only until very lightly browned, turning often. Place the browned strips in a bowl; set aside. Add 1 additional tablespoon butter to the skillet; melt and spread to cover the bottom of the skillet. Place the remaining ½ tenderloin strips in skillet; sprinkle with the remaining ½ salt and pepper. Sauté lightly and add to the bowl of browned tenderloin strips; set aside.

Reduce the skillet heat to medium-low (300° F. in an electric skillet). When the skillet cools to the reduced temperature, add 3 table-spoons butter; melt and spread to cover the bottom of the skillet. Add the shallots and mushrooms; sauté 3 minutes or until the mushrooms give up their juices, stirring often. Turn off the skillet heat (or remove the skillet from the heat). Leave the shallots and mushrooms in the skillet; set aside.

Add the sherry to the Medium White Sauce; stir to blend and set aside. Pour 12 cups water into a small kettle; cover and bring to a boil over high heat. Add the noodles; cook, uncovered, in boiling water for about 10 minutes until tender (page 283), stirring often.

Meanwhile, add the white sauce mixture to the skillet containing the shallots and mushrooms; stir to combine. Over low heat (250° F. in an electric skillet), heat the mixture through and completely deglaze the skillet (use a spatula to scrape the bottom of the skillet, if necessary). Do not allow the mixture to boil. Add the sour cream; stir until well blended, but do not allow to boil or simmer. Add the tenderloin strips; stir to combine. Heat the mixture through, but continue not to allow it to boil or simmer; cover and keep warm.

When the noodles are tender, drain in a colander; return the noodles to the kettle and rinse in very hot water. Drain the noodles well in a

(Recipe continues on next page)

colander and return to the kettle. Add 2 tablespoons melted butter and toss until the noodles are evenly coated. Place servings of noodles on individual plates; spoon generous amounts of Beef Stroganoff over the noodles.

SERVES 8

VARIATION: Beef Stroganoff may be served over Boiled Rice (page 272) rather than noodles.

ROAST BEEF TENDERLOIN WITH MUSHROOM SAUCE

1 whole beef tenderloin with the small, narrow end trimmed off* (about 4 to 4½ pounds)
1 recipe Beef Gravy/Sauce with Mushrooms (page 376)

Trimming the narrow end off the tenderloin will make the piece of meat more uniform in thickness to achieve uniform doneness when roasted. Have the butcher remove the tough, silver-colored, membranous tissue over the top of the tenderloin.

Preheat the oven to 425° F.

Place the tenderloin on a wire rack in a shallow roasting pan. Insert a meat thermometer into the center of the thickest part of the meat. Roast, uncovered, adding no water, until the thermometer reaches 140° F. (rare), about 45 to 55 minutes (see Note). Remove the tenderloin from the oven when the thermometer reaches 5° F. below the desired temperature, as the meat will continue cooking.

Place the tenderloin on a cutting board and lay a piece of aluminum foil lightly over the top of the meat to help keep it hot. Do not crimp the foil around the tenderloin, as the intensity of the retained heat may cause the meat to continue cooking beyond the desired doneness. Prepare the Beef Gravy/Sauce with Mushrooms; keep hot in the pan.

Cut the tenderloin into ½-inch slices; place 1 or 2 slices on warm, individual dinner plates or arrange all the slices on a warm serving platter. Pour the hot sauce into a sauceboat and pass at the table.

NOTE: While beef tenderloin is traditionally served rare because many diners consider this tender, deluxe cut of meat to be at the height of succulence at this doneness, it may be served more done, if preferred, for reasons of taste or food safety (see Meat Safety, page 157). To roast beef tenderloin to stages of doneness greater than rare, use the following guide:

Doneness	Thermometer Reading
Medium Rare	150° F.
Medium	160° F
Well Done	170° F

SERVES 8 (⅓ TO ½ POUND PER PERSON)

SIEGFRIED'S FLANK STEAK ROULADE

Siegfried Hoerner, one of those to whom this cookbook is dedicated, brought this great meat dish from his German homeland. Not only is it a standard fare with his family in Stuttgart, but it is popular throughout Germany. When you cut the rolled meat to serve it, the attractive and appealing filling is revealed.

1½ to 2 pounds flank steak, scored (page 26) on one side
1 pound lean, pure ground beef
½ teaspoon dried leaf rosemary
2 tablespoons snipped, fresh parsley
¼ teaspoon ground nutmeg
1 teaspoon salt
½ teaspoon pepper
1 extra-large egg
1 to 2 carrots, pared
1 to 2 stalks celery
3 extra-large eggs, hard-cooked (page 264)
2 tablespoons vegetable shortening

1 cup chopped onions (about 1 medium onion)
1 carrot, pared and sliced
8 whole black peppercorns
½ cup water
½ cup beef broth, homemade (page 87) or commercially canned
½ cup dry red wine
2 pounds medium-small red potatoes, pared (optional)
Salt and pepper to season potatoes
2 tablespoons all-purpose flour
½ teaspoon salt

Place the flank steak, scored side down, on a large board or other large, flat surface. Using a rolling pin, roll the steak to approximately ¼-inch thickness. After rolling, the steak should measure at least 9 × 11 inches; set aside.

In a large mixing bowl, place the ground beef, rosemary, parsley, nutmeg, 1 teaspoon salt, ½ teaspoon pepper, and 1 egg; using a large, metal mixing spoon, break up the ground beef and stir until the ingredients are evenly combined. Spoon the ground beef mixture over the steak; using a small, narrow spatula, spread evenly to within ¼ inch of the edges of the steak. Using your hands, pat the ground beef mixture medium firmly; set aside.

Cut the carrots and celery lengthwise into quarters or halves, depending upon size. At one of the short ends of the steak, place the carrot and celery strips, end to end, in 4 alternating rows across the 9-inch width of the steak (1 row end-to-end carrots, 1 row end-to-end celery; repeat the 2 rows). Arrange the 3 hard-cooked eggs (uncut) in a row, end to end, across the 9-inch width of the steak, on top of, and centered on, the 4 rows of carrot and celery strips.

Starting from the short end of the steak on which the carrots, celery, and eggs are arranged, roll the steak, moderately tightly, jelly-roll fashion. (The eggs, surrounded by carrots and celery, will form the center of the roll.) Using cotton string, tie the roulade securely; set aside.

In an electric skillet or a heavy skillet on the range, melt the vegetable shortening over

medium-high heat (380° F. in an electric skillet). Tilt the skillet back and forth to completely cover the bottom with the melted shortening. Place the roulade in the skillet; brown well on all sides. Transfer the browned roulade to a heavy roaster. Reduce the skillet heat to low (250° F. in an electric skillet). Place the onions, sliced carrots, and peppercorns around the meat in the roaster; set aside.

Preheat the oven to 325° F.

When the skillet cools to the reduced temperature, pour ½ cup water into the skillet and deglaze. Add the beef broth and red wine; stir until blended. Pour the skillet liquid over the meat. Cover the roaster. Bake for 1 hour. Place the potatoes (if included) around the meat; salt and pepper the potatoes very lightly. Cover the roaster. Bake for an additional 1 hour.

When done, transfer the roulade and potatoes to a baking pan; cover with aluminum foil to keep warm. Press the sauce in the roaster through a food mill (see Note). Pour the sauce into a small saucepan. Add the flour and ½ teaspoon salt; stir until completely smooth. Bring the sauce to a boil over medium heat, stirring constantly. Then, reduce the heat to very low, cover the saucepan, and keep the sauce warm over warm heat. Remove the string from the roulade; slice about ⅜ inch thick (thick enough to retain the design of the egg and vegetable center). Arrange the sliced roulade and potatoes on individual dinner plates or a serving plate. Pour the sauce into a sauceboat and pass at the table.

NOTE: If a food mill is not available, the sauce may be strained in a sieve. If desired, after straining the sauce, the peppercorns may be removed and the strained vegetables may be chopped finely and returned to the sauce.

SERVES 8

VARIATION: Follow the recipe with the following exceptions: Spread ¼ cup German-style brown mustard with horseradish flavor, in a medium-thin layer over the steak to within ¼ inch of the edges before adding the ground beef mixture.

(Recipe continues on next page)

After adding the ground beef mixture, place 3 slices of bacon, side by side, across one of the short ends of the steak (3 rows of bacon). Arrange the 4 rows of carrot and celery strips on top of the bacon, adding 2 rows of dill pickles, sliced lengthwise in uniform size with the carrot and celery strips. Arrange the rows in the following order: carrots, dill pickles, celery; repeat the 3 rows. Place a row of hard-cooked eggs on top, as in the above recipe.

CHICKEN-FRIED STEAK

This recipe for Chicken-Fried Steak—a classic Middle America dish—is from The Windrow restaurant located in Creston, Iowa, where both my parents were raised. The restaurant gets its name from a term used in farming. Formerly, all mowed hay was raked into long rows, called "windrows," to dry before it was baled or stored. Nowadays, much hay is put up using systems and new machinery which do not always involve windrowing.

½ cup all-purpose flour
1 tablespoon seasoned salt, homemade
 (page 58) or commercial*
¼ teaspoon garlic powder
¼ teaspoon white pepper
1 extra-large egg
2 tablespoons whole milk
6 top round steaks (about 2 pounds total)
 cut ½ inch thick, then put through a
 tenderizer 4 times by the butcher
1 tablespoon vegetable oil
1 tablespoon butter
1 recipe Milk Gravy (page 375) (optional)

If commercial seasoned salt is used, select one which does not include monosodium glutamate as an ingredient.

Preheat the oven to 275° F.

In a small mixing bowl, place the flour, seasoned salt, garlic powder, and white pepper; stir to combine. Sprinkle the flour mixture over a 1-foot-square piece of waxed paper; set aside. In a small mixing bowl, place the egg and milk; using an electric mixer or a table fork, beat until blended. Pour the egg mixture into a pie pan; set aside. Dredge both sides of the steaks in the flour mixture; shake off the excess. Dip the steaks in the egg mixture; then, redredge in the flour mixture. Place the coated steaks on a clean piece of waxed paper; set aside.

In an electric skillet or a large, heavy skillet on the range, heat the vegetable oil over medium heat (360° F. in an electric skillet). Tilt the skillet back and forth to completely cover the bottom with the oil. Add the butter; melt and spread over the bottom of the skillet. Place the steaks in the skillet; fry 3 to 4 minutes on each side until well browned and cooked through, turning once.

Place the fried steaks, single layer, in a shallow pan; cover loosely with aluminum foil. Place the pan in the warm oven to keep the steaks hot while making Milk Gravy. Serve the gravy over or under the steaks, or pass at the table.

SERVES 6

ACCOMPANIMENT SUGGESTION: Mashed Potatoes (page 332) are traditionally served with Chicken-Fried Steak, in which case the gravy is usually passed at the table.

DRIED BEEF GRAVY

½ cup all-purpose flour
¾ teaspoon salt
½ teaspoon white pepper
¼ cup (4 tablespoons) butter
5 ounces dried beef, cut into 1-inch-square
 pieces
1 quart whole milk

In a small bowl, place the flour, salt, and white pepper; stir to combine; set aside. In a large, heavy skillet, melt the butter over medium heat. Do not allow the butter to brown. Place the dried beef in the skillet; stir until the dried beef is coated with butter. Remove the skillet from the heat.

Sprinkle the flour mixture over the dried beef; stir until the dried beef is coated with the flour mixture and no lumps remain. Add the milk and return the skillet to the heat. Cook the dried beef mixture until the gravy thickens and is just under boiling, stirring constantly. Do not allow the mixture to boil.

SERVES 6

SERVING SUGGESTIONS: Serve over Mashed Potatoes (page 332), toasted and buttered English muffins, or boiled white rice (page 272).

ROUND STEAK BRAISED WITH ONIONS

Top round steak, a less-expensive cut of meat, is transformed into luscious dining when braised slowly with onions. It would be hard to find a more typical Midwest meat and potatoes dish.

1 top round steak, ¾ inch thick (about 1⅓ pounds)
¾ teaspoon salt
¼ teaspoon pepper
¼ cup all-purpose flour
1 tablespoon plus 2 teaspoons vegetable shortening
1 cup hot water
1 pound onions, sliced ¼ inch thick and separated into rings (about 2 large onions)
1 cup hot water
1 pound red potatoes, unpared, sliced ⅜ inch thick (about 3 large potatoes)
⅛ teaspoon pepper
Additional water, if necessary
½ 1-ounce package onion soup mix

Using a sharp knife, slit the fat every 2 inches around the edge of the steak, being careful not to penetrate the flesh, which would cause a loss of meat juices during cooking. Place the steak on a piece of waxed paper; set aside.

In a small sauce dish, place ¾ teaspoon salt and ¼ teaspoon pepper; stir to combine. Sprinkle ½ of the salt and pepper mixture over the steak; then sprinkle ½ of the flour over the steak. Using your hand, spread the flour over the entire top surface of the steak. Turn the steak over and repeat the procedure, using the remaining salt and pepper mixture and flour; set aside.

In an electric skillet or a large, heavy skillet on the range, melt the vegetable shortening over high heat (400° F. in an electric skillet). Tilt the skillet back and forth to completely cover the bottom with the melted shortening. Place the steak in the skillet, letting the excess flour fall onto the waxed paper. Brown the steak well, about 6 minutes on the first side and 5 minutes on the second side.

Reduce the skillet heat to very low (210° F. in an electric skillet). When the skillet cools to the reduced temperature, pour 1 cup hot water around (not over) the steak. Cover the skillet tightly; simmer the steak for ½ hour. Then, place the onions over and around the steak. Pour an additional 1 cup hot water around the steak and onions; cover and simmer for ½ hour.

Place overlapping sliced potatoes around the steak and onions. If necessary, add additional hot water to keep a small amount of water in the skillet. Sprinkle ⅛ teaspoon pepper over the potatoes. Sprinkle the soup mix over the meat, onions, and potatoes. Cover and simmer for an additional ½ hour (see Note).

To serve, place the steak on a serving platter; spoon the onions and natural sauce over the steak. Arrange the potatoes around the steak. If desired, the potatoes may be served with the bottom, browned side up.

NOTE: If necessary, add water periodically during cooking to retain a small amount of water on the bottom of the skillet. To achieve a rich flavor and deep brown color, allow the water in the skillet to reduce to a thick, brown sauce at least once during the cooking process, being careful not to allow the sauce to burn.

SERVES 4

BROILED STEAK

Steaks for broiling: tenderloin (fillet and filet mignon), top loin, porterhouse, T-bone, rib eye, rib, sirloin, and chuck eye. 1½ inches is the preferable thickness for most broiled steaks*
Salt or garlic salt (optional)
Pepper (optional)

Of course, these steaks vary in size naturally, due to their cut. Generally, a full steak should be served to each person, except in the case of sirloin steak—a large steak which is cut into individual servings after broiling. On average, people eat 6 to 8 ounces of steak; however, on occasion some will eat up to a 16-ounce steak.

Preheat the broiler.

To prepare the steaks for broiling, trim away the excess fat. To prevent the steaks from curling during broiling, slit the remaining fat at 2-inch intervals around the edges of the steaks, being careful not to penetrate the flesh, causing loss of meat juices.

Place the steaks on an ungreased broiler rack over the broiler pan. If desired, *just prior to broiling,* the steaks may be lightly seasoned with salt or garlic salt, and pepper.

Broil the steaks 4 inches from the heat. Turn the steaks only once during broiling, using tongs (a fork will pierce the meat and cause loss of juice). Broil the steaks 2 minutes longer on the first side than on the second side. The size, and amount of bone and fat vary considerably among steaks; therefore, prescribed broiling times are only approximate (see following chart). Use an instant thermometer (page 44) to test for doneness. Or test for doneness by slitting the steak near the bone, using a sharp, thin-bladed knife. For steaks with no bone, make a slit in the center of the steak.

Approximate Broiling Times

Doneness	Minutes	
	1st Side	2nd Side
1½-INCH-THICK STEAKS		
Rare*	9	7
Medium Rare	11	9
Medium	12	10
Well Done	14	12
1-INCH-THICK STEAKS		
Rare*	6	3
Medium Rare	7	5
Medium	8	6
Well Done	11	9

* There is some bacterial risk when beef is consumed rare (140° F.) (see Meat Safety, page 157).

ACCOMPANIMENT SUGGESTIONS

• Place a cold Onion Butter star (page 369) or Garlic Butter ball (page 368) atop each hot steak before serving, or pass molded Garlic Butter at the table. Do not season the steaks otherwise.

• Béarnaise Sauce (page 366) is a nice accompaniment for tenderloin steak. No other seasonings should be used on the steak.

BEEF BRISKET

1 5- to 6-pound beef brisket
1 1.1-ounce package beefy onion soup mix
¼ teaspoon pepper
1 12-ounce bottle or can beer
¾ cup home-canned Chili Sauce (page 783) or 1 12-ounce bottle commercial chili sauce
¼ cup cornstarch

Preheat the oven to 325° F.

Place the brisket in a heavy roaster; set aside. In a small mixing bowl, place the soup mix and pepper; stir to combine; set aside. Pour the beer over the brisket in the roaster. Use the entire bottle/can of beer even though the beer may partially cover the meat. Sprinkle the top of the brisket evenly with the onion soup mixture. Pour the chili sauce back and forth evenly over the onion soup mixture. Bake, covered, 5 to 6 hours (1 hour per pound of brisket). Do not baste.

Remove the brisket from the roaster and cover with aluminum foil to keep warm. Strain the roaster drippings in a sieve. Measure 2 cups strained drippings and pour into a small saucepan, reserving the remaining drippings; set aside. Place the cornstarch in a glass jar or plastic container with a secure lid; set aside. Measure ½ cup reserved drippings (add water, if necessary, to make ½ cup liquid); add to the cornstarch in the jar/container. Cover and shake vigorously until blended. Add to the drippings in the saucepan; stir to blend. Cook over medium heat until thickened, stirring constantly; cover and keep warm over very low heat.

Slice the brisket ½ inch thick and place on a serving plate. Serve the sauce in a gravy boat.

SERVES 12

SERVING SUGGESTIONS: Small Yukon Gold potatoes, unpared and steamed (page 302); Mashed Potatoes (page 332); or Mashed Potatoes in a Casserole (page 333) make a good accompaniment for this meat dish.

RIB ROAST (STANDING OR ROLLED)

1 standing or rolled rib roast (allow approximately ½ pound per serving)
Salt (optional)
Pepper (optional)

Preheat the oven to 325° F.

Place the roast, fat side up, on a wire rack in a shallow roasting pan. Salt and pepper the meat, if desired. Insert a meat thermometer to the center of the meat, making certain that the tip of the thermometer is not touching a bone. Do not add water or any other liquid to the meat; do not cover the meat or pan. Roast for approx-

imately the following lengths of time, depending upon the size and shape of the meat and individual ovens:

Approximate Roasting Times

Doneness	Thermometer Reading	Approx. Minutes per Pound
STANDING RIB ROAST		
Rare*	140° F.	18 to 20
Medium Rare	150° F.	20 to 25
Medium	160 °F.	25
Well Done	170 °F.	30
ROLLED RIB ROAST		
Rare*	140° F.	23 to 28
Medium Rare	150° F.	28 to 30
Medium	160 °F.	30 to 35
Well Done	170 °F.	35 to 40

There is some bacterial risk when beef is consumed rare (140° F.) (see Meat Safety, page 157).

Do not baste the meat. When the roast is close to reaching the desired thermometer reading, press the thermometer deeper into the meat. Very often, the thermometer reading will then fall due to a dislocation of the thermometer during roasting. Because the meat will continue roasting after it is removed from the oven, remove the roast from the oven when the thermometer registers 5° F. below the desired temperature. Transfer the roast to a heated platter and cover it loosely with aluminum foil. Let the roast stand about 15 minutes before carving, to achieve easier and neater slicing.

SERVING SUGGESTIONS

• Serve with Beef Gravy (page 376) made from drippings in the roasting pan.

• Serve with natural juices (au jus) and with freshly shredded horseradish (page 46) over individual servings of meat or served as a garnish on each plate.

• Serve Popovers (page 454) as an accompaniment, in which case the roast should be served with natural juices rather than Beef Gravy.

POT ROAST WITH VEGETABLES

A mainstay for Sunday dinner—and the leftovers are a boon when it's time to make Monday and Tuesday nights' dinners.

2 tablespoons vegetable shortening, divided
1 4- to 5-pound boneless beef chuck roast
¼ teaspoon salt, divided
¼ teaspoon pepper, divided
1½ pounds russet potatoes (about 4 to 5 medium potatoes)
6 medium-sized carrots
3 medium-sized yellow onions
Salt and pepper
1 recipe Pot Roast Gravy (page 376)

Preheat a large, deep electric skillet (see Note) to 400°F. (high heat). Add 1 tablespoon shortening. Tilt the skillet back and forth to completely cover the bottom with the melted shortening. Place the roast in the skillet; sprinkle with ⅛ teaspoon salt and ⅛ teaspoon pepper. Brown the roast *well* on the bottom and all short sides. Add the remaining 1 tablespoon shortening. Turn the roast over; sprinkle with the remaining ⅛ teaspoon salt and the ⅛ teaspoon pepper; brown the top (which now becomes the bottom of the roast). Brown the roast until a *very deep brown* on all sides, just short of burning (about 20 minutes total browning time). Deep browning enhances the flavor of the meat and gravy. It is important to brown *all* sides of the roast to seal in the natural juices. Use tongs to turn the meat; piercing the meat with a fork will cause loss of juice from the meat. When browning the short sides of the roast, it may be necessary to hold the meat in position with the tongs.

After the roast has been browned, reduce the skillet heat to 220°F. (very low heat). When the skillet cools to the reduced temperature, pour hot water around (not over) the roast to a depth of about ⅜ inch. Cover the skillet and slowly simmer the roast 45 minutes per pound, adding additional water if necessary.

Meanwhile, pare and cut the potatoes widthwise in half or into thirds, depending upon the size of the potatoes. As the potatoes are prepared, place them in a large bowl of cold water to prevent discoloration; set aside. Pare the carrots (page 45). Cut the carrots in half widthwise; then cut lengthwise in half or into fourths, depending upon the size of the carrots; set aside. Cut off the ends of the onions and peel; set aside.

One hour before the roast is done, arrange the vegetables around the meat. Salt and pepper the vegetables lightly. To achieve especially rich, brown gravy, allow the liquid in the skillet to reduce to a thick, brown sauce before adding the vegetables; watch carefully to prevent the sauce from burning. After adding the vegetables, add the water to restore the liquid to ⅜-inch depth. Then, allow the liquid to reduce again, which will brown the vegetables and enrich their flavor.

When done, place the pot roast and vegetables on a serving platter; cover with aluminum foil to keep warm. Prepare Pot Roast Gravy and serve in a gravy boat at the table.

NOTE: Pot Roast with Vegetables may be prepared in a large, heavy-bottomed, tightly covered, conventional skillet on the range. The skillet must be deep enough and the lid high enough to accommodate the meat with the lid tightly covering the skillet.

SERVES 6

SUGGESTIONS FOR USING LEFTOVER POT ROAST

- Use leftover meat and potatoes to make Hash (page 172).

- Use leftover meat to make delicious Beef Salad Sandwiches (page 351).

SAUERBRATEN WITH POTATO DUMPLINGS

In German, "sauerbraten" means "marinated roast." And marinate it does!—for 3 full days before you cook it. I won a blue ribbon for this dish in the ethnic cooking division at the 1988 Iowa State Fair.

1 4-pound boned rump roast
4 bay leaves
½ teaspoon whole black peppercorns
2 large onions, sliced thinly
2 tablespoons sugar
8 whole cloves
1 small carrot, pared and minced
1 teaspoon salt
1 teaspoon mustard seed
½ cup dry red wine
1 cup water
1½ cups red wine vinegar
2 tablespoons all-purpose flour
1½ teaspoons salt
⅛ teaspoon ground pepper
¼ cup vegetable shortening
1 large onion, sliced thinly
6 whole cloves
½ teaspoon whole black peppercorns
½ teaspoon mustard seeds
⅓ cup rolled gingersnap crumbs
Additional salt (optional)
1 recipe Potato Dumplings (page 334)

Place the roast in a large, round baking dish; set aside. In a medium mixing bowl, place the bay leaves, ½ teaspoon peppercorns, 2 sliced onions, sugar, 8 whole cloves, carrot, 1 teaspoon salt, 1 teaspoon mustard seed, and red wine; stir to combine; set aside. Into a small saucepan, pour the water and vinegar; bring to a boil over high heat. Add to the wine mixture; stir to blend. Pour the wine mixture over the roast and let stand several minutes until cool. Then, cover and refrigerate for 3 days, turning the roast twice each day.

Remove the roast from the marinade and dry with paper towels; set aside. Strain the marinade through a sieve; set aside. In a small sauce dish, place the flour, 1½ teaspoons salt, and ground pepper; stir to combine. Sprinkle the flour mixture over a piece of waxed paper; dredge the roast in the flour mixture. In a deep electric skillet (or a Dutch oven on the range), melt the vegetable shortening over high heat (400° F. in an electric skillet). Tilt the skillet back and forth to completely cover the bottom with the melted shortening. Place the roast in the skillet, letting the excess flour fall onto the waxed paper. Brown the roast well on all sides.

Reduce the skillet heat to very low (220° F. in an electric skillet). When the skillet cools to the reduced temperature, pour ¾ cup of the marinade over the roast. Cover and refrigerate the remaining marinade. Arrange 1 sliced onion over and around the roast. Add 6 whole cloves, ½ teaspoon peppercorns, and ½ teaspoon mustard seed to the marinade around the roast. Cover the skillet and simmer the roast for 3½ to 4 hours, or until the meat is tender, adding a little additional marinade, if necessary.

Place the roast on a warm platter; cover loosely with aluminum foil; let stand. Strain the skillet drippings through a sieve. Pour the strained drippings into a gravy skimmer (page 23; see Note). Let stand 2 minutes. Pour off the drippings and discard the fat; return ⅓ cup drippings to the skillet. Add the gingersnap crumbs; stir to combine. Slowly add 2 cups reserved marinade (add water, if necessary, to measure 2 cups liquid); stir to blend. Bring to a boil over medium-low heat (300° F. in an electric skillet) and cook until thickened, stirring constantly. Add additional salt, if desired.

Slice the roast and arrange on a warm serving platter. Spoon some gingersnap gravy over the meat and pour the remainder into a gravy boat to pass at the table. Arrange Potato Dumplings around the Sauerbraten.

NOTE: If a gravy skimmer is not available, pour the strained drippings into a regular 1-cup glass liquid measuring cup. Let stand about 2 minutes until the fat rises to the top. Using a baster, draw off the fat and discard.

SERVES 8 TO 10

BRAISED SHORT RIBS WITH DILLED POTATOES

Short ribs are cut from the ends of standing rib roasts. Have the butcher cut them to the specifications suggested in the recipe.

3½ pounds short ribs, 2 × 3½ to 4 inches
   (1 to 1¾ inches thick)
⅔ cup vegetable oil
⅓ cup red wine vinegar
1 teaspoon Worcestershire sauce
¼ teaspoon salt
¼ teaspoon pepper
1 tablespoon vegetable shortening
½ cup chopped onions
½ teaspoon whole black peppercorns
¾ cup water
2 pounds whole, small potatoes, pared
Salt
1 recipe Cream Gravy (page 375)
1 teaspoon snipped, fresh dillweed

Place the short ribs, single layer, in an 8 × 8-inch ungreased baking dish; set aside. In a glass jar or plastic container with a secure lid, place the vegetable oil, vinegar, Worcestershire sauce, ¼ teaspoon salt, and ¼ teaspoon pepper. Cover and shake vigorously until blended; pour over the meat. Cover with plastic wrap; refrigerate for 1 hour, turning the meat over after 30 minutes.

In an electric skillet or a large, heavy skillet on the range, melt the vegetable shortening over high heat (400°F. in an electric skillet). Tilt the skillet back and forth to completely cover the bottom with the melted shortening. Lift the short ribs out of the marinade and place them in the skillet. (Do not wipe the marinade off the meat.) Discard the remaining marinade. Brown the meat well on all 4 sides. Reduce the skillet heat to very low (210°F. in an electric skillet).

When the skillet cools to the reduced temperature, scatter the onions and peppercorns around (not over) the meat. Pour ¾ cup water around the meat. Cover the skillet; simmer slowly for 2¼ hours, adding additional water if

necessary. After 1¼ hours cooking time, place the potatoes on the bottom of the skillet around the short ribs. Sprinkle each potato with a dash of salt. Turn the potatoes after 30 minutes cooking time to achieve more even browning.

When done, the meat will be very tender and may fall off the bone of some pieces when removed from the skillet. Place the short ribs in the center of a large serving platter and arrange the potatoes around the meat; cover with aluminum foil to keep warm while making the gravy.

Pour the drippings from the skillet into a bowl; measure 1 tablespoon drippings and pour back into skillet. Increase the skillet heat to medium-low (325°F. in an electric skillet) and make Cream Gravy. Strain the gravy in a sieve. Pour the strained gravy into a gravy boat and serve at the table. Remove the foil from the meat and potatoes platter; sprinkle dillweed over the potatoes. Serve immediately.

SERVES 4

ACCOMPANIMENT SUGGESTIONS: Glazed Carrots (page 313) and Sliced Tomatoes and Lettuce Salad (page 122) complement this dish well.

BROILED GROUND BEEF PATTIES

The simple addition of onions, an egg, catsup, and other seasonings elevate this easy-to-fix ground beef fare from ordinary to praiseworthy family dining.

1 pound lean, pure ground beef
¼ cup finely chopped onions
1 extra-large egg
2 tablespoons tomato catsup, home canned
   (page 781) or commercially canned
¼ teaspoon salt
⅛ teaspoon pepper
Dash of garlic powder

Preheat the broiler.

In a medium mixing bowl, place the ground beef, onions, egg, catsup, salt, pepper, and garlic powder; using a large, metal mixing spoon, break up the ground beef and stir until the ingredients are combined evenly. Form into four 1-inch-thick patties and place on an ungreased broiler rack over the broiler pan.

Broil 6 inches from the heat for the following times, depending upon the desired doneness, turning only once.

Broiling Times

| Doneness | Minutes | |
	1st Side	2nd Side
Medium	8	6
Well Done	12	8

SERVES 4

ACCOMPANIMENT SUGGESTIONS: At the table, pass Zucchini Relish (page 778), Bell Pepper Relish (page 779), or Chili Sauce (page 783).

HAMBURGER STUFF

Oh, so simple, but oh, so good! This kid- and adult-pleaser, an invention of my mom's, and, for lack of a formal name, has always been called "Hamburger Stuff" in our family.

1 pound lean, pure ground beef
1½ pounds coarsely ground potatoes
   (about 3 large potatoes)
¾ cup coarsely ground onions
1 teaspoon salt
½ teaspoon pepper
1½ cups water
1 recipe (¼ cup) Buttered Cracker Crumbs
   (page 49)

Preheat the oven to 350° F. Grease a 2-quart round baking dish; set aside.

Place the ground beef in a large, heavy skillet; lightly brown the meat over medium to medium-low heat. Remove from the heat. Add the potatoes, onions, salt, and pepper; stir to combine. Add 1½ cups water; stir to combine.

Turn the ground beef mixture into the prepared baking dish. Sprinkle the crumbs evenly over the top. Bake, uncovered, for 45 minutes.

SERVES 6

SERVING SUGGESTION: At the table, pass home-canned (page 783) or commercially canned chili sauce.

MOTHER'S MEAT LOAF

1 16-ounce can commercial whole, peeled
   tomatoes or 1 pint home-canned
   Tomatoes (page 736)
1½ pounds lean, pure ground beef
½ teaspoon salt
⅛ teaspoon pepper
¾ cup chopped onions
30 Ritz crackers, rolled finely
2 extra-large eggs
1 recipe Catsup Sauce (page 362)

Preheat the oven to 325° F. Grease a 6 × 10-inch baking dish; set aside.

Drain the tomatoes *well,* reserving the juice for other uses. In a large bowl, place the tomatoes, ground beef, salt, pepper, onions, crackers, and eggs; using a large, metal mixing spoon, combine thoroughly, breaking the tomatoes into small pieces. Form the mixture into an oval loaf and place it in the prepared baking dish. Bake, uncovered, 1 hour.

Meanwhile, make the Catsup Sauce; set aside. After baking 1 hour, remove the meat loaf from the oven and spoon approximately ½ of the hot Catsup Sauce evenly over the top of the loaf. Return the meat loaf to the oven and bake, uncovered, an additional 15 minutes.

To serve, cut the meat loaf into ⅝-inch slices widthwise; then, cut the loaf in half lengthwise, creating 2 pieces of meat loaf per slice. Serve 2 pieces, overlapping, on each plate. Reheat the remaining hot Catsup Sauce, pour into a sauceboat, and pass at the table.

SERVES 8

SURPRISE CENTER MEAT LOAVES

2 pounds lean, pure ground beef
⅔ cup chopped green bell peppers
2 extra-large eggs
½ garlic clove, pressed
½ cup tomato catsup, home canned
   (page 781) or commercially canned
2 tablespoons horseradish mustard
2 teaspoons dried parsley
½ teaspoon dried leaf oregano
1 teaspoon salt
¼ teaspoon pepper
2½ cups fresh, whole-wheat bread crumbs
   crumbled by hand (page 48)
4 ounces sharp cheddar cheese, cut into 21
   cubes

Preheat the oven to 325°F. Grease seven 2¼ × 4¼-inch mini loaf pans; set aside.

In a large mixing bowl, place the ground beef, green peppers, eggs, garlic, catsup, mustard, parsley, oregano, salt, pepper, and bread crumbs; using a large, metal mixing spoon, break up the ground beef and combine the ingredients well. Spoon ½ of the meat mixture proportionally into the prepared loaf pans. Using a teaspoon and a cutting motion, distribute the mixture lightly in the bottom of the pans. Do not pack. Place 3 cheese cubes lengthwise down the center of each loaf. Spoon the remaining ½ meat mixture evenly into the pans. Using the teaspoon, distribute the mixture over the pans, making certain that the cheese cubes are entirely covered. Using the back of the teaspoon, *lightly* press the loaves into the pans and smooth the tops of the loaves. Pressing the mixture too tightly into the pans will result in overly compact loaves. Bake the meat loaves, uncovered, for 50 minutes.

To serve, run a thin, sharp knife around the inside edges of each loaf. Remove the loaves from the pans with a small, narrow spatula. Serve one mini meat loaf per person.

SERVES 7

SERVING SUGGESTIONS: Garnish the plates with sprigs of fresh parsley and pass chili sauce (home canned, page 783, or commercially canned) at the table.

ALTERNATIVE BAKING PROCEDURE: This recipe may be baked in one 5 × 9-inch loaf pan. Follow the assembly procedure in the recipe, arranging the cheese cubes randomly in 3 rows of 7 cubes each down the center portion of the loaf. Random placement of the cubes within each row will help assure the presence of cheese in each slice of baked meat loaf. Bake for 1 hour at 325°F.

SERVES 7 TO 8

HASH

2½ cups cold, coarsely chopped, cooked
   roast beef, pork, or lamb
2½ cups cold, coarsely chopped, cooked
   potatoes (about 2 medium potatoes)
1¼ cups chopped onions (about 1 medium
   onion)
¼ cup all-purpose flour
¾ teaspoon salt
¼ teaspoon pepper
½ cup whole milk
2 tablespoons vegetable oil
Sprigs of fresh parsley for decoration
Tomato catsup, home canned (page 736) or
   commercially canned
Bell Pepper Relish (page 779) (optional)

In a large mixing bowl, place the meat, potatoes, and onions; set aside. In a small bowl, place the flour, salt, and pepper; stir to combine. Add the milk; stir until smooth. Add the flour mixture to the mixing bowl containing the meat, potatoes, and onions; stir to combine; set aside.

In a large, *heavy-bottomed* skillet, heat the vegetable oil over low heat. Add the meat mixture in an even layer and cook, uncovered, over *low* heat, for 20 minutes. Cover and cook an additional 10 minutes. During the entire cooking time, do not turn the hash or stir, but intermittently run a small spatula under the hash to loosen it and help keep it from sticking to the bottom of the skillet.

When nicely brown and cooked, use a large spatula to fold half of the hash over the other half. Lift to a serving the plate; decorate the plate with parsley. At the table, pass the catsup and/or Bell Pepper Relish.

SERVES 6

ALICE'S MEAT AND TATER PIE

Alice Dalbey Bernstein is one of my closest, lifelong friends. In fact, our families' association predates Alice and me—her parents and my mother attended Drake University together. Now living in Baltimore with her husband, Neil, Alice served this yummy dish—a definite reflection of her Midwest heritage—when I was there on a visit. She served it with a crisp, green salad at her always impeccably set dining room table before we headed, with friends, to watch a national tennis tournament. It seemed just the right menu for the occasion. Of course I asked for and received the recipe, which I now pass on with Alice's permission.

1 pound lean, pure ground beef
½ cup whole milk
1 1-ounce package onion soup mix
⅛ teaspoon pepper
⅛ teaspoon ground allspice
Pastry for 1 9-inch, 2-crust pie (Pastry Piecrust, page 460)
1 12-ounce package frozen hash brown potato patties, thawed
½ cup shredded onions
1 cup tomato catsup, home canned (page 781), or commercially canned, warmed

Preheat the oven to 350° F.

In a medium bowl, place the ground beef, milk, soup mix, pepper, and allspice; using a large, metal mixing spoon, break up the ground beef and stir until the ingredients are well combined; set aside. Line a 9-inch pie pan with pastry for the bottom crust. Spoon the meat mixture evenly over the bottom-crust pastry;

lightly pat. With your fingers, separate the potatoes and crumble them evenly over the meat mixture. Spoon the onions over the potatoes. Slit and arrange the top piecrust. Flute the edge. Bake for 1 hour and 10 minutes. Pass warmed catsup at the table.

SERVES 6

VARIATIONS: Substitute chili sauce (home canned, page 783, or commerically canned), unheated, or Bell Pepper Relish (page 779), unheated, for the warmed catsup.

MEAT AND POTATO PATTIES

Here's a simple way to convert leftover roast (of any kind) and mashed potatoes into a new dish. Sometimes this dish is as popular at the dinner table as the original meal served the night before.

3 cups cold, coarsely ground (page 49), cooked roast beef, pork, veal, or lamb
½ medium onion, coarsely ground
1½ cups cold mashed potatoes
1 extra-large egg
¾ teaspoon salt
¼ teaspoon pepper
1 tablespoon vegetable oil
1 tablespoon butter

In a medium mixing bowl, place the meat, onions, potatoes, egg, salt, and pepper; stir to combine. Using a ½ cup measuring cup, measure level ½ cups of the meat mixture; with your hands, form the portions into patties and place on a piece of waxed paper; set aside.

In a heavy-bottomed skillet, heat the vegetable oil over medium heat. Tilt the skillet back and forth to completely cover the bottom with the oil. Add the butter; spread to blend with the oil. Place the patties in the skillet; sauté until the patties are brown and the onions in them are cooked. Turn once. Serve the patties directly on individual dinner plates or place them on a serving platter.

MAKES 7 PATTIES

BEEF AND BISCUIT CASSEROLE

1 pound lean, pure ground beef
½ cup chopped onions
1 8-ounce can commercial tomato sauce
¼ cup tomato catsup, home canned (page 781) or commercially canned
½ teaspoon salt
⅛ teaspoon pepper
½ teaspoon dried leaf basil
4 ounces Colby cheese, sliced
1 recipe Baking Powder Biscuits (page 446) (see Variation, below)

Preheat the oven to 400°F.

In an electric skillet or a heavy skillet on the range, begin browning the ground beef over medium-low heat (325°F. in an electric skillet). Using a large, metal mixing spoon, break up the ground beef as it cooks, and stir often. When the ground beef releases enough fat to cover the bottom of the skillet, add the onions. Continue cooking until the ground beef and onions are nicely browned. Turn off the heat and allow the skillet to cool slightly. Then, add the tomato sauce, catsup, salt, pepper, and basil; stir to combine.

In an ungreased 1½-quart round baking dish, place, alternately, 3 layers of the ground beef mixture and 2 layers of cheese slices (beginning and ending with the meat mixture). Bake, uncovered, for 10 minutes.

Remove the baking dish from the oven. Increase the oven temperature to 450°F. Arrange 8 unbaked Baking Powder Biscuits, nearly touching, around the edge of the baking dish, over the ground beef mixture. Arrange the remaining biscuits, nearly touching, in an ungreased round cake pan. Place the baking dish and pan of extra biscuits in the oven. Bake, uncovered, for 10 to 12 minutes until the biscuits are lightly golden.

SERVES 6

VARIATION: For faster preparation, substitute 1 7.5-ounce tube of refrigerated biscuits for the homemade Baking Powder Biscuits. After adding the biscuits to the baking dish, bake for 8 to 10 minutes. (Check the biscuit-tube label for suggested oven temperature and baking time.)

GROUND SIRLOIN-NOODLE CASSEROLE

1 tablespoon butter
1¼ pounds ground sirloin
¾ cup chopped onions
¾ teaspoon salt
½ teaspoon pepper
1 cup chopped celery
2 tablespoons butter
1 cup sliced, fresh mushrooms
¼ cup dry white wine
1½ recipes Medium White Sauce (page 366)
2 teaspoons instant beef bouillon granules
¼ cup freshly grated Parmesan cheese (page 46)
10 cups water
8 ounces wide egg noodles
1 tablespoon butter, melted
1 recipe (¼ cup) Buttered Cracker Crumbs (page 49)

In an electric skillet or a skillet on the range, melt 1 tablespoon butter over medium heat (350°F. in an electric skillet). Tilt the skillet back and forth to completely cover the bottom with the melted butter. Add the ground sirloin and start to brown it, breaking up the meat with a large, metal mixing spoon, and stirring often. When the meat is slightly brown, add the onions, salt, and pepper. Continue cooking and stirring until the meat is well browned. Turn off the heat under the skillet. Add the celery and stir to combine; cover the skillet and let stand.

In a small, heavy skillet, melt 2 tablespoons butter over medium heat. Place the mushrooms in the skillet; sauté 3 minutes until the mushrooms give up their juices, stirring often. Remove from the heat; let stand until cooled slightly. Add the wine and stir in; cover and set aside.

Make the Medium White Sauce; remove from the heat. Add the bouillon granules; stir until dissolved. Add the Parmesan cheese; stir to blend. Add the mushroom mixture; stir until the liquids are blended; cover and set aside.

Preheat the oven to 350°F. Butter a 2-quart round baking dish; set aside.

Pour 10 cups water into a kettle; cover and bring to a boil over high heat. Add the noodles and boil, uncovered, until tender (about 10 minutes), stirring often. Drain the noodles in a colander. Return the noodles to the cooking kettle; rinse in hot water. Drain the noodles well in the colander.

Place the noodles in a large mixing bowl. Add 1 tablespoon melted butter; toss to coat. Add the ground sirloin mixture and white sauce mixture; stir and fold until evenly combined. Turn the mixture into the prepared baking dish. Sprinkle the crumbs evenly over the top. Bake, uncovered, for 30 minutes.

SERVES 8 GENEROUSLY

STUFFED CABBAGE LEAVES

1 pound lean, pure ground beef
½ cup raw long-grain rice (not instant)
2 extra-large eggs
1 cup minced onions (about 1 medium onion)
2 tablespoons snipped, fresh parsley
¾ teaspoon dried leaf thyme
½ teaspoon salt
¼ teaspoon pepper
1 large head cabbage
1 large onion, sliced
2 28-ounce cans commercial whole, peeled, tomatoes, undrained, or 7 cups (1¾ quarts) home-canned Tomatoes (page 736), undrained
1 15-ounce can commercial tomato sauce
¾ cup freshly squeezed, strained lemon juice (about 2 large lemons)
⅓ cup packed light brown sugar

½ teaspoon salt
¼ teaspoon pepper
⅛ teaspoon ground nutmeg

In a large mixing bowl, place the ground beef, rice, eggs, minced onions, parsley, thyme, ½ teaspoon salt, and ¼ teaspoon pepper; using a large, metal mixing spoon, break up the ground beef and combine the ingredients well. Cover with plastic wrap; set aside.

Wash the cabbage; remove and discard the outer leaves. Using a paring knife, cut out as much of the cabbage core as possible without cutting into the leaves. Fill an 8-quart kettle ¾ full of hot water; cover and bring to a boil over high heat. Remove the cover and dip the cabbage head into the boiling water. After *a few seconds,* remove the cabbage from the kettle with a slotted spoon and place it on several layers of paper towels. With your hands, remove as many whole leaves as will easily separate from the head (usually 2 or 3), being careful not to tear the leaves. Place the separated leaves on several layers of dry paper towels. Redip the cabbage head in boiling water and repeat the process until a total of 17 cabbage leaves has been removed. As the leaves are removed, it will likely be necessary to cut out the remainder of the cabbage core which had previously been too deep in the head for careful removal.

Blanch the leaves (page 44) 3 minutes, in batches. Drain well on several layers of paper towels. Arrange 5 of the smaller, less green leaves over the bottom of a heavy 8-quart roaster; set aside. Place ¼ cup of the ground beef mixture in the center (cupped side) of each of 11 or 12 of the remaining cabbage leaves. Fold the 2 sides of each leaf over the meat mixture; then, from the thick end of the cabbage leaves, loosely roll the leaves. Place the cabbage rolls, seam down, over the cabbage leaves in the bottom of the roaster. (It will be necessary to arrange some of the rolls in 2 layers.) Distribute the onion slices over the cabbage rolls; set aside.

Preheat the oven to 375°F.

Place the undrained tomatoes in a large

(Recipe continues on next page)

saucepan; using a metal mixing spoon, break the tomatoes into large chunks. Add the tomato sauce and lemon juice; stir to blend. Cover the saucepan; bring the tomato mixture to a boil over medium-high heat. Ladle the mixture over the onion slices and cabbage rolls in the roaster. Cover the roaster; set aside. In a small mixing bowl, place the brown sugar, ½ teaspoon salt, ¼ teaspoon pepper, and nutmeg; stir to combine. Sprinkle over all in the roaster. Bake, covered, for 1 hour. Then, baste lightly. Bake, *uncovered,* for an additional 2 hours, basting lightly after 1 hour of baking. Baste lightly again before serving.

SERVES 8

STUFFED GREEN PEPPERS

½ cup raw long-grain rice, regular or
  instant
4 large green bell peppers
1 6-ounce can commercial tomato paste
¾ cup water
1 tablespoon tomato catsup, home canned
  (page 781) or commercially canned
1 tablespoon cider vinegar
1 tablespoon packed dark brown sugar
1 tablespoon onion juice (page 45) or
  1 teaspoon onion powder
¼ teaspoon salt
⅛ teaspoon pepper
Dash of ground cinnamon
1 pound lean, pure ground beef
½ cup finely chopped celery
¼ cup finely chopped onions
½ teaspoon salt
⅛ teaspoon garlic salt
⅓ cup water

Boil the rice (see page 272 for boiling *regular* long-grain rice; follow the package instructions for cooking *instant* rice); set aside. Wash the green peppers. Cut a thin slice off the top of the peppers; carefully remove the seeds and inner, white parts of the flesh. In a large kettle, bring sufficient water to a boil, over high heat, as will

cover the peppers. Place the peppers in the boiling water; cover the kettle and reduce the heat slightly. Boil the peppers 5 minutes. Drain the peppers upside down on several layers of paper towels.

In a medium saucepan, place the tomato paste, water, catsup, vinegar, brown sugar, onion juice, ¼ teaspoon salt, pepper, and cinnamon. Cover the pan. Over medium-low heat, simmer the mixture for 10 minutes. Meanwhile, in a large mixing bowl, place the ground beef, celery, onions, ½ teaspoon salt, and garlic salt; using a large, metal mixing spoon, break up the ground beef and combine the ingredients well.

Preheat the oven to 350° F. Lightly grease an 8 × 8-inch baking dish; set aside.

Stuff the cavities of the green peppers with the meat mixture, patting lightly and filling to slightly above the top of the peppers. Place the stuffed peppers in the prepared baking dish. Pour ½ of the tomato paste mixture over the tops of the peppers (some of the mixture will trickle down the sides of the peppers). Cover the remaining ½ of the tomato paste mixture, and set aside. Pour ⅓ cup water into the bottom of the baking dish. Bake the stuffed peppers for 1 hour and 10 minutes.

At serving time, heat the remaining ½ of the tomato paste mixture over medium-low heat; pour into a sauce dish and pass at the table.

SERVES 4

STUFFED ONIONS

6 extra-large Vidalia or Texas super sweet
  onions* (about 5½ to 6 pounds onions)
2 tablespoons butter
4 ounces (about 1½ cups) coarsely-
  chopped, fresh mushrooms
1 tablespoon butter
½ pound lean, pure ground beef
1 teaspoon salt
¼ teaspoon pepper
¼ teaspoon ground thyme
1 tablespoon dried parsley

1 extra-large egg, slightly beaten
½ cup finely crumbled, fresh, whole-wheat bread crumbs (page 48)
½ cup drained whole-kernel corn, home canned (page 751), frozen and cooked, or commercially canned
2 tablespoons freshly grated Parmesan cheese (page 46)
1 cup beef broth, homemade (page 87) or commercially canned

These suggested kinds of onions are exceptionally sweet and lend themselves especially well to this dish.

To prepare each onion, cut a slice off the stem end, exposing approximately 2½ inches diameter of onion surface. (This will be the top of the stuffed onion.) Then, cut a small slice off the root end, parallel with the first cut, to form a flat surface upon which the onion can stand steadily. Cut off the ends of the removed slices, peel, and reserve the usable onion slices. Peel the skin and outer layer of the onions.

Using a grapefruit knife, cut a circle in the flesh on the top of each onion, leaving a ½-inch outer edge. Using a melon baller, carefully scoop out the onion flesh, leaving a shell approximately ½ inch thick on the sides of the onion and slightly thicker on the bottom. The shell must be thick enough to be firm and retain its shape. Reserve the scooped-out onion flesh.

Place the onion shells in a large kettle; add hot water to cover. Cover the kettle. Bring the onion shells to a boil over high heat; reduce the heat slightly, and boil gently 7 minutes. Immediately remove the shells from the boiling water, and drain upside down on several layers of paper towels. Chop the reserved onion slices and flesh; measure 2 cups chopped onions; set aside.

In an electric skillet or a large, heavy skillet on the range, melt 2 tablespoons butter over medium-low heat (300° F. in an electric skillet). Tilt the skillet back and forth to completely cover the bottom with the melted butter. Place the mushrooms in the skillet; sauté lightly (about 5 minutes). Using a slotted spoon, remove the mushrooms from the skillet and place in a small bowl; set aside. Add 1 tablespoon butter to the skillet. When the butter melts, add the ground beef and 2 cups chopped reserved onions, salt, and pepper. Increase the skillet heat to medium (350° F. in an electric skillet). Brown the meat and onions well, using a large, metal mixing spoon to break up the meat and turn the mixture often. When browned, spoon the meat and onion mixture into a large mixing bowl.

Preheat the oven to 350° F. Butter liberally a 7 × 11-inch baking dish; set aside.

Add the mushrooms, thyme, parsley, egg, bread crumbs, and corn to the meat mixture; stir until combined well. Using a tablespoon, fill the onion shells with the meat mixture, packing fairly solidly and mounding the stuffing slightly above the top of the onions. Sprinkle 1 teaspoon Parmesan cheese over the stuffing in each onion. Arrange the stuffed onions in the prepared baking dish. Pour the beef broth around the onions. Bake, uncovered, for 1 hour. Baste the onions 3 or 4 times during baking.

To serve, place 1 Stuffed Onion on each of 6 individual dinner plates. Pour the drippings from the baking dish into a gravy boat and pass at the table.

SERVES 6

Other Beef Recipes

Veal

....

BREADED VEAL CUTLETS WITH LEEKS AND SHIITAKE MUSHROOMS

1 cup commercially packaged corn flake crumbs or 5 cups corn flakes crumbed in a food processor or blender (page 49)

½ teaspoon salt

¼ teaspoon white pepper

1 extra-large egg

2 tablespoons whole milk

1 ¾-inch thick, boneless veal loin strip with the back strap removed (about 2 pounds), cut widthwise into 6 pieces

1 tablespoon vegetable oil

1 tablespoon butter

2 tablespoons butter

¾ cup leeks thinly sliced widthwise (about 2 medium leeks)

3½ ounces sliced, fresh shiitake mushrooms (about 2 cups)

2 recipes Extra-Thin White Sauce (page 366), substituting 1½ cups whole milk and ½ cup chicken broth (homemade [page 88] or commercially canned) for 2 cups whole milk

EARLY IN THE DAY (see Note): Butter a 7 × 11-inch baking dish; set aside.

In a small bowl, place the corn flake crumbs, salt, and white pepper; stir to combine. Sprinkle the mixture over a 1-foot-square piece of waxed paper; set aside. In a small mixing bowl, place the egg and 2 tablespoons milk; using an electric mixer or a table fork, beat until blended. Pour the egg mixture into a pie pan. Dredge each piece of veal in the corn flake crumbs mixture; then, dip in the egg mixture to coat; dredge again in the corn flake crumbs mixture and place on a clean piece of waxed paper. Let stand for 5 minutes.

In a large electric skillet or a heavy-bottomed skillet on the range, heat the vegetable oil over medium heat (350° F. in an electric skillet). Using a spatula, spread the oil over the bottom of the skillet. Add 1 tablespoon butter. Tilt the skillet back and forth to blend the butter with the oil. Place the cutlets in the skillet; sauté 4 to 5 minutes on each side until deeply browned. Arrange, single-layer, in the prepared baking dish. Let cool slightly; then, cover tightly with aluminum foil and refrigerate.

In a medium, heavy-bottomed skillet, melt 2 tablespoons butter over medium heat. Be careful not to let the butter brown. Add the leeks and mushrooms; sauté for 5 to 6 minutes, turning often and not allowing them to brown; set aside. Make the Extra-Thin White Sauce. Add the sautéed leeks and mushrooms plus the pan juices to the white sauce; stir to combine. Cover the saucepan and refrigerate.

1¼ HOURS BEFORE SERVING: Preheat the oven to 325° F.

Mound the white sauce mixture over the veal cutlets. Cover the baking dish lightly with aluminum foil. Bake for 1 hour.

To serve, place the Breaded Veal Cutlets on 6 individual dinner plates. Pour the remaining sauce in the baking dish into a sauceboat; pass at the table.

NOTE: The reason for preparing this dish early in the day is to allow the white sauce mixture to become slightly firm under refrigeration, making it possible to mound the mixture over the cutlets before baking. This procedure eliminates the need for basting and results in a greater quantity of the white sauce mixture remaining on top of the cutlets during baking, thus improving their flavor and appearance.

SERVES 6

Veal

• RETAIL CUTS •
WHERE THEY COME FROM
HOW TO COOK THEM

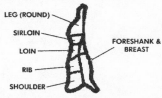

LEG (ROUND)
SIRLOIN
LOIN
RIB
SHOULDER
FORESHANK & BREAST

RIB

Rib Roast
Roast

Boneless Rib Roast
Roast

Crown Roast
Roast

Boneless Rib Chop
Braise, Panfry, Broil

Rib Chop
Braise, Panfry, Broil

Short Ribs
Braise, Cook in Liquid

SHOULDER

Blade Roast
Braise, Roast

Arm Roast
Braise, Roast

Blade Steak
Braise, Panfry

Arm Steak
Braise, Panfry

Boneless Shoulder Arm Roast
Braise, Roast

Boneless Shoulder Eye Roast
Braise, Roast

LEG (ROUND)

Boneless Rump Roast
Braise, Roast

Round Steak
Braise, Panfry

Top Round Steak
Braise, Panfry

Leg Cutlet
Braise, Panfry, Broil

FORESHANK & BREAST

Breast
Braise, Roast

Boneless Breast Roast
Braise, Roast

Cross Cut Shank
Braise, Cook in Liquid

Riblet
Braise, Cook in Liquid

Shank
Braise, Cook in Liquid

LOIN

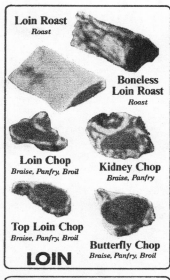

Loin Roast
Roast

Boneless Loin Roast
Roast

Loin Chop
Braise, Panfry, Broil

Kidney Chop
Braise, Panfry

Top Loin Chop
Braise, Panfry, Broil

Butterfly Chop
Braise, Panfry, Broil

SIRLOIN

Sirloin Roast
Roast

Boneless Sirloin Roast
Roast

Sirloin Steak
Braise, Panfry, Broil

Top Sirloin Steak
Braise, Panfry, Broil

OTHER CUTS

Veal for Stew
Braise, Cook in Liquid

Ground Veal
Panfry, Broil

Cubes for Kabobs
Braise

Cubed Steak
Braise, Panfry

THIS CHART APPROVED BY
NATIONAL LIVE STOCK & MEAT BOARD

NATIONAL LIVE STOCK
MB
AND MEAT BOARD

VEAL OR CALF'S LIVER WITH BACON AND ONIONS

¼ cup all-purpose flour
½ teaspoon salt
¼ teaspoon pepper
1 pound veal or calf's liver, cut ⅜ inch thick
8 slices (about ½ pound) bacon
1 large onion, thinly sliced and separated into rings
⅛ teaspoon salt
Dash of pepper
1 tablespoon butter, if necessary

In a small mixing bowl, place the flour, ½ teaspoon salt, and ¼ teaspoon pepper; stir to combine. Sprinkle the flour mixture over a piece of waxed paper. Dredge both sides of the liver in the flour mixture; set aside.

In an electric skillet or a heavy-bottomed skillet on the range, fry the bacon over medium-low heat (320° F. in an electric skillet); drain between several layers of paper towels. Place the onions in the skillet. Sprinkle ⅛ teaspoon salt and a dash of pepper over the onions. Sauté the onions 3 minutes only, turning occasionally. Move the onions to one side of the skillet and place the liver directly on the bottom of the skillet. If necessary, add 1 tablespoon butter for sufficient grease to sauté the liver. Sauté the liver for 4 to 5 minutes, turning once. Continue sautéing and turning the onions alongside the liver. When done, the liver should be nicely browned on the outside and delicately pink on the inside. Do not overcook, as this will cause toughness.

To serve, pile the onions on the liver and place the bacon next to the liver on the plate.

SERVES 4

VARIATION ~ **WITHOUT BACON:** Follow the recipe through the dredging of the liver. Omit the bacon. In an electric skillet or a heavy-bottomed skillet on the range, heat 1 tablespoon vegetable oil over medium-low heat (320° F. in an electric skillet); using a spatula, spread the vegetable oil over the bottom of the skillet. Add 1 tablespoon butter. Tilt the skillet back and forth to blend the butter with the oil. Place the onions in the skillet and resume following the recipe. Add 1 additional tablespoon butter to the skillet just before adding the liver for sautéing.

VEAL TENDERLOIN ROULADES WITH WILD RICE

1 pound fresh spinach
⅓ pound ground veal
⅓ pound mild Italian sausage
⅓ pound lean, pure ground beef
1 2-ounce jar sliced pimientos, drained (2 tablespoons)
1 cup fresh, white bread crumbs (page 48)
½ teaspoon salt
½ teaspoon dried leaf marjoram
1 extra-large egg
4 veal tenderloins, ⅔ to ¾ pound each, pounded to ¼-inch thickness
1 tablespoon vegetable shortening
2½ cups chicken broth, homemade (page 88) or commercially canned, divided
¼ cup all-purpose flour
½ cup dry white wine
1¼ cups raw wild rice, cooked (page 276)

Cut the stems off the spinach leaves; discard the stems. Wash the spinach leaves twice; then, place in a large kettle and add water to cover. Cover the kettle. Bring the spinach to a boil over high heat. Reduce the heat and simmer for 4 minutes. Drain the spinach well in a colander; with your hand, press the spinach to remove as much liquid as possible. Using a sharp knife, chop the spinach finely. Measure ½ cup chopped spinach.

In a medium mixing bowl, place ½ cup spinach, ground veal, Italian sausage, ground beef, pimientos, bread crumbs, salt, marjoram, and egg; using a large, metal mixing spoon, break up the ground meats and combine the ingredients well. Set aside.

Place the tenderloins on a piece of waxed paper. Divide the meat mixture into fourths and place ¼ of the mixture on each tenderloin. Distribute the mixture over the surface of the tenderloins; pat down well with the back of a spoon to within ⅜ inch of the edges of the tenderloins. Roll the tenderloins short side to short side. With cotton string, securely tie each roulade twice widthwise to hold it closed; then, tie it lengthwise around the ends and widthwise around the center, as you would tie a package (see illustration).

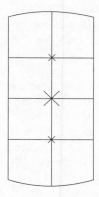

Preheat the oven to 325° F.

In an electric skillet or a heavy skillet on the range, melt the vegetable shortening over medium heat (350° F. in an electric skillet). Using a spatula, spread the melted shortening over the entire bottom of the skillet. Place the roulades in the skillet; brown well on all sides. Place the roulades in a heavy roaster, arranging them single layer, seams down; set aside. Reduce the skillet heat to very low (220° F. in an electric skillet). When the skillet cools to the reduced temperature, pour 1 cup chicken broth into the skillet and deglaze completely. Pour the skillet liquid over the roulades. Cover the roaster. Bake the roulades for 1 hour, basting 2 or 3 times during the baking period.

Remove the roaster from the oven and baste the roulades. Transfer the roulades to a plate or pan; cover lightly with aluminum foil. Pour the roaster drippings into a 2-cup glass measuring cup. Add enough chicken broth to measure 2 cups liquid; pour into a medium saucepan; set aside. Return the roulades to the roaster; cover to keep warm.

In a small glass jar or plastic container with a secure lid, place the flour and ½ cup chicken broth; cover and shake vigorously until blended. Add the flour mixture to the drippings and broth in the saucepan; stir to blend. Place the saucepan over medium heat and cook the gravy mixture until thick, stirring continuously. Add the wine; heat through. Remove the wine gravy from the heat and strain in a sieve, if necessary; keep warm.

Remove the roulades from the roaster. Remove the strings and cut the roulades into ½-inch slices widthwise. On a serving platter or on individual dinner plates, arrange the roulade slices on a bed of hot wild rice. Pour the wine gravy into a gravy boat and pass at the table.

SERVES 8

SERVING SUGGESTIONS: Decorate the serving platter with a cluster of Tomato Roses and Rosebuds (page 405) nestled in sprigs of flat-leafed parsley. If the roulade is served on individual plates, decorate each plate with one Tomato Rose arranged on one or two small sprigs of flat-leafed parsley.

VEAL PICCATA WITH THYME

½ cup all-purpose flour
1 teaspoon salt
½ teaspoon white pepper
10 slices (about 2¼ pounds) veal top round, cut ¼ inch thick; then, each slice cut in half widthwise to make 20 pieces
1 to 2 tablespoons vegetable oil
1 to 2 tablespoons butter
1¾ cups homemade Chicken Broth (page 88) or 1 14½-ounce can commercial chicken broth, divided
¼ cup dry white wine
1 tablespoon fresh thyme leaves
¼ cup freshly squeezed, strained lemon juice
¼ cup dry white wine
Thin slices of lemon for garnish

In a small mixing bowl, place the flour, salt, and white pepper; stir to combine. Sprinkle the flour mixture over a piece of waxed paper. Dredge the veal pieces lightly in the mixture; shake to remove all excess flour, and place, single layer, on a clean piece of waxed paper. Measure 2 tablespoons of the remaining flour mixture (add additional flour, if necessary) and place in a small glass jar or plastic container with a secure lid; cover and set aside.

In an electric skillet or a large, heavy-bottomed skillet on the range, heat 1 tablespoon vegetable oil over medium-low heat (320° F. in an electric skillet), being careful not to let the heat become warmer. Using a spatula, spread the vegetable oil over the entire bottom of the skillet. Add 1 tablespoon butter. Tilt the skillet back and forth to blend the butter with the oil. Place veal pieces, single layer, a few at a time, in the skillet; sauté about 5 minutes (2 to 3 minutes on each side) until very lightly golden. Place the sautéed veal pieces in a large, shallow pan and set aside. Add 1 additional tablespoon vegetable oil and 1 additional tablespoon butter during sautéing, if necessary. After all the pieces of veal

have been sautéed, reduce the skillet heat to very low (220° F. in an electric skillet).

When the skillet has cooled to the reduced temperature, return all the veal pieces to the skillet; set aside. Into a small mixing bowl, pour ½ cup chicken broth and ¼ cup white wine; stir to blend. Pour the wine mixture carefully over the veal. Sprinkle the thyme over and around the veal. Cover the skillet. Cook the veal for 15 minutes. Add ½ cup additional chicken broth if liquid depletes during cooking. Do not turn the meat. (See Note.)

Place the veal in a shallow pan; cover lightly with aluminum foil and keep warm. Retain very low skillet heat (220° F. in an electric skillet). Pour ½ cup chicken broth, lemon juice, and ¼ cup white wine into the skillet; using a large, metal mixing spoon, stir and scrape until the skillet is completely deglazed. Strain the skillet liquid through a sieve; pour the strained liquid into a small saucepan; set aside.

Add ¼ cup chicken broth to the 2 tablespoons reserved flour; cover the jar/container and shake briskly until blended. Add the flour mixture to the strained skillet juices in the saucepan; stir to blend. Place the saucepan over medium heat. Bring the mixture to a boil, stirring constantly. Boil for 2 minutes, continuing to stir constantly. Remove the sauce from the heat.

To serve, arrange 3 pieces of veal, overlapping slightly, on 6 individual dinner plates (there will be 2 extra pieces). Spoon the sauce over the veal on each plate. Garnish the plates with thin lemon slices.

NOTE: At this point in the preparation, the skillet may be turned off or removed from the heat and the veal may be left in the covered skillet for up to 1 hour until the recipe is completed shortly before serving. In this case, the veal must be reheated in the skillet over very low heat before proceeding with the recipe.

SERVES 6

Pork

CROWN ROAST OF PORK FILLED WITH FRESH MIXED VEGETABLES ROSEMARY

1 8- to 10-pound crown roast of pork, with backbone removed*
¼ teaspoon pepper
1 teaspoon snipped, fresh rosemary
1 cup German Spätlese wine,** divided
2 recipes Pork Wine Gravy using German Spätlese wine** (page 377)
1 recipe Mixed Fresh Vegetables with Rosemary (page 322)
4½ pounds Oven-Browned Potatoes (page 334)
Tomato Roses (page 405) for decoration
Sprigs of fresh rosemary for decoration

Have the butcher remove the backbone from the meat before he makes the crown roast. Order the exact number of ribs you want in the roast—1 rib per diner plus 2 extra ribs for big eaters. An 18-rib crown roast of pork weighs about 8¾ pounds and will serve 16.

**German Kabinett or American Johannisberg Riesling wine may be substituted.*

Preheat the oven to 325° F.

Place the roast on a wire rack in a shallow roasting pan. Sprinkle the inside of the crown and the outside of the roast with the pepper and rosemary. Cover the ends of the rib bones firmly with aluminum foil to prevent overbrowning. Insert a meat thermometer into the center of the thickest part of the roast near the base, making certain that the tip of the thermometer is not touching a bone. Roast, uncovered, until the thermometer reaches 160° F. for medium doneness (approximately 20 to 25 minutes per pound) (see Note). Remove the roast from the oven when the temperature reaches 5° F. below the desired temperature, as the meat will continue cooking. After roasting 1 hour, carefully pour ½ cup wine over the roast. After roasting an additional 45 minutes, pour the remaining ½ cup wine over the roast. After roasting another 45 minutes, baste the roast with pan juices.

When the thermometer has reached the desired temperature, remove the roast from the oven and place it into the center of a large, round serving platter. Cover lightly with aluminum foil to keep warm. Make the Pork Wine Gravy.

To serve, remove the aluminum foil from the roast and rib bones. Fill the crown with the mixed vegetables; place the remaining mixed vegetables in a vegetable serving dish. Place white paper frilled booties over each rib bone. Arrange the potatoes around the roast. Decorate the platter with Tomato Roses and sprigs of fresh rosemary. Cut and serve the roast at the table. Cut between each rib bone and serve 1 rib chop to each diner. Pass the Pork Wine Gravy in a gravy boat.

NOTE: For well done, roast until the thermometer reaches 170° F. (approximately 25 to 30 minutes per pound).

SERVES 16

ACCOMPANIMENT SUGGESTION: Scalloped Apples (page 345) make an excellent side dish.

Pork

• RETAIL CUTS •
WHERE THEY COME FROM
HOW TO COOK THEM

LEG
SIDE
LOIN
ARM SHOULDER
BLADE SHOULDER

LEG/HAM

Leg Cutlet
Panfry, Braise, Broil, Panbroil

Top Leg (Inside) Roast
Roast, Braise

Smoked Ham
Roast

Smoked Ham Shank Portion
Roast

Smoked Ham Center Slice
Broil, Panbroil, Panfry, Roast

Smoked Ham Rump Portion
Roast

Canned Ham
Roast

Sliced Ham
Panfry, Panbroil, Braise

Boneless Smoked Ham
Roast

LOIN

Blade Chop
Braise, Broil, Panbroil, Panfry

Rib Chop
Broil, Panbroil, Panfry, Braise

Top Loin Chop
Broil, Panbroil, Panfry, Braise

Loin Chop
Broil, Panbroil, Panfry, Braise

Sirloin Chop
Braise

Butterfly Chop
Broil, Panbroil, Panfry, Braise

Sirloin Cutlet
Braise, Broil, Panbroil, Panfry

Back Ribs
Roast, Broil, Braise, Cook in Liquid

Country-Style Ribs
Roast, Braise, Broil, Cook in Liquid

Tenderloin
Roast, Braise, (Slices: Panfry, Braise)

Center Rib Roast
Roast

Top Loin Roast (Double)
Roast

Blade Roast
Roast, Braise

Boneless Blade Roast
Roast, Braise

Sirloin Roast
Roast

Center Loin Roast
Roast

Crown Roast
Roast

Smoked Loin Chop
Roast, Broil, Panbroil, Panfry

Boneless Sirloin Roast
Roast

Canadian-Style Bacon
Roast, Broil, Panbroil, Panfry

SHOULDER

Blade Roast
Roast, Braise

Blade Steak
Braise, Broil, Panbroil, Panfry

Boneless Blade Roast
Roast, Braise

Smoked Shoulder Roll
Roast, Cook in Liquid

Boneless Arm Picnic Roast
Roast, Braise

Smoked Hocks
Braise, Cook in Liquid

Smoked Picnic
Roast, Cook in Liquid

SIDE

Spareribs
Roast, Broil, Cook in Liquid, Braise

Sliced Bacon
Panfry, Broil, Roast (Bake)

THIS CHART APPROVED BY
NATIONAL LIVE STOCK & MEAT BOARD

OTHER CUTS

Cubed Steak
Braise, Panbroil, Panfry

Pork Pieces
Braise, Cook in Liquid

Cubes for Kabobs
Broil, Braise

Ground Pork
Broil, Panbroil, Panfry, Roast (Bake)

Sausage Links
Braise, Panfry, Roast

IOWA PORK CHOPS

Known throughout the Midwest as the Iowa Pork Chop or the Iowa Chop, this thick, flavorful, and tender cut of pork is like a steak. Specifically, Iowa Pork Chops are center-cut loin pork chops cut 1¼ to 1½ inches thick. They may be prepared in any way desired. During the winter, when it's too cold for outdoor grilling, I like to fix them in this traditional way. When the weather is warmer, these succulent chops are incredibly delicious prepared outdoors on the grill (see Grilled Iowa Pork Chops, page 251). Iowa Chops are so named because Iowa produces more pork than any other state.

4 Iowa Pork Chops (center-cut loin pork
    chops, 1¼ to 1½ inches thick)
Salt
Pepper
All-purpose flour
2 tablespoons vegetable shortening
¼ cup water

Place the pork chops on a piece of waxed paper. Sprinkle the chops lightly on both sides with salt and pepper. Sprinkle flour liberally over the chops. Using your hand, spread the flour over the entire top surface of the chops. Turn the chops over and repeat the procedure; set aside.

Preheat an electric skillet or a heavy skillet on the range to medium–high heat (380°F. in an electric skillet). Melt the shortening in the skillet. Tilt the skillet back and forth to completely cover the bottom with the melted shortening. Shake the excess flour off the chops and place them in the skillet. Brown for about 10 minutes on each side, turning once. Reduce the skillet heat to very low (220°F. in an electric skillet). When the skillet cools to the lower temperature, add the water. Cover tightly and cook for 30 minutes.

SERVES 4

ACCOMPANIMENT SUGGESTIONS:
- Serve with Mashed Potatoes (page 332) and Milk Gravy (page 375). The gravy should be served on the mashed potatoes, not over or under the pork chops.
- Ten minutes before the pork chops are done, place unpared, cored, fresh apple slices, or fresh or canned pineapple slices in the skillet and brown for 5 minutes on each side. Serve as a garnish on the plates.
- Serve with homemade Plain Applesauce (page 344).
- Serve Rhubarb–Strawberry Conserve (page 761) or Grape Conserve (page 760) as a garnish.

BARBECUED LOIN BACK RIBS

6 pounds pork loin back ribs (baby backs)*
1 recipe Barbecue Sauce (page 360),
    divided

*Have the butcher remove the fell (a thin, tough membrane) from the bony side of the ribs.

Preheat the oven to 400°F.

Cut each side of ribs in half, or leave whole. Place the ribs, bony side down, in a heavy roaster. Bake, uncovered, for 30 minutes. Remove the roaster from the oven; reduce the oven heat to 325°F. Using a baster, draw off and discard the excess fat in the roaster.

Pour ½ of the Barbecue Sauce over the ribs, lifting them with a fork to make certain that all the ribs are coated with sauce. Bake, covered, for 30 minutes. Then, baste each piece of ribs. Bake, covered, for an additional 30 minutes. Pour an additional ¼ of the Barbecue Sauce over the ribs; bake, covered, for an additional 1 hour, basting twice. Pour the remaining ¼ of the Barbecue Sauce over the ribs; bake, uncovered, for an additional 30 minutes, basting after 15 minutes baking time. (Leave the ribs bony side down during the entire baking time.)

SERVES 6
(ALLOW 1 POUND RIBS PER DINER)

LOIN OF PORK

For perfect pork, cook it to 160°F. (medium doneness). For more on this subject, see page 157.

½ teaspoon ground sage
½ teaspoon Hungarian paprika
½ teaspoon dry mustard
¼ teaspoon salt
⅛ teaspoon pepper
1 4- to 5-pound center-cut, boneless, *double* pork loin, tied at 1½-inch intervals

Preheat the oven to 325°F.

In a small sauce dish, place the sage, paprika, dry mustard, salt, and pepper; stir to combine; set aside. Place the roast on a wire rack in a shallow roasting pan. Rub the sage mixture over the top of the roast. Insert a meat thermometer into the center of the roast. Roast the meat, uncovered, until the thermometer reaches 160°F. for medium doneness (approximately 30 minutes per pound) (see Note). Remove the roast from the oven when the thermometer reaches 5°F. below the desired temperature, as the meat will continue cooking.

When the meat thermometer has reached the desired temperature, remove the roast from the oven and cover loosely with aluminum foil; let stand 15 minutes.

To serve, place the sliced or unsliced roast on a warm serving platter.

NOTE: For well done, roast until the thermometer reaches 170°F. (approximately 30 to 35 minutes per pound).

A 4-POUND PORK LOIN SERVES 8 TO 12

SINGLE PORK LOIN: To prepare 1 4- to 5-pound center-cut, boneless, single pork loin, tie at 3-inch intervals. Follow the recipe, above, for double pork loin, with the following alterations in roasting times: To reach an internal temperature of 160°F. (medium done), roast approximately 20 minutes per pound. To reach an internal temperature of 170°F. (well done), roast approximately 25 minutes per pound.

LOIN OF PORK NATURAL JUICE OR GRAVY: To serve loin of pork natural juice, deglaze the roasting pan with 1 cup water; strain the pan juices through a sieve and serve in a small sauceboat. To serve loin of pork gravy, follow the recipe for Roast Pork Gravy (page 377).

Loin of Pork with Brandied Apples

1 recipe Loin of Pork (above)
¼ cup packed light brown sugar
¼ cup granulated sugar
½ teaspoon ground cinnamon
¼ teaspoon ground mace
2 pounds Golden Delicious apples (4 medium-large apples)
1 tablespoon freshly squeezed, strained lemon juice
2 teaspoons vegetable oil
2 tablespoons butter
1 teaspoon cornstarch
2 teaspoons good brandy

30 MINUTES BEFORE LOIN OF PORK IS DONE: In a small mixing bowl, place the brown sugar, granulated sugar, cinnamon, and mace; stir to combine; set aside. Wash, quarter, and core the apples; do not pare. Slice the apples ¼ inch thick; place in a large mixing bowl. Sprinkle the lemon juice over the apples; toss to coat. Add the sugar mixture; toss until the apples are coated; set aside.

Pour the vegetable oil into a medium, heavy-bottomed skillet; using a spatula, distribute the oil over the entire bottom. Place the skillet over medium-high heat. Add the butter. Tilt the skillet back and forth to blend the butter with the oil. Place the apples in the skillet; sauté for 12 minutes until tender, turning intermittently. Remove the skillet from the heat and let the sautéed apples stand, uncovered, in the skillet.

While the Loin of Pork is standing for 15 minutes after removal from the oven, reheat the sautéed apples. Then, using a slotted spoon, transfer the apples to a mixing bowl; cover lightly and set aside. Pour about ¼ cup juice from the skillet into a small mixing bowl; add the cornstarch and stir until blended. Add the cornstarch mixture to the remaining juice in the skillet; stir to blend. Place over medium heat and cook until the mixture thickens, stirring constantly. Add the brandy; heat through. Pour over the apples; toss lightly.

To serve, surround the sliced or unsliced roast on the serving plate with the brandied apples. This recipe makes enough brandied apples to serve as a garnish with the Loin of Pork. If larger portions are desired, double the recipe.

WITH A 4-POUND PORK LOIN, SERVES 8 TO 12

SPARERIBS AND SAUERKRAUT

2 racks (about 6 pounds) pork spareribs
  with brisket removed*
2 tablespoons butter
1 large onion, sliced and separated into
  rings
1 cup water
½ teaspoon salt
½ teaspoon pepper
1½ pounds russet potatoes, pared and cut in
  half or into thirds, depending upon size
1 quart home-canned Sauerkraut (page
  734) or 32 ounces commercial, fresh
  sauerkraut
1 tablespoon caraway seed
1 tablespoon packed light brown sugar
2 cups pared, quartered, cored, and sliced
  Golden Delicious apples (about 1 large or
  2 medium-small apples)
Paprika for decoration

  Have the butcher cut each rack into 3 approximately equal pieces.

Parboil (page 24) the spareribs for 10 minutes in a large kettle to remove fat and tenderize. Drain the spareribs; set aside.

Preheat the oven to 350° F.

In a large, heavy roaster, melt the butter over medium-high heat. Tilt the roaster back and forth to completely cover the bottom with the melted butter. Add the onions; sauté until well browned (about 10 minutes), turning often. Remove from the heat; let the roaster stand until cooled slightly. Add 1 cup water to the roaster; stir briefly to combine with the onions; set aside.

In a small sauce dish, place the salt and pepper; stir to combine; set aside. Place the spareribs in the roaster, meaty side up. Sprinkle the combined salt and pepper over each of the 6 pieces of spareribs. Cover the roaster. Bake the spareribs for 1 hour.

Place the potatoes around and over the spareribs; cover the roaster. Bake an additional 1 hour. Meanwhile, in a colander, drain the sauerkraut well. In a large mixing bowl, place the drained sauerkraut, caraway seed, and brown sugar; stir to combine. Cover with plastic wrap; set aside. Near the end of the second hour of baking the spareribs, prepare the apples and add to the sauerkraut mixture; stir to combine. Cover and set aside.

After 2 hours of baking the spareribs, remove the roaster from the oven. Remove the potatoes from the roaster and place in a bowl. Move the spareribs to one side of the roaster. Place the sauerkraut mixture on the other side of the roaster next to the spareribs. Return the potatoes to the roaster, placing them around and over the spareribs. Cover the roaster. Bake for an additional 1 hour.

To serve, place 1 piece of the spareribs on each of 6 individual dinner or oval steak plates. Place 1 or 2 potato pieces on each plate next to the spareribs. Sprinkle the potatoes lightly with paprika for decoration. Remove the remaining potatoes from the roaster and place in a bowl. Stir the sauerkraut together with the onions and juices in the bottom of the roaster. Using a large, slotted spoon, place a serving of drained sauerkraut on each plate. Place the remaining drained sauerkraut in a serving bowl; arrange the remaining potatoes around the periphery of the bowl over the sauerkraut. Pass at the table for additional helpings.

SERVES 6

PORK AND NOODLES CASSEROLE WITH SAGE-Y RED SAUCE

1 pound lean, ground pork
1 15-ounce can commercial tomato sauce
2 teaspoons dried leaf sage
2 teaspoons dried parsley
¾ teaspoon salt
⅛ teaspoon black pepper
Dash of cayenne pepper*
15 ounces ricotta cheese
¼ cup commercial sour cream
¼ cup finely chopped onions
2 tablespoons snipped, fresh chives
2 tablespoons finely chopped green bell
  peppers
8 cups water
8 ounces (about 4 cups) egg noodles
2 tablespoons butter, melted
Sprig of fresh sage for decoration (optional)

For more spicy flavor, use ⅛ teaspoon cayenne pepper.

In a large, heavy-bottomed skillet, brown the ground pork well over medium heat, using a large, metal mixing spoon to break up the meat and stir often. Remove from the heat. When cooled slightly, add the tomato sauce, sage, parsley, salt, black pepper, and cayenne pepper; stir to combine; set aside. In a medium bowl, place the ricotta cheese, sour cream, onions, chives, and green peppers; stir until completely combined; set aside.

Preheat the oven to 375°F. Butter a 7×11-inch baking dish; set aside.

In a large saucepan, bring 8 cups water to a boil over high heat. Add the noodles and boil until just tender (about 8 minutes), stirring frequently. Drain the noodles in a sieve and rinse well under hot, running water. Rinse and dry the saucepan in which the noodles were cooked; return the noodles to the saucepan. Drizzle the melted butter over the noodles; using a wooden spoon, toss to coat.

Place ½ of the noodles in the prepared baking dish; distribute evenly over the bottom of the dish. Spoon the ricotta cheese mixture over the noodles and spread evenly. Add the remaining ½ noodles; distribute evenly over the ricotta cheese mixture. Spoon the meat mixture evenly over all. Bake, uncovered, for 30 minutes. Cut into 8 servings. Decorate with a sprig of fresh sage, if available. Serve with a spatula.

SERVES 8

BISCUITS AND GRAVY MADEIRA

1 recipe raw sausage mixture (page 189)
  (do not make sausage mixture into
  patties and do not cook)
½ cup all-purpose flour
½ teaspoon salt
½ teaspoon pepper
1 cup whole milk
¼ cup (4 tablespoons) butter
2 cups homemade Beef Broth (page 87)
  or 1 14½-ounce can commercial beef
  broth
1 cup whole milk
¼ cup Madeira wine
1 recipe Baking Powder Biscuits (page 446)

Place the sausage mixture in an electric skillet or a large, heavy skillet on the range over medium-low heat (300°F. in an electric skillet). Using a large, metal mixing spoon, break up the sausage mixture into small pieces as it cooks and stir often. Cook the sausage until completely done, with no pink remaining, and browned slightly. When done, reduce the skillet heat to very low (210°F. in an electric skillet). Using a slotted spoon, remove the sausage from the skillet and place it in a small mixing bowl; set aside. In a small glass jar or plastic container with a secure lid, place the flour, salt, and pepper; stir to combine. Add 1 cup milk; cover and shake vigorously until blended; set aside.

When the skillet cools to the reduced temperature, add the butter. When the butter melts, add the beef broth and deglaze the skillet completely. Add 1 cup milk, Madeira wine, and the flour mixture; stir to blend. Bring the mixture to a simmer, stirring constantly (increase the heat very slightly, if necessary). Simmer the mixture 2 minutes, until thick and blended, stirring continuously. Add the sausage and stir to combine; heat through (see Note).

Make the Baking Powder Biscuits as near serving time as possible and serve piping hot in a cloth-lined roll basket. Serve the gravy in an appropriate serving bowl or tureen with a large serving ladle. To eat this dish, diners split 1 or 2 biscuits in half, place the biscuit halves open-faced on their plates, and ladle gravy over the top.

NOTE: At this point in the procedure, the Gravy Madeira may be refrigerated in a covered container and reheated in a skillet at serving time.

SERVES 4

SAUSAGE PATTIES

1 pound ground pork
1½ teaspoons ground sage
¾ teaspoon dried, leaf summer savory
¾ teaspoon salt
¼ teaspoon pepper
Dash of cayenne pepper

Place the ground pork in a medium mixing bowl; set aside. In a small mixing bowl, place the sage, summer savory, salt, pepper, and cayenne pepper; stir to combine. Add the sage mixture to the ground pork; using your hands, mix until thoroughly combined. Pat the mixture in the bottom of the mixing bowl; using a knife, cut into 6 even portions. Using your hands, shape 6 patties ¾ inch thick and 2½ inches in diameter.

Place the patties in an ungreased, 9-inch, heavy-bottomed skillet. Over medium-low heat, fry the patties for 18 minutes, turning once after the first 10 minutes of frying. After frying 18 minutes, cover the skillet and continue cooking for an additional 5 minutes. The patties should be fried to a dark brown, but should not

be crispy or burned. They should be well done with no pink remaining.

SERVES 3 TO 6

SMOKED PORK CHOPS WITH PRUNE-APPLE STUFFING

2 pounds yams
6 smoked rib pork chops, 1 to 1¼ inches thick
⅓ cup bite-sized pitted prunes cut into ⅜-inch cubes
1½ cups pared, quartered, cored, and chopped Golden Delicious apples
2 tablespoons packed light brown sugar
2 tablespoons ginger preserves
2 tablespoons freshly squeezed orange juice
1 teaspoon finely grated orange rind (page 47)
1 tablespoon vegetable shortening
1 tablespoon butter
½ cup water
Dash of salt
Dash of white pepper

Using a vegetable brush, scrub the yams. Place the unpared yams in a large saucepan; add hot water to cover. Cover the saucepan. Bring the yams to a boil over high heat; reduce the heat and cook at a low boil for 15 minutes. Drain the yams and place on a wire rack; let stand to cool. Then, peel the yams, removing the thin layer of flesh under the skin to reveal the bright orange flesh. Cut the yams widthwise into approximately 2-inch slices; set aside.

Using a sharp knife, slit each pork chop laterally through the center from the meaty side to ½ inch from the bone edge to form a pocket; set aside. In a small mixing bowl, place the prunes, apples, brown sugar, ginger preserves, orange juice, and orange rind; stir to combine. Fill the pockets in the pork chops with the prune mixture. Break 6 toothpicks in half and

(Recipe continues on next page)

skewer each pocket closed with 2 toothpick halves; set aside.

Preheat the oven to 350° F.

In an electric skillet or a large, heavy-bottomed skillet on the range, melt the shortening over medium heat (350° F. in an electric skillet). Using a spatula, spread the melted shortening over the entire bottom of the skillet. Add the butter. Tilt the skillet back and forth to blend the butter with the melted shortening. Place the pork chops in the skillet; brown on both sides, turning once (about 7 to 8 minutes on each side). Place the chops in a heavy roaster; set aside. Reduce the skillet heat to very low (220° F. in an electric skillet).

When the skillet cools to the reduced temperature, pour ½ cup water into the skillet and deglaze. Pour the skillet liquid over and around the chops. Arrange the yams around the chops. Sprinkle the yams with a dash of salt and white pepper. Cover the roaster.

Bake the pork chops and yams for 35 minutes, basting twice during baking and again just before serving. *Remove all toothpicks before serving.* Pour the drippings in the roaster into a gravy boat and pass at the table as additional sauce for the yams. (If necessary, strain the sauce in a sieve.)

SERVES 6

BUTCHER'S PLATTER WITH SAUERKRAUT

1 2⅓- to 2½-pound smoked pork shank, cut into 4 serving pieces
1 recipe Sauerkraut (page 310), substituting 1 cup cooking liquid from smoked pork shank for 1 cup commercial vegetable broth
1½ pounds medium to small red potatoes
6 smoked bratwurst
¼ cup whole milk
2 tablespoons bacon grease or lard
German-style mustard, such as horseradish mustard

Horseradish, homemade (page 46) or commercially canned

EARLY IN THE DAY (OR 4 HOURS BEFORE SERVING): Place the pork shank in a large kettle; add water to cover. Cover the kettle. Bring the pork shank to a boil over high heat; reduce the heat to low and simmer for 2 hours. Remove the kettle from the heat; uncover and let stand until the pork shank and broth cool slightly. Then, cover the kettle and refrigerate (leaving the pork shank and broth in the kettle).

Prepare the sauerkraut through thickening of the sauerkraut liquid (using 1 cup cooking liquid from the smoked pork shank), but do not drain. Cover the saucepan and refrigerate the sauerkraut.

45 MINUTES BEFORE SERVING: Scrub the potatoes well, using a vegetable brush. Place the unpared potatoes in a large saucepan; add hot water to cover. Cover the saucepan. Bring the potatoes to a boil over high heat; reduce the heat and simmer until tender (about 20 minutes). Drain well and dry; keep warm. (The potatoes will be served unpeeled.)

20 MINUTES BEFORE SERVING: Place the kettle containing the pork shank and broth over medium heat to reheat. Place the bratwurst in an uncovered saucepan of boiling water. Turn off the heat under the saucepan; let the bratwurst stand in the hot water about 7 minutes.

Pour the milk into a small, shallow pan; roll the bratwurst in the milk to fully coat; set aside. In a small, heavy-bottomed skillet, heat the bacon grease over medium heat. Tilt the skillet back and forth to completely cover the bottom with the grease. Place the bratwurst in the skillet and fry until evenly brown on all sides (about 10 minutes).

Meanwhile, reheat the sauerkraut; then drain, reserving the liquid. Cover to keep hot.

TO SERVE: Cover the bottom of a large, heated platter with the drained sauerkraut. Place the *drained* pork shank and bratwurst on top of the sauerkraut. Arrange the potatoes around the edge of the platter or serve in a separate serving bowl. Pass the mustard and horseradish in appropriate serving dishes at the table.

SERVES 4

VARIATIONS: Ham, various kinds of encased wursts, fresh pork, or boiled beef may be served in substitution for, or in addition to, smoked pork shank and smoked bratwurst.

ACCOMPANIMENT SUGGESTIONS: Serve with Cucumber Salad (page 131), pumpernickel bread, and beer.

BEDEVILED BACON

Here's a classy, unusual way to prepare bacon for serving as a side dish at brunches and special breakfasts. The spicy seasoning also makes this an ideal choice for adding zing to wintertime waffle dinners.

12 slices (½ to ¾ pound) thick bacon
1 extra-large egg
1 teaspoon prepared mustard
¼ teaspoon cayenne pepper
1 teaspoon cider vinegar
¾ cup commercial cracker meal

Cut the bacon slices in half widthwise; set aside. In a small mixing bowl, place the egg, mustard, cayenne pepper, and vinegar; using an electric mixer, beat on medium speed until blended and smooth. Pour the egg mixture into a pie pan; set aside.

Sprinkle the cracker meal over a 1-foot-square piece of waxed paper; set aside. Dip the bacon pieces in the egg mixture; then, dredge lightly in the cracker meal and place, single layer, on ungreased broiler racks over broiler pans. Let stand 15 minutes.

Meanwhile, preheat the oven to 350° F.

Bake the bacon for 18 to 20 minutes. Watch carefully during the last few minutes of baking, as the bacon can overbrown quickly at the end of the baking period.

SERVES 6

HAM BAKED IN SHERRY SAUCE

1 8- to 9-pound full-muscle,* boneless, best-quality, fully cooked ham**
1½ cups cream sherry
1 cup (½ pint) apricot jam, home canned (page 747) or commercially canned
1 cup honey
2 tablespoons cornstarch
¼ teaspoon ground cinnamon
2 cups cream sherry

  Some retail hams consist of smaller pieces of meat pressed together with water and formed. Full-muscle hams are whole, uncut-up sections of meat.

  **To prepare a 3½- to 4-pound piece of ham, halve the recipe ingredients and reduce the initial baking period from 2 hours to 1½ hours. (Maintain the final baking period of 50 minutes to 1 hour.)*

Preheat the oven to 325° F.

Place the ham in a shallow baking dish. Pour 1½ cups sherry over the ham. Bake, uncovered, for 2 hours, basting occasionally.

Meanwhile, in a medium saucepan, place the apricot jam, honey, cornstarch, cinnamon, and 2 cups sherry; stir to combine. Cook the mixture over medium heat until clear and slightly thickened, stirring constantly; cover and set aside.

At the end of the 2-hour baking period, pour the sherry sauce over the ham. Bake, uncovered, for an additional 50 minutes to 1 hour, basting at least twice.

To serve, slice the ham and arrange on a serving platter. Spoon hot sherry sauce from the baking dish into a sauceboat and pass at the table.

EACH POUND OF HAM SERVES 4

TRADITIONAL BAKED HAM

1 8- to 9-pound full-muscle,* boneless,
  best-quality, fully cooked ham
Whole cloves
1 15¼-ounce can commercial sliced
  pineapple in pineapple juice
1 cup packed light brown sugar
2 tablespoons prepared mustard
1 tablespoon reserved pineapple juice
Maraschino cherries, cut in half lengthwise

*Some retail hams consist of smaller pieces of
meat pressed together with water and formed.
Full-muscle hams are whole, uncut-up sections
of meat.*

Preheat the oven to 350° F.

Using a sharp knife, score the ham by making
diagonal cuts, about ⅛ inch deep at ¾-inch
intervals, in 2 directions over the surface of the
ham, forming a diamond pattern. Insert a whole
clove in the ham at each point where the scor-
ing lines cross. Wrap and seal the ham in heavy-
duty aluminum foil; place in a shallow baking
pan. Bake for 3 hours.

Meanwhile, near the end of the 3-hour baking period, drain the pineapple in a sieve, reserving the juice. Set the juice aside. Place the
pineapple slices in a bowl; cover and set aside. In
a medium bowl, place the brown sugar, mustard,
and 1 tablespoon reserved pineapple juice; stir
until blended; set aside. (Reserve the remaining
pineapple juice for other uses.)

When the ham has baked 3 hours, remove it
from the oven. Reduce the oven temperature to
325° F. Open the aluminum foil and place the
pineapple slices, single layer, on top of the ham,
securing the slices with short toothpicks, if
necessary. (Reserve any remaining pineapple
slices for other uses.) Place a maraschino cherry
half, cut side down, in the center of each pineapple slice. Pour the brown sugar mixture over
the ham.

Return the ham to the oven, leaving the
aluminum foil open. Bake an additional 30 minutes, basting 3 or 4 times. *Before serving, remove
any toothpicks which may have been used to secure the
pineapple slices.*

EACH POUND OF HAM SERVES 4

HAM AND YAM CASSEROLE

1½ pounds yams
2 cups fully cooked ham cut into bite-sized
  pieces
1½ cups pared, quartered, cored, and sliced
  Golden Delicious apples
¼ teaspoon salt
¼ teaspoon paprika
½ cup packed light brown sugar
2 tablespoons bourbon
2 tablespoons butter

Using a vegetable brush, scrub the yams well.
Place the unpared yams in a large saucepan; add
hot water to cover. Cover the saucepan. Bring
the yams to a boil over high heat; reduce the
heat to medium and cook at a low boil for 15
minutes. Drain the yams and place them on a
wire rack; let stand until cool.

Preheat the oven to 350° F. Butter a 2-quart
round baking dish; set aside.

Peel the yams, removing the thin layer of flesh
directly beneath the skin to reveal the bright
orange flesh. Slice the yams ¾ inch thick (about
4 cups sliced yams). Arrange ½ of the yams in
the bottom of the prepared baking dish. Distribute the ham evenly over the yams; then, distribute the apples evenly over the ham. Arrange
the remaining yams over the apples; sprinkle
with salt and paprika; set aside. In a small mixing bowl, place the brown sugar and bourbon;
stir to combine. Sprinkle the brown sugar mixture evenly over the ingredients in the baking
dish. Dot with butter.

Bake, covered, for 20 minutes. Baste; then
bake, uncovered, for an additional 25 minutes.
Baste and serve.

SERVES 6

HAM STEAK WITH GLAZED PINEAPPLE

1 2-pound center-sliced, smoked ham
　steak, ¾ to 1 inch thick
1 tablespoon vegetable shortening
Glazed Pineapple (recipe follows)
Sprigs of fresh parsley for decoration

In an electric skillet or a heavy skillet on the range, melt the shortening over medium-low heat (330° F. in an electric skillet). Using a spatula, spread the melted shortening over the entire bottom of the skillet. Place the ham steak in the heated skillet; fry 8 minutes on each side (16 minutes total), turning once. Serve on a platter with Glazed Pineapple. Decorate with sprigs of parsley.

SERVES 4

Glazed Pineapple

1 8-ounce can commercial, unsweetened
　pineapple slices in pineapple juice
　(4 slices)
2 tablespoons packed light brown sugar
1 teaspoon vegetable oil
2 teaspoons butter

Drain the pineapple in a sieve, reserving the juice. Set the pineapple aside. Measure 2 tablespoons reserved juice and place in a small mixing bowl. (Reserve the remaining pineapple juice for other uses.) Add the brown sugar to the 2 tablespoons pineapple juice; stir to combine; set aside.

In a medium-small, heavy skillet, heat the vegetable oil over medium-high heat. Using a spatula, spread the vegetable oil over the entire bottom of the skillet. Add the butter. Tilt the skillet back and forth to blend the butter with the oil. Arrange the pineapple slices, single layer, in the skillet. Spoon the brown sugar mixture over the pineapple; sauté for 10 minutes, turning once or twice with a spatula.

HAM LOAF WITH HORSERADISH SAUCE

1 16-ounce can whole, peeled commercial
　tomatoes or 1 pint home-canned
　Tomatoes (page 736)
1 pound ground, fully cooked ham
½ pound lean, pure ground beef
½ pound lean, ground pork
2 cups bran flakes, rolled (about 1 cup
　rolled flakes)
3 extra-large eggs
¾ cup chopped onions
½ cup chopped green bell peppers
¼ teaspoon pepper
1 recipe Horseradish Sauce (page 361)

Preheat the oven to 350° F. Grease a 9 × 13-inch baking dish; set aside.

In a sieve, drain the tomatoes well; reserve the juice for other uses. In a large mixing bowl, place the drained tomatoes, ground ham, ground beef, ground pork, bran flakes crumbs, eggs, onions, green peppers, and pepper; using a large, metal mixing spoon, break up the ground meats and combine the ingredients well. Using your hands, form the meat mixture into an oval loaf and place it in the prepared dish. Bake, uncovered, for 1½ hours.

To serve, place the ham loaf on a warm, oval serving platter. Cut the loaf into ⅝-inch slices widthwise; then, cut the loaf in half lengthwise, creating 2 pieces of ham loaf per slice. Supply a small serving spatula or a serving fork for serving the ham loaf slices. Pass the Horseradish Sauce in a sauce dish at the table.

SERVES 8

GLAZED HAM LOAF

1½ pounds ground, fully cooked ham
½ pound lean, ground pork
½ pound lean, pure ground beef
22 graham cracker squares, rolled finely
   (about 1⅔ cups)
1 cup whole milk
2 extra-large eggs
¼ teaspoon pepper
Glaze (recipe follows)

Preheat the oven to 350° F. Grease a 9 × 13-inch baking dish; set aside.

In a large mixing bowl, place the ground ham, ground pork, ground beef, graham cracker crumbs, milk, eggs, and pepper; using a large, metal mixing spoon, break up the ground meats and combine the ingredients well. Using your hands, form the meat mixture into an oval loaf and place it in the prepared dish. Bake, uncovered, for 1 hour.

Meanwhile, make the glaze; cover and set aside. When the ham loaf has baked 1 hour, remove it from the oven. Using a baster, draw off and discard any excess fat which has accumulated on the bottom of the dish. Pour the glaze over the loaf and continue baking, uncovered, for ½ hour, basting at least 3 times.

To serve, cut the ham loaf into ⅝-inch slices widthwise; then, cut the loaf in half lengthwise, creating 2 pieces of ham loaf per slice. Serve 2 pieces overlapping, on each individual plate. Spoon a little glaze over the ham loaf slices. Pour the remaining glaze into a sauceboat and pass at the table.

SERVES 8

Glaze

1 cup packed dark brown sugar
2 tablespoons dry mustard
½ cup red wine vinegar
½ cup water
Dash of ground cloves

In a small mixing bowl, place the brown sugar, dry mustard, vinegar, water, and cloves; stir to combine. Do not cook.

ACCOMPANIMENT SUGGESTION: Serve with Carrot Puree (page 311). To serve, place the uncut ham loaf on a serving platter. Using a decorating bag fit with large open-star tip number 8B (page 383), pipe small servings of Carrot Puree on the platter around the ham loaf. Decorate the platter with sprigs of fresh parsley. Cut the ham loaf at the table. Provide the server with a small spatula for use in transferring the decorative portions of Carrot Puree from the serving platter to individual dinner plates.

HAM AND POTATO CROQUETTES

1 pound (about 2 large) russet potatoes,
   pared and cut into thirds
1 tablespoon butter
¼ cup whole milk
4 cups ground, fully cooked ham
1 tablespoon dried parsley
½ teaspoon salt
¼ teaspoon pepper
⅓ cup shredded onions
2 extra-large eggs
2 tablespoons water
1 cup fine Dried Bread Crumbs (page 48)
¼ cup (4 tablespoons) butter, melted
1 recipe Parsley Sauce (page 363)
   (optional)

Place the potatoes in a large saucepan; add hot water to cover. Cover the saucepan. Bring the potatoes to a boil over high heat. Reduce the heat and cook the potatoes at a low boil until tender (about 25 minutes); drain well. Add 1 tablespoon butter and milk to the potatoes; using an electric mixer, beat on high speed to mash. In a large mixing bowl, place the potatoes, ham, parsley, salt, pepper, and onions; using a mixing spoon, stir to combine; set aside.

Preheat the oven to 350°F. Grease a 9 × 13-inch baking pan; set aside.

Place eggs in a small mixing bowl; using an electric mixer, beat lightly on medium speed. Add 2 tablespoons water; beat to blend; set aside. Sprinkle the crumbs over a piece of waxed paper; set aside.

Form cone-shaped croquettes, using ⅓ cup of the ham mixture for each croquette. A small, ⅓-cup-capacity funnel simplifies this task and helps in making uniformly shaped croquettes. Fill the funnel with the mixture; tap out on a clean sheet of waxed paper and roll lightly to make a smooth croquette surface. Dip the croquettes in the egg mixture; then, roll all sides in the crumbs. (The entire surface of the croquettes, including the base, should be coated with the egg mixture and crumbs.) Place the croquettes, upright, in the prepared baking pan, with the base of the cones on the pan bottom. Bake the croquettes for 15 minutes. Remove from the oven and brush the croquettes carefully with melted butter. Return to the oven and bake for an additional 20 minutes. May be served with Parsley Sauce or alone.

MAKES 12 CROQUETTES; SERVES 6

TO DEEP-FAT FRY CROQUETTES: Bread the croquettes by rolling them in the Dried Bread Crumbs, then dipping them in the egg mixture, and rolling them again in the bread crumbs. Fry the croquettes in deep fat for about 2 minutes, or until golden brown, at 380°F. Drain on several layers of paper towels.

HAM PINWHEELS WITH CHEESE SAUCE

¼ cup plus 2 tablespoons (6 tablespoons) butter, softened
¼ cup plus 1 tablespoon prepared mustard
3 cups ground, fully cooked ham
1 recipe Baking Powder Biscuits dough (page 446)
1 recipe Cheese Sauce (page 367)

Preheat the oven to 450°F. Grease two 7 × 11-inch shallow baking pans; set aside.

In a medium mixing bowl, place the butter and mustard; stir to blend. Add the ham; stir to combine; set aside. Make the Baking Powder Biscuit dough. Using a stockinet-covered and lightly-floured rolling pin (page 54), roll out the biscuit dough on a floured pastry cloth to a rectangle approximately 12 × 15 inches. (The biscuit dough will be a little less than ¼ inch thick.)

Spread the ham mixture evenly over the dough. Starting from one of the short sides of the rectangle, roll the dough and ham mixture jelly-roll fashion. With a sharp, thin-bladed knife, cut the 15-inch-long roll into ten 1½-inch slices. Place the pinwheels on the floured pastry cloth. Using a small, floured spatula, flatten each pinwheel to about 1-inch thickness. Place the pinwheels in the prepared baking pans.

Bake the pinwheels for 12 to 15 minutes. Pass warm Cheese Sauce at the table.

SERVES 8 TO 10

Other Pork Recipes

Deluxe Eggplant Stuffed with Ham (page 318)
Eggplant and Ham Casserole (page 318)
Gary's Hickory-Smoked Pork Ribs (page 252)
Grilled Iowa Pork Chops (page 251)
Ham Salad Sandwiches (page 352)
Hot Roast Pork Sandwiches with Chutney (page 353)
Pigs in a Cornfield (page 315)
Mushroom and Cheese-Filled Porkburgers (page 254)
Pork Chop Dinner in Foil (page 299)
Pork Roast with Tangy Rosemary Sauce (page 253)
Pork Salad Sandwiches (page 351)
Scalloped Potatoes with Ham (page 330)

Lamb

BABY LAMB CHOPS

Baby (spring) loin lamb chops, 1¼ to 1½ inches thick (about ⅓ pound per chop)
1 garlic clove
Dash of garlic salt (optional)

Preheat the broiler.

Using a small, sharp knife, slit the fat on the sides of each chop 2 or 3 times at 1-inch intervals to prevent the meat from curling during broiling. When slitting the fat, be careful not to penetrate the meat flesh, causing loss of meat juices. Rub the broiler rack with a small piece of fat; place the rack over the broiler pan. Cut the garlic clove in half lengthwise. Rub both sides of the chops with the cut sides of the garlic. Arrange the chops on the broiler rack; sprinkle lightly with garlic salt, if desired.

Broil the chops 3 inches from the heat. For medium-done chops, broil 6 minutes on each side. For medium-rare chops, broil 5 minutes on each side. For rare chops (see Note), broil 4 minutes on each side. For well-done chops, broil 7 to 8 minutes on each side.

NOTE: There is some bacterial risk when lamb is consumed rare (140° F.) (see Meat Safety, page 157).

ROAST LEG OF LAMB WITH MINT JELLY GLAZE

Shank half of a leg of lamb (4 to 5 pounds)*
1 large garlic clove, cut into 5 slices
½ teaspoon salt
¼ teaspoon pepper
¼ cup mint jelly, home canned (page 742) or commercially canned
⅛ teaspoon garlic salt
1 recipe Roast Lamb Gravy (page 377)
Peppermint Pears, home canned (page 729) or commercially canned, for garnish
Additional mint jelly, if desired

To roast a full leg of lamb, follow this recipe, making no changes, including ingredient amounts.

Preheat the oven to 325° F.

Using a small knife, cut 5 small gashes, equally spaced, around the top and sides of the lamb. Insert one garlic slice in each gash. If the end of the leg bone has been stripped of meat, cover the bone with aluminum foil to prevent over-browning. Place the lamb, fat side up, on a wire rack in a shallow roasting pan. Sprinkle salt and pepper over the roast. Insert a meat thermometer into the center of the lamb, making certain that the tip of the thermometer is not touching the bone.

Place the lamb, uncovered, in the oven. For well-done lamb, roast until the meat thermometer reaches 170° F. (about 30 to 35 minutes per pound). For medium-done lamb, roast until the meat thermometer reaches 160° F. (about 25 to 30 minutes per pound). For medium-rare lamb, roast until the meat thermometer reaches 150° F. (about 20 to 25 minutes per pound). Remove the lamb from the oven when the thermometer reaches 5° F. below desired temperature, as the meat will continue cooking.

(Recipe continues on page 198)

Lamb

• RETAIL CUTS •
WHERE THEY COME FROM
HOW TO COOK THEM

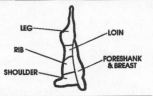

LEG — LOIN
RIB — FORESHANK & BREAST
SHOULDER

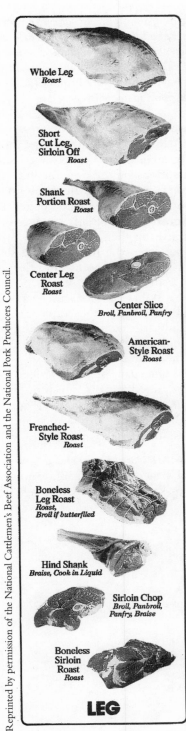

Whole Leg
Roast

Short Cut Leg, Sirloin Off
Roast

Shank Portion Roast
Roast

Center Leg Roast
Roast

Center Slice
Broil, Panbroil, Panfry

American-Style Roast
Roast

Frenched-Style Roast
Roast

Boneless Leg Roast
Roast, Broil if butterflied

Hind Shank
Braise, Cook in Liquid

Sirloin Chop
Broil, Panbroil, Panfry, Braise

Boneless Sirloin Roast
Roast

LEG

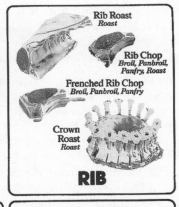

Rib Roast
Roast

Rib Chop
Broil, Panbroil, Panfry, Roast

Frenched Rib Chop
Broil, Panbroil, Panfry

Crown Roast
Roast

RIB

Loin Roast
Roast

Loin Chop
Broil, Panbroil, Panfry

Double Loin Chop
Broil, Panbroil, Panfry

LOIN

Square-Cut Shoulder, Whole
Roast, Braise

Pre-Sliced Shoulder
Roast, Braise

Boneless Shoulder Roast
Roast, Braise

Neck Slice
Braise, Cook in Liquid

Blade Chop
Braise, Broil, Panbroil, Panfry

Arm Chop
Braise, Broil, Panbroil, Panfry

SHOULDER

Shank
Braise, Cook in Liquid

Spareribs
Braise, Broil, Roast

Boneless Rolled Breast
Roast, Braise

Riblets
Braise, Cook in Liquid, Broil

FORESHANK & BREAST

Lamb for Stew
Braise, Cook in Liquid

Cubes for Kabobs
Broil, Braise

Ground Lamb
Broil, Panbroil, Roast (Bake)

OTHER CUTS

THIS CHART APPROVED BY
NATIONAL LIVE STOCK & MEAT BOARD

30 MINUTES BEFORE LAMB IS DONE: In the a small saucepan, place the mint jelly and garlic salt; heat over low heat until the jelly melts, stirring occasionally. Brush the mint glaze over the lamb 3 times during the last 20 minutes of roasting.

TO SERVE LEG OF LAMB: When the meat thermometer registers 5° F. below the desired temperature, remove the lamb from the oven and place it on a platter; cover loosely with aluminum foil to keep warm while making Roast Lamb Gravy. The lamb may be sliced at the table or in the kitchen. Garnish the platter with Peppermint Pears. Pour the gravy into a gravy boat and pass at the table. Unmelted mint jelly may be served at the table, if desired.

SERVES 6

DAY 2 LEG OF LAMB

This dish reflects a common way Midwest cooks turn leftover roast (beef, veal, pork, or lamb), gravy, and vegetables into a tasty new dish for dinner the next evening. In the case of this recipe, there are no leftover vegetables from the preparation of Roast Leg of Lamb with Mint Jelly Glaze (page 196), so newly cooked carrots, mushrooms, and onions are combined with the leftover lamb and gravy.

1¼ cups carrots, pared and sliced ⅛ inch
    thick (about 3 carrots)
2 tablespoons butter
1½ cups sliced, fresh mushrooms
2 tablespoons butter
1 cup coarsely chopped onions
1 garlic clove, pressed
4 cups cold, cubed, cooked Leg of Lamb
    (page 196)
2 cups leftover Roast Lamb Gravy
    (page 377)*

*If there are less than 2 cups of leftover gravy, place ½ cup of the liquid in which the carrots were cooked, and 1 tablespoon flour in a small glass jar or plastic container with a secure lid; cover and shake vigorously until blended. Add to all the ingredients before heating (double the liquid and flour, if needed).

Boil the carrots (page 302); drain (reserve the liquid, if needed [see Note, above]). Set the carrots aside. In a small, heavy-bottomed skillet, melt 2 tablespoons butter over medium heat. Tilt the skillet back and forth to completely cover the bottom with the melted butter. Place the mushrooms in the skillet; sauté until the mushrooms give up their juices (about 5 minutes). Remove from the heat. Using a slotted spoon, remove the mushrooms from the skillet and place in a small bowl; set aside.

Return the skillet to medium heat; add 2 tablespoons butter. When the butter melts, add the onions and garlic; sauté until the onions are transparent and tender (about 5 minutes). Remove from the heat.

In a heavy saucepan, place the cubed lamb, lamb gravy, drained carrots, mushrooms, and onion mixture; stir to combine. Place over medium-high heat; bring to a simmer and cook for 2 minutes, stirring intermittently.

SERVING SUGGESTIONS: Serve Day 2 Leg of Lamb over Mashed Potatoes (page 332), egg noodles (page 283), or Perfect Boiled Rice (page 272).

Poultry and Stuffings (Dressings)

I had a hankering for good old-fashioned fried chicken—the kind that has a rich brown, piquant coating which faintly glistens as it's served straight from the heavy frying pan. But it was only May, and our family's annual Fourth of July fried chicken–potato salad–cherry pie picnic was two months away.

My impatient taste buds triggered a memory recall of the Minburn Cafe, one of those tiny, folksy Midwest eateries where years before I had occasionally gone with my parents for farm-style Sunday chicken dinners—always topped off with a piece of melt-in-your-mouth home-made pie. A telephone call heralded the good news that Shirlie and Keith Simmer were still serving those down-home noon dinners.

Keith told me that after the many hardworking years operating the cafe (Shirlie's mother, Nellie Mishler, opened it in 1947), they had slowed the pace a bit by closing on Sundays. Thursdays were now fried chicken day—from 10:30 A.M. until 2:00 P.M. He advised getting there early before the chicken runs out.

It was a soul-satisfying, comfortable forty-minute drive from my home on the outskirts of West Des Moines to Minburn, Iowa, population 390. If you looked closely, you could see the corn which had pushed just above the coal-black soil to soak in the brilliant midmorning sun. I rolled the window down and let the sweet-smelling breeze whip through my hair as my eyes drank in the beauty of the land, flat in all directions to the horizon.

When I was young, our family constantly drove these country roads back and forth to our Dallas County farms, but somehow I never appreciated the beauty of it all then. Perhaps it was all too close and too familiar. Perhaps it takes sixty years of living and seeing and experiencing to truly recognize beauty.

I arrived at 10:45. The sign CAFE was faded and slightly battered with the scars of time but, like an old trooper, came shining through. Nothing had changed. It was like opening a scrapbook to reminisce over old black-and-white snapshots taken with a Kodak box camera. Shirlie, who had arrived at 4:30 A.M. to bake the pies, greeted a few other early arrivals and me at the door. She seated us at the same chrome and Formica tables I remembered. Keith, who was doing the cooking, left the chicken unattended long enough to come around the corner and add his low-keyed welcome to the informal group of friends and neighbors who had begun to gather in the small dining room. Shirlie and Keith had no other help; they were the alpha and omega of the operation, and I marveled.

In the intervening thirty or more years since my last fried chicken dinner at the Minburn Cafe, I had had the good fortune to eat in some of the finest restaurants in this country and Europe—dining experiences which will remain highlights of my life. In New York, lunches at La Grenouille and dinners at La Côte Basque and Lutèce; lunch at Claridges in London; elegant dinners at the Paris Ritz, fittingly begun with Dom Pérignon; and meals in the rustic Alpine ambience of the Goldener Hirsch in Salzburg. The food I was about to eat, the aggregate experience of the occasion, and the lessons gained, would add the Minburn Cafe to this special list of restaurants where I have enjoyed some of the most memorable meals of a lifetime. At the Minburn Cafe, simplicity became elegance; humble sincerety became grace; plain, wonderful cooking became exquisite cuisine.

As I relished each bite of the unmistakably homemade coleslaw, with that just right combination of salt, pepper, and sugar sparingly mixed with the mayonnaise dressing, the remainder of the five tables filled with friendly folks who all greeted each other and me as Shirlie informally led them to their respective places. There are no strangers in small Midwest places like the Minburn Cafe. You leave pretense at the door and talk about the need for a good rain to germinate the corn not up yet; you chat with Shirlie—as she delivers the heaping plates of food—as unreservedly as if she were your mother serving dinner at the big kitchen table; and mainly, you talk with the other diners about the wonderful food and how you're all eating too much but you don't care—it's worth it. You have the distinct feeling that anyone in that room would come to your aid—a stranger—as if you were family. You sense a deep-seated goodness about these people —an implacable, righteous value system sometimes thought to be in jeopardy of burial in the rubble of civilization's selfishness and greed.

When Keith sent my man-sized plate of food from the kitchen, it was exactly what my deprived palate needed to cure its fried chicken nostalgia—four huge pieces, two white and two dark, including a leg; mashed potatoes and gravy; and baked beans. Of course, I couldn't begin to eat it all, especially with pie coming up, but I did devour the leg and one juicy breast as well as a plentiful amount of the potatoes and beans.

The pie that followed had the makings of one of those stories you repeat over and over again to family and friends for the rest of your life. All four kinds Shirlie had baked that morning were among my favorites: black raspberry, rhubarb, apple, and banana cream. I opted for the black raspberry which had been made from berries given to Shirlie by a friend last year during the raspberry season. Shirlie had frozen them for later use. Simply put, that was the best piece of black raspberry pie I have ever eaten or ever expect to eat. The filling, thickened with flour, was of perfect consistency—not gluelike, yet not runny, causing the slice to lose its shape. And the crust was perfection—the epitome of flakiness, baked to the very second of proper doneness.

As I began to realize how much I had eaten and how full I was, slices of banana cream arrived at the next table. One glimpse was enough

Grant Wood, *Dinner for Threshers*. Fine Arts Museums of San Francisco. Gift of Mr. and Mrs. John D. Rockefeller 3rd, 1979.7.105.

to cause me to lose any discipline I might have had left, not to speak of decorum, and I asked Shirlie if she could spare a piece of banana cream in light of the other customers yet to be served dessert, probably all of whom would qualify as "Die for Pie" people. With no hesitation, which helped relieve my sheepish guilt, she placed an unforgettable piece of banana cream in front of me. I polished it off, not leaving a crumb, and tried to recollect, without success, any other occasion on which I had eaten two pieces of pie at a single meal.

Not too many years have flown by since many a Midwesterner enjoyed similar fried chicken banquets with regularity. Chicken every Sunday was a standard block in the patchwork quilt of Midwest life, and for good reason. Farm women, with few exceptions, raised chickens to supply eggs for their own kitchens and to sell the oversupply in town for what was called "egg money"—traditionally their own cash to spend on little extras and to save for purchasing Christmas presents and the like. Equally important, chickens were a convenient, inexpensive source of fresh, appetizing meat for the table. A few hours before mealtime, rural cooks simply made a trip to the chicken coop or farmyard where they caught and whisked away to kill, pluck, and dress one or more plump birds, depending upon the number of hungry diners scheduled to put their feet under the table.

At harvesttime, when neighboring farmers worked as one group, going from farm to farm to carry out the gargantuan task of getting the crops in, many chickens and a whole lot of mashed potatoes and gravy were required to stage the colossal midday meals prepared by farmwives for the hungry crew.

In those days, occasionally I would be visiting my grandparents at haying or threshing time and would help set the table, pare potatoes, or carry out other rudimentary kitchen tasks. It was a long morning of nonstop work to meet the noon deadline, when we ushered unbelievable quantities of luscious food to the table, including homemade bread or rolls and gigantic pieces of blue ribbon-quality pies and cakes for dessert. After the men had returned to the field, reenergized for the afternoon of taxing physical labor, Grandmother, the one or two other wives who were helping her, and I would clear one end of the table and sit down to eat and catch our breath. Since dishwashers still were only unlikely, futuristic contraptions promised by faraway people who were thought not to have their feet on terra firma, the dishwashing went well into the afternoon.

One of my favorite pictures is Grant Wood's *Dinner for Threshers* because his portrayal is so true to life in so much of the detail. The scene startlingly resembles my grandparents' farm with the red barn trimmed in white outside the side entrance to the house. Just as the picture depicts, Grandmother would place a washbowl and a big pitcher of water on the washstand on the porch for the men to wash their hands and faces (and usually their arms, after which they would ordinarily roll down and button their sleeves before sitting at the table). Grandma also unfailingly had horse pictures on the walls, always hung a little too high (so they wouldn't get bumped). But my favorite part of this picture is use of the pump organ stool for a chair at the table—so very, very typical.

One dissimilarity is the chickens scratching in the barnyard. Grandma was extremely critical of this practice and schooled us emphatically that chickens should be confined to the chicken house and special yard fenced in with chicken wire. (Many farm families allowed their chickens to run loose and, in part, forage for themselves because this practice seemed to result in deeper yellow-orange egg yolks.)

Although the visualization did not come off Grant Wood's brush, you could safely bet your egg money that a big platter of fried chicken would be in view if the farmer sitting on the organ stool would lean to one side.

Threshers' noonday dinners became a thing of the past when big, modern farm equipment was rolled into machine sheds. Modern technology has brought many radical changes to farming and farm life, marked by much larger, more specialized farms. As farming becomes big business, fewer families living in modern farm homes raise chickens for their own consumption.

Although the Sunday fried chicken tradition had become securely vested in city and town life by those who had migrated from the farm, calorie/saturated fat/cholesterol awareness has taken its toll on this farmland custom. When contemporary, health-conscious town and country Heartlanders occasionally decide to jump the track and prepare fried chicken with all the trimmings, what used to be an ambrosial but normal meal becomes more of a special occasion.

Exit fried chicken; enter skinless, boneless chicken breasts. Most Americans, including those who hail from the Midwest, have taken to these touted saints of nutrition with such voraciousness, it gives pause to wonder if one morning we will all wake up cackling and crowing. But chicken breasts are reasonably priced, easy to prepare, and versatile, combining well with a host of diverse seasonings and foods. Ballyhooed for their rock-bottom calories and saturated fat (see the chart, page 156), we are creatively using skinless chicken breasts in salads, pasta dishes, sandwiches, and casseroles, as well as gobbling

them up solo. They are good eating without guilt.

One of the old chicken favorites which has transcended time by safely clearing the nutrition hurdle is Chicken and Noodles (page 210). As popular now as it was at the beginning of the century, it is made with skinless baked chicken, broth, and noodles. The dish seems downright avant-garde when called "pasta." Also high on the list of poultry perennials, the still delicious standby Chicken Salad (page 140) continues to weather every gastronomic and nutrition storm, and is continually reinvented in new guises.

A forgotten old-timer due for a revival in this boneless chicken era is Scalloped Chicken (page 210). For readers under forty who may not have encountered this delicious repast, it is on the order of a combined chicken and dressing dish which is baked. Appropriate for family dining, luncheons, and informal buffet suppers, it is cut into squares and served with a spatula.

Roast Stuffed Turkey (page 212) is part and parcel of Thanksgiving, and in a big share of Midwest homes, it highlights the Christmas meal as well. Shortly after Rudolph guides Santa's sleigh off the rooftop, the mother of the house is up stuffing and trussing the big bird to get it in the oven for the several hours of roasting before the scheduled dinner. By the time the children awaken and race to the tree to see what marvelous toys await them and to see if Santa drank the milk and ate the cookies left for him on the hearth, you can already catch an occasional whiff of the turkey floating through the house like vapor from a magic lamp.

Thanksgiving and Christmas turkeys are calculatedly large in proportion to the number of diners to assure ample leftovers for an encore feast the following day and lunch sandwiches thereafter until the bones are picked clean.

In most corners of the Heartland, stuffing is called "dressing." It is traditionally made with dried bread cubes, celery, onions, and lots of sage, preferably grown in last summer's garden and fastidiously dried, crushed, and stored in an airtight container kept in a cool place to safely lock in the pungent flavor (Sage Dressing, page 215).

However, holiday dressing ingredients definitely are a family thing, passed on from generation to generation as surely as the family farm. Oysters are a prerequisite for dressing in some homes, while siblings in other households are brought up on dressing made with corn bread. Wild rice and chestnut dressings are less frequently spooned from turkeys roasted in the Midland, although new-generation cooks seem to deviate more daringly from old family cooking stencils, introducing interesting and tasty combinations of dressing makin's to the surprise, and often delight, of modern families.

The exclusive relegation of turkey to holiday meals is going by the wayside as turkey breasts are aligning with chicken breasts in everyday-eating popularity. Turkey is now more frequently substituted for chicken in salads and casseroles for a change of pace.

Domestic ducks, geese, pheasants, and quail are rather infrequently served in the Midwest, due in part to the fact that this is prime game-bird country, and Heartlanders are accustomed to eating the real McCoy available in the wild.

Poultry and Stuffings (Dressings) Safety

All poultry sold commercially in the United States must be officially inspected by the Food Safety and Inspection Service of the U.S. Department of Agriculture to ensure that it is wholesome, properly labeled, and not adulterated. Proper handling by the consumer is equally important to ensure that safe poultry is served at the table. To help inform consumers, the USDA requires that safe handling and cooking instructions be placed on all packages of raw poultry, including any poultry product not considered ready-to-eat.

For further assistance, consumers may call the U.S. Department of Agriculture's Meat and Poultry Hotline at 800-535-4555 (in Washing-

ton, D.C., call 202-720-3333), Monday through Friday, 10:00 A.M.–4:00 P.M. Eastern time.

The following are basic guidelines for the safe storage, handling, and cooking of poultry:

• Cook poultry to the following internal temperatures:

Poultry Product	Internal Temperature and Indication
Whole poultry	180° F.—Juices run clear when thigh is pierced with a fork; legs move easily; meat is fork-tender
Poultry breasts, roasts	170° F.—Juices run clear; meat is fork-tender
Poultry thighs, drumsticks, and wings	Cook until juices run clear

• Use a meat thermometer to accurately gauge the internal temperature of whole poultry (see page 44) and poultry breasts (roasts).

Although poultry technically is safe when cooked to an internal temperature of 160° F., most people do not consider the texture or taste to be as palatable as when cooked to the temperatures given above. Always cook ground poultry to 165° F. because bacteria can spread throughout ground poultry during processing.

• Keep raw poultry stored in the refrigerator at 40° F. or below, or in the freezer at 0° F. or below. Cook fresh poultry within 1 or 2 days or freeze it.

• Thaw poultry in the refrigerator, in the microwave oven (see Food Safety: Microwave Ovens, page 31, for procedural information), or in cold water, changing the water every 30 minutes. Do not thaw poultry at room temperature on the kitchen counter or in the sink because surface bacteria on thawed portions of the poultry can multiply to illness-causing levels before inner portions have thawed.

Poultry thawed in the refrigerator may be kept refrigerated 1 to 2 days after thawing. Poultry thawed in the microwave oven or in cold water should be cooked immediately after thawing.

Keep poultry thawed in cold water in a leakproof package or a zipper-seal plastic bag during thawing to prevent bacteria in the surrounding environment from being introduced into the food, and to prevent the poultry tissues from absorbing water, resulting in a watery product.

- Thoroughly rinse raw, thawed poultry under cold, running water, and dry it with paper towels before cooking.

- Throw away poultry packaging material.

- Completely cook poultry at one time. Do not partially cook it, refrigerate it, and then complete the cooking at a later time.

- Stuff whole poultry *just before* cooking. Mix dry stuffing (dressing) ingredients with other stuffing (dressing) ingredients, such as butter and broth, just before stuffing the bird. Stuff the bird fairly loosely, as the stuffing (dressing) will expand during cooking. Cook stuffing (dressing) in the bird or separately, to 165° F.; use a meat thermometer or instant thermometer to check the temperature.

- Place cooked poultry on a clean platter, not on the unwashed platter that held the raw poultry.

- Refrigerate poultry within 2 hours after cooking. Remove the stuffing (dressing) from the bird and refrigerate it in a separate container. For quicker cooling, it is best to remove the meat from the bones before refrigeration. If there is a large quantity of leftover poultry, store it in several shallow containers to expedite cooling.

- Use refrigerated, leftover poultry and stuffing (dressing) within 3 to 4 days, or freeze these foods. If leftover poultry is covered with gravy or broth, use it within 1 to 2 days or freeze it. Eat cooked leftover poultry cold, or reheat it to at least 165° F. (steaming hot).

- Wash your hands with soap and hot water before and after handling raw or cooked poultry. Wash kitchen tools and equipment, cutting boards and other work surfaces, sink, and faucet handles with hot, soapy water after they come in contact with raw or cooked poultry, and before they come in contact with other food.

Chicken

COOKED CHICKEN
For Salads and Other Dishes

4 pounds split chicken breasts *with* skin*
(may have attached ribs)
1 tablespoon butter, melted

While the breast is the most desirable chicken part to use in salads and most dishes, any other parts of choice may be substituted. Baking chicken pieces with the skin on and then removing the skin after baking results in more moist cut-up chicken.

Preheat the oven to 350° F.

Wash the chicken under cold, running water and place it between several layers of paper towels to dry. When dry, place the chicken breasts, single layer, skin side up, in an ungreased 9 × 13-inch baking dish. Brush the chicken with the melted butter. Cover the baking dish tightly with aluminum foil, leaving space between the foil and the chicken. Bake for 1¼ hours, until fork-tender.

While the chicken is hot, remove the skin and bones; discard. Place the breasts in a container or bowl; cover and refrigerate. When the chicken is cold, cut into desired pieces.

MAKES ABOUT 4 CUPS COOKED, CUT-UP CHICKEN

BAKED CUT-UP CHICKEN

3 to 4 pounds cut-up chicken with skin
  (chicken parts of choice)
2 tablespoons butter
1/8 teaspoon salt
Dash of white pepper
2 teaspoons snipped, fresh summer savory
  or 3/4 teaspoon dried leaf summer savory

Preheat the oven to 350° F. Butter lightly a
9 × 13-inch baking dish.

Wash the chicken pieces under cold, running
water and place them between several layers of
paper towels to dry. When dry, place the chicken
pieces, single layer, skin side down, in the prepared baking dish. Dot the chicken with the
butter.

Bake the chicken, uncovered, for 30 minutes.
Turn the chicken pieces over; sprinkle with salt,
pepper, and savory. Bake, uncovered, for an
additional 30 minutes, until fork-tender.

SERVES 6 TO 8

CHICKEN BREASTS STUFFED WITH SPINACH AND MUSHROOMS

A nice party-time entrée for luncheons or dinners.

8 whole, boneless chicken breasts *with* skin,
  cut in half lengthwise
1 1/2 pounds fresh spinach
3 tablespoons butter
2/3 cup finely chopped onions
8 ounces finely chopped, fresh mushrooms
1 tablespoon dry white wine
1/3 cup Ritz cracker crumbs (about 8 finely
  rolled crackers)
1 extra-large egg, slightly beaten
2 teaspoons freshly squeezed, strained
  lemon juice
1/2 cup fresh parsley leaves (stems removed)
1 teaspoon dried leaf tarragon
3/4 teaspoon salt
1/4 teaspoon pepper
1/4 cup (4 tablespoons) butter, melted

Wash the chicken breasts under cold, running
water and place them between several layers of
paper towels to dry; set aside.

Cut the stems off the spinach leaves; discard
the stems. Wash the spinach leaves twice. Place
the spinach in a large kettle and add water to
cover. Cover the kettle. Bring the spinach to a
boil over high heat. Reduce the heat and simmer 4 minutes. Drain the spinach in a colander;
with your hand, press the spinach to remove as
much liquid as possible. Using a sharp knife,
chop the spinach (about 1 cup cooked and
chopped spinach); set aside.

Preheat the oven to 350° F. Butter a 9 × 13-
inch baking dish; set aside.

In a heavy-bottomed skillet, melt 3 tablespoons butter over medium-high heat. Tilt the
skillet back and forth to completely cover the
bottom with the melted butter. Place the onions
in the skillet; sauté 1 minute. Then, add the
mushrooms; sauté an additional 4 minutes, until
very little liquid remains in the skillet. Remove
the skillet from the heat and let cool slightly.
Add the white wine and stir in; set aside. In a
large mixing bowl, place the spinach, onion
mixture, crumbs, egg, lemon juice, parsley, tarragon, salt, pepper, and 1/4 cup melted butter; stir
until well combined; set aside.

Using your fingers, open a 2 1/2-inch-wide
pocket between the skin and flesh on the side
opposite the cut side of each chicken breast.
Stuff the pocket of each breast with 1 heaping
tablespoon of stuffing. Pull the skin over the
stuffing and under the side of each breast; secure
with half a toothpick. Tuck the extra skin on
both ends of each breast under the breast and
place, single layer, in the prepared baking dish.

Bake the chicken breasts, uncovered, for 50
minutes. *Remove the toothpicks before serving.*

SERVES 16

ACCOMPANIMENT SUGGESTION: Serve with Baked
Rice (page 275).

CHICKEN DIVAN

A true American classic that continues to thread across the generations—you just can't go wrong serving Chicken Divan, for luncheons, dinners, suppers, buffets, and family meals.

1 recipe (4 pounds) Cooked Chicken breasts (page 204) skinned, boned (if any bones), and refrigerated. Reserve and refrigerate baking-dish juices in a separate, covered bowl
7 cups fresh broccoli spears
2 recipes Thick White Sauce (page 366), substituting 1 cup whole milk and 1 cup chicken broth for 2 cups whole milk
1 cup Miracle Whip salad dressing
3 tablespoons freshly squeezed, strained lemon juice
½ teaspoon curry powder
2 tablespoons freshly grated Parmesan cheese (page 46)

Preheat the oven to 350° F. Butter lightly a 9 × 13-inch baking dish; set aside.

Cut the cold chicken breasts widthwise into ³⁄₁₆-inch slices; arrange in the bottom of the prepared baking dish; set aside. Steam the broccoli spears (page 302) until just tender (about 5 minutes). Place the steamed broccoli spears in a colander and rinse under cold, running water to stop the cooking; let stand to drain well.

Skim the congealed fat off the top of the cold, chicken baking-dish juices and discard; use the remaining chicken broth to make Thick White Sauce (see recipe ingredients, above). If necessary, add homemade (page 88) or commercially canned chicken broth to make 1 cup broth. Add the salad dressing, lemon juice, and curry powder to the white sauce; using a handheld electric mixer, beat on low speed only until blended and smooth. Set aside.

Arrange the drained broccoli spears over the chicken in the baking dish. Pour the white sauce mixture evenly over the broccoli spears. Sprinkle the Parmesan cheese evenly over all. Bake,

uncovered, until the Chicken Divan bubbles (about 30 minutes).

SERVES 8

SESAME CHICKEN BREASTS

2 whole, skinless, boneless chicken breasts, cut in half lengthwise (1 to 1¼ pounds total chicken breasts)
⅓ cup chicken broth, homemade (page 88) or commercially canned
¼ cup dry white wine
1 tablespoon freshly squeezed, strained lemon juice
1 tablespoon minced green onions (scallions), white part only
2 teaspoons honey
2 teaspoons extra-virgin olive oil
1 tablespoon butter
½ teaspoon lemon pepper, divided
2 tablespoons dry white wine
½ teaspoon cornstarch
1 teaspoon toasted sesame seeds (page 50)

Wash the chicken breasts under cold, running water and place them between several layers of paper towels to dry; set aside. In a small mixing bowl, place the chicken broth, ¼ cup white wine, lemon juice, onions, and honey; stir to combine. Cover with plastic wrap and set aside.

In a large, heavy-bottomed skillet, heat the olive oil over medium-high heat. Using a spatula, spread the olive oil over the entire bottom of the skillet. Add the butter. Tilt the skillet back and forth to blend the butter with the oil. Place the chicken breasts, single layer, skin side down, in the skillet. Sprinkle ¼ teaspoon of the lemon pepper over the breasts. Sauté the chicken breasts 3 minutes. Turn the breasts over and sprinkle with the remaining ¼ teaspoon lemon pepper. Sauté the breasts 3 minutes on the second side. Reduce the heat to low. Remove the skillet from the heat and let cool slightly. Then, pour the chicken broth mixture around (not over) the breasts.

Cover the skillet and place over low heat. Bring the chicken breasts to a simmer; simmer gently 5 minutes. Do not overcook the breasts, causing them to become tough.

Place the chicken breasts on a platter and cover with aluminum foil to keep warm. Increase the heat under the skillet to high; cook until the skillet liquid reduces to about ⅔ cup. Meanwhile, in a small sauce dish, place 2 tablespoons white wine and cornstarch; stir until blended. Add the cornstarch mixture to the reduced skillet liquid; continue cooking until the sauce thickens, stirring continuously. Spoon the sauce over the chicken breasts; then, sprinkle the sesame seeds over top.

SERVES 4

CHICKEN BREASTS BAKED IN SHERRY SAUCE

4 whole, skinless, boneless chicken breasts, cut in half lengthwise (2 to 2½ pounds total chicken breasts)
3 tablespoons butter
3 tablespoons all-purpose flour
½ teaspoon celery salt
⅛ teaspoon white pepper
3 tablespoons butter
1 cup whole milk
8 ounces commercial sour cream
1 tablespoon butter
¼ cup minced celery
3 tablespoons minced leeks
1 tablespoon butter
¾ cup sliced, fresh mushrooms
1 teaspoon dried leaf chervil
¼ cup dry sherry

Preheat the oven to 325° F. Butter very lightly a 9 × 13-inch baking dish; set aside.

Wash the chicken breasts under cold, running water and place them between several layers of paper towels to dry; set aside.

In an electric skillet or a large, heavy-bottomed skillet on the range, melt 3 tablespoons butter over medium-low heat (320° F. in an electric skillet). Tilt the skillet back and forth to completely cover the bottom with the melted butter. Place the chicken breasts in the skillet; brown lightly (2 minutes on each side). Drain the browned chicken breasts on 3 layers of paper towels. Then, arrange the chicken breasts, single layer, in the prepared baking dish; set aside.

In a small sauce dish, place the flour, celery salt, and white pepper; stir to combine; set aside. In a medium saucepan, melt 3 tablespoons butter over low heat. Remove from the heat. Add the flour mixture; stir until perfectly smooth. Add the milk; stir to combine. Place the saucepan over medium-low heat; cook the mixture until thick and just under boiling, stirring constantly. Do not allow the mixture to boil. Remove from the heat. Add the sour cream; stir until smooth and blended; set aside.

In a small, heavy-bottomed skillet, melt 1 tablespoon butter over medium heat. Do not let the butter brown. Place the celery in the skillet; sauté 4 minutes (do not brown). Remove from the heat. Using a slotted spoon, remove the sautéed celery (excluding pan juices) from the skillet and add to the sour cream mixture; set aside. Place the leeks in the skillet used for sautéing the celery; sauté 3 minutes over medium heat (do not brown). Remove from the heat. Using a slotted spoon, remove the sautéed leeks (excluding pan juices) from the skillet and add to the sour cream mixture; set aside.

Add 1 tablespoon butter to the skillet used for sautéing the celery and leeks. Melt the butter over medium heat. Place the mushrooms in the skillet; sauté 3 minutes, until the mushrooms give up their juices (do not brown). Add the mushrooms and pan juices, and the chervil and sherry to the sour cream mixture; stir until all ingredients are combined. Pour evenly over the chicken breasts. Bake, uncovered, for 40 minutes.

SERVES 8

SERVING SUGGESTION: Serve the chicken breasts on individual dinner plates over Perfect Boiled Rice (page 272). Spoon additional sherry sauce from the baking dish over all.

ROSEMARY CHICKEN BREASTS WITH RED RASPBERRY SAUCE

I hope you try (and like) this contemporary chicken breast recipe. It blends red raspberry vinegar, chicken broth, crème de cassis, and honey in a luscious sauce punctuated with whole, fresh raspberries. The sauce is spooned over boneless chicken breasts which have been sautéed over fresh rosemary.

2 whole, skinless, boneless chicken breasts, cut in half lengthwise (1 to 1 1/4 pounds total chicken breasts)
2/3 cup chicken broth, homemade (page 88) or commercially canned
3 tablespoons red raspberry vinegar
1 tablespoon crème de cassis (page 21)
2 tablespoons honey
2 teaspoons cornstarch
1/4 teaspoon salt
1/8 teaspoon white pepper
1 tablespoon vegetable oil
1 tablespoon butter
1 teaspoon snipped, fresh rosemary
5 drops liquid red food coloring (optional)
1/2 cup fresh red raspberries, washed and well drained
4 sprigs of fresh rosemary for decoration

Wash the chicken breasts under cold, running water and place them between several layers of paper towels to dry; set aside. In a small saucepan, place the chicken broth, vinegar, crème de cassis, honey, cornstarch, salt, and white pepper; stir until blended; set aside.

In a large, heavy-bottomed skillet, heat the vegetable oil over medium-high heat. Using a spatula, spread the vegetable oil over the entire bottom of the skillet. Add the butter. Tilt the skillet back and forth to blend the butter with the oil. Sprinkle the rosemary evenly over the bottom of the skillet. Then, place the chicken breasts, single layer, skin side down, in the skillet. Sauté the breasts 3 minutes on each side, until cooked through, turning once.

Meanwhile, place the saucepan containing the raspberry vinegar mixture over medium heat; bring the mixture to a low boil, stirring constantly. Boil the mixture 5 minutes until clear, thickened, and slightly reduced, stirring often. Remove from the heat; add the food coloring (if used) and stir until blended. Add the raspberries; return to medium heat, and quickly heat through without stirring, to prevent breaking up the raspberries. Remove from the heat; cover to keep warm and set aside.

After the chicken breasts have been sautéed 3 minutes on each side, remove from the heat; cover and let stand 1 minute. To serve, place the chicken breasts on individual dinner plates. Carefully spoon the raspberry sauce over each chicken breast. Decorate each plate with a sprig of fresh rosemary.

SERVES 4

CHICKEN THIGHS WITH PEACH-APRICOT GLAZE

3 1/2 to 4 pounds chicken thighs* with skin
2 tablespoons butter
1/3 cup peach jam, home canned (page 750) or commercially canned
1/3 cup apricot jam, home canned (page 747) or commercially canned
2 teaspoons cider vinegar
2 teaspoons soy sauce
1 teaspoon dry mustard

*Any other chicken parts of choice may be substituted.

Preheat the oven to 350°F. Butter lightly a 9 × 13-inch baking dish; set aside.

Wash the chicken thighs under cold, running water and dry between several layers of paper towels. Place the chicken thighs, single layer, skin side down, in the prepared baking dish; dot with the butter. Bake, uncovered, for 40 minutes.

Meanwhile, in a small mixing bowl, place the peach jam, apricot jam, vinegar, soy sauce, and dry mustard; stir until evenly combined.

After 40 minutes baking, turn the chicken over and spoon ½ of the jam mixture (glaze) over the thighs. Bake, uncovered, for an additional 10 minutes. Spoon the remaining ½ glaze over the thighs. Bake for an additional 10 minutes, until fork-tender.

SERVES 6 TO 8

CHICKEN À LA KING

This is one of those grand old dishes which never goes out of style. The origin of this refined chicken fare is a matter of debate. However, published records verify its existence in the early twentieth century, and some argue that it dates back to the last quarter of the nineteenth century. One thing we can say with certainty: it will remain popular into the twenty-first century!

3 tablespoons butter
3 cups sliced, fresh mushrooms (about 8 ounces mushrooms)
2 tablespoons very finely chopped onions
½ cup all-purpose flour
1 teaspoon salt
¼ teaspoon white pepper
½ cup (¼ pound) butter
2 cups (1 pint) half-and-half
2 cups chicken broth, homemade (page 88) or commercially canned
4 cups cold, cooked, skinless chicken-breast meat cut into bite-sized pieces (cook and prepare about 4 pounds split chicken breasts *with* skin [may have attached ribs], page 204)
1 4 ounce jar sliced pimientos, drained and coarsely chopped (¼ cup)
2 extra-large egg yolks, slightly beaten
2 tablespoons dry sherry

In a medium, heavy-bottomed skillet, melt 3 tablespoons butter over medium heat. Tilt the skillet back and forth to completely cover the bottom with the melted butter. Place the mushrooms in the skillet; sauté until the mushrooms give up their juices (about 7 minutes). Using a slotted spoon, remove the mushrooms from the skillet and place them in a small mixing bowl; set aside. Add the onions to the skillet; sauté lightly for about 2 minutes. Do not allow the onions to brown. Add the onions and skillet liquid to the sautéed mushrooms in the mixing bowl; set aside.

In a small mixing bowl, place the flour, salt, and white pepper; stir to combine; set aside. In a large saucepan, melt ½ cup butter over low heat. Remove from the heat. Add the flour mixture and stir until perfectly smooth. Add the half-and-half and chicken broth; stir to combine. Place the saucepan over medium heat; cook the mixture until thick and just *under* a simmer, stirring constantly. Remove from the heat. Add the mushroom mixture, chicken, and pimientos; stir to combine. Return to medium heat; heat through but do not allow the mixture to simmer. (At this point, the saucepan may be covered and the chicken mixture refrigerated until shortly before serving time.)

Just prior to serving time, heat the chicken mixture over medium-low heat, stirring often. Spoon about ¾ cup of the hot chicken mixture over the egg yolks in a small bowl; stir in. Add the egg yolk mixture to the chicken mixture; stir well to blend. While stirring constantly, continue cooking over medium-low heat until the mixture thickens slightly more from addition of the egg yolks, but do not allow it to simmer (about 3 minutes). Add the sherry; stir to blend. Serve immediately.

SERVES 8

SERVING SUGGESTIONS: Serve over Puff Pastry Shells (Patty Shells) (page 470), Perfect Boiled Rice (page 272), or Mashed Potatoes (page 332).

CHICKEN AND NOODLES

2 tablespoons butter
8 ounces sliced, fresh mushrooms (about 3 cups)
2 cups chicken broth, homemade (page 88) or commercially canned, divided
1 tablespoon all-purpose flour
1 teaspoon salt
½ teaspoon pepper
12 cups water
12 ounces egg noodles
4 cups cold, cooked, skinless white and dark chicken meat cut into bite-sized pieces (cook and prepare about 4 pounds chicken pieces *with* skin, page 204)
2 tablespoons butter, melted

In a medium, heavy-bottomed skillet, melt 2 tablespoons butter over medium heat. Tilt the skillet back and forth to completely cover the bottom with the melted butter. Place the mushrooms in the skillet; sauté until the mushrooms give up their juices (about 5 minutes). Do not let the butter or mushrooms brown. Set aside.

Pour about ⅓ cup of the chicken broth into a small glass jar or plastic container with a secure lid. Add the flour. Cover and shake vigorously until blended and smooth; set aside. In a large saucepan, place the remaining 1⅔ cups chicken broth, salt, and pepper; bring the mixture to a boil over medium-high heat. Add the flour mixture; stir to blend. Return to a simmer and cook until the mixture thickens slightly (about 2 minutes), stirring continuously. Remove from the heat; cover and set aside.

Pour 12 cups water into a small kettle or large saucepan; cover and bring to a boil over high heat. Add the noodles; boil, uncovered, until the noodles are tender (about 10 minutes), stirring often. Meanwhile, add the chicken to the broth mixture and heat through over medium-low heat, stirring often.

Drain the noodles in a sieve; return the noodles to the kettle and rinse in very hot water. Drain the noodles again in the sieve. Return the well-drained noodles to the kettle. Add 2 tablespoons melted butter and toss until the noodles are evenly coated. Add the hot chicken mixture and mushrooms with pan liquids; toss lightly to combine.

SERVES 8

TRADITIONAL SERVING ACCOMPANIMENTS: Chicken and Noodles are traditionally served with Mashed Potatoes (page 332). Diners spoon Chicken and Noodles over their Mashed Potatoes. Baking Powder Biscuits (page 446) also are a favorite accompaniment.

SCALLOPED CHICKEN

When I was a young camper at Clearwater Camp on Tomahawk Lake near Minocqua, Wisconsin, this was my all-time favorite Sunday-noon dinner dish, which was often served by the fabulous cook, Andy.

4 cups cold, cooked, skinless, white and dark chicken meat cut into bite-sized pieces (cook and prepare about 4 pounds chicken parts *with* skin, page 204)
3½ cups chicken broth, homemade (page 88) or commercially canned
⅓ cup chopped celery
½ cup finely chopped onions
1 teaspoon dried leaf thyme
½ teaspoon salt
¼ teaspoon pepper
4 extra-large eggs, slightly beaten
2 tablespoons butter
2 cups sliced, fresh mushrooms (5 to 6 ounces mushrooms)
3 cups small, fresh bread cubes, ½ white and ½ whole wheat*
2 recipes Medium White Sauce (page 336), substituting 1 cup whole milk and 1 cup chicken broth (homemade, page 88, or commercially canned) for 2 cups whole milk

All white or all whole-wheat fresh bread cubes may be used.

Preheat the oven to 350° F. Grease a 9 × 13-inch baking dish; set aside.

In a large mixing bowl, place the chicken, 3½ cups chicken broth, celery, onions, thyme, salt, pepper, and eggs; do not mix; set aside. In a small skillet, melt the butter over low heat. Tilt the skillet back and forth to completely cover the bottom with the melted butter. Place the mushrooms in the skillet; sauté slowly until the mushrooms give up their juices (about 5 minutes). Keep the heat low to prevent the butter from browning. Add the mushrooms and skillet juices to the chicken mixture. Add the bread cubes. Using a large mixing spoon, fold all the ingredients together; turn into the prepared baking dish and spread evenly. Bake, uncovered, for 45 minutes.

Meanwhile, make the Medium White Sauce.

To serve, cut the Scalloped Chicken into square servings. Using a spatula, place 1 serving on each individual plate. Pour the hot white sauce into a sauce dish and pass at the table.

SERVES 12

FRIED CHICKEN

This is a very popular way to prepare fried chicken in the Midwest (and the way our family has fixed it for three generations). After frying the chicken in vegetable oil and butter over high heat to as deep a brown as possible, reduce the heat to low, pour off all but a little of the skillet liquid, and cover. After cooking 1 hour undisturbed (don't turn the pieces), the chicken will be succulent and tender, with a deep, rich outer flavoring.

Tip: When I'm preparing a large quantity of Fried Chicken for our family's annual Fourth of July picnic, I take the electric skillet to the garage and do the browning out there on a table covered with paper towels to keep the spattering out of the kitchen. (When you fry chicken over high heat to achieve deep browning, there is considerable and unavoidable spattering). Then, I bring the skilletful of browned chicken back into the house for the final hour of cooking.

1 3- to 4-pound chicken (fryer), cut up
½ cup all-purpose flour
1½ teaspoons salt
¼ teaspoon pepper
1 teaspoon paprika
¼ cup vegetable oil
1 tablespoon butter

Wash the chicken pieces under cold, running water and place them between several layers of paper towels to dry; set aside. In a small mixing bowl, place the flour, salt, pepper, and paprika; stir until combined thoroughly. Sprinkle the flour mixture over a piece of waxed paper; dredge the chicken pieces in the mixture. Shake the chicken pieces to remove excess flour and place, single layer, on a clean piece of waxed paper; set aside.

Preheat an electric skillet or a large, heavy-bottomed skillet on the range to high heat (400° F. in an electric skillet). Pour the vegetable oil into the skillet. Tilt the skillet back and forth to completely cover the bottom with the vegetable oil. Add the butter; spread to blend the butter with the oil. Place the chicken pieces, single layer, in the skillet; fry until a deep golden brown (about 10 to 15 minutes), turning once or twice. Reduce the skillet heat to low (250° F. in an electric skillet); pour off excess liquid, if necessary, to leave about ¼ inch liquid in the skillet. Cover the skillet and cook the chicken 1 hour, until fork-tender.

NOTE: When browning larger quantities of chicken, it may be necessary intermittently to add more vegetable oil and butter to the skillet. In the final recipe step, pile all of the browned chicken in the skillet, cover, and cook for 1 hour at 250° F., until fork-tender.

SERVES 4 TO 5

SERVING SUGGESTIONS

• In the summer, serve with Potato Salad (page 133). During warm months, Fried Chicken may be served at room temperature or chilled. Wonderful for picnics.

(Recipe continues on next page)

- In the winter, serve with Mashed Potatoes (page 332) and Milk Gravy (page 375). The gravy should be served on the Mashed Potatoes, and should not be served over or under the Fried Chicken. Spiced Peaches (page 774) are an excellent accompaniment.

BARBECUED CHICKEN

1 3-pound chicken (fryer), cut up
2 tablespoons butter
1¼ cups Barbecue Sauce (page 360), divided

Preheat the oven to 350°F. Butter the bottom and 2 inches up the side of a Dutch oven.

Wash the chicken pieces under cold, running water and place them between several layers of paper towels to dry. When dry, place the chicken pieces, skin side down, in the prepared Dutch oven; dot with the butter.

Bake the chicken, uncovered, for 30 minutes. Turn the chicken pieces over; Bake, uncovered, for an additional 30 minutes. Reduce the oven heat to 325°F. Pour ¾ cup of the Barbecue Sauce over the chicken; cover and bake for 30 minutes. Then, pour the remaining ½ cup Barbecue Sauce over the chicken; uncover and bake for an additional 30 minutes, until fork-tender.

SERVES 6

Other Chicken Recipes

Chicken Salad (page 140)
Hot Chicken Salad (page 141)
Mesquite-Grilled Chicken Breasts (page 254)
Mesquite-Grilled Chicken Salad (page 141)
Plain Grilled Chicken Breasts (page 255)
Rotisserie Chicken with Orange-Ginger Glaze (page 256)
Warm Chicken-Vegetable Salad with Pistachio Nuts and Raspberry Vinaigrette Dressing (page 142)

Turkey

ROAST STUFFED TURKEY

1 6- to 24-pound dressed turkey, fresh or frozen (allow 1 pound per serving for birds 12 pounds or under, and ¾ pound per serving for birds over 12 pounds)
Dressing (stuffing) of choice (page 215)
Vegetable oil
Turkey Gravy (or Turkey Giblet Gravy) (page 378)

TO THAW FROZEN TURKEY: Although a whole turkey purchased frozen may safely be thawed in the refrigerator, in cold water, or in the microwave oven, I prefer thawing in the refrigerator. Procedures for all 3 methods of thawing follow.

To thaw in the refrigerator, keep the turkey wrapped and place it in a pan; let stand about 24 hours for each 5 pounds of turkey. Let large turkeys stand a maximum of 5 days in the refrigerator. The giblets and neck are customarily packed in the neck and body cavities of frozen turkeys. They may be removed from the cavities near the end of the thawing period to expedite complete thawing of the bird. If desired, the giblets and neck may be refrigerated and reserved for use in Giblet Gravy.

To thaw in cold water, make certain that the turkey is in a leakproof package or a zipper-seal plastic bag. This prevents bacteria in the surrounding environment from being introduced into the food, and prevents the poultry tissues from absorbing water, resulting in a watery product. Change the cold water every 30 minutes. Approximately 30 minutes per pound of turkey are required for thawing. After thawing in cold water, the turkey should be cooked immediately.

To thaw in the microwave oven, consult the manufacturer's instructions for the size turkey that will fit into your oven, the minutes per pound and power level to use for thawing. Turkeys thawed in the microwave must be cooked immediately after thawing (see Microwave Ovens, page 31, for further information on this food safety guideline).

TO REFRIGERATE FRESH TURKEY: A whole turkey purchased fresh (not frozen) may safely be refrigerated up to 2 days before roasting.

TO PREPARE THE TURKEY FOR ROASTING: *Do not stuff the turkey until immediately before roasting.* When ready to roast the turkey, rinse the outside and cavities of the bird under cold, running water. Cut away and discard any fat remaining on the bird. Place the turkey on several layers of paper towels to drain. Using additional paper towels, pat the outside and cavities dry.

To stuff the turkey, stand the bird on its tail end in a large bowl; using a tablespoon, stuff the neck cavity loosely with dressing. Pull the neck skin over the dressing and fasten it to the body with a poultry skewer. Turn the bird and place the neck end in the bowl; stuff the body cavity loosely with dressing. It is important to stuff the dressing fairly loosely in the bird because dressing expands during cooking.

Remove the turkey from the bowl and lay the bird, breast side up, on a piece of waxed paper or directly on a clean work surface. Pull the legs close to the body and tie the ends together with cotton string. If the tail has been left on the bird, tie the legs to the tail to partially close the body cavity. Some frozen turkeys are packed with a metal clamp to secure the legs, in which case it is not necessary to tie the legs with string. Fold the wings under the bird to provide a platform for roasting.

Place the turkey, breast side up, on a wire rack in a shallow roasting pan. Brush all the exposed surfaces of the bird with vegetable oil. Insert a meat thermometer into one of the inner thigh areas near the breast, making certain the tip of the thermometer is not touching bone. While many commercial turkeys are packed with a disposable thermometer preinserted into the breast which is designed to pop up when the bird is done, a standard meat thermometer, inserted into the thickest part of the thigh at the time the turkey is placed in the oven for roasting, is considered a more reliable means of determining doneness. Also, a standard meat thermometer makes it possible to know how close the turkey is to being done—an aid in timing preparation of the remainder of the meal.

TO ROAST THE TURKEY: Preheat the oven to 325° F.

Cover the turkey loosely with extra-heavy aluminum foil, leaving space between the bird and the foil. Lightly tuck the foil around the front, back, and sides of the bird. Do not add water to the pan. Roast the turkey until the meat thermometer reaches 180° F. and the juices run clear, which will take the following approximate time:

Approximate Roasting Times

Turkey Weight	Hours
6–8 pounds	3–3½
8–12 pounds	3½–4½
12–16 pounds	4½–5½
16–20 pounds	5½–6
20–24 pounds	6–6½

The roasting time may vary up to 30 minutes, depending upon the bird and the oven. Use the meat thermometer to check the temperature of the dressing. The center of the dressing inside the bird (or in a separate baking dish) must reach a temperature of 165° F. for food safety.

Remove the aluminum foil about 30 minutes before the turkey is done to complete the browning of the bird.

When done, remove the turkey from the oven and place it on a serving platter or carving board; cover loosely with aluminum foil and let it stand 10 minutes before carving. Meanwhile, make the Turkey Gravy (or Giblet Gravy). Remove all the dressing from the neck and body cavities before carving the turkey. Pour the gravy into a gravy boat and pass at the table.

(Recipe continues on next page)

TRADITIONAL ACCOMPANIMENT: Mashed Potatoes (page 332) are traditionally served with turkey at holiday meals.

ROAST UNSTUFFED TURKEY: Follow the Roast Stuffed Turkey recipe, above, omitting the dressing (stuffing). Roast the turkey until the meat thermometer reaches 180° F., which will take the following approximate time:

Approximate Roasting Times

Turkey Weight	Hours
6–8 pounds	2½–3
8–12 pounds	3–4
12–16 pounds	4–5
16–20 pounds	5–5½
20–24 pounds	5½–6

ROAST TURKEY BREAST

1 5- to 7-pound fresh (or frozen and
   thawed) turkey breast
Vegetable oil

Preheat the oven to 325° F.

Brush the turkey breast with vegetable oil. Insert the meat thermometer to the center of the breast. Wrap and seal the breast in extra-heavy aluminum foil, with the face of the meat thermometer on the outside of the foil for viewing. Place on a wire rack in a shallow roasting pan.

Roast the turkey breast until the meat thermometer reaches 170° F. (about 2 to 2¾ hours). Open the aluminum foil about 30 minutes before the breast is done and baste 2 times with drippings.

SERVES 12

PRONTO SPICY TURKEY TENDERLOINS

1 8-ounce jar (about 1 cup) commercially
   canned mild salsa
2 tablespoons dry red wine
1 tablespoon peach jam, home canned
   (page 750) or commercially canned
¼ teaspoon salt
¾ cup zucchini cut into ½-inch cubes
⅔ cup sliced, fresh mushrooms
1 tablespoon vegetable oil
2 5- to 7-ounce turkey tenderloins
½ teaspoon cornstarch

In a medium mixing bowl, place the salsa, wine, jam, and salt; stir to combine. Add the zucchini and mushrooms; stir to combine; set aside. In a medium, heavy-bottomed skillet, heat the vegetable oil over medium heat. Using a spatula, spread the vegetable oil over the entire bottom of the skillet. Place the tenderloins in the skillet; sauté 3 minutes on each side, until lightly browned. Remove the skillet from the heat and let stand until cooled slightly. Reduce the range heat to medium-low.

When the skillet cools, pour the salsa mixture over the tenderloins. Cover the skillet and place over medium-low heat. Bring the tenderloins to a simmer and simmer 12 to 18 minutes (depending upon the thickness of the tenderloins), until no pink color remains in the turkey meat. Remove the skillet from the heat.

Using a spatula, place the tenderloins on individual plates or on a serving plate. Using a slotted spoon, lift the remaining vegetables from the sauce in the skillet and place over the tenderloins. Cover the tenderloins lightly with aluminum foil to keep warm. Add the cornstarch to the sauce in the skillet; stir vigorously until completely blended. Place the skillet over medium heat; bring the sauce to a boil, stirring constantly. Boil for about 30 seconds until the sauce thickens, stirring continuously. Spoon the sauce over the turkey tenderloins and vegetables.

SERVES 2

Other Turkey Recipes

Arabesque Turkey Salad (page 142)

Stuffings (Dressings)

SAGE DRESSING

7 cups Dried Bread Cubes (page 48),
  ½ white and ½ whole wheat*
1 cup medium-finely chopped celery
¾ cup chopped onions
1 tablespoon plus 2 teaspoons coarsely
  crushed dried leaf sage
1 teaspoon salt
¼ teaspoon pepper
¼ teaspoon poultry seasoning
½ cup (¼ pound) butter, melted
1 cup hot water

  *Although not as desirable in my opinion, all
  white or all whole-wheat Dried Bread Cubes
  may be used.

In a very large mixing bowl, place the bread cubes, celery, onions, sage, salt, pepper, and poultry seasoning; stir to combine. Add the butter; toss to coat the ingredients. Drizzle the water evenly over the mixture; toss lightly to moisten.

MAKES ENOUGH DRESSING TO STUFF THE NECK AND BODY CAVITIES OF AN 8-POUND TURKEY (SEE NOTE). OR, PLACE THE UNBAKED DRESSING IN A BUTTERED 2-QUART ROUND BAKING DISH AND BAKE, COVERED, FOR 30 MINUTES AT 350°F. (MAY BE BAKED FOR 45 MINUTES AT 325°F.)

NOTE: For dressing to stuff a larger turkey, increase the recipe ingredients proportionately.

CHESTNUT DRESSING: Shell and skin 2 dozen medium to large chestnuts (page 51). Measure 1½ cups skinned chestnuts. Boil the chestnuts (page 51) and drain; let stand to cool. Chop the chestnuts coarsely; set aside.

Follow the Sage Dressing recipe, above, adding the chopped chestnuts to the ingredients after adding the onions.

OYSTER DRESSING: Follow the Sage Dressing recipe, above, reducing the dried leaf sage to 2 teaspoons and reducing the hot water to ¾ cup. Add 1 pint shucked, raw oysters, drained (see Note) and chopped coarsely, to the ingredients after adding the onions. The drained oyster liquor may be heated and substituted for part of the water, if desired.

NOTE: If desired, reserve the drained liquor for use in the dressing.

CORN BREAD DRESSING

1 recipe Corn Bread (page 441)
1 cup chicken broth, homemade (page 88) or commercially canned
1 cup chopped celery with leaves
1 cup chopped onions
5 slices bacon, fried, drained between paper towels, and crumbled
¼ cup (4 tablespoons) butter, melted
2 extra-large eggs, beaten
1 teaspoon dried leaf thyme (or 1 tablespoon finely snipped, fresh thyme)
½ teaspoon poultry seasoning
½ teaspoon salt
⅛ teaspoon pepper

After baking the Corn Bread, let it stand, uncovered, for 5 hours to dry. Crumble the dried corn bread. Measure 6 cups crumbled corn bread and place in a large mixing bowl; set aside. Pour the broth into a medium saucepan. Cover the saucepan. Bring the broth to a boil over high heat. Add the celery and onions. Cover the saucepan and reduce the heat. Simmer the broth mixture 5 minutes. Remove from the heat; let stand to cool.

Sprinkle the crumbled bacon over the corn bread; set aside. Add the butter, eggs, thyme, poultry seasoning, salt, and pepper to the cooled broth mixture; stir well. Pour the broth mixture evenly over the corn bread and bacon; toss lightly to combine.

MAKES ENOUGH DRESSING TO STUFF THE NECK AND BODY CAVITIES OF AN 8-POUND TURKEY (SEE NOTE). OR, PLACE THE UNBAKED DRESSING IN A BUTTERED 2-QUART ROUND BAKING DISH AND BAKE, COVERED, FOR 40 MINUTES AT 325°F.

NOTE: For dressing to stuff a larger turkey, increase recipe the ingredients proportionately.

WILD RICE DRESSING

⅓ cup raw wild rice, cooked in homemade (page 87) or commercially canned beef broth (page 276).
4 slices bacon, cut widthwise into ½-inch pieces
½ cup chopped onions
1¼ cups sliced, fresh mushrooms
½ cup chopped celery
1 cup Dried Bread Crumbs (page 48)
½ teaspoon dried leaf thyme
½ teaspoon dried leaf sage
½ teaspoon salt
⅛ teaspoon pepper
¼ cup beef broth, homemade (page 87) or commercially canned

Place the cooked wild rice in a large mixing bowl; set aside. In a small, heavy-bottomed skillet, fry the bacon over medium heat until crisp, but not too brown. Using a slotted spoon, remove the bacon from the skillet and place in the bowl containing the wild rice; set aside. Place the onions and mushrooms in the skillet; fry in the bacon grease, over medium heat, until the onions are translucent and the mushrooms give up their juices (about 5 minutes). Using a slotted spoon, remove the onions and mushrooms from the skillet and add to the wild rice. Add the celery, crumbs, thyme, sage, salt, and pepper; stir to combine all the ingredients. Add ¼ cup beef broth; stir to combine.

MAKES ENOUGH DRESSING TO STUFF THE NECK AND BODY CAVITIES OF A 6-POUND BIRD (SEE NOTE). OR, PLACE THE UNBAKED DRESSING IN A BUTTERED 1½-QUART ROUND BAKING DISH AND BAKE, COVERED, FOR 30 MINUTES AT 350°F. (MAY BE BAKED FOR 45 MINUTES AT 325°F.)

NOTE: For dressing to stuff a larger bird, increase the recipe ingredients proportionately.

Fish and Shellfish

Fish

No doubt about it—fishing is a primary hobby in the Midwest. In support of this sweeping statement, the Iowa Department of Natural Resources estimates that 1 in 3 Iowans fishes within the state borders—a typical pattern in most Midwest states, where anglers cut across all age, income, gender, and vocational groups.

Despite the diversity of their demographics, Heartland fishermen have one unmistakable characteristic in common—they are avid! Geared with skillfully rigged lures, dogged determination fuels their relentless pursuit of that big, evasive one lurking below the surface.

It all starts about kindergarten age, when sandy-haired, freckle-faced kids dangle their legs over the end of the boat dock at the family's cottage on the lake, and their grandfather gives the first instruction on how to equip their fishing pole with a bobber and thread a squirmy worm on the hook. The heart-pounding thrill of catching that first mess of little bluegills—just enough for dinner—and the adulation from Grandma as she places the big platter on the table, seem to hook these neophytes on a life path of fishing.

Once inextricably caught in this lifetime fishing net, there is a predictable order of events. From worms, little fishing rookies quickly progress to casting for bass with Hula Poppers—to trolling for walleyes with a Rapala Shad Rap on the end of their line—to acquiring an ice auger, portable ice-fishing house, and space heater (allowing nothing so trivial as the weather to interrupt this fishing focus)—to planning annual spring fishing trips bound for rushing trout streams where they put to the test the array of flies they have been hand-tying all winter long on the kitchen table—to purchasing a summer home for retirement on a fish-laden lake—to escorting their grandchildren down to the dock for their ceremonial fishing initiation.

This typical scenario explains why much of the fish eating in the Midwest has centered on the varieties caught by family and friends—especially prior to recent years, when commercial fresh fish were rarely available in consumer markets.

Indisputably, most people consider walleyes to be the choice indigenous Midwest fish. They definitely are in the same class with Dover sole, and are one of the primary fish veteran anglers go after. The white, sweet flesh of walleyes makes delectable dining, and the ⅓- to ½-pound dressed fillets make perfect individual servings. While this is a common size, walleyes up to 4 pounds, yielding larger fillets, are often caught, and trophies up to 8 or more pounds are sometimes the prize of an unforgettable day of fishing.

Other excellent Midwest fish for eating are sauger; crappies; bass; perch; rainbow, brook, and brown trout; lake trout; and catfish. Northern pike, plentiful in the north lake country, are large and fun to catch, and are mild flavored, but their boniness often saves their lives. Many a true-blue walleye fishing enthusiast carefully removes the hook from the mouths of these long, speckled fighters and delivers them back to the water to swim away. In defense of Northerns, when they are caught in very cold water, their nice, white flesh retains its shape nicely after cooking, making them a good choice for Fish Chowder (page 96).

There was a day when Midwest fishing was concentrated on (if not confined to) the natural lakes, rivers, and streams of Minnesota, Wisconsin, and Michigan; the Mississippi, Missouri, and other large rivers; and the Great Lakes bordering Midwestern states. However, that picture has changed radically in recent decades with the building of big reservoirs and the implementation of other dam projects which have created large bodies of water for soil and water conservation, flood control, power generation, and re-creational purposes. The successful stocking of these waters with fish by state natural resource departments, as well as their stocking and regulation of streams suitable for trout, have created outstanding fishing in all Midwest states.

The favored way of preparing freshly caught Midwest fish has been, and continues to be, panfried or deep-fat fried. There is some variation as to type of breading used. My preference is for dipping fillets in seasoned egg, dredging them in cornflake crumbs, and panfrying them lightly in half vegetable oil and half butter. Boy, are they good! See the recipe for Panfried Fish Fillets on page 224. This recipe calls for a minimum of frying fat (2 tablespoons), and I personally think the results are better than when more fat is used or when the fish are deep-fat fried.

Broiling and baking are also wonderful ways to prepare fish caught in Midwest waters. Both cooking methods accommodate a myriad of interestingly flavored sauces—either spooned over the fish at the time of serving, or cooked with the fish. One of the beauties of fish is their compatibility with such a variety of diverse foods, flavors, and seasonings, as exemplified by the recipes for Broiled Walleye Fillets with Caper Sauce (page 224) and Perch Fillets with Hazelnuts and White Wine (page 221), as well as other recipes in this chapter.

A fish course, served after the first course and before the main course, is seldom served in Middle America, even at very formal dinners. While cocktail forks for use in eating certain shellfish dishes are often found in silver chests, most Midwest households are not equipped with fish knives and forks.

In recent years, Midwest consumption of fish has burgeoned far beyond the stringers-full filleted on the fish-cleaning table behind the garage. Two reasons are apparent: (1) fresh fish of many kinds are now more readily available at the retail level across the Mid-American states, and (2) more fish, in general, are included in home menus today because fish are low in saturated fat and cholesterol and are a good source of protein. Midlanders need no longer tote salmon home from trips to the west coast in order to prepare fresh, poached or grilled salmon steaks. And an old Midwest favorite, Salmon Loaf (page 224), now often made with fresh salmon, has taken on new life.

Whether caught with your own rod and reel or purchased at the fish market, freshness is the unequivocal key to good-tasting fish. That strong, disagreeable, fishy smell signals less-than-fresh fish. The sooner fish is eaten after caught, the better. In earlier days when my husband and I did considerable primitive canoe tripping in Minnesota and Canada with our good friends, Prudy and John Leachman, our usual morning routine started with the men paddling out early to catch fish for breakfast while Prudy and I built the fire, pared potatoes, unpacked eggs for frying, and made a big pot of coffee. On lucky mornings, we would have walleyes, cleaned only minutes before frying with the potatoes and eggs. When fried that fresh, fish curls slightly. Those of you who have experienced this sensational fish treat will, I'm sure, join me in shouting to the heavens, "Now, *that's* fish!!"

Shellfish

Situated in the center of our expansive country, Midwest inlanders are pretty much deprived of fresh shellfish, most of which come from coastal waters. Although bubbling lobster tanks are featured in scattered restaurants and retail fish markets, and fresh clams and mussels are sometimes spotted heaped on crushed ice in fish market display cases, much of the shellfish available in the Heartland is, or has been, frozen.

I think it is safe to speculate that shrimp is generally the most relished shellfish in this neck of the woods. A group of friends can gobble up an astounding amount of steaming, boiled shrimp placed in a big bowl in the center of the table. At such informal occasions, the peeling and deveining of these incredibly lush morsels is left to each diner. Set a generous sauce dish of zippy, home-made Cocktail Sauce (page 361) at each person's place (there's nothing worse than not enough sauce), toss a green salad, offer pilsner glasses of beer or nice-sized glasses of white wine, and voilà!—a meal fit for a king (or queen).

In addition to the spices, beer added to the water in which shrimp are boiled imparts a subtle, elegant flavor. Once the shrimp are dropped into this epicurean brew, don't take your eyes off the kettle because overcooking will cause shrimp to become tough. Cook them only until they turn pink and curl (about 2 to 5 minutes) (see Boiled Shrimp, page 229).

For as long as I can remember, fried (deep-fat) shrimp have been a highly popular entrée on Midwest restaurant menus. Once upon a time, fried sea scallops were almost as popular, but they seem to be less frequently offered in recent years. Bay scallops seldom appear on Midland menus.

When it comes to shellfish, oysters have the most historic foothold in the Midwest. Oddly enough, oysters were a delicacy purveyed to the pioneering frontier when other more basic items were often in short supply. A fondness for oysters has held fast through the generations, expressed most profusely at Christmastime, when Oyster Stew (page 103), Scalloped Oysters (page 228), and Oyster Dressing (page 215) pay homage to this heritage. Unfortunately, fresh, unshucked oysters are hard to come by across much of the Midwest, and generally can be found only in select seafood restaurants and oyster bars in larger cities.

Whole fresh lobsters, lobster tails, and lobster salad are not served as commonly in the Midwest as in some other parts of the country. Availability is, again, a deterrent. Alaskan king crab legs are occasionally found on menus, sometimes paired with steak. Frozen crab legs are available in larger supermarkets for home preparation. In the more rural sections of the Midwest, crabmeat salad has not hit the stride it enjoys in the larger metropolitan areas. Encounters with imitation crabmeat—a poor substitute for the real thing—can be a source of consternation.

Except in clam chowder, clams are served with relative infrequency, and mussels—fairly new to the Midwest—are eaten even less often.

When all is said and done, one can summarize by saying that shellfish—not indigenous to the Heartland—play second fiddle to meats, poultry, and fish throughout most of the Midwest.

Fish and Shellfish Safety

To help ensure against foodborne illnesses, the following procedures should be practiced when securing, storing, handling, and cooking fish and shellfish:

- Oysters, scallops, clams, and mussels are molluscan shellfish. They are filter feeders that process large quantities of water. Illness-causing bacteria and viruses may be present in shellfish harvested in polluted waters which have not been certified as safe, and the safety of waters can change from day to day. Therefore, it is very important to purchase mollusks and other shellfish from reputable sources.

- Fully cook fish and shellfish. Cook fish, filleted or whole, to an internal temperature of 160° F. At this temperature, the flesh is opaque and it flakes easily when pricked with a sharp fork. Cook shellfish to an internal temperature of 160° F. (steaming hot). The flesh should be opaque. To check the internal temperature of fish and shellfish, use an instant thermometer (page 44).

- Refrigerate raw fish and shellfish at 40° F. or below for only 1 to 2 days before cooking or freezing. Freeze at 0° F. or below.

- Thaw frozen fish and shellfish in the refrigerator or in the microwave oven (see Food Safety: Microwave Ovens, page 31, for procedural information), not on the kitchen counter or in the sink.

- Before cooking, rinse raw fish and shellfish under cold, running water, and dry with paper towels.

- Throw away fish and shellfish packaging material.

- Place cooked fish and shellfish on a clean platter, not on an unwashed platter which held the raw product.

- Wash your hands with soap and hot water before and after handling raw and cooked fish or shellfish. Wash kitchen tools and equipment, cutting boards and other work surfaces, sink, and faucet handles with hot, soapy water after they come in contact with raw or cooked fish or shellfish, and before they come in contact with other food.

Fish

BAKED BASS WITH MUSTARD-WINE SAUCE

2 pounds bass fillets
½ cup whole milk
½ teaspoon salt
¾ cup Dried Bread Crumbs (page 48)
¼ cup (4 tablespoons) butter, melted
Mustard-Wine Sauce (recipe follows)

Preheat the oven to 425° F. Grease a 10½ × 15-½-inch shallow baking (cookie) pan; set aside. Wash the fillets under cold, running water and place them between several layers of paper towels to dry; set aside. In a small, flat-bottomed dish or a pie pan, place the milk and salt; stir to blend; set aside. Sprinkle the bread crumbs over a piece of waxed paper; set aside. Dip the fillets in the milk mixture; then, dredge in the crumbs until fully coated. Place the fillets, single layer, in the prepared baking pan; drizzle with the butter.

Bake for 15 to 20 minutes, or until the fish flakes easily when pricked with a sharp fork. Place the fillets on individual plates or on a serving platter; spoon hot Mustard-Wine Sauce over top.

SERVES 4

Mustard-Wine Sauce

3 tablespoons all-purpose flour
$\frac{1}{4}$ teaspoon dry mustard
$\frac{1}{8}$ teaspoon white pepper
2 teaspoons sugar
$\frac{1}{4}$ cup (4 tablespoons) butter
$\frac{1}{2}$ cup water (or fish stock)
$\frac{1}{2}$ cup dry white wine
1 tablespoon prepared mustard

In a small sauce dish, place the flour, dry mustard, white pepper, and sugar; stir to combine; set aside. In a small saucepan, melt the butter over low heat. Remove from the heat. Add the flour mixture; stir until perfectly smooth. Add the water. Cook over medium-low heat until the mixture thickens, stirring continuously. Add the wine and prepared mustard; stir to blend. Heat through, stirring constantly.

VARIATION: Substitute white Rhine wine for dry white wine and omit the sugar.

PERCH FILLETS WITH HAZELNUTS AND WHITE WINE

Fishermen friends are always asking me for new and different ways to prepare their stringers of fish. They seem to like this one a lot. I hear reports of their taking the chopped hazelnuts, white wine, and chives along on fishing trips to Minnesota and Canada so they can prepare the dish after a good day's catch. Any type of mild fish fillets may be used with this recipe.

2 pounds perch fillets
$\frac{1}{3}$ cup all-purpose flour
$\frac{1}{2}$ teaspoon salt
$\frac{1}{2}$ cup chopped hazelnuts (page 50)
$\frac{1}{4}$ cup (4 tablespoons) butter
$\frac{1}{4}$ cup dry white wine
1 tablespoon snipped, fresh chives

Preheat the oven to 450° F. Grease liberally a $10\frac{1}{2} \times 15\frac{1}{2}$-inch shallow baking (cookie) pan; set aside.

Wash the fillets under cold, running water and place them between several layers of paper towels to dry; set aside. In a small sauce dish, place the flour and salt; stir to combine. Sprinkle the flour mixture over a piece of waxed paper. Dredge the fillets in the flour mixture. Shake off excess flour and place the fillets, single layer, in the prepared baking pan. Distribute the chopped hazelnuts evenly over the fillets; set aside.

In a tiny saucepan, melt the butter over low heat; add the wine and stir to blend. Spoon the wine mixture over the fillets. Distribute the chives evenly over the fillets.

Bake the fillets for 12 to 15 minutes, or until the fish flakes easily when pricked with a sharp fork. Remove from the oven and spoon the pan juices over the fillets.

SERVES 4

BAKED WALLEYE DELUXE

2 pounds walleye fillets (about 4 fillets)
½ cup Caesar salad dressing, homemade
    (including anchovy mixture and
    Parmesan cheese—see Caesar Salad,
    page 122) or commercially canned
2 cups finely rolled potato chips
¼ cup freshly grated Parmesan cheese
    (page 46)
1 cup finely shredded, extra-sharp cheddar
    cheese
1 tablespoon finely snipped, fresh parsley
¼ teaspoon paprika

Preheat the oven to 450° F. Grease liberally a
10½ × 15½-inch shallow baking (cookie) pan;
set aside.

Wash the fillets under cold, running water and
place them between several layers of paper towels to dry; set aside. Pour the salad dressing into
a shallow, flat-bottomed, glass dish such as a pie
pan; set aside. Sprinkle the rolled potato chips
over a piece of waxed paper; set aside.

Dip the fillets in the salad dressing; then,
dredge in the potato chips until fully coated.
Place the fillets, single layer, in the prepared baking pan. Sprinkle the Parmesan cheese over the
fillets; then, distribute the cheddar cheese evenly
over the fillets. Scatter the parsley over the cheddar cheese. Using your fingers, sprinkle the
paprika lightly over all.

Bake for 12 to 15 minutes, or until the fish
flakes easily when pricked with a sharp fork.

SERVES 4

BROILED FISH FILLETS

This is a basic recipe for broiling fish fillets.

1½ to 2 pounds walleye, sauger, crappie,
    bass, perch, sole, or other fish fillets
¼ cup freshly squeezed, strained lemon
    juice
3 tablespoons butter
Paprika
Lemon wedges for garnish
1 recipe Tartar Sauce (page 361) (optional)

Preheat the broiler.

Wash the fillets under cold, running water and
place them between several layers of paper towels to dry. When dry, arrange the fillets, single
layer, in the bottom of a broiler pan (remove and
do not use the perforated rack over the broiler
pan). Pour the lemon juice over the fillets; dot
with the butter and sprinkle lightly with paprika.

Broil the fillets 4 inches from the heat about 5
to 7 minutes, or until the fish flakes easily when
pricked with a sharp fork. As a general guide,
broil fillets 5 minutes per ½ inch of thickness
measured at the thickest part of the fish to be
cooked. Small, thin fillets require less cooking
time. Baste the fillets with the pan juices halfway
through broiling. Do not turn the fillets.

When done, place the fillets on individual
plates. Garnish the plates with lemon wedges. If
desired, Tartar Sauce may be passed at the table.

SERVES 4

BROILED FISH FILLETS AMANDINE

2 tablespoons butter
⅓ cup sliced, unblanched almonds
Dash of salt
Dash of white pepper

In a small, heavy-bottomed skillet, melt the butter over medium heat. Tilt the skillet back and
forth to completely cover the bottom with the
melted butter. Place the almonds, salt, and white

pepper in the skillet; sauté 3 minutes; set aside and keep warm.

Follow the Broiled Fish Fillets recipe, above. After the fillets have been broiled and removed from the broiler pan, add the hot sautéed almonds and skillet liquid to the pan juices in the broiler pan; stir to combine and spoon over the fillets after placing them on individual plates.

FILLET OF SOLE WITH LIME SAUCE

Midwesterners frequently travel to southern climes in the winter to escape the cold weather. Time spent in Florida visiting my parents who wintered there, was the inspiration for this recipe, which features a lime sauce, a somewhat different way of serving the wonderful Florida fish: red snapper, flounder, and grouper.

2 pounds sole fillets* (about 4 fillets)
¼ cup freshly squeezed, strained lime juice
3 tablespoons butter
Lime Sauce (recipe follows)
Grooved Lime Twists (page 401) for
    decoration
Sprigs of watercress for decoration

Fillets of any mild fish, such as red snapper, flounder, or grouper, may be substituted.

Preheat the broiler.

Wash the fillets under cold, running water and place them between several layers of paper towels to dry. When dry, arrange the fillets, single layer, in the bottom of a broiler pan (remove and do not use the perforated rack over the broiler pan). Pour the lime juice over the fillets; dot with the butter.

Broil the fillets, 4 inches from the heat, for 5 to 7 minutes, or until the fish flakes easily when pricked with a sharp fork. Baste the fillets with the pan juices after 3 minutes of broiling. Do not turn the fillets.

When done, place the fillets on individual plates; spoon the Lime Sauce over the fish (or, spoon the Lime Sauce onto the plates and place the fillets over the sauce). Decorate the plates with Grooved Lime Twists and sprigs of watercress.

SERVES 4

Lime Sauce

2 tablespoons all-purpose flour
¼ teaspoon salt
⅛ teaspoon white pepper
2 tablespoons butter
1 cup half-and-half
2 egg yolks, beaten
¼ cup dry white wine
2 tablespoons freshly squeezed, strained
    lime juice

In a small sauce dish, place the flour, salt, and white pepper; stir to combine; set aside. In a small saucepan, melt the butter over low heat. Remove from the heat. Add the flour mixture; stir until perfectly smooth. Add the half-and-half; stir to combine. Place over medium-low heat and cook until the mixture thickens, stirring constantly. Add about 2 tablespoons of the hot half-and-half mixture to the egg yolks; stir in. Add the egg yolk mixture to the hot half-and-half mixture and cook until thickened (about 3 minutes), stirring constantly. Add the wine and lime juice; stir to blend. Heat through.

ACCOMPANIMENT SUGGESTIONS
• Colorful steamed vegetables, such as miniature carrots (page 302) and small green beans

• New Potatoes (without parsley; page 331)

• Braised Celery (page 314)

BROILED WALLEYE FILLETS WITH CAPER SAUCE

2 pounds walleye fillets (about 4 fillets)
¼ cup freshly squeezed, strained lemon juice
3 tablespoons butter
¼ teaspoon celery salt
1 recipe Caper Sauce (page 363)

Preheat the broiler.

Wash the fillets under cold, running water and place them between several layers of paper towels to dry. When dry, arrange the fillets, single layer, in the bottom of a broiler pan (remove and do not use the perforated rack over the broiler pan). Pour the lemon juice over the fillets; dot with the butter and sprinkle with the celery salt.

Broil the fillets, 4 inches from the heat, for 5 to 7 minutes, or until the fish flakes easily when pricked with a sharp fork. Baste the fillets with the pan juices after 3 minutes of broiling. Do not turn the fillets. When done, place the fillets on individual plates; spoon the Caper Sauce over the fish.

SERVES 4

PANFRIED FISH FILLETS

2 pounds walleye, sauger, crappie, bass, or perch fillets
1 extra-large egg
¼ teaspoon salt
⅛ teaspoon pepper
1½ cups commercial cornflake crumbs or 7½ cups cornflakes, crumbed (page 49)
1 tablespoon vegetable oil
1 tablespoon butter

Wash the fillets under cold, running water and place them between several layers of paper towels to dry; set aside. In a flat-bottomed dish or a pie pan, place the egg, salt, and pepper; using a

table fork, beat well; set aside. Sprinkle the cornflake crumbs over a piece of waxed paper; set aside. Dip the fillets in the egg mixture; then, dredge in the crumbs until fully coated. Place the dredged fillets on a clean piece of waxed paper; set aside.

Preheat an electric skillet or a large, heavy-bottomed skillet on the range to medium-high heat (380° F. in an electric skillet). Place the vegetable oil in the skillet. Using a spatula, spread the vegetable oil over the entire bottom of the skillet. Add the butter. Tilt the skillet back and forth to blend the butter with the oil. Place the fillets, single layer, in the skillet. Fry the fillets 4 minutes on each side, turning only once. Small, thin fillets require less cooking time. The fish is done when it flakes easily when pricked with a sharp fork. Do not overcook. Add additional vegetable oil and butter during frying, if necessary. Place the fillets directly on individual plates.

SERVES 4

TRADITIONAL ACCOMPANIMENTS: Panfried Fish Fillets are traditionally served with American Fries (page 330). Tartar Sauce (page 361) is usually passed at the table for diners who wish it, and the fish plates are often garnished with lemon wedges.

SALMON LOAF

2 cups Cold Poached Salmon Steaks (page 225) cut into chunks, or 1 14¾-ounce can commercial red sockeye salmon
1 tablespoon freshly squeezed, strained lemon juice
2 tablespoons butter, melted
2 extra-large eggs, or 1 extra-large egg if using canned salmon
20 Ritz crackers, rolled finely
2 tablespoons hot water

Preheat the oven to 350° F. Butter an 8 × 8-inch or a 6 × 10-inch baking dish; set aside.

Place the salmon (and all salmon juices, if using canned salmon) in a medium mixing bowl. Using your fingers and a small paring knife, carefully remove and discard all the skin and bones. Then, using your fingers, flake the salmon. Add the lemon juice, butter, eggs (1 egg if using canned salmon), and rolled crackers; stir to combine. Shape into a round or oval loaf and place in the prepared baking dish. Pour 2 tablespoons hot water around (not over) the loaf. Bake, uncovered, 35 minutes.

SERVES 4

ACCOMPANIMENT SUGGESTION: At the table, serve Dilled Creamed Peas (page 327) or plain Creamed Peas (page 327) for diners to ladle over the Salmon Loaf slices.

POACHED SALMON STEAKS

1 cup chopped onions
2 stalks celery with leaves, cut into ½-inch slices
1 carrot, pared and cut into ⅛-inch slices
4 sprigs of fresh parsley
1 bay leaf
6 whole black peppercorns
1 whole clove
1 teaspoon salt
¼ teaspoon dried leaf thyme
½ cup dry white wine
¼ cup cider vinegar
6 cups water
4 fresh salmon steaks, 1 inch thick
Sprigs of fresh watercress or parsley for decoration
1 recipe Hollandaise Sauce (page 367)

In a large saucepan, place the onions, celery, carrots, 4 sprigs parsley, bay leaf, peppercorns, clove, salt, thyme, wine, vinegar, and water; stir to combine. Cover the saucepan. Bring the mixture to a boil over high heat; reduce the heat and simmer 20 minutes. Pour the mixture into

a large skillet; cover and set aside. Wrap each salmon steak in 2 layers of damp cheesecloth (do not tie with string); set aside.

Over high heat, bring the mixture in the skillet to a boil. Lower the salmon steaks into the mixture; cover the skillet and return the mixture to a low boil. Reduce the heat and simmer 10 minutes. When properly done, the salmon steaks should flake when pricked with a sharp fork.

Using a spatula, remove the steaks from the skillet; unwrap. With the aid of a small paring knife, carefully remove the skin around the steaks. (Discard the mixture in which the steaks were poached.)

Using the spatula, place the salmon steaks on individual plates. Decorate the plates with sprigs of watercress or parsley. Pass Hollandaise Sauce in an attractive sauce dish at the table.

SERVES 4

ACCOMPANIMENT SUGGESTIONS: Serve with Baked Cucumbers (page 317) and plain, steamed new potatoes (page 328) which may be peeled or left unpeeled.

COLD POACHED SALMON STEAKS

Lemon wedges for garnish
Sprigs of watercress for decoration
1 recipe Green Sauce (Sauce Verte) (page 364)

Follow the Poached Salmon Steaks recipe, above, through poaching the steaks. Then, place the wrapped salmon steaks in a flat dish; cover and refrigerate until cold. When ready to serve, unwrap the steaks; carefully remove the skin and place the steaks on individual plates. Garnish the plates with lemon wedges and decorate with sprigs of watercress. Serve with Green Sauce (Sauce Verte) on the side.

ACCOMPANIMENT SUGGESTION: Serve with Cucumber Salad (page 131).

DEVILED TUNA ON PATTY SHELLS

Puff Pastry Shells, often called Patty Shells, make delightful, flaky, cups for creamed foods, such as this Deviled Tuna or Chicken à la King (page 209). As the name implies, Puff Pastry Shells are made of puff pastry (the recipe for making them on page 470 uses frozen puff pastry). When time doesn't permit making Patty Shells, serve the Deviled Tuna on toast.

3 tablespoons all-purpose flour
1 teaspoon dry mustard
1 teaspoon onion powder
¾ teaspoon salt
¼ teaspoon white pepper
3 tablespoons butter
2 cups whole milk
½ teaspoon Worcestershire sauce
1 6-ounce can solid, white albacore tuna, packed in water, drained and broken into large chunks
2 extra-large eggs, hard-cooked (page 264) and chopped coarsely
6 Patty Shells (page 470), warm
2 teaspoons finely snipped, fresh parsley for garnish

In a small mixing bowl, place the flour, dry mustard, onion powder, salt, and white pepper; stir to combine; set aside. In a small saucepan, melt the butter over low heat. Remove from the heat. Add the flour mixture; stir until perfectly smooth. Add the milk; stir to combine. Place over medium-low heat; cook until the mixture thickens and is just under boiling, stirring constantly. Remove from the heat. Add the Worcestershire sauce; stir until blended. Add the tuna and eggs; stir to evenly distribute. Return to medium-low heat; stir until the mixture is hot. Do not allow to boil.

Place 1 warm Patty Shell on each of 6 individual plates. Spoon Deviled Tuna over the Patty Shells; sprinkle with snipped parsley to garnish.

SERVES 6

VARIATION: Serve the Deviled Tuna over toast rather than over Patty Shells.

Other Fish Recipes

Fish Chowder (page 96)
Marinated Fish Steaks (page 257)
Kathy Griffin's Orange Roughy Parmesan (page 258)
Tuna-Almond Luncheon Salad (page 143)
Tuna-Noodle Casserole (page 297)
Tuna Salad Sandwiches (page 352)

Shellfish

SHRIMP CURRY

Authentic Shrimp Curry of this type contains fresh coconut milk which is made by processing the liquid and meat of coconuts. In most parts of the country, it is impractical to rely on the availability of usable fresh coconuts; however, the substitution of cream of coconut and coconut-flavored milk, as called for in this recipe, achieves a similar flavor and consistency.

½ teaspoon finely grated fresh ginger (page 46)
½ teaspoon ground turmeric
½ teaspoon ground cardamom
½ teaspoon ground cinnamon
½ teaspoon ground cloves
1 teaspoon salt
¼ cup (4 tablespoons) butter
2½ cups finely chopped onions (about 2 large onions)
1 cup commercially canned cream of coconut*
1 cup Coconut-Flavored Milk (recipe follows)

1½ pounds raw, unshelled 26- to 30-sized shrimp, boiled, shelled, and deveined (page 229)
1½ cups raw long-grain white rice (not instant), boiled (page 272)

Available in the mixed beverage or baking section of the supermarket.

CONDIMENTS
Chutney (the primary condiment served with Shrimp Curry), home canned (page 776) or commercially canned
Raisins, dark and/or golden
Finely chopped, preserved kumquats, commercially canned
Shredded coconut
Salted peanuts
Finely chopped, crystallized ginger
Pickled pearl onions, commercially canned
Snipped, fresh parsley
Fresh tomatoes, blanched (page 44), peeled, quartered, seeded and cored (page 45), and chopped
Chopped, hard-cooked eggs (page 264)
Chopped sweet pickles
Grated lemon rind

In a small sauce dish, place the ginger, turmeric, cardamom, cinnamon, cloves, and salt; set aside. In a large, heavy-bottomed skillet, melt the butter over medium heat. Tilt the skillet back and forth to completely cover the bottom with the melted butter. Place the onions in the skillet; sauté until golden (about 10 minutes). Be careful not to burn the butter nor to brown the onions too deeply. Add the spice mixture and continue cooking for about 2 minutes, stirring constantly. Remove the skillet from the heat and let stand to cool slightly. Then, add the cream of coconut and coconut-flavored milk; stir in well.

Return the skillet to medium heat. Bring the mixture to a low simmer; cook for 3 to 5 minutes, until the mixture thickens slightly. Add the shrimp and heat through only. The shrimp will become tough if allowed to cook beyond heating.

To serve, place the Shrimp Curry and rice in separate serving bowls. Diners spoon the Shrimp Curry over rice. Place a medium sauce dish of chutney and small sauce dishes of at least 5 additional condiments in the center of the table so diners may conveniently and intermittently spoon various condiments over portions of their Shrimp Curry. For a dazzling table, serve all of the condiments. If more than 6 diners are seated at the table, provide 2 sets of condiments.

SERVES 4

Coconut-Flavored Milk

1 cup whole milk
1 cup packed, raw, chip coconut (unsweetened)

Pour the milk into a small saucepan; heat to just under boiling over medium-low heat. Add the coconut; stir to combine. Cover the saucepan; turn off the heat, but leave the saucepan on the burner. Let stand 30 minutes.

Place the mixture in a blender beaker; process to liquify. Strain the mixture through 4 layers of damp cheesecloth secured in a sieve over a deep pan. Wring the cheesecloth to press out as much milk as possible; discard the unstrained pieces of coconut. Refrigerate the coconut-flavored milk in a covered container up to 2 days, ready for use.

ACCOMPANIMENT SUGGESTIONS: For a meal planned around Shrimp Curry, serve Hearts of Palm-Persimmon Salad (page 123) for a first course. Pass warm Deluxe Sesame Seed Crackers (page 449) with the Shrimp Curry course. For dessert, serve Fresh Fruit Compote (page 346) and Macadamia Nut Cookies (page 619).

BAKED SCALLOPS WITH SHERRIED GARLIC BUTTER

1½ pounds sea scallops
¼ cup (4 tablespoons) butter
2 garlic cloves, pressed
4 ounces sliced, fresh mushrooms
¼ cup thinly sliced green onions
   (scallions), white part only
1 tablespoon dry sherry
Paprika for decoration

Preheat the oven to 400° F.

Wash the scallops under cold, running water to remove any sand in the crevices; place them between 3 layers of paper towels to dry; set aside. In a medium, heavy-bottomed skillet, melt the butter over medium heat. Tilt the skillet back and forth to completely cover the bottom with the melted butter. Place the garlic, mushrooms, and onions in the skillet; sauté until the mushrooms give up their juices (about 3 minutes), being careful not to let the butter or vegetables brown. Remove from the heat. Add the sherry; stir in.

Using a slotted spoon, remove the *mushrooms* from the skillet and distribute evenly over the bottoms of four 5-inch-diameter by 1-inch-deep round baking dishes appropriate for serving. (Don't worry if some of the sautéed onions and garlic are spooned out and distributed with the mushrooms.) Set the baking dishes aside. Place the scallops in the skillet containing the onions and garlic; stir to coat with the mixture in the skillet.

Using the slotted spoon, remove the coated scallops from the skillet and arrange over the mushrooms, distributing them evenly among the 4 baking dishes. Spoon the remaining skillet mixture evenly over the scallops in each dish. Sprinkle with paprika.

Bake the scallops, uncovered, for 15 minutes. Place each baking dish on a doily-lined, salad-sized plate. Provide a cocktail fork and a fish knife (or other small knife) with each diner's table service.

SERVES 4

SCALLOPED OYSTERS

¼ cup plus 1 tablespoon (5 tablespoons)
   butter
½ cup (about 10) coarsely rolled saltines
½ cup fine Dried Bread Crumbs
   (page 48)
1 pint medium-sized, shucked, raw oysters
¼ cup half-and-half
¼ teaspoon ground nutmeg
¾ teaspoon dried leaf oregano
½ teaspoon salt
⅛ teaspoon pepper
1 tablespoon snipped, fresh parsley
Paprika

Preheat the oven to 325° F. Butter a 1-quart round baking dish; set aside.

In a small saucepan, melt the butter over low heat. Remove from the heat. Add the saltines and bread crumbs; stir to combine; set aside. Drain the oysters in a sieve, reserving the liquor. Set the oysters aside. Measure ¼ cup oyster liquor and pour into a small mixing bowl. Add the half-and-half; stir until blended; set aside. In a small sauce dish, place the nutmeg, oregano, salt, and pepper; stir to combine; set aside.

Place ½ of the oysters in the prepared baking dish. Sprinkle ½ of the nutmeg mixture over the oysters. Spoon ⅓ of the crumb mixture evenly over the seasoned oysters. Repeat the layers. Pour the half-and-half mixture evenly over the layers. Add a final layer of crumbs. Scatter the parsley over the top; sprinkle with paprika. Bake, uncovered, for 45 minutes.

SERVES 4

BOILED SHRIMP

4 pounds raw, unshelled shrimp
1 3-ounce bag shrimp boil spice*
1 12-ounce bottle or can beer

*Ready-filled bags of shrimp boil spice may be
purchased commercially.

Rinse the shrimp under cold, running water; set
aside. Into a deep kettle, pour enough water to
generously cover the shrimp when they are
added later. Place the shrimp boil spice in the
kettle. Cover the kettle and bring the mixture to
a boil over high heat. Add the beer; cover and
return to a boil. Add the shrimp and simmer,
uncovered, 2 to 5 minutes, until the shrimp are
pink and curled. *Do not overcook,* as this will result
in tough shrimp. Immediately drain the shrimp
in a colander to retard further cooking.

To serve Boiled Shrimp as a main course, see
the procedure below. If Boiled Shrimp are to
be used in the preparation of another recipe,
such as Shrimp Curry, Shrimp Cocktail, or
other shrimp dishes, hot or cold, proceed to
shell and devein the shrimp (procedure follows), or refrigerate the boiled, unshelled
shrimp for later preparation.

TO SERVE BOILED SHRIMP AS A MAIN COURSE:
Boiled shrimp may be served hot or cold as a
main course. To serve, heap drained, unpeeled
shrimp into a large bowl and place it in the center of the dining table. If serving a number of
people at a large table, divide the shrimp into 2
bowls for convenient access by diners throughout the meal.

Let each diner shell and devein his or her own
shrimp. Provide a small knife with each diner's
table service for this purpose, and set the table
with a bowl at each diner's place for discarded
shrimp shells and veins. Provide each diner with
a generous amount of Cocktail Sauce (page
361) served in an individual ramekin or small

sauce dish. A Boiled Shrimp meal is informal
luxury!

ONE POUND RAW, UNSHELLED SHRIMP SERVES 3

TO SHELL AND DEVEIN SHRIMP: To shell shrimp,
place your thumb between the swimmerettes
(small appendages under the abdomen) and pull
off the shell. The tail may be left on or removed.
To remove the black vein which runs along the
center of the back, use a paring knife to make a
1/8-inch cut at the head end of the shrimp. Pull
the vein toward the tail and remove.

BOILED WHOLE LOBSTERS

For average servings, allow one 1- to 2-pound
lobster per person. Avid lobster gourmands with
hearty appetites may prefer larger lobsters.

Pour sufficient water into a large kettle to
completely cover the lobsters when they are
added later; cover and bring to a rapid boil over
high heat. Plunge the live lobsters headfirst into
the boiling water. Cover the kettle. When the
water returns to a rapid boil, boil 1- to 2-pound
lobsters 10 to 15 minutes. If the water begins to
boil over during cooking, remove the kettle
cover briefly to release steam. Do not boil more
lobsters at a time than can be well covered with
the boiling water. When done, the shells will be
bright red and the meat will be opaque. Place
the cooked lobsters on 4 layers of paper towels
to drain. Using kitchen scissors or a sharp knife,
slit the underside of the lobsters from end to
end. Serve the lobsters with individual, small
ramekins of Clarified Butter (page 370) and
lemon wedges. Provide a lobster cracker, cocktail fork, and lobster pick (if available) for each
diner.

BOILED LOBSTER TAILS
Lobster Meat for Salads and Other Dishes

Purchase African or American lobster tails in the shell weighing about 8 ounces each. Thaw the tails if frozen. Rinse the lobster tails under cold, running water. Drop the tails into a kettle of rapidly boiling water over high heat. When the water returns to a rapid boil, boil the lobster tails, uncovered, about 1 minute per ounce of tail (boil 8-ounce lobster tails about 8 minutes). When done, the shells will be bright red and the meat will be opaque. Place the cooked lobster tails, shell side up, on 4 layers of paper towels to drain.

When cooled sufficiently to handle, use a small knife and kitchen scissors to cut away the underside membrane on each lobster tail. With your fingers, pull the meat from the shells. Place the lobster meat in a bowl or plastic container; cover and refrigerate. Or, proceed to prepare the cooked lobster meat for use in a recipe.

BOILED ALASKAN KING CRAB LEGS
Crabmeat for Salads and Other Dishes

Purchase Alaskan king crab legs. Thaw the crab legs if frozen.

If the crab legs are uncooked, rinse them under cold, running water. Drop the crab legs into a kettle of rapidly boiling water over high heat. When the water returns to a rapid boil, boil the crab legs, uncovered, 5 minutes. *If the crab legs have been precooked,* rinse them under cold, running water and boil them only 3 minutes.

Place the cooked crab legs on 4 layers of paper towels to drain.

When cooled sufficiently to handle, cut the crab leg shells with a small, sharp knife. Use your fingers and a small fork or lobster pick to pull the crabmeat from the shells. Place the crabmeat in a bowl or plastic container; cover and refrigerate. Or, proceed to prepare the cooked crabmeat for use in a recipe.

ONE POUND UNSHELLED ALASKAN KING CRAB LEGS YIELDS ABOUT 2 CUPS FINELY CHOPPED CRABMEAT

Other Shellfish Recipes

Corn-Oyster Casserole (page 317)
Crabmeat Louis (page 145)
Crabmeat Salad (page 145)
Grilled Lobster Tails Basted with Tarragon Butter Sauce (page 258
Lobster-Avocado Salad (page 147)
Lobster Salad (page 146)
Molded Shrimp and Cucumber Ring (page 144)
Oyster Stew (page 103)
Seafood Mosaic (page 146)
Shrimp Luncheon Salad with Fresh Green Beans and Sherried Dressing (page 143)

Wild Game

TO A WATERFOWL

Whither, midst falling dew,
While glow the heavens with the last steps of day,
Far, through their rosy depths, dost thou pursue
*   Thy solitary way?*

Vainly the fowler's eye
Might mark thy distant flight to do thee wrong,
As, darkly seen against the crimson sky,
*   Thy figure floats along.*

Seek'st thou the plashy brink
Of weedy lake, or marge of river wide,
Or where the rocking billows rise and sink
*   On the chafed ocean-side?*

There is a Power whose care
Teaches thy way along that pathless coast —
The desert and illimitable air —
*   Lone wandering, but not lost.*

All day thy wings have fanned,
At that far height, the cold, thin atmosphere,
Yet stoop not, weary, to the welcome land,
*   Though the dark night is near.*

And soon that toil shall end;
Soon shalt thou find a summer home, and rest,
And scream among thy fellows; reeds shall bend,
*   Soon, o'er thy sheltered nest.*

Thou'rt gone, the abyss of heaven
Hath swallowed up thy form; yet, on my heart
Deeply has sunk the lesson thou hast given,
*   And shall not soon depart.*

He who, from zone to zone,
Guides through the boundless sky thy certain flight,
In the long way that I must tread alone,
*   Will lead my steps aright.*

WILLIAM CULLEN BRYANT

In the early spring and late fall, Midwesterners fall asleep and awake to the assuring, honking of geese on their semiannual journeys between their breeding grounds in Canada—as far north as within the Arctic Circle—and their winter habitat—as far south as Central America. The endurance of these wondrous birds and the mystery of their precision compasses continue to bewilder scientists despite decades of study and conjecture.

Traveling hundreds or, commonly, thousands of miles each way, North American geese have for centuries followed specific routes, using one of the four migratory waterfowl flyways on this continent. One of these flyways, the Mississippi flyway, cuts directly through the heart of the Midwest, and another, the Central flyway, encompasses the most westerly tier of Midwest states.

With the precision of trained mechanics, these ingenious wildfowl prepare for their flights by donning a new set of feathers, which they fastidiously preen, oil, and arrange, and by fueling up for the long trips by storing additional fat on their bodies. They wing their way through the heavens at speeds of 40 to 55 miles per hour, nonstop for hours at a time, braving the travails of storms, ice, and fatigue which exact a deadly toll. They stop at the same locations, year in and year out, to feed and rest, and they terminate their flights in the very same nesting areas in the north and wintering places in the south as the generations before them. They mate for life and fly with their new offspring, tending to the well-being of their young ones until they are able to fend for themselves.

Their V formations covering the sky high above the earth and the unfathomable sight of tens of thousands of magnificent snow geese feeding and resting during their clockwork stop at the DeSoto National Wildlife Refuge on the Missouri River near Blair, Nebraska, are among that golden handful of incredible glimpses of nature's wonders experienced during one's lifetime which are seen with the eyes and which touch the soul, but defy description with mere words.

At times when the struggling of humanity around the globe appears overwhelming, and mankind's seeming loss of direction generates a sense of futility, my faith in the order of it all is restored by contemplating the miraculous, changeless migration of the geese. To me, it has always been sufficient proof of an omniscient power immutably committed to universal organization. The geese are messengers of many lessons for man.

What, then, is the justification for hunting such creatures so masterfully crafted by Providence? How can we truly relish the meals which result?

Kahlil Gibran answered these questions with ethereal majesty:

Would that you could live on the fragrance of the earth, and like an air plant be sustained by the light.

But since you must kill to eat, and rob the newly born of its mother's milk to quench your thirst, let it then be an act of worship. . . .

When you kill a beast say to him in your heart, "By the same power that slays you, I too am slain; and I too shall be consumed.

For the law that delivered you into my hand shall deliver me into a mightier hand.

Your blood and my blood is naught but the sap that feeds the tree of heaven."

KAHLIL GIBRAN
Excerpt from "On Eating and Drinking"
The Prophet

Our Midwest forefathers hunted for the purpose of food. Just as waterfowl are endowed with remarkable instincts engraved upon their genes which guide them, day and night, over the same invisible highways in the sky back to their homes, so, too, man's genes seem to harbor the once life-sustaining drive to hunt. It is packaged in modern-day life as a hobby—a sport—and it is widespread in the Heartland. Based on a 1996 national survey by the United States government (see Sources Consulted, page 842), over 27 percent of the Iowa adult male population hunts. Interestingly, unlike fishing, few

United States Department of the Interior • Fish and Wildlife Service

Bob Hines.

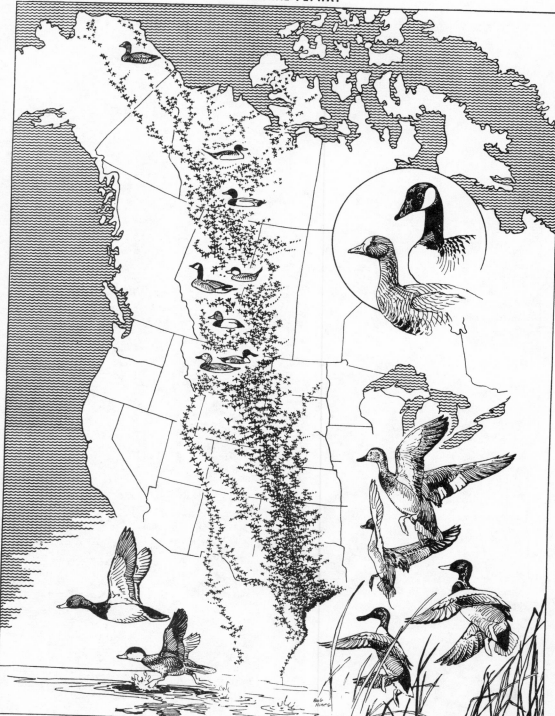

United States Department of the Interior • Fish and Wildlife Service

women hunt, although a female hunter can be spotted now and then among a group of tan-clad shooters walking a cornfield to flush pheasants. My own mother was a world champion skeet shooter, although she seldom hunted.

Were it not for the sustained interest in hunting, it is highly probable that our large populations of waterfowl, upland game birds, and game animals would be in grave jeopardy. Hunters have been the backbone of active, effective conservation programs to preserve this continent's wild game. Substantial amounts of private money and time support voluntary organizations such as the Izaak Walton League, the National Wild Turkey Federation, Whitetails Unlimited, Pheasants Forever, and many other organizations committed to conserving and perpetuating our nation's rich endowment of game birds and animals. Ducks Unlimited, one of the largest of these groups, works to restore and build natural wetland areas for migratory waterfowl in Canada and the northern prairie states, as well as in their wintering areas in the Gulf states and Mexico. This laudable program has helped counter the continual drainage of natural wetlands—the nesting places of many ducks and geese—mainly by farming interests seeking to produce more tillable land.

Hunting regulations and game management by state and federal agencies also have played prominent roles in protecting nature's creatures of the land, sky, and waters. Hunting seasons and bag limits are determined each year based upon wild game populations. A single year of drought or flooding can be devastating to birds and animals dependent upon the wild for their food, water, and nesting protection.

While scales weighing contemporary hunter motivation would, in all probability, tip on the side of "sport," there is substantial counterbalance on the "food" side. Game dinners are a bite out of Midwest living. In the face of our stressfully paced, mechanized lives, they harken us back to one of the basic formulas governing existence: the securing of food to sustain life.

Midwesterners have a reputation for being very practical, no-nonsense people. Perhaps this characteristic derives from living in the open spaces, close to the earth, where nature is more easily observed and where the production of livestock and crops for the nation's and the world's food supply is of central concern. Game dinners are humbling reminders that we are dependent upon the food provided by nature.

Hunting for the sole purpose of sport becomes slaughter and violates ethical propriety; bagged game should be cleaned with care, prepared with thought, and eaten with pleasure.

Despite the encroachment of agriculture and a more dense populace, large numbers of nonmigratory upland birds, deer, and other wild game still inhabit the Midwest and are visible even to those who do not hunt. From my vantage point at this typewriter—on the outskirts of West Des Moines, Iowa—the brilliant red and blue-green plumage of rooster pheasants caught my eye several times this past winter as they foraged with hens in the stubbles of the soybean field across the road. And one morning, close to Christmas, my heart skipped a beat as I happened to catch the spectacular sight of a big buck deer darting with incredible speed across the backyard and into the driveway, headed for a nearby wooded area inhabited by many deer.

One of the most unusual close-up glances of game birds I have ever experienced occurred this past April, during the time when the sky, high above, was filled with migrating waterfowl. I heard the very loud, clear honking of geese, dissimilar to the familiar, distant orchestra of honking usually heard during the migratory season. I reached the kitchen window just in time to see three enormous Canada geese fly within a few feet of where I was standing. For some reason, they had dropped out of their formation. Perhaps one of them was sick, or perhaps it was a pair stopping to rest with their first-year offspring who was too tired to continue. They flew off at a very low level toward that wooded area where the deer dwell, and I never saw them again.

In addition to the ducks and geese which are called in by hunters from blinds along the Mis-

PHEASANT DISTRIBUTION AND ABUNDANCE
As Hens Per Square Mile of North America in Spring 1986

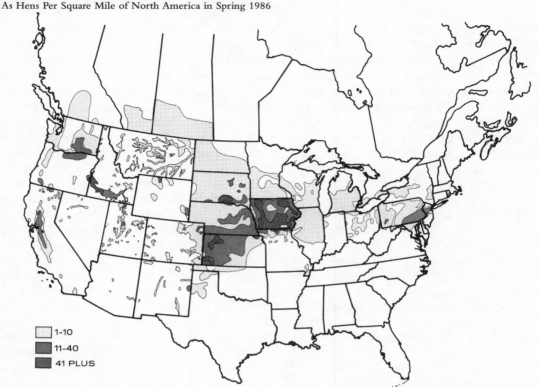

1-10

11-40

41 PLUS

Dahlgren, Robert B. "Distribution and Abundance of the Ring-Necked Pheasant in North America." In *PHEASANTS: Symptoms of Wildlife Problems on Agricultural Land: Proceedings of a Symposium Held at the 49th Midwest Fish and Wildlife Conference in Milwaukee, Wisconsin, December 8, 1987,* edited by Diana L. Hallet, William R. Edwards, and George V. Burger. Bloomington, Indiana: The Northcentral Section of The Wildlife Society, 1988, 34.

sissippi, Missouri, Illinois, and other rivers, as well as reservoirs and sloughs in the flyway corridors, pheasant, quail, wild turkeys, Hungarian partridge, and rabbits are also brought home in significant numbers. Less frequently, grouse and prairie chickens cross hunters' paths, providing pleasurable variation in the traditional game fare.

As shown on the map above, the core of the North American pheasant distribution lies in the Midwest. The Iowa Department of Natural Resources estimates that over 1.4 million pheasants were taken in Iowa by hunters in 1996—far and away the most bagged bird or animal in that state. Their plentifulness is not the only reason for their popularity. Perhaps more important is their unsurpassed rich flavor and tenderness which equate to luxurious dining.

Among waterfowl, game gourmands generally consider mallard ducks and Canada and white-fronted geese the supreme species for eating.

Midwest venison is known for its exceptional palatability, attributable to the fact that in addition to their customary browsing diet, Heartland deer feed on corn, soybeans, and other feed grains and legume crops grown in this agricultural area. This translates into high-quality meat, as with cattle and hogs. While whitetails are found in large numbers in nearly all parts of the continental United States, two Midwest states, Michigan and Wisconsin, ranked among the top five states in estimated 1997 deer populations, based on a national survey published in *Bowhunter* magazine (see Sources Consulted, page 842). In that year, 1,600,000 of these nimble animals were estimated to have populated Michigan, giving the state third place ranking in the nation behind Texas and Mississippi.

I grew up with hunting, and the resultant family meals of quail, duck, geese, and pheasant prepared with excellence by my mother. She often created memorable dinner parties when good friends were invited to share in the choice fare. Our traditionally copious supply and variety of game for dining is currently well maintained by my brother, whose intense interest and considerable expertise in hunting keep our freezers well stocked. In fact, he provided all the game for testing the recipes presented in this chapter.

Not only in our family, but in families all across the Midwest, hunters and the hunting ritual remain undaunted. On this open prairie where you can see the sun rise and set, when you wake up to find frost on the pumpkin and when the milkweed pods overflow with downy fuzzies which dance across the meadows on the wings of the autumn breeze, men's fancies turn to hunting. It is time to oil the shotgun, brush up on duck-calling skills, patch any tiny leaks in the waders, and buy a new fluorescent orange cap.

Even Prince, the English pointer in the backyard kennel, senses the impending excitement, impatiently awaiting the signal to jump into the metal dog carrier in the back of the Suburban, ready to head for his favorite activity. Hunting is in his genes, as Mother Nature imbued him with the instinctual finesse to find quail by scent and to hold them at point until his master quietly steals from behind and flushes the birds.

You know that some wonderful game dinners —ceremonies of life in the Midwest—are not too many weeks away.

BAKED PHEASANT

1 2- to 3-pound wild pheasant, skinned or
  unskinned, and dressed (page 22)
1 recipe Wild Rice Dressing (page 216)
2 slices bacon
¼ cup beef broth, homemade (page 87) or
  commercially canned

Wash the pheasant, inside and outside, under cold, running water. Using a paring knife, remove and discard most of the fat and any remaining gunshot, bits of feathers, and pinfeathers (if unskinned). Using paper towels, dry the pheasant on the outside and in the body cavity (also the neck cavity, if unskinned).

Preheat the oven to 325° F.

Stuff the cavity(ies) of the bird loosely with Wild Rice Dressing (see Note 1); truss (page 26) and set aside. Cut the bacon slices in half widthwise. Cover the pheasant breast with the bacon slices; set aside.

Lay a large piece of extra-heavy aluminum foil over a wire rack in a shallow roasting pan. Place the pheasant, breast up, on the aluminum foil. Cover the sharp ends of the poultry skewers (if used) with small pieces of aluminum foil to prevent piercing of the foil wrapping. Cup the aluminum foil around the sides of the pheasant. Pour the beef broth over the pheasant, retaining the broth within the foil. Seal the pheasant and beef broth in the aluminum foil.

Bake the pheasant for 2 hours. Then, open the foil to expose the breast. If the pheasant is unskinned, the bacon slices may be removed to allow the breast to brown for a more attractive appearance. (Before serving the pheasant, discard the bacon or reserve it for other uses.) Bake for an additional 30 minutes (see Note 2).

NOTE 1: Any remaining dressing may be placed in a buttered, round baking dish and baked, covered, for 45 minutes at 325° F. or 30 minutes at 350° F. Serve as additional dressing with the pheasant.

NOTE 2: Allow the pheasant to bake the full 2½ hours even though, in all likelihood, this baking time will exceed the time required for the bird to reach an internal temperature of 180° F., the recommended temperature for doneness of whole poultry (including game birds) (page 203). Game birds generally must be cooked longer than domestic poultry to achieve the desired doneness.

SERVES 4

WILD PHEASANT
WITH PORT WINE SAUCE

1 wild pheasant, plucked (not skinned),
   dressed (page 22), and cut into serving
   pieces
1 cup chicken broth, homemade (page 88)
   or commercially canned
½ cup port wine
1 bay leaf
½ cup all-purpose flour
1 teaspoon salt
¼ teaspoon pepper
2 tablespoons vegetable oil
2 tablespoons butter
½ cup currant jelly
1 teaspoon prepared mustard
1 teaspoon finely grated orange rind
   (page 47)

Wash the pheasant pieces under cold, running water. Using a paring knife, remove any remaining gunshot, bits of feathers, and pinfeathers. Place the pheasant pieces between several layers of paper towels to dry; set aside.

In a small mixing bowl, place the chicken broth, wine, and bay leaf; stir to combine; set aside. In another small mixing bowl, place the flour, salt, and pepper; stir to combine. Sprinkle the flour mixture over a piece of waxed paper. Dredge the pheasant pieces in the flour mixture and place on a clean piece of waxed paper; set aside.

Preheat an electric skillet or a large, heavy-bottomed skillet on the range to high heat (400° F. in an electric skillet). Place the vegetable oil in the skillet. Tilt the skillet back and forth to completely cover the bottom with the vegetable oil. Add the butter; spread to blend with the oil. Place the pheasant pieces, single layer, in the skillet and brown well on all sides (about 10 to 15 minutes). Reduce the skillet heat to very low (220° F. in an electric skillet). When the skillet cools to the reduced temperature, add the wine mixture. Cover and simmer for 1 hour, or until the pheasant is tender.

Meanwhile, in a small mixing bowl, place the jelly, mustard, and orange rind; stir to combine; set aside. When the pheasant is done, remove it from the skillet and arrange on a heated platter; cover with aluminum foil to keep warm. Place the jelly mixture in the skillet; stir until the jelly dissolves and blends with the skillet juices. Pour the sauce over the pheasant.

SERVES 3 OR 4

HUNGARIAN PARTRIDGE
GRAND MARNIER WITH
ORANGE-WILD RICE STUFFING

Native to Eurasia, Hungarian or gray partridge (Perdix perdix) were introduced to the United States in the late 1700's by Benjamin Franklin's son-in-law, who released some of the birds on his land in New Jersey. Numerous generally unsuccessful attempts were made to establish Hungarian partridge in many parts of this country in the early 1900's. However, through continual stocking attempts over the years, Hungarian partridge gradually have been established in North America, most successfully on the northern Great Plains which includes the western portion of the Midwest. (A hunting season for Hungarian partridge was established in Iowa in 1963.)

While Hungarian partridge are increasing in number, they are far less prevalent in the Midwest than ring-necked pheasants and bobwhite quail which, like Hungarian partridge, are members of the Phasianidae *family of gallinaceous birds. Gallinaceous birds are ground birds which feed on insects, grain, seeds, berries, and buds. They burst into rapid flight, but do not fly long distances. Hungarian partridge resemble quail, with a short tail and similar-looking head, but they are larger than quail, averaging about 10 inches long, which makes them especially nice for serving.*

1½ cups raw wild rice
1¾ cups homemade Beef Broth (page 87)
   or 1 14½-ounce can commercial beef
   broth
10 wild Hungarian partridge, dressed
⅓ cup finely diced orange peel
½ cup water
⅛ teaspoon ground nutmeg
10 slices bacon
1¾ cups homemade Beef Broth (page 87)
   or 1 14½-ounce can commercial beef
   broth
½ cup Grand Marnier
1½ cups freshly squeezed, strained orange
   juice, divided
¼ cup cornstarch
Salt (optional)
White pepper (optional)

Cook the wild rice in 1¾ cups beef broth (see page 276 for procedure). If necessary, add additional broth or water to the rice during cooking.

Wash the partridge, inside and outside, under cold, running water. Using a paring knife, remove any remaining gunshot, bits of feathers, and pinfeathers (if unskinned). Drain the partridge on several layers of paper towels.

Preheat the oven to 350° F.

In a tiny saucepan, place the orange peel and ½ cup water. Bring the mixture to a simmer over medium heat; reduce the heat and simmer, uncovered, 5 minutes. Remove from the heat; drain well in a small sieve. Add the drained orange peel and nutmeg to the rice; stir to combine. Spoon the orange–wild rice stuffing into the cavities of the partridge and pack lightly. With cotton string, tie the ends of the legs of each bird together; then run the string around the body of each bird and tie securely.

Cut the bacon slices in half widthwise; place 2 half slices over the breast of each partridge. Place the birds, single layer, breast up, in 1 or 2 heavy roasters; set aside. In a small mixing bowl, place 1¾ cups beef broth and the Grand Marnier; stir to blend. Pour over the partridge. Cover and bake for 2¼ hours, basting occasionally (see Note).

Remove the roaster(s) from the oven and transfer the birds to a large pan. Remove the bacon slices from the partridge and reserve. Cut and remove the string from the birds. Replace the bacon slices on the breasts of the partridge. Cover the pan with aluminum foil to keep the birds warm.

Strain the roaster juices in a sieve; then, pour into a medium saucepan. Add *1 cup* orange juice; stir to blend; set aside. In a small glass jar or plastic container with a secure lid, place the cornstarch and the remaining ½ cup orange juice; cover and shake vigorously until blended and smooth; set aside. Place the saucepan containing the roaster-juice mixture over medium heat. Bring the mixture to a simmer, stirring constantly. Add sufficient cornstarch mixture to bring the sauce to a medium-thin consistency, stirring continuously.

If commercial beef broth has been used, it is not necessary to add salt and white pepper to the sauce; if homemade broth has been used, the addition of salt and white pepper may be required, depending upon the seasoning of the broth and individual taste preference.

To serve, place 1 partridge on each individual dinner plate. Ladle a small amount of the sauce over the birds and pass the remainder in a sauceboat at the table.

NOTE: Allow the partridge to bake the full 2¼ hours even though, in all likelihood, this baking time will exceed the time required for the birds to reach an internal temperature of 180° F., the recommended temperature for doneness of whole poultry (including game birds) (page 203). Game birds generally must be cooked longer than domestic poultry to achieve the desired tenderness.

ALLOW 2 PARTRIDGE FOR DINERS WITH BIG APPETITES AND 1 FOR DINERS WITH LIGHTER APPETITES

SERVING SUGGESTION: Garnish the plates with Orange Baskets (page 401) filled with Gooseberry Conserve (page 759) or cranberry relish.

WILD DUCK WITH MERLOT WINE SAUCE

The mallard is generally considered to be the most desirable species of duck for dining from the Midwest fly-ways. Mallards are among the larger ducks and are sur-face feeders. Surface-feeding ducks, sometimes called "dabblers," seldom dive. Rather, they feed in shallow water or on dry land and are primarily vegetarians, although they eat some insects, small fish, and mollusks.

2 wild ducks, plucked (not skinned) and
    dressed (page 22)
2 small celery stalks with green leaves
2 medium carrots, pared
1 medium onion, quartered
2 sprigs of dried sage (or 1 tablespoon plus
    1 teaspoon dried leaf sage)
1½ cups merlot wine
¼ cup cognac
8 ounces fresh mushrooms, sliced (3 cups)
½ cup chopped onions
2 tablespoons snipped, fresh parsley
½ teaspoon salt
¼ teaspoon pepper
2 tablespoons all-purpose flour
½ cup merlot wine

Preheat the oven to 375° F.

Wash the ducks, inside and outside, under cold, running water. Using a paring knife, remove any remaining gunshot, bits of feathers, and pinfeathers. Using paper towels, dry the ducks on the outside and in the cavities. In the body cavity of each duck, place 1 celery stalk, 1 carrot, 2 quarters of the onion, and 1 sprig dried sage (or 2 teaspoons dried leaf sage).

Place the ducks, side by side, on a large piece of extra-heavy aluminum foil. Wrap the ducks loosely in the foil and place them on a wire rack in a shallow roasting pan. Bake the ducks for 45 minutes.

Meanwhile, in a medium mixing bowl, place 1½ cups merlot wine, cognac, mushrooms, ½ cup chopped onions, parsley, salt, and pepper; stir to combine; set aside.

After the ducks have baked for 45 minutes, remove them from the oven. Reduce the oven temperature to 325° F. Using a baster, remove and discard any fat which has accumulated in the bottom of the foil. Pour the wine mixture over the ducks, retaining the mixture within the foil. Pull the foil back over the birds, leaving a slight opening at the top. Return the ducks to the oven.

Bake the ducks until cooked medium (160° F. internal temperature) to medium rare (150° F. internal temperature), depending upon prefer-ence (see Note) (about 30 minutes to 1 hour additional baking time, depending upon the size of the ducks and doneness preference), basting frequently.

When done, place the ducks on a cutting board, reserving the wine mixture in the alu-minum foil. Remove and discard the vegetables and sage sprigs in the duck cavities. Using game shears, cut each duck in half lengthwise; cover with aluminum foil to keep warm.

Pour the wine mixture from the aluminum foil into a small saucepan; place over low heat. In a small glass jar or plastic container with a secure lid, place the flour and ½ cup merlot wine; cover and shake vigorously until blended. Add to the wine mixture in the saucepan; stir to blend. Increase the heat to medium-high; bring the sauce to a boil, stirring constantly. Reduce the heat to medium and cook 1 min-ute, until the sauce thickens, stirring continu-ously. Remove from the heat and cover.

Arrange the duck halves on a warm serving platter, or place on 4 individual dinner plates. Ladle a moderate amount of the wine sauce over the duck halves and pass the remaining sauce in a sauceboat at the table.

NOTE: While there are several schools of thought regarding the degree of doneness at which wild duck is best eaten, I side with the major-ity of duck hunters/connoisseurs who maintain that duck is at its height of flavor and succu-lence when served on the medium-rare side. There is some bacterial risk to consuming duck cooked to less than 160° F. internal temperature.

SERVES 4

BAKED GOOSE WITH APRICOT-COGNAC DRESSING

1 5- to 8-pound wild goose, plucked (not skinned) and dressed (page 22)
6 ounces chopped, dried apricots (about 1 cup)
3 cups small, fresh, whole-wheat bread cubes (about 5 slices bread; use crusts)
½ cup chopped onions
1 cup unpared, quartered, cored, and chopped Granny Smith apple (about 1 small apple)
½ teaspoon salt
¼ teaspoon pepper
¼ cup (4 tablespoons) butter, melted
2 tablespoons cognac, divided
4 slices bacon
¼ cup beef broth, homemade (page 87) or commercially canned
¼ cup cognac
1 recipe Apricot Sauce (page 365)

Wash the goose, inside and outside, under cold, running water. Using a paring knife, remove any remaining gunshot, bits of feathers, and pin-feathers. Cut away and discard as much fat as possible from the cavity. Using paper towels, dry the goose on the outside and in the cavities; set aside or cover and refrigerate until ready to roast.

Preheat the oven to 325°F.

Prepare the dressing just before stuffing and roasting the goose as follows: in a large mixing bowl, place the apricots, bread cubes, onions, apples, salt, and pepper. Pour the melted butter and 2 tablespoons cognac over the ingredients; toss lightly to combine. Stuff the neck and body cavities of the goose loosely with dressing (see Note 1). Using poultry skewers and cotton string, close the cavities. Tie the ends of the legs together to hold them close to the body. With a sharp fork, prick the breast of the goose 8 times to allow fat to drain during baking. Cut the bacon slices in half widthwise. Cover the goose breast with the bacon slices; set aside.

Lay a large piece of extra-heavy aluminum foil over a wire rack in a shallow roasting pan. Place the goose, breast up, on the aluminum foil. Cover the sharp ends of the poultry skewers with small pieces of aluminum foil to prevent piercing of the foil wrapping; set aside. In a small bowl, pour the beef broth and 2 tablespoons cognac; stir to blend; set aside. Cup the aluminum foil around the sides of the goose. Pour the beef broth mixture over the goose, retaining the mixture within the foil. Seal the goose and beef broth mixture in the aluminum foil.

Bake the goose for 40 minutes *per pound* (see Note 2). Do not baste. After 1½ hours of baking, open the foil and pour *1 tablespoon* of the cognac over the goose breast; reseal the foil. Repeat the procedure after an additional 1 hour of baking. One-half hour before the goose is done, open the foil to expose the breast; the bacon slices may be left on the breast or removed. The bacon slices help retain moisture; however, if the goose is to be served uncarved at the table, removal of the bacon slices will allow the breast to brown for a more attractive appearance. (Before serving the goose, discard the bacon or reserve it for other uses.)

To serve, spoon hot Apricot Sauce over individual servings of sliced goose. Pass additional Apricot Sauce in a sauce dish at the table.

NOTE 1: Any remaining dressing may be placed in a buttered, round baking dish and baked, covered, for 45 minutes at 325°F. or 30 minutes at 350°F. Serve as additional dressing with the goose.

NOTE 2: Allow the goose to bake the full 40 minutes per pound even though, in all likelihood, this baking time will exceed the time required for the bird to reach an internal temperature of 180°F., the recommended temperature for doneness of whole poultry (including game birds) (page 203). Game birds generally must be cooked longer than domestic poultry to achieve the desired tenderness.

SERVES 6 TO 10, DEPENDING UPON SIZE OF GOOSE

WILD GOOSE PÂTÉ

4 cups (1 pound) ground (use coarse grinder blade, page 49), cooked wild goose (page 241)
1 pound ground pork
½ pound ground ham
2 extra-large eggs
¼ cup whipping cream, unwhipped
¼ cup cognac
½ cup finely chopped onions
2 tablespoons finely snipped, fresh parsley
1 garlic clove, pressed
2 tablespoons all-purpose flour
¾ teaspoon salt
¾ teaspoon pepper
½ teaspoon ground thyme
¼ teaspoon ground cinnamon
½ pound thickly sliced side pork

ASPIC
½ cup cold water
2 teaspoons (1 envelope) unflavored gelatin
1 cup Clarified Beef Broth (page 88), divided
2 tablespoons cognac, divided
1 tablespoon snipped, fresh parsley
Snipped, fresh parsley for garnish (optional)
Cornichon* Pickle Fans (page 402) for garnish
Small, thin slices pumpernickel bread

*A type of pickle.

Set out two 3¾ × 7½ × 2¼-inch loaf pans. Cut 2 pieces of white, corrugated cardboard (cake board) *slightly* smaller in length and width than the top of the loaf pans. Cover the boards smoothly with aluminum foil; set aside. Preheat the oven to 350° F.

In a large mixing bowl, place the goose, pork, and ham; stir until well combined. Place about ⅓ of the meat mixture in a blender or food processor. Add the eggs, whipping cream, cognac, onions, parsley, and garlic. Using the blender or food processor, puree the mixture. Add the pureed mixture to the remaining meat

mixture in the mixing bowl; stir to combine; set aside. In a small sauce dish, place the flour, salt, pepper, thyme, and cinnamon; stir to combine. Add the flour mixture to the meat mixture; stir until thoroughly combined; set aside.

Line the loaf pans with the side pork, laying the pork slices, single layer, widthwise across the bottom of the pans and up the sides, letting the ends of the pork slices hang over the sides of the pans. Pack the meat mixture into the pork-lined pans. Use the back of a tablespoon to smooth the top of the mixture in each pan. Fold overlapping pork slices neatly over the meat mixture in each pan. Cover the pans tightly with heavy-duty aluminum foil. Place the loaf pans of pâté in a 9 × 13-inch baking pan. Pour very hot, but not boiling, water into the baking pan to approximately ½ the height of the loaf pans. Bake for 2 hours.

Remove the pans of pâté from the hot water and place on a wire rack. Remove the aluminum foil from the tops of the pans and discard. Place the foil-covered boards directly on the hot pâté in each pan. Place weights, such as heavy canned goods, directly on top of the foil-covered boards. Let stand 15 minutes. Then, transfer the wire racks holding the weighted pâtés to the refrigerator; let stand 8 hours or overnight. Weighting the pâtés during the cooling period will make them firmer in consistency and easier to slice.

After cooling, remove the weights and foil-covered boards. Run a sharp, thin-bladed knife around the inside edges of the pans. To unmold the pâtés, cover the tops of the pans with a large piece of plastic wrap; place a wire rack over 1 pan at a time and invert. Wrap the pâtés in the plastic wrap and refrigerate.

Then, wash, dry, and lightly oil (page 109) the 2 loaf pans in which the pâtés were baked; set aside, and proceed to make the aspic.

Pour ½ cup cold water into a small bowl; sprinkle the gelatin over the water; let stand 15 minutes. In a very small saucepan, place ¼ cup plus 2 teaspoons of the beef broth. Cover and refrigerate the remaining beef broth. Place the saucepan over high heat and bring the beef broth mixture to a boil. Remove from the heat. Add 3 tablespoons of the gelatin mixture; stir until completely dissolved. Cover the remaining gelatin mixture; set aside at room temperature. Let the beef broth mixture stand until lukewarm. Then, add 1 tablespoon of the cognac; stir to blend. Pour the beef broth mixture (aspic) over the bottoms of the 2 prepared loaf pans, dividing the mixture evenly between the pans. Refrigerate until the aspic is partially set. Distribute the snipped parsley evenly over the partially set aspic in the 2 pans; refrigerate until completely set (about 3 hours).

Unwrap the pâtés and carefully place them in the loaf pans over the set gelatin. Place the pâtés in the loaf pans as they were baked (do not invert the pâtés in the pans). Refrigerate the pâtés.

Pour the remaining, refrigerated beef broth into a small saucepan; bring to a boil over high heat. Remove from the heat. Add the remaining gelatin mixture; stir until completely dissolved. Let stand until lukewarm. Add the remaining 1 tablespoon cognac; stir to blend. Pour the aspic around and over the pâtés. Aspic should entirely cover the sides of the pâtés. Refrigerate until completely set (about 5 hours). Then, cover lightly with aluminum foil. Keeps in the refrigerator up to 3 days.

To unmold, remove the foil cover and follow the directions for unmolding small, individual salad molds (page 109). Using a sharp, thin-bladed knife, cut each pâté into 16 slices. To serve as a first-course appetizer, arrange 2 slices on each individual plate. Sprinkle snipped parsley sparingly over the pâté slices, if desired. Garnish the plates with Cornichon Pickle Fans. Arrange pumpernickel bread on a bread tray and pass at the table.

SERVES 16

WILD DUCK PÂTÉ: Substitute cooked wild duck for cooked wild goose.

VENISON PÂTÉ: Substitute cooked venison for cooked wild goose.

WILD TURKEY BREAST OVER RICE WITH SPICED GRAPE SAUCE

The native North American wild turkey (Meleagris gallopavo) is the source of all domesticated turkeys, which explains why wild and domestic turkeys look very much alike. The Eastern wild turkey (Meleagris gallopavo silvestris), one of the subspecies of the North American wild turkey, was the turkey of the Pilgrims and became our symbol of Thanksgiving.

Thanks to the efforts of state departments of natural resources, biologists, and the National Wild Turkey Federation, the North American wild turkey population has been regenerated. By about the early 1970's, wild turkeys had multiplied in the Midwest to the point that there was a harvestable population for hunting (beyond the protected breeding population).

Although wild turkeys roost in trees, they are incredibly fast ground runners, which accounts for their highly muscled legs (which do not make the best eating). While our family occasionally roasts a whole wild turkey on Thanksgiving to authentically celebrate the day, more often we prepare only the good-tasting, more tender breast.

1 8-pound wild turkey breast, skinned
¼ cup (4 tablespoons) butter, melted
¼ cup chicken broth, homemade (page 88) or commercially canned
2 cups raw long-grain rice (not instant), boiled (page 272)
Spiced Grape Sauce (recipe follows)

Preheat the oven to 325° F.

Wash the turkey breast under cold, running water. Using a paring knife, remove any remaining gunshot and bits of feathers; dry with paper towels. Place the breast in the center of a large piece of extra-heavy aluminum foil. Cup the foil around the sides of the breast. Brush the breast with the melted butter. Pour the chicken broth around the base of the breast, retaining the broth within the foil. Seal the breast and chicken broth in the aluminum foil.

(Recipe continues on next page)

Place on a wire rack in a shallow roasting pan. Bake for 4 hours (30 minutes per pound), basting occasionally (see Note).

To serve, slice the breast thinly and serve over the rice. Spoon the Spiced Grape Sauce over the turkey breast slices and pass the remaining sauce in a sauce dish at the table.

NOTE: Allow the breast to bake the full 30 minutes per pound even though, in all likelihood, this baking time will exceed the time required for the breast to reach an internal temperature of 170° F., the recommended temperature for doneness of whole poultry breasts (including game birds) (page 203). Game birds generally must be cooked longer than domestic poultry to achieve the desired tenderness.

SERVES 16

VARIATION: To prepare this recipe using domestic turkey breast, roast the turkey breast following the recipe for Roast Turkey Breast on page 214. Otherwise, follow this recipe for preparation of the rice and Spiced Grape Sauce, and for serving.

Spiced Grape Sauce

4 cups seedless white grapes cut in half lengthwise
6 2½-inch pieces of stick cinnamon
12 whole cloves
4 cups water
1 cup (½ pound) butter
2 tablespoons plus 2 teaspoons cornstarch
⅛ teaspoon ground cloves
2 cups white German Rhine wine or American Johannisberg Riesling
1 cup finely chopped celery hearts
½ cup chopped, fresh mushrooms

In a large saucepan, place the grapes, stick cinnamon, cloves, and water. Cover the saucepan. Bring the mixture to a boil over high heat; reduce the heat and simmer 5 minutes. Drain the mixture in a colander. Remove and discard the cinnamon sticks and cloves; set the grapes aside.

Melt the butter in a clean, dry, large saucepan over low heat. Remove from the heat. Add the cornstarch and ground cloves; stir until the mixture is perfectly smooth. Add the wine, celery, and mushrooms; stir to combine. Bring the mixture to a low simmer over medium heat, stirring constantly; simmer 5 minutes, stirring continuously. Add the drained grapes; heat through.

MAKES ABOUT 8 CUPS

QUAIL IN NESTS

Several species of quail are native to North America; however, only the bobwhite quail (Colinus virginianus) is found in the Midwest. Bobwhite quail are named after their call which sounds like "bob-bob-white." Mottled reddish brown in color, bobwhites nest under brush and in other ground cover, and roost there in groups called coveys. They are small birds, about 8 inches long and only 4 to 6 ounces dressed for cooking. This recipe was the winner of the Game Wardens' Wild Game Cook-Off at the 1990 Iowa State Fair.

½ cup dry white wine
1 cup chopped, fresh mushrooms
12 wild quail, dressed (page 22)
½ cup all-purpose flour
1 teaspoon salt
¼ teaspoon pepper
1 tablespoon vegetable oil
2 tablespoons butter, divided
¼ cup finely chopped shallots
1¾ cups homemade Chicken Broth (page 88) or 1 14½-ounce can commercial chicken broth
¾ cup pared and finely shredded carrots
2 tablespoons snipped, fresh parsley
2 tablespoons finely chopped celery
1 leafy celery-stalk top, chopped
Additional dry white wine, if necessary
½ teaspoon salt
⅛ teaspoon pepper
¼ cup all-purpose flour
½ cup water
12 Nests (recipe follows)

EARLY IN THE DAY: In a small glass bowl, place ½ cup wine and the mushrooms; cover with plastic wrap and refrigerate. Wash the quail, inside and outside, under cold, running water. Using a paring knife, remove any remaining gunshot, bits of feathers, and pinfeathers (if unskinned). Dry the quail on several layers of paper towels.

Slightly cross the legs of each bird and secure the legs close to the body with cotton string wrapped around the ends of the legs and around the bird; tie securely. Arrange the quail, single layer, on several layers of paper towels placed in the bottom of a flat baking dish. Cover the baking dish tightly with plastic wrap; refrigerate until ready to begin cooking the quail, allowing sufficient time for the birds to thoroughly drain.

2½ HOURS BEFORE SERVING TIME: In a small bowl, place ½ cup flour, 1 teaspoon salt, and ¼ teaspoon pepper; stir to combine. Sprinkle the flour mixture over a piece of waxed paper. Dredge the quail in the flour mixture and place on a clean piece of waxed paper; set aside.

Preheat an electric skillet or a heavy skillet on the range to medium-low to medium (330° F. in an electric skillet). Place the vegetable oil in the skillet. Using a spatula, spread the vegetable oil over the entire bottom of the skillet. Add 1 tablespoon of the butter. Tilt the skillet back and forth to blend the butter with the oil. (The vegetable oil will help prevent the butter from burning.) Place the quail in the skillet and brown on all sides (approximately 30 minutes). Handle the quail carefully to prevent the string from becoming loose. If necessary, add the remaining 1 tablespoon butter to the skillet during browning. When a nice, deep brown, remove the quail from the skillet and arrange, single layer, breast up, in the center of a heavy roaster; set aside. Reduce the skillet heat to very low (220° F. in an electric skillet) and let the skillet cool slightly.

Preheat the oven to 350° F.

Place the shallots in the skillet to simmer just a bit as the skillet continues to lose heat. When the skillet cools to the reduced temperature, add the chicken broth and deglaze. Add the refriger-ated wine and mushroom mixture, carrots, parsley, chopped celery, and chopped celery top; heat through, but do not allow to boil. Spoon the entire skillet mixture over and around the quail.

Cover the roaster and bake the quail 1½ hours. Baste the quail after the first 30 minutes of baking; then, baste every 20 minutes. Add a little additional dry white wine (or water), if necessary (see Note). Meanwhile, prepare the Nests and cover tightly with aluminum foil; place in a shallow baking pan, ready to toast just before serving.

NOTE: Allow the quail to bake the full 1½ hours even though, in all likelihood, this baking time will exceed the time required for the birds to reach an internal temperature of 180° F., the recommended temperature for doneness of whole poultry (including game birds) (page 203). Game birds generally must be cooked longer than domestic poultry to achieve the desired doneness.

SERVING TIME: Remove the quail from the roaster and place them in a baking pan. Leave the strings on the birds and cover the birds with aluminum foil to keep them warm; set aside.

Preheat the broiler.

Press the roaster juices and vegetables through a food mill; then, pour into a small saucepan. Add ½ teaspoon salt and ⅛ teaspoon pepper; stir to combine; set aside. In a small jar or plastic container with a secure lid, place ¼ cup flour and ½ cup water; cover and shake vigorously until well blended. Add about ½ of the flour mixture to the roaster-juice mixture in the saucepan; stir to blend. Bring the mixture to a boil over medium heat, stirring constantly and adding additional flour mixture, if needed, to achieve medium-thin consistency. Remove from the heat and strain the sauce through a sieve. Return the sauce to the pan; cover and keep warm.

Toast the Nests under the broiler until light brown. Remove the strings from the quail. Fit 1 quail into each hot, toasted Nest. Place 1 Quail in Nest on each individual dinner plate. Ladle

(Recipe continues on next page)

the sauce moderately over all. Pour the remaining sauce into a gravy boat and pass at the table.

SERVES 6 TO 12 (QUAIL ARE TINY AND MANY DINERS WILL EAT 2)

Nests

2 large loaves French bread
½ cup (¼ pound) butter, softened
½ teaspoon dried parsley
½ teaspoon dried leaf basil

Select bread slightly larger in diameter than the size of the quail; use only the large center sections of the loaves. Cut 12 slices of bread 1½ inches thick. With your fingers, carefully pull out pieces of bread from the center portion of each slice to form a nest about 1 inch deep, leaving about ½ inch of bread at the base of the Nest. Butter the entire top side of each Nest, including the inside and top edge. Sprinkle the entire top side of each Nest with the parsley and basil. Follow the recipe for completion of the Nests.

ACCOMPANIMENT AND SERVING SUGGESTIONS: Pecan Wild Rice (page 276) is a perfect complement to Quail in Nests. Spread a generous bed of Pecan Wild Rice over a large serving platter. Arrange the Quail in Nests on the rice. Garnish the platter with Artichoke Bottoms Filled with Tiny Vegetables (page 396) and decorate the platter with A Bunch of Whole Miniature Carrots (page 398). Pour all of the sauce into a gravy boat and pass at the table.

Other Wild Game Recipes

Wine-Marinated Venison Steaks (page 259)

Outdoor Cooking

From the arrival of the first robin until the sumacs surrender their scarlet leaves to foreboding fall winds, there's a whole lotta outdoor cooking goin' on in Milwaukee, Wisconsin; Smithton, Missouri; Minot, North Dakota; Anderson, Indiana; and all points in between.

Rolling the grill out of the garage and wiping off Winter's dusty shroud, checking out the charcoal supply, and locating the long-handled tongs in readiness for grilling the season's first steaks or hamburgers under the setting sun are Midwest rites of spring. It is a heartening precursor to the other good things just around the corner—golf, Bermuda shorts, sailing, horse shows, and pancake breakfasts in the woods.

This is not to ignore the dedicated few who shovel a path through the snow to roast the Christmas turkey on the outdoor grill. But most of us prefer to light our winter fires in the family room fireplace, cozy up to the hearth, and nibble on a piece of warm mincemeat pie as we watch the crackling fire ebb to pulsating red coals. Nevertheless, gas-flame grills, in particular, make year-round outdoor cooking feasible for people who have protected porches and for those who live in the southerly reaches of the Heartland, where Old Man Winter is less harsh.

To north woods fishermen and canoe trippers, "outdoor cooking" connotes shore lunches, when fallen pine and birch logs are chopped to build an open fire, and brown, prickly needles, gathered by the handsful under soaring, green pine trees, serve as kindling, and when the morning's walleye catch is filleted for frying with potatoes in a heavy cast-iron skillet as soon as the fire calms down a bit. After such an in-comparable midday feast, a short snooze is in order, with your back propped against a big tree and the scent of pine comin' on the breeze.

But the recipes in this book have been crafted for outdoor cooking on man-made grills which are adaptable to most any setting. From the simple, charcoal, kettle type to the big, pricey, gas-fueled models with all the sophisticated trappings, these "now" requisites fill the sum-mer, locust-humming Midwest air with that dis-tinct, incredible aroma of something wonderful grilling. In backyards, and on patios, decks, porches, and driveways in cities, towns, and on farms, grilling is definitely hot! And the portable models are on the go in vans, station wagons, and recreational vehicles headed for picnics in state parks, cookouts on riverbanks, and Little League baseball games.

CONTEMPORARY GRILLERS

This outdoor cooking craze is hardly unique to the Midwest. It prevails from sea to shining sea for good reason. Grilling of meats results in a singular, luscious flavor which cannot be dupli-cated by any other cooking method, and few homes are equipped to grill food indoors. In the wintertime, many snowbelt steak zealots get their T-bone fixes at their favorite steak houses where bona fide indoor grills are standard equipment.

Another reason for the universal appeal of cooking outdoors is that it puts the quietus on slaving over a hot stove on a summer evening, when you could be out watering the snapdrag-ons—droopy from the searing afternoon sun—while the charcoal is readying in the grill. Plus—not a small consideration—the cleanup is a breeze.

About forty to fifty years ago, when outdoor grilling burst into popularity, in part due to effi-cient, reasonably priced grilling equipment becoming more readily available, it was gener-ally customary for the man of the house to take charge of grilling while the woman of the house prepared the rest of the meal. Grilling was a man's world. In that era, when most Midwest husbands did not cook, and housewives were four-star generals over the pots and pans, many males received their cooking baptism at the out-door grill, discovering for the first time the sat-isfaction and fun of cookery. To a great extent, Midwest men still hold sway when it comes to the Weber, but by no means is outdoor cooking the exclusive men's club it used to be (nor is indoor cooking only a woman's purview nowadays).

While grilled steaks and hamburgers continue to dominate the outdoor cooking scene, the ver-satility of present-day grilling equipment has expanded outdoor cooking to encompass addi-tional cooking methods other than plain grilling.

Today, beautifully prepared roasts, hams, and turkeys cooked by indirect heat are proudly marched to the kitchen for carving by apron-clad grillers who have mastered this technique. On other occasions, golden-brown chickens, self-basting on efficient rotisseries, whet the appetites of hungry onlookers as orange-ginger glaze is brushed on the birds just minutes before serving (Rotisserie Chicken with Orange-Ginger Glaze, page 256). And hickory-smoked barbecued ribs, lazily cooked all afternoon in special smokers, automatically transform any get-together into a memorable summer dining experience (Gary's Hickory-Smoked Pork Ribs, page 252).

Outdoor grills have proven user-friendly when it comes to the preparation of a wide vari-ety of foods which reflect changes in population eating habits. Increasingly, skinless, boneless chicken breasts and thick fish steaks—often marinated to add special flavors and succulence—appear on the outdoor-cooking bill of fare. Lobster tails, pork chops, wild game, and veg-etables also join the outdoor-cooking cavalcade with more regularity. The fact that grilling is one of the lower-fat cooking methods recom-mended by the National Cholesterol Education Program of the National Heart, Lung, and Blood Institute has added momentum to the trend toward greater diversity in the types of food now popularly grilled in the open air.

Meat Safety for Outdoor Cooking

For basic principles on the safe storage, handling, and cooking of meat, see Meat Safety, page 157. The following are additional safety guidelines which specifically pertain to cooking meat outdoors:

- Marinate meat in a glass dish in the refrigerator, not on the kitchen counter. When preparing marinade, reserve any portion needed for basting or making a sauce; then, combine the remaining marinade with the raw meat. Do not baste meat cooking on the grill with marinade which has been in contact with raw meat unless it has been boiled.

- Wash forks, tongs, brushes, and other tools which come in contact with raw meat in hot, soapy water before reusing them to handle cooked meat.

- When cooking meat ahead in a conventional or microwave oven (see Note), cook it completely to ensure that bacteria throughout the meat are destroyed. Then, quickly cool the cooked meat in the refrigerator. Later, the meat can safely be reheated on the grill to add that distinctive barbecue flavor.

It is safe to partially cook meat in the oven or microwave, or to parboil it to reduce outdoor cooking time, only if—after partially cooking or parboiling—the meat *immediately* goes on the grill.

- In hot weather of 85° F. or above, do not leave meat out more than 1 hour before cooking and 1 hour after cooking. It is best to take raw meat directly from the refrigerator (or cooler, if picnicking) to the grill. Immediately refrigerate leftovers.

- Cook meat to the safe internal temperatures specified in Meat Safety, page 157, but be careful not to overcook meat on the outdoor grill. Remove visible fat from raw meat before placing it on the grill to avoid flare-ups. Do not consume charred meat.

- Place cooked meat on a clean platter, not on the unwashed platter which held the raw meat.

- Clean the grill after each use.

For further information and answers to specific questions regarding the safe cooking of meat outdoors, call the U.S. Department of Agriculture's Meat and Poultry Hotline at 800-535-4555 (in Washington, D.C., call 202-720-3333), Monday through Friday, 10:00 A.M.–4:00 p.m. Eastern time.

NOTE: See Food Safety: Microwave Ovens, page 31, for information on safe microwave cooking.

BARBECUE SAUCE FOR OUTDOOR COOKING

1 tablespoon extra-virgin olive oil
1 tablespoon butter
¾ cup finely ground (page 49) onions
  (about 1 large onion)
1 large garlic clove, pressed
1 14-ounce bottle (about 1½ cups)
  commercial hot catsup
½ cup red wine vinegar
½ cup dry red wine
¼ cup unsulphured molasses
3 tablespoons freshly squeezed, strained
  lemon juice
3 tablespoons Worcestershire sauce
2 tablespoons horseradish mustard
2 tablespoons chili powder
2 teaspoons ground cumin
½ teaspoon celery salt
½ teaspoon dry mustard
½ teaspoon salt
¼ teaspoon pepper
8 dashes Tabasco pepper sauce
1 tablespoon cornstarch
1 tablespoon red wine vinegar

In a medium-large, deep, heavy-bottomed, non-aluminum saucepan, heat the olive oil over medium heat. Tilt the saucepan back and forth to completely cover the bottom with the olive oil. Add the butter; spread to blend with the oil. Place the onions and garlic in the saucepan; sauté 10 minutes, stirring and turning often. Remove from the heat. Add the catsup, ½ cup vinegar, wine, molasses, lemon juice, Worcestershire sauce, horseradish mustard, chili powder, cumin, celery salt, dry mustard, salt, pepper, and pepper sauce; stir to combine. Place over medium heat; bring the mixture to a simmer, stirring often. Reduce the heat and simmer, uncovered, 30 minutes, stirring frequently. Remove from the heat; set aside.

In a very small sauce dish, place the cornstarch and 1 tablespoon vinegar; stir until perfectly smooth. Add to the barbecue sauce mixture; stir to blend. Place over medium heat and bring to a simmer, stirring constantly. Reduce the heat and simmer 5 minutes, stirring nearly constantly as the sauce thickens. Remove from the heat; cool slightly. Pour the Barbecue Sauce into a heatproof quart jar (such as a canning jar); cover and refrigerate.

MAKES ABOUT 2¼ CUPS

Beef

GRILLED STEAK

Steaks for grilling: tenderloin fillet (and
  filet mignon), top loin, porterhouse, rib
  eye, T-bone, rib, sirloin, and chuck eye*
Salt or garlic salt (optional)
Pepper (optional)

1½ inches is the preferable thickness for most grilled steaks, depending upon the cut.

Trim away the excess fat from the edges of the steaks. To prevent the steaks from curling during grilling, slit the remaining fat at 2-inch intervals around the edges of the steaks, being careful not to penetrate the flesh, causing loss of meat juices. If desired, *just prior to grilling,* the steaks may be seasoned lightly with salt or garlic salt, and pepper.

Place the steaks on the cooking grate in an outdoor grill, about 4 inches above medium-hot coals (the coals should be covered with a thin layer of ash). Grill the steaks uncovered. Use tongs (a fork will pierce the meat and cause loss of juice) to turn the steaks only once, grilling 2 minutes longer on the first side than on the second side. While the length of grilling time depends not only upon the desired doneness but also upon the size of the steaks, the temperature of the coals, and the weather, the following time chart may serve as a guideline for grilling 1½-inch steaks:

Approximate Grilling Times

	Minutes	
Doneness	1st Side	2nd Side
1½-INCH-THICK STEAKS		
Rare*	9	7
Medium Rare	11	9
Medium	13	11
Well Done	16	14

There is some bacterial risk when beef is consumed rare (140°F.) (see Meat Safety, page 157).

To grill 1-inch-thick steaks, deduct approximately 5 minutes total from the above grilling times.

Use an instant thermometer (page 44) to test for doneness. Or, test for doneness by slitting the steak near the bone, using a sharp, thin-bladed knife. For steaks with no bone, make a slit in the center of the steak.

GRILLED HAMBURGER STEAK

2¼ pounds lean, pure ground beef
¾ cup finely chopped onions
1 extra-large egg
½ teaspoon salt
¼ teaspoon pepper
6 slices bacon
Chili sauce, home canned (page 783) or commercially canned

In a large mixing bowl, place the ground beef, onions, egg, salt, and pepper; using a large, metal mixing spoon, break up the ground beef and combine all the ingredients well. Form the ground beef mixture into 6 1-inch-thick patties. Wrap a strip of bacon around each patty and secure with half a toothpick.

Place the hamburger steaks on the cooking grate in an outdoor charcoal or gas grill, about 4 inches above *hot* coals (the coals should be barely covered with ash). Grill the hamburger steaks uncovered. For medium-done hamburger steaks, grill for 3 minutes. Turn the hamburger steaks and grill for 10 minutes. Then, turn and grill for an additional 10 minutes. For well-done hamburger steaks, turn again and grill another 7 minutes.

Carefully remove the toothpicks before serving. Pass the chili sauce in a sauce dish at the table.

SERVES 6

Pork

GRILLED IOWA PORK CHOPS

As prepared and served annually at the Iowa State Fair by the Iowa Pork Producers. They use Seven Seas Viva Italian salad dressing when grilling these awesome chops.

8 Iowa Pork Chops (center-cut pork loin chops, 1¼ to 1½ inches thick)
Garlic salt
1 8-ounce bottle commercial Italian salad dressing (see headnote)

Place the pork chops on the cooking grate in an outdoor charcoal or gas grill, 4 to 6 inches above medium-hot coals (the coals should be covered with a thin layer of ash). Grill the pork chops for 15 minutes, uncovered. Then, sprinkle the chops lightly with garlic salt. Using a brush, cover the

(Recipe continues on next page)

surface of the chops with salad dressing. Turn the chops and immediately repeat the garlic salt and salad dressing additions on the second side of the chops. Grill the chops, uncovered, for an additional 10 minutes or until the internal temperature reaches 160° F. (medium done) (Turn the chops only once.)

SERVES 8

GARY'S HICKORY SMOKED PORK RIBS

10 to 11 pounds (about 6 racks) pork loin back (baby back) ribs*
8 hickory wood chunks approximately 1 × 1 × 2 inches each
2 recipes Barbecue Sauce for Outdoor Cooking (page 250)

Have the butcher remove the fell (a thin, tough membrane) from the bony side of the ribs.

THE SMOKER: Use a manufactured smoker (rather than a homemade device) which utilizes charcoal for the heat source rather than electricity or gas (see Note). The use of charcoal will result in better-flavored ribs. Select a smoker which has a water pan inside the unit. Because smoked ribs are cooked over a long period of time on low heat, evaporating water from a water pan will retard drying of the ribs. The smoker should have a thermometer with a gauge visible when the smoker is closed.

NOTE: To use an electric or gas smoker, follow the manufacturer's instructions.

TO PREPARE THE SMOKER: Follow the smoker manufacturer's instructions carefully. A large quantity of charcoal is required—approximately 3 gallons in most smokers which accommodate 10 to 12 pounds of loin back ribs. Place the hickory wood chunks in a clean bowl of water and soak them *at least* 1 hour (the longer, the better) before starting the charcoal fire.

Unlike lighting charcoal for most outdoor cooking, when all of the briquets are started at the same time, to prepare the charcoal for cooking ribs in a smoker, apply starter fluid only to the center portion of the charcoal and ignite. The fire will spread slowly outward over the charcoal, thus maintaining relatively steady heat during the long, slow cooking process. Let the charcoal burn approximately 15 minutes until the ignited briquets are white around the edges. It is important that all of the starter fluid be completely burned off before placing the ribs in the smoker to avoid an undesirable flavor in the smoked meat.

Place the water pan near the charcoal so the heat will expedite the evaporation process. Fill the pan completely with cool water. One 12-ounce bottle or can of beer, or 8 ounces of dry red wine, may be substituted for part of the water in the water pan; however, these beverages will impart a distinctly different flavor to the ribs which some diners do not consider desirable.

Place 4 soaked hickory wood chunks over the ignited briquets. (Do not use more than 4 hickory chunks at this point, as more chunks might cause too much flaming.)

TO COOK THE RIBS: Using a pastry brush, apply a generous but not excessive amount of Barbecue Sauce to the meaty side of the ribs. Then, place the ribs, bony side down, on the grills or racks in the smoker. Close the smoker. The smoking/cooking time will be approximately 4 to 5 hours, depending upon the heat in the smoker and the outdoor temperature. Ribs can be cooked on a cold, winter day if the smoker is in an area protected from the wind.

The temperature inside the smoker may vary satisfactorily within the range of 225 to 260° F. *Do not* open the smoker during the entire smoking/cooking period unless the temperature inside the smoker drops below 225° F. In such case, open the smoker to stir the fire and/or add a few charcoal briquets if needed. If it is necessary to open the smoker to recharge the fire, add boiling water to fill the water pan; 2 to 4 of the remaining soaked hickory wood chunks may be placed on the fire if increased hickory flavor is desired. Do not open the smoker for the purpose of filling the water pan, even if you suspect that the water has entirely evaporated.

The ribs are ready to serve when removed from the smoker. The meat will be pinkish red in color. Additional hot Barbecue Sauce may be passed at the table.

SERVES 10 (ALLOW 1 POUND RIBS PER DINER)

PORK ROAST WITH TANGY ROSEMARY SAUCE

Until I began writing this cookbook, our family had never tackled the preparation of a roast on the outdoor grill. I guess we had always envisioned it a demanding task with questionable results. We were wrong! Once you take a few minutes to learn the procedure for roasting by indirect heat on the grill, you find that it's quite simple. The roasts are not only reliably cooked, but they have a unique, tantalizing flavor not achievable in the kitchen oven. Add a sauce, such as the rosemary sauce in this recipe, and you have phenomenal eating with little effort. Roasts prepared on the grill are great to serve when you gather family or friends for a weekend meal in the summertime.

½ cup tomato catsup, home canned (page 781) or commercially canned
¼ cup red wine vinegar
2 tablespoons packed dark brown sugar
2 teaspoons dried leaf rosemary
1 garlic clove, pressed
1 3- to 4-pound boneless pork rib-end roast, tied every 1¼ inches

EARLY IN THE DAY: In a small mixing bowl, place the catsup, vinegar, brown sugar, rosemary, and garlic; stir until well combined. Cover and refrigerate.

TO PREPARE THE OUTDOOR GRILL FOR INDIRECT COOKING: Purchase ready-made, or construct out of extra-heavy aluminum foil, a shallow, aluminum foil drip pan slightly larger than the area under the roast during grilling. Place the drip pan on the center of the fuel grate. Al-though not necessary, if you have them, attach 2 charcoal rails to the outside wires along both sides of the fuel grate (1 rail on each outside wire). These rails will help contain the charcoal when added.

Then, mound a plentiful and equal amount of charcoal along both of the long sides of the drip pan on the outside of the pan (*or*, along the outside of the rails). Remove the drip pan from the grill and set aside.

25 MINUTES BEFORE COMMENCING TO COOK THE ROAST (ABOUT 2 HOURS BEFORE SERVING): Ignite the coals and let them burn about 25 minutes until they are lightly coated with gray ash. Then, replace the drip pan on the fuel grate. Place the cooking grate in the grill, about 4 inches above the coals.

Place the roast on an outdoor-grill roast holder (a V-shaped wire rack available where outdoor cooking equipment is sold). Insert a meat thermometer to the center of the roast. Place the holder containing the roast on the cooking grate directly above the drip pan. Using a brush, generously baste the roast with the rosemary sauce. Cover the grill.

Roast the meat for 1 to 1¾ hours, until the meat thermometer reaches 160° F. for medium doneness (see Note), brushing the roast with the rosemary sauce every 20 minutes. Remove the roast from the grill when the thermometer reaches 5° F. below the desired temperature, as the meat will continue cooking. The length of cooking time depends upon the desired doneness, the size of the roast, and the heat of the coals. If the grill contains a thermometer, try to maintain a grill temperature of 325 to 350° F. If the grill temperature begins to drop, carefully tap some of the ash off the coals with a long-handled implement or add a few more charcoal briquets.

When the roast has reached the desired doneness, remove it from the grill and let it stand 5 to 10 minutes before slicing.

NOTE: For well done, roast until the thermometer reaches 170° F.

A 4-POUND ROAST SERVES 8

MUSHROOM AND CHEESE-FILLED PORKBURGERS

As enamored of hamburgers as we Americans are, it's a wonder that more of us haven't discovered equally delicious porkburgers! While pork tenderloins are among the Midwest's favorite sandwiches, you don't often find porkburgers sizzling on outdoor grills or listed on restaurant menus. That is bound to change! These sensational-tasting burgers are made with plain ground pork (not pork sausage, which is highly seasoned ground pork). They are prepared exactly the same way as hamburgers and should be cooked to the same degree of doneness (medium [160° F.] or well-done [170° F.]). Here is a snazzy way to prepare grilled porkburgers adapted from an Iowa Pork Producers Association recipe. You sandwich mushrooms, green onions, and Swiss cheese between two ground pork patties and seal the edges. Diners will be delightfully surprised to find the hidden treasure of savories when they take the first bite.

1 tablespoon butter
1 cup sliced, fresh mushrooms
1½ pounds extra-lean, ground pork
1 teaspoon garlic salt
¼ teaspoon pepper
¼ cup thinly sliced green onions (scallions)
4 ounces (1 cup) shredded Swiss cheese

FIVE HOURS BEFORE GRILLING: In a small, heavy-bottomed skillet, heat the butter over medium heat. Tilt the skillet back and forth to completely cover the bottom with the melted butter. Place the mushrooms in the skillet; sauté lightly only until the mushrooms give up their juices (2 or 3 minutes); set aside.

In a large mixing bowl, place the ground pork, garlic salt, and pepper; using a large, metal mixing spoon, break up the ground pork and stir until the ingredients are well combined. With the back of the mixing spoon, pat the ground pork mixture into the bottom of the bowl; using a knife, cut the mixture into 8 equal portions. Using your hands, roll each portion into a ball and place on a piece of waxed paper. Pat out each ball into a patty about 4 inches in diameter. Using a slotted spoon, distribute the mushrooms equally over 4 of the patties to within ½ inch of the outer edges. Distribute the onions equally over the mushrooms. Scatter the cheese equally over the onions. Place each of the 4 unfilled patties over one of the filled patties. Pinch the edges of the patties together to seal.

Place the filled patties on a tray lined with plastic wrap; cover tightly with the plastic wrap. Refrigerate for at least 4 hours to chill well so the porkburgers will hold their shape during grilling.

TO GRILL THE PORKBURGERS: Place the porkburgers on the cooking grate in an outdoor grill, about 4 inches above *medium* coals (the coals should glow through a layer of ash). Grill the porkburgers, uncovered, for 15 minutes on the first side; turn once and grill for 8 minutes on the second side, until no pink meat remains.

SERVES 4

Chicken

MESQUITE-GRILLED CHICKEN BREASTS

3 whole, skinless, boneless chicken breasts, cut in half lengthwise (1½ to 2 pounds total)
8 mesquite wood chips approximately 1 × 1 × 2 inches each

Wash the chicken breasts under cold, running water. Cut away any remaining fat on the breasts. Place the breasts between several layers of paper towels to dry. When dry, place the breasts in a flat-bottomed dish; cover and refrigerate.

Place the wood chips in a large, clean bowl or pan. Cover the chips with water; let stand at least 30 minutes. Meanwhile, ignite the charcoal in the outdoor grill; let stand about 30 minutes until the coals are medium hot (the coals should be covered with a thin layer of ash). Distribute the medium-hot coals, single layer, over the fuel grate. Drain the wood chips; distribute them over the coals. (If using a gas grill, consult the manufacturer's instructions for using wood chips.)

Spray the clean, cold, outdoor-grill cooking grate with nonstick cooking spray. Just before commencing to grill the chicken breasts, place the cooking grate in the grill, about 4 inches above the coals. Place the chicken breasts on the cooking grate and grill, uncovered, for 4 to 5 minutes per side, depending upon the size of the breasts, the temperature of coals, and the weather. Do not overcook the chicken breasts as they will become tough and dry. Serve hot or refrigerate, covered, for use in other recipes.

SERVES 6

PLAIN GRILLED CHICKEN BREASTS: Follow the Mesquite-Grilled Chicken Breasts recipe, above, eliminating the mesquite wood chips.

GRILLED CHICKEN BREASTS WITH FRESH SUMMER SAVORY AND TOASTED WALNUTS

3 tablespoons finely minced leeks (about 1 leek) (see recipe procedures, below)
2 teaspoons butter
1½ cups chicken broth, homemade (page 88) or commercially canned
2 teaspoons fresh, snipped summer savory
2 teaspoons white balsamic vinegar
2 teaspoons honey

1 teaspoon cornstarch
¼ teaspoon finely grated fresh ginger
¼ teaspoon salt
⅛ teaspoon white pepper
¼ cup broken English walnuts, toasted (page 50)
4 Plain Grilled Chicken Breasts (left column)
Sprigs of fresh summer savory for decoration

Trim away and discard the root end and leaves of the leek, leaving only the white and greenish white parts. Slice the leek in half lengthwise and wash it well, making certain all sand has been washed away. Mince the leek finely. Measure 3 tablespoons minced leeks and place in a small sauce dish; set aside.

In a small, heavy-bottomed saucepan, melt the butter over medium-low heat. Add the minced leeks and sauté about 5 minutes, until the leeks are softened. Do not allow the leeks to brown. Remove from the heat. Add the chicken broth; stir to combine. Cover the saucepan. Over high heat, bring the chicken broth mixture to a boil. Uncover the saucepan and reduce the heat to medium. Cook the mixture at a gentle boil until reduced to about 1 cup (about 15 minutes). Remove from the heat.

To the reduced chicken broth mixture, add the summer savory, vinegar, honey, cornstarch, ginger, salt, and white pepper; stir well to combine. Over medium heat, bring the mixture to a gentle boil, stirring constantly. Boil the mixture 5 minutes to blend the flavors and thicken the mixture, continuing to stir constantly. Remove from the heat. Add the walnuts to the hot chicken broth mixture just before serving; stir to combine.

Place the hot Plain Grilled Chicken Breasts on 4 individual plates or on a serving platter. Spoon the sauce over the chicken breasts. Decorate with sprigs of fresh summer savory.

SERVES 4

ROTISSERIE CHICKEN WITH ORANGE-GINGER GLAZE

1 to 3 3-pound whole chickens (fryers)*
1 tablespoon vegetable oil per chicken
½ cup orange marmalade, home canned
   (page 762) or commercially canned
2 teaspoons ground ginger
2 tablespoons tomato catsup, home canned
   (page 781) or commercially canned
¼ cup vegetable oil

If cooking only 1 chicken, cut the glaze ingredients in half (use ¼ cup orange marmalade, 1 teaspoon ginger, 2 tablespoons catsup, and 2 tablespoons vegetable oil).

TO PREPARE THE GRILL AND FIRE: Prepare the outdoor grill for cooking the chicken(s) indirectly by placing a drip pan(s) on the fuel grate, under the rotisserie spit where the chicken(s) will be mounted, and by mounding a generous and equal amount of charcoal briquets on either side of the drip pan(s) on the outside of the pan(s). The coals should be about 6 inches from the spit. Remove the drip pan(s) from the grill and set aside.

Ignite the coals and let them burn about 25 minutes until they are lightly coated with gray ash. Then, replace the drip pan(s) in the grill.

TO PREPARE THE CHICKEN(S) FOR THE ROTIS-SERIE: To prepare each chicken, wash, inside and outside, under cold, running water. Using paper towels, dry the outside and cavities of the chicken. Cut away and discard the neck skin if it has been left on the chicken. Secure the wings close to the body by placing heavy cotton string under the back of the bird widthwise, pulling it tightly around the bird, looping each end of the string around one of the wings, and tying the string over the breast. For further security, the string may be pulled around the body and wings again (omitting looping the wings) and tied over the breast. Leave the string ends uncut.

Insert the spit through the chicken lengthwise, and firmly insert the holding fork into the front end of the bird; tighten the holding-fork screw. Then, insert the second holding fork into the tail end of the bird and tighten the holding-fork screw. Wrap another piece of string around the tail and pull crosswise over the spit to secure the tail to the spit. Loop the ends of the string around the crossed legs of the bird and tie securely. Leave the string ends uncut. Then, pull the wing and leg strings together and tie. Repeat the mounting procedure if cooking 2 or 3 chickens (using 2 holding forks per chicken).

Center the chicken(s) evenly on the spit. Brush each chicken generously with about 1 tablespoon vegetable oil.

NOTE: The procedure for mounting 1 or more chickens on a spit vary with the size and make of the grill. Check the manufacturer's instructions for specific information on using your grill for rotisserie cooking.

TO COOK THE CHICKEN(S): When the coals are ready and the drip pan(s) has been replaced in the grill, mount the spit holding the chicken(s) on the rotisserie and cover the grill. The grill temperature should be about 350° F. (medium heat). Rotate the chicken(s) on the rotisserie about 1 to 1¼ hours, until an instant thermometer (page 44) inserted to the center of the thickest part of the breast registers 180° F. If the cooking time exceeds 1 hour, add some additional briquets. It is not necessary to brush additional vegetable oil on the chicken(s) during cooking as it (they) will self-baste.

Meanwhile, in a small mixing bowl, place the marmalade, ginger, catsup, and ¼ cup vegetable oil; stir until blended. When the chicken reaches 180° F. internal temperature, brush the marmalade mixture over the entire body of the bird(s) as it (they) rotates. Then, cover the grill and let the chicken(s) rotate about 1½ minutes. Repeat this glazing procedure 2 more times (about 5 minutes total time for the glazing process), being watchful not to allow the glazed chicken(s) to overbrown.

Remove the chicken(s) from the spit. Remove and discard the string. Using poultry shears or a sharp knife, cut the chicken(s) in half lengthwise. For smaller portions, cut each half in two widthwise.

ONE CHICKEN SERVES 2 TO 4 PERSONS

TO COOK THE CHICKEN(S) ON A ROAST HOLDER: Rather than cooking the chicken(s) on a rotisserie, 1 or 2 chickens may be cooked and glazed on an outdoor-grill roast holder. See the recipe for Pork Roast with Tangy Rosemary Sauce (page 253) for preparation of the outdoor grill and placement of the roast holder.

To prepare each chicken, wash, inside and outside, under cold, running water. Using paper towels, dry the outside and cavities of the chicken. Cut away and discard the neck skin if it has been left on the chicken. Fold the wings under the back. Cross the legs and tie them together securely with cotton string. Brush the bird with vegetable oil as in the rotisserie recipe above. Place the bird, breast up, on the roast holder. Insert a meat thermometer into one of the inner thigh areas near the breast, making certain the tip of the thermometer is not touching bone.

When the coals are ready, place the roast holder containing the chicken(s) on the cooking grate directly above the drip pan. Cover the grill and cook for approximately the same period of time as in the rotisserie recipe. Do not turn the chicken(s). When the internal temperature reaches 180° F., remove the meat thermometer. Glaze the accessible parts of chicken(s) 3 times, following the procedure in the rotisserie recipe.

Fish

MARINATED FISH STEAKS

6 salmon, tuna, swordfish, or halibut steaks, 1 inch thick
1 cup freshly squeezed, strained orange juice
¼ cup freshly squeezed, strained lemon juice
¼ cup extra-virgin olive oil
¼ cup tomato catsup, home canned (page 781) or commercially canned
¼ cup low-sodium soy sauce
2 tablespoons snipped, fresh parsley
1 tablespoon snipped, fresh marjoram
½ teaspoon white pepper
Lemon wedges for garnish

Wash the fish steaks under cold, running water and place them between several layers of paper towels to dry; set aside. In a quart jar or plastic container with a secure lid, place the orange juice, lemon juice, olive oil, catsup, soy sauce, parsley, marjoram, and white pepper; cover and shake vigorously until blended and smooth. Pour ¼ cup of the mixture (marinade) into a small glass jar or plastic container; cover, refrigerate, and reserve for later use during grilling. Set the remaining marinade aside.

Arrange the fish steaks, single layer, in a flat-bottomed, glass baking dish. Pour the set-aside, remaining marinade over the fish; cover tightly with plastic wrap and refrigerate for 30 minutes. Turn the fish over; cover and refrigerate an additional 30 minutes.

Meanwhile, ignite the charcoal in the outdoor grill; let stand about 30 minutes until the coals

(Recipe continues on next page)

are medium-hot (the coals should be covered with a thin layer of ash). Distribute the medium-hot coals, single layer, over the fuel grate.

Spray the clean, cold, outdoor-grill cooking grate and an outdoor-cooking spatula with nonstick cooking spray. Just before commencing to grill the fish steaks, place the cooking grate in the grill, about 4 inches above the coals. Remove the fish steaks from the marinade and place them on the cooking grate. Discard the marinade. Grill the steaks, uncovered, for 5 minutes. Brush the tops of the steaks lightly with a small amount of the ¼ cup reserved, refrigerated marinade. Using the sprayed spatula, carefully turn the steaks over; grill an additional 5 minutes, until the fish flakes easily when pricked with a sharp fork. Guard against overcooking by staying at the grill while the steaks are cooking. Fish overcooks and chars very easily.

To serve, garnish the serving platter or individual dinner plates with lemon wedges.

SERVES 6

KATHY GRIFFIN'S ORANGE ROUGHY PARMESAN

You never know where or when you'll find a fabulous recipe. This one turned up when I was waiting in the examination room for my dermatologist. His nurse, Kathy, noticed that I was writing recipes on my ever-present yellow legal pad, and we began talking about this cookbook. I could tell instantly that she was a good cook. Here is one of the excellent recipes she shared that day.

4 (about 2 pounds) orange roughy fillets*
1 cup freshly grated Parmesan cheese
  (page 46)
¼ teaspoon salt
¼ teaspoon white pepper
1 cup thinly sliced leeks
2 tablespoons butter
1 tablespoon capers

*Any mild fish fillets may be substituted.

Wash the fillets under cold, running water and place them between several layers of paper towels to dry; set aside. In a small mixing bowl, place the Parmesan cheese, salt, and white pepper; stir to combine; set aside.

Place the fillets, single layer, in the center of a large piece of extra-heavy aluminum foil. Distribute the leeks equally over the fillets; dot with the butter. Scatter the capers equally over the fillets. Spoon the Parmesan cheese mixture evenly over all.

Seal the fillets tightly in the aluminum foil; carefully place on the cooking grate in the outdoor cooking grill, about 4 inches above hot coals (the coals should be barely covered with ash). Grill, uncovered, for 10 minutes. Do not turn.

SERVES 4

Shellfish

GRILLED LOBSTER TAILS BASTED WITH TARRAGON BUTTER SAUCE

6 African or American lobster tails in the
  shell (about 8 ounces each)
1 recipe Tarragon Butter Sauce (recipe
  follows)
1 cup Clarified Butter (page 370)

If purchased frozen, thaw the lobster tails. Using a small knife and kitchen scissors, cut away and discard the underside hard membrane. Rinse under cold, running water and place, shell side up, on 2 layers of paper towels to drain.

Insert a long, metal skewer (see Note) lengthwise through each tail to prevent curling during grilling. Or, with your hands, bend each tail backward to crack the shell in several places. Place the tails, shell side down, in a pan; brush generously with Tarragon Butter Sauce.

Spray the clean, cold, outdoor-grill cooking grate with nonstick cooking spray. Just before commencing to grill the lobster tails, place the cooking grate in the grill. Place the lobster tails, shell side up, directly on the grill grate, about 4 inches above medium-hot coals (the coals should be covered with a thin layer of ash). Grill the tails, uncovered, for 7 minutes. Turn the tails over (to shell side down). Brush the tails generously with Tarragon Butter Sauce and continue brushing intermittently with the sauce (use all of the sauce) as the tails grill for 10 minutes on the second side. Exact grilling time depends upon the size of the lobster tails, the temperature of coals, the grill, and the weather. The tails are done when the shells are bright red and the meat is opaque.

Serve 1 lobster tail per person. Place an individual, small ramekin of Clarified Butter on each plate.

NOTE: If using wooden skewers, soak the skewers at least 15 minutes in water before inserting in the lobster tails to help prevent burning on the grill.

SERVES 6

Tarragon Butter Sauce

½ cup (¼ pound) butter
¼ cup freshly squeezed, strained lemon juice
¼ teaspoon dried leaf tarragon
½ teaspoon onion powder

Melt the butter in a small saucepan. Add the lemon juice, tarragon, and onion powder; stir to combine. Keep warm over very low heat.

ACCOMPANIMENT SUGGESTIONS: Serve Grilled Lobster Tails with Rice Pilaf (page 274), Carrots Cosmopolitan (page 312), and a tossed green salad (page 124).

Wild Game

WINE-MARINATED VENISON STEAKS

4 venison steaks, ½ inch thick
2 cups blackberry wine*
2 teaspoons dried leaf oregano
2 bay leaves
½ teaspoon whole black peppercorns
¼ cup extra-virgin olive oil
1 recipe Onion Butter stars (page 369)

If blackberry wine is not available, port wine may be substituted.

18 TO 24 HOURS BEFORE GRILLING THE STEAKS: Wash the steaks under cold, running water and place between several layers of paper towels to dry. When dry, trim away all the fat and connective tissue. Place the steaks in an 8 × 8-inch glass baking dish; set aside. In a small mixing bowl, place the wine, oregano, bay leaves, and peppercorns; stir to combine. Pour the wine mixture over the steaks; the steaks must be entirely covered with liquid. If necessary, add additional wine. Cover the baking dish securely with plastic wrap. Refrigerate 18 to 24 hours. The steaks should not be marinated longer than 24 hours.

30 MINUTES BEFORE GRILLING THE STEAKS: Remove the steaks from the refrigerator. Remove the steaks from the marinade and place them on several layers of paper towels. Pat the steaks dry. Do not remove any leaf oregano which may remain on the surface of the steaks after drying. Discard the marinade; wash and dry the baking dish. Return the steaks to the baking dish; brush

(Recipe continues on next page)

generously on both sides with olive oil. Let stand, uncovered, at room temperature until grilled.

TO GRILL THE STEAKS: Place the steaks on the outdoor-grill cooking grate, about 4 inches above hot coals (the coals should be barely covered with ash). Grill the steaks, uncovered, for 14 minutes on the first side; turn and grill for an additional 10 minutes on the second side, until well done (see Note). Transfer the steaks to warmed plates and place an Onion Butter star atop each steak. Serve immediately.

NOTE: Venison steaks may be cooked medium (160°F.); however, I believe the flavor of venison is enhanced by cooking it well done (170°F.). In addition, the meat is more tender when cooked until well done.

SERVES 4

ACCOMPANIMENT SUGGESTION: Potato Pancakes with Lingonberries (page 335) are an excellent taste and visual complement to Wine-Marinated Venison Steaks.

Vegetables

ONIONS IN FOIL

FOR EACH INDIVIDUAL SERVING
1 medium onion
1 tablespoon Italian salad dressing, homemade (page 148) or commercially bottled
¼ teaspoon Worcestershire sauce
Dash of salt
Dash of pepper
2 teaspoons butter

Cut off and discard each end of the onion. Peel the onion and remove the outer layer. Partially quarter the onion by making two cuts at right angles from the top through ¾ of the onion (leaving the bottom ¼ of the onion uncut). Place the onion in the center of two layers of heavy-duty aluminum foil cut 12 inches square. Carefully spread the onion slightly apart. Pour the salad dressing and Worcestershire sauce into the center of the onion. Sprinkle the center lightly with salt and pepper. Place the butter pat inside the onion. Seal the onion and seasonings tightly in the foil. With your hands, press the foil against the onion to form a ball shape.

To cook on an outdoor covered grill, place the onions on the cooking grate, about 4 inches above hot coals (the coals should be barely covered with ash). Cover the grill and cook about 35 minutes, turning the onions to a new side every 5 minutes.

To cook on an uncovered, open grill, place the onions directly on the hot coals and roast for about 25 minutes, turning the onions to a new side every 5 minutes. Begin checking the onions for doneness about 8 minutes before the end of the cooking period. Exact cooking time depends upon the size of the onions, the temperature of coals, the grill, and the weather.

VARIATION: Add a pinch of snipped, fresh oregano or dried leaf oregano to the seasonings placed in the onion before sealing in aluminum foil.

Other Outdoor Cooking Recipes

Mesquite-Grilled Chicken Salad (page 141)
Warm Chicken-Vegetable Salad with Pistachio Nuts and Raspberry Vinaigrette Dressing (page 142)

Eggs

P oor Richard's proverb "Early to bed and early to rise, makes a man healthy, wealthy, and wise" is still a cornerstone of the Midwest work ethic. The call to "rise 'n shine" echoes across the prairie at an hour some people would consider incredibly early—5:00 or 6:00 A.M. is not uncommon.

If you live on a farm, the early-morning cacophony of cattle bawling to be fed and hogs banging their feeder lids is a reliable alarm clock signaling the start of dawn, or predawn, morning chores. Midwestern town and city dwellers' body clocks have remained set on farm time, resulting in the business day beginning and ending early all across the central time zone. Part and parcel of this early-morning regimen is a hearty breakfast. After all, it's a long time until lunch (or dinner, as the noon meal is called in many farm homes).

Town or country, no matter what else graces the breakfast plate, eggs are the centerpiece— most often fried, scrambled, or "poached" in a special poaching pan with egg cups. In city eateries, omelets are offered with increased frequency on breakfast menus.

Business at breakfast is definitely in vogue, with many a transaction finalized over eggs and a selected assortment of complementary standbys—most notably, American fries, pancakes, waffles, French toast, muffins, baking powder biscuits, cinnamon rolls, toast, ham, sausage, bacon, and, every now and then, steak.

Probably a holdover from earlier rural days when all farms had chickens and, therefore, an abundant egg supply, the last cup of breakfast coffee doesn't necessarily mark the end of the day's egg consumption. Eggs find their way into food served at all hours of the day and in all settings. For example, take deviled eggs (you can hardly find a Midwesterner who isn't crazy about them). They turn up everywhere from fancy cocktail parties where the tangy, golden fillings have been fastidiously swirled into the egg whites and chapeaued with dainty garnish, to Labor Day picnics where the cook's thumb served as piping tool and paprika is the decoration.

Little wonder that palates enamored of deviled eggs find the same chemistry with egg salad sandwiches, the old, but far from passé, favorite. I can still resurrect that unmistakable smell of egg salad which suddenly permeated the Greenwood elementary school lunchroom when we all unsnapped the lunch boxes our mothers had packed before we left for school. We've eaten those great-tasting sandwiches into adulthood and still relish them as much as we did in third grade.

In most Middle-American households, brunch for friends or a family holiday breakfast automatically triggers plans for an out-of-the-ordinary, egg-intensive casserole. Two suggested recipes for such occasions are found in this chapter: Brunch Eggs (page 265) and Eggsotic Eggs (page 268).

Falling into the category of simple, down-home cooking are fried egg sandwiches (with catsup, of course) which are regularly ordered by weary travelers in roadside cafés, and are the "old-reliable" of late-night snacks. In a pinch, they can be supper if a meeting causes you to miss the family meal. Even those who can't cook much can make them. And—putting all nutrition considerations aside—they're still best when made with buttered, very soft, white, commercial bread.

Of course, with scads of baking and cooking going on in the Midland, jillions of eggs lose their identity each day in breads, cakes, cookies, meat loaves, and casserole dishes.

While eggs have been somewhat out of favor in recent years because of cholesterol fallout, the new finding that eggs aren't such a culprit after all is music to the ears of egg-loving Midwesterners. According to the National Heart, Lung, and Blood Institute (see Note), four egg yolks a week, including egg yolks in cooked and processed foods, are entirely within recommended parameters for healthy adults. (Egg whites contain no cholesterol.) Pass the deviled eggs, please.

NOTE: See Sources Consulted, page 842, for the complete bibliographical reference.

Egg Sizes

Commercial eggs are sold in six sizes: jumbo, extra large, large, medium, small, and peewee. In the preparation of many foods, it is important to use the size of eggs specified in the recipes. With few exceptions, the recipes in *The Blue Ribbon Country Cookbook* call for extra-large eggs.

Egg Safety

The chance of contracting the illness salmonellosis from raw or undercooked eggs is very minimal. Only a very small percentage of eggs (liberally estimated at 0.005 percent, or 1 in 20,000 eggs produced nationally) might contain the bacteria *Salmonella enteritidis*. The bacteria is inside the egg shell, and scientists as yet have been unable to discover how contamination occurs.

While salmonellosis is an uncomfortable illness, it is usually of short duration and is rarely life-threatening. However, some groups of people are particularly vulnerable to the infection. Those at high risk are very young persons, elderly people, pregnant women (because of risk to the fetus), and persons with serious illnesses or weakened immune systems.

Most cases of salmonellosis have been traced to foods other than eggs; namely, chicken, fish, and beef, as well as to human carriers and to cross-contamination via food preparers, kitchen tools, and other foods during preparation.

Refrigeration of eggs at 40° F. or below limits the growth of *Salmonella enteritidis,* and the organism is destroyed when eggs are cooked to a temperature of 160° F. The number of *Salmonella enteritidis* bacteria in freshly laid, contaminated eggs is probably very small; therefore, with proper refrigeration, handling, and cooking of these eggs, there is a good chance that the bacteria will not multiply sufficiently to cause sickness in healthy people.

While *Salmonella enteritidis* may be found in both the yolk and white of eggs, egg whites do not support the growth of the bacteria well, whereas egg yolks provide a good environment for multiplication of the bacteria. Therefore, the inclusion of uncooked, refrigerated egg whites in properly refrigerated foods might be considered a low risk for healthy people. A cautionary note heads recipes in *The Blue Ribbon Country Cookbook* which contain uncooked egg whites. Foods in *The Blue Ribbon Country Cookbook* containing egg yolks should be cooked according to the recipe procedures and the guidelines in this section.

Adherence to the following guidelines will help assure the safe purchase, storage, handling, and cooking of eggs:

- Purchase only refrigerated, grade A or AA eggs with clean, uncracked shells.

  There is no difference in nutritional value between infertile and fertile eggs or between white-shelled and brown-shelled eggs. Shell color results from hen breed.

  Yolk color (pale yellow to deep yellow) results from the type of feed consumed by the hen and is not an indication of nutritional content.

- Keep eggs refrigerated at 40° F. or below. Refrigerate eggs as soon as possible after purchase.

  It is best to refrigerate eggs in their carton on an inside shelf of the refrigerator rather than to transfer them to the special egg container in the door of some refrigerators. Repeated opening of the refrigerator door risks fluctuation in the temperature of eggs stored in the door. Storage in the carton helps prevent loss of moisture and carbon dioxide from eggs. This is especially applicable with frost-free refrigerators.

- Do not wash eggs before storing or using them. Eggs are washed as a part of commercial processing; therefore, it is unnecessary to rewash them.

- Raw eggs may safely be kept refrigerated at home up to 3 weeks. Hard-cooked eggs, unpeeled or peeled, may safely be kept refrigerated up to 1 week after cooking.

- When recipes call for the use of raw eggs at room temperature, eggs may be left at room temperature up to 2 hours, including preparation time.

- Cooked eggs and cooked dishes containing eggs should not be unrefrigerated for more than 2 hours (not including cooking time). Refrigerate leftover food containing eggs immediately after serving. When refrigerating large amounts of hot, egg-containing food, place smaller portions in shallow containers for quicker cooling.

  Hard-cooked Easter eggs should not be consumed if unrefrigerated for more than 2 hours.

- Do not eat raw egg yolks or foods containing raw egg yolks. Homemade foods which often contain raw egg yolks are: eggnog, Caesar salad, ice cream, mayonnaise, and hollandaise sause. When made commercially, these foods contain pasteurized eggs. Pasteurization of eggs destroys microorganisms which are present, including *Salmonella enteritidis.*

  For complete safety, do not eat raw egg whites; however, refrigerated raw egg whites in properly refrigerated foods might be considered a low risk for healthy people (see paragraph 5 of this section).

  Make homemade eggnog, ice cream, and like foods using a cooked custard base. (A pasteurized liquid egg product may be used; however, many of the liquid egg products currently available on the retail market contain

98 percent to 99 percent egg white and no egg yolk. When using pasteurized egg products, carefully follow the package instructions for storage and handling to prevent contamination and spoilage.)

Do not eat uncooked cake batter or cookie dough containing raw eggs, or taste partially cooked foods containing eggs.

- Cook eggs until the whites are completely set and the yolks begin to thicken. The yolks need not be cooked until they are hard. Cook scrambled eggs and omelets until no visible liquid egg remains. Cook fried eggs on both sides or in a covered frying pan, or baste the eggs. For the greatest safety, and especially when preparing eggs for high-risk groups, cook eggs until both the whites and yolks are completely firm.

Under all circumstances, cook egg yolks and food containing egg yolks to a temperature of 160° F. An instant thermometer (page 44) is an efficient, easy way to gauge the temperature of eggs or dishes containing eggs while they are cooking. Baked goods reach a temperature of more than 160° F. when fully cooked. Soft custards reach a temperature above 160° F. when the mixtures coat a metal spoon.

- A blood spot in an egg does not affect its safety or nutritional value. Simply use a clean teaspoon to remove it, if desired.

- The cord-type parts of an egg white, called the chalazae, are perfectly edible and do not interfere with the beating of egg whites. The chalazae function to hold the egg yolk in the center of the egg white. Thick chalazae are an indication of an egg's freshness and high quality.

- Wash your hands with soap and hot water before and after they come in contact with eggs or food containing eggs. Wash kitchen tools and equipment, work surfaces, sink, and faucet handles with hot, soapy water after they come in contact with eggs or food containing eggs, and before they come in contact with other food.

For answers to further questions pertaining to egg safety, call the U.S. Department of Agriculture's Meat and Poultry Hotline at 800-535-4555 (in Washington, D.C., call 202-720-3333), Monday through Friday, 10:00 A.M.–4:00 P.M. Eastern time.

TO COOK EGGS IN THE SHELL

HARD-COOKED EGGS: Purchase eggs 5 to 7 days prior to hard-cooking because very fresh, hard-cooked eggs are difficult to peel. To hard-cook eggs, place the eggs in a saucepan and cover with cold water. Cover the pan. Over medium-high heat, bring the eggs to just boiling. Turn off the heat, but leave the covered pan on the burner. If the eggs continue to boil, remove the pan from the burner for a few moments until the burner cools slightly. Let extra-large eggs stand in the hot water 15 minutes. (Decrease or increase the standing time by 3 minutes per egg size [see Egg Sizes, page 262].) Drain immediately and run cold water over the eggs in the saucepan for about 30 seconds. Drain; refill the saucepan with fresh, cold water. Let the eggs stand in the cold water 15 minutes. Drain; place the eggs in a covered container and refrigerate. Peel when ready to use.

Hard-cooking eggs at too high a temperature, or for too long a time at a low temperature, causes the whites to become tough and rubbery and the yolks to become tough and to possibly darken on the surface.

It is important to cool the eggs in cold water immediately after cooking to help prevent the shells from sticking to the cooked egg whites, making peeling difficult. Quickly cooling hard-cooked eggs also helps prevent the yolk surfaces from darkening.

SOFT-COOKED EGGS: Follow the procedure for Hard-Cooked Eggs, above, letting extra-large eggs stand in the hot water from 3 to 5 minutes, depending upon desired softness. Drain immediately and run cold water over the eggs in the saucepan for about 30 seconds until cool enough to handle.

TO SERVE SOFT-COOKED EGGS: To serve a soft-cooked egg in a small ramekin or other sauce-type serving dish, use a sharp knife to break the shell in half widthwise around the egg. Cut the egg in half where the shell was broken. Using a teaspoon, scoop the egg from each shell half into the dish.

To serve a soft-cooked egg in an egg cup, place the unshelled egg, small end down, in the egg cup. Using egg scissors—sometimes called an egg topper—made especially for the purpose (see illustration), cut the shell circularly near the top of the large end of the egg. (If you don't have egg scissors, use a butter knife to tap around the top of the egg and crack the shell.) Using a sharp knife, cut off the top of the egg at the place where the shell was cut (or cracked). Discard the egg top. Supply a small teaspoon for the diner to eat the egg directly from the shell.

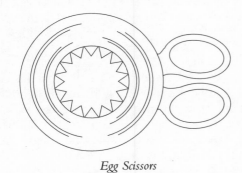

Egg Scissors

BRUNCH EGGS

2 cups (8 ounces) shredded, sharp cheddar cheese
2 tablespoons butter
2 tablespoons butter
2 cups sliced, fresh mushrooms
8 ounces commercial sour cream
2 teaspoons Worcestershire sauce
1 cup half-and-half
2 tablespoons Dijon mustard
¼ teaspoon salt
¼ teaspoon white pepper
1 dozen extra-large eggs
1 2-ounce jar chopped pimientos, drained (2 tablespoons)
2 tablespoons freshly grated Parmesan cheese (page 46)

Preheat the oven to 325° F. Butter a 9 × 13-inch baking dish.

Distribute the cheese evenly over the bottom of the prepared baking dish; dot with 2 tablespoons butter; set aside. In a small, heavy-bottomed skillet, melt 2 tablespoons butter over medium heat. Tilt the skillet back and forth to completely cover the bottom with the melted butter. Place the mushrooms in the skillet; sauté until the mushrooms give up their juices and the pan liquid reduces to a small quantity covering the bottom of the skillet (about 6 to 7 minutes). In a small mixing bowl, place the mushrooms and remaining pan liquid, sour cream, and Worcestershire sauce; stir to combine.

Spoon the mushroom mixture over the shredded cheese and butter in the baking dish; using a small, narrow spatula, spread evenly; set aside. In a small mixing bowl, place the half-and-half, mustard, salt, and white pepper; stir to combine. Pour ½ of the mustard mixture evenly over the mushroom mixture in the baking dish. Set the remaining ½ of the mustard mixture aside.

Place the eggs in a medium mixing bowl; using an electric mixer, beat slightly on medium speed. Add the pimientos; stir to evenly distribute. Pour the egg mixture over the mustard mixture in the baking dish. Pour the remaining ½ of the mustard mixture evenly over the egg mixture. Sprinkle the Parmesan cheese over all. Bake, uncovered, for 45 minutes, until set.

Using a sharp, thin-bladed knife, cut the Brunch Eggs into serving pieces. Remove the serving pieces from the baking dish with a spatula.

SERVES 8 TO 10

SCRAMBLED EGGS WITH FRESH SAVORY

4 extra-large eggs
¼ cup plus 1 tablespoon whole milk
Dash of salt
1 tablespoon butter
1 teaspoon finely snipped, fresh savory

In a small mixing bowl, place the eggs, milk, and salt; set aside. In a medium skillet, melt the butter over medium to medium-high heat. While the butter is melting, beat the egg mixture very vigorously with a table fork. When the butter just begins to sizzle (do not let it brown, even faintly), beat the egg mixture again and immediately pour it into the skillet. It is important to beat the egg mixture right up to the moment of pouring it into the skillet to produce light and airy scrambled eggs.

After pouring the egg mixture into the skillet, sprinkle it evenly with the savory. Let the egg mixture cook undisturbed until it begins to congeal around the edge of the skillet. Then, using the table fork or a spatula, turn the egg mixture over to expose the uncooked portions to the direct heat of the skillet. After a few seconds, move and turn the egg mixture again. Continue moving and turning the mixture until no visible liquid egg remains. Minimum movement and turning of the mixture will produce the lightest scrambled eggs. Do not allow the eggs to brown at all. Serve immediately.

SERVES 2 OR 3, DEPENDING UPON APPETITES

TO REDUCE OR INCREASE THE RECIPE: The recipe may be reduced to as little as 1 egg (use 1 tablespoon plus 1 teaspoon milk, a dash of salt, ¼ teaspoon savory, and about 2 teaspoons butter to grease a small skillet), or the recipe may be increased for more servings.

VARIATIONS
• To make plain scrambled eggs, eliminate the savory.

• Substitute ¼ cup fried and drained bacon pieces for the savory.

FRIED EGGS

1 tablespoon butter, bacon drippings, or sausage drippings
4 extra-large eggs
1 tablespoon water

In a 9-inch, heavy-bottomed skillet, melt 1 tablespoon butter over medium heat. If bacon or sausage has just been fried in the skillet, pour the drippings into a small, heatproof bowl. Using a spatula, scrape away and discard any meat particles remaining on the bottom of the skillet. Measure 1 tablespoon of the drippings and return to the skillet; omit the butter. Tilt the skillet back and forth to completely cover the bottom with the melted butter or drippings.

When the fat is sizzling, break the eggs, one at a time, into the skillet. Avoid placing the eggs in the skillet before the fat is hot, as the egg whites will not begin to solidify quickly enough to prevent them from spreading too thinly. When the egg whites have partially solidified, add 1 tablespoon water to the skillet and cover. The steam resulting from the addition of the water will help cook the tops of the eggs without turning them over.

After adding the water and covering the skillet, avoid removing the lid to check the eggs as much as possible, as the steam will escape each time the lid is removed, and the cooking of the top of the eggs will be interrupted. For medium-well doneness, cook the eggs a total of about 5 minutes. When done, serve immediately.

MAKES 4 FRIED EGGS

NOTE: Adjust the size of the skillet and the amount of fat and water to the number of eggs to be fried. Adjust the cooking time to the preference for doneness of eggs (see Egg Safety, page 262).

DEVILED EGGS

1½ dozen small eggs *or* 1 dozen extra-
  large eggs, hard-cooked (page 264)
¼ teaspoon salt
⅛ teaspoon white pepper
½ teaspoon dry mustard
1 teaspoon sugar
1 tablespoon prepared mustard
⅓ cup Miracle Whip salad dressing
Paprika and/or single, fresh parsley leaves
  for decoration

Peel the eggs (see Note 1). Cut the eggs in half lengthwise (see Note 2). Remove the yolks and place them in a small mixing bowl; place the egg whites on a piece of waxed paper and set aside. Using a table fork, mash the egg yolks against the side of the mixing bowl until they are of fine consistency. *Then,* add the salt, white pepper, dry mustard, sugar, prepared mustard, and salad dressing; using a spoon, stir until blended well.

Using a decorating bag fit with large open-star tip number 6B (page 383), fill the egg whites with the egg-yolk mixture (see Note 3). For simple decoration, sprinkle the egg-yolk fillings with paprika or decorate the top of each filling with a tiny, fresh parsley leaf.

NOTE 1: To peel a hard-cooked egg, softly tap it against the kitchen sink rim to crack the shell. Then, using your fingers, carefully peel away the shell, taking care not to nick the egg white.

NOTE 2: The eggs may be cut widthwise if preferred. Deviled Eggs cut widthwise may be cut sawtooth fashion.

NOTE 3: The egg whites may be filled using a table knife. Then, using your thumb, pat the egg-yolk mixture smoothly into the yolk cavities.

**MAKES 3 DOZEN SMALL OR 2 DOZEN EXTRA-
LARGE DEVILED EGGS**

ALTERNATIVE DECORATIONS

- Decorate each Deviled Egg with a thin slice of cold, Boiled Shrimp (page 229), about ½ inch long, and 3 capers. Six medium shrimp will decorate 3 dozen Deviled Eggs.

- Arrange a tiny sprig of fresh dillweed and 3 capers on top of the egg-yolk filling in each Deviled Egg.

- Decorate the Deviled Eggs with caviar, pieces of smoked salmon, thin slices of stuffed olives, strips of pimiento, or slices of truffles.

EGGS GOLDENROD

Eggs Goldenrod is an old dish which is equally appropriate for sophisticated or simple dining. It is nice to serve for a late-night buffet supper, a brunch, or a family lunch.

2 recipes Medium White Sauce (page 366),
  adding 1 teaspoon sugar, ¾ teaspoon dry
  mustard, and a dash of cayenne pepper to
  the total flour mixture for 2 recipes
6 extra-large eggs, hard-cooked
4 slices warm, white toast,* buttered
Sprigs of fresh parsley for garnish

  **Whole-wheat toast may be substituted.*

Prepare the Medium White Sauce; cover and set aside. Peel the eggs. Remove and reserve 2 egg yolks. Chop coarsely the remainder of the eggs, including the 2 extra egg whites; set aside. Grate the 2 reserved egg yolks finely; set aside. Add the chopped eggs to the white sauce; stir to combine. Over medium-low heat, heat the white sauce mixture through, but do not allow it to boil.

Place 1 piece of toast on each of 4 individual plates. Spoon the white sauce mixture over the toast. Sprinkle the grated egg yolks over the white sauce mixture. Decorate the plates with parsley sprigs.

SERVES 4

EGGSOTIC EGGS

10 extra-large eggs, hard-cooked (page 264)
2 14-ounce cans commercial artichoke
  bottoms, drained
3 recipes Thin White Sauce (page 366),
  adding 1½ teaspoons dry mustard and
  1½ teaspoons sugar to the total flour
  mixture for 3 recipes
½ cup Miracle Whip salad dressing
4 ounces dried beef, cut into ¾-inch
  squares
½ pound carrots, pared, sliced ¼ inch
  thick, boiled (page 302), and drained
2 ounces (¾ cup) sliced, fresh mushrooms
2 recipes 4½-Inch-Square Puff Pastry
  Shells (page 470) (16 Puff Pastry Shells)
Garnish (optional; instructions follow)

Butter a 7 × 11-inch baking dish; set aside.

Use 10 yolks and 9 whites of the 10 hard-cooked eggs to make 18 Deviled Eggs (reserve the remaining egg white for other uses). Follow the Deviled Eggs recipe on page 267, using the same amount of ingredients (other than the eggs) as for 1 dozen extra-large eggs, and omitting the decoration. Cut the eggs widthwise in sawtooth fashion. Use large open-star tip number 6B (page 383) to fill the eggs; set aside.

Place 17 artichoke bottoms, stem side down, in the prepared baking dish (reserving 1 artichoke bottom for garnish). If necessary, cut a small slice off the stem side of the artichoke bottoms so they stand stably in the baking dish. Place 1 Deviled Egg in each artichoke bottom (reserving 1 Deviled Egg for garnish). If necessary, trim a small slice off the bottom of the Deviled Eggs so they rest securely in the artichoke bottoms; set aside.

Preheat the oven to 350° F.

Make the Thin White Sauce; remove from the heat. Add the salad dressing; using a handheld electric mixer, beat on high speed until blended. Add the dried beef, carrots, and mushrooms; stir to combine. Pour the dried beef mixture over the Deviled Eggs and artichokes in the baking dish. Arrange the partial garnish, if used (see Garnish instructions that follow). Bake, uncovered, for 30 minutes.

Remove from the oven and arrange the remainder of the garnish, if used. Serve Eggsotic Eggs at the table or on the buffet, placing 1 hot Puff Pastry Shell on each individual plate, and spooning 1 artichoke bottom and Deviled Egg with dried beef sauce into each shell.

SERVES 8 (2 FOR EACH DINER)

GARNISH (see illustration)
1 artichoke bottom, reserved from recipe,
  above
1 Deviled Egg, reserved from recipe, above
Carrots, pared and boiled (page 302); then,
  cut julienne (page 23) into 20 2-inch-
  long sticks
Individual pieces of dried beef, rolled
  tightly and cut into 12 1¾-inch-long
  rolls
Vegetable oil
Small sprigs of fresh parsley leaves
1 Cutout Tomato Star (page 405)

Eggsotic Eggs Garnish

Before baking the Eggsotic Eggs, place an artichoke heart in the center of the filled baking dish; place the Deviled Egg in the artichoke bottom. Alternate the carrot strips and dried-beef rolls in spoke-like fashion around the artichoke bottom. Brush all the garnish very lightly with vegetable oil.

After baking, arrange the parsley sprigs around the Deviled Egg and place the Cutout Tomato Star in the center of the Deviled Egg filling.

Other Egg Recipes

Rice and Beans

Rice

Provisions were often in short supply on the Midwest frontier, especially during the cold, winter months when boats could not navigate the icy rivers and the horse-drawn supply wagons did not run. Because settlers could grow their own potatoes easily and well in this part of the country, and because they could be stored successfully for winter consumption, potatoes were the carbohydrate staple of Midwest pioneers. When rice was available for purchase, pioneer women commonly used it to make rice pudding. They made it without eggs, which were often scarce in the early days of settlement. (See the recipe for Old-Fashioned Rice Pudding, page 655.)

Today, Missouri is the only Midwest state producing rice commercially, with about 3 percent of the U.S. total. Because inhabitants of the agriculturally oriented Midwest historically have centered their diets around the wide variety of products grown here, rice generally has not been a food prepared and eaten in great quantities by most Midwesterners. Although potatoes are not one of the largest present-day Midwest commodities (21 percent of the national total is produced here), they have retained their role as a primary energy source in the Heartland diet. In Mid-America—dyed-in-the-wool potato country—only in recent years has rice occasionally nudged potatoes from their time-honored place on dinner plates.

The intrusion of rice into hallowed potato space on contemporary Midwest plates is occurring not so much because greater numbers of people prefer the taste of rice over potatoes, but more because of perceived healthy diet considerations. Actually, potatoes have fewer calories and less fat than rice, as shown in the table at the bottom of the page.

Potatoes, however, are generally prepared and/or eaten with added ingredients which drive up the calorie-fat-cholesterol intake, whereas rice is often prepared and served without such malefactors. In fact, the form, consistency, and taste of rice make it a perfect companion for mixing with nearly any steamed vegetable, or with lean meat, poultry, fish, or shellfish. Look for a continued rise in the Midwest popularity charts for this type of rice dish. Broccoli-Rice Casserole (page 273) and Spanish Rice (page 275), long-standing Midwest favorites, will predictably remain ever popular.

Wild rice, the delicacy which grows in the shallow water along the shores of the lakes and streams in Minnesota and Wisconsin, actually is not a rice at all. It is the grain of a tall, aquatic grass (*Zizania aquatica*) which is not related to rice (*Orysa sativa*). Wild rice, also know as Indian rice, water rice, and water oats, was a staple of the American Indians who lived in these regions, and Indian wars were fought for control of the wild rice producing areas.

The Indians ate wild rice with game—a taste-pleasing combination which has stood the test of time. Across the Midwest, wild game is still very commonly served with wild rice. For current-day recipes which team game birds with wild rice, see Hungarian Partridge Grand Marnier with Orange–Wild Rice Stuffing (page 238), Baked Pheasant (page 237) stuffed with Wild Rice Dressing (page 216), and Quail in Nests (page 244) which the recipe suggests be served over a bed of Pecan Wild Rice (page 276).

Due to the difficulty of harvesting, drying, threshing, and winnowing native wild rice by hand, and the erratic crop supply from year to year, wild rice has been a very expensive, luxury food. Especially in commercial eating establishments, wild rice frequently has been served in combination with white rice to make the treasured bounty go further. By custom, travelers to Minnesota and Wisconsin have purchased a supply of these prized grains to take advantage of lower price and, in some years, availability at all. However, that picture is changing. In recent years, wild rice has become a commercial product harvested primarily in cultivated paddies, and it is becoming more readily available in supermarkets at a price within reach, though still approximately three times the cost of white rice.

Natural complements to wild rice include bacon, onions, mushrooms, and nuts, which frequently appear in ingredient lists in wild rice recipes (see Wild Rice with Bacon and Onions, page 277, and Wild Rice Casserole, page 276.) Newer wild rice dishes receiving the Midwest thumbs-up are Wild Rice Soup (page 95) and Wild Rice Salad (page 134) which joins wild rice with several vegetables as well as mandarin oranges.

PER ½ CUP EDIBLE PORTION

	Calories	Fat (grams)	Carbohydrate (grams)	Protein (grams)
Boiled White Rice, long grain	103	.22	22.26	2.12
Boiled Potatoes, without skins	67	.08	15.61	1.33

Sources: USDA Agriculture Handbooks 8–20, 1991 Supplement; and 8–11, 1984.

Beans

Beans are standard Midwest fare, mainly served baked or in bean soup. You would be hard pressed to attend a potluck picnic, family re-union, or summer barbecue without spying at least one pot of deep brownish red baked beans (the result of slow, low-temperature baking) with an onion and a few bacon strips visible on top, adding to that one-of-a-kind flavor (Baked Beans, page 277). Most grassroots Midwestern-ers resist any attempt by experimental cooks to change or sophisticate this old-fashioned style of making these rich, succulent beans. They are hard to better!

So well seated are baked beans on our family's list of inveterate favorites, the truth is you will always find a casserole of them among the nu-merous side dishes on our Thanksgiving and Christmas tables. Like many other Midlanders, baked beans are caviar to my brother, who picked up the penchant by osmosis from our father. In our family, that unforgettable smell permeating the house before holiday feasts is a blend of turkey, sage dressing, and baked beans, and I am the first to admit that those darned beans are a worthy complement to traditional turkey dinners. There would be a void on my Thanksgiving plate without them.

Year in and year out, Midwest palates are mad about Bean Soup, usually served as the main course with corn bread. (It makes my mouth water to write about it.) The recipe for this tan-talizing dish on page 89, is my mother's. While I concede daughterly bias, I think it is the best bean soup I've ever tasted. Her secrets: always use Great Northern beans, never soak the beans prior to cooking because it will cause them to become mushy, use pork shank and hock (plain ham will not infuse that unique flavor), never add salt until the end of cooking because it will toughen the beans, and include her special ingredient—brown sugar.

While the famous U.S. Senate dining room bean soup is wonderful and warrants its fame, I think Mother's version presents mighty tough competition.

Rice

PERFECT BOILED RICE

For the fluffiest, driest rice imaginable, try this recipe—it really isn't difficult. Once you make boiled rice this way, you will see how easy it is to do and how wonderful the results are.

2 quarts water
1 teaspoon salt
1 cup raw long-grain rice (not instant)

In a kettle or large saucepan, bring the water and salt to a boil over high heat. Add the rice gradually so the water continues to boil. Boil briskly, uncovered, for 20 minutes until the rice is completely tender, stirring occasionally.

Turn the rice into a sieve and rinse it under hot, running water. Place a clean, cotton tea towel, folded into several layers, over the sieve and rice; set aside. Pour very hot water (from the teakettle) into a large saucepan; place the covered sieve in the saucepan *over* the hot water. Make certain that the rice is not touching the water. Do not place the saucepan over heat.

In about 15 minutes, the rice will be fluffy and dry, ready for serving.

MAKES ABOUT 3¹/₂ CUPS

BROCCOLI-RICE CASSEROLE

2½ cups water
1 cup raw long-grain rice (not instant)
1 tablespoon butter
4 cups fresh broccoli flowerets
1½ recipes Thick White Sauce (page 366)
2 teaspoons instant chicken bouillon
    granules
¼ teaspoon celery salt
1 8-ounce jar Cheez Whiz pasteurized
    process cheese sauce
1 tablespoon butter
¾ cup chopped onions
1 tablespoon butter
¼ cup coarsely chopped, fresh mushrooms
¼ cup sliced, then quartered, fresh
    mushrooms
4 ounces (1 cup) shredded, mild cheddar
    cheese

Pour 2½ cups water into a medium saucepan. Cover the saucepan and bring the water to a boil over high heat. Add the rice and butter; stir to combine. Cover the saucepan. Reduce the heat and simmer the rice 20 minutes, stirring occasionally. Remove from the heat; let stand, covered, 5 minutes or until all the water is absorbed.

Steam the broccoli flowerets (page 302) 3 minutes. Immediately remove the steamer basket (or top of the steamer pan) containing the broccoli from the saucepan (or bottom of the steamer pan). Leave the broccoli in the steamer basket (pan) and rinse it under cold, running water to stop the cooking; set aside.

Make the Thick White Sauce. Remove from the heat. Add the bouillon granules and celery salt; stir until the granules dissolve. Then, add the process cheese sauce and stir until blended; cover and set aside.

Preheat the oven to 350° F. Grease a 7 × 11-inch baking dish; set aside.

In a small, heavy-bottomed skillet, melt 1 tablespoon butter over medium to medium-high heat. Tilt the skillet back and forth to completely cover the bottom with the melted butter.

Place the onions in the skillet; sauté 5 minutes until pale golden. Add the onions to the white sauce mixture; stir to combine; cover and set aside.

In a clean, small, heavy-bottomed skillet, melt 1 tablespoon butter over medium heat. Place ¼ cup chopped mushrooms and ¼ cup sliced, then quartered mushrooms in the skillet; sauté 3 minutes. Add the sautéed mushrooms and pan liquids to the white sauce mixture; stir to combine; set aside. Drain any water remaining on the rice. Add the white sauce mixture to the rice; stir until combined; set aside.

Arrange the broccoli over the bottom of the prepared baking dish. Spoon the rice mixture evenly over the broccoli. Scatter the shredded cheese over the top. Bake, uncovered, for 30 minutes.

SERVES 14

RICE IN RING MOLD

A lovely way to serve rice.

1½ cups raw long-grain rice (not instant)
2 tablespoons butter, melted
2 tablespoons snipped, fresh parsley
2 tablespoons pine nuts

Butter a 1-quart ring mold; set aside.

Boil the rice, following the procedure in the recipe for Perfect Boiled Rice (page 272). Place the hot, boiled rice in a medium mixing bowl. Add the butter, parsley, and pine nuts; toss until evenly combined. Place the rice mixture in the prepared ring mold; press lightly into the mold. Let stand about 2 minutes. Invert the mold onto a warm, flat serving platter.

SERVES 6

RICE PILAF

Pilaf (also called pilaff, pilau, and pilaw) is a dish of Middle East origin which has been known to the English-speaking world since at least as far back as the seventeenth century. Although it has enjoyed popularity in the southern part of the United States for decades (there, usually called pilau and often pronounced "perlew"), and ethnic groups across the nation have perpetuated traditional versions of the dish, pilaf has undergone a general, American reincarnation in recent years.

While there are many ways to prepare it, pilaf is most commonly made with rice that is first browned in butter or oil and then cooked in broth with seasonings and, often, vegetables. When meat, fowl, fish, or shellfish are added, it becomes a main dish. The version that follows is meant to be a side dish; however, it can be converted into a main dish by adding cooked beef, veal, or lamb.

¼ cup (4 tablespoons) butter
1 cup raw long-grain rice (not instant)
1 tablespoon butter
⅓ cup chopped celery
1 tablespoon butter
½ cup chopped leeks (white and greenish white parts)
¾ cup chopped, fresh mushrooms
1 tablespoon chopped celery leaves
¼ teaspoon salt
⅛ teaspoon pepper
1¾ cups homemade Chicken Broth (page 88) or 1 14½-ounce can commercial chicken broth
½ cup dry white wine
2 tablespoons snipped, fresh parsley

In a small, heavy-bottomed skillet, melt ¼ cup butter over medium heat. Place the rice in the skillet; sauté 5 minutes until it is a deep caramel color, stirring often. Place the rice in a large saucepan; set aside.

Wipe the skillet with a paper towel. Place 1 tablespoon butter in the skillet; melt the butter over medium heat. Tilt the skillet back and forth to completely cover the bottom with the melted butter. Place the celery in the skillet; sauté 4 minutes, stirring occasionally. Do not let the celery brown. Place the sautéed celery in the saucepan containing the rice; set aside. Add 1 tablespoon butter to the skillet; melt the butter over medium heat. Spread the melted butter over the skillet bottom. Place the leeks and mushrooms in the skillet; sauté 3 minutes, stirring often. Do not let the leeks and mushrooms brown. Add the sautéed leeks and mushrooms with pan juices to the rice. Add the celery leaves, salt, pepper, broth, and wine to the rice; stir to combine all the ingredients in the saucepan. Cover the saucepan.

Bring the rice mixture to a boil over high heat; reduce the heat to low and simmer 20 minutes, stirring occasionally. Most of the liquid will have been absorbed. Remove from the heat; uncover. Quickly add the parsley and stir to evenly distribute. Place a clean, cotton tea towel, folded into several layers, over the pan. Make certain that the entire pan is covered. Move the saucepan to the back of the range (not over direct heat) and let stand 10 minutes or more until no liquid remains. Then, if not served immediately, the saucepan may be placed in a warm (not hotter) oven for a brief period of time to keep the Rice Pilaf warm. Remove the tea towel and place the regular cover on the saucepan before placing it in the oven.

SERVES 6

SPANISH RICE

Serve a tossed salad alongside this dish, and you have a meal. Well, almost. Some of us dessert lovers will want a brownie to top it off.

1 pound lean, pure ground beef
1 tablespoon butter
1 cup chopped onions
1 cup chopped green bell peppers
1 garlic clove, pressed
½ cup water
1 28-ounce can commercial whole, peeled tomatoes, undrained, or 1 quart home-canned whole, peeled Tomatoes (page 736), undrained
¾ teaspoon dried leaf oregano
¾ teaspoon chili powder
1 teaspoon sugar
¾ teaspoon salt
½ teaspoon pepper
2 dashes Tabasco pepper sauce
1¼ cups uncooked instant rice

Place the ground beef in an electric skillet or a large, heavy-bottomed skillet on the range. Brown the ground beef over medium to medium-low heat (340°F. in an electric skillet) until the meat loses its red color. Using a large, metal mixing spoon, break up the ground beef as it browns. Add the butter, onions, green peppers, and garlic; continue cooking until the onions and green peppers are tender but barely browned. Remove the skillet from the heat and let the mixture cool slightly. Then, add the water, tomatoes, oregano, chili powder, sugar, salt, pepper, and pepper sauce; using the mixing spoon, break the tomatoes into small chunks and stir to combine the ingredients.

Return the skillet heat to medium to medium-low (340°F. in an electric skillet). Bring the mixture to a boil. Add the rice; stir to combine. Remove from the heat. Cover the skillet and let stand 7 minutes undisturbed. Then, stir the mixture. If the liquid has not been completely absorbed, simmer the mixture, uncovered, over low heat (250°F. in an electric skillet) until the liquid has been reduced sufficiently to achieve the desired consistency of the mixture. Spanish Rice should be moist but not runny.

SERVES 6

BAKED RICE

When time is a factor, one would be hard-pressed to find a more simple rice recipe than this one. It's mighty good, too—one of those "put it in a dish, put it in the oven, and it comes out great" miracle dishes. We all love them!

1¼ cups raw long-grain rice (not instant)
4 cups homemade Chicken Broth (page 88) or 2 14½-ounce cans commercial chicken broth*
1 medium bay leaf
3 dashes Tabasco pepper sauce
⅛ teaspoon white pepper
¼ cup plus 2 tablespoons (6 tablespoons) butter, melted

*Beef broth may be substituted for chicken broth if the rice is to be served as an accompaniment to a meat dish.

Preheat the oven to 350°F. Butter a 2-quart round baking dish or a 7 × 11-inch baking dish; set aside.

In a large mixing bowl, place the rice, broth, bay leaf, pepper sauce, white pepper, and butter; stir to combine. Pour the mixture into the prepared baking dish. Bake, uncovered, for 1 hour, until the rice is tender and golden. Stir once or twice during the early part of baking before the rice begins to set.

SERVES 8

VARIATION: Add ¼ cup thinly sliced green onions (scallions) when combining all the ingredients.

TO COOK WILD RICE

Place the raw wild rice in a sieve. Wash the rice *well* under cold, running water. Place the rice in a saucepan; cover with water ½ inch above the rice. Cover the saucepan. Bring the rice to a boil over high heat; reduce the heat and simmer 35 minutes, or until all the rice has opened. The water will have been all, or nearly all, absorbed. Stir the rice 2 or 3 times during the cooking period, adding a little additional water if necessary. Wild rice is done when all the kernels have opened.

When the rice is done, remove the saucepan from the heat and move it to the back of the range. Let stand, covered, 1 hour or more to allow any remaining water to be absorbed by the rice.

Just before serving, warm the rice, covered, over very low heat.

1¼ CUPS RAW WILD RICE YIELDS ABOUT 4 CUPS COOKED RICE

VARIATION: Wild rice may be cooked in beef broth or chicken broth rather than water. For 1¼ cups raw wild rice, cook in 2 cups broth. It generally takes longer for wild rice to open when cooked in broth. Add more broth during cooking if necessary.

PECAN WILD RICE

1¼ cups raw wild rice
2 cups chicken broth, homemade
  (page 88) or commercially canned
3 tablespoons butter
½ cup chopped pecans
¾ cup chopped onions
½ teaspoon salt
2 tablespoons snipped, fresh parsley

Cook the wild rice in the chicken broth (see To Cook Wild Rice, above); set aside.

In a small, heavy skillet, melt the butter over medium heat. Tilt the skillet back and forth to completely cover the bottom with the melted butter. Place the pecans and onions in the skillet; sauté lightly until the onions are tender, being careful not to let the butter burn. Add the salt and parsley; stir to combine. Remove from the heat. Add the pecan mixture, including the pan juices, to the wild rice; stir to combine.

SERVES 7 TO 8

WILD RICE CASSEROLE

1½ cups raw wild rice
1 pound sliced bacon
1 tablespoon instant chicken bouillon
  granules
⅓ cup boiling water
¾ cup chopped onions
1 cup sliced, fresh mushrooms
8 ounces commercial sour cream
¼ cup Worcestershire sauce
2 tablespoons butter, melted
½ teaspoon salt
¼ teaspoon freshly ground pepper
⅓ cup slivered almonds

Cook the wild rice (in water, see To Cook Wild Rice, above); set aside.

Preheat the oven to 350° F. Butter a 2-quart round baking dish; set aside.

In a large, heavy-bottomed skillet, fry the bacon over medium heat until crisp; drain well between paper towels. With your fingers, break the bacon into small pieces; set aside. Place the bouillon granules in ⅓ cup boiling water; stir until dissolved; set aside.

In a large mixing bowl, place the wild rice, bacon pieces, bouillon, onions, mushrooms, sour cream, Worcestershire sauce, melted butter, salt, pepper, and almonds; stir until combined. Place the mixture in the prepared baking dish. Bake, uncovered, for 1 hour.

SERVES 8

WILD RICE WITH BACON AND ONIONS

1¼ cups raw wild rice
¼ pound (5 slices) bacon, cut widthwise
   into 1-inch pieces
1¼ cups chopped onions

Cook the wild rice (in water, see To Cook Wild Rice, page 276); set aside.

In a medium, heavy-bottomed skillet, fry the bacon pieces over medium heat until crisp. Using a slotted spoon, remove the bacon from the skillet and add to the wild rice; set aside. Place the onions in the skillet; fry in the bacon grease over medium heat until tender and golden in color (about 5 minutes). Add the onions and remaining skillet grease to the wild rice; stir to combine the ingredients. Then, heat the wild rice mixture, covered, over warm heat, stirring 2 or 3 times.

Wild Rice with Bacon and Onions may be prepared up to 1 day before serving and refrigerated in the covered saucepan. Before heating the cold rice mixture over warm heat, add a very small amount of water to barely cover the bottom of the pan.

SERVES 8

Other Rice Recipes

Wild Rice Salad (page 134)
Wild Rice Soup (page 95)

Beans

BAKED BEANS

⅔ cup packed dark brown sugar
1 teaspoon dry mustard
1 31-ounce can Van Camp's pork and
   beans, undrained
½ cup tomato catsup, home canned
   (page 736) or commercially canned
1 medium onion
2 slices bacon, cut in half widthwise

Preheat the oven to 325°F. Grease a 1½-quart round baking dish; set aside.

In a small mixing bowl, place the brown sugar and dry mustard; stir to combine; set aside. Spoon ½ of the pork and beans into the prepared baking dish. Sprinkle ½ of the brown sugar mixture evenly over the beans. Repeat the layers with the remaining ½ pork and beans and ½ brown sugar mixture. Pour the catsup back and forth over the top of the beans and brown sugar mixture; using a small, narrow spatula, spread evenly to cover the surface of the beans and brown sugar mixture.

Place the onion in the center of the dish over the catsup. Arrange the bacon slices over the catsup. Bake, uncovered, for 2½ hours.

SERVES 8

CALICO BEANS

Perfect for taking to a potluck.

1 pound lean, pure ground beef
½ teaspoon salt
¼ teaspoon pepper
½ pound sliced bacon
½ cup chopped onions
1 31-ounce can commercial pork and
    beans, undrained
1 15½-ounce can commercial dark red
    kidney beans, drained
1 15½-ounce can commercial butter beans,
    undrained
½ cup packed dark brown sugar
¼ cup granulated sugar
1 teaspoon dry mustard
⅓ cup tomato catsup, home canned
    (page 781) or commercially canned
2 tablespoons dark molasses

Preheat the oven to 325° F. Grease a 3-quart round baking dish; set aside.

In a large, heavy-bottomed skillet, place the ground beef, salt, and pepper. Over medium to medium-low heat, brown the ground beef lightly. Using a large, metal mixing spoon, break up the ground beef as it browns. Spoon the browned ground beef into a very large mixing bowl; set aside.

Cut 4 slices of bacon widthwise into 1-inch pieces; add to the ground beef; set aside. Cut the remaining slices of bacon widthwise into 1-inch pieces and place in the skillet used to brown the ground beef; fry lightly over medium to medium-low heat. Using a slotted spoon, remove the bacon from the skillet and add to the ground beef; set aside. Place the onions in the skillet used to fry the bacon; brown lightly in the bacon grease over medium heat. Using the slotted spoon, remove the onions from the skillet and add to the ground beef. Add the pork and beans, kidney beans, and butter beans to the ground beef. Do not stir; set aside.

In a small mixing bowl, place the brown sugar, granulated sugar, and dry mustard; stir to combine. Add the catsup and molasses to the sugar mixture; stir until well combined. Add the sugar mixture to the ground beef and beans; using a large, wooden mixing spoon, stir and fold until all the ingredients are combined and evenly distributed. In the stirring process, try to avoid cutting the beans with the spoon.

Turn the mixture into the prepared baking dish. Bake for 2 hours, covered. Then, remove the cover and continue baking, uncovered, for an additional 1½ hours.

SERVES 12

ACCOMPANIMENT SUGGESTIONS

- In the summer, serve with Corn on the Cob (page 315), Potato Salad (page 133), and Marinated Cucumbers and Onions (page 130). For dessert, serve a compote of fresh, summer fruit, and Peanut Cookies (page 628).

- In the winter, serve with Iowa Pork Chops (page 185), Coleslaw (page 133), and Deviled Eggs (page 267). For dessert, serve Apple Pie (page 476) à la mode.

BAKED BEANS AND POLISH SAUSAGE WITH SAUERKRAUT AND APPLESAUCE

1 16-ounce can commercial pork and beans
2 cups home-canned Sauerkraut (page 734), drained, or 16 ounces commercial, fresh sauerkraut, drained
2 cups homemade extra-thick Plain Applesauce (page 244), or 1 15-ounce jar or can commercial plain applesauce
⅓ cup packed dark brown sugar
¼ teaspoon ground allspice
½ pound (2 to 4, depending upon size) Polish sausages, sliced ⅜ inch thick

Preheat the oven to 325°F. Grease a 1½-quart round baking dish; set aside.

In a large mixing bowl, place the pork and beans, sauerkraut, and applesauce; stir to combine; set aside. In a small mixing bowl, place the brown sugar and allspice; stir to combine. Add the brown sugar mixture to the bean mixture; stir to combine. Add the Polish sausage slices; stir until evenly distributed. Place the mixture in the prepared baking dish. Bake, uncovered, for 2 hours.

SERVES 8

Other Bean Recipes

Bean Soup (page 89)
Lima Bean and Ground Sirloin Casserole (page 295)
Succotash (page 323)
Ten-Bean Soup (page 90)

Pasta

W hat, really, is pasta? Literally, "pasta" is an Italian word meaning "paste." Pasta is the paste (or dough) used to make a group of products which are also called pasta. The word "pasta" also is used to designate a dish which contains a pasta product as well as other food.

Pasta is made in both dried and fresh forms. It is made with either semolina or bread-type flour, such as unbleached or bleached all-purpose flour, which is combined with a liquid—usually water and/or eggs—and sometimes olive oil or vegetable oil, salt, and coloring and flavoring (commonly, spinach is used to produce a green color; tomatoes or beet juice, a red hue; carrots, orange; and squid ink, charcoal gray).

Semolina, used in making the best quality dried pasta, is the crushed endosperm (the large center portion of cereal grains) of durum, a hard, high-protein species of wheat. Semolina produces a superior dried pasta which holds its shape during cooking better than dried pasta made with bread-type flour. Fresh pasta is ordinarily made with unbleached or bleached all-purpose flour and eggs. Sometimes, small quantities of olive oil or vegetable oil and/or water, plus salt, are included.

Dried pasta stores satisfactorily up to one year if wrapped securely or kept in a tightly covered container. Fresh pasta must be kept under refrigeration and used within 4 days, or it may be frozen for up to 6 months.

While some gastronomists classify noodle-like products made with rice or soy flour as pasta, I prefer to limit the nomenclature "pasta" to noodle/macaroni-like products made from a flour derived from wheat which is mixed with a liquid to make a dough. For example, although couscous, popularly used in North African cooking, is granular semolina, it is not made by mixing the semolina with a liquid and forming it into a dough; therefore, I do not categorize this product as pasta.

There are approximately 150 sizes and shapes of pasta. See page 282 for pictures of some of the most popular types. Some are designed to contain fillings and some are crafted to combine well with different sauces. Thicknesses vary for adaptability to a broad spectrum of dishes, and some appear to be the result of creative whimsy for eye appeal, diversion, and eating fun.

It is now generally believed that pasta was first made in Sicily during the latter part of the Roman Empire. The Romans used Sicily for the cultivation of their wheat, and, reportedly, the surplus supply of ground wheat was preserved by mixing it with water and drying it in the sun. There is documentation that fresh pasta was made in central and northern Italy as far back as the Middle Ages. However, it was not until the early nineteenth century, when factory-made dried pasta came into production, that pasta began to gain in popular usage as the first course in Italian meals. It was well into the century before the custom spread to the northerly sections of Italy.

Three authentic Italian pasta dishes from the old country, handed down in the family of my wonderful Italian neighbor, Grace Montognese, are included in this chapter: Braciole (page 287), Italian-style Spaghetti and Meatballs (page 288), and Pasta Ripiena (page 284). Under her close guidance and supervision, Grace taught me how to make these absolutely delicious dishes which, after testing and quickly sampling, I straightway delivered across the street for her final approval. I hope that you enjoy making these Italian specialties and that your family and dining guests take pleasure in eating them. Thanks, Grace, for sharing them with all of us!

Macaroni and noodles have been standbys in Midwest home-style dining for decades; however, formerly they were not usually thought of as "pasta." Macaroni and Cheese (page 285),

Macaroni Salad (page 139), and Macaroni-Beef Casserole (page 290) are old reliables in the middle states. The same holds true for Chicken and Noodles (page 210) and Beef and Noodles (page 158), both ingrained in Heartland diets for aeons, with predictably clear sailing far into the future. In earlier years, fresh noodles regularly were made from scratch by fine, old-time Midwest cooks. With the momentum of the current pasta vogue, homemade noodles are turning up again with surprising frequency.

"Noodles," as the term is used in traditional Midwest cookery, means "egg noodles." As implied, eggs are used in making them. Egg noodles are thin (although they are sometimes made thicker), ribbonlike strips of pasta which usually range in width from about $3/16$ to $3/8$ inch. Dried commercial egg noodles are short in length and often curly.

Noodles are a favored ingredient in Mid-America main-dish casseroles because they combine so excellently with most meats, fish, shellfish, and vegetables, as well as many sauces. Exemplifying this diversity are casserole recipes in this book in which noodles complement ground beef (Ground Sirloin-Noodle Casserole, page 174), ground pork (Pork and Noodles Casserole with Sage-y Red Sauce, page 188), ring bologna (Ring Bologna Casserole, page 297), and tuna (Tuna-Noodle Casserole, page 297).

While pasta is certainly not new under the sun (as we have seen), contemporary usage of the word "pasta," as a dish, often connotes new combinations of pasta with foods and sauces which are usually—though not always—designed to be healthful and light.

Pasta's trendiness stems from the fact that it is a food high in complex carbohydrates and generally low in saturated fat and total fat. Along with bread, cereal, and rice, pasta is specifically named in the food group from which Americans are advised to eat the most daily servings on the U.S. government's 1992 Food Guide Pyramid (see pages 790–792). Of course, all the ingredients, including the sauce, in a particular pasta dish must be taken into account when figuring the total nutritive value of that dish. For

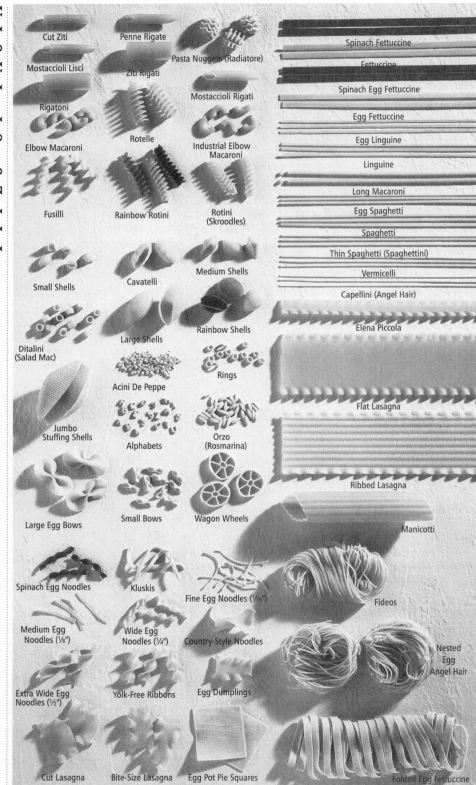

TYPES OF PASTA

- Cut Ziti
- Penne Rigate
- Pasta Nuggets (Radiatore)
- Mostaccioli Lisci
- Ziti Rigati
- Mostaccioli Rigati
- Rigatoni
- Rotelle
- Industrial Elbow Macaroni
- Elbow Macaroni
- Fusilli
- Rainbow Rotini
- Rotini (Skroodles)
- Small Shells
- Cavatelli
- Medium Shells
- Large Shells
- Rainbow Shells
- Ditalini (Salad Mac)
- Acini De Peppe
- Rings
- Alphabets
- Orzo (Rosmarina)
- Jumbo Stuffing Shells
- Large Egg Bows
- Small Bows
- Wagon Wheels
- Spinach Egg Noodles
- Kluskis
- Fine Egg Noodles (1/16")
- Medium Egg Noodles (1/8")
- Wide Egg Noodles (1/4")
- Country-Style Noodles
- Extra Wide Egg Noodles (1/2")
- Yolk-Free Ribbons
- Egg Dumplings
- Cut Lasagna
- Bite-Size Lasagna
- Egg Pot Pie Squares

- Spinach Fettuccine
- Fettuccine
- Spinach Egg Fettuccine
- Egg Fettuccine
- Egg Linguine
- Linguine
- Long Macaroni
- Egg Spaghetti
- Spaghetti
- Thin Spaghetti (Spaghettini)
- Vermicelli
- Capellini (Angel Hair)
- Elena Piccola
- Flat Lasagna
- Ribbed Lasagna
- Manicotti
- Fideos
- Nested Egg Angel Hair
- Folded Egg Fettuccine

Picture Courtesy of Creamette Pasta.

instance, it should be remembered that sauces containing large amounts of butter and cream are high in saturated fat, and that pasta made with eggs contains cholesterol.

Although Midwesterners, especially those outside the major cities, seem to be marching in the new-style pasta caravan at a somewhat slower cadence than on the east and west coasts, the pace is picking up. Stay tuned.

Carnival Salad (page 138), Chicken and Broccoli Pasta, with variations (page 287), and Rainbow Pasta Dinner (page 292) are main-course pasta dishes with the new twist. Pasta lends itself well to creative cookery, so seize the moment and come up with your very own inventions using original combinations of pastas, vegetables, herbs, meats, and what have you, to the delight of your diners.

TO COOK DRIED PASTA

In a large, covered kettle or saucepan, bring sufficient water to a boil, over high heat, as will cover by 2 inches the quantity of pasta to be cooked (approximately 5 quarts of water per pound of pasta). Salt may be added optionally to the water (up to 1 tablespoon per pound of pasta). When the water comes to a rolling boil, uncover the kettle and add the pasta all at once. Cook the pasta uncovered. Return the water (with pasta) to a rolling boil, stirring frequently to prevent the pasta from sticking to the kettle and the pieces of pasta from sticking together. Keep the cooking temperature sufficiently high during the cooking process to retain a rapid boil. Continue to stir frequently during the cooking process. Cook the pasta until it reaches the desired tenderness (approximately 8 to 15 minutes) depending upon the type of pasta and the amount being cooked. Thinner pasta and lesser quantities of pasta require less cooking time.

To check for doneness, use a spoon to cut a piece of the pasta against the inside of the kettle. When done, pasta should be firm and retain its shape but cut easily. Do not overcook. When done, drain the pasta in a colander or sieve and rinse it under hot, running water. Drain well. Rinse the cooking kettle with hot water and dry the kettle. Return the pasta to the kettle. Melted butter may be added and tossed with the pasta to prevent the pasta from sticking together and to add flavor (about 2 tablespoons of butter per pound of pasta). Or, add the desired sauce and toss. If pasta is to be served cold, rinse it in cold water, drain well, and return it to a cold kettle.

The quantity of pasta required per serving varies widely with the dish to be served and the appetites of the diners; however, ⅛ to ¼ pound per serving is an average range for pasta-intensive dishes.

FETTUCCINE ALFREDO

Main dish, side dish, or first course, this one's rich beyond reason. (Every now and then we're entitled to throw open the gate.) My introduction to this dish was in Rome in 1954, when it was tossed high above the pasta bowl and served by the *Alfredo.*

1 pound fettuccine, cooked, rinsed in hot water, and drained (left column)
1 cup (½ pint) whipping cream, unwhipped
½ teaspoon white pepper
¼ teaspoon salt
½ cup (¼ pound) butter, melted
2 cups freshly grated Parmesan cheese (page 46)

After cooking, rinsing, and draining the fettuccine, return the hot fettuccine to the rinsed and dried cooking kettle; cover and set aside. Pour the whipping cream into a small saucepan; warm over low heat. Remove from the heat and add the white pepper and salt; stir to combine. Add the cream mixture and butter to the fettuccine; toss until the pasta is evenly coated. Add the Parmesan cheese; toss *well*. Turn into a warm, pasta serving bowl; serve immediately.

**SERVES 4 AS A MAIN DISH OR
6 AS A SIDE DISH OR FIRST COURSE**

(Recipe continues on next page)

- After adding the Parmesan cheese and tossing, add 6 slices bacon, fried crisply, drained, and crumbled; toss until evenly distributed. Or, sprinkle the crumbled bacon over the top of the dish before serving.

- After adding the Parmesan cheese and tossing, add 1½ cups small broccoli flowerets, steamed (page 302) 3 minutes; toss carefully to evenly distribute.

PASTA RIPIENA

½ pound lean, pure ground beef
¾ cup freshly grated Romano cheese (page 46)
½ cup commercially packaged, seasoned, Italian-style bread crumbs
1 tablespoon plus 1 teaspoon snipped, fresh basil
1 large garlic clove, pressed
½ teaspoon salt
¼ teaspoon pepper
2 extra-large eggs
2 tablespoons whole milk
½ cup extra-virgin olive oil
2 garlic cloves, pressed
½ cup water
1 12-ounce can commercial tomato paste
1 8-ounce can commercial tomato sauce
2¾ cups water
1 tablespoon plus 1 teaspoon snipped, fresh basil
½ bay leaf
½ teaspoon salt
¼ teaspoon pepper
3 extra-large eggs, hard-cooked (page 264)
2 quarts water
8 ounces rigatoni
⅔ cup freshly grated Romano cheese (page 46), divided
1 cup shredded, mild cheddar cheese, divided

In a medium mixing bowl, place the ground beef, ¾ cup Romano cheese, bread crumbs, 1 tablespoon plus 1 teaspoon basil, 1 large pressed garlic clove, ½ teaspoon salt, ¼ teaspoon pepper, eggs, and milk. Using a large, metal mixing spoon, break up the ground beef and stir until the ingredients are completely combined and evenly distributed. Using a 1-inch trigger scoop or melon baller to apportion the meat mixture, roll tiny, 1-inch meatballs in your hands and set aside on a piece of waxed paper. (Makes about 5 dozen meatballs.)

In an electric skillet or a large, heavy-bottomed skillet on the range, heat the olive oil over medium heat (350° F. in an electric skillet). Brown ⅓ of the meatballs at a time in the hot olive oil, turning them several times with a very small spatula to achieve even browning and retain their round shape. (It is difficult to turn more than ⅓ of the meatballs at a time in a timely manner.) When properly browned, the meatballs should be medium brown in color and not crusty. Place the browned meatballs in a bowl; cover and refrigerate.

Heat the skillet in which the meatballs were browned to medium heat (350° F. in an electric skillet), leaving the olive oil and pan juices in the skillet. Place the 2 pressed garlic cloves in the skillet; sauté the garlic about 1 minute until very slightly browned. Reduce the skillet heat to low (250° F. in an electric skillet).

When the skillet cools to the reduced temperature, pour ½ cup water into the skillet and completely deglaze. Pour the skillet liquid into a large (about 8-quart), heavy-bottomed kettle. Add the tomato paste and tomato sauce; stir until the olive oil is completely blended. Add 2¾ cups water, 1 tablespoon plus 1 teaspoon basil, ½ bay leaf, ½ teaspoon salt, and ¼ teaspoon pepper; stir well to blend and combine.

Cover the kettle; bring the sauce to a fast *simmer* over medium-high heat, stirring often. Reduce the heat to low and maintain a fast simmer. Cook for 1 hour, stirring frequently and keeping the vent on the kettle lid open. If the lid does not have a vent, tilt the lid to partially cover the kettle during the last 15 minutes of cooking.

Add the meatballs to the sauce in the kettle; using a wooden spoon to help avoid cutting the meatballs, stir to combine. Cover the kettle and continue simmering the mixture for 1 additional hour, stirring often. Continue to keep the lid vent open, or tilt the kettle lid during the last 15 minutes of cooking. If the sauce reduces to the desired thickness before the cooking time has elapsed, close the vent on the lid and keep the kettle tightly covered except when stirring. A small amount of water may be added if necessary. When the cooking time has elapsed, remove from the heat. Remove and discard the bay leaf. Cover the kettle and set aside.

Peel the eggs. Cut three ⅜-inch egg slices for decoration; set aside. Chop the remaining eggs; set aside. Pour 2 quarts water into a medium kettle. Cover the kettle and bring the water to a rolling boil over high heat. Drop the rigatoni into the boiling water and boil, uncovered, 12 to 14 minutes, until tender, stirring frequently. Do not overcook. Drain the rigatoni in a colander. Return the rigatoni to the kettle in which it was cooked; add hot water to rinse. Drain well in the colander. Turn the rigatoni into a large mixing bowl. Add ½ cup of the sauce (no meatballs) from the kettle and 2 tablespoons of the Romano cheese; toss to combine; set aside.

In an ungreased, 2½-quart, 3-inch-deep, rectangular baking casserole, place ½ cup of the sauce (no meatballs) from the kettle; spread to thinly cover the bottom of the casserole. Add ½ of the rigatoni mixture; spread evenly. Sprinkle ½ of the remaining Romano cheese over the rigatoni mixture. Distribute ½ of the cheddar cheese over the Romano cheese. Spoon ½ of the chopped eggs evenly over the cheddar cheese. Add ½ of the meatballs and ½ of the remaining sauce; distribute evenly. Repeat the layers of rigatoni mixture, Romano cheese, cheddar cheese, chopped eggs, meatballs, and sauce, using the remainder of the ingredients. Decoratively arrange the 3 reserved egg slices on top and in the center of the casserole.

Bake, uncovered, for 25 minutes, or until just hot. If the casserole has been refrigerated prior to baking, the baking time will be slightly longer.

SERVES 6 OR 7

MACARONI AND CHEESE

2 quarts water
7 ounces (about 1¾ cups) small elbow
  macaroni
⅓ cup diced green bell peppers
1 4-ounce jar pimientos, drained and
  chopped (¼ cup)
1 12-ounce can (1½ cups) evaporated milk
½ teaspoon salt
½ pound pasteurized process sharp
  American cheese, cut into approximately
  ½-inch cubes
2 teaspoons Worcestershire sauce
½ teaspoon dry mustard

Preheat the oven to 350° F. Grease a 2-quart round baking dish; set aside.

Pour 2 quarts water into a medium kettle; cover the kettle and bring the water to a rolling boil over high heat. Drop the macaroni into the boiling water and boil, uncovered, 8 to 10 minutes, until tender, stirring frequently. Do not overcook. Drain the macaroni in a colander; rinse under hot, running water and drain well. Turn the macaroni into a large mixing bowl. Add the green peppers and pimientos; toss to distribute evenly. Place the macaroni mixture in the prepared baking dish; set aside.

In a small saucepan, place the evaporated milk and salt; stir to combine. Place the saucepan, uncovered, over medium heat; scald the milk (page 25). Remove from the heat. Add the cheese, Worcestershire sauce, and dry mustard. Place over low heat and stir until the cheese melts and the mixture is completely blended. Do not allow the mixture to boil. Pour the cheese mixture evenly over the macaroni. Bake, uncovered, for 25 minutes.

SERVES 8

CHICKEN-MACARONI LOAF
Served Cold

In warm weather, serve attractive-looking slices of this cold loaf as the main dish for luncheons or light family dinners. Whatever the weather, it makes an innovative first course, even for more formal occasions.

¼ cup all-purpose flour
1 teaspoon salt
½ teaspoon white pepper
¼ cup (4 tablespoons) butter
½ cup minced onions
¾ cup sliced, small, fresh mushrooms
¾ cup whole milk
½ cup chicken broth, homemade
  (page 88) or commercially canned
1 tablespoon prepared mustard
4 ounces pasteurized process American
  cheese, cut into approximately ½-inch
  cubes
7 ounces (2 cups) small elbow macaroni,
  cooked in salted water (page 283), rinsed
  in cold water, and drained
2 cups cooked, skinless chicken-breast meat
  (page 204) diced ¼ inch square
1 extra-large egg, slightly beaten
1 2-ounce jar sliced pimientos, drained and
  diced (2 tablespoons)
Sprigs the of fresh parsley for decoration

Preheat the oven to 350° F. Using Special Grease (page 56), grease well a 3⅝ × 10¼ × 2⅝-inch-deep, preferably nonstick, baking pan with straight (not slanted) sides; set aside.

In a small mixing bowl, place the flour, salt, and white pepper; stir to combine; set aside. In a medium, heavy-bottomed saucepan, melt the butter over medium heat. Place the onions and mushrooms in the saucepan; sauté lightly 5 minutes. Remove from the heat. Add the flour mixture and stir until completely blended with the butter, with no flour lumps remaining. Add the milk, broth, and mustard; stir to combine. Return the saucepan to medium heat; cook the mixture until thickened and just under boiling,

stirring constantly. Do not allow the mixture to boil. Remove from the heat and reduce the heat to low. Add the cheese. Place the saucepan over low heat; stir the mixture continuously until the cheese has melted, intermittently pressing the cheese cubes against the pan with the back of the spoon to expedite melting. Do not allow the mixture to boil. Remove from the heat and set aside.

In a large mixing bowl, place the macaroni, chicken, and egg; toss lightly until evenly distributed. Add the pimientos and cheese sauce; stir well to combine. Place in the prepared baking pan. Bake, uncovered, for 40 minutes. Remove from the oven and place on a wire rack; let stand to cool slightly. Then, refrigerate until completely cold. When cold, cover with aluminum foil.

To serve, carefully run a sharp, thin-bladed knife around the inside edges of the pan to loosen the sides of the Chicken-Macaroni Loaf from the pan. Place a cold serving platter (or cutting board) over the top of the pan. Holding the pan and platter (board) securely together, invert to release the loaf onto the platter (board). If the loaf does not release onto the platter (board), place a hot, moist tea towel over the bottom of the pan, leaving the pan inverted on the platter (board); let stand briefly. If the loaf does not release, remove the tea towel. Then, hold the pan and platter (board) securely together and shake them up and down to facilitate release of the loaf onto the platter (board). Using a sharp knife, slice the loaf into approximately ⅞-inch-wide servings. Serve on the platter or individual plates. Decorate the platter or individual plates with parsley sprigs.

SERVES 11 TO 12

CHICKEN AND BROCCOLI PASTA

2 cups rotini, cooked, rinsed in hot water,
and drained (page 283)
¼ cup (4 tablespoons) butter
1 cup (½ pint) whipping cream, unwhipped
⅛ teaspoon salt
½ teaspoon white pepper
2 cups freshly grated Parmesan cheese
(page 46)
2 cups cooked, skinless chicken-breast meat
cut into bite-sized pieces (page 204), hot
2 cups hot, steamed broccoli flowerets
(page 302)
1 cup sliced, fresh mushrooms (uncooked)
Additional freshly grated Parmesan cheese
(page 46)

After cooking, rinsing, and draining the rotini,
return the hot rotini to the rinsed and dried
cooking kettle. Add the butter, whipping cream,
salt, white pepper, and 2 cups Parmesan cheese;
using a wooden mixing spoon, toss to combine.
Add the hot chicken, hot broccoli, and mushrooms; toss lightly to evenly distribute. Pass additional Parmesan cheese at the table.

SERVES 4

VARIATIONS
• Substitute the following meat and vegetable
combinations, or other combinations of
your choice, for the chicken, broccoli, and
mushrooms, making the substitutions in
amounts and proportions to suit your taste
preferences:

~ Crisply fried bacon pieces, cooked peas,
and cooked carrot slices.

~ Bite-sized pieces of medium-rare beef tenderloin (see Meat Safety, page 157), steamed
zucchini sliced ½ inch thick and cut in half,
and fresh tomato pieces with seeds and
cores removed (page 45).

~ Hot ring bologna slices, cooked green
beans, and bite-sized pieces of steamed red
bell peppers.

• Substitute spinach or rainbow rotini for the
plain rotini.

GRACE MONTOGNESE'S BRACIOLE
Italian Steak Rolls

STEAK ROLLS
4 boneless, top round steaks, about
½ pound each, cut ¼ inch thick
6 slices bacon
1 cup minced celery hearts (with leaves)
(page 21)
¾ cup freshly grated Romano cheese
(page 46)
¾ cup commercially packaged, seasoned,
Italian-style bread crumbs
1 large or 2 small garlic cloves, pressed
1 teaspoon dried leaf basil
1 tablespoon plus 1 teaspoon finely
snipped, fresh parsley
½ teaspoon salt
¼ teaspoon pepper
2 extra-large eggs

SAUCE
2 cups water
3 cups water
2 18-ounce cans commercial tomato paste
1 15-ounce can commercial tomato sauce
1 garlic clove, pressed
1 bay leaf
1 teaspoon dried leaf basil
½ teaspoon dried leaf oregano
1 teaspoon dried parsley
½ teaspoon salt
¼ teaspoon pepper

PASTA
1 pound linguini
¾ cup freshly grated Romano cheese,
(page 46), divided
Additional freshly grated Romano cheese
(page 46)

(Recipe continues on next page)

Cut each round steak in half widthwise. Using a sharp knife, slit any fat on the sides of the meat diagonally at 2-inch intervals, being careful not to cut into the flesh (causing loss of meat juice); set aside. Cut major portions of fat from the bacon. Place the bacon fat in an electric skillet or a large, heavy-bottomed skillet on the range. Melt the bacon fat over low heat (250° F. in an electric skillet). Meanwhile, cut the remaining bacon into ¼-inch-square pieces. In a large mixing bowl, place the bacon, celery, ¾ cup Romano cheese, bread crumbs, 1 large or 2 small pressed garlic cloves, 1 teaspoon basil, fresh parsley, ½ teaspoon salt, ¼ teaspoon pepper, and eggs; stir until thoroughly combined; set aside.

Remove the skillet from heat. Using a slotted spoon, remove the unmelted bacon pieces from the skillet and discard. Set the skillet aside (do not remove the bacon grease).

Lay the 8 pieces of round steak on a piece of waxed paper resting on a flat work surface. Spoon the bacon mixture, evenly divided, onto the meat pieces. Using a spoon, spread the bacon mixture evenly over each piece of meat to within ½ inch of the edges. Roll each piece of meat widthwise, jelly-roll fashion, and tie securely with cotton string, making certain the filling is sealed in; set aside.

Heat the skillet containing the bacon grease to medium (350° F. in an electric skillet). When hot, place the braciole (steak rolls) in the skillet; brown well on all sides (about 15 minutes). Add some olive oil to the skillet if additional fat is needed. When brown, place the braciole in a flat pan and reduce the skillet heat to low (250° F. in an electric skillet).

When the skillet cools to the reduced temperature, add 2 cups water and deglaze completely. Pour the skillet liquid into a large, *heavy-bottomed* kettle. To the kettle, add 3 cups water and the tomato paste, tomato sauce, 1 pressed garlic clove, bay leaf, 1 teaspoon basil, oregano, dried parsley, ½ teaspoon salt, and ¼ teaspoon pepper; stir to combine. Bring the sauce to a simmer over medium-high heat, stirring constantly. Reduce the heat to low and add the braciole; cover and simmer slowly 2½

hours. During the cooking period, occasionally run a large mixing spoon or spatula under the braciole to help prevent them from sticking to the bottom of the kettle.

20 MINUTES BEFORE SERVING TIME: Cook the linguini, rinse in hot water, and drain (page 283). Return the hot linguine to the rinsed and dried cooking kettle; cover to keep warm; set aside. Remove the braciole from the kettle and carefully remove the string. Place the braciole on a heated serving platter; cover with aluminum foil to keep warm.

Add 3 cups of the cooked sauce and ½ cup of the Romano cheese to the linguini; toss to combine and turn into a warm, pasta serving bowl. Sprinkle the remaining ¼ cup Romano cheese over the linguini. Cover the Romano cheese with an additional 1 cup sauce; *do not toss.* Spoon some sauce over the braciole. Serve the braciole and linguini at the table. Pass additional Romano cheese in an appropriate serving dish, and additional sauce in a sauce dish.

SERVES 8

GRACE'S SPAGHETTI AND MEATBALLS

MEATBALLS
1½ cups commercially packaged, seasoned, Italian-style bread crumbs
2 cups freshly grated Romano cheese (page 46)
1 tablespoon dried, leaf basil
¾ teaspoon salt
¼ teaspoon pepper
¾ pound lean, pure ground beef
¼ pound lean, ground pork
4 extra-large eggs
⅓ cup whole milk
2 garlic cloves, pressed
2 tablespoons snipped, fresh parsley
¼ cup vegetable oil

In a large mixing bowl, place the bread crumbs, Romano cheese, basil, salt, and pepper; stir to combine. Add the ground beef, ground pork, eggs, milk, garlic, and parsley. Using a large, metal mixing spoon, break up the ground meat and stir until the ingredients are evenly combined. Turn the mixture into an 8 × 8-inch baking dish; pat evenly into the bottom of the dish. Using a small knife, cut the mixture into 16 equal portions. Using your hands, roll each portion into a compact meatball and set aside on a piece of waxed paper.

In an electric skillet or a large, heavy-bottomed skillet on the range, heat the vegetable oil over medium-high heat (375° F. in an electric skillet). Place the meatballs in the skillet and brown about 10 minutes, until medium brown in color but not crusty, turning often to retain their round shape. Place the browned meatballs in a bowl; cover and refrigerate.

TOMATO SAUCE
½ cup extra-virgin olive oil
2 garlic cloves, pressed
2 12-ounce cans commercial tomato paste
2 8-ounce cans commercial tomato sauce
6 cups water
1 teaspoon dried, leaf sweet basil
1 teaspoon dried leaf oregano
1 bay leaf
1 teaspoon salt

Heat the olive oil in a 6- to 8-quart, heavy-bottomed kettle over medium-high heat. Place the garlic in the kettle; brown about 2 minutes in the hot oil. Remove the kettle from the heat and allow the oil to cool slightly. Then, add the tomato paste and tomato sauce; stir until the olive oil is completely blended. Add the water, basil, oregano, bay leaf, and salt; stir until well combined. Cover the kettle; bring the sauce to a fast *simmer* over medium-high heat, stirring often. Reduce the heat to low and maintain a fast simmer. Cook for 1 hour, stirring frequently and keeping the vent on the kettle lid open. If the lid does not have a vent, tilt the lid to par-

tially cover the kettle during the last 15 minutes of cooking.

Add the meatballs to the sauce in the kettle. Cover the kettle and continue simmering the mixture for an additional 1 hour, stirring often. Use a wooden mixing spoon to stir, and stir in a circular motion to help prevent cutting the meatballs. Continue to keep the lid vent open, or tilt the kettle lid during the last 15 minutes of cooking. If the sauce reduces to the desired thickness before the cooking time has elapsed, close the vent on the lid and keep the kettle tightly covered except when stirring. A small amount of water may be added if necessary. If the sauce is slightly thin at the end of the cooking period, remove the cover and continue simmering for a few minutes until it is reduced to the desired consistency. Remove from the heat and cover; set aside.

SPAGHETTI
1 pound spaghetti

Cook the spaghetti (page 283); drain in a sieve. Rinse under hot, running water; drain well in the sieve. (Do not add butter.)

TO SERVE
1¾ cups freshly grated Romano cheese (page 46), divided

Place the spaghetti in the bottom of a large, warm pasta bowl. Sprinkle ¾ cup of the Romano cheese over the spaghetti; set aside. Carefully remove the meatballs from the tomato sauce and place in a bowl; cover to keep warm and set aside. Ladle 1 cup of the sauce into a small sauce dish to serve at the table as extra sauce; cover to keep warm and set aside.

Pour all but approximately 1½ cups of the remaining sauce over the spaghetti and cheese; toss until evenly combined. Sprinkle ¼ cup of the Romano cheese over the spaghetti mixture. Arrange the meatballs on top of the spaghetti mixture toward one side of the bowl (to retain an uncovered surface of spaghetti for serving).

(Recipe continues on next page)

Spoon the remaining 1½ cups sauce over all. Place the remaining ¾ cup Romano cheese in an appropriate serving dish to pass at the table.

SERVES 8

ACCOMPANIMENT SUGGESTIONS: Spaghetti and meatballs are traditionally served with an all-green lettuce and vegetable salad (page 124) tossed with Italian Salad Dressing (page 148), and Garlic Bread (page 368).

LASAGNA

⅓ pound Italian sausage
⅔ pound lean, pure ground beef
1 garlic clove, pressed
1 tablespoon snipped, fresh parsley
1 tablespoon snipped, fresh basil
1 teaspoon salt
1 16-ounce can commercial crushed tomatoes, undrained
1 12-ounce can commercial tomato paste
3 cups small curd, cream-style cottage cheese
2 extra-large eggs, beaten
1 teaspoon salt
½ teaspoon pepper
2 tablespoons snipped, fresh parsley
½ cup freshly grated Parmesan cheese (page 46)
10 ounces lasagna, cooked, rinsed in hot water, and drained (page 283)
1 pound mozzarella cheese, sliced very thinly

In an electric skillet or a large, heavy-bottomed skillet on the range, place the Italian sausage, ground beef, and garlic over medium heat (350°F. in an electric skillet). Brown the meat, using a large, metal mixing spoon to break up the meat as it browns. Reduce the heat to very low (220°F. in an electric skillet). When the skillet cools to the reduced temperature, add the 1 tablespoon parsley, basil, 1 teaspoon salt, tomatoes, and tomato paste; stir to combine.

Simmer, uncovered, 30 minutes, until the sauce is thick, stirring occasionally.

Preheat the oven to 375°F. Grease a 9 × 13-inch baking dish; set aside.

In a medium bowl, place the cottage cheese, eggs, 1 teaspoon salt, pepper, 2 tablespoons parsley, and Parmesan cheese; stir to combine; set aside. Arrange ½ of the cooked lasagna, single layer, in the bottom of the prepared baking dish. Spread ½ of the cottage cheese mixture evenly over the lasagna. Arrange ½ of the mozzarella cheese slices over the cottage cheese mixture. Spread ½ of the meat sauce over the cheese slices. Repeat the layers, using the remaining ½ of the ingredients.

Bake, uncovered, for 30 minutes. Remove from the oven and let stand 15 minutes to allow the Lasagna to set slightly. To serve, cut the Lasagna into 12 square servings with a sharp knife. Use a small spatula to remove the servings from the baking dish.

SERVES 12

MACARONI-BEEF CASSEROLE

1 tablespoon vegetable shortening
1 pound lean, pure ground beef
1 cup chopped green bell peppers
1 cup chopped onions
1 teaspoon salt
⅛ teaspoon pepper
1 10-ounce package frozen sweet corn
2 quarts water
1 teaspoon salt
1½ cups elbow macaroni
1 16-ounce can commercial whole, peeled tomatoes, undrained, or 1 pint home-canned Tomatoes (page 736), undrained
1 10¾-ounce can condensed tomato soup

In an electric skillet or a large, heavy-bottomed skillet on the range, melt the vegetable shortening over medium heat (350°F. in an electric skillet). Tilt the skillet back and forth to completely cover the bottom with the melted shortening.

Place the ground beef in the skillet and begin to brown. Using a large, metal mixing spoon, break up the ground beef as it heats and browns. When the meat begins to lose its red color, add the green peppers, onions, salt, and pepper; stir to combine and continue browning. When the meat is brown and the vegetables are cooked lightly, remove from the heat; set aside. Cook the corn, following directions on the package; drain in a sieve and set aside.

Preheat the oven to 350° F. Grease a 2-quart round baking dish; set aside.

Pour 2 quarts water into a medium kettle; add 1 teaspoon salt and stir to combine. Cover the kettle and bring the salted water to a rolling boil over high heat. Drop the macaroni into the boiling water and boil, uncovered, 10 minutes, until tender, stirring frequently. Do not overcook. Drain the macaroni in a colander; rinse under hot, running water and drain well; set aside.

Add the tomatoes to the ground beef mixture; using a metal mixing spoon, break the tomatoes into small chunks. Add the tomato soup; stir to blend and combine the ingredients. Add the corn and macaroni; toss carefully to evenly distribute. Turn the mixture into the prepared baking dish. Bake, covered, for 35 minutes.

SERVES 8

VARIATIONS

- Prior to baking, top the casserole with freshly grated Parmesan cheese (page 46), or shredded cheddar or mozzarella cheese.

- Substitute cooked green beans or carrots for the corn, or use one or both of them in combination with the corn (decreasing the amount of corn proportionately).

ISABEL'S NOODLE KUGEL

Noodle Kugel is a classic Jewish side dish that I first enjoyed at Isabel and Stan Levin's home. Isabel serves other versions of noodle kugel made with fruits, raisins, and additional sugar or preserves as dessert.

⅓ cup sugar*
1 teaspoon ground cinnamon**
1 teaspoon salt
8 ounces commercial sour cream
1 cup small curd, cream-style cottage cheese
4 quarts water
12 ounces extra-wide egg noodles
3 tablespoons butter, melted
4 extra-large eggs, beaten
3 tablespoons cornflake crumbs, commercially packaged or crumbed in a blender or food processor (page 49)
3 tablespoons butter

The sugar may be increased to ½ cup, if desired.

**The cinnamon may be increased to 1¼ teaspoons, if desired.*

Preheat the oven to 350° F. Butter a 9 × 13–inch baking dish; set aside.

In a medium mixing bowl, place the sugar, cinnamon, and salt; stir to combine. Add the sour cream and cottage cheese; stir to combine; set aside.

Pour 4 quarts water into a medium kettle; cover and bring the water to a boil over high heat. Drop the noodles into the boiling water and boil, uncovered, about 10 minutes, until just tender, stirring frequently. Do not overcook. Drain the noodles in a sieve; rinse under hot, running water and drain well. Rinse and dry the cooking kettle; return the noodles to the kettle. Add 3 tablespoons melted butter; toss until the noodles are evenly coated. Add the sour cream mixture and eggs; stir to combine.

Turn the noodle mixture into the prepared baking dish; spread evenly. Sprinkle the cornflake crumbs over the top. Dot with 3 tablespoons butter. Bake for 20 minutes. Then, cover loosely with aluminum foil and bake an additional 15 minutes, until fully set.

Using a sharp knife, cut the Noodle Kugel into 15 servings. Use a small spatula to remove the servings from the baking dish.

SERVES 15

RAINBOW PASTA DINNER

4 slices bacon, cut widthwise into 1-inch pieces
1 large onion, chopped (about 1½ cups)
1 green bell pepper, diced (about 1¼ cups)
1 pound lean, pure ground beef
1 teaspoon salt
¼ teaspoon pepper
2 16-ounce cans commercial, whole, peeled tomatoes, undrained, or 1 quart home-canned Tomatoes (page 736), undrained
1 teaspoon dried leaf basil
¼ teaspoon dried leaf oregano
1 teaspoon sugar
¾ cup chili sauce, home canned (page 783) or commercially canned
1 16-ounce can commercial wax beans, drained, or 1 pint home-canned Wax Beans (page 733), drained
2 quarts water
8 ounces rainbow rotini (also known as garden rotini)

In an electric skillet or a large, heavy-bottomed skillet on the range, fry the bacon pieces over medium-low heat (300° F. in an electric skillet), until cooked but not overly crisp. Using a slotted spoon, remove the bacon from the skillet and place in a small bowl; set aside. Place the onions and green peppers in the skillet; fry in the bacon grease over medium-low heat (300° F. in an electric skillet), until the onions are lightly browned. Add the ground beef, salt, and pepper. Using a large, metal mixing spoon, break up the ground beef and stir to combine with the onions and peppers. Continue frying over medium-low heat (300° F. in an electric skillet), until the ground beef is medium browned.

Reduce the skillet heat to very low (215° F. in an electric skillet). When the skillet cools to the reduced temperature, add the bacon, tomatoes, basil, oregano, sugar, and chili sauce. Using the large, metal mixing spoon, break the tomatoes into bite-sized chunks; stir to combine all the ingredients. Cover the skillet and simmer the mixture 25 minutes, stirring occasionally. Then, uncover the skillet and continue simmering about 10 to 15 minutes, until the mixture is reduced to a thick consistency. The mixture should not be runny; however, it should not be reduced to a pasty consistency. Add the wax beans; heat through.

Meanwhile, pour 2 quarts water into a medium kettle. Cover the kettle and bring the water to a rolling boil over high heat. Drop the rotini into the boiling water and boil, uncovered, 10 to 12 minutes, until tender, stirring occasionally. Drain the rotini in a colander; rinse under hot, running water and drain well.

Add the rotini to the ground beef mixture; toss lightly to combine. Serve in a large bowl.

SERVES 8

Other Pasta Recipes

One-Dish Meals

What constitutes a one-dish meal? That depends. Are you talking breakfast, lunch, or dinner? Do you mean the main meal of the day or a lesser one? Is nutritional value a factor?

To an extent, it hinges on the point of view of the diner. Vegetarians would have a perspective, and I suppose someone might sit down to a big plateful of baked beans and call it a meal.

For the purposes of this chapter, I am talking about the primary meal of the day, be it dinner or lunch—in most cases, dinner. Strictly speaking, the one dish should contain three types of food: (1) *meat, poultry, or fish* (or a substitute protein, such as a legume, cheese, or nuts), (2) *a carbohydrate,* such as potatoes, rice, or pasta, and (3) *a vegetable* (besides potatoes or a legume).

Having said that, if you investigate the recipes in this chapter, you will find some exceptions. Two other criteria were applied before placement in the one-dish cubbyhole:

1. With the addition of a salad, does the dish make a complete meal tastewise?
2. Does the composition of the dish permit it to look sufficient standing alone on the plate?

These last two measures throw a curve of arbitrariness into our otherwise clear-cut definition.

Since we are already into the gray area, let me muddy the water a little more. Stuffed Green Peppers (page 176) fits our principal definition of a one-dish meal to a T, with ground beef, rice, and plenty of vegetables; however, I have selected to leave this dish in the meats chapter because it seems to me that a stuffed green pep-per—no matter how delicious—would look mighty lonely alone on the plate. On the other hand, if you would place a nice serving of tossed green salad on the *same* plate, the visual effect would be agreeably sufficient.

Conversely, one or two dishes included in this chapter may not contain precisely all three types of food designated for a one-dish meal, but they seem substantial and complete enough to slip by.

Not to exclude any borderline candidates for one-dish meal distinction, and to take differing opinions into account, at the end of the chapter there is a list of recipes found in other chapters that might be considered close contenders. (Cookbook writing can be complex.)

Enough of this minutia! Putting aside debate and hairsplitting over labels, most cooks re-sponsible for daily family meals will rally around the proposition that one-dish meals are a boon. They can usually be prepared ahead of time, people of all ages are crazy about them, the kitchen looks neat and orderly before and after the meal (sans beaucoup pots and pans, the cleanup is a breeze), and there is often enough left over for dinner the next evening (or the evening after next if your family is finicky about eating the same fare twice in a row).

One-dish meals are frequently casseroles which go from the oven directly to the table for serving family style. Most—though not all—of the recipes in this chapter are of that type.

Casseroles—one-dish and otherwise—are right up there with apple pie when it comes to the foods most associated with Midwest home cooking. And what could be better tasting? You rarely can find anything close to one of these savorous concoctions on a restaurant menu—not these luscious, mystifying conglomerates which only mothers know how to mastermind.

When newlyweds make those predictable calls home to ask Mom how to make a certain yearned-for dish, you can bank on it—if they dial a Midwest area code, chances are excellent the inquiry will be about a favorite casserole. When a television commentator asked a young soldier from Indiana, who was stationed in the Middle East during Desert Storm, what he most missed about not being home on Christmas Day, he replied, "Mom's Broccoli-Rice Casse-role" (see page 273).

One of the most popular picks of first-time cooks across the Heartland—after conquest of egg salad sandwiches and macaroni and cheese out of the box—is Tuna-Noodle Casserole (page 297), probably because the tuna and peas come out of cans and it's not hard learning how to cook noodles. New cook or pro, it's a great-tasting one-dish meal to place in the middle of the table!

One-dish meals are not necessarily quick to prepare. While most of them can be prepared in advance, some are a lark and others take some doing. In the lark category is Dinner-in-a-Hurry Casserole (page 296). An easier one-dish meal would be hard to find since it leans almost entirely on prepared foods. Martha Cotter's Seven-Layer Dinner (page 298) which, with the exception of one can of tomatoes, utilizes only fresh foods, runs into considerably more prepa-ration time.

Foods recruited for service in Midwest one-dish casseroles run the gamut from artichokes to zucchini. You name it, it has probably found its way into one of these incredible edibles at one time or another. To get an idea of the infinite variety of foods which turn up in Midland one-dishers, peruse a Nebraska or Missouri church cookbook, or cruise past the red-checkered, end-to-end picnic tables at a July family reunion in Wooster, Ohio, or Junction City, Kansas.

Once you get the hang of it, you'll be com-ing up with your own marvelous originals which your children or grandchildren will one day want to find out how to make. No doubt about it—these Midwest everything-in-one-dish miracles are worth writing home about!

BAKED CABBAGE WITH HAMBURGER

Believe it or not, this recipe is from my grandmother's cookbook. One might easily think it had been expressly tailored to twenty-first-century informal dining.

1 small head of cabbage, cored
1 pound lean, pure ground beef
1 extra-large egg
2 tablespoons whole milk
2 tablespoons all-purpose flour
¾ cup coarsely chopped onions
⅛ teaspoon dry mustard
½ teaspoon salt
¼ teaspoon pepper
1 tablespoon butter, melted
Dash of ground nutmeg
Chili sauce, home canned (page 783) or
    commercially canned

Preheat the oven to 350° F.

Place the cabbage in the center of a roaster or Dutch oven; set aside. In a large mixing bowl, place the ground beef, egg, milk, flour, onions, dry mustard, salt, and pepper. Using a large, metal mixing spoon, break up the ground beef and stir until the ingredients are evenly combined. Spoon the ground beef mixture around the cabbage. Bake, covered, for 1¼ hours, until the cabbage is tender and the ground beef mixture is well done.

Place the cabbage in the center of a serving plate and surround it with the ground beef mixture. Just before serving, drizzle the melted butter over the cabbage and sprinkle the cabbage lightly with a dash of nutmeg.

To serve, cut the cabbage into 4 wedges and place 1 wedge on each of 4 dinner plates. Using a spoon, place ¼ of the ground beef mixture next to and touching the cabbage wedge on each plate. Place the chili sauce in a sauce dish and pass at the table.

SERVES 4

LIMA BEAN AND GROUND SIRLOIN CASSEROLE

1¾ cups dried baby lima beans
1 pound ground sirloin
1 teaspoon salt
¼ teaspoon pepper
1 teaspoon dry mustard
1 16-ounce can commercial whole, peeled
    tomatoes, undrained, or 1 pint home-
    canned Tomatoes (page 736), undrained
½ cup chili sauce, home canned (page 783)
    or commercially canned
1 tablespoon packed light brown sugar
1 teaspoon dried leaf basil
½ bay leaf
3½ cups sliced yellow onions separated
    into rings

Wash and sort the beans; place them in a large mixing bowl. Cover the beans with cold water and soak them overnight (or about 8 hours).

Preheat the oven to 325° F. Grease a 3-quart round baking dish; set aside.

Drain the beans and set aside. In a large mixing bowl, place the ground sirloin, salt, pepper, and dry mustard; using a large, metal mixing spoon, break up the ground sirloin and stir until the ingredients are evenly combined; set aside. In a medium mixing bowl, place the tomatoes, chili sauce, brown sugar, basil, and bay leaf; using a tablespoon, break the tomatoes into coarse pieces and stir to combine the ingredients; set aside.

In the prepared baking dish, layer in the following order: ½ of the beans, ½ of the ground sirloin mixture, ½ of the onion rings, and ½ of the tomato mixture. Repeat the layers, using the remaining ½ of the ingredients. Bake, covered, for 3 hours.

SERVES 8

LAYERED ZUCCHINI CASSEROLE

1 pound (1 large) zucchini, unpared, sliced ⅛ inch thick

2 cups thyme croutons (see Herb Croutons, page 48)

1 large onion, sliced as thinly as possible

½ medium green bell pepper, sliced lengthwise ⅛ inch thick

¾ pound (2 medium) fresh tomatoes, blanched (page 44), peeled, and sliced ¼ inch thick

1 extra-large egg

1 teaspoon dried leaf basil

½ teaspoon dry mustard

½ teaspoon salt

¼ teaspoon pepper

6 slices bacon, cut widthwise into 1-inch pieces

6 ounces Swiss cheese, thinly sliced

1 recipe (¼ cup) Buttered Cracker Crumbs (page 49)

1 tablespoon freshly grated Parmesan cheese (page 46)

Preheat the oven to 350° F. Butter a 7 × 11-inch baking dish; set aside.

Steam the zucchini (page 302) 3 minutes. Immediately remove the steamer basket containing the zucchini from the pan. Leave the zucchini in the steamer basket and rinse it under cold, running water to stop the cooking. Drain *well;* set aside.

In the bottom of the prepared baking dish, distribute the croutons evenly. Over the croutons, layer in the following order: the steamed zucchini, onions, green peppers, and tomatoes; set aside. In a small mixing bowl, place the egg, basil, dry mustard, salt, and pepper; using a handheld electric mixer, beat lightly on medium speed. Pour the egg mixture evenly over the tomato layer in the baking dish. Arrange the bacon, then the Swiss cheese, in layers over the top. Bake, uncovered, for 15 minutes.

Meanwhile, in a small mixing bowl, place the crumbs and Parmesan cheese; stir to combine; set aside. At the end of the 15-minute baking period, remove the baking dish from the oven. Increase the oven temperature to 375° F. Sprinkle the crumb mixture evenly over the top of the casserole; return it to the oven and bake, uncovered, an additional 30 minutes.

Remove the baking dish from the oven; place it on a wire rack and let stand 3 minutes. Using a sharp knife, cut the Layered Zucchini Casserole into 8 serving pieces. Use a spatula to remove the servings from the baking dish.

SERVES 6 TO 8

DINNER-IN-A-HURRY CASSEROLE

1 pound lean, pure ground beef

1 1-ounce package onion soup mix

1 10¾-ounce can commercial, condensed cream of celery soup (undiluted)

1 10-ounce package frozen tiny peas, uncooked

1 1-pound package frozen Tater Tots potatoes, uncooked

Preheat the oven to 350° F. Grease a 2-quart round baking dish.

In the prepared baking dish, layer in the following order: the ground beef, onion soup mix, celery soup, peas, and potatoes. Bake, covered, for 1 hour.

SERVES 6

RING BOLOGNA CASSEROLE

1 1-pound ring of beef bologna
2 recipes Medium White Sauce (page 366)
1 10¾-ounce can commercial, condensed
   cream of mushroom soup (undiluted), or
   1 recipe Cream of Mushroom Soup
   (page 89)
4 cups water
1 tablespoon plus 1 teaspoon instant beef
   bouillon granules
5 ounces kluski egg noodles*
2 cups finely chopped onions (about 1 large
   onion)
1 tablespoon snipped, fresh parsley
½ cup fresh green beans cut into 1-inch
   pieces, cooked (page 305) and drained
2 tablespoons Buttered Bread Crumbs
   (page 49)

*If kluski egg noodles are not available, regular
thin, narrow egg noodles may be substituted.*

Preheat the oven to 325°F. Butter a 2-quart
round baking dish; set aside.

Slice the bologna ¼ inch thick; peel off the
casing. Cut each slice into quarters; set aside. Prepare the Medium White Sauce. Add the mushroom soup; stir to blend. Cover and set aside.

Pour 4 cups water into a large saucepan; bring
to a boil over high heat. Add the bouillon granules; stir until dissolved. Add the noodles and
cook, uncovered, in the boiling bouillon until
tender, stirring often. Drain the noodles in a
sieve; return the noodles to the saucepan and
rinse in hot water. Drain the noodles again in
the sieve; set aside.

To the white sauce mixture, add the bologna,
noodles, onions, parsley, and green beans; stir
and fold until combined and evenly distributed.
Turn the mixture into the prepared baking dish.
Sprinkle the crumbs evenly over the top. Bake,
uncovered, for 1 hour.

SERVES 6

VARIATION: Substitute bratwurst for the ring beef
bologna.

TUNA-NOODLE CASSEROLE

2 tablespoons butter
½ cup chopped onions
⅓ cup chopped celery
1 cup sliced, fresh mushrooms
1 recipe Thin White Sauce (page 366),
   increasing the pepper to ¼ teaspoon
½ cup mayonnaise
½ teaspoon soy sauce
½ teaspoon dry mustard
8 ounces (4 cups) egg noodles, cooked,
   rinsed in hot water, and drained (page
   283)
1 9-ounce can solid, white albacore tuna,
   packed in water
1 15¼-ounce can commercial peas, drained
1 recipe (¼ cup) Buttered Cracker Crumbs
   made with saltines (page 49)

In a small, heavy-bottomed skillet, melt the butter over medium heat. Tilt the skillet back and
forth to completely cover the bottom with the
melted butter. Place the onions and celery in the
skillet; sauté lightly 2 minutes. Add the mushrooms; sauté 1 minute. Do not allow the vegetables to brown. Set aside.

Preheat the oven to 350°F. Butter a 2-quart
round baking dish; set aside.

Make the Thin White Sauce. Add the mayonnaise, soy sauce, and dry mustard; using a handheld electric mixer, beat over low heat until
smooth. Add the mushroom mixture with pan
juices; stir to combine. Remove from the heat
and set aside.

Turn the drained noodles into a large mixing
bowl. Add the white sauce mixture; toss to
combine; set aside. Drain the tuna; cut into generous chunks. Add the tuna chunks and drained
peas to the noodle mixture; using a wooden
mixing spoon, toss carefully to avoid crushing
the tuna and peas.

Turn the mixture into the prepared baking
dish. Sprinkle the crumbs evenly over the top.
Bake, uncovered, for 35 minutes.

SERVES 8

MARTHA COTTER'S SEVEN-LAYER DINNER

¼ cup raw long-grain rice (not instant)
6 slices thick bacon
1 recipe Cream of Mushroom Soup*
   (page 89)
1 pound lean, pure ground beef
½ teaspoon ground marjoram
¼ teaspoon salt
⅛ teaspoon pepper
1 14½-ounce can commercial whole,
   peeled tomatoes or 1 pint home-canned
   Tomatoes (page 736)
1 teaspoon dried leaf basil
¼ teaspoon salt
⅛ teaspoon pepper
2 cups sliced, raw russet potatoes
¼ teaspoon salt
⅛ teaspoon pepper
¾ cup chopped onions
½ cup diced green bell peppers
1 cup fresh green beans cut into
   1½-inch pieces

*1 10¾-ounce can commercial, condensed
cream of mushroom soup (undiluted) may be
substituted.*

Boil the rice (page 272); set aside. Cut the bacon widthwise into 1-inch pieces. In a medium skillet, *partially* fry the bacon over medium heat, to extract some of the fat. Using a slotted spoon, remove the bacon from the skillet and place in a small bowl; cover and set aside. Make the Cream of Mushroom Soup; cover and refrigerate.

Preheat the oven to 350° F. Butter a 2½-quart, 3½-inch-deep baking casserole with straight sides; set aside.

In a medium mixing bowl, place the ground beef, marjoram, ¼ teaspoon salt, and ⅛ teaspoon pepper; using a large, metal mixing spoon, break up the ground beef and stir until the ingredients are evenly combined. Cover the ground beef mixture and set aside. Drain the tomatoes in a

sieve; reserve the drained juice for other uses. Place the tomatoes in a medium mixing bowl; using the edge of a tablespoon, break the tomatoes into coarse pieces. Do not drain off the juice which accumulates from breaking up the tomatoes. To the tomatoes, add the basil, ¼ teaspoon salt, and ⅛ teaspoon pepper; stir to combine; cover and set aside. In the prepared baking casserole, layer in the following order, the:

   Potatoes
   ¼ teaspoon salt (sprinkle over the potatoes)
   ⅛ teaspoon pepper (sprinkle over the potatoes)
   Onions
   Bacon
   Ground sirloin mixture (drop chunks evenly over the bacon layer)
   Rice
   Green peppers
   Green beans

Pour the tomato mixture and accumulated juice evenly over the green beans. Spoon the Cream of Mushroom Soup evenly over all. Bake, covered, for 45 minutes. Uncover and bake for an additional 30 minutes.

SERVES 6 GENEROUSLY

PORK CHOP DINNER IN FOIL

A fun, one-dish meal. Take the aluminum-foil bundles directly from the oven to the picnic table on the patio or in the yard (or on the porch, balcony, or terrace if you're an apartment dweller) and delight in winsome outdoor dining with simplicity. Toss an uncomplicated green salad and if you're in the mood, pour glasses of red wine.

1 tablespoon vegetable shortening
4 loin pork chops, 1¼ inches thick
Salt and pepper to taste
4 ears of sweet corn
4 medium to small red potatoes
1 large onion, cut into 8 slices
1 teaspoon dried dillweed
Salt
¼ cup (4 tablespoons) butter

Cut four 14 × 18-inch pieces of heavy-duty aluminum foil; set aside.

Preheat an electric skillet or a large, heavy-bottomed skillet on the range to medium-high (380°F. in an electric skillet). Melt the shortening in the skillet. Tilt the skillet back and forth to completely cover the bottom with the melted shortening. Place the pork chops in the skillet; sprinkle lightly with salt and pepper to taste. Brown the pork chops well (about 10 minutes on each side), turning once. Place 1 pork chop and 1 ear of corn in the center of each piece of foil; set aside.

Preheat the oven to 350°F.

Pare the potatoes and slice each potato widthwise about ³⁄₁₆ inch thick. Next to each pork chop, place the slices of 1 potato overlapping in a fan shape. On each sheet of foil, tuck 1 slice of onion under all the slices of potato and 1 slice of onion between the slices in the middle of the potato. Sprinkle the potatoes and onions on each sheet of foil with ¼ of the dillweed and a dash of salt. Dot the potatoes, onions, and corn with the butter (1 tablespoon per foil dinner).

Wrap and seal each foil bundle tightly, leaving the pork chops, corn, and potatoes and onions flat on the bottom of the aluminum foil (do not roll the bundle contents). Place the bundles, single layer, on 1 or 2 shallow cookie pans. Bake for 1 hour, until the potatoes and onions are tender, and the pork chops have reached an internal temperature of at least 160°F. as gauged on an instant thermometer (page 44). Unwrap the foil and transfer the dinners from the foil to individual dinner plates.

SERVES 4

Other One-Dish Meal Recipes

Vegetables

Midwinter, when the allure of the first gentle, fairyland snowfalls has long faded from the memory, and unremitting blizzards pack cutting winds which penetrate the very marrow of the bones, the arrival of the first seed catalog— plucked from the ice-crusted mailbox—is like a miracle tonic.

That harbinger of spring, with its enticing pictures of scarlet tomatoes and electric-colored zinnias painted by the rays of July's flaming sun, bolts the winter doldrums into excited planning for the coming season's vegetable and flower gardens.

Soon, flats of catalog-ordered seeds sprouting tiny green leaves will be sunning in the house through southerly windows as Mother Nature performs her wondrous feat. As soon as the last frost has been shooed away by warm spring breezes, the healthy little Rutger's and Super Sioux tomato plants, as well as the green and yellow bell peppers, the cucumbers, and the herbs will be transplanted in the outdoor garden to thrive in the rich soil and soak up the heavenly rains.

This spring seed ritual is as old as the Midwest. In settlement days, vegetable gardens (then, principally the domain of farmwives) were a primary source of family food—fresh during the growing season and canned for the long winter ahead. Gardens and canning continued to be an imperative of Midwest farm life well into the twentieth century. Although generally no longer a necessity, beautiful vegetable gardens are still proudly maintained by many, if not most, Mid-American farm families.

Even among those who no longer farm, attachment to the soil has persisted in the Midwest lineage and is manifested in profuse vegetable gardening, now pursued mostly as a hobby. Many city and town dwellers who are pressed for garden space try to squeeze at least a couple of tomato and green pepper plants into the corner of their yards. The claim that the taste of store-bought tomatoes bears precious little resemblance to the homegrown ones goes virtually unchallenged in these parts.

Gardenless folks crowd to city and town farmers' markets, where truck gardeners bring their fresh produce to sell. These festive marketplaces jump with activity in the early morning hours when pickup trucks roll in from across the countryside with freshly picked vegetables and fruits, while eager customers stand on the curbs sipping coffee, munching on homemade cinnamon rolls, and chatting with friends as they wait for the good earth's bounty to be unloaded.

Midwesterners are hallmarked vegetable buffs! In concert with Heartlanders' farming heritage, vegetables have continued to play a key role in their dietary and nutritional patterns. In days past, it was a rare dinner without potatoes and another vegetable served family style at the table. With the new wave of calorie consciousness, potatoes (especially with gravy or toppings) are sometimes absent, but vegetables continue to mainstream. Interlinked is the galaxy of vegetable salads so typical of Midwest dining.

From the annual high of savoring the first radishes from the garden (you can't resist pulling a few even though they're not quite large enough yet) to the last day of canning, when jars of End-of-Garden Relish are lifted from the canner, Midwest cooks turn their harvest into a continuous stream of interesting vegetable dishes. They stew, bake, cream, steam, boil, fry, puree, grill, and braise their veggies. And their flair for preparing scalloped vegetables as well as other diverse vegetable casseroles is a Midwest cooking marvel. With pints and quarts of summer garden freshness stored in jars in the basement (as well as in freezers), they keep their wonderful vegetable band playing well into the winter.

Nearly all vegetables flourish in the fertile Midwest ground. Besides potatoes (see pages 270–271), green and wax beans, carrots, bell peppers, onions, leaf lettuce, cucumbers, peas, tomatoes, and squash are among the most popular homegrown vegetable fare. But the more unusual also are grown frequently, and serve as the basis for stylish gourmet dishes. Stewed Rutabagas with Root Vegetables (page 338), Kohlrabi with Tarragon (page 320), Fennel and Tomatoes Braised in Wine (page 319), and Bok Choy Roulades (page 307) are among the recipes in this chapter which exemplify imaginative Midwest gardening translated into fashionable cuisine.

Of course, the Heartland is famous for its sweet corn. Farmers allocate a few rows alongside their field corn for the planting of an ample quantity of their favorite variety. (Field corn, the Midwest's primary crop, is utilized for animal nutrition and for conversion to a myriad of products, such as cooking oil, syrups, and starches.)

In the summer, when fresh corn is in season, it is a shame to deviate from the simplest and best way to prepare these Midwest kernels of gold; i.e., pick, shuck, boil 5 minutes, and eat on the cob slathered with butter. The least amount of time allowed to elapse between the picking and the eating, the better.

Later, when the straw-colored cornstalks have been converted to Halloween porch decorations, Midland cooks open canned jars or freezer containers of cream-style or whole-kernel corn to prepare yummy casseroles of Scalloped Corn (page 315) or Corn Pudding (page 316) for dinner on brisk fall evenings. A peek into a Minnesota or South Dakota kitchen might reveal Squaw Corn (page 316) being whipped up for a quick, easy dinner; and Corn-Oyster Casserole (page 317) is sure to be among the Thanksgiving meal plans in many a home across Illinois and Nebraska. It's wonderful with turkey.

My friend Patty Davis is creator of one of the most delicious corn dishes I have ever tasted (Patty Davis's Scalloped Corn, page 316), and it's suitable for company fare as well as family meals. Our mutual friend, Nancy Amend, executes this peerless dish with enviable finesse, and religiously serves it with pheasant—shot by husband, Dick—at their annual, fall game-dinner parties. Pheasant and Patty Davis's Scalloped Corn can only be described as a food marriage made in heaven.

Heading the list of exotic Midwest specialty vegetables are morel mushrooms. These wild, indigenous morsels are to the Midwest what truffles are to France. They are gathered each year by ardent mushroom marauders who traipse to their secret places in the woods for these prizes—primarily for their own consumption, though occasionally, if you are lucky, you can land a small box in a good produce market for a goodly price—about $20 a pound. Though not as choice, some dried morels are available all year round at approximately $11 an *ounce*. For those who happen to be among the fortunate few to fall heir to some of these hard to come by, fresh delicacies, a recipe for sautéing them in white wine is given in this chapter. Such a dining occasion calls for a prime steak and the uncorking of a special bottle of wine held in reserve for such a dining regale.

Steamed Vegetables

Most vegetables better retain their nutrients, flavor, and shape if steamed rather than boiled. To steam vegetables, pour about ¾ inch water in a saucepan. Place a steamer basket in the saucepan and arrange raw, prepared vegetables in the basket. Cover the saucepan. Bring the water to a boil over high heat; reduce the heat to low and steam the vegetables over briskly simmering water until they reach the desired doneness.

Steamer pans with a removable, perforated top section which fits into the bottom pan (like a double boiler) are also available.

For maximum nutrient and flavor retention, vegetables should be cooked until just tender

but still firm. Overcooking vegetables is a common error. Nowadays, vegetables generally are not cooked as long as they were in years past.

Boiled Vegetables

Some especially firm vegetables, such as potatoes (except very small new potatoes), carrots, turnips, parsnips, and kohlrabi, are more satisfactorily cooked by boiling rather than steaming because it is difficult to get these vegetables done in a timely manner by steaming.

To boil vegetables, place the prepared vegetables in a saucepan; cover the vegetables with hot water. Cover the saucepan. Bring the vegetables to a boil over high heat; reduce the heat to medium and boil the vegetables until the desired doneness.

Asparagus Spears (page 303), Green and Wax Beans (page 305), and Beets (page 306) are among other vegetables generally cooked by boiling. Corn on the Cob is most commonly and best prepared by boiling (page 315).

Miniature Vegetables

Miniature (or baby) vegetables are colorful on the plate, fun to eat, and easy to prepare. They are served at posh dinner parties and are equally popular with family meal planners, who utilize them to add variety and spark to everyday fare.

Most appealing and fashionable when served in mixed combinations, it is left to the cook's imagination to combine varieties of miniatures which mingle compatible flavors and are color-coordinated with the rest of the meal. For example, carrots, turnips, scallopini, and tiny, red cocktail tomatoes might be served with Roast

Beef Tenderloin (page 162), while yellow sunburst squash, leeks, kohlrabi, and eggplants could be selected to accompany Baked Walleye Deluxe (page 222).

The favored way of preparing miniature vegetables is simply to steam them and toss them lightly in butter. It would defeat the uniqueness of these special little morsels to bury their cunningness in sauces—they are sufficient unto themselves. Because the skins of miniatures are often thicker than their full-sized counterparts, the steaming time required to tenderize these small vegetables is often longer than might be expected. For example, while full-sized green zucchini sliced ¼ inch thick steam to tenderness in 3 minutes, miniature zucchini require a full 5 minutes of steaming to reach a palatable level of doneness. Steaming times for the various varieties of miniatures are left to the vigilant cook watching over the steamer.

Miniature vegetables are available in specialty food stores and are turning up with more frequency in produce departments of top-line supermarkets. They can be specially ordered by most produce purveyors. Among the kinds of miniature vegetables available are the following:

Artichokes
Beets
Belgian Endive
Bok Choy
Broccoli
Carrots
Cauliflower
Corn
Eggplants
Kohlrabi
Leeks
Potatoes
Squash (scallopini, green summer, yellow sunburst, yellow crookneck, green zucchini, and yellow zucchini)
Tomatoes (yellow teardrop and red cocktail [tiny cherry])
Turnips

Asparagus

ASPARAGUS SPEARS

Asparagus spears are generally cooked by boiling because long spears will not lay flat in most household-sized steamers. To prepare the spears for boiling, break one spear (of typical size to the remainder of the spears) in your hands to determine the natural breaking point, above which the spear will be tender. Cut the remaining spears uniformly in this length.

To boil the asparagus, pour about ½ inch water into a skillet large enough in diameter to accommodate the spears to be cooked. Cover the skillet. Bring the water to a boil over high heat. Place the spears in the skillet; reduce the heat to medium. Cover the skillet. Return the water to a simmer and cook the asparagus about 3 minutes, depending upon their size.

To serve, drain the asparagus well and brush with a small amount of melted butter.

ASPARAGUS SPEARS AMANDINE

1 tablespoon butter, melted
¼ cup sliced almonds, toasted (page 50)
1¼ pounds fresh asparagus spears, cooked (see Asparagus Spears, above)

Melt the butter in a tiny saucepan. Add the toasted almonds and stir to coat. Arrange the cooked asparagus spears in a vegetable serving dish or on individual serving plates. Spoon the almonds and remaining butter over the asparagus.

SERVES 4

ASPARAGUS CUSTARD

2 cups fresh asparagus pieces cut diagonally
  into 1½-inch lengths
3 slices bacon, cut widthwise into 6 pieces
3 extra-large eggs
¼ teaspoon white pepper
1 teaspoon Worcestershire sauce
1 cup whole milk, scalded (page 25)
1 cup Fresh Bread Crumbs (page 48)
1 cup finely shredded Colby cheese

Preheat the oven to 325°F. Butter a 1½-quart
round baking dish; set aside.

Pour about ½ inch water into a medium
saucepan; bring to a boil over high heat. Place
the asparagus pieces in the saucepan; reduce the
heat to medium. Cover the saucepan. Return to
a simmer and cook the asparagus 5 minutes.
Drain the asparagus thoroughly in a colander;
set aside. In a small, heavy skillet, fry the bacon
pieces over medium heat until partially cooked;
drain between several layers of paper towels and
set aside.

Place the eggs in a medium mixing bowl;
using an electric mixer, beat slightly on medium
speed. Add the white pepper and Worcestershire
sauce; stir to combine. Slowly add the scalded
milk to the egg mixture, stirring constantly. Add
the asparagus, bread crumbs, and cheese; stir to
combine. Place the mixture in the prepared baking dish. Top with the bacon pieces.

Place the baking dish in a 9 × 13-inch baking
pan; then, pour very hot, but not boiling, water
into the pan to approximately ½ the height of
the baking dish. Bake, uncovered, for 1 hour, or
until a table knife inserted near the center of the
Asparagus Custard comes out clean.

SERVES 6

DIVINE BAKED ASPARAGUS

1 pound fresh asparagus spears
1½ recipes Medium White Sauce
  (page 366)
2 ounces finely shredded Swiss cheese
  (about ½ cup)
2 ounces crumbled Maytag blue cheese
  (about ½ cup)
¾ cup sliced almonds
1 recipe (¼ cup) Buttered Cracker Crumbs
  (page 49)

Wash the asparagus; trim off the lower "woody"
portions of the spears. Cut the spears into 2½-
inch lengths. Place the asparagus in a medium
saucepan; add water to cover. Cover the
saucepan. Bring the asparagus to a boil over high
heat; reduce the heat and simmer 10 minutes. It
is important to cook the asparagus this length of
time in order to extract sufficient water from the
spears to avoid a thin, runny, final baked dish.
Drain the cooked asparagus well in a colander.

Preheat the oven to 350°F. Butter a 6 × 10-
inch baking dish; set aside.

Prepare the Medium White Sauce; remove
from the heat. Add the Swiss cheese and blue
cheese; stir until the cheeses have melted and
the sauce is smooth. (To facilitate the melting
process, the sauce may be stirred over low heat
if care is taken not to allow the sauce to reach a
simmer.) When the cheeses have melted, add the
almonds; stir to combine; set aside.

Arrange the asparagus pieces evenly in the
prepared baking dish. Pour the cheese sauce
evenly over the asparagus; top with the crumbs.
Bake, uncovered, for 30 minutes. The mixture
will be bubbly and the crumbs golden.

SERVES 6

Green and Wax Beans

TO COOK AND SERVE GREEN AND WAX BEANS

Wash the beans well, using a vegetable brush if necessary. Cut or snap off the ends and pull off the strings along both sides of the pods if the strings are large and tough. Leave the beans whole, or cut or snap into uniform lengths of choice. Place the prepared beans in a saucepan and cover with water. Add salt if desired. Cover the saucepan and bring the beans to a boil over high heat. Reduce the heat and simmer 10 minutes or until the beans reach the desired tenderness. To serve, drain the beans, add butter, and toss.

GREEN BEAN CASSEROLE

2 9-ounce packages frozen French-cut green beans
½ cup reserved liquid from cooked and drained green beans
¾ cup shredded Colby cheese
1 10¾-ounce can commercial, condensed cream of mushroom soup (undiluted)
¼ cup finely chopped onions
1 2-ounce jar pimientos, drained and chopped (2 tablespoons)
¾ cup commercially canned French-fried onions

Preheat the oven to 350° F. Grease a 6 × 10-inch baking dish; set aside.

Cook the green beans, following instructions on the packages. Drain the beans in a sieve, reserving ½ cup cooking liquid. In a large mixing bowl, place the green beans, ½ cup reserved cooking liquid, cheese, mushroom soup, chopped onions, and pimientos. Turn the mixture into the prepared baking dish. Bake, uncovered, for 25 minutes. Top with the French-fried onions and return to the oven to bake for an additional 5 minutes.

SERVES 8

GREEN BEANS WITH BACON AND ONIONS

5 slices bacon, cut widthwise into 1-inch pieces
½ cup chopped onions
½ teaspoon salt
⅛ teaspoon pepper
2 teaspoons tarragon vinegar
½ teaspoon dried leaf tarragon
1¼ pounds fresh green beans, cooked (left column) and hot

In a small, heavy-bottomed skillet, fry the bacon pieces over medium heat until crisp. Using a slotted spoon, remove the bacon from the skillet and place in a small bowl (do not drain the fried bacon); set aside. Place the onions in the skillet used to fry the bacon; fry in the bacon grease over medium heat until tender (about 5 minutes). Remove the skillet from the heat. Let the skillet (with onions) stand until cooled to a low temperature. Then, place the bacon, salt, pepper, vinegar, and tarragon in the cooled skillet with the onions; stir to combine; set aside.

Drain the hot, cooked green beans. Pour the bacon and onions mixture over the beans and toss lightly to combine.

SERVES 8

GREEN BEANS WITH MARJORAM

1 pound green beans
2 packed tablespoons finely snipped, fresh
　marjoram or 2 teaspoons dried leaf
　marjoram
1 tablespoon butter

Follow To Cook and Serve Green and Wax
Beans procedure (page 305), adding the marjoram to the saucepan containing the beans and
water before cooking. To serve, drain the beans,
add the butter, and toss.

SERVES 4

Beets

TO COOK AND
SERVE BEETS

Trim away a portion of the stems and roots of
beets, *leaving 1 inch of the stems and 1 inch of the
roots on the beets.* Discard the portions of stems
and roots trimmed away. Using a vegetable
brush, scrub the beets thoroughly. Place the
beets in a saucepan; add water to cover. Cover
the saucepan. Bring the beets to a boil over high
heat. Reduce the heat and cook at a low boil for
½ to 1 hour (depending upon the size and age
of the beets), until tender. Drain the beets.

When cool enough to handle, cut off the
remaining stems and roots of the beets. Then,
slip the skins off the beets. Leave the beets whole
or slice, dice, or cut them julienne (page 23). To
serve, drizzle a small amount of melted butter
over the beets and toss gently.

HARVARD BEETS

*Although this recipe's name would appear to indicate
its origin, such may not be the case. There is a school
of thought (no pun intended) that insists these beets
derived their name from the fact that they share the
same color as Harvard's football jerseys. Apparently,
rivalry generated another dish called "Yale Beets." It
is made exactly like Harvard Beets except orange juice
is substituted for the vinegar and 1½ teaspoons of
lemon juice are added. To date, I have found no inter-
pretation of the implications of these ingredient substitutions (if there are any) and I shall not venture one.*

*Others who dig into this sort of food lore argue that
the dish was served in a mid-nineteenth-century
Boston restaurant by the name of Harwood's and that
the Russian proprietor, having difficulty with English,
pronounced the name of his restaurant more like
"Harvard."*

4 cups cooked fresh beets (see To Cook . . .
　Beets, left column) sliced ³⁄₁₆ inch thick,
　reserving cooking liquid, or 2 16-ounce
　cans commercial sliced beets, drained,
　reserving liquid
¼ cup sugar
2 tablespoons cornstarch
¼ teaspoon ground cloves
¼ cup plus 2 tablespoons cider vinegar
2 tablespoons butter

Measure 1¼ cups reserved beet liquid; set aside.
In a medium-large saucepan, place the sugar,
cornstarch, and cloves; stir to combine. Add 1¼
cups reserved beet liquid and the vinegar; stir to
blend. Place the saucepan over medium-high
heat and cook the mixture until thick and
translucent (about 7 minutes), stirring constantly. Remove from the heat. Add the butter;
stir until dissolved. Add the beets and stir to
combine; heat through.

SERVES 6

Bok Choy

Bok choy or pak choi *(Brassica chinensis)* resembles a bunch of celery in form, with rather wide, thick, white stalks and broad, glossy, dark green leaves (see illustration). Bok choy is a standard vegetable in Oriental diets, and is sometimes known as "Chinese cabbage." However, this name can lead to confusion, because napa and michihli cabbages (types of *Brassica pekinensis*) are most often, if not generally, also called "Chinese cabbage." Napa and michihli cabbages resemble a tight bunch of leaf-type lettuce. Michihli cabbage is longer and more slender in form than napa cabbage. The leaves of both are comparatively thin, crinkled looking, and pale green. A knowledgeable produce department manager and the accompanying illustration will help distinguish bok choy from napa and michihli cabbages in case of question.

BOK CHOY ROULADES

This recipe uses only bok choy leaves. Use the remaining stalks in a stir-fry, or split the stalks in half lengthwise, then cut the split stalks into 2-inch-long pieces and stuff them to make a refreshingly different, crunchy hors d'oeuvre (see Bok Choy Stuffed with Red Caviar, page 66).

1½ dozen medium to thin, fresh asparagus
    spears
4 thin carrots
6 leafy bok choy stalks
3 extra-large eggs, hard-cooked (page 264)
    and sliced
1 recipe Mustard Hollandaise Sauce
    (page 367), warm

Wash the asparagus spears. Cut the spears to a uniform length of about 5 inches; set aside. Pour about ½ inch water into a skillet large enough in diameter to accommodate the spears.

Cover the skillet. Bring the water to a boil over high heat. Place the spears in the skillet; reduce the heat to medium. Cover the skillet. Return the water to a simmer and simmer the spears about 2 minutes, until just tender; drain immediately and set aside.

Pare the carrots and cut them into 5-inch lengths. Quarter each carrot lengthwise. Place the carrots in a saucepan; add water to cover. Cover the saucepan. Bring the carrots to a boil over high heat. Reduce the heat to medium and simmer the carrots until tender but still rigid (about 3 to 5 minutes). Drain well; set aside.

Cut the large green leaves off the bok choy stalks at the place the stalks turn white. Reserve the white stalks for other uses. Wash the bok choy leaves. Lay the leaves flat in a large kettle; add water to cover. Cover the kettle. Bring the leaves to a boil over high heat; reduce the heat and simmer for 3 minutes or until the leaves are tender but retain their shape. Carefully remove the bok choy leaves from the kettle and place them between paper towels to drain.

Then, widthwise across each leaf, near the cut end, place 3 asparagus spears, 2 carrot strips, and 2 egg slices. (Reserve the remaining egg slices for other uses.) Starting from the cut end, roll each leaf jelly-roll fashion. The asparagus spears and carrots should show on the ends of the roulades. Place the roulades, seam down, in a pan over hot water until ready to serve. Finely dice the remaining cooked carrots for garnish; set aside.

To serve, spoon the warm Mustard Hollandaise Sauce over each roulade and garnish the top with the diced carrots.

SERVES 6

Bok Choy

Broccoli

BROCCOLI CASSEROLE

8 cups fresh broccoli stalks cut 3 inches long and slit 2 or 3 times (see recipe procedures, below, for preparation)
1 recipe Cream of Mushroom Soup (page 89) or 1 10¾-ounce can commercial, condensed cream of mushroom soup (undiluted)
8 ounces commercial sour cream
½ cup chopped celery
1 2-ounce jar pimientos, drained and chopped (2 tablespoons)
1 cup shredded, sharp cheddar cheese
¼ teaspoon salt
¼ teaspoon pepper
¼ cup Whole-Wheat Onion Crumbs (recipe follows)

Preheat the oven to 350° F. Grease a 6 × 10-inch baking dish; set aside.

Cut off and discard the lower portion of the broccoli stalks, leaving 3-inch-long spears. Wash the broccoli. Cut each broccoli spear lengthwise 2 or 3 times to form uniformly slit stalks with flowerets about 1 inch in diameter. Steam the spears (page 302) until just tender (about 4 minutes). In the prepared baking dish, arrange the spears in overlapping rows to cover the bottom of the dish; set aside.

In a medium mixing bowl, place the soup, sour cream, celery, pimientos, cheese, salt, and pepper; stir well to combine. Spoon the mixture evenly over the broccoli spears, taking care to cover all the spears. Spread the mixture to the sides of the dish. Sprinkle the Whole-Wheat Onion Crumbs over the top. Bake, uncovered, for 30 minutes. The mixture will be bubbly and the crumbs will be lightly browned.

SERVES 6 TO 8

Whole-Wheat Onion Crumbs

¼ cup (4 tablespoons) butter, melted
2 teaspoons finely grated onions
1 cup coarse, dried, whole-wheat bread crumbs (page 48)

Melt the butter in a small saucepan over medium-low heat. Place the onions in the saucepan; sauté lightly. Remove from the heat; add the crumbs and stir until the crumbs are evenly coated with the butter mixture (see Note).

NOTE: Only ¼ cup Whole-Wheat Onion Crumbs is called for in the Broccoli Casserole recipe above. Freeze the remaining crumbs in a tightly covered, labeled, pint jar. These crumbs freeze nicely for convenient future use to top casseroles.

VEGETABLE MEDLEY: Follow the Broccoli Casserole recipe, above, substituting 8 cups steamed (page 302), mixed, fresh, cauliflower flowerets, Brussels sprouts, asparagus spears cut into 2-inch lengths, pearl onions, and broccoli (or any combination thereof) for 8 cups broccoli spears. Vegetable Medley is especially nice if you double the recipe and use a 9 × 13-inch baking dish.

BROCCOLI PUREE

2 pounds fresh broccoli
3 tablespoons butter, melted
2 tablespoons whipping cream, unwhipped
¼ teaspoon ground marjoram
¼ teaspoon salt
¼ teaspoon pepper

Cut off and discard the lower portion of the broccoli stalks. Wash the broccoli. Cut the flowerets off the stems; set the flowerets aside. Slice the stems ½ inch thick and place in a large saucepan; add water to cover. Cover the saucepan. Bring the sliced stems to a boil over high heat; reduce the heat and cook at a low boil 15 minutes. Add the flowerets; boil an additional

10 minutes. Drain the stems and flowerets well in a colander.

In a blender (see Note), place the stems and flowerets. Add the butter, whipping cream, marjoram, salt, and pepper; process until pureed. Broccoli Puree may be reheated in the top of a double boiler over simmering water. To serve, spoon into a small serving dish.

NOTE: If a blender is not available, a food processor may be used.

MAKES 2 CUPS PUREE

Brussels Sprouts

DINNER BRUSSELS SPROUTS

4 cups fresh Brussels sprouts, trimmed
1¾ cups homemade Chicken Broth (page 88) or 1 14½-ounce can commercial chicken broth
¼ teaspoon salt
⅛ teaspoon pepper
2 tablespoons butter

In a medium saucepan, place the Brussels sprouts, broth, salt, and pepper. Cover the saucepan. Bring the mixture to a boil over high heat. Reduce the heat and simmer until the Brussels sprouts are just tender and still bright green in color (about 7 minutes, depending on the size of the Brussels sprouts). Using a slotted spoon, remove the Brussels sprouts from the saucepan and place in a bowl; cover and keep warm. Boil the Brussels sprouts cooking liquid, uncovered, in the saucepan until reduced to about ½ cup. Add the butter and melt; stir to blend. Return the Brussels sprouts to the saucepan and heat through; toss well with the broth mixture.

Using a slotted spoon, place the Dinner Brussels Sprouts in a serving dish or on individual dinner plates.

SERVES 6

CREAMED BRUSSELS SPROUTS WITH CHESTNUTS

1½ pounds fresh Brussels sprouts, trimmed
1 recipe Medium White Sauce (page 366)
½ cup finely shredded Swiss cheese
¼ teaspoon ground sage
1½ cups shelled, skinned, and boiled whole chestnuts (page 51) or 1 8-ounce jar commercial, roasted whole chestnuts

Steam the Brussels sprouts (page 302); drain well in a colander; set aside. In a medium saucepan, prepare the Medium White Sauce. Add the cheese and sage; stir until the cheese has melted and the mixture is smooth; cover and set aside. If using canned chestnuts, drain the chestnuts in a colander; rinse and redrain. Add the Brussels sprouts and whole chestnuts to the cheese sauce; heat through over low heat. Do not allow to boil.

SERVES 8

VARIATION: The chestnuts may be chopped before adding to the cheese sauce.

Cabbage

BRAISED CABBAGE

Why don't we prepare this good-tasting, easy-to-fix dish more often? Maybe it's already in your current, standard repertoire. But if it isn't, and if you're seeking new menu ideas for retrieval from one of those cooking ruts into which we all slip, consider adding this to your rescue list of recipes.

¼ cup (4 tablespoons) butter
1 2-pound head cabbage, cored and sliced
 ¼ inch thick
⅔ cup chicken broth, homemade
 (page 88) or commercially canned
¼ teaspoon salt
¼ teaspoon white pepper
½ teaspoon sugar
Ground nutmeg

In an electric skillet or a heavy-bottomed skillet on the range, melt the butter over medium-low heat (260° F. in an electric skillet). Place the cabbage in the skillet; sauté 2 minutes, turning the cabbage often with a spatula. Cover the skillet. Cook the cabbage 7 minutes, turning occasionally. Add the broth. Cover the skillet and braise the cabbage 5 minutes, until just tender. Avoid overcooking. Add the salt, white pepper, and sugar; toss to combine.

Place ½ of the Braised Cabbage in a serving bowl; sprinkle moderately with nutmeg. Add the remaining ½ of the Braised Cabbage; sprinkle nutmeg lightly over the top.

SERVES 8

SAUERKRAUT

Even if you think you don't like sauerkraut, give it another try using this recipe. Home-canned or fresh sauerkraut is on a much higher echelon than most commercially canned sauerkraut, and the added ingredients in this recipe blend to deliver a gourmet-like flavor you may not have expected possible in a sauerkraut dish.

1 quart home-canned Sauerkraut (page
 734) or 32 ounces commercial, fresh
 sauerkraut
2 tablespoons bacon grease
1 large onion, chopped (about 1¼ cups)
1 cup commercially canned vegetable broth
1¼ cups Riesling wine
1 tablespoon dried juniper berries
¼ teaspoon caraway seed
¼ teaspoon dried leaf marjoram
¼ teaspoon dried leaf thyme
½ bay leaf
1 tablespoon all-purpose flour
2 tablespoons water

In a sieve, drain the sauerkraut well. Place the drained sauerkraut in a large, heavy-bottomed saucepan; set aside. In a small, heavy-bottomed skillet, melt the bacon grease over medium heat. Place the chopped onions in the skillet; sauté only until a very pale, golden color (about 5 minutes). Using a slotted spoon, remove the onions from the skillet and add to the sauerkraut. Add the broth and wine to the sauerkraut; stir to combine; set aside.

Using slightly dampened cheesecloth, make a cheesecloth bag (page 44) filled with the juniper berries, caraway seed, marjoram, thyme, and bay leaf; add to the sauerkraut mixture and press under the surface of the sauerkraut. Cover the saucepan. Bring the sauerkraut mixture to a simmer over medium-high heat. Reduce the heat to low and simmer 45 minutes, stirring occasionally.

Remove the cheesecloth bag from the saucepan and discard. In a very small glass jar or plastic container with a secure lid, place the flour and 2 tablespoons water; cover and shake vigorously until blended and smooth. Add to the sauerkraut mixture; stir to blend. Simmer the sauerkraut mixture 2 minutes, until the liquid is slightly thickened, stirring constantly. Remove from the heat. If not serving immediately, cover the saucepan and let stand up to 2 hours before serving time. Otherwise, refrigerate. This sauerkraut may be made and refrigerated up to 2 days before serving.

Near serving time, reheat the Sauerkraut over medium heat, stirring often. At serving time, drain the Sauerkraut in a sieve, reserving the liquid to use in reheating any leftover Sauerkraut. Keeps in the refrigerator up to 4 days from the time it is made.

SERVES 8 AS A SIDE DISH OR 6 WHEN SERVED WITH A SAUERKRAUT-INTENSIVE ENTRÉE

RED CABBAGE WITH RED WINE

1 cup water
1 2½-pound head red cabbage, shredded
1 cup dry red wine, such as Cabernet Sauvignon, divided
2 large Golden Delicious apples, pared, quartered, cored, and sliced
¼ cup packed light brown sugar
1½ teaspoons all-purpose flour
1 teaspoon salt
Dash of pepper
¼ cup cider vinegar
3 tablespoons butter, melted

Pour 1 cup water into a medium kettle. Cover the kettle and bring the water to a boil over high heat. Place the cabbage in the kettle; cover and reduce the heat. Simmer the cabbage 15 minutes. Then, add ½ cup of the wine; simmer, covered, 5 minutes. Add the apples; simmer, covered, 5 minutes. Add the remaining ½ cup of wine; simmer, covered, 5 minutes, or until the cabbage is tender.

Meanwhile, in a small mixing bowl, place the brown sugar, flour, salt, and pepper; stir to combine. Add the vinegar and butter; stir to blend and combine. When the cabbage is tender, add the brown sugar mixture and stir well; simmer, uncovered, 5 minutes, stirring often.

SERVES 6 TO 8

Carrots

CARROT PUREE

1 pound carrots, pared and sliced ½ inch thick
1 medium onion, quartered
¼ teaspoon celery salt
⅛ teaspoon white pepper
Dash of ground nutmeg
1 tablespoon butter, softened
1 tablespoon cream or whole milk
Ground nutmeg for garnish

In a medium saucepan, place the carrots and onions; add water to cover. Cover the saucepan. Bring the carrots and onions to a boil over high heat. Reduce the heat and simmer briskly until the carrots are *very* tender (about 20 minutes). Drain the carrots and onions in a sieve; remove the onions and reserve for other uses.

In a blender (see Note), place the carrots, celery salt, white pepper, nutmeg, butter, and cream; process until pureed. To serve, spoon the Pureed Carrots into a serving dish and sprinkle a little nutmeg on top for garnish. Or, using a decorating bag fit with large open-star tip number 8B (page 383), pipe a decorative portion of Pureed Carrots onto each individual plate.

NOTE: If a blender is not available, a food processor may be used.

SERVES 4

CARROTS COSMOPOLITAN

This dish is similar to a soufflé.

1½ pounds carrots, pared and sliced
  ½ inch thick
2 tablespoons packed light brown sugar
¼ teaspoon ground mace
¾ teaspoon salt
¼ teaspoon white pepper
3 tablespoons finely grated onions
3 extra-large eggs, room temperature
3 tablespoons butter, melted
1¾ cups whole milk
1 cup Dried Bread Crumbs (page 48)

Place the carrots in a medium saucepan; add water to cover. Cover the saucepan. Bring the carrots to a boil over high heat. Reduce the heat and cook at a low boil until the carrots are very tender (about 20 minutes); drain in a colander. In a food processor (see Note), puree the carrots in thirds (about 2¼ cups total pureed carrots). In a large mixing bowl, place the pureed carrots, brown sugar, mace, salt, white pepper, and onions; stir to combine. (At this point, the mixture may be covered and refrigerated up to 24 hours. Remove from the refrigerator 1 hour before ready to complete the recipe preparation, and let stand at room temperature.)

Preheat the oven to 325° F. Butter a 2-quart round baking dish; set aside.

Just before ready to bake the dish, separate the eggs, placing the yolks in a small mixing bowl and the whites in a medium mixing bowl. Set the egg whites aside. Using an electric mixer, beat the egg yolks on medium speed. Add the egg yolks, butter, milk, and crumbs to the carrot mixture; stir until combined; set aside. Using the electric mixer, with clean, dry, beater blades, beat the egg whites on high speed until soft peaks hold. Add the beaten egg whites to the carrot mixture; using a large spoon, fold in until just combined. Turn the mixture into the prepared baking dish. Bake, uncovered, for 45 minutes.

NOTE: If a food processor is not available, a blender may be used.

SERVES 10

DILLED CARROT CASSEROLE

2 pounds carrots, pared and sliced
  diagonally ½ inch thick (about 4½ cups)
4 ounces shredded, sharp cheddar cheese
  (about 1 cup)
1½ recipes Dill Croutons (see Herb
  Croutons, page 48)
2 extra-large eggs
½ teaspoon salt
¼ cup half-and-half
¼ cup (4 tablespoons) butter, melted

Preheat the oven to 350° F. Butter a 6 × 10-inch baking dish; set aside.

Place the carrots in a large saucepan; add water to cover. Cover the saucepan. Bring the carrots to a boil over high heat; reduce the heat and simmer the carrots 10 minutes, until just tender. Drain the carrots thoroughly in a colander. Return the drained carrots to the saucepan. Add the cheese and croutons; toss until evenly distributed. Turn the mixture into the prepared baking dish; spread evenly; set aside.

Place the eggs in a small mixing bowl; using an electric mixer, beat slightly on medium speed. Add the salt, half-and-half, and butter; beat only until blended. Pour evenly over the carrot mixture. Bake, uncovered, for 25 minutes, until lightly brown.

SERVES 8

GLAZED CARROTS

1 pound carrots
2 tablespoons butter
¼ cup packed light brown sugar

Pare the carrots. Cut the carrots in half width-wise; then, cut each carrot half lengthwise in half or into fourths, depending upon the size of the carrot. Place the carrots in a large saucepan; add water to cover. Cover the saucepan. Bring the carrots to a boil over high heat. Reduce the heat and simmer the carrots briskly 10 minutes, until just tender. Drain the carrots in a colander. Return the drained carrots to the saucepan; cover and set aside on the back of the range (*not over heat*).

Melt the butter in a small saucepan over low heat. Add the brown sugar; stir continuously until the brown sugar warms, dissolves some, and completely blends with the butter. Pour the brown sugar mixture over the carrots; using a wooden spoon, toss carefully to coat. Cover and place over *warm* (not hotter) heat; let stand 5 minutes. Watch carefully—if the brown sugar commences to burn or the carrots begin to brown, immediately remove from the heat. During the 5-minute standing time, the brown sugar will fully dissolve and the glaze will become thin for better coverage of the carrots. Toss again before serving.

SERVES 6

GLAZED CARROTS WITH KUMQUATS

2 pounds fresh, baby carrots
1 10-ounce jar preserved kumquats
3 tablespoons packed light brown sugar
1 tablespoon honey
1 teaspoon finely grated orange rind
1 tablespoon freshly squeezed orange juice
1 tablespoon butter, melted
¼ teaspoon salt
Small sprigs of fresh parsley for decoration

Preheat the oven to 350° F. Butter a 6 × 10-inch baking dish; set aside.

Pare the carrots; boil until tender (page 302). Drain the carrots in a colander; set aside. Drain the kumquats in a sieve, reserving the syrup. Set the kumquats aside. Measure ⅓ cup reserved kumquat syrup and pour into a small mixing bowl. Add the brown sugar, honey, orange rind, orange juice, butter, and salt; stir to combine; set aside.

Set aside 2 kumquats for decoration. Using a sharp, thin-bladed knife, cut the remaining kumquats lengthwise into sixths; remove the seeds. Place the kumquats in a bowl; set aside. Arrange the carrots in rows in the bottom of the prepared baking dish. Distribute the cut kumquats evenly over the carrots. Pour the brown sugar mixture evenly over all.

Bake, uncovered, for 20 minutes, until well heated. Baste before serving. Decorate the corner of the baking dish with the 2 whole kumquats and the parsley sprigs.

SERVES 8

Celery

CELERY BAKED IN ALMOND SAUCE

5 cups celery sliced ½ inch thick (about
   1 bunch celery; select celery with narrow
   stalks)
2 recipes Medium White Sauce (page 366),
   substituting 1½ cups whole milk and
   ½ cup reserved celery cooking liquid
   (see recipe procedures, below) for 2 cups
   whole milk; substituting ¾ teaspoon salt
   for 1 teaspoon salt; and using white
   pepper
2 chopped, leafy celery tops
¼ cup slivered almonds, toasted (page 50)
½ cup finely chopped onions
1 2-ounce jar pimientos, drained and
   chopped (2 tablespoons)
1 tablespoon butter
2 tablespoons Dried Bread Crumbs
   (page 48)
2 tablespoons chopped, toasted (page 50)
   slivered almonds

Place the celery in a saucepan; add water to
cover. Cover the saucepan. Bring the celery to a
boil over high heat. Reduce the heat and simmer 10 minutes, until the celery is just tender.
Drain the celery in a colander, reserving ½ cup
cooking liquid. Return the drained celery to the
saucepan; cover and set aside.

Preheat the oven to 350° F. Butter a 1½-quart
round baking dish; set aside.

Make the Medium White Sauce; remove from
the heat. Add the celery tops, ¼ cup almonds,
onions, and pimientos; stir to combine. Add the
white sauce mixture to the celery; stir to combine. Place the celery mixture in the prepared
baking dish; set aside.

In a small saucepan, melt the butter over low
heat. Remove from the heat; add the bread
crumbs and 2 tablespoons chopped almonds; stir
until the crumbs and almonds are evenly coated

with butter. Sprinkle the crumb mixture evenly
over the celery mixture. Bake, uncovered, for 25
minutes. The mixture will be bubbly and the
crumb topping will be golden.

SERVES 10

BRAISED CELERY

1 bunch celery
3 tablespoons butter
2 tablespoons finely chopped onions
¼ teaspoon salt
⅛ teaspoon white pepper
1 cup beef broth, homemade (page 87) or
   commercially canned
1 tablespoon cornstarch
Additional beef broth, homemade
   (page 87) or commercially canned,
   if necessary
1 tablespoon chopped pimientos

Trim away the heavy root end, a small portion of
the tops of the stalks, and the leaves from the celery. Wash the celery stalks individually and dry
with a clean tea towel or paper towels. Cut the
celery-heart stalks and inner stalks into 2-inch
lengths; reserve the remaining stalks. Measure
4 cups cut celery pieces. If necessary, cut and use
the reserved celery stalks to make 4 cups celery
pieces, utilizing the innermost stalks first. The
celery pieces should be fairly uniform in width.
If some pieces are too wide, cut in half lengthwise. Set 4 cups celery pieces aside. (Reserve the
remaining celery stalks for other uses.)

In a medium, heavy-bottomed skillet, melt
the butter over medium heat. Tilt the skillet
back and forth to completely cover the bottom
with the melted butter. Place the celery pieces,
onions, salt, and white pepper in the skillet;
sauté 5 minutes, being careful not to let the butter burn. Reduce the heat to low. When the
skillet cools slightly, add the beef broth. Cover
the skillet and simmer the mixture 10 minutes.
Remove from the heat. Using a slotted spoon,

remove the celery pieces from the skillet and place in a bowl; set aside.

Add the cornstarch to the liquid in the skillet; stir until smooth. Place the skillet over low heat and cook the mixture until thickened, stirring constantly. The mixture should be quite thick; however, if it appears to be overly thick, add a bit more beef broth. Add the celery pieces and heat through. Add the pimientos; stir to evenly distribute.

SERVES 6

Corn

TO COOK AND SERVE CORN ON THE COB

For flavor perfection, Corn on the Cob should be eaten within half a day after the sweet corn is picked in the field or garden. While only a few lucky people can enjoy this gastronomic pleasure, it points out the critical importance of freshness when selecting sweet corn for preparation. Purchase fresh, *unshucked* corn. The kernels should spurt milk when pierced with a fingernail.

Shuck the corn just before cooking. Remove all silk and cut off both ends of the ears with a sharp knife. Cook the corn just before serving; do not cook it in advance. Drop the ears into a kettle of plain (unsalted) boiling water. Boil until the milk in the kernels is just set—5 to 6 minutes. Immediately remove the corn from the boiling water and place it momentarily on several layers of paper towels to drain. Serve immediately. Small handles with pins, available commercially, may be inserted at both ends of the ears before serving, adding to the ease and pleasure of eating Corn on the Cob. At the table, pass an ample amount of melted butter with a small brush for application to the ears. Some diners lightly salt Corn on the Cob after applying butter.

SCALLOPED CORN

1 15-ounce can commercial cream-style corn or 1 pint home-canned Cream-Style Corn (page 733)
3 tablespoons finely chopped onions
1 2-ounce jar pimientos, drained and coarsely chopped (2 tablespoons)
24 Ritz crackers, rolled medium-coarsely (1 cup)
1 extra-large egg, beaten
¼ cup whole milk
¼ teaspoon salt
Dash of pepper
2 teaspoons butter

Preheat the oven to 350°F. Butter a 1-quart round baking dish; set aside.

In a medium mixing bowl, place the corn, onions, pimientos, cracker crumbs, egg, milk, salt, and pepper; stir to combine. Place the mixture in the prepared baking dish. Dot with the butter. Bake, uncovered, for 30 minutes. The top will be faintly brown around the very edge and the mixture will be thick.

SERVES 6

PIGS IN A CORNFIELD

1 teaspoon vegetable shortening
8 (¾ pound) link pork sausages

In a medium, heavy-bottomed skillet, melt the shortening over medium-high heat; using a spatula, spread the melted shortening over the entire bottom of the skillet. Place the sausages in the skillet; brown on all sides (about 10 minutes). Drain the sausage well between paper towels. Cut each link widthwise into sixths; set aside. Follow the Scalloped Corn recipe, above, adding the sausage pieces to the ingredients before combining them.

SERVES 6

PATTY DAVIS'S SCALLOPED CORN

3 11-ounce cans Niblets whole-kernel, golden sweet corn, drained
1 cup (½ pint) whipping cream, unwhipped
⅓ cup commercial sour cream
¼ teaspoon salt
¼ teaspoon pepper
22 very coarsely crushed saltines (crush in your hands) (about 1⅔ cups saltines)
1 cup sliced, fresh mushrooms
2 tablespoons butter

Preheat the oven to 350°F. Butter a 2-quart round baking dish; set aside.

In a large mixing bowl, place the corn, whipping cream, sour cream, salt, pepper, crushed saltines, and mushrooms; stir to combine. Turn the mixture into the prepared baking dish. Using the back of a spoon, push any visible mushroom slices beneath the surface of the mixture. Dot with the butter. Bake, uncovered, for 35 minutes. The mixture will be bubbly around the edge of the casserole.

SERVES 10

CORN PUDDING

4 extra-large eggs
½ teaspoon salt
⅛ teaspoon white pepper
1 teaspoon sugar
2 cups whole milk, scalded (page 25)
2 tablespoons butter
1 15¼-ounce can commercial whole-kernel corn, drained, or 1 pint home-canned Whole-Kernel Corn (page 731), drained
⅓ cup finely shredded, mild cheddar cheese

Preheat the oven to 325°F. Butter lightly a 2-quart round baking dish; set aside.

Place the eggs in a medium mixing bowl; using an electric mixer, beat slightly on medium speed. Add the salt, white pepper, and sugar; stir to combine; set aside. After scalding the milk, remove it from the heat and add the butter; stir until the butter melts. Add the milk mixture *slowly* to the egg mixture, stirring constantly. Add the corn and cheese; stir to combine. Pour into the prepared baking dish.

Place the baking dish in a 9 × 13-inch baking dish; then, pour very hot, but not boiling, water into the pan to approximately ½ the height of the baking dish. Bake, uncovered, for 1 hour, or until a table knife inserted near the center of the Corn Pudding comes out clean.

SERVES 6

SQUAW CORN

4 slices bacon, cut widthwise into 1-inch pieces
4 extra-large eggs
⅛ teaspoon salt
1 15-ounce can commercial cream-style corn or 1 pint home-canned Cream-Style Corn (page 733)

In a medium, heavy-bottomed skillet, fry the bacon over medium heat until crisp. Meanwhile, in a medium mixing bowl, place the eggs and salt; using an electric mixer, beat well. Add the corn to the egg mixture; using a spoon, stir and fold to combine. When the bacon is crisp, add the corn mixture to the skillet. Using a small spatula, turn the mixture intermittently until the eggs are cooked (about 10 minutes).

SERVES 4

SERVING SUGGESTIONS: Serve Squaw Corn for an informal brunch, a late informal supper, or for a quick and tasty dinner main course.

CORN-OYSTER CASSEROLE

2 15-ounce cans commercial cream-style
   corn or 2 1-pint jars home-canned
   Cream-Style Corn (page 733)
1/3 cup finely chopped onions
2 cups coarsely rolled saltines (about 36
   saltines)
3 extra-large eggs, slightly beaten
1/4 cup (4 tablespoons) butter, melted
1/4 cup half-and-half
1/2 teaspoon salt
1/4 teaspoon pepper
1 quart medium-sized shucked oysters, well
   drained
1 recipe (1/4 cup) Buttered Cracker Crumbs
   (page 49)

Preheat the oven to 350° F. Butter well a 3-quart
round baking dish; set aside.

In a large mixing bowl, place the corn,
onions, rolled saltines, eggs, butter, half-and-
half, salt, and pepper; stir to combine. Spoon 1/3
of the mixture into the prepared baking dish.
Dot the mixture with 1/2 of the oysters. Repeat
the layers. Then, add a layer of the remaining 1/3
of the corn mixture. Top with the buttered
crumbs. Bake, uncovered, for 1 hour.

SERVES 10

Cucumbers

BAKED CUCUMBERS

2 1/2 pounds (about 3 large) seedless
   cucumbers
2 tablespoons butter
1 teaspoon cornstarch
1 tablespoon snipped, fresh dillweed
1/2 teaspoon salt
1/4 teaspoon white pepper
2 tablespoons dry white wine
1 recipe (1/4 cup) Buttered Bread Crumbs
   (page 49)

Preheat the oven to 350° F. Butter an 8 × 8-inch
baking dish; set aside.

Pare the cucumbers (page 45); slice 1/2 inch
thick. Measure 7 cups cucumber slices and place
them in a large saucepan. (Reserve any remaining cucumber slices for other uses.) Add hot
water to cover the cucumber slices in the saucepan. Cover the saucepan. Bring the cucumbers
to a boil over high heat. Reduce the heat and
simmer 10 minutes, until the cucumbers are
very tender. Drain the cucumbers in a colander;
let stand to cool slightly.

In a tiny saucepan, melt the butter over warm
heat. Remove from the heat. Add the cornstarch; stir until completely blended, with no
lumps remaining. Then, add the dillweed, salt,
and white pepper; stir to combine. Add the
wine; stir in and set aside.

Place the cucumbers in the prepared baking
dish. Pour the wine mixture evenly over the
cucumbers. Just before baking, sprinkle the
crumbs over the top. Bake, uncovered, for 30
minutes. The crumb topping will be golden.

SERVES 10

Eggplant

DELUXE EGGPLANT STUFFED WITH HAM

Church cookbooks are often like forgotten treasure chests full of precious gems. They are repositories of many wonderful recipes which deserve broader publication. The recipe that follows is adapted from a recipe which appeared in a 1976 cookbook published by the women of Plymouth Congregational United Church of Christ, Des Moines, Iowa, our family's church. The cookbook recipe bears the name of Martha Lenhart, wife of our senior minister at the time. Hints for serving are provided in the headnote preceding the recipe: "Good for a luncheon dish, served with tomato aspic or tossed salad."

1 small (¾ to 1 pound) eggplant
2 tablespoons butter
¾ cup chopped onions
1 small garlic clove, pressed
⅓ cup chopped green bell peppers
2 tablespoons butter
1 cup sliced, fresh mushrooms
¼ teaspoon salt
⅛ teaspoon pepper
¼ teaspoon dried leaf thyme
1 cup ham cubes cut ½ inch square from a
    ¼-inch slice of fully cooked ham (about
    ⅓ pound of ham)
¼ cup grated Colby cheese
½ cup hot water

Wash the eggplant and dry. Trim off the stem end. Cut the eggplant in half lengthwise; using a paring knife and spoon, cut and scoop out the pulp, leaving a ½-inch shell. Cut the pulp into approximately ½-inch cubes; set aside. Place the eggplant shells in a skillet; add about ½ inch water. Cover the skillet. Bring the eggplant shells to a boil over high heat. Reduce the heat and simmer about 5 minutes, *only* until the shells are just tender. Further cooking will cause the shells to lose their shape after they are stuffed.

Remove the shells from the skillet; place on several layers of paper towels and set aside.

Preheat the oven to 375° F.

In a heavy-bottomed skillet, melt 2 tablespoons butter over medium heat. Tilt the skillet back and forth to completely cover the bottom with the melted butter. Place the onions, garlic, and green peppers in the skillet; brown lightly. Using a slotted spoon, remove the vegetables from the skillet and place in a bowl; set aside. Melt an additional 2 tablespoons butter in the skillet. Place the cubed eggplant pulp, mushrooms, salt, pepper, and thyme in the skillet; sauté until the mushrooms give up their juices and the pulp is tender (about 6 minutes), stirring frequently. Remove from the heat. Add the onion mixture and ham cubes; stir to combine.

Spoon the mixture into the eggplant shells and distribute grated cheese over the stuffing. Place the stuffed shells in a baking dish and pour ½ cup hot water into the dish. Bake, uncovered, for 20 minutes, until the stuffing is hot.

SERVES 2

EGGPLANT AND HAM CASSEROLE: Follow the Deluxe Eggplant Stuffed with Ham recipe, above, except: after trimming off the stem end of the eggplant, pare and cube the entire eggplant. Sauté the entire cubed eggplant with the mushrooms. Turn the completed ham mixture into a greased 1-quart round baking dish. Distribute the cheese over the top. Bake, uncovered, for 20 minutes at 375° F.

SERVES 2

EGGPLANT PARMESAN

2 1- to 1¼-pound eggplants
½ cup commercially packaged cornflake
    crumbs or 2½ cups cornflakes, crumbed
    (page 49)
½ cup freshly grated Parmesan cheese
    (page 46)
½ teaspoon salt
⅛ teaspoon white pepper

1 extra-large egg
2 tablespoons vegetable oil
1 tablespoon butter
Additional butter, if necessary
1 recipe Tomato Sauce (page 362), warm
Additional freshly grated Parmesan cheese

Wash the eggplants and dry. Trim off the stem ends. Cut the eggplants widthwise into ½-inch slices. Pare the skin from the eggplant slices; set aside. In a small bowl, place the crumbs, ½ cup Parmesan cheese, salt, and white pepper; stir to combine. Scatter the crumb mixture over a piece of waxed paper; set aside. Place the egg in a pie pan or other flat-bottomed dish; using a table fork, beat well; set aside.

In an electric skillet or a large, heavy-bottomed skillet on the range, heat the vegetable oil over medium heat (350° F. in an electric skillet). Tilt the skillet back and forth to completely cover the bottom with the oil. Add the butter; spread to blend with the oil. Dip the eggplant slices in the egg, covering the edges as well as both sides; then, dredge the edges and both sides in the crumb mixture. Place the eggplant slices in the skillet and sauté, one layer at a time, 4 minutes on each side, until tender and well browned. Turn only once; add more butter if necessary.

Place the sautéed eggplant slices on individual plates or on a serving plate and spoon warm Tomato Sauce over the top. At the table, pass additional Parmesan cheese to sprinkle over the sauce.

SERVES 8

SERVING SUGGESTIONS
- Serve as a main course, accompanied by an all-green Tossed Salad (page 124) and Toasted Garlic Bread (page 428).

- Serve as a side dish.

SAUTÉED EGGPLANT: Follow the Eggplant Parmesan recipe, above, substituting an additional ½ cup cornflake crumbs for ½ cup freshly grated Parmesan cheese and omitting the Tomato Sauce and additional freshly grated Parmesan cheese.

Fennel

FENNEL AND TOMATOES BRAISED IN WINE

1 medium (½ to ¾ pound after removing stalks) fennel bulb
1 tablespoon extra-virgin olive oil
2 tablespoons butter
⅓ cup sliced leeks (white and greenish white parts only) (about 1 leek)
¼ teaspoon fennel seed
¼ teaspoon salt
⅛ teaspoon white pepper
1 cup dry white wine
½ pound tomatoes, blanched (page 44), stemmed, peeled, quartered, seeded and cored (page 45), and coarsely chopped (about ¾ cup)
¾ cup sliced, fresh mushrooms

Cut away the stalks and leaves from the fennel bulb. (Reserve the stalks and leaves for other uses.) Cut a thin slice off the root end of the bulb and discard. Remove and discard the outer layer of the bulb if the surface contains any brown spots. Wash the bulb and dry it. Cut the bulb in half vertically through the root end. Using a small paring knife, remove and discard the core from both halves of the bulb. Chop each bulb half coarsely; set aside.

Preheat an electric skillet or a large, heavy-bottomed skillet on the range to medium heat (350° F. in an electric skillet). Add the olive oil; tilt the skillet back and forth to completely cover the bottom with the oil. Add the butter; quickly spread to blend with the oil. Place the fennel and leeks in the skillet; sauté until lightly brown (about 5 minutes), stirring and turning often. Reduce the heat to low (220° F. in an electric skillet).

When the skillet cools to the reduced temperature, add the fennel seed, salt, white pepper,

(Recipe continues on next page)

and wine; stir to combine. Cover the skillet and simmer the fennel mixture 10 minutes, stirring about 2 times. Add the tomatoes and mushrooms; cover and simmer an additional 5 minutes.

SERVES 2 TO 3

Kohlrabi

While kohlrabi somewhat resembles the turnip in shape and texture, most of the similarities between these vegetables stop there. Kohlrabi is milder and sweeter in flavor than the turnip, and is not a root vegetable. In fact, kohlrabi is the bulbous *stem* of the plant, and grows just above the ground. The leaves grow directly from the bulbous stem, giving kohlrabi that knobby appearance. Kohlrabi may be pale green or purple in color, although the variety carried in the produce market I frequent is consistently the pale green type. Kohlrabi is a member of the same species *(Brassica oleracea)* as head cabbage, Brussels sprouts, broccoli, cauliflower, kale, and collards. (The turnip is a member of a different species, *Brassica rapa.*)

To call kohlrabi a new vegetable would be grossly inaccurate; however, it is comparatively "new" insofar as general availability in many Midwest produce markets, and inclusion in standard Midwest cooking. In addition to serving it cooked, kohlrabi may be pared and used raw (diced, shredded, or cut julienne) in salads, or as a crudité (page 21) with dips on an hors d'oeuvre tray. Nutritionally, kohlrabi is a superb source of potassium and vitamin C.

KOHLRABI WITH TARRAGON

8 ounces commercial sour cream
1 tablespoon all-purpose flour
½ teaspoon dried leaf tarragon
1½ pounds kohlrabi (about 6 medium kohlrabi)
3 tablespoons butter
¼ cup water
½ teaspoon salt

In a small mixing bowl, place the sour cream, flour, and tarragon; stir to combine. Cover and set aside. Wash the kohlrabi; cut off the ends and pare, completely removing the rather thick, fibrous layer of flesh underneath the outer skin. Cut the kohlrabi into ½-inch cubes; set aside.

In a large, heavy-bottomed skillet, melt the butter over low heat. Tilt the skillet back and forth to completely cover the bottom with the melted butter. Place the kohlrabi in the skillet and sauté over low heat 3 minutes. Add the water and salt; cover and cook over low heat 15 minutes, until just tender, turning intermittently. There should be little or no water left in the skillet at the end of the cooking period. Add the sour cream mixture; stir to combine with the kohlrabi. Then, cook over low heat about 2 minutes until the sour cream mixture is hot and fairly thick, stirring constantly.

SERVES 6

Mixed Vegetables

SNAPPY STIR-FRY VEGETABLES

1 medium (½ to ¾ pound after removing
   stalks) fennel bulb
1 cup carrots, pared and sliced diagonally
   ⅛ inch thick
1 cup coarsely chopped onions
¾ cup coarsely chopped red bell peppers
⅛ pound (about 1 cup) snow peas
¼ cup salted, whole cashews
¼ cup Sherried Dressing with Fennel and
   Thyme (page 149)
1 teaspoon cornstarch
2 tablespoons vegetable oil
½ teaspoon salt
½ teaspoon white pepper
½ recipe Perfect Boiled Rice (page 272)

Cut away the stalks and leaves from the fennel
bulb. (Reserve the stalks and leaves for other
uses.) Cut a thin slice off the root end of the
bulb and discard. Remove and discard the outer
layer of the bulb if the surface contains any
brown spots. Wash the bulb and dry it. Cut the
bulb in half vertically through the root end.
Using a small paring knife, remove and discard
the core from both halves of the bulb. Cut each
bulb half widthwise into ⅜-inch slices; place in
a small bowl and set aside.

Place the carrots, onions, and peppers in separate bowls; set aside. Remove the ends and
strings from the snow peas (page 327); wash and
dry. Place the snow peas in a separate bowl; set
aside. Measure the cashews; place in a separate
bowl; set aside. In a small sauce dish, place the
sherried dressing and cornstarch. Using a small
fork (such as a salad fork), beat until the cornstarch blends with the dressing; set aside.

Preheat a wok, electric skillet, or large, heavy-
bottomed skillet on the range to medium-high
heat (370° F. if using a wok or electric skillet).
Add the vegetable oil. Tilt the wok or skillet
back and forth to completely cover the sides and
bottom of the wok or the bottom of the skillet
with hot oil. Place the fennel and carrots in the
wok or skillet; stir-fry (page 26) 2 minutes (see
Note), using a spatula to move and turn the vegetables almost constantly to prevent them from
scorching. Add the onions and red peppers; stir-
fry an additional 3 minutes, continuing to move
and turn the vegetables. Add the snow peas, salt,
and white pepper; stir to combine. Reduce the
heat to low (240° F. if using a wok or electric
skillet). Cover the wok or skillet. Let the vegetables cook 1 minute without uncovering.

Uncover the wok or skillet. Using the spatula,
move the vegetables to one side of the wok or
skillet. Pour the cornstarch mixture into the center of the wok or skillet; heat and cook briefly
until the mixture thickens, using a mixing spoon
to stir constantly. Then, using the mixing spoon,
combine the cornstarch mixture and vegetables.
Add the cashews; stir only until evenly distributed. When done, the vegetables should be
crispy-tender.

Spoon Snappy Stir-Fry Vegetables over rice
on individual plates or spoon the vegetables and
rice into separate serving bowls to pass at the
table.

NOTE: A digital timer which indicates seconds is
helpful in achieving optimum results with stir-
fry dishes since the cooking times are so brief,
making the time spans difficult to gauge without a precise timekeeper.

**SERVES 2 AS A MAIN COURSE OR
4 AS A SIDE DISH (ELIMINATE THE RICE)**

MIXED FRESH VEGETABLES WITH ROSEMARY

1 red bell pepper
6 carrots
1 small head cauliflower
2 medium kohlrabi
10 ounces pearl onions
2 medium green zucchini
1 medium yellow zucchini
½ cup (¼ pound) butter
1 tablespoon fresh, snipped rosemary or
   1 teaspoon dried leaf rosemary

TO PREPARE THE VEGETABLES: Prepare the vegetables separately to preserve their individual colors and flavors. For steaming and boiling procedures, see Steamed Vegetables and Boiled Vegetables (page 302). After each vegetable is prepared, drain in a colander. Rinse under cold, running water to stop the cooking. Drain well. Place in a separate zipper-seal plastic bag and refrigerate. Prepare the vegetables as follows:

Red Bell Pepper: Cut lengthwise into ¼-inch strips. Cut away all white flesh. Cut each strip widthwise into 3 pieces. Steam 3 minutes.

Carrots: Cut off the ends and pare. Cut diagonally into ⅜-inch slices. Boil 5 minutes in water to cover.

Cauliflower: Cut into bite-sized flowerets. Steam 3 minutes.

Kohlrabi: Cut off the ends and pare. Cut into ¾-inch cubes. Boil 15 minutes in water to cover.

Pearl Onions: Peel (page 45). Steam 3 minutes.

Zucchini: Cut off the ends. Cut into ¼-inch slices. Steam 2 minutes.

TO SERVE: When ready to serve, place all the prepared vegetables in a very large mixing bowl.

With your hands, toss carefully until evenly distributed. Place the mixed vegetables in the top of a large steamer pan. Steam *only* until hot. Meanwhile, in a small saucepan, melt the butter over low heat. Add the rosemary and stir to combine; set aside.

Turn the hot vegetables into a very large mixing bowl. Pour the butter mixture over the vegetables; using a wooden mixing spoon, toss lightly.

SERVES 16

VEGETABLE VARIATIONS: Any combination of vegetables may be used. Among other vegetables which might be included in a mixed vegetable combination are the following:

Asparagus: Cut into 1-inch pieces. Simmer 1 minute in water to cover.

Green, Yellow, and Purple Bell Peppers: Follow preparation of Red Bell Peppers.

Broccoli: Cut into bite-sized flowerets. Steam 3 minutes.

Small Brussels Sprouts: Trim off the stem ends. Steam 6 minutes.

Celery: Cut diagonally into ⅜-inch slices. Steam 5 minutes.

Snow Peas: Snip off the ends and pull off the strings along both sides of the pods. Steam 3 minutes.

Cherry Tomatoes: Add raw when heating the mixed vegetables before serving.

SEASONING VARIATIONS: Mixed Fresh Vegetables may be served plain, without the enhancement of butter and herbs or may be seasoned with butter or herbs alone. When butter is used, the following herbs, fresh or dried, may be substituted for rosemary: basil, chives, dillweed, marjoram, savory, tarragon, and thyme. When butter is not used, the vegetables may be seasoned with the same herbs, but the herbs should be fresh.

SUCCOTASH

2 ounces cured salt pork, cut into 4 pieces
½ cup water
¼ teaspoon salt
⅛ teaspoon pepper
1 teaspoon sugar
1 10-ounce package frozen baby
  lima beans
1 10-ounce package frozen whole-kernel
  corn
½ cup half-and-half
2 tablespoons butter

In a medium saucepan, place the salt pork, water, salt, pepper, sugar, and frozen lima beans. Cover the saucepan. Bring the mixture to a boil over high heat. Reduce the heat and simmer 15 minutes. Add the frozen corn. Cover the saucepan and return the mixture to a simmer; cook 4 minutes. Drain well, leaving the mixture in the saucepan. Remove and discard the salt pork.

Add the half-and-half and butter to the lima bean–corn mixture. Cover the saucepan and place over low heat. Heat the Succotash through, stirring intermittently to blend and combine the ingredients.

SERVES 6

BUFFET VEGETABLES

Asparagus
Small Brussels sprouts
Carrots
Kohlrabi
Frozen peas
Cherry tomatoes
Yellow zucchini
Butter, melted
Snipped, fresh chives

TO PREPARE THE VEGETABLES: Prepare the vegetables separately to preserve their individual colors and flavors. For steaming and boiling procedures, see Steamed Vegetables and Boiled Vegetables (page 302).

Asparagus: Cut into 2-inch pieces. Simmer 2 minutes in water to cover.

Small Brussels sprouts: Trim off the stem ends. Steam 6 minutes.

Carrots: Cut off the ends and pare. Cut julienne (page 23) into 1½-inch strips. Boil 3 minutes in water to cover.

Kohlrabi: Cut off the ends and pare. Cut into ¾-inch cubes. Boil 15 minutes in water to cover.

Peas: Add the frozen peas to the cooked carrots. Continue cooking only until the peas are hot.

Cherry tomatoes: Steam 1 minute.

Yellow zucchini: Cut off the ends. Cut into ¼-inch slices. Steam 2 minutes.

Cook (or reheat, if previously prepared) all the vegetables separately just before arranging in the serving dish. Thoroughly drain the vegetables which have been cooked in water; namely, the asparagus, carrots and peas, and kohlrabi. Return the kohlrabi to the saucepan; add melted butter and snipped chives; toss.

Arrange the vegetables diagonally in a 9 × 13-inch baking dish, using a piece of white, corrugated cardboard (cake board) to contain previously arranged vegetables as the next strip of vegetables is added (see illustration). After the vegetables are arranged in the baking dish, brush them generously with butter. Place the baking dish in an attractive silver or basket-type serving holder. Place on the buffet table.

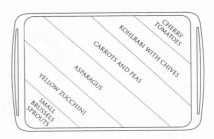

VEGETABLE BUNDLES

12 narrow carrot strips, 3 inches long (pare
   carrots; cut into 3-inch lengths; then, cut
   lengthwise into quarters or sixths,
   depending upon size of carrots)
12 small diameter, fresh green beans
   (remove ends and strings [page 305]; cut
   into 3-inch lengths)
12 small diameter, fresh asparagus spears
   (cut into 3-inch lengths, using the top
   ends only)
Green leek tops from 1 leek
1 tablespoon butter, melted

Place the carrot strips in a small saucepan; add
water to cover. Cover the saucepan. Bring the
carrots to a boil over high heat; reduce heat
slightly and boil 3 minutes. Drain the carrots in
a colander; place under cold, running water to
stop the cooking. Set the carrots aside on a flat
work surface, handling carefully to prevent
tearing.

Boil and process the green beans, using the
same boiling time and procedures as with the
carrots. Boil and process the asparagus spears,
boiling only 1 minute, but otherwise following
the same procedures as with the carrots.

Process the leek tops to make them pliable
(page 401); avoid overprocessing, causing leek
tops to become too limp and, thus, unmanage-
able. Using an X-Acto knife, cut four ¼-inch-
wide strips (ribbons) from the leek tops; let
stand.

On a flat work surface, arrange 4 bundles of
vegetables, each containing 3 carrot strips, 3
green beans, and 3 asparagus spears. (If the green
beans and/or asparagus spears are somewhat
large in diameter, reduce the number of carrot
strips and/or green beans and/or asparagus
spears in each bundle to 2, if desired.) Place each
bundle of vegetables across the center of 1 leek
ribbon. Tie each bundle together with the leek
ribbon, making a single tie. (It is difficult to tie
a complete bow without tearing the leek ribbon.) Using kitchen scissors, trim the ends of

the leek ribbons, leaving an attractive length of
ribbon ends on the bundles.

Carefully, place the Vegetable Bundles in the
top of a large steamer pan. Immediately before
serving, steam bundles about *1 minute,* only until
warm. Then, using a soft brush, lightly brush the
bundles with melted butter to bring out the
color of the vegetables and make them glisten.

MAKES 4 VEGETABLE BUNDLES

Mushrooms

CREAMED MUSHROOMS

1 tablespoon butter
½ cup chopped onions
¼ teaspoon salt
⅛ teaspoon white pepper
1 tablespoon butter
¾ pound large, fresh mushrooms, sliced
2 tablespoons all-purpose flour
1 cup (½ pint) whipping cream,*
   unwhipped
2 tablespoons dry vermouth
8 ounces angel-hair pasta (capellini),
   cooked, rinsed in hot water, and drained
   (page 283)

Half-and-half may be substituted.

In a small to medium, heavy-bottomed skillet,
melt 1 tablespoon butter over medium heat. Tilt
the skillet back and forth to completely cover
the bottom with the melted butter. Place the
onions, salt, and white pepper in the skillet;
sauté the onions until translucent, but not
brown. Add 1 tablespoon butter and the mushrooms; continue sautéing until the mushrooms
give up their juices. Remove from the heat.
With a slotted spoon, remove the mushrooms
and onions from the skillet and place in a bowl;
set aside.

Add the flour to the liquid in the skillet; stir

until completely smooth. Add the whipping cream and vermouth; stir to blend. Return the skillet to medium heat; cook the mixture until it thickens, stirring constantly. Add the mushrooms and onions; stir to combine; heat through. Serve Creamed Mushrooms over angel-hair pasta.

SERVES 4

VARIATION: Substitute ¾ cup raw long-grain rice, cooked (page 272) or 8 ounces medium to narrow egg noodles, cooked, rinsed in hot water, and drained (page 283) for the angel-hair pasta.

SERVING SUGGESTIONS
- Serve on a brunch menu or as a luncheon main dish.

- Serve as an accompaniment to beef, veal, Baked Cut-up Chicken (page 205), or Roast Turkey Breast (page 214).

- Serve as a first-course appetizer. Spoon Creamed Mushrooms (substitute small mushrooms for the large mushrooms called for in recipe) into the center of tiny, unmolded, 3½-inch individual ring molds of rice (follow the Rice in Ring Mold recipe and procedure [page 273], eliminating the pine nuts).

MOREL MUSHROOMS SAUTÉED IN WHITE WINE

The morel is a prized variety of mushroom found only in the wild, and is gathered in parts of the Midwest. In delicacy, desirability, and rarity, morels can be likened to fresh European truffles.

½ pound fresh morel mushrooms
4 cups cold water
1 tablespoon salt
1 extra-large egg
¼ teaspoon salt
⅛ teaspoon pepper

½ cup all-purpose flour
1 tablespoon vegetable oil
2 tablespoons butter
1 small garlic clove, pressed
2 tablespoons dry white wine

Clean the mushrooms well under cold, running water to remove soil and ants and other insects. In a large mixing bowl, place 4 cups cold water and 1 tablespoon salt; stir until the salt dissolves. Place the mushrooms in the salt solution; soak 15 minutes to remove any remaining insects. Drain the mushrooms; rinse well in clear water. Drain on several layers of paper towels. Trim off the bottoms of the stems and slice the mushrooms in half lengthwise; set aside.

In a small bowl, place the egg, ¼ teaspoon salt, and pepper; using a table fork, beat well; set aside. Sprinkle the flour over a piece of waxed paper; set aside. Dip the mushroom halves in the egg mixture and then dredge in the flour. Place the dredged mushrooms on a clean piece of waxed paper; set aside.

In a medium, heavy-bottomed skillet, heat the vegetable oil over medium heat. Using a spatula, spread the vegetable oil over the entire bottom of the skillet. Add the butter. Tilt the skillet back and forth to blend the butter with the oil. Place the mushrooms and garlic in the skillet; sauté 7 minutes until golden brown, keeping the heat low enough to prevent the oil and butter from burning. Reduce the heat; add the white wine and heat through, stirring to blend the wine with the pan juices and to coat the mushrooms with the wine sauce.

SERVES 4

SERVING SUGGESTIONS
- Especially good spooned over beef steaks or slices of beef tenderloin.

- Serve on the same plate, or as a side dish, with veal and wild game.

Onions

FRENCH-FRIED ONION RINGS

1½ pounds yellow onions (about 3 large
   onions)
½ cup all-purpose flour
¾ teaspoon salt
½ teaspoon white pepper
½ cup whole milk
1 extra-large egg, slightly beaten
1 tablespoon vegetable oil
1 quart vegetable oil

Cut off the ends and peel the onions. Cut the
onions into ³⁄₁₆-inch uniform slices. Carefully
separate all the rings, reserving the tiny center
rings for other uses; set aside. In a medium mixing bowl, place the flour, salt, and white pepper;
stir to combine. Add the milk, egg, and 1 tablespoon vegetable oil. Using an electric mixer,
beat on low speed only until smooth; set aside.

Pour 1 quart vegetable oil into a deep-fat
fryer or an electric skillet; preheat the oil to
375° F. Drop a handful of onion rings into the
batter. Using a cooking fork, turn the rings until
they are completely coated. Using the fork,
remove the rings from the batter and hold the
rings over the mixing bowl briefly until the
excess batter drips back into the bowl. Drop
the coated rings into the hot oil. Repeat the
coating process with additional raw onion rings,
but drop only enough onion rings into the oil
to maintain a single layer in the fryer (or skillet).
Fry the rings about 4 minutes until they reach a
light golden color. Using the fork, remove the
fried onion rings from the fryer (or skillet) and
place, single layer, on 3 layers of paper towels to
drain. Place a single layer of paper towels over
the onion rings to help absorb the oil and keep
the rings hot.

Repeat the process until all the rings have
been fried. Drain batches of the fried rings on
fresh, unsaturated paper towels to achieve maximum absorbency. French-Fried Onion Rings
should be served as grease-free as possible.

Serve the onion rings immediately while hot.
If necessary, drained onion rings may be placed
in a 9 × 13-inch baking pan and placed, *uncovered,* in a 300° F. oven to keep hot; however,
French-Fried Onion Rings are best when not
held.

SERVES 4

CREAMED ONIONS

1¼ pounds pearl onions
1 recipe Thin White Sauce (page 366), hot
Paprika for decoration

Peel the onions (page 45) and the trim ends.
Steam the onions (page 302) until tender. Add
the onions to the hot Thin White Sauce; stir to
combine. Serve in small sauce dishes. Sprinkle
sparingly with paprika.

SERVES 6

Peas

CREAMED PEAS

1 10-ounce package frozen peas
1 recipe Medium White Sauce (page 366),
    hot

Cook the peas briefly, following the directions
on the package. Drain well in a sieve; set aside.
In a medium saucepan, make the Medium
White Sauce. Add the peas to the hot white
sauce; stir lightly until the peas are evenly
distributed.

SERVES 4

DILLED CREAMED PEAS: Follow the Creamed
Peas recipe, above, adding ½ teaspoon dried
dillweed to the white sauce and stirring to combine before adding the peas.

PEAS WITH MUSHROOMS AND SHALLOTS

1 tablespoon butter
½ cup sliced, fresh mushrooms
3 tablespoons minced shallots
2 teaspoons dry sherry
½ cup water
2 teaspoons instant chicken bouillon
    granules
1 10-ounce package frozen peas

In a small, heavy-bottomed skillet, melt the butter over medium heat. Tilt the skillet back and
forth to completely cover the bottom with the
melted butter. Place the mushrooms and shallots
in the skillet; sauté 3 minutes. Remove from the
heat; let stand until the skillet cools slightly.

Then, add the sherry; stir to blend with the
pan juices; set aside.

Pour ½ cup water into a medium to small
saucepan. Cover the saucepan and bring the
water to a boil over high heat. Add the bouillon
granules; stir until dissolved. Add the peas.
Cover the saucepan and bring the peas to a simmer. Reduce the heat and simmer 2 minutes.
Drain the peas in a sieve.

Return the drained peas to the saucepan. Add
the mushroom and shallot mixture, including
the pan juices; stir to combine.

SERVES 4

MINTED PEAS

1 10-ounce package frozen peas
2 teaspoons butter
1 tablespoon finely snipped, fresh mint
    leaves

Cook the peas briefly, following the directions
on the package; drain well. Add the butter and
mint leaves; toss lightly until the butter melts
and the ingredients are combined.

SERVES 4

TO COOK AND SERVE SNOW PEAS

Wash the pods. Remove the ends of the pods
and the strings along both sides of the pods.
Steam (page 302) 3 minutes. Snow Peas are
served in the pods. A small amount of butter may
be tossed with the peas before serving, if desired.

TO COOK AND SERVE SUGAR SNAP PEAS

Follow the procedures for cooking and serving
snow peas (see To Cook and Serve Snow Peas,
above), except steam Sugar Snap Peas about 4
minutes or until just tender.

Potatoes

TO COOK AND SERVE BOILED POTATOES

Boiled potatoes may be served as such, or they are often used in the preparation of other dishes such as Potato Salad and Potato Dumplings. Potatoes may be boiled either pared or unpared.

BOILED PARED POTATOES: Using a vegetable parer, remove all skin and eyes from the potatoes. Immediately drop each pared potato into a saucepan of cold water. Immersion in cold water will prevent pared potatoes from discoloring. Pared potatoes may be retained in cold water 1 hour or so without harm to the product. If the potatoes are especially large, they may be cut in half or into thirds, depending upon how the boiled potatoes will be used.

When ready to boil the potatoes, drain the cold water and replace it with hot water to cover. Cover the saucepan. Bring the potatoes to a boil over high heat; reduce the heat to medium and boil moderately until the potatoes are tender when pierced with a sharp fork (about 25 minutes, depending upon the size of the potatoes). Avoid overcooking, causing the potatoes to fragment and become mushy. When done, remove from heat and drain the potatoes immediately to avoid sogginess.

As a side dish, boiled potatoes are traditionally served with butter, gravy, natural meat juice, or sauce.

BOILED UNPARED POTATOES: Using a vegetable brush, scrub the potatoes well. Place the unpared, whole (uncut) potatoes in a saucepan and add hot water to cover. Cover the saucepan. Boil the potatoes, following the procedure for Boiled Pared Potatoes, above. When done, drain the potatoes immediately. If the potatoes are to be cooled for use in another dish, place them on wire racks. When cool enough to handle or when completely cool, the potatoes may be peeled, using a small paring knife. If the potatoes

are to be sliced or cut in other exacting shapes, allow them to cool completely before peeling and slicing or cutting. Cool potatoes can be cut more uniformly and are less likely to fragment.

If not allowed to overcook, potatoes boiled unpared retain their shape and cohesion after peeling. This is important if the cooked potatoes are to be sliced or otherwise cut into uniform pieces. When potatoes are boiled *after* paring, the outside portion of the potatoes is prone to become somewhat soft and borderline mealy by the time the center is fully cooked—a quality not intolerable for dishes such as Mashed Potatoes but unsatisfactory for cooked potatoes which are to be sliced or otherwise cut for use in such dishes as Potato Salad where symmetry is important.

Boiled, unpared red potatoes retain their shape especially well after peeling; therefore, they are an excellent variety to use in Potato Salad. In contrast, russet potatoes are softer and are the more desirable variety to use in making Baked Potatoes and Mashed Potatoes.

TO COOK AND SERVE STEAMED POTATOES

Small, new potatoes may be steamed, pared or unpared. See Steamed Vegetables (page 302) for the procedure.

BAKED POTATOES

Uniformly sized russet potatoes

Preheat the oven to 450° F.

Using a vegetable brush, scrub the potatoes well; dry with paper towels. Wrap each potato tightly in a single layer of aluminum foil. Place the wrapped potatoes directly on the center rack in the oven. Bake for 45 to 60 minutes, depending upon size of the potatoes (see Note).

To serve, remove and discard the aluminum foil. Using a sharp paring knife, cut a cross in the top of each potato. Press the ends of each potato toward the center to open the cross and force some of the cooked potato flesh through the opening.

NOTE: Potatoes may be baked at a lower temperature for a longer period of time.

ACCOMPANIMENT SUGGESTIONS: Serve butter, sour cream, finely snipped chives, crumbled cooked bacon, chopped green onions, grated cheddar cheese, or any combination (or all) of these items to top the potatoes. Pass the topping(s) at the table, allowing diners to add their own.

TWICE-BAKED POTATOES

2 pounds russet potatoes, baked (see Baked
 Potatoes, page 328) (4 large potatoes)
2 tablespoons snipped, fresh chives
2 tablespoons butter, melted
½ cup finely shredded, extra-sharp cheddar
 cheese
Paprika for decoration

Immediately after baking the potatoes, remove the aluminum foil. Using a small, sharp knife, cut a thin slice lengthwise off the top of each potato. Using a teaspoon, carefully remove the cooked potato flesh from each potato, leaving a ⅛-inch lining of potato flesh adhering to the skin for stability of the shell. Place the potato flesh in a large mixing bowl; set aside. Set the shells aside. Using the teaspoon, remove the potato flesh from the cutaway slices and add it to the mixing bowl containing the potato flesh; discard the skin.

Mash the potato flesh, following the recipe for Mashed Potatoes (page 332). Add the chives to the mashed potatoes; using a mixing spoon, stir until evenly distributed.

Preheat the oven to 400° F.

Using a teaspoon and your thumb, *lightly* pack the mashed potatoes into the potato shells, rounding slightly. Smooth the tops of the mashed potatoes with your thumb. Then, draw the edge of the teaspoon diagonally across the mashed potatoes several times to make parallel rows of slight indentations.

Replace the stuffed potatoes loosely in the pieces of aluminum foil used for baking, but leave the tops of the potatoes uncovered; place in a shallow baking dish (see Note).

Pour the melted butter over the mashed potatoes. Bake, uncovered, for 25 minutes. Remove from the oven and distribute the shredded cheese over the mashed potatoes. Sprinkle the paprika over the cheese. Bake for an additional 3 minutes, until the cheese melts.

NOTE: At this point, the baking dish may be covered with plastic wrap and set aside or refrigerated for completion of the potatoes before serving later in the day.

SERVES 4

VARIATION: Substitute minced onions for the chives.

DECORATION SUGGESTION: For a more decorative appearance, reserve a portion of the mashed potatoes when packing the shells. Using a decorating bag fit with large open-star tip number 8B (page 383), pipe the reserved mashed potatoes in an attractive pattern over the top of the packed potatoes.

Eliminate making indentations in the mashed potatoes with the teaspoon. Include the addition of melted butter. The addition of shredded cheese is optional. Paprika decoration is also optional. If cheese is not added, eliminate the additional 3 minutes baking time. Instead, the potatoes may be browned quickly under the broiler, about 5 inches from the heat, if desired.

AMERICAN FRIES

1 tablespoon vegetable oil
2 tablespoons butter
2 pounds red potatoes, pared, quartered, and sliced ⅜ inch thick (about 6 medium-large potatoes)
1½ cups coarsely chopped onions
½ teaspoon salt
¼ teaspoon pepper

In an electric skillet or a large, heavy-bottomed skillet on the range, heat the vegetable oil over medium heat (350° F. if using an electric skillet). Using a spatula, spread the vegetable oil over the entire bottom of the skillet. Add the butter. Tilt the skillet back and forth to blend the butter with the oil.

Place the potatoes in the skillet; fry, uncovered, 8 minutes, turning often. Add the onions; fry an additional 5 minutes, turning intermittently to achieve even browning. Reduce the skillet heat to medium-low (280° F. if using an electric skillet). Cover the skillet and continue cooking the potatoes and onions 10 minutes, until tender, turning occasionally.

SERVES 4

SCALLOPED POTATOES

2 pounds red potatoes (about 6 medium potatoes)
2 recipes Medium White Sauce (page 366), warm
⅓ cup chopped onions
1 cup (4 ounces) shredded Colby cheese

Pare the potatoes and retain in a large bowl of cold water to prevent discoloration; set aside. Make 2 recipes of Medium White Sauce; cover and set aside.

Preheat the oven to 350° F. Grease a 2-quart round baking dish; set aside.

Slice each potato as follows: cut the potato in half lengthwise; while holding the potato halves together, roll the potato one-quarter turn and cut the potato halves lengthwise in half or into thirds, depending upon the size of the potato. While continuing to hold the potato together, cut it widthwise into ¼-inch slices. Place ½ of the sliced potatoes in the prepared baking dish; distribute ½ of the chopped onions evenly over the potatoes. Scatter ½ of the shredded cheese evenly over the onions; cover with ½ of the warm white sauce. Repeat the layers, using the remaining ½ of the ingredients.

Cover and bake for 1 hour. Uncover and continue baking until nicely browned (about 15 minutes).

SERVES 6

SCALLOPED POTATOES WITH HAM: Cut fully cooked ham into 1½ cups of ⅜-inch cubes. Follow the Scalloped Potatoes recipe, above, distributing ½ of the ham cubes over each of the 2 potato layers. Bake in a greased 2½-quart round baking dish.

ALLEGRO SCALLOPED POTATOES

In music, "allegro" means to play the composition at a quick tempo and merrily, definitions which connote the speed and pleasure with which this amazing potato casserole is prepared. The recipe relies heavily on prepared foods, but don't be turned off. They'll shout "Bravissimo!" when you serve it.

1 10¾-ounce can commercial, condensed cream of chicken soup (undiluted)
8 ounces commercial sour cream
1 2-pound bag frozen hash brown potatoes, thawed
1 cup chopped onions
½ teaspoon salt
¼ teaspoon white pepper
8 ounces sharp cheddar cheese, shredded (about 2 cups)
1 tablespoon plus 2 teaspoons butter

Paprika for decoration
Sprigs of fresh parsley for decoration

Preheat the oven to 350° F. Butter well a 7 × 11-inch baking dish; set aside.

In a medium mixing bowl, place the chicken soup and sour cream; stir to combine; set aside. In the prepared baking dish, layer in the following order: ½ of the potatoes, ½ of the onions, ½ of the salt, ½ of the white pepper, ½ of the sour cream mixture (spread as evenly as possible), and ½ of the cheese. Repeat the layers, using the remaining ½ of the layered ingredients. Dot with the butter. Sprinkle the paprika lightly over the top (see Note).

Bake, uncovered, for 1 hour. When done, the top should be slightly browned. Decorate with the parsley sprigs.

NOTE: At this point, the baking dish may be covered with plastic wrap and the Allegro Scalloped Potatoes refrigerated for baking and serving later in the day.

SERVES 10

SERVING SUGGESTION: A convenient and very tasty dish to serve at buffets.

NEW POTATOES WITH PARSLEY

2 pounds small, new, red potatoes
3 tablespoons butter
1½ teaspoons freshly squeezed, strained lemon juice
2 tablespoons finely snipped, fresh parsley

Using a vegetable brush, scrub the potatoes well. Place the potatoes in a saucepan; add hot water to cover. Cover the saucepan. Bring the potatoes to a boil over high heat; reduce the heat to medium and boil moderately until the potatoes are tender when pierced with a sharp fork (about 20 minutes). Drain the potatoes; let stand until cool enough to handle.

Meanwhile, in a tiny saucepan, melt the butter over low heat. Remove from the heat. Add the lemon juice and parsley; stir to combine; set aside. Peel the potatoes and place them in a mixing bowl. Drizzle the parsley mixture over the potatoes; using a wooden mixing spoon, toss to coat the potatoes. To serve, turn into a serving bowl.

SERVES 6

CREAMED NEW POTATOES AND PEAS WITH SNIPPED CHIVES

2 pounds small, new, red potatoes
1 10-ounce package frozen, tiny peas
1½ recipes Thin White Sauce (page 366), hot
1 tablespoon snipped, fresh chives

Using a vegetable brush, scrub the potatoes well. Place the potatoes in a large saucepan; add hot water to cover. Cover the saucepan. Bring the potatoes to a boil over high heat; reduce the heat to medium and boil moderately until the potatoes are tender when pierced with a sharp fork (about 20 minutes). Drain the potatoes; let stand until cool enough to handle.

Meanwhile, cook the peas briefly, following the directions on the package; set aside. Peel the potatoes and place in a mixing bowl; cover with aluminum foil to keep warm. Drain the peas and add to the potatoes; using a wooden mixing spoon, toss very gently and turn into a serving bowl. Pour the hot Thin White Sauce over the potatoes and peas; sprinkle with the chives.

SERVES 8

MASHED POTATOES

2 pounds russet potatoes (about 4 large
  potatoes)
3 tablespoons butter
¾ teaspoon salt
¼ cup whole milk
1 tablespoon butter

Pare the potatoes carefully, removing all skin and
eyes. Immediately after paring each potato, place
it in a large saucepan filled with cold water to
prevent discoloration. Cut each pared potato
into thirds and return to the cold water. Pared
potatoes may be retained in cold water 1 hour
or so before cooking.

When ready to cook the potatoes, drain the
cold water and replace with hot water to cover.
Cover the saucepan. Bring the potatoes to a boil
over high heat; reduce the heat to medium and
boil moderately until potatoes are tender when
pierced with a sharp fork (about 25 minutes).
Avoid overcooking, causing the potatoes to fragment and become mushy. Overcooked potatoes
can result in watery mashed potatoes which lack
the desired lightness and fluffiness.

Drain the potatoes *well,* leaving them in the
saucepan in which they were cooked to help
retain heat. Add 3 tablespoons butter, salt, and
milk. Using an electric mixer, beat the potato
mixture on high speed until completely smooth
and fluffy, with *no lumps* (see Note).

Spoon the Mashed Potatoes into a serving
bowl and top with a generous pat of butter
(about 1 tablespoon).

NOTE: Mashed Potatoes are best when served
immediately after mashing; however, they may
be held for a short period of time by covering
the pan and placing it in a larger pan of hot
water over low heat.

SERVES 6

ACCOMPANIMENT SUGGESTIONS
• Serve with gravy or natural meat juice passed
  at the table in a gravy boat.

• Certain dishes, such as Beef and Noodles
  (page 158), Chicken and Noodles (page 210),
  and Dried Beef Gravy (page 164), are traditionally served over Mashed Potatoes.

MASHED POTATO PATTIES

3 cups cold, leftover mashed potatoes
1 extra-large egg
1 teaspoon vegetable oil
1 tablespoon butter

In a medium mixing bowl, place the mashed
potatoes and egg; using a fork or a handheld
electric mixer, mix until smooth. Using a ½-
cup measuring cup, measure ½-cup portions of
the potato mixture and shape into thick patties
with your hands; place the patties on a plate or
in a shallow pan; set aside.

In a medium, heavy-bottomed skillet, heat
the vegetable oil and butter over medium heat.
Tilt the skillet back and forth to completely
cover bottom with the blend of oil and butter.
When the oil and butter *begin* to sizzle, carefully
place the patties in the skillet, using a small spatula. Fry the patties, uncovered, until nicely
browned and heated through, turning once.

MAKES 6 PATTIES

SERVING NOTE: Mashed Potato Patties are generally not served with gravy, although they may
be. If desired, gravy may be passed at the table
for diners who wish to ladle it over their potato
patty.

MASHED POTATOES IN A CASSEROLE

A great dish for parties and buffets!

4 pounds russet potatoes (about 8 large
    potatoes)
8 ounces commercial sour cream
8 ounces cream cheese, softened
2 tablespoons butter
2 teaspoons finely snipped, fresh parsley

Pare the potatoes carefully, removing all skin and eyes. Immediately after paring each potato, place it in a very large saucepan filled with cold water to prevent discoloration. Cut each potato into thirds and return to the cold water. Drain the cold water and replace with hot water to cover. Cover the saucepan. Bring the potatoes to a boil over high heat; reduce the heat to medium and boil moderately until the potatoes are tender when pierced with a sharp fork (about 25 minutes).

When the potatoes are nearly done, preheat the oven to 325° F. Butter a 9 × 13-inch baking dish; set aside.

When the potatoes are done, drain *well,* leaving them in the saucepan in which they were cooked to help retain the heat. To the potatoes, add the sour cream and cream cheese. Using an electric mixer, beat the potato mixture on high speed until completely smooth, with *no lumps.*

Spoon the mashed potatoes into the prepared baking dish. With the back of a tablespoon, fashion attractive peaks in the top of the potatoes. Dot with butter in the little valleys formed between the peaks. Sprinkle parsley evenly over the potatoes. Cover with aluminum foil (see Note) and bake until heated thoroughly (about 20 to 25 minutes depending upon whether or not the casserole has been refrigerated).

NOTE: After covering the mashed potatoes with aluminum foil, the dish may be refrigerated up to 24 hours before baking.

SERVES 12

DUCHESS POTATOES

Potato finery for the main-course plate at an elegant dinner party.

2 extra-large eggs
¾ teaspoon salt
2½ pounds russet potatoes, pared, boiled,
    and drained (page 328) (about 4 very
    large potatoes)
3 tablespoons butter
3 tablespoons butter, melted

Preheat the oven to 350° F. Butter one 9 × 13-inch baking dish and one 6 × 10-inch baking dish; set aside.

In a small mixing bowl, place the eggs and salt; using an electric mixer, beat slightly on medium speed. To the drained potatoes, add the egg mixture and 3 tablespoons butter. Using the electric mixer, beat the potato mixture on high speed until completely smooth, with *no lumps.*

Using a decorating bag fit with large open-star tip number 8B (page 383), pipe about 20 rosettes (page 390) of the potato mixture, side by side but not touching, onto the prepared baking dishes. Drizzle 3 tablespoons melted butter over the rosettes. Bake, uncovered, 10 minutes. Brown the Duchess Potatoes quickly under the broiler, about 5 inches from the heat. Use a small spatula to carefully transfer the Duchess Potatoes from the baking dishes onto individual plates or a serving platter.

SERVES 10

OVEN-BROWNED POTATOES

Small, new, russet or red potatoes
Butter
Vegetable oil
Pan drippings

Using a vegetable brush, scrub the potatoes well; do not pare. Place the potatoes in a saucepan; add hot water to cover. Cover the saucepan. Bring the potatoes to a boil over high heat; reduce the heat to medium and boil moderately 10 minutes, until *just tender* (the potatoes will cook further during browning). Drain the potatoes; place them on a wire rack and let stand until cool enough to handle (or, optionally, until completely cool).

Preheat the oven to 350° F. Butter a shallow baking pan large enough to accommodate, single layer, the number of potatoes to be oven browned; set aside.

Peel the potatoes and place in the prepared baking pan (see Note 1). Add enough equal amounts of butter and vegetable oil to the bottom of the baking pan to very thinly cover the pan bottom when the butter melts. If roasting meat simultaneously, spoon some of the meat-pan drippings over the potatoes for flavor and to enhance browning. (Be sure to leave sufficient drippings in the meat pan to make gravy, if planned.) (See Note 2.)

Place the potatoes in the oven and brown for 25 minutes. Turn the potatoes over; baste with pan drippings and continue browning an additional 20 minutes.

NOTE 1: After the potatoes have been peeled and placed in the prepared baking pan, the baking pan may be tightly covered with plastic wrap and the potatoes refrigerated up to 24 hours before completion of cooking.

NOTE 2: Although the boiled and peeled potatoes may be browned in the bottom of a pan in which meat is being roasted rather than in a separate baking pan, meats are generally roasted on a wire rack which does not leave sufficient space on the bottom of the pan to place the potatoes. If the potatoes are browned in the meat pan (or in a separate baking pan) in a 325° F. oven, allow an additional 15 minutes (1 hour total) for browning.

POTATO DUMPLINGS

3 pounds red potatoes
3 extra-large eggs
¾ cup regular (not instant) Cream of Wheat cereal, uncooked, or ¾ cup raw farina
1¼ cups all-purpose flour
1¼ teaspoons salt
¾ teaspoon sugar
¼ teaspoon ground nutmeg
¼ teaspoon ground cinnamon
Water
Salt
Crumb Topping (recipe follows)

Pare and boil the potatoes (page 328). Drain the potatoes well and press them through a ricer into a large mixing bowl; set aside. Place the eggs in a small mixing bowl; using an electric mixer, beat slightly on medium speed. Add the Cream of Wheat, flour, salt, sugar, nutmeg, and cinnamon; stir to combine. Add the egg mixture to the potatoes; stir until well combined.

With floured hands, make uniform balls about 1¾ inches in diameter and place on a piece of waxed paper. If the potato mixture is too sticky for easy handling, roll the balls lightly in a small amount of flour as you form them. Set aside.

Pour at least 3 quarts water into a large kettle. Add 1 teaspoon salt for each quart of water. Cover the kettle and bring the salted water to a boil over high heat. Drop the dumplings into the boiling water and simmer, uncovered, 20 minutes. Adjust the heat to maintain a simmer. Lift the dumplings out with a slotted spoon. Sprinkle Crumb Topping on each dumpling.

SERVES 10

Crumb Topping

3 tablespoons butter
2 tablespoons finely minced onions
½ cup fine, Dried Bread Crumbs (page 48)

In a small, heavy-bottomed skillet, melt the butter over medium heat. Place the onions in the skillet; sauté briefly (about 5 minutes), until tender. Add the crumbs and brown lightly.

POTATO PANCAKES WITH LINGONBERRIES

2 pounds russet potatoes (about 4 large
   potatoes)
¼ cup all-purpose flour
¾ teaspoon salt
¼ teaspoon pepper
½ teaspoon ground nutmeg
2 extra-large eggs
½ cup medium-grated onions (about
   1 medium onion)
1 tablespoon vegetable oil
2 tablespoons butter
1 tablespoon vegetable oil
2 tablespoons butter
1 cup commercially canned wild
   lingonberries in sugar

Pare the potatoes. Immediately after paring each potato, place it, whole, in a large mixing bowl of cold water to prevent discoloration; set aside. In a small mixing bowl, place the flour, salt, pepper, and nutmeg; stir to combine; set aside. Place the eggs in a medium mixing bowl; using an electric mixer, beat on medium speed only until the whites and yolks are blended. Add the flour mixture; beat only until blended. Add the onions; beat briefly to combine; set aside.

Remove one potato from the water and pat it dry with paper towels or a clean tea towel. Grate the potato coarsely. Place the grated potato in a sieve over a deep pan. With the back of your hand, press the grated potato to extract as much

liquid as possible. Immediately add the drained potatoes to the egg mixture; stir until the potatoes are thoroughly coated. Repeat the procedure with the 3 remaining potatoes, processing only 1 potato at a time to help prevent the potatoes from turning brown. Set the potato batter aside.

Preheat an electric skillet or a large, heavy-bottomed skillet on the range to medium-high heat (380° F. in an electric skillet). Place 1 tablespoon vegetable oil in the skillet. Using a spatula, spread the vegetable oil over the entire bottom of the skillet. Add 2 tablespoons butter. Tilt the skillet back and forth to blend the butter with the oil. When the oil and butter sizzle, use a ¼-cup measuring cup to drop 4 or 5 even, ¼ cups of potato batter, uniformly distributed, onto the hot skillet surface. Using a spatula, flatten each mound of batter into a pancake approximately 4 inches in diameter. Fry the pancakes 2 minutes, until the bottoms are golden brown; turn once and fry the second side an additional 2 minutes.

Arrange the potato pancakes on a warm platter and place, uncovered, in a warm oven while frying the remaining pancakes.

Blend an additional 1 tablespoon vegetable oil and 2 tablespoons butter in the skillet before frying the remaining potato pancakes.

Serve the pancakes immediately. Place the lingonberries in a small, crystal serving dish; let each diner spoon lingonberries over his/her potato pancakes at the table.

MAKES ABOUT 10 PANCAKES

POTATO PANCAKES WITH APPLESAUCE: Follow the Potato Pancakes with Lingonberries recipe, above, substituting 1 cup Plain Applesauce (page 344) for 1 cup lingonberries.

Yams

In the United States, the vegetable we call a "yam" is a variety of sweet potato. True yams are botanically unrelated to sweet potatoes, and are widely grown and consumed in the tropics. They are available in this country principally in Latin markets. Though a national misnomer, the yams called for in this cookbook are the sweet potato variety.

What we usually label a "sweet potato" has light yellow skin, with flesh that is pale yellow in color, and when cooked, is dry and mealy in texture. Yams have copper-colored skin and deep orange flesh which is moist and sweet when cooked. I personally prefer the texture and rich flavor of yams over sweet potatoes, and admit to being further swayed by their beautiful, intense orange color.

BAKED YAMS

Uniformly sized yams
Butter
Salt
Pepper

Preheat the oven to 350° F.

Using a vegetable brush, scrub the yams well; dry them with paper towels. Wrap each yam tightly in a single layer of aluminum foil. Place the wrapped yams directly on the center rack in the oven. Bake for 45 to 50 minutes, depending upon the size of the yams, until fork-tender.

To serve, remove and discard the aluminum foil. Using a sharp paring knife, cut a cross in the top of each yam. Press the ends of each yam toward the center to open the cross and force some of the cooked yam flesh through the opening. Tuck a pat of butter slightly into the exposed flesh on the top of each yam. Pass additional butter at the table. Set the table with salt and pepper for use by diners who wish to add these seasonings to their Baked Yams.

CINNAMON YAM BALLS

3 pounds yams (about 6 medium yams)
¾ teaspoon salt
¼ teaspoon pepper
½ teaspoon ground cinnamon
2 tablespoons butter, melted
10 marshmallows
3 tablespoons butter
¼ cup light corn syrup
1 cup packed light brown sugar
½ cup chopped pecans

Using a vegetable brush, scrub the yams well. Place the unpared yams in a large saucepan; add hot water to cover. Cover the saucepan. Bring the yams to a boil over high heat; reduce the heat to medium and cook at a low boil about 15 minutes, until the yams are just tender. The cooking time will depend upon the size of the yams. Drain the yams; place them on a wire rack and let stand until cool enough to handle.

Peel the yams, removing the thin layer of flesh directly beneath the skin to reveal the bright orange flesh, and place them in a large mixing bowl. Add the salt, pepper, cinnamon, and 2 tablespoons melted butter. Using an electric mixer, beat the yam mixture on medium-high speed until smooth and fluffy; set aside.

Preheat the oven to 350° F. Butter a 9 × 13-inch baking dish; set aside.

With your hands, roll the yam mixture around each marshmallow, making 10 yam balls, each about 2¼ inches in diameter. Place the yam balls, side by side but not touching, in the prepared baking dish; set aside.

In a small saucepan, melt 3 tablespoons butter over low heat. Add the corn syrup and brown sugar; stir to combine. Cook over low heat only until the mixture is smooth and blended, stirring constantly. Pour the corn syrup mixture evenly over the yam balls; sprinkle with the chopped pecans. Bake, uncovered, for 20 minutes.

SERVES 10

CANDIED YAMS

3 pounds yams (about 6 medium yams)
¼ teaspoon salt
½ cup packed light brown sugar
2 tablespoons butter
⅓ cup dark corn syrup
1 cup miniature marshmallows

Using a vegetable brush, scrub the yams well. Place the unpared yams in a large saucepan; add hot water to cover. Cover the saucepan. Bring the yams to a boil over high heat; reduce the heat to medium and cook at a low boil about 15 minutes, until the yams are just tender. The cooking time will depend upon the size of the yams. Avoid overcooking, causing the yams to become mushy. Drain the yams; place on a wire rack to cool.

Butter a 7 × 11-inch baking dish; set aside.

Peel the cooled yams, removing the thin layer of flesh directly beneath the skin to reveal the bright orange flesh. Cut the yams widthwise into 1½-inch chunks and arrange, single layer, in the prepared baking dish.

IMMEDIATELY BEFORE BAKING: Preheat the oven to 350° F. Sprinkle the salt over the yams. Then, distribute the brown sugar over the yams and dot with the butter. Drizzle the syrup back and forth over top. Immediately place the yams in the oven and bake, uncovered, for 20 minutes. Remove from the oven and baste. Scatter the marshmallows evenly over the yams. Bake an additional 5 minutes. Baste and serve.

SERVES 10

TO PREPARE CANDIED YAMS IN ADVANCE: Up to 1 day before serving, Candied Yams may be prepared through arranging them in the baking dish. Cover the dish with plastic wrap and refrigerate until ready to bake. Do not add the topping until immediately before baking. Placing the topping on Candied Yams in advance of baking will result in the brown sugar dissolving and sinking to the bottom of the baking dish

together with the syrup, adversely affecting the final quality of the glaze.

CANDIED YAMS WITH GOOSEBERRIES

½ cup gooseberry jam, home canned (page 755) or commercially canned
¼ cup packed light brown sugar
¼ teaspoon ground mace
2 tablespoons butter

Follow the Candied Yams recipe, above, through the sprinkling of salt over the yams. Then, discontinue following the recipe and proceed, as follows: In a small bowl, place the gooseberry jam, brown sugar, and mace; stir to combine. *Immediately before baking,* spoon the gooseberry jam mixture over the yams. Dot with the butter. Bake, uncovered, for 25 minutes.

SERVES 10

YAMS GRAND MARNIER WITH CRANBERRIES AND KUMQUATS

2 pounds yams (about 4 medium yams)
1¼ cups sugar
½ teaspoon ground cinnamon
½ teaspoon ground nutmeg
¼ teaspoon ground mace
1 12-ounce package fresh cranberries, washed and sorted (about 3½ cups)
⅓ cup kumquats halved lengthwise, seeded, and finely sliced widthwise
½ cup pecan halves
3 tablespoons Grand Marnier liqueur

Using a vegetable brush, scrub the yams well. Place the unpared yams in a large saucepan; add hot water to cover. Cover the saucepan. Bring the yams to a boil over high heat; reduce the heat to medium and cook at a low boil about 15 minutes, until the yams are just tender. The cooking time will depend upon the size of the

(Recipe continues on next page)

yams. Avoid overcooking, causing the yams to become mushy. Drain the yams; place them on a wire rack and let stand until cool.

Peel the cooled yams, removing the thin layer of flesh directly beneath the skin to reveal the bright orange flesh. Cut the yams widthwise into 1½-inch chunks; set aside.

Preheat the oven to 375° F. Butter one 1½-quart round baking dish *and* one 2-quart round baking dish; set aside.

In a large mixing bowl, place the sugar, cinnamon, nutmeg, and mace; stir to combine. Add the cranberries, kumquats, and pecans; stir to combine. Turn the cranberry mixture into the prepared 1½-quart baking dish; spread evenly. Bake, uncovered, for 30 minutes.

Remove the cranberry mixture from the oven. Add the Grand Marnier liqueur; stir to combine. Into the prepared 2-quart baking dish, spoon a small amount of the cranberry mixture to cover the bottom of the dish. Arrange the yams evenly over the cranberry mixture in the bottom of the 2-quart baking dish. Spoon the remaining cranberry mixture over the yams.

Cover and bake for 15 minutes, until heated through.

SERVES 8

Rutabagas

While rutabagas and turnips are related and share many characteristics, they are actually separate species in the same botanical genus as cabbage (*Brassica*). The common variety of rutabagas (also known as yellow turnips) has yellow flesh and light gold skin which changes to a deep purple mottled with green at the stem end, while bulbous turnips have white flesh and white skin which blends into a pretty purplish rose color at the top. The purple-hued parts of rutabagas and turnips are the parts which grow above the ground. Rutabagas are larger than turnips and have firmer flesh. Their distinct flavor is somewhat sweeter than that of turnips.

STEWED RUTABAGAS WITH ROOT VEGETABLES

Our family has always enjoyed the taste of rutabagas and I commonly serve them as a wintertime main course, using this recipe. A tossed, green salad and coarse, dark bread are good accompaniments, followed by fruit for dessert.

1¼ cups whole milk
1¼ cups water
¾ teaspoon salt
¼ teaspoon white pepper
4 cups pared rutabagas, cut into ½-inch cubes (about 1½ pounds rutabagas)
1 cup pared, sliced carrots
½ pound pared, red potatoes cut into ½-inch cubes
¾ cup sliced leeks (white and greenish white parts only) (1 large or 2 medium leeks)
¼ cup coarsely diced green bell peppers
⅓ cup sliced celery
2 tablespoons butter
¼ pound pasteurized process American cheese, shredded
¼ cup rolled saltines (5 saltines)

In a large saucepan, place the milk, water, salt, and white pepper; stir to blend. Bring the mixture to a simmer over medium heat. Add the rutabagas, carrots, potatoes, leeks, green peppers, and celery; stir to combine. Cover the saucepan and return the mixture to a simmer. Reduce the heat and cook about 20 minutes, until the vegetables are tender. Add the butter, cheese, and saltines. Stir gently over low heat until the cheese melts.

SERVES 4 AS A MAIN COURSE OR 8 AS A SIDE DISH

SERVING SUGGESTIONS: Serve in soup bowls as a main course or in sauce dishes as a side dish.

Spinach

TO COOK AND SERVE SPINACH

Remove from the spinach and discard the stems and any yellow leaves. Wash the spinach leaves twice, making certain that all the sand has been removed. Place the spinach leaves in a large kettle; add water to cover. Cover the kettle. Bring the spinach to a boil over high heat; reduce the heat and simmer 4 minutes. Drain the spinach well in a colander.

Chop the spinach on a cutting board and place in a mixing bowl. Add 1 tablespoon plus 1 teaspoon melted butter per pound of raw spinach used. Toss to coat the spinach. If necessary, rewarm the spinach in a covered saucepan over very low heat, stirring often.

Serve family style in a vegetable dish or in individual sauce dishes. Garnish with hard-cooked egg slices (page 264). Serve with lemon wedges or pass a cruet of cider vinegar at the table.

1 POUND OF RAW SPINACH SERVES 2 OR 3

Squash

BAKED ACORN SQUASH

Acorn squash are also known as Des Moines squash. They are commonly dark green and often mottled with orange. There is also an all-orange variety of acorn squash called Gold Acorn squash. Des Moines squash and Gold Acorn squash are similar in flavor.

2 acorn squash
1 tablespoon plus 1 teaspoon butter, softened
Salt (optional)
½ cup packed dark brown sugar
¼ cup (4 tablespoons) butter

Preheat the oven to 400° F.

Wash the squash; dry them with paper towels. Using a large, sharp, rigid knife, cut the squash in half lengthwise. Using a tablespoon, scrape out and discard the seeds and stringy centers of the squash. Brush the yellow flesh of each squash half (including the top rims) generously with 1 teaspoon butter. Lightly sprinkle salt over the flesh, if desired. Place the squash, cut side down, in a 9 × 13-inch ungreased baking dish. Bake, uncovered, for 30 minutes.

Remove the squash from the oven and reduce the oven temperature to 350° F. Using a spatula, turn the squash cut side up. Place 2 tablespoons packed brown sugar and 1 tablespoon butter in the cavity of each squash half. Return the squash to the oven and bake, uncovered, for an additional 15 to 30 minutes, depending upon the size of the squash. Bake the squash until the flesh is fork-tender and the top rim of each squash half is golden brown. Be careful not to overbake. Serve 1 squash half per person.

SERVES 4

VARIATION: When baking Gold Acorn Squash, substitute light brown sugar for the dark brown sugar.

ZUCCHINI WITH WALNUTS

1 teaspoon vegetable oil
1½ tablespoons butter
¾ pound green and yellow zucchini (1 medium zucchini of each color), sliced ¼ inch thick
⅓ cup shallots thinly sliced and separated into rings
3 tablespoons water
2 tablespoons dry red wine
¼ cup broken English walnuts

In a medium, heavy-bottomed skillet, heat the vegetable oil over medium heat. Using a spatula,

(Recipe continues on next page)

spread the vegetable oil over the entire bottom of the skillet. Add the butter. Tilt the skillet back and forth to blend the butter with the oil. Place the zucchini and shallots in the skillet; sauté until lightly brown (about 5 minutes). Reduce the heat to low. When the skillet cools slightly, add the water and wine; stir to blend. Simmer the mixture 3 minutes to reduce the liquid. Add the walnuts; stir to combine; heat through.

SERVES 4

Tomatoes

TOMATO BASKETS OF VEGETABLES

6 medium-sized, firm but ripe tomatoes
¾ cup freshly grated Parmesan cheese
 (page 46)
½ teaspoon lemon pepper
6 Vegetable Bundles, each containing 2
 carrots, 2 green beans, and 2 asparagus
 spears (page 324)
½ cup water
½ cup frozen tiny peas
½ cup frozen corn
1 teaspoon dried leaf basil
1 tablespoon butter, melted
¼ teaspoon salt
2 tablespoons butter, melted

Blanch the tomatoes (page 44) about 30 seconds and peel. Using a sharp knife, slice ¼ to ½ inch off the stem end of each tomato, creating a flat surface on the top of each tomato. Using a grapefruit knife, carefully carve out and discard the center of each tomato, leaving ½ inch flesh around the periphery and bottom of each tomato to form a basket. Remove and discard any remaining seed pouches.

Sprinkle 2 teaspoons Parmesan cheese evenly around the inside of each tomato. Sprinkle lemon pepper in each tomato, proportionately dividing the ½ teaspoon among the 6 tomatoes. Place a Vegetable Bundle in each tomato, leaning it against the side of the basket. (When making the Vegetable Bundles, the length of the vegetables will depend upon the size of the tomatoes; the bundles should stand attractively above the edge of the tomatoes, but must be short enough to stand securely.) Set aside.

Pour ½ cup water into a small saucepan. Cover the saucepan and bring the water to a boil over high heat. Place the peas, corn, and basil in the saucepan; cover and bring to a high simmer. Reduce the heat and simmer 2 minutes. Drain the vegetables well in a sieve; then, return them to the saucepan. Add 1 tablespoon melted butter and the salt; using a wooden spoon, toss carefully until combined. Using a teaspoon, fill the baskets with the peas and corn mixture. Place the Tomato Baskets in the top of a large steamer pan.

JUST BEFORE SERVING: Steam the Tomato Baskets *about 1 to 2 minutes only,* until warm. Then, immediately remove the top section of the steamer from the bottom pan. Using a soft brush, brush melted butter over the tomatoes, Vegetable Bundles, and peas and corn mixture. Serve immediately. If the Tomato Baskets are steamed too long or stand in a hot steamer after being warmed, the tomatoes will lose their basket shape and may even fall apart.

SERVES 6

SERVING SUGGESTIONS: A handsome and tasty complement to meat dishes, especially beef, veal, and lamb.

SCALLOPED TOMATOES

1 pint home-canned Tomatoes (page 736),
   undrained, or 1 16-ounce can commercial
   whole, peeled tomatoes, undrained
1 tablespoon butter
½ cup minced onions
¼ cup finely chopped celery
¼ cup Dried Bread Crumbs (page 48)
1 tablespoon finely snipped, fresh parsley
½ teaspoon sugar
⅛ teaspoon pepper
¼ teaspoon salt (omit if commercially
   canned tomatoes contain salt)
1 tablespoon butter, melted
1¼ cups tarragon croutons (see Herb
   Croutons, page 48)

Preheat the oven to 350° F. Butter a 1-quart
round baking dish; set aside.

Place the undrained tomatoes in a medium
mixing bowl. Using a small knife, cut the tomatoes into quarters or eighths, depending upon
their size. (The tomatoes should be in large
chunks.) Set aside. In a small, heavy-bottomed
skillet, melt 1 tablespoon butter over medium
heat. Tilt the skillet back and forth to completely
cover the bottom with the melted butter. Place
the onions and celery in the skillet; sauté lightly
(about 5 minutes); do not brown. Using a slotted spoon, remove the onions and celery from
the skillet and place in the bowl containing the
tomatoes; stir to combine; set aside.

In a small mixing bowl, place the crumbs,
parsley, sugar, pepper, and salt (if used); stir to
combine. Add 1 tablespoon melted butter; stir to
combine. Add the crumb mixture to the tomato
mixture; stir to combine.

Spoon ½ of the tomato mixture into the prepared baking dish (see Note). Scatter ½ of the
croutons evenly over the tomato mixture. Repeat the layers, using the remaining ½ of the
tomato mixture and croutons. Bake, uncovered,
for 25 minutes. The mixture will be bubbly.

SERVES 6

NOTE: Do not assemble the ingredients in the
baking dish until shortly before baking so the
croutons will remain whole.

STEWED TOMATOES

1 pint home-canned Tomatoes (page 736),
   undrained, or 1 16-ounce can commercial
   whole, peeled tomatoes, undrained
1 tablespoon finely chopped onions
1 tablespoon finely chopped green bell
   peppers
2 medium-sized, fresh basil leaves, finely
   snipped
¼ teaspoon sugar
⅛ teaspoon salt
Dash of pepper
Dash of ground nutmeg

Place the undrained tomatoes in a medium
saucepan. Using a small knife, cut the tomatoes
into quarters or eighths, depending upon their
size. (The tomatoes should be in large chunks.)
Add the onions, green peppers, basil, sugar, salt,
pepper, and nutmeg; stir to combine. Cover the
saucepan and bring the mixture to a boil over
medium-high heat. Reduce the heat to low and
simmer 10 minutes, until the onions and green
peppers are tender. Serve in individual sauce
dishes.

SERVES 4

Other Vegetable Recipes

Fruits

Midwest woods, pastures, and marshes are the berries! In these tranquil oases, blueberries, cranberries, gooseberries, black and red raspberries, strawberries, elderberries, blackberries, mulberries, currants, dewberries, saskatoonberries, buffaloberries, nannyberries, huckleberries, and a number of other edible berries still grow in the wild.

On dewy summer mornings, Heartland jam and jelly makers and pie bakers don their long-sleeved shirts and head for the brambles near a meadowlark-inhabited pasture. It's time for their annual pilgrimage to pick raspberries for a day of canning and baking, silhouetting their mothers and grandmothers before them.

The white, puffy kite tail trailing a 747 jet high above and the drone of a modern farm tractor in a nearby field would seem to render the berry-gathering venture an anachronism. But in Middle America—particularly the rural expanses—people continue to live in a pleasant blend with nature while pursuing contemporary lives embellished with modern conveniences and primed with the technical knowledge of the day. Gathering wild raspberries to make jam and a Master of Agriculture degree are not a dichotomy—they interweave to make the fabric of the Midwest lifestyle. Passionate efforts pervade to preserve the integrity of the Midwest environment so this desirable way of life can be perpetuated.

In spite of the encroachment of agriculture and industry, nature continues to serve up a myriad of wild fruits—in addition to berries—for contemporary Heartlanders to harvest and savor: wild plums for jam and butter; crab apples for pickling and jelly; wild blackcherries for jelly and wine; hawthorn fruit for fresh eating and jelly; grapes, chokecherries, and ground-cherries for jelly and jam; pawpaws for breads, cookies, and ice cream; and persimmons for immediate eating and use in breads, pies, and puddings.

While the thrill and enchantment of reaping these treasures in the wild have made gathering expeditions an enduring activity, nowadays most of the fruit picked by hand for private, home consumption is grown domestically. Farm families and suburbanites alike plant and tend apple, cherry, peach, pear, and other fruit trees, and their gardens often include strawberry patches, raspberry bushes, and grapevines. In addition, commercial apple orchards and U-Pick fields of lush strawberries and raspberries dot the countryside and provide a source of homegrown fruit for ardent canners (and those with big freezers) who need large quantities, and for city dwellers and others who do not maintain fruit trees and gardens.

Of course, a plethora of exquisite fruits grown in other parts of the United States and around the world are available in Midland produce markets and play an important part in established eating patterns. For example, Colorado peaches are especially prized here for canning, freezing, pies, homemade ice cream, and just plain good eating.

Apples are the most widespread fruit grown commercially in the Heartland. Among a lengthy list of varieties successfully grown here, many people, including this writer, consider Jonathans the forerunner for eating. When you pick one off the tree, polish it to a luster on your jeans, and bite into it, the firm, supremely flavored flesh snaps, releasing luscious juice which begins to roll down your cheeks. Could it have been a Jonathan that Eve presented to Adam?

In the light of such exquisite quality, you may wonder why only 9 percent of the nation's commercial apple supply comes from Midwest orchards. Three factors seem to be at play. First, Midland farmers, stewards of huge tracts of our country's most fertile land, have traditionally raised grains and legumes, a great deal of which is fed to livestock for the production of meat and other animal by-products. Second, outside the metropolitan areas, the Midwest generally lacks a sufficiently dense population to maintain labor-intensive fruit farming. Third, many kinds of fruit trees are in jeopardy of survival through frigid winters which often bring with them heavy ice and snow storms. These considerations, as well as a relatively short growing season, account for the fact that fruit is not one of the Midwest's largest commercial commodities.

Even though Michigan—fruit standard-bearer among the twelve Midwest states—ranked fifth in the nation in 1996 cash receipts for fruits and nuts, only 6 percent of that state's total cash receipts for agricultural commodities derived from these food products. But this is not to minimize the importance of delicious Michigan fruit in our nation's fruit supply. Connoisseurs across the continent nab Michigan blueberries and cherries when they hit greengrocers' display counters. Also, excellent peaches, apricots, nectarines, and grapes hail from the Wolverine State.

Another important American fruit thrives in the northerly reaches of the Midwest. When Thanksgiving rolls around, check your package of fresh cranberries. It may have come from northern Wisconsin, where approximately one-third of the U.S. cranberry crop is produced.

In gauging the role of fruit in Midwest eating, readers should not be misled by the relative brevity of this chapter. It doesn't take a recipe in a cookbook to enjoy most fruit at its finest—fresh and ripened to its height of flavor, texture, and juiciness. Across the Heartland, fresh fruit for dessert is a standard, and gorgeous compotes of beautiful, kaleidoscopic fruits elicit raves from families and epicures alike (see Fresh Fruit Compote, page 346).

A goodly amount of Midwest fresh fruit lands between flaky crust in out-of-this-world homemade pies, and in cobblers and other dreamy desserts. For instance, spring is typified by rosy red rhubarb pies fresh from the oven, and a host of cobbler-like rhubarb desserts often served with vanilla ice cream or topped with a generous dollop of whipped cream (see Rhubarb Rapture, page 754). And most Mid-America cooks don't let autumn slip by without making Apple Crisp (page 649) at least once.

Midwesterners' fondness for canned fruit remains on a continuum from two or three generations ago, when it was a necessary mainstay in farm family diets, to now, when home-canned fruit is considered delectable gourmet fare. Peaches, applesauce, apricots, plums, pears, and berries are "put by" in the kitchens of modern-day canners who take pleasure in preparing and serving fine food and who pursue canning primarily as a hobby. Jelly, jam, preserves, and conserve makers utilize gallons of fresh, summer fruit to stock their larders with row after row of filled jars in a rainbow of breathtaking colors, ready for winter dining and holiday gift giving.

Opening these jars of Mother Earth's bounty in January is an infallible way to lift sagging winter spirits. The "whisssh" of a newly opened jar of black raspberry jam releases that heavenly aroma of raspberries, as pungent as the morning the berries were picked and dropped in the pail on the gatherer's arm.

AMBROSIA

Ambrosia, the food of the Greek and Roman gods, is an appropriate name for this time-honored dessert, which apparently dates back to the nineteenth century. Worthy creations are awarded permanence.

4 medium-large oranges, sectioned
  (page 47)
Juice of 1 medium-large orange
⅓ cup flaked coconut
3 bananas

In a medium mixing bowl, place the orange sections, orange juice, and coconut. Just before serving, slice the bananas and add to the mixture; using a wooden mixing spoon, stir to combine. Spoon into crystal fruit dishes.

SERVES 8

CINNAMON APPLESAUCE

A fixture in Midwest cooking.

2 pounds cooking apples (about 5 large
  apples) (McIntosh is an excellent variety
  for applesauce)
⅔ cup water*
½ cup sugar
1 teaspoon freshly squeezed, strained lemon
  juice
½ teaspoon ground cinnamon

  **Reduce the water to ½ cup for extra-thick
  applesauce.*

Wash the apples. Pare, quarter, and core the apples. In a large saucepan, place the apples and water. Cover the saucepan. Bring the apples to a boil over high heat. Reduce the heat and simmer 15 to 20 minutes, or until the apples are tender, stirring occasionally. Add the sugar and stir constantly until dissolved. Add the lemon juice and cinnamon; stir to blend and combine. Remove from the heat.

Some varieties of apples remain in whole pieces after cooking, while other varieties puree when stirred during the cooking process. After the applesauce is made, press it through a food mill if desired.

MAKES ABOUT 3 CUPS

PLAIN APPLESAUCE: Follow the Cinnamon Applesauce recipe, above, eliminating the ground cinnamon.

SCALLOPED APPLES

¼ cup granulated sugar
¼ cup packed light brown sugar
1 tablespoon plus 2 teaspoons all-purpose flour
¼ teaspoon ground cinnamon
¼ teaspoon ground nutmeg
¼ teaspoon ground mace
8 cups Golden Delicious apples, pared, quartered, cored, and sliced ⅛ inch thick (about 6 medium apples), divided
2 tablespoons freshly squeezed, strained lemon juice, divided
2 tablespoons cognac
4 cups dried raisin bread cubes (page 48), divided
¼ cup plus 2 tablespoons (6 tablespoons) butter, melted
½ cup chopped, unsalted peanuts
2 tablespoons butter

Preheat the oven to 350° F. Butter a 7 × 11-inch baking dish; set aside.

In a small mixing bowl, place the granulated sugar, brown sugar, flour, cinnamon, nutmeg, and mace; stir to combine; set aside.

Pare, quarter, core, and slice 4 cups apples; place in a large mixing bowl. Sprinkle 1 tablespoon lemon juice over the apples; toss to coat. Prepare the remaining 4 cups sliced apples; add to the mixing bowl containing the sliced apples. Sprinkle the remaining 1 tablespoon lemon juice over the apples; toss to coat. Sprinkle the cognac over the apples; toss to combine. Sprinkle the sugar mixture over the apples; toss to coat. Cover with plastic wrap; set aside.

Place the bread cubes in a large mixing bowl; drizzle the melted butter evenly over the top. Toss until the bread cubes are coated. Arrange ½ of the bread cubes evenly over the bottom of the prepared baking dish. Spoon the apple mixture evenly over the bread cubes. Scatter the peanuts evenly over the top. Dot with 2 tablespoons butter.

Cover the baking dish with aluminum foil.

Bake for 45 minutes. Remove from the oven. Remove the foil and spoon the remaining ½ bread cubes evenly over the top of the apple mixture. Bake, *uncovered,* for an additional 15 minutes.

SERVES 12

FRESH PEARS STUFFED WITH RUM-FLAVORED RICOTTA CHEESE

A sublime dessert.

15 ounces ricotta cheese
3 tablespoons light rum
1 tablespoon honey
6 large, ripe Comice or Bartlett pears
2 tablespoons freshly squeezed, strained lemon juice
½ teaspoon powdered instant coffee (to powder instant coffee, process in blender*)
12 sprigs of fresh mint for decoration

*If a blender is not available, a food processor may be used; however, it is difficult to achieve a fine powder using a food processor.

In a blender (see Note), place the ricotta cheese, rum, and honey; process in the blender until smooth. Place the cheese mixture in a small bowl; cover and refrigerate until cold.

Just before serving, cut the pears in half lengthwise; core and pare. Immediately after coring and paring each pear half, brush it lightly with lemon juice to prevent discoloration. Spoon about 2 tablespoons of the cheese mixture over the core cavity area of each pear half. Sprinkle the instant coffee over the cheese mixture on each pear half. Place each pear half on a small plate and decorate each plate with a sprig of mint. Serve immediately. Provide a small knife and fork with each diner's table service.

NOTE: If a blender is not available, a food processor may be used.

SERVES 12

FRESH FRUIT COMPOTE

1½ cups freshly squeezed orange juice
1 red apple, unpared, quartered, cored, and sliced
1 Granny Smith apple, unpared, quartered, cored, and sliced
1 ripe, juicy pear, pared, quartered, cored, and sliced
1 banana, peeled and sliced
1 large red grapefruit, peeled and sectioned (page 47)
2 large oranges, peeled and sectioned (page 47)
½ small cantaloupe, pared, cut lengthwise into 1-inch-wide strips, and sliced
½ small honeydew melon, pared, cut lengthwise into 1-inch-wide strips, and sliced
⅔ fresh pineapple, pared, cored, sliced, and cut into bite-sized pieces
1½ cups seedless, red grapes
1½ cups strawberries, hulled (page 23) and cut in half lengthwise
2 kiwis, ends trimmed (cut away the core at the stem end), pared, and sliced ¼ inch thick

Pour the orange juice into a large mixing bowl. Prepare the apples, pear, and banana, and mix with the orange juice as they are prepared to prevent discoloration. Prepare the remaining ingredients and add to the mixing bowl; wait to combine until all the fruit has been prepared to help avoid tearing the fruit pieces by over-handling.

Using a wooden spoon, combine the fruit carefully and turn into a glass compote or bowl. To serve, ladle the fruit into crystal sherbet glasses or sauce dishes at the table. Place on small, doily-lined plates.

SERVES 12

OPTIONAL GARNISH: The kiwi slices may be reserved and used to garnish the compote by overlapping them around the edge of the bowl. Additional kiwi slices may be required.

ACCOMPANIMENT SUGGESTION: At the table, pass a beautiful plate on which is arranged one or more of the following cookies: Scotch Shortbread (page 639), Butterscotch Icebox Cookies (page 644), or Lace Cookies (page 627).

UGLI FRUIT, KIWI, AND STRAWBERRY DESSERT SUITE

Ugli (pronounced "ugly") is the trademark name of a Jamaican fruit believed to be a cross between a tangerine and a grapefruit (or, some authorities say, a pomelo). While its thick, somewhat loose-fitting skin of lime green to light orange color may not be superglamorous, the ultra-juicy citrus fruit it encases is a radiant yellow-orange and anything but ugly. Ugli fruit ranges in size from a good-sized orange to a large grapefruit, and its flavor is best described as acid-sweet. Peel it and eat it like a tangerine, or cut it in half and eat it as you would a grapefruit. The recipe that follows calls for the fruit to be sectioned. Available from December to about May, Ugli fruit is a superior, change-of-pace citrus for use in both desserts and salads. It is sometimes known as "uniq" fruit.

1 large Ugli fruit
2 kiwis
½ pound fresh strawberries
4 small sprigs of fresh mint for decoration

Peel the Ugli fruit; remove all remaining white membrane. Section the Ugli fruit (page 47), retaining all juice; set aside. Trim off both ends of the kiwis and cut away the core at the stem end. Pare the kiwis and slice them widthwise ¼ inch thick; set aside. Wash the strawberries; using a strawberry huller, remove the hulls (page 23). Cut the strawberries in half lengthwise; set aside.

Artistically arrange the prepared fruit in 4 crystal sherbet glasses. Pour the reserved Ugli fruit juice over the fruit in each glass. Decorate each serving with a small sprig of fresh mint and place it on a small, doily-lined plate.

SERVES 4

ACCOMPANIMENT SUGGESTIONS: *ACCOMPANIMENT SUGGESTIONS:* Place 2 Coconut Macaroons (page 611), Frosted Orange Cookies (page 615), or Almond-Butter Puffs (page 608) on the doily-lined plate under each serving; or, arrange all 3 types of cookies on a lovely plate and pass at the table.

HOT CURRIED FRUIT

1 17-ounce can commercial unpeeled apricot halves
1 16½-ounce can commercial pitted Royal Anne white cherries
1 16-ounce can commercial sliced pears
1 16-ounce can commercial cling peach halves
1 15¼-ounce can commercial pineapple chunks
1 17-ounce can commercial figs
1 16½-ounce can commercial white grapes
1 16-ounce can commercial pitted dark sweet cherries
1 16½-ounce can commercial gooseberries
1 cup packed light brown sugar
1 tablespoon curry powder
½ teaspoon ground ginger
2 tablespoons cornstarch
½ cup (¼ pound) butter

Preheat the oven to 350°F. Butter a 10 × 15-inch (4-quart) baking dish; set aside.

In a sieve, drain the apricots, Royal Anne cherries, pears, peaches, and pineapple chunks, reserving the mixed juice. Place the drained fruit in a very large mixing bowl; set aside. Measure 1½ cups reserved mixed juice; set aside. (Reserve any remaining mixed juice for other uses.) Then, drain the figs, grapes, and dark cherries; if desired, reserve the juices from these fruits for other uses. Add the drained fruit to the mixing bowl containing the first-drained fruit. Using a wooden mixing spoon, *carefully* combine the fruits. Turn the mixed fruits into the prepared baking dish. Drain the gooseberries and carefully distribute them over the mixed fruit; set aside.

In a small mixing bowl, place the brown sugar, curry powder, ginger, and cornstarch; stir to combine; set aside. In a small saucepan, melt the butter over low heat. Remove from the heat; add the brown sugar mixture and stir well. Add the 1½ cups reserved mixed juice; stir to combine. Cook the fruit juice mixture over medium heat until smooth and thick, stirring continuously. Pour the mixture evenly over the fruit (see Note). Bake, uncovered, 35 minutes, until completely heated and bubbly.

NOTE: At this point, the baking dish may be covered with plastic wrap and the curried fruit refrigerated up to 24 hours prior to baking. (Bake uncovered.)

SERVES 16

SERVING SUGGESTIONS
• An excellent brunch dish.

• Serve with ham, poultry, and game birds.

BROILED GRAPEFRUIT

3 large red grapefruit
3 maraschino cherries, cut in half lengthwise
2 tablespoons packed light brown sugar
2 tablespoons pure maple syrup
2 tablespoons butter, melted
2 tablespoons cream sherry (optional)

Preheat the broiler.

Cut the grapefruit in half and remove the seeds. Using a grapefruit knife, cut around the meat in each grapefruit section to loosen the fruit from the membrane. Arrange the grapefruit halves in a shallow, flat-bottomed baking dish. Place half a cherry, skin side up, in the center of each grapefruit half. Sprinkle 1 teaspoon brown sugar over each grapefruit half. Then, drizzle 1 teaspoon maple syrup evenly over each half. Lightly brush 1 teaspoon melted

(Recipe continues on next page)

butter over each grapefruit half, *including the rind and the cherry.*

Broil the grapefruit, 4 inches from the heat, about 8 minutes, until golden. Watch the grapefruit closely. If they begin to overbrown, immediately remove them from the broiler. When done, remove the grapefruit from the broiler and drizzle 1 teaspoon sherry over each grapefruit half. Serve on small plates or in small sauce dishes. Place either the small plates or sauce dishes containing the Broiled Grapefruit on slightly larger, doily-lined service plates.

SERVES 6

SERVING SUGGESTION: This is nice served as a first course on a brunch or holiday breakfast menu.

BAKED BRANDIED ORANGES

4 small, seedless, thin-skinned oranges
2 tablespoons Grand Marnier liqueur
8 small, seedless, red grapes for garnish
1 kiwi for garnish
1½ cups sugar
1 tablespoon butter

Wash the oranges, removing any stickers and stamped-on brand names or other markings (use a small amount of kitchen cleanser on a damp sponge; then, rinse the oranges well).

Bring a covered kettle of water to a boil over high heat. Drop the oranges into the boiling water and boil briskly, uncovered, for 20 minutes, or until the skins are tender when pierced with a sharp fork. Turn the oranges often during cooking. Using a slotted spoon, remove the oranges from the boiling water and place them on several layers of paper towels. Reserve 1 cup of the water in which the oranges were boiled.

Preheat the oven to 400° F. Butter a 9¾ × 9¾ × 2-inch-deep baking dish (with cover); set aside.

When the oranges are cool enough to handle, carefully trim away the stem ends. Cut the oranges in half widthwise. Carefully cut out most of the central white pith at the center of each half. Arrange the orange halves, cut side up, in the prepared baking dish. Drizzle ¾ teaspoon Grand Marnier liqueur over the flesh of each orange half. Place a grape in the center of each half; set aside.

Trim off both ends of the kiwi and cut away the core at the stem end. Pare the kiwi and slice it widthwise ³⁄₁₆ inch thick. Select the 4 largest slices; reserve the remaining slices for other uses. Cut each of the 4 retained slices in half. Using an X-Acto knife or a small paring knife, make a crescent-shaped cut in the center of each piece of kiwi to cut away the white center flesh. Fit a piece of kiwi around the grape on each orange half; set aside.

In a small saucepan, place the sugar and the 1 cup reserved water in which the oranges were boiled. Bring to a boil over medium-high heat, stirring constantly until the sugar dissolves; boil 3 minutes. Pour the hot sugar mixture over the oranges. Place 2 small pieces of butter on each orange half (about ⅓ teaspoon per half).

Cover the baking dish and bake the oranges for 40 minutes, until translucent, basting twice. Baste again before serving.

At their own option, diners may eat only the orange flesh which separates easily from the skin with the aid of a knife and fork, or they may eat the tender orange skin as well as the flesh.

SERVES 8

SERVING SUGGESTIONS: Serve as an accompaniment/garnish with ham, pork, and wild game dishes.

BAKED FRUIT

12 bite-sized pitted prunes
1 cup water
1 20-ounce can commercial crushed pineapple, undrained
4 ounces shredded, medium cheddar cheese (1 cup)
½ cup sugar

3 tablespoons all-purpose flour
¼ teaspoon salt
¼ teaspoon ground allspice
4 commercially canned, unpeeled apricot
   halves, cut into thirds vertically
1 cup Plain Croutons (page 48)

In a small saucepan, place the prunes and water. Bring the prunes to a boil, uncovered, over high heat; reduce the heat and simmer 1 minute. Remove from the heat. Cover the saucepan and let the prunes stand to cool.

Preheat the oven to 350° F. Butter a 6 × 10-inch baking dish; set aside.

In a medium mixing bowl, place the pineapple, cheese, sugar, flour, salt, and allspice; stir to combine. Turn the mixture into the prepared baking dish. Press the prunes and apricots lightly and decoratively into the pineapple mixture in the following pattern:

Make 6 rows of fruit across the 6-inch (narrow) way of the dish, using 2 prunes and 2 pieces of apricot in each row, and alternating the fruit, as follows:

First row—prune, apricot, prune, apricot
Second row—apricot, prune, apricot, prune
Repeat the 2 rows twice (see illustration).

Arrange the apricot pieces diagonally, skin side up.

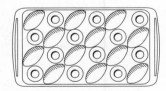

Scatter the Plain Croutons evenly over the top. Bake, uncovered, for 30 minutes.

SERVES 8

SERVING SUGGESTIONS
 • A delicious accompaniment for ham, pork, and chicken.

 • An excellent side dish for a buffet brunch.

Other Fruit Recipes

NOTE: Recipes for breads, sauces, beverages, additional pies, cakes, and cookies, and other items which include fruit may be found in the index.

Sandwiches

I t's a foregone conclusion that, from coast to coast, more hamburgers and hotdogs find their way between halves of buns than any other sandwich filling. Ham and cheese, BLT (bacon, lettuce, and tomato), peanut butter and jelly, and tuna salad would be safely among the beloved warhorses vying for position on the runners-up tally.

Halfway between our shores, there are some other venerated fillings close to sandwich lovers' hearts. I would put money on egg salad for the winner in this category. (See pages 261–262 for more about this darling of the Midwest Dagwoods.) Tying for my bet to place in this Heartland sandwich derby would be meat salad and cold meat loaf. A U.S. Department of Agriculture nationwide survey* shows that more meat is consumed per household in the Midwest than in any other region of the country. The abundance of leftover beef and pork roasts and hams have traditionally been ground with sweet pickles and onions, and mixed with mayonnaise and other seasonings to make incredibly tasty lunch sandwiches, while cold meat loaf, catsup (or chili sauce), and leaf lettuce are the fixings for a Heartland Hall of Famer.

If you select the fillings and condiments judiciously, sandwiches can be 4-star healthful eating, helping to meet many of the recommended daily requirements on the U.S. government's 1992 Food Guide Pyramid (page 790). Sandwiches can be as trendy and attractive as your imagination lets them be. So have fun! Assemble smart, with-it combinations of foods and seasonings between slices of interesting breads and rolls for fashionable meals. Scan the dozens of sandwich ideas in this chapter to get your creative juices going.

*USDA Food Consumption Survey 1977–78. Reports H-7, H-8, and H-10, 1983.

Cold Sandwiches

BEEF SALAD SANDWICHES

Meat salad—one of the best sandwich fillings ever concocted. If you don't happen to have a meat grinder (page 49), it's worth acquiring one if only to make these delicious sandwiches from your leftover meats. (For additional meat salad sandwich recipes, see Pork Salad Sandwiches [right column] and Ham Salad Sandwiches [page 352].)

1½ cups cold, ground, cooked roast beef
    (use the coarse blade on the meat
    grinder*; page 49)
¼ cup ground onions (about 1 small
    onion)
¼ cup chopped sweet gherkin pickles
2 tablespoons pickle juice (from jar of
    sweet gherkin pickles)
¼ teaspoon salt
⅛ teaspoon pepper
¼ cup Miracle Whip salad dressing
6 slices whole-wheat bread, homemade
    (page 419) or commercially baked
3 sandwich-sized pieces of leaf lettuce

*If a meat grinder is not available, a food
 processor may be used, although the results
 will not be as satisfactory (see pages 49–50).
 If using a food processor, drop the meat into
 the feeding tube in batches, removing each
 batch from the work bowl before proceeding to
 the next batch. The onions may be processed in
 one batch.*

In a medium mixing bowl, place the roast beef, onions, pickles, pickle juice, salt, pepper, and salad dressing; stir until well combined. Spread the beef salad equally on 3 slices of bread. Arrange 1 piece of leaf lettuce over the beef salad in each sandwich. Cover the sandwiches with the remaining 3 slices of bread. Cut the sandwiches in half diagonally.

MAKES 3 SANDWICHES

PORK SALAD SANDWICHES

3 cups cold, ground, cooked pork (use
    the coarse blade on the meat grinder*;
    page 49)
⅓ cup sweet pickle relish, including some
    of the pickle juice
½ cup Miracle Whip salad dressing
10 slices of at least 2 breads of choice, such
    as oat bran bread, onion bread, and
    Honey-Seed Bread (page 421) (an even
    number of slices of each kind of bread)
Sandwich-sized lettuce leaves of at least
    2 varieties

*If a meat grinder is not available, a food
 processor may be used, although the results
 will not be as satisfactory (see pages 49–50).
 If using a food processor, drop the meat into
 the feeding tube in batches, removing each
 batch from the work bowl before proceeding to
 the next batch.*

In a medium mixing bowl, place the pork, pickle relish, and salad dressing; stir to combine. Turn the pork salad into a serving bowl. Arrange the bread in a bread cloth on a bread tray. Place the lettuce leaves on a small, separate serving plate or arrange them around a serving plate under the bowl of pork salad. Let the diners make their own sandwiches.

MAKES 5 SANDWICHES (2½ CUPS PORK SALAD)

HAM SALAD SANDWICHES

1 pound (4 cups) cold, ground, fully
  cooked ham (use the coarse blade on the
  meat grinder*; page 49)
1/3 cup sweet pickle relish
2 tablespoons snipped, fresh chives
1 cup Miracle Whip salad dressing
12 slices bread of choice
6 sandwich-sized pieces of leaf lettuce

*If a meat grinder is not available, a food
processor may be used, although the results
will not be as satisfactory (see pages 49–50).
If using a food processor, drop the meat into
the feeding tube in batches, removing each
batch from the work bowl before proceeding to
the next batch.*

In a medium mixing bowl, place the ham, pickle
relish, chives, and salad dressing; stir to combine.
Spread the ham salad equally on 6 slices of
bread. Arrange 1 piece of lettuce over the ham
salad in each sandwich. Cover the sandwiches
with the remaining 6 slices of bread. Cut the
sandwiches in half diagonally.

MAKES 6 SANDWICHES (3 CUPS HAM SALAD)

EGG SALAD SANDWICHES

4 extra-large eggs, hard-cooked (page 264),
  cold, and coarsely chopped
1 teaspoon prepared mustard
1/2 teaspoon sugar
1/4 teaspoon white pepper
1/4 cup Miracle Whip salad dressing
4 slices bread of choice
Boston lettuce

In a medium mixing bowl, place the eggs, mustard, sugar, white pepper, and salad dressing; stir
to combine. Spread the egg salad equally on 2
slices of bread. Arrange the lettuce leaves over
the egg salad in each sandwich. Cover the sandwiches with the remaining 2 slices of bread. Cut
the sandwiches in half diagonally.

MAKES 2 SANDWICHES

TUNA SALAD SANDWICHES

1 6-ounce can solid, white albacore tuna,
  packed in water, drained
1 extra-large egg, hard-cooked (page 264),
  cold, and medium-coarsely chopped
1/4 cup chopped celery
1/4 cup chopped sweet gherkin pickles
1/3 cup Miracle Whip salad dressing
6 slices bread of choice
3 sandwich-sized pieces of red-tip leaf
  lettuce

In a medium mixing bowl, place the tuna, egg,
celery, pickles, and salad dressing. Using the
edge of a tablespoon, break the tuna into small
chunks; then, stir to combine the ingredients.
Spread the tuna salad equally on 3 slices of
bread. Arrange 1 piece of lettuce over the tuna
salad in each sandwich. Cover the sandwiches
with the remaining 3 slices of bread. Cut the
sandwiches in half diagonally.

MAKES 3 SANDWICHES

Hot Sandwiches

CORNED BEEF AND SWISS CHEESE FRENCH-TOASTED SANDWICHES

2 extra-large eggs
2 tablespoons whole milk
¼ teaspoon salt
1 tablespoon plus 1 teaspoon Dijon mustard
8 slices white bread, homemade (page 419) or commercially baked
½ pound thinly sliced, cooked corned beef
½ pound medium-thinly sliced Swiss cheese
2 tablespoons butter

In a small mixing bowl, place the eggs, milk, and salt; using a table fork, beat until blended. Pour the egg mixture into a pie pan; set aside. Spread 1 teaspoon mustard on each of 4 slices of bread. Arrange ¼ of the corned beef over the mustard in each sandwich. Then, place ¼ of the Swiss cheese over the corned beef in each sandwich. Cover the sandwiches with the remaining 4 slices of bread.

In an electric skillet or a heavy-bottomed skillet on the range, heat the butter over medium-low heat (330° F. if using an electric skillet). Tilt the skillet back and forth to completely cover the bottom with the melted butter. Dip both sides of each sandwich in the egg mixture and place in the skillet. Fry 4 to 5 minutes on each side until medium brown, turning once. Cut each sandwich in half diagonally. Serve immediately.

MAKES 4 SANDWICHES

HOT ROAST PORK SANDWICHES WITH CHUTNEY

1 pound leftover cold, cooked Loin of Pork (page 186)
1 teaspoon vegetable oil
1 tablespoon butter, divided
4 onion buns, split
2 tablespoons butter for buns
¼ cup chutney, home canned (page 776) or commercially canned

Preheat the broiler.

Slice the cold roast pork very thinly; set aside. In a heavy-bottomed skillet, heat the vegetable oil over medium heat. Using a spatula, spread the vegetable oil over the entire bottom of the skillet. Add about 1½ teaspoons butter. Tilt the skillet back and forth to blend the butter with the oil. Place the slices of roast pork in batches, single layer, in the skillet; sauté very lightly (about 1 minute on each side), turning once and adding the remaining 1½ teaspoons butter to the skillet as needed. Place the sautéed slices in a covered pan to keep warm.

Meanwhile, butter both halves of the split onion buns, using about ¾ teaspoon butter per bun half. Place the bun halves in a shallow pan and toast under the broiler, 6 inches from the heat. Arrange the sautéed roast pork slices, evenly divided, on the bottom half of each hot, toasted bun. Chop the chutney, if necessary, and spread 1 tablespoon generously over the pork slices on the bottom halves of the buns. Cover the sandwiches with the top halves of the buns. Serve immediately.

MAKES 4 SANDWICHES

PRESTO BARBECUED WIENERS ON TOASTED BUNS

Make these dolled-up weiners the focal point of a quick family dinner.

1 cup tomato catsup, home canned (page 781) or commercially canned (a little less than 1 12-ounce bottle)
2 teaspoons dark corn syrup
2 teaspoons Worcestershire sauce
1 teaspoon chili powder
¼ teaspoon dry mustard
¼ teaspoon onion powder
Dash of cayenne pepper
Dash of ground mace
½ cup water
1 pound (8 to 10) wieners (any style)
Wiener buns, split
Butter

In a medium saucepan, place the catsup, syrup, Worcestershire sauce, chili powder, dry mustard, onion powder, cayenne pepper, mace, and water; stir to blend. Place the saucepan, uncovered, over medium-high heat; bring the catsup mixture (barbecue sauce) to a simmer. Add the wieners and return to a simmer, uncovered. Lower the heat and simmer, uncovered, 20 minutes, turning the wieners and stirring intermittently.

Preheat the broiler.

When nearly ready to serve, butter both halves of the split wiener buns. Place both halves of the buns in a shallow pan and toast under the broiler, 6 inches from the heat. Place 1 or 2 toasted bun halves on each plate and 1 wiener on each half. Spoon the barbecue sauce over all. The number of servings depends upon the style and number of wieners purchased and the appetites of the diners.

SLOPPY JOES

3 pounds lean, pure ground beef
¾ cup finely chopped onions (about 1 large onion)
1 large garlic clove, pressed
1 29-ounce can commercial tomato sauce
¼ cup commercial hot catsup
⅛ teaspoon (10 dashes) Tabasco pepper sauce
16 onion buns, split

In an electric skillet or a heavy-bottomed skillet on the range, place the ground beef, onions, and garlic; brown the ingredients over medium-low heat (325° F. if using an electric skillet). heat. Reduce the skillet heat to very low (220° F. if using an electric skillet). When the skillet cools to the reduced temperature, add the tomato sauce, catsup, and pepper sauce; stir to combine. Cover the skillet and simmer the mixture 10 minutes. Spoon the mixture over the bottom halves of the split onion buns. Cover the sandwiches with the top halves of the buns.

MAKES 16 SANDWICHES

OPEN-FACED GRILLED CHEESE SANDWICHES

Eyes light up when they spy these inviting open-faced sandwiches on the lunch table. To my taste, they're better than customary close-faced grilled cheese sandwiches and they're a snap to make to boot. You don't have to get out the skillet or griddle as you do when making the close-faced type. You just pop the bread in the toaster, add the butter and cheese, and scoot the sandwiches under the broiler—one of those cases when simpler is better.

Whole-wheat bread, homemade (page 419) or commercially baked
Butter, softened
Colby cheese, sliced ¼ inch thick

Preheat the broiler.

Toast the bread (both sides) in a toaster; spread with the butter. Cover the buttered toast with a single layer of cheese slices. Broil the open-faced sandwiches, 6 inches from the heat, until the cheese is soft and slightly melted. Watch carefully to prevent the edges of the toast from overbrowning.

SERVING SUGGESTION: Grilled Cheese Sandwiches are wonderful when spread thinly with any kind of jelly. Let diners spread their own.

VARIATIONS: Rye or white bread, and Swiss or any type of cheddar cheese may be substituted. Rye bread and Swiss cheese make a particularly tasty combination. Do not use pasteurized process cheese as a substitute.

36 Additional Sandwich Ideas

MEAT SANDWICHES

COLD MEAT SANDWICHES

Cooked Baked Ham (page 192), Swiss cheese, and leaf lettuce on a poppy seed bun spread with Dijon mustard and/or mayonnaise.

BLT (bacon, lettuce, and tomato) Variation: Grilled Canadian bacon, spinach leaves, and sliced yellow tomatoes on an onion roll spread with Thousand Island Dressing (page 147).

Braunschweiger and French onion sour cream on pumpernickel bread.

Cold, cooked Loin of Pork (page 186), watercress, and soft cream cheese with pineapple on a potato roll.

Cold, cooked Meat Loaf (page 171), tomato catsup or chili sauce, and leaf lettuce (optional) on white bread.

Cooked corned beef, shredded red cabbage, and beer mustard on caraway rye bread.

Salami, provolone, and stone-ground mustard on dark rye bread.

Cold, cooked Leg of Lamb (page 196) and fresh mint leaves on thinly sliced, buttered white toast spread sparingly with Green Sauce (page 364).

Sliced ring bologna, mild cheddar cheese, and sweet gherkin pickles sliced lengthwise, on a large, soft, split bread stick, with condiments of choice.

Tongue, horseradish mustard, and red-tip leaf lettuce on Milwaukee rye bread.

Spinach Salad Sandwich: Spinach leaves, fried bacon pieces, sliced fresh mushrooms, and slices of Hard-Cooked Egg (page 264) on egg bread spread with Miracle Whip salad dressing which has been mixed with a small amount of Basic Vinaigrette Dressing (page 152).

Traditional Club Sandwich: Spread mayonnaise sparingly on 3 thin slices of white or whole-wheat toast. On the mayonnaise side of the first piece of toast, place cold, sliced turkey breast and fried, drained bacon strips; cover with the second piece of toast, mayonnaise side up. Add sliced tomatoes and leaf lettuce; cover with the third piece of toast, mayonnaise side down. Cut the sandwich into triangular quarters and skewer each quarter with a cellophane-frilled toothpick.

HOT MEAT SANDWICHES

French Dip: Thinly sliced Rib Roast (page 167) on a French roll; jus (natural pan juices) on the side for dipping.

Grilled Hamburger Steak (page 251) and Bell Pepper Relish (page 779) on a whole-wheat bun.

Broiled Ground Beef Patty without onions (page 170), thinly sliced Swiss cheese, and sautéed onions on grilled rye bread. (Place the broiled beef patty on a slice of rye bread; top with the Swiss cheese. Place under the broiler briefly, until the cheese melts. Spoon the onions over the meat and cheese; cover with the top bread slice. Grill both sides of the sandwich in a lightly oiled and buttered skillet.)

Sliced meatballs with tomato sauce (see Grace's Spaghetti and Meatballs, page 288) and thinly sliced mozzarella cheese on a hoagie bun. Wrap in aluminum foil and heat in a preheated 350° F. oven.

POULTRY SANDWICHES

COLD POULTRY SANDWICHES

Sliced turkey breast (pages 212, 214, and 243), alfalfa sprouts, and Curried Mayonnaise Dressing (page 154) on a croissant.

Sliced, wild pheasant (pages 237 and 238) and Belgian endive on a croissant spread with Orange Butter (page 369).

Sliced, smoked breast of turkey, medium-mild Muenster cheese, and Boston lettuce on sourdough bread.

HOT POULTRY SANDWICHES

Plain or Mesquite-Grilled Chicken Breast (pages 254–255), sliced avocados, and sliced tomatoes on a sourdough bun lightly spread with lemon pepper–flavored mayonnaise.

Sliced Barbecued Chicken with extra barbecue sauce (page 212) and thinly sliced cheddar cheese on a wiener bun. Wrap in aluminum foil and heat in a preheated 350° F. oven.

FISH SANDWICHES

COLD FISH SANDWICHES

Cold, flaked Poached Salmon Steak (page 225), watercress, and Green Sauce (page 364) on dill bread.

Greek Salad Sandwich: Sliced tomatoes and green bell pepper rings, both marinated in Basic Vinaigrette Dressing (page 152) and then drained slightly; anchovies; fresh, ripe Greek olives, pitted and sliced; crumbled feta cheese; and romaine lettuce on a split roll. Before capping the sandwich, dip the cut surface of the top roll half in the marinade.

HOT FISH SANDWICHES

Hot (or cold) Broiled Crappie Fillet (page 222), capers, and Bibb lettuce on a whole-wheat bagel spread with smoked salmon–flavored soft cream cheese.

Hot, Panfried Walleye Fillet (page 224) and Louis Dressing (page 151) on a white mountain roll.

VEGETABLE SANDWICHES

COLD VEGETABLE SANDWICHES

Green bell pepper rings, sliced seedless cucumbers, minced celery, and green pepper mustard on a sesame seed bun.

Shredded carrots, minced celery, and chopped red bell peppers, all lightly mixed with lemon juice–spiked mayonnaise, on muesli bread.

Sliced radishes; steamed and cooled Snow Peas (page 327); and cooked, well-drained, and cooled Wax Beans (page 305) on stone-ground whole-wheat bread spread with Onion Butter (page 369).

Sliced tomatoes; sliced yellow zucchini; and tiny, fresh broccoli flowerets on oat bran bread spread with mayonnaise which has been mixed with a small amount of Italian Salad Dressing (page 148).

PEANUT BUTTER SANDWICHES

COLD PEANUT BUTTER SANDWICHES
Creamy peanut butter and Grape Conserve (page 760) on raisin bread.

HOT PEANUT BUTTER SANDWICHES
Chunky peanut butter and sliced bananas on a hot, toasted and buttered, honey-wheat English muffin, or on hot, toasted and buttered cinnamon bread.

BREAKFAST SANDWICHES

COLD BREAKFAST SANDWICHES
Sliced, fresh strawberries and strawberry yogurt between two cooled Waffle quarters (page 456).

HOT BREAKFAST SANDWICHES
Eggs Benedict Sandwich: Fried Canadian bacon, poached egg, and Hollandaise Sauce (page 367) on a large, toasted English muffin.

Fried Egg (page 266) and fried, well-drained bacon on a toasted and buttered cheddar cheese English muffin.

Hot Sausage Patty (page 189) and a slice of Colby–Monterey Jack cheese on a large, buttered Baking Powder Biscuit (page 446). Wrap in aluminum foil and heat in a pre-heated 350° F. oven.

Small omelet on a toasted bagel which has been buttered and sprinkled with ground cinnamon and sugar (see Cinnamon Toast, page 430).

Sauces and Gravies

What is the difference between sauce and gravy—those two works of culinary art which often upstage the principal food they are cast to support? Theoretically, gravy is a type of sauce; however, its ingredients are so prescribed and its use so pervasive as to warrant its own designation.

Sauce is a fluid of any texture made from any food(s) and usually thickened. It usually is served over—rarely under in the Midwest—a food, or it may be combined with a food(s) as a flavor complement.

Gravy is a usually smooth fluid made from meat or poultry juices and particles remaining in the pan after browning and/or cooking, combined with a liquid—usually broth, water, milk, or wine—and thickened with flour or sometimes cornstarch. It usually is served over —rarely under in the Midwest—potatoes and/or meat or poultry as a flavor complement.

Lying between the east and west coasts is a wide buffer of beautiful agricultural land which holds the added distinction of being world-class gravy country. Midwesterners earned their credentials as master gravy makers through long experience. About the time your primary focus was on memorizing the multiplication tables, your mother would beckon you to the stove and hand you the big mixing spoon with clear instructions to stir the gravy continuously and energetically while she mashed the potatoes. It might have been forgivable to slip through the cracks of Midwest life without acquiring the skill of making cinnamon rolls, but any Heartlander worth his or her salt in the kitchen did not want to suffer the humiliation of serving lumpy gravy. Not in this land of milk and honey and fine livestock, where every dinner was planned around meat, potatoes, and gravy.

But nothing stays the same. Sometimes, very desirable, time-honored things are superseded by other things perceived to be even more desirable or important in the overview. I'm afraid that is what is happening to mashed potatoes and gravy. It is tough to face—head-on—the reality that Midwest gravy making has peaked. While there is still plenty of that deep brown, complex-tasting, smooth-as-silk comfort food ladled over fluffy mashed potatoes, its heyday is somewhere in the past tense.

The fact of the matter is, machines have taken up where mashed potatoes and gravy left off. It doesn't take as many calories to operate a John Deere 7800 tractor pulling a Vermeer round bailer as it did to pitch hay in the August sun. In addition to the calorie consideration, saturated fat and cholesterol have undermined our romance with gravy even though our love for it is undying.

Things taken for granted and then denied become more appreciated. Mashed potatoes and gravy have been elevated to a pedestal reserved for treasured foods prepared on special occasions and savored by the bite.

HOW MIDWEST SAUCES AND GRAVIES ARE USED

Because the quality of Midwest meat is so superior, only now and then are gravies and sauces served over the best cuts, such as steaks and chops. Flavor additions can interfere with the full, exquisite taste of the superb meat itself. A rose is a rose.

But there are certainly exceptions to this broad-sweeping statement. To illustrate, one of my standard meat offerings when company is invited for dinner is roast beef tenderloin served with a gravy-type mushroom sauce enhanced with a bit of sherry (Roast Beef Tenderloin with Mushroom Sauce, page 162). But I always serve

the sauce at the table, which permits meat purists to quietly pass the sauceboat on to the next diner without ladling so much as a smidgen over their not-to-be-adulterated slices of beef.

Midwest-style meat sauces are often the straight, natural pan juices remaining in the skillet or roaster after braising, baking, or roasting. A good example is Swiss Steak (page 160), that succulent dish in which the tomatoes, onions, carrots, celery, golden raisins, and herbs blend with the meat juices over the long baking time to brew a wonderful sauce which needs only to be strained before pouring it into the sauceboat.

In some cases, a gravy or sauce is part and parcel of a traditional dish. A vinegar-flavored gravy, often thickened with gingersnap crumbs, is always served with Sauerbraten (page 169), and, of course, it is mandatory that Barbecued Ribs (pages 252 and 185) be smoked or baked in a Barbecue Sauce (pages 250 and 360), with additional sauce usually passed at the table. Sometimes, general diner consensus formulated over the years establishes the felicitous teaming of sauces with certain meats. Raisin Sauce (page 365) over baked ham comes to mind, as well as Horseradish Sauce (page 361) over ham loaf.

As for vegetables, Hollandaise Sauce (page 367) and cheese sauces (pages 367 and 368) trickle over asparagus, broccoli, and cauliflower with regularity in the Heartland. White Sauce (page 366) often transforms plain vegetables into cream style, or joins forces with vegetables, together with other foods and special seasonings, in baked casserole dishes, such as Divine Baked Asparagus (page 304), Celery Baked in Almond Sauce (page 314), and ever-wonderful Scalloped Potatoes (page 330).

Strictly speaking, Jellied Cranberry Sauce (page 364) is not a sauce because it is not fluid; however, its classification is a dilemma. It doesn't qualify as a relish because it contains no vinegar, it lacks the translucency to be a jelly, it is too important on the plate to be labeled a garnish, yet it is not quite important enough to be called a dish. However one may categorize it, it is divine stuff—shimmery out of a fancy mold, gorgeous in color, smooth and tender as it is spooned onto the plate, and perfect for adding just the right amount of tart, fruity flavor to complement delicately flavored turkey and sage dressing.

If I may express a personal bias, I think that cranberry sauce in the jellied form, made by pressing the cranberries through a food mill, is not only more elegant than the saucy type, in which the cranberries are left whole, but also, is a more pleasing texture—and taste—adjunct to traditional poultry fare. In smooth jellied cranberry sauce, the cranberry skins are removed and the remaining tartness of the cranberries is distributed throughout the sauce, mollifying the stark sharpness of the berries to create a more sophisticated flavor. However you prefer it, it's marvelous sauce, made in sundry ways in the Midwest since the pioneers found cranberries growing profusely in the wild across Minnesota, Wisconsin, and Michigan.

Until about midway through the twentieth century, even Midwest farmers not engaged in dairy farming commonly kept a milk cow or two to supply milk for their own family's consumption. This resulted in luxurious amounts of the richest cream you can imagine which was hand-cranked into unforgettable ice cream in the summer and beat into heaps of whipped cream for cakes, pies, and other desserts in the winter. Although a wide array of sauces flows over desserts in the Heartland, none has outflanked the perpetual popularity of real Whipped Cream (page 373), lightly sweetened, and flavored with vanilla. At the end of the twentieth century, Midwesterners are still riding the whipped cream wave, even though the cream now usually comes from cartons rather than their own barns.

Savory Sauces

BARBECUE SAUCE

This barbecue sauce is not precooked. It is for use with indoor cooking recipes which call for the sauce to be poured over meat, poultry, or wild game which is then baked at medium to medium-low heat for an extended period of time. For a precooked barbecue sauce to use for outdoor cooking on the grill or in the smoker, see Barbecue Sauce for Outdoor Cooking (page 250).

2 cups tomato catsup, home canned (page 781) or commercially canned
¾ cup chili sauce, home canned (page 783) or commercially canned
⅔ cup packed dark brown sugar
½ cup red wine vinegar
⅓ cup freshly squeezed, strained lemon juice
3 tablespoons Heinz 57 Sauce
3 tablespoons prepared mustard
2 tablespoons Worcestershire sauce
1 tablespoon very finely grated onions
1 tablespoon vegetable oil
1 teaspoon dry mustard
1 teaspoon celery salt
1 teaspoon pepper
½ teaspoon dried leaf thyme
Dash of Tabasco pepper sauce
¾ cup beer

In a medium mixing bowl, place the catsup, chili sauce, brown sugar, vinegar, lemon juice, Heinz 57 Sauce, prepared mustard, Worcestershire sauce, onions, vegetable oil, dry mustard, celery salt, pepper, thyme, pepper sauce, and beer; using an electric mixer, beat on medium speed until well blended. *Do not cook* the Barbecue Sauce before use in recipes. Place the sauce in a glass jar; cover tightly and refrigerate up to 2 weeks.

MAKES 5¼ CUPS

VARIATION: For more spicy Barbecue Sauce, substitute commercially canned hot tomato catsup for standard tomato catsup.

SERVING SUGGESTIONS: Use this Barbecue Sauce to make Barbecued Loin Back Ribs (page 185), Barbecued Chicken (page 212), and barbecued butterfly pork chops.

COCKTAIL SAUCE

A Midwest favorite sauce for shrimp, whether served cold or deep-fat fried.

1 cup commercial chili sauce
¼ cup *well-drained,* packed, prepared horseradish, homemade (page 46) or commercially canned
2 teaspoons finely grated onions
2 teaspoons celery seed
2 teaspoons celery salt
2 teaspoons Worcestershire sauce
½ teaspoon garlic salt
½ teaspoon salt
¼ teaspoon pepper
5 dashes of Tabasco pepper sauce
¼ cup sugar

In a small mixing bowl place the chili sauce, horseradish, onions, celery seed, celery salt, Worcestershire sauce, garlic salt, salt, pepper, pepper sauce, and sugar; stir well to combine. Place the sauce in a glass jar; cover tightly and refrigerate at least 2 days to blend flavors before serving. Keeps up to 2 weeks in the refrigerator.

MAKES ABOUT 1½ CUPS

HORSERADISH SAUCE

A dreamy, light sauce wonderfully served through the years with ham loaf (see Ham Loaf with Horseradish Sauce, page 193). It is also well paired with beef and fresh pork.

This recipe is from my grandmother's cookbook where it appeared in her own handwriting. The cultural heritage of food is exemplified by the fact that recipes for Horseradish Sauce in current cookbooks are very similar to hers. My grandmother's life spanned the years 1880 to 1945.

2 tablespoons well-drained, packed, prepared horseradish, homemade (page 46) or commercially canned
¼ teaspoon salt
½ cup whipping cream, whipped (with no additions)

Add the horseradish and salt to the whipped cream; fold to combine. Serve immediately or cover and refrigerate up to 3 hours.

Just before serving, lightly fold the sauce again, and spoon it attractively into a small, crystal serving dish.

MAKES ABOUT 1 CUP

TARTAR SAUCE

½ cup Miracle Whip salad dressing
3 tablespoons sweet pickle relish
3 tablespoons minced onions

In a small mixing bowl place the salad dressing, sweet pickle relish, and onions; stir to combine.

In a covered glass jar or plastic container, Tartar Sauce keeps up to 2 weeks in the refrigerator.

SERVES 4 AS A CONDIMENT FOR FISH OR SHELLFISH

TOMATO SAUCE

3¼ pounds ripe tomatoes (4 cups pulp; see
  recipe procedures below)
2 tablespoons butter
1 cup finely chopped onions (about 1 large
  onion)
1 large garlic clove, pressed
2 tablespoons butter
1 cup finely chopped, fresh mushrooms
  (about 4 ounces mushrooms)
1 teaspoon dried leaf oregano
1 tablespoon finely snipped, fresh parsley
1 bay leaf
6 whole cloves, in cheesecloth bag
  (page 44)
1¼ teaspoons salt
¼ teaspoon pepper
2 teaspoons sugar
2 tablespoons all-purpose flour
2 tablespoons water

Wash the tomatoes. Blanch the tomatoes (page
44) 1 minute; stem, peel, quarter, seed and core
(page 45). Pour off the surplus juice and reserve
for other uses. Process the tomatoes in a blender
(see Note), *in thirds,* for about 2 seconds, only.
The pulp should contain very small chunks of
tomatoes. Be careful not to totally liquefy the
tomatoes. Measure 4 cups pulp; set aside.

In a large, heavy-bottomed saucepan, melt 2
tablespoons butter over medium heat. Place the
onions and garlic in the saucepan; sauté until
translucent and tender but not brown. Spoon
the onion mixture into a small bowl; set aside.
Place an additional 2 tablespoons butter in the
saucepan. Add the mushrooms and sauté over
medium heat until they give up their juices.
Remove from the heat; let stand until the mushrooms cool slightly.

Then, add the tomato pulp, onion mixture,
oregano, parsley, bay leaf, cheesecloth bag of
cloves, salt, pepper, and sugar to the saucepan
containing the mushrooms; stir to combine.
Return the saucepan to medium heat; cover and
bring the mixture to a boil. Reduce the heat

and simmer the mixture slowly for 45 minutes.
Remove from the heat. Remove and discard the
bay leaf and cheesecloth bag of cloves. Set aside.

In a small glass jar or plastic container with a
secure lid, place the flour and water; cover and
shake vigorously until blended and smooth.
Add the flour mixture to the mixture in the
saucepan; stir to combine. Place the saucepan
over low heat; return the mixture to a low boil
and cook 3 minutes, until thickened, stirring
constantly. In a covered glass jar or plastic container, Tomato Sauce keeps up to 1 week in the
refrigerator.

NOTE: If a blender is not available, process the
tomatoes in 1-cup batches in a food processor,
pulsing until the pulp contains very small
chunks of tomatoes. Be careful not to totally liquefy the tomatoes.

MAKES ABOUT 4 CUPS

SERVING SUGGESTIONS
• Use in Italian dishes (see Eggplant Parmesan,
  page 318).

• Serve over vegetables such as zucchini, green
  beans, or mixed vegetables.

• Use in pasta dishes.

• Use in casseroles.

CATSUP SAUCE

1 cup tomato catsup, home canned
  (page 781) or commercially canned
1 tablespoon prepared mustard
2 tablespoons packed dark brown sugar

In a small saucepan, place the catsup, mustard,
and brown sugar; stir to combine. Place the
saucepan over low heat and bring the mixture to
a simmer, stirring frequently. Keeps, covered, up
to 1 week in the refrigerator.

MAKES ABOUT 1 CUP

SERVING SUGGESTIONS

- Spread over beef and pork during the last 15 minutes of cooking (see Mother's Meat Loaf, page 171).

- Serve warm in a sauce dish at the table for diners to use on hamburgers, porkburgers, hotdogs, and roast pork.

DILL SAUCE

1 cup mayonnaise
2 tablespoons dry white wine
1 teaspoon white wine Worcestershire sauce
1 teaspoon sugar
3 dashes of Tabasco pepper sauce
1 teaspoon snipped, fresh dillweed

In a small mixing bowl, place the mayonnaise, white wine, white wine Worcestershire sauce, sugar, and pepper sauce; using an electric mixer, beat on medium-high speed until smooth and blended. Add the dillweed; using a spoon, stir until evenly combined. In a covered glass jar or plastic container, Dill Sauce keeps up to 2 days in the refrigerator.

MAKES ABOUT 1 CUP

SERVING SUGGESTIONS

- Serve with cold or hot fish and shellfish.

- Serve with cold lamb or veal sandwiches.

PARSLEY SAUCE

3 tablespoons finely snipped, fresh parsley or 1 tablespoon dried parsley
¼ teaspoon celery salt
1 recipe Medium White Sauce (page 366)

Add the parsley and celery salt to hot Medium White Sauce; stir to combine. Best when served immediately or soon after making; however, it may be refrigerated in a covered container up to 2 days.

MAKES ABOUT 1 CUP

SERVING SUGGESTIONS

- Serve over boiled and then peeled small, new, red potatoes (page 331).

- Serve with Broiled Fish Fillets (page 222).

CAPER SAUCE

¼ cup (4 tablespoons) butter
½ teaspoon cornstarch
1 tablespoon vinegar drained from bottled capers
2 tablespoons drained, bottled capers (page 21)
2 tablespoons snipped, fresh parsley
1 tablespoon freshly squeezed, strained lemon juice
1 tablespoon dry white wine
Dash of cayenne pepper

In a small saucepan, melt the butter over low heat. Remove from the heat. Add the cornstarch; stir until blended. Then, add the vinegar, capers, parsley, lemon juice, wine, and cayenne pepper; stir to blend and combine. Place over medium heat and cook the sauce until slightly thickened, stirring constantly. Serve immediately or refrigerate in a covered glass or plastic container up to 4 hours. Reheat if not served immediately.

MAKES ABOUT ½ CUP (ENOUGH TO SPOON OVER 4 ½-POUND FISH FILLETS)

SERVING SUGGESTION: Serve over broiled fish fillets (see Broiled Walleye Fillets with Caper Sauce, (page 224).

GREEN SAUCE (SAUCE VERTE)

This lovely green-colored sauce is traditionally served with Cold Poached Salmon Steaks. It may also accompany cold lobster and other cold shellfish, and poached, broiled, or baked fish served cold.

1 cup mayonnaise
2 teaspoons dry white wine
1 tablespoon finely snipped, fresh parsley
2 teaspoons finely snipped, fresh dillweed
1 teaspoon finely snipped, fresh chives

In a small blender beaker or a small food processor, place the mayonnaise, white wine, parsley, dillweed, and chives. Process until the herbs are chopped as finely as possible. In a covered glass or plastic container, Green Sauce keeps up to 2 days in the refrigerator.

JELLIED CRANBERRY SAUCE

2 12-ounce packages (7 cups) fresh
  cranberries
2 cups water
3⅓ cups sugar

Wash and sort the cranberries. In an 8-quart, heavy-bottomed saucepan, place the cranberries and water. Cover the saucepan and bring the cranberries to a boil over high heat. Reduce the heat to medium and simmer the cranberries about 3 minutes, until the skins burst and the berries are soft, stirring occasionally. Press the cranberries and liquid through a food mill; set aside.

Clean the saucepan and pour the pressed cranberries into the pan. Add the sugar; stir well to combine. Over high heat, bring the mixture to a boil, stirring constantly. Attach a candy thermometer to the saucepan. Boil the mixture until it reaches 8° F. above the boiling point of water (page 712) and begins to sheet (page 738) (about 7 minutes), stirring continuously. Remove from the heat; using a metal spoon, quickly skim the foam (if any) off the top of the cranberry sauce and discard. *Immediately* pour the cranberry sauce (there will be about 4 cups) into 1 or more ungreased molds. Place the mold(s) carefully on a wire cookie rack; let stand 30 minutes to cool the cranberry sauce partially. Then, refrigerate, uncovered. When the cranberry sauce is completely cooled and set, cover the molds with plastic wrap.

Unmold just before serving. To unmold, insert a paring knife about 1 inch into the outer edge of the mold at 3 approximately equidistant places. Place a flat serving plate on top of the mold; hold the plate and mold together and invert. If the sauce does not unmold, lift the inverted mold slightly and insert a paring knife along the edge of the mold at one place until the sauce releases. Do not unmold Jellied Cranberry Sauce by placing the mold in warm water or applying warm towels to the mold.

Keep up to 2 days molded in the refrigerator. After unmolding and serving, leftover Jellied Cranberry Sauce may be covered and refrigerated up to 5 days, although it will weep.

MAKES ABOUT 4 CUPS

SERVING SUGGESTIONS
- A traditional accompaniment for holiday roast turkey.

- Excellent with all fowl.

APRICOT SAUCE

6 ounces dried apricots (about 1 cup
  packed dried apricots)
2 cups water
½ cup sugar
1 tablespoon cornstarch
2 tablespoons freshly squeezed, strained
  lemon juice
⅛ teaspoon ground cloves
1 tablespoon cognac

In a small saucepan, place the apricots and water.
Cover the saucepan. Bring the apricots to a boil
over high heat; reduce the heat and simmer 15
minutes. Place the apricots and cooking liquid
in a blender (see Note); process until pureed; set
aside.

In a clean, dry, small saucepan, place the sugar,
cornstarch, lemon juice, and cloves; stir until
completely smooth and blended. Add about ½
cup of the pureed apricots; stir to blend. Add the
remainder of the pureed apricots; stir until
blended. Over medium-low heat, cook the apricot mixture until clear and thick (about 6 minutes), stirring constantly. At this point, the sauce
may be placed in a covered jar or plastic container and refrigerated up to 1 day before serving. Just before serving, reheat the sauce over
low heat. Add the cognac and stir to blend.

NOTE: If a blender is not available, a food processor may be used.

MAKES ABOUT 2½ CUPS

SERVING SUGGESTIONS: Nice with goose (see
Baked Goose with Apricot-Cognac Dressing,
page 241), duck, and ham.

RAISIN SAUCE

*Raisin Sauce is simply too good to be forgotten, but
you can hardly find a recipe for it in current cookbooks.
There seems to be no rhyme or reason for this in light
of the fact that Raisin Sauce's extended relationship
with ham has long been recognized as a shining example of the perfect food couple!*

1 cup water
⅓ cup golden raisins
⅓ cup currants
3 tablespoons packed dark brown sugar
⅛ teaspoon ground ginger
⅛ teaspoon salt
1 tablespoon plus 2 teaspoons cornstarch
¼ cup port wine
1 tablespoon red wine vinegar
¼ cup water

Pour 1 cup water into a small saucepan. Cover
the saucepan and bring the water to a boil over
high heat. Remove from the heat. Place the
raisins and currants in the saucepan of hot water.
Cover the saucepan and let the raisins and
currants stand to plump 30 minutes.

In a small mixing bowl, place the brown
sugar, ginger, salt, and cornstarch; stir to combine. Add the wine, vinegar, and ¼ cup water;
stir until smooth. Add to the raisin-water mixture; stir to mix. Place over medium heat and
cook until the sauce thickens, stirring continuously. Serve hot. In a covered glass jar or plastic
container, Raisin Sauce keeps up to 1 week in
the refrigerator.

MAKES ABOUT 1¼ CUPS

VARIATION: ⅔ cup regular raisins may be substituted for the golden raisins and currants.

MEDIUM WHITE SAUCE

White sauce is one of the most frequently used sauces in Midwest cooking. Rarely is this sauce used alone. Rather, white sauce is ordinarily combined with other foods in dishes such as casseroles, creamed vegetables, and cream soups, and is used in making other sauces. Recipes for 5 thicknesses of white sauce are given here. Selection of thickness depends upon use of the sauce; however, Medium White Sauce is used most often.

Properly made white sauce is smooth, with absolutely no lumps. If the simple procedures are followed, completely smooth white sauce will result every time.

2 tablespoons all-purpose flour
½ teaspoon salt
⅛ teaspoon white pepper or black pepper
2 tablespoons butter
1 cup whole milk

In a small sauce dish, place the flour, salt, and pepper; stir to combine; set aside. In a small saucepan, melt the butter over low heat. Remove from the heat. Add the flour mixture and stir until the mixture is perfectly smooth. Add the milk; stir to mix. Place over medium-low heat. Cook until the mixture thickens and is just under boiling (about 8 minutes), stirring constantly. Do not allow the mixture to boil. Best when used immediately or soon after making; however, white sauce may be refrigerated in a covered container up to 2 days.

MAKES ABOUT 1 CUP

THIN WHITE SAUCE: Follow the Medium White Sauce recipe, above, increasing the milk to 1¼ cups. Makes about 1¼ cups.

EXTRA-THIN WHITE SAUCE: Follow the Medium White Sauce recipe, above, decreasing the flour and butter to 1 tablespoon each. Makes about 1 cup.

THICK WHITE SAUCE: Follow the Medium White Sauce recipe, above, increasing the flour and butter to 3 tablespoons each. Makes slightly more than 1 cup.

EXTRA-THICK WHITE SAUCE: Follow the Medium White Sauce recipe, above, increasing the flour and butter to ¼ cup each. Makes about 1¼ cups.

BÉARNAISE SAUCE

A classic French sauce.

¼ cup white wine tarragon vinegar
1 shallot, chopped
1 teaspoon snipped, fresh chervil*
1 teaspoon snipped, fresh tarragon**
⅛ teaspoon white pepper
3 extra-large egg yolks
1 tablespoon whipping cream, unwhipped
¾ cup (¼ pound plus 4 tablespoons) butter, melted
2 teaspoons very finely snipped, fresh parsley

If fresh chervil is not available, a generous ¼ teaspoon dried leaf chervil may be substituted.

**If fresh tarragon is not available, a generous ¼ teaspoon dried leaf tarragon may be substituted.*

In a small blender beaker (or a small food processor), place the vinegar, shallots, chervil, tarragon, and white pepper; process on high speed until the herbs are chopped as finely as possible. Place the mixture in a very small saucepan. Place the saucepan over medium-low heat and simmer the mixture until it is reduced by half. (The mixture will be quite thick.) Pour the mixture into the top of a double boiler; cover and let stand until cooled to room temperature.

Then, add the egg yolks and whipping cream; using a handheld electric mixer, beat on low speed until blended. Place the top of the double boiler in the bottom pan *over* (not touching) hot (*not boiling*) water. Place over low heat. Add the melted butter *very gradually* to the egg yolk mixture while beating continuously with the electric mixer on low speed and watching carefully that the water does not boil. Continue beating until the sauce is thick and shiny like mayonnaise. Add the parsley; stir to combine. Serve immediately.

If the sauce should curdle, add an additional 1 to 2 tablespoons cold whipping cream and beat well, using the electric mixer.

MAKES ABOUT 1 CUP

SERVING SUGGESTIONS: Serve on beef, particularly broiled beef tenderloin steak (see Broiled Steak, page 166); poached, baked, or broiled fish fillets or steaks; and steamed or boiled vegetables compatible with tarragon (see Herb Chart, pages 40–43).

HOLLANDAISE SAUCE

3 extra-large egg yolks
1 tablespoon whipping cream, unwhipped
¼ teaspoon salt
Dash of cayenne pepper
1 tablespoon freshly squeezed, strained lemon juice
½ cup (¼ pound) butter, melted

In the top of a double boiler, place the egg yolks, whipping cream, salt, cayenne pepper, and lemon juice; using a handheld electric mixer, beat on medium speed until blended. Place the top of the double boiler in the bottom pan *over* (not touching) hot (*not boiling*) water. Place over low heat. Add the melted butter *very gradually* to the egg yolk mixture while beating continuously with the electric mixer on medium speed and watching carefully that the water does not boil. Continue beating until the sauce thickens. Serve immediately.

To hold the sauce for a very short period of time, place lukewarm water in the bottom pan of the double boiler; cover the top of the double boiler and let the sauce stand over the water. If the sauce should curdle, add an additional 1 to

2 tablespoons cold whipping cream and beat well, using the electric mixer.

MAKES ABOUT ¾ CUP

MUSTARD HOLLANDAISE SAUCE: Follow the Hollandaise Sauce recipe, above, adding 1 teaspoon prepared mustard to the egg yolk mixture ingredients after adding the lemon juice.

SERVING SUGGESTIONS
• Serve over boiled or steamed asparagus, broccoli, and cauliflower.

• Serve with Poached Salmon Steaks (page 225).

• Serve with eggs Benedict.

CHEESE SAUCE

1 recipe Thin White Sauce (page 366)
¼ teaspoon dry mustard (optional)
½ teaspoon Worcestershire sauce (optional)
1 cup shredded, mild cheddar cheese*

*For a stronger, more tangy cheese flavor, substitute sharp cheddar cheese for mild cheddar cheese.

When making the Thin White Sauce, stir the dry mustard into the flour mixture and add the Worcestershire sauce to the milk. When the white sauce has thickened, remove from the heat and add the cheese; stir until melted and blended. Best when served immediately or soon after making; however, Cheese Sauce may be refrigerated in a covered container up to 2 days.

MAKES ABOUT 1¾ CUPS

SERVING SUGGESTIONS
• Serve over cauliflower, broccoli, and asparagus.

• Serve over ham (see Ham Pinwheels with Cheese Sauce (page 195).

HOT SWISS CHEESE SAUCE

2 tablespoons butter
1 tablespoon grated onions
3 tablespoons all-purpose flour
¾ cup plus 2 tablespoons half-and-half
¼ cup whipping cream
2 teaspoons instant chicken bouillon
   granules
1 cup (4 ounces) shredded Swiss cheese
½ cup freshly grated Parmesan cheese
   (page 46)
2 teaspoons dry sherry

In a medium, heavy-bottomed saucepan, melt the butter over medium heat. Place the onions in the saucepan; sauté 2 minutes. Do not allow the butter to brown. Remove from the heat.

Place the flour in the saucepan; stir until blended with the pan juices. Add the half-and-half, whipping cream, and bouillon granules; stir to combine. Return the saucepan to medium heat and cook the mixture until thickened, stirring constantly. Do not allow the mixture to boil. Reduce the heat to medium-low. Add the Swiss cheese and Parmesan cheese to the mixture; stir until the cheeses melt and the mixture is blended and smooth (about 10 minutes). Add the sherry; stir to blend. Best when served immediately or soon after making.

MAKES ABOUT 1½ CUPS

SERVING SUGGESTIONS

• Serve (hot) as a dip for cold shrimp (see Shrimp with Dips, page 62).

• Serve over Baked Potatoes (page 328).

• Serve over Dinner Brussels Sprouts (page 309) or in a sauce dish next to Buffet Vegetables (page 323).

GARLIC BUTTER

½ cup (¼ pound) butter, softened
4 medium to large garlic cloves, pressed

In a small mixing bowl, place butter and garlic; stir well to combine. Pack soft Garlic Butter into a fancy, small mold; cover with plastic wrap and refrigerate until hardened. To unmold, briefly dip the mold in warm water and invert onto a small serving plate; refrigerate until completely hardened. Then, cover with plastic wrap and refrigerate until ready to serve. Keeps in the refrigerator for the same length of time as plain butter (see the expiration date on the butter carton).

MAKES 8 1-TABLESPOON SERVINGS

GARLIC BUTTER BALLS: Cover the bowl of soft Garlic Butter with plastic wrap and place in the refrigerator; let stand until slightly hardened. Then, using a 1-inch melon baller, scoop out balls of Garlic Butter and drop them into a bowl of ice water as they are made, to retain their shape. Dip the melon baller in hot water before scooping out each ball. Garlic Butter balls may be refrigerated in the ice water until served or, when hardened, they may be transferred to a plate, covered with plastic wrap, and stored in the refrigerator. Garlic Butter Balls may be ribbed (see Ribbed Butter Balls, page 396).

MAKES 8 1-TABLESPOON SERVINGS

SERVING SUGGESTION: Serve with Broiled Steak (page 166) or Grilled Steak (page 250).

SERVING ALTERNATIVES

• **GARLIC BREAD:** Cut a 1-pound loaf of Italian or French bread into ¾-inch slices, cutting almost through the loaf, but leaving the slices attached (about 16 slices). Using 1 recipe of Garlic Butter (not molded or made into Garlic Butter Balls), butter generously 1 side of each slice. Wrap the loaf in aluminum foil and just before serving, heat, in a preheated 350° F. oven until hot (about 5 minutes). To serve, remove the hot loaf from the aluminum foil and place it in a long, napkin-lined basket. Diners pull off slices.

- Use Garlic Butter (not molded or made into Garlic Butter Balls) to make Toasted Garlic Bread (page 428).

ONION BUTTER

Onion Butter may be used to make attractive garnishes which melt to add a delicious flavor enhancement to foods.

¼ cup (4 tablespoons) butter, softened
2 teaspoons freshly squeezed, strained
    lemon juice, room temperature
1 teaspoon fresh onion juice (page 45)
1 teaspoon finely snipped, fresh parsley
⅛ teaspoon white pepper

In a small mixing bowl; place the butter, lemon juice, onion juice, parsley, and white pepper; stir until blended and smooth. Using a decorating bag fit with large open-star tip number 6B (page 383), pipe stars (page 389) of Onion Butter onto waxed paper; refrigerate until completely hardened. Then, place the Onion Butter stars on a flat plate; cover with plastic wrap and refrigerate until ready to serve.

MAKES 6 ONION BUTTER STARS

SERVING SUGGESTIONS

- Place 1 Onion Butter star on individual, piping-hot steaks (see Broiled Steak, page 166, and Grilled Steak, page 250) and serve immediately.

- Place 1 or more Onion Butter stars on serving dishes of steamed or boiled vegetables such as green beans, asparagus, carrots, peas, and mixed vegetables.

SERVING ALTERNATIVES

- Use Onion Butter to make unribbed or ribbed butter balls (see Garlic Butter Balls, page 368).

- Pack soft Onion Butter into a small sauce dish or fancy mold; cover with plastic wrap and refrigerate until hardened. To unmold, briefly dip the sauce dish or mold in warm water and invert onto a small serving plate; refrigerate until completely hardened. Then, cover with plastic wrap and refrigerate until ready to serve. Or, before serving, use a small, sharp, thin-bladed knife dipped in hot water to slice the unmolded butter attractively. Place 1 piece of the butter on each hot steak or other food before zipping to the table.

MAKES 4 1-TABLESPOON SERVINGS

ORANGE BUTTER

½ cup (¼ pound) butter, softened
1 teaspoon finely grated orange rind
    (page 47)
⅛ teaspoon orange extract

In a small mixing bowl, place the butter, orange rind, and orange extract; using an electric mixer, beat on high speed to combine and blend. Using a spoon, pile the Orange Butter attractively into a small serving bowl and refrigerate; cover with plastic wrap when hardened. Keeps in the refrigerator for the same length of time as plain butter (see the expiration date on butter carton).

MAKES 8 1-TABLESPOON SERVINGS

SERVING SUGGESTIONS: Serve with breads, such as Mincemeat Bread with Orange Butter (page 436), Whole-Wheat Orange Bread (page 440), Baking Powder Biscuits (page 446), Waffles (page 456), Cranberry-Orange Muffins (page 445), Oat Bran Muffins (page 444), Soy Whole-Wheat Muffins (page 444), 100% Whole-Wheat Muffins (page 443), and toast.

SERVING ALTERNATIVES

- After mixing the Orange Butter, use a decorating bag fit with large open-star tip number 6B (page 383) to pipe 8 Orange Butter

(Recipe continues on next page)

rosettes (page 390) onto waxed paper; refrigerate until completely hardened. Then, place the Orange Butter rosettes on a flat plate; cover with plastic wrap and refrigerate until ready to serve.

- Use Orange Butter to make Ribbed (or unribbed) Butter Balls (page 396).

MAKES 8 1-TABLESPOON SERVINGS

CLARIFIED BUTTER

Clarified butter is also called "drawn butter."

In a small saucepan, melt the butter over low heat. Remove the butter from the heat and let stand about 3 minutes until the white milk solids settle on the bottom of the pan. Using a tablespoon, skim off and discard the fat floating on the melted butter. Then, using a baster, draw off the clear, yellow clarified butter, being careful not to disturb the solids on the pan bottom. As the Clarified Butter is drawn off, place it in a clean, small saucepan. Place over low heat to warm.

The milk solids in regular butter cause it to burn at a low temperature; therefore, removal of the milk solids permits Clarified Butter to be used for cooking at higher temperatures without burning. However, Clarified Butter is less flavorful than regular butter. Elimination of the milk solids allows tightly covered Clarified Butter to be safely refrigerated for several months.

**1½ CUPS (¾ POUND) OF REGULAR BUTTER
MAKES ABOUT 1 CUP OF CLARIFIED BUTTER**

SERVING SUGGESTIONS: Boiled or grilled whole lobsters or lobster tails are traditionally served with small, individual ramekins of warm Clarified Butter (see Boiled Whole Lobsters, page 229, and Grilled Lobster Tails Basted with Tarragon Sauce, page 258). Diners dunk bites into the Clarified Butter.

1 CUP OF CLARIFIED BUTTER MAKES 6 SERVINGS

Other Savory Sauce Recipes

Barbecue Sauce for Outdoor Cooking (page 250)

Dessert Sauces

CARAMEL SAUCE

¼ cup (4 tablespoons) butter
1 cup packed light brown sugar
½ cup light corn syrup
½ cup dark corn syrup
½ cup whipping cream, unwhipped
½ teaspoon pure vanilla extract

In a small saucepan, melt the butter over low heat. Remove from the heat. Add the brown sugar, light corn syrup, and dark corn syrup; stir to combine. Bring the mixture to a boil over medium heat, stirring constantly; boil 2 minutes, stirring intermittently. Remove from the heat. Add the whipping cream and vanilla; stir until blended. Let stand until cooled slightly. Then, place the Caramel Sauce in a pint jar; cover and refrigerate up to 1 week.

To serve over ice cream and many desserts (see Baked Nutmeg Bananas with Ice Cream and Caramel Sauce, page 670), place the Caramel Sauce in a small saucepan over warm heat. Warm only until thinned to the consistency of a fudge sauce, stirring often. Caramel Sauce may also be served hot, in which case it will be of thinner consistency.

MAKES ABOUT 2 CUPS

HOT FUDGE

½ cup semisweet chocolate chips
2 tablespoons butter
½ cup sugar
1 5-ounce can (about ⅔ cup) evaporated
   milk
1 teaspoon pure vanilla extract

In the top of a double boiler, place the chocolate chips and butter. Place the top of the double boiler over (not touching) hot water in the bottom pan. Melt the chocolate chips and butter, stirring until completed blended. Add the sugar and evaporated milk; stir to combine. Place the double boiler over medium-high heat and bring the water in the bottom pan to a boil. Reduce the heat slightly and cook the chocolate mixture over (not touching) boiling water 15 minutes, until thick, stirring constantly.

Remove the top of the double boiler from the bottom pan and place on a wire rack. Add the vanilla; stir until blended. Store, covered, in the refrigerator up to 1 week. To serve, reheat in the top of the double boiler over boiling water. Serve over ice cream.

MAKES 1¼ CUPS (ABOUT 6 SERVINGS)

HOT BUTTERSCOTCH FUDGE: Follow the Hot Fudge recipe, above, substituting ½ cup butterscotch chips for ½ cup semisweet chocolate chips, and substituting ½ cup packed light brown sugar for ½ cup (granulated) sugar. After adding the brown sugar and evaporated milk, use a handheld electric mixer to beat the mixture on low speed during the first few minutes of cooking, until the mixture is completely smooth. Butterscotch chips may become grainy during the melting process, but will smooth out when beat with the sugar and evaporated milk.

CHOCOLATE SAUCE

¼ cup unsweetened cocoa powder
¾ cup sugar
¼ cup light corn syrup
¼ cup water
⅛ teaspoon salt
¾ cup whipping cream, unwhipped
1 teaspoon pure vanilla extract

In a 2½ quart, heavy-bottomed saucepan, place the cocoa, sugar, syrup, water, and salt; stir to combine. Place the saucepan over medium heat; stir the mixture constantly until the sugar dissolves. Then, attach a candy thermometer to the saucepan. Bring the mixture to a boil over medium heat and cook, without stirring, until the temperature reaches 230° F. (about 5 minutes boiling time). Remove from the heat and detach the thermometer. Add the whipping cream and vanilla; stir until blended. Refrigerate, covered, up to 1 week.

MAKES 1½ CUPS (8 3-TABLESPOON SERVINGS)

SERVING SUGGESTIONS: Serve warm or cold over ice cream, cake, or other desserts.

MAPLE BRANDY SAUCE

1 cup pure maple syrup
2 tablespoons butter
2 tablespoons brandy

In a very small saucepan, heat the syrup to nearly boiling over medium heat. Add the butter and brandy; stir until the butter melts and the ingredients are fully blended. Remove from the heat and serve immediately, or let stand to cool slightly and then pour the Maple Brandy Sauce into a pint jar. Cover and refrigerate up to 1 week.

MAKES ENOUGH SAUCE FOR 8 TO 10 SERVINGS

SERVING SUGGESTIONS: Serve hot Maple Brandy Sauce over vanilla, butter pecan, or butter brickle ice cream.

LEMON SAUCE

1 tablespoon cornstarch
½ cup sugar
Dash of salt
Dash of ground nutmeg
1 cup boiling water
2 tablespoons butter
2 tablespoons plus 1½ teaspoons freshly
    squeezed, strained lemon juice
1 drop yellow liquid food coloring

In a small saucepan, place the cornstarch, sugar, salt, and nutmeg; stir to combine. Add 1 cup boiling water; stir to blend. Cook the mixture over medium heat until thick and translucent, stirring constantly. Remove from the heat. Add the butter, lemon juice, and food coloring; stir until the butter melts and the ingredients blend. Serve warm or cold. In a covered glass jar, Lemon Sauce keeps up to 3 days in the refrigerator.

MAKES ABOUT 1¼ CUPS

SERVING SUGGESTIONS
- Serve cold Lemon Sauce or Lemon Sauce with Raisins (see recipe, below) over bread pudding (see Bread Pudding with Lemon Sauce, page 660).

- Serve warm Lemon Sauce over Apple Brown Betty (page 650).

- Serve warm or cold Lemon Sauce over cake such as Gingerbread (page 544).

LEMON SAUCE WITH RAISINS: In a small saucepan, place ½ cup raisins and ½ cup water. Cover the saucepan. Bring the raisins to a boil over high heat. Remove from the heat; let the raisin mixture stand, covered, until cool. Then, drain the raisins well in a sieve. Add the raisins to completed Lemon Sauce (see recipe, above); stir to evenly distribute.

CUSTARD SAUCE

Also known as stirred custard, soft custard, and boiled custard, the sublime richness of this versatile sauce adds an elegant touch to the many desserts it enhances. Custard Sauce plays a major role in certain traditional, notable desserts, such as Snow Pudding (page 660) and floating island. Spooned over fresh fruit, gelatin, or cake, it turns a good dessert into a special one. Especially children are fond of it served alone.

3 extra-large egg yolks
3 tablespoons sugar
⅛ teaspoon salt
1 cup half-and-half
1 cup whole milk
1 teaspoon pure vanilla extract

Place the egg yolks in the top of a double boiler; using a handheld electric mixer, beat slightly on medium-high speed. Add the sugar and salt; stir to combine; set aside.

Into a small saucepan, pour the half-and-half and milk; place over medium heat and scald (page 25). Pour about ½ cup of the scalded milk mixture into the egg yolk mixture; stir quickly to blend. Then, pour about ½ cup additional scalded milk mixture into the egg yolk mixture; stir to blend. Pour the remaining scalded milk mixture into the egg yolk mixture; stir to blend.

Place the top of the double boiler containing the egg yolk mixture over (not touching) hot (not boiling) water in the bottom pan. While stirring constantly and watching carefully to keep the water in the bottom pan at just below the boiling point, cook the mixture until it coats the spoon (about 10 to 12 minutes). Remove the top of the double boiler from the bottom pan. Add the vanilla; stir until blended. Pour the Custard Sauce into a bowl; let stand on a wire rack for a few minutes, until cooled slightly. Then, refrigerate; cover when completely cool. Keeps up to 3 days in the refrigerator.

MAKES ABOUT 2¼ CUPS

RUM SAUCE

1 cup sugar
2 tablespoons plus 1 teaspoon cornstarch
⅛ teaspoon salt
1 cup water
¼ cup (4 tablespoons) butter
Dash of ground mace
¼ cup dark rum

In a small saucepan, place the sugar, cornstarch, and salt; stir to combine. Add the water; stir to mix. Cook the mixture over medium-high heat until thick and translucent, stirring constantly. Remove from the heat. Add the butter and mace; stir until the butter melts. Add the rum; stir until completely blended. Serve Rum Sauce warm or cold. To heat, return the sauce to medium heat; stir until warm. Do not bring to a boil. In a covered glass jar, Rum Sauce keeps up to 1 week in the refrigerator.

MAKES ABOUT 1¾ CUPS

SERVING SUGGESTIONS

- Serve warm Rum Sauce and Rum-Raisin Sauce (see recipe below) over cake such as Gingerbread (page 544).

- Serve cold Rum Sauce on spumoni ice cream. Serve cold Rum-Raisin Sauce (see recipe, below) on vanilla ice cream.

RUM-RAISIN SAUCE: In a small saucepan, place 1 cup raisins and 1¼ cups water. Cover the saucepan. Bring the raisins to a boil over high heat. Remove from the heat; let the raisin mixture stand, covered, until cool.

Then, drain the raisins in a sieve, reserving the liquid. Set the raisins aside. Strain the raisin liquid through a piece of damp cotton flannel secured, napped side up, in a small sieve over a bowl (see Note); set aside.

Follow the Rum Sauce recipe, above, substituting ¾ cup sugar for 1 cup sugar, and substituting the strained raisin liquid (no need to measure) for 1 cup water. Add the raisins after the rum has been blended into the sauce; stir to evenly distribute. Warm the sauce, following the procedure in the Rum Sauce recipe.

NOTE: If a piece of cotton flannel is not available, 4 layers of damp, *untreated* cheesecloth may be substituted and secured in the sieve.

WHIPPED CREAM

1 cup (½ pint) whipping cream
2 tablespoons granulated sugar
1 teaspoon pure vanilla extract

Pour the whipping cream into a cold (previously refrigerated), medium-small mixing bowl. Using an electric mixer, beat the cream on medium-high speed until it begins to stiffen. Reduce the mixer speed to medium-low. Add the sugar and vanilla; continue beating the cream until stiff but still soft and fluffy.

While the mixer is beating the cream, intermittently run a rubber spatula against the edge of the mixing bowl to move the cream in the outer portions of the bowl toward the center, helping to assure that all the cream is evenly beaten.

Watch the cream very carefully as it nears the desired stiffness, as overbeaten whipping cream turns to butter in the blink of an eye, making it less appealing in appearance and texture. Reducing the mixer speed to low in the final moments of beating helps keep the cream more controllable.

Whipped Cream is best when served immediately after whipping; however, it may be covered and kept in the refrigerator about 2 to 3 hours before liquid begins to accumulate in the bottom of the bowl and the Whipped Cream begins to stiffen. When serving Whipped Cream which has been prepared in advance, spoon it off the top to avoid including any liquid which may have accumulated at the bottom of the bowl. From a food safety standpoint, Whipped Cream may be kept refrigerated for as many days as the

(Recipe continues on next page)

cream would have stayed fresh before it was whipped; however, stored Whipped Cream continues to lose its fluffiness as liquid steadily drains to the bottom of the storage container.

MAKES 2 CUPS

DECORATOR WHIPPED CREAM

1 cup (½ pint) whipping cream
¼ cup powdered sugar
1 teaspoon clear vanilla
Paste food coloring (when coloring is used)

Pour the whipping cream into a cold (previously refrigerated), medium-small mixing bowl. Using an electric mixer, beat the cream on medium-high speed until it begins to stiffen. Reduce the mixer speed to medium-low. Add the powdered sugar, vanilla, and paste food coloring (if used); continue beating the cream until stiff but still soft and fluffy.

While the mixer is beating the cream, intermittently run a rubber spatula against the edge of the mixing bowl to move the cream in the outer portions of the bowl toward the center, helping to assure that all the cream is evenly beaten.

Watch the cream very carefully as it nears the desired stiffness, as overbeaten whipping cream turns to butter in the blink of an eye, making it less appealing in appearance and texture. Reducing the mixer speed to low in the final moments of beating helps keep the cream more controllable.

WHEN TO USE DECORATOR WHIPPED CREAM: Use Decorator Whipped Cream when whipped cream of a stiffer consistency than regular whipped cream (see Whipped Cream, page 373) is desired or required. The stiffer consistency of Decorator Whipped Cream is achieved by the substitution of powdered sugar or granulated sugar, which is used in most traditional whipped cream. Use Decorator Whipped Cream to frost pies and cakes, and to pipe whipped cream dec-

orations using a decorating bag and tips (page 383). Decorator Whipped Cream may also be used for general purposes if you prefer it.

It is necessary that whipped cream used to pipe decorations be firm bodied to retain precise, sharp, piped decorative designs. When used to pipe decorations, Decorator Whipped Cream should be whipped to just under the point of turning to butter. Also, it is important to use paste food coloring rather than liquid food coloring to retain maximum stiffness.

For use in frosting pies and cakes, and piping decorations, Decorator Whipped Cream should be whipped immediately before using. For best results, it should be applied to the food product within 2 to 3 hours of serving time to avert any seepage of liquid from the whipped cream.

ORANGE DECORATOR WHIPPED CREAM: Follow the Decorator Whipped Cream recipe, substituting ¼ teaspoon orange extract and ¾ teaspoon clear vanilla for 1 teaspoon clear vanilla. Using orange paste food coloring, tint the whipped cream pale orange.

CHOCOLATE DECORATOR WHIPPED CREAM: Follow the Decorator Whipped Cream recipe, adding 2 tablespoons unsweetened cocoa powder to the whipping cream after adding the powdered sugar and vanilla.

Gravies

MILK GRAVY

Even though this gravy is commonly known as "cream gravy," it is more often made with whole milk than with cream nowadays. I have written a separate recipe for Cream Gravy (see right column) which uses half-and-half and requires only half the amount of flour for thickening as that needed for Milk Gravy. These two gravies may be used interchangeably. Most people consider Milk Gravy plenty rich and tasty for general use. When you want a superluxurious gravy for entertaining or otherwise, go for the Cream Gravy, calories and all.

Milk Gravy (or Cream Gravy) is the traditional—and best—gravy to serve over mashed potatoes when panfried chicken (see Fried Chicken, page 211) or pork chops (see Iowa Pork Chops, page 185) are the main fare. It is also the gravy which accompanies Chicken Fried Steak (page 164). This versatile gravy may be made with equal success using the skillet drippings and meat particles after panfrying or braising pork, veal, poultry, wildfowl, or beef.

¼ cup all-purpose flour
½ teaspoon salt
¼ teaspoon pepper
1 cup whole milk
1 cup whole milk

In a pint jar or a plastic container with a secure lid, place the flour, salt, pepper, and 1 cup milk; cover and shake vigorously until blended and smooth; set aside.

Then, pour 1 cup milk into the skillet in which the meat was cooked. Over very low heat (220° F. if using an electric skillet), deglaze the skillet. Add the flour mixture; stir well to blend. Increase the skillet heat to medium (350° F. if

using an electric skillet). Bring the gravy to a brisk simmer, stirring constantly. Simmer the gravy 1 minute, stirring continuously. Serve immediately.

MAKES ABOUT 2 CUPS

CREAM GRAVY

Cream Gravy may be used interchangeably with Milk Gravy. See the headnote under the recipe for Milk Gravy, left column, for a description of the many uses for this wonderful gravy. The recipe for Braised Short Ribs with Dilled Potatoes on page 170 specifically uses Cream Gravy and calls for it to be strained after making for perfect smoothness, which I find more suitable with the dilled, unmashed potatoes.

2 tablespoons all-purpose flour
½ teaspoon salt
¼ teaspoon pepper
1 cup half-and-half
1 cup half-and-half

In a pint jar or a plastic container with a secure lid, place the flour, salt, pepper, and 1 cup half-and-half; cover and shake vigorously until blended and smooth; set aside.

Then, pour 1 cup half-and-half into the skillet in which the meat was cooked. Over very low heat (220° F. if using an electric skillet), deglaze the skillet. Add the flour mixture; stir well to blend. Increase the skillet heat to medium (350° F. if using an electric skillet). Bring the gravy to a brisk simmer, stirring constantly. Simmer the gravy 1 minute, stirring continuously. Serve immediately.

MAKES ABOUT 2 CUPS

BEEF GRAVY

¼ cup plus 2 teaspoons flour
½ teaspoon salt
¼ teaspoon pepper
1 cup cold water
¼ cup skimmed drippings from beef
    roasting pan (see recipe procedures
    below)
1 cup hot water

In a pint jar or a plastic container with a secure lid, place the flour, salt, pepper, and 1 cup cold water; cover and shake vigorously until blended and smooth; set aside.

Pour the drippings from the beef roasting pan into a gravy skimmer (page 23); let stand 2 minutes. Pour off the drippings; discard the fat (see Note 1). Measure ¼ cup skimmed drippings and pour into a medium saucepan; set aside.

Pour 1 cup hot water into the beef roasting pan; place over medium heat. Using a metal mixing spoon, scrape the bottom of the roasting pan until completely deglazed. Pour the roasting pan liquid into the saucepan containing the measured drippings. Add the flour mixture. Stir to blend the ingredients. Place over medium heat. While stirring constantly, bring the gravy to a boil and boil 2 minutes (see Note 2). Pour the gravy into a gravy boat and serve immediately.

NOTE 1: If a gravy skimmer is not available, pour the drippings into a regular 1-cup glass measuring cup with a pouring spout. Let stand about 2 minutes until the fat rises to the top. Using a baster, draw off the fat and discard.

NOTE 2: If the gravy does not appear dark enough, ¼ teaspoon Kitchen Bouquet browning and seasoning sauce may be stirred in.

MAKES ABOUT 2¼ CUPS

BEEF GRAVY/SAUCE WITH MUSHROOMS: In a small, heavy-bottomed skillet, melt 2 tablespoons butter over medium heat. Place 4 ounces fresh mushrooms, sliced ⅛ inch thick (about 1½ cups), in the skillet; sauté until the mushrooms give up their juices (about 5 minutes). Remove from the heat; set aside.

To make Beef *Gravy* with Mushrooms, follow the Beef Gravy recipe, above. Add the mushrooms and pan juices to the gravy; stir to combine and blend. Add 1 tablespoon dry sherry; stir to blend.

To make Beef *Sauce* with Mushrooms, follow the Beef Gravy recipe, above, reducing the flour to ¼ cup. Add the mushrooms and pan juices; stir to combine and blend. Add 1 tablespoon dry sherry; stir to blend.

BEEF WINE GRAVY: Follow the Beef Gravy recipe, above, substituting ¼ cup red or white wine for ¼ cup of the cold water. If wine is used in the preparation of the beef dish with which this gravy will be served, the flavor of the served fare usually will be enhanced if the same wine used in cooking the meat is used in the gravy.

POT ROAST GRAVY

¼ cup all-purpose flour
½ teaspoon salt
¼ teaspoon pepper
½ cup cold water
1½ cups skillet juices plus hot water

In a small glass jar or plastic container with a secure lid, place the flour, salt, pepper, and ½ cup cold water; cover and shake vigorously until blended and smooth; set aside.

Pour the juices from the skillet in which the pot roast was cooked into a 2-cup glass measuring cup with a pouring spout; add hot water to make 1½ cups liquid. Return the skillet juices plus added water to the skillet. Over very low heat (220° F. if using an electric skillet) deglaze the skillet. Add the flour mixture; stir to blend well with the skillet liquid. Increase the skillet heat to medium-low (325° F. if using an electric skillet). Bring the gravy to a simmer, stirring constantly. Simmer the gravy 2 to 3 minutes, stirring continuously.

MAKES ABOUT 2 CUPS

ROAST PORK GRAVY

¼ cup all-purpose flour
½ teaspoon salt
¼ teaspoon pepper
1 cup cold water
1 cup hot water

In a pint jar or a plastic container with a secure lid, place the flour, salt, pepper, and 1 cup cold water; cover and shake vigorously until blended and smooth; set aside.

Using a baster, draw off and discard any excess fat in the pork roasting pan. Pour 1 cup hot water into the roasting pan; place over medium heat. Using a metal mixing spoon, scrape the bottom of the roasting pan until completely deglazed. Strain the roasting pan liquid through a sieve. Pour the strained liquid into a medium saucepan. Add the flour mixture; stir to blend. Place over medium-high heat. While stirring constantly, bring the gravy to a boil and boil 2 minutes. Pour the gravy into a gravy boat and serve immediately.

MAKES ABOUT 2 CUPS

PORK WINE GRAVY: Follow the Roast Pork Gravy recipe, above, substituting ¼ cup red or white wine for ¼ cup of the cold water. If wine is used in the preparation of the pork dish with which this gravy will be served, the flavor of the served fare usually will be enhanced if the same wine used in cooking the meat is used in the gravy.

ROAST LAMB GRAVY

¼ cup all-purpose flour
½ teaspoon garlic salt
½ teaspoon salt
⅛ teaspoon pepper
½ cup cold water
¼ cup skimmed drippings from lamb roasting pan (see recipe procedures below)
1½ cups hot water

In a small glass jar or plastic container with a secure lid, place the flour, garlic salt, salt, pepper, and ½ cup cold water; cover and shake vigorously until blended and smooth; set aside.

Pour the drippings from the lamb roasting pan into a gravy skimmer (page 23); let stand 2 minutes. Pour off the drippings; discard the fat (see Note 1). Measure ¼ cup skimmed drippings and pour into a medium saucepan; set aside.

Pour 1½ cups hot water into the lamb roasting pan; place over medium heat. Using a metal mixing spoon, scrape the bottom of the roasting pan until completely deglazed. Strain the roasting pan liquid through a piece of damp cotton flannel secured, napped side up, in a sieve over a bowl (see Note 2). Pour the strained juices into the saucepan containing the measured drippings. Add the flour mixture. Stir to blend the ingredients. Place over medium heat. Bring the gravy to a brisk simmer, stirring constantly. Simmer the gravy 1 minute, stirring continuously. Pour the gravy into a gravy boat and serve immediately.

NOTE 1: If a gravy skimmer is not available, pour the drippings into a regular 1-cup glass measuring cup with a pouring spout. Let stand about 2 minutes until the fat rises to the top. Using a baster, draw off the fat and discard.

NOTE 2: If a piece of cotton flannel is not available, 4 layers of damp, *untreated* cheesecloth may be substituted and secured in the sieve.

MAKES ABOUT 2¼ CUPS

TURKEY GRAVY

½ cup all-purpose flour
1 teaspoon salt
½ teaspoon pepper
4 cups (1 quart) whole milk, divided
½ cup skimmed drippings from turkey
 roasting pan (see recipe procedures
 below)

When the turkey is nearly done, place the flour, salt, pepper, and about 1 cup of the milk in a pint jar or a plastic container with a secure lid; cover and shake vigorously until blended and smooth; set aside. Pour the remaining milk in a medium saucepan. Warm the milk (do not allow it to boil) over medium-low heat to help quicken the gravy-making process after the turkey is out of the oven.

Pour the drippings from the turkey roasting pan into a gravy skimmer (page 23); let stand 2 minutes. Pour off the drippings; discard the fat (see Note). Measure ½ cup skimmed drippings and add to the warm milk; stir to blend. Add the flour mixture; stir to blend. Increase the heat to medium. Bring the gravy to a brisk simmer, stirring constantly. Simmer the gravy 1 minute, stirring continously. Pour the gravy into a gravy boat and serve immediately.

NOTE: If a gravy skimmer is not available, pour the drippings into a regular 1- or 2-cup glass measuring cup with a pouring spout. Let stand about 2 minutes until the fat rises to the top. Using a baster, draw off the fat and discard.

MAKES ABOUT 4½ CUPS

TURKEY GIBLET GRAVY

Turkey giblets (heart, gizzard, and liver)
 and neck
1 celery stalk including leaves, chopped
 coarsely
1 small onion, sliced thinly
3 whole black peppercorns
1 recipe Turkey Gravy (left column)

THE DAY BEFORE SERVING OR EARLY IN THE DAY OF SERVING: Wash the giblets and neck under cold, running water. Dry the liver between paper towels. Place the dried liver on a plate; cover and refrigerate. In a large saucepan, place the heart, gizzard, neck, celery, onions, and peppercorns; add water to cover. Cover the saucepan; bring the mixture to a boil over high heat. Reduce the heat and simmer 1 hour, or until the giblets and neck are tender. Remove the meat from the saucepan and place it in a colander to drain; set aside. Add the liver to the broth in the saucepan; simmer 25 minutes, or until tender.

Meanwhile, remove the meat from the neck bone; discard the bone. Chop the heart, gizzard, and neck meat finely; place in a container; cover and refrigerate. When the liver is done, place it in the colander to drain. Chop the liver finely; place it in the container containing the other chopped meats; cover and refrigerate.

JUST BEFORE SERVING: Make the Turkey Gravy. Add the chopped giblets and neck meat; heat through and serve.

Other Gravy Recipes

Dried Beef Gravy (page 164)
Biscuits and Gravy Madeira (page 188)

Garnishes and Decorations

The Pleasure of Dining

"Life is what you make it." Yes and no. We have control over much of our destiny through our attitudes about work and play, perseverance, integrity, learning, discipline, and caring. But the mysterious factors—fate, luck, and perhaps, reasons of the soul—all beyond our understanding and manipulation—interweave our lives. No matter what our circumstances, we do possess, to a great extent, the option of adopting a lifestyle of civility, orderliness, cleanliness, respect, happiness, and beauty. Financial status, education, and position have surprisingly little to do with living a life of basic grace and refinement. Means do not dictate true style.

Rich or poor, we all must eat to live. The consumption of food can be reduced to the chore of eating out of necessity, or it can be elevated to the pleasure of dining. For most of us, to eat or to dine is our daily choice.*

A family of humble means may sit down together at a neatly set kitchen table for a dinner of broiled ground beef patties, fresh green beans, and baked potatoes, while another family of greater wherewithal may dine on sliced beef tenderloin, asparagus amandine, and duchess potatoes served in their spacious dining room. However, there may be considerable commonality between the two tables in addition to the good balance and nutrition of both these meals. Both meals may be served in an organized fashion, pleasant conversation about the day's activities may be carried on by each family, simple good manners may prevail, and all family members may remain at both tables until the meals have been completed.

* In no way are these statements and thoughts meant to overlook the plight of the thousands of homeless, handicapped, aged, and ill persons who are dependent upon others for the maintenance of dignified lives.

Today, with working mothers and busy schedules, mealtimes are often one of the few times an active family has the opportunity to be together. Meals provide scheduled times on a regular basis when successes, problems, and questions, no matter how great or how small, may be shared and discussed. Many children raised in homes where planned meals, with all family members present, were the norm, attest to the fact that much of their home training in life values took place through relaxed discussions at mealtimes. Prioritizing scarce time to include nutritious breakfasts enjoyed together as a family could play a role in ironing out some of the difficulties the American family is facing, not to mention the health benefits to be derived.

Viewed from the proper perspective, daily mealtimes can be mini vacations from the routine and responsibilities of life. Giving thought to the preparation of attractive, interesting food, plus concern and study about nutrition and its effect on how we feel, work, and look, can have life-enriching and healthful results. The preparation and presentation of attractive food for our families, our friends, and ourselves should be an established habit—a part of life which helps make each day and each meal special and worthwhile.

Even if you live alone, the table can be set, the candles can be lit, and appealing food can delight your palate as you listen to beautiful music or enjoy the company of your favorite television commentators as they tell you about the happenings of the day. Luxuriate for the moment! Rest for fifteen minutes after dinner. Then, you're ready to tackle the work brought home from the office, tend to household tasks, or read until it's time to go to bed. Day after day of yogurt out of the container for lunch and frozen dinners eaten on a bare kitchen counter contribute to a monotonous, uninteresting, unhealthy lifestyle and person.

I had a friend who used to say, "I like good food in small quantities." Well said. An observation can be made that the habit of volume eating is too prevalent in many parts of the Midwest, especially among people who pursue sedentary occupations. The attitude toward eating should be transformed from "filling up" to "savoring flavor." Eating more slowly and truly tasting the flavor of the food in our mouths can make it much easier to stop when enough has been consumed to meet nutritional requirements.

Beautification of the food we eat is a natural manifestation of civilized life. Through the ages, people have turned to the arts as mediums for self-expression and for the enrichment of their lives and environment. Satisfying color and texture combinations of decorously arranged foods gratify our sense of beauty and balance as well as our sense of taste. Garnishes and decorations can lift the most simple fare out of the ordinary. Whether a spray of fresh, dark green watercress or a picturesque arrangement of red and yellow tomato roses, each can render a plate of food beautiful, fascinating, or fun.

Assigning importance to the presentation of food has crescendoed in recent years, reaching fortissimo in some of the newer restaurants and cafés in New York and California. Finer restaurants and private clubs in Chicago, Minneapolis, Cleveland, and other large Midwest cities are following suit. Adding substantial impetus are the glossy pages of food magazines filled cover to cover with pictures of inviting food glamorously presented—all of which are influencing home cooks to focus more and more on this dimension.

Garnishes and decorations should complement food, not detract from it or supplant it. Decorating a plate can be carried to extremes and become an end unto itself. The most beautiful, artistic decorations do not mollify ho-hum food.

Although the terms "garnish" and "decoration" are commonly used interchangeably within the context of food, I make a distinction between the two, defining each, as follows:

Garnish is a small quantity of food, artistically cut, sculpted, and/or arranged on an individual or serving plate of food as an adjunct to enhance the overall appearance of the plate and as a flavor-complement to the primary food.

Decoration is a very small embellishment of food or edible flowers placed or arranged on primary food or garnish, or otherwise placed on individual or serving plates of food for the purpose of adding color, flair, and general eye appeal.

A piped deviled egg and carrot curls arranged on the edge of a Lobster-Avocado Salad (page 147) luncheon plate are examples of garnish. A tiny parsley leaf or a sprinkle of paprika on top of the deviled egg filling are examples of decoration. The assignment of one of these descriptions depends upon the quantity of food used and its purpose. Garnish generally employs a larger quantity of food than decoration. Sometimes there is a thin line between the two. If a few chocolate curls are arranged on the top of a frosted cake primarily for looks, they are a decoration. If the white frosting on a chocolate cake is covered with shaved chocolate to add flavor as well as artistic appeal, the shavings would be defined as garnish.

Whether or not a cook chooses to make a definition distinction between these two types of food ornamentation is, of course, a matter of personal choice. The ornamental enhancement of food is the important consideration, not what it may be labeled.

This chapter contains instructions for making thirty-eight doable garnishes and decorations which can change the complexion of served food from pedestrian to classy.

It can be as simple as surprising the family with a Radish Fan (page 403) doing a balancing act on top of their tossed salads. Or, flabbergast them with a gorgeous Cucumber Rose (page 399) and sprig of fresh dill in the center of a summertime bowl of Cucumber Salad (page 131). For a weekend informal lunch on the patio, make Sweet Pickle Fans (page 402) and Celery Brushes (page 399), and arrange them nattily on a platter of cold cuts and cheeses. It will almost seem like a party!

Even if it's a busy Wednesday evening after taking the kids to Cub Scouts and piano lessons, a crispy sprig of parsley next to the heated left-over meat loaf, and a tiny jar of sliced pimientos added to the canned corn warming on the stove can help change the meal from eating to dining.

Grilled steak dinners—always a treat—become even more tantalizing when a Baked Tomato Parmesan (page 404) is nestled beside the Twice-Baked Potato (page 329) on each plate just as the sizzling T-bones are rushed to the kitchen from the grill. Before the plates are hurried to the table, place a sprig of fresh cilantro next to each tomato and top each steak with a pretty Onion Butter star (page 369). Then, listen for the X's and O's.

From breakfast for one to black-tie dinner for one hundred—and all the meals in between—may your dining be pleasurable!

Edible Flowers

Gracing the center of the table, flowers lend majesty to dining. Edible flowers can also be exquisite decoration for the food to be savored. With new emphasis on the art of food presentation, guests in fashionable restaurants and at special dinner parties are delighting more frequently in beautifully arranged plates of food made even more breathtaking by the final, sophisticated touch of real, edible flowers.

Flowers would probably bejewel food more often if cooks had more information about the varieties which are edible. As we all know, many flowers are poisonous—among the winsome blossoms on the **poisonous** list are buttercup *(Ranunculus acris),* daffodil *(Narcissus pseudonarcissus),* lily of the valley *(Convallaria majalis),* and sweet pea *(Lathyrus odoratus).* You must know what you are doing before venturing into the garden or woods, or onto the lawn to pick flowers for human consumption. One must be absolutely sure about the safety of a flower before placing it on a plate of food. *Nonedible flowers should never be used for decorating food,* even if diners are forewarned.

Availability of flowers suitable for food is also

a factor. Avant-garde cooks with a green thumb as well as an artistic flair are not only cultivating their own herb gardens, but also are tending beds of edible flowers for last-minute picking to glamorize wonderful food (see Nasturtium Salad, page 132).

A formidable barrier to flower feasting is pollution. Flowers which have been sprayed with chemical insecticides or fertilizers should not be eaten, even if they have been washed beforehand. This caveat rules out flowers commercially purchased at a florist or greenhouse. As the use of edible flowers for food grows more widespread, some varieties may become available at organic food stores or in produce markets. However, one would want assurance that they had been raised for human consumption and had not been subjected to chemical sprays. For all practical purposes, the only safe sources for edible posies are your own controlled garden and yard (provided the yard is free from pets).

Another warning must be passed along: some people are allergic to flowers. Persons subject to food allergies are best advised not to eat flowers. Whatever one's predisposition to allergies, the conservative approach is recommended for everyone eating a flower variety for the first time. Excitement over the newfound adventure of food beautification with blossoms can prompt initiates to go overboard. While it is tempting to astonish your family or friends with an unexpected, virtual bouquet salad of ravishing flowers, sound counsel suggests that such a spectacular splash be prefaced with a series of taste testings comprised of a couple of small blossoms, or two or three large petals at a time as complements to the regular daily fare.

Even when you have studied your lesson and have decided upon a specific edible flower variety for inclusion in a dish, you must be certain that the flowers ushered into the kitchen are, in fact, the intended ones. *The only safe way to identify flowers suitable for eating is by botanical name.* Common names are insufficient. A wide variety of flowers is often known by a single, common name. For example, while daylilies *(Hemerocallis fulva)* are edible, a false assumption that most or all "lilies" are edible could lead to disaster. Tiger lilies *(Lilium lancifolium)* are among members of the lily family which are poisonous. If in doubt, don't experiment.

All of the foregoing admonitions are not intended to discourage culinary pacesetters from exploring the realm of edible flowers. Although a relatively new form of artistic culinary expression in modern American home cooking, flower cookery is ancient in practice. The use of edible flowers in cooking is meritorious and safe if properly studied and pursued.

The following flowers, listed by both their common and botanical names, are among those safe for decorating food and for consumption by most healthy people:

Apple (*Malus spp.*)
Calendula (*Calendula officinalis*)
Chrysanthemum (*Chrysanthemum ×
    morifolium*)
Dandelion, plus leaves (*Taraxacum officinale*)
Daylily, flowers only; not the tubers (roots)
    (*Hemerocallis fulva*)
Elderberry (*Sambucus canadensis* [deep purple
    to black fruit] and *S. caerulea* [dark blue to
    black fruit]) (**not** *S. pubens* [red fruit])
Johnny-jump-up *(Viola tricolor)*
Mustard (*Brassica nigra, B. hirta, B. juncea,*
    and *B. rapa*)
Nasturtium, plus leaves (*Tropaeolum majus*)
Pansy (*Viola × Wittrockiana*)
Pink (*Dianthus spp.*)
Redbud (*Cercis canadensis*)
Red Clover (*Trifolium pratense*)
Rose, wild and domestic (*Rosa spp.*)
Squash Blossoms (*Cucurbita spp.*)
Violet, plus leaves (*Viola odorata*)

In addition to this partial list of edible flowers, the blossoms of most herbs used in cooking are edible. However, for peak flavor, herbs should not be allowed to bloom (see To Dry Herbs, page 39), so diligent herb gardeners snip the flower buds from their herb plants as soon as they appear. Even so, among dedicated herbalists, there has emerged a *corps d'elite* who know they can have their herbs and eat the flowers too. Alongside their fastidiously pruned herbs, they allow a plant or two of each variety to bloom—providing showstopping dazzlers for dishes flavored with leaves from their well-groomed, neighboring kin. One can often catch sight of herb blossoms nowadays floating in stunning bottles of upscale herb vinegars displayed in gourmet food stores.

The following are some of the herbs whose flowers are safely edible by most healthy people:

Basil (*Ocimum basilicum*)
Chervil (*Anthriscus cerefolium*)
Chives (*Allium schoenoprasum*)
Coriander (*Coriandrum sativum*)
Dill (*Anethum graveolens*)
Fennel (*Foeniculum vulgare*)
Marjoram (*Origanum majorana* and *Origanum vulgare*)
Mint (*Mentha spp.*)
Oregano (*Origanum vulgare subsp. birtum*)
Rosemary (*Rosmarinus officinalis*)
Sage (*Salvia officinalis*)
Thyme (*Thymus vulgaris*)

The preparation of edible flowers for consumption varies with the flower. While violets, Johnny-jump-ups, pansies, and nasturtiums may be eaten in their entirety (see Sugared Violets, page 408), only the petals of large calendulas, chrysanthemums, and roses are eaten. Further, the white, lower portion of the petals of chrysanthemums, pinks, roses, and certain other flowers can be bitter tasting and is often trimmed away. Especially when preparing larger flowers for eating, the pistils, stamens, and sepals (see illustration) should be removed.

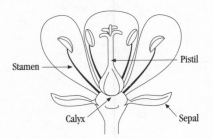

Food safety and sanitation considerations dictate that flowers be washed before being served as food; however, no matter how careful one may be, washing compromises the fresh, velvety appearance of most delicate blossoms. In the interest of public safety, I prescribe that all edible flowers be washed before being served as food. I admit to breaking this rule on occasion because I use edible flowers only from my own garden and yard, where I know they have not been subject to chemical contaminants (except natural air pollutants and the chance of wild animal pollution). In the kitchen, I meticulously examine each blossom for insects and bits of dust or dirt. (Here in the Midwest, the tiniest speck of our coal black soil resting on a vivid flower petal is easily spotted.)

Visual ballistics—from glitter to high drama—undoubtedly are the attraction when it comes to playing matchmaker between food and flower. But flavor is not to be underestimated when orchestrating harmonious unions between food and flower eligibles. Flowers have individual flavors ranging from sweet to spicy to pungent, and vary in degree of flavor intensity from mild to strong. Successful food-flower marriages are arranged by creative, knowledgeable, and adventuresome cooks.

Using a Decorating Bag to Pipe Garnishes and Decorations

Acquiring the know-how to use a decorating bag pays off in beautiful food—as elegant to behold as it is felicitious to eat. Attractively presented food charms, tempts, and just seems to taste better.

Any interested cook can learn to pipe professional-looking borders around a cake and turn out "almost too good-looking to eat" roses to decorate the top—or, to put the finishing touch on a knockout meat platter or tantalizing casserole by piping a generous zigzag ring of fluffy mashed potatoes around the edge. There are 3 requirements: some competent instruction, good equipment, and *practice.*

My advice is to enroll in a cake-decorating class. Continuing education programs and private cooking schools often offer such courses. Also, Wilton Enterprises sponsors cake-decorating courses in many locales across the country (see Note). Use of a decorating bag can be learned most expeditiously and satisfactorily through classes which incorporate both teacher demonstration and student practice, followed by lots of practice at home.

This section contains a brief introduction to the use of a decorating bag, as well as pictures and instructions for piping a few of the basic borders, designs, and flowers.

NOTE: For class locations and schedules, call 800-942-8881.

BASIC EQUIPMENT

Good-quality equipment is essential to obtain the desired results. Sweet Celebrations Inc. and Wilton Enterprises are excellent sources for decorating equipment and supplies (see page 850 for addresses and telephone numbers). Wilton equipment and supplies are carried by retail stores in many areas.

Tip numbers called for in the instructions below and in recipes in this book are standard Wilton tip numbers. The same numbers apply to tips available from Sweet Celebrations Inc.—the difference in sizes between the two tip lines is negligible.

The following basic equipment is needed to pipe the garnishes and decorations pictured and described later in this section:

Polyester decorating bags in 8-inch, 10-inch, and 12-inch sizes
Couplers
Tips in assorted sizes

Tip storage box (to help prevent bending and denting of tips)
8-inch narrow, straight spatula
1½-inch flower nail
Pair of small scissors
4½-inch-long piece of ¼-inch dowel, sharpened in a pencil sharpener
Waxed paper cut into 2-inch squares
Paste food coloring in assorted colors
Toothpicks
Small and medium plastic containers with secure lids (for tinting and refrigerating icing)
Piping gel (to use when piping Holly Leaves; instructions, below)
Decorating turntable (see illustration, page 573)
Tip brush (to help clean tips)

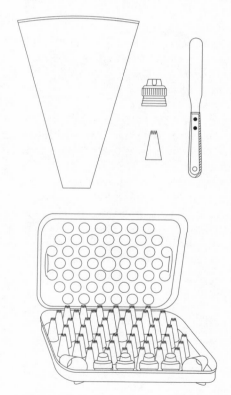

Top, clockwise from left: *Polyester decorating bag; Coupler; 8-inch narrow, straight spatula; and Tip.* Bottom: *Tip storage box.*

CARE OF EQUIPMENT

All decorating equipment should be stored in a special box or drawer to keep it in good condition, and for ready access when decorating is on the cooking agenda.

Tips should be stored in a tip storage box (see illustration) to help prevent them from becoming bent or dented. Bends or dents in tips can distort piped shapes.

Decorating bags, tips, couplers, and other decorating equipment should be washed in very hot, soapy water after use to remove all grease. Turn decorating bags inside out to thoroughly scrub the inside surfaces; then, reverse the bags and scrub the outside surfaces. Rinse the bags thoroughly in very hot water and dry them with a clean tea towel. Place each dried decorating bag tentlike over a wineglass or other tall, narrow glass and let it stand until completely dry before re-storing.

Use a special tip brush to assist in removing icing from the inside of tips. Then, wash the tips in very hot, soapy water, handling them with care. Rinse and dry the tips. Then, let them stand in a safe spot until completely dry before re-storing them in the tip storage box.

ICING CONSISTENCY

While several types of icing and techniques may be employed to frost and decorate cakes, this section is confined to the use of buttercream-type icing. This type of icing generally is used when learning to decorate, and is preferred, in general, by many people (including me) because of its good taste and very edible consistency, and because of the ease with which it is made and handled.

Proper icing consistency is critical to achieving success with cake frostings and decorations. Although a wide variety of recipes for buttercream-type icings may be used, it is recommended that cooks new to decorating use one of the following icing recipes developed especially for decorating:

Cake Decorators' White Icing (page 576)
Cake Decorators' Buttercream Icing (page 576)
Cake Decorators' Chocolate Icing (page 577)

These icings are excellent for frosting cakes to be decorated, as well as for the decorations themselves, because they apply nicely and make it possible to achieve a very smooth cake finish which is desirable when the surface is to be decorated. When an abundance of flowers, leaves, and other piped decorations and/or writing will be used to bedeck a cake, a smooth frosting finish is a necessity. See To Frost a Cake, page 573, for techniques to produce a smoothly frosted cake.

Different decorations require different icing consistencies. Thin icing is needed for writing, printing, stems, and leaves. Icing of medium consistency is used to pipe most borders. Stiff icing is necessary for piping roses. The three cake decorators' icings listed above are readily adaptable to various consistencies. To ·stiffen these icings, add additional powdered sugar; to make them thinner, add additional water.

When beating the ingredients to make icing for piped decorations, use an electric mixer speed no greater than medium-high and beat the icing only until blended and creamy. This will help diminish the incorporation of air bubbles, allowing a smoother, more continuous flow of the icing when piping.

Cake Decorators' White Icing is the warhorse of cake decorating. Made with vegetable shortening (no butter) and powdered sugar (no unsweetened cocoa powder), its consistency is particularly efficient, reliable, and adaptable. Because it is pure white, it is generally used when the icing for decorations is to be tinted.

Sometimes, more than one kind of icing is used on a cake. For example, a cake may be frosted with Cake Decorators' Chocolate Icing, piped with top and bottom borders of the same chocolate icing, and decorated with a bouquet of colorful flowers made with tinted Cake Decorators' White Icing.

CONSISTENCY OF OTHER PIPED FOODS

The same general techniques used for piping icing are used to pipe other foods. With some experience in working with a decorating bag comes the adeptness to adjust the consistency of foods to be piped. Oftentimes, it is a matter of on-the-spot trial and error. Different foods and different tips call for varied consistencies.

A number of recipes in this book suggest piping borders and other decorations using whipped cream. Whipped cream must be very thick and stable to be piped successfully. The recipe for Decorator Whipped Cream (page 374) is recommended for use in piping. This recipe produces a more stable whipped cream because it uses powdered sugar for sweetening rather than granulated sugar. When Decorator Whipped Cream is beaten as thickly as possible without allowing it to turn to butter, it holds piped shapes and patterns very well without the use of added gelatin for a stabilizer. This is especially true if, after piping, the decorated food is refrigerated for a brief period before being served.

Two flavored Decorator Whipped Cream recipes are found in this book: Orange Decorator Whipped Cream, and Chocolate Decorator Whipped Cream (page 374). Other flavored and tinted Decorator Whipped Creams may be created by using these recipes as ingredient guides.

TO TINT ICING

Paste food coloring is used to tint icing for piped decorations because it does not add liquid to change the icing consistency. Also, it is highly concentrated, so *very little* is required.

Before using paste food coloring, use a toothpick to stir the coloring in the jar. If the coloring dries out, use a few drops of glycerin (a cake-decorating supply) to restore its heavy-creamy consistency.

To tint icing, add a tiny amount of coloring to mixed icing by dipping the end of a clean toothpick into the coloring and then into the icing. Use the electric mixer to blend the color into the icing. Or, if mixing several colors of icing, place appropriate amounts of white icing in small, individual plastic containers. Then, use clean toothpicks to add coloring to the icing in each container, and vigorously stir with separate spoons until fully blended. Blend the coloring into the icing after only 1 addition of color, as paste food coloring is very concentrated. If more intense color is desired, use a *clean* toothpick to add additional coloring. Do not dip a toothpick which has been in contact with icing back into the jar of food coloring.

Substitute Cake Decorators' Chocolate Icing for dark brown colors. For best results in mixing black icing, add black paste food coloring to Cake Decorators' Chocolate Icing.

Buttercream-type icings tinted with paste food coloring continue to intensify and darken in color for about 1 to 2 hours after mixing. Keep in mind that, as a general rule, pastel decorations are more appetizing than intensely colored decorations.

PREPARING THE DECORATING BAG

Use of a coupler allows several different-sized tips to be used on a single, filled decorating bag. A coupler also helps stabilize the tip position and flow of icing. For this latter reason, use of a coupler—even when only one color of icing will be piped—is recommended.

A coupler consists of two parts: the base, which fits inside the decorating bag, and the ring, which screws onto the base on the outside of the decorating bag to hold the tip in place (see illustration, below).

When a coupler is used, it is usually necessary to trim the tip of a new decorating bag to make the opening at the narrow end of the bag large enough to accommodate the coupler. It is important to trim the tip of the decorating bag methodically, as follows: Place the base of the coupler in the decorating bag, narrow end first, and push it into the tip of the bag as far as you can. Then, using a pencil, mark the place on the outside of the bag where the bottom thread of the coupler base pushes against the bag. Remove the coupler base from the bag, and cut across the decorating bag at the marked place, thus making a larger opening in the bag.

Place the coupler base back in the decorating bag, and push the narrow end through the opening at the narrow end of the bag. Place the tip to be used over the exposed portion of the coupler and screw the ring onto the coupler base to hold the tip in place.

To change tips, simply unscrew the coupler ring; remove the tip and replace it with another tip; then, screw the ring back onto the coupler.

TO FILL THE DECORATING BAG

To fill the decorating bag, first fold the sides of the bag down to form a cuff and open the bag. Then, using an 8-inch narrow, straight spatula, fill the bag no more than half full of icing. Unfold the cuff. Holding the bottom of the bag with one hand, use your free hand to twist the top portion of the bag, sealing in the icing and forcing it toward the bottom of the bag. When this procedure is followed, no icing will get on the hands of the decorator or ooze out over the top of the bag while in the process of piping.

TO HOLD AND USE THE DECORATING BAG

Use both hands when decorating—for steadiness. Clasp the filled decorating bag firmly between your right thumb and index finger around the twisted portion at the top of the bag. Place the other 3 fingers of your right hand on the surface of the bag. This position allows you to keep the decorating bag sealed and also control the pressure and flow of the icing through the tip. Position your left hand near the bottom of the bag and use it to help guide the bag.

Before commencing to pipe with a newly filled decorating bag, hold the bag as described in the preceding paragraph and force the icing (or other food) to the narrow end of the bag. Then, pipe the icing (or other food) onto a piece of waxed paper until the bag "burps," releasing any air trapped in the bag during filling. This procedure will help assure a steady flow of icing (or other food) when piping.

Most garnishes and decorations are piped with the decorating bag held at a 90-degree angle to the surface being piped (perpendicular to the surface) or at a 45-degree angle to the surface being piped (halfway between perpendicular and horizontal to the surface; see illustration).

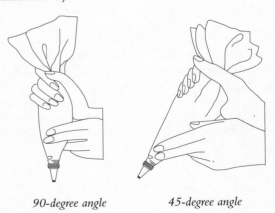

90-degree angle   *45-degree angle*

Pressure control is a key element in the use of a decorating bag. Different pressures are required to execute different decorations and effects. Very often, single strokes require variations of pressure as they are piped.

Pressure is controlled by your right-hand grip of the decorating bag. The amount of pressure and the steadiness of pressure regulate the size and uniformity of the decorations. Squeezing the bag with prescribed amounts of pressure, holding pressure steady, and relaxing or stopping pressure at the right times are important skills in producing piped decorations. Pressure-control dexterity is gained through practice and experience.

Proper bag position, pressure, and hand-arm movement must be simultaneously discharged when using a decorating bag. A new initiate may liken this feat to rubbing the top of the head and the stomach in opposite circles at the same time; however, focused students soon get the hang of it. Practice makes perfect.

LEFT-HANDED DECORATORS

If you are left-handed, grip the decorating bag with your left hand and guide the bag with your right hand. Use opposite hands called for in the instructions. When the instructions call for holding the top of the bag to the right, hold it to the left. Except when writing and printing, decorate from the right to the left rather than from the left to the right as with right-handed persons. When using a decorating turntable, rotate it counterclockwise. When piping a flower on a flower nail, rotate the nail clockwise in your right hand as you use your left hand to pipe. When piping roses on a stick, use tip number 97 rather than tip number 61, and rotate the stick counterclockwise as you use your left hand to pipe.

To Pipe Various Basic Decorations

DECORATIONS PIPED WITH ROUND TIPS

WRITING AND PRINTING

Use tip numbers 1 through 4 and thin icing consistency. Pipe freehanded or, if desired, use a toothpick or pattern press to draw guidelines to follow.

TO WRITE: Hold the bag at a 45-degree angle to the surface with the back of the bag to the right. The tip should lightly touch the surface as you write. Move your whole arm to write effectively with icing.

TO PRINT: Hold the bag at a 45-degree angle to the surface with the tip resting lightly on the surface. Hold the back of the bag to the right for horizontal lines and toward you for vertical lines. With steady, even pressure, squeeze out a straight line, lifting the tip off the surface to let the icing string drop. Be sure to stop squeezing before you lift the tip to end the line so a tail doesn't form.

STEMS: Use tip numbers 1 through 4 and thin icing consistency. Hold the bag at a 45-degree angle to the surface with the back of the bag to the right. Touch the tip lightly to the surface to attach the icing as you start to squeeze, but lift the tip ever so slightly above the surface as you draw out your stem so it will be rounded rather than flat. To end the line, stop squeezing and pull the tip along the surface.

DOTS: For tiny dots, use tip numbers 1 and 2 and thin icing consistency. Hold the bag at a 90-degree angle to the surface with the tip slightly above the surface. Squeeze the bag to pipe the desired dot.

For larger dots, use wider diameter round tips and medium icing consistency. Hold the bag at a 90-degree angle to the surface with the tip slightly above the surface. Squeeze the bag and keep the point of the tip in the icing until the dot is the desired size. Stop the pressure and pull the tip away. If needed or desired, use the tip to remove the point on the dot, or smooth the top of the dot with your finger which has been dipped in cornstarch. For very large dots or balls, lift the tip as you squeeze to allow greater icing buildup.

DECORATIONS PIPED WITH STAR TIPS

Star tips create some of the most popular decorations, including stars; rope, zigzag, and shell borders; and rosettes. The most often used star tips are numbers 13 through 22. Star tips range in size from small to extra large. For deep-ribbed decorations, use tip numbers 24, 25 through 31, 133, and 195. Large star tips include numbers 32, 96, 4B, 6B, and 8B. Fine-cut star tips include numbers 362 through 364, 172, and 199.

STARS

Use medium icing consistency. Hold the bag at a 90-degree angle to the surface with the tip slightly above the surface. Squeeze the bag to form a star. Then, stop the pressure and pull the tip away. Increase or decrease the pressure to change the star size. An entire cake or just one area may be covered with stars made very close together so no cake shows between the stars. Use the triple-star tip or one of the large star tips to save time.

TO PIPE STAR FLOWERS: Use medium icing consistency. Hold the bag at a 90-degree angle to the surface with the tip slightly above the surface. Squeeze the bag and keep the tip in the icing until star petals are formed. Stop the pressure and pull the tip away. Using tip number 2 or 3, add dots in the center of the flower.

ROPE BORDERS

Use medium icing consistency. Hold the bag at a 45-degree angle to the surface with the back of the bag pointing over your right shoulder. Touch the tip to the surface. While squeezing the bag, move the tip down, up and around to the right, forming a slight S curve. Stop the pressure and pull the tip away. Then, tuck the tip under the bottom arch of the first S and repeat the procedure. Continue joining S curves to form the rope.

ZIGZAG BORDERS

Use medium icing consistency. Hold the bag at a 45-degree angle to the surface so the back of the bag points to the right, and your fingers gripping the bag are facing you. Allow the tip to touch the surface lightly. Steadily squeeze the bag and move your hand in a tight side-to-side motion. To end, stop the pressure and pull the tip away.

SHELL BORDERS

Use medium icing consistency. Hold the bag at a 45-degree angle to the surface with the back of the bag toward you and the tip slightly above the surface. Squeeze with heavy pressure and lift the tip slightly as icing builds and fans out into a full base. Gradually relax the pressure as you pull the tip slightly toward you and lower the tip until it touches the surface, making the tail. Stop the pressure completely and pull the tip away. Start each new shell slightly behind the tail of the previous shell.

REVERSE SHELL BORDERS

Use medium icing consistency. Hold the bag at a 45-degree angle to the surface with the back of the bag toward you and the tip slightly above the surface. Squeeze the bag and let the icing fan out as if you were making a typical shell (see instructions for Shell Borders above). Then, swing the tip around to the left in a semicircular motion as you relax the pressure to form the tail of the shell. Stop the pressure and pull the tip away. Continue repeating the procedure, alternating directions, for a series of reverse shells.

ROSETTES

Rosettes may be used as individual decorations, or contiguous rosettes may be used as a border.

Use medium icing consistency. Hold the bag at a 90-degree angle to the surface with the tip slightly above the surface. Squeeze the bag and move your hand to the left, up and around in a circular motion to the starting point. Stop the pressure and pull the tip away. For a fancy effect, decorate the center with a small star.

DECORATIONS PIPED WITH DROP FLOWER TIPS

Drop flowers are the easiest flowers to pipe. The number of openings on the end of the tip determines the number of petals the flower will have. Small tips include numbers 107, 108, 129, 224, and 225. Medium tips include numbers 109, 131, 140, 190, 191, and 193 through 195. For large flowers, use tip numbers 1B, 1C, 1E, 1G, 2C, 2D, 2E, and 2F.

DROP FLOWERS

Use slightly stiffer than medium icing consistency. Hold the bag at a 90-degree angle to the surface with the tip touching the surface. Squeeze the bag to form a flower. Then, stop the pressure and pull the tip away.

SWIRLED DROP FLOWERS

Swirled drop flowers cannot be made directly on a cake or other food surface. Pipe swirled drop flowers on waxed paper and let them stand until air-dried. Then, using a small spatula, loosen the flowers from the waxed paper and position them on the cake or other food surface with your hand.

Use slightly stiffer than medium icing consistency. Hold the bag at a 90-degree angle to the surface. Turn your wrist to the left (counterclockwise) as far as possible. Lightly touch the tip to the surface. As you squeeze out the icing, slowly return your wrist to its normal position. Then, stop the pressure and lift the tip away. Using tip number 2 or 3, pipe a single dot or several small dots in the center of the flower.

DECORATIONS PIPED WITH LEAF TIPS

The V-shaped opening of leaf tips gives piped leaves pointed ends. Make small leaves with center veins using tip numbers 65s and 65 through 70. For large leaves with center veins, use tip numbers 112, 113, and 115. Other popular tip numbers are 73, 75, 326, 349, and 352.

BASIC LEAVES

Use thin icing consistency. Hold the bag at a 45-degree angle to the surface with the back of the bag toward you. Touch the tip lightly to the surface, with the wide opening parallel to the surface. Squeeze the bag and hold the tip in place to let the icing fan out to form a base. Then, relax and stop the pressure as you pull the tip toward you and draw the leaf to a point.

HOLLY LEAVES

Using a pastry brush, coat the inside of the decorating bag with a thin layer of piping gel before filling the bag with icing of thin consistency. Hold the bag at a 45-degree angle to the surface with the back of the bag toward you. Touch the tip lightly to the surface, with the wide opening parallel to the surface. Squeeze the bag hard to build up a base, and at the same time, lift the tip slightly. Then, move the bag up and down in a series of quick motions to produce a ruffle effect. Then, relax and stop the pressure as you pull the tip toward you and draw the leaf to a point. Before the icing begins to set, place the tip of a toothpick into the icing near the center vein of the leaf and pull up and out from the center to form the points of the leaf. (Lining the bag with piping gel results in an icing consistency more adaptable to forming leaf points.)

POINSETTIAS

Use tip number 352 and thin to medium icing consistency. Hold the bag at a 45-degree angle to the surface with the back of the bag toward you. Touch the tip lightly to the surface, with the wide opening parallel to the surface. To pipe the first leaf-shaped petal, squeeze the bag hard to build up a base, and at the same time, lift the tip slightly. Then, relax and stop the pressure as you pull the tip toward you and draw the leaf to a point. Pipe 5 additional leaf-shaped petals evenly spaced in a circle. Add 6 smaller leaf-shaped petals on top of, and between, the large ones. Using tip number 2, pipe several small dots in the center of the poinsettia.

TO PIPE ROSES AND ROSEBUDS

ROSES

A flower nail is used when piping most roses. For medium roses, use a 1½-inch flower nail. For small roses, a 1¼-inch flower nail may be used. For large roses, a 2- or 3-inch flower nail will be required. Use stiff icing consistency.

The key to making any flower on a flower nail is to coordinate the turning of the nail with the formulation of a petal. Hold the stem of the nail between your left thumb and index finger, so you can turn the flat nailhead at the same time you are piping a flower with your right hand.

THE BASE

Use a 1½-inch flower nail and tip number 12. (Use tip number 10 for smaller-sized roses.) Attach a 2-inch square piece of waxed paper to the nailhead with a dot of icing. Hold the bag at a 90-degree angle to the nailhead with the tip slightly above the center of the nailhead. Squeeze with heavy pressure, keeping the bottom of the tip in the icing until you have made a full, round base. Ease the pressure as you raise the tip up and away from the nailhead, narrowing the base to a dome head. The base is very important for successful rose making. Be sure that it is secure to the nail and can support all the petals.

THE CENTER BUD

Use tip number 104. (For small roses, use tip numbers 101s and 101 through 103. For large roses, use tip numbers 124 through 127. For giant roses, use tip number 127D.) Hold the bag at a 45-degree angle to the nailhead with the narrow end of the tip up. Position the tip with the wide end just below the top of the dome and the narrow end pointed in slightly. The back of the bag should be pointed over your shoulder. Now you must do 3 things simultaneously: squeeze the bag, turn the nail counterclockwise, and pull the tip up and away from the top of the dome, stretching the icing into a ribbon band. Relax the pressure as you bring the band of icing down around the dome, overlapping the point at which you started.

FIRST ROW OF 3 PETALS

Hold the bag at a 45-degree angle to the nailhead with the narrow end of tip number 104 up. Touch the wide end of the tip to the midpoint of the bud base. The back of the bag should be pointed over your shoulder. Squeeze the bag and turn the nail counterclockwise as you move the tip up and back down to the midpoint of the bud base, forming the first petal of the rose. Then, start slightly behind the end of the first petal and pipe the second petal, following the same procedure as for the first petal. Start slightly behind the end of the second petal and add a third petal, ending the third petal overlapping the starting point of the first petal.

SECOND ROW OF 5 PETALS

Touch the wide end of tip number 104 slightly below the center of a petal in the first row, angling the narrow end of the tip out slightly more than for the first row of petals. Squeeze the bag and turn the nail counterclockwise as you move the tip up and back down to form the first petal in the second row. Then, start slightly behind the end of the first petal in the second row and pipe the second petal in the second row. Repeat the procedure for a total of 5 petals, ending the fifth petal overlapping the starting point of the first petal in the second row.

THIRD ROW OF 7 PETALS

Touch the wide end of tip number 104 below the center of a petal in the second row, angling the narrow end of the tip out slightly more than for the second row of petals. Squeeze the bag and turn the nail counterclockwise as you move the tip up and back down to form the first petal in the third row. Repeat the procedure followed for the second row, piping a total of 7 petals in the third row.

Slip the square of waxed paper with the completed rose off the flower nail and place it on a flat surface. Let it stand until the rose is air-dried. Then, carefully lift the rose from the waxed paper square and position it on the cake or other food surface with your hand. If butter is an ingredient in the icing used to pipe the rose, refrigerate the rose on the waxed paper square after piping.

Alternatively, the rose may be transferred directly from the flower nail to the cake or other food surface by sliding an open pair of small scissors directly under the freshly piped rose and gently lifting the flower off the waxed paper square and flower nail. Position the rose on the cake or other food surface by slowly closing the scissors and using the stem of the flower nail to guide the base of the rose.

TO PIPE SMALL ROSES ON A STICK

Small roses may be piped more quickly using a stick rather than following the flower nail procedure. This method is particularly useful when large quantities of small roses are required; for example, when using roses to decorate cookies.

To prepare the stick, cut a ¼-inch dowel into a piece 4½ inches long. Then, sharpen one end of the cut piece in a pencil sharpener as you would a pencil. Use tip number 61 and stiff icing consistency. Hold the bag at a 45-degree angle to the stick with the narrow end of the tip up. Position the tip with the wide end just below the tip of the stick and the narrow end pointed in slightly. While squeezing the bag and turning the stick *clockwise,* pipe 3 contiguous bands of icing around the stick from the point downward. This procedure covers the end of the stick with 1 layer of icing, which will serve as the base of the rose.

THE CENTER BUD: Follow the procedure for piping the center bud of a rose on a flower nail (see Roses, page 392), except turn the stick *clockwise.*

FIRST ROW OF 3 PETALS: Follow the procedure for piping the first row of 3 petals of a rose on a flower nail (see Roses, page 392), except turn the stick *clockwise.*

SECOND ROW OF 5 PETALS: Follow the procedure for piping the second row of 5 petals of a rose on a flower nail (see Roses, page 392), except turn the stick *clockwise.*

Generally, a third row of 7 petals is not piped on small stick roses; however, if somewhat larger roses are desired, a third row of 7 petals may be added.

To remove a freshly piped rose from the stick, place a pair of small scissors around the stick and under the base of the rose. Gently move the scissors upward, removing the rose from the stick. The piped rose may be immediately positioned on the cake or other food surface, using the stick to guide the rose off the scissors. Or, use the stick to guide the rose off the scissors onto waxed paper and let the rose stand to air-dry.

ROSEBUDS

Pipe the rosebuds directly onto the cake, candy, or other food surface. Use tip numbers 101 through 104 for the petals, depending upon the size of rosebud desired. Use tip numbers 1 through 3 for the calyx and sepals (see illustration, page 383), depending upon the size of the piped petals.

PETALS: Use tip number 104 and stiff icing consistency. To make the base petal, hold the bag at a 45-degree angle to the surface so the back of the bag points over your shoulder, and your fingertips gripping the bag are facing you. Touch the wide end of the tip to the surface and point the narrow end to the right. Squeeze the bag and move the tip forward ¼ inch along the surface; hesitate so the icing fans out, and then move the tip back to the original position, stopping the pressure about halfway back.

To make an overlapping center petal, hold the bag in the same position as for the base petal, with the wide end of the tip touching the inside right edge of the base petal and the narrow end pointing slightly up above the base petal. Squeeze the bag and lift the tip slightly. Continue squeezing as the icing catches the inside edge of the base petal and rolls to form an interlocking center petal. Stop the pressure; touch the wide end of the tip back down to the surface and pull the tip away.

CALYX AND SEPALS: Use tip number 3 and thin icing consistency. To pipe the calyx, hold the bag at a 45-degree angle to the base of the bud with the back of the bag toward you. Touch the tip to the bottom of the bud. Squeeze the bag and pull the tip up and away from the bud, relaxing the pressure as you draw the calyx to a point.

Start in the same position as for the calyx to pipe the center sepal. Squeeze the bag and let the icing build up. Then, begin to lift the bag up and away from the flower. Stop the pressure as you pull away to form the point of the sepal. Repeat the procedure, piping 1 sepal on the left and 1 sepal on the right of the center sepal.

TO PIPE LEAVES INSTEAD OF A CALYX AND SEPALS: If preferred, pipe 2 small leaves near the bottom of the bud instead of piping a calyx with sepals. Use tip numbers 65 through 67, depending upon the size of the piped petals, and follow the procedure for piping Basic Leaves, page 391.

Photographs and accompanying edited instructions courtesy of Wilton Enterprises.

BUTTER ROSES

They're butter with beauty and class.

1 cup (½ pound) cold butter

Cut the butter into approximately 16 pieces and drop into a blender beaker. Let stand, uncovered, for about 35 minutes until the butter softens just enough to process in the blender. (The butter must be very stiff to pipe successful roses.)

Process the butter in the blender until smooth.

Pipe roses, following the instructions on pages 392–393, using tip number 12 for the bases, and tip number 104 for the center buds and the petals. Place the waxed paper squares holding the piped roses on a flat plate and immediately refrigerate, uncovered. When the roses have hardened, cover them lightly with plastic wrap.

Immediately before serving peel away the waxed paper and place the roses on individual bread and butter plates, or on a flat-bottomed butter server or serving plate.

MAKES ABOUT 1 DOZEN

BUTTER CURLS

A quick-and-easy way to add further glamour to your dinner party table. You'll need a butter curler (see illustration) and a little bit of practice using it.

1 ¼-pound stick butter

Ten minutes before making Butter Curls, remove the butter from the refrigerator and place it on a flat-bottomed plate; set aside. (The butter should be only slightly soft to make well-shaped Butter Curls.)

Line the bottom of another flat-bottomed plate with waxed paper cut to the size of the bottom of the plate so it lays flat; set aside.

To make the curls, dip the butter curler (see illustration) into a glass of hot water. Shake the excess water off the curler. While holding the butter stick steady with the thumb of one hand, pull the curler toward you, down the length of the butter stick, pressing the curler gently and evenly into the butter.

With your fingers, remove the Butter Curl from the curler and, if necessary, make any slight adjustments in the shape of the curl. Then, place the Butter Curl, seam down and single layer, on the waxed paper-lined plate. Redip the curler into the hot water before making each Butter Curl.

Refrigerate the Butter Curls, uncovered, until hardened. Then, cover with plastic wrap.

Immediately before serving, arrange the Butter Curls, single layer, on a cold serving plate; provide a small fork, such as an olive or pickle fork, for serving. Or, place 1 Butter Curl on each diner's bread and butter plate.

MAKES ABOUT 10 USABLE BUTTER CURLS

FLUTED BUTTER WEDGES

When you want generous servings of butter that still look genteel.

Dip a fluted garnishing cutter (see illustration, page 128) into hot water. Using the warm garnishing knife, cut a ⅜-inch-wide slice of butter widthwise from an uncut pound of butter. Dip a sharp, thin-bladed, standard knife into the hot water. Using the warm standard knife, cut the fluted slice of butter in half diagonally (see illustration).

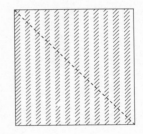

Using a small spatula, place the 2 Fluted Butter Wedges on a flat plate lined with waxed paper. Repeat the process, dipping the knives into hot water before each cut. Cover the Fluted Butter Wedges with plastic wrap and refrigerate until immediately prior to serving.

1 FLUTED BUTTER WEDGE MAKES 1 SERVING

Butter Curler

RIBBED BUTTER BALLS

A showy way to serve butter.

Place an uncut pound of butter or a ¼-pound stick of butter on a flat plate. Let the butter stand at room temperature until *slightly* soft.

Use a ⅞-inch Westmark brand butter-ball cutter or a 1-inch melon baller to cut the butter balls. Dip the cutter into boiling hot water before making each cut. To cut evenly shaped balls, press the blade face of the cutter into the slightly softened butter and then turn the cutter evenly while continuing to press. Immediately place the cut balls in a bowl of ice water.

To rib the butter balls, remove them from the ice water and roll them, one at a time, between 2 ribbed butter paddles (see illustration). Drop the Ribbed Butter Balls back into the ice water or place them, single layer, on a flat plate lined with waxed paper; refrigerate. Cover with plastic wrap when the butter fully hardens.

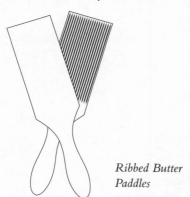

Ribbed Butter Paddles

VARIATION: Use specially blended butter, such as Onion Butter or Orange Butter (page 369), which has been refrigerated to harden in a wide, shallow bowl.

HERBED BUTTER BALLS: Sprinkle very finely snipped, fresh parsley (or other fresh herb) over a small piece of waxed paper; set aside.

Follow the Ribbed Butter Balls recipe, above. After rolling the butter balls between the ribbed butter paddles, roll the Ribbed Butter Balls in the parsley (or other herb). Place the Herbed Butter Balls, single layer, on a flat plate lined with waxed paper; refrigerate. Cover with plastic wrap when the butter fully hardens.

ARTICHOKE BOTTOMS FILLED WITH BROCCOLI AND CARROT PUREES

For your fanciest dinner party, garnish beef, veal, lamb, fish, or poultry plates with this exquisite savory.

Drain commercially canned artichoke bottoms. Steam (page 302) the artichoke bottoms until heated. Remove the artichokes from the steamer and brush the surfaces very lightly with melted butter.

Using a demitasse spoon, fill ½ of each artichoke bottom with warm Broccoli Puree (page 308) and the other ½ with warm Carrot Puree (page 311).

ARTICHOKE BOTTOMS FILLED WITH TINY VEGETABLES

A slightly less formal garnish than Artichoke Bottoms Filled with Broccoli and Carrot Purees (see above), but supremely elegant.

Steam (page 302), briefly and separately, frozen tiny peas; uniformly chopped red bell peppers; and peeled, tiny pearl onions (page 45). Place all the vegetables in a mixing bowl and toss lightly with a small amount of melted butter for sheen and flavor; keep warm.

Drain commercially canned artichoke bottoms. Steam the artichoke bottoms until heated. Remove the artichokes from the steamer and brush the surfaces very lightly with melted butter. Using a teaspoon, carefully fill the artichoke bottoms with the mixed vegetables.

SERVING SUGGESTIONS: Serve with Roast Beef Tenderloin with Mushroom Sauce (page 162),

Broiled Filet Mignon (page 166), Baby Lamb Chops (page 196), Loin of Pork (page 186), and Poached Salmon Steaks (page 225).

VARIATION: Artichoke bottoms may be filled with any combination of tiny, whole vegetables and/or uniformly chopped vegetables (or any single, tiny or chopped vegetable) in coordination with the flavor and color of the food to be garnished.

APPLE-LINGONBERRY GARNISH

This outstanding garnish is a borrowed idea from Switzerland and Austria, where it is most often served on plates with wild game.

2 cups cold water
¾ teaspoon white vinegar
¾ teaspoon salt
2 cups hot water
1¼ cups sugar
1 2-inch piece stick cinnamon
1 whole clove
Up to 6 medium to large Golden Delicious apples
Commercially canned wild lingonberries in sugar

In a medium mixing bowl, place 2 cups cold water, vinegar, and salt; stir until the salt dissolves; set aside.

In a medium saucepan, place 2 cups hot water and sugar. Bring the mixture to a boil over high heat, stirring constantly until the sugar dissolves. When the mixture boils, add the stick cinnamon and the clove; reduce the heat and cover the saucepan. Simmer the mixture briskly for 5 minutes. Remove from the heat; set aside.

Wash and dry the apples. Using a sharp, thin-bladed knife, cut a ⅝-inch-wide slice lengthwise from 2 opposite sides of one of the apples (see illustration A).

Illustration A

With a 2-inch, round, fluted cutter, cut 1 fluted apple circle from each of the 2 slices of apple. Using a ¾- to ⅝-inch round, plain (unfluted) cutter, press the cutter ¼ inch deep into the center of each fluted apple circle and then withdraw the cutter. (Do not cut completely through the fluted apple circles.) (See illustration B.)

Illustration B

Using a tiny, ⅜-inch melon baller, carefully scoop out the apple flesh from the center circles to ¼ inch below the top apple surface, to form a cup in each fluted apple circle. As they are prepared, drop the carved apple circles into the vinegar mixture to prevent discoloration. Repeat the process until the desired number of apple circles has been carved.

Drain and rinse the apple circles twice in clear water; set aside. Remove the cinnamon stick and clove from the syrup. Quickly bring the syrup to a boil over high heat. Drop 1 layer of apple circles at a time into the boiling syrup; boil 3 for minutes (no more). Using a slotted spoon,

(Recipe continues on next page)

remove the apple circles from the syrup and drain, upside down, on 2 layers of paper towels. When drained, place the apple circles, single layer, on a flat plate; cover tightly with plastic wrap and refrigerate. If serving Apple-Lingonberry Garnish with a hot dish, remove the apple circles from the refrigerator 1 hour before serving time to allow the apple circles to reach room temperature.

Drain the lingonberries directly on 4 layers of paper towels. Shortly before serving, use a demitasse spoon to fill the cups in the apple circles with the drained lingonberries. Avoid filling the cups too far in advance, as the lingonberries may bleed into the apples.

MAKES UP TO 12

SERVING SUGGESTION: Serve with wild game, pork chops and roasts, lamb, and poultry.

CARROT CURLS

Select bright orange, medium to large, uniformly sized carrots. Cut off both ends of the carrots, cutting off enough of the small, pointed root ends to make each carrot fairly uniform in diameter. Pare the carrots. Cut a thin slice lengthwise off each carrot, creating a flat surface on which the carrots can rest solidly while cutting curls.

Place 1 carrot on a cutting board. Hold the carrot firmly with one hand. With the other hand, draw a *sharp* vegetable parer down the length of the carrot, cutting a thin strip. Roll the the carrot strip loosely around your finger to make a curl; place a toothpick through the curled carrot to secure. Repeat the process.

Place the Carrot Curls in a bowl of cold water and ice cubes; refrigerate a few hours or overnight to set the curls. Shortly before serving, drain the Carrot Curls on paper towels; *remove the toothpicks.*

SERVING SUGGESTIONS

• Makes attractive, informal garnish for tossed vegetable salads, sandwich platters, and cold luncheon plates.

• Adds color and dimension to a relish tray.

CARROT BOWS

Guests are sure to take note of this extra-special carrot decoration on their dinner salad or luncheon plates, or when used to embellish serving platters.

Follow the procedure for making Carrot Curls, left column, through cutting thin strips of carrots.

Using a sharp knife, trim each strip to make it uniform in width. Tie a knot in the center of each strip, making a bow. Using kitchen scissors, cut the ends of the bows diagonally in the shape of an inverted V, in the same manner as trimming the ends of ribbons.

Place the Carrot Bows in a bowl of cold water and ice cubes; refrigerate for a few hours or overnight to set the bows. Shortly before serving, drain the Carrot Bows on paper towels.

A BUNCH OF WHOLE, MINIATURE CARROTS

Trim miniature carrots, leaving ½ to 1 inch of the green stems attached (length of the retained stems depends upon the size of the carrots). Pare the carrots using the scraping method if carrots are very tiny (page 45).

Boil or steam (page 302) the carrots briefly. If the carrots are boiled, drain them in a colander.

Brush the carrots lightly with melted butter for sheen, and arrange them in a fan-shaped bunch on a platter or on individual plates of food. To decorate most platters, either 5 or 3 carrots make an attractive display; however, any number of carrots may be used (odd numbers usually look best).

CELERY BRUSHES

A splashy rendition of celery sticks.

Use small to medium stalks of celery, or cut large stalks in half lengthwise. Cut the stalks widthwise into 3½- to 5-inch pieces, depending upon the end effect desired.

Using a small, sharp knife, make parallel, lengthwise cuts through each celery piece, leaving ½ inch of the piece uncut and intact at one end. The more narrow the pieces are cut, the more fringelike will be the final appearance. Place the cut Celery Brushes in a bowl of cold water and ice cubes; refrigerate for several hours or overnight to open, curl, and set the brushes. Shortly before serving, drain the Celery Brushes on paper towels.

SERVING SUGGESTIONS
• Serve as a crudité (page 21).

• Use as a garnish for serving platters or individual plates.

CUCUMBER ROSES

This could become one of your favorite food decorations to make. One of these in the center of an hors d'oeuvre tray of Cucumber Wheels (page 67) and other goodies makes a real statement.

Cut 10 paper-thin slices from an unpared, seedless cucumber. Make 1 cut in each slice from the center to the edge. With 1 slice, make a tight cone to form the center of the rose. Build the rose with the remainder of the slices, overlapping them progressively looser. Secure the finished rose with 2 small toothpicks.

For food safety, remove the toothpicks from Cucumber Roses before placing them on individual plates of food. If one or more Cucumber Roses is used to decorate a serving platter, remove the toothpicks if there is any chance that the Cucumber Rose(s) will be eaten.

GROOVED CUCUMBER SLICES

Simple to make but you'll need a channel knife (see illustration). Use the grooved slices in salads or for garnish.

Run a channel knife (see illustration) lengthwise down an unpared, seedless cucumber. Continue cutting grooves at even intervals around the entire cucumber. Then, slice the cucumber widthwise.

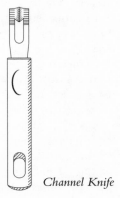

Channel Knife

MARINATED DRIED ITALIAN OLIVES

1 pound dried Italian olives
1 garlic clove, quartered lengthwise
Freshly ground pepper
1⅓ cups extra-virgin olive oil

Place the olives in a quart jar, distributing the garlic clove quarters evenly in the olives. Grind pepper over the top. Pour the olive oil into the jar to cover the olives. Place a lid on the jar. Refrigerate the olives and let stand at least 2 days before serving. Before serving, drain the olives well. Keep leftover olives refrigerated.

MAKES 1 POUND

GREEN ONION BRUSHES

Onion Brushes are principally for decoration since only ½ inch of the white root end, the part of green onions (scallions) most commonly eaten, is left uncut. Tucked between raw vegetables on a relish tray, or arranged with other food decorations on the corner of a buffet salad, the deep green, frilly appearance of Green Onion Brushes provides a stylish accent. P.S. They're a breeze to make.

Select large to medium green onions (scallions). Cut away the root ends 1½ inches from the point where the green stems commence to branch away from the solid part of the onions; reserve the root ends for other uses. Wash the onions. Remove and discard the outer layer of the onions if coarse and/or slightly discolored. Trim off enough of the green, stem ends to leave the onions about 4 inches in length.

On a cutting board, using a small, sharp knife, make straight cuts lengthwise through each onion, starting ½ inch from the root end and cutting through the green, stem end. (Leave ½ inch of the root end uncut.) Make several of these cuts through each onion, making the strips as thin as possible. Place the cut Green Onion Brushes in a bowl of cold water and ice cubes; refrigerate for 1 hour to curl the brushes. Shortly before serving, drain the Green Onion Brushes on paper towels.

MULTICOLORED GREEN ONION FLOWERS

Add patriotic fireworks to the platter of Deviled Eggs (page 267) you take to the Fourth of July picnic with red, white, and blue Onion Flowers. Everyone will get a bang out of it!

A technique similar to that used in making Green Onion Brushes (left column) is used to make Multicolored Green Onion Flowers. Select large to medium green onions (scallions). Trim off the root ends, leaving as much of the white part of the onions as possible. Then, trim off enough of the green, stem ends to leave the onions about 4 inches in length. Remove and discard the outer layer of onions if coarse and/or slightly discolored.

On a cutting board, using a small, sharp knife, make straight cuts lengthwise through each onion, starting ½ inch from the green, *stem* end and cutting through the white, root end. (Leave ½ inch of the green, stem end uncut.) Make several of these cuts through each onion, making the strips as thin as possible; set aside.

Pour 4 cups cold water into a medium stainless steel or glass bowl. Add 2 teaspoons liquid food coloring; stir to blend. Add a few ice cubes to the bowl. Immerse the cut onions in the colored water. Place a plate or small, glass baking dish cover over the water and ice cubes in the bowl to function as a weight, keeping the onions completely submerged in the colored water. Refrigerate 24 hours, until the onion flowers are colored and curled. Shortly before serving, drain the onion flowers on paper towels.

Make Green Onion Flowers of as many different colors as desired to decorate serving plates and food displays. For more intense colors, increase the liquid food coloring to 1 tablespoon.

TO CUT LEAVES, STEMS, AND DESIGNS FROM LEEK TOPS

You'll find many applications for softened, carvable leek tops. Although a small, sharp paring knife may be used for the cutting, an X-Acto knife produces better results. I recommend adding one of these knives to your collection of kitchen tools (they're available at art supply stores) for use in making food decorations as well as accomplishing other cooking tasks such as cutting corrugated cardboard cake circles.

Cut the green tops from the leeks. Wash the tops and drop them into a large saucepan of boiling water; let stand briefly until the leek tops are soft and pliable. Place 2 layers of paper towels on a wooden cutting board. Spread the softened leek tops flat on the paper towels.

Using an X-Acto knife, cut desired leaves, stems, or other designs from the leek tops.

LEMON, LIME, AND ORANGE TWISTS

We often see these popular citrus twists decorating all kinds of foods, from pies (see Daiquiri Pie, page 500) to fruit salads, and have been served them as decoration on plates of food ranging from breakfast omelets (usually Orange Twists) to fish entrées (see Fillet of Sole with Lime Sauce, page 223). Here's how to make them in 3 short sentences (and you can make them just about as quickly).

Thinly slice widthwise an unpeeled lemon, lime, or orange. Make 1 cut in each slice from the center to the edge. Hold each slice on either side of the cut and twist in opposite directions.

VARIATION ~ GROOVED TWISTS: Prior to slicing the fruit, use a channel knife (see illustration, page 399) to cut equidistant grooves lengthwise from end to end around the fruit.

ORANGE BASKETS

Here's an idea for your next bridge (or other) luncheon: Fill daintily carved Orange Baskets with miniature pieces of fresh fruit and tie the handles with ribbons cut from leek tops (left column). Place one of these handsome baskets of fruit on each guest's plate next to Chicken Salad (page 140). Pass miniature Caramel Rolls (page 427) if you like. For a grand finale, serve stunning pieces of Black Forest Pie decorated with Chocolate Scrolls (page 488).

Select bright orange, symmetrical, uniformly sized oranges. The selected size is dependent upon how the Orange Baskets will be used. Wash the oranges, removing any stickers and stamped-on brand names or other markings (use a small amount of kitchen cleanser on a damp sponge; then, rinse the oranges well). Dry the oranges.

To make each Orange Basket, place the orange on a cutting board, with the stem and blossom ends horizontal to the board. Using a small, sharp, thin-bladed knife, make 2 parallel cuts, ⅜ inch apart, centered on the top of the orange, cutting downward *halfway* through the fruit to form the basket handle. Then, for medium to large oranges (see Note), make a horizontal cut starting ½ inch up from the base of the basket handle and continuing horizontally around the orange to the opposite side of the handle, being careful not to cut through the handle. Remove the cutaway orange piece and reserve for other uses. Repeat the same cut on the other side of the handle and remove the cutaway piece (see illustration A).

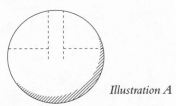

Illustration A

(Recipe continues on next page)

Using a grapefruit knife, cut the orange pulp in the basket away from the white peel membrane. Then, using a grapefruit spoon or a teaspoon, carefully remove the pulp, reserving it for other uses. Using a sharp paring knife, cut a sawtooth edge around the top edge of the basket, cutting each tooth ½ inch deep and ½ inch wide at the base (see illustration B).

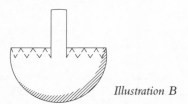

Illustration B

NOTE: For small oranges, make all the dimensions proportionately smaller.

SERVING SUGGESTIONS

• Fill Orange Baskets with fresh fruit; a conserve to accompany meat, poultry, or wild game (see Serving Suggestion, page 239); or a small serving of a fruit salad, such as Twenty-four Hour Salad (page 112) or Apple Salad (page 110). Depending upon the filling, a bow fashioned from green leek tops (page 401) or made with regular material ribbon may be tied to one side of each basket handle. Place an Orange Basket on each diner's plate as a stunning garnish.

• Fill Orange Baskets with sherbet (page 26) or sorbet (page 26) and serve for dessert.

VARIATION: The basket handles may be eliminated.

PICKLE FANS

Using a small, sharp, thin-bladed knife, cut thin, parallel slices lengthwise in a small pickle, cutting only to about ½ inch from one end of the pickle. (One end of the pickle will be uncut.) Using your fingers, spread the slices to form a fan.

Repeat the procedure to make additional Pickle Fans. If the pickles are large enough, the portion to be sliced may be pared very thinly prior to slicing for a more attractive final appearance.

SERVING SUGGESTIONS

• Use as garnish when serving sandwiches.

• Serve on cheese platters.

• Serve cornichon (a type of pickle) Pickle Fans as the traditional garnish for pâtés.

BELL PEPPER LEAVES AND FLOWER PETALS

Leaves and flower petals may be cut from green, red, yellow, orange, and purple bell peppers.

Use bell peppers. Wash the peppers; cut them lengthwise into quarters or sixths, depending upon the size of the peppers. Cut away the seeds and inner white parts of the flesh. Place the pepper sections in a saucepan (use a separate saucepan for each color of peppers); add water to cover. Cover the saucepan. Bring the peppers to a boil over high heat; reduce the heat slightly and boil about 8 minutes, until the skins peel off easily. Drain the peppers. Peel the pepper sections. Place the pepper sections on a cutting board and carefully flatten them.

Using small leaf- and petal-shaped cutters or an X-Acto knife, cut out leaves and petals. Flower stems may also be cut from green peppers.

SERVING SUGGESTIONS

• Use to decorate the tops of vegetable and meat casseroles (after baking) and vegetable salads.

• Use as decoration directly on individual plates containing meats, fish, poultry, vegetables, or vegetable salad.

• Use to decorate raw vegetable platters.

PINEAPPLE TULIPS

Using a sharp, thin-bladed paring knife or an X-Acto knife, cut very thin tulip stems from deep green celery stalks. With scissors, fashion leaves from the green, leafy celery tops. Cut the tulip blossoms from thin slices of fresh pineapple. To intensify the yellow color, dip the Pineapple Tulip blossoms in a small sauce dish of water to which a few drops of liquid yellow food coloring have been added. Remove the blossoms from the sauce dish and place them on a paper towel to drain.

Carefully arrange the tulip parts on the food to be decorated. Pineapple blossoms may also be tinted red or orange.

SERVING SUGGESTION: Nice for decorating molded fruit salads which contain pineapple.

RADISH FANS

A fresh idea for serving some of the big crop of radishes from your garden. Or, select bright red radishes at your produce market especially for making these artful fans.

Select long, oval-shaped radishes to make Radish Fans. Wash the radishes; using a small, very sharp, thin-bladed knife, cut off both the stem and root ends. Make thin, parallel cuts *widthwise* down the entire length of each radish, cutting almost through the radish, but leaving the thin "slices" attached.

Place the cut radishes in a bowl of cold water and ice cubes; refrigerate a few hours or overnight. The radishes will open to simulate fans.

RADISH GYROSCOPES

Kids will love these atop their salads and will call them "cool."

Wash the radishes and slice off both the stem and root ends. Using a sharp, thin-bladed knife, slice the radishes widthwise $\frac{1}{16}$ to $\frac{1}{8}$ inch thick. Make a cut from the center of each slice to the edge. Make a second cut $\frac{1}{16}$ to $\frac{1}{8}$ inch from, and parallel to, the first cut. Make a tiny cut at the center of the radish slice between the two parallel cuts; remove and discard the little piece which has been cut out (see illustration A).

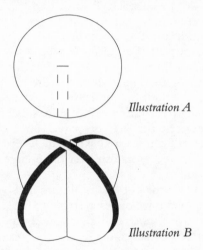

Illustration A

Illustration B

Fit 2 cut radish slices together at the points where the cutouts have been made to form a Radish Gyroscope (see illustration B). Fit the remaining radish slices together.

RADISH ROSES

These are always eye appealing to serve (see illustration on page 379). The tool suggested under Alternative, below, makes quick work out of attractive Radish Roses.

Select large, round radishes to make Radish Roses. Wash the radishes. Using a small, very sharp, thin-bladed knife, cut off the stem end of each radish, thus making a small, flat surface on which the finished rose can stand. Then, cut a tiny slice off the root end of each radish, leaving a small, white "dot" on top of each red radish.

To make each Radish Rose, cut 5, thin, evenly sized petals from the skin around the radish, as follows: cut the petals downward from the top of the radish, leaving a tiny bit of red radish skin around the center white "dot," and cutting the petals almost to the base (stem end) of the radish, but leaving them securely attached. If desired, cut 5, thin, small inner petals between the 5 large petals, cutting the small petals from the red skin which remains on the body of each radish after the 5 large petals have been cut.

Place the cut Radish Roses in a bowl of cold water and ice cubes; refrigerate for several hours or overnight. The petals will open to form attractive vegetable garnishes resembling red roses.

ALTERNATIVE: Westmark manufactures a small, combination tool which cuts Radish Roses as well as sawtooth edging on citrus fruit. Using the tool, good-looking Radish Roses are cut quickly and uniformly with a single clamping action. The cut roses should be placed in ice water and refrigerated, following the same procedure as with hand-cut Radish Roses.

STRAWBERRY FANS

Strawberry Fans look great as garnish on a summer luncheon plate featuring cold or hot poultry. And they're often the perfect decorative complement for fruit salads and desserts.

Select and wash attractive strawberries. Using a sharp, thin-bladed, paring knife, make ⅛-inch, parallel cuts lengthwise down the strawberries toward the stem end, but do not cut completely through the strawberries (the "slices" will remain attached to the stem end of the berries). With your fingers, carefully spread the slices on each strawberry in the shape of a fan.

The stems and/or green, leafy sepals may be left on the strawberries or they may be removed prior to "slicing." Do not remove the inner, center pith of the berries; if removed, the "slices" will not be firm enough to hold their shape and stay together.

BAKED TOMATOES PARMESAN

3 medium-sized, firm tomatoes, unpeeled
1 recipe (¼ cup) Buttered Cracker Crumbs made with Ritz crackers (page 49)
1 tablespoon freshly grated Parmesan cheese (page 46)
2 teaspoons finely snipped, fresh parsley
¼ teaspoon dried leaf basil or ¾ teaspoon finely snipped, fresh basil

Preheat the oven to 350° F.

Wash the tomatoes. Cut the tomatoes in half widthwise. Cut a thin slice off the ends of the tomatoes to make a platform on which the tomatoes can stand firmly and evenly. Place the tomato halves in an ungreased 8 × 8-inch baking dish or pan; set aside.

In a small mixing bowl, place the cracker crumbs, Parmesan cheese, parsley, and basil; stir to combine. Spoon the cheese mixture over the top of each tomato half. Using the back of a teaspoon, press the cheese mixture evenly over the top of each tomato half.

Bake the tomato halves, uncovered, for 25 minutes. Then, place them briefly under the broiler, 6 inches from the heat, until lightly brown.

MAKES 6

SERVING SUGGESTIONS: A natural accompaniment for steaks. Also nice with Brunch Eggs (page 265).

TOMATO ROSES

This is one of the most beautiful and revered food decorations.

Using a small, sharp, thin-bladed knife, pare a medium tomato in the same manner that you would pare an apple, starting at the blossom end and cutting a *thin,* ¾-inch-wide strip of peel in circular fashion around the tomato, ending at the stem end.

Cut the peel into 3-inch-long pieces. With the first 3-inch piece of peel from the blossom end of the tomato, make a tight cone, flesh side in, which will form the center of the rose. While still holding the center cone, wrap another 3-inch strip of peel around the cone. (The beginning of the second strip should overlap the end of the first strip.) Then, lay the rose facedown on a wooden board and continue wrapping the strips of peel (the rose petals) around the outside of the rose, with increasing looseness to form an open rose. The beginning of each strip should overlap the end of the previous strip. Secure the petals with one or more small toothpicks. Using a spatula, turn the rose upright. Place the Tomato Roses on a flat plate; cover loosely with plastic wrap and refrigerate until serving time. *Before placing Tomato Roses on individual plates or serving plates, carefully remove all toothpicks to assure food safety.*

TOMATO ROSEBUDS: Following the procedure for making a Tomato Rose, above, cut 2 thin, ½ × 2½-inch strips of tomato peel. Use one of the strips to form a tightly coiled center of the rosebud, and the other strip to form tight petals.

SERVING SUGGESTION: Use Tomato Roses and Tomato Rosebuds to decorate individual plates, and serving platters and dishes of meats, poultry, fish, salads, and vegetables. They are also becoming as decoration on hors d'oeuvre trays. The use of one Tomato Rose and one Tomato Rosebud together makes a particularly effective decoration. To enhance the look, arrange small sprigs of fresh coriander, watercress, or parsley around the tomatoes. Or, using a small, sharp paring knife or an X-Acto knife, cut the blossom (not stem) end of steamed, chilled, unbuttered snow peas (page 327) in the shape of a W to simulate a ribbon. Trim away the stem ends. Then, tuck two "ribbons," in the fashion of ribbon streamers, under each rose or combination rose-rosebud.

CUTOUT TOMATO STARS

To make tiny cutout stars and other designs out of tomatoes, blanch (page 44) a firm, bright red tomato 30 to 45 seconds. Immediately immerse the tomato in cold water to stop the cooking. Carefully stem, peel, quarter, and seed and core (page 45) the tomato. Cut away the protruding inside tomato flesh to make the remaining flesh even in thickness. If necessary, cut away additional inside flesh so the remaining flesh is not only even, but somewhat thinner.

Press the tomato flesh flat on a wooden cutting board. Using a tiny star cutter (or a cutter of any desired design), cut the Tomato Stars.

Using a small spatula, move the cutout stars from the cutting board to the desired positions for food decoration or to a flat plate for later use. To store, cover with plastic wrap and refrigerate.

(Recipe continues on next page)

- Use cutouts of any design to decorate deviled eggs, dips, molded vegetable salads, casseroles (after baking), and other foods and dishes.

- Use cutouts in combination with other decorative foods to fashion flowers and other designs.

YELLOW ZUCCHINI RINGS FILLED WITH BASIL JELLY

8 unpared, yellow zucchini slices ¼ inch thick and 1¾ to 2 inches in diameter
4 to 6 teaspoons Basil Jelly (page 745)
16 to 24 small Johnny-jump-up blossoms (page 382) (optional)

Steam the zucchini slices (page 302) 3 minutes. Immediately remove the steamer basket containing the zucchini slices from the pan. Leave the zucchini slices in the steamer basket and rinse them under cold, running water to stop the cooking. Drain well.

On a cutting board, use a sharp paring knife to carefully cut around the periphery of the center seed section of each zucchini slice, cutting entirely through the slice. Remove and discard the center seed section of each slice, leaving the slice in the form of a ring. Briefly place the rings, single layer, on 2 layers of paper towels to drain further. Then, place the rings, single layer, in a flat-bottomed dish or plate; cover with plastic wrap. If the finished zucchini rings will be served within 2 hours, let them stand to cool to room temperature. Otherwise, place the rings in the refrigerator and remove them from the refrigerator about 1 hour before serving to allow them to warm to room temperature.

At serving time, arrange 1 zucchini ring to one side of each individual, main-course plate. Using a ½-teaspoon measuring spoon or a demitasse spoon, carefully place ½ to ¾ teaspoon (depending upon the diameter of the zucchini rings) Basil Jelly in the center hole of each zucchini ring. The jelly should mound slightly above the top surface of the rings. (Do not prewarm the plates, causing the jelly to melt quickly.) Decoratively arrange 2 or 3 (depending upon the size of the blossoms and the diameter of the zucchini rings) Johnny-jump-up blossoms contiguously on the outside edge of a section of each zucchini ring.

MAKES 8

VARIATIONS
- Substitute green zucchini for yellow zucchini.

- Substitute another jelly compatible with the food being served for Basil Jelly; for example, Mint Jelly (page 742) with lamb, onion jelly with pork, crab apple jelly with chicken, and currant jelly with pheasant, quail, and grouse.

- Substitute another edible flower (page 382) in color harmony with the zucchini and jelly selected and the food being served.

CHOCOLATE CURLS

A striking decoration/garnish atop cakes, pies, and other desserts. It usually takes some practice to get the hang of making Chocolate Curls. If your first attempts don't satisfy you, break up the practice curls and use as Shaved Chocolate (see page 408).

Make Chocolate Curls from a 3-ounce or larger bar of high-quality milk chocolate. The secret to making Chocolate Curls is to have the chocolate at the proper temperature—soft enough to be pliable, but not so soft that the curls will not hold their shape. One way to warm the chocolate to the desired temperature of about 80° F., is to unwrap it, place it on a piece of aluminum foil on the middle shelf of the oven, turn on the oven light, and close the oven door. The heat of the oven light will usually be sufficient to warm the chocolate within a few minutes.

Then, if using a 3-ounce chocolate bar, cut the bar in half lengthwise, using a thin, sharp knife. If using a different-sized piece of chocolate, cut it into 1½-inch-wide lengths. To help achieve precision cuts, warm the knife blade before each cut by dipping it into a tall glass of very hot water and then wiping the blade completely dry.

Place a piece of waxed paper on a cutting board, a piece of marble, or a smooth countertop. Place 1 of the pieces of chocolate, smooth side up, near the edge of the cutting board, marble, or countertop. Dip a sharp vegetable parer into the glass of very hot water and wipe it completely dry. Hold the chocolate strip in place with the thumb of one hand over a paper towel (to prevent the heat of your hand from melting the chocolate). With the other hand, *firmly* press and pull the vegetable parer toward you down the strip of chocolate to form a curl. Place a toothpick through the inside of the curl and transfer the curl to a clean piece of waxed paper. Repeat the process, dipping the vegetable parer in hot water and wiping it dry before cutting each curl. Rewarm the chocolate if necessary. Refrigerate the Chocolate Curls a few minutes, until firm, before using.

NARROW CHOCOLATE CURLS: Warm the chocolate bar, following the procedure given in the Chocolate Curls recipe, above. Do not cut the chocolate into strips. Hold the entire chocolate bar in one hand with a paper towel. Using the other hand, *firmly* press and pull a warmed and dried, sharp vegetable parer toward you down the *narrow edge* of the bar to form small curls. Place the curls on a clean piece of waxed paper; refrigerate until firm.

CHOCOLATE SCROLLS

The scroll pattern shown in this recipe was designed especially to garnish Black Forest Pie (page 488); however, the same pattern may be used on other whipped cream-frosted or -garnished chocolate pies and cakes.

Scroll pattern
1 4-ounce German's sweet cooking
   chocolate bar

Trace the scroll pattern (see the pattern below) 8 times on a piece of tissue paper; tape the tissue paper to a white, corrugated cardboard cake board. Tape waxed paper to the corrugated board over the tissue paper; set aside.

Break the chocolate into pieces and place in a tiny saucepan. Hold the tiny saucepan over (not touching) hot (not boiling) water in a small saucepan; stir until the chocolate completely melts. Refrigerate the tiny saucepan containing the melted chocolate for a few minutes until the chocolate cools to the consistency for piping.

Then, using a decorating bag fit with small round tip number 3 (page 383), pipe 8 Chocolate Scrolls on the waxed paper, following the lines in the patterns. Carefully place the board with the piped scrolls in the refrigerator for several minutes. *Refrigerate only until the scrolls are cool and set.*

With a thin spatula, remove the scrolls from the waxed paper and place them flat, single layer,

(Recipe continues on next page)

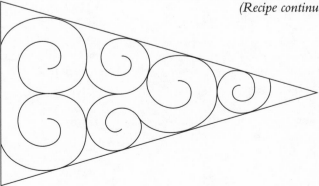

Scroll Design (actual size)

on clean waxed paper lining an airtight container. Store in a cool, dry place.

MAKES 8

VARIATIONS: Follow the above procedure to pipe other designs and decorations in chocolate.

SHAVED CHOCOLATE

Use the type and size of chocolate bar described in the procedures for making Chocolate Curls (see page 406). Do not warm the chocolate. To make Shaved Chocolate, the chocolate should be quite cool. Hold the chocolate bar in one hand with a paper towel. Using an unwarmed, sharp vegetable parer in the other hand, cut irregular chocolate shavings from the edges of the bar. Place the shavings on a clean piece of waxed paper and refrigerate. Or, if the shavings will not be used the day they are made, place them in a small container and cover tightly; refrigerate until ready to use.

SUGARED VIOLETS

Freshly picked violets
1 extra-large egg white
½ cup superfine sugar*

> *If superfine sugar is not available, process regular granulated sugar in a blender or food processor until fine.*

Leave the stems on the violets. Carefully check each violet, making certain that it is free from any insects or specks of dust or dirt. After checking, place the violets, single layer, on a paper towel; set aside.

Separate the egg white into a small sauce dish. Using a table fork, beat the egg white only slightly, until smooth; set aside. Place a small, finely meshed hand strainer on a piece of waxed paper. Pour part of the sugar into the strainer; set aside.

With one hand, hold a single violet by the stem. With the other hand, use a small, soft, number 3 watercolor brush to paint first the back and then the front of the violet with the egg white. While continuing to hold the violet, use the strainer to sprinkle a thin layer of sugar first over the back and then the front of the violet. Make sure all surfaces of the violet are sugared. If a spot has been missed, repaint the spot with egg white and sprinkle it with additional sugar. Lay the Sugared Violets, single layer, on a clean spatter screen (see illustration); let stand 24 hours to dry.

Spatter Screen

Then, using a thin spatula, carefully remove the Sugared Violets from the spatter screen and place them, single layer, on waxed paper in an airtight container. Freeze until ready to use. The stems may be cut off with a small pair of scissors at the time the violets are used. Violets are edible (see Edible Flowers, page 381).

SERVING SUGGESTIONS: Use to decorate pies (see Apricot Chiffon Pie with Sugared Violets, page 499); cakes; cookies; ice cream, sherbets, and sorbets; salads; and trays of hors d'oeuvres or tea sandwiches.

OTHER EDIBLE FLOWERS WHICH MAY BE SUGARED: Johnny-jump-up (*Viola tricolor*), pansy (*Viola × Wittrockiana*), pink (*Dianthus spp.*), sweetheart rose (*Rosa spp.*), and petals of a rose (*Rosa spp.*) are among other edible flowers which may be sugared.

TINTED COCONUT

For use on cakes, pies, cookies, and other desserts. Go easy with the coloring—pale colors are generally the most appealing to diners.

1 7-ounce package (about 2⅔ cups)
    flaked coconut
½ teaspoon water
Liquid or paste food coloring

Place the coconut in a medium mixing bowl; set aside. Place the water in a small sauce dish. Add a few drops of liquid food coloring or, using a toothpick, add a small amount of paste food coloring; stir until blended. Drizzle the water mixture over the coconut; stir until the coconut is evenly tinted. Cover tightly until ready for use.

MAKES ENOUGH TO COVER THE TOP AND SIDES OF A FROSTED, 2-LAYER, 10-INCH ROUND CAKE

Other Garnish Recipes

Baked Brandied Oranges (page 348)
Bok Choy Stuffed with Red Caviar
    (page 66)
Cherry Tomatoes Stuffed with Curried
    Chicken Salad (page 68)
Cucumber Wheels (page 67)
Deviled Eggs (page 267)
Miniature Vegetables, steamed (page 302)
Petite Potatoes (page 68)
Stuffed Fennel Sticks (page 69)
Vegetable Bundles (page 324)

Other Decoration Recipes

To Make an Ice Ring (page 694)

Breads and Rolls

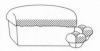

Since prehistoric times, bread has remained the primal staff of life. It is believed that nearly 12,000 years ago, in Neolithic times, primitive man made the first bread, probably of crushed grain mixed with water, which was most likely placed on heated stones and covered with hot ashes to bake.

The harvesting and grinding of wheat and the mixing and baking of bread were portrayed in paintings on the walls of ancient Egyptian tombs, and it was the Egyptians who eventually discovered that fermented wheat dough produced a lighter loaf of baked bread.

By the early Greek and Roman days, public bakeries (bakehouses) had begun to be established, and by approximately 100 B.C., it is said that there were 258 public bakehouses in Rome. Over the succeeding 2,000 years, bread has continued to be a dominant food in mankind's diet.

In 1992, the significant role of bread in the nutrition of Americans was refueled and ignited for launching into the next millennium when the U.S. Department of Agriculture released the new Food Guide Pyramid (see page 790) which illustrates the most up-to-date recommendations for healthful eating based on the latest research. Breads, cereals, rice, and pasta—all grain foods—make up the food group forming the base layer of the pyramid, from which we are advised to eat the greatest number of daily servings—6 to 11.

Americans will gladly oblige this health mandate insofar as bread is concerned, owing to the fact that bread's long evolution with man has resulted in one of our most marvelous-tasting, satisfying, and diverse foods.

On the cutting edge of this bread-making odyssey is the Midwest, home of the bread and roll all-stars who compete for top honors every year at the state fairs. At these annual "you have to see it to believe it" events, the best of the best whisk from the oven their prize loaves, rolls, biscuits, buns, muffins, sweet breads, and other aromatic goodies and rush them to be judged in an incredibly lengthy list of classes. For instance, at the 1997 Iowa State Fair, an astronomical 126 separate bread and roll classes were on the slate (plus 32 classes in the junior and intermediate divisions). That's a mighty lot of sensational breadstuff, and it included many specialties less frequently made at home, such as scones, pita bread, hot cross buns, and bread sticks.

The high point of this bake-off extravaganza is the annual cinnamon roll judging. (Heartlanders have an incurable crush on cinnamon rolls!) The standing-room-only crowd of drooling cinnamon-roll-aholics who gather for this derby must content themselves with feasting on the spectacle with their eyes—at least until the enviable ribbon winners have been announced, after which there is a mass sprint to the cinnamon roll stand located near the Bill Riley Stage.

With full appreciation of the fact that some Midlanders will label any criticism whatsoever of Midwest cinnamon rolls "sacrilege" or, at best, "utter impropriety," I will bravely venture out on a shaky limb and express the opinion that the lighter-than-a-cloud cinnamon rolls with the gorgeously gooey frosting at the state fair cinnamon roll stand and elsewhere in these parts, are frequently too generous in size (or should I let my hair down and say outrageously humongous?) nowadays. Could it be an obsession gone overboard? Or, is it a case of the eyes of the bakers being too big for the breadbaskets of the noshers? Nah, I guess not. Not when 99 percent of us red-blooded Midwesterners succumb to the temptation of these outsized monarchs of the munchies and somehow down every crumb with no remorse.

First cousins to cinnamon rolls are affectionately called "sticky rolls" in most corners of the Midwest. More formally, they are known as caramel rolls or caramel-pecan rolls. Basically, you make them exactly like cinnamon rolls, brushing the rolled-out dough with melted butter, sprinkling it with a cinnamon-sugar mixture, then rolling it jelly-roll fashion and slicing it. At this point, the kissing cousins part company, and sticky rolls are baked over a rich, buttery, brown sugar syrup which optionally may be covered with pecans. After baking, the pans are inverted and lifted off these golden charmers which have already filled the kitchen with that ineffable aroma.

Across the Heartland, miniature-sized sticky rolls as well as some quick breads are often served with certain luncheon main courses, notably cold poultry and fruit salads. Imaginative combinations of flours, fruits, vegetables, and flavorings have earned Midwest loaves of quick bread a great culinary distinction. People still love the old-time favorites, date nut bread, banana bread, and Pumpkin Bread (page 437), but au courant quick breads, such as Apricot Bread (page 432), Mincemeat Bread with Orange Butter (page 436), and Lemon Bread (page 435), have added flair to this versatile category of breads. Sometimes, just the right quick bread can be the taste complement you are searching for to serve with a dinner main course. For example, thin slices of Whole-Wheat Prune Bread (page 440) with Baked Pheasant, and Cranberry Nut Bread (page 434) with Loin of Pork.

Like loaves of quick bread, the range of tantalizing Heartland muffins has reached well beyond the tried-and-true blueberry and cornmeal standards. At a leisurely breakfast this weekend, throw your family for a loop with Lingonberry-Oat Bran Muffins (page 445). Whether your breakfast fare is continental or he-man style with eggs, bacon, and American Fries (page 330), these tasties will give your breakfast pizzazz and get the day off to a flying start. Or, for a touch of quick-bread elegance of a different type, tiptoe to the kitchen while the family is still fast asleep and whip up Marie Dalbey's Sour Cream Coffee Cake (page 452).

(After this peerless breakfast offering, ask any favor and it will be granted.)

While we're on the subject of breakfast, Midwest hands clap for pancakes, waffles, and doughnuts for the A.M. meal. And every once in a while, especially on cold winter evenings when the winds off Lake Michigan threaten to frostbite unprotected faces along the Chicago shore, Waffles (page 456) served with Sausage Patties (page 189) hit the spot for a homey dinner.

Any account of Midwest bread and roll conventions would be incomplete without heavily underscoring the hallowed niche baking powder biscuits occupy in the Midland food heritage. Since frontier days, so fundamental and ingrained have biscuits been in the diet of this agricultural region, they deservedly could be named folk bread of the Heartland.

Properly made, baking powder biscuits are so light they are in virtual danger of floating off your plate before you split them open, add a dab of butter, and take that first lush bite. My mother was a world-class master at making light biscuits (see her recipe on page 446). She taught that, like piecrust, the best baking powder biscuits are made with lard and that the dough should be manipulated in the manner I have recorded in the recipe procedures.

In addition to being a traditional breakfast bread, petite, airy biscuits are a grand complement to poultry as well as many meat dishes, and are perfectly acceptable and appropriate to serve with dinner. Biscuits sometimes take their place at the dinner table arranged like a string of pearls around the edge of main-dish casseroles (see Beef and Biscuit Casserole, page 174). Of relatively recent vintage across Middle America is the widespread popularity of biscuits and gravy, an old southern dish which worked its way north primarily via chain breakfast restaurants. I have taken the liberty of somewhat gentrifying this stick-to-your-ribs dish by adding a touch of Madeira. (Don't tell the traditionalists until the compliments are all in from around the table.) (See the recipe on page 188.)

Unlike New York City and other places where baguettes and other wonderful hard rolls are very often the choice for dinner, soft rolls predominate at the dinner hour in the Midwest. Even what are labeled "Hard Rolls" in good bakeries usually have comparatively soft crusts. In the Heartland, velvety Butterhorn, Cloverleaf, and Parker House Dinner Rolls (page 423) are all made from the same yeast dough, and differ only in the way the dough is shaped before the final rising and baking. When the silver roll basket is passed again at the table, it is hard to resist slipping your fingers under the warm bread cloth to quietly steal yet another one of these fluffy gossamers.

Yeast Breads and Rolls

Yeast is a microscopic plant. When used in making breads and rolls, the dough is leavened with carbon dioxide gas formed when the yeast cells metabolize fermentable sugars present in the dough.

In addition to yeast, flour, liquid, and salt are requisite ingredients in yeast dough. Sugar, fat, and eggs are optional ingredients; however, sugar and fat are generally included. The proportions of these ingredients, temperature, and the manner of mixing and handling the dough are all critical factors in the production of high-quality yeast breads and rolls.

Light, finely grained, and uniformly brown yeast breads which send forth that heavenly aroma as they bake in the oven are primarily the result of the application of good chemistry. Though not represented as a chemistry lesson on yeast breads and rolls, the suggestions and instructions given in this discussion and in the recipes in *The Blue Ribbon Country Cookbook* are based on the chemistry principles operative in yeast-bread and -roll baking. Bread-making hobbyists find the study of yeast-bread chemistry not only interesting, but also helpful in turning out superior products.

YEAST

Yeast used in making breads and rolls is available commercially in three forms: compressed cakes, active dry granules, and fast-rise dry granules. The yeast-bread and -roll recipes in this cookbook call for active dry yeast. Active dry yeast is most commonly purchased in ¼-ounce packets · containing about 2¼ teaspoons of granular yeast. The packets should be stored in a cool, dry place, and used before their expiration date. Open packets should be stored in an airtight container in the refrigerator.

Active dry yeast should be dissolved in water rather than milk or some other liquid. The temperature of the water is *critical,* and should be 110° to 115° F. It is important to use a food or yeast thermometer, or the temperature probe of a microwave oven to assure proper water temperature. Temperatures lower than 105° F. will cause the diffusion of a substance from the yeast which will adversely affect the volume and quality of the bread. Temperatures much higher than 115° F. will impair the yeast, and at 130° F., the yeast cells cannot survive.

FLOUR

Wheat flour (white or whole wheat) is a necessary ingredient in yeast breads and rolls because it is the only type of flour rich in the thick and elastic gluten. Gluten is an elastic protein which develops into strands in yeast dough as it is mixed with liquid and kneaded. Developed gluten surrounds and holds the bubbles of carbon dioxide as they form in the dough, and the gluten stretches to contain the carbon dioxide gas bubbles as they expand. This is how yeast dough rises. While other types of flour, such as rye, barley, and soy, may be used successfully in yeast breads, they must be used in combination with wheat flour.

All-purpose white flour is the most widely used flour for making yeast breads at home. Bread flour, a hard-wheat flour especially rich in strong gluten, is a choice product for bread making, and produces bread of particularly high volume and superb texture. *The Blue Ribbon Country Cookbook* bread recipes call for the use of bread flour although all-purpose flour may be used in substitution.

Recipes for yeast breads and rolls generally prescribe a range of flour quantity. This is because flour varies in moisture content and capacity to hold added liquid. The less the amount of flour used in proportion to liquid, the softer the baked product will be. Dough for rolls and most sweet breads should be as soft as will permit kneading, to produce light, fluffy end products; therefore, a minimum amount of flour in proportion to liquid should be incorporated into these products. Most nonsweet yeast breads are made with a medium-stiff dough, achieved by the incorporation of a somewhat greater proportion of flour to liquid. Some coarse breads require a stiffer dough to produce the desired texture.

As a general rule, the less the amount of flour used, within the quantity range given in a recipe, the better. Enough flour must be added to prevent the dough from being too sticky to handle and knead, but too much flour will result in heavy, compact baked goods. When stirring flour into yeast dough during the last phase of mixing, add the flour gradually and with special caution.

After the dough is mixed, cover the bowl with a tea towel and let the dough stand 5 minutes to allow time for the flour to take up additional liquid. This will decrease the stickiness of the dough, helping to make it manageable with the least amount of additional flour required.

Then, turn the mixed dough onto a *lightly floured* pastry cloth (page 54) or wooden board. Roll the dough in the flour on the cloth or board to lightly coat the entire outside surface, making it easier to knead. Knead with lightly floured hands. If your hands become sticky, flour them again. As the gluten develops during kneading, the dough will become less sticky. If the dough is too sticky to be manageable, add some flour during kneading; however, the total amount of flour in the dough should not exceed the maximum amount of flour specified in the recipe. Ideally, little additional flour should be added during kneading. No flour should be added to the dough after it has risen, as this may cause streaking and coarseness in the finished product.

LIQUID

Milk is the most common liquid used in making yeast breads and rolls. It should be scalded (page 25). Unscalded milk causes sticky dough and coarse, low-volume bread.

Plain water and potato water are also frequently used liquids in yeast breads and rolls. (It is interesting to note that milk is 87.69 percent water.) Breads made with potato water have slightly greater volume and a characteristic flavor, moistness, and tenderness.

Salt, sugar, and fat specified in yeast-bread and -roll recipes are added to the scalded milk, or other hot liquid, to be dissolved and blended. This liquid mixture should be cooled to 80 to 85° F. (to measure, use a food thermometer or the temperature probe of a microwave oven which registers temperatures at least as low as 75° F.) before adding the dissolved yeast and first portion of flour for mixing.

SALT

Besides providing flavor, salt has important functions in the formulation of yeast dough. With-out salt, yeast dough becomes sticky and difficult to handle. Also, salt assists in controlling the yeast's production of carbon dioxide and flavor-producing components. Slowing the production of carbon dioxide helps prevent overexpansion and rupture of the air cells, adversely affecting the bread's texture. The amount of salt called for in a yeast-bread or -roll recipe should not be altered. To do so would interfere with the balance of ingredients and likely result in an inferior product.

SUGAR

In addition to adding flavor, sugar aids in raising yeast dough by providing a ready supply of food for the yeast, which results in the production of carbon dioxide gas bubbles. Sugar also helps attain beautiful browning.

FAT

Fat functions to make yeast products more tender. It also plays a role in browning as well as adding flavor. Further, fat increases the length of time yeast products remain fresh.

EGGS

Eggs not only enrich the taste of yeast breads and rolls, but also add color and provide additional protein to contribute to improved texture.

KNEADING DOUGH

Both mixing and kneading develop the gluten in yeast dough. Kneading should be done gently, yet firmly. If dough is treated too roughly, the strands of gluten will be broken. When this happens, the surface of the dough will appear rough.

To knead, start by flattening the dough slightly with your hands. Pull the far side of the dough toward you, folding the dough in half.

Then, with your hands rounded over the dough, push the dough with the heels of your hands. Turn the dough one-quarter of the way around and repeat. Short, firm strokes are the most effective. Short pauses between the strokes, which allow time for the dough to relax, contribute to achieving the best dough elasticity.

Kneading by hand should be continued for at least the full time specified in a recipe. While dough may be over-kneaded, under-kneading is a common mistake in yeast-bread making. Dough may be hand-kneaded considerably longer than the time specified in most recipes before reaching the point of being overworked. Sweet dough requires more mixing and kneading than nonsweet dough because the high proportion of sugar in sweet dough causes the flour to be slower to absorb water.

Properly kneaded dough loses its stickiness. It will be smooth and elastic, and will be filled with tiny gas bubbles which can be seen beneath the surface.

RAISING DOUGH

Yeast dough must be risen in a bowl large enough to accommodate a doubling of the dough bulk. Use a pastry brush to lightly grease the bowl with vegetable shortening. After placing the dough in the bowl, turn the dough over so all surfaces of the dough are greased. Place a clean tea towel over the bowl to prevent the surface of the dough from crusting during the rising period.

Under perfect bread-making conditions, the dough and the place dough is set to rise, both will be at 80° F., the optimum temperature for the fermentation of yeast dough. 78 to 82° F. is the ideal temperature range for prime fermentation. While most recipes (including those in *The Blue Ribbon Country Cookbook*) call for yeast dough to be risen in a "warm" place, it is well to remember that 80° F. is less than body temperature, but warmer than the usual room temperatures for both heating and air conditioning. "Warm" is relative.

When yeast dough rises in too warm a location, it rises too quickly, causing the bread or rolls to have a yeasty, unmellowed flavor, as well as poor texture. Yeast dough will rise at temperatures lower than 78° F.; however, fermentation proceeds slowly. The risk for detrimental effects on rising dough is greater when the temperature of the rising location is too high than when it is too low.

Yeast dough should rise in a location free from drafts. The oven is an excellent place. If the oven temperature is lower than 80° F., turning on the oven light in advance will generally increase the oven warmth to the desired temperature. If necessary, the oven light may be left on while the dough is rising in order to maintain the proper temperature.

Some bakers like to maintain an 80° F. oven by half-filling a 9×13-inch baking pan with hot water and placing it on the lower rack of the oven directly beneath the bowl of unshaped dough or pan(s) of shaped dough. Usually, the baking pan must be refilled with hot water before each rising. Sometimes it is also necessary to refill the pan with hot water during the rising.

The time it takes for yeast dough to rise depends upon the temperatures of the dough and the rising location, as well as the proportions of yeast and other ingredients in the dough.

Yeast dough should rise until approximately doubled in bulk. If dough over-rises, the gluten strands overstretch, causing an elasticity loss which cannot be regained after punching down. Dough allowed to over-rise after it is shaped may flatten during baking due to inability of the overstretched gluten to contain the gas bubbles as they continue to expand during the initial baking period. Low-volume, heavy baked goods are also the consequence of under-risen dough, due to the crumb setting during baking before the gas bubbles expand adequately to obtain a light, nicely risen baked product.

Hard-wheat flour, such as bread flour, contains very strong gluten, producing yeast dough which can withstand the stress of expanding carbon dioxide bubbles better than dough made with softer wheat flour which contains weaker gluten. All-purpose flour is a blend of high-gluten hard wheat and low-gluten soft wheat. While all-purpose flour is an excellent choice for use in home-baked yeast breads and rolls, it is better to let dough made with all-purpose flour rise to just under double in bulk as a precaution against over-rising. The resiliency of the gluten in dough made with bread flour warrants allowing the dough to rise until slightly more than double in bulk. A second rising before shaping produces bread with greater volume and a better, less yeasty flavor.

To test rising dough for doubling in bulk, lightly and rather quickly press two fingers approximately ½ inch into the center of the dough. If the dents remain after withdrawing your fingers, the dough has risen sufficiently. If the indentations fill in rapidly, the dough needs to rise further.

PUNCHING DOUGH DOWN

After the dough has doubled in bulk, it is punched down. Punching dough down has several purposes. Among them, it helps prevent the gluten strands surrounding the carbon dioxide gas bubbles from becoming overstretched. Also, punching down subdivides the gas bubbles into smaller bubbles, resulting in a more evenly textured baked product. Additionally, punching the dough down allows the yeast cells to come in contact with additional food for the production of further carbon dioxide.

After yeast dough has been punched down, it is important to handle it gently to avoid tearing, packing, or otherwise injuring the strands of gluten which have been separated by gas bubbles.

To punch dough down, press your fist into the center of the dough in the bowl. Lift the edges of the dough from the sides of the bowl and pull them to the center. Then, turn the dough over in the bowl.

If a recipe calls for a second rising of the dough before shaping, re-cover the bowl and let the dough rise again in the selected rising place (80° F.). A second rising before shaping will take less time (usually about one-half the time) than required for the first rising. After a second rising, punch the dough down, following the same procedure as after the first rising.

After punching the dough down following the second rising, or following the first rising if a second rising is not used, turn the dough onto the pastry cloth or wooden board, cover it with a tea towel, and let it rest for 10 minutes. Resting the dough at this point makes the subsequent shaping easier.

SHAPING DOUGH

For directions on how to shape bread loaves, see To Shape Loaves of Yeast Bread (page 417). Instructions for shaping various kinds of rolls are given in the procedures for each roll recipe in this book.

After the dough has been shaped, cover the baking pans of shaped bread or roll dough with a tea towel and place the pans in the 80° F. rising location. Let the shaped dough rise until nearly doubled in bulk. When the dough holds a slight indentation after pressing it lightly with your finger, it is ready for baking.

BAKING

Throughout the baking process, temperature continues to play a major role in the production of yeast breads and rolls.

When exposed to oven heat, yeast breads and rolls rise very rapidly until they reach an internal temperature of 131° F. Heat causes accelerated production of carbon dioxide in the dough, resulting in the quickened expansion of the gas bubbles. Simultaneously, the gluten surrounding the expanding gas bubbles becomes less able to withstand the pressure because heat causes the dough to become more fluid. High-quality yeast bread results when the yeast ceases to produce carbon dioxide, the dough sets, and the cells begin to leak gas *before* the gas bubbles become overinflated and begin to rupture, *but not before* the bubbles inflate sufficiently to result in a light, evenly textured baked product. Correct oven temperature is a key factor in achieving this objective.

Normally sized bread loaves should be baked in the center of a preheated oven. Most loaves of bread are properly baked at 375 or 400°F. If a bread loaf threatens to become overbrown during baking, a very loose cap of aluminum foil may be placed lightly over the top of the loaf.

Rich yeast breads and rolls, such as sweet rolls, brown more easily due to the higher ratio of sugar in the dough, and are usually baked at 350 or 375°F. The lesser volume of dough in rolls allows them to be baked at slightly lower temperatures without impairing the quality. However, when oven temperatures are too low, both yeast breads and yeast rolls will overinflate before the dough sets.

If yeast dough is overinflated before it is placed in the oven, further intense inflation generated by the heat will ultimately create an irregular texture, and may cause a bread loaf to flatten and extend over the sides of the pan as a result of gas bubbles rupturing before the crumb has set. When underinflated dough is placed in the oven, the dough will set before the gas bubbles expand sufficiently, thus producing baked goods that are dense and low in volume.

It is difficult to tell when a loaf of bread is done. A golden-brown crust does not always equate to an adequately baked interior. While the age-old test of thumping the loaf with your finger and listening for the hollow sound signaling doneness is not without merit, that sound is not a foolproof sign that the bread is done. Proper oven temperature, heed to baking time, and experience are the most valid factors in determining the doneness of bread loaves. Rolls can generally be judged done when they are golden brown.

When done, baked bread should be removed from the pan immediately and placed on a wire rack, away from drafts, to cool. If left in the pan after baking, steam is apt to cause the bread to become soggy. If bread is left to cool on a wire rack in a drafty location, the crust is in jeopardy of cracking.

To Shape Loaves of Yeast Bread

When a recipe calls for the yeast dough to be divided into portions for two or more loaves, use a sharp, thin-bladed knife to cut the dough. Shape each portion into a ball. Then, shape each ball of dough, as follows:

LOAVES TO BE BAKED IN LOAF PANS

PATTING METHOD: Pat the dough into an oblong loaf with a nicely rounded top. The loaf should be approximately the length of the loaf pan in which it will be baked. Gently pull and stretch the dough downward along the sides of the loaf, fashioning a smooth, rounded loaf. Tuck the excess dough under the loaf; seal any pleats or prominent creases on the underside of the loaf by pinching the dough together with your fingers. Place the shaped loaf in the greased loaf pan. The ends of the loaf should touch the short sides of the pan. If they don't, pat the dough gently until the ends touch the pan.

ROLLING METHOD: Some bread bakers prefer to shape bread loaves by rolling the dough. To shape a loaf of bread to be baked in a 5 × 9-inch loaf pan using the rolling method, place the dough on a *lightly floured* pastry cloth (page 54) or wooden board; using a *lightly floured* rolling pin, roll the dough into an 8 × 12-inch rectangle. Then, use your hands to tightly roll the dough, short side to short side, jelly-roll fashion, using your fingers to seal the dough after each turn. After the dough is completely rolled, seal the seam by pinching the dough together with your fingertips. Press down on each end of the dough to form a flat, sealed strip at both ends of the loaf. Fold the end strips under the loaf. Place the dough, seam down, in the greased loaf pan, making sure that the ends of the loaf touch the short sides of the pan, and making any needed adjustments to shape an attractive, symmetrical loaf.

The rolling method of shaping helps prevent holes in the baked bread by rolling excess air out of the dough; however, you can sometimes see the roll pattern in the baked crumb, which may or may not be objectionable to the bread baker. The patting method and rolling method are equally acceptable methods of shaping bread loaves entered in state fair food competition.

FREESTANDING LOAVES TO BE BAKED ON COOKIE PANS

OBLONG LOAVES: Freestanding oblong loaves may be shaped using either the Patting Method or the Rolling Method (see Loaves to Be Baked in Loaf Pans, page 417).

If using the Patting Method, pat the dough into an oblong loaf with greater width and height in the center part of the loaf, and with tapered ends. Proceed as for shaping Loaves to Be Baked in Loaf Pans using the Patting Method (see page 417). Place the shaped, freestanding loaf on a greased cookie pan.

If using the Rolling Method, follow the procedure for Shaping Loaves to Be Baked in Loaf Pans using the Rolling Method (see page 417). Before placing the rolled loaf on a greased cookie pan, shape the loaf to have greater width and height in the center, with tapered ends.

ROUND LOAVES: Freestanding round loaves must be shaped by patting. Fashion the ball of dough into a round loaf of desired diameter with a well-rounded crown. While turning the loaf, gently pull and stretch the dough downward and under the loaf to achieve a smooth finish and good symmetry. Pinch together any pleats or prominent creases on the bottom of the loaf which were created in the shaping process. Place the shaped loaf on a greased cookie pan.

To Store and Freeze Yeast Breads and Rolls

Yeast breads and rolls begin to go stale very shortly after baking, even when they have been properly stored. Consensus among food chemists has not been fully reached as to all the chemical reasons for this propensity to staleness. Stale yeast breads and rolls become more unpliable and crumbly, with leatherlike crust and a changed flavor.

STORING

After newly baked yeast breads and rolls have cooled completely, place them in zipper-seal plastic bags, with as little air as possible trapped inside the bags. Store yeast breads and rolls at room temperature even though mold is likely to grow on them if stored too long at high temperatures. Refrigeration accelerates staleness in baked yeast breads and rolls despite the fact that it may help to forestall the growth of mold. It is best to freeze yeast breads and rolls which will not be consumed within 2 or 3 days.

FREEZING

For best results in freezing yeast breads and rolls, freeze them as soon as they have cooled thoroughly after baking. Place the baked products in special zipper-seal plastic *freezer* bags (they are heavier than regular zipper-seal plastic bags), and force as much air as possible out of the bags before sealing. Store yeast breads and rolls in the freezer at 0° F. or below, up to 3 months.

To thaw frozen yeast breads and rolls, leave them sealed in the zipper-seal plastic freezer bags and let them stand at room temperature 1 hour or more, until thawed. Do not apply frosting to breads and rolls before freezing. Frost breads and rolls after they have been removed from the freezer and have thawed completely.

Yeast Breads

WHITE BREAD

1½ cups whole milk
½ cup vegetable shortening, room
    temperature
½ cup sugar
1¾ teaspoons salt
2 ¼-ounce packets (about 1 tablespoon
    plus 1½ teaspoons) active dry yeast
½ cup warm water (110 to 115° F.)
2 extra-large eggs, room temperature
7 to 7½ cups bread flour, divided

In a small saucepan, scald the milk over medium heat (page 25). Remove from the heat. Add the vegetable shortening, sugar, and salt; stir until blended. Pour the milk mixture into a large mixing bowl; let stand until the mixture cools to 80 to 85° F. Meanwhile, in a small bowl, sprinkle the yeast over ½ cup warm water (110 to 115° F.); stir until completely dissolved.

To the cooled milk mixture, add the yeast mixture, eggs, and 2 cups of the flour. Using an electric mixer, beat the mixture on low speed until combined; then, beat the mixture on medium speed until smooth (about 2 minutes). Using a large mixing spoon, gradually stir in enough of the remaining flour to form a soft dough that does not adhere to the sides of the bowl. Cover the bowl with a clean tea towel; let the dough stand 5 minutes.

Turn the dough onto a lightly floured (use bread flour) pastry cloth (page 54) or wooden board. Roll the dough on the cloth or board to lightly cover the entire outside surface with flour. Knead the dough until smooth and satiny (about 10 minutes).

Place the dough in a clean, greased bowl; turn the dough over so all surfaces are greased. Cover the bowl with the tea towel. Let the dough rise in a warm place (80° F.) until doubled in bulk (about 1½ hours).

Punch the dough down. Cover the bowl with the tea towel. Let the dough rise again in the warm place (80° F.) until doubled in bulk (about 45 minutes).

Punch the dough down. Turn the dough onto the pastry cloth or wooden board; cover with the tea towel. Let the dough rest 10 minutes. Meanwhile, grease two 5 × 9-inch loaf pans; set aside.

Using a sharp, thin-bladed knife, cut the dough in half. Shape each half of the dough into a loaf (page 417) and place in a prepared loaf pan. Cover the pans with tea towels. Let the bread rise in the warm place (80° F.) until doubled in bulk (about 45 minutes).

Preheat the oven to 375° F.

Bake the bread loaves for 35 minutes, or until done. Immediately remove the bread from the pans and place them on wire racks to cool.

MAKES 2 LOAVES

WHOLE-WHEAT BREAD

2 ¼-ounce packets (about 1 tablespoon
    plus 1½ teaspoons) active dry yeast
½ cup warm water (110 to 115° F.)
⅓ cup plus 1 tablespoon honey
¼ cup vegetable shortening, room
    temperature
2¾ teaspoons salt
1¾ cups warm water (80 to 85° F.)
3 cups whole-wheat flour
3½ to 4 cups bread flour
Butter, softened

In a large mixing bowl, sprinkle the yeast over ½ cup warm water (110 to 115° F.); stir until completely dissolved. Add the honey, vegetable shortening, salt, 1¾ cups warm water (80 to 85° F.), and the whole-wheat flour. Using an electric mixer, beat the mixture on low speed until combined; then, beat the mixture on medium speed until smooth (about 2 minutes). Using a large mixing spoon, gradually stir in

(Recipe continues on next page)

enough of the bread flour to form a dough that does not adhere to the sides of the bowl. Cover the bowl with a clean tea towel; let the dough stand 5 minutes.

Turn the dough onto a lightly floured (use bread flour) pastry cloth (page 54) or wooden board. Roll the dough on the cloth or board to lightly cover the entire outside surface with flour. Knead the dough until smooth and elastic (about 10 minutes).

Place the dough in a clean, greased bowl; turn the dough over so all surfaces are greased. Cover the bowl with the tea towel. Let the dough rise in a warm place (80° F.) until doubled in bulk (about 1 to 1¼ hours).

Punch the dough down. Turn the dough onto the pastry cloth or wooden board; cover with the tea towel. Let the dough rest 10 minutes. Meanwhile, grease two 5 × 9-inch loaf pans; set aside.

Using a sharp, thin-bladed knife, cut the dough in half. Shape each half of the dough into a loaf (page 417) and place in a prepared loaf pan. Brush the tops of the bread loaves with softened butter. Cover the pans with tea towels. Let the bread rise in the warm place (80° F.) until doubled in bulk (about 1 hour).

Preheat the oven to 375° F.

Bake the bread loaves for 40 to 50 minutes, or until done. Immediately remove the bread from the pans and place them on wire racks to cool.

MAKES 2 LOAVES

LIMPA
Swedish Rye Bread

Swedish baked goods are among the world's finest, and limpa is one of the breads for which Sweden's baking artisans are best known. This wonderful rye bread may be flavored with one or more of the following: caraway seed, anise seed, fennel seed, cumin, orange rind, and lemon rind. The recipe that follows uses caraway seed. Some recipes for limpa include molasses as a sweet ingredient along with brown sugar. Limpa means "loaf" in Swedish.

½ cup water
¼ cup packed light brown sugar
2 teaspoons vegetable shortening
2 teaspoons salt
2 teaspoons caraway seed
1 cup water
½ cup warm water (110 to 115° F.)
1 ¼-ounce packet (about 2¼ teaspoons) active dry yeast
4 cups bread flour, divided
2 cups rye flour, divided

In a small saucepan, place ½ cup water, brown sugar, vegetable shortening, salt, and caraway seed. Bring the mixture to a boil over high heat, stirring constantly; reduce the heat and simmer gently 5 minutes, stirring intermittently. Remove from the heat and pour the mixture into a large mixing bowl. Add 1 cup water and stir to blend; let stand until the mixture cools to 80 to 85° F. Meanwhile, pour ½ cup warm water (110 to 115° F.) into a small bowl. Sprinkle the yeast over the water; stir until completely dissolved.

To the cooled brown sugar mixture, add the yeast mixture and 2 cups of the bread flour; using a standard-sized electric mixer, beat on low speed until combined. Add the remaining 2 cups of the bread flour; beat on medium speed until smooth (about 2 minutes). Using a large mixing spoon, gradually stir in 1½ cups of the rye flour. Cover the bowl with a clean tea towel; let the dough stand 5 minutes.

Sprinkle ¼ cup of the rye flour over a pastry cloth (page 54) or wooden board. Turn the dough onto the floured cloth or board. Roll the dough on the board cloth or to lightly cover the entire outside surface with flour. Knead the dough until smooth and satiny (about 10 minutes). If the dough feels sticky and too soft, knead in a part or all of the remaining ¼ cup rye flour.

Place the dough in a clean, greased bowl; turn the dough over so all surfaces are greased. Cover the bowl with the tea towel. Let the dough rise in a warm place (80° F.) until doubled in bulk (about 1¼ hours).

Punch the dough down. Cover the bowl with

the tea towel. Let the dough rise again in the warm place (80° F.) until doubled in bulk (about 1 hour).

Punch the dough down. Turn the dough onto the pastry cloth or wooden board; cover with the tea towel. Let the dough rest 10 minutes. Meanwhile, lightly grease a $12 \times 18 \times 1$-inch cookie pan; set aside.

Using a sharp, thin-bladed knife, cut the dough in half. Shape each half of the dough into a ball (see Round Loaves, page 418). Place the balls of dough 4 inches apart on the prepared cookie pan. If desired, make 3 or 4 parallel cuts about ½ inch deep across the top of each loaf, using a sharp knife. Cover the loaves with the tea towel. Let the bread rise in the warm place (80° F.) until doubled in bulk (about 1 hour).

Preheat the oven to 375° F.

Bake the bread loaves for 45 to 50 minutes, until a rich brown color. Immediately remove the bread loaves from the pan and place them on wire racks to cool.

MAKES 2 LOAVES

VARIATIONS

- For a shiny crust, brush the tops of the loaves with whole milk or slightly beaten egg white after the bread has fully baked. Then, return the bread to the oven for an additional 2 minutes.

- Shape the dough into 2 regular, oblong-shaped loaves (page 417) and place in 2 greased 5×9-inch loaf pans.

HONEY-SEED BREAD

2 ¼-ounce packets (about 1 tablespoon
   plus 1½ teaspoons) active dry yeast
½ cup warm water (110° to 115° F.)
⅓ cup honey
¼ cup vegetable shortening
1 tablespoon salt
2 tablespoons poppy seed
1 tablespoon sesame seed
2 teaspoons caraway seed

1¾ cups warm water (80 to 85° F.)
3 cups whole-wheat flour
¼ cup raw, hulled (unsalted) sunflower
   seeds
3½ to 4 cups bread flour

In a large mixing bowl, sprinkle the yeast over ½ cup warm water (110° to 115° F.); stir until completely dissolved. Add the honey, vegetable shortening, salt, poppy seed, sesame seed, caraway seed, 1¾ cups warm water (80° to 85° F.), and the whole-wheat flour. Using an electric mixer, beat the mixture on low speed until combined; then, beat the mixture on medium speed until smooth (about 2 minutes). Add the sunflower seeds; using a large mixing spoon, stir to evenly distribute. Using the mixing spoon, gradually stir in enough of the bread flour to form a dough that does not adhere to the sides of the bowl. Cover the bowl with a clean tea towel; let the dough stand 5 minutes.

Turn the dough onto a lightly floured (use bread flour) pastry cloth (page 54) or wooden board. Roll the dough on the cloth or board to lightly cover the entire outside surface with flour. Knead the dough until smooth and elastic (about 10 minutes).

Place the dough in a clean, greased bowl; turn the dough over so all surfaces are greased. Cover the bowl with the tea towel. Let the dough rise in a warm place (80 to 85° F.) until doubled in bulk (about 1 hour).

Punch the dough down. Turn the dough onto the pastry cloth or wooden board; cover with the tea towel. Let the dough rest 10 minutes. Meanwhile, grease two 5×9-inch loaf pans; set aside.

Using a sharp, thin-bladed knife, cut the dough in half. Shape each half of the dough into a loaf (page 417) and place in a prepared loaf pan. Cover the pans with tea towels. Let the bread rise in the warm place (80° F.) until doubled in bulk (about 1 hour).

Preheat the oven to 375° F.

Bake the bread loaves for 40 to 50 minutes, or until done. Immediately remove the bread from the pans and place them on wire racks to cool.

MAKES 2 LOAVES

PAT BERRY'S JULEKAKE
Norwegian Christmas Bread

Blue ribbon awarded to Pat Berry, 1989 Iowa State Fair.

Pat Berry is a supreme baker of yeast breads and rolls, for which she has won countless blue ribbons at the Iowa State Fair. Her presentations of Julekake are beautiful to behold. Pat now serves as a judge at the fair, and I always enjoy judging classes with her because of her broad cooking knowledge backed up by practical, applied experience.

4 ounces (½ cup) red candied cherries, cut in half
4 ounces (½ cup) green candied cherries, cut in half
½ cup golden raisins
¾ cup English walnuts, cut or broken to about ³⁄₁₆ inch diameter (optional)
5½ to 6½ cups bread flour, divided
2 ¼-ounce packets (about 1 tablespoon plus 1½ teaspoons) active dry yeast
1 teaspoon salt
1 teaspoon ground cardamom
½ teaspoon ground cinnamon
1 cup whole milk
1 cup water
½ cup plus 3 tablespoons (¼ pound plus 3 tablespoons) butter
¼ cup honey
3 large eggs, room temperature
Glaze (recipe follows)
Additional red candied cherries, green candied cherries, and English walnuts (if used in bread) for garnish

In a small mixing bowl, place ½ cup red candied cherries, ½ cup green candied cherries, ½ cup raisins, and ¾ cup walnuts. Sprinkle 1 tablespoon plus 2 teaspoons of the flour over the fruits and nuts; stir until separated and combined; set aside.

In a large mixing bowl, place 2 cups of the flour, yeast, salt, cardamom, and cinnamon; stir well to combine; set aside. In a small saucepan, place the milk, 1 cup water, and butter. Over medium heat, heat the mixture to 110 to 115° F., stirring intermittently.

To the yeast mixture, add the warm milk mixture, honey, and eggs. Using an electric mixer, beat the mixture on low speed until combined; then, beat the mixture on medium speed 3 minutes. Add the fruit and nut mixture; using a large mixing spoon, stir to combine. Using the mixing spoon, gradually stir in 3 to 3½ cups additional flour to form a soft dough. Cover the bowl with the clean tea towel; let the dough stand 5 minutes.

Turn the dough onto a lightly floured (use bread flour) pastry cloth (page 54) or wooden board. Roll the dough on the cloth or board to lightly cover the entire outside surface with flour. Knead in ½ to 1 cup additional flour until the dough is smooth and elastic (about 8 to 10 minutes).

Place the dough in a clean, greased bowl; turn the dough over so all surfaces are greased. Cover the bowl with the tea towel. Let the dough rise in a warm place (80° F.) until doubled in bulk (about 55 to 60 minutes).

Punch the dough down. Turn the dough onto the pastry cloth or wooden board; cover with the tea towel. Let the dough rest 10 minutes. Meanwhile, grease two 10½ × 15½ × 1-inch cookie pans; set aside.

Using a sharp, thin-bladed knife, cut the dough into 3 equal parts. Shape each piece of dough into a ball (see Rounded Loaves, page 418). Place 2 balls of dough on one of the prepared cookie pans, and 1 ball of dough on the other prepared cookie pan. Using your hand, flatten the balls slightly. Cover the loaves with tea towels. Let the bread rise in the warm place (80° F.) until doubled in bulk (about 45 minutes).

Preheat the oven to 350° F.

Bake the bread loaves for 30 to 35 minutes, or until done. The loaves will be only very lightly brown when done. Immediately remove the bread loaves from the pans and place them on wire racks; let stand until completely cool.

Drizzle Glaze over the cooled loaves. Garnish the loaves attractively with red candied cherries, green candied cherries, and walnuts (if used in the bread).

MAKES 3 LOAVES

Glaze

1½ cups powdered sugar
2½ teaspoons whole milk
¼ teaspoon almond extract

In a small mixing bowl, place the powdered sugar, milk, and almond extract; using an electric mixer, beat on high speed until blended and smooth.

TO FREEZE JULEKAKE: This bread freezes well. Freeze the loaves, unglazed and ungarnished, in separate zipper-seal plastic freezer bags. Glaze and garnish the loaves after they have completely thawed.

Yeast Rolls

DINNER ROLLS

Butterhorn Rolls, Cloverleaf Rolls, and Parker House Rolls (see recipes, below) differ from each other only in the way they are shaped. The same dough (see Dinner Rolls recipe, below) is used to make all 3 types of rolls. The shapes of Cloverleaf Rolls and Butterhorn Rolls generally would be considered more formal than the more conventional shape of Parker House Rolls.

¾ cup whole milk
¼ cup plus 2 tablespoons (6 tablespoons) butter
¼ cup sugar
1 teaspoon salt
2 ¼-ounce packets (about 1 tablespoon plus 1½ teaspoons) active dry yeast
½ cup warm water (110 to 115° F.)
2 extra-large eggs, room temperature

5¾ to 6¼ cups sifted all-purpose flour (sift before measuring), divided
Butter, melted

In a small saucepan, scald the milk over medium heat (page 25). Remove from the heat. Add ¼ cup plus 2 tablespoons butter, sugar, and salt; stir until blended. Pour the milk mixture into a large mixing bowl; let stand until the mixture cools to 80 to 85° F. Meanwhile, in a small bowl, sprinkle the yeast over ½ cup warm water (110 to 115° F.); stir until completely dissolved.

To the cooled milk mixture, add the yeast mixture, eggs, and 2 cups of the flour. Using an electric mixer, beat the mixture on low speed until combined; then, beat the mixture on medium speed 2 minutes. Using a large mixing spoon, gradually stir in enough of the remaining flour to form a dough that does not adhere to the sides of the bowl. Cover the bowl with a clean tea towel; let the dough stand 5 minutes.

Turn the dough onto a lightly floured pastry cloth (page 54) or wooden board. Roll the dough on the cloth or board to lightly cover the entire outside surface with flour. Knead the dough until smooth and elastic (about 8 minutes). The dough should be very soft.

Place the dough in a clean, greased bowl; turn the dough over so all surfaces are greased. Cover the bowl with the tea towel. Let the dough rise in a warm place (80° F.) until doubled in bulk (about 1 to 1½ hours).

Punch the dough down. Turn the dough onto the pastry cloth or wooden board; cover with the tea towel. Let the dough rest 10 minutes. Follow the procedures, below, for shaping the type of dinner rolls desired.

After shaping the rolls, use a soft brush to brush them very lightly with melted butter. Cover the pans of rolls with tea towels. Let the rolls rise in the warm place (80° F.) until nearly doubled in bulk (about 30 to 45 minutes).

Preheat the oven to 375° F.

Bake the rolls for 10 to 12 minutes. Immedi-

(Recipe continues on next page)

ately remove the rolls from the pans and place them on wire cookie racks. Serve immediately or let stand on wire racks until completely cool. Store, single layer, in an airtight container. Dinner Rolls (including all configurations) should be served hot in a roll basket (wicker, silver, or otherwise) lined and covered with a bread cloth to keep them warm. To heat rolls baked in advance and cooled, wrap them in airtight aluminum foil and place in a preheated 350° F. oven for 5 to 8 minutes.

MAKES 24 TO 32 ROLLS

BUTTERHORN ROLLS: Follow the Dinner Rolls recipe, above, through resting the dough for 10 minutes after punching it down. Grease lightly four 10½ × 15½ × 1-inch cookie pans; set aside.

Using a sharp, thin-bladed knife, cut the dough in half. Using a lightly floured rolling pin, roll each half of the dough into a 12-inch-diameter circle. Using a soft pastry brush, brush 1 tablespoon melted butter over each circle of dough. Cut each circle of dough into 16 equal wedges. Roll each wedge, starting with the wide end. Place the rolls, pointed end down, 2 inches apart on the prepared cookie pans. Resume following the procedures in the Dinner Rolls recipe to conclusion.

MAKES 32

CLOVERLEAF ROLLS: Follow the Dinner Rolls recipe, above, through resting the dough for 10 minutes after punching it down. Grease lightly 24 3 × 1-inch muffin-pan cups; set aside.

Using a sharp, thin-bladed knife, cut the dough into 4 equal pieces. Shape each piece of dough into long rolls 1 inch in diameter. Cut each roll widthwise into 1-inch pieces. Gently pull and stretch the dough downward and under each piece of dough to form a uniform ball with a smooth top. Place 3 dough balls, smooth side up, in each prepared muffin-pan cup. Resume following the procedures in the Dinner Rolls recipe to conclusion.

MAKES 24

PARKER HOUSE ROLLS: Follow the Dinner Rolls recipe, above, through resting the dough for 10 minutes after punching it down. Grease lightly four 10½ × 15½ × 1-inch cookie pans; set aside.

Using a sharp, thin-bladed knife, cut the dough in half. Using a lightly floured rolling pin, roll each half of the dough to ¼-inch thickness. Using a floured, 2½-inch round cutter, cut the dough into rounds. Wipe and reflour the cutter between each cut. Reroll and cut the excess dough until all the dough is used.

Using a soft brush, brush the dough rounds with melted butter (you will need about 2 tablespoons melted butter). Using the dull side of a table knife blade, make a crease, slightly off center, across each round. Fold the large side of each round over the small side, overlapping slightly. With your fingers, firmly press the folded edge (where you made the crease) of each round. Place the rolls 2 inches apart on the prepared cookie pans. Resume following the procedures in the Dinner Rolls recipe to conclusion.

MAKES 30

HOT CROSS BUNS

Although Hot Cross Buns, piped with a white frosting cross, are a traditional roll served by Christians during the Easter season, the affiliation of cross-marked bread with religion predates Christianity. It is said that the Greeks and Romans ate bread marked with a cross at public sacrifices and that the pagan Saxons ate cross-marked bread to honor their goddess of light, Eostre. Further, it is believed that the Mexican and Peruvian peoples participated in a similar custom using cross bread. The Saxons probably introduced cross-marked bread to England, where in pre-Christian times it was made to honor the goddess of spring. Early Christians adopted the bread since it bore the cross, the symbol of their faith. The tradition migrated to the United States with the English settlers.

Hot Cross Buns contain currants (or raisins), spices,

and sometimes candied citron. They are served at breakfast, coffee, and brunch, and with certain luncheon menus.

¾ cup whole milk
½ cup (¼ pound) butter
⅓ cup sugar
1 teaspoon salt
1 ¼-ounce packet plus ¼ teaspoon (about 2½ teaspoons) active dry yeast
¼ cup warm water (110 to 115° F.)
1 extra-large egg, room temperature
¾ teaspoon ground cinnamon
3½ to 4 cups sifted all-purpose flour (sift before measuring), divided
⅔ cup currants
2 ounces (¼ cup) finely diced candied citron
1 extra-large egg white, room temperature
1 teaspoon water (approximately 80° F.)
½ recipe untinted Confectioners' Frosting (page 579)

In a small saucepan, scald the milk over medium heat (page 25). Remove from the heat. Add the butter, sugar, and salt; stir until blended. Pour the milk mixture into a large mixing bowl; let stand until the mixture cools to 80 to 85° F. Meanwhile, in a small bowl, sprinkle the yeast over ¼ cup warm water (110 to 115° F.); stir until completely dissolved.

To the cooled milk mixture, add the yeast mixture, 1 egg, cinnamon, and 2 cups of the flour. Using an electric mixer, beat the mixture on low speed until combined; then, beat the mixture on medium speed 2 minutes. Add the currants and citron; using a large mixing spoon, stir to combine. Using the mixing spoon, gradually stir in enough of the remaining flour to form a dough that does not adhere to the sides of the bowl.

Place the dough in a clean, lightly greased bowl; turn the dough over so all surfaces are greased. Cover the bowl with a clean tea towel. Let the dough rise in a warm place (80° F.) until doubled in bulk (about 1¼ to 1½ hours).

Punch the dough down. Turn the dough onto a lightly floured pastry cloth (page 54) or wooden board; cover with the tea towel. Let the dough rest 10 minutes. Meanwhile, grease lightly two 10½ × 15½ × 1-inch cookie pans; set aside.

Knead the dough 2 minutes. Using a lightly floured rolling pin, roll the dough to ¾-inch thickness. Using a lightly oiled, 2-inch round cutter, cut the dough into rounds and place them 1½ inches apart on the prepared cookie pans. Intermittently wipe and reoil the cutter. Reroll and cut the excess dough until all the dough is used; set aside.

In a small sauce dish, place 1 egg white and 1 teaspoon water (approximately 80° F.); using a table fork, beat slightly. Using a soft brush, brush a thin layer of egg white mixture over the tops of the dough rounds (buns). Cover the pans of buns with tea towels. Let the buns rise in the warm place (80° F.) until nearly doubled in bulk (about 45 minutes to 1 hour).

Preheat the oven to 350° F.

Bake the buns for 15 minutes. Immediately remove the buns from the pans and place them on wire cookie racks; let stand to cool slightly. While the buns are still warm, use a decorating bag fit with tip number 7 (page 383) to pipe a cross of Confectioners' Frosting on the top of each bun. Serve immediately. Or, let the unpiped buns stand on the wire racks until completely cool; then store, single layer, in an airtight container. Just before serving, wrap the buns in airtight aluminum foil and warm in a preheated 350° F. oven for about 5 minutes. Then, pipe crosses on the buns and serve.

MAKES 2 DOZEN

CINNAMON ROLLS

¾ cup whole milk
½ cup (¼ pound) butter
½ cup sugar
1 teaspoon salt
2 ¼-ounce packets (about 1 tablespoon
    plus 1½ teaspoons) active dry yeast
½ cup warm water (110° to 115° F.)
2 extra-large eggs, room temperature
1 teaspoon pure vanilla extract
5¾ to 6¼ cups sifted all-purpose flour
    (sift before measuring), divided
¾ cup sugar
1 tablespoon ground cinnamon
3 tablespoons butter, melted
1 recipe untinted Confectioners' Frosting
    (page 579)

In a small saucepan, scald the milk over medium heat (page 25). Remove from the heat. Add ½ cup butter, ½ cup sugar, and salt; stir until blended. Pour the milk mixture into a large mixing bowl; let stand until the mixture cools to 80 to 85° F. Meanwhile, in a small bowl, sprinkle the yeast over ½ cup warm water (110 to 115° F.); stir until completely dissolved.

To the cooled milk mixture, add the yeast mixture, eggs, vanilla, and 2 cups of the flour. Using an electric mixer, beat the mixture on low speed until combined; then, beat the mixture on medium speed 2 minutes. Using a large mixing spoon, gradually stir in enough of the remaining flour to form a dough that does not adhere to the sides of the bowl. Cover the bowl with a clean tea towel; let the dough stand 5 minutes.

Turn the dough onto a lightly floured pastry cloth (page 54) or wooden board. Roll the dough on the cloth or board to lightly cover the entire outside surface with flour. Knead the dough until smooth and elastic (about 10 minutes). The dough should be very soft.

Place the dough in a clean, greased bowl; turn the dough over so all surfaces are greased. Cover the bowl with the tea towel. Let the dough rise in a warm place (80° F.) until doubled in bulk (about 1 to 1½ hours).

Punch the dough down. Turn the dough onto the pastry cloth or wooden board; cover with the tea towel. Let the dough rest 10 minutes. Meanwhile, in a small bowl, place ¾ cup sugar and cinnamon; stir to combine; set aside. Grease well two 9-inch or three 8-inch round baking pans; set aside.

Using a sharp, thin-bladed knife, cut the dough in half. Using a lightly floured rolling pin, roll each half of the dough into an 8 × 12-inch rectangle. Using a soft brush, brush 1½ tablespoons melted butter over each rectangle of dough. Sprinkle ½ of the cinnamon mixture evenly over each rectangle. Roll each rectangle, long side to long side, jelly-roll fashion. With your fingers, pinch the seam to seal. Cut each roll of dough widthwise into twelve 1-inch slices. Place the dough slices, cut side down, in the prepared baking pans. Cover the pans of rolls with the tea towel. Let the rolls rise in the warm place (80° F.) until nearly doubled in bulk (about 30 to 40 minutes).

Preheat the oven to 375° F.

Bake the rolls for 20 to 25 minutes. Remove from the oven and place the pans of rolls on wire racks; cool 5 minutes. Remove the rolls from the pans and place them on wire racks over waxed paper. Frost moderately warm rolls with Confectioners' Frosting. Serve the rolls immediately or let them stand until completely cool. Store, single layer, in a airtight container.

MAKES 2 DOZEN

SERVING ALTERNATIVE: Cool and store the rolls unfrosted. Immediately before serving, wrap the rolls in airtight aluminum foil and heat in a preheated 350° F. oven for about 5 minutes. Then, frost and serve warm.

VARIATION: After sprinkling ½ of the cinnamon mixture over each rectangle of dough, distribute ⅓ cup raisins evenly over each rectangle before rolling jelly-roll fashion.

CARAMEL ROLLS (STICKY ROLLS)

I like to serve Caramel Rolls warm in the morning with breakfast, midmorning coffee, and brunch, and at midday with cold, salad luncheons. As an accompaniment to hot luncheons and on most other occasions (Midwesterners sometimes eat Caramel Rolls with dinner), I prefer them at room temperature. Some diners prefer always to eat them warm.

1 recipe Cinnamon Rolls (page 426)
2 tablespoons butter
¾ cup packed light brown sugar
2 tablespoons light corn syrup
¾ cup broken pecans or pecan halves (optional)
3 tablespoons butter, melted

Follow the Cinnamon Rolls recipe through combining the sugar and cinnamon. Then, butter generously two 9-inch or three 8-inch round baking pans; set aside.

In a small saucepan, melt 2 tablespoons butter over low heat. Remove from the heat. Add the brown sugar and corn syrup; stir to combine. Return to low heat; cook the brown sugar until blended, stirring constantly. Pour the mixture, evenly divided, into the prepared baking pans. Divide the pecans between (among) the pans and distribute them evenly over the brown sugar mixture; set aside.

Using a sharp, thin-bladed knife, cut the dough in half. Using a lightly floured rolling pin, roll each half of the dough into an 8 × 12-inch rectangle. Using a soft brush, brush 1½ tablespoons melted butter over each rectangle of dough. Sprinkle ½ of the cinnamon mixture evenly over each rectangle. Roll each rectangle, long side to long side, jelly-roll fashion. With your fingers, pinch the seam to seal. Cut each roll of dough widthwise into twelve 1-inch slices. Place the dough slices, cut side down, directly on the brown sugar mixture in the pans. Cover the pans of rolls with the tea towel. Let the rolls rise in the warm place (80° F.) until nearly doubled in bulk (about 30 to 45 minutes).

Preheat oven to 375° F.

Bake the rolls for 20 to 25 minutes. Remove from the oven and place the pans of rolls on wire racks; cool 5 minutes. Remove the rolls from the pans by inverting the pans onto wire racks over waxed paper. Serve the rolls immediately or let them stand, sticky side up, on the wire racks until completely cool. (Eliminate the Confectioners' Frosting used in the Cinnamon Rolls recipe.) Store the rolls, single layer, in an airtight container. Serve Caramel Rolls sticky side up.

MAKES 2 DOZEN

SERVING SUGGESTIONS: Caramel Rolls may be served warm or at room temperature (see headnote). To reheat, wrap the rolls in airtight aluminum foil and place them in a preheated 350° F. oven for about 5 minutes.

Toast

TOASTED BACON BREAD

½ cup (¼ pound) butter, softened
1 1-pound loaf Italian or French bread, sliced ¾ inch thick (about 16 slices)
½ pound bacon, fried crisply, drained well between paper towels, and crumbled

Spread butter generously on one side of each bread slice. Place the buttered slices, single layer, in 1 or more large, shallow baking pan(s). Scatter the crumbled bacon evenly over the slices. Cover the pan(s) tightly with aluminum foil; set aside until a few minutes before serving time.

Near serving time, preheat the broiler.

Uncover the pan(s) of bacon bread and place under the broiler, about 6 inches from the heat. Leave under the broiler until the bread is toasted to a light brown (about 2 to 3 minutes). Watch very carefully. Serve immediately in a cloth-lined breadbasket.

MAKES ABOUT 16 SLICES

TOASTED GARLIC BREAD

1 recipe Garlic Butter (page 368), not molded
1 1-pound loaf Italian or French bread, sliced ¾ inch thick (about 16 slices)

Spread Garlic Butter generously on one side of each bread slice. Place the buttered slices, single layer, in 1 or more large, shallow baking pan(s). Cover the pan(s) tightly with aluminum foil; set aside until a few minutes before serving time.

Near serving time, preheat the broiler.

Uncover the pan(s) of garlic bread and place under the broiler, about 6 inches from the heat. Leave under the broiler until the bread is toasted to a light brown (about 2 to 3 minutes). Watch very carefully. Serve immediately.

MAKES ABOUT 16 SLICES

SERVING SUGGESTION: Serve with Grace's Spaghetti and Meatballs (page 288) as well as many other Italian dishes.

TOASTED HERB BREAD

½ cup (¼ pound) butter, softened
1 tablespoon finely snipped, fresh parsley leaves
1 tablespoon finely snipped, fresh chives
1 1-pound loaf French bread, sliced 1 inch thick (about 12 slices)

In a small bowl, place the butter, parsley, and chives; stir to combine. Spread evenly on one side of each bread slice. Place the bread slices, single layer, in 1 or more large, shallow baking pan(s). Cover the pan(s) tightly with aluminum foil; set aside until a few minutes before serving time.

Near serving time, preheat the broiler.

Uncover the pan(s) of herb bread and place under the broiler, about 6 inches from the heat. Leave under the broiler until the bread bubbles and browns (about 2 to 3 minutes). Watch carefully. Serve immediately.

MAKES ABOUT 12 SLICES

VARIATIONS: Fresh parsley or chives may be used singly or in combination with 1 or more of the following herbs: basil, chervil, dill, fennel, marjoram, rosemary, tarragon, and thyme. Combine 2 well-packed tablespoons of finely snipped, fresh herbs with each ½ cup softened butter.

Dried herbs may also be used. Use 2 teaspoons dried herbs to each ½ cup butter. When using dried herbs, soak the measured herbs in 1 tablespoon lemon juice for 5 minutes; then press out most of juice before combining with the softened butter.

TOASTED SESAME BREAD

¼ cup (4 tablespoons) butter, softened
1 tablespoon Dijon mustard
1 tablespoon finely snipped, fresh parsley leaves
1 teaspoon grated onions
2 teaspoons sesame seed
1 1-pound loaf French bread, sliced ½ inch thick (about 24 slices)

Preheat the broiler.

In a small mixing bowl, place the butter, mustard, parsley, onions, and sesame seed; stir to combine. Spread the mixture thinly on one side of each bread slice. Place the bread slices, single layer, in 1 or more large, shallow baking pan(s).

Place the pan(s) under the broiler, about 6 inches from the heat. Leave under the broiler until the bread bubbles and browns (about 2 to 3 minutes). Watch carefully. Serve immediately.

MAKES ABOUT 24 SLICES

TOASTED PARMESAN-PARSLEY BREAD

My favorite bread to serve with steaks and pork chops. People go for toasted breads on a dinner menu, and this one especially seems to hit the spot.

½ cup (¼ pound) butter, softened
1 1-pound loaf French bread, sliced ¾ inch thick (about 16 slices)
¾ cup freshly grated Parmesan cheese (page 46)
¼ cup finely snipped, fresh parsley leaves

Spread butter generously on one side of each bread slice. Place the buttered slices, single layer, in 1 or more large, shallow baking pan(s). Using a teaspoon, sprinkle Parmesan cheese over the buttered slices (use all of the cheese). Using your fingers, distribute the parsley evenly over the Parmesan cheese on the slices. Cover the pan(s) tightly with aluminum foil; set aside until a few minutes before serving time.

Near serving time, preheat the broiler.

Uncover the pan(s) of parmesan-parsley bread and place under the broiler, about 6 inches from the heat. Leave under the broiler until the bread is bubbly and lightly browned (about 2 to 3 minutes). Watch carefully. Serve immediately in a covered breadbasket.

MAKES ABOUT 12 SLICES

FRENCH TOAST

2 extra-large eggs
2 tablespoons whole, lowfat, or fat-free (skim) milk
⅛ teaspoon salt
Dash of pepper
1 tablespoon butter
4 slices French bread, ¾ to 1 inch thick
Butter
Pure maple syrup, hot

In an 8-inch round or square baking pan, place the eggs, milk, salt, and pepper; using a table fork, beat the mixture until blended.

Preheat an electric skillet, griddle, or regular skillet on the range to medium heat (350° F. in an electric skillet). Melt 1 tablespoon butter in the skillet. Using a spatula, spread the butter over the entire bottom of the skillet.

Using a fork, dip 1 bread slice at a time in the egg mixture, covering both sides of the bread generously with the mixture. Immediately after dipping each slice of bread in the egg mixture, place it in the skillet. Sizzle the dipped bread slices a few minutes on each side, until a deep, golden brown. Turn only once. Serve immediately. Pass generous portions of butter and hot syrup at the table for diners to first butter their French Toast and then pour syrup over top.

SERVES 2

VARIATION: Any type of white or whole-wheat bread may be substituted for French bread. Bread used to make French Toast need not be as thick as designated in the above recipe.

SERVING SUGGESTION: Powdered sugar may be sprinkled sparingly on top of French Toast before serving (primarily as a decoration).

MILK TOAST

1 teaspoon sugar
¼ teaspoon ground cinnamon
1 tablespoon plus 1 teaspoon butter, softened
2 slices white, whole-wheat, or raisin toast, hot
1⅓ cups whole, lowfat, or fat-free (skim) milk, hot

In a small sauce dish, place the sugar and cinnamon; stir to combine; set aside. Spread ½ of the butter on each slice of hot toast. Sprinkle the cinnamon mixture equally over the buttered toast. Cut each slice of toast twice, diagonally from corner to corner, to make 4 triangular pieces.

Place 4 toast quarters in each of 2 warmed soup or chowder bowls. Pour ½ of the hot milk over the toast in each bowl. Serve *immediately* before the toast becomes soggy.

SERVES 2

CINNAMON TOAST: Follow the Milk Toast recipe, above, through sprinkling the toast with the cinnamon mixture. (Eliminate milk from the recipe.) Cut the Cinnamon Toast in half diagonally, and serve in lieu of plain toast.

SAUTÉED TOAST POINTS

6 slices very thin, white bread
2 tablespoons butter

Trim the crusts from the bread slices. Cut each slice twice, diagonally from corner to corner, to make 4 triangular bread points.

Preheat an electric skillet or a skillet on the range to medium-low heat (300° F. in an electric skillet). Melt the butter in the skillet. Using a spatula, spread the butter over the entire bottom of the skillet. Place the bread points, single layer, in the skillet. Sauté both sides of the bread points until a deep golden brown, turning once. Remove the toast points from the skillet and place on wire cookie racks; let stand, uncovered, until serving time.

MAKES 2 DOZEN

VARIATIONS: One tablespoon finely snipped, fresh basil, parsley, or dill (or 1 teaspoon of any 1 of these herbs, dried) may be mixed with the butter in the skillet prior to sautéing the toast points.

SERVING SUGGESTIONS: Serve with hot hors d'oeuvres, first-course appetizers, soups, and salads.

Yeast Doughnuts

RAISED DOUGHNUTS

1 cup whole milk
½ cup sugar
1 teaspoon salt
1 ¼-ounce packet (about 2¼ teaspoons) active dry yeast
¼ cup warm water (110° to 115° F.)
4½ cups sifted all-purpose flour (sift before measuring), divided
¼ cup vegetable shortening, softened
2 extra-large eggs, room temperature
½ teaspoon ground nutmeg
About 4 pounds vegetable shortening for frying

In a small saucepan, scald the milk over medium heat (page 25). Remove from the heat. Add the sugar and salt; stir until blended. Pour the milk mixture into a large mixing bowl; let stand until the mixture cools to 80° to 85° F. Meanwhile, in a small bowl, sprinkle the yeast over ¼ cup warm water (110° to 115° F.); stir until completely dissolved.

To the cooled milk mixture, add the yeast mixture and 2¼ cups of the flour. Using an electric mixer, beat the mixture on low speed until combined; then, beat the mixture on medium speed until well blended and smooth (about 2 minutes). Cover the bowl with a clean tea towel. Let the yeast mixture rise in a warm place (80° F.) about 1 hour.

Then, place ¼ cup vegetable shortening in a small mixing bowl; using an electric mixer, cream well on high speed. Add the eggs, one at a time, beating well on high speed after each addition. Add the egg mixture to the yeast mixture; using the electric mixer, beat on medium-high speed until combined; set aside. Sift the remaining 2¼ cups flour with the nutmeg. Using a large mixing spoon, gradually stir the flour mixture into the yeast mixture. Cover the bowl with the tea towel; let the dough stand 5 minutes.

Turn the dough onto a lightly floured pastry cloth or wooden board (page 54). Roll the dough on the cloth or board to lightly cover the entire outside surface with flour. Knead the dough well (about 8 minutes).

Place the dough in a clean, greased bowl; turn the dough over so all surfaces are greased. Cover the bowl with the tea towel. Let dough rise in the warm place (80° F.) until doubled in bulk (about 1 hour).

Turn the dough onto the pastry cloth or wooden board. Using a stockinet-covered, then lightly floured rolling pin (page 54), roll the dough to ¾-inch thickness. Using a 2¾-inch, floured doughnut cutter, cut out the doughnuts and place them on a very lightly floured wooden board. Gather the remaining dough into a ball; roll out again and cut. Repeat until all the dough is used. Cover the doughnuts with the tea towel. Let the doughnuts rise in a warm place (80° F.) until doubled in bulk (about 45 minutes).

In a deep-fat fryer or deep electric skillet, heat about 4 pounds vegetable shortening to 370° F. The melted shortening should be at least 1¼ inches deep. Using a spatula, carefully place the

doughnuts, *raised side down,* in the hot shortening. Fry the doughnuts 40 seconds on each side, turning once by slipping a cooking fork under the doughnuts, one at a time (do not pierce), and turning them over. Fry no more than 4 doughnuts at a time in order to control the frying time and keep the temperature of the shortening as stable as possible.

When done, place the fork under the doughnuts, one at a time, and remove from the shortening. Place the doughnuts on wire racks covered with paper towels to drain. To sugar or glaze the doughnuts, see the procedures below.

MAKES 2 DOZEN

TO SUGAR THE DOUGHNUTS: Place ¼ cup sugar in a zipper-seal plastic bag. Place the warm doughnuts, one at a time, in the bag; seal and shake carefully until evenly coated.

TO GLAZE THE DOUGHNUTS

1 pound (4 cups) powdered sugar
¼ cup plus 2 tablespoons water
1 teaspoon pure vanilla extract

Allow the Raised Doughnuts to completely cool. Then, in a medium mixing bowl, place the powdered sugar, water, and vanilla; using an electric mixer, beat on high speed only until blended and smooth. Place the glaze in a small, flat pan. Dip both sides of the doughnuts in the glaze to cover all surfaces and place the doughnuts on wire racks to dry.

Quick Breads

TO TEST QUICK BREAD LOAVES FOR DONENESS

The standard procedure employed to test quick bread loaves for doneness is to insert a wooden toothpick into the center of the bread. If the toothpick comes out clean, the bread is judged to be done. This is the same method commonly used to determine the doneness of cakes.

Many quick bread loaves include a relatively large quantity of fruit or vegetable pieces which can make testing for their doneness a bit tricky. When withdrawn from a perfectly done loaf of quick bread, the testing toothpick may appear damp if it happened to have penetrated a nice, juicy piece of fruit, such as cranberry or apple. A second test in a different location on the bread may help the baker discern if the dampness of, or residue on, the first testing toothpick was due to the fruit/vegetable or less-than-done batter.

TO REMOVE QUICK BREAD LOAVES FROM LOAF PANS

Place the loaf pan of baked quick bread on a wire rack immediately after removing it from the oven. Let the bread stand exactly 10 minutes (use a timer) to cool. Then, carefully run a sharp, thin-bladed knife around the inside edges and to the bottom of the loaf pan to loosen the bread from the sides of the pan. Place a second wire rack over the pan. Securely hold both wire racks over and under the pan, and quickly invert them. The bread will fall from the pan onto the lower wire rack. Remove the top wire rack and carefully lift the pan off the bread.

To return the bread to its upright position, lightly place the extra wire rack on the exposed bottom side of the bread. Hold both wire racks and invert. Remove the top wire rack.

Let the bread stand on the wire rack until completely cool. Wrap the bread in airtight aluminum foil or place it in a properly sized, airtight container.

ABOUT THE CRACKING OF QUICK BREAD LOAVES

The top of quick bread loaves often cracks, which is normal and should not concern the baker. The cracking is caused by the center of the bread continuing to rise after the top crust sets.

Many state fair blue ribbons are placed across cracks in the top of loaves of quick bread.

Breads

APRICOT BREAD

1 6-ounce package dried apricots (about 1 cup packed apricots)
½ cup golden raisins
1 medium orange
2 cups all-purpose flour
2 teaspoons baking powder
½ teaspoon baking soda
½ teaspoon salt
1 extra-large egg
1 cup sugar
1 teaspoon pure vanilla extract
2 tablespoons butter, melted
½ cup broken pecans

Place the apricots in a small saucepan. Pour boiling water over the apricots to cover. Cover the saucepan; let stand until the apricot mixture cools. Place the raisins in a separate, small sauce-pan; follow the same procedure as for the apricots.

Preheat the oven to 350° F. Grease lightly a 5 × 9-inch loaf pan on the bottom and *only* 1 inch up the sides; set aside.

Drain the cooled apricots in a sieve, reserving the juice. Using a sharp knife, dice the apricots approximately ¼ inch square; set aside. Drain the cooled raisins in a sieve; set aside. Grate finely (page 47) the rind of the orange; set aside. Then, squeeze the juice from the orange and add enough of the reserved apricot juice to make 1 cup liquid; set aside.

Onto waxed paper, sift together the flour, baking powder, baking soda, and salt; set aside.

Place the egg in a large mixing bowl. Using an electric mixer, beat the egg briefly on high speed. Add the sugar and beat well on high speed. Add the orange rind, vanilla, and butter; beat on high speed until combined and blended. Add, alternately, the flour mixture in thirds, and the orange juice mixture in halves, beating on low speed after each addition only until blended. Add the apricots, raisins, and pecans; using a large mixing spoon, fold in until evenly distributed.

Spoon the batter into the prepared loaf pan. Using a small, narrow spatula, lightly and quickly spread the batter evenly in the pan. Bake for 50 minutes, or until a wooden toothpick inserted into the center of the loaf comes out clean.

Remove the bread from the oven and place on a wire rack; cool 10 minutes. Remove the bread from the pan (page 428); let stand on a wire rack until completely cool. Wrap in air-tight aluminum foil.

MAKES 1 LARGE LOAF

CARROT-SPICE BREAD

2 cups sifted all-purpose flour (sift before measuring)
2 teaspoons baking powder
1 teaspoon baking soda
⅛ teaspoon salt
1 teaspoon ground cinnamon
¾ cup granulated sugar
¼ cup packed light brown sugar
¾ cup sunflower oil
2 extra-large eggs
¾ teaspoon pure vanilla extract
1 cup finely shredded carrots (about 3 medium carrots)
¾ cup broken English walnuts

Preheat the oven to 350° F. Grease lightly a 5 × 9-inch loaf pan on the bottom and *only* 1 inch up the sides; set aside.

Onto waxed paper, sift together the flour, baking powder, baking soda, salt, and cinnamon; set aside.

In a large mixing bowl, place the granulated sugar, brown sugar, and sunflower oil; using an electric mixer, beat well on high speed. Add the eggs, one at a time, beating well on high speed after each addition. Add the vanilla; beat until well blended. Add ½ of the flour mixture; beat on low speed only until blended; repeat the procedure with the remaining ½ of the flour. Add the carrots and walnuts; using a large mixing spoon, quickly fold in until evenly distributed.

Pour the batter into the prepared loaf pan. Using a small spatula, spread the batter evenly in the pan. Bake 50 minutes, or until a wooden toothpick inserted into the center of the loaf comes out clean.

Remove the bread from the oven and place on a wire rack; cool 10 minutes. Remove the bread from the pan (page 428); let stand on a wire rack until completely cool. Wrap in air-tight aluminum foil.

MAKES 1 LARGE LOAF

CRANBERRY NUT BREAD

An all-occasion holiday bread for breakfast, coffees, brunches, luncheons, and teas, and with selected dinner menus.

2 cups fresh cranberries, coarsely ground (page 49) (about 1 cup ground cranberries)
¼ cup sugar
3 cups sifted all-purpose flour (sift before measuring)
1 tablespoon plus 1 teaspoon baking power
¼ teaspoon salt
1 extra-large egg
1 cup sugar
2 tablespoons butter, melted
1 cup whole milk
½ cup chopped pecans

Preheat the oven to 350° F. Grease lightly a 5 × 9-inch loaf pan on the bottom and *only* 1 inch up the sides; set aside.

Place the ground cranberries in a small mixing bowl. Add ¼ cup sugar; stir to combine; set aside. Onto waxed paper, sift together the flour, baking powder, and salt; set aside.

In a large mixing bowl, place the egg and 1 cup sugar; using an electric mixer, beat well on high speed. Add the butter; beat on high speed until blended. Add, alternately, the flour mixture in thirds, and the milk in halves, beating on low speed after each addition only until blended. Add the cranberry mixture and pecans; using a large mixing spoon, fold in until evenly distributed.

Pour the batter into the prepared loaf pan. Using a small, narrow spatula, spread the batter evenly in the pan. Bake for 50 minutes, or until a wooden toothpick inserted into the center of the loaf comes out clean.

Remove the bread from the oven and place on a wire rack; cool 10 minutes. Remove the bread from the pan (page 428); let stand on a wire rack until completely cool. Wrap in airtight aluminum foil.

MAKES 1 LARGE LOAF

DUTCH APPLE BREAD

This luscious-tasting and -looking bread is a specialty in Holland Dutch communities. When I go to Pella, Iowa, I always bring home a loaf or two of fantastic Apple Bread from the Jaarsma Bakery.

2 cups sifted all-purpose flour (sift before measuring)
2 teaspoons baking powder
½ teaspoon salt
1 cup *unpared*, quartered, and cored apples diced ⅜ inch square
½ cup (¼ pound) butter, softened
1 cup sugar
2 extra-large eggs
1 teaspoon pure vanilla extract
2 tablespoons whole milk
⅓ cup broken pecans
Glaze (recipe follows)

Preheat the oven to 350° F. Grease lightly a 5 × 9-inch loaf pan on the bottom and *only* 1 inch up the sides; set aside.

Reserve 3 tablespoons of the measured flour in a small sauce dish; set aside. Onto waxed paper, sift together the remaining flour, baking powder, and salt; set aside. Prepare the apples and place them in a small mixing bowl; set aside.

In a large mixing bowl, place the butter and sugar; using an electric mixer, cream well on high speed. Add the eggs, one at a time, beating well on high speed after each addition. Add the vanilla and milk; beat until blended; set aside.

Add the pecans to the apples; sprinkle the reserved 3 tablespoons flour over top and toss quickly to coat. Add the apple mixture and flour mixture to the egg mixture; using a large mixing spoon, fold in only until the flour is dampened and the apples and pecans are evenly distributed.

Spoon the batter into the prepared loaf pan. Using a small, narrow spatula, spread the batter evenly in the pan. Bake for 45 minutes, or until a wooden toothpick inserted into the center of the loaf comes out clean.

Remove the bread from the oven and place on a wire rack; cool 10 minutes. Remove the bread from the pan (page 428) and place on a wire rack over waxed paper; let stand until completely cool.

Then, pour the Glaze over the bread, allowing it to drip down the sides; let stand until the glaze is dry. Place the bread in an airtight container or wrap in aluminum foil.

MAKES 1 LARGE LOAF

Glaze

½ cup powdered sugar
2 tablespoons butter, melted
2 teaspoons water

In a small mixing bowl, place the powdered sugar, butter, and water; using an electric mixer, beat on high speed only until smooth.

LEMON BREAD

1 cup broken pecans
2 cups sifted all-purpose flour (sift before measuring)
2 teaspoons baking soda
½ teaspoon salt
1 cup (½ pound) butter, softened
2 cups sugar
4 extra-large eggs
1 teaspoon lemon extract
1 teaspoon finely grated lemon rind
1 cup buttermilk
Glaze (recipe follows)

Preheat the oven to 350° F. Grease lightly two 4½ × 8½-inch loaf pans on the bottoms and *only* 1 inch up the sides; set aside.

Place the pecans in a small mixing bowl. Sprinkle 1 tablespoon of the measured flour over the pecans; toss until evenly dusted; set aside. Onto waxed paper, sift together the remaining flour, baking soda, and salt; set aside.

In a large mixing bowl, place the butter and sugar; using an electric mixer, beat on high speed until light and creamy. Add the eggs, one at a time, beating well on high speed after each addition. Add the lemon extract and lemon rind; beat on high speed until fluffy. Add, alternately, the flour mixture in fourths, and the buttermilk in thirds, beating on low speed after each addition only until blended. Add the pecans; using a large mixing spoon, fold in only until evenly distributed.

Spoon the batter equally into the prepared loaf pans. Using a small, narrow spatula, spread the batter evenly in the pans. Bake for 50 minutes, or until a wooden toothpick inserted into the center of the loaves comes out clean.

Remove the bread from the oven and place on wire racks; cool 10 minutes. Remove the bread from the pans (page 428) and place on wire racks over waxed paper; let stand while preparing the glaze.

Spoon warm Glaze, a little at a time, over the warm bread. Using a soft brush, spread the glaze evenly over the top of the bread and brush the glaze on the sides of the bread; let stand until completely cool. Wrap the loaves separately in airtight aluminum foil.

MAKES 2 MEDIUM LOAVES

Glaze

1 cup sugar
⅓ cup freshly squeezed, strained lemon juice (about 2 lemons)

In a small saucepan, place the sugar and lemon juice; stir to combine. Over medium-high heat, heat the lemon mixture only until the sugar melts, stirring constantly.

SERVING SUGGESTIONS: A nice breakfast, brunch, or tea bread.

MINCEMEAT BREAD
WITH ORANGE BUTTER

Baked in a ring mold, this bread looks nice served at buffet-style coffees, breakfasts, and brunches. It's especially inviting and appropriate around the holidays.

1¾ cups sifted all-purpose flour (sift before measuring)
1 tablespoon baking powder
½ teaspoon salt
¼ teaspoon ground cinnamon
⅛ teaspoon ground nutmeg
2 extra-large eggs
¼ cup whole milk
3 tablespoons butter, melted
½ cup packed dark brown sugar
1 cup mincemeat, home canned (page 726) or commercially canned
2 ounces finely diced candied orange peel (about ¼ cup packed candied orange peel), homemade (page 685) or commercial
1 recipe Orange Butter (page 369) or Ribbed Orange Butter Balls (page 396)

Preheat the oven to 350°F. Grease and flour an 8-inch ring mold; set aside.

Onto waxed paper, sift together the flour, baking powder, salt, cinnamon, and nutmeg. Place the flour mixture in a medium mixing bowl. Using a tablespoon, make a well in the center of the flour mixture; set aside.

Place the eggs in a medium-small mixing bowl. Using an electric mixer, beat the eggs slightly on medium speed. Add the milk, butter, and brown sugar; beat on medium speed only until blended. Add the mincemeat and candied orange peel; using a tablespoon, stir to combine. Pour the mincemeat mixture, all at once, into the well in the flour mixture; using a small mixing spoon, stir and fold *only* until the flour disappears and the mincemeat and candied orange peel are evenly distributed.

Spoon the batter into the prepared ring mold. Using a small, narrow spatula, spread the batter evenly in the ring mold. Bake for 45 minutes, or until a wooden toothpick inserted into the bread comes out clean.

Remove the bread from the oven and place on a wire rack; let stand 10 minutes. Then, carefully run a sharp, thin-bladed knife around the outer and inner edges of the ring mold to loosen the bread. Place a second wire rack over the top of the ring mold; hold both wire racks securely and invert. Remove the top wire rack and carefully lift the ring mold off the bread. The bread may be reinverted or left as is with the bottom side up. Let the bread stand on a wire rack until completely cool.

Using 2 spatulas, transfer the bread to a 10-inch corrugated cardboard cake circle; place in an airtight cake container.

To serve, slice the bread ring, leaving it in place on the cake circle. Place the cake circle on a cake stand or serving tray. Place a serving bowl of Orange Butter or Ribbed Orange Butter Balls in the center of the bread ring.

MAKES ABOUT 20 SLICES

POPPY SEED BREAD
WITH ORANGE GLAZE

3 cups all-purpose flour
1½ teaspoons baking powder
1 teaspoon salt
1½ cups sugar
½ cup plus 2 tablespoons vegetable oil
½ cup (¼ pound) butter, melted
3 extra-large eggs
1½ teaspoons pure vanilla extract
1½ teaspoons almond extract
2 tablespoons poppy seed
1½ cups whole milk
Orange Glaze (recipe follows)

Preheat the oven to 340°F. Grease lightly two 4½ × 8½-inch loaf pans on the bottoms and *only* 1 inch up the sides; set aside (see Note).

Onto waxed paper, sift together the flour, baking powder, and salt; set aside.

In a large mixing bowl, place the sugar and vegetable oil; using an electric mixer, beat well on high speed. Add the butter; beat on high speed until blended. Add the eggs, one at a time, beating well on high speed after each addition. Add the vanilla, almond extract, and poppy seed; beat to blend and combine. Add, alternately, the flour mixture in thirds, and the milk in halves, beating on low speed after each addition only until blended.

Pour the batter equally into the prepared loaf pans. Using a small, narrow spatula, spread the batter evenly in the pans. Bake for 1 hour, or until a wooden toothpick inserted into the center of the loaves comes out clean.

Remove the bread from the oven and place on wire racks; cool 10 minutes. Remove the bread from the pans (page 428) and place on wire racks over waxed paper. Immediately pour the hot Orange Glaze over the tops of the loaves, letting it trickle down the sides. Use a soft brush to spread the glaze over the entire top of the loaves; let stand until completely cool. Wrap the loaves separately in airtight aluminum foil.

NOTE: One 4 × 16-inch loaf pan may be substituted for two 4½ × 8½-inch loaf pans.

MAKES 2 MEDIUM LOAVES (OR 1 LONG LOAF IF 4 BY 16-INCH LOAF PAN IS USED)

Orange Glaze

¾ cup sugar
2 tablespoons plus 2 teaspoons freshly
   squeezed, strained orange juice
½ teaspoon almond extract

In a small saucepan, place the sugar and orange juice; stir together. Over medium–high heat, bring the mixture to a boil, stirring constantly. Remove from the heat. Add the almond extract; stir to blend.

PUMPKIN BREAD

Definitely one of the Midwest's best-loved quick breads. It goes with fall and the Halloween and Thanksgiving seasons.

3⅓ cups all-purpose flour
2 teaspoons baking soda
1½ teaspoons salt
1 teaspoon ground cinnamon
1 teaspoon ground nutmeg
3 cups sugar
1 cup vegetable oil
4 extra-large eggs
1 16-ounce can commercial pumpkin
⅔ cup water

Preheat the oven to 350° F. Grease lightly two 5 × 9-inch loaf pans on the bottoms and *only* 1 inch up the sides; set aside.

Onto waxed paper, sift together the flour, baking soda, salt, cinnamon, and nutmeg; set aside.

In a large mixing bowl, place the sugar and vegetable oil; using an electric mixer, beat on high speed until light and well blended. Add the eggs, one at a time, beating well on high speed after each addition. Add the pumpkin and water; beat until completely blended. Add the flour mixture in halves, beating on low speed after each addition only until blended.

Pour the batter equally into the prepared loaf pans. Using a small, narrow spatula, spread the batter evenly in the pans. Bake for 1 hour, or until wooden toothpick inserted into center of the loaves comes out clean.

Remove the bread from the oven and place on wire racks; cool 10 minutes. Remove the bread from the pans (page 428); let stand on wire racks until completely cool. Wrap the loaves separately in airtight aluminum foil.

MAKES 2 LARGE LOAVES

RHUBARB BREAD

1½ cups fresh rhubarb diced ¼ inch square
2½ cups all-purpose flour
1 teaspoon baking powder
1 teaspoon baking soda
½ teaspoon salt
½ cup granulated sugar
1 teaspoon ground cinnamon
1 tablespoon butter, melted
1½ cups packed light brown sugar
⅔ cup vegetable oil
1 extra-large egg
1 teaspoon pure vanilla extract
1 cup buttermilk
½ cup broken pecans

Preheat the oven to 350°F. Grease lightly two 4½ × 8½-inch loaf pans on the bottoms and *only* 1 inch up the sides; set aside.

Wash the rhubarb; dry between paper towels. Dice the rhubarb and place it in a medium mixing bowl; set aside. Reserve 2 tablespoons of the measured flour in a small sauce dish; set aside. Onto waxed paper, sift together the remaining flour, baking powder, baking soda, and salt; set aside. In a small mixing bowl, place the granulated sugar and cinnamon; stir to combine. Add the butter and stir until crumbly; set aside.

In a large mixing bowl, place the brown sugar and vegetable oil; using an electric mixer, beat well on high speed. Add the egg and vanilla; beat on high speed until the mixture is well blended. Add, alternately, the flour mixture in thirds, and the buttermilk in halves, beating on low speed after each addition only until blended; set aside. Add the pecans to the rhubarb; stir until evenly combined. Sprinkle the 2 tablespoons reserved flour over the rhubarb mixture; toss to coat. Add the rhubarb mixture to the batter; fold in until the rhubarb and pecans are evenly distributed.

Spoon the batter equally into the prepared loaf pans. Using a small, narrow spatula, spread the batter evenly in the pans. Using a tablespoon, sprinkle the cinnamon mixture evenly over the batter. Bake for 50 minutes, or until a wooden toothpick inserted into the center of the loaves comes out clean.

Remove the bread from the oven and place on wire racks; cool 10 minutes. Remove the bread from the pans (page 428); let stand on wire racks until completely cool. Wrap the loaves separately in airtight aluminum foil.

MAKES 2 MEDIUM LOAVES

SERVING SUGGESTIONS: Rhubarb Bread, with its sweet, crumbly topping, is perfect for breakfast or brunch, or with a salad luncheon.

JANET STERN'S MANDEL (ALMOND) BREAD

An utterly exquisite bread for luncheons and teas.

3 cups all-purpose flour
1 tablespoon baking powder
1 teaspoon salt
¼ cup vegetable shortening
¼ cup (4 tablespoons) butter, softened
1 cup sugar
3 extra-large eggs, room temperature
2 teaspoons pure vanilla extract
½ cup chopped blanched almonds (chop slivered blanched almonds)
All-purpose flour
⅓ cup sugar
¾ teaspoon ground cinnamon
2 tablespoons butter, melted

Preheat the oven to 350°F. Using vegetable shortening, grease an insulated cookie sheet (see Note); set aside.

Onto waxed paper, sift together 3 cups flour, baking powder, and salt; set aside.

In a large mixing bowl, place the vegetable shortening, ¼ cup butter, and 1 cup sugar; using an electric mixer, cream well on high speed. Add the eggs, one at a time, beating well on high speed after each addition. Add the vanilla; beat until thoroughly blended. Add ½ of the flour mixture; beat on low speed only until blended. Add the remaining ½ of the flour mixture and almonds; beat on low speed only until the flour mixture is blended.

Spoon ⅓ of the dough onto a well-floured pastry cloth (page 54); sprinkle the dough very lightly with flour (use only enough flour to permit handling of the dough). With floured hands, quickly shape the dough into a soft roll about 9 inches long. Place the roll to one side of the prepared cookie sheet. Following the same procedure, shape 2 more rolls, using the remaining dough. Space the 3 rolls, side by side, on the cookie sheet. Bake for 25 minutes.

Meanwhile, in a small mixing bowl, place the ⅓ cup sugar and cinnamon; stir to combine; set aside. After baking for 25 minutes, remove the bread from the oven. Using a spatula, immediately transfer the bread to a large wooden board covered with aluminum foil. Brush 2 tablespoons melted butter over the entire surface of the bread except the bottom of the loaves. Sprinkle the cinnamon mixture liberally (use all of the mixture) over the loaves and roll the loaves in the mixture which falls onto the aluminum foil. Spoon any mixture remaining on the foil onto the top of the loaves.

Then, using a sharp, thin-bladed knife, cut each loaf diagonally into 1-inch slices (about 7 to 8 slices per loaf). Using the spatula, return the cut loaves to the cookie sheet. Push each loaf together to close any space between the slices (to prevent drying). Bake for an additional 5 minutes at 350°F.

Using a spatula, remove the loaves from the cookie sheet and place them on wire cookie racks; let stand until cool. When cool, immediately wrap the loaves separately in airtight aluminum foil.

NOTE: Although not as satisfactory, a standard cookie sheet may be used if an insulated cookie sheet is not available.

MAKES ABOUT 2 DOZEN SLICES

SERVING SUGGESTIONS: Serve as a breakfast, brunch, or salad-luncheon bread. Or, cut the slices thinner and serve as a tea bread.

ZUCCHINI BREAD

The popularity of this bread can be attributed not only to its super taste, but to the big supply of zucchini from Midwest vegetable gardens.

3 cups all-purpose flour
1 teaspoon baking powder
1 teaspoon baking soda
1 teaspoon salt
1 teaspoon ground cinnamon
2 cups sugar
1 cup vegetable oil
3 extra-large eggs
2 teaspoons pure vanilla extract
3 cups unpared, cored, and coarsely
   shredded fresh zucchini
1 cup broken pecans
1 cup flaked coconut

Preheat the oven to 325°F. Grease lightly two 5 × 9-inch loaf pans on the bottoms and *only* 1 inch up the sides; set aside.

Onto waxed paper, sift together the flour, baking powder, baking soda, salt, and cinnamon; set aside.

In a large mixing bowl; place the sugar and vegetable oil; using an electric mixer, beat on high speed until light and well blended. Add the eggs, one at a time, beating well on high speed after each addition. Add the vanilla; beat until well blended. Add the flour mixture in halves, beating on low speed after each addition only until blended. Add the zucchini, pecans, and coconut; using a large mixing spoon, fold in until evenly distributed.

Pour the batter equally into the prepared loaf pans. Using a small, narrow spatula, spread the batter evenly in the pans. Bake for 1 hour, or until a wooden toothpick inserted into the center of the loaves comes out clean.

Remove the bread from the oven and place on wire racks; cool 10 minutes. Remove the bread from the pans (page 428); let stand on wire racks until completely cool. Wrap the loaves separately in airtight aluminum foil.

MAKES 2 LARGE LOAVES

WHOLE-WHEAT ORANGE BREAD

¾ cup broken English walnuts
½ cup golden raisins
1½ cups all-purpose flour
¾ cup whole-wheat flour
1 teaspoon baking powder
1 teaspoon baking soda
¼ teaspoon salt
1 teaspoon ground cinnamon
½ teaspoon ground ginger
½ cup (¼ pound) butter, softened
⅔ cup sugar
¼ cup honey
2 extra-large eggs
1 tablespoon finely grated orange rind
½ cup freshly squeezed, strained orange
  juice

Preheat the oven to 325° F. Grease lightly a 5 × 9-inch loaf pan on the bottom and *only* 1 inch up the sides; set aside.

In a small mixing bowl, place the walnuts and raisins; set aside. In a medium mixing bowl, place the all-purpose flour and whole-wheat flour; stir to combine. Sprinkle 2 tablespoons of the flour mixture over the walnut mixture; toss to coat; set aside. Onto waxed paper, sift together the remaining flour mixture, baking powder, baking soda, salt, cinnamon, and ginger; set aside.

In a large mixing bowl, place the butter, sugar, and honey; using an electric mixer, cream well on high speed. Add the eggs, one at a time, beating well on high speed after each addition. Add the orange rind; beat the mixture until light and fluffy. Add, alternately, the flour mixture in fourths, and the orange juice in thirds, beating on low speed after each addition only until blended. Add the walnut mixture; using a large mixing spoon, fold in until evenly distributed.

Pour the batter into the prepared loaf pan. Using a small, narrow spatula, lightly and quickly spread the batter evenly in the pan. Bake for 1 hour, or until a wooden toothpick inserted into the center of the loaf comes out clean.

Remove the bread from the oven and place on a wire rack; cool 10 minutes. Remove the bread from the pan (page 428); let stand on a wire rack until completely cool. Wrap in airtight aluminum foil.

MAKES 1 LARGE LOAF

WHOLE-WHEAT PRUNE BREAD

A full-flavored bread particularly good for serving in the fall and winter.

1 12-ounce package bite-sized pitted
  prunes
1½ cups water
½ cup reserved prune juice
1½ cups whole-wheat flour
1 teaspoon baking powder
1 teaspoon baking soda
¼ teaspoon salt
2 tablespoons butter, softened
½ cup sugar
1 extra-large egg
1 cup homemade sour milk (page 58)

In a small saucepan, place the prunes and water; cover and bring to a boil. Reduce the heat and simmer the prunes 2 minutes. Remove from the heat; let stand to cool (covered).

When cool, drain the prunes well in a sieve, reserving the juice. Measure 1 cup cooked prunes; grind coarsely (page 49); set aside. Measure ½ cup reserved prune juice; set aside. (Reserve the remaining prunes and juice for other uses.)

Preheat the oven to 350° F. Grease lightly a 5 × 9-inch loaf pan on the bottom and *only* 1 inch up the sides; set aside.

Onto waxed paper, sift together the flour, baking powder, baking soda, and salt; set aside.

In a medium mixing bowl, place the butter and sugar; using an electric mixer, cream well on high speed. Add the egg; beat well on high speed. Add approximately ¼ of the flour mixture; beat on low speed only until blended. Add ½ cup prune juice; beat on low speed only until blended. Add, alternately, the remaining flour mixture in thirds, and the sour milk in halves, beating after each addition only until blended. Add 1 cup ground prunes; using a large mixing spoon, fold in until evenly distributed.

Pour the batter into the prepared loaf pan. Using a small, narrow spatula, spread the batter evenly in the pan. Bake for 50 to 55 minutes, or until a wooden toothpick inserted into the center of the loaf comes out clean.

Remove the bread from the oven and place on a wire rack; cool 10 minutes. Remove the bread from the pan (page 428); let stand on a wire rack until completely cool. Wrap in airtight aluminum foil.

MAKES 1 LARGE LOAF

CORN BREAD

Midwest-style corn bread, thick in shape and made with yellow cornmeal, flour, and a bit of sugar (among other ingredients) has been a fixture in Heartland diets since the pioneer days.

Corn is truly the American grain. It is exclusively indigenous to North and South America. In fact, North American corn dates back to at least 2000 B.C. New World explorers learned about corn from the Indians for whom it was a staple, cultivated crop. From the Indians, the settlers learned to grind corn and use it to make corn bread or "Indian bread" as it was called then. Today, nearly four hundred years later, it can be said that corn bread is universally enjoyed across the Midwest—not surprising since the Midwest, sometimes referred to as the "Corn Belt," is where about 40 percent of the world's corn is grown.

Corn Bread is easy and reliable to make. You can whip up a world-class pan of this American classic at the same time you prepare dinner.

1 cup yellow cornmeal
1 cup all-purpose flour
3 tablespoons sugar
1 tablespoon plus 1 teaspoon baking powder
¾ teaspoon salt
1 extra-large egg
1½ cups whole milk
¼ cup (4 tablespoons) butter, melted

Preheat the oven to 425° F. Grease lightly an 8 × 8-inch baking pan on the bottom and *only* ½ inch up the sides; set aside.

Onto waxed paper, sift together the cornmeal, flour, sugar, baking powder, and salt. Place the cornmeal mixture in a medium mixing bowl; stir to combine. Using a tablespoon, make a well in the center of the cornmeal mixture; set aside.

Place the egg in a small mixing bowl. Using an electric mixer, beat the egg slightly on medium speed. Add the milk and butter; beat on medium speed only until blended. Pour the egg mixture, all at once, into the well in the cornmeal mixture; using a small mixing spoon, stir and fold *only* until the cornmeal mixture is dampened. The batter will be lumpy.

Pour the batter into the prepared baking pan. Using a small, narrow spatula, lightly and quickly spread the batter evenly in the pan. Bake for 20 minutes.

Remove the Corn Bread from the oven and place on a wire rack. Cut into 9 pieces. Serve hot (see Note).

NOTE: Corn Bread may be cooled in the pan, then covered with aluminum foil, and reheated before serving.

SERVES 9

SERVING SUGGESTIONS
• Serve with plenty of butter. Many Midwesterners also enjoy jellies and jams with Corn Bread.

• A natural accompaniment for Bean Soup (page 89).

AMERICAN INDIAN FRY BREAD

Fry bread is a specialty of several American Indian peoples, including the Ojibway or Ojibwa (also known as Chippewa) Indians in the Minnesota region of the Midwest. The bread dough, made of flour, baking powder, salt, milk or water, and sometimes sugar, is rolled into thin circles and then is deep-fat fried. It is usually served with honey or some other sweet spread. I prefer fry bread made without sugar as an ingredient, and like to spread butter over my serving of the bread before adding honey, jam, or jelly. Our family enjoys eating American Indian Fry Bread with dinner.

2¼ cups all-purpose flour
1½ teaspoons baking powder
⅛ teaspoon salt
¾ cup plus 1 tablespoon whole milk, warm
Vegetable oil for frying

Onto waxed paper, sift together the flour, baking powder, and salt. Place the flour mixture in a medium mixing bowl. Add the warm milk; stir in quickly. Turn the mixture onto a lightly floured pastry cloth (page 54); knead until smooth (about 4 minutes).

Using a sharp, thin-bladed knife, cut the dough in half. Using a stockinet-covered, then lightly floured rolling pin (page 54), roll each half of the dough into a circle ⅛ inch thick; let stand.

Pour 1 inch of vegetable oil into a large electric skillet; heat to 380° F. (medium-high heat). Fry the circles, one at a time, in the hot oil. Fry 2 minutes on each side, turning once. Drain on paper towels. To serve, diners tear off portions of the bread at the table. Serve with butter; and honey, jams, and jellies.

SERVES 4

VARIATION: Cut the kneaded dough into 4 parts. Roll and fry each part, following the procedures in the recipe. Serve each diner 1 whole portion of fry bread.

SERVES 4

BROWN BREAD

½ cup chopped dates
½ cup broken English walnuts
1½ cups whole-wheat flour
½ cup all-purpose flour
2 teaspoons baking soda
¼ teaspoon salt
1½ cups packed dark brown sugar
1 extra-large egg
1½ cups buttermilk
1 tablespoon plus 2 teaspoons vegetable oil

Preheat the oven to 350° F. Grease lightly a 5 × 9-inch loaf pan on the bottom and *only* 1 inch up the sides; set aside.

In a small mixing bowl, place the dates and walnuts; stir to combine; set aside. Sprinkle 1 tablespoon of the measured whole-wheat flour over the date-nut mixture; stir until evenly dusted; set aside. Onto waxed paper, sift together the remaining whole-wheat flour, the all-purpose flour, baking soda, and salt. Place the flour mixture in a large mixing bowl. Using a tablespoon, make a well in the center of the mixture; set aside.

Place the egg in a small mixing bowl. Using an electric mixer, beat the egg slightly on medium speed. Add the buttermilk and vegetable oil; beat on medium speed only until blended. Pour the egg mixture, all at once, into the well in the flour mixture. Using a large mixing spoon, stir and fold *only* until the flour disappears. Add the date-nut mixture; quickly fold in until evenly distributed.

Spoon the batter into the prepared loaf pan. Using a small, narrow spatula, lightly and quickly spread the batter evenly in the pan. Bake for 50 to 55 minutes, or until a wooden toothpick inserted into the center of the loaf comes out clean.

Remove the bread from the oven and place on a wire rack; cool 10 minutes. Remove the bread from the pan (page 428); let stand on a wire rack until completely cool. Wrap in airtight aluminum foil.

MAKES 1 LARGE LOAF

Muffins

CORNMEAL MUFFINS

1 cup yellow cornmeal
1 cup all-purpose flour
1 tablespoon plus 1 teaspoon baking
  powder
½ teaspoon salt
1 extra-large egg
1¼ cups whole milk
¼ cup (4 tablespoons) butter, melted

Preheat the oven to 400° F. Using Special Grease (page 56) (see Note), grease twelve 3 × 1-inch muffin-pan cups; set aside.

Onto waxed paper, sift together the cornmeal, flour, baking powder, and salt. Place the cornmeal mixture in a medium mixing bowl. Using a tablespoon, make a well in the center of the cornmeal mixture; set aside.

Place the egg in a small mixing bowl. Using an electric mixer, beat the egg slightly on medium speed. Add the milk and butter; beat on medium speed only until blended. Pour the egg mixture, all at once, into the well in the cornmeal mixture; using a small mixing spoon, stir and fold *only* until the cornmeal mixture is dampened. The batter will be lumpy.

Using 2 tablespoons (1 to transport the batter and 1 to push the batter from the filled tablespoon), spoon the batter into the prepared muffin-pan cups. Each cup will be nearly full. Bake for 12 to 13 minutes.

Immediately remove the baked muffins from the cups by inverting the pan(s). Serve the muffins hot, or let them cool on wire racks.

NOTE: Although not as satisfactory, vegetable shortening may be substituted for Special Grease.

MAKES 12

100% WHOLE-WHEAT MUFFINS

2 cups whole-wheat flour
1 tablespoon plus 1 teaspoon baking
  powder
½ teaspoon salt
¼ cup sugar
2 extra-large eggs
1 cup whole milk
¼ cup butter, melted, *or* ¼ cup vegetable
  shortening, melted

Preheat the oven to 400° F. Using Special Grease (page 56) (see Note), grease twelve 3 × 1-inch muffin-pan cups; set aside.

Onto waxed paper, sift together the flour, baking powder, salt, and sugar. Place the flour mixture in a medium mixing bowl. Using a tablespoon, make a well in the center of the flour mixture; set aside.

Place the eggs in a small mixing bowl. Using an electric mixer, beat the eggs slightly on medium speed. Add the milk and butter; beat on medium speed only until blended. Pour the egg mixture, all at once, into the well in the flour mixture; using a small mixing spoon, stir and fold *only* until the flour disappears. The batter will be lumpy.

Using 2 tablespoons (1 to transport the batter and 1 to push the batter from the filled tablespoon), spoon the batter into the prepared muffin-pan cups. Each cup will be about ⅔ full. Bake for 15 minutes.

Immediately remove the baked muffins from the muffin-pan cups by inverting the pan(s). Serve the muffins hot, or let them cool on wire racks.

NOTE: Although not as satisfactory, vegetable shortening may be substituted for Special Grease.

MAKES 12

SOY WHOLE-WHEAT MUFFINS

I think you will like the flavor of these muffins which combine soy flour with whole-wheat flour.

½ cup soy flour
1½ cups whole-wheat flour
1 tablespoon baking powder
½ teaspoon salt
2 tablespoons sugar
1 extra-large egg
1 cup whole milk
3 tablespoons vegetable oil

Preheat the oven to 400° F. Using Special Grease (page 56) (see Note), grease ten 3 × 1-inch muffin-pan cups; set aside.

Onto waxed paper, sift together the soy flour, whole-wheat flour, baking powder, salt, and sugar. Place the flour mixture in a medium mixing bowl. Using a tablespoon, make a well in the center of the flour mixture; set aside.

Place the egg in a small mixing bowl. Using an electric mixer, beat the egg slightly on medium speed. Add the milk and vegetable oil; beat on medium speed only until blended. Pour the egg mixture, all at once, into the well in the flour mixture; using a small mixing spoon, stir and fold *only* until the flour disappears. The mixture will be lumpy.

Using 2 tablespoons (1 to transport the batter and 1 to push the batter from the filled tablespoon), spoon the batter into the prepared muffin-pan cups. Each cup will be nearly full. Bake for 12 to 15 minutes.

Immediately remove the baked muffins from the muffin-pan cups by inverting the pan(s). Serve the muffins hot, or let them cool on wire racks.

NOTE: Although not as satisfactory, vegetable shortening may be substituted for Special Grease.

MAKES 10

OAT BRAN MUFFINS

1 cup all-purpose flour
1¼ teaspoons baking soda
¼ teaspoon salt
3 tablespoons sugar
1 cup oat bran
2 extra-large eggs
8 ounces commercial sour cream
¼ cup whole milk
3 tablespoons butter, melted, *or* 3 tablespoons vegetable oil

Preheat the oven to 400° F. Using Special Grease (page 56) (see Note), grease ten 3 × 1-inch muffin-pan cups; set aside.

Onto waxed paper, sift together the flour, baking soda, salt, and sugar. Place the flour mixture in a medium mixing bowl. Add the oat bran; stir to combine. Using a tablespoon, make a well in the center of the flour mixture; set aside.

Place the eggs in a small mixing bowl. Using an electric mixer, beat the eggs slightly on medium speed. Add the sour cream, milk, and butter; beat on medium speed only until blended. Pour the egg mixture, all at once, into the well in the flour mixture; using a small mixing spoon, stir and fold *only* until the flour disappears. The batter will be lumpy.

Using 2 tablespoons (1 to transport the batter and 1 to push the batter from the filled tablespoon), spoon the batter into the prepared muffin-pan cups. Each cup will be nearly full. Bake for 15 minutes.

Immediately remove the baked muffins from the muffin-pan cups by inverting the pan(s). Serve the muffins hot, or let them cool on wire racks.

NOTE: Although not as satisfactory, vegetable shortening may be substituted for Special Grease.

MAKES 10

LINGONBERRY-OAT BRAN MUFFINS

Good tasting, good-looking, and good for you. Who could ask for anything more?

1 recipe Oat Bran Muffins, above
½ cup plus 2 tablespoons commercially canned wild lingonberries in sugar

Follow the Oat Bran Muffins recipe through the mixing of the ingredients. Fill the muffin-pan cups half full of the batter. Using a teaspoon, make a well in the center of the batter in each muffin-pan cup. Place 1 tablespoon lingonberries in each well. Spoon the remaining batter equally into the muffin-pan cups. Each cup will be nearly full. Resume following the Oat Bran Muffins recipe for baking.

CRANBERRY-ORANGE MUFFINS

1 tablespoon plus 1 teaspoon finely ground orange peel (requires about 1 medium orange) (see recipe procedures below)
2 cups fresh cranberries
2 cups all-purpose flour
1 tablespoon plus 1 teaspoon baking powder
½ teaspoon salt
¼ cup sugar
2 extra-large eggs
1 cup whole milk
3 tablespoons butter, melted, *or* 3 tablespoons vegetable oil
½ cup broken pecans

Preheat the oven to 400° F. Using Special Grease (page 56) (see Note), grease twelve 3 × 1-inch muffin-pan cups; set aside.

Wash the orange; dry it. Using a sharp paring knife, thinly pare the orange, removing *only* the orange-colored outer peel, including as little of the white peel membrane as possible. Using a meat grinder fit with a fine blade (page 49),

grind the peel. Measure 1 tablespoon plus 1 teaspoon finely ground peel; set aside.

Wash the cranberries; drain well in a sieve. Grind the cranberries finely in the meat grinder; drain in a sieve; set aside.

Onto waxed paper, sift together the flour, baking powder, salt, and sugar. Place the flour mixture in a medium mixing bowl. Using a tablespoon, make a well in the center of the flour mixture; set aside.

Place the eggs in a small mixing bowl. Using an electric mixer, beat the eggs slightly on medium speed. Add the milk and butter; beat on medium speed only until blended. Pour the egg mixture, all at once, into the well in the flour mixture; using a small mixing spoon, make 3 or 4 folding strokes until the egg mixture begins to mix with the flour mixture. Add the orange peel, cranberries, and pecans; fold and stir *only* until the flour disappears (and the fruit and nuts are evenly distributed). The batter will be lumpy.

Using 2 tablespoons (1 to transport the batter and 1 to push the batter from the filled tablespoon), spoon the batter into the prepared muffin-pan cups. Each cup will be nearly full. Bake for 15 minutes.

Immediately remove the baked muffins from the muffin-pan cups by inverting the pan(s). Serve the muffins hot, or let them cool on wire racks.

NOTE: Although not as satisfactory, vegetable shortening may be substituted for Special Grease.

MAKES 12

BANANA MUFFINS

1½ cups all-purpose flour
1 teaspoon baking soda
1 teaspoon ground nutmeg
¾ cup sugar
1 cup mashed, very ripe bananas (about 2 large bananas)
1 extra-large egg
½ cup (¼ pound) butter, melted
1 teaspoon pure vanilla extract

Preheat the oven to 350° F. Using Special Grease (page 56) (see Note), grease twelve 3 × 1-inch muffin-pan cups; set aside.

Onto waxed paper, sift together the flour, baking soda, nutmeg, and sugar. Place the flour mixture in a medium mixing bowl. Using a tablespoon, make a well in the center of the flour mixture; set aside.

Peel the bananas; slice them into a small mixing bowl. Using a fork, mash the bananas (the bananas will be slightly lumpy); measure and set aside.

Place the egg in a small mixing bowl. Using an electric mixer, beat the egg slightly on medium speed. Add the butter and vanilla; beat on medium speed only until blended. Add the bananas; using a spoon, stir to combine. Pour the egg mixture, all at once, into the well in the flour mixture; using a small mixing spoon, stir and fold *only* until the flour disappears. The batter will be lumpy.

Using 2 tablespoons (1 to transport the batter and 1 to push the batter from the filled tablespoon), spoon the batter into the prepared muffin-pan cups. Each cup will be about ⅔ full. Bake for 15 to 18 minutes.

Immediately remove the baked muffins from the muffin-pan cups by inverting the pan(s). Serve the muffins hot, or let them cool on wire racks.

NOTE: Although not as satisfactory, vegetable shortening may be substituted for Special Grease.

MAKES 12

Biscuits

BAKING POWDER BISCUITS

2 cups sifted all-purpose flour (sift before measuring)
1 tablespoon plus 1 teaspoon baking powder
½ teaspoon salt
¼ cup plus 2 tablespoons refrigerated lard
¾ cup whole milk, cold

Preheat the oven to 400° F.

Onto waxed paper, sift together the flour, baking powder, and salt. Place the flour mixture in a medium mixing bowl. Using a table knife, quickly cut the measured lard into approximately nickel-sized (irregular) chunks and drop them onto the flour mixture. Using a pastry blender, cut the lard into the flour mixture until the mixture is the texture of coarse cornmeal. Using a table fork, make a well in the center of the flour mixture. Pour the milk, all at once, into the well in the flour mixture. Using the fork, stir with 25 to 30 strokes, until the flour mixture is dampened and the dough stiffens. (Biscuit dough is stirred and manipulated more than muffin batter.)

Turn the dough onto a *lightly floured* pastry cloth (page 54) or wooden board. Knead (page 23) about 20 times until the dough is cohesive and manageable. Using a *lightly floured* rolling pin, roll the dough to ½-inch thickness. Using a floured, 2-inch biscuit cutter, cut the biscuits with a straight up and down motion, dipping the cutter in flour between each cut. Wipe the cutter intermittently with a paper towel when the dough begins to cling to it. Place the cut biscuits on an ungreased cookie sheet (preferably, an insulated cookie sheet). Gather the remaining dough and knead briefly; reroll and cut additional biscuits. Repeat the procedure until all the dough is used. Bake for 12 minutes, until the biscuits are lightly brown.

When done, immediately remove the biscuits from the cookie sheet to prevent the bottoms from overbrowning on the hot, cookie-sheet surface. Place the biscuits in a cloth-lined roll basket for immediate serving. If serving at a later time, place the biscuits on a wire cookie rack to cool. When cool, promptly arrange them, single layer, in an airtight container. Just before serving, reheat the biscuits in a microwave oven, or wrap them in airtight aluminum foil and heat them in a preheated 350° F. oven.

MAKES 14

OLD-FASHIONED SERVING SUGGESTION: Set the table with a bread and butter plate at each diner's place. The diner splits a biscuit in half, places it open-faced on the bread and butter plate, then generously butters each half and pours hot maple syrup over top. This dish is eaten with a fork.

(When Baking Powder Biscuits were on my mother's family dinner menu, no matter how the biscuits were otherwise eaten with the meal, at least one biscuit always was savored this way by each of us.)

OLD-FASHIONED (BISCUIT-STYLE) SHORTCAKES

2 cups sifted all-purpose flour (sift before measuring)
1 tablespoon plus 1 teaspoon baking powder
1/2 teaspoon salt
1/4 cup sugar
1 extra-large egg, cold
1/2 cup whole milk, cold
1/4 cup plus 2 tablespoons refrigerated lard
Additional lard (about 1 teaspoon) for top of shortcakes

Preheat the oven to 450° F.

Onto waxed paper, sift together the flour, baking powder, salt, and sugar. Place the flour mixture in a medium mixing bowl; set aside. In a small mixing bowl, place the egg and milk; using an electric mixer, beat on medium speed until blended; set aside.

Using a table knife, quickly cut the measured lard into approximately nickel-sized (irregular) chunks and drop them onto the flour mixture. Using a pastry blender, cut the lard into the flour mixture until the mixture is the texture of coarse cornmeal. Using a table fork, make a well in the center of the flour mixture. Pour the egg mixture, all at once, into the well in the flour mixture. Using the fork, stir with 25 to 30 strokes, until the flour mixture is dampened and the dough stiffens.

Turn the dough onto a *lightly floured* pastry cloth (page 54) or wooden board. Knead (page 23) about 20 times until the dough is cohesive and manageable. Using a *lightly floured* rolling pin, roll the dough to 1/2-inch thickness. Using a floured, 2 1/2-inch biscuit cutter, cut the shortcakes with a straight up and down motion, dipping the cutter in flour between each cut. Wipe the cutter intermittently with a paper towel when the dough begins to cling to it. Place the cut shortcakes on an ungreased cookie sheet (preferably, an insulated cookie sheet). Gather the remaining dough and knead briefly; reroll and cut additional shortcakes. Repeat the procedure until all the dough is used. Using a knife, lay about 1/8 teaspoon of lard on top of each shortcake. Bake for 11 to 12 minutes, until the shortcakes are lightly brown.

When done, immediately remove the shortcakes from the cookie sheet and place them on a wire cookie rack; let stand until lukewarm or completely cool, depending upon how the shortcakes are to be served. If allowed to completely cool, promptly arrange the shortcakes, single layer, in an airtight container.

MAKES 8

OLD-FASHIONED STRAWBERRY SHORTCAKE

In the Midwest, three different types of cakes are used to make strawberry shortcake: Old-Fashioned (Biscuit-Style) Shortcake (page 447), Sponge-Style Shortcake (page 558), and Angel Food Cake (page 555). The recipe that follows is for strawberry shortcake made with biscuit-style shortcakes. (Old-Fashioned [Biscuit-Style] Shortcakes are accurately defined as biscuits rather than cakes.)

While there are many Old-Fashioned (Biscuit-Style) Shortcake advocates, Sponge-Style Shortcake or Angel Food Cake is generally preferred by most contemporary strawberry shortcake enthusiasts.

2 pints fresh strawberries
¼ cup sugar
1 recipe Old-Fashioned (Biscuit-Style) Shortcakes (page 447), lukewarm*
¼ cup (4 tablespoons) butter, melted (optional)
1 recipe Whipped Cream (page 373)

Shortcakes may be served completely cool, if preferred.

Wash and hull the strawberries (page 23). Reserve 8 whole strawberries for garnishing the tops of the shortcakes. Place ½ of the remaining berries in a flat-bottomed pan and crush them with a potato masher; place in a medium mixing bowl; set aside. Slice the remaining berries lengthwise ⅜ inch thick; add to the crushed berries. Add the sugar; stir to combine; set aside.

Using a sharp, thin-bladed knife, split the lukewarm shortcakes in half lengthwise. Lightly brush the melted butter over the cut side of the bottom halves of the shortcakes, and place them on individual serving plates. Spoon ½ of the strawberries equally over the bottom halves of the shortcakes. Place the top halves of the shortcakes over the berries. Spoon the remaining ½ of the berries eually over the tops of the shortcakes. Spoon a generous dollop of Whipped Cream over each shortcake and garnish with a whole strawberry.

SERVES 8

OLD-FASHIONED PEACH, RASPBERRY, OR BLUEBERRY SHORTCAKE: Follow the Old-Fashioned Strawberry Shortcake recipe, above, substituting peaches, raspberries, or blueberries for the strawberries. Prepare the fruit as follows:

PEACHES: Wash, blanch (page 44) 30 seconds; peel, halve, pit, and quarter. Slice the peach quarters ⅜ inch thick. Using a potato masher, crush ½ of the peach slices. Leave the remaining ½ of the slices intact.

RASPBERRIES OR BLUEBERRIES: Wash and drain. Using a potato masher, crush ½ of the berries. Leave the remaining ½ of the berries whole.

Dumplings

DUMPLINGS

2 cups sifted all-purpose flour (sift before measuring)
1 tablespoon plus 1 teaspoon baking powder
½ teaspoon salt
3 tablespoons refrigerated vegetable shortening
1 cup whole milk, cold

Onto waxed paper, sift together the flour, baking powder, and salt. Place the flour mixture in a medium mixing bowl. Using a table knife, quickly cut the measured shortening into approximately dime-sized (irregular) chunks and drop them onto the flour mixture. Using a pastry blender, cut the shortening into the flour mixture until the mixture is the texture of coarse cornmeal. Using a table fork, make a well in the center of the flour mixture. Pour the milk, all at once, into the well in the flour mixture. Using a small mixing spoon, stir and fold until combined.

Drop the batter by the tablespoonful onto the top of boiling broth or stew. Cover the kettle; reduce the heat slightly but keep the liquid bubbling. Cook 15 minutes. *Do not lift the cover while the Dumplings are cooking—not even to peek.*

Remove from the heat. Uncover the kettle. Using a small spatula, remove the Dumplings and place them, single layer, in a pan; cover to keep warm.

MAKES 10

HERB DUMPLINGS: Follow the Dumplings recipe, above, sprinkling 1 tablespoon finely snipped, fresh parsley and ¼ teaspoon dried leaf summer savory over the sifted flour mixture in the mixing bowl. Using a small mixing spoon, lightly combine the herbs with the flour mixture. Then, add the shortening and proceed to follow with the Dumplings recipe.

 THYME DUMPLINGS: Follow the Herb Dumplings recipe, above, substituting ¾ teaspoon finely snipped, fresh thyme for ¼ teaspoon dried summer savory.

Crackers

DELUXE CRACKERS

A breeze to prepare and nice to serve when entertaining.

Small, plain water crackers
Butter, softened

Preheat the broiler.

Spread the crackers very thinly with butter and place them in a shallow baking pan. Place under the broiler, about 6 inches from the heat. Leave the crackers under the broiler until the butter bubbles well (about 1 minute). Watch carefully.

Serve warm.

DELUXE SESAME SEED CRACKERS: Follow the Deluxe Cracker recipe, above, substituting small water crackers with sesame seeds for the small, plain water crackers.

SERVING SUGGESTIONS: Serve with soups, first-course appetizers, salads, and hors d'oeuvres.

ELEGANT CRACKERS

A step up from Deluxe Crackers (see preceding recipe), but more involved and time-consuming to prepare.

Ice cubes and water
1 dozen saltines
3 tablespoons butter, melted

Preheat the oven to 375° F.

Butter lightly the bottom of a 9 × 13-inch baking pan; set aside.

Place the ice cubes and water in a large mixing bowl to ⅔ full. Float the crackers, 4 at a time, in the ice water. Using a slotted spatula, push the crackers under the surface of the water to immerse them briefly; then, let the crackers float in the water for a *few seconds* until puffy but not falling apart. Using the spatula, carefully remove the crackers from the water and place them, single layer (do not overlap), in the prepared pan.

Using a soft brush, brush the top of the crackers with butter. Bake for 15 minutes.

Remove the crackers from the oven. Reduce the oven heat to 275° F. Brush the crackers with additional butter; bake for an additional 15 minutes, until a deep brown color. Using a spatula, place the crackers on waxed paper to cool. Store in an airtight container.

SERVING SUGGESTIONS: Serve with soups and salads.

RICE CRACKERS

1 cup all-purpose flour
¼ teaspoon salt
¼ teaspoon white pepper
½ cup (¼ pound) butter, softened
1½ cups very finely shredded, extra-sharp
   cheddar cheese
1 cup Rice Krispies cereal

Preheat the oven to 350° F. Grease lightly cookie sheets; set aside.

Onto waxed paper, sift together flour, salt, and white pepper; set aside.

In a medium mixing bowl, place the butter and cheese; using an electric mixer, beat on high speed until creamy. Add the flour mixture; continue beating on high speed until the mixture is of a creamy consistency. Add the Rice Krispies; using a spoon, stir to evenly combine.

Using a 1-inch trigger scoop or melon baller, scoop portions of the dough and roll 1-inch balls of dough in your hands; place them about 2½ inches apart on the prepared cookie sheets. With the heel of your hand, flatten the balls to 2-inch-diameter crackers. Bake for 12 minutes.

Using a thin spatula, carefully transfer the crackers to waxed paper; let stand until completely cool. Store in an airtight container in single layers separated by sheets of plastic wrap.

MAKES ABOUT 3½ DOZEN

SERVING SUGGESTION: Serve with thin soups.

CHEESE STRAWS

Look no further if you're searching for the ultimate gourmet cracker to serve with a thin soup as an introduction to a beautiful dinner. These Cheese Straws are rich, delicate, and in tune with polished dining.

1 cup sifted all-purpose flour (sift before
   measuring)
¼ teaspoon salt
½ cup (¼ pound) butter, softened
1 cup finely shredded, sharp cheddar cheese
3 tablespoons freshly grated Parmesan
   cheese (page 46)

Preheat the oven to 350° F.

Onto waxed paper, sift together the flour and salt; set aside.

Place the butter in a small mixing bowl; using an electric mixer, cream on high speed. Add the cheddar cheese; beat on high speed until well combined. Add the Parmesan cheese; continue beating on high speed until fluffy. Add the flour mixture; beat on medium speed until well blended.

Using a decorating bag fit with large (⅝ inch wide) basket-weave tip number 2B (page 383), pipe 2-inch-long, ribbed sticks onto ungreased cookie sheets. Bake for 10 to 12 minutes.

Using a thin spatula, place the Cheese Straws on waxed paper; let stand until completely cool. Store in an airtight container.

MAKES 6 DOZEN ¾-INCH-WIDE CHEESE STRAWS

ALTERNATIVE BAKING METHOD: Use a cookie press fit with a ribbon disc to press 2-inch-long, ribbed sticks onto the cookie sheets.

MAKES 3 DOZEN 1½-INCH-WIDE CHEESE STRAWS

SERVING SUGGESTION: Serve with soup appetizer courses.

Coffee Cake

CINNAMON COFFEE CAKE

Coffee cake is a choice selection for serving with break-fast, morning coffee, and brunch (provided the menu includes one or more explicitly breakfast main dishes). It is grand to serve when a morning meeting is held at your house.

1½ cups sifted all-purpose flour (sift before
    measuring)
2 teaspoons baking powder
½ cup sugar
½ teaspoon salt
3 tablespoons butter, softened
1 extra-large egg
½ cup whole milk
Cinnamon Topping (recipe follows)
2 tablespoons butter

Preheat the oven to 375° F. Using Special Grease (page 56) (see Note), grease an 8 × 8-inch baking pan; set aside.

Onto waxed paper, sift together the flour, baking powder, sugar, and salt. Place the flour mixture in a medium mixing bowl. Using a table knife, cut the 3 tablespoons softened butter into about 6 chunks and drop onto the flour mixture. Using a pastry blender, cut the butter into the flour mixture until the mixture is the texture of cornmeal. Using a table fork, make a well in the center of the flour mixture; set aside.

Place the egg in a small mixing bowl. Using an electric mixer, beat the egg slightly on medium speed. Add the milk; beat on medium speed only until blended. Pour the egg mixture, all at once, into the well in the flour mixture; using a small mixing spoon, stir and fold *only* until the flour disappears. The batter will be lumpy and sticky.

Spoon the batter into the prepared baking pan. Using a small, narrow spatula, quickly spread the batter evenly in the pan. Sprinkle the

Cinnamon Topping evenly over the batter; dot with 2 tablespoons butter. Bake for 20 minutes. Serve hot. Cut into 9 pieces.

NOTE: Although not as satisfactory, vegetable shortening may be substituted for Special Grease.

SERVES 9

VARIATION: Add ½ teaspoon pure vanilla extract to the small mixing bowl after adding ½ cup whole milk. Then, proceed to beat only until blended.

Cinnamon Topping

¼ cup sugar
1 teaspoon ground cinnamon

In a small mixing bowl, place the sugar and cinnamon; stir to combine.

APPLE COFFEE CAKE

1 recipe Cinnamon Coffee Cake, above
1½ cups pared, quartered, cored, and thinly
    sliced cooking apples, such as Golden
    Delicious (about 1 large apple)

Follow the Cinnamon Coffee Cake recipe through spreading the batter in the baking pan. Then, distribute the apples evenly over the batter. Sprinkle Cinnamon Topping evenly over the apples; dot with 2 tablespoons butter. Bake for 25 minutes at 375° F.

**CRUMB COFFEE CAKE
(STREUSEL KAFFEEKUCHEN)**

1 recipe Cinnamon Coffee Cake, above
Crumb Topping (recipe follows)

Follow the Cinnamon Coffee Cake recipe through mixing the batter. Spoon ½ of the batter into the prepared baking pan. Using a small, narrow spatula, spread the batter evenly in the pan. Sprinkle ½ of the Crumb Topping over the

(Recipe continues on next page)

batter. Spoon the remaining ½ batter over the Crumb Topping. Using the small spatula, spread the batter as evenly as possible over the topping. Sprinkle the remaining ½ Crumb Topping over the batter. (Eliminate the Cinnamon Topping and 2 tablespoons of butter for dotting the coffee cake called for in the Cinnamon Coffee Cake recipe.) Bake for 20 to 25 minutes at 375° F.

VARIATION: Place all the batter in the baking pan; halve the Crumb Topping recipe and sprinkle it evenly over the batter.

Crumb Topping

½ cup packed light brown sugar
2 tablespoons all-purpose flour
1 tablespoon ground cinnamon
½ cup chopped pecans
2 tablespoons butter, melted

In a small mixing bowl, place the brown sugar, flour, cinnamon, and pecans; stir to combine. Add the butter; stir until combined.

MARIE DALBEY'S SOUR CREAM COFFEE CAKE

A truly deluxe coffee cake baked in a springform pan.

¾ cup chopped pecans
¼ cup plus 2 tablespoons sugar
½ teaspoon ground cinnamon
2 cups sifted all-purpose flour (sift before measuring)
1 teaspoon baking powder
½ teaspoon salt
1 cup (½ pound) butter, softened
1½ cups sugar
2 extra-large eggs
8 ounces commercial sour cream
1¼ teaspoons pure vanilla extract

Preheat the oven to 350° F. Using Special Grease (page 56) (see Note), grease a 9 × 3-inch springform pan; set aside.

In a small bowl, place the pecans, ¼ cup plus 2 tablespoons sugar, and cinnamon; stir to combine; set aside. Onto waxed paper, sift together the flour, baking powder, and salt; set aside.

In a large mixing bowl, place the butter and 1½ cups sugar; using an electric mixer, cream on high speed. While continuing to beat on high speed, add the eggs, one at a time; beat until blended and fluffy. Add the sour cream and vanilla; beat until well blended. Add the flour mixture in halves, beating on low speed after each addition only until blended.

Spoon ½ of the batter into the prepared springform pan; spread with a small, narrow spatula, slightly mounding the batter toward the center of the pan. Sprinkle ½ of the pecan mixture evenly over the batter. Spoon the remaining ½ of the batter into the pan; spread, using the previous procedure. Sprinkle with the remaining ½ pecan mixture. Bake for 50 minutes, or until a wooden toothpick inserted into the center of the coffee cake comes out clean. *Caution:* Do not open the oven door until at least 45 minutes baking time has elapsed, as opening the oven door sooner may cause this delicate coffee cake to fall.

Remove the coffee cake from the oven and place on a wire rack; cool 10 minutes. Then, carefully run a sharp, thin-bladed knife around the inside edge of the pan; remove the sides of the pan. Leave the coffee cake on the bottom of the pan and serve warm.

NOTE: Although not as satisfactory, vegetable shortening may be substituted for Special Grease.

SERVES 12

Doughnuts

CAKE DOUGHNUTS

3½ cups all–purpose flour
2 teaspoons baking powder
1 teaspoon baking soda
½ teaspoon salt
¼ teaspoon ground cinnamon
¼ teaspoon ground nutmeg
2 extra-large eggs
1 cup sugar
2 tablespoons vegetable shortening, melted
 and cooled slightly
½ teaspoon pure vanilla extract
¾ cup buttermilk
About 4 pounds vegetable shortening for
 frying

Onto waxed paper, sift together the flour, baking powder, baking soda, salt, cinnamon, and nutmeg; set aside.

Place the eggs in a large mixing bowl. Using an electric mixer, beat the eggs well on medium speed. Add the sugar, 2 tablespoons melted vegetable shortening, and vanilla; beat well on high speed. Add the buttermilk; beat on high speed until blended. Add the flour mixture all at once; beat on low speed only until blended and smooth. Cover the bowl; refrigerate the dough at least 2 hours.

Turn the dough onto a lightly floured pastry cloth (page 54). Using a stockinet-covered, then lightly floured rolling pin (page 54), roll the dough to ⅜-inch thickness. Using a 2¾-inch, floured doughnut cutter, cut out the doughnuts and place them on lightly floured cookie sheets. Dip the cutter in flour before cutting each doughnut. Intermittently, remove the excess dough which accumulates around the cutting edge of the doughnut cutter. Gather the remaining dough into a ball; roll out again and cut. Repeat until all the dough is used. Handle the dough as little as possible.

In a deep-fat fryer or deep electric skillet, heat about 4 pounds vegetable shortening to 370° F. The melted shortening should be at least 1¼ inches deep. Do not commence to fry the doughnuts until the 370° F. temperature has been reached.

Using a spatula, lift the doughnuts from the cookie sheets and place them in the hot shortening. Fry the doughnuts about 1½ minutes on each side, turning once by slipping a cooking fork under the doughnuts, one at a time, and turning them over. Fry no more than 6 doughnuts at a time in order to control the frying time and keep the temperature of the shortening as stable as possible.

When done, place the fork under the doughnuts, one at a time, and remove them from the shortening. Place the doughnuts on wire racks covered with paper towels to drain. To sugar, or frost and garnish the doughnuts, see the recipes, below.

MAKES ABOUT 2 DOZEN

CINNAMON-SUGAR DOUGHNUTS

½ cup granulated sugar
1 teaspoon ground cinnamon
1 recipe Cake Doughnuts, above

In a small bowl, place the sugar and cinnamon; stir until evenly combined. Place the cinnamon mixture in a zipper-seal plastic bag. Place the *warm* doughnuts, one at a time, in the bag; seal and shake carefully until evenly coated. Place the coated doughnuts on wire racks; let stand until completely cool.

POWDERED SUGAR DOUGHNUTS

½ cup powdered sugar
1 recipe Cake Doughnuts, above

Place the powdered sugar in a zipper-seal plastic bag. Place *cool* doughnuts, one at a time, in the bag; seal and shake carefully until fully coated.

(Recipe continues on next page)

VANILLA-FROSTED DOUGHNUTS

1 recipe Ornamental Vanilla Frosting
    (page 584)
1 recipe Cake Doughnuts, above

Using a small, narrow, tapered spatula, frost the tops of *cool* doughnuts and place them on wire racks until the frosting cools. Frosts 1 dozen doughnuts only.

Immediately after frosting the doughnuts, before the frosting dries, one of the following may be sprinkled on the frosting:

Flaked coconut
Chopped pecans, almonds, or hazelnuts
    (page 50)
Nonpareils (page 24)

When the frosting cools and dries, store the doughnuts in an airtight container.

CHOCOLATE-FROSTED DOUGHNUTS

1 recipe Ornamental Chocolate Frosting
    (page 584)
1 recipe Cake Doughnuts, above

Follow the Vanilla–Frosted Doughnuts recipe, above, for frosting procedures, garnishing suggestions, and storage instructions.

Popovers

POPOVERS

3 extra-large eggs
1⅓ cups whole milk
¼ teaspoon salt
1 tablespoon butter, melted
1⅓ cups all-purpose flour

Butter 6 popover-pan cups (see Note); set aside.

Place the eggs in a medium mixing bowl. Using an electric mixer, beat the eggs slightly on medium speed. Add the milk, salt, and butter; beat on medium speed until blended. Add the flour; beat on low speed only until blended. Avoid overbeating.

Using 2 tablespoons (1 to transport the batter and 1 to push the batter from the filled tablespoon), fill the prepared popover-pan cups half full of batter. Place in a *cold* oven. Turn on the oven to 450° F. and bake the popovers 15 minutes. Reduce the oven heat to 350° F. and bake the popovers an additional 15 to 20 minutes. When done, the Popovers will be crisp on the outside and moist on the inside. Serve hot.

NOTE: I prefer the type of popover pan with cups measuring about 2½ inches wide and 2½ inches deep which are separated by wires. If a popover pan is not available, custard cups may be substituted.

MAKES 6

SERVING SUGGESTION: Traditionally served with Rib Roast (Standing or Rolled) (page 167).

Pancakes and Waffles

PANCAKES GEORGE

From the golden recipe book of George Dinsdale, Omaha, Nebraska, who was a culinarian par excellence.

1¼ cups sifted all-purpose flour (sift before measuring)
1½ teaspoons baking powder
½ teaspoon baking soda
½ teaspoon salt
1 tablespoon sugar
1 extra-large egg
1 tablespoon plus 2 teaspoons vegetable oil
1½ cups buttermilk
1 teaspoon butter
Butter
Pure maple syrup, hot

Onto waxed paper, sift together the flour, baking powder, baking soda, salt, and sugar. Place the flour mixture in a medium mixing bowl. Using a tablespoon, make a well in the center of the flour mixture; set aside.

Immediately prior to baking the pancakes, place the egg in a small mixing bowl. Using an electric mixer, beat the egg slightly on medium speed. Add the vegetable oil and buttermilk; beat on medium speed only until blended. Pour the egg mixture, all at once, into the well in the flour mixture; using a small mixing spoon, stir and fold *only* until the flour disappears. The batter will be lumpy.

Preheat an electric skillet, a griddle, or a large, heavy-bottomed skillet on the range to medium-high (375° F. in an electric skillet).

Place 1 teaspoon butter in the skillet; using a spatula, spread the melted butter over the entire bottom of the skillet. Using a large mixing spoon, spoon the batter onto the sizzling skillet, cooking two or three 5-inch pancakes at a time. Using the spatula, turn pancakes *once* when bubbles form and break on the top of the batter, and the underside of the pancakes is browned (cook about 1½ minutes on each side). Serve immediately.

Do not add additional butter to the skillet as you cook the rest of the pancakes even though the skillet appears to be ungreased—it is not necessary. In fact, pancakes cooked subsequent to the first batch on the skillet are considered by most pancake devotees to be superior to the first batch cooked in the freshly added butter.

Pass generous portions of butter and hot, pure maple syrup at the table for diners to place on top of their pancakes.

The recipe may be doubled.

MAKES ABOUT NINE 5-INCH PANCAKES

NOTE
- Pancake batter should be made immediately prior to cooking the pancakes. The quality of the batter deteriorates if it stands too long or is stored in the refrigerator.

- To enjoy pancakes at their best, they should be eaten immediately as they come off the skillet; therefore, it is preferable that pancakes be cooked after the diners are seated at the table. Necessarily, this means that the cook eats last.

BLUEBERRY PANCAKES: Wash fresh blueberries; spread on paper towels to dry. Follow the Pancakes George recipe, above, sprinkling blueberries on the pancakes immediately after the batter is spooned onto the skillet. Then, resume following the cooking and serving procedures in the Pancakes George recipe (see Note, below).

STRAWBERRY PANCAKES: Wash and hull fresh strawberries (page 23); dry between paper towels. Quarter or slice the berries, depending upon size. Follow the Pancakes George recipe, above, sprinkling strawberries on the pancakes immediately after the batter is spooned onto the skillet. Then, resume following the cooking and serving procedures in the Pancakes George recipe (see Note, below).

(Recipe continues on next page)

PINEAPPLE PANCAKES: Drain commercially canned, unsweetened pineapple slices in a colander; reserve the juice for other uses. Dry the slices between paper towels. Follow the Pancakes George recipe, above, placing 1 pineapple slice in the center of each pancake immediately after the batter is spooned onto the skillet. Then, resume following the cooking and serving procedures in the Pancakes George recipe (see Note, below).

NOTE: When baking pancakes with added fruit, add about 1 teaspoon additional butter to the skillet to prevent the fruit from sticking. The addition of fruit generally necessitates a slight increase in the cooking time for pancakes.

WAFFLES

2 cups all-purpose flour
1 tablespoon baking powder
½ teaspoon salt
1 tablespoon plus 1 teaspoon sugar
3 extra-large eggs, room temperature
1⅔ cups whole milk
¼ cup plus 2 tablespoons butter, melted
  and cooled slightly
Butter
Pure maple syrup, hot

Onto waxed paper, sift together the flour, baking powder, salt, and sugar. Place the flour mixture in a large mixing bowl. Using a tablespoon, make a well in the center of the flour mixture; set aside.

Separate the eggs, placing the whites in a medium-small mixing bowl and the yolks in a small mixing bowl; set the egg whites aside. Using an electric mixer, beat the egg yolks slightly on medium speed. Add the milk and butter; beat on medium speed only until blended; set aside. Using the electric mixer fit with clean, dry beater blades, beat the egg whites on high speed until stiff but still moist and glossy; set aside.

Pour the milk mixture, all at once, into the well in the flour mixture; using a large mixing spoon, stir and fold *only* until the flour disappears. The batter will be lumpy. Add the egg whites; using the mixing spoon, fold in quickly, leaving marble-sized clumps of egg whites in the batter.

Cook the waffles in an electric waffle iron, following the instructions from the manufacturer. Waffles should be cooked until they stop steaming—about 3 minutes. Set the table with plenty of butter and hot, pure maple syrup.

MAKES 7 AVERAGE-SIZED WAFFLES

NOTE: While waffles are best when served directly off the waffle iron, cooked waffles may be placed, single layer, on wire racks resting on cookie sheets or cookie pans, and kept warm for a short period of time in a 275° F. oven. If a portion or all of the waffles are to be served directly off the waffle iron, they are served at informal meals when the cook stations himself/herself at the waffle iron and eats last. The usual courtesy of waiting until everyone is served before diners commence eating is best dispensed with at most waffle meals.

SERVING SUGGESTIONS: Waffles may be served for breakfast, brunch, or casual dinners. Serve them with Canadian bacon, ham, sausage, regular bacon, or Bedeviled Bacon (page 191). Additionally, Fried Eggs (page 266) or poached eggs are an excellent accompaniment.

TO FREEZE WAFFLES: Place cooked waffles on wire racks; let stand until cool. Stack up to 3 waffles on a large piece of freezer paper, placing smaller pieces of freezer paper between the waffles. Wrap the stack of waffles airtightly in the freezer paper and seal with freezer tape. Place the package of waffles in a zipper-seal plastic freezer bag; store in the freezer.

To heat for serving, break off quarters or halves of frozen waffles and heat in a conventional toaster. Or, heat frozen, whole waffles, or frozen quarters or halves of waffles, in a microwave oven.

WHOLE-WHEAT WAFFLES: Follow the Waffles recipe, above, substituting 1 cup whole-wheat flour and 1 cup all-purpose flour for 2 cups all-purpose flour.

Fritters

CORN FRITTERS

1 cup all-purpose flour
1 teaspoon baking powder
¾ teaspoon salt
1 tablespoon plus 1 teaspoon sugar
2 extra-large eggs
¼ cup whole milk
2 tablespoons butter, melted
1½ cups drained whole-kernel corn, home canned (page 731) or commercially canned
2 tablespoons vegetable oil
1 teaspoon butter

Onto waxed paper, sift together the flour, baking powder, salt, and sugar. Place the flour mixture in a medium mixing bowl. Using a tablespoon, make a well in the center of the flour mixture; set aside.

Place the eggs in a small mixing bowl. Using an electric mixer, beat the eggs well on medium speed. Add the milk and butter; beat on medium speed until blended; set aside. Add the corn; stir in.

Preheat an electric skillet or a large, heavy-bottomed skillet on the range to medium-high (380° F. in an electric skillet).

Pour the egg mixture, all at once, into the well in the flour mixture; using a small mixing spoon, fold in only until the mixture is blended and the corn is evenly combined; set aside. Place the vegetable oil in the skillet. Tilt the skillet back and forth to completely cover the bottom with the oil. Add 1 teaspoon butter; spread to blend with the oil. When the grease sizzles, drop heaping tablespoonsful of batter onto the skillet. Fry the fritters about 5 minutes, turning once.

MAKES 10

SERVING SUGGESTIONS
- Serve Corn Fritters with butter and hot, pure maple syrup as a main course, accompanied by bacon, ham, or sausage.

- Make small, dollar-sized Corn Fritters and serve themm without butter and syrup, as an accompaniment to ham, pork, and lamb dishes.

APPLE FRITTERS: Follow the Corn Fritters recipe, above, substituting 1½ cups pared, quartered, cored, and coarsely diced (page 22) Golden Delicious or other cooking apples for the corn. Using a small hand strainer, sprinkle powdered sugar over the fried fritters. Serve with or without butter and hot, pure maple syrup.

Pies and Tarts

They say that absence makes the heart grow fonder. But the cravings of former Midwesterners for homemade Heartland pie are matched by the ongoing love affair Midwest inhabitants have with these choice treats.

When you venture too far away, searches for a slice of pie like the kind you savored in the Midwest often end in disappointment. It's hard to duplicate that flaky crust, so tender it breaks when your fork barely touches it. And how can you equal those fillings of apples just picked in the orchard by the farmhouse, or that special chocolate cream with mounds of pouffy, golden meringue?

It is not nostalgia playing tricks. One of the Midwest's greatest contributions to the culinary world is its pies. Not to say that there aren't pockets of superb pie bakers in other places, but masterful pie baking in the central states is uniquely widespread. No matter where you may find yourself in these twelve states, a piece of unforgettable pie is not far away.

Many business people who travel the Midwest organize their itineraries around lunchtime pie feasts in small towns—the places pie people most often sleuth. Small cafés on town squares where gifted pie ladies arrive early every morning (except Sunday) to turn out pecan, sour cream raisin, lemon meringue, butterscotch, and a host of other popular winners are the all-time favorite hot spots for pie gourmands.

There for lunch, the consumption of a hot roast beef sandwich or some other time-honored, rural main-fare dish—no matter how delicious—is a mere formality, and quickly dispensed with to get to the main event: pie. Maybe even two pieces if you're by yourself and no one will ever know.

World-class crust is the first thing that sets Midwest pies apart from most others. Usually made with lard, it is mixed with the expertise of a rocket scientist. And the heavenly fillings are virtually peerless. No canned pie fillings or packaged pudding mixes in those hallowed kitchens next to the lunch counter! Just country-fresh eggs and milk, big canisters full of flour and sugar, and juicy, fresh peaches ready for blanching, peeling, and slicing.

While Midwest farmwives have long enjoyed accolades for their breads, cakes, and cookies, pies are their pièce de résistance. In earlier days, the baking of pies on Saturday for Sunday noon dinner following church was a weekly event. This ritual carried over to subsequent generations, even when descendants became city dwellers. My mother-in-law, who was Holland Dutch and grew up on a farm near Sully, Iowa, always baked a pie—usually cherry—for the main Sunday meal. When I was married, my husband expected the same offering each Sunday, which is how I gained early experience with pastry.

Holiday meals in the Midwest traditionally include pie. At Thanksgiving, it is pumpkin. At Christmas, pumpkin and mincemeat. In our family, pie shares the holiday meal spotlight with turkey. In fact, we have always scheduled our holiday meals no earlier than 5:00 P.M. so the pies can be made and cooled that very day—no day-old pie for this clan.

There is always plenty of preholiday discussion (if not friendly arguing) over what kind(s) of pie will be served other than pumpkin. (The latter is not even up for discussion.) Since the family pie-baking baton has been passed from my mother to me, I dutifully execute the majority-vote outcome. At this writing (December 6), two pumpkins and one cherry have just been devoured at Thanksgiving. My nephew complains that he was denied banana cream for Thanksgiving by a close vote, and demands this be included on December 25. My brother wants another cherry pie made with the cherries picked from the tree in his yard last summer and frozen specifically for the occasion. As of now, it's one pumpkin, one banana cream, and one

cherry, with the decision to forgo mincemeat this year.

Do you get the drift? Pie is a centerpiece in Midwest fare. Good pie bakers are clearly placed on a "pastry pedestal" by family and friends. I wouldn't go so far as to say that people would marry for it, but serving up a piece of your heartthrob's favorite pie at the end of a candlelight dinner doesn't hurt. Good pie definitely has an avenue to every Midwesterner's heart.

To Cut and Serve Pies and Tarts

If a pie has been baked with an attractive lattice top, or has been otherwise decorated in a particularly appealing way, it is inviting to show the pie at the table before returning to the kitchen to cut it. Diners eat with their eyes as well as their palates. A tart may be displayed by removing the rim of the pan and placing the tart on a raised stand. (Leave the tart on the pan bottom.)

Use a medium to small, sharp, thin-bladed knife to cut pies and tarts. Wipe both sides of the blade on a damp sponge before each cut. When cutting, take care to cut completely through the crust—on the bottom and side of the pan as well as the fluted edge—so the slices will be neat and unfrayed when removed from the pan.

Cut meringue-topped pies with a wet blade to prevent the meringue from sticking to the knife. Dip the knife blade into a glass of tepid water, shake off the excess water (safely away from the pie), make a cut, wipe the blade on a damp sponge and repeat.

To cut ice cream pies, dip the knife blade into a glass of very hot water. Wipe the blade on a damp sponge to remove excess water; then, make one cut in the pie. Dip the blade into the hot water and wipe it on the sponge before making each cut. For very neat, even pieces of pie, go over the cuts a second time.

Use a wedge-shaped pie spatula to remove cut

pie slices from the pie pan and tart slices from the tart pan bottom. Place slices on individual serving plates.

Standard pies in 8- or 9-inch pie pans cut into 7 servings. Standard pies in 10-inch pie pans cut into 8 servings. Cheese pies in 9-inch pie pans cut into 9 servings. Ice cream pies in 9-inch pie pans cut into 10 servings. Tarts in 9-inch tart pans cut into 9 servings.

Pastry

PASTRY PIECRUST

Best Pastry Piecrust, 1988 Iowa State Fair.

MAKES ENOUGH PASTRY PIECRUST FOR:

- Two 8- or 9-inch pie shells

- One 8- or 9-inch two-crust pie

- One 8- or 9-inch lattice-top pie

2½ cups sifted all-purpose flour (sift before measuring)
1 teaspoon salt
¾ cup refrigerated lard
⅓ cup refrigerated water

Onto waxed paper, sift together the flour and salt. Place the flour mixture in a large mixing bowl. Using a pastry blender, cut ⅔ of the lard into the flour mixture until the mixture is the texture of cornmeal. Cut in the remaining ⅓ of the lard until the size of peas. Move the mixture to one side of the bowl. Sprinkle 2 or 3 teaspoons of the water over the mixture. Using the back of a table fork, lightly rake the moistened portion of the mixture to the other side of the

bowl. Repeat the procedure until all the water has been added. Mix and handle the pastry as little as possible. With floured hands, form the pastry into 2 balls (don't worry if the pastry doesn't hold together well) and wrap each pastry ball fairly tightly in plastic wrap.

In your hands, quickly press 1 wrapped ball of pastry somewhat firmly to form a more solid ball. Then, leaving the pastry ball wrapped, use your hands to flatten the pastry ball into a round, pattylike shape about 3½ to 4 inches in diameter. Next, smooth the edges of the wrapped pastry as much as you can, under the constraints of quick, *minimal* handling, to help lessen splitting of the edge of the pastry when it is rolled. Immediately refrigerate the shaped, wrapped portion of the pastry. Repeat the procedure with the second ball of pastry. These procedures should all be done as fast as possible to minimize the handling of the pastry.

After about 30 minutes of refrigeration, remove one of the portions of pastry from the refrigerator (see Note). Unwrap the pastry and place it on a lightly floured pastry cloth (page 54). Let the pastry stand 1 minute or so, just until it is soft enough to roll.

Using a stockinet-covered, then lightly floured rolling pin (page 54), roll the pastry on the pastry cloth, rolling from the center to the edge, until the pastry is 1½ inches greater in diameter than the inverted pie pan to be used. Carefully run a thin spatula around and under the edge of the pastry to loosen it from the pastry cloth. Fold the pastry in half. Move the folded pastry to the ungreased pie pan, situating the fold across the center of the pan. Unfold the pastry and fit it into the pan. Do not stretch the pastry. If it is necessary to patch the pastry, place a scrap of rolled pastry over the place to be patched and lightly press the edges to seal. Then, using your finger, lightly moisten the seam with cold water.

Continue the recipe, below, according to the type of pie to be baked.

NOTE: There are two purposes for brief refrigeration of the pastry: (1) to recool the lard, and (2) to allow a little time for the moisture in the pastry to be assimilated by the flour more evenly, thereby making the pastry easier to roll and handle.

BAKED PIE SHELL: Preheat the oven to 425°F.

Using kitchen scissors, trim the edge of the pastry to 1 inch beyond the edge of the pan. Roll the edge of the pastry *under,* evenly along the top of the pan rim. Roll small sections of pastry at a time. After rolling a section, press the pastry together to form a uniform, continuous edge in the shape of a triangular peak over and around the pie pan rim. Then, flute the edge by flouring the end of a table knife handle and pressing it into the outside of the triangular pastry edge and against the thumb and index finger of your other hand on the inside of the triangular pastry edge to form a V. Repeat, making contiguous V's around the pan.

Using a table fork, prick the pastry every 1 inch around the side of the pan and every 1½ to 1¾ inches on the bottom of the pan. Bake for 10 to 12 minutes. If any bubbles form in the pastry after a few minutes of baking, prick them with a fork. Cool on a wire rack.

MAKES ENOUGH PASTRY FOR TWO 8- OR 9-INCH PIE SHELLS

NOTE: If only one pie shell is needed, the recipe may be halved; or, prepare the second pie shell for baking, then cover it with plastic wrap and freeze it. Remove the pie shell from the freezer 5 minutes before baking.

UNBAKED PIE SHELL: Follow the Baked Pie Shell procedure, above, omitting the pricking of the pastry and the baking.

TWO-CRUST PIE: Using kitchen scissors, trim the unbaked bottom-crust pastry evenly with the edge of the pan. Lay a piece of plastic wrap over the pastry-lined pan to prevent the pastry from drying; set aside. Remove the second portion of pastry from the refrigerator. Unwrap the pastry and place it on the lightly floured pastry cloth. Let the pastry stand 1 minute or so, just until soft enough to roll. Using the stockinet-covered, then lightly floured rolling pin, roll the top-crust pastry on the pastry cloth to about 1½ inches greater in diameter than an inverted pie pan of the same size as the one being used for the pie. Let the rolled pastry stand on the pastry cloth; cover it lightly with a piece of plastic wrap.

Remove the plastic wrap covering the pie pan and fill the pie, following a specific pie recipe. Remove the plastic wrap from the rolled top-crust pastry. Carefully run a thin spatula around and under the edge of the pastry to loosen it from the pastry cloth. Fold the pastry in half. Using a small, sharp knife, make several slits through both halves of the pastry near the folded edge to allow steam to escape during baking. Slits may be made evenly or in a decorative design.

Move the top-crust pastry to the filled pie and unfold. Using kitchen scissors, trim the top-crust pastry to ½ inch beyond the edge of the pan. Fold the edge of the top-crust pastry *under* the edge of the bottom-crust pastry along the top of the rim, and press the pastry together to form a uniform, continuous edge in the shape of a triangular peak over and around the pie pan rim. Flute the edge (follow the Baked Pie Shell procedures, left column). Bake according to a specific pie recipe.

MAKES ENOUGH PASTRY FOR ONE 8- OR 9-INCH TWO-CRUST PIE

LATTICE-TOP PIE: Using kitchen scissors, trim the unbaked bottom-crust pastry to ½ inch beyond the edge of the pan. Lay a piece of plastic wrap over the pastry-lined pan to prevent the pastry from drying; set aside. Remove the second portion of pastry from the refrigerator. Unwrap the pastry and place it on the lightly floured pastry cloth. Let the pastry stand 1 minute or so, just until soft enough to roll. Using the stockinet-covered, then lightly floured rolling pin, roll the top-crust pastry on the pastry cloth to about 1½ inches greater in diameter than an inverted pie pan of the same size as the one being used for the pie. Using a sharp, thin-bladed, floured knife, cut 14 strips of pastry ⅝ inch wide. Wipe the knife with a paper towel and reflour before each cut. Let the cut pastry stand on the pastry cloth; cover lightly with a piece of plastic wrap.

Remove the plastic wrap covering the pie pan and fill the pie, following a specific pie recipe. Remove the plastic wrap covering the pastry strips. Place the 2 longest pastry strips crosswise across the center of the pie. Arrange 3 strips on each side of, and parallel to, the lower center strip, carefully folding back the intersecting center strip before adding every other new strip to create a weave. Then, arrange 3 strips on each side of, and parallel to, the other center strip, folding back every other intersecting strip to form a weave (see illustration).

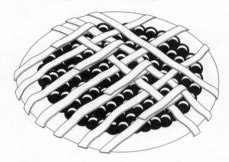

Using kitchen scissors, trim the lattice strips to ½ inch beyond the edge of the pan. Roll the bottom-crust pastry *over* the lattice strips along the top of the rim, and press the pastry together to form a uniform, continuous edge in the shape of a triangular peak over and around the pie pan rim. Flute the edge (follow the Baked Pie Shell procedures, page 461). Bake according to a specific pie recipe.

MAKES ENOUGH PASTRY FOR ONE 8- OR 9-INCH LATTICE-TOP PIE

1½ RECIPES OF PASTRY PIECRUST

3¼ cups plus 2 tablespoons sifted
  all-purpose flour (sift before measuring)
1½ teaspoons salt
1 cup plus 2 tablespoons refrigerated lard
½ cup refrigerated water

Follow the Pastry Piecrust recipe procedures.

MAKES ENOUGH PASTRY FOR ONE 8- OR 9-INCH TWO-CRUST PIE PLUS ONE 8- OR 9-INCH BAKED PIE SHELL

NOTE: For a wonderful snack, form a ball out of any leftover pastry; roll and place it on a cookie sheet or on the bottom of a pie pan. Using a table fork, prick the pastry every 1½ to 1¾ inches. Sprinkle the pastry with combined ground cinnamon and sugar (¼ teaspoon ground cinnamon per 1 teaspoon sugar). To bake, follow the Baked Pie Shell procedures, above. Cool on a wire rack and break off pieces as eaten.

PASTRY PIECRUST TART SHELLS

Pastry Piecrust may be used to make tart shells of various sizes. These pastry shells are used to make tarts which are just small, standard pies. See page 510 for an explanation of the difference between pastry piecrust tarts and classical tarts. A recipe for Classical Tart Pastry may be found on page 468.

1 recipe Pastry Piecrust (page 460; see
  recipe procedures, below)

Bake the tart shells in small aluminum tart pans measuring about 3 to 4½ inches in diameter, with *slanted* sides (like miniature pie pans). Aluminum-foil pans are not satisfactory.

Preheat the oven to 425°F.

Follow the Pastry Piecrust recipe through rolling the first portion of pastry as for a standard-sized pie. Invert a tart pan on, and near the edge of, the rolled pastry. Using a sharp, flour-dipped knife, cut a circle of pastry greater in diameter than the inverted pan, allowing sufficient pastry to fit into the pan and flute an edge proportionate in size to the small tart pan. Follow the Pastry Piecrust procedures for transferring and fitting the cutout pastry into the ungreased tart pan. Follow the Baked Pie Shell procedures (page 461) for forming and fluting the edge, and for pricking the pastry. The size of the V's in the fluting should be smaller, and the space between pricks in the pastry should be less than for a standard pie, and should be gauged in proportion to the size of the tart pan.

Cut and fit into the tart pans as many pastry circles as possible from the rolled pastry. Then, quickly gather the pastry scraps and lightly press them into a ball; reroll and cut additional circles. Roll the second portion of pastry and repeat the procedure. Unavoidably, the pastry rolled more than once will not be as flaky and tender as the pastry rolled only one time.

Bake the tart shells for approximately 10 minutes, depending upon the size of the pans. Watch carefully. If any bubbles form in the pastry after a few minutes of baking, prick them with a fork. The tart shells will be lightly brown when done. Cool on wire racks.

Baked Pastry Piecrust Tart Shells may be removed from the pans before or after filling. If the filling is heavy, it is safer to leave the shells in the pans until filled to avoid the risk of breaking the fragile crust even though filled tart shells are more difficult to remove from the pans. If the planned filling is light, the shells may be carefully removed from the pans after cooling and before filling.

SECRETS FOR MAKING SUCCESSFUL PASTRY PIECRUST

Many cooks consider good pastry piecrust to be one of the most difficult of all culinary undertakings. When piecrust ingredients are mixed to the optimum consistency for the production of first-class crust, the dough does not hold together well, making it difficult to gather and roll. In addition, humidity, room temperature, temperature of ingredients, and other factors affect the flour and fat, causing piecrust dough to be somewhat different each time you make it.

Nevertheless, these hurdles in no way should frighten away those who wish to master the challenge. As with most things, piecrust expertise takes study, patience, and practice, practice, practice. The satisfaction derived when family and friends rave about the incredibly luscious slice of pie you have placed in front of them, will more than offset the effort.

Many users of this cookbook are already accomplished piecrust bakers. For those readers desirous of joining the ranks, it is suggested that the recipe for Pastry Piecrust (page 460) be studied and followed carefully. The following additional hints and explanations should be of further assistance.

- The best pastry piecrust is made with lard. Fat acts to shorten the strands of gluten (the derivation of the term "shortening") in piecrust dough, thereby making the crust more tender. Lard is composed of relatively short-chain fatty acids which cover the gluten better than the longer-chain fatty acids found in hydrogenated vegetable shortening. By covering more area of gluten, short-chain fatty acids provide more tenderness.

  In addition, lard adds the piquant flavor often associated with choice, homemade piecrust—a flavor which cannot be duplicated with other types of fat.

  Commercial lard is readily available in most supermarkets. (If a baker does not wish to use lard, vegetable shortening may be substituted.)

- Use *cold* lard and water. Keep both refrigerated, even after measuring, until added to the piecrust mixture. Piecrust is made flaky, in part, by bits and pieces of lard melting during baking which create air spaces throughout the baked pastry. Warm lard will blend with the flour and not retain its particle integrity. Warm water will cause the lard to soften when added to the pastry mixture.

- From beginning to end, handle piecrust pastry *as little as possible*. In every step of the pastry-making procedure, this is one of the keys to retaining the distinct pieces of lard in the pastry and to preventing the lard from melting.

- Measure piecrust ingredients precisely. The ratio of ingredients is critical. Occasionally, a very slight variation in the amount of water called for in the recipe may be warranted. In a dry climate, and when the flour has low moisture content, it may be necessary to increase the water by 1 or 2 teaspoons in order to hold the dough together and roll it out without undue cracking. In addition, sometimes bits of unmoistened dough gravitate to the bottom of the bowl during mixing and remain there after the dough is gathered into balls, in which case a tiny amount of additional water may be sprinkled over the dry particles in the bottom of the bowl. Using a fork, stir the mixture briefly; then, gather it and add it to the remainder of the dough.

In humid weather, slightly less water may be necessary than called for in the recipe. In any case, use only enough water to make workable dough. Too much water will cause the crust to be tough.

- Cut the measured lard into chunks about the diameter of a quarter before adding to the flour mixture. This will speed the cutting-in process and help achieve even distribution of the lard in the pastry.

- To cut the lard into the flour, use a pastry blender with thin, round wires (see illustration). This simple tool allows the greatest control of the cutting-in process.

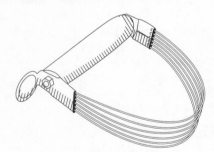

Pastry Blender

Hold the pastry blender firmly and use rapid, circular reverse folding-in motions. In other words, press the pastry blender against the front bottom of the mixing bowl to cut the lard, then push the blender away from you, about ⅔ of the way across the bottom of the bowl, and bring it up over the mixture and back toward you in a circular motion.

Simultaneously, turn the mixing bowl with your free hand. Quickly cutting in the lard, using rapid motions, will keep the pastry light and airy.

Small chunks of lard will usually adhere to the wires of the pastry blender at the beginning of the cutting-in process. Use a table knife to release lard stuck in the wires, and drop it back into the pastry mixture.

- It is critical to first cut in ⅔ of the lard until the mixture is the texture of cornmeal, and then to cut in the remaining ⅓ of the lard until the size of peas. The cornmeal texture is necessary for cohesion of the dough; the pea-sized pieces are necessary for flakiness. Follow closely the procedure for mixing the pastry ingredients described in the recipe for Pastry Piecrust (page 460).

- Piecrust dough of the best consistency tends to fall apart somewhat as it is gathered and formed into a ball and after the dough is placed on the pastry cloth. Cooks new to piecrust making will think the dough is too dry. However, when you commence to roll the dough, it will cohere and roll out smoothly. If the dough cracks throughout and does not hold together when rolled, it is, in fact, not moist enough. Experience is the best teacher in judging how much water to add when mixing the dough, though this is one of the biggest challenges even for expert piecrust bakers. Because of the necessity for handling the dough as little as possible, a significant measure of flakiness will be sacrificed if rolled-out dough is gathered, remixed, and rerolled.

- Roll the dough on a lightly floured pastry cloth, using a stockinet-covered, then lightly floured rolling pin (see To Use a Pastry Cloth and a Stockinet-Covered Rolling Pin, page 54).

- Roll out the dough with as few strokes as possible. Start by lightly rolling the dough to further flatten it. If needed, smooth the edges again with your hands, but only to the extent that you can do so speedily and with minimal touching of the pastry. Then, roll from the center of the dough to the edge. Let up on the pressure slightly as you reach the edge. This will help prevent the edge both from splitting and becoming too thin; however, it is virtually impossible to eliminate all edge splitting.

When a split occurs in the edge of the pastry during the rolling process, stop rolling and cut a small piece of pastry from any protruding edge of the circle of pastry. Place the cutaway piece of pastry over the split, like a patch. Carefully roll over the patch once or twice, rolling parallel with the pastry edge nearest the patch rather than rolling outward from the center. This is usually sufficient to bind the patch to the pastry without the use of water as a sealer. Final rolling of the entire pastry circle will often totally blend the patch with the remainder of the pastry, making the patched section indistinguishable.

(To illustrate the edge-splitting problem, some seasoned entrants in state fair pie competitions make 1½ recipes of dough when preparing a pie for entry. The extra dough allows the entrant to roll out a larger circle of pastry than required and cut off a significant amount of edge, thus averting the possible need to patch the edge which might be noticed by a perceptive judge.)

• Use dull, metal pie pans, such as those made of anodized aluminum. Shiny pie pans reflect heat, making it more difficult to produce properly browned, nonsoggy, bottom crusts. On the other hand, very dark pie pans should be avoided because they contribute to over-browning. Do not use nonstick, slick-coated pie pans. Glass pie plates are acceptable to use because they absorb and distribute heat evenly; however, I prefer to use metal pie pans.

• After unfolding the pastry in the pie pan, fit it gently against the bottom and sides of the pan. Avoid stretching the pastry, which will cause it to shrink when baked. To prevent stretching, after unfolding, use one hand to lift the edge of the pastry which overhangs the pan (relieving the tautness), while fitting the pastry into the pan with the other hand. When fitting, do not press the pastry against the pan, but gently ease it into place, trying to make sure that it touches the bottom and side of the pan, and that no air pockets are trapped between the pastry and the pan. These procedures will help prevent pie shells from blistering during baking and help keep the pastry lining the side of the pie pan from slipping down during baking.

Properly pricking the bottom and sides of pie shells with a fork before baking is also an important factor in holding the pastry in place. Pricking helps prevent pockets of steam from forming between the crust and the pie pan.

Some recipes advocate the use of weights, such as beans, to hold pie shell pastry in place during baking. This procedure is counterproductive to attaining the flaky crust the baker is so laboriously trying to achieve. Flakiness results from air spaces in the baked crust; weights delete air spaces.

• To mold a fluted pastry edge on *baked and unbaked pie shells,* use your fingers to roll small sections of the overhanging pastry (about 1½ inches at a time) *under* (not over), until the rolled section is situated over the top of the pie pan rim. (The pastry seam will be *under* the rolled edge and not visible.)

Immediately after rolling a section of overhanging pastry, lightly mold it with your fingers into an upright triangular peak situated directly over the rim of the pan. Repeat the rolling and molding procedure around the pie, trying to make the continuous triangular peak as uniform in size and shape as possible.

If a section of overhanging pastry seems too long or too thick as you roll and mold the pastry around the pan, trim some of it away with kitchen scissors before commencing to roll that particular section. Should a section of overhanging pastry be too short or too thin, carefully hold a small, extra piece of rolled-out pastry *under* the overhanging pastry and roll the extra pastry into the roll.

Follow the procedures in Baked Pie Shell

(page 461) to flute the molded triangular pastry peak around the pie pan, taking care to keep the fluted pastry edge directly on *top* of the rim. If the fluted pastry edge hangs over the outside of the pie pan rim, it will most likely sag over the edge of the pan during baking. Conversely, if the fluted pastry edge is too close to the inside of the pan, it may cause both the fluted edge and the pastry against the side of the pan to slip downward into the pan during baking.

• To mold a fluted pastry edge on a *two-crust pie,* fold the overhanging upper-crust pastry *under* the bottom-crust pastry, which has been trimmed evenly with the edge of the pie pan (see procedures for Two-Crust Pie, page 461). After all the overhanging upper-crust pastry has been folded under the bottom-crust pastry, use your fingers to lightly mold the pastry around the edge of the pan into an upright triangular peak situated *directly over* the rim of the pan, pressing the 2 crusts together to seal. Then, flute the triangular pastry peak. The technique for molding the triangular peak on a two-crust pie is similar to that employed when preparing a baked pie shell; the procedure for fluting is identical (see Baked Pie Shell, page 461).

• To mold a fluted pastry edge on a *lattice-top pie,* roll the overhanging bottom-crust pastry *over* the overhanging lattice strips. (Roll the edge pastry in the opposite direction from rolling the edge on a baked pie shell or a two-crust pie.) As the bottom-crust pastry and lattice strips are rolled together, gently pull the lattice strips taut to help prevent them from sinking beneath the surface of the pie filling near the outer edge of the pie. At the same time, keep the ends of the lattice strips in their straight lines as the overhanging bottom-crust pastry is rolled over them. This can be slightly tricky, since the lattice strips, laid at right angles, must be molded angularly to form the circular edge around the pan, but the know-how will be acquired after practicing a few times.

After all the edge pastry has been rolled, use your fingers to lightly mold an upright triangular peak situated *directly over* the rim of the pan, pressing the bottom-crust pastry and the lattice-top pastry together. Then, flute the triangular pastry peak, following the procedure in Baked Pie Shell (page 461). Contrary to baked pie shells and two-crust pies, the pastry seam on the edge of a lattice-top pie is visible at the inner base of the triangular pastry peak. Fluting helps disguise the seam.

• While edge pastry must be handled more than the pastry in the rest of a pie, the cardinal rule still prevails: handle pastry as little and as quickly as possible to retain optimal flakiness. It helps to rinse your hands in cold water (wipe them completely dry) before flouring them to handle pastry. Warm hands melt the pieces of lard you are trying to retain in the pastry before baking.

• When the pie filling is to be baked in the pie, it should not be added until the last possible moment to best preserve the composition integrity of the bottom crust. Filling allowed to stand in unbaked bottom-crust pastry can cause the bottom crust to become soggy and lose much of its flakiness. At best, the bottom crust of a baked filled pie is not as flaky as the top and edge crust due to the moisture and weight of the filling on the bottom pastry during baking.

When making a two-crust or lattice-top pie, prepare the filling before commencing to mix the pastry (pastry ingredients may be premeasured, of course). Roll and fit the bottom-crust pastry in the pie pan. Then, lay a piece of plastic wrap over the pan to prevent the pastry from drying out. Quickly roll the top-crust pastry (and cut strips if making a lattice-top pie). Lay a piece of plastic wrap over the rolled top-crust pastry. *Then,* place the filling in the pastry-lined pan, arrange the top-crust pastry and flute the edge as expeditiously as possible. Immediately place the pie in a thoroughly preheated oven, being careful not to tilt the pie in transit, causing the filling to wash against the edge.

- Pastry-crust pies should be served the same day they are baked. Pastry crust is never as good as it is in the immediate few hours after a pie has cooled. Moisture absorbed from the pie filling and refrigeration (if required) causes the crust to lose a measure of its crispness, lightness, and flakiness. For the very best results, freshly baked pies not requiring refrigeration should be kept uncovered on wire racks—for total circulation—in a relatively cool, dry part of the house until served. Covering pies or leaving them in a steamy kitchen will allow moisture to infuse the crust. (I keep baked pies which do not require refrigeration on wire racks on the dining-room buffet until mealtime.)

    Cream and custard pies must be served soon after they have cooled; otherwise, they must be refrigerated for food safety. Therefore, timing of the baking or filling of these pies must be gauged to the planned serving time if refrigeration is to be avoided. This timing factor becomes even more critical with meringue-topped pies, which not only should be eaten the day they are made, but also should not be refrigerated before serving, if possible. Refrigeration causes meringue to become tough and to shrink.

    Of course, some types of pastry-crust pies require refrigeration before serving; for example, pies topped or decorated with whipped cream, and chiffon pies which all must be refrigerated to set and to retain the consistency of their fillings. Such pastry-crust pies should be stored in the refrigerator *uncovered* on a wire rack until serving time. This allows more air to circulate around the crust and generally leads to less moisture absorption than when covered. Of course, make certain that other foods stored in the refrigerator are covered to avoid the transfer of other food flavors to the pie. Whipped cream topping and decoration are especially prone to this hazard.

- If a pastry-crust pie requiring refrigeration must be made the day before serving, store it in the refrigerator on a wire rack placed in a plastic pie container. Tilt the container cover to allow for some air circulation and prevent the surface of the pie filling from drying out. Under any circumstance, whipped cream topping and decoration should be applied near the time of serving to avert the possibility of the whipped cream weeping onto the filling.

- If time restrictions require it, pastry pie shells may be baked the day before they are filled and served if they are stored at room temperature in an airtight container standing on a wire rack. Some quality will be sacrificed.

- *Unbaked* pastry pie shells may be frozen (see the Note under Baked Pie Shell, page 461); however, when baked, the crust will be less flaky and slightly tough.

- After serving, most leftover fruit pies may be stored at room temperature for 1 or 2 days. Loosely covering them in a plastic pie container will help prevent the filling from drying out. All other leftover pies should be covered and refrigerated.

TO MAKE ALUMINUM FOIL EDGE-COVERS FOR PIES

When a pie requires a lengthy period of baking, its fluted pastry edge usually overbrowns if not covered with aluminum foil during part of the baking time.

To make a foil edge-cover, cut aluminum foil into three 4 × 12-inch pieces, and one 4 × 4-inch piece. Staple the pieces together to form one continuous 4-inch-wide strip. Then, staple the two ends together to form a circle. Stand the aluminum foil circle around a 9-inch pie pan. Using your hands, *very loosely* crinkle the foil around the rim of the pie pan, fashioning a cover which can be easily dropped over the edge of pies without damaging the pastry.

TO DECORATE PASTRY PIECRUST

CUTOUT PASTRY DECORATIONS: To decorate the top of Pastry Piecrust (page 460) with applied, cutout pastry decorations, roll the pastry as for piecrust. Using flour-dipped, small cutters in the design of stars, flowers, leaves, letters of the alphabet, or other designs, carefully cut out desired pastry designs. Wipe the cutters with a paper towel and reflour before each cut. Or, using a flour-dipped X-Acto knife, cut out pastry of your own design.

Place an egg white in a small sauce dish; using a table fork, beat until foamy. Using a small, soft watercolor brush, apply a small amount of the egg white to the back of each pastry cutout and arrange on the surface of the *unbaked* pastry to be decorated, pressing softly to cement. No alteration in baking time or procedure is required. Follow the recipe for the item being prepared.

EGG WHITE GLAZE: Place an egg white in a small sauce dish; using a table fork, beat until foamy. Using a very soft brush, lightly apply a thin layer of egg white over the *unbaked* pastry, omitting any fluted edge. No alteration in baking time or procedure is required. Bake according to the recipe for the item being prepared. When the pastry has reached the desired golden color during baking, cover it lightly with a piece of aluminum foil and continue baking.

SUGAR GLAZE: Using your fingers or a very small spoon (such as a demitasse spoon), sprinkle sanding sugar (see Note) or granulated sugar over the top crust of a two-crust pie or the lattice crust of a lattice-top pie (omitting the fluted edge) 10 minutes prior to completion of baking. No alteration in baking time or procedure is required. Return the pastry to the oven and bake, uncovered, at the temperature called for in the recipe.

Sugar glaze adds a special glisten to two-crust and lattice-top fruit pies—that final touch which makes a beautifully made pie even more appealing.

NOTE: Sanding sugar has crystals larger in size than granulated sugar, and is often used by professional bakers to decorate the tops of cookies, pastry, and other baked items. Sanding sugar makes a particularly noticeable and handsome decoration. In addition to white, it is available in a host of nice colors. Your local baker may be a source for sanding sugar, or it can be ordered from Sweet Celebrations Inc. (see Product Sources, page 849).

CLASSICAL TART PASTRY

Classical Tart Pastry differs considerably from Pastry Piecrust (page 460) in the ingredients used, the techniques employed, and the texture after baking. Baked Classical Tart Pastry is similar in consistency and taste to a rich cookie. Baked in special tart pans with removable rims, it is used when making classical tarts (see pages 510–511 for more information). Recipes for classical tarts, using this recipe, may be found on pages 512–515.

1 cup plus 1 tablespoon sifted all-purpose flour (sift before measuring)
2 tablespoons sugar
½ teaspoon salt
¼ cup plus 2 tablespoons (6 tablespoons) butter, softened
2 extra-large egg yolks, slightly beaten with a fork
½ teaspoon pure vanilla extract

Set out a 9-inch tart pan with a removable, perpendicular, ⅞-inch-high, fluted rim.

Onto waxed paper, sift together the flour, sugar, and salt. Place the flour mixture in a medium mixing bowl. Using a tablespoon, make a well in the center of the flour mixture. Place the butter, egg yolks, and vanilla in the well. Using an electric mixer, beat on medium speed *only until all the ingredients are combined;* guard against overbeating.

Using floured hands, quickly gather the pastry into a ball, handling as little as possible. Using a stockinet-covered, then lightly floured rolling pin (page 54), roll the pastry on a lightly floured pastry cloth (page 54) to 1 inch greater in diameter than the inverted tart-pan rim. Carefully run a thin spatula around and under the edge of the pastry to loosen it from the pastry cloth.

Place the ungreased, inverted tart pan (bottom and rim) on the center of the pastry. Place a wire rack over the inverted tart pan. With both hands, hold the wire rack and the pastry cloth (pulled somewhat tautly); invert quickly. Carefully peel the pastry cloth off the pastry.

With floured hands, quickly and gently fit the pastry into the pan. Pull the extra pastry overlapping the pan back into the pan and press it into the pastry lining the pan rim, thereby making the pastry lining the rim of the pan slightly thicker than the pastry on the bottom of the pan. As you press the extra pastry against the inside of the pan rim, mold the top of the pastry to make it flat and even with the top of the rim. Do not be concerned if the rim of the pan cuts through some of the pastry when inverting the tart pan. If this happens, simply press the severed portions of pastry into the inside of the pan rim, smoothing it into the pastry lining.

Using a table fork, prick the pastry on the *bottom* of the pan at 1-inch intervals in a circle around the periphery of the pan, about ⅛ inch from the edge. Then, prick the remainder of the pastry on the *bottom* of the pan at 1½- to 1¾-inch intervals (see illustration). Do not prick the side pastry. Refrigerate the tart shell, uncovered, for 1½ hours.

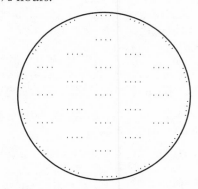

Preheat the oven to 350°F.

Remove the tart pan from the refrigerator and place it on a wire rack. Leave the tart pan on the wire rack and immediately place the tart pan *and* rack in the oven on the middle shelf. Bake for 13 to 15 minutes, until golden brown. If any bubbles form in the pastry on the bottom of the pan after a few minutes of baking, prick them with a fork. If any pastry on the sides of the pan falls down, use a table fork to press it back into the pan rim.

Place the baked tart shell on a wire rack to cool. (To avoid scorching the countertop, use a wire rack different from the one used under the tart pan during baking.) Do not remove the pan rim until just before serving or displaying the tart. This will help prevent the side pastry from breaking off when handling and filling the tart shell. Always leave the pan bottom under the tart.

MAKES ONE 9-INCH CLASSICAL TART SHELL

TARTLET SHELLS

Made in teeny tartlet tins, these pastry shells are usually artistically filled and decorated with tantalizing hors d'oeuvre savories or seductive dessert dainties.

3 ounces cream cheese, softened
½ cup (¼ pound) butter, softened
¼ teaspoon salt
1 cup plus 2 tablespoons all-purpose flour

Preheat the oven to 400°F.

Place the cream cheese in a small mixing bowl; using an electric mixer, beat on high speed until creamy. Add the butter and salt; continue beating on high speed until blended. Add the flour; using a spoon, stir to combine.

With floured hands, form the dough into ¾-inch-diameter balls. Press each pastry ball firmly into the bottom and sides of an ungreased, tiny 1¾-inch fluted tartlet tin with slanted sides, molding the pastry to make it flat and even with the top edge of the tin. Using a small fork, prick the pastry in each tartlet tin twice.

Place the pastry-lined tartlet tins on a cookie pan (with 1-inch sides). Bake the Tartlet Shells for 11 to 12 minutes, or until golden in color. Remove from the oven and place the cookie pan on a wire rack. Cool the Tartlet Shells

(Recipe continues on next page)

2 minutes. Remove the shells from the tins by inverting them, one at a time, in your hands. Place the Tartlet Shells on waxed paper; let stand until completely cool. Store the Tartlet Shells, single layer, in an airtight container until ready to fill.

MAKES ABOUT 3 DOZEN

SERVING SUGGESTIONS: These Tartlet Shells contain no sugar and may be filled with either nonsweet or sweet foods.

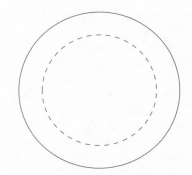

PUFF PASTRY SHELLS (PATTY SHELLS)

These pretty-looking, flaky, individual "containers" or shells made of puff pastry are filled with creamed poultry, shellfish, fish, meat, egg, or vegetable refinements and are often served as the main course for luncheons, brunches, or late suppers (see Chicken à la King, page 209; Deviled Tuna on Patty Shells, page 226; and Eggsotic Eggs, page 268). Commercial, frozen puff pastry makes light work of these poufy niceties.

1 17¼-ounce package (2 sheets) frozen
  puff pastry
2 extra-large egg yolks
2 teaspoons half-and-half

Remove the frozen pastry sheets from the sealed inner package and let them stand, folded, at room temperature 30 minutes to thaw. Meanwhile, in a small sauce dish, place the egg yolks and half-and-half; using a table fork, beat to blend; set aside.

Preheat the oven to 350° F.

On a lightly floured pastry cloth (page 54), carefully unfold the pastry sheets. Using a stockinet-covered, then lightly floured rolling pin (page 54), roll each pastry sheet to a 9½ × 9½-inch square. Using a floured, 3-inch round cutter, cut 9 pastry circles from each sheet of pastry. Then, using a floured, 2⅛-inch round cutter, cut an inner circle ⅔ through the pastry on each 3-inch circle (see illustration).

Place the 18 pastry circles on an ungreased cookie sheet. Using a soft brush, brush the *top* of the circles lightly with the egg yolk mixture. Do not allow the egg yolk mixture to drip down the sides of the pastry, as the mixture will act as an adhesive and prevent the pastry from rising evenly. Using a table fork, prick each pastry circle several times. Bake for 18 to 20 minutes, or until golden in color.

Immediately upon removal from the oven, use a small, thin-bladed knife to loosen and help remove the inner circles which were cut ⅔ through the pastry on each pastry circle. A base of pastry will remain within each circle. The removed inner circles may be retained and used as lids on filled Puff Pastry Shells, if desired. Remove any damp pastry which may remain on the underside of the pastry lids. Carefully place the Puff Pastry Shells and lids on wire cookie racks; let stand until completely cool. Store, uncovered, if the shells will be used within 12 hours; otherwise, store in a container with the cover ajar to permit the circulation of air.

MAKES 1½ DOZEN 3½-INCH-ROUND PUFF PASTRY SHELLS (PATTY SHELLS)

4½-INCH-SQUARE PUFF PASTRY SHELLS: Follow the Puff Pastry Shells (Patty Shells) recipe, above, through rolling each pastry sheet to a 9½ × 9½ square.

Preheat the oven to 350° F.

Using a sharp, thin-bladed, floured knife and a ruler to measure, cut four 4-inch squares of pastry from each pastry sheet. Place the 8 pastry squares on an ungreased cookie sheet. Using a soft brush, brush the *top* (not the sides) of the squares lightly with the egg yolk mixture. From the remaining rolled pastry, cut:

16 pastry strips, ⅜ inch wide by 4 inches long; and
16 pastry strips, ⅜ inch wide by 3¼ inches long.

See illustration A for cutting each pastry sheet.

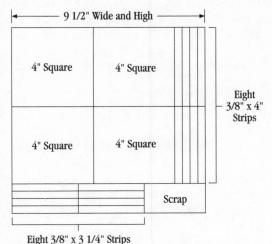

Illustration A

Lay two 4-inch pastry strips and two 3¼-inch pastry strips flat on top of each 4-inch pastry square along all 4 edges (see illustration B).

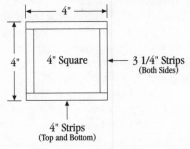

Illustration B

The pastry strips should abut but not overlap. Using a soft brush, brush the *top* (not the sides) of the strips lightly with the egg yolk mixture. Using a table fork, prick the bottoms of the squares several times. Bake for 18 to 20 minutes,

or until golden in color. Check after 5 minutes of baking; if the bottoms of the shells have puffed up, prick the puffed areas with a fork.

When done, use a thin spatula to carefully place the shells on wire cookie racks to cool. Follow the Puff Pastry Shells (Patty Shells) recipe for storage procedure.

MAKES EIGHT 4½-INCH-SQUARE PUFF PASTRY SHELLS (PATTY SHELLS)

Other Piecrusts

UNBAKED GRAHAM CRACKER CRUST

⅓ cup packed light brown sugar
½ teaspoon ground cinnamon
1½ cups rolled graham cracker crumbs (about 20 graham cracker squares)
¼ cup plus 2 tablespoons (6 tablespoons) butter, melted

Butter well a 9–inch pie pan; set aside.

In a medium mixing bowl, place the brown sugar and cinnamon; stir to combine. Add the graham cracker crumbs; stir until well combined. Add the melted butter; stir until the mixture is crumbly in texture.

Place the crumb mixture in the bottom of the prepared pie pan. With the back of a tablespoon, press the mixture firmly and evenly over the bottom and side of the pie pan. As you press the crumb mixture against the side of the pan near the rim, use the index finger of your free hand to push the mixture against the back of the tablespoon and mold the top edge of the crust

(Recipe continues on next page)

compactly in a low triangular shape slanted slightly inward. The top edge should not be left frayed, allowing loose crumbs to fall onto the filling when the pie is filled or when it is cut for serving. (Do not cover the top of the pie pan rim with the mixture.)

Refrigerate the crust; let stand in the refrigerator at least 15 minutes before filling. (This crust may be baked after filling if called for in a recipe.)

BAKED GRAHAM CRACKER CRUST

Crumb crusts are light years easier to make than Pastry Piecrust, and they're scrumptious when matched with appropriate fillings. Two of my favorite pies using the Baked Graham Cracker Crust recipe that follows are Graham Cracker Fudge Pie (page 487) and Glazed Fresh Blueberry Pie (page 478).

1½ cups rolled graham cracker crumbs
    (about 20 graham cracker squares)
¼ cup granulated sugar
¼ cup plus 2 tablespoons (6 tablespoons)
    butter, softened

Preheat the oven to 350° F.

In a medium mixing bowl, place the graham cracker crumbs and sugar; stir to combine. Cut the butter into approximately 8 pieces and drop into the bowl containing the graham cracker crumb mixture. Using a pastry blender, cut the butter into the crumb mixture until the mixture is crumbly in texture.

Place the crumb mixture in the bottom of an ungreased 9-inch pie pan. With the back of a tablespoon, press the mixture firmly and evenly over the bottom and side of the pie pan. As you press the crumb mixture against the side of the pan near the rim, use the index finger of your free hand to push the mixture against the back of the tablespoon and mold the top edge of the crust compactly in a low triangular shape slanted slightly inward. The top edge should not be left frayed, allowing loose crumbs to fall onto the

filling when the pie is filled or when it is cut for serving. (Do not cover the top of the pie pan rim with the mixture.)

Bake the crust for 8 minutes. Baking causes very little change in the appearance of the crust. Remove the piecrust from the oven and place on a wire rack to cool before filling.

BAKED NUTMEG GRAHAM CRACKER CRUST: Follow the Baked Graham Cracker Crust recipe, above, adding ½ teaspoon ground nutmeg to the mixing bowl containing the graham cracker crumbs and sugar before stirring to combine.

MERINGUE PIE SHELL

4 extra-large egg whites, room temperature
¼ teaspoon cream of tartar
1 cup superfine sugar

Preheat the oven to 275° F. Butter *well* a 9-inch pie pan; set aside.

In a medium mixing bowl, place the egg whites and cream of tartar; using an electric mixer, beat on high speed until soft peaks hold. While continuing to beat on high speed, very gradually sprinkle the sugar over the egg white mixture. Beat until the sugar completely dissolves and the meringue is stiff but still glossy (about 3 minutes, after commencing to add the sugar).

Using a small, narrow spatula, spread the meringue evenly on the bottom and up the sides (not on the rim) of the prepared pie pan, reserving enough meringue to pipe a border, if desired.

If a piped border is planned, the meringue up the side of the pan should be ½ inch thick with a flat, smooth, top edge, even with the rim. Using a decorating bag fit with medium-large open-star tip number 32 (page 383), pipe a zigzag border (page 389) of meringue on top of the ½-inch meringue edge. Do not pipe the border on the rim of the pie pan.

Bake the meringue shell for 55 minutes.

When done, the meringue will be ivory colored and crusty. It is normal if the meringue cracks slightly. Cool the shell on a wire rack in a non-humid place away from drafts.

MAKES ONE 9-INCH PIE SHELL

Meringue Pie Topping

3 extra-large egg whites, room temperature
¼ teaspoon cream of tartar
Dash of salt
½ teaspoon clear vanilla
¼ cup plus 2 tablespoons superfine sugar

Preheat the oven to 350°F.

Place the egg whites in a medium mixing bowl; using an electric mixer, beat on high speed until foamy. Add the cream of tartar and salt; continue beating on high speed until soft peaks hold. Add the vanilla. While continuing to beat on high speed; very gradually add the sugar. Beat until the sugar dissolves and the meringue is stiff but still glossy (about 2½ minutes after commencing to add the sugar).

Spoon part of the meringue onto the outer portions of slightly cooled filling (see Note) in a 9-inch pie pan. Using a small, narrow spatula, spread the meringue around the edge of the pie, making certain that it touches the inner edge of the piecrust to seal the meringue and help prevent shrinkage. Mound the remainder of the meringue in the center of the pie. Using the spatula, briefly spread the meringue to distribute the topping symmetrically. Then, using the back of the spatula, swirl the meringue to form attractive peaks.

Bake the meringue-topped pie for 5 minutes. Reduce the heat to 325°F. and continue baking for 7 to 10 minutes, until the meringue is golden. If the meringue reaches the desired golden color prior to baking 12 minutes, turn off the oven and leave the pie in the oven until 12 minutes have elapsed.

Remove the pie from the oven and place on a wire rack in a fairly warm location away from drafts; let stand until cool.

NOTE: The filling should still be quite warm when the meringue topping is added. This will help assure that the underside of the meringue cooks and does not weep onto the filling.

When making meringue to top a cream-type pie, let the cooked filling cool slightly on a wire rack before pouring it into the pie shell. Let the filled pie shell stand on a wire rack while immediately proceeding to make the meringue. Some degree of flakiness is sacrificed when pastry piecrust is filled with a warm to hot filling, but that is the unavoidable nature of meringue-topped pies.

**MAKES ENOUGH MERINGUE TO TOP
ONE 9-INCH PIE**

VARIATIONS

- Ingredient amounts for Meringue Pie Topping for one 8-inch pie, or for use with pie recipes calling for 2 extra-large egg yolks in the filling:

2 extra-large egg whites, room temperature
¼ teaspoon cream of tartar
Dash of salt
¼ teaspoon clear vanilla
¼ cup superfine sugar

Follow the Meringue Pie Topping recipe procedures, above.

**MAKES ENOUGH MERINGUE TO TOP
ONE 8-INCH PIE**

- Ingredient amounts for Meringue Pie Topping for one 10-inch pie, or for use with pie recipes calling for 4 extra-large egg yolks in the filling:

4 extra-large egg whites, room temperature
½ teaspoon cream of tartar
⅛ teaspoon salt
½ teaspoon clear vanilla
½ cup superfine sugar

Follow the Meringue Pie Topping recipe procedures, above.

**MAKES ENOUGH MERINGUE TO TOP
ONE 10-INCH PIE**

GINGERSNAP CRUST

1⅓ cups finely rolled gingersnap crumbs
   (about twenty 2-inch gingersnap cookies)
¼ cup plus 2 tablespoons (6 tablespoons)
   butter, softened

Preheat the oven to 350° F.

Place the gingersnap crumbs in a medium mixing bowl. Cut the butter into approximately 8 pieces and drop into the bowl containing the gingersnap crumbs. Using a pastry blender, cut the butter into the crumbs until the mixture is crumbly in texture.

Place the crumb mixture in the bottom of an ungreased 9-inch pie pan. With the back of a tablespoon, press the mixture firmly and evenly over the bottom and side of the pie pan. As you press the crumb mixture against the side of the pan near the rim, use the index finger of your free hand to push the mixture against the back of the tablespoon and mold the top edge of the crust compactly in a low triangular shape slanted slightly inward. The top edge should not be left frayed, allowing loose crumbs to fall onto the filling when the pie is filled or when it is cut for serving. (Do not cover the top of the pie pan rim with the mixture.)

Bake the crust for 8 minutes. Baking causes very little change in the appearance of the crust. Remove the piecrust from the oven and place on a wire rack to cool before filling.

MAKES ONE 9-INCH PIE SHELL

10-INCH GINGERSNAP CRUST PIE SHELL

1¾ cups finely rolled gingersnap crumbs
   (about 26 2-inch gingersnap cookies)
½ cup (¼ pound) butter, softened

Follow the Gingersnap Crust recipe, above, substituting a 10-inch pie pan for a 9-inch pan.

MAKES ONE 10-INCH PIE SHELL

UNBAKED VANILLA WAFER CRUST

Ice cream pies frequently are made using crumb crusts. The pleasingly rich vanilla flavor of this crumb crust pairs well with butter brickle ice cream and a touch of chunky peanut butter in Peanut Butter Brickle Ice Cream Pie (page 671) to create a just-right, refreshing finale to a substantial dinner.

1½ cups rolled vanilla wafer crumbs (about
   33 vanilla wafers)
1 teaspoon pure vanilla extract
¼ cup plus 2 tablespoons (6 tablespoons)
   butter, melted

Place the vanilla wafer crumbs in a medium mixing bowl; set aside. Add the vanilla to the melted butter; stir to blend. Pour the butter mixture over the crumbs; stir until the mixture is crumbly in texture.

Place the crumb mixture in the bottom of an ungreased 9-inch pie pan. With the back of a tablespoon, press the mixture firmly and evenly over the bottom and side of the pie pan. As you press the crumb mixture against the side of the pan near the rim, use the index finger of your free hand to push the mixture against the back of the tablespoon and mold the top edge of the crust compactly in a low triangular shape slanted slightly inward. The top edge should not be left frayed, allowing loose crumbs to fall onto the filling when the pie is filled or when it is cut for serving. (Do not cover the top of the pie pan rim with the mixture.)

Refrigerate the crust; let stand in the refrigerator at least 15 minutes before filling.

MAKES ONE 9-INCH PIE SHELL

Pies

TYPES OF DESSERT PIES

Dessert pies may be classified into the following seven general types based upon their fillings:

FRUIT PIES: Standard fruit pies are filled with whole, sliced, or cut-up fruit—usually fresh—sweetened with sugar and thickened with flour, cornstarch, or quick-cooking tapioca. Most are baked with 2 crusts.

Another type of fruit pie consists of a baked pie shell in which fresh fruit is arranged and then covered with a sweet, translucent glaze. Whipped cream is often piped decoratively over portions of the glaze.

CREAM PIES: Cream pies have a soft, pudding-type filling made with egg yolks, milk, sugar, and flavoring, and thickened with cornstarch or flour. Fruits, such as bananas or peaches, may be mixed with the cream filling. Cooked cream pie fillings are poured into baked pie shells and are generally topped with meringue or whipped cream.

CUSTARD PIES: Custard pies are simply custards baked in a pie shell. The basic custard ingredients are eggs, milk, sugar, and flavoring. Other ingredients, such as pumpkin or fruits, may be added.

SYRUP-BASED NUT PIES: Syrup-based nut pies are made with syrup or molasses, eggs, butter, sugar, flavoring, and nuts. The fillings bake to a transparent, jellylike consistency, and the nuts rise to cover the top of the pies. Pecan pie is the best known example of this type of pie.

CHIFFON PIES: Chiffon pies are light, airy pies made by folding stiffly beaten egg whites—and sometimes whipped cream, as well—into a very thick mixture of egg yolks, unflavored gelatin, sugar, flavoring, and milk or other liquid, which has been cooked in a double boiler and cooled to room temperature. Pieces of fruit or other additions may also be folded into the filling. Chiffon filling is usually piled high in the pie shell and is often topped with whipped cream.

CHEESE PIES: Dessert cheese pies most often have as principal ingredients, cream cheese, eggs, sugar, and flavoring, which are beaten only until blended and smooth. The cheese filling is usually baked in a graham cracker crust which lines a standard pie pan, or occasionally, a springform pan. Or, the filling may be baked in a pastry shell. Fresh fruit, such as berries, is commonly arranged over the chilled filling and then covered with a translucent glaze. Some cheese pies are made with cottage cheese.

CHEESE PIE CONTRASTED WITH CHEESECAKE: While, very commonly, no distinction is made between cheese pie and cheesecake, I distinguish between the two by ascribing the following characteristics to cheesecake: Cheesecake

- Is deeper in size than cheese pie and is most always baked in a springform pan.

- Usually has a very thin crust of either a special pastry or finely ground crumbs which are often, though not always, made with zwieback.

- Often has flour as an ingredient.

- Commonly has a baked sour cream topping or is served with a fruit sauce spooned over individual servings.

(See page 662 for Cheesecake recipe.)

ICE CREAM PIES (SEE PAGE 671 FOR RECIPES): Ice cream pies consist of ice cream—plain, mixed with other ingredients, or layered with other fillings—frozen in a crumb crust or a baked pastry shell. They may be topped with crumbs, meringue, or various garnishes and decorations such as whipped cream, chopped nuts, and fruit. The toppings are added before the pie is frozen or at serving time, depending upon the type.

Fruit Pies

APPLE PIE

The All-American pie!

¾ cup sugar
2 tablespoons plus 2 teaspoons all-purpose
  flour
1 teaspoon ground cinnamon
¼ teaspoon ground nutmeg
Dash of salt
7 cups Golden Delicious apples sliced
  ⅛ inch thick (about 6 medium apples)
Pastry Piecrust for 1 9-inch lattice-top pie
  (page 460)*
2 tablespoons butter
Sanding sugar (see Sugar Glaze, page 468)
  or granulated sugar to decorate lattice
  crust

*If desired, a plain top crust may be substituted
for a lattice top (see Two-Crust Pie, page 461).*

In a small mixing bowl, place ¾ cup sugar, flour, cinnamon, nutmeg, and salt; stir to combine; set aside. Wash the apples. Pare, quarter, core, and slice the apples. Measure 7 cups sliced apples and place in a large mixing bowl. Sprinkle the sugar mixture over the apples; using a mixing spoon, toss lightly until the apple slices are coated. Let the apple mixture stand.

Preheat the oven to 400°F.

Prepare the pastry. Line the pie pan with the bottom-crust pastry. Lay a piece of plastic wrap lightly over the pie pan to prevent the pastry from drying; set aside. Roll the top-crust pastry; cut 14 pastry strips. Leave the cut strips on the pastry cloth; cover lightly with a piece of plastic wrap; let stand.

Remove the plastic wrap covering the pie pan. Spoon the apple mixture evenly over the bottom-crust pastry; dot with butter. Remove the plastic wrap covering the pastry strips.

Arrange the lattice-top pastry on the pie and flute the edge.

Bake the pie for 1 hour. After 15 minutes baking, drop an aluminum foil edge-cover (page 467) over the fluted edge of the pie to prevent overbrowning. After 25 minutes total baking, rotate the pie 180 degrees in the oven to help achieve even browning. When the lattice crust reaches the desired golden color (after approximately 25 minutes total baking), lay a piece of aluminum foil loosely over the entire pie (including the foil edge-cover). After 50 minutes total baking, remove the foil from the top and edge of the pie. Then, remove the pie from the oven. Using your fingers or a very small spoon (such as a demitasse spoon), sprinkle the sanding sugar lightly over the lattice crust. Do not sprinkle the sugar over the fluted edge of the pie. Return the pie to the oven and bake for 10 additional minutes.

When done, remove the pie from the oven and place on a wire rack to cool.

MAKES ONE 9-INCH PIE; 7 SERVINGS

SERVING SUGGESTIONS

• Drape a thin slice of yellow cheddar cheese over one side of each piece of pie after placing the pie servings on individual plates; or,

• Place a scoop of vanilla ice cream (homemade, page 669, or commercial) next to each pie slice.

CRAN-APPLE PIE

1½ cups fresh cranberries, washed
5½ cups Golden Delicious apples sliced
  ⅛ inch thick (about 5 medium apples)
Pastry Piecrust for 1 9-inch two-crust pie
  (page 460)

Follow the Apple Pie recipe, above, substituting 1½ cups fresh cranberries and 5½ cups apples for the 7 cups apples. Make a regular top crust rather than a lattice-top crust.

MAKES ONE 9-INCH PIE; 7 SERVINGS

APPLE CRUMB PIE

Satisfy your sweet tooth with this delectable change-of-pace apple pie. Don't forget the ice cream. Apple Crumb Pie and vanilla ice cream are a duet!

²⁄₃ cup granulated sugar
3 tablespoons all-purpose flour
¾ teaspoon ground cinnamon
6 cups Golden Delicious apples sliced
   ⅜ inch thick (about 5 medium apples)
½ cup (¼ pound) butter
1 cup all-purpose flour
½ cup packed light brown sugar
½ teaspoon ground cinnamon
1 9-inch unbaked Pastry Piecrust pie shell
   (page 460)

In a small mixing bowl, place the granulated sugar, 3 tablespoons flour, and ¾ teaspoon cinnamon; stir to combine; set aside. Wash the apples. Pare the apples and place in a large bowl of cold water as they are pared to help prevent discoloration. Quarter and core the apples. Cut each quarter in half lengthwise and slice ⅜ inch thick. Measure 6 cups sliced apples and place in a large mixing bowl. Sprinkle the sugar mixture over the apples; using a mixing spoon, toss lightly until the apple slices are coated. Let the apple mixture stand.

Preheat the oven to 400°F.

Remove the butter from the refrigerator; set aside. In a medium mixing bowl, place 1 cup flour, brown sugar, and ½ teaspoon cinnamon; stir to combine. Cut the butter into approximately 8 pieces and drop onto the flour mixture. Using a pastry blender, cut the butter into the flour mixture until the mixture is the consistency of coarse crumbs; set aside.

Spoon the apples and accumulated juice evenly into the pie shell. Using a tablespoon, sprinkle the flour mixture evenly over the apples, being careful not to sprinkle the mixture on the fluted edge of the piecrust. If this should

occur, use a very soft brush to brush the flour mixture off the fluted edge.

Bake the pie for 50 to 55 minutes. After 15 minutes baking, drop an aluminum foil edge-cover (page 467) over the fluted edge of the pie to prevent overbrowning. Lay a piece of aluminum foil loosely over the entire pie (including the foil edge-cover). After 15 additional minutes baking, rotate the pie 180 degrees in the oven to help achieve even browning. After 40 minutes total baking, check the brownness of the fluted edge. Remove the foil from the top and edge of the pie if the fluted edge needs further browning. Bake for 10 to 15 additional minutes.

When done, remove the pie from the oven and place on a wire rack to cool.

MAKES ONE 9-INCH PIE; 7 SERVINGS

SERVING SUGGESTION: Serve warm with a scoop of vanilla ice cream (homemade, page 669, or commercial).

BLUEBERRY PIE

¾ cup sugar
3 tablespoons all-purpose flour
4 cups fresh blueberries
Pastry Piecrust for 1 9-inch two-crust pie
  (page 460)
2 tablespoons butter
Sanding sugar (see Sugar Glaze, page 468)
  or granulated sugar to decorate top crust

In a small mixing bowl, place ¾ cup sugar and flour; stir to combine; set aside. Wash and sort the blueberries; drain in a colander. Measure 4 cups blueberries and place in a large mixing bowl. Sprinkle the sugar mixture over the blueberries; using a mixing spoon, toss lightly until the blueberries are coated. Let the blueberry mixture stand.

Preheat the oven to 400°F.

Prepare the pastry. Line the pie pan with the bottom-crust pastry. Lay a piece of plastic wrap lightly over the pie pan to prevent the pastry from drying; set aside. Roll the top-crust pastry. Leave the top-crust pastry on the pastry cloth; cover lightly with a piece of plastic wrap; let stand.

Remove the plastic wrap covering the pie pan. Spoon the blueberry mixture evenly over the bottom-crust pastry; dot with butter. Remove the plastic wrap covering the top-crust pastry. Fold and slit the top-crust pastry; arrange on the pie and flute the edge.

Bake the pie for 45 minutes. After 15 minutes baking, drop an aluminum foil edge-cover (page 467) over the fluted edge of the pie to prevent overbrowning. After 25 minutes total baking, rotate the pie 180 degrees in the oven to help achieve even browning. If the top crust reaches the desired golden color prior to completion of baking, lay a piece of aluminum foil loosely over the entire pie (including the foil edge-cover). After 35 minutes total baking, remove the foil from the top (if used) and edge of the pie. Then, remove the pie from the oven. Using your fingers or a very small spoon (such as a demitasse spoon), sprinkle the sanding sugar lightly over the top crust. Do not sprinkle the sugar over the fluted edge of the pie. Return the pie to the oven and bake for 10 additional minutes.

When done, remove the pie from the oven and place on a wire rack to cool.

MAKES ONE 9-INCH PIE; 7 SERVINGS

GLAZED FRESH BLUEBERRY PIE

½ cup sugar
3 tablespoons cornstarch
½ teaspoon ground cinnamon
⅛ teaspoon salt
1 cup water
1 quart fresh blueberries,* divided
2 tablespoons freshly squeezed, strained
  lemon juice
1 9-inch Baked Graham Cracker Crust pie
  shell (page 472)
1 recipe Decorator Whipped Cream
  (page 374)

Two pints home-canned Blueberries (page 714) or commercially canned blueberries may be substituted for fresh blueberries. Drain the canned blueberries in a sieve, reserving the juice. Substitute blueberry juice for water in the above recipe ingredients, adding water, if necessary, to make 1 cup liquid. Do not add any blueberries to the glaze mixture during the cooking process; add all of the blueberries after removing the mixture from the heat and stirring in the lemon juice.

In a medium saucepan, place the sugar, cornstarch, cinnamon, and salt; stir to combine. Add the water; stir well. Bring the cornstarch mixture to a simmer over medium heat, stirring constantly. Add 1 cup blueberries. Return the mixture to a simmer and cook until thick and translucent (about 2 minutes), stirring continuously. Remove from the heat and place the saucepan on a wire rack.

Add the lemon juice; stir to blend. Add the remaining 3 cups blueberries; stir to evenly distribute. Let the mixture stand until cooled to room temperature.

Spoon the blueberry mixture into the pie shell; using a small, narrow spatula, spread smoothly. Refrigerate until the filling is cold and set.

Using a decorating bag fit with large open-star tip number 6B (page 383) decorate the top of the pie with piped Decorator Whipped Cream, allowing some of the blueberry filling to show. Refrigerate the pie and keep stored in the refrigerator.

MAKES ONE 9-INCH PIE; 7 SERVINGS

ALTERNATIVE TOPPING: Using a small, narrow spatula, spread Decorator Whipped Cream evenly over the entire surface of the filling. Decorate the top of the pie with fresh blueberries.

CHERRY PIE

Across America, cherry pie is associated with George Washington, "The Father of His Country." Serving cherry pie in February is one of the ways we celebrate Washington's birthday and honor our first president.

In the Midwest, cherry pie is also a celebratory food on another important national holiday, the Fourth of July, and for two well-founded reasons: at that time of the summer, the tart, bright red cherries used in making cherry pies are ripe and ready for picking off the cherry trees growing in town and city yards, and on farms. Plus, the brilliant red color of the fruit, which fades little with the baking, becomes part of the decoration on picnic tables parading red, white, and blue.

4 cups pitted, tart, fresh (or frozen and thawed) red cherries
1⅓ cups sugar*
2 tablespoons quick-cooking tapioca
Dash of salt
Pastry Piecrust for 1 9-inch lattice-top pie (page 460)**
2 tablespoons butter, melted
Sanding sugar (see Sugar Glaze, page 468) or granulated sugar to decorate lattice crust

*Use 1½ cups sugar if the cherries are especially tart.

**If desired, a plain top crust may be substituted for a lattice top (see Two-Crust Pie, page 461).

In a medium mixing bowl, place the cherries, 1⅓ cups sugar, tapioca, and salt; stir to combine. Let the cherry mixture stand.

Preheat the oven to 400° F.

Prepare the pastry. Line the pie pan with the bottom-crust pastry. Lay a piece of plastic wrap lightly over the pie pan to prevent the pastry from drying; set aside. Roll the top-crust pastry; cut 14 pastry strips. Leave the cut strips on the pastry cloth; cover lightly with a piece of plastic wrap; let stand.

Add the butter to the cherry mixture; stir to blend the liquids. Remove the plastic wrap covering the pie pan. Spoon the cherry mixture over the bottom-crust pastry, distributing the cherries evenly over the entire bottom of the pastry-lined pie pan. Remove the plastic wrap covering the pastry strips. Arrange the lattice-top pastry on the pie and flute the edge.

Bake the pie for 45 minutes. After 15 minutes baking, drop an aluminum foil edge-cover (page 467) over the fluted edge of the pie to prevent overbrowning. After 25 minutes total baking, rotate the pie 180 degrees in the oven to help achieve even browning. If the lattice crust reaches the desired golden color prior to completion of baking, lay a piece of aluminum foil loosely over the entire pie (including the foil edge-cover). After 35 minutes total baking, remove the foil from the top (if used) and edge of the pie. Then, remove the pie from the oven. Using your fingers or a very small spoon (such as a demitasse spoon), sprinkle the sanding sugar lightly over the lattice crust. Do not sprinkle the sugar over the fluted edge of the pie. Return the pie to the oven and bake for 10 additional minutes.

When done, remove the pie from the oven and place on a wire rack to cool.

MAKES ONE 9-INCH PIE; 7 SERVINGS

GOOSEBERRY-DATE PIE

Gooseberries are old hat to most Midwest natives, who have eaten them in pies for as long as they can remember. Gooseberries are small, very tart green berries which develop reddish purple tinges when they ripen. They are gathered mainly in the wild, where they grow on prickly bushes. In the early summer, I often gather wild raspberries with my friend, Betty Baker, who several years ago divulged to me her secret gathering place. As we head into the woods, we always take along an extra pail for gooseberries, which we find in most years. (Sometimes weather conditions affect the wild berry crop.)

4½ cups fresh gooseberries*
½ cup sugar
2 tablespoons cornstarch
1 teaspoon ground cinnamon
¼ teaspoon salt
1 cup cooking juice from gooseberries
1 cup seeded dates cut into pieces (cut
    medium-sized dates into eighths)
    or 1 cup commercially packaged
    prechopped dates
1 9-inch baked Pastry Piecrust pie shell
    (page 460)
1 recipe Decorator Whipped Cream (page
    374)

*If fresh gooseberries are not available, 2 16½-ounce cans of commercial gooseberries may be substituted. Drain the gooseberries well in a sieve, reserving 1 cup syrup to use in substitution for 1 cup cooking juice from gooseberries in the recipe ingredients above.

Wash and sort the gooseberries. Place the gooseberries in a medium saucepan; add water to cover. Cover the saucepan. Bring the gooseberries to a low simmer over medium-low heat; uncover and simmer 3 minutes. Drain the gooseberries in a sieve, reserving the juice. Measure 1 cup reserved juice; set aside. Place the drained gooseberries in a medium mixing bowl; set aside.

In a small saucepan, place the sugar, cornstarch, cinnamon, and salt; stir to combine. Add the 1 cup reserved cooking juice from the gooseberries; stir well. Bring the cornstarch mixture to a boil over medium heat, stirring constantly. Reduce the heat and continue boiling until the mixture is thick and translucent (about 2 minutes), stirring continuously. Remove from the heat. Add the dates and the hot, cornstarch mixture to the gooseberries; using a wooden mixing spoon, stir carefully, only until combined. Place the mixing bowl containing the gooseberry-date filling on a wire rack; let stand until lukewarm.

Spoon the lukewarm gooseberry-date filling evenly into the pie shell; let stand on a wire rack until completely cool.

Shortly before serving, pipe a lattice pattern and border on the top of the pie (see pages 389–390 for border pictures and procedures), using a decorating bag fit with medium-large open-star tip number 32 (page 383) and filled with Decorator Whipped Cream. Refrigerate the pie until served.

MAKES ONE 9-INCH PIE; 7 SERVINGS

GOOSEBERRY PIE

6 cups fresh gooseberries*
¾ cup sugar

*If fresh gooseberries are not available, 3 16½-ounce cans of commercial gooseberries may be substituted. Drain the gooseberries well in a sieve, reserving 1 cup syrup in substitution for 1 cup cooking juice from gooseberries in the Gooseberry-Date Pie recipe. Substitute ⅔ cup sugar (rather than substituting ¾ cup sugar) for ½ cup sugar in the Gooseberry-Date Pie recipe.

Follow the Gooseberry-Date Pie recipe, above, substituting 6 cups fresh gooseberries for 4½ cups fresh gooseberries, and ¾ cup sugar for ½ cup sugar. Eliminate the dates.

MAKES ONE 9-INCH PIE; 7 SERVINGS

PEACH PIE

Without a doubt, fresh Peach Pie is one of the high points of summer dining. When your eyes catch sight of the golden peaches peaking through the tender lattice crust, anticipation of that soothing, yet fruity, taste seems to have a near-tranquilizing effect.

½ cup sugar
3 tablespoons all-purpose flour
¼ teaspoon ground cinnamon
5 cups peeled, halved, pitted, quartered, and sliced fresh peaches
1 tablespoon freshly squeezed, strained lemon juice
Pastry Piecrust for 1 9-inch lattice-top pie (page 460)*
2 tablespoons butter
Sanding sugar (see Sugar Glaze, page 468) or granulated sugar to decorate lattice crust

If desired, a plain top crust may be substituted for a lattice top (see Two-Crust Pie, page 461).

In a small mixing bowl, place ½ cup sugar, flour, and cinnamon; stir to combine; set aside. Wash the peaches; peel, halve, pit, quarter, and slice. Measure 5 cups sliced peaches and place in a large mixing bowl. Sprinkle lemon juice over the sliced peaches 2 or 3 times during preparation to prevent discoloration. Add any remaining lemon juice; using a wooden mixing spoon, stir *carefully* to assure that all the peach slices are coated with lemon juice. Sprinkle the sugar mixture evenly over the peaches; toss lightly. Let the peach mixture stand.

Preheat the oven to 400°F.

Prepare the pastry. Line the pie pan with the bottom-crust pastry. Lay a piece of plastic wrap lightly over the pie pan to prevent the pastry from drying; set aside. Roll the top-crust pastry; cut 14 pastry strips. Leave the cut strips on the pastry cloth; cover lightly with a piece of plastic wrap; let stand.

Remove the plastic wrap covering the pie pan. Spoon the peach mixture evenly over the bottom-crust pastry; dot with butter. Remove the plastic wrap covering the pastry strips. Arrange the lattice-top pastry on the pie and flute the edge.

Bake the pie for 45 minutes. After 15 minutes baking, drop an aluminum foil edge-cover (page 467) over the fluted edge of the pie to prevent overbrowning. After 25 minutes total baking, rotate the pie 180 degrees in the oven to help achieve even browning. If the lattice crust reaches the desired golden color prior to completion of baking, lay a piece of aluminum foil loosely over the entire pie (including the foil edge-cover). After 35 minutes total baking, remove the foil from the top (if used) and edge of the pie. Then, remove the pie from the oven. Using your fingers or a very small spoon (such as a demitasse spoon), sprinkle the sanding sugar lightly over the lattice crust. Do not sprinkle the sugar over the fluted edge of the pie. Return the pie to the oven and bake for 10 additional minutes.

When done, remove the pie from the oven and place on a wire rack to cool.

MAKES ONE 9-INCH PIE; 7 SERVINGS

PEACH–RED RASPBERRY PIE

3½ cups peeled, halved, pitted, quartered, and sliced fresh peaches
1½ cups fresh red raspberries

Follow the Peach Pie recipe, above, substituting 3½ cups sliced peaches and 1½ cups red raspberries for 5 cups sliced peaches. Keep the sliced peaches and raspberries in separate bowls. Sprinkle the entire sugar mixture over the sliced peaches; add no sugar mixture to the raspberries.

To fill the pie, spoon ½ of the peach mixture evenly over the bottom-crust pastry. Distribute the raspberries evenly over the peach layer. Spoon the remaining ½ of the peach mixture evenly over the raspberries.

FRESH PEAR PIE

While pears are a fairly common fruit used in making tarts, pear pies are not frequently encountered. If you're wondering whether Pear Pie is really good and whether you should try one, the answers are "yes" and "yes."

½ cup granulated sugar
2 tablespoons quick-cooking tapioca
½ teaspoon ground cinnamon
Dash of ground mace
8 cups cold water
1 tablespoon white vinegar
1 tablespoon salt
4 to 5 large, fresh Bartlett pears (5 cups sliced pears; see recipe procedures below)
3 tablespoons freshly squeezed, strained lemon juice
½ cup (¼ pound) butter
¾ cup all-purpose flour
½ cup packed light brown sugar
½ teaspoon ground ginger
1 9-inch unbaked Pastry Piecrust pie shell (page 460)

In a small mixing bowl, place the granulated sugar, tapioca, cinnamon, and mace; stir to combine; set aside. In a small kettle or large mixing bowl, place 8 cups water, vinegar, and salt; stir until the salt dissolves; set aside.

Wash, halve, core, and pare the pears. As the pear halves are prepared, drop them into the vinegar solution to prevent discoloration. Drain and rinse the pear halves twice. Then, carefully place the pears in a colander to fully drain. Cut the pear halves in half lengthwise. Slice each pear quarter widthwise into ⅜-inch slices. Measure 5 cups sliced pears and place in a large mixing bowl. Sprinkle the lemon juice over the pears; using a wooden mixing spoon, toss to coat all slices. Add the tapioca mixture; toss until the pear slices are coated. Let the pear mixture stand for 15 minutes.

Preheat the oven to 375° F.

While the pear mixture is standing, remove the butter from the refrigerator; set aside. In a medium mixing bowl, place the flour, brown sugar, and ginger; stir to combine. Cut the butter into approximately 8 pieces and drop onto the flour mixture. Using a pastry blender, cut the butter into the flour mixture until the mixture is the consistency of very coarse crumbs; set aside.

Spoon the pear slices and accumulated juice evenly into the pie shell, mounding the pear slices slightly in the center of the pie. Using a tablespoon, sprinkle the flour mixture evenly over the pears, being careful not to sprinkle the mixture on the fluted edge of the piecrust. If this should occur, use a very soft brush to brush the flour mixture off the fluted edge. The flour mixture should cover all the pears and be slightly mounded in the center of the pie.

Bake the pie for 50 minutes. After 15 minutes baking, drop an aluminum foil edge-cover (page 467) over the fluted edge of the pie to prevent overbrowning. After 25 minutes total baking, rotate the pie 180 degrees in the oven to help achieve even browning. When the topping on the pie reaches the desired brownness, lay a piece of aluminum foil loosely over the entire pie (including the foil edge-cover). After 40 minutes total baking, check the brownness of the fluted edge. Remove the foil from the top and edge of the pie if the fluted edge needs further browning. Bake for 10 additional minutes.

When done, remove the pie from the oven and place on a wire rack to cool.

MAKES ONE 9-INCH PIE; 7 SERVINGS

SERVING SUGGESTIONS
- Serve warm with a small scoop of vanilla ice cream (homemade, page 669, or commercial).

- Serve at room temperature topped with a dollop of Whipped Cream (page 373).

RHUBARB PIE

Rhubarb Pie: an old-time (and modern-time, too) pie rite of spring—the season when you have more rhubarb growing than you know what to do with. This does not mean to infer that Rhubarb Pie is remotely inferior, only that you might wish the generous bounty were harvestable over a longer period of time so you could spread out the joy of eating fresh rhubarb dishes. The availability hurdle is cleared by some rhubarb fanciers who wash, cut, and freeze part of their abundant crop in zipper-seal plastic freezer bags for later delivery in off-season rhubarb desserts.

1²/₃ cups sugar
¹/₃ cup all-purpose flour
¹/₂ teaspoon ground nutmeg
4 cups fresh (or frozen) rhubarb cut into
    ¹/₂-inch lengths
Pastry Piecrust for 1 9-inch two-crust pie
    (page 460)
2 tablespoons butter

In a medium mixing bowl, place the sugar, flour, and nutmeg; stir to combine; set aside. Place the rhubarb in a large mixing bowl. Sprinkle the sugar mixture over the rhubarb; using a mixing spoon, toss lightly until the rhubarb is coated. Let the rhubarb mixture stand for 15 minutes.

Preheat the oven to 400° F.

While the rhubarb mixture is standing, prepare the pastry. Line the pie pan with the bottom-crust pastry. Lay a piece of plastic wrap lightly over the pie pan to prevent the pastry from drying; set aside. Roll the top-crust pastry. Leave the top-crust pastry on the pastry cloth; cover lightly with a piece of plastic wrap; let stand.

Remove the plastic wrap covering the pie pan. Spoon the rhubarb mixture over the bottom-crust pastry, distributing the rhubarb evenly; dot with butter. Remove the plastic wrap covering the top-crust pastry. Fold and slit the top-crust pastry; arrange on the pie and flute the edge.

Bake the pie for 40 to 50 minutes. After 15 minutes baking, drop an aluminum foil edge-cover (page 467) over the fluted edge of the pie to prevent overbrowning. After 25 minutes total baking, rotate the pie 180 degrees in the oven to help achieve even browning. If the top crust reaches the desired golden color prior to completion of baking, lay a piece of aluminum foil loosely over the entire pie (including the foil edge-cover). After 35 minutes total baking, remove the foil from the top (if used) and edge of the pie. Bake for 5 to 10 additional minutes.

When done, remove the pie from the oven and place on a wire rack to cool.

MAKES ONE 9-INCH PIE; 7 SERVINGS

SERVING SUGGESTIONS
- Serve with a scoop of vanilla ice cream (homemade, page 669, or commercial).

- Top each slice of pie with a generous dollop of Whipped Cream (page 373).

STRAWBERRY-RHUBARB PIE

1 cup sugar
¼ cup plus 1 tablespoon all-purpose flour
1 tablespoon plus 1 teaspoon cornstarch
½ teaspoon ground mace
2 cups hulled (page 23), halved or
    quartered (depending upon size) fresh
    strawberries
2 cups fresh rhubarb cut into ¾-inch
    lengths
Pastry Piecrust for 1 9-inch lattice-top pie
    (page 460)*
1 5-ounce can (½ cup plus 2 tablespoons)
    evaporated milk
Sanding sugar (see Sugar Glaze, page 468)
    or granulated sugar to decorate lattice
    crust

*If desired, a plain top crust may be substituted
for a lattice top (see Two-Crust Pie, page
461).*

In a small mixing bowl, place 1 cup sugar, flour, cornstarch, and mace; stir to combine; set aside. In a large mixing bowl, place the strawberries and rhubarb; stir until evenly distributed; set aside.

Preheat the oven to 400° F.

Prepare the pastry. Line the pie pan with the bottom-crust pastry. Lay a piece of plastic wrap lightly over the pie pan to prevent the pastry from drying; set aside. Roll the top-crust pastry; cut 14 pastry strips. Leave the cut strips on the pastry cloth; cover lightly with a piece of plastic wrap; let stand.

Add the evaporated milk to the sugar mixture; stir until completely blended; set aside. Remove the plastic wrap covering the pie pan. Spoon the strawberry-rhubarb mixture evenly over the bottom-crust pastry. Pour the evaporated milk mixture evenly over the strawberries and rhubarb in the pie. Remove the plastic wrap covering the pastry strips. Arrange the lattice-top pastry on the pie and flute the edge.

Bake the pie for 55 minutes. After 15 minutes baking, drop an aluminum foil edge-cover (page 467) over the fluted edge of the pie to prevent overbrowning. After 25 minutes total baking, rotate the pie 180 degrees in the oven to help achieve even browning. If the lattice crust reaches the desired golden color prior to the completion of baking, lay a piece of aluminum foil loosely over the entire pie (including the foil edge-cover). After 45 minutes total baking, remove the foil from the top (if used) and edge of the pie. Then, remove the pie from the oven. Using your fingers or a very small spoon (such as a demitasse spoon), sprinkle the sanding sugar lightly over the lattice crust. Do not sprinkle the sugar over the fluted edge of the pie. Return the pie to the oven and bake for 10 additional minutes.

When done, remove the pie from the oven and place on a wire rack to cool.

MAKES ONE 9-INCH PIE; 7 SERVINGS

GLAZED STRAWBERRY PIE

Huge, gorgeous strawberries arranged under shiny glaze with no-holds-barred amounts of whipped cream piped like white puffy clouds on the top—all of this makes a spring and summertime pie indulgence that is too satisfying to resist.

8 cups (about 2¼ pounds) hulled (page
    23), whole, fresh strawberries
¾ cups sugar
3 tablespoons cornstarch
½ cup plus 2 tablespoons water
12 drops red liquid food coloring
1 9-inch baked Pastry Piecrust pie shell
    (page 460)
1 recipe Decorator Whipped Cream
    (page 374)

Place 2 cups of the strawberries in a blender beaker; using the blender, puree; set aside. Distribute the remaining 6 cups strawberries on paper towels to completely drain; set aside.

In a medium saucepan, place the sugar and cornstarch; stir to combine. Add the water; stir well. Add the pureed strawberries; stir to combine. Bring the strawberry mixture to a boil over medium heat, stirring constantly. Reduce the heat and continue boiling and stirring until the mixture is thick and translucent (about 2 minutes). Remove from the heat and place the saucepan on a wire rack. Add the food coloring; stir until evenly blended. Let the mixture stand to cool slightly, stirring occasionally.

Meanwhile, arrange the whole strawberries, stem end down, in the pie shell. If the strawberries are especially large, cut them in half lengthwise, and arrange them, cut-side down, in the pie shell. Slightly mound the strawberries in the center of the pie for a more attractive final appearance.

Pour the cooked strawberry mixture evenly over the strawberries in the pie shell; refrigerate until cold.

Using a decorating bag fit with large open-star tip number 6B (page 383), pipe two wide, continuous borders of Decorator Whipped Cream on top of the pie around the outside edge (see pages 389–390 for pictures and procedures for borders), leaving the center portion of the pie free of topping. Refrigerate the pie and keep stored in the refrigerator.

MAKES ONE 9-INCH PIE; 7 SERVINGS

ALTERNATIVE GARNISH: If a decorating bag is not available, spoon small, uniform mounds of the Decorator Whipped Cream around the edge of the pie.

RASPBERRY PIE

¾ cup sugar
3 tablespoons cornstarch
⅛ teaspoon salt
5 cups fresh red or black raspberries
Pastry Piecrust for 1 9-inch two-crust pie
   (page 460)
2 tablespoons butter
Sanding sugar (see Sugar Glaze, page 468)
   or granulated sugar to decorate top crust

In a small mixing bowl, place ¾ cup sugar, cornstarch, and salt; stir to combine; set aside. Using gentle handling to retain the wholeness of the raspberries, rinse, drain in a colander, and measure the berries. Place the raspberries in a large mixing bowl. Sprinkle the sugar mixture evenly over the berries; using a wooden mixing spoon, toss *minimally* to coat the berries. Let the raspberry mixture stand.

Preheat the oven to 400°F.

Prepare the pastry. Line the pie pan with the bottom-crust pastry. Lay a piece of plastic wrap lightly over the pie pan to prevent the pastry from drying; set aside. Roll the top-crust pastry. Leave the top-crust pastry on the pastry cloth; cover lightly with a piece of plastic wrap; let stand.

Remove the plastic wrap covering the pie pan. Turn the raspberry mixture into the bottom-crust pastry; using the wooden mixing spoon, spread the raspberries carefully and evenly. Dot the raspberry filling with butter. Remove the plastic wrap covering the top-crust pastry. Fold and slit the top-crust pastry; arrange on the pie and flute the edge.

Bake the pie for 45 minutes. After 15 minutes baking, drop an aluminum foil edge-cover (page 467) over the fluted edge of the pie to prevent overbrowning. After 25 minutes total baking, rotate the pie 180 degrees in the oven to help achieve even browning. If the top crust reaches the desired golden color prior to completion of baking, lay a piece of aluminum foil loosely over the entire pie (including the foil edge-cover). After 35 minutes total baking, remove the foil from the top (if used) and edge of the pie. Then, remove the pie from the oven. Using your fingers or a very small spoon (such as a demitasse spoon), sprinkle the sanding sugar lightly over the top crust. Do not sprinkle the sugar over the fluted edge of the pie. Return the pie to the oven and bake for 10 additional minutes.

When done, remove the pie from the oven and place on a wire rack to cool.

MAKES ONE 9-INCH PIE; 7 SERVINGS

FRESH PLUM PIE

1 cup sugar
¼ cup cornstarch
1 teaspoon ground cinnamon
5 cups fresh, pitted plums cut into quarters
    or sixths lengthwise, depending upon size
Pastry Piecrust for 1 9-inch two–crust pie
    (page 460)
2 tablespoons butter
Sanding sugar (see Sugar Glaze, page 468)
    or granulated sugar to decorate top crust

In a medium saucepan, place 1 cup sugar, corn-starch, and cinnamon; stir to combine. Add the plums; stir to combine. Bring the plum mixture to a simmer over medium heat, stirring con-stantly. Reduce the heat to medium-low and cook until the mixture is thick and translucent, stirring continuously. Remove from the heat; set aside.

Preheat the oven to 400° F.

Prepare the pastry. Line the pie pan with the bottom-crust pastry. Lay a piece of plastic wrap lightly over the pie pan to prevent the pastry from drying; set aside. Roll the top-crust pastry. Leave the top-crust pastry on the pastry cloth; cover lightly with a piece of plastic wrap; let stand.

Remove the plastic wrap covering the pie pan. Spoon the plum mixture evenly over the bottom-crust pastry; dot with butter. Remove the plastic wrap covering the top-crust pastry. Fold and slit the top-crust pastry; arrange on the pie and flute the edge.

Bake the pie for 45 minutes. After 15 minutes baking, drop an aluminum foil edge-cover (page 467) over the fluted edge of the pie to prevent overbrowning. After 25 minutes total baking, rotate the pie 180 degrees in the oven to help achieve even browning. If the top crust reaches the desired golden color prior to completion of baking, lay a piece of aluminum foil loosely over the entire pie (including the foil edge-cover). After 35 minutes total baking, remove the foil from the top (if used) and edge of the pie. Then, remove the pie from the oven. Using your fin-gers or a very small spoon (such as a demitasse spoon), sprinkle the sanding sugar lightly over the top crust. Do not sprinkle the sugar over the fluted edge of the pie. Return the pie to the oven and bake for 10 additional minutes.

When done, remove the pie from the oven and place on a wire rack to cool.

MAKES ONE 9-INCH PIE; 7 SERVINGS

BRANDIED MINCEMEAT PIE

Homemade mincemeat is in a class by itself. Plan ahead for the next holiday season and make your own special mincemeat (see Brandied Mincemeat, page 726) to serve in this traditional pie. Use the remain-der of your canned or frozen mincemeat for gift giving, and for making Mincemeat Cookies (page 621) and Mincemeat–Rum Ice Cream Pie (page 671) later in the winter.

Pastry Piecrust for 1 9-inch two–crust pie
    (page 460)
1 quart home-canned or home-frozen
    Brandied Mincemeat (page 726)
1 extra-large egg white

Preheat the oven to 400° F.

Line the pie pan with the bottom-crust pas-try. Lay a piece of plastic wrap lightly over the pie pan to prevent the pastry from drying; set aside. Roll the top-crust pastry. Leave the top-crust pastry on the pastry cloth; cover lightly with a piece of plastic wrap; let stand.

Remove the plastic wrap covering the pie pan. Spoon the mincemeat evenly over the bottom-crust pastry. Remove the plastic wrap covering the top-crust pastry. Fold and slit the top-crust pastry; arrange on the pie and flute the edge; set aside.

Place the egg white in a small sauce dish; using a table fork, beat until foamy. Using a very soft brush, apply lightly a thin layer of egg white over the top-crust pastry, *omitting* the fluted edge.

Bake the pie for 45 minutes. After 15 minutes baking, drop an aluminum foil edge-cover (page

467) over the fluted edge of the pie to prevent overbrowning. After 25 minutes total baking, rotate the pie 180 degrees in the oven to help achieve even browning. When the top of the pie reaches the desired golden color, lay a piece of aluminum foil loosely over the entire pie (including the foil edge-cover). After 40 minutes total baking, remove the foil from the top and edge of the pie. Bake for 5 additional minutes.

When done, remove the pie from the oven and place on a wire rack. Serve at room temperature or hot (cut slices may be heated in a microwave oven). Store leftover pie in the refrigerator. If the pie is baked well in advance of serving, it should be refrigerated since it contains meat.

MAKES ONE 9-INCH PIE; 7 SERVINGS

HOLIDAY DECORATION: The top crust of the pie may be decorated with cutout pastry stars applied prior to baking the pie. See To Decorate Pastry Piecrust (page 467) for instructions.

Cream Pies

GRAHAM CRACKER FUDGE PIE

"Calling all chocolate lovers!" Satisfy your craving with this super-duper pie which borders on a confection. The recipe came from longtime friend Dora Smith who lives in Melcher, Iowa. The tattered card bearing this recipe has been in my recipe box ever since Dora served this awesome pie at a party years ago. I've served it over and over. How can such a phenomenal pie be so easy to make? Don't ask—just enjoy! (I cut this rich 9-inch pie into 8 servings rather than the usual 7.)

½ cup whole milk
6 1.45-ounce (8.7 ounces total) Hershey's
   milk chocolate with almond bars, broken
   into chunks
28 large marshmallows

1 cup (½ pint) whipping cream, unwhipped
1 9-inch Baked Graham Cracker Crust pie
   shell (page 472)
1 recipe Decorator Whipped Cream
   (page 374)
Shaved Chocolate (page 408) for
   decoration

In the top of a double boiler, place the milk, chocolate bar chunks, and marshmallows. Place the top of the double boiler over (not touching) hot (not simmering) water in the bottom pan on the range. Stir continuously until the chocolate and marshmallows melt and the mixture blends.

Remove the top of the double boiler from the bottom pan and place it on a wire rack. Let the mixture stand until cooled to room temperature, stirring occasionally.

Meanwhile, pour 1 cup whipping cream into a medium-small mixing bowl. Using an electric mixer, beat the cream on medium-high speed until it begins to stiffen. Reduce the mixer speed to medium-low and continue beating the cream until stiff, but still soft and fluffy; cover and refrigerate.

When the chocolate mixture cools to room temperature, add the whipped cream; fold in. Pour the filling mixture into the pie shell; using a small, narrow spatula, spread evenly, slightly mounding the mixture in the center of the pie. Refrigerate the pie until the filling is cold and set.

Then, spoon the Decorator Whipped Cream over the top of the pie; using the small, narrow spatula, spread evenly and smoothly over the entire surface of the filling. Sprinkle the Shaved Chocolate over the top. Refrigerate the pie and keep stored in the refrigerator.

MAKES ONE 9-INCH PIE; 8 SERVINGS

BLACK FOREST PIE

A glamorous pie.

3 ounces (3 squares) unsweetened
    chocolate
¼ cup water
2 extra-large eggs, slightly beaten
Dash of salt
½ cup (¼ pound) butter, softened
¾ cup sugar
1 teaspoon pure vanilla extract
1 9-inch baked Pastry Piecrust pie shell
    (page 460)
1 recipe Cherry Glaze (recipe follows)
1 recipe Decorator Whipped Cream (page
    374)
6 Chocolate Scrolls (page 407) (optional)
Shaved Chocolate (page 408)

In the top of a double boiler, place the chocolate and water. Place the top of the double boiler
over (not touching) hot (not simmering) water
in the bottom pan on the range. Stir the
chocolate-water mixture until the chocolate
melts and blends with the water.

Add the eggs and salt. Using a handheld electric mixer, beat the mixture on low speed until
the mixture reaches 160° F. Use a candy thermometer to assure the proper temperature. When
the mixture reaches 160° F., immediately remove
the top of the double boiler from the bottom
pan and place it in a bowl of cold water to cool
the mixture quickly. Using the electric mixer,
intermittently beat the mixture on low speed
until it cools to room temperature—*not cooler.*

Meanwhile, in a medium mixing bowl, place
the butter and sugar; using a standard-sized electric mixer, beat 4 minutes on high speed to
cream well. Add the chocolate mixture and
vanilla; continue beating on high speed until the
mixture is completely blended and fluffy.

Turn the mixture into the pie shell; using a
small, narrow spatula, spread smoothly. Refrigerate the pie until the filling is cold and set.

Then, spoon the Cherry Glaze, cooled to

room temperature, evenly over the cold chocolate pie filling. Refrigerate until the glaze is cold
and set.

Using a decorating bag fit with large open-
star tip number 6B (page 383) and filled with
Decorator Whipped Cream, pipe a border and
decorative center on the top of the pie (see
pages 389–390 for pictures and procedures). The
Cherry Glaze should remain visible between the
whipped cream border and the center.

Arrange the Chocolate Scrolls (if used) at
even intervals in spokelike fashion around the
pie, pressing one of the long edges of each scroll
into the whipped cream border and center to
hold it in place. The wide end of the scrolls
should be pressed into the border, and the narrow, pointed end should be pressed into the
center.

Sprinkle the Shaved Chocolate sparingly on
the whipped cream between the scrolls in the
center of the pie (see illustration). Refrigerate
the pie and keep stored in the refrigerator.

MAKES ONE 9-INCH PIE; 7 SERVINGS

Black Forest Pie

Cherry Glaze

2 cups pitted, tart, fresh (or frozen and
    thawed) red cherries
⅓ cup sugar
2 tablespoons plus 2 teaspoons cornstarch
¼ teaspoon almond extract

In a medium mixing bowl, place the cherries and sugar; stir to combine. Let stand at room temperature until the sugar dissolves and the cherries give juice.

Pour the juice off the cherries, reserving the juice. Set the drained cherries aside. Measure 1 cup reserved juice (add water, if necessary, to make 1 cup liquid). Pour the juice into a small saucepan. Add the cornstarch; stir to combine. Bring the juice mixture to a simmer over medium heat and cook until thick and translucent (about 2 minutes), stirring constantly. Remove from the heat and place the saucepan on a wire rack.

Add the almond extract; stir until blended. Add the cherries; stir to combine. Let the mixture stand until cooled to room temperature.

BUTTERSCOTCH PIE

One of my all-time favorite pies.

1½ cups packed light brown sugar
¼ cup all-purpose flour
3 tablespoons cornstarch
¼ teaspoon salt
3 extra-large egg yolks
2 cups whole milk, scalded (page 25)
1 tablespoon butter
1 teaspoon pure vanilla extract
1 9-inch baked Pastry Piecrust pie shell
  (page 460)
1 recipe Decorator Whipped Cream (page
  374) *or* 1 recipe Meringue Pie Topping
  (use 3 extra-large egg whites; page 473)

In a medium mixing bowl, place the brown sugar, flour, cornstarch, and salt; stir to combine; set aside.

Place the egg yolks in the top of a double boiler. Using a handheld electric mixer, beat the egg yolks slightly on medium speed. Add the flour mixture; beat on medium speed until combined. Add about ⅓ cup of the hot, scalded milk; beat on medium speed to blend. While beating continuously, slowly add the remaining scalded milk. Place the top of the double boiler over low boiling water in the bottom pan. Cook the mixture until thick (about 10 minutes), constantly beating with the electric mixer on low speed or stirring with a spoon.

Remove the top of the double boiler from the bottom pan and place it on a wire rack. Add the butter and vanilla; stir until blended.

Proceed, following one of the alternatives below:

WHIPPED CREAM TOPPING (My preferred topping): Let the butterscotch mixture stand until cooled to room temperature, stirring occasionally. If the mixture becomes slightly lumpy, beat briefly with the electric mixer on low speed until smooth.

Spoon the butterscotch mixture into the pie shell; using a small, narrow spatula, spread evenly. Refrigerate the pie until the filling is cold and set.

Then, spoon the Decorator Whipped Cream over the top of the pie; using a small, narrow spatula, spread evenly and smoothly over the entire surface of the filling. Refrigerate the pie and keep stored in the refrigerator.

MERINGUE TOPPING: Let the butterscotch mixture stand only until cooled slightly. Pour the warm to hot butterscotch mixture into the pie shell; using a small, narrow spatula, spread evenly. Cover the filling with the Meringue Pie Topping and bake, following the Meringue Pie Topping recipe.

Remove the pie from the oven and place it on a wire rack in a fairly warm location away from drafts; let stand until cool. Serve soon after cool; otherwise, the pie must be refrigerated and kept stored in the refrigerator.

MAKES ONE 9-INCH PIE; 7 SERVINGS

CHOCOLATE CREAM PIE

1 cup sugar
⅓ cup all-purpose flour
¼ teaspoon salt
3 extra-large egg yolks
2¼ cups whole milk, scalded (page 25)
2½ ounces (2½ squares) unsweetened
  chocolate, cut into pieces
2 tablespoons butter
1 teaspoon pure vanilla extract
1 9-inch baked Pastry Piecrust pie shell
  (page 460)
1 recipe Meringue Pie Topping (use
  3 extra-large egg whites; page 473)

In a small mixing bowl, place the sugar, flour, and salt; stir to combine; set aside.

Place the egg yolks in the top of a double boiler. Using a handheld electric mixer, beat the egg yolks slightly on medium speed. Add the flour mixture; beat on medium speed until combined. Add about ⅓ cup of the hot, scalded milk; beat on medium speed to blend. While beating continuously, slowly add the remaining scalded milk. Add the chocolate; stir to combine (it is not necessary to stir until the chocolate dissolves). Place the top of the double boiler over low boiling water in the bottom pan. Cook the mixture 15 minutes, until thick and smooth, beating with the electric mixer on low speed during the first 5 minutes of cooking, and stirring continuously with a spoon during the last 10 minutes of cooking. If lumps form during the last 10 minutes of cooking, beat intermittently with the electric mixer.

Remove the top of the double boiler from the bottom pan and place it on a wire rack. Add the butter and vanilla; stir until blended. Let the mixture stand only until cooled slightly. Then, using the electric mixer, beat briefly on low speed until smooth.

Pour the warm to hot chocolate mixture into the pie shell; using a small, narrow spatula, spread the filling, slightly mounding it in the center of the pie. Cover the filling with the Meringue Pie Topping and bake, following the Meringue Pie Topping recipe.

Remove the pie from the oven and place it on a wire rack in a fairly warm location away from drafts; let stand until cool. Serve soon after cool; otherwise, the pie must be refrigerated and kept stored in the refrigerator.

MAKES ONE 9-INCH PIE; 7 SERVINGS

VARIATION: Chocolate Cream Pie may be topped with 1 recipe Decorator Whipped Cream (page 374) rather than Meringue Pie Topping.

After the additions of butter and vanilla to the cooked filling, let the mixture stand until cooled to room temperature, stirring occasionally. Then, using the electric mixer, beat briefly on low speed until smooth.

Spoon the filling mixture into the pie shell; using a small, narrow spatula, spread evenly. Refrigerate the pie until the filling is cold and set.

Then, spoon the Decorator Whipped Cream over the top of the pie; using a small, narrow spatula, spread smoothly over the entire surface of the filling. The pie may be decorated with Shaved Chocolate (page 408) distributed over the whipped cream topping. Refrigerate the pie and keep stored in the refrigerator.

COCONUT CREAM PIE

½ cup plus 1 tablespoon sugar
¼ cup cornstarch
¼ teaspoon salt
2¼ cups whole milk
3 extra-large egg yolks, slightly beaten
2 tablespoons butter
1 teaspoon pure vanilla extract
¾ cup shredded coconut
1 9-inch baked Pastry Piecrust pie shell
  (page 460)
1 recipe Meringue Pie Topping (use
  3 extra-large egg whites; page 473)
3 tablespoons shredded coconut

In the top of a double boiler, place the sugar, cornstarch, and salt; stir to combine. Add the milk; stir well. Place the top of the double boiler over boiling water in the bottom pan. Cook the cornstarch mixture until thick (about 8 minutes), constantly beating with a handheld electric mixer on low speed or stirring with a spoon. Add about ½ cup of the hot cornstarch mixture to the egg yolks and quickly stir in. Then, add the egg yolk mixture to the remaining cornstarch mixture and stir vigorously to blend. Cook the mixture 2 minutes, beating constantly with the electric mixer on low speed.

Remove the top of the double boiler from the bottom pan and place it on a wire rack. Add the butter and vanilla; using the electric mixer, beat on low speed until blended. Let the filling mixture stand only until cooled slightly, stirring occasionally. Then, add ¾ cup coconut; stir to combine.

Pour the warm to hot filling mixture into the pie shell; using a small, narrow spatula, spread evenly. Cover the filling with the Meringue Pie Topping. Sprinkle 3 tablespoons coconut over the meringue. Bake, following the Meringue Pie Topping recipe.

Remove the pie from the oven and place it on a wire rack in a fairly warm location away from drafts; let stand until cool. Serve soon after cool; otherwise the pie must be refrigerated and kept stored in the refrigerator.

MAKES ONE 9-INCH PIE; 7 SERVINGS

BANANA CREAM PIE

2 bananas

Follow the Coconut Cream Pie recipe, above, through slightly cooling the filling. Eliminate the coconut.

Spoon a small amount of warm to hot filling into the pie shell to cover the bottom of the crust. Slice 1 banana evenly over the filling in the pie shell; cover the banana slices with ½ of the remaining filling. Slice the second banana evenly over the filling in the pie; cover the banana slices with the remaining filling. Cover

the filling with the Meringue Pie Topping. Eliminate the coconut garnish. Bake, following the Meringue Pie Topping recipe.

Remove the pie from the oven and place it on a wire rack in a fairly warm location away from drafts; let stand until cool. Serve soon after cool; otherwise, the pie must be refrigerated and kept stored in the refrigerator.

MAKES ONE 9-INCH PIE; 7 SERVINGS

VARIATION: Banana Cream Pie may be topped with 1 recipe Decorator Whipped Cream (page 374) rather than Meringue Pie Topping.

After the additions of butter and vanilla to the cooked filling, let the mixture stand until cooled to room temperature, stirring occasionally. Then, using the electric mixer, beat briefly on low speed until smooth.

Fill the pie shell, following the procedure in the Banana Cream Pie recipe. Refrigerate the pie until the filling is cold and set.

Then, spoon the Decorator Whipped Cream over the top of the pie; using a small, narrow spatula, spread smoothly over the entire surface of the filling. Refrigerate the pie and keep stored in the refrigerator.

PEACH CREAM PIE

1 9-inch baked Gingersnap Crust pie shell (page 474)
2 cups peeled, halved, pitted, quartered, and sliced fresh peaches
1 recipe Decorator Whipped Cream (page 374)

Follow the Coconut Cream Pie recipe, above, through the additions of butter and vanilla to the cooked filling. Let the filling mixture stand until cooled to room temperature, stirring occasionally. Then, using the electric mixer, beat briefly on low speed until smooth. Eliminate the coconut.

Substitute the Gingersnap Crust pie shell for the baked Pastry Piecrust pie shell. Assemble the filling and peaches in the pie shell, following the procedure in the Banana Cream Pie recipe,

(Recipe continues on next page)

above, substituting 1 cup sliced peaches for each banana. Eliminate the Meringue Pie Topping. Refrigerate the pie until the filling is cold and set.

Then, spoon the Decorator Whipped Cream over the top of the pie; using a small, narrow spatula, spread smoothly over the entire surface of the filling. Refrigerate the pie and keep stored in the refrigerator.

MAKES ONE 9-INCH PIE; 7 SERVINGS

FRENCH SILK PIE

In years past, French Silk Pie contained uncooked eggs; however, new food safety guidelines caution against eating raw eggs (see Egg Safety, page 262). I reworked the outdated method of making French Silk Pie and devised this recipe, which calls for cooking the eggs in the chocolate mixture to 160° F., the recommended safe temperature to which eggs should be cooked. I don't think any of the desirable texture and flavor of the original French Silk Pie has been sacrificed with the change in preparation procedure. Hope you agree.

3 ounces (3 squares) unsweetened
   chocolate
⅓ cup water
3 extra-large eggs, slightly beaten
⅛ teaspoon salt
¾ cup (¼ pound plus 4 tablespoons)
   butter, softened
1 cup sugar
1¼ teaspoons pure vanilla extract
1 9-inch baked Pastry Piecrust pie shell
   (page 460)
1 recipe Decorator Whipped Cream
   (page 374)
Chocolate Curls (page 406) for decoration

In the top of a double boiler, place the chocolate and water. Place the top of the double boiler over (not touching) hot (not simmering) water in the bottom pan on the range. Stir the chocolate-water mixture until the chocolate melts and blends with the water.

Add the eggs and salt. Using a handheld electric mixer, beat the mixture on low speed until the mixture reaches 160° F. Use a candy thermometer to assure the proper temperature. When the mixture reaches 160° F., immediately remove the top of the double boiler from the bottom pan and place it in a bowl of cold water to cool the mixture quickly. Using the electric mixer, intermittently beat the mixture on low speed until it cools to room temperature—*not cooler.*

Meanwhile, in a medium mixing bowl, place the butter and sugar; using a standard-sized electric mixer, beat 4 minutes on high speed to cream well. Add the chocolate mixture and vanilla; continue beating on high speed until the mixture is completely blended and fluffy.

Turn the mixture into the pie shell; using a small, narrow spatula, spread smoothly. Refrigerate the pie until the filling is cold and set.

Then, spoon the Decorator Whipped Cream over the top of the pie, reserving enough whipped cream to pipe a border. Using the small, narrow spatula, spread the whipped cream smoothly over the entire surface of the chocolate filling. Using a decorating bag fit with medium-large open-star tip number 32 (page 383), pipe a rope border (page 389) of Decorator Whipped Cream around the edge of the filling. Arrange the Chocolate Curls over the top of the pie. Refrigerate the pie and keep stored in the refrigerator.

MAKES ONE 9-INCH PIE; 7 SERVINGS

LEMON ANGEL PIE

Angel pies, which are made with Meringue Pie Shells, could not have been more appropriately named. They are truly heavenly—especially Lemon Angel Pie, the best-known angel pie. The light, mildly crunchy meringue shell and pleasantly tart lemon filling spread with a layer of whipped cream and sprinkled with pale yellow coconut translate into a perfect summer luncheon dessert.

4 extra-large egg yolks
½ cup sugar
¼ cup freshly squeezed, strained lemon
  juice
2 teaspoons finely grated lemon rind (page
  47) (rind of about 2 lemons)
2 recipes Decorator Whipped Cream
  (page 374)
1 9-inch baked Meringue Pie Shell
  (page 472)
½ cup pale yellow Tinted Coconut
  (page 409)

Place the egg yolks in a small mixing bowl. Using a standard-sized electric mixer, beat the egg yolks on high speed 4 minutes, until thick and lemon colored. In the top of a double boiler, place the beaten egg yolks, sugar, lemon juice, and lemon rind; stir to combine. Place the top of the double boiler over (not touching) simmering water in the bottom pan. Cook the lemon mixture until thick (about 7 to 8 minutes), beating continuously with a handheld electric mixer on the lowest speed. When done, the mixture will very softly mound when spooned.

Remove the top of the double boiler from the bottom pan and refrigerate it until the lemon mixture cools to slightly under room temperature.

Then, spoon ½ of the Decorator Whipped Cream into the Meringue Pie Shell; using a small, narrow spatula, spread evenly. Spoon the lemon mixture over the whipped cream in the pie shell; using a clean, small, narrow spatula, spread evenly. Spoon the remaining ½ of the whipped cream over the lemon mixture; using a clean, small, narrow spatula, spread evenly. Refrigerate the pie, uncovered; let stand at least 6 hours before serving.

Just before cutting and serving, sprinkle the Tinted Coconut evenly over the top of the pie. Keep the pie stored in the refrigerator.

MAKES ONE 9-INCH PIE; 7 SERVINGS.

VARIATION: Just before filling the Meringue Pie Shell, fold ¾ of the Decorator Whipped Cream

into the lemon mixture. Spoon the lemon mixture into the pie shell; using a small, narrow spatula, spread evenly. Refrigerate the pie until the filling is cold and set. Then, spoon the remaining ¼ of the Decorator Whipped Cream over the pie filling; using a small, narrow spatula, spread evenly. Refrigerate the pie until the whipped cream topping sets. Sprinkle the Tinted Coconut evenly over the top of the pie just before cutting and serving. Keep the pie stored in the refrigerator.

LEMON MERINGUE PIE

1 cup sugar
¼ cup plus 2 teaspoons cornstarch
Dash of salt
1⅓ cups cold water
3 extra-large egg yolks, slightly beaten
¼ cup freshly squeezed, strained lemon
  juice
1 tablespoon butter
1 teaspoon finely grated lemon rind (page
  47) (rind of about 1 lemon)
1 8-inch baked Pastry Piecrust pie shell
  (page 460)
1 recipe Meringue Pie Topping (use 3
  extra-large egg whites; page 473)

In a medium saucepan, place the sugar, cornstarch, and salt; stir to combine. Add the water; stir well. Bring the cornstarch mixture to a boil over medium heat, stirring constantly. Reduce the heat and cook the mixture until thick (about 3 minutes), stirring continuously. Add about ½ cup of the hot cornstarch mixture to the egg yolks and quickly stir in. Then, add the egg yolk mixture and lemon juice to the remaining cornstarch mixture and stir vigorously to blend. Return the mixture to a low boil and cook 2 minutes, stirring constantly.

Remove the saucepan from the heat and place it on a wire rack. Add the butter and lemon

(Recipe continues on next page)

rind; stir to blend and combine. Let the lemon mixture stand only until cooled slightly, stirring occasionally.

Pour the warm to hot lemon mixture into the pie shell; using a small, narrow spatula, spread evenly. Cover the filling with the Meringue Pie Topping and bake, following the Meringue Pie Topping recipe.

Remove the pie from the oven and place it on a wire rack in a fairly warm location away from drafts; let stand until cool. Serve soon after cool; otherwise, the pie must be refrigerated and kept stored in the refrigerator.

MAKES ONE 8-INCH PIE; 7 SERVINGS

ORANGE MERINGUE PIE

This is similar to Lemon Meringue Pie but less tart.

1 cup sugar
½ cup all-purpose flour
2 tablespoons cornstarch
¼ teaspoon salt
1 cup freshly squeezed, strained orange juice
1 cup water
3 extra-large egg yolks, slightly beaten
2 tablespoons finely grated orange rind (page 47)
2 tablespoons freshly squeezed, strained lemon juice
1 9-inch baked Pastry Piecrust pie shell (page 460)
1 recipe Meringue Pie Topping (use 3 extra-large egg whites; page 473)

In the top of a double boiler, place the sugar, flour, cornstarch, and salt; stir to combine. Add the orange juice and water; stir well. Place the top of the double boiler over boiling water in the bottom pan. Cook the orange mixture until it begins to thicken, continuously stirring with a spoon or beating with a handheld electric mixer on the lowest speed. If stirring the mix-

ture with a spoon, intermittent beating of the mixture with an electric mixer will help keep the mixture smooth, without lumps. Add about ½ cup of the hot orange mixture to the egg yolks and quickly stir in. Then, add the egg yolk mixture and orange rind to the remaining orange mixture and stir vigorously to blend and combine. Continue cooking the orange mixture 5 minutes, constantly stirring or beating with the electric mixer on low speed.

Remove the top of the double boiler from the bottom pan and place it on a wire rack. Add the lemon juice; using the electric mixer, beat on low speed until blended. Let the orange mixture stand only until cooled slightly, stirring occasionally.

Pour the warm to hot orange mixture into the pie shell; using a small, narrow spatula, spread evenly. Cover the filling with the Meringue Pie Topping and bake, following the Meringue Pie Topping recipe.

Remove the pie from the oven and place it on a wire rack in a fairly warm location away from drafts; let stand until cool. Serve soon after cool; otherwise, the pie must be refrigerated and kept stored in the refrigerator.

MAKES ONE 9-INCH PIE; 7 SERVINGS

PRUNE MERINGUE PIE

⅓ cup sugar
2 tablespoons cornstarch
¼ teaspoon salt
2 cups (1 pint) half-and-half
2 extra-large egg yolks, slightly beaten
2 tablespoons butter
1½ teaspoons pure vanilla extract
1¼ cups bite-sized pitted prunes cut into approximately ⅜-inch cubes
1 9-inch baked Pastry Piecrust pie shell (page 460)
1 recipe Meringue Pie Topping (use 3 extra-large egg whites; page 473)

In the top of a double boiler, place the sugar, cornstarch, and salt; stir to combine. Add the half-and-half; stir well. Place the top of the double boiler over boiling water in the bottom pan. Cook the cornstarch mixture until thick (about 7 minutes), constantly stirring with a spoon or beating with a handheld electric mixer on the lowest speed. Add about ½ cup of the hot cornstarch mixture to the egg yolks and quickly stir in. Then, add the egg yolk mixture to the remaining cornstarch mixture and stir vigorously to blend. Cook the mixture 2 minutes, beating constantly with the electric mixer on low speed.

Remove the top of the double boiler from the bottom pan and place it on a wire rack. Add the butter and vanilla; using the electric mixer, beat on low speed until blended. Let the filling mixture stand only until cooled slightly, stirring occasionally. Add the prunes; stir until evenly distributed.

Pour the warm to hot prune mixture into the pie shell; using a small, narrow spatula, spread evenly. Cover the filling with the Meringue Pie Topping and bake, following the Meringue Pie Topping recipe.

Remove the pie from the oven and place it on a wire rack in a fairly warm location away from drafts; let stand until cool. Serve soon after cool; otherwise, the pie must be refrigerated and kept stored in the refrigerator.

MAKES ONE 9-INCH PIE; 7 SERVINGS

SOUR CREAM RAISIN PIE

A Midwest oldie with a big fan club that never diminishes in number.

¾ cup raisins,* plumped (page 46)
⅔ cup sugar
1 teaspoon ground cinnamon
½ teaspoon ground cloves
3 extra-large egg yolks
8 ounces commercial sour cream
1 8-inch baked Pastry Piecrust pie shell (page 460)
1 recipe Meringue Pie Topping (use 3 extra-large egg whites; page 473)

  **The raisins may be chopped, if desired (page 45).*

Plump the raisins and drain in a sieve; set aside. In a small mixing bowl, place the sugar, cinnamon, and cloves; stir to combine; set aside.

Place the egg yolks in the top of a double boiler. Using a handheld electric mixer, beat the egg yolks slightly on medium speed. Add the sour cream; using a spoon, stir vigorously until blended. Add the sugar mixture; stir to combine. Place the top of the double boiler over simmering water in the bottom pan. Cook the mixture until thick (about 7 minutes), stirring constantly.

Remove the top of the double boiler from the bottom pan and place it on a wire rack. Add the raisins; stir until evenly distributed. Let the mixture stand only until cooled slightly, stirring occasionally.

Pour the warm to hot raisin mixture into the pie shell; using a small, narrow spatula, spread evenly. Cover the filling with the Meringue Pie Topping and bake, following the Meringue Pie Topping recipe.

Remove the pie from the oven and place it on a wire rack in a fairly warm location away from drafts; let stand until cool. Serve soon after cool; otherwise, the pie must be refrigerated and kept stored in the refrigerator.

MAKES ONE 8-INCH PIE; 7 SERVINGS.

Custard Pies

PUMPKIN PIE

½ cup packed light brown sugar
½ cup granulated sugar
½ teaspoon salt
1¼ teaspoons ground cinnamon
1 teaspoon ground ginger
½ teaspoon ground cloves
½ teaspoon ground nutmeg
1½ cups commercially canned pumpkin
1 cup whole milk
1 5-ounce can (½ cup plus 2 tablespoons) evaporated milk
3 extra-large eggs, slightly beaten
1 9-inch unbaked Pastry Piecrust pie shell (page 460)
1 recipe Whipped Cream (page 373)

Preheat the oven to 400° F.

In a medium mixing bowl, place the brown sugar, granulated sugar, salt, cinnamon, ginger, cloves, and nutmeg; stir to combine. Add the pumpkin; stir vigorously until well blended. Add the whole milk, evaporated milk, and eggs; stir until blended and smooth. Pour the pumpkin mixture into the pie shell.

Bake the pie for 15 minutes. Reduce the oven temperature to 350° F. and continue baking for 45 additional minutes, or until a table knife inserted into the pumpkin filling halfway between the edge and the center of the pie comes out clean.

Remove the pie from the oven and place it on a wire rack to cool. To serve, spoon a large dollop of the Whipped Cream on top of each pie slice. After serving, leftover pie must be refrigerated.

MAKES ONE 9-INCH PIE; 7 SERVINGS

CUSTARD PIE

Baking the pie shell for 7 minutes prior to adding the custard filling, as called for in the recipe that follows, helps reduce the perennial custard pie problem of a soggy bottom crust. Avoiding use of a shiny metal pie pan which reflects the heat will also aid in overcoming the soggy bottom crust difficulty when making custard pies (see page 465 for more on this subject).

Some custard pie bakers advocate baking the pie shell and the custard in separate pie pans and then slipping the baked custard into the baked pie shell. This procedure never appealed to me as a very viable way to beat the soggy bottom crust problem, but some may find it workable.

4 extra-large eggs
⅔ cup sugar
½ teaspoon salt
1½ teaspoons pure vanilla extract
1 9-inch unbaked Pastry Piecrust pie shell (page 460), pricked on the side and bottom (see Baked Pie Shell, page 461, for pricking procedure)
2½ cups whole milk, scalded (page 25)
Ground nutmeg

Preheat the oven to 425° F.

Place the eggs in a medium mixing bowl. Using an electric mixer, beat the eggs slightly on medium speed. Add the sugar, salt, and vanilla; using a spoon, stir until blended; set aside.

Place the unbaked pie shell in the oven and bake for 7 minutes. If any bubbles form in the pastry after a few minutes of baking, prick them with a fork. Meanwhile, scald the milk and pour it slowly into the egg mixture, stirring constantly.

After baking for 7 minutes, remove the pie shell from the oven and place it on a wire rack. Reduce the oven temperature to 350° F. Pour the egg mixture into the pie shell; sprinkle the egg mixture filling with the nutmeg.

Bake the pie for 30 minutes, or until a table knife inserted into the custard filling halfway between the edge and the center of the pie comes out clean. The custard will continue cooking after removal of the pie from the oven, and the center of the pie will fully set. Over-baking will cause the custard to become porous and watery.

Remove the pie from the oven and place it on a wire rack. Let the pie stand until cool; then, refrigerate it immediately. Keep the pie stored in the refrigerator.

MAKES ONE 9-INCH PIE; 7 SERVINGS

SERVING SUGGESTION: Cooled Custard Pie may be garnished with Decorator Whipped Cream (page 374) spooned or piped (using a decorating bag fit with a tip of choice, page 383) over the top. The whipped cream may be sprinkled with ground nutmeg for decoration.

RHUBARB CUSTARD PIE

1⅓ cups sugar
¼ teaspoon salt
¼ teaspoon ground nutmeg
4 cups fresh rhubarb cut into ¾-inch
  lengths
1 tablespoon all-purpose flour
3 extra-large eggs
¼ cup half-and-half
½ teaspoon pure vanilla extract
1 9-inch unbaked Pastry Piecrust pie shell
  (page 460), pricked on the side and
  bottom (see Baked Pie Shell, page 461,
  for pricking procedure)

Preheat the oven to 425° F.

In a small mixing bowl, place the sugar, salt, and nutmeg; stir to combine; set aside. Place the rhubarb in a large mixing bowl. Sprinkle the flour over the rhubarb; toss to coat; set aside.

Place the eggs in a small mixing bowl. Using an electric mixer, beat the eggs slightly on medium speed. Add the half-and-half and vanilla; stir to blend. Add the sugar mixture; stir to combine; set aside.

Place the unbaked pie shell in the oven and bake for 5 minutes. If any bubbles form in the pastry after a few minutes of baking, prick them with a fork. Then, remove the pie shell from the oven and place it on a wire rack; let stand. Reduce the oven temperature to 350° F. Pour the egg mixture over the rhubarb; stir to combine. Spoon the rhubarb mixture evenly into the pie shell.

Bake the pie for 50 to 55 minutes, or until the custard is set. When the fluted edge of the piecrust reaches the desired golden color, cover it with an aluminum foil edge-cover (page 467) to prevent overbrowning. During the last 15 minutes of baking, a piece of aluminum foil may be laid loosely over the entire pie (including the foil edge-cover) to prevent the top of the pie from overbrowning.

When the pie is done, remove the foil from the top (if used) and edge of the pie. Then, remove the pie from the oven and place it on a wire rack. Let the pie stand until cool; then, refrigerate it immediately. Keep the pie stored in the refrigerator.

MAKES ONE 9-INCH PIE; 7 SERVINGS

SERVING SUGGESTION: After the pie has thoroughly cooled in the refrigerator, use a decorating bag fit with large open-star tip number 6B (page 383) and filled with Decorator Whipped Cream (page 374) to pipe attractive garnish on the top of the pie (see pages 388–394 for pictures and procedures).

Syrup-Based Nut Pies

PECAN PIE

4 extra-large eggs
¾ cup sugar
¼ teaspoon salt
1 cup light corn syrup
¼ cup plus 2 tablespoons (6 tablespoons) butter, melted
1 9-inch unbaked Pastry Piecrust pie shell (page 460)
2 cups (8 ounces) uniformly sized pecan halves
1 tablespoon butter, melted

Preheat the oven to 400°F.

Place the eggs in a medium mixing bowl. Using an electric mixer, beat the eggs slightly on medium speed. Add the sugar and salt; beat on medium speed to combine. Add the syrup and 6 tablespoons melted butter; beat until blended. Pour the mixture into the pie shell.

Bake the pie for 10 minutes. Meanwhile, place the pecan halves in a small mixing bowl. Pour 1 tablespoon melted butter over the pecans; toss to coat, being careful not to break or nick the pecans.

After baking for 10 minutes, remove the pie from the oven and place it on a wire rack. Reduce the oven temperature to 350°F. Arrange the pecan halves, side by side in concentric circles, on top of the pie.

Return the pie to the oven and bake for 35 minutes, or until a table knife inserted into the filling halfway between the edge and the center of the pie comes out clean. The filling will continue cooking after removal of the pie from the oven, and the center of the pie will fully set.

Remove the pie from the oven and place it on a wire rack to cool. Serve the pie at room temperature. After serving, leftover pie should be refrigerated.

MAKES ONE 9-INCH PIE; 7 SERVINGS

VARIATIONS: For a quicker but less decorative way to make this Pecan Pie, do not coat the pecans with 1 tablespoon melted butter, or otherwise use the 1 tablespoon butter in the recipe. Add the *uncoated* pecan halves to the egg mixture after all the other ingredients have been blended; using a spoon, stir and fold until the pecans are evenly distributed.

Pour the pecan mixture into the pie shell. Bake the pie at 350°F. for 45 to 50 minutes, or until the filling is set. During baking, the pecan halves will rise to the top of the filling in a random pattern.

BLACK WALNUT PIE: Follow the Pecan Pie recipe, substituting 1 cup dark corn syrup for 1 cup light corn syrup and substituting 2 cups very coarsely broken black walnuts for 2 cups pecan halves. Follow the procedure in Variations, above.

CHOCOLATE PECAN PIE

People who like both pecan pie and chocolate flavor will experience double delight when they savor this double delicious Chocolate Pecan Pie.

¾ cup sugar
1¼ cups dark corn syrup
2 ounces (2 squares) unsweetened chocolate
¼ cup (4 tablespoons) butter
4 extra-large eggs, slightly beaten
1 tablespoon Myers's (dark) rum
2 cups (8 ounces) pecan halves
1 9-inch unbaked Pastry Piecrust pie shell (page 460)
1 recipe Whipped Cream (page 373)

Preheat the oven to 375°F.

In a medium saucepan, place the sugar and syrup; stir to combine. Slowly bring the syrup mixture to a boil over medium-low heat, stirring constantly. Remove from the heat. Add the chocolate and butter; stir until melted and blended. Add about ½ cup of the hot chocolate mixture to the eggs and quickly stir in. Then, add the egg mixture to the remaining chocolate mixture; using a handheld electric mixer, beat on low speed only until blended. Add the rum; using a spoon, stir to blend. Add the pecans; stir to combine. Pour the mixture into the pie shell.

Place the pie in the oven and immediately reduce the oven temperature to 350° F. Bake the pie for 45 to 50 minutes, or until a table knife inserted into the filling halfway between the edge and the center of the pie comes out clean. The filling will continue cooking after removal of the pie from the oven, and the center of the pie will fully set.

Remove the pie from the oven and place it on a wire rack to cool. Serve the pie at room temperature, with a dollop of the Whipped Cream spooned on top of each slice. After serving, left-over pie should be refrigerated.

MAKES ONE 9-INCH PIE; 7 SERVINGS

Chiffon Pies

APRICOT CHIFFON PIE WITH SUGARED VIOLETS

This elegant-looking and -tasting pie is suitable for elaborate dinners and luncheons.

Note: This recipe contains uncooked egg whites (see page 262).

1 6-ounce package dried apricots (about 1 cup packed apricots)
¾ cup water
¼ cup sugar
¼ teaspoon salt
2 teaspoons (1 envelope) unflavored gelatin
3 extra-large eggs, room temperature, separated

2 tablespoons freshly squeezed, strained lemon juice
¼ cup whipping cream, unwhipped
5 drops almond extract
½ cup sugar
1 8-inch baked Pastry Piecrust pie shell (page 460)
1 recipe Decorator Whipped Cream (page 374)
3 dozen Sugared Violets (page 408)

In a small saucepan, place the apricots and ¾ cup water; cover and let stand 1 hour. Then, bring the covered apricot mixture to a boil over high heat; reduce the heat and simmer 12 minutes. Place the apricots and cooking liquid in a blender beaker; using the blender, puree. Measure 1 cup pureed apricots and set aside. (Reserve any remainder for other uses.)

In a small mixing bowl, place ¼ cup sugar, salt, and gelatin; stir to combine; set aside. Place the egg yolks in the top of a double boiler. Using a handheld electric mixer, beat the egg yolks slightly on medium speed. Add the 1 cup pureed apricots and lemon juice; using a spoon, stir to blend. Add the sugar mixture; stir to combine. Place the top of the double boiler over boiling water in the bottom pan. Cook the apricot mixture until thick (about 5 minutes), stirring constantly.

Remove the top of the double boiler from the bottom pan; refrigerate only until the mixture does not feel warm, stirring occasionally during the cooling period.

Meanwhile, pour ¼ cup whipping cream into a small mixing bowl. Using the electric mixer fit with clean, dry blades, beat the cream on medium-high speed until it begins to stiffen. Reduce the mixer speed to medium-low. Add the almond extract; continue beating the cream until stiff, but still soft and fluffy. Cover and refrigerate.

When the apricot mixture has cooled, immediately remove it from the refrigerator; set aside. Place the egg whites in a large mixing bowl. Using a standard-sized electric mixer, beat the

(Recipe continues on next page)

egg whites on high speed until soft peaks hold. While continuing to beat on high speed, very gradually add ½ cup sugar and continue beating the egg white mixture until stiff, but still moist and glossy. Pour the apricot mixture over the egg white mixture. Add the almond-flavored whipped cream. Using a large mixing spoon, fold together.

Turn the filling mixture into the pie shell; using a small, narrow spatula, spread evenly. Refrigerate the pie until the filling is cold and set.

Then, using a decorating bag fit with medium open-star tip number 21 (page 383) and filled with Decorator Whipped Cream, pipe a border of rosettes (page 390) around the edge of the pie, and a circle of swags in the center of the pie. Place a Sugared Violet on top of each rosette, and arrange a few Sugared Violets artistically on the whipped cream swags. Refrigerate the pie and keep stored in the refrigerator.

MAKES ONE 8-INCH PIE; 7 SERVINGS

ALTERNATIVE TOPPING: Using the small, narrow spatula, spread the Decorator Whipped Cream attractively over the entire pie filling. Cut the pie into 7 servings and arrange 5 Sugared Violets on each serving.

DAIQUIRI PIE

A warm-weather pie, coinciding with the time daiquiris are served.

Note: This recipe contains uncooked egg whites (see page 262).

3 tablespoons cold water
2 teaspoons (1 envelope) unflavored gelatin
4 extra-large eggs, room temperature, separated
½ cup sugar
Dash of salt
2 teaspoons finely grated lime rind (page 47)
¼ cup freshly squeezed, strained lime juice

½ cup light rum
5 drops green liquid food coloring (optional)
½ cup sugar
1 9-inch baked Pastry Piecrust pie shell (page 460)
1 recipe Decorator Whipped Cream (page 374)
7 Lime Twists (page 401) for decoration

Pour 3 tablespoons cold water into a small sauce dish. Sprinkle the gelatin over the water; let stand 15 minutes.

Place the egg yolks in the top of a double boiler. Using a handheld electric mixer, beat the egg yolks slightly on medium speed. Add ½ cup sugar, salt, lime rind, lime juice, and the gelatin mixture; stir to combine. Place the top of the double boiler over boiling water in the bottom pan. Cook the lime mixture until very thick (about 7 minutes), stirring constantly.

Remove the top of the double boiler from the bottom pan and place it on a wire rack; let stand until the lime mixture cools to room temperature, stirring intermittently. (The lime mixture may be refrigerated to hasten cooling; however, watch carefully to prevent it from becoming too cool and gelling; stir intermittently.)

When the lime mixture has cooled to room temperature, add the rum and food coloring; stir until completely blended; set aside. Place the egg whites in a large mixing bowl. Using a standard-sized electric mixer, beat the egg whites on high speed until soft peaks hold. While continuing to beat on high speed, very gradually add ½ cup sugar and continue beating the egg white mixture until stiff, but still moist and glossy. Pour the lime mixture over the egg white mixture; using a large mixing spoon, fold in.

Turn the filling mixture into the pie shell; using a small, narrow spatula, spread smoothly. Refrigerate the pie until the filling is cold and set.

Then, spoon the Decorator Whipped Cream over the top of the pie; using the small, narrow spatula, spread attractively over the entire surface of the filling. Arrange the 7 Lime Twists uniformly around the top of the pie in such a way that 1 Twist will be centered on the top of each of 7 slices of pie. (Or, place 1 Lime Twist on the top of each serving of pie after it is cut.) Refrigerate the pie and keep stored in the refrigerator.

MAKES ONE 9-INCH PIE; 7 SERVINGS

BLACK BOTTOM PIE

Note: This recipe contains uncooked egg whites (see page 262).

¼ cup cold water
2 teaspoons (1 envelope) unflavored gelatin
1½ ounces (1½ squares) unsweetened chocolate
4 extra-large eggs, room temperature
½ cup sugar
1 tablespoon plus 1 teaspoon cornstarch
2 cups whole milk, scalded (page 25)
1 teaspoon pure vanilla extract
1 10-inch baked Gingersnap Crust pie shell (page 474)
2 tablespoons Myers's (dark) rum
½ cup sugar
½ recipe Decorator Whipped Cream (page 374)
Shaved Chocolate (page 408) for decoration

Pour ¼ cup water into a small sauce dish. Sprinkle the gelatin over the water; set aside. Cut the unsweetened chocolate into small pieces; place in a small mixing bowl; set aside. Separate the eggs, placing the egg whites in a large mixing bowl and the egg yolks in a small mixing bowl. Set the egg whites aside. Using an electric mixer, beat the egg yolks slightly on medium speed; set aside.

In the top of a double boiler, place ½ cup sugar and cornstarch; stir to combine. Add the scalded milk; stir well. Place the top of the double boiler over boiling water in the bottom pan.

Cook the cornstarch mixture until it thickens (about 5 minutes), stirring constantly.

Remove the entire double boiler pan from the heat; let stand. Add about ½ cup of the hot cornstarch mixture to the egg yolks and quickly stir in. Then, add the egg yolk mixture to the remaining cornstarch mixture and stir vigorously to blend. Return the entire double boiler pan to the heat. While stirring constantly, cook the mixture over simmering water until the mixture coats a spoon (about 2 minutes).

Remove the entire double boiler pan from the heat. Add 1 measured cup of the hot cornstarch mixture to the chocolate pieces; stir until the chocolate melts. Add the vanilla; stir until blended.

Pour the chocolate mixture into the pie shell. Place the pie on a wire rack; set aside.

Add the gelatin mixture to the remaining cornstarch mixture; stir until the gelatin fully dissolves. Remove the top of the double boiler from the bottom pan and place it on a wire rack. Add the rum; stir until well blended. Let the rum mixture stand until cooled to room temperature, stirring occasionally. (The rum mixture may be refrigerated to expedite cooling; however, watch carefully to prevent it from becoming too cool and gelling; stir intermittently.)

Then, using the electric mixer fit with clean, dry blades, beat the egg whites on high speed until soft peaks hold. While continuing to beat on high speed, very gradually add ½ cup sugar and continue beating the egg white mixture until stiff, but still moist and glossy. Pour the rum mixture over the egg white mixture; using a large mixing spoon, fold in, carefully and quickly.

Place the egg white mixture over the chocolate layer in the pie shell; using a small, narrow spatula, spread evenly. Refrigerate the pie until the filling is cold and set.

Then, using a decorating bag fit with large open-star tip number 6B (page 383) and filled with Decorator Whipped Cream, pipe a shell border (page 389) around the edge of the pie and a large rosette (page 390) in the center of

(Recipe continues on next page)

the pie. Scatter the Shaved Chocolate over the pie filling between the piped whipped cream border and the center. Refrigerate the pie and keep stored in the refrigerator.

MAKES ONE 10-INCH PIE; 8 SERVINGS

ALTERNATIVE TOPPING: Spoon the Decorator Whipped Cream over the top of the pie; using the small, narrow spatula, spread smoothly over the entire surface of the filling. Decorate with the Shaved Chocolate, if desired.

EGGNOG CHIFFON PIE

An elegant holiday menu item with a modern tone.

Note: This recipe contains uncooked egg whites (see page 262).

¼ cup cold water
1 tablespoon (exactly) unflavored gelatin
4 extra-large eggs, room temperature
¼ cup sugar
¼ teaspoon salt
1¼ cups whole milk, scalded (page 25)
⅓ cup light rum (or 2 teaspoons rum flavoring)
½ teaspoon ground nutmeg
½ cup sugar
1 9-inch Baked Nutmeg Graham Cracker Crust pie shell (page 472)
1 recipe Decorator Whipped Cream (page 374)
Ground nutmeg for decoration

Pour ¼ cup cold water into a small sauce dish. Sprinkle the gelatin over the water; let stand 15 minutes. Separate the eggs, placing the egg whites in a large mixing bowl and the egg yolks in a small mixing bowl. Set the egg whites aside. Using an electric mixer, beat the egg yolks slightly on medium speed; set aside.

In the top of a double boiler, place ¼ cup sugar, salt, and hot, scalded milk; stir well to combine. Add about ½ cup of the hot milk

mixture to the egg yolks and quickly stir in. Then, add the egg yolk mixture to the remaining milk mixture and stir vigorously to blend. Place the top of the double boiler over simmering water in the bottom pan. Cook the mixture 3 minutes, stirring constantly. (The mixture will be slightly thickened.) Do not overcook the mixture, causing it to curdle (see Note).

Remove the top of the double boiler from the bottom pan and place it on a wire rack. Add the gelatin mixture to the hot mixture; stir until the gelatin fully dissolves. Add the rum and ½ teaspoon nutmeg; stir until well blended and combined. Refrigerate the rum mixture and stir intermittently until the mixture mounds when dropped from the spoon (about 1½ hours). Be careful not to let the mixture fully set.

Remove the rum mixture from the refrigerator. Using a handheld electric mixer, beat the mixture briefly on high speed until smooth; set aside.

Using the electric mixer fit with clean, dry blades, beat the egg whites on high speed until soft peaks hold. While continuing to beat on high speed, very gradually add ½ cup sugar and continue beating the egg white mixture until stiff, but still moist and glossy. Pour the rum mixture over the egg white mixture; using a large mixing spoon, fold in.

Turn the filling mixture into the pie shell; using a small, narrow spatula, spread smoothly, mounding slightly in the center of the pie. Refrigerate the pie until the filling is cold and set.

Then, spoon the Decorator Whipped Cream over the top of the pie; using the small, narrow spatula, spread attractively over the entire surface of the filling. Sprinkle the nutmeg sparingly over the whipped cream topping. Refrigerate the pie and keep stored in the refrigerator.

NOTE: Despite careful timing, if the mixture should begin to curdle, immediately remove the top of the double boiler from the bottom pan and beat the mixture until smooth, using a handheld electric mixer on high speed.

MAKES ONE 9-INCH PIE; 7 SERVINGS

OPTIONAL DECORATION: Reserve ½ of the Decorator Whipped Cream. Using the small, narrow spatula, spread the remaining ½ of the Decorator Whipped Cream smoothly over the pie filling. Sprinkle the nutmeg sparingly over the center ⅔ of the whipped cream-topped pie. Using a decorating bag fit with medium-large open-star tip number 32 (page 383) and filled with the reserved Decorator Whipped Cream, pipe 2 small, contiguous shell borders (page 389) around the edge of the pie, over the whipped cream topping.

MELINDA'S PUMPKIN CHIFFON PIE

This is a rich, smashing alternative to conventional pumpkin pie.

Note: This recipe contains uncooked egg whites (see page 262).

¼ cup whole milk
2 teaspoons (1 envelope) unflavored
  gelatin
3 extra-large eggs, room temperature,
  separated
¾ cup packed light brown sugar
½ teaspoon salt
1 teaspoon ground cinnamon
½ teaspoon ground nutmeg
¼ teaspoon ground ginger
½ cup whole milk
1¼ cups commercially canned pumpkin
½ cup granulated sugar
1 9-inch Baked Graham Cracker Crust pie
  shell (page 472)
1 recipe Decorator Whipped Cream
  (page 374)
Ground nutmeg for decoration

Pour ¼ cup milk into a small sauce dish. Sprinkle the gelatin over the milk; let stand for 15 minutes.

Place the egg yolks in the top of a double boiler. Using a handheld electric mixer, beat the egg yolks slightly on medium speed. Add the brown sugar, salt, cinnamon, ½ teaspoon nutmeg, and the ginger; stir to combine. Add ½ cup milk; stir well. Place the top of the double boiler over simmering water in the bottom pan. Cook the mixture until thick (about 8 minutes), alternately and constantly stirring with a spoon and beating with the electric mixer on low speed. Add the gelatin mixture; stir until well blended.

Remove the top of the double boiler from the bottom pan and place it on a wire rack. Add the pumpkin; stir until evenly blended. Refrigerate the pumpkin mixture until cooled to room temperature.

Then, remove the pumpkin mixture from the refrigerator; set aside. Place the egg whites in a large mixing bowl. Using a standard-sized electric mixer, beat the egg whites on high speed until soft peaks hold. While continuing to beat on high speed, very gradually add ½ cup granulated sugar and continue beating the egg white mixture until stiff, but still moist and glossy. Pour the pumpkin mixture over the egg white mixture; using a large mixing spoon, fold in.

Turn the filling mixture into the pie shell; using a small, narrow spatula, spread evenly, mounding slightly in the center of the pie. Refrigerate the pie until the filling is cold and set.

Reserve a portion of the Decorator Whipped Cream; using the small, narrow spatula, swirl the remainder over the pie filling. Using a decorating bag fit with large open-star tip number 6B (page 383) and filled with the reserved Decorator Whipped Cream, pipe a zigzag border (page 389) around the pie. Using your fingers, sprinkle the nutmeg very sparingly over the center of the pie. Refrigerate the pie and keep stored in the refrigerator.

To serve, cut smaller than usual pieces of this rich pie.

MAKES ONE 9-INCH PIE; 8 OR 9 SERVINGS

LEMON CHIFFON PIE

I have served this pie more often at dinner parties than any other pie. It is my favorite, and it won the blue ribbon for Best Chiffon Pie, at the 1988 Iowa State Fair.

Note: This recipe contains uncooked egg whites (see page 262).

⅓ cup cold water
2¼ teaspoons (exactly) unflavored gelatin
4 extra-large eggs, room temperature, separated
1 teaspoon finely grated lemon rind (page 47) (rind of about 1 lemon)
3 tablespoons freshly squeezed, strained lemon juice
Dash of salt
½ cup sugar
½ cup sugar
1 9-inch baked Pastry Piecrust pie shell (page 460)
1 recipe Decorator Whipped Cream (page 374)

Pour ⅓ cup cold water into a small sauce dish. Sprinkle the gelatin over the water; let stand 15 minutes.

In the top of a double boiler, place the egg yolks, lemon rind, lemon juice, and salt; using a handheld electric mixer, beat slightly on medium speed. Add ½ cup sugar; beat on low speed to blend. Place the top of the double boiler over boiling water in the bottom pan. Cook the lemon mixture until very thick (about 5 minutes), stirring constantly. Add the gelatin mixture; stir until completely dissolved and blended.

Remove the top of the double boiler from the bottom pan; refrigerate until the lemon mixture cools to room temperature, stirring occasionally.

Then, remove the lemon mixture from the refrigerator; set aside. Place the egg whites in a large mixing bowl. Using a standard-sized electric mixer, beat the egg whites on high speed until soft peaks hold. While continuing to beat on high speed, very gradually add ½ cup sugar and continue beating the egg white mixture until stiff, but still moist and glossy. Pour the lemon mixture over the egg white mixture; using a large mixing spoon, fold in.

Using the mixing spoon, pile the filling mixture high into the pie shell, mounding in the center; using a small, narrow spatula, smooth the surface. Refrigerate the pie until the filling is cold and set.

Then, spoon Decorator Whipped Cream over the pie filling; using the small, narrow spatula, spread smoothly. Refrigerate the pie and keep stored in the refrigerator.

MAKES ONE 9-INCH PIE; 7 SERVINGS

OPTIONAL DECORATION: Reserve a portion of the Decorator Whipped Cream; using a small, narrow spatula, spread the remainder smoothly over the top of the pie. Using paste food coloring, tint part of the reserved whipped cream pale yellow. Fit 2 decorating bags with medium-large open-star tips number 32 (page 383). Fill 1 decorating bag with white whipped cream and the other with pale yellow whipped cream. Pipe a white, shell border around the edge of the pie and a large rosette in the center of the pie. Then, pipe pale yellow decorations of choice on the pie. (See pages 389–390 for illustrations and procedures for the shell border, the rosette, and other decorations.)

PINEAPPLE CHIFFON PIE

Note: This recipe contains uncooked egg whites (see page 262).

1 8¼-ounce can commercial crushed
    pineapple in heavy syrup
⅓ cup cold water
1 tablespoon (exactly) unflavored gelatin
4 extra-large eggs, room temperature,
    separated
⅓ cup granulated sugar
¼ teaspoon salt
1 tablespoon freshly squeezed, strained
    lemon juice
1 cup (½ pint) whipping cream, unwhipped
½ cup granulated sugar
1 9-inch baked Pastry Piecrust pie shell
    (page 460)
2 tablespoons powdered sugar
½ teaspoon pure vanilla extract

Place the crushed pineapple, including the syrup, in a blender beaker; using the blender, puree; set aside. Pour ⅓ cup cold water into a small sauce dish. Sprinkle the gelatin over the water; let stand 15 minutes.

Place the egg yolks in the top of a double boiler. Using a handheld electric mixer, beat the egg yolks slightly on medium speed. Add ⅓ cup granulated sugar, salt, lemon juice, and pureed pineapple; beat on low speed to blend. Place the top of the double boiler over boiling water in the bottom pan. Cook the pineapple mixture until thick (about 5 minutes), stirring constantly. Add the gelatin mixture; stir until well blended.

Remove the top of the double boiler from the bottom pan; refrigerate until the pineapple mixture is slightly cooler than room temperature, stirring occasionally.

Meanwhile, pour the whipping cream into a medium mixing bowl. Using a standard-sized electric mixer, beat the cream on medium-high speed until it begins to stiffen. Reduce the mixer speed to medium-low and continue beat-ing the cream until stiff, but still soft and fluffy; cover and refrigerate.

When the pineapple mixture has cooled to slightly cooler than room temperature, remove it from the refrigerator; set aside. Place the egg whites in a large mixing bowl. Using the standard-sized electric mixer fit with clean, dry blades, beat the egg whites on high speed until soft peaks hold. While continuing to beat on high speed, very gradually add ½ cup granulated sugar and continue beating the egg white mixture until stiff, but still moist and glossy. Spoon ½ of the whipped cream over the egg white mixture. Cover and refrigerate the remaining ½ of the whipped cream. Pour the pineapple mixture over the egg white mixture and whipped cream; using a large mixing spoon, quickly fold together.

Turn the filling mixture into the pie shell; using a small, narrow spatula, spread evenly, mounding slightly in the center of the pie. Refrigerate the pie until the filling is cold and set.

Then, remove the reserved ½ of the whipped cream from the refrigerator. Add the powdered sugar and vanilla; using the standard-sized electric mixer fit with clean, dry blades, beat *briefly* on low speed to blend. Spoon the whipped cream over the pie filling; using a small, narrow spatula, spread smoothly and evenly. Refrigerate the pie and keep stored in the refrigerator.

MAKES ONE 9-INCH PIE; 7 SERVINGS

OPTIONAL DECORATION: Using paste food coloring, tint ½ recipe Decorator Whipped Cream (page 374) pale yellow. Using a decorating bag fit with medium-large open-star tip number 32 (page 383) and filled with the tinted Decorator Whipped Cream, decorate the whipped cream-topped pie with piped rosettes (page 390) and/or swags.

REGAL GRAPE CHIFFON PIE

Note: This recipe contains uncooked egg whites (see page 262).

4 cups stemmed Concord grapes
$1/3$ cup sugar
$1/4$ teaspoon salt
1 tablespoon (exactly) unflavored gelatin
4 extra-large eggs, room temperature, separated
2 tablespoons freshly squeezed, strained lemon juice
$1/2$ cup whipping cream, unwhipped
$1/3$ cup sugar
1 9-inch baked Pastry Piecrust pie shell (page 460)
1 recipe Decorator Whipped Cream (page 374)
Violet-colored paste food coloring (optional)

Place small bunches of the grapes in a colander; wash under running cold water. Stem the grapes, selecting out only the fully ripened, unblemished fruit. Measure 4 cups stemmed grapes. Place the grapes in a large, flat-bottomed pan; using a potato masher, crush the grapes slightly. Place the crushed grapes in a heavy-bottomed kettle. Bring the grapes to a simmer over high heat, stirring constantly. Reduce the heat and cover the kettle. Cook the grapes at a low simmer 10 minutes, stirring frequently.

Press the cooked grapes through a food mill to remove the seeds, pressing through as much of the skins as possible. Measure $1/2$ cups grape puree; set aside. (Reserve any remaining puree for other uses.)

In a small mixing bowl, place $1/3$ cup sugar, salt, and gelatin; stir to combine; set aside.

Place the egg yolks in the top of a double boiler. Using a handheld electric mixer, beat the egg yolks slightly on medium speed. Add the $1/2$ cups grape puree and lemon juice; using a spoon, stir until blended. Add the gelatin mixture; stir to combine. Place the top of the dou-

ble boiler over boiling water in the bottom pan. Cook the grape mixture until thick (about 8 minutes), stirring constantly.

Remove the top of the double boiler from the bottom pan and place it on a wire rack. Let stand until the grape mixture cools slightly; then, refrigerate until the grape mixture cools to room temperature, stirring occasionally.

Meanwhile, pour $1/2$ cup whipping cream into a small mixing bowl. Using a standard-sized electric mixer, beat the cream on medium-high speed until it begins to stiffen. Reduce the mixer speed to medium-low and continue beating the cream until stiff, but still soft and fluffy; cover and refrigerate.

When the grape mixture has cooled to room temperature, remove it from the refrigerator; set aside. Place the egg whites in a large mixing bowl. Using the standard-sized electric mixer fit with clean, dry blades, beat the egg whites on high speed until soft peaks hold. While continuing to beat on high speed, very gradually add $1/3$ cup sugar and continue beating the egg white mixture until stiff, but still moist and glossy. Add the whipped cream and grape mixture to the egg white mixture; using a large mixing spoon, carefully fold together only until the mixtures are combined and the color is uniform.

Turn the filling mixture into the pie shell; using a small, narrow spatula, spread evenly, mounding slightly in the center of the pie. Refrigerate the pie until the filling is cold and set.

Then, make the Decorator Whipped Cream and tint $1/2$ of it pale violet to match the pie filling. Using a small, narrow spatula, frost the entire pie filling evenly and smoothly with the white whipped cream. Using a decorating bag fit with medium-large open-star tip number 32 (page 383) and filled with the tinted whipped cream, decorate the top of the frosted pie with a piped border of rosettes (page 390) and a piped ring of swags around the center of the pie. Refrigerate the pie and keep stored in the refrigerator.

MAKES ONE 9-INCH PIE; SERVES 7

TANGERINE CHIFFON PIE

Just the name of this pie sounds inviting, and the results fulfill expectations.

Note: This recipe contains uncooked egg whites (see page 262).

1¼ cup freshly squeezed, strained tangerine juice (about 8 medium-sized Clementine tangerines [mandarins]*), divided
2½ teaspoons (exactly) unflavored gelatin
2 teaspoons finely grated tangerine rind (page 47)
1 tablespoon freshly squeezed, strained lemon juice
2 tablespoons sugar
¼ teaspoon salt
4 extra-large eggs, room temperature, separated
Orange-colored paste food coloring
⅓ cup sugar
1 9-inch baked Pastry Piecrust pie shell (page 460)
1 recipe Orange Decorator Whipped Cream (page 374)
1 11-ounce can commercial mandarin orange segments, well drained

Clementine is a variety of mandarins; however, mandarins are popularly known as tangerines in the United States. If Clementine tangerines are not available, any other variety of tangerines may be substituted.

Pour ¼ cup tangerine juice into a small sauce dish. Sprinkle the gelatin over the juice; let stand 15 minutes.

In the top of a double boiler, place the remaining 1 cup tangerine juice, tangerine rind, lemon juice, 2 tablespoons sugar, salt, and egg yolks; using a handheld electric mixer, beat on medium speed until well combined. Place the top of the double boiler over boiling water in the bottom pan. Cook the tangerine mixture until thick (about 8 minutes), stirring constantly. Add the gelatin mixture; stir until completely dissolved and blended.

Remove the top of the double boiler from the bottom pan and place it on a wire rack. Add a *very small* amount of orange food coloring; using the electric mixer, beat on medium speed until the mixture is uniformly colored. Refrigerate the tangerine mixture until slightly cooler than room temperature, stirring occasionally.

Then, remove the tangerine mixture from the refrigerator; set aside. Place the egg whites in a large mixing bowl. Using a standard-sized electric mixer, beat the egg whites on high speed until soft peaks hold. While continuing to beat on high speed, very gradually add ⅓ cup sugar and continue beating the egg white mixture until stiff, but still moist and glossy. Pour the tangerine mixture over the egg white mixture; using a large mixing spoon, quickly fold in until evenly combined.

Spoon the tangerine mixture into the pie shell; using a small, narrow spatula, spread smoothly, mounding in the center of the pie. Refrigerate the pie until the filling is cold and set.

Then, spoon the Orange-Flavored Decorator Whipped Cream over the pie filling; using a small, narrow spatula, spread attractively over the pie. Place the mandarin orange segments randomly over the whipped cream topping. (Reserve the remaining mandarin orange segments for other uses.) Refrigerate the pie and keep stored in the refrigerator.

MAKES ONE 9-INCH PIE; 7 SERVINGS

KAHLÚA PIE

Note: This recipe contains uncooked egg whites (see page 262).

½ cup strong coffee, cold
2 teaspoons (1 envelope) unflavored gelatin
4 extra-large eggs, room temperature, separated
⅓ cup sugar
Dash of salt
3 tablespoons Kahlúa (page 23)
3 tablespoons Irish whiskey
½ cup whipping cream, unwhipped
⅓ cup sugar
1 9-inch Baked Nutmeg Graham Cracker Crust pie shell (page 472)
1 recipe Decorator Whipped Cream (page 374)
Powdered instant coffee for decoration (to powder instant coffee process in blender*)

If a blender is not available, a food processor may be used; however, it is difficult to achieve a find powder using a food processor. Reserve any remaining powdered instant coffee for other uses, such as flavoring whipped cream (see Filling recipe, page 561).

Pour the coffee into a small sauce dish. Sprinkle the gelatin over the coffee; let stand 15 minutes.

Place the egg yolks in the top of a double boiler. Using a handheld electric mixer, beat the egg yolks slightly on medium speed. Add ⅓ cup sugar, salt, and gelatin mixture; using the electric mixer, beat briefly on low speed until blended. Place the top of the double boiler over boiling water in the bottom pan. Cook the mixture until very thick (about 7 minutes), stirring constantly.

Remove the top of the double boiler from the bottom pan and place it on a wire rack. Add the Kahlúa and Irish whiskey; using the electric mixer, beat on low speed only until blended. Refrigerate the Kahlúa mixture until lukewarm,

stirring occasionally; do not allow the mixture to gel.

Meanwhile, pour ½ cup whipping cream into a small mixing bowl. Using a standard-sized electric mixer, beat the cream on medium-high speed until it begins to stiffen. Reduce the mixer speed to medium-low and continue beating the cream until stiff, but still soft and fluffy; cover and refrigerate.

When the Kahlúa mixture cools to lukewarm, remove it from the refrigerator; set aside. Place the egg whites in a large mixing bowl. Using the standard-sized electric mixer fit with clean, dry blades, beat the egg whites on high speed until soft peaks hold. While continuing to beat on high speed, very gradually add ⅓ cup sugar and continue beating the egg white mixture until stiff, but still moist and glossy. Add the whipped cream and Kahlúa mixture to the egg white mixture; using a large mixing spoon, fold together.

Spoon the filling mixture into the pie shell; using a small, narrow spatula, spread evenly and smoothly, mounding slightly in the center of the pie. Refrigerate the pie until the filling is cold and set.

Then, using a decorating bag fit with large open-star tip number 6B (page 383), pipe a reverse shell border (page 390) of Decorator Whipped Cream around the edge of the pie and in a small circle around the center of the pie. Sprinkle the powdered instant coffee sparingly over the piped whipped cream. Refrigerate the pie and keep stored in the refrigerator. Cut the pie into 8 servings, as it is very rich.

MAKES ONE 9-INCH PIE; 8 SERVINGS

ALTERNATIVE TOPPING: Spoon the Decorator Whipped Cream over the top of the pie; using a small, narrow spatula, spread evenly over the entire surface of the filling. Sprinkle the powdered instant coffee over the whipped cream topping.

Cheese Pies

CHERRY CHEESE PIE

For years, I made these Cherry Cheese Pies at Christmastime and delivered them to close friends for their holiday dining. If you decide to do the same, coax your commercial baker into selling you pie containers. Just before you leave to deliver your goodies, place the pies in the containers and decorate the tops with a few red and green satin ribbons. Once you initiate this tradition, your friends will hope for repeat performances year after year.

12 ounces cream cheese, softened
½ cup sugar
2 extra-large eggs
½ teaspoon pure vanilla extract
1 9-inch Unbaked Graham Cracker Crust
    pie shell (page 471)
Cherry Topping (recipe follows)

Preheat the oven to 350° F.

In a medium mixing bowl, place the cream cheese and sugar; using an electric mixer, beat on high speed only until the mixture is completely smooth. Stop the electric mixer. Add the eggs and vanilla; beat on medium speed only until blended. Pour the cheese mixture into the pie shell.

Bake the pie for 30 minutes, until set. Remove the pie from the oven and place it on a wire rack. Let stand to cool slightly; then refrigerate.

When the pie is cold, make the Cherry Topping. When the topping has cooled, remove the pie from the refrigerator and spoon the topping over the cheese filling. Distribute the cherries and glaze evenly over the pie. Refrigerate the pie. Allow the topping to set before serving. Keep the pie stored in the refrigerator.

MAKES ONE 9-INCH PIE; 9 SERVINGS

NOTE: Cherry Cheese Pie may be made the day before serving. It keeps very well for 2 or 3 days.

Cherry Topping

2 cups pitted, tart, fresh red cherries (or 1
    1-pound bag frozen red cherries, thawed)
½ cup juice drained from cherries
2 tablespoons sugar
1 tablespoon cornstarch
¼ teaspoon almond extract
Red liquid food coloring (optional)

Drain the cherries well in a sieve, reserving the juice. Measure ½ cup reserved juice, adding water, if necessary, to make ½ cup liquid; set aside.

In a small saucepan, place the sugar and cornstarch; stir to combine. Add the ½ cup reserved juice; stir well. Bring the mixture to a simmer over medium heat, stirring constantly. Simmer the mixture until thick and translucent (about 1½ minutes), stirring continuously. Remove from the heat and place the saucepan on a wire rack. Add the cherries and almond extract; stir to combine. Add a few drops of red food coloring; stir to blend. Let the mixture stand to cool until close to room temperature.

OPTIONAL DECORATION: After the Cherry Topping has set, pipe small, contiguous rosettes (page 390) around the edge of the pie, using a decorating bag fit with medium-small open-star tip number 18 (page 383) and filled with 8 ounces of soft-style cream cheese.

STRAWBERRY CHEESE PIE

1 recipe Cherry Cheese Pie (recipe, above)
Strawberry Topping (recipe follows)

Follow the Cherry Cheese Pie recipe, substituting Strawberry Topping for Cherry Topping.

(Recipe continues on next page)

Strawberry Topping

4 cups fresh strawberries cut in half,
  lengthwise
2 tablespoons sugar
2 teaspoons cornstarch
Red liquid food coloring (optional)

Arrange 2½ cups of the strawberries, cut-side
down, in concentric circles on top of the cold
cheese pie; refrigerate.

Place the remaining 1½ cups of the strawberries in a blender beaker; using the blender,
puree. Strain the pureed strawberries through a
piece of damp cotton flannel secured, napped
side up, in a sieve over a bowl. Measure ½ cup
strawberry juice, adding water, if necessary, to
make ½ cup liquid; set aside.

In a small saucepan, place the sugar and cornstarch; stir to combine. Add the ½ cup strawberry juice; stir well. Bring the mixture to a
simmer over medium heat, stirring constantly.
Simmer the mixture until thick and translucent
(about 1½ minutes), stirring continuously.
Remove from the heat and place the saucepan
on a wire rack. Add a few drops of red food coloring; stir to blend. Let the mixture stand to
cool slightly.

Spoon the slightly cooled glaze evenly over
the cold pie. Refrigerate the pie and keep stored
in the refrigerator.

MAKES ONE 9-INCH PIE; 9 SERVINGS

RED RASPBERRY CHEESE PIE

1 recipe Strawberry Cheese Pie (recipe,
  above)
4 cups whole, fresh red raspberries

Follow the Strawberry Cheese Pie recipe, substituting 4 cups red raspberries for 4 cups strawberries. Cover the top of the cheese pie with
raspberries arranged, stem end down, in concentric circles. Puree the remainder of the raspberries in a blender and follow the Strawberry
Topping recipe, using the same juice, sugar, and

cornstarch quantities. The addition of red food
coloring is optional.

MAKES ONE 9-INCH PIE; 9 SERVINGS

BLUEBERRY CHEESE PIE

1 recipe Strawberry Cheese Pie (recipe,
  above)
4 cups whole, fresh blueberries

Follow the Strawberrry Cheese Pie recipe, substituting 4 cups blueberries for 4 cups strawberries. Cover the top of the cheese pie with a
single layer of blueberries. Puree the remainder
of the blueberries in a blender and follow the
Strawberry Topping recipe, using the same juice,
sugar, and cornstarch quantities. Eliminate the
food coloring.

MAKES ONE 9-INCH PIE; 9 SERVINGS

Tarts

TYPES OF DESSERT TARTS

The word "tart" is used to describe two types of
pastry desserts. Neither type rivals standard pie
in popularity across the Midwest.

CLASSICAL TARTS: Classical tarts are European-
style, pielike pastries made with a rich, buttery,
single crust similar in composition and texture
to a cookie. The sides of the crust are short in
height (about ¾ to 1 inch), often fluted, and are
perpendicular to the bottom of the tart. Classical tarts are commonly made in special, round
tart pans with removable bottoms. These special

pans are available in many sizes. Classical tarts also may be made in a flan ring placed on a cookie sheet, which serves as the bottom of the pan. Flan rings are available in round, rectangular, and square shapes.

Classical tarts are generally filled with large pieces of artistically arranged poached or fresh fruit which are covered with a translucent glaze. Often, the fruit is arranged over a medium-thin layer of cream filling (commonly, vanilla flavor) spread over the bottom of the crust.

In the Midwest, classical tarts are most often prepared by people with recent European backgrounds or by native Midwesterners who have discovered these exquisite pastries in their travels abroad or in European restaurants in this country.

SMALL, STANDARD PIES: The word "tart" is commonly used to describe individual serving-sized standard pies made in regular, small pie pans of 3 to 4½ inches diameter with slanted sides. The crusts and fillings for these tarts are identical to those used in making standard-sized pies. They are simply prepared in small pie pans.

VANILLA CREAM TART FILLING

Classical tarts often contain a layer of rich vanilla cream underneath a top layer of beautifully arranged glazed fruit (see Classical Tarts, page 510). The recipe for vanilla cream that follows is especially for that use. It is made more rich than the vanilla cream used in making standard cream pies such as Coconut Cream Pie (page 490) and Banana Cream Pie (page 491), by substituting half-and-half for whole milk, and by using proportionately more egg yolks, sugar, and flavoring. This Vanilla Cream Tart Filling recipe is called for in the recipes for Apple Tart (page 512), Pear Tart (page 513), Strawberry Tart (page 513), and Three-Fruit Tart with Peach Schnapps Glaze (page 515).

⅓ cup sugar
2 tablespoons plus 2 teaspoons cornstarch
⅛ teaspoon salt
1 cup half-and-half
3 extra-large egg yolks, slightly beaten
2 teaspoons butter
1½ teaspoons pure vanilla extract
¼ teaspoon almond extract

In the top of a double boiler, place the sugar, cornstarch, and salt; stir to combine. Add the half-and-half; stir well. Place the top of the double boiler over boiling water in the bottom pan. Cook the cornstarch mixture until very thick (about 4 to 5 minutes), constantly beating with a handheld electric mixer on low speed or stirring with a spoon. Add about ⅓ cup of the hot cornstarch mixture to the egg yolks and quickly stir in. Then, add the egg yolk mixture to the remaining cornstarch mixture and stir vigorously to blend. Cook the mixture 2 minutes, beating constantly with the electric mixer on low speed.

Remove the top of the double boiler from the bottom pan and place it on a wire rack. Add the butter and vanilla; using the electric mixer, beat on medium speed until blended. Refrigerate the mixture until cooled to room temperature, stirring occasionally.

Then, remove the mixture from the refrigerator. Spoon the mixture into the baked tart shell, following the procedures in a particular tart recipe.

Tarts containing Vanilla Cream Tart Filling must be kept refrigerated.

MAKES ENOUGH FOR USE IN ONE 9-INCH TART

APPLE TART

Exercise your artistic inclinations by creating a picture-perfect arrangement of apples on this exquisite tart (see illustration, page 458).

8 cups cold water
1 tablespoon white vinegar
1 tablespoon salt
1 pound Golden Delicious apples (about 3 large apples)*
5 cups water
1 cup sugar
1 9-inch baked Classical Tart Pastry shell (page 468)
1 recipe Vanilla Cream Tart FIlling (page 511)
1 tablespoon cold water
1½ teaspoons (exactly) unflavored gelatin
1 teaspoon sugar
½ teaspoon arrowroot (page 19)
½ cup apple jelly, home canned (page 739) or commercially canned
1 recipe Decorator Whipped Cream (page 374)
Ground cinnamon for garnish

Home-canned Apples (page 712) may be substituted (no additional cooking is required; they are ready for slicing).

THE DAY BEFORE SERVING: In a small kettle or large mixing bowl, place 8 cups cold water, vinegar, and salt; stir until the salt dissolves; set aside. Wash the apples; pare and immediately drop them into the vinegar solution to prevent discoloration. Quarter and core the apples, continuing to retain the prepared fruit in the vinegar solution; set aside.

In a large saucepan, place 5 cups water and 1 cup sugar; stir to combine. Bring the mixture to a boil over high heat, stirring until the sugar dissolves. Reduce the heat and simmer the syrup 3 minutes, stirring occasionally. Then, increase the heat to high and return the syrup to a full boil.

Meanwhile, drain the apples and *thoroughly rinse* them twice in cold water. Place the rinsed apples in the boiling syrup. When the syrup returns to a boil, boil the apples 5 minutes, using a wooden mixing spoon to turn the apples occasionally.

Drain the apples in a colander, reserving the syrup. Run cold water over the apples to stop the cooking. Place the drained apples in a bowl or plastic storage container. Let the apples stand, uncovered, until cooled to nearly room temperature. Let the reserved syrup stand in a separate container, also to cool to nearly room temperature. When the apples and syrup have cooled, pour the syrup over the apples; cover and refrigerate.

The Classical Tart Pastry shell may be baked the day before serving, if desired. If baked a day in advance, let the baked tart shell stand on a wire rack until completely cool. Then, place the tart shell (pan rim and bottom *unremoved*) in an airtight container; store at room temperature.

THE DAY OF SERVING: Make the Vanilla Cream Tart Filling. Spoon the room-temperature filling into the baked tart shell, leaving the removable rim on the tart pan; using a small, narrow spatula, spread evenly. Refrigerate, uncovered, until the filling is cold and set.

Drain the apple quarters in the colander, reserving the syrup for other uses. Place the drained apples between 3 layers of paper towels to dry. On a cutting board, using a small, sharp, thin-bladed knife, carefully cut the apple quarters *lengthwise* into thin, uniform slices ¼ inch thick on the outside, wide edge of the slices. Arrange the apple slices in 2 concentric circles over the cream tart filling, overlapping the slices and completely covering the filling; set aside.

Place 1 tablespoon cold water in a small sauce dish. Sprinkle the gelatin over the water; let stand 15 minutes to soften. In a separate small sauce dish, place 1 teaspoon sugar and the arrowroot; stir to combine; set aside.

Place the apple jelly in a small saucepan. Bring the jelly to a boil over medium heat, stirring constantly. Boil 1 minute only, stirring continuously. Remove from the heat and add the gelatin mixture; stir until completely dissolved and blended. Immediately add the arrowroot mixture; stir briefly until blended and thick.

Drizzle the apple jelly glaze over the tart, being careful not to get glaze on the tart shell edge. Using a soft brush, spread the glaze completely over the apples and any tiny portions of cream filling showing between the apple slices. Refrigerate the tart, uncovered.

Remove the tart pan rim just before serving or briefly displaying the tart before serving; leave the pan bottom under the tart. To serve, place a slice of Apple Tart toward one side of each individual serving plate. Using a decorating bag fit with large open-star tip number 6B (page 383), pipe Decorator Whipped Cream in a line of continuous swirls down the side of each serving plate, parallel to, but not touching the tart slice. Sprinkle cinnamon sparingly over the whipped cream. Cover and refrigerate the leftover tart on the pan bottom.

MAKES ONE 9-INCH TART; 9 SERVINGS

PEAR TART

3 medium, ripe, fresh Bartlett pears*
Ground nutmeg for garnish

*Home-canned Plain Pears (page 723) or Pears Amaretto (page 723) may be substituted (no additional cooking is required; they are ready for slicing).

Follow the Apple Tart recipe, above, substituting fresh pears for fresh apples. Wash, halve, core, and pare the pears; immediately dropping them into the vinegar solution. Cook the pears single layer. Slice the pears lengthwise. Substitute nutmeg for cinnamon to garnish the whipped cream.

MAKES ONE 9-INCH TART; 9 SERVINGS

STRAWBERRY TART

1 recipe Vanilla Cream Tart Filling (page 511)
1 9-inch baked Classical Tart Pastry shell (page 468)
1 recipe Strawberry Topping (page 510)

Spoon the room-temperature Vanilla Cream Tart Filling into the baked tart shell, leaving the removable rim on the tart pan; using a small, narrow spatula, spread evenly. Refrigerate, uncovered, until the filling is cold and set.

Follow the Strawberry Topping recipe to arrange the strawberries over the cold cream filling in the tart shell, and to prepare and apply the glaze. Refrigerate the tart, uncovered, allowing sufficient time for the glaze to set before serving.

Remove the tart pan rim just before serving or briefly displaying the tart before serving; leave the pan bottom under the tart. Cover and refrigerate the leftover tart on the pan bottom.

MAKES ONE 9-INCH TART; 9 SERVINGS

GRAPEFRUIT AND ORANGE TART

2 cups red grapefruit sections with juice
  (page 47) (about 3 large grapefruit)
3 tablespoons sugar
1 cup orange sections with juice (page 47)
  (about 3 medium-large oranges)
1 tablespoon sugar
1 9-inch baked Classical Tart Pastry shell
  (page 468)
⅔ cup ground English walnuts (page 50)
Freshly squeezed, strained orange juice
1 cup sugar
3 tablespoons cornstarch
Dash of salt
1 tablespoon butter
¼ teaspoon clear vanilla
1 recipe Whipped Cream (page 373)

THE NIGHT BEFORE SERVING: Section the grapefruit; measure 2 cups grapefruit sections and
place in a glass bowl. With your hands, squeeze
the juice from the unused grapefruit parts into
the bowl containing the grapefruit sections.
Sprinkle 3 tablespoons sugar over the grapefruit
sections; cover with plastic wrap and refrigerate.
Following the same procedure, prepare 1 cup
orange sections and juice, placing them in a separate glass bowl and sprinkling with 1 tablespoon sugar.

THE DAY OF SERVING: Leave the removable rim
on the tart pan containing the baked tart shell.
Sprinkle the ground walnuts over the bottom of
the tart shell. Using the back of a spoon or your
hand, carefully pat the walnuts into the tart shell;
set aside.

Remove the grapefruit and orange mixtures
from the refrigerator. If sugar remains on top of
either mixture, stir with a wooden mixing
spoon, being careful not to tear the fruit sections. Drain the grapefruit and orange sections,
side by side, in a colander, reserving the juice
and letting it mix in a bowl under the colander.
Strain the reserved juice in a sieve. Strain
enough additional freshly squeezed orange juice

to measure 1¼ cups total strained juice; set
aside.

In a small saucepan, place the 1 cup sugar,
cornstarch, and salt; stir to combine. Add the 1¼
cups strained juice; stir well. Bring the juice
mixture to a simmer over medium heat, stirring
constantly. Simmer the mixture until thick and
translucent (about 2 minutes), stirring continuously. Remove from the heat and place the
saucepan on a wire rack. Add the butter and
vanilla; stir until completely blended. Let the
juice glaze stand only a few minutes until cooled
slightly.

Then, spoon sufficient juice glaze into the tart
shell to generously cover the walnuts and provide an even base for the fruit sections to be
arranged on top; set the remaining juice glaze
aside.

Arrange the grapefruit sections, slightly overlapping, around the outside of the tart, with the
ends of the sections pointing toward the rim and
the center of the tart. Arrange the orange sections in similar fashion in a concentric circle
around the center of the tart (see illustration).

Spoon sufficient juice glaze over the tart to
glaze the fruit sections and fill any spaces between the sections, being careful not to get glaze
on the tart shell edge. (Reserve any remaining
juice glaze for other uses.) Let the tart stand
on a wire rack in a cool, dry place until cool
and set.

Remove the tart pan rim just before serving

or briefly displaying the tart before serving; leave the pan bottom under the tart. Place the Whipped Cream in an attractive bowl; pass at the table for diners to spoon a dollop over or beside their individual tart servings. Cover and refrigerate the leftover tart on the pan bottom.

MAKES ONE 9-INCH TART; 9 SERVINGS

THREE-FRUIT TART WITH PEACH SCHNAPPS GLAZE

Food, like music, can evoke warm memories of past happy events. Tarts like this one remind me of the beautiful tarts savored on wonderful trips to France, Switzerland, and Austria.

1 recipe Vanilla Cream Tart Filling
   (page 511)
1 9-inch baked Classical Tart Pastry shell
   (page 468)
1 16-ounce can commercial sliced, yellow
   cling peaches
1 16-ounce can commercial sliced Bartlett
   pears
1 17-ounce can commercial unpeeled
   apricot halves
½ cup peach jam, home canned (page 750)
   or commercially canned
2 teaspoons peach schnapps

Spoon the room-temperature Vanilla Cream Tart Filling into the baked tart shell, leaving the removable rim on the tart pan; using a small, narrow spatula, spread evenly. Refrigerate, uncovered, until the filling is cold and set.

Separately, drain the peaches, pears, and apricots in a colander, being careful not to tear the fruit. Place the drained fruit between 3 layers of paper towels to further drain and dry.

Over the cream filling in the tart shell, arrange attractively the peach slices, pear slices, and apricot halves, in that order, each in a concentric circle beginning at the outside edge of the tart; set aside.

Place ½ cup peach jam in a small saucepan; bring the jam just to boiling over medium-low heat, stirring constantly. Strain the hot jam through a sieve. Measure ¼ cup strained jam and place in a tiny, clean saucepan. Over low heat, heat the strained jam until warm, stirring constantly. Remove from the heat and add the peach schnapps; stir until blended.

Spoon the peach schnapps glaze evenly over the tart, being careful not to get glaze on the tart shell edge. If necessary, use a small, very soft brush to spread the glaze over all exposed portions of the fruit and cream filling. Refrigerate the tart, uncovered, allowing sufficient time for the glaze to set before serving.

Carefully remove the tart pan rim just before serving or briefly displaying the tart before serving; leave the pan bottom under the tart. Cover and refrigerate the leftover tart on the pan bottom.

MAKES ONE 9-INCH TART; 9 SERVINGS

Cakes and Frostings

THE MIDWEST CAKEWALK

Mixers are whirring, the flour is flying,
Eggs are cracked by the dozen,
Vanilla and spice waft the whole biosphere,
Midwest kitchens are buzzin'.

Mothers yell warnings, "Don't run in the house,
You'll test my dear, patient lovin'!
Play Nintendo or scoot out the door,
'Cause I have a cake in the oven."

Sour Cream Spice Cakes with raisins and nuts
Spew from Ohio galleys,
While Oatmeal Cakes from the Hoosier State
Number far too many to tally.

Michigan apples fill Applesauce Cakes,
It's hickory nuts in Missouri,
Rhubarb is Illinois' "piece of cake,"
Will there be enough? Not to worry.

Sheet cakes, layer cakes, Bundt, and loaf,
Fill pans across the Dakotas.
"Calories," you say? Who gives a hoot?
For now, au revoir to the quotas.

Cherries and pineapple star in Nebraska,
Upside-Down Cake's the heroine, sorta.
Wisconsin Frauen mix cherries mit kirsch,
*They're making Schwarzwälder Kirschtorte. ***

Gingerbread rates in the Sunflower State,
Chiffon's a North Star State hit,
Angel Food's cool where Tall Corn doth rule,
With berries, they eat every bit.

They're all the best from the great Midwest,
But no matter the countless they bake,
Across this mighty, big stretch of land,
It's chocolate that e'er "takes the cake."

* Black Forest Cherry Torte (page 570)

Cakes

TYPES OF CAKES

Cakes may be classified into the following nine general types based upon their form or content:

LAYER CAKES: Layer cakes consist of individually baked cakes—usually two or three—of the same size which are stacked, with frosting or a thickened filling spread between the layers. The top and side of layer cakes are often frosted and then may be garnished or decorated with frosting designs, nuts, coconut, chocolate curls, other food products, or edible flowers.

SHEET CAKES: Sheet cakes are single-layer cakes which are generally baked in a 2-inch-deep pan. When baked at home, they are often cooled and frosted in the baking pan, remaining in the pan until cut and served. After cooling, sheet cakes may be cut into individual servings which are then iced on the top and sides. Petits fours are an example.

LOAF AND BUNDT CAKES: Loaf and Bundt cakes are deep, unlayered cakes baked in a loaf pan, Bundt pan, ring mold pan, or tube pan. Cakes in this classification usually include among their contents traditional cake ingredients; i.e., fat, sugar, eggs, flour, leaven, liquid, and flavoring.

ANGEL FOOD CAKES: Angel food cakes are very light, airy, tall cakes made with many egg whites, cake flour, sugar, cream of tartar, and flavoring, with air and steam serving as the primary leavening agents. Angel food cakes contain no shortening. They are usually baked in a special tube pan with a removable bottom and tube section, and cooling legs.

SPONGE CAKES: Sponge cakes are similar to angel food cakes in that they have a light, airy consistency and contain similar ingredients, including no shortening. They differ from angel food cakes in that they have egg yolks and a small amount of water as ingredients, and contain fewer egg whites. Like angel food cakes, air and steam are the primary leavening agents in sponge cakes; however, baking powder may be included, if desired. While often baked in a tube pan, sponge cakes are baked in a cookie pan when used in making jelly rolls, Yule logs, and similar cakes. They also may be baked in other types of pans when called for in recipes for particular style cakes.

CHIFFON CAKES: Chiffon cakes are a cousin of sponge cakes. In addition to the ingredients in sponge cakes, chiffon cakes include vegetable oil as an added ingredient, and they always contain baking powder. Due to the inclusion of oil, the egg whites in chiffon cakes must be beaten until extraordinarily stiff. Chiffon cakes are generally baked in a tube pan.

FRUITCAKES: Fruitcakes are dense, heavy cakes whose primary ingredients are a selected combination of candied fruits, raisins, nuts, dates, figs, and other dried fruits bound together with a minimum amount of cake batter. These rich cakes are best when aged in liquor-soaked cloths, and are generally baked in loaf or tube pans. Fruitcakes are traditionally served during the Christmas holiday season.

TORTES: Tortes are elegant, delicate cakes usually containing many eggs and, often, ground nuts and/or bread crumbs in substitution for part or all of the flour. Tortes generally consist of several layers of cake often infused with liqueur. Among the ingredients frequently included in the fillings between the layers are jam, whipped cream, and finely chopped nuts. Or, a buttercream frosting may be used to sandwich the layers. Tortes are commonly iced with a buttercream frosting or a glaze, and then decorated ornately.

CUPCAKES: Cupcakes are small, round, single serving–sized cakes baked in muffin-pan cups which are greased or lined with paper baking cups. Most standard cake batters may be used to make cupcakes. The tops of cupcakes are usually frosted with a buttercream frosting. They frequently are decorated with chopped or whole nuts, coconut, nonpareils (page 24), crushed candy, piped frosting, or other decorations compatible with the cake flavor, frosting, and serving occasion.

SECRETS FOR BAKING SUCCESSFUL CAKES

I would like to help dispel the modern notion that cakes come from boxes. The truth is, cakes result from the mixing and baking of proportionate amounts of certain ingredients such as flour, sugar, eggs, leavening, milk, flavoring, and, commonly, fat.

Contrary to the impression held by some, cakes made with fresh ingredients are quick and easy to prepare from scratch. And the delectable results are umatched by anything to be found in the colorful boxes on aisle 4.

The hardest, most time-consuming part about baking a cake is frosting it—especially layer cakes (see To Frost a Cake, page 573). But the task of frosting must be accomplished whether the icing comes from a plastic container off the shelf or from a bowl of fluffy sweetness made at home almost before the baker can say "Jack Robinson." Luscious frosting is not difficult to make. Why not spend the time spreading one's own superior product?

Primed with the requisite equipment, proper ingredients, an understanding of a few simple basics of preparation, and a reliable recipe, any cook rapidly can learn to turn out gratifying, praiseworthy fare for the cake stand.

To label the following information "secrets" is really a misnomer. What follows are some of the fundamental principles and procedures in baking good cakes based on food science and practical experience gained through decades of American cake baking. The pointers and suggestions given here are in addition to those found within the recipes and in other articles in this chapter.

EQUIPMENT
Proper equipment has much to do with the outcome of a cake. Accumulate the right equipment before expending the energy and quelling the enthusiasm for cake baking on a predictable failure due to faulty equipment.

The following basic equipment will take the baker through years of blue ribbon cake baking:

• A standard-sized, substantial, upright electric mixer.

• Top-quality, anodized aluminum cake pans of various sizes.

Wilton Enterprises carries an excellent line of cake pans available in many stores and by mail order. A nearly inexhaustible line of high-grade cake pans of every size and description also can be found in the Sweet Celebrations Inc. catalog. (See Product Sources, page 850, for addresses and telephone numbers.)

Do not use cake pans with nonstick or slick-coated surfaces often displayed in cookware sections. Also, dark-colored pans should not be used because they absorb heat too readily and cause overbrowning. Shiny, stainless steel pans are not good selections because they do not conduct heat well.

• A level, calibrated oven.

Most modern ranges are made with leveling feet. The installation manual accompanying the range describes how to adjust them to achieve a level oven.

A properly calibrated oven is a must. Temperature control is all-important to successful cake baking. In fact, accurate temperature control is critical to all baking and cooking.

While oven thermometers are helpful in determining the accuracy of oven temperature, I have found that the most satisfactory and reliable way to calibrate an oven is to call the consumer service number of the range manufacturer and have an experienced person sent to do it professionally. Even new ranges require oven calibration.

• Fundamental measuring utensils (see To Measure Ingredients, page 51).

- A regular-sized (preferably 5-cup) sifter and a 1-cup sifter (see To Sift Flour, page 56).

- A pastry brush, flour scoop, regular-sized rubber spatula, large mixing spoon, timer, large spatula, and sharp, thin-bladed knife; stainless steel mixing bowls; waxed paper; bake-even cake strips (see To Use Bake-Even Cake Strips, page 521); regular tableware knives (for leveling measured dry ingredients) and tablespoons and teaspoons (for mixing); long, wooden toothpicks; 3 wire racks; and frosting tools (page 573).

Assemble all the needed equipment before commencing to measure and mix the ingredients for a cake.

PROPER INGREDIENTS

- Use only fresh, high-quality ingredients (see Notes about Recipe Ingredients, page 18).

- Review the recipe well in advance of preparing a cake, making sure that all the necessary ingredients are on hand.

- Have all the cake ingredients at room temperature before starting to combine them.

Depending upon the kitchen temperature, remove butter or vegetable shortening from the refrigerator about 2 hours in advance of commencing to mix a cake.

Remove eggs from the refrigerator 1 hour in advance. Let the eggs stand in the shells and break them immediately before adding them to the batter. If the recipe calls for the eggs to be separated, place the part of the eggs not immediately used in the batter (usually the whites) in a bowl and cover with plastic wrap. Let stand at room temperature until used, a short time later, in the preparation of the batter.

I do not like to let milk, half-and-half, or cream stand unrefrigerated too long, so I remove from the refrigerator and measure any of these required products immediately after assembling the needed equipment for baking the cake, then return the unneeded portion to the refrigerator. By the time the liquid ingredient is added to the batter, it will have warmed considerably, albeit not quite to room temperature.

TIPS FOR MIXING AND BAKING SHORTENED CAKES (CAKES CONTAINING FAT) (SEE NOTE, PAGE 521)

- Before commencing to mix a cake:
  ~ Complete any required preparation of ingredients (such as chopping nuts).
  ~ Measure all ingredients (except vanilla or other such liquid flavoring, which can readily be measured when added to the batter).
  ~ Prepare the cake pan(s).
  ~ Sift the flour (usually with added leavening and salt).

- When you begin to mix the cake, proceed uninterrupted until the cake(s) is(are) in the oven.

- When the electric mixer is running during the mixing process, use a rubber spatula to scrape the side of the mixing bowl, moving the batter from the side to the center of the bowl as the mixer is beating. This helps assure even mixture of the ingredients. I like to hold the spatula in one hand while manually controlling the turning of the mixing bowl with the other hand.

- It is highly important to cream the fat and sugar adequately. Creaming incorporates air, helping to produce light cakes. When sufficiently creamed, the fat-sugar mixture will be fluffy and light.

- If more than one whole egg (or egg yolk) is called for, add the eggs (or egg yolks) one at a time and beat very well after adding each. This procedure achieves thorough blending of the whole eggs (or egg yolks) with the creamed fat and sugar, and effects further aeration of the batter.

- After adding vanilla (or other flavoring), beat the batter well on medium-high speed, not only to blend the flavoring, but also to incorporate as much additional air as possible into the batter before adding the flour mixture and liquid.

- Add the sifted flour mixture and liquid alternately, usually in fourths and thirds, depending on the recipe, always beginning and ending with the dry ingredients (flour mixture). Use a flour scoop to transport estimated portions of the flour mixture from the waxed paper to the mixing bowl. When measuring the liquid before commencing to mix the cake (described, above), my preference is to use fractional measuring cups (and measuring spoons, if required) for measuring, and then to pour the measured liquid into a glass measuring cup with a pouring spout. The glass measuring cup makes estimated additions of liquid to the batter more efficient and the pouring spout reduces the risk of spilling measured liquid.

  After each addition of both the flour mixture and the liquid, beat the batter on low speed only until the added flour mixture or liquid is blended. On my mixer, I use speed 2 and beat approximately 20 seconds after adding ¼ of the flour mixture for an average-sized cake, and approximately 12 seconds after adding ⅓ of the liquid. Of course, these numbers will vary, depending upon the mixer and the volume of ingredients.

  After all the flour mixture and liquid additions have been made and blended, beat the batter *very briefly* (about 20 seconds) on low speed, but slightly faster than the speed used after the flour mixture and liquid additions. I use speed 3 on my electric mixer. The purpose of this final, short beating is to help make certain that all ingredients are evenly blended.

- Many cake recipes call for the eggs to be separated and the egg whites to be beaten and folded into the cake batter as the last procedure in mixing. Beaten egg whites lose their volume quickly when left to stand; therefore, when beaten egg whites are to be incorporated into cake batter, they should not be beaten until the remainder of the batter has been mixed. Unless a kitchen is equipped with 2 standard-sized electric mixers, it is necessary that the beater blades be removed from the mixer, thoroughly washed and dried, and reinserted into the mixer before beating the egg whites. (Do not use a blender or food processor for beating egg whites.)

  Beat the egg whites on high speed until soft peaks hold. Soft peaks of beaten egg whites bend to the side when the beater blades are lifted from the egg whites. Continue beating the egg whites on high speed while simultaneously and *very slowly* sprinkling the measured sugar over the egg white mixture. Beat the egg white mixture until stiff peaks hold, but the mixture is still moist and glossy. Stiff peaks of beaten egg whites remain upright when the beater blades are lifted from the mixture. Sugar is usually added to the egg whites during beating to help stabilize the foam and to produce a mixture consistency which allows the beaten egg whites to be more readily folded into the batter.

  Using a large mixing spoon, fold the egg white mixture into the batter with care, but quickly, to minimize the loss of air (see definition of "Fold," page 22).

- If baking a layer cake, use a large mixing spoon to place large spoonsful of the batter *alternately* into the prepared cake pans. By following this procedure, approximately equal amounts of batter will be placed in each pan, resulting in uniformly sized cake layers. Then, use a small, narrow spatula (see illustration, page 573) to lightly and quickly spread the batter in the pans, mounding the batter ever so slightly in the center.

- Bake the cake(s) on the center shelf of the preheated oven. Do not open the oven door until near the end of the baking period, as the cooling effect on the batter may cause the cake to fall. Jolts to the oven may also cause a cake to fall (see the second verse of the poem introducing this chapter).

- Near the end of the baking time, check the cake for doneness. Avoid overbaking. Cakes dry when left in the oven for even a few minutes after they are done.

NOTE: Mixing and baking procedures for other types of cakes, such as angel food and sponge cakes, are found in the recipe procedures for those cakes.

RELIABLE RECIPES

The ingredients must be balanced properly to produce a successful cake; therefore, accurate measuring is very important. Carefully measure the ingredients and closely follow the procedures given in the cake recipes in this chapter or in other tested recipes, applying generally accepted principles of skillful cake baking. Wonderful cakes will be the reward!

TO USE BAKE-EVEN CAKE STRIPS*

A level top surface can be maintained on most cakes during baking by wrapping bake-even cake strips around the outside of the cake pans prior to baking. A level top surface is required on lower layers of layered cakes and on the tops of cakes to be decorated with piped frosting. Bake-even cake strips work by helping to control heat distribution in the pan during baking.

To use bake-even cake strips, immerse them in cold water and let them stand at least 5 minutes. Just before commencing to mix the ingredients to bake a cake, remove the strips from the water and run them tightly between your index and middle fingers to extract excess water. (Do not wring the strips.)

Wrap one strip, aluminized side out, tightly around the *outside* of each prepared cake pan. Overlap the strip ends and secure with a pin supplied in the package with the strips. Bake-even cake strips are available in several lengths; however, they may be overlapped and pinned together around larger pans. Overlapping of the strips does not interfere with their performance efficiency.

A product of Wilton Enterprises (see Product Sources, page 850).

Spoon the batter into the pans and bake the cakes as usual. Remove the strips immediately after removing the cakes from the oven and placing them on wire racks. Follow the standard procedure of letting the cakes stand 10 minutes on wire racks to partially cool before removing them from the pans. Hang the strips on a towel bar to completely dry before refolding them for storage. They may be reused over and over.

Use of bake-even cake strips generally makes it unnecessary to level cakes after baking.

Bake-even cake strips fit best around 2-inch-deep cake pans with straight (not slanted) sides. They should not be used around cakes which contain large proportions of ground nuts and/or bread crumbs in substitution for part, or all, of the flour (as in many tortes). These cakes do not develop crowns during baking

Cake recipes in the chapter indicate when the use of bake-even cake strips is recommended.

TO LEVEL A BAKED CAKE

When a baked cake is to be used as a lower layer of a finished cake, or when the top layer of a cake is to be piped with decoration, it is necessary that the top surface of the cake be flat and level. If baking has produced a crown on the cake, it must be removed to achieve the needed level surface (see Note).

To level a cake, place it on a corrugated cardboard cake circle. Place the cake circle (with cake) on a decorating turntable. (See illustration, page 573.) While slowly rotating the turntable with one hand, move a serrated knife horizontally back and forth in sawing motions across the top of the cake to remove the crown. The crown should be removed at eye level to assure that the finished cake surface is parallel with the bottom of the cake.

Or, to level a cake with greater ease and accuracy, cake levelers are commercially available from Sweet Celebrations Inc. and Wilton Enterprises (see Product Sources, page 850). Cake levelers horizontally level cakes or split them into layers with precision. These simple kitchen tools adjust to desired heights and operate as a saw which is pulled through the cake. Cake levelers are available in several styles, varying in cost from reasonable to pricey.

NOTE: Special bake-even cake strips may be placed on cake pans prior to baking most cakes to produce cakes without crowns (see To Use Bake-Even Cake Strips, page 521).

TO SPLIT A CAKE INTO LAYERS

Baked cakes may be split horizontally to make 2 or more layers. Cakes with several thin layers are most often made by splitting each of 2 or 3 baked cake layers in half to make 4 or 6 layers, respectively.

To split a cake into layers, a procedure similar to that used to level a baked cake is employed (see To Level a Baked Cake, page 521). Follow the same procedure for placing the cake to be split on a corrugated cardboard cake circle and then on a decorating turntable. Level the top of the cake, if required, as described above. Then, with the knife blade parallel to the bottom of the cake, hold a serrated knife against the side of the cake at the place where you wish to make the cut. To split the cake, move the knife back and forth in sawing motions while slowly rotating the turntable with your other hand. As in leveling a cake, a cake should be split at eye level to help assure that it is cut parallel with the bottom of the cake.

After making the cut, carefully slide a corrugated cardboard cake circle between the split layers and remove the top layer.

As described in To Level a Baked Cake, a cake leveler kitchen tool also may be used to split cakes into layers.

TO CUT AND SERVE CAKES

After taking the time to bake and carefully frost a delectable cake, the same diligence should be applied to cutting and serving it in order to ren-der the individual servings as tantalizing as the whole, uncut cake.

Proper, meticulous cake cutting takes a little time and patience. Pride in the professional-looking results will deem the bit of extra effort well worth it. As my wonderful first-grade teacher, Miss Cameron, engraved on our minds: "Anything worth doing, is worth doing well."

TO CUT ROUND LAYER CAKES AND TORTES: Dip a sharp, *thin-bladed* knife into a tall glass or pitcher of hot water. Shake off the excess water (away from the cake) and make a cut from the center to the edge of the cake. Hold the knife at a slight angle (handle upward) when you cut into the cake so the point of the knife will cut down the center and to the bottom of the cake in a straight, vertical line; then, pull the knife handle fully downward to complete the cut. This procedure will help assure a pointed, unfrayed edge at the center end of the cut piece.

After making the cut, wipe the knife on a damp sponge or cloth, redip the knife in hot water, shake off the excess water, and make the second cut. Repeat the procedure for each cut.

Exercise care to make the cuts at right angles to the bottom of the cake so the slices will not be slanted. Also, gauge the cuts to make sure that servings arriving at the table are uniform in size (unless a family member requests a smaller—or larger—piece).

Cut the number of pieces to be served before removing any of the servings from the cake. Use a triangular pie/cake server to remove the cut slices. Carefully push the server under the bottom of a cake slice all the way to the center; lift straight up and transfer the cut piece to an individual serving plate.

TO CUT SHEET CAKES AND SQUARE LAYER CAKES: To achieve servings of uniform size, hold a ruler against the edges of the cake pan (or close to the edges of the cake, if it has been removed from the pan) and make tiny marks in the frosting with the point of a sharp knife at measured places along the edges of the cake where you wish to make cuts. Before marking, you must decide what size pieces you desire and do some arithmetic vis-à-vis the pan size.

Measure and mark all four sides of the cake. Shortcutting the process by marking only two sides of the cake, more often than not results in slightly slanted cut lines, producing irregular pieces of cake.

To cut marked cakes, dip a sharp, *thin-bladed* knife into a tall glass or pitcher of hot water. Shake off the excess water (away from the cake) and, in a nonstop motion, make a cut from one side of the cake to the opposite side. Do not use back-and-forth sawing motions when cutting, or lift the knife from the cake before the full cut is made. These actions will cause raggedy frosting edges as well as possible crumbling of the cut edges of the cake. After making the cut, wipe the knife on a damp sponge or cloth, redip the knife in hot water, shake off the excess water, and make the next cut. Repeat the procedure for each cut.

When cutting rectangular sheet cakes, make the lengthwise cuts before the widthwise cuts. By following this sequence, the cake will be more stable when the long, more difficult cuts are made. If cutting a cake in the pan, run the knife along the inside edges of the pan to loosen the cake from the pan *after* making the other cuts. By loosening the cake from the pan last, the cake will better hold its position when making the previous cuts.

To remove the cut pieces from the pan (or cake board), use a small spatula as close to the size of the cut pieces of cake as possible. Push the spatula completely under a cut piece of cake and lift straight upward to remove.

TO CUT LOAF AND BUNDT CAKES: Dip a sharp, *thin-bladed* knife into a tall glass or pitcher of hot water. Shake off the excess water (away from the cake) and make a single cut in the cake. Wipe the knife on a damp sponge or cloth, redip the knife in hot water, shake off the excess water, and make the second cut. Repeat the procedure for each cut. Cut the number of pieces to be served before removing any of the servings from the cake.

Remove cut slices from the cake using a spatula or pie/cake server appropriate for the size and shape of the cut pieces.

TO CUT ANGEL FOOD CAKES, SPONGE CAKES, AND CHIFFON CAKES: To cut the first slice of cake, dip a pronged cake cutter (see illustration) into a small, deep pan of hot water. Shake off the excess water (away from the cake) and plunge the cutter into the cake where you wish to make a cut. Pull the cutter straight up and out of the cake. Wipe the cutter on a damp sponge or cloth. Redip the cutter in hot water, shake off the excess water, and plunge the cutter into the cake where you wish to make the second cut for the first slice. Pull the cutter straight up and out of the cake.

Then, dip a long, sharp, *thin-bladed* (nonserrated) knife into a tall glass or pitcher of hot water and shake off the excess water (away from the cake). Using light, sawing motions with the knife, complete the cuts at the two places pierced with the cutter. Use a triangular pie/cake server to remove the first cut slice from the cake.

Wipe the pronged cake cutter on a damp sponge or cloth, redip the cutter in hot water, shake off the excess water, and plunge the cutter into the cake where you wish to make the next cut. Leaving the cutter in the cake, rotate the top of the cutter away from the cake to break the next slice from the cake. Transfer the cut slice to an individual serving plate. Wipe the cutter, redip it in hot water, and shake off the excess water before piercing the cake and breaking away each slice.

Pronged Cake Cutter

If a pronged cake cutter is not available, slices may be cut using light, sawing motions with a long, sharp, *thin-bladed* (nonserrated) knife. Wipe the knife on a damp sponge or cloth, dip the knife in hot water, and shake off the excess water before making each cut.

TO CUT FRUITCAKES: For precision pieces, fruitcakes should be refrigerated and chilled before slicing. Dip a sharp, *thin-bladed* knife into a tall glass or pitcher of hot water, shake off the excess water (away from the cake), and make a cut. Wipe the knife on a damp sponge or cloth, re-dip the knife in hot water, shake off the excess water, and make the second cut. Repeat the procedure for each subsequent cut. Cut the number of pieces to be served before removing any of the servings from the cake.

SERVINGS

While the number of servings from a particular-sized cake depends upon how the cake will be served, the dining occasion, the appetites of the diners, and the richness and nature of the cake, the following may serve as general guidelines:

Cake Description	Number of Servings
2- or 3-layer, 8-inch round or square cake	10
2- or 3-layer, 9-inch round or square cake	12
2- or 3-layer, 10-inch round or square cake	16
7 × 11-inch sheet cake	12
9 × 13-inch sheet cake	15
5 × 9-inch loaf cake	12
10-inch Bundt cake	14
10 × 4-inch tube-pan angel food, sponge, or chiffon cake	12
8-inch round torte	12
9-inch round torte	14

Layer Cakes

TO REMOVE LAYER CAKES FROM CAKE PANS

Immediately upon removing from the oven, place baked layer cakes on separate wire racks. Remove the bake-even cake strips, if used, from the pans (page 521). Let the cakes stand in the pans exactly 10 minutes (use a timer) to partially cool.

Then, carefully run a sharp, thin-bladed knife around the inside edge of the pans to completely loosen the side of the cakes from the pans. Place a wire rack over one of the pans. Firmly hold both the wire rack under the pan and the wire rack over the pan and, in a single motion, invert the wire racks (and pan). The cake will drop onto the lower rack provided the right type of pan has been used (see Equipment, page 18) and properly prepared, and the cake has been correctly baked.

Remove the upper wire rack and carefully lift the pan off the cake. Lightly place the extra wire rack over the exposed bottom side of the cake, hold the wire racks on both sides of the cake, and invert to return the cake to its upright position. Remove the upper wire rack and let the cake stand on the lower wire rack. Repeat the procedure with the other layer(s).

Let the cakes stand on the wire racks until completely cool. Then, immediately frost the cake (see To Frost a Cake, page 573), or place the layers on separate corrugated cardboard cake circles and store in separate airtight cake containers to prevent drying.

Follow the recipe procedures for removal of other types of cakes from their pans.

WHITE CAKE

2½ cups sifted cake flour (sift before
    measuring)
1 tablespoon plus ¼ teaspoon baking
    powder
½ teaspoon salt
⅔ cup vegetable shortening, softened
1¼ cups sugar
1½ teaspoons clear vanilla
1 cup whole milk
4 extra-large egg whites, room temperature
¼ cup sugar
Frosting of choice (see Frosting Suggestion,
    below)

Preheat the oven to 375° F. Grease well and flour
lightly two 8 × 2-inch *or* two 9 × 1½- or 2-inch
round cake pans; set aside (see Note).

Onto wax paper, sift together the flour, baking powder, and salt; set aside.

In a large mixing bowl, place the vegetable
shortening and 1¼ cups sugar; using an electric
mixer, cream well on medium-high speed. Add
the vanilla; continue beating on medium-high
speed until blended. Add, alternately, the flour
mixture in fourths, and the milk in thirds, beating on low speed after each addition only until
blended; set aside.

Place the egg whites in a large mixing bowl.
Using the electric mixer fit with clean, dry
blades, beat the egg whites on high speed until
soft peaks hold. While continuing to beat on
high speed, very gradually add ¼ cup sugar and
continue beating the egg white mixture until
stiff, but still moist and glossy. Add the egg white
mixture to the cake batter; using a large mixing
spoon, fold in.

Using the large mixing spoon, spoon the batter equally into the 2 prepared cake pans. Using
a small, narrow spatula, lightly and quickly
spread the batter evenly in the pans. Bake the
cakes for 17 to 18 minutes, or until a wooden
toothpick inserted into the center of the cakes
comes out clean.

Remove the cakes from the oven and place
on wire racks; let stand to cool 10 minutes.
Remove the cakes from the pans (page 520); let
stand on wire racks until completely cool.

Then, frost between the layers, and the top
and side of the cake with frosting of choice (see
To Frost a Cake, page 573). Let the cake stand
until the frosting sets. Then, place the cake in an
airtight container.

NOTE: Do not wrap bake-even cake strips (page
521) around the cake pans when using this
recipe.

**MAKES ONE 8- OR 9-INCH, 2-LAYER ROUND CAKE;
10 SERVINGS**

FROSTING SUGGESTION: This cake was a blue ribbon winner frosted with Fluff Frosting (page
583) garnished with Pink-Tinted Coconut
(page 409). Immediately after frosting the cake
with Fluff Frosting, spoon Tinted Coconut
(pink or another color of choice) over the top
and side of the cake, pressing the coconut lightly
into the frosting with your hand only until it
holds in place. Let the cake stand 1 hour to allow
the frosting to dry slightly. Then, place the cake
in an airtight container.

3-LAYER WHITE CAKE

3¾ cups sifted cake flour (sift before
    measuring)
1 tablespoon plus 1¾ teaspoons baking
    powder
¾ teaspoon salt
1 cup vegetable shortening, softened
1¾ cups plus 2 tablespoons sugar
2¼ teaspoons clear vanilla
1½ cups whole milk
6 extra-large egg whites, room temperature
¼ cup plus 2 tablespoons sugar

Follow the procedures in the White Cake
recipe, above, using three 8 × 2-inch *or* three
9 × 1½- or 2-inch round cake pans and the
ingredient amounts for a 3-Layer White Cake.

**MAKES ONE 8- OR 9-INCH, 3-LAYER ROUND CAKE;
10 OR 12 SERVINGS**

SHADOW CAKE

A shadow of mellifluous chocolate trickling down over billowy, white Boiled Frosting gives this gorgeous, delectable cake its name. Underneath the picturesque frosting, a white middle layer "shadows" two chocolate outer ones (see illustration, page 516).

3 tablespoons sugar
¼ teaspoon baking soda
¼ teaspoon salt
2½ ounces (2½ squares) unsweetened chocolate
¼ cup boiling water
2½ cups sifted cake flour (sift before measuring)
2½ teaspoons baking powder
½ teaspoon salt
½ cup (¼ pound) butter, softened
1 cup sugar
1 extra-large egg plus 2 extra-large egg yolks
1½ teaspoons pure vanilla extract
¾ cup whole milk
1 recipe Boiled Frosting (page 578)
2 ounces (2 squares) unsweetened chocolate
2 teaspoons butter

Preheat the oven to 350°F. Using Special Grease (page 56), grease three 8 × 2-inch round cake pans (see Note); set aside. Place 3 bake-even cake strips (page 521) in cold water; let stand.

In a small sauce dish, place 3 tablespoons sugar, baking soda, and ¼ teaspoon salt; stir to combine; set aside.

Place 2½ ounces chocolate in the top of a double boiler over (not touching) simmering water in the bottom pan. Melt the chocolate, stirring constantly. Add the sugar mixture; stir to combine. Remove the top of the double boiler from the bottom pan. Add the boiling water to the chocolate mixture; stir until blended; set aside.

Onto waxed paper, sift together the flour, baking powder, and ½ teaspoon salt; set aside.

Extract the excess water from the bake-even cake strips. Wrap and pin the strips around the prepared cake pans; set aside.

In a large mixing bowl, place the butter and 1 cup sugar; using an electric mixer cream well on medium-high speed. Add the whole egg and egg yolks, one at a time, beating well on medium-high speed after each addition. Add the vanilla; continue beating on medium-high speed until light and fluffy. Add, alternately, the flour mixture in fourths, and the milk in thirds, beating on low speed after each addition only until blended. Using a large mixing spoon, spoon ⅓ of the cake batter into 1 prepared cake pan. Using a small, narrow spatula, lightly and quickly spread the batter evenly in the pan; set aside.

Add the chocolate mixture to the remaining batter; using the electric mixer, beat on low speed only until blended. Using a clean, large mixing spoon, spoon the batter equally into the 2 remaining prepared cake pans; using a clean, small, narrow spatula, spread the batter evenly in the pans. Bake the cakes for 20 to 25 minutes, or until a wooden toothpick inserted into the center of the cakes comes out clean.

Remove the cakes from the oven and place on wire racks; remove the cake strips. Let the cakes stand to cool 10 minutes. Remove the cakes from the pans (page 520); let stand on wire racks until completely cool.

Then, with the Boiled Frosting, frost between the layers of the cake, using the light-colored cake as the center layer (see To Frost a Cake, page 573); frost the top of the cake quite smoothly; frost the sides of the cake and then swirl the *side* frosting attractively (see To Swirl Frosting, page 575). Let the cake stand until the frosting sets.

Then, in a tiny saucepan, place 2 ounces chocolate and 2 teaspoons butter. Melt the chocolate and butter over *warm* (no hotter) heat, stirring constantly and until completely blended. Cool the chocolate mixture *slightly*. Using a tablespoon, spoon the chocolate mixture onto the top of the cake and let it trickle down the sides. Let the cake stand until the chocolate topping sets. Then, place the cake in an airtight container.

NOTE: Although not as satisfactory, the pans may be greased and floured in substitution for using Special Grease.

MAKES ONE 8-INCH, 3-LAYER ROUND CAKE; 10 SERVINGS

OPTIONAL DECORATION: For additional elegance, decorate the top of the cake with 3 fresh, white roses placed in the center (see Edible Flowers, page 381).

WHITE AND CHOCOLATE 2-LAYER CAKE

To satisfy all preferences, this cake sports one white layer and one chocolate layer, and uses both white and chocolate frostings.

2 tablespoons sugar
¼ teaspoon baking soda
2 ounces (2 squares) unsweetened
   chocolate
3 tablespoons boiling water
Ingredients for 1 recipe White Cake
   (page 525) (see recipe procedures, below)
½ recipe Cake Decorators' White Icing
   (page 576)
½ recipe Cake Decorators' Chocolate Icing
   (page 577)

Preheat the oven to 375° F. Grease well and flour lightly two 8 × 2-inch round baking pans; set aside (see Note).

In a small sauce dish, place the sugar and baking soda; stir to combine; set aside. Place the chocolate in a tiny saucepan. Hold the tiny pan over (not touching) low simmering water in a small saucepan until the chocolate melts, stirring intermittently. Remove the tiny pan from the heat. Add the baking soda mixture to the melted chocolate; stir to combine. Add the boiling water; stir until blended; set aside.

Follow the White Cake recipe through the additions of the flour mixture and milk. Using a large mixing spoon, spoon the cake batter equally into 2 medium mixing bowls. Add the chocolate mixture to one of the bowls of batter; using the electric mixer, beat on low speed only until completely blended; set aside.

Follow the White Cake recipe to beat 4 egg whites, adding ¼ cup sugar. Using a table knife, cut the beaten egg white mixture in half. Quickly and carefully spoon ½ of the egg white mixture into each bowl of batter. Using a separate, large mixing spoon for each bowl, fold in.

Spoon each bowl of batter into one of the prepared cake pans. Using a small, narrow spatula, lightly and quickly spread the batter evenly in one of the pans. Then, clean and dry the spatula, and spread the batter in the second pan. Bake the cakes for 17 to 18 minutes, or until a wooden toothpick inserted into the center of the cakes comes out clean.

Remove the cakes from the oven and place on wire racks; let stand to cool 10 minutes. Remove the cakes from the pans (page 520); let stand on wire racks until completely cool.

Then, frost between the layers of the cake with the Cake Decorators' White Icing, using the chocolate cake as the bottom layer (see To Frost a Cake, page 573). Frost the top and sides of the cake with the Cake Decorators' Chocolate Icing. Let the cake stand until the frosting sets. Then, place the cake in an airtight container.

NOTE: Do not wrap bake-even cake strips (page 521) around the cake pans when using this recipe.

MAKES ONE 8-INCH, 2-LAYER ROUND CAKE; 10 SERVINGS

OPTIONAL DECORATION: Reserve a portion of both the Cake Decorators' White Icing and the Cake Decorators' Chocolate Icing to decorate the cake. Fit 2 decorating bags each with a medium open-star tip number 21 (page 383). Fill one of the bags with Cake Decorators' White

(Recipe continues on next page)

Icing, and the other bag with Cake Decorators' Chocolate Icing. Pipe a shell border (page 389) around the bottom and top of the cake, alternating white and chocolate shells. Arrange piped, white roses (pages 392–393) on the top of the cake. Using medium leaf tip number 67, pipe chocolate leaves (page 391) around the roses.

CHECKERBOARD CAKE

Each slice looks like a chocolate and yellow cake checkerboard. A special Checkerboard Cake Set (three 9-inch round baking pans and a divider), available commercially, is required to make this fun dessert.

2½ ounces (2½ squares) unsweetened chocolate
4 cups sifted cake flour (sift before measuring)
3 tablespoons plus 2 teaspoons baking powder
1 teaspoon salt
¾ cup (¼ pound plus 4 tablespoons) butter, softened
2 cups sugar
2 extra-large eggs
2 teaspoons pure vanilla extract
1½ cups plus 2 tablespoons whole milk
1 recipe Cake Decorators' Chocolate Icing (page 577)

Preheat the oven to 350° F. Grease and flour lightly the three 9-inch round cake pans in a Checkerboard Cake Set (see headnote); set aside.

Place the chocolate in a tiny saucepan. Hold the tiny pan over (not touching) low simmering water in a small saucepan until the chocolate melts, stirring intermittently. Remove the tiny pan from the heat; set aside.

Onto waxed paper, sift together the flour, baking powder, and salt; set aside.

In a large mixing bowl, place the butter and sugar; using an electric mixer, cream well on medium-high speed. Add the eggs, one at a time, beating well on medium-high speed after

each addition. Add the vanilla; beat on medium-high speed until light and fluffy. Add, alternately, the flour mixture in fourths, and the milk in thirds, beating on low speed after each addition only until blended.

Using a large mixing spoon, spoon slightly less than ½ of the cake batter into a medium mixing bowl; set aside. Add the melted chocolate to the remaining batter; using the electric mixer, beat on low speed until blended.

Place the checkerboard cake divider in one of the prepared cake pans (the top layer of the cake). The divider separates the cake into 3 sections (see illustration A).

Illustration A

Use one hand to press down on the divider and hold it firmly against the bottom of the pan to help prevent seepage of batter between the sections. Using a tableware teaspoon, carefully spoon chocolate batter into the outside and the center sections of the pan until approximately ½ full. Using a small, narrow spatula spread the batter evenly. Then, using a clean teaspoon, spoon yellow batter into the middle section of the pan until approximately ½ full. Using a clean, small, narrow spatula, spread the batter evenly. All batter in the pan should be the same depth.

Remove the divider; rinse and dry it. Wipe off any excess batter around the inside edge of the pan; carefully regrease (but don't reflour) the edge of the pan, if necessary, taking care not to touch the batter with grease.

Repeat the exact procedure to fill the second pan with batter (the bottom layer of the cake).

Using the same procedure, fill the third pan (the middle layer of the cake), placing the yellow batter in the outside and the center sections, and the chocolate batter in the middle section.

Bake the cakes for 18 to 20 minutes, or until a wooden toothpick inserted into the center of the cakes comes out clean.

Remove the cakes from the oven and place on wire racks; let stand to cool 10 minutes. Remove the cakes from the pans (page 520); let stand on wire racks until completely cool.

Frost between the layers of the cake with the Cake Decorators' Chocolate Icing, using the layer with yellow cake in the outside and center sections as the middle layer. Then, frost the top and side of the cake as smoothly as possible with Cake Decorators' Chocolate Icing (see To Frost a Cake, page 573). Let the cake stand until the frosting sets. Then, place the cake in an airtight container. When the cake is served, each slice will look like a checkerboard (see illustration B).

Illustration B

MAKES ONE 9-INCH, 3-LAYER ROUND CAKE; 12 SERVINGS

OPTIONAL DECORATION
½ recipe Cake Decorators' Buttercream Icing (page 576)

Before frosting the cake, reserve 1½ cups of the Cake Decorators' Chocolate Icing; set aside. After frosting the cake, let the cake stand only until the frosting partially sets.

Then, using a 1-inch-square cookie cutter (see Note), lightly mark rows of squares in the frosting over the entire top surface of the cake. Using a decorating bag fit with very small round tip number 2 (page 383) and filled with Cake Decorators' Buttercream Icing, outline every other square. Using the same icing and small round tip number 5, fill in alternate out-

lined squares, in checkerboard fashion. To finish the cake, use a decorating bag fit with medium open-star tip number 21 and filled with the reserved Cake Decorators' Chocolate Icing to pipe shell borders (page 389) around the bottom and top of the cake. Let the cake stand until the frosting sets. Then, place the cake in an airtight container.

NOTE: If not available commercially, the cutter may be made from a suitable gauge of aluminum flashing material available at hardware stores.

CHOCOLATE CAKE

Lion among cakes!

3 ounces (3 squares) unsweetened chocolate
2 cups sifted cake flour (sift before measuring)
1 teaspoon baking soda
½ teaspoon salt
½ cup (¼ pound) butter *or* vegetable shortening, softened
1½ cups sugar
2 extra-large eggs
1 teaspoon pure vanilla extract
1 cup whole milk
1 recipe Chocolate Frosting (page 580)
Chocolate Curls (page 406) for decoration

Preheat the oven to 350° F. Using Special Grease (page 56), grease two 8 × 2-inch round cake pans (see Note); set aside. Place 2 bake-even cake strips (page 521) in cold water; let stand.

Place the chocolate in a tiny saucepan. Hold the tiny pan over (not touching) low simmering water in a small saucepan until the chocolate melts, stirring intermittently. Remove the tiny pan from the heat; set aside.

Onto waxed paper, sift together the flour, baking soda, and salt; set aside.

Extract the excess water from the bake-even

(Recipe continues on next page)

cake strips. Wrap and pin the strips around the prepared cake pans; set aside.

In a large mixing bowl, place the butter and sugar; using an electric mixer, cream well on medium-high speed. Add the eggs, one at a time, beating well on medium-high speed after each addition. Add the vanilla and melted chocolate; beat on medium-high speed until completely blended. Add, alternately, the flour mixture in fourths, and the milk in thirds, beating on low speed after each addition only until blended.

Using a large mixing spoon, spoon the cake batter equally into the 2 prepared cake pans. Using a small, narrow spatula, lightly and quickly spread the batter evenly in the pans. Bake the cakes for 25 minutes, or until a wooden toothpick inserted into the center of the cakes comes out clean.

Remove the cakes from the oven and place on wire racks; remove the cake strips. Let the cakes stand to cool 10 minutes. Remove the cakes from the pans (page 520); let stand on wire racks until completely cool.

Then, frost between the layers, and the top and side of the cake with the Chocolate Frosting (see To Frost a Cake, page 573). Let the cake stand until the frosting sets. Then, place the cake in an airtight container.

NOTE: Although not as satisfactory, the pans may be greased and floured in substitution for using Special Grease.

MAKES ONE 8-INCH, 2-LAYER ROUND CAKE; 10 SERVINGS

VARIATION: A frosting of choice may be substituted for the Chocolate Frosting.

CHOCOLATE BANANA CAKE WITH BANANA-NUT FROSTING

Chocolate adds a new twist to this banana cake.

2 cups sifted cake flour (sift before measuring)

1½ teaspoons baking powder
¾ teaspoon baking soda
¾ teaspoon salt
¾ cup mashed bananas (see procedures, below) (about 2 very ripe bananas)
2 ounces (2 squares) unsweetened chocolate
½ cup (¼ pound) butter *or* vegetable shortening, softened
1½ cups packed light brown sugar
¾ cup homemade sour milk (page 58)
2 extra-large eggs
1 teaspoon pure vanilla extract
1 recipe Banana-Nut Frosting (page 581)
Pecan halves for decoration

Preheat the oven to 350° F. Using Special Grease (page 56), grease two 8 × 2-inch round cake pans (see Note 1); set aside (see Note 2).

Onto waxed paper, sift together the flour, baking powder, baking soda, and salt; set aside. Slice the bananas into a medium-small mixing bowl; using a table fork, mash well. Measure ¾ cup mashed bananas; set aside.

Place the chocolate in a tiny saucepan. Hold the tiny pan over (not touching) low simmering water in a small saucepan until the chocolate melts, stirring intermittently. Remove the tiny pan from the heat; set aside.

In a large mixing bowl, place the butter and brown sugar; using an electric mixer, beat well on medium-high speed. Add the eggs, one at a time, beating well on medium-high speed after each addition. Add the vanilla; continue beating on medium-high speed until light and fluffy. Add the bananas; beat well. Add the melted chocolate; beat until blended. Add, alternately, the flour mixture in fourths, and the sour milk in thirds, beating on low speed after each addition only until blended.

Using a large mixing spoon, spoon the cake batter equally into the 2 prepared cake pans. Using a small, narrow spatula, lightly and quickly spread the batter evenly in the pans. Bake the cakes for 30 minutes, or until a wooden toothpick inserted into the center of the cakes comes out clean.

Remove the cakes from the oven and place on wire racks; let stand to cool 10 minutes. Remove the cakes from the pans (page 520); let stand on wire racks until completely cool.

Then, frost between the layers, and the top and side of the cake with the Banana-Nut Frosting (see To Frost a Cake, page 573). Arrange the pecan halves, side by side widthwise, on top of the cake around the outer edge. Let the cake stand until the frosting sets. Then, place the cake in an airtight container.

NOTE 1: Although not as satisfactory, the pans may be greased and floured in substitution for using Special Grease.

NOTE 2: Do not wrap bake-even cake strips (page 521) around the cake pans when using this recipe.

MAKES ONE 8-INCH, 2-LAYER ROUND CAKE; 10 SERVINGS

GERMAN CHOCOLATE CAKE

Sweet chocolate and frosting loaded with coconut and pecans distinguish this 3-layer, ever-popular cake. By tradition, the side of German Chocolate Cake usually is not frosted.

1 4-ounce German's sweet cooking chocolate bar, broken into several pieces
½ cup water
2¼ cups sifted cake flour (sift before measuring)
1½ teaspoons baking soda
½ teaspoon salt
¾ cup (¼ pound plus 4 tablespoons) butter, softened
1¼ cups sugar
4 extra-large eggs, room temperature, separated
1½ teaspoons pure vanilla extract
1 cup buttermilk
¼ cup sugar
1 recipe Coconut-Pecan Frosting I (page 582)

Preheat the oven to 350° F. Using Special Grease (page 56), grease three 8 × 2-inch round cake pans (see Note); set aside. Place 3 bake-even cake strips (page 521) in cold water; let stand.

In a small saucepan, place the chocolate pieces and water; place over medium-low heat and stir continuously until the chocolate melts. Remove from the heat; let stand to cool to room temperature.

Onto waxed paper, sift together the flour, baking soda, and salt; set aside.

Extract the excess water from the bake-even cake strips. Wrap and pin the strips around the prepared cake pans; set aside.

In a large mixing bowl, place the butter and 1¼ cups sugar; using an electric mixer, cream well on medium-high speed. Add the egg yolks, one at a time, beating well on medium-high speed after each addition. The batter should be very light and fluffy. Add the vanilla and melted chocolate; beat on medium-high speed until completely blended. Add, alternately, the flour mixture in fourths, and the buttermilk in thirds, beating on low speed after each addition only until blended; set aside.

Place the egg whites in a large mixing bowl. Using the electric mixer fit with clean, dry blades, beat the egg whites on high speed until soft peaks hold. While continuing to beat on high speed, very gradually add ¼ cup sugar and continue beating the egg white mixture until stiff, but still moist and glossy. Add the egg white mixture to the cake batter; using a large mixing spoon, fold in. (If the bowl in which the batter was mixed is not large enough, quickly and carefully transfer the batter to a larger mixing bowl before adding the egg white mixture.)

Using the large mixing spoon, spoon the batter equally into the 3 prepared cake pans. Using a small, narrow spatula, lightly and quickly spread the batter evenly in the pans. Bake the cakes for 30 minutes, or until a wooden toothpick inserted into the center of the cakes comes out clean.

Remove the cakes from the oven and place on wire racks; remove the cake strips. Let the

(Recipe continues on next page)

cakes stand to cool 10 minutes. Remove the cakes from the pans (page 520); let stand on wire racks until completely cool.

Then, frost between the layers, and the top, *but not the side,* of the cake with the Coconut-Pecan Frosting I (see To Frost a Cake, page 573). Let the cake stand until the frosting sets. Then, place the cake in an airtight container and refrigerate.

NOTE: Although not as satisfactory, the pans may be greased and floured in substitution for using Special Grease.

MAKES ONE 8-INCH, 3-LAYER ROUND CAKE; 10 SERVINGS

YELLOW CAKE

In contrast to White Cake, which uses egg whites and vegetable shortening to maintain its pure whiteness, Yellow Cake contains egg yolks and butter, which give this cake its warm, sunny hue. While Chocolate Frosting is customarily used on Yellow Cake, as called for in the recipe that follows, other frostings may be substituted, if you prefer (see Variation, below).

3 cups sifted cake flour (sift before measuring)
1 tablespoon plus ¾ teaspoon baking powder
¾ teaspoon salt
½ cup (¼ pound) butter
1½ cups sugar
2 extra-large eggs
1½ teaspoons pure vanilla extract
1 cup whole milk
1 recipe Chocolate Frosting (page 580), *or* other frosting of choice

Preheat the oven to 350° F. Using Special Grease (page 56), grease two 9 × 2-inch round cake pans (see Note); set aside. Place 2 bake-even cake strips (page 521) in cold water; let stand.

Onto waxed paper, sift together the flour, baking powder, and salt; set aside.

Extract the excess water from the bake-even cake strips. Wrap and pin the strips around the prepared cake pans; set aside.

In a large mixing bowl, place the butter and sugar; using an electric mixer, cream well on medium-high speed. Add the eggs, one at a time, beating well on medium-high speed after each addition. Add the vanilla; continue beating on medium-high speed until very light and fluffy. Add, alternately, the flour mixture in fourths, and the milk in thirds, beating on low speed after each addition only until blended.

Using a large mixing spoon, spoon the cake batter equally into the 2 prepared cake pans. Using a small, narrow spatula, lightly and quickly spread the batter evenly in the pans. Bake the cakes for 18 to 20 minutes, or until a wooden toothpick inserted into the center of the cakes comes out clean.

Remove the cakes from the oven and place on wire racks; remove the cake strips. Let the cakes stand to cool 10 minutes. Remove the cakes from the pans (page 520); let stand on wire racks until completely cool.

Then, frost between the layers, and the top and side of cake with the Chocolate Frosting (see To Frost a Cake, page 573). Let the cake stand until the frosting sets. Then, place the cake in an airtight container.

NOTE: Although not as satisfactory, the pans may be greased and floured in substitution for using Special Grease.

MAKES ONE 9-INCH, 2-LAYER ROUND CAKE; 12 SERVINGS

VARIATION: Add ¾ teaspoon lemon extract after adding the vanilla. Frost the cake with 1 recipe Lemon Buttercream Frosting (page 577).

BURNT-SUGAR CAKE

A longtime member of the cake hall of fame, Burnt-Sugar Cake's seductive, caramelized flavor continues to win its well-deserved praise and adoration.

2½ cups sifted cake flour (sift before measuring)
1 tablespoon baking powder
1 cup cold water
¼ cup cool Burnt-Sugar Syrup (recipe follows)
½ cup (¼ pound) butter, softened
1¼ cups sugar
2 extra-large eggs, room temperature, separated
1 teaspoon pure vanilla extract
¼ cup sugar
1 recipe Burnt-Sugar Frosting (page 578)

Preheat the oven to 350° F. Using Special Grease (page 56), grease two 9 × 2-inch round cake pans (see Note); set aside. Place 2 bake-even cake strips (page 521) in cold water; let stand.

Onto waxed paper, sift together the flour and baking powder; set aside. Into a small mixing bowl, pour the cold water and Burnt-Sugar Syrup; stir until blended; set aside.

Extract the excess water from the bake-even cake strips. Wrap and pin the strips around the prepared cake pans; set aside.

In a large mixing bowl, place the butter and 1¼ cups sugar; using an electric mixer, cream well on medium-high speed. Add the egg yolks, one at a time, beating well on medium-high speed after each addition. Add the vanilla; continue beating on medium-high until the batter is fluffy. Add, alternately, the flour mixture in fourths, and the burnt-sugar mixture in thirds, beating on low speed after each addition only until blended; set aside.

Place the egg whites in a medium mixing bowl. Using the electric mixer fit with clean, dry blades, beat the egg whites on high speed until soft peaks hold. While continuing to beat on high speed, very gradually add ¼ cup sugar

and continue beating the egg white mixture until it is stiff and cuts with a table knife, but is still moist and glossy. Add the egg white mixture to the cake batter; using a large mixing spoon, fold in.

Using the large mixing spoon, spoon the batter equally into the 2 prepared cake pans. Using a small, narrow spatula, lightly and quickly spread the batter evenly in the pans. Bake the cakes for 25 minutes, or until a wooden toothpick inserted into the center of the cakes comes out clean.

Remove the cakes from the oven and place on wire racks; remove the cake strips. Let the cakes stand to cool 10 minutes. Remove the cakes from the pans (page 520); let stand on wire racks until completely cool.

Then, frost between the layers, and the top and side of the cake with the Burnt-Sugar Frosting (see To Frost a Cake, page 573). Let the cake stand until the frosting sets. Then, place the cake in an airtight container.

NOTE: Although not as satisfactory, the pans may be greased and floured in substitution for using Special Grease.

MAKES ONE 9-INCH, 2-LAYER ROUND CAKE; 12 SERVINGS

Burnt-Sugar Syrup

⅔ cup sugar
⅔ cup boiling water

Place the sugar in a small, heavy saucepan over medium heat. Melt the sugar, stirring constantly. Continue stirring until the melted sugar is deep brown in color. Remove from the heat. Add the boiling water; stir until completely blended. Return the saucepan to medium heat. Bring the mixture to a boil and cook, without stirring, until the mixture is the consistency of syrup and reduced to ½ cup. Remove from the heat and cool at room temperature.

MAKES ½ CUP, ENOUGH FOR USE IN THE BURNT-SUGAR CAKE, ABOVE, AND 1 RECIPE OF BURNT-SUGAR FROSTING (PAGE 578).

HARVEST MOON CAKE

I resurrected this recipe from Mother's old three-ring recipe book (a treasure trove, believe me). She says Harvest Moon Cake was popular when she was young (that would have been in the 1930's). Why this grand-tasting cake made with brown sugar has been in hibernation is hard to fathom. The frosting, which matches the cake in color and name, is really Seven-Minute Frosting made with brown sugar rather than granulated sugar. I can't figure out how this cake got its name because it is very light brown in color—not gold, the color associated with the full harvest moon.

3 cups sifted cake flour (sift before
   measuring)
1 tablespoon baking powder
¼ teaspoon salt
¾ cup (¼ pound plus 4 tablespoons)
   butter, softened
1 cup plus 2 tablespoons packed light
   brown sugar
3 extra-large egg yolks
1½ teaspoons pure vanilla extract
1 cup whole milk
1 recipe Harvest Moon Frosting (page 579)
⅓ cup sliced, unblanched almonds, toasted
   (page 50) and chopped (page 50)

Preheat the oven to 350° F. Using Special Grease (page 56), grease two 8 × 2-inch round cake pans (see Note); set aside. Place 2 bake-even cake strips (page 521) in cold water; let stand.

Onto waxed paper, sift together the flour, baking powder, and salt; set aside.

Extract the excess water from the bake-even cake strips. Wrap and pin the strips around the prepared cake pans; set aside.

In a large mixing bowl, place the butter and brown sugar; using an electric mixer, cream well on medium-high speed. Add the egg yolks, one at a time, beating on medium-high speed after each addition. Add the vanilla; continue beating until completely blended. Add, alternately, the flour mixture in fourths, and the milk in thirds, beating on low speed after each addition only until blended.

Using a large mixing spoon, spoon the cake batter equally into the 2 prepared cake pans. Using a small, narrow spatula, lightly and quickly spread the batter evenly in the pans. Bake the cakes for 20 to 25 minutes, or until a wooden toothpick inserted into the center of the cakes comes out clean.

Remove the cakes from the oven and place on wire racks; remove the cake strips. Let the cakes stand to cool 10 minutes. Remove the cakes from the pans (page 520); let stand on wire racks until completely cool.

Then, frost between the layers, and the top and side of the cake with the Harvest Moon Frosting (see To Frost a Cake, page 573).

Sprinkle the chopped almonds in the form of a circle to resemble a full moon on the top of the cake. The perimeter of the moon should be about 1 inch from the outside edge of the cake. To achieve a well-formed moon with a sharp edge, make a stencil by using an X-Acto knife to cut a 6-inch-diameter circle out of the center of an 8-inch-diameter corrugated cardboard cake circle. With one hand, hold the stencil close to the frosting surface and, with the other hand, sprinkle the almonds evenly inside the circle.

Let the cake stand until the frosting sets. Then, place the cake in an airtight container.

NOTE: Although not as satisfactory, the pans may be greased and floured in substitution for using Special Grease.

**MAKES ONE 8-INCH, 2-LAYER ROUND CAKE;
10 SERVINGS**

CARROT CAKE

2 cups sifted all-purpose flour (sift before measuring)
1¾ teaspoons baking soda
1 teaspoon ground cinnamon
½ teaspoon salt
2 cups sugar
1½ cups vegetable oil
4 extra-large eggs
1 teaspoon pure vanilla extract
3 cups pared and medium-finely shredded carrots
1 cup broken pecans
Cream Cheese Frosting (recipe follows)

Preheat the oven to 350°F. Grease and lightly flour two 9 × 2-inch round cake pans; set aside.

Onto waxed paper, sift together the flour, baking soda, cinnamon, and salt. Place the flour mixture in a large mixing bowl. Add the sugar; using a large mixing spoon, stir to combine. Using the mixing spoon, make a well in the center of the flour mixture.

Pour the vegetable oil, all at once, into the well in the flour mixture; using an electric mixer, beat on medium-high speed until blended. While continuing to beat on medium-high speed, add the eggs, one at a time, beating after each addition until blended. Add the vanilla; beat on medium-high speed until blended. Add the carrots; beat on medium speed until evenly combined. Add the pecans; using the large mixing spoon, stir and fold until evenly distributed.

Using the large mixing spoon, spoon the cake batter equally into the 2 prepared cake pans. Using a small, narrow spatula, lightly and quickly spread the batter evenly in the pans. Bake the cakes for 35 minutes, or until a wooden toothpick inserted into the center of the cakes comes out clean.

Remove the cakes from the oven and place on wire racks; let stand to cool 10 minutes. Remove the cakes from the pans (page 520); let stand on wire racks until completely cool.

Then, frost between the layers, and the top and side of the cake with the Cream Cheese Frosting (see To Frost a Cake, page 573). Let the cake stand until the frosting sets. Then, place the cake in an airtight container and store in the refrigerator.

MAKES ONE 9-INCH, 2-LAYER ROUND CAKE; 12 SERVINGS

Cream Cheese Frosting

8 ounces cream cheese, softened
½ cup (¼ pound) butter, softened
1 teaspoon pure vanilla extract
1 pound (4 cups) powdered sugar
½ cup chopped pecans
½ cup raisins, quartered

In a medium mixing bowl, place the cream cheese and butter; using an electric mixer, beat on high speed until completely blended and smooth. Add the vanilla; beat on medium-high speed until blended. Add the powdered sugar; mix on low speed and then beat on medium-high speed only until blended and fluffy. Add the pecans and raisins; using a large spoon, stir until evenly distributed.

OPTIONAL DECORATION

¼ recipe Cake Decorators' White Icing (page 576)
Orange and leaf green paste food coloring

Tint ½ of the Cake Decorators' White Icing orange and the remaining ½ of the icing leaf green (see To Tint Icing, page 386). Place the orange-tinted icing in a decorating bag fit with small round tip number 5 (page 383) and the leaf green–tinted icing in a decorating bag fit with very small round tip number 2.

Pipe 5 or more orange carrots with green, leafy tops around the top of the cake, with the small end of the carrots pointing toward the center of the cake.

PINK CHAMPAGNE CAKE

This fashionable Midwest cake derives its name more from its color and elegance than from the champagne it contains. Actually, only 1 tablespoon of champagne is used in the custard filling, and none is included among the other cake ingredients. That leaves the remainder of the bottle to pour into fluted champagne glasses and raise in a toast to a luxurious dessert.

2¼ cups sifted cake flour (sift before
    measuring)
1 tablespoon baking powder
¾ teaspoon salt
1 cup superfine sugar
⅓ cup vegetable oil
½ cup whole milk
2 extra-large eggs, room temperature,
    separated
1 teaspoon clear vanilla
1 dot, pink paste food coloring
½ cup whole milk
½ cup superfine sugar
Champagne Custard Filling (recipe follows)
1 recipe Cake Decorators' White Icing
    (page 576)
Pink paste food coloring

Preheat the oven to 325° F. Grease well and flour lightly two 9 × 2-inch round cake pans; set aside. Place 2 bake-even cake strips (page 521) in cold water; let stand.

Onto waxed paper, sift together the flour, baking powder, and salt.

Extract the excess water from the bake-even cake strips. Wrap and pin the strips around the prepared cake pans; set aside.

Place the flour mixture in a large mixing bowl. Add 1 cup sugar; using a large mixing spoon, stir to combine. Using the mixing spoon, make a well in the center of the flour mixture.

Pour the vegetable oil and ½ cup milk into the well in the flour mixture; using an electric mixer, beat on medium speed until blended. Add the egg yolks, one at a time, beating well on medium-high speed after each addition. Add the vanilla, dot of pink food coloring (use a toothpick), and ½ cup milk; continue beating on medium-high speed until well blended; set aside.

Place the egg whites in a large mixing bowl. Using the electric mixer fit with clean, dry blades, beat the egg whites on high speed until soft peaks hold. While continuing to beat on high speed, very gradually add ½ cup sugar and continue beating the egg white mixture until stiff, but still moist and glossy. Add the egg white mixture to the cake batter; using a large mixing spoon, fold in until blended and the color is even.

Using the large mixing spoon, spoon the batter equally into the 2 prepared cake pans. Using a small, narrow spatula, lightly and quickly spread the batter evenly in the pans. Bake the cakes for 30 to 35 minutes, or until a wooden toothpick inserted the into center of the cakes comes out clean.

Remove the cakes from the oven and place on wire racks; remove the cake strips. Let the cakes stand to cool 10 minutes. Remove the cakes from the pans (page 520); let stand on wire racks until completely cool.

Then, spread the Champagne Custard Filling between the cake layers (see To Frost a Cake, page 573); set aside. Reserve 1½ cups of the Cake Decorators' White Icing. Tint the remainder of the icing pale pink (see To Tint Icing, page 386). Use the pink-tinted icing to frost smoothly the top and side of the cake. Using a decorating bag fit with medium open-star tip number 19 (page 383), pipe a shell border (page 389) of the reserved white icing around the bottom of the cake, and a reverse shell border (page 390) of the reserved white icing around the top edge of the cake.

Let the cake stand until the frosting sets. Then, place the cake in an airtight container and store in refrigerator.

**MAKES ONE 9-INCH, 2-LAYER ROUND CAKE;
12 SERVINGS**

Champagne Custard Filling

¼ cup granulated sugar
1 tablespoon plus 2 teaspoons cornstarch
Dash of salt
⅔ cup whole milk
1 extra-large egg yolk, slightly beaten
2 teaspoons butter
½ teaspoon pure vanilla extract
2 tablespoons butter, softened
1 cup powdered sugar
Dash of salt
½ teaspoon pure vanilla extract
1 tablespoon champagne
1¼ teaspoons cognac
¾ cup powdered sugar

In the top of a double boiler, place the granulated sugar, cornstarch, and dash of salt; stir to combine. Add the milk; stir well. Place the top of the double boiler over simmering water in the bottom pan. Cook the mixture until thick (about 2 to 3 minutes), constantly beating with a handheld electric mixer on low speed or stirring with a spoon. Add about ¼ cup of the hot cornstarch mixture to the egg yolk and quickly stir in. Then, add the egg yolk mixture to the remaining cornstarch mixture and stir vigorously to blend. Cook the mixture 2 minutes, beating constantly with the electric mixer on low speed.

Remove the top of the double boiler from the bottom pan and place on a wire rack. Add 2 teaspoons butter and ½ teaspoon vanilla; using the electric mixer, beat on low speed until blended. Let the custard mixture stand until cooled to room temperature, stirring occasionally.

Then, in a small mixing bowl, place 2 tablespoons softened butter, 1 cup powdered sugar, dash of salt, ½ teaspoon vanilla, champagne, and cognac; using the electric mixer, beat on high speed until blended and fluffy. Add the custard mixture and ¾ cup powdered sugar; beat on high speed until blended.

LADY BALTIMORE CAKE

This is a cake with a history, although that history has several versions. The gist of the story is that the cake was baked by a Charleston, South Carolina, lady for Owen Wister, a novelist who then described the cake in his 1906 book Lady Baltimore. *While there are varying accounts of the cake's origin, everyone agrees on how it should be made: It is a three-layer white cake filled with figs, raisins, nuts, and candied cherries in white Boiled Frosting, all of which is iced with the remainder of the frosting. It's a glamorous, wonderful delicacy!*

1 recipe Boiled Frosting (page 578)
½ cup chopped dried figs (page 45)
½ cup chopped raisins (page 45)
4 ounces (½ cup) red candied cherries, chopped (page 45)
½ cup broken English walnuts
Baked cake layers for one 8-inch, 3-layer White Cake (page 525), substituting 1 teaspoon clear vanilla and ½ teaspoon almond extract for 1½ teaspoons clear vanilla
2 tablespoons chopped raisins
3 tablespoons chopped English walnuts
2 tablespoons quartered, red candied cherries

In a medium mixing bowl, place 2 cups of the Boiled Frosting, figs, ½ cup chopped raisins, 4 ounces chopped cherries, and ½ cup walnuts; stir to combine and evenly distribute the fruits and nuts. Spread the frosting mixture between the cake layers, but not on the top or side of the cake (see To Frost a Cake, page 573). Using the remaining plain Boiled Frosting, frost the top and side of the cake.

Sprinkle the top of the cake with 2 tablespoons chopped raisins and 3 tablespoons chopped walnuts. Then, randomly distribute 2 tablespoons quartered cherries over the top of the cake. Let the cake stand until the frosting sets. Then, place the cake in an airtight container.

MAKES ONE 8-INCH, 3-LAYER ROUND CAKE; 10 SERVINGS

PRUNELLA CAKE WITH HICKORY NUTS AND CREAMY CINNAMON FROSTING

Interesting ingredients join superbly in this outstanding cake.

1 cup soft prunes diced ¼ inch square
  (purchase bite-sized, pitted prunes to
  dice)
1⅓ cups all purpose flour
½ teaspoon baking powder
½ teaspoon baking soda
½ teaspoon ground cinnamon
½ teaspoon ground nutmeg
½ teaspoon ground allspice
½ teaspoon salt
½ cup vegetable shortening, softened
1 cup sugar
2 extra-large eggs
⅔ cup homemade sour milk (page 58)
1 recipe Creamy Cinnamon Frosting
  (page 578)
1½ cups broken hickory nuts*

*English walnuts may be substituted if hickory nuts are not available.

Preheat the oven to 350° F. Using Special Grease (page 56), grease two 8 × 2-inch round cake pans (see Note); set aside. Place 2 bake-even cake strips (page 521) in cold water; let stand.

Place the prunes in a small mixing bowl. Sprinkle 1 tablespoon of the measured flour over the prunes; stir until the prunes are evenly dusted; set aside. Onto waxed paper, sift together the remaining flour, baking powder, baking soda, cinnamon, nutmeg, allspice, and salt; set aside.

Extract the excess water from the bake-even cake strips. Wrap and pin the strips around the prepared cake pans; set aside.

In a large mixing bowl, place the vegetable shortening and sugar; using an electric mixer, cream well on medium-high speed. While continuing to beat on medium-high speed, add the eggs, one at a time, and beat until fluffy. Add, alternately, the flour mixture in fourths, and the sour milk in thirds, beating on low speed after each addition only until blended. Add the prunes; using a large mixing spoon, quickly fold in.

Using the large mixing spoon, spoon the cake batter equally into the 2 prepared cake pans. Using a small, narrow spatula, lightly and quickly spread the batter evenly in the pans. Bake the cakes for 25 minutes, or until a wooden toothpick inserted into the center of the cakes comes out clean.

Remove the cakes from the oven and place on wire racks; remove the cakes strips. Let the cakes stand to cool 10 minutes. Remove the cakes from the pans (page 520); let stand on wire racks until completely cool.

Then, frost the cake between the layers, on the top, and, generously, on the side with the Creamy Cinnamon Frosting, reserving some of the frosting to later decorate the top of the cake. Apply the frosting as smoothly as possible (see To Frost a Cake, page 573).

Press a small handful of hickory nuts, one by one, into the frosting around the side of the cake until the side is covered with nuts. Using a decorating bag fit with medium open-star tip number 21 (page 383) and filled with the reserved frosting, pipe a shell border (page 389) around the top edge of cake. Then, using large drop flower tip number 2D, pipe a large drop flower decoration (page 390) in the center of cake and smaller dropflower decorations spaced evenly around the top of the cake between the border and the center decoration. Place a small piece of broken hickory nut in the center of each of the smaller drop flower decorations. Let the cake stand until frosting sets. Then, place the cake in an airtight container.

NOTE: Although not as satisfactory, the pans may be greased and floured in substitution for using Special Grease.

MAKES ONE 8-INCH, 2-LAYER ROUND CAKE; 10 SERVINGS

WHIPPED CREAM CAKE WITH CRÈME DE MENTHE FROSTING

I decided to try making a whipped cream cake when I noticed it listed among the cake classes to be judged at the 1990 Iowa State Fair. After studying about whipped cream cakes, and two or three testings, I wrote the recipe that follows. I'm happy to report that the end result garnered a blue ribbon.

3 cups sifted cake flour (sift before measuring)
1 tablespoon baking powder
½ teaspoon salt
1½ cups sugar
1½ cups whipping cream, unwhipped
1½ teaspoons pure vanilla extract
3 extra-large eggs, room temperature
1 recipe Crème de Menthe Whipped Cream Frosting (page 582)
Sprig(s) of fresh mint leaves for decoration

Preheat the oven to 350° F. Grease well and flour lightly two 8 × 2-inch round cake pans; set aside. Place 2 bake-even cake strips (page 521) in cold water; let stand.

Onto waxed paper, sift together the flour, baking powder, salt, and sugar; set aside.

Pour the whipping cream into a medium mixing bowl. Using an electric mixer, beat the cream on medium-high speed until it begins to stiffen. Reduce the mixer speed to medium-low. Add the vanilla and continue beating the cream until stiff, but still soft and fluffy; cover and refrigerate.

Extract the excess water from the bake-even cake strips. Wrap and pin the strips around the prepared cake pans; set aside.

Place the eggs in a small mixing bowl. Using the electric mixer fit with clean, dry blades, beat the eggs on high speed 5 minutes, until thick and lemon colored; set aside. Turn the whipped cream into a large mixing bowl. Pour the beaten eggs over the whipped cream; using a large mix-ing spoon, fold in thoroughly but quickly. Sprinkle the flour mixture, about 1 cup at a time, over the whipped cream mixture and fold in after each addition, using the large mixing spoon.

Using the large mixing spoon, spoon the cake batter equally into the 2 prepared cake pans. Using a small, narrow spatula, lightly and quickly spread the batter evenly in the pans. Bake the cakes for 25 to 30 minutes, or until a wooden toothpick inserted into the center of the cakes comes out clean.

Remove the cakes from the oven and place on wire racks; remove the cake strips. Let the cakes stand to cool 10 minutes. Remove the cakes from the pans (page 520); let stand on wire racks until completely cool.

Then, frost between the layers, and the top and side of cake with the Crème de Menthe Whipped Cream Frosting (see To Frost a Cake, page 573). Place the cake in an airtight container and store in the refrigerator.

Just before displaying the cake prior to serving, place a sprig of mint leaves in the center of the cake; or, place slices of cake on individual plates and decorate each plate with a small sprig of mint leaves.

MAKES ONE 8-INCH, 2-LAYER ROUND CAKE; 10 SERVINGS

VARIATIONS

- For an attractive holiday cake, decorate the cake with red maraschino cherries which have been cut in half lengthwise, then rinsed under cold, running water and dried between paper towels. Add small sprigs of fresh mint leaves, if desired.

- Frost the cake with Whipped Cream–Coconut Frosting (page 581).

SPICE CAKE

Caramel Frosting and chopped hazelnuts top this two-layer Spice Cake.

2¼ cups sifted cake flour (sift before
   measuring)
1 teaspoon baking powder
1 teaspoon baking soda
½ teaspoon salt
1 teaspoon ground cinnamon
¼ teaspoon ground nutmeg
¼ teaspoon ground cloves
½ cup (¼ pound) butter, softened
¾ cup granulated sugar
⅔ cup packed light brown sugar
3 extra-large eggs
1 cup buttermilk
1 recipe Caramel Frosting (page 580)
3 tablespoons chopped hazelnuts
   (page 50)

Preheat the oven to 350° F. Using Special Grease (page 56), grease two 9 × 2-inch round cake pans (see Note); set aside. Place 2 bake-even cake strips (page 521) in cold water; let stand.

Onto waxed paper, sift together the flour, baking powder, baking soda, salt, cinnamon, nutmeg, and cloves; set aside.

Extract the excess water from the bake-even cake strips. Wrap and pin the strips around the prepared cake pans; set aside.

In a large mixing bowl, place the butter, granulated sugar, and brown sugar; using an electric mixer, beat on medium-high speed until creamed. Add the eggs, one at a time, beating well on medium-high speed after each addition. Add, alternately, the flour mixture in fourths, and the buttermilk in thirds, beating on low speed after each addition only until blended.

Using a large mixing spoon, spoon the cake batter equally into the 2 prepared cake pans. Using a small, narrow spatula, lightly and quickly spread the batter evenly in the pans. Bake the cakes for 30 minutes, or until a

wooden toothpick inserted into the center of the cakes comes out clean.

Remove the cakes from the oven and place on wire racks; remove the cake strips. Let the cakes stand to cool 10 minutes. Remove the cakes from the pans (page 520); let stand on wire racks until completely cool.

Then, frost between the layers, and the top and side of cake with the Caramel Frosting (see To Frost a Cake, page 573). Sprinkle the chopped hazelnuts over the top of the cake. Let the cake stand until the frosting sets. Then, place the cake in an airtight container.

NOTE: Although not as satisfactory, the pans may be greased and floured in substitution for using Special Grease.

MAKES ONE 9-INCH, 2-LAYER ROUND CAKE; 12 SERVINGS

VARIATION: Powdered Sugar Frosting (page 580) is also excellent on Spice Cake.

Sheet Cakes

APPLESAUCE CAKE WITH VANILLA SAUCE

A delicious, golden oldie from the recipe file of Ada Goreham, originally from Grinnell, Iowa, and mother of Dee Staples, my sister-in-law.

1 cup golden raisins, plumped (page 46)
½ cup broken pecans
2 cups sifted cake flour (sift before
   measuring)
1 teaspoon baking soda
¼ teaspoon salt
¾ teaspoon ground cinnamon
½ teaspoon ground nutmeg
½ teaspoon ground cloves
⅓ cup vegetable shortening, softened

1 cup sugar
1 extra-large egg
1½ cups puree-style, unsweetened, Plain Applesauce, homemade (page 344) or commercially canned
Vanilla Sauce (recipe follows)

Drain the plumped raisins in a sieve; distribute over paper towels to dry.

Preheat the oven to 350° F. Using Special Grease (page 56), grease a 7 × 11 × 2-inch baking pan (see Note); set aside.

In a small mixing bowl, place the dry raisins and pecans; stir to combine; set aside. Sprinkle 1 tablespoon of the measured flour over the raisin-pecan mixture; stir until evenly dusted; set aside. Onto waxed paper, sift together the remaining flour, baking soda, salt, cinnamon, nutmeg, and cloves; set aside.

In a large mixing bowl, place the vegetable shortening and sugar; using an electric mixer, cream well on medium-high speed. Add the egg; beat well on medium-high speed. Add, alternately, the flour mixture in fourths, and the applesauce in thirds, beating on low speed after each addition only until blended.

Pour the cake batter into the prepared baking pan. Using a small, narrow spatula, lightly and quickly spread the batter evenly in the pan. Bake the cake for 30 to 35 minutes, or until a wooden toothpick inserted into the center of the cake comes out clean.

Remove the cake from the oven and place on a wire rack. Serve the cake warm, with the warm Vanilla Sauce spooned over individual servings.

NOTE: Although not as satisfactory, the pan may be greased and floured in substitution for using Special Grease.

MAKES ONE 7 × 11-INCH SHEET CAKE; 12 SERVINGS

Vanilla Sauce

½ cup sugar
2 tablespoons cornstarch
¼ teaspoon salt
2 cups water
¼ cup (4 tablespoons) butter
2 teaspoons clear vanilla

In a small saucepan, place the sugar, cornstarch, and salt; stir to combine. Add the water; stir well. Bring the mixture to a full boil over medium heat, stirring constantly. Reduce the heat and cook the mixture until thick, stirring continuously. Remove from the heat. Add the butter and vanilla; stir until blended. Serve warm.

RHUBARB CAKE

When rhubarb is cut and brought into the house for the preparation of eagerly awaited rhubarb dishes, it's a sure sign that spring has arrived at last. When most Midwesterners see the rosy red stalks being washed and cut in the kitchen, they anticipate delighting in pies, crunchy desserts, and quick breads (see Rhubarb Pie, page 483; Strawberry-Rhubarb Pie, page 484; Rhubarb Rapture, page 654; and Rhubarb Bread, page 438). For variety during the next rhubarb-feasting season, surprise everyone with this tasty Rhubarb Cake with tantalizing Buttercream Frosting.

2 cups cake flour
1 teaspoon baking soda
¼ teaspoon salt
½ cup (¼ pound) butter, softened
1½ cups sugar
1 extra-large egg
1¼ teaspoons pure vanilla extract
1 cup whole milk
2 cups fresh rhubarb, diced ¼ inch square
1 recipe Buttercream Frosting (page 577)

(Recipe continues on next page)

Preheat the oven to 350° F. Using Special Grease (page 56), grease a 7 × 11 × 2-inch baking pan (see Note); set aside.

Reserve 1 tablespoon of the measured flour in a small sauce dish. Onto waxed paper, sift together the remaining flour, baking soda, and salt; set aside.

In a large mixing bowl, place the butter and sugar; using an electric mixer, cream well on medium-high speed. Add the egg and vanilla; beat on medium-high speed until light and fluffy. Add, alternately, the flour mixture in fourths, and the milk in thirds, beating on low speed after each addition only until blended; set aside.

Place the rhubarb in a medium mixing bowl. Sprinkle the 1 tablespoon reserved flour over the rhubarb; toss until the rhubarb is coated. Add the rhubarb to the cake batter; using a large mixing spoon, fold in only until evenly distributed.

Turn the batter into the prepared baking pan. Using a small, narrow spatula, lightly and quickly spread the batter evenly in the pan. Bake the cake for 40 to 45 minutes.

Remove the cake from the oven and place on a wire rack to cool.

When completely cool, leave the cake in the pan and frost it with the Buttercream Frosting. Let the cake stand until the frosting sets. Then, cover the cake with aluminum foil.

NOTE: Although not as satisfactory, the pan may be greased and floured in substitution for using Special Grease.

**MAKES ONE 7 × 11-INCH SHEET CAKE;
12 SERVINGS**

FRUIT COCKTAIL CAKE

1 16-ounce can commercial fruit cocktail in heavy syrup
2 cups all-purpose flour
2 teaspoons baking soda
2 tablespoons butter, softened
1½ cups sugar
2 extra-large eggs
1 recipe Coconut-Pecan Frosting II (page 582)

Preheat the oven to 350° F. Using Special Grease (page 56), grease a 9 × 13 × 2-inch baking pan (see Note); set aside.

Drain the fruit cocktail in a sieve, reserving the syrup. Place the fruit in a small mixing bowl and pour the syrup into a glass measuring cup with pouring spout; set aside.

Reserve 2 tablespoons of the measured flour in a small sauce dish; set aside. Onto waxed paper, sift together the remaining flour and baking soda; set aside.

In a large mixing bowl, place the butter and sugar; using an electric mixer, beat on medium-high speed until the mixture is the texture of crumbs. Add the eggs, one at a time, beating well on medium-high speed after each addition. Add, alternately, the flour mixture in fourths, and the fruit syrup in thirds, beating on low speed after each addition only until blended; set aside.

Sprinkle the 2 tablespoons reserved flour over the fruit and quickly toss to coat. Add the fruit to the cake batter; using a large mixing spoon, fold in only until evenly distributed.

Pour the batter into the prepared baking pan. Using a small, narrow spatula, lightly and quickly spread the batter evenly in the pan. Bake the cake for 30 minutes.

Remove the cake from the oven and place on a wire rack; let stand to cool 30 minutes. While the cake is still warm, frost it in the pan with the Coconut-Pecan Frosting II. Let the cake stand on the wire rack until completely cool. Then, cover the cake with aluminum foil or a baking pan cover.

NOTE: Although not as satisfactory, the pan may be greased and floured in substitution for using Special Grease.

MAKES ONE 9 × 13-INCH SHEET CAKE; 18 SERVINGS

PINEAPPLE UPSIDE-DOWN CAKE

1 20-ounce can commercial pineapple slices in unsweetened pineapple juice
½ cup juice drained from pineapple slices
2 tablespoons plus 2 teaspoons butter
½ cup packed dark brown sugar
3 red maraschino cherries, cut in half lengthwise
1¼ cups sifted all-purpose flour (sift before measuring)
2 teaspoons baking powder
¼ cup plus 2 tablespoons (6 tablespoons) butter, softened
½ cup sugar
1 extra-large egg
1 teaspoon pure vanilla extract
1 recipe Whipped Cream (page 373)

Preheat the oven to 350° F.

Drain the pineapple slices well in a sieve, reserving the juice. Measure ½ cup of the reserved pineapple juice. Set the pineapple slices and reserved juice aside.

Place 2 tablespoons plus 2 teaspoons butter in an *ungreased* 8 × 8 × 2-inch baking pan. Place the baking pan over warm heat; let stand until the butter melts. Remove from the heat. Tilt the pan back and forth to spread the melted butter over the entire bottom of the pan. Sprinkle the brown sugar evenly over the butter in the bottom of the pan. Over the brown sugar, arrange 1 pineapple slice near each of the corners of the pan, and 1 pineapple slice in the center of the pan. Place ½ of a maraschino cherry, cut side

up, in the center of each pineapple slice. If desired, an additional ¼ slice of pineapple and 1 maraschino cherry half may be placed on each side of the pan between the slices, allowing each serving of cake to be topped with pineapple and a cherry half when the cake is cut into 9 servings; set aside.

Onto waxed paper, sift together the flour and baking powder; set aside.

In a medium mixing bowl, place ¼ cup plus 2 tablespoons butter and sugar; using an electric mixer, cream well on medium-high speed. Add the egg; beat on medium-high speed until fluffy. Add the vanilla; continue beating on medium-high speed until well blended. Add, alternately, the flour mixture in thirds, and the reserved pineapple syrup in halves, beating on low speed after each addition only until blended.

Using a large mixing spoon, spoon the cake batter over the pineapple slices in the bottom of the pan. Using a small, narrow spatula, spread the batter evenly over the entire bottom of the pan, being careful not to disturb the arrangement of the pineapple slices and cherries. Bake the cake for 40 minutes.

Remove the cake from the oven and place on a wire rack; let stand to cool 10 minutes. Then, run a sharp, thin-bladed knife along the inside edges of the cake pan. Invert the cake onto a serving plate. Carefully lift the pan off the cake. Let the cake stand until completely cool. Then, cover the cake with an airtight dome or place it in an airtight container.

Pass the Whipped Cream in an inviting serving bowl at the table.

MAKES ONE 8-INCH-SQUARE SHEET-TYPE CAKE; 9 SERVINGS

WACKY CAKE

So unorthodox are the mixing procedures for this fun cake, it has been dubbed "Wacky Cake." Who has ever heard of making holes in the flour mixture in the pan and pouring a different ingredient into each of them? Well, it works. When you're looking for a little cooking levity, you're sure to get a kick out of baking this good-tasting, maverick cake.

1½ cups cake flour
1 teaspoon baking soda
½ teaspoon salt
3 tablespoons unsweetened cocoa powder
1 cup sugar
1 tablespoon cider vinegar
1 teaspoon pure vanilla extract
¼ cup plus 2 tablespoons (6 tablespoons)
  butter, melted
1 cup water
½ recipe Buttercream Frosting (page 577)
  or ½ recipe Chocolate Frosting
  (page 580)

Preheat the oven to 350° F.

Into an *ungreased* 8 × 8 × 2-inch baking pan, sift together the flour, baking soda, salt, cocoa, and sugar; using a small, narrow spatula, spread evenly in the pan. Using a tablespoon, make 2 small holes and 1 large hole in the flour mixture, making the holes in a triangular pattern around the central part of the cake pan. Into 1 of the small holes, pour the vinegar. Into the other small hole, pour the vanilla. Into the large hole, pour the melted butter. Pour 1 cup water over all. Using a tablespoon, stir and beat the mixture well, until blended. The cake batter will be very slightly lumpy.

Using a damp sponge, remove the excess batter from the sides of the pan above the batter. Bake the cake for 30 minutes, or until a wooden toothpick inserted into the center of the cake comes out clean.

Remove the cake from the oven and place on a wire rack to cool.

When completely cool, leave the cake in the pan and frost it with the Buttercream Frosting or the Chocolate Frosting. Let the cake stand until the frosting sets. Then, cover the cake with aluminum foil.

MAKES ONE 8-INCH-SQUARE SHEET CAKE; 10 SERVINGS

GINGERBREAD

Counter the cool breezes of fall and the winds of winter with warm pieces of gingerbread, enhanced, if you like, with Rum or Lemon Sauce spooned over the top.

1 cup water
2 teaspoons baking soda
2½ cups sifted all-purpose flour (sift before
  measuring)
1 teaspoon ground ginger
1 teaspoon ground cinnamon
1 teaspoon ground cloves
½ teaspoon ground allspice
½ cup (¼ pound) butter, softened
½ cup sugar
1 cup light molasses
2 extra-large eggs

Preheat the oven to 350° F. Grease and flour lightly a 7 × 11 × 2-inch baking pan; set aside.

Pour 1 cup water into a very small saucepan. Bring the water to a boil over high heat. Remove from the heat. Add the baking soda; stir to dissolve; set aside.

Onto waxed paper, sift together the flour, ginger, cinnamon, cloves, and allspice; set aside.

In a large mixing bowl, place the butter and sugar; using an electric mixer, cream well on medium-high speed. Add the molasses; beat on medium-high until blended. Add the eggs, one at a time, beating well on medium-high speed after each addition. Add, alternately, the flour mixture in fourths, and the baking soda mixture in thirds, beating on low speed after each addition only until blended.

Pour the Gingerbread batter into the prepared pan. Using a small, narrow spatula, lightly and quickly spread the batter evenly in the pan. Bake the Gingerbread for 35 to 40 minutes, or until a wooden toothpick inserted into the center of the Gingerbread comes out clean.

Remove the Gingerbread from the oven and place on a wire rack to cool. When completely cool, cover the Gingerbread with aluminum foil.

MAKES ONE 7 × 11-INCH SHEET CAKE; 12 SERVINGS

SERVING SUGGESTIONS

- Spoon warm Rum Sauce (page 373) or Lemon Sauce (page 372) over individual servings.

- Serve Gingerbread with a generous dollop of Whipped Cream (page 373) on each slice.

SOUR CREAM SPICE CAKE

Here is the recipe for one of the cakes my mother made the most often when we were kids. It was—and still is—my brother's favorite.

3 cups all-purpose flour
2 teaspoons baking soda
½ teaspoon cream of tartar
½ teaspoon salt
2 teaspoons ground cinnamon
½ teaspoon ground cloves
½ teaspoon ground nutmeg
1 cup raisins, plumped (page 46), drained, and dried between several layers of paper towels
1 cup broken English walnuts
2 cups sugar
2 cups homemade sour cream (page 58)
4 extra-large eggs
1 recipe Powdered Sugar Frosting (page 580)

Preheat the oven to 350° F. Using Special Grease (page 56), grease a 9 × 13 × 2-inch baking pan (see Note); set aside.

Reserve 1 tablespoon of the measured flour in a small sauce dish. Onto waxed paper, sift together the remaining flour, baking soda, cream of tartar, salt, cinnamon, cloves, and nutmeg; set aside.

In a medium mixing bowl, place the raisins and walnuts. Sprinkle the 1 tablespoon reserved flour over the raisins and walnuts; toss until lightly dusted and evenly distributed; set aside.

In a large mixing bowl, place the sugar and sour cream; using an electric mixer, blend well on medium-high speed. Add the eggs, one at a time, beating well on medium-high speed after each addition. Continue beating the mixture on medium-high until fluffy. Add the flour mixture; beat on low speed only until well blended. Add the raisins and walnuts; using a large mixing spoon, fold in.

Turn the cake batter into the prepared baking pan. Using a small, narrow spatula, lightly and quickly spread the batter evenly in the pan. Bake the cake for 30 to 35 minutes, or until a wooden toothpick inserted into the center of the cake comes out clean.

Remove the cake from the oven and place on a wire rack to cool.

When completely cool, leave the cake in the pan and frost it with the Powdered Sugar Frosting. Let the cake stand until the frosting sets. Then, cover the cake with aluminum foil or a baking pan cover.

NOTE: Although not as satisfactory, the pan may be greased and floured in substitution for using Special Grease.

MAKES ONE 9 × 13-INCH SHEET CAKE; 15 SERVINGS

OATMEAL CAKE

A rich, lush, dessert-type cake.

1½ cups water
1 cup quick-cooking rolled oats, uncooked
1½ cups sifted cake flour (sift before measuring)
1 teaspoon baking soda
½ teaspoon salt
1 teaspoon ground cinnamon
½ cup vegetable shortening, softened
1 cup granulated sugar
1 cup packed light brown sugar
2 extra-large eggs
Topping (recipe follows)
¾ cup whipping cream, unwhipped
1 tablespoon granulated sugar
½ teaspoon pure vanilla extract

Preheat the oven to 325° F. Using Special Grease (page 56), grease a 9 × 13 × 2-inch baking pan (see Note); set aside.

Pour 1½ cups water into a medium saucepan; bring the water to a boil over high heat. Add the oats; stir to combine. Remove from the heat; let stand.

Onto waxed paper, sift together the flour, baking soda, salt, and cinnamon; set aside.

In a large mixing bowl, place the vegetable shortening, 1 cup granulated sugar, and brown sugar; using an electric mixer, cream well on medium-high speed. Add the eggs, one at a time, beating well on medium-high speed after each addition. Add the flour mixture; beat on low speed only until blended. Add the oatmeal mixture; beat on low speed only until combined.

Pour the cake batter into the prepared baking pan. Using a small, narrow spatula, lightly and quickly spread the batter evenly in the pan. Bake the cake for 35 minutes, or until a wooden toothpick inserted into the center of the cake comes out clean.

Remove the cake from the oven and place on a wire rack. Increase the oven temperature to 400° F. Spoon the Topping over the hot cake in the pan; using the small spatula, spread as evenly as possible, being careful not to crush the cake. Return the cake to the oven; bake for 8 additional minutes.

Remove the cake from the oven and place on the wire rack; let stand until completely cool. Then, cover the cake with aluminum foil or a baking pan cover.

Shortly before serving, pour the whipping cream into a small mixing bowl. Using the electric mixer fit with clean, dry blades, beat the cream on medium-high speed until it begins to stiffen. Reduce the mixer speed to medium-low. Add 1 tablespoon granulated sugar and vanilla; continue beating the cream until stiff, but still soft and fluffy; cover and refrigerate. Spoon a small dollop of whipped cream over individual pieces of Oatmeal Cake at serving time.

NOTE: Although not as satisfactory, the pan may be greased and floured in substitution for using Special Grease.

MAKES ONE 9 × 13-INCH SHEET CAKE; 15 SERVINGS

Topping

½ cup (¼ pound) butter
½ cup packed light brown sugar
¼ cup whipping cream, unwhipped
1 teaspoon pure vanilla extract
1 cup chopped pecans
1 cup flaked coconut

In a small saucepan, melt the butter over low heat. Remove from the heat. Add the brown sugar; using an electric mixer, beat on medium speed until blended. Add the whipping cream and vanilla; beat to blend. Add the pecans and coconut; using a spoon, stir until evenly combined.

COLA CAKE

Would you believe? Your favorite cola is an ingredient in both this yummy chocolate cake and its nutty, chocolate frosting. Wonders never cease.

2 cups cake flour
2 cups sugar
1/2 cup (1/4 pound) butter
1 cup Coca-Cola Classic cola *or* regular
   Pepsi-Cola cola
3 tablespoons unsweetened cocoa powder
1/2 cup buttermilk
2 extra-large eggs, well beaten
1 teaspoon baking soda
1 teaspoon pure vanilla extract
1 1/2 cups miniature marshmallows
Cola Icing (recipe follows)

Preheat the oven to 350° F. Using Special Grease (page 56), grease a 9 × 13 × 2-inch baking pan (see Note); set aside.

Onto waxed paper, sift together the flour and sugar. Place the flour mixture in a large mixing bowl; set aside.

In a small saucepan, place the butter, cola, and cocoa; stir. Bring the cola mixture to the boiling point over medium heat, stirring constantly. Pour the cola mixture over the flour mixture; using an electric mixer, beat well on medium-high speed. Add the buttermilk, eggs, baking soda, vanilla, and marshmallows; beat well.

Pour the cake batter into the prepared baking pan. Using a small, narrow spatula, lightly and quickly spread the batter evenly in the pan. Bake the cake for 40 minutes, or until a wooden toothpick inserted into the center of the cake comes out clean.

Remove the cake from the oven and place on a wire rack. Spread the Cola Icing over the *hot* cake in the pan. Let the cake stand on the wire rack until completely cool. Then, cover the cake with aluminum foil or a baking pan cover.

NOTE: Although not as satisfactory, the pan may be greased and floured in substitution for using Special Grease.

**MAKES ONE 9 × 13-INCH SHEET CAKE;
15 SERVINGS**

Cola Icing

1 pound (4 cups) powdered sugar
1/2 cup (1/4 pound) butter
1/4 cup plus 2 tablespoons Coca-Cola
   Classic cola *or* regular Pepsi-Cola cola
3 tablespoons unsweetened cocoa powder
1 cup chopped pecans

Place the powdered sugar in a medium mixing bowl; set aside. In a small saucepan, place the butter, cola, and cocoa; stir. Bring the cola mixture to the boiling point over medium heat, stirring constantly. Pour the hot cola mixture over the powdered sugar; using an electric mixer, beat on high speed only until well blended and fluffy.

AUNT TELL'S DEVIL'S FOOD CAKE

My Aunt Fauntell, who lived in Creston, Iowa, was an excellent cook. This was her specialty cake—always known as "Aunt Tell's Cake" in our family (when we were little, my brother and I couldn't pronounce her name, so we called her "Aunt Tell").

2 cups sifted cake flour (sift before measuring)
1 teaspoon baking soda
¼ teaspoon salt
½ cup (¼ pound) butter, softened
1¼ cups sugar
3 extra-large eggs, room temperature, separated
1 teaspoon pure vanilla extract
½ cup unsweetened cocoa powder
1 cup cold water
½ cup sugar
1 recipe Chocolate Frosting (page 580)

Preheat the oven to 350° F. Using Special Grease (page 56), grease a 9 × 13 × 2-inch baking pan (see Note); set aside.

Onto waxed paper, sift together the flour, baking soda, and salt; set aside.

In a large mixing bowl, place the butter and 1¼ cups sugar; using an electric mixer, cream well on medium-high speed. Add the egg yolks, one at a time, beating well on medium-high speed after each addition. Add the vanilla; continue beating on medium-high speed until completely blended. Add the cocoa; beat on medium-high speed until blended. Add, alternately, the flour mixture in fourths, and the water in thirds, beating on low speed after each addition only until blended; set aside.

Place the egg whites in a large mixing bowl. Using the electric mixer fit with clean, dry blades, beat the egg whites on high speed until soft peaks hold. While continuing to beat on high speed, gradually add ½ cup sugar and continue beating the egg white mixture until stiff, but still moist and glossy. Add the egg white

mixture to the cake batter; using a large mixing spoon, fold in.

Using the large mixing spoon, spoon the batter into the prepared baking pan. Using a small, narrow spatula, lightly and quickly spread the batter evenly in the pan. Bake the cake for 30 minutes, or until a wooden toothpick inserted into the center of the cake comes out clean.

Remove the cake from the oven and place on a wire rack to cool.

When completely cool, leave the cake in the pan and frost it with the Chocolate Frosting. Let the cake stand until the frosting sets. Then, cover the cake with aluminum foil or a baking pan cover.

NOTE: Although not as satisfactory, the pan may be greased and floured in substitution for using Special Grease.

MAKES ONE 9 × 13-INCH SHEET CAKE; 15 SERVINGS

VARIATION: If a white frosting is desired, frost with Marshmallow Cloud Frosting (page 584).

Loaf and Bundt Cakes

JERRI GOREHAM'S CHOCOLATE-NUT BUNDT CAKE

Jerri Goreham, an Iowa relative who now lives in La Jolla, California, is a cookbooknik with an unfathomable collection. Wherever she goes, it's a good bet that she will return home with one or more additions to her ever-increasing library. But you won't find this recipe in any bound book on Jerri's shelves—it was passed down from her mother who hailed from Tipton, Iowa.

1 cup plus 2 tablespoons water
1 cup chopped dates
2 cups sifted all-purpose flour (sift before
    measuring)
1 teaspoon baking soda
1 tablespoon unsweetened cocoa powder
1 12-ounce package (2 cups) semisweet
    chocolate chips
1 cup broken pecans
1 cup (½ pound) butter, softened
1 cup sugar
2 extra-large eggs
1 teaspoon pure vanilla extract
2 recipes Chocolate Glaze (page 585)

Preheat the oven to 350° F. Using Special Grease (page 56), grease a 10-inch (12-cup) Bundt pan (see Note); set aside.

Pour 1 cup plus 2 tablespoons water into a small saucepan. Bring the water to a boil over high heat. Remove from the heat. Add the dates and stir to combine; let stand until cool.

Reserve 1 tablespoon of the measured flour in a small sauce dish. Then, onto waxed paper, sift together the remaining flour, baking soda, and cocoa; set aside. In a medium mixing bowl, place the chocolate chips and pecans. Sprinkle the 1 tablespoon reserved flour over the chocolate chips and pecans; toss until lightly dusted and evenly distributed; set aside.

In a large mixing bowl, place the butter and sugar; using an electric mixer, beat on medium-high speed until light and fluffy. Add the eggs, one at a time, beating well on medium-high speed after each addition. Add the vanilla; continue beating on medium-high speed until blended. Add, alternately, the flour mixture in fourths, and the date mixture (including the liquid) in thirds, beating on low speed after each addition only until blended; set aside. Measure ½ cup of the chocolate chip–pecan mixture; set aside. Add the remaining chocolate chip–pecan mixture to the cake batter; using a large mixing spoon, fold in.

Using the large mixing spoon, spoon the cake batter into the prepared Bundt pan. Scatter the ½ cup reserved chocolate chip–pecan mixture evenly over the batter. Bake the cake for 40 to 45 minutes, or until a wooden toothpick inserted into the cake comes out clean. (*Caution*: If the testing toothpick pierces chocolate chips or dates when inserted into the cake, the toothpick may not be clean when removed from cake even though the cake crumb is done.)

Remove the cake from the oven and place on a wire rack; let stand to cool 10 minutes. Very carefully, run a small, sharp, thin-bladed knife around the inside edge of the pan ⅛ inch below the top surface of the cake. Place a wire rack over the cake pan and invert. Carefully lift the pan off the cake. Let the cake stand on the wire rack until completely cool.

Then, place the wire rack holding the cake on a piece of waxed paper. Using a teaspoon, spoon the Chocolate Glaze over the top of the cake, letting it trickle down the sides. Let the cake stand until the glaze sets. Then, transfer the cake to a perfectly flat serving plate or a corrugated cardboard cake circle. Cover the cake with an airtight dome or place it in an airtight container.

NOTE: Although not as satisfactory, the pan may be greased and floured in substitution for using Special Grease.

MAKES ONE 10-INCH BUNDT CAKE; 14 SERVINGS

VARIATION: The cake may be topped with sprinkled powdered sugar rather than the Chocolate Glaze. Place 1 tablespoon powdered sugar in a small hand strainer and sprinkle the powdered sugar evenly over the top of the cool cake.

SERVING SUGGESTIONS
- Serve with Vanilla Ice Cream, homemade (page 669) or commercial.

- Pass an attractive serving bowl of Whipped Cream (page 373) at the table.

MARBLE CAKE

This distinctive cake is made in a loaf pan to give it greater depth for showing off the swirls of chocolate and white cake. Served slices are most appealing.

1 tablespoon plus 1 teaspoon sugar
⅛ teaspoon baking soda
1½ ounces (1½ squares) unsweetened chocolate
2 tablespoons boiling water
1⅔ cups sifted cake flour (sift before measuring)
2¼ teaspoons baking powder
½ teaspoon salt
½ cup vegetable shortening, softened
¾ cup sugar
1 teaspoon clear vanilla
⅔ cup whole milk
3 extra-large egg whites, room temperature
¼ cup sugar
1 recipe Chocolate Frosting (page 580)

Preheat the oven to 350° F. Grease and flour lightly a 5 × 9 × 2¾-inch loaf pan; set aside.

In a small sauce dish, place 1 tablespoon plus 1 teaspoon sugar and baking soda; stir to combine; set aside. Place the chocolate in a tiny saucepan. Hold the tiny pan over (not touching) low simmering water in a small saucepan until the chocolate melts, stirring intermittently. Remove the tiny pan from the heat. Add the baking soda mixture to the melted chocolate; stir to combine. Add the boiling water; stir until blended; set aside.

Onto waxed paper, sift together the flour, baking powder, and salt; set aside.

In a large mixing bowl, place the vegetable shortening and ¾ cup sugar; using an electric mixer, beat on medium-high speed until fluffy. Add the vanilla; beat on medium-high speed until blended. Add, alternately, the flour mixture in fourths, and the milk in thirds, beating on low speed after each addition only until blended. Using a large mixing spoon, carefully spoon ½ of the cake batter into another large mixing bowl. Add the chocolate mixture to one of the bowls of batter; using the electric mixer, beat on low speed only until blended; set aside.

Place the egg whites in a medium mixing bowl. Using the electric mixer fit with clean, dry blades, beat the egg whites on high speed until soft peaks hold. While continuing to beat on high speed, very gradually add ¼ cup sugar and continue beating the egg white mixture until stiff, but still moist and glossy. Using a table knife, cut the egg white mixture in half. Quickly and carefully, spoon ½ of the egg white mixture over the white batter, and the remaining ½ of the egg white mixture over the chocolate batter. Using separate, large mixing spoons, fold in.

Alternately place large spoons of white and chocolate batter side by side in the prepared loaf pan. Zigzag a table knife through the batter (to the bottom of the pan) to create a marble effect in the baked cake. Using a small, narrow spatula, lightly even the top of the batter in the pan. Bake the cake for 45 minutes, or until a wooden toothpick inserted into the center of the cake comes out clean.

Remove the cake from the oven and place on a wire rack; let stand to cool 10 minutes. Remove the cake from the pan, following the same procedure as for removing a layer cake from a cake pan (page 520); let stand on the wire rack until completely cool.

Then, frost the top and sides of the cake with the Chocolate Frosting (see To Frost a Cake, page 573). Let the cake stand until the frosting sets. Then, cover the cake with an airtight dome or place it in an airtight container.

MAKES ONE 5 × 9-INCH LOAF CAKE; 12 SERVINGS

OPTIONAL DECORATION

1 recipe Ornamental Vanilla Frosting made with whole milk (page 584)
1 recipe Chocolate Glaze (page 585)

Immediately after frosting the cake with the Chocolate Frosting, fit 2 decorating bags each with a small round tip number 2 (page 383). Fill one of the bags with Ornamental Vanilla Frosting and the other with Chocolate Glaze. Then, pipe vanilla and chocolate swirls randomly, but artistically, over the top of the cake. Lastly, pipe a shell border (page 389) of Chocolate Frosting around the bottom and top of the cake, using a decorating bag fit with medium open-star tip number 21 (reserve sufficient Chocolate Frosting before frosting the cake).

MILKY WAY CAKE

Ridiculously rich; incredibly luscious.

3 cups sifted all-purpose flour (sift before
    measuring)
½ teaspoon baking soda
8 2.15-ounce Milky Way candy bars
½ cup (¼ pound) butter
½ cup (¼ pound) butter, softened
2 cups sugar
4 extra-large eggs
1¼ cups buttermilk
1 cup broken pecans
1 recipe Supreme Chocolate Icing
    (page 585)

Preheat the oven to 325° F. Using Special Grease (page 56), grease a 10 × 4-inch tube pan (see Note 1); set aside.

Onto waxed paper, sift together the flour and baking soda; set aside.

In the top of a double boiler, place the Milky Way bars and ½ cup butter. Place the top of the double boiler over (not touching) simmering water in the bottom pan. Stir the candy-butter mixture until melted and completely blended. (The mixture will be thick.) Remove the top of the double boiler from the bottom pan; set aside.

In a large mixing bowl, place ½ cup softened butter and sugar; using an electric mixer, cream well on medium-high speed. Add the eggs, one at a time, beating well on medium-high speed after each addition. Add, alternately, the flour mixture in fourths, and the buttermilk in thirds, beating on low speed after each addition only until blended. Add the chocolate mixture; beat on medium speed only until blended. Add the pecans; using a large mixing spoon, fold in.

Turn the cake batter into the prepared tube pan. Using a small, narrow spatula, lightly and quickly spread the batter evenly in the pan. Bake the cake for 1 hour and 10 to 15 minutes. When done, this cake will be dense and very slightly moist. Insert a long, wooden toothpick into the cake to help determine doneness.

Remove the cake from the oven and place the upright pan on a wire rack; let stand to cool 15 minutes. Then, carefully run a sharp, thin-bladed knife around the inside edge of the pan (not around the tube) to loosen the cake. Place a 12-inch corrugated cardboard cake circle over the top of the pan (see Note 2). Hold the cake circle and the pan together securely and invert. Carefully lift the pan off the cake. Place the cake circle (and cake) on the wire rack; let stand until the cake is completely cool.

Then, frost the top and side of the cake with the Supreme Chocolate Icing. Let the cake stand until the frosting sets. Then, place the cake in an airtight container.

NOTE 1: Although not as satisfactory, the pan may be greased and floured in substitution for using Special Grease.

NOTE 2: If a corrugated cardboard cake circle is not available, a perfectly flat serving plate may be substituted.

MAKES ONE 10 × 4-INCH TUBE CAKE; 20 SERVINGS

SERVING SUGGESTION: A small scoop of vanilla ice cream complements Milky Way Cake well. Serve the ice cream next to the cake (not on top).

POUND CAKE

Pound cake is an old, historic cake which derives its name from the traditional ingredients; 1 pound each of butter, flour, sugar, and eggs (plus flavoring, such as lemon or vanilla extract, or mace). The following recipe makes an authentic pound cake with the exception that I have taken the liberty of adding a bit of baking powder (only 1 teaspoon) for added leavening. For flavoring, I like the combination of vanilla and lemon extract; however, the baker may adjust the flavoring to suit his/her personal preferences.

Although small versions of Pound Cake are often baked in loaf pans, the original, full-sized Pound Cake is traditionally baked in a tube pan.

1 pound butter (2 cups), softened to cool room temperature (about 70° F.)
1 pound cake flour (4½ cups sifted cake flour; sift before measuring)
1 pound sugar (2¼ cups)
1 pound eggs (7 extra–large eggs), room temperature
1 teaspoon baking powder
1 teaspoon pure vanilla extract
1 teaspoon lemon extract

Place the butter in a very large mixing bowl; set aside.

Preheat the oven to 325° F. Grease and flour a 10 × 4-inch tube pan; set aside.

Onto waxed paper, sift together the flour and baking powder; set aside.

Using an electric mixer, cream the butter on medium–high speed. While continuing to beat on medium–high speed, add the sugar in fourths, creaming well after each addition (about 5 minutes total beating time to add and cream the sugar). While continuing to beat on medium-high, add the eggs, one at a time, beating well after each addition (about 5 minutes total beating time to add the eggs). Add the vanilla and lemon extract; beat on medium–high speed until blended. Add the flour mixture in fourths, beating on low speed after each addition only until blended (about 5 minutes total beating time to add the flour mixture).

Using a large mixing spoon, spoon the cake batter into the prepared tube pan. Using a small, narrow spatula, lightly and quickly spread the batter evenly in the pan. Bake the cake for 1 hour to 1 hour and 10 minutes, or until a long, wooden toothpick inserted into the cake comes out clean.

Remove the cake from the oven and place the upright pan on a wire rack; let stand to cool 15 minutes. Then, carefully run a sharp, thin-bladed knife around the inside edge of the pan (not around the tube) to loosen the cake. Place a 12-inch corrugated cardboard cake circle over the top of the pan (see Note). Hold the cake circle and the pan together securely and invert. Carefully lift the pan off the cake. Place the cake circle (and cake) on wire rack; let stand until the cake is completely cool. Then, place the cake in an airtight container.

NOTE: If a corrugated cardboard cake circle is not available, a perfectly flat serving plate may be substituted.

MAKES ONE 10 × 4-INCH TUBE CAKE; 20 SERVINGS

OPTIONAL DECORATION: When cool, the cake may be dusted with powdered sugar, if desired. Place 1 tablespoon powdered sugar in a small hand strainer and sprinkle the powdered sugar over the top of the cake.

SCRIPTURE CAKE

Scripture Cake is so named because it is made from ingredients referred to in the Bible.

1½ cups sifted all-purpose flour (sift before measuring) (1 Kings 4:22)

2 teaspoons baking powder (1 Corinthians 5:6)

2 teaspoons ground cinnamon (1 Kings 10:10)

1 teaspoon ground nutmeg (1 Kings 10:10)

½ teaspoon ground ginger (1 Kings 10:2)

½ teaspoon ground cloves (1 Kings 10:2)

⅛ teaspoon salt (Leviticus 2:13)

2 cups chopped, dried figs (1 Samuel 30:12)

2 cups chopped, unblanched almonds (chop slivered, unblanched almonds; page 50) (Genesis 43:11)

2 cups raisins (1 Samuel 30:12)

½ cup (¼ pound) butter, softened (Judges 5:25)

1⅔ cups sugar (Jeremiah 6:20)

2 tablespoons honey (Exodus 16:31)

6 extra-large eggs, room temperature, separated (Isaiah 10:14)

½ cup whole milk (Judges 4:19)

⅓ cup sugar (Jeremiah 6:20)

1 tablespoon powdered sugar for decoration

Preheat the oven to 300° F. Using Special Grease (page 56), grease a 10-inch (12-cup) Bundt pan (see Note 1); set aside.

Reserve 3 tablespoons of the measured flour in a small sauce dish; set aside. Then, onto waxed paper, sift together the remaining flour, baking powder, cinnamon, nutmeg, ginger, cloves, and salt; set aside. In a medium mixing bowl, place the figs, almonds, and raisins; stir to combine. Sprinkle the 3 tablespoons reserved flour over the fig mixture; toss until well dusted; cover and set aside.

In a large mixing bowl, place the butter, 1⅔ cups sugar, and honey; using an electric mixer, cream well on medium-high speed. Add the egg yolks, one at a time, beating well on medium-high speed after each addition. Add, alternately, the flour mixture in fourths, and the milk in thirds, beating on low speed after each addition only until blended; set aside.

Place the egg whites in a large mixing bowl. Using the electric mixer fit with clean, dry blades, beat the egg whites on high speed until soft peaks hold. While continuing to beat on high speed, very gradually add ⅓ cup sugar and continue beating the egg white mixture until stiff, but still moist and glossy; set aside. Add the fig mixture to the flour batter; using a large mixing spoon, fold in only until evenly distributed. Add the egg white mixture; quickly fold in.

Using the large mixing spoon, spoon the cake batter into the prepared Bundt pan. Bake the cake for 1 hour and 50 minutes, or until a wooden toothpick inserted into the cake comes out clean. (*Caution:* If the testing toothpick happens to pierce a piece of fruit when inserted into cake, the toothpick may not be clean when removed from cake even though the cake crumb is done.)

Remove the cake from the oven and place on a wire rack; let stand to cool 10 minutes. Very carefully, run a small, sharp, thin-bladed knife around the inside edge of the pan ⅛ inch below the top surface of the cake. Place a 10- or 12-inch corrugated cardboard cake circle over the top of the pan (see Note 2). Hold the cake circle and the pan together securely and invert. Carefully lift the pan off the cake. Place the cake circle (and cake) on a wire rack; let stand until the cake is completely cool.

Then, place the powdered sugar in a small hand strainer and sprinkle over the top of the cake. Place the cake in an airtight container.

NOTE 1: Although not as satisfactory, the pan may be greased and floured in substitution for using Special Grease.

NOTE 2: If a corrugated cardboard cake circle is not available, a perfectly flat serving plate may be substituted.

MAKES ONE 10-INCH BUNDT CAKE; 14 SERVINGS

Angel Food Cakes

ANGEL FOOD CAKE

Lighter-than-a-feather Angel Food Cake has been popular and fashionable in America since the last quarter of the nineteenth century when this sublimely delicious repast provided a propitious way to put extra egg whites to use. (This recipe calls for 1½ cups of egg whites.)

Although it was the sweet taste and satiny texture that won Angel Food Cake permanence in the best-loved desserts inner circle, present-day health awareness has harkened Angel Food Cake center stage, owing to the absence of egg yolks and shortening among its ingredients. Burdened with no cholesterol whatsoever, and virtually no fat (just 1 gram in the cake flour), this culinary centenarian is as "in" as any cake could hope to be. But don't forget: there are 193 calories in each piece of this food fit for the angels (when a 10-inch cake is cut into 12 servings). Nothing is perfect.

1 cup sifted cake flour (sift before
    measuring)
1 cup superfine sugar
1½ cups egg whites (about 10 extra-large
    egg whites*), room temperature
1½ teaspoons cream of tartar
½ teaspoon salt
1 teaspoon pure vanilla extract
½ teaspoon almond extract
½ cup superfine sugar

About 12 large egg whites.

Preheat the oven to 350°F.

Onto waxed paper, sift together the flour and 1 cup sugar 4 times. (If you are using a triple sifter [page 57] go ahead and sift the flour mixture 4 times through the triple sifter.) Return the sifted flour mixture to the top of the sifter; set aside.

Place the egg whites in an extra-large mixing bowl. Using an electric mixer, beat the egg whites on high speed until foamy. Add the

cream of tartar and salt; continue beating on high speed just until soft peaks hold. Add the vanilla and almond extract. While beating on medium speed, very gradually sprinkle ½ cup sugar over the egg white mixture; beat only until the sugar is blended.

If necessary, use a large rubber spatula to quickly and carefully push the egg white mixture into a larger mixing bowl for more expeditious folding in of the flour mixture, which is the next procedure.

Sift the flour mixture in fourths over the egg white mixture, using a large mixing spoon to fold in after each addition only until the flour disappears.

Push the cake batter into an *ungreased* 10 × 4-inch tube pan with a removable bottom. Using a small, narrow spatula, lightly and quickly smooth the top of the batter. Then, carefully run a narrow, rubber spatula once around the center of the batter in the pan to remove any large air pockets. Place the cake on the lowest shelf in the oven. Bake the cake for 40 minutes, or until a long, wooden toothpick inserted into the cake comes out clean.

Remove the cake from the oven. Immediately invert the pan and let it stand on the cooling legs until the cake is *completely cool* (about 2 hours). If the pan does not have cooling legs, place the center tube over the neck of a bottle and let the cake stand until cool.

When the cake is cool, carefully run a very sharp, very thin-bladed knife in a continuous motion first around the inside edge and then around the center tube of the pan to loosen the cake. Hold the knife against the side of the pan (and the center tube) to help prevent tearing the cake. Avoid up-and-down, sawing motions, which will spoil the outside appearance of the cake. Lift the center tube section, with the cake, out of the pan. Then, run the knife around the bottom of the tube section under the cake. Invert the cake onto a 12-inch corrugated cardboard cake circle or a perfectly flat serving plate. Carefully lift the tube section off the cake. Place the cake in an airtight container.

MAKES ONE 10 × 4-INCH TUBE CAKE; 12 SERVINGS

GEORGE WASHINGTON ICEBOX CAKE

Made-to-order for serving on George Washington's Birthday, this decorative cake derives its name from the generous amount of maraschino cherries used in making it. But it's perfectly suitable for serving any time of the year.

¾ cup red maraschino cherries cut in half lengthwise, divided
1 Angel Food Cake (page 554) *or* 1 Sponge Cake (page 556)
1½ recipes Decorator Whipped Cream (page 374)
1 7-ounce package (2⅓ cups) shredded coconut, divided
¾ cup broken English walnuts
1 recipe Decorator Whipped Cream (page 374)

Place the maraschino cherries in a sieve; rinse under cold, running water. Place the cherries, single layer, between several layers of paper towels; let stand to dry.

With your fingers, tear the cake into pieces approximately 1 to 1½ inches square and place them in a large mixing bowl. Add 1½ recipes of Decorator Whipped Cream, 1⅓ cups of the coconut (cover the remaining coconut and set aside), ½ cup of the maraschino cherries (cover the remaining maraschino cherries and refrigerate), and all of the walnuts. Using a large mixing spoon, fold together carefully.

Transfer the mixture to a large mixing bowl approximately 9 inches in diameter which has been lined with plastic wrap. Using the back of the mixing spoon, press the mixture lightly into the bowl; cover with plastic wrap and refrigerate at least 6 hours.

Invert the bowl onto a flat serving plate. Lift the bowl off the cake and peel off the plastic wrap.

Frost the cake with 1 recipe of Decorator Whipped Cream. Spoon the remaining 1 cup of coconut over the entire cake, using your hand to lightly press the coconut into the whipped cream to hold it in place. Then, lightly press the remaining ¼ cup maraschino cherries randomly into the whipped cream frosting. Refrigerate the cake.

This cake is eye-appealing and should be served at the table. To serve, use a sharp, thin-bladed knife to cut 12 wedge-shaped servings. Using a triangle pie/cake server, remove the servings from the cake and place them, cut side down, on individual serving plates.

SERVES 12

STRAWBERRY "SHORTCAKE" (WITH ANGEL FOOD CAKE)

Angel Food Cake is often substituted for Old-Fashioned (Biscuit-Style) Shortcake (page 447) or Sponge-Style Shortcake (page 558) when serving Strawberry Shortcake. (See the headnote for Old-Fashioned Strawberry Shortcake, page 448.)

2 pints fresh strawberries
12 whole, fresh strawberries for garnish (in addition to the 2 pints)
1 recipe Angel Food Cake (page 554)
2 recipes Whipped Cream (page 373)

Wash the 2 pints strawberries; using a strawberry huller, remove the hulls (page 23). Cut the hulled strawberries in half or into quarters lengthwise, depending upon the size of the berries; place in a bowl and set aside. Wash and hull the 12 whole strawberries; place in a bowl and set aside.

Cut the Angel Food Cake into 12 servings and place each serving on an individual dessert plate. Spoon about ⅓ cup of the sliced, fresh strawberries over each serving of cake. Top each serving with a generous dollop of the Whipped

(Recipe continues on next page)

Cream. Place 1 of the whole strawberries atop the Whipped Cream on each serving.

SERVES 12

VARIATIONS: Fresh raspberries, blueberries, or sliced peaches may be substituted for the strawberries.

Sponge and Chiffon Cakes

SPONGE CAKE

2¼ cups sifted cake flour (sift before measuring)
½ teaspoon salt
8 extra-large eggs,* room temperature, separated
1¾ cups superfine sugar
½ cup plus 2 tablespoons water
1 tablespoon freshly squeezed, strained lemon juice
1½ teaspoons very finely grated lemon rind (page 47)
1 teaspoon pure vanilla extract
1½ teaspoons cream of tartar
½ cup superfine sugar

If extra-large eggs are not available, 10 large eggs may be substituted.

Preheat the oven to 325° F.

Onto waxed paper, sift together the flour and salt; set aside.

Place the egg yolks in a medium mixing bowl. Using an electric mixer, beat the egg yolks on high speed about 8 minutes, until very thick and butter colored. While continuing to beat the egg yolks on high speed, very gradually add 1¾ cups sugar (about 3 minutes additional beating time). Add the water, lemon juice, lemon rind, and vanilla; beat on high speed until blended. Transfer the egg yolk mixture to a large mixing bowl. Add the flour mixture in thirds, using a large mixing spoon to fold in after each addition only until the flour disappears; set aside.

Place the egg whites in a large mixing bowl. Using the electric mixer fit with clean, dry blades, beat the egg whites on high speed until foamy. Add the cream of tartar; continue beating on high speed until soft peaks hold. While continuing to beat on high speed, very gradually add ½ cup sugar and continue beating the egg white mixture until stiff, but still moist and glossy. Quickly, with as little disturbance as possible to the mixture, transfer the egg white mixture to an extra-large mixing bowl. Pour the egg yolk mixture back and forth over the egg white mixture; using the large mixing spoon, fold in carefully and quickly.

Pour the cake batter into an *ungreased* 10 × 4-inch tube pan with a removable bottom. Using a small, narrow spatula, lightly spread the batter evenly in the pan. Then, carefully run a narrow, rubber spatula once around the center of the batter in the pan to remove any large air pockets. Bake the cake for 50 to 60 minutes. When done, the inside of the cracks on the top of the cake will appear dry, not moist, and the cake will spring back when pressed lightly with your finger.

Remove the cake from the oven. Immediately invert the pan and let it stand on the cooling legs until the cake is *completely cool* (about 2 hours). If the pan does not have cooling legs, place the center tube over the neck of a bottle and let the cake stand until cool.

When the cake is cool, carefully run a sharp, very thin-bladed knife in a continuous motion first around the inside edge and then around the center tube of the pan to loosen the cake. Hold the knife against the side of the pan (and the center tube) to help prevent tearing the cake. Avoid up-and-down, sawing motions, which will spoil the outside appearance of the cake. Lift the center tube section, with the cake, out of the pan. Then, run the knife around the bottom of the tube section under the cake. Invert the cake onto a 12-inch corrugated cardboard cake circle or a perfectly flat serving plate. Carefully lift the tube section off the cake. Place the cake in an airtight container.

MAKES ONE 10 × 4-INCH TUBE CAKE; 12 SERVINGS

SERVING SUGGESTIONS

- Serve plain.
- Spoon fresh fruit over individual servings; top with Whipped Cream (page 373).
- Spoon Glaze (page 585) over the top of the cake and let it trickle down the sides.

LEMON-FILLED SPONGE CAKE

1 baked Sponge Cake (recipe, above)
Lemon Filling (recipe follows)
1½ recipes Lemon Buttercream Frosting
    (page 577)

Using a serrated knife or a cake leveler, split the Sponge Cake in half horizontally, making 2 layers (see To Split a Cake into Layers, page 522). Using a large spatula, carefully transfer the top layer to another 12-inch corrugated cardboard cake circle.

Spoon the cold Lemon Filling over the bottom cake layer. Using a small, narrow spatula, spread the filling evenly to within ¼ inch of the outside and inside edges of the cake. Using the large spatula, position the top layer of the cake over the Lemon Filling.

Frost the top and side of the cake with the Lemon Buttercream Frosting (see To Frost a Cake, page 573). Let the cake stand until the frosting sets. Then, place the cake in an airtight container and refrigerate. Use light, sawing motions with a sharp, very thin-bladed knife to cut the cake into serving portions.

Lemon Filling

¾ cup sugar
¼ cup all-purpose flour
⅛ teaspoon salt
1 extra-large egg
3 tablespoons water
2 tablespoons butter
¼ cup freshly squeezed, strained lemon
    juice
½ teaspoon finely grated lemon rind
    (page 47)

In a small mixing bowl, place the sugar, flour, and salt; stir to combine; set aside.

Place the egg in the top of a double boiler; using a handheld electric mixer, beat well on medium-high speed. Add the water; beat on medium-high speed until blended. Add the flour mixture; using a spoon, stir to combine. Place the top of the double boiler over boiling water in the bottom pan. Cook the mixture until very thick (about 8 minutes), constantly stirring with a spoon or beating with the electric mixer on low speed.

Remove the top of the double boiler from the bottom pan and place on a wire rack; using the electric mixer, beat briefly on medium speed to remove any lumps. Add the butter, lemon juice, and lemon rind; beat on medium speed until blended and combined.

Let the Lemon Filling stand on the wire rack until cooled slightly. Then, place a piece of plastic wrap directly on the filling and refrigerate. Wait until the filling is cold before using it to fill the cake. Cakes filled with Lemon Filling must be kept refrigerated.

SPONGE-STYLE SHORTCAKES

½ cup sifted cake flour (sift before measuring)
½ teaspoon baking powder
⅛ teaspoon salt
3 extra-large eggs,* room temperature, separated
½ teaspoon pure vanilla extract
¼ teaspoon very finely grated lemon rind (page 47)
1 teaspoon freshly squeezed, strained lemon juice
¼ cup superfine sugar
¼ teaspoon cream of tartar
¼ cup superfine sugar

If extra-large eggs are not available, 4 large eggs may be substituted.

Preheat the oven to 325° F. Grease well and flour lightly twelve 3½-inch-diameter by 1-inch-deep shortcake pan molds. (Shortcake pans sometimes contain 6 molds for individual shortcakes. In such case, 2 pans will be required.)

Onto waxed paper, sift together the flour, baking powder, and salt. Return the sifted flour mixture to the top of the sifter; set aside.

Place the egg yolks in a small mixing bowl. Using an electric mixer, beat the egg yolks on high speed 5 minutes, until thick and lemon colored. Add the vanilla, lemon rind, and lemon juice; beat on high speed until blended. While continuing to beat the egg yolk mixture on high speed, very gradually add ¼ cup sugar; beat 1 additional minute after adding the sugar. *Sift* the flour mixture over the egg yolk mixture; using a mixing spoon, fold in only until the flour disappears; set aside.

Place the egg whites in a large mixing bowl. Using the electric mixer fit with clean, dry blades, beat the egg whites on high speed until foamy. Add the cream of tartar; continue beating on high speed until soft peaks hold. While continuing to beat on high speed, very gradually add ¼ cup sugar and continue beating the egg white mixture until stiff, but still moist and glossy. Pour the egg yolk mixture back and forth over the egg white mixture; using a large mixing spoon, fold in carefully and quickly.

Spoon the cake batter into the 12 prepared shortcake pan molds. Using a small, narrow spatula, lightly and quickly spread the batter evenly to within about ⅜ inch of the top of each mold. Bake the shortcakes 10 minutes, until the top surface of the cakes springs back when touched lightly.

Remove the pans from the oven and place on wire racks. *Immediately* run a small, sharp, thin-bladed knife around the inside edge of each mold to loosen the shortcakes. Place a wire rack over one pan at a time and invert to unmold the shortcakes. Let the shortcakes stand on wire racks only until cool.

Meanwhile, cut a piece of waxed paper to fit the bottom of an airtight storage container. Place the waxed paper in the storage container and dust the waxed paper with a small amount of powdered sugar to prevent the shortcakes from sticking to it. The small amount of powdered sugar which will adhere to the bottoms of the shortcakes during storage will also prevent them from sticking to the serving plates. Place the cooled shortcakes in the storage container and cover tightly.

MAKES TWELVE 3½ × 1-INCH SHORTCAKES; 12 SERVINGS

STRAWBERRY SPONGE-STYLE SHORTCAKE

Strawberry Shortcake also may be made using Old-Fashioned (Biscuit-Style) Shortcake (page 447) or Angel Food Cake (page 555) instead of Sponge-Style Shortcake. (See the headnote for Old-Fashioned Strawberry Shortcake, page 448)

2 pints fresh strawberries
12 baked Sponge-Style Shortcakes (left column)
2 recipes Whipped Cream (page 373)

Wash the strawberries; using a strawberry huller, remove the hulls (page 23). Reserve 12 uniform, whole strawberries and cut the remainder in half or into quarters lengthwise, depending upon the size of the berries; place in a bowl and set aside. Place the shortcakes on individual dessert plates. Spoon the sliced strawberries equally over the shortcakes. Top each serving with a generous dollop of the Whipped Cream. Place 1 of the reserved whole strawberries atop the Whipped Cream on each serving.

SERVES 12

VARIATIONS: Fresh raspberries, blueberries, or sliced peaches may be substituted for the strawberries.

JELLY ROLL

Jelly rolls are a traditional cake dating back to the middle 1800's. They consist of a thin sponge cake rolled, historically, around a jelly filling and sprinkled with powdered sugar. When sliced for serving, the attractive pinwheel design is revealed. A wide variety of fillings is used nowadays in jelly rolls, ranging from jams to fruited frostings and flavored whipped cream (see Filling Suggestions, below).

¾ cup sifted cake flour (sift before
    measuring)
1 teaspoon baking powder
¼ teaspoon salt
4 extra-large eggs,* room temperature,
    separated
1 teaspoon pure vanilla extract
½ cup superfine sugar
¼ cup superfine sugar
Powdered sugar
1½ cups jelly, jam, frosting, or other filling
    (see Filling Suggestions, below)

  *If extra-large eggs are not available, 5 large
  eggs may be substituted.*

Preheat the oven to 350° F. Grease and flour lightly a 10½ × 15½ × 1-inch jelly-roll (cookie) pan. Line the bottom of the pan with waxed paper. Grease the waxed paper; set aside.

Onto a piece of clean waxed paper, sift together the flour, baking powder, and salt. Return the sifted flour mixture to the top of the sifter; set aside.

Place the egg yolks in a small mixing bowl. Using an electric mixer, beat the egg yolks on high speed 5 minutes, until thick and lemon colored. Add the vanilla; beat on high speed until blended. While continuing to beat the egg yolk mixture on high speed, very gradually add ½ cup sugar and continue beating until completely blended and creamy. *Sift* the flour mixture over the egg yolk mixture; using a mixing spoon, fold in only until the flour disappears; set aside.

Place the egg whites in a large mixing bowl. Using the electric mixer fit with clean, dry blades, beat the egg whites on high speed until soft peaks hold. While continuing to beat on high speed, very gradually add ¼ cup sugar and continue beating the egg white mixture until stiff, but still moist and glossy. Pour the egg yolk mixture back and forth over the egg white mixture; using a large mixing spoon, fold in carefully and quickly.

Turn the cake batter into the prepared jelly-roll pan. Using a large, narrow spatula, carefully spread the batter evenly over the pan. Bake the cake for 10 to 12 minutes, until the top surface of the cake springs back when touched lightly.

Meanwhile, lay a clean kitchen hand towel on a flat surface and dust it with sifted powdered sugar (page 57); let stand.

Remove the cake from the oven and place on a wire rack. *Immediately* run a sharp, thin-bladed knife along the inside edges of the pan to loosen the cake. Place the dusted hand towel over the cake pan, dusted side down. Pull the towel tautly over the pan and invert the towel and pan. Lay the inverted towel and pan on the flat surface. Lift the pan off the cake and peel the waxed paper off the bottom of the cake. Beginning at one of the short sides of the cake, roll the warm

(Recipe continues on next page)

cake and towel together. Place the rolled cake on a wire rack, seam down, and let stand until completely cool.

Then, unroll the cake. Spoon teaspoonsful of jelly evenly over the surface of the cake. Using a small, narrow spatula, lightly spread the jelly to within ¼ inch of the edges of the cake. Roll the cake short side to short side (without the towel). Using a small hand strainer, dust the top of the Jelly Roll with additional powdered sugar. Cover tightly until serving time.

SERVES 10

FILLING SUGGESTIONS: Any jelly, jam, conserve, flavored whipped cream, or frosting may be used to fill the Jelly Roll. Nuts; chopped, fresh or canned fruits; or candied fruits may be used in combination with any whipped cream or frosting. The following are a few suggested fillings:

- Red Raspberry Jelly (page 744)

- Apricot Jam (page 747)

- Rhubarb-Strawberry Conserve (page 761)

- 1½ recipes Chocolate Decorator Whipped Cream (page 374). ¾ cup chopped pecans may be folded into the whipped cream, if desired.

- 1 8-ounce can commercial crushed pineapple, well drained, combined with 1 recipe Buttercream Frosting (page 577).

YULE LOG
Bûche de Noël

In many parts of the United States, this cake is known by its French name: Bûche de Noël. The English translation is Yule log, the name by which this famous French Christmas cake is best known in the Midwest. The cake is made to resemble the Yule log, which in earlier times was placed in the fireplace on Christmas Eve to serve as the foundation for the fire. Often, Yule log cakes are piped and decorated to further carry out the holiday theme.

1 baked Jelly Roll cake without filling (page 559), roll cake in hand towel and let stand until completely cool)
Filling (recipe follows)
1 recipe Mocha Buttercream Frosting (page 578), reserving ¾ cup frosting before adding cocoa and coffee to remainder of frosting
¼ recipe Cake Decorators' White Icing (page 576) for decoration
Ivory, bright red, kelly green, and yellow-orange paste food coloring

Cut an 8 × 14-inch piece of corrugated cardboard cake board; set aside.

Unroll the Jelly Roll and towel. Using a very sharp, thin-bladed knife, cut a 1-inch strip of cake off one of the short sides of the Jelly Roll. Cut the strip in half widthwise; roll each half and secure with a toothpick. Then, unroll the strips and spread them with Filling. Reroll the strips and resecure with toothpicks; place in a zipper-seal plastic bag and refrigerate. (These 2 pieces will later be attached to the Yule Log to simulate branch stumps.)

Spoon the remainder of the Filling over the Jelly Roll. Using a small, narrow spatula, spread the filling evenly to within ¼ inch of the edges of the cake. Roll the cake short side to short side (without the towel). Place the cake, seam down, on the cut piece of corrugated cardboard cake board. Slip strips of waxed paper under the bottom edges of the Jelly Roll to prevent unwanted frosting from getting on the exposed border of the cake board when frosting the Yule Log; set aside.

Using ivory-colored paste food coloring, tint the ¾ cup reserved light-colored Mocha Buttercream Frosting to simulate the inner color of cut logs; cover and set aside. Using a small, narrow spatula, frost the log, except the ends, with the dark-colored Mocha Buttercream Frosting, reserving a small amount of the frosting. Apply the frosting liberally and smoothly. Then, pull a wide-toothed decorating comb (see illustration, page 569) down the length of the log several times and contiguously until the entire log is grooved to simulate bark; set aside.

Remove the 2 rolled cake strips from the refrigerator. Using a very sharp, thin-bladed knife, cut a thin triangular piece off one of the ends of each strip (see illustration). Discard (or eat) the cutaway triangular pieces.

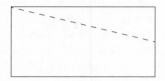

Apply a very generous amount of the reserved dark-colored Mocha Buttercream Frosting to the surface from which the triangular piece was cut away on each rolled strip. Press the frosted surface of one of the rolled strips into the frosting on one side of the log to affix the rolled strip to the log and simulate a branch stump. Affix the other rolled strip to the opposite side, and at the opposite end, of the log. Then, apply the reserved dark-colored Mocha Buttercream Frosting only to the *edge* (the bark) of the stumps. Run the decorating comb around the frosting on the edge of the stumps in a single, circular motion.

Using a clean, small, narrow spatula, frost the ends of the log and stumps with the light-colored Mocha Buttercream Frosting, making circular swirls with the spatula to simulate the rings of a cut log.

With quick motions, pull the strips of waxed paper from under the Yule Log. Make any necessary, small repairs to the frosting around the bottom of the log. Refrigerate the Yule Log until the frosting sets.

To decorate the Yule Log (see illustration), use paste food coloring to tint portions of the Cake Decorators' White Icing bright red, kelly green, and yellow-orange (for the center of the poinsettias). Place each of the 3 tinted icings in a separate decorating bag. Fit the decorating bags (page 383) with the numbered tips indicated below, and pipe the word "Noel" in red across the log; then, decorate the Yule Log with

piped holly (green leaves and red berries) and poinsettias (red petals, 3 yellow-orange dots in center of petals, and green leaves) (see Writing and Printing, page 388; Holly Leaves, page 391; and Poinsettias, page 391, for piping procedures).

"Noel"—small round tip number 3
Holly—medium leaf tip number 68 (leaves) and small round tip number 3 (berries)
Poinsettias—medium leaf tip number 352 (petals), tiny round tip number 2 (center dots), and small leaf tip number 66 (leaves)

Yule Log

Refrigerate the Yule Log and let the frosting decorations set before serving. Keep the Yule Log refrigerated.

SERVES 10

Filling

1½ recipes Decorator Whipped Cream (page 374)
2 teaspoons unsweetened cocoa powder
2 teaspoons powdered instant coffee (to powder instant coffee, process in blender*)

If a blender is not available, a food processor may be used; however, it is difficult to achieve a fine powder using a food processor. Reserve any remaining powdered instant coffee for other uses.

When preparing the Decorator Whipped Cream, add the cocoa and powdered instant coffee after adding the powdered sugar; cover and refrigerate.

BOSTON CREAM PIE

Although called a "pie," this lush dessert bears no resemblance to one. Boston Cream Pie is definitely a cake, made with two layers of sponge cake and a rich custard filling. The top of this yummy creation is iced with a thin chocolate coating, which I allow to trickle down the sides. By any name, it's really good!

1 cup sifted cake flour (sift before
    measuring)
1 teaspoon baking powder
¼ teaspoon salt
3 extra-large eggs,* room temperature
1 cup superfine sugar
½ teaspoon finely grated lemon rind
    (page 47)
2 teaspoons freshly squeezed, strained
    lemon juice
¼ cup plus 2 tablespoons hot (not scalded)
    milk
Custard Filling (recipe follows)
1 recipe Chocolate Coating (page 586)
Chocolate Curls (page 406)

    If extra-large eggs are not available, 4 large eggs may be substituted.

Preheat the oven to 350° F. Line the bottoms of 2 *ungreased* 8-inch round cake pans with waxed paper; set aside.

Onto a piece of waxed paper, sift together the flour, baking powder, and salt; set aside.

Place the eggs in a large mixing bowl. Using an electric mixer, beat the eggs on high speed 5 minutes, until very thick. While continuing to beat on high speed, very gradually add the sugar. Add the lemon rind and lemon juice; beat on high speed until combined and blended. Add the flour mixture in fourths, using a large mixing spoon to fold in after each addition only until the flour disappears. Add the milk all at once; using the large mixing spoon, quickly fold and stir in.

Using the large mixing spoon, spoon the cake batter equally into the 2 prepared cake pans. Using a small, narrow spatula, lightly and quickly spread the batter evenly in the pans. Bake the cakes for 20 minutes, until the top surface of the cake springs back when touched lightly.

Remove the cakes from the oven and place on wire racks; let stand in the pans until completely cool.

Then, run a sharp, thin-bladed knife around the inside edge of the pans to loosen the cakes. Invert one cake (the bottom layer) onto a perfectly flat serving plate; carefully lift the pan off the cake and peel the waxed paper off the bottom of the cake. Invert the other cake onto a wire rack and follow the same procedure.

Spoon the Custard Filling over the bottom cake layer on the serving plate. Using a small, narrow spatula, spread the filling evenly to within ¼ inch of the outside edge of the cake. Using a large spatula, position the top layer of the cake, bottom side up, over the Custard Filling.

Spoon the Chocolate Coating over the cake and let it run down the sides. If necessary, use a clean, small, narrow spatula to help spread the Chocolate Coating over the entire edge of the cake. Carefully wipe any excess Chocolate Coating off the serving plate. Decorate the top of the cake with the Chocolate Curls. Let the cake stand until the Chocolate Coating sets. Then, place the cake in an airtight container and refrigerate.

MAKES ONE 8-INCH, 2-LAYER ROUND CAKE; 10 TO 12 SERVINGS

Custard Filling

¾ cup half-and-half
¼ cup sugar
⅛ teaspoon salt
¼ cup half-and-half
2 tablespoons cornstarch
2 egg yolks, slightly beaten
¾ teaspoon pure vanilla extract
½ cup whipping cream, unwhipped

Pour ¾ cup half-and-half into a medium saucepan; place over medium heat and let stand until bubbles begin to form around the edge of the pan. Add the sugar and salt; stir until dissolved. Remove from the heat; cover and set aside.

In a small mixing bowl, place ¼ cup half-and-half and cornstarch; stir until smooth and blended. Add the egg yolks; stir to blend. Add about ⅓ cup of the hot half-and-half mixture to the egg mixture; stir to blend. Add the egg mixture to the remaining, hot half-and-half mixture; stir until blended. Over medium-low heat, cook the mixture until it thickens, stirring constantly.

Remove the custard mixture from the heat and place on a wire rack. Add the vanilla; stir until blended. Let the custard mixture stand until cooled slightly; then, refrigerate until cooled to room temperature, stirring occasionally.

Meanwhile, pour the whipping cream into a small mixing bowl. Using an electric mixer, beat the cream on medium-high speed until it begins to stiffen. Reduce the mixer speed to medium-low and continue beating the cream until stiff, but still soft and fluffy; cover and refrigerate.

When the custard mixture cools to room temperature, add the whipped cream; using a mixing spoon, fold in. Cover and keep refrigerated.

ORANGE-COCONUT CHIFFON CAKE

When a professional baker invented chiffon cake in the late 1940's, it was all the rage, and it has stood the test of a half-century's time. Similar to a sponge cake, chiffon cake includes vegetable oil as an added ingredient, and it always contains baking powder (see Types of Cakes, page 517). The light texture, refreshing orange flavor, flaky coconut appliqué, and subdued color of this Orange-Coconut Chiffon Cake make for a perfect summertime dessert.

2¼ cups sifted cake flour (sift before measuring)
1 tablespoon baking powder
1 teaspoon salt
1½ cups superfine sugar
½ cup vegetable oil

6 extra-large egg yolks,* room temperature
¼ cup finely grated orange rind (page 47) (rind of about 3 extra-large oranges)
¾ cup freshly squeezed, strained orange juice
½ teaspoon pure vanilla extract
1 cup egg whites (about 7 extra-large egg whites**), room temperature
½ teaspoon cream of tartar
1 recipe Orange Fluff Frosting (page 583), tinted *very pale* orange
1 recipe Tinted Coconut (page 409), tinted light orange
Orange-colored paste food coloring (to tint Orange Fluff Frosting and Tinted Coconut)

If extra-large egg yolks are not available, 7 large egg yolks may be substituted.

**About 8 large egg whites.*

Preheat the oven to 325° F.

Onto waxed paper, sift together the flour, baking powder, salt, and sugar. Place the flour mixture in a large mixing bowl. With a large mixing spoon, make a well in the center of the flour mixture. Into the well, place the vegetable oil, egg yolks, orange rind, orange juice, and vanilla; using an electric mixer, beat on medium speed until well blended and very smooth; set aside.

Place the egg whites in a large mixing bowl. Using the electric mixer fit with clean, dry blades, beat the egg whites on high speed until foamy. Add the cream of tartar; continue beating on high speed until the egg white mixture is *very stiff* and dry. (Do not worry about overbeating.) Pour the egg yolk mixture back and forth over the egg white mixture; using a large mixing spoon, fold in carefully and quickly.

Pour the cake batter into an *ungreased* 10 × 4-inch tube pan with a removable bottom. Using a small, narrow spatula, lightly spread the batter evenly in the pan. Bake the cake for 50 to 55 minutes, or until a long, wooden toothpick inserted into the cake comes out clean.

(Recipe continues on next page)

Remove the cake from the oven. Immediately invert the pan and let it stand on the cooling legs until the cake is *completely cool* (about 2 hours). If the pan does not have cooling legs, place the center tube over the neck of a bottle and let the cake stand until cool.

When the cake is cool, carefully run a very sharp, very thin-bladed knife in a continuous motion first around the inside edge and then around the center tube of the pan to loosen the cake. Hold the knife against the side of the pan (and the center tube) to help prevent tearing the cake. Avoid up-and-down, sawing motions, which will spoil the outside appearance of the cake. Lift the center tube section, with the cake, out of the pan. Then, run the knife around the bottom of the tube section under the cake. Invert the cake onto a 12-inch corrugated cardboard cake circle or a perfectly flat serving plate. Carefully lift the tube section off the cake.

Frost the top and side of the cake with the Orange Fluff Frosting (see To Frost a Cake, page 573). Immediately after frosting the cake, spoon the Tinted Coconut over the top and side of the cake, pressing the coconut lightly into the frosting on the side of the cake with your hand only until it holds in place. Let the cake stand 1 hour to allow the frosting to dry slightly. Then, place the cake in an airtight container.

MAKES ONE 10×4-INCH TUBE CAKE; 12 SERVINGS

Fruitcakes

TRADITIONAL HOLIDAY FRUITCAKE

Get in the holiday spirit early by making this exquisite fruitcake. You may make it in either 7 small loaf pans (for gift giving) or 1 large tube pan. The cakes (or cake) are wrapped in cognac-soaked cloths and left to season for 6 weeks before serving.

8 ounces (1 cup) candied pineapple slices sliced thinly
8 ounces (1 cup) diced candied orange peel
8 ounces (1 cup) diced candied citron
4 ounces (½ cup) red candied cherries, cut in half
4 ounces (½ cup) green candied cherries, cut in half
1 8-ounce package pitted dates, quartered (1 cup packed dates)
1 8-ounce package dried figs, stems removed and cut into eighths (1 cup packed figs)
1 15-ounce box (2½ cups) raisins
1 cup currants
1 cup coarsely broken pecans
1 cup coarsely broken English walnuts
2 cups sifted all-purpose flour (sift before measuring)
2 teaspoons baking powder
1 teaspoon salt
1 teaspoon ground allspice
½ teaspoon ground cloves
½ teaspoon ground nutmeg
¼ cup freshly squeezed, strained orange juice
¼ cup cognac
1 cup (½ pound) butter, softened
½ cup sugar
½ cup honey
5 extra-large eggs
2¼ cups cognac, divided
½ cup light corn syrup

DECORATION INGREDIENTS

4 ounces (½ cup) red candied cherries
4 ounces (½ cup) candied pineapple slices
   cut into wedges
35 pecan halves (5 per fruitcake)

Cut seven 13-inch-square pieces of clean, dry, white cotton cloth; set aside.

Prepare the fruits and nuts (the first 11 ingredients); set aside in separate, covered bowls.

Preheat the oven to 275° F. Grease seven 3 × 5¾ × 2⅛-inch loaf pans; set aside.

Reserve ¾ cup of the measured flour in a small mixing bowl; set aside. Onto waxed paper, sift together the remaining flour, baking powder, salt, allspice, cloves, and nutmeg; set aside.

Place the prepared fruits and nuts (the first 11 ingredients) in an extra-large mixing bowl or kettle. Sprinkle the ¾ cup reserved flour over the fruits and nuts; mix with your hands until the fruits and nuts are coated with flour and evenly distributed; set aside.

In a small mixing bowl, pour the orange juice and ¼ cup cognac; stir to blend; set aside.

In a large mixing bowl, place the butter and sugar; using an electric mixer, cream well on medium-high speed. Add the honey and beat on medium-high speed until fluffy. Add the eggs, one at a time, beating well on medium-high speed after each addition. Add, alternately, the flour mixture in fourths, and the orange juice mixture in thirds, beating on low speed after each addition only until blended. Pour the cake batter over the fruits and nuts mixture; using a large mixing spoon, fold and stir until combined.

Spoon the fruitcake batter equally into the 7 prepared loaf pans. With the back of a tablespoon, smooth lightly the top of the batter in the pans. Place the fruitcakes on the middle shelf in the oven. Then, place a 7 × 11 × 2-inch pan of very hot (not boiling) water (from the teakettle) on the oven shelf beneath the fruitcakes. Bake the fruitcakes for 1½ hours. When done, the cakes will spring back when pressed lightly with your finger.

Remove the fruitcakes from the oven and place on wire racks; let stand in the pans until *completely* cool.

Then, carefully run a sharp, thin-bladed knife along the inside edges of the pans to loosen the cakes. Remove the fruitcakes from the pans by inverting the pans, one at a time, in your hand or onto a wire rack. Let the cakes stand in the upright position.

Pour ¾ cup cognac into a large mixing bowl. Place the 7 pieces of cut cotton cloth in the bowl and saturate them in the cognac. Wrap each fruitcake in one of the cognac-soaked cloths. Then, wrap each fruitcake in airtight aluminum foil lined with plastic wrap. Place the fruitcakes, single layer, on a tray or cookie pan and store in a cool place such as the basement.

In 7 days, unwrap the fruitcakes; place the cloths in a large mixing bowl and sprinkle them with ½ cup cognac. Rewrap the fruitcakes, as before, and re-store them. Repeat the process of unwrapping the fruitcakes, resoaking the cloths, rewrapping the fruitcakes, and re-storing them 2 additional times at 7- to 10-day intervals.

Six weeks after baking, unwrap the fruitcakes, leaving the cloths wrapped around the sides of the fruitcakes to prevent them from drying while glazing and decorating the tops of the cakes.

Place the syrup in a very small saucepan. Over medium-low heat, heat the syrup until warm. Using a soft brush, paint the top of the fruitcakes with warm syrup. Arrange the red candied cherries, candied pineapple wedges, and pecan halves in a design or randomly on the top of the fruitcakes. Then, brush warm syrup on all sides of the decorations and brush a second layer of syrup on the remaining undecorated portions of the top of the cakes. Let the fruitcakes stand 45 minutes for the glaze to dry. Remove the cloths wrapped around the sides of the fruitcakes and store the fruitcakes in airtight containers or wrap them in plastic wrap.

(Recipe continues on next page)

See To Cut Fruitcakes (page 524) for the procedure to cut the fruitcakes into serving portions.

MAKES SEVEN 1-POUND FRUITCAKES; 8 SERVINGS PER FRUITCAKE

ALTERNATIVE BAKING PAN: Traditional Holiday Fruitcake may be baked in a 10 × 4-inch tube pan with a removable bottom. Grease the pan; line the pan with aluminum foil, fitting the foil as smoothly as possible to the pan to prevent creases in the cake. Then, grease the aluminum foil. Bake the fruitcake for 3 hours at 275° F.

Remove the fruitcake from the oven and place on a wire rack; let stand upright in the pan until *completely* cool.

When cool, remove the fruitcake from the pan by lifting out the center tube section and then lifting the cake off the tube section. Carefully remove the aluminum foil and place the fruitcake on a *flat,* nonmetallic plate or tray.

Use one 22-inch-square piece of clean, dry, white cotton cloth for saturating in cognac and wrapping the fruitcake. (If necessary, the fruitcake may be left on the plate or tray if it is too difficult to transport the fruitcake and place it on the soaked cloth. Wrap the soaked cloth snugly around the fruitcake on the plate or tray.)

MAKES ONE 7-POUND FRUITCAKE; 56 SERVINGS

WHITE FRUITCAKE

Lightly hued fruits and nuts combine in a white batter to give this fruitcake a contemporary look. (Don't tell, but White Fruitcake is not a new cake by any means.)

8 ounces (1 cup) candied pineapple slices sliced thinly
4 ounces (½ cup) diced candied lemon peel
4 ounces (½ cup) diced candied orange peel
4 ounces (½ cup) diced candied citron
1 15-ounce box (2½ cups) golden raisins
1 6-ounce package dried apricots (about 1 cup packed apricots), each half cut into quarters
½ cup flaked coconut
1 cup coarsely chopped, slivered blanched almonds (chop with a knife)
1 cup coarsely chopped Brazil nuts (chop with a knife)
2¾ cups sifted all-purpose flour (sift before measuring)
2 teaspoons baking powder
1 cup (½ pound) butter, softened
1 cup sugar
2 tablespoons freshly squeezed, strained lemon juice
1 tablespoon grated orange rind (page 47)
⅓ cup whole milk
7 extra-large egg whites, room temperature
½ cup sugar
2½ dozen whole, blanched almonds for decoration
6 pieces diced candied citron for decoration
2 tablespoons honey
1 extra-large egg white
2¼ cups dry sherry, divided

Cut one 22-inch-square piece of clean, dry, white cotton cloth; set aside.

Prepare the fruits and nuts (the first 9 ingredients); set aside in separate, covered bowls.

Preheat the oven to 275° F. Grease a 10 × 4-inch tube pan with a removable bottom. Then, line the pan with aluminum foil, fitting the foil as smoothly as possible to the pan to prevent creases in the cake. Grease the aluminum foil; set aside.

Reserve ¾ cup of the measured flour in a small mixing bowl. Onto waxed paper, sift together the remaining flour and baking powder; set aside.

Place the prepared fruits and nuts (the first 9 ingredients) in an extra-large mixing bowl or kettle. Sprinkle the ¾ cup reserved flour over the fruits and nuts; mix with your hands until the fruits and nuts are coated with flour and evenly distributed; set aside.

In a large mixing bowl, place the butter and

1 cup sugar; using an electric mixer, cream well on medium-high speed. Add the lemon juice and orange rind; beat on medium-high to blend and combine. Add, alternately, the flour mixture in fourths, and the milk in thirds, beating on low speed after each addition only until blended. Pour the cake batter over the fruits and nuts mixture; using a large mixing spoon, fold and stir until combined; set aside.

Place the egg whites in a large mixing bowl. Using the electric mixer fit with clean, dry blades, beat the egg whites on high speed until soft peaks hold. While continuing to beat on high speed, very gradually add ½ cup sugar and continue beating the egg white mixture until stiff, but still moist and glossy. Add the egg white mixture to the fruitcake batter; using a large mixing spoon, fold in as quickly and carefully as possible.

Spoon the batter into the prepared tube pan. Using a small, narrow spatula, smooth lightly the top of the batter in the pan. Place the fruitcake on the middle shelf in the oven. Then, place a 7 × 11 × 2-inch pan of very hot (not boiling) water (from the teakettle) on the oven shelf beneath the fruitcake. Bake the fruitcake for 2¼ hours.

Remove the fruitcake from the oven and place on a wire rack. Immediately decorate the top of the fruitcake with 6 daisies, each fashioned from 5 almonds for petals and 1 piece of diced candied citron for the center; set aside. In a small mixing bowl, place the honey and 1 egg white; using a table fork, beat until slightly frothy. Using a soft brush, glaze the top of the fruitcake (including the decoration) with the egg white mixture. Return the fruitcake to the oven and bake for 45 additional minutes. When done, the cake will spring back when pressed lightly with your finger.

Remove the fruitcake from the oven and place on a wire rack; let stand upright in the pan until *completely* cool.

When cool, remove the fruitcake from the pan by lifting out the center tube section and then lifting the cake off the tube section. Carefully remove the aluminum foil and place the

fruitcake on a *flat,* nonmetallic plate or tray; set aside.

Pour ¾ cup sherry into a large mixing bowl. Place the piece of cut cotton cloth in the bowl and saturate it in the sherry. Wrap the fruitcake in the sherry-soaked cloth (see Note). Then, wrap the fruitcake in airtight aluminum foil lined with plastic wrap. Place the fruitcake on a tray or cookie pan and store in a cool place such as the basement.

In 7 days, unwrap the fruitcake; place the cloth in a large mixing bowl and sprinkle it with ½ cup sherry. Rewrap the fruitcake, as before, and re-store it. Repeat the process of unwrapping the fruitcake, resoaking the cloth, rewrapping fruitcake, and re-storing it 2 additional times at 7- to 10-day intervals.

Six weeks after baking, unwrap the fruitcake. Store in an airtight container in the refrigerator.

NOTE: If necessary, the fruitcake may be left on the plate or tray if it is too difficult to transport the fruitcake and place it on the soaked cloth. Wrap the soaked cloth snugly around the fruitcake on the plate or tray.

MAKES ONE 6-POUND FRUITCAKE; 48 SERVINGS

ALTERNATIVE BAKING PANS: White Fruitcake may be baked in 6 greased 3 × 5¾ × 2⅛-inch loaf pans (eliminate the aluminum foil lining). Bake the fruitcakes for 1 hour at 275° F. Then, immediately decorate and glaze the fruitcakes. Bake for 30 additional minutes at 275° F.

Remove the fruitcakes from the oven and place on wire racks; let stand in the pans until *completely* cool.

Then, carefully run a sharp, thin-bladed knife along the inside edges of the pans to loosen the cakes. Remove the fruitcakes from the pans by inverting the pans, one at a time, in your hand or onto a wire rack. Let the cakes stand in the upright position.

Use six 13-inch-square pieces of clean, dry, white cotton cloth for saturating in sherry and wrapping the fruitcakes.

MAKES SIX 1-POUND FRUITCAKES; 8 SERVINGS PER FRUITCAKE

Tortes

JOY MCFARLAND'S MILE-HIGH TORTE

Blue ribbon awarded to Joy McFarland, 1992 Iowa State Fair.

Joy McFarland is one of the prodigious winners of blue ribbons at the Iowa State Fair. This divine entry of hers not only won a blue ribbon at the 1992 Iowa State Fair, but also was named Best Overall Cake at the fair that year. Joy and her husband, David, farm near Ellston, Iowa, and are one of the state's largest breeders of purebred Angus cattle.

2¼ cups cake flour
2 teaspoons baking soda
⅛ teaspoon salt
½ cup (¼ pound) butter, softened
2 cups packed light brown sugar
3 extra-large eggs
1 teaspoon pure vanilla extract
3 1-ounce packages Choco Bake chocolate
8 ounces commercial sour cream
1 cup water
½ cup seedless red raspberry jam
6 tablespoons Chambord raspberry
   liqueur, divided
Raspberry Frosting (recipe follows)
Fresh red raspberries for decoration
Chocolate Curls (page 406) for decoration
Additional seedless red raspberry jam for
   glazing raspberries

Preheat the oven to 350° F. Using Special Grease (page 56), grease three 8 × 2-inch round cake pans (see Note 1); set aside. Place 3 bake-even cake strips (page 521) in cold water; let stand (see Note).

Onto waxed paper, sift together the flour, baking soda, and salt; set aside.

Extract the excess water from the bake-even cake strips. Wrap and pin the strips around the prepared cake pans; set aside.

In a large mixing bowl, place the butter and brown sugar; using an electric mixer, cream well on medium-high speed. While continuing to beat on medium-high speed, add the eggs one at a time; beat until fluffy. Add the vanilla and Choco Bake; beat on medium-high speed until completely blended. Add the sour cream; beat on medium-high speed until blended. Add, alternately, the flour mixture in fourths, and the water in thirds, beating on low speed after each addition only until blended.

Using a large mixing spoon, spoon the cake batter equally into the 3 prepared cake pans. Using a small, narrow spatula, lightly and quickly spread the batter evenly in the pans. Bake the cakes for 25 minutes, or until a wooden toothpick inserted into the center of the cakes comes out clean.

Remove the cakes from the oven and place on wire racks; remove the cake strips. Let the cakes stand to cool 10 minutes. Remove the cakes from the pans (page 520); let stand on wire racks until completely cool.

If necessary, level the cakes to remove the crowns (page 521) (if bake-even cake strips were not used).

To assemble, fill, and frost the torte (procedure to follow), follow the techniques described in To Frost a Cake (page 573). Assemble all 3 cake layers *underside up* to provide spongelike surfaces which will absorb the liqueur filling when added.

In a small saucepan, melt ½ cup raspberry jam over low heat; set aside. Slowly drizzle 2 tablespoons of the Chambord evenly over the bottom torte layer; let stand a few moments until the Chambord soaks in. Spread ½ of the melted raspberry jam over the bottom torte layer. Then, carefully spread 1 cup of the Raspberry Frosting over the jam. Place the middle torte layer evenly over the bottom layer. Repeat the filling and frosting procedure.

Place the top torte layer evenly over the middle layer. Drizzle the remaining 2 tablespoons Chambord over the top layer. (Melted raspberry jam is *not* applied to the top layer.) Frost the top and side of the torte with Raspberry Frosting.

Decorate the top of the torte with the fresh red raspberries and Chocolate Curls. In a small saucepan, melt a small amount of additional raspberry jam over low heat. Using a small, soft watercolor brush, paint the fresh raspberries with the melted jam to glaze them. Let the torte stand until the frosting sets. Then, place the torte in an airtight container and refrigerate.

NOTE 1: Although not as satisfactory, the pans may be greased and floured in substitution for using Special Grease.

NOTE 2: The use of bake-even cake strips is optional with this recipe, but it is recommended in order to achieve evenly topped torte layers which do not require leveling.

MAKES ONE 8-INCH, 3-LAYER ROUND TORTE; 12 SERVINGS

Raspberry Frosting

2 cups (1 pound) butter, softened
2 pounds (8 cups) powdered sugar
¾ cup unsweetened cocoa powder
1 cup (½ pint) whipping cream, unwhipped
¼ cup Chambord raspberry liqueur

Place the butter in a very large mixing bowl; using an electric mixer, beat on medium-high speed until fluffy. Add the powdered sugar, cocoa, whipping cream, and Chambord. Beat on low speed until partially mixed; then, beat on medium speed only until blended and fluffy.

OPTIONAL FROSTING DECORATION: After frosting smoothly the side of the torte, immediately run a decorating comb (see illustrations) around the side frosting to form small, parallel lines of decorative frosting ridges.

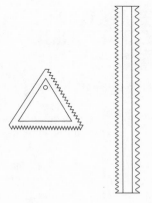

Two Styles of Decorating Combs

Using a decorating bag fit with medium open-star tip number 21 (page 383), pipe a shell border (page 389) of Raspberry Frosting around the bottom and top of the torte. (When frosting the torte, reserve about 1½ cups of the Raspberry Frosting for piping the borders.) Arrange a circle of fresh red raspberries around the top of the torte close to, but not touching, the shell border. Then, pipe an additional shell border of Raspberry Frosting (using tip number 21) around the torte, inside the circle of raspberries. Place a large raspberry in the center of the torte and arrange Chocolate Curls, in spoke fashion, around it (see illustration). Glaze the raspberries, following the procedure in the recipe.

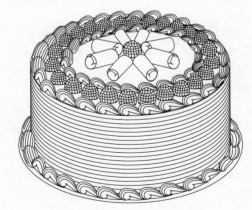

Joy McFarland's Mile-High Torte

BLACK FOREST CHERRY TORTE
Schwarzwälder Kirschtorte

This is one of the great, grand German desserts from the Black Forest region where tart, red cherries grow. Between the three layers of this infatuating chocolate cake is a lush cherry filling spiked with Kirschwasser (cherry brandy). More Kirschwasser flavors the whipped cream swirled lavishly over the top. As a final indulgence, shaved chocolate and maraschino cherries are added as adornment to the whipped cream. It's fun to make and glorious to eat!

3 ounces (3 squares) unsweetened
   chocolate
¼ cup sugar
½ cup whole milk
2¼ cups sifted cake flour (sift before
   measuring)
1 teaspoon baking soda
½ teaspoon salt
½ cup (¼ pound) butter, softened
1¼ cups sugar
3 extra-large eggs
1 teaspoon pure vanilla extract
1 cup whole milk
Cherry Filling (recipe follows)
Kirschwasser Whipped Cream (recipe
   follows)
Shaved Chocolate (page 408)
Maraschino cherries, rinsed, drained, and
   dried between paper towels, for
   decoration

Preheat the oven to 350° F. Using Special Grease (page 56), grease three 8 × 2-inch round cake pans (see Note); set aside. Place 3 bake-even cake strips (page 521) in cold water; let stand.

In the top of a double boiler, place the chocolate, ¼ cup sugar, and ½ cup milk. Place the top of the double boiler over (not touching) simmering water in the bottom pan. Stir the mixture constantly until the chocolate melts and the mixture is completely blended and smooth.

Remove the top of the double boiler from the bottom pan; set aside.

Onto waxed paper, sift together the flour, baking soda, and salt; set aside.

Extract the excess water from the bake-even cake strips. Wrap and pin the strips around the prepared cake pans; set aside.

In a large mixing bowl, place the butter and 1¼ cups sugar; using an electric mixer, beat on medium-high speed until light and fluffy. Add the eggs, one at a time, beating well on medium-high speed after each addition. Add the chocolate mixture and vanilla; beat on medium-high speed until blended. Add, alternately, the flour mixture in fourths, and 1 cup milk in thirds, beating on low speed after each addition only until blended.

Using a large mixing spoon, spoon the cake batter equally into the 3 prepared cake pans. Using a small, narrow spatula, lightly and quickly spread the batter evenly in the pans. Bake the cakes for 25 minutes, or until a wooden toothpick inserted into the center of the cakes comes out clean.

Remove the cakes from the oven and place on wire racks; remove the cake strips. Let the cakes stand to cool 10 minutes. Remove the cakes from the pans (page 520); let stand on wire racks until completely cool.

Then, spread ½ of the Cherry Filling between the bottom and middle torte layers; spread the remaining ½ of the Cherry Filling between the middle and top torte layers (see To Frost a Cake, page 573). Spread the Kirschwasser Whipped Cream attractively over the top of the torte, leaving the side of the cake unfrosted.

Decorate the top of the torte with the Shaved Chocolate and the maraschino cherries. Place the torte in an airtight cake container and refrigerate.

NOTE: Although not as satisfactory, the pans may be greased and floured in substitution for using Special Grease.

**MAKES ONE 8-INCH, 3-LAYER ROUND TORTE;
12 SERVINGS**

Cherry Filling

2 cups pitted, tart, fresh (or frozen and
   thawed) red cherries
1 cup plus 3 tablespoons sugar
1 cup juice drained from cherries
3 tablespoons cornstarch
Red liquid food coloring (optional)
¼ cup Kirschwasser (cherry brandy;
   page 23)

Cut the cherries in half lengthwise, and place in
a medium mixing bowl. Add the sugar and stir to
combine; let stand 1 hour, stirring occasionally.

Drain the cherries in a sieve, reserving the
juice. Measure 1 cup reserved juice, adding
water, if necessary, to make 1 cup liquid. Place
the cherries in a medium saucepan. Add the 1
cup reserved juice and cornstarch; stir to combine. Bring the cherry mixture to a simmer over
medium heat and cook until thick and translucent, stirring constantly.

Remove the saucepan from the heat and place
on a wire rack. Add a few drops of food coloring (if used); stir until evenly blended. Add the
Kirschwasser; stir to blend. Let the Cherry Filling stand until cooled to room temperature
before spreading.

Kirschwasser Whipped Cream

1 cup (½ pint) whipping cream
⅓ cup powdered sugar, sifted (page 57)
1 tablespoon plus 2 teaspoons Kirschwasser
   (cherry brandy; page 23)

Pour the whipping cream into a cold (previously refrigerated), medium-small mixing bowl.
Using an electric mixer, beat the cream on
medium-high speed until it begins to stiffen.
Reduce the mixer speed to medium-low. While
continuing to beat, sprinkle the powdered sugar
over the cream. Then, sprinkle in the Kirschwasser. Continue beating the cream until stiff
but still soft and fluffy.

HAZELNUT TORTE

*This famous old-world torte is a good example of a
European baking procedure which uses large quantities of ground nuts in combination with flour. Sometimes, European-style baked goods are made with
ground nuts and no flour at all (see Zimtsterne cookies, page 637).*

¾ pound (about 2¼ cups) shelled
   hazelnuts, toasted and skinned (page 50)
¾ cup sifted cake flour (sift before
   measuring)
¾ teaspoon powdered instant coffee (to
   powder instant coffee, process in
   blender*)
¾ teaspoon unsweetened cocoa powder
9 extra-large eggs,** room temperature,
   separated
1 cup superfine sugar
1½ teaspoons Myers's (dark) rum
1½ teaspoons finely grated lemon rind
   (page 47)
1 teaspoon pure vanilla extract
½ cup superfine sugar
Hazelnut Frosting (recipe follows)
3 tablespoons toasted, skinned, and
   chopped hazelnuts for decoration (chop
   with a knife)

 *If a blender is not available, a food processor
  may be used; however, it is difficult to achieve
  a fine powder using a food processor. Reserve
  any remaining powdered instant coffee for
  other uses, such as flavored whipped cream
  (see Filling recipe, page 561).*

 **If extra-large eggs are not available, 12 large
  eggs may be substituted.*

In a food processor, process ¾ pound hazelnuts
for *a few seconds* until ground. Be careful not to
overprocess, reducing the nuts to butter. Set the
ground nuts aside.

(Recipe continues on next page)

Preheat the oven to 350°F. Grease the bottoms of two 9-inch springform pans; set aside (see Note).

Onto waxed paper, sift together the flour, coffee, and cocoa. Place the flour mixture in a medium mixing bowl. Add the ground hazelnuts; stir to combine; set aside.

Place the egg yolks in a large mixing bowl. Using an electric mixer, beat the egg yolks on high speed about 8 minutes, until very thick and butter colored. While continuing to beat the egg yolks on high speed, very gradually add 1 cup sugar (about 3 minutes additional beating time). Add the rum, lemon rind, and vanilla; beat on high speed 2 additional minutes, until very thick. Add the flour mixture in thirds, using a large mixing spoon to fold in after each addition only until the flour disappears; set aside.

Place the egg whites in a large mixing bowl. Using the electric mixer fit with clean, dry blades, beat the egg whites on high speed until soft peaks hold. While continuing to beat on high speed, very gradually add ½ cup sugar and continue beating the egg white mixture until stiff, but still moist and glossy. Pour the egg yolk mixture back and forth over the egg white mixture; using the large mixing spoon, fold in carefully and quickly.

Pour ⅓ of the cake batter into one of the prepared springform pans. Pour the remaining ⅔ of the batter into the other springform pan. Using a small, narrow spatula, lightly spread the batter evenly in the pans. Then, carefully run a narrow, rubber spatula once in a circle around the batter in each pan halfway between the edge and the center of the pans to remove any large air pockets. Bake the cakes for 20 to 25 minutes, or until the cakes spring back when touched lightly with your finger. (The thicker cake will take longer to bake.)

Remove the cakes from the oven and place on wire racks; let the cakes stand in the pans until completely cool.

When the cakes are cool, run a sharp, very thin-bladed knife in a continuous motion around the inside edge of the pans to loosen the cakes. Then, remove the sides of the pans. Invert each cake onto a wire rack and carefully remove the pan bottoms. Split the thicker cake in half horizontally to form 2 layers (see To Split a Cake into Layers, page 522). (The thinner, single cake is the third layer.)

Reserve about 1½ cups of the Hazelnut Frosting to decorate the torte. With the remainder of the frosting, frost between the layers, and the top and side of the torte (see To Frost a Cake, page 573). Sprinkle the 3 tablespoons chopped hazelnuts over the top of the torte. With the 1½ cups reserved Hazelnut Frosting, pipe rope borders (page 389) around the bottom and top of the torte using a decorating bag fit with medium open-star tip number 21 (page 383). Let the torte stand until the frosting sets. Then, place the torte in an airtight container and refrigerate.

NOTE: Do not wrap bake-even cake strips (page 521) around the cake pans when using this recipe.

MAKES ONE 9-INCH, 3-LAYER ROUND TORTE; 14 SERVINGS

Hazelnut Frosting

¼ pound (about ¾ cup) shelled hazelnuts, toasted and skinned (page 50)
1 cup sugar
¾ teaspoon cornstarch
8 extra-large egg yolks*
1 cup (½ pint) whipping cream, unwhipped
2¾ teaspoons pure vanilla extract
2 cups (1 pound) butter

  *If extra-large egg yolks are not available,
   9 large egg yolks may be substituted.

In a food processor, process the hazelnuts for *a few seconds* until ground. Be careful not to over-process, reducing the nuts to butter. Set the ground nuts aside. In a small mixing bowl, place the sugar and cornstarch; stir to combine; set aside.

Place the egg yolks in a medium mixing bowl. Using an electric mixer, beat the egg yolks on high speed about 8 minutes, until very thick and butter colored. While continuing to beat the egg yolks on high speed, very gradually add the sugar mixture; beat until blended. While continuing to beat on high speed, gradually add the whipping cream; beat until blended. With the aid of a rubber spatula, place the egg yolk mixture in the top of a double boiler. Place the top of the double boiler over simmering water in the bottom pan. Cook the egg yolk mixture until thick (about 15 to 20 minutes), stirring constantly.

Remove the top of the double boiler from the bottom pan and place it on a wire rack. Add the vanilla; stir until blended. Let the mixture stand until cooled slightly; then, refrigerate until cold, stirring occasionally.

Remove the butter from the refrigerator and place it in a large mixing bowl; let stand 5 minutes only. Using the electric mixer fit with clean, dry blades, beat the butter on high speed until fluffy. Add the cold egg yolk mixture; beat on high speed until well blended. Add the ground hazelnuts; beat to combine. Use the Hazelnut Frosting immediately. Food frosted with Hazelnut Frosting must be kept refrigerated.

Frostings

TO FROST A CAKE

EQUIPMENT FOR FROSTING A CAKE
With the following items, you will be well equipped to frost most types of cakes made in the home kitchen (see illustration):

Corrugated cardboard cake circles and
    boards
1 decorating turntable
1 8-inch, narrow, angled spatula
1 12-inch, narrow, angled spatula

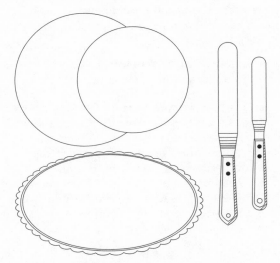

Clockwise from bottom: *Decorating Turntable; Corrugated Cardboard Cake Circles; 12-Inch Narrow, Angled Spatula; and 8-Inch Narrow, Angled Spatula.*

The above equipment is available from Wilton Enterprises and Sweet Celebrations Inc. (see Product Sources, page 850, for addresses and telephone numbers).

FROSTING CONSISTENCY

Proper frosting consistency is critical to the successful frosting of a cake. With a tinge of facetiousness, the instruction is: "Frosting should not be too thick, nor should it be too thin." Frosting which is too thick will not spread easily and attractively, and will pull at the surface of the cake, causing crumbling. Frosting which is too thin will run, and cannot be spread thick enough to smoothly cover the cake. Extremely thin frosting may permeate the cake, causing soggy texture.

The knack of achieving correct frosting consistency is gained by experience—trial and error. Reliable, tested frosting recipes generally produce frostings of satisfactory consistency; however, factors such as room temperature, softness of the butter or shortening, and humidity may create the need for tiny adjustments to thicken or thin the frosting.

Bowls of frosting should be covered immediately after making and should be kept covered as much as possible during the frosting process to prevent drying.

STEPS PREPARATORY TO FROSTING (other than sheet cakes frosted in the baking pan)

1. If frosting a layered cake, level the lower layer(s) if necessary (see To Level a Baked Cake, page 521). Level the top layer if necessary or required because of planned decoration. Some cakes frosted more informally—for example, with swirls of Boiled Frosting (page 578) or Seven-Minute Frosting (page 579)—may be considered more eye-appealing if the top layer has an unleveled crown.

2. Brush the cake surfaces lightly with a soft pastry brush to remove any loose crumbs which would otherwise mingle with the frosting as it is applied.

3. Place the lower layer of the cake (or the entire cake, if not layered) on a corrugated cardboard cake circle (or board) which is approximately 2 inches greater in diameter (or length and width) than the diameter (or length and width) of the cake; in other words, use a 10-inch cake circle under an 8-inch round cake. (While it is strongly recommended that a cake circle [or board] be used to achieve good results and for ease of handling, a *perfectly flat* plate with little or no rim may be substituted.)

4. Place the cake circle which holds the lowest cake layer (or the entire single-layered cake) on a decorating turntable. Slip three 4-inch × 1-foot strips of waxed paper under the bottom edge of the cake around the cardboard cake circle to prevent unwanted frosting from getting on the exposed border of the cake circle during the frosting process. The waxed paper will be removed after the cake is frosted.

FROSTING PROCEDURE

To help prevent cake crumbs from mixing with the frosting as it is applied, always keep the spatula on the frosting and avoid letting it touch the surface of the cake.

To frost the lower layer of a cake, place tablespoonful of frosting (or other filling) over the central surface of the cake. Using the small spatula, spread the frosting very evenly and smoothly to within ¼ inch of the outside edge of the cake. The weight of the top layer(s) will press the frosting to the edge of the cake. It is important to maintain an even thickness of frosting between the layers and to finish the surface smoothly in order to produce a symmetrical cake which does not tilt. Carefully place the top (or next) cake layer over the frosting (or filling) covering the bottom layer, taking great care to position it evenly over the bottom layer. Repeat the process if stacking more than 2 layers. If desired, the top cake layer may be inverted, thereby positioning the bottom side of the layer at the top of the whole cake to provide a smoother surface for frosting.

Spoon frosting over the top of the cake; using the large spatula, spread the frosting evenly over the top surface, pushing the surplus frosting over the edge and down the side of the cake.

Using the small spatula, transport frosting from the bowl to the side of the cake, spreading small vertical areas at a time. Then, if a smooth finish is desired, hold the small spatula in a stationary, vertical position perpendicular to the cardboard cake circle and lightly against the frosting on the side of the cake. Slowly turn the decorating turntable; return excess frosting accumulated on the spatula to the bowl.

Finally, if a smooth finish is desired on the top of a level-topped cake, make fan-type sweeping motions with the edge of the large spatula from the top edge of the cake toward the center, returning any excess frosting to the bowl. Rotate the decorating turntable before making each sweep. Then, using either the large or small spatula, smooth the frosting in the center of the cake. As a last step, very lightly pull the edge of the large spatula over the entire top of the cake. If the frosting on the cake becomes too dry and unpliable before the finishing process is completed, intermittently dip the spatula in very hot water and wipe it dry as you hurry to complete the smoothing procedure. The heat of the spatula will help soften the frosting. Or, with extreme care, the spatula may be left slightly damp after dipping in the hot water. The tiny bit of water will thin the surface of the frosting, making it easier to rework, and also will help restore a shiny finish. *This technique should not be used on frostings which contain egg whites.*

To achieve a smooth frosting finish employing the techniques described above, a buttercream-style frosting is generally used.

After the top and side of the cake are frosted, use quick motions to pull the strips of waxed paper from under the cake. Make any necessary small repairs to the frosting around the bottom of the cake. Make certain that the frosting on the side of the cake touches the cake circle in order to completely seal the cake with frosting to prevent loss of moisture. This also can be accomplished by piping a border around the bottom of the cake (see pages 389–390 for illustrations and procedures for piping borders). Piping borders around the bottom and top of a cake not only endows it with a professional flair, but also helps mask any flaws in the application of frosting.

Allow the newly frosted cake to stand for a short time until the frosting sets; then, place it in an airtight cake container. Leave the frosted cake on the cake circle throughout, including serving.

For an even more perfect job of frosting, first frost the cake with a very thin layer of frosting to contain the crumbs. Let the frosting dry for a few minutes before applying the main layer of frosting.

To achieve a completely smooth finish to the frosting on the top of the cake, which is especially desirable if the cake is to be decorated with piped flowers and/or lettering, or other piped frosting decorations, let the newly frosted cake stand only until the frosting is dry to touch. Then, place a piece of parchment baking paper or a paper towel over the top of the cake. Lightly roll a pizza roller back and forth over the parchment or paper towel to smooth the frosting surface. Or, draw the edge of the large spatula lightly across the parchment or paper towel to achieve the same result. This smoothing procedure should be used only on buttercream-style frostings. It is particularly effective when Cake Decorators' Icing (page 576) has been used to frost the cake. The consistency of some frostings is not conducive to the successful application of this smoothing procedure.

TO SWIRL FROSTING: The consistency of Boiled Frosting (page 578), Seven-Minute Frosting (page 579), and other frostings made with beaten egg whites lends itself best to a swirled finish. In fact, these frostings, skillfully applied in swirls, can render a cake almost too glamorous to eat! Most buttercream-style frostings also can be swirled successfully.

While frostings made with beaten egg whites generally are not used when a smooth finish is desired, there are exceptions. For example, the recipe for Shadow Cake (page 526) calls for Boiled Frosting to be applied smoothly to the top of the cake and swirled on the sides.

(Recipe continues on next page)

For a swirled frosting finish, spoon frosting over the top of the cake. Using the small spatula, spread the frosting to cover the top surface. Then, use the small spatula to sculpt quick, random C's on the frosting surface. Additional portions of frosting may be added as you sculpt the C's to produce a decorative, symmetrical appearance.

Use the small spatula to apply frosting over small vertical areas at a time on the side of the cake. After applying the frosting to each small area, swirl the frosting just applied.

When the cake is completely frosted, do any necessary touching up with further swirls and added bits of frosting where needed.

CAKE DECORATORS' ICINGS

Use Cake Decorators' Icings to pipe flowers and other decorations, including lettering, for/on cakes. Also use Cake Decorators' Icings to frost such decorated cakes, as a very smooth finish can be achieved with this icing. A flat, smooth frosting surface on which to apply piped icing decorations is essential to produce an attractive and professional-looking decorated cake. (See To Frost a Cake, page 573, for procedures.)

Cake Decorators' White Icing

½ cup nonfat dry milk
½ cup cool water
½ teaspoon clear vanilla
½ teaspoon almond extract
1 teaspoon salt
1⅓ cups vegetable shortening, softened
2 pounds (8 cups) powdered sugar
Paste food coloring (optional)

In a large mixing bowl, place the dry milk, water, vanilla, almond extract, and salt; stir until completely blended. Add the vegetable shortening and powdered sugar; using an electric mixer, beat on medium-high speed only until blended and creamy.

To tint the icing, use a toothpick to add a tiny amount of paste food coloring; beat the icing on medium-high speed only until the color is evenly blended.

Use the frosting immediately or place it in an airtight plastic storage container and refrigerate. Keeps well up to one week in the refrigerator.

MAKES ENOUGH TO FROST BETWEEN THE LAYERS, AND THE TOP AND SIDES, AND TO DECORATE ONE 2- OR 3-LAYER, 8- OR 9-INCH ROUND OR SQUARE CAKE

¼ RECIPE CAKE DECORATORS' WHITE ICING (MINUS ALMOND EXTRACT FOR SMALL DECORATING TASKS)

2 tablespoons dry milk
2 tablespoons cool water
¼ teaspoon clear vanilla
¼ teaspoon salt
¼ cup plus 1 tablespoon plus 1 teaspoon vegetable shortening, softened
2 cups powdered sugar

Use a small mixing bowl and follow the recipe.

Cake Decorators' Buttercream Icing

⅔ cup (¼ pound plus 2 tablespoons plus 2 teaspoons) butter, softened
⅔ cup vegetable shortening, softened

Follow the Cake Decorators' White Icing recipe, above, substituting ⅔ cup butter and ⅔ cup vegetable shortening for 1⅓ cups vegetable shortening. (In general, Cake Decorators' *White* Icing should be used when the icing is to be tinted.)

Cake Decorators' Chocolate Icing

¼ cup nonfat dry milk
½ cup cool water
1 teaspoon pure vanilla extract
1 cup (½ pound) butter, softened
2 pounds (8 cups) powdered sugar
1 cup unsweetened cocoa powder

In a small mixing bowl, place the dry milk, water, and vanilla; stir until completely blended; set aside. In a large mixing bowl, place the butter, powdered sugar, cocoa, and dry milk mixture; using an electric mixer, beat on medium–high speed only until blended and creamy.

Use the frosting immediately or place it in an airtight plastic storage container and refrigerate. Keeps well up to one week in the refrigerator.

MAKES ENOUGH TO FROST BETWEEN THE LAYERS, AND THE TOP AND SIDES, AND TO DECORATE ONE 2- OR 3-LAYER, 8- OR 9-INCH ROUND OR SQUARE CAKE

BUTTERCREAM FROSTING

½ cup (¼ pound) butter, softened
1 pound (4 cups) powdered sugar
¼ teaspoon salt
2 teaspoons pure vanilla extract
¼ cup half-and-half

In a medium mixing bowl, place the butter, powdered sugar, salt, vanilla, and half-and-half. Using an electric mixer, beat the mixture on medium–high speed only until blended and fluffy.

MAKES ENOUGH TO FROST BETWEEN THE LAYERS, AND THE TOP AND SIDES OF ONE 2-LAYER, 8- OR 9-INCH ROUND OR SQUARE CAKE, OR THE TOP OF ONE 9 × 13-INCH SHEET CAKE

LEMON BUTTERCREAM FROSTING

½ cup (¼ pound) butter, softened
1 pound (4 cups) powdered sugar
¼ cup freshly squeezed, strained lemon
  juice
¼ teaspoon lemon extract
Lemon-colored paste food coloring

In a medium mixing bowl, place the butter, powdered sugar, lemon juice, and lemon extract. Using an electric mixer, beat the ingredients on low speed to combine; then, increase the mixer speed to medium–high and continue beating only until blended and smooth. To lightly tint the frosting, use a toothpick to add a tiny amount of paste food coloring; beat the frosting on medium–high speed only until the color is evenly blended.

If thinner frosting is desired, add water, 1 or 2 teaspoons at a time, until the desired consistency is achieved.

MAKES ENOUGH TO FROST BETWEEN THE LAYERS, AND THE TOP AND SIDES OF ONE 2-LAYER, 8- OR 9-INCH ROUND OR SQUARE CAKE, OR THE TOP OF ONE 9 × 13-INCH SHEET CAKE

MOCHA BUTTERCREAM FROSTING

½ cup (¼ pound) butter, softened
1 pound (4 cups) powdered sugar
¼ teaspoon salt
½ teaspoon pure vanilla extract
2 tablespoons half-and-half
1 tablespoon unsweetened cocoa powder
2 tablespoons strong, brewed coffee, room
temperature

In a medium mixing bowl, place the butter, powdered sugar, salt, vanilla, half-and-half, cocoa, and coffee. Using an electric mixer, beat the mixture on medium-high speed only until blended and fluffy.

MAKES ENOUGH TO FROST BETWEEN THE LAYERS, AND THE TOP AND SIDES OF ONE 2-LAYER, 8- OR 9-INCH ROUND OR SQUARE CAKE, THE TOP OF ONE 9×13-INCH SHEET CAKE, OR THE SIDE OF ONE ROLLED 10½×15½-INCH JELLY-ROLL CAKE

CREAMY CINNAMON FROSTING

1 pound plus 1 cup (5 cups) powdered
  sugar
1½ teaspoons ground cinnamon
½ teaspoon salt
½ cup vegetable shortening
¼ cup plus 2 tablespoons half-and-half
1¼ teaspoons pure vanilla extract

In a medium mixing bowl, place the powdered sugar, cinnamon, salt, vegetable shortening, half-and-half, and vanilla. Using an electric mixer, beat the mixture on medium-high speed only until smooth and creamy.

MAKES ENOUGH TO FROST BETWEEN THE LAYERS, AND THE TOP AND SIDES, AND TO DECORATE ONE 2-LAYER, 8- OR 9-INCH ROUND OR SQUARE CAKE, OR THE TOP OF ONE 9×13-INCH SHEET CAKE

BOILED FROSTING

Note: This recipe contains uncooked egg whites (see page 262).

2¼ cups sugar
1 cup water
2 tablespoons light corn syrup
⅛ teaspoon salt
3 extra-large egg whites, room temperature
1 teaspoon clear vanilla

In a large, heavy saucepan, place the sugar, water, syrup, and salt; stir to combine. Over low heat, stir the mixture until the sugar dissolves. Attach a candy thermometer. Increase the heat to medium-high. Bring the mixture to a boil and cook, *without stirring,* until the temperature reaches 240° F. (see Note).

Meanwhile, place the egg whites in a large mixing bowl. Using an electric mixer, beat the egg whites on high speed until stiff peaks hold; let stand.

When the syrup reaches 240° F. (see Note), remove from the heat and detach the thermometer. While beating constantly with the electric mixer on high speed, *slowly* trickle the hot syrup into the beaten egg whites. Add the vanilla and continue beating on high speed until the frosting is thick enough to hold stiff peaks.

NOTE: This temperature is for use at sea-level locations. To adjust the temperature for preparation of this recipe at higher elevations, see Boiled Candies and Frostings, page 35.

MAKES ENOUGH TO FROST BETWEEN THE LAYERS, AND THE TOP AND SIDES OF ONE 2- OR 3-LAYER, 8- OR 9-INCH ROUND OR SQUARE CAKE, OR THE TOP OF ONE 9×13-INCH SHEET CAKE

BURNT-SUGAR FROSTING: Follow the Boiled Frosting recipe, above, substituting ¼ cup Burnt-Sugar Syrup (page 533) for 2 tablespoons light corn syrup.

CONFECTIONERS' FROSTING

1 pound (4 cups) powdered sugar
¼ cup plus 1 tablespoon half-and-half
2 teaspoons clear vanilla
Paste food coloring (optional)

In a medium mixing bowl, place the powdered sugar, half-and-half, and vanilla; using an electric mixer, beat on medium-high speed only until well blended. To tint the frosting, use a toothpick to add a tiny amount of paste food coloring. Using a spoon, stir the frosting vigorously until the color is completely blended and uniform.

Use the frosting immediately. While using the frosting, place a piece of plastic wrap over half of the bowl to help keep the frosting moist.

MAKES ENOUGH TO FROST 5 DOZEN LARGE COOKIES; TO DECORATE 15 DOZEN MEDIUM COOKIES; OR TO FROST 2 DOZEN CINNAMON ROLLS

SERVING SUGGESTIONS

- Use plain or tinted Confectioners' Frosting to frost cutout cookies which will be decorated with colored sugar, nonpareils (page 24), and other edible decorations (see To Decorate Cutout Cookies, page 635).

- Use Confectioners' Frosting to pipe decorations on cookies (see Gingerbread People, page 634, and Mincemeat Cookies, page 621).

SEVEN-MINUTE FROSTING

1¾ cups sugar
½ cup cold water
1 tablespoon light corn syrup
2 extra-large egg whites, room temperature
⅛ teaspoon salt
1 teaspoon clear vanilla

In the top of a double boiler with at least an 8-cup (top pan) capacity, place the sugar, water, syrup, egg whites, and salt; using a handheld electric mixer, beat 1 minute on high speed. Place the top of the double boiler over (not touching) boiling water in the bottom pan. While beating constantly with the electric mixer on high speed, cook the mixture 7 minutes, or until stiff peaks hold. If the frosting threatens to spill over the edge of the double boiler top pan during the cooking process, spoon some of the frosting out of the pan and discard. (This recipe makes ample frosting for the cakes whose recipes in *The Blue Ribbon Country Cookbook* specify its use.)

Remove the top of the double boiler from the bottom pan and transfer the frosting mixture to a large mixing bowl. Add the vanilla. Using a standard-sized electric mixer, beat the frosting on high speed until stiff enough to spread.

MAKES ENOUGH TO FROST BETWEEN THE LAYERS, AND THE TOP AND SIDES OF ONE 2-LAYER, 8- OR 9-INCH ROUND OR SQUARE CAKE, OR THE TOP OF ONE 9 × 13-INCH SHEET CAKE

SUGGESTION FOR USE OF LEFTOVER FROSTING: This recipe makes a generous amount of frosting. Leftover frosting may be used to frost commercially purchased vanilla or chocolate wafers. Top each frosted wafer with a pecan half, an English walnut half, or a hazelnut.

HARVEST MOON FROSTING: Follow the Seven-Minute Frosting recipe, above, substituting 1¾ cups packed light brown sugar for 1¾ cups granulated sugar, and substituting 1 teaspoon pure vanilla extract for 1 teaspoon clear vanilla.

CHOCOLATE FROSTING

This wonderful, basic Chocolate Frosting recipe is my mother's. I've enjoyed it my whole life on cakes, brownies, and cookies, and have never found a better chocolate buttercream frosting. The fresh, strong, brewed coffee in this frosting gives it a richness and depth of flavor which make it a standout. (Be sure to use real butter.)

1 pound (4 cups) powdered sugar
⅓ cup unsweetened cocoa powder
½ cup (¼ pound) butter, melted
¼ cup strong, brewed coffee, room temperature
2 teaspoons pure vanilla extract

In a medium mixing bowl, place the powdered sugar, cocoa, butter, coffee, and vanilla. Using an electric mixer, beat the mixture on high speed only until completely smooth.

MAKES ENOUGH TO FROST BETWEEN THE LAYERS, AND THE TOP AND SIDES OF ONE 2-LAYER, 8- OR 9-INCH ROUND OR SQUARE CAKE, THE TOP OF ONE 9×13-INCH SHEET CAKE, THE TOP AND SIDES OF ONE 5×9-INCH LOAF CAKE, OR 7 DOZEN MEDIUM COOKIES

CARAMEL FROSTING

¾ cup (¼ pound plus 4 tablespoons) butter
1½ cups packed light brown sugar
⅓ cup half-and-half
3¼ cups powdered sugar, sifted (page 57)

In a medium-small, heavy saucepan, melt the butter over low heat. Add the brown sugar; stir to combine. Over medium heat, bring the brown sugar mixture to a boil, stirring constantly. Boil the mixture 2 minutes, stirring continuously. Remove from the heat. Add the half-and-half; stir vigorously to blend. Return the mixture to a boil over medium heat, stirring constantly. Remove from the heat.

Leave the brown sugar mixture in the saucepan and refrigerate it until the mixture is cooled to slightly warm (about 40 minutes), stirring intermittently.

Then, remove the mixture from the refrigerator; set aside. Place the powdered sugar in a medium mixing bowl. Add the brown sugar mixture; using an electric mixer, beat on medium-high speed only until blended and smooth.

MAKES ENOUGH TO FROST ONE 2-LAYER, 8- OR 9-INCH ROUND OR SQUARE CAKE, OR THE TOP OF ONE 9×13-INCH SHEET CAKE

POWDERED SUGAR FROSTING

A primary frosting used in the Midwest to frost cakes and cookies.

1 pound (4 cups) powdered sugar
¼ cup plus 2 tablespoons (6 tablespoons) butter, melted
¼ cup half-and-half *or* whole milk
2 teaspoons clear vanilla

In a medium mixing bowl, place the powdered sugar, butter, half-and-half (or milk), and vanilla. Using an electric mixer, beat the mixture on medium-high speed only until blended and fluffy.

MAKES ENOUGH TO FROST BETWEEN THE LAYERS, AND THE TOP AND SIDES OF ONE 2-LAYER, 8- OR 9-INCH ROUND OR SQUARE CAKE, THE TOP OF ONE 9×13-INCH SHEET CAKE, OR 7 DOZEN MEDIUM COOKIES

ORANGE FROSTING

2 cups powdered sugar
2 tablespoons butter, melted
2 tablespoons freshly squeezed, strained
    orange juice
1 tablespoon very finely grated orange rind
    (page 47)
Orange-colored paste food coloring
    (optional)

In a medium mixing bowl, place the powdered sugar, butter, orange juice, orange rind, and a tiny amount of food coloring (if used). Using an electric mixer, beat the mixture on medium-high speed only until blended and smooth.

MAKES ENOUGH TO FROST 6 DOZEN MEDIUM COOKIES. DOUBLE THE RECIPE TO FROST BETWEEN THE LAYERS, AND THE TOP AND SIDES OF ONE 2-LAYER, 8- OR 9-INCH ROUND OR SQUARE CAKE, OR THE TOP OF ONE 9 × 13-INCH SHEET CAKE

BANANA-NUT FROSTING

1 pound (4 cups) powdered sugar
¼ cup plus 2 tablespoons (6 tablespoons)
    butter, melted
¼ cup half-and-half
1½ teaspoons clear vanilla
¼ teaspoon banana flavoring
½ cup chopped pecans

In a medium mixing bowl, place the powdered sugar, butter, half-and-half, vanilla, and banana flavoring. Using an electric mixer, beat the mixture on medium-high speed only until blended and smooth. Add the pecans; beat on medium speed until evenly distributed.

MAKES ENOUGH TO FROST BETWEEN THE LAYERS, AND THE TOP AND SIDES OF ONE 2-LAYER, 8- OR 9-INCH ROUND OR SQUARE CAKE, OR THE TOP OF ONE 9 × 13-INCH SHEET CAKE

WHIPPED CREAM-COCONUT FROSTING

1 cup (½ pint) whipping cream
¼ cup powdered sugar
½ teaspoon clear vanilla
½ cup shredded coconut

Pour the whipping cream into a cold (previously refrigerated), medium-small mixing bowl. Using an electric mixer, beat the cream on medium-high speed until it begins to stiffen. Reduce the mixer speed to medium-low. Add the powdered sugar and vanilla; continue beating the cream until stiff but still soft and fluffy.

Frost the top and sides of a white or yellow cake with the whipped cream. Then, sprinkle the coconut on the frosted top and sides of the cake, pressing the coconut lightly into the frosting on the sides of the cake with your hand only until it holds in place. Refrigerate the cake after frosting.

MAKES ENOUGH TO FROST THE TOP AND SIDES OF ONE 1-LAYER, 8- OR 9-INCH ROUND OR SQUARE CAKE

VARIATION: After applying the coconut to the frosted cake, garnish the top of the cake with fresh raspberries, strawberries, or blueberries, or in combination.

NOTE: To frost between the layers, and the top and sides of one 2-layer, 8- or 9-inch round or square cake, double the recipe. Use coconut between the layers as well as on top of the cake. Use fruit only on the top of the cake (see Variation, above).

COCONUT-PECAN FROSTING I

½ cup (¼ pound) butter
1 cup sugar
1 cup evaporated milk
3 extra-large egg yolks, slightly beaten
1 teaspoon pure vanilla extract
1¼ cups flaked coconut
1 cup chopped pecans

In a small saucepan, melt the butter over low heat. Add the sugar, evaporated milk, and egg yolks. Increase the heat to medium; cook the mixture until thick (about 10 minutes), stirring constantly. Do not allow the mixture to boil.

Remove the saucepan from the heat and place on a wire rack. Add the vanilla; stir until blended. Add the coconut and pecans; stir to combine. Let stand until the frosting is cooled to spreading consistency, stirring occasionally. Cakes frosted with Coconut–Pecan Frosting I must be kept refrigerated.

MAKES ENOUGH TO FROST BETWEEN THE LAYERS, AND THE TOP OF ONE 3-LAYER, 8-INCH ROUND OR SQUARE CAKE, OR THE TOP OF ONE 9 × 13-INCH SHEET CAKE

COCONUT-PECAN FROSTING II

½ cup (¼ pound) butter
¾ cup sugar
½ cup evaporated milk
1 teaspoon pure vanilla extract
1 cup flaked coconut
1 cup broken pecans

In a small saucepan, melt the butter over low heat. Remove from the heat. Add the sugar and evaporated milk; stir to combine. Bring the mixture to a rapid boil over medium–high heat, stirring constantly. Reduce the heat slightly and continue boiling rapidly 5 minutes, stirring continuously.

Remove the saucepan from the heat. Add the vanilla; stir to blend. Add the coconut; stir to combine. Then, add the pecans; stir to combine.

MAKES ENOUGH TO FROST THE TOP OF ONE 9 × 13-INCH SHEET CAKE

CRÈME DE MENTHE BUTTER FROSTING

½ cup (¼ pound) butter, softened
1 pound (4 cups) powdered sugar
¼ cup plus 2 tablespoons green crème de menthe

In a medium mixing bowl, place the butter, powdered sugar, and crème de menthe. Using an electric mixer, beat the mixture on medium-high speed only until blended and fluffy.

MAKES ENOUGH TO FROST BETWEEN THE LAYERS, AND THE TOP AND SIDES OF ONE 2-LAYER, 8- OR 9-INCH ROUND OR SQUARE CAKE, OR THE TOP OF ONE 9 × 13-INCH SHEET CAKE

SERVING SUGGESTIONS
- Particularly good with chocolate cake. The frosted cake may be decorated with Chocolate Curls (page 406).

- Makes a nice green frosting for Christmas and St. Patrick's Day cakes and cookies.

CRÈME DE MENTHE WHIPPED CREAM FROSTING

2½ cups miniature marshmallows
⅓ cup whole milk
¼ cup green crème de menthe
2 cups (1 pint) whipping cream
½ cup powdered sugar, sifted (page 57)

In a medium saucepan, place the marshmallows and milk. Over medium heat, stir the mixture constantly until the marshmallows *completely* melt (about 5 minutes). Remove the saucepan from the heat and place on a wire rack. Let the mixture stand until cooled to room temperature, stirring occasionally.

Then, add the crème de menthe; stir until completely blended; set aside. Pour the whipping cream into a cold (previously refrigerated), medium mixing bowl. Using an electric mixer, beat the cream on medium–high speed until it begins to stiffen. Reduce the mixer speed to medium–low. Add the powdered sugar; continue beating the cream until stiff but still soft and fluffy.

Pour the crème de menthe mixture back and forth over the whipped cream; using a mixing spoon, fold in until evenly blended. Refrigerate the cake after frosting.

MAKES ENOUGH TO FROST BETWEEN THE LAYERS, AND THE TOP AND SIDES OF ONE 2- OR 3-LAYER, 8- OR 9-INCH ROUND OR SQUARE CAKE

HONEY–CREAM CHEESE FROSTING

3 ounces cream cheese, softened
2 teaspoons honey
1 teaspoon clear vanilla
¾ cup powdered sugar

Place the cream cheese in a small mixing bowl. Using an electric mixer, beat the cream cheese on high speed until creamy. Add the honey and vanilla; beat on medium–high speed until blended. Add the powdered sugar; beat on medium–high speed until smooth.

Place the uncovered food frosted with Honey–Cream Cheese Frosting in the refrigerator; let stand 2 hours, until the frosting sets. (Even when set, this frosting is slightly soft.) Then, cover the food and store in the refrigerator for food safety due to the ingredient, cream cheese.

MAKES ENOUGH TO DECORATE 5 DOZEN MEDIUM COOKIES

SERVING SUGGESTION: Using a decorating bag fit with small round tip number 2 (page 383), pipe close, parallel stripes of Honey–Cream Cheese Frosting back and fourth across the tops of cookies for an attractive decoration.

FLUFF FROSTING

Note: This recipe contains uncooked egg whites (see page 262).

1 cup plus 2 tablespoons light corn syrup
2 extra-large egg whites, room temperature
⅛ teaspoon salt
1¼ teaspoons clear vanilla

Place the syrup in a small saucepan. Bring the syrup to a boil over medium heat, stirring constantly. Remove from the heat; set aside.

Place the egg whites in a medium mixing bowl. Using an electric mixer, beat the egg whites on high speed until stiff peaks hold. Add the salt and vanilla. While continuing to beat on high speed, pour the hot syrup in a slow, steady stream into the egg white mixture and continue beating until the frosting is fluffy and of spreading consistency.

MAKES ENOUGH TO FROST BETWEEN THE LAYERS, AND THE TOP AND SIDES OF ONE 8- OR 9-INCH ROUND OR SQUARE CAKE, THE TOP OF ONE 9×13-INCH SHEET CAKE, OR THE TOP AND SIDES OF ONE 10×4-INCH TUBE CAKE

ORANGE FLUFF FROSTING: Follow the Fluff Frosting recipe, with the following modifications:

After removing the syrup from the heat, use a toothpick to add a tiny amount of orange-colored paste food coloring; stir to blend. Reduce the clear vanilla to ¾ teaspoon and add 1 teaspoon orange extract.

MARSHMALLOW CLOUD FROSTING

Note: This recipe contains uncooked egg whites (see page 262).

1 cup sugar
¼ teaspoon cream of tartar
⅛ teaspoon salt
⅓ cup water
2 extra-large egg whites, room temperature
1 cup miniature marshmallows
1 teaspoon clear vanilla

In a small, heavy saucepan, place the sugar, cream of tartar, salt, and water; stir to combine. Over low heat, stir the mixture until the sugar dissolves. Attach a candy thermometer. Increase the heat to medium-high. Bring the mixture to a boil and cook, *without stirring,* until the temperature reaches 240° F. (see Note).

Meanwhile, place the egg whites in a medium mixing bowl. Using an electric mixer, beat the egg whites on high speed until stiff peaks hold; let stand.

When the syrup reaches 240° F. (see Note), remove from the heat and detach the thermometer. Immediately add the marshmallows; stir quickly to dissolve the marshmallows and blend with the syrup. While beating constantly with the electric mixer on high speed, *slowly* trickle the hot marshmallow syrup into the beaten egg whites. Add the vanilla and continue beating on high speed until the frosting is thick enough to hold stiff peaks.

NOTE: This temperature is for use at sea-level locations. To adjust the temperature for preparation of this recipe at higher elevations, see Boiled Candies and Frostings, page 35.

MAKES ENOUGH TO FROST BETWEEN THE LAYERS, AND THE TOP AND SIDES OF ONE 2-LAYER, 8- OR 9-INCH ROUND OR SQUARE CAKE, OR THE TOP OF ONE 9 × 13-INCH SHEET CAKE

ORNAMENTAL VANILLA FROSTING

1½ cups powdered sugar
1 teaspoon clear vanilla
1 tablespoon plus 1 teaspoon water

In a small mixing bowl, place the powdered sugar, vanilla, and water. Using an electric mixer, beat the mixture on medium-high speed only until blended and smooth.

MAKES ENOUGH TO FROST 1 DOZEN CAKE DOUGHNUTS

SERVING SUGGESTION: Use Ornamental Vanilla Frosting to pipe stripes and other simple line-type decorations over cakes, bars, and other cookies.

VARIATION: Whole milk may be substituted for the water.

ORNAMENTAL CHOCOLATE FROSTING

1 cup powdered sugar
2 tablespoons butter
1½ ounces (1½ squares) unsweetened chocolate
2 tablespoons hot water
½ teaspoon pure vanilla extract

Place the powdered sugar in a small mixing bowl; set aside. In a tiny saucepan, place the butter and chocolate. Hold the tiny pan over (not touching) low simmering water in a small saucepan until the butter and chocolate melt, stirring intermittently. Remove the tiny pan from the heat and stir the melted butter and chocolate vigorously until blended.

Add the chocolate mixture, hot water, and vanilla to the powdered sugar. Using an electric mixer, beat the mixture on medium-high speed only until blended and smooth.

MAKES ENOUGH TO FROST 1 DOZEN CAKE DOUGHNUTS

SUPREME CHOCOLATE ICING

2½ cups sugar
1 cup evaporated milk
1 6-ounce package (1 cup) semisweet
   chocolate chips
1 cup marshmallow cream
½ cup (¼ pound) butter

Butter the sides of a medium-large, heavy-bottomed saucepan. Place the sugar and milk in the saucepan; stir to combine. Bring the mixture to a boil over medium heat, stirring constantly. Attach a candy thermometer. Continue boiling the mixture until the temperature reaches 234°F. (see Note), stirring often.

Remove the saucepan from the heat; detach the thermometer. Add the chocolate chips, marshmallow cream, and butter; using a spoon, stir vigorously until all the ingredients completely melt and the icing is perfectly smooth.

Place the saucepan on a wire rack; let the icing stand to cool at room temperature, stirring occasionally to break up the crust which forms on the top of the icing. To achieve a smooth appearance on a frosted cake, cool the icing to lukewarm.

When cooled to lukewarm, carefully pour the icing over the top and edge of the cake, letting it trickle down the side. Using a small, narrow spatula, apply additional icing to any remaining unfrosted sections on the side of the cake. Cut away extra icing which trickles onto the serving plate or waxed paper covering the corrugated cardboard cake circle (board) around the bottom of the cake.

NOTE: This temperature is for use at sea-level locations. To adjust the temperature for preparation of this recipe at higher elevations, see Boiled Candies and Frostings, page 35.

MAKES ENOUGH TO FROST THE TOP AND SIDES OF ONE 10 × 4-INCH TUBE CAKE

VARIATION: To use Supreme Chocolate Icing to frost a cake in the conventional manner; that is, by spreading the icing with a spatula, allow the icing to cool to room temperature before spreading.

SUGGESTION FOR USE OF LEFTOVER ICING: Leftover icing may be used to frost commercially purchased vanilla or chocolate wafers. Pecan halves may be placed on the top of each frosted cookie.

GLAZE

1½ cups powdered sugar
1 tablespoon plus 2 teaspoons water
1 teaspoon clear vanilla

In a medium mixing bowl, place the powdered sugar, water, and vanilla. Using an electric mixer, beat the mixture on low speed until the powdered sugar is moistened; then, increase the mixer speed to high and continue beating only until blended and smooth.

MAKES ENOUGH TO GLAZE 4 DOZEN LARGE COOKIES

CHOCOLATE GLAZE

2 ounces (2 squares) semisweet chocolate
2 teaspoons butter

In the top of a double boiler, place the chocolate and butter. Place the top of the double boiler over (not touching) hot (not boiling) water in the bottom pan; stir constantly until the chocolate and butter melt and blend.

TO USE CHOCOLATE GLAZE FOR PIPING: If Chocolate Glaze is to be used for decorative piping, allow it to cool to a workable consistency.

MAKES ENOUGH TO DECORATE ONE 10-INCH BUNDT CAKE OR ONE 5 × 9-INCH LOAF CAKE

CHOCOLATE COATING

2 ounces (2 squares) semisweet chocolate
2 tablespoons butter
3 tablespoons half-and-half
1 cup sifted powdered sugar (page 57) (sift before measuring)
½ teaspoon pure vanilla extract

In the top of a double boiler, place the chocolate and butter. Place the top of the double boiler over (not touching) hot (not boiling) water in the bottom pan; stir constantly until the chocolate and butter melt and blend. Add the half-and-half; continue stirring until blended and warm.

Remove the top of the double boiler from the bottom pan. Add the powdered sugar and vanilla; using a spoon, stir until blended and smooth.

MAKES ENOUGH TO COAT THE TOP OF ONE 8-INCH ROUND OR SQUARE CAKE

Cookies

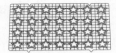

Across the Midwest, Grandma's cookie jar is not a relic immortalized only in fairy tales. It is live and well—just ask the grandchildren. Kids are in seventh heaven when they peek under the lid and discover a treasure trove of chocolate chip, oatmeal, or peanut butter morsels.

While the sweet smell of all kinds of irresistible baked goods seems to permeate the Heartland air, it doesn't take a scientific study to conclude that more cookies issue from Midwest ovens than any other kind of dessert goodie. Just about anyone who cooks at all bakes cookies—if only at Christmastime, when cookie-baking frenzy sets in.

It boggles the mind to think how many millions of cookies are baked from Ohio through Nebraska in the month of December. This once-a-year cookie bake-off is the time when ethnic cookies reflecting a family's origin are made, full tilt. The tattered recipes, in an ancestor's handwriting, are pulled from the recipe box and faithfully followed, as they have been for decades. Scandinavians climb up on the kitchen stool to reach the very top shelf of the cupboard, where the special iron used to make Krumkake is stored, while families of Scotch heritage make plans to bake traditional Scotch Shortbread (page 639).

In German households, the antique, wooden Springerle (page 636) molds brought from Germany by an earlier-generation family member are unwrapped early in the season, since these picturesque, old-world cookies must be made ahead to allow enough time for ripening in the tins. Closer to Christmas, Zimtsterne (Cinnamon Stars) (page 637) and Lebkuchen (page 600) will be added to the annual selection.

Holiday cookie baking is often a shared family event, when mothers, daughters, and granddaughters (and now sometimes fathers, sons, and grandsons) work together, starting early in the morning and baking all day, with flour sifting and oven watching interspersed with pauses for coffee, chatting, and testing the results of the year's undertakings.

Near Christmas Day, knocks begin to be heard at the back door, when friends and neighbors bring platters of the scrumptious cookies they have made. The exchange of cookies is as much a part of Christmas as holly. There is always much discussion and critiquing when the whole family samples the array. Of course, none ever tastes as good as the ones Mom made.

Mother love and cookies are inextricably bound, and the making of traditional favorites calls up wonderful, warm memories of years past. When young newlyweds begin baking the cookies their mothers made, it seems to help establish a real home.

If one were to poll Midwesterners, asking, "What is the most popular cookie in the Midwest among people of all ages?," I think the overwhelming majority would answer, "Brownies." Besides being a regular for family desserts, Brownies (page 602) turn up at chili dinners, church socials, and football tailgate parties, and make standard appearances in lunch boxes and on fishing trips. The best ones have thick, chocolate frosting, and most have nuts, unless they're baked for children. For some reason, many kids do not care for nuts.

In the bar cookie category, Lemon Bars (page 593) would probably rank second in popularity to Brownies, followed by Pumpkin Bars (page 592). Though it is very risky to begin naming cookie favorites because so many kinds are made and there is such a variance in family tastes, some of the other cookies fancied by many Midwesterners are: Snickerdoodles (page 630), Butterscotch Icebox Cookies (page 644), Frosted Chocolate Cookies (page 615), Old-Fashioned Sugar Cookies (page 633), Pineapple Cookies with Powdered Sugar Frosting (page 620), and the list could go on and on.

This chapter offers eighty-four recipes which are just a drop in the luscious Midwest cookie bucket, but they were selected to be representative of the gigantic Midwest cookie universe.

TYPES OF COOKIES

Cookies may be classified into the following six general types based upon the process by which they are made:

BAR COOKIES: Bar cookies are dense, moist, and usually cakelike. The batter/dough is spread/pressed into a pan, baked, and cut into rectangles, squares, or triangles when cool.

DROP COOKIES: The dough of drop cookies is scooped from the mixing bowl in a spoon, trigger scoop, or melon baller and dropped or pushed with a second spoon onto cookie sheets for baking.

MOLDED COOKIES: Molded cookies are shaped usually in the hands and usually before baking. Many are rolled into balls and placed on cookie sheets for baking. In some instances, the balls of dough are then flattened or pressed in various ways. The dough of some types of molded cookies is rolled into pencil-like sticks and then twisted into various shapes. Certain cookies, such as Lace Cookies (page 627), are molded into prescribed shapes after baking.

ROLLED COOKIES: The dough of rolled cookies is gathered into a ball, rolled out with a rolling pin, and cut into cookies, generally using cookie cutters. Sometimes the dough is chilled to facilitate rolling and cutting.

REFRIGERATOR COOKIES: Refrigerator cookie dough is shaped into large, thick rolls (usually about 1 to 2 inches in diameter), wrapped in plastic wrap, and refrigerated overnight or until completely cold. The rolls are then sliced into cookies and baked on cookie sheets.

PRESSED COOKIES: Pressed cookies are made by forcing the dough through a cookie press fit with disks of various designs and shapes, or by piping the dough with a decorating bag fit with selected tips, onto cookie sheets for baking.

SECRETS FOR BAKING SUCCESSFUL COOKIES

- Bake cookies (except bar cookies, of course) on shiny, aluminum cookie sheets without sides. Pans with sides deflect oven heat. Insulated cookie sheets help prevent the bottoms of cookies from overbrowning. Bake bar cookies in good-quality aluminum pans. (Wilton Enterprises [see Product Sources, page 850] carries excellent aluminum baking pans.) Do not use nonstick cookie sheets or baking pans.

- Take pains to make cookies uniform in size. Not only are they more attractive-looking, but also, they bake more uniformly.

- To prevent the cookie dough from drying, keep the mixing bowl of dough covered with aluminum foil or plastic wrap when not filling cookie sheets with batches of cookies for baking.

- Bake cookies in the *top half* of the oven to prevent the bottoms from becoming too brown. In most standard ovens with four shelf positions, bake cookies at the *second* shelf position from the top.

- Use a timer when baking cookies, and watch the cookies closely while they are baking. Avoid the pitfall of filling cookie sheets when you should be watching the cookies baking in the oven. The baking of attractive, uniform cookies requires time and concentration.

- Use a thin, sharp, medium to small spatula to remove baked cookies from cookie sheets. Use of the proper spatula will prevent the bottoms of baked cookies from crumbling when they are transferred from the cookie sheets for cooling.

- Cool baked cookies on pieces of waxed paper spread on the kitchen counter, or on wire cookie racks, depending upon the type of cookie. Most cookies are best cooled on waxed paper because the bottoms remain perfectly flat during the cooling process. Certain special cookies such as Kringla (page 623) and Lace Cookies (page 627) preferably are cooled on wire cookie racks which allow the air to circulate around all surfaces of the cookies. Special wire cookie racks are made with close-set wires strung in the pattern of small squares which provide even support for small cookies. The wires on general utility wire racks are set too far apart to provide uniform support under warm cookies.

- After removing baked cookies from a cookie sheet, immediately scrape the cookie sheet, while it is still hot, with a wide spatula to remove crumbs and excess grease. Then, wipe the cookie sheet with a paper towel. Place the cookie sheet in a cool place such as the basement to hasten cooling. Wait until the cookie sheet is *completely cool* before filling it with another batch of cookies for baking. Regrease the cookie sheet, if necessary.

- As soon as baked cookies have cooled thoroughly, arrange them, single layer with plastic wrap between the layers, in an airtight container.

- Cookie sheets and baking pans should be washed by hand to retain their finish for even baking results. Insulated cookie sheets should not be immersed in water.

TO GREASE COOKIE SHEETS

To bake most cookies, either soft vegetable shortening or vegetable oil should be used to grease the cookie sheets. To apply vegetable shortening, use a pastry brush to spread a light, even coat over the surface of the cookie sheets. To use vegetable oil, pour a very small amount from the bottle directly onto the cookie sheets;

then, use a pastry brush to spread evenly. Wipe away any excess oil with a paper towel.

To bake certain cookies, Special Grease (page 56) is recommended for greasing the cookie sheets because of its particular nonstick attribute; however, Special Grease is not recommended for general use in the baking of most cookies (see When To Use Special Grease, page 56).

Parchment baking paper is sometimes used to line cookie sheets in lieu of greasing. When used in the baking of appropriate cookies, it helps prevent the bottoms from overbrowning. Parchment baking paper affords the additional advantage of producing baked cookies with no trace of grease residue on the bottoms.

Cookie recipes in *The Blue Ribbon Country Cookbook* specify when other than vegetable shortening or vegetable oil is recommended for greasing the cookie sheets. Of course, some cookies are baked on ungreased cookie sheets.

Depending upon the cookies, it is often necessary to very lightly regrease the cookie sheets after baking each batch (see Secrets for Baking Successful Cookies, page 589).

Bar Cookies

TO GREASE BAKING PANS FOR BAR COOKIES

Unless otherwise specified in the recipe, use vegetable shortening to grease baking pans for baking bar cookies.

TO CUT AND SERVE BAR COOKIES

After investing the time to bake a pan of delicious-tasting bars, it is worth the extra effort to cut them in an eye-appealing way. For very uniform, professional-looking bars, use a ruler to determine the exact places for cutting. Carefully hold the ruler against the edges of the bak-

ing pan and, with the point of a sharp knife, make tiny marks along the top edges of the bars where you plan to cut. Mark all four sides of the bars to help prevent making slanted cuts.

To cut marked bars, dip a sharp, *thin-bladed* knife into a tall glass of hot water. Then, partially dry the knife on a damp sponge or cloth. In a nonstop motion, make a cut from one side of the bars to the opposite side. Do not use back-and-forth sawing motions to cut, or lift the knife from the bars before the full cut is made. After making each cut, wipe the knife blade clean on the damp sponge or cloth, redip the knife in hot water, and partially dry it on the damp sponge or cloth. If the pan is rectangular, make the long cuts first; then, make the short cuts. Make each cut twice to assure precision cutting.

After making the cuts across the pan in both directions, run the knife along the inside edges of the pan to loosen the sides of the bars from the pan. If the sides are not loosened until last, the bars will not shift as readily during cutting, making it easier to cut straight lines.

To remove the cut bars from the pan, use a small spatula as close in size to the bars as possible. Push the spatula completely under one bar at a time and lift straight upward to remove.

RAISIN BARS

1 14-ounce can (1¼ cups) sweetened condensed milk
2 teaspoons finely grated lemon rind (page 47) (rind of about 2 lemons)
1 tablespoon freshly squeezed, strained lemon juice
1 12-ounce box (2 cups) raisins
1 cup all-purpose flour
½ teaspoon baking soda
¼ teaspoon salt (optional)
2½ cups Quaker MultiGrain cereal, uncooked (found at the supermarket with the oatmeal)
1½ cups broken pecans

1 cup (½ pound) margarine, softened
1⅓ cups packed light brown sugar
1½ teaspoons pure vanilla extract

In a medium, heavy-bottomed saucepan, place the condensed milk, lemon rind, and lemon juice; stir to blend and combine. Over medium heat, scald the milk mixture (page 25), stirring constantly. Remove from the heat. Add the raisins; stir to combine. Cover and let stand until cooled to room temperature.

Preheat the oven to 350° F. Grease a 9 × 13 × 2-inch baking pan; set aside.

Onto waxed paper, sift together the flour, baking soda, and salt (if included); set aside. In a medium mixing bowl, place the MultiGrain and pecans; stir until evenly distributed; set aside.

In a large mixing bowl, place the margarine and brown sugar; using an electric mixer, beat on medium-high speed until fluffy. Add the vanilla; beat on medium-high speed until blended. Add the flour mixture; beat on low speed only until blended. Add the pecan mixture; using a large mixing spoon, stir until evenly combined and crumbly.

Reserve 2 cups of the MultiGrain mixture; spoon the remaining mixture into the prepared baking pan. Using the back of a tablespoon, press the mixture evenly into the bottom of the pan. Pour the raisin mixture back and forth over the MultiGrain mixture in the baking pan. Using a large, narrow spatula, spread the raisin mixture to within ½ inch of the sides of the pan. Sprinkle the 2 cups reserved MultiGrain mixture over the raisin mixture; pat lightly with the back of the tablespoon. Bake for 30 minutes, until lightly golden.

Remove from the oven and place the baking pan on a wire rack. Let stand until the uncut bars completely cool.

Then, cut into 45 bars (page 586). Arrange the bars in an airtight container.

MAKES 45

DATE BARS

Date Bars, packed with dates and English walnuts and sprinkled with powdered sugar, are as old as the hills but every bit as good and voguish today as they were way back when. Mother added the recipe that follows to her recipe notebook before I was born, and I continue to whip up this family favorite to the present time.

1 cup all-purpose flour
1 teaspoon baking powder
⅛ teaspoon salt
¼ teaspoon ground cloves
¼ teaspoon ground cinnamon
3 extra-large eggs
1 cup sugar
1 teaspoon pure vanilla extract
2 8-ounce packages chopped dates (2 cups packed dates)
1 cup chopped English walnuts
3 tablespoons powdered sugar

Preheat the oven to 325° F. Grease a 9 × 13 × 2-inch baking pan; set aside.

Onto waxed paper, sift together the flour, baking powder, salt, cloves, and cinnamon; set aside.

Place the eggs in a large mixing bowl. Using an electric mixer, beat the eggs well on medium-high speed. Add the sugar and vanilla; beat well on medium-high speed. Add the flour mixture; beat on low speed only until blended. Add the dates and walnuts; using a large mixing spoon, stir and fold in.

Using the large mixing spoon, spoon the batter into the prepared baking pan. Using a large, narrow spatula, quickly spread the batter evenly in the pan. Bake for 25 minutes, until golden and the bars just begin to pull away slightly from the sides of the pan.

Remove from the oven and place the baking pan on a wire rack. Let stand until the uncut bars completely cool.

(Recipe continues on next page)

Then, place the powdered sugar in a small hand strainer. Sprinkle the powdered sugar over the uncut bars. Cut into forty 1 × 2-inch bars (page 586). Arrange the bars in an airtight container.

MAKES 40

OPTIONAL DECORATION: Using your fingers, sprinkle a faint amount of ground cinnamon on each bar.

PUMPKIN BARS WITH CASHEW FROSTING

Pumpkin Bars are "Midwest" through and through. In this recipe, cashews complement the pumpkin flavor to give the traditional cream cheese frosting a new and delicious twist.

2 cups all-purpose flour
2 teaspoons baking soda
¼ teaspoon salt
1½ teaspoons ground cinnamon
½ cup (¼ pound) butter, melted
2 cups sugar
½ cup vegetable oil
4 extra-large eggs
1 15-ounce can commercial pumpkin
Cashew Frosting (recipe follows)

Preheat the oven to 350° F. Using Special Grease (page 56), grease a 10½ × 15½ × 1-inch cookie pan (see Note); set aside.

Onto waxed paper, sift together the flour, baking soda, salt, and cinnamon; set aside.

In a large mixing bowl, place the butter, sugar, and vegetable oil; using an electric mixer, beat well on medium-high speed. Add the eggs, one at a time, beating well on medium-high speed after each addition. Add the pumpkin; beat on medium-high speed until completely blended. Add the flour mixture in halves, beating on low speed after each addition only until blended.

Using a large mixing spoon, spoon the batter into the prepared cookie pan. Using a large, narrow spatula, quickly spread the batter evenly in the pan. Bake for 25 minutes, or until a wooden toothpick inserted into the center comes out clean.

Remove from the oven and place the cookie pan on a wire rack. Let stand until the uncut bars completely cool.

Then, frost smoothly the uncut bars in the pan with the Cashew Frosting. Place the uncut bars, uncovered, in the refrigerator; let stand only until the frosting sets.

Cut into 48 bars (page 586). Arrange the bars in an airtight container and keep refrigerated.

NOTE: Although not as satisfactory, the pan may be greased and floured in substitution for using Special Grease.

MAKES 48

Cashew Frosting

3 ounces cream cheese, softened
¼ cup (4 tablespoons) butter, softened
1 tablespoon plus 2 teaspoons whole milk
1 teaspoon pure vanilla extract
3 cups powdered sugar
½ cup chopped, unsalted cashews

In a medium mixing bowl, place the cream cheese and butter; using an electric mixer, beat on high speed until blended and smooth. Add the milk and vanilla; beat on medium-high speed until creamy. Add the powdered sugar; beat on medium-high speed until fluffy. Add the cashews; beat on medium speed only until combined.

SERVING SUGGESTION: At Thanksgiving time, for something different or to serve a large gathering, serve Pumpkin Bars with Cashew Frosting instead of traditional Pumpkin Pie (see menu, pages 828–829).

LEMON BARS

Lemon lovers go for these. A generous measure of coconut gives these Lemon Bars an extra-special flavor and sets them apart from usual renditions.

½ cup (¼ pound) butter
1 cup sifted all-purpose flour (sift before measuring)
¼ cup powdered sugar
2 extra-large eggs
1 cup granulated sugar
2 teaspoons finely grated lemon rind (page 47) (rind of about 2 lemons)
3 tablespoons freshly squeezed, strained lemon juice
2 tablespoons all-purpose flour
⅛ teaspoon salt
1 cup shredded coconut
2 tablespoons powdered sugar
Lemon zest (page 46) for decoration (optional)

Preheat the oven to 350° F. Butter lightly an 8 × 8 × 2-inch baking pan; set aside.

Remove the butter from the refrigerator; let stand. Onto waxed paper, sift together 1 cup flour and ¼ cup powdered sugar. Place the flour mixture in a medium mixing bowl. Using a knife, cut the butter into approximately 8 pieces and drop into the bowl containing the flour mixture. Using a pastry blender, cut the butter into the flour mixture until approximately ⅔ of the mixture is the texture of coarse cornmeal and ⅓ of the mixture is the size of small peas.

Turn the mixture into the prepared baking pan. Using the back of a tablespoon, pat the mixture evenly and firmly into the bottom of the pan. Bake for 10 minutes. The crust will be pale and unbrowned.

Remove from the oven and place the baking pan on a wire rack. Let stand until the baked crust completely cools.

Then, preheat the oven to 350° F.

Carefully rebutter lightly the sides of the baking pan *above* the baked crust; set aside.

Place the eggs in a medium mixing bowl. Using an electric mixer, beat the eggs well on medium-high speed. Add the granulated sugar, lemon rind, and lemon juice; beat well on medium-high speed. Add 2 tablespoons flour and salt; beat until blended. Add the coconut; using a large mixing spoon, fold in.

Pour the lemon mixture over the baked crust in the pan. Bake for 25 minutes. The edges will be lightly browned.

Remove from the oven and place the baking pan on the wire rack; let stand. Place 2 tablespoons powdered sugar in a small hand strainer. Sprinkle the powdered sugar over the hot lemon bars to evenly dust the surface. Return the lemon bars to the oven; bake for an additional 2 minutes.

Remove from the oven and place the baking pan on the wire rack. Let stand until the uncut bars completely cool.

Then, cut into 18 bars (page 586). Arrange the bars in an airtight container. The top of each bar may be decorated with a few tiny pieces of lemon zest, if desired.

MAKES 18

3-LAYER CHERRY CHIP BARS

All kinds of new chips, from raspberry to peanut butter to mint can be found in the baking aisle of supermarkets today. This recipe features cherry-flavored chips which combine in the middle layer of the bars with crushed pineapple and coconut for a summery, even Hawaiian-like, flair.

Note: This recipe contains an uncooked egg white (see page 262).

BOTTOM LAYER
1 cup (½ pound) butter
2 cups all-purpose flour
¼ cup plus 2 tablespoons powdered sugar

(Recipe continues on next page)

Remove 1 cup butter from the refrigerator and let stand 10 minutes before use in the recipe.

Preheat the oven to 350°F.

In a medium mixing bowl, place 2 cups flour and ¼ cup plus 2 tablespoons powdered sugar; stir to combine. Using a knife, cut the butter into approximately tablespoon-sized pieces and drop into the bowl containing the flour mixture. Using a pastry blender, cut the butter into the flour mixture until the mixture is the texture of coarse cornmeal.

Turn the mixture into an ungreased 9 × 13 × 2-inch baking pan. Using a tablespoon, spread the mixture evenly over the bottom of the pan. Then, with lightly floured hands, pat the mixture tightly into the bottom of the pan. Bake for 15 minutes, until lightly golden.

Remove from the oven and place the baking pan on a wire rack. Let stand until the baked crust completely cools.

MIDDLE LAYER

1 cup (6 ounces) cherry baking chips
¾ cup flaked coconut
2 tablespoons all-purpose flour
¼ cup plus 2 tablespoons all-purpose flour
1 teaspoon baking powder
¼ teaspoon salt
4 extra-large eggs
1⅔ cups granulated sugar
2 teaspoon pure vanilla extract
1 8¼-ounce can commercial crushed pineapple, drained

Preheat the oven to 350°F. Butter lightly the sides of the baking pan *above* the baked crust; set aside.

In a small mixing bowl, place the cherry chips and coconut; sprinkle 2 tablespoons flour over top. Using a tablespoon, toss to coat the cherry chips and coconut; set aside. Onto waxed paper, sift together ¼ cup plus 2 tablespoons flour, baking powder, and salt; set aside.

Place the eggs in a large mixing bowl. Using an electric mixer, beat the eggs well on medium-high speed. Add the granulated sugar and vanilla; beat on medium-high speed until

blended. Add the flour mixture; beat on low speed only until blended. Add the cherry chip mixture and drained pineapple; using a large mixing spoon, fold in until evenly combined.

Pour the batter over the baked crust in the pan. Using a small, narrow spatula, quickly spread the batter evenly. Bake for 30 minutes, until golden.

Remove from the oven and place the baking pan on the wire rack. Let stand until the uncut bars completely cool.

TOP LAYER (FROSTING)

2 cups powdered sugar
2 tablespoons butter, melted
2 tablespoons maraschino cherry juice (pour off juice from commercially canned red maraschino cherries)
1 extra-large egg white

In a medium mixing bowl, place 2 cups powdered sugar, 2 tablespoons butter, cherry juice, and egg white. Using the electric mixer fit with clean, dry blades, beat the mixture on high speed until smooth.

Spoon the frosting over the Middle Layer in the pan. Using a large, narrow spatula, spread the frosting evenly. Let the uncut bars stand until the frosting sets.

Then, cut into 35 bars (page 586). Arrange the bars in an airtight container and keep refrigerated.

MAKES 35

OPTIONAL DECORATION: Each bar may be decorated with ¼ red candied cherry.

ROSE LEE'S APRICOT BARS

Talk about melt-in-your-mouth goodies . . . Rose Lee Pomerantz baked these bars for a press party we held years ago to unveil a new apartment building built by her husband, Marvin, my brother, and my husband. They were such a smash hit, they nearly upstaged the beautiful building.

½ cup (¼ pound) butter
1 6-ounce package (about 1 packed cup) dried apricots
1 cup sifted all-purpose flour (sift before measuring)
¼ cup granulated sugar
⅓ cup sifted all-purpose flour (sift before measuring)
½ teaspoon baking powder
¼ teaspoon salt
2 extra-large eggs
1 cup packed light brown sugar
½ teaspoon pure vanilla extract
½ cup broken pecans
2 tablespoons powdered sugar

Preheat the oven to 350° F.

Remove the butter from the refrigerator; set aside. Cut the apricots into small pieces approximately ¼ inch square (page 45); set aside.

In a large mixing bowl, place 1 cup flour and granulated sugar; stir to combine. Using a knife, cut the butter into approximately 10 pieces and drop into the bowl containing the flour mixture. Using a pastry blender, cut the butter into the flour mixture until the mixture is the texture of coarse cornmeal.

Turn the mixture into an ungreased 9 × 13 × 2-inch baking pan. Using the back of a tablespoon and your hand, press the mixture evenly into the bottom of the pan. Bake for 15 minutes, until lightly golden.

Remove from the oven and place the baking pan on a wire rack; let stand. Leave the oven on at 350° F.

Onto waxed paper, sift together ⅓ cup flour, baking powder, and salt; set aside.

Place the eggs in a large mixing bowl. Using an electric mixer, beat the eggs well on medium-high speed. While continuing to beat on medium-high speed, gradually add the brown sugar. Add the vanilla; beat on medium-high speed until completely blended. Add the flour mixture; beat on low speed only until blended. Add the apricots and pecans; using a large mixing spoon, fold in until evenly distributed; set aside.

Butter lightly the sides of the baking pan *above* the baked crust. Pour the batter over the baked crust. Using a small, narrow spatula, spread the batter evenly. Bake for 20 to 25 minutes, until lightly golden.

Remove from the oven and place the baking pan on the wire rack. Let stand until the uncut bars completely cool.

Then, place the powdered sugar in a small hand strainer. Sprinkle the powdered sugar evenly over the uncut bars. Cut into 27 bars (page 586). Arrange the bars in an airtight container.

MAKES 27

JANHAGEL KOEKJES
Johnny Buckshot Cookies

Janhagel Koekjes are a historical Holland Dutch cookie named after mercenary soldiers, nicknamed Jan Hagels, who were hired by the Dutch. The chopped almonds sprinkled over the top of these cookies are said to resemble buckshot.

2 cups all-purpose flour
¼ teaspoon baking soda
¼ teaspoon salt
1 cup (½ pound) butter, softened
2 cups sugar
1 extra-large egg, separated
¾ teaspoon sugar
¾ teaspoon ground cinnamon
¾ cup chopped, slivered blanched almonds (page 50)

(Recipe continues on next page)

Preheat the oven to 350°F. Grease a 10½ × 15½ × 1-inch cookie pan; set aside.

Onto waxed paper, sift together the flour, baking soda, and salt; set aside.

In a large mixing bowl, place the butter and 2 cups sugar; using an electric mixer, cream well on medium-high speed. Add the egg yolk; beat on medium-high speed until very light and fluffy. Add the flour mixture; using a pastry blender, cut the butter mixture into the flour mixture.

Using a large mixing spoon, spoon the dough into the prepared cookie pan. With your hands, spread the dough and press as evenly as possible into the bottom of the pan; set aside. Place the egg white in a small sauce dish. Using a table fork, beat the egg white slightly until frothy. Using a soft pastry brush, brush the egg white over the dough in the cookie pan; set aside. Place ¾ teaspoon sugar and cinnamon in a small sauce dish; stir to combine. Using a teaspoon, sprinkle the cinnamon mixture over the egg-brushed dough. Then, sprinkle the almonds evenly over the top. Press the almonds very lightly into the dough. Bake for 20 minutes, until lightly golden.

Remove from the oven and place the cookie pan on a wire rack. While warm, cut the uncut baked cookies into 48 small squares (page 586). Remove the cookies from the pan and place on wire cookie racks; let stand until completely cool.

Then, arrange the cookies in an airtight container.

MAKES 48

BUTTERSCOTCH MAGIC BARS WITH BRAZIL NUTS

This is an adaptation of the old, familiar recipe for Magic Bars, sometimes called "Hello Dollies" in regional cookbooks. I have no idea why these bars were dubbed Hello Dollies in some circles, but I do know why they were called "magic." Houdini would have had his hands full coming up with an easier, more mystifying way to materialize a delicious bar cookie. You simply place the six ingredients directly in the pan, in layers, and bake. I have used butterscotch chips rather than chocolate chips which are often called for in these recipes, and have specified Brazil nuts for the nut layer.

At Christmastime, my grandmothers and mother always placed on the coffee table or a side table a wooden nut dish full of mixed, unshelled nuts. These nut dishes were made with a center wooden post covered on top with a piece of metal on which the snacker cracked the nuts with a matching wooden mallet resembling a gavel. You supplied nut dishes with a nut pick and sometimes a small, metal nutcracker for those who preferred that method of cracking over the mallet mode (if you weren't careful, your fingers holding a nut on the post could be hit by the mallet). There were always almonds, pecans, hazelnuts (filberts), English walnuts, and Brazil nuts in the Christmas nut bowl. The Brazil nuts were the big ones and the hardest to crack.

½ cup (¼ pound) butter
20 graham cracker squares, rolled finely (about 1½ cups crumbs)
1 14-ounce can (1¼ cups) sweetened condensed milk
1 cup (6 ounces) butterscotch chips
1 cup chopped Brazil nuts (page 50)
1 cup flaked coconut

Preheat the oven to 325°F.

Place the butter in a 9 × 13 × 2-inch baking pan. Place the baking pan in the oven to melt the butter. Watch carefully and do not allow the butter to brown. Remove from the oven. Tilt the pan back and forth to completely cover the bottom with the melted butter.

Spoon the graham cracker crumbs evenly over the butter; using the back of a tablespoon, press to form a compact and even layer. Pour the condensed milk evenly over the crumbs. If necessary, use a small, narrow spatula to carefully distribute the milk over the entire surface of the crumbs.

Sprinkle the butterscotch chips evenly over the condensed milk. Then, spoon the nuts evenly over the surface. Sprinkle the coconut evenly over the top. Bake for 30 minutes, until lightly browned.

Remove from the oven and place the baking pan on a wire rack. Let stand until the uncut bars completely cool.

Then, cut into 30 bars (page 586). Arrange the bars in an airtight container.

MAKES 30

BLACK WALNUT BARS

These distinctively flavored native American nuts, plentiful across the central and eastern parts of the Midwest, have a very difficult shell to crack, otherwise they would surely be used more often in cookies, cakes, and other foods. Another deterrent is the thick, chartreuse-colored husks in which the shells are encased. Many Midwesterners have found that the easiest way to remove these husks is to let the walnuts stand for a period of time after gathering and then to run them through an old-fashioned, hand-cranked, or a motor-driven corn sheller. After removal of the husks, various devices are employed to crack the ultrahard shells. For a number of years, a man sold a viselike apparatus for this purpose at the Iowa State Fair, but I haven't seen him there the last few years.

Shelled, native black walnuts are occasionally found at farmers' markets or in produce sections of local supermarkets. In the past few years, commercial black walnuts have become available in the regular section where nuts are displayed at the supermarket. When you locate and invest in good black walnuts (or gather and shell them yourself), store them in the freezer to retain their freshness (see To Store Nuts, page 51).

2¾ cups sifted all-purpose flour (sift before measuring)
2½ teaspoons baking powder
¾ teaspoon salt
¾ cup (¼ pound plus 4 tablespoons) butter, melted
1 pound light brown sugar (2¼ cups packed sugar)
3 extra-large eggs
½ teaspoon pure vanilla extract
½ teaspoon black walnut flavoring
1 cup broken black walnuts
1 6-ounce package (1 cup) semisweet chocolate chips

Preheat the oven to 350° F. Grease a 10½ × 15½ × 1-inch cookie pan; set aside.

Onto waxed paper, sift together the flour, baking powder, and salt; set aside.

In a large mixing bowl, place the butter and brown sugar; using an electric mixer, beat well on medium-high speed. Add the eggs, one at a time, beating well on medium-high speed after each addition. Add the vanilla and walnut flavoring; beat on medium-high speed until fluffy. Add the flour mixture; beat on low speed only until blended. Add the walnuts and chocolate chips; using a large mixing spoon, fold in until evenly distributed.

Turn the batter into the prepared cookie pan. Using a large, narrow spatula, quickly spread the batter evenly in the pan. Bake for 20 minutes, or until a wooden toothpick inserted into the center comes out clean.

Remove from the oven and place the cookie pan on a wire rack. Let stand until the uncut bars completely cool.

Then, cut into 48 bars (page 586). Arrange the bars in an airtight container.

MAKES 48

TRAIL MIX BARS

Pack along these nourishing bars, chockful of healthful ingredients, when you head for a hike in the woods. (But don't let the name of these bars confine the pleasure of eating them only to outdoor occasions.)

1 cup commercially packaged trail mix (fruits and nuts)
⅔ cup sifted whole wheat flour (sift before measuring)
½ teaspoon baking powder
½ teaspoon baking soda
½ cup (¼ pound) margarine, softened
⅓ cup packed light brown sugar
½ cup honey
1 extra-large egg
1 teaspoon pure vanilla extract
1 cup quick-cooking rolled oats, uncooked

Preheat the oven to 350° F. Grease a 9 × 13 × 2-inch baking pan; set aside.

Place the trail mix in a small mixing bowl. Sprinkle 2 teaspoons of the measured flour over the trail mix; stir to coat the trail mix; set aside. Onto waxed paper, sift together the remaining flour, baking powder, and baking soda; set aside.

In a large mixing bowl, place the margarine and brown sugar; using an electric mixer, beat on medium-high speed until creamed. Add the honey; beat on medium-high speed until well blended. Add the egg and vanilla; continue beating on medium-high speed until blended. Add the flour mixture; beat on low speed only until blended. Add the oats; beat on low speed only until combined. Add the trail mix; using a large mixing spoon, fold in.

Using a large mixing spoon, spoon the batter into the prepared baking pan. Using a large, narrow spatula, quickly spread the batter evenly in the pan. Bake for 20 minutes, or until a wooden toothpick inserted into the center comes out clean.

Remove from the oven and place the baking pan on a wire rack. Let stand until the uncut bars completely cool.

Then, cut into 30 bars (page 586). Arrange the bars in an airtight container.

MAKES 30

DREAM BARS

½ cup (¼ pound) butter
1 cup all-purpose flour
½ cup packed light brown sugar
2 extra-large eggs
1 cup packed light brown sugar
1 teaspoon pure vanilla extract
1 tablespoon all-purpose flour
½ teaspoon baking powder
Dash of salt
1 cup shredded coconut
1 cup chopped pecans

Remove the butter from the refrigerator and let stand 5 minutes before use in the recipe.

Preheat the oven to 350° F.

Onto waxed paper, sift together 1 cup flour and ½ cup brown sugar. Place the flour mixture in a large mixing bowl. Using a knife, cut the butter into approximately 8 pieces and drop into the bowl containing the flour mixture. Using a pastry blender, cut the butter into the flour mixture until the mixture is the texture of coarse cornmeal interspersed with some pieces the size of small peas.

Turn the mixture into an ungreased 9 × 13 × 2-inch baking pan. Using the back of a tablespoon and your hand, pat the mixture evenly into the bottom of the pan. Bake for 10 minutes.

Remove from the oven and place the baking pan on a wire rack; let stand for approximately 3 to 5 minutes.

Meanwhile, place the eggs in a medium mixing bowl. Using an electric mixer, beat the eggs well on medium-high speed. Add 1 cup brown sugar; beat on medium-high speed until well blended. Add the vanilla, 1 tablespoon flour, baking powder, and salt; beat on medium speed only until blended.

Using a large mixing spoon, spoon the mixture over the baked crust. Using a small, narrow spatula, spread the mixture evenly. Bake for 20 minutes, or until a wooden toothpick inserted into the center comes out clean.

Remove from the oven and place the baking pan on the wire rack. Let stand until the uncut bars completely cool.

Then, cut into 44 bars (page 586). Arrange the bars in an airtight container.

MAKES 44

HONEY-HAZELNUT STRIPS

2 cups all-purpose flour
½ teaspoon baking powder
½ teaspoon baking soda
¼ teaspoon salt
1 teaspoon ground cinnamon
¼ teaspoon ground cloves
¾ cup (¼ pound plus 4 tablespoons) butter, softened
¾ cup sugar
2 extra-large egg yolks
¾ cup honey
¾ cup chopped hazelnuts (page 50)

Preheat the oven to 325° F. Grease a 9 × 13 × 2-inch baking pan; set aside.

Onto waxed paper, sift together the flour, baking powder, baking soda, salt, cinnamon, and cloves; set aside.

In a large mixing bowl, place the butter and sugar; using an electric mixer, cream well on medium-high speed. Add the egg yolks; beat on medium-high speed until well blended. Add the honey; continue beating on medium-high speed until very fluffy. Add the flour mixture; beat on low speed only until blended. Add the hazelnuts; beat on low speed only until combined and evenly distributed.

Using a large mixing spoon, spoon the batter into the prepared baking pan. Using a large, narrow spatula, quickly spread the batter evenly in the pan. Bake for 40 minutes, or until the top is lightly brown. Be careful not to overbake; Honey-Hazelnut Strips should be moist and chewy on the inside.

Remove from the oven and place the baking pan on a wire rack. Let stand until the uncut strips completely cool.

Then, cut into fifty-one ¾ × 3-inch strips (page 586). Arrange the strips in an airtight container or leave the cut strips in the baking pan and cover tightly with aluminum foil or a baking pan cover.

MAKES 51

OPTIONAL FROSTING DECORATION
½ recipe Confectioners' Frosting (page 579)

Using a decorating bag fit with small round tip number 2 (page 383), pipe narrow lines (page 388) of Confectioners' Frosting crisscrossed diagonally over the entire surface of cool, uncut Honey-Hazelnut Strips. Pipe the lines about ⅜ inch apart (see illustration).

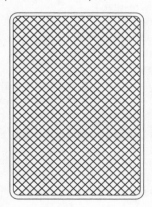

When the frosting is just dry, cut into strips. Do not allow the frosting to become too dry and hardened before cutting the strips, as this may cause the frosting to crack when cut, detracting from the appearance of the design.

LEBKUCHEN
Spiced Honey Cake

Notwithstanding the renowned, international reputation of Bavaria's age-old specialties, Weisswurst (veal sausage) and beer, Nuremberg's Lebkuchen probably is the masterpiece which has captured the region's greatest culinary fame. In medieval times, Nuremberg was a center of spice trade, and there was an abundance of honey available from Franconia in the northern part of Bavaria. Access to spices and honey, key ingredients in Lebkuchen, prompted creation of this legendary Deutschland classic.

2¼ cups sifted all-purpose flour (sift before measuring)
½ teaspoon baking soda
½ teaspoon ground cinnamon
½ teaspoon ground cloves
½ teaspoon ground allspice
¼ teaspoon ground nutmeg
½ cup warm, very strong, brewed coffee (double strength)
½ cup honey
¼ cup vegetable shortening
½ cup packed dark brown sugar
1 extra-large egg
2 ounces (¼ cup) diced candied citron
2 ounces (¼ cup) diced candied orange peel
2 ounces (¼ cup) diced candied lemon peel
¾ cup finely chopped, sliced unblanched almonds
Orange Glaze (recipe follows)

Preheat the oven to 350° F. Grease a 10½ × 15½ × 1-inch cookie pan; set aside.

Onto waxed paper, sift together the flour, baking soda, cinnamon, cloves, allspice, and nutmeg; set aside. In a small mixing bowl, place the coffee and honey; stir to blend; set aside. In a medium mixing bowl, place the vegetable shortening and brown sugar; using an electric mixer, beat on medium-high speed until creamed. Add the egg; continue beating on medium-high speed until well blended. Add, alternately, the flour mixture in fourths, and the honey mixture in thirds, beating on low speed after each addition only until blended. Add the citron, orange peel, lemon peel, and almonds; using a large mixing spoon, fold in until evenly distributed.

Using the large mixing spoon, spoon the batter into the prepared cookie pan. Using a large, narrow spatula, quickly spread the batter evenly in the pan. Bake for 20 minutes, or until a wooden toothpick inserted into the center comes out clean.

Remove from the oven and place the cookie pan on a wire rack. Let stand until the uncut Lebkuchen completely cools.

Then, drizzle the Orange Glaze over the uncut Lebkuchen; using a soft pastry brush, spread the glaze over the entire top surface. Before the glaze completely dries, cut the Lebkuchen into forty-two 1½ × 2½-inch bars (page 586); let stand until the glaze dries. Then, arrange the bars in an airtight container.

MAKES 42

Orange Glaze

1½ cups powdered sugar
3 tablespoons water
½ teaspoon orange extract

In a small mixing bowl, place the powdered sugar, water, and orange extract. Using an electric mixer, beat the mixture on medium-high speed until smooth.

HOLIDAY DECORATION: Cut green candied cherries and red candied cherries in the fashion of holly leaves and berries. Immediately after cutting the Lebkuchen and before the glaze completely dries, arrange the cut cherries in the form of a holly sprig on the top of each bar.

CHARLOTTE'S BUTTER RUM CHEESE BARS

A native of Montgomery County, Ohio, Charlotte Watkins is one wonderful cook! Charlotte once served these too luscious for words bars at the end of a fabulous dinner, and I took home the recipe, which still stands in my recipe box. These scrumptious bars took the red ribbon in the always large, two-layer bar class at the 1992 Iowa State Fair.

BOTTOM LAYER
1 cup all-purpose flour
¼ teaspoon cream of tartar
¼ teaspoon baking soda
¼ cup (4 tablespoons) butter, softened
½ cup packed light brown sugar
½ extra-large egg (slightly beat 1 egg; use ½) *or* 1 small (no larger) egg
¼ teaspoon pure vanilla extract
¼ cup broken pecans

Preheat the oven to 350° F. Butter lightly a 7 × 11 × 2-inch baking pan; set aside.

Onto waxed paper, sift together the flour, cream of tartar, and baking soda; set aside.

In a medium mixing bowl, place the butter and brown sugar; using an electric mixer, beat on medium-high speed until creamed. Add ½ egg and vanilla; beat on medium-high speed until fluffy. Add the flour mixture; beat on low speed only until blended. Add the pecans; using a mixing spoon, fold in until evenly distributed.

Turn the mixture into the prepared baking pan. With lightly floured hands, pat the mixture evenly into the bottom of the pan. Bake for 15 minutes.

Remove from the oven and place the baking pan on a wire rack. Let stand until the bottom layer of the bars completely cools.

TOP LAYER
8 ounces cream cheese, softened
½ cup granulated sugar
1 extra-large egg
1 teaspoon rum flavoring
¼ teaspoon pure vanilla extract
2½ dozen unblemished pecan halves

When the bottom layer of the bars has completely cooled, preheat the oven to 375° F.

In a small mixing bowl, place the cream cheese and granulated sugar; using the electric mixer fit with clean, dry blades, beat on high speed until creamed. Add the egg and rum flavoring; beat on medium-high speed until blended and smooth.

Spoon the cream cheese mixture over the bottom layer of the bars. Using a small, narrow spatula, spread the cream cheese mixture evenly. Bake for 20 minutes, until lightly golden.

Remove from the oven and place the baking pan on the wire rack. Let stand until the uncut bars cool slightly. Then, refrigerate, uncovered, and on a wire rack, at least 1 hour.

Cut into 30 bars (page 586). Decorate the top of each bar with a pecan half. Arrange the bars in an airtight container and keep refrigerated.

MAKES 30

HOLIDAY DECORATION: For the holidays, decorate the top of each bar with ½ red candied cherry rather than ½ pecan.

CRÈME DE MENTHE BARS

These pretty to look at bars feature a chocolate-flavored bottom layer and a green-hued, crème de menthe–flavored top layer made with cream cheese. Yum! The top layer is unbaked, simplifying the preparation. To further fancify the appearance of these minty bars, pipe a crisscross chocolate decoration on top, as described and illustrated below.

BOTTOM LAYER
1 cup all-purpose flour
½ cup unsweetened cocoa powder
1 cup (½ pound) butter, softened
2 cups sugar
4 extra-large eggs, beaten
2 teaspoons pure vanilla extract

(Recipe continues on next page)

Preheat the oven to 375° F. Grease a 9 × 13 × 2-inch baking pan; set aside.

Onto waxed paper, sift together the flour and cocoa; set aside.

In a large mixing bowl, place the butter and sugar; using an electric mixer, cream well on medium-high speed. Add the eggs; continue beating on medium-high speed until well blended. Add the vanilla; beat on medium-high speed until blended. Add the flour mixture in halves, beating on low speed after each addition only until blended.

Using a large mixing spoon, spoon the batter into the prepared baking pan. Using a large, narrow spatula, spread the batter evenly in the pan. Bake for 20 minutes, or until a wooden toothpick inserted into the center comes out clean.

Remove from the oven and place the baking pan on a wire rack. Let stand until the bottom layer of the bars completely cools.

TOP LAYER
3 ounces cream cheese, softened
¼ cup (4 tablespoons) butter, softened
1 pound (4 cups) powdered sugar
¼ cup green crème de menthe

In a medium mixing bowl, place the cream cheese and butter; using the electric mixer fit with clean, dry blades, beat on high speed until blended and smooth. Add the powdered sugar and crème de menthe; beat on low speed to combine; then, beat on medium-high speed until completely blended.

Spoon the crème de menthe mixture over the bottom layer of the bars. Using a large, narrow spatula, spread the crème de menthe mixture evenly. Let stand only until the top layer sets.

DECORATION
½ cup (3 ounces) semisweet chocolate chips
2 tablespoons butter

In the top of a double boiler place the chocolate chips and butter. Place the top of the double boiler over (not touching) hot (not simmering)

water in the bottom pan. Stir the chocolate chips and butter until melted and blended.

Remove the top of the double boiler from the bottom pan. Using a decorating bag fit with small round tip number 3 (page 383), pipe the chocolate mixture in a diagonal crisscross pattern (page 388) over the top of the second layer. Pipe the lines about ½ inch apart (see illustration).

Refrigerate the uncut bars, uncovered, until set. Then, cut into 32 bars (page 586). Arrange the bars in an airtight container and keep refrigerated.

MAKES 32

FROSTED BROWNIES

Brownies probably go unchallenged as America's number one bar cookie. This version, with a thick layer of frosting, carries chocolate extravagance to the limit.

1¼ cups sifted all-purpose flour (sift before measuring)
½ teaspoon baking powder
½ teaspoon salt
4 ounces (4 squares) unsweetened chocolate
1 cup (½ pound) butter
2 cups sugar
4 extra-large eggs
1 teaspoon pure vanilla extract
1 cup broken English walnuts
1 recipe Chocolate Frosting (page 580)

Preheat the oven to 375° F. Grease a 9 × 13 × 2-inch baking pan; set aside.

Onto waxed paper, sift together the flour, baking powder, and salt; set aside.

In the top of a double boiler, place the chocolate and butter. Place the top of the double boiler over (not touching) simmering water in the bottom pan. Stir the chocolate and butter constantly until melted and blended.

Remove the top of the double boiler from the bottom pan. Add the sugar; stir to combine. Transfer the chocolate mixture to a large mixing bowl. Add the eggs, one at a time, beating well with an electric mixer on medium-high speed after each addition. Add the vanilla; continue beating on medium-high until well blended. Add the flour mixture; beat on low speed only until blended. Add the walnuts; using a large mixing spoon, fold in.

Pour the batter into the prepared baking pan. Using a large, narrow spatula, lightly and quickly spread the batter evenly in the pan. Bake for 20 minutes, or until a wooden toothpick inserted into the center comes out clean (see Note).

Remove from the oven and place the baking pan on a wire rack. Let stand until the uncut brownies completely cool.

Then, frost the brownies in the pan with the Chocolate Frosting. Let the brownies stand until the frosting sets.

Then, cut into 33 bars (page 586). Arrange the brownies in an airtight container.

NOTE: For more moist brownies, bake for about 17 minutes, or until a wooden toothpick inserted into the center comes out barely moist.

MAKES 33

CREAM CHEESE BROWNIES

8 ounces cream cheese, softened
½ cup sugar
2 extra-large eggs
1 teaspoon pure vanilla extract
1 recipe Frosted Brownies, above (see recipe procedures, below)

Preheat the oven to 350° F. (see Note). Grease a 9 × 13 × 2-inch baking pan; set aside.

In a medium-small mixing bowl, place the cream cheese and sugar; using an electric mixer, beat on high speed until creamy and *completely* smooth. Add the eggs, one at a time, beating well on medium-high speed after each addition. Add the vanilla; beat on medium-high speed until well blended; set aside.

Follow the recipe for Frosted Brownies through spreading the brownie batter in the baking pan. Then, slowly pour the cream cheese mixture back and forth over the brownie batter. If necessary, use a small, narrow spatula to spread the cream cheese mixture over any uncovered portion of the brownie batter. Bake for 30 to 35 minutes, until lightly golden.

Remove from the oven and place the baking pan on a wire rack. Let stand only until the uncut brownies completely cool. Then, cover and refrigerate.

When cold, frost the brownies in the pan with the Chocolate Frosting. Let the brownies stand only until the frosting sets. Then, cover the uncut brownies tightly with aluminum foil or a baking pan cover, and store in the refrigerator.

Before serving, cut into 33 bars (page 586). Keep stored in the refrigerator.

NOTE: Note the different baking temperature from Frosted Brownies, above.

MAKES 33

OPTIONAL DECORATION: After the Chocolate Frosting sets, pipe stripes (page 388) of Ornamental Vanilla Frosting (page 584) back and forth over the Chocolate Frosting, using a decorating bag fit with small round tip number 2 (page 383). Cover and store in the refrigerator. Let the piped decoration set well before cutting into bars.

MARBLE BROWNIES
WITH FEATHER ICING

These fancy, fancy brownies with chocolate and white marbling and feathered icing carry traditional brownies to new heights. They're haute enough to be served on most any occasion.

1½ cups chopped English walnuts
1½ cups sifted cake flour (sift before measuring)
½ teaspoon baking powder
½ teaspoon salt
2 ounces (2 squares) unsweetened chocolate
1 cup (½ pound) butter, softened
1⅔ cups sugar
4 extra-large eggs, room temperature, separated
2 teaspoons pure vanilla extract
⅓ cup sugar
Chocolate Icing (recipe follows)
White Icing (recipe follows)

Preheat the oven to 350° F. Grease a 9 × 13 × 2-inch baking pan; set aside.

Place the walnuts in a small mixing bowl. Sprinkle 2 teaspoons of the measured flour over the walnuts; toss until well coated; set aside. Onto waxed paper, sift together the remaining flour, baking powder, and salt; set aside.

Place the chocolate in a tiny saucepan. Hold the tiny pan over (not touching) low simmering water in a small saucepan until the chocolate melts, stirring intermittently. Remove the tiny pan from the heat; set aside.

In a large mixing bowl, place the butter and 1⅔ cups sugar; using an electric mixer, beat on medium-high speed until fluffy. Add the egg yolks, one at a time, beating well on medium-high after each addition. Add the vanilla; beat on medium-high speed until blended. Add the flour mixture; beat on low speed only until blended. Add the walnuts; using a large mixing spoon, stir and fold in until evenly distributed.

Using the large mixing spoon, spoon ½ of the batter into another large mixing bowl. Add the melted chocolate to one of the bowls of batter; using the electric mixer, beat on low speed only until blended; set aside.

Place the egg whites in a medium mixing bowl. Using the electric mixer fit with clean, dry blades, beat the egg whites on high speed until soft peaks hold. While continuing to beat on high speed, very gradually add ⅓ cup sugar and continue beating the egg white mixture until stiff, but still moist and glossy.

Using a table knife, cut the beaten egg white mixture in half. Quickly and carefully spoon ½ of the egg white mixture over the white batter, and the remaining ½ of the egg white mixture over the chocolate batter. Using separate mixing spoons, fold the egg white mixture into the 2 batters.

Alternately place heaping tablespoons of white and chocolate batter side by side in the prepared baking pan. Zigzag a table knife through the batter to create a marble effect in the baked brownies. Using a small, narrow spatula, lightly even the top of the batter in the pan. Bake for 30 minutes, or until a wooden toothpick inserted into the center comes out clean.

Remove from the oven and place the baking pan on a wire rack. Let stand until the uncut brownies completely cool.

For Feather Icing, spoon the Chocolate Icing over the cooled, uncut brownies in the pan. Using a small, narrow spatula, quickly spread the icing evenly. Using a decorating bag fit with small round tip number 3 (page 383) and filled with White Icing, immediately pipe even, parallel lines (page 388) of White Icing, ⅝ inch apart, on top of the Chocolate Icing widthwise across the brownies. Immediately, starting at one of the short sides of the pan, lightly draw a table knife over the surface of the icing, in parallel lines 1¼ inches apart, lengthwise across the brownies. Turn the pan, and starting from the other short side, draw the knife over the surface of the icing, in parallel lines 1¼ inches apart, centered between the lines pulled from the opposite side. In other words, pull parallel lines ⅝ inch apart, in alternate directions lengthwise across the brownies, to produce a feathered effect with the White Icing (see illustration). Wipe the knife on a damp sponge after pulling each line. Avoid pressing the knife deeply into the Chocolate Icing when making the lines. It is necessary to work quickly before the icing sets.

Let the uncut brownies stand in the pan on the wire rack until the icing completely sets.

Then, cut into 48 approximately square bars (page 586). Arrange the brownies in an airtight container.

MAKES 48

VARIATION: Marble Brownies may be frosted with the Chocolate Icing alone, eliminating the White Icing and feathering.

Chocolate Icing

3 cups powdered sugar
¼ cup unsweetened cocoa powder
¼ cup plus 2 tablespoons (6 tablespoons) butter, melted
3 tablespoons plus 1 teaspoon warm, strong, brewed coffee
1 teaspoon pure vanilla extract

In a medium mixing bowl, place the powdered sugar, cocoa, butter, coffee, and vanilla. Using an electric mixer, beat the mixture on medium-high speed only until completely smooth.

White Icing

¾ cup powdered sugar
2¼ teaspoons water
½ teaspoon clear vanilla

In a small mixing bowl, place the powdered sugar, water, and vanilla. Using an electric mixer, beat the mixture on medium-high speed only until completely smooth.

GRAHAM CRACKER GOODIES

Good after-school snacks.

¾ cup packed light brown sugar
¼ teaspoon ground cinnamon
½ cup (¼ pound) butter, melted
⅓ cup chopped pecans
30 graham cracker squares

Preheat the oven to 350° F.

In a medium-small mixing bowl, place the brown sugar and cinnamon; stir to combine. Add the butter; stir well. Add the pecans; stir until evenly combined.

Spread the brown sugar mixture over the center of the graham cracker squares (the topping will spread to cover the graham crackers during baking).

Place the graham crackers on ungreased cookie sheets. Bake for 10 minutes.

Using a thin spatula, place the baked Graham Cracker Goodies on waxed paper to cool.

MAKES 30

SAINT AND SINNER CRUNCHIES

1 cup sugar
1 cup light corn syrup
2 tablespoons butter
1 7-ounce package (about 6 cups) Special
    K cereal
1 12-ounce jar (about 1½ cups) chunky
    peanut butter
1 12-ounce package (2 cups) semisweet
    chocolate chips
1 cup (6 ounces) butterscotch chips
2 teaspoons butter

Butter a 10½ × 15½ × 1-inch cookie pan; set
aside.

In a large saucepan, place the sugar, syrup, and
2 tablespoons butter; stir to combine. Bring the
mixture to a boil over medium heat, stirring
constantly. Remove from the heat. Add the
cereal; stir until well coated. Add the peanut
butter; stir to combine.

Turn the mixture into the prepared cookie
pan. Using the back of a tablespoon, pat the
mixture evenly into the bottom of the pan; set
aside.

In the top of a double boiler, place the chocolate chips and butterscotch chips. Place the top
of the double boiler over (not touching) hot
(not simmering) water in the bottom pan. Stir
continuously to expedite the melting of the
chips and to blend. Add 2 teaspoons butter; stir
until melted and blended.

Pour the chocolate mixture back and forth
over the cereal mixture in the cookie pan. Using
a small, narrow spatula, spread the chocolate
mixture evenly. Refrigerate the uncut Saint and
Sinner Crunchies, uncovered, until set.

Then, cut into seventy 1½-inch squares (page
586). Cover the cookie pan tightly with aluminum foil. Store either in the refrigerator or at
room temperature.

MAKES 70

COLETTE WORTMAN'S DANISH PUFF

These Danish Puffs are nothing short of exquisite!

PASTRY
½ cup (¼ pound) butter or margarine
1 cup sifted all-purpose flour (sift before
    measuring)
2 tablespoons refrigerated water

Remove the butter from the refrigerator and let
stand 10 minutes before use in the recipe. Grease
a cookie sheet (preferably an insulated cookie
sheet); set aside.

Resift the flour into a medium mixing bowl.
Using a knife, cut the butter into approximately
8 pieces and drop into the bowl containing the
flour. Using a pastry blender, cut the butter into
the flour until the mixture is the texture of
cornmeal interspersed with some pieces the size
of small peas.

Tilt the mixing bowl and gently shake the
flour mixture to one side of the bowl. Sprinkle
about 1½ teaspoons of the water over the mixture; using a table fork, lightly rake the moistened portion of the mixture to the other side of
the bowl. Repeat the procedure until all the
water has been added.

With floured hands, divide the pastry in half.
On the prepared cookie sheet and with floured
hands, pat each ½ of the dough into a long,
3 × 12-inch strip. Lay a piece of plastic wrap
lightly over the pastry; set aside.

TOPPING
1 cup sifted all-purpose flour (sift before
    measuring)
½ cup (¼ pound) butter or margarine
1 cup water
1 teaspoon almond extract
3 extra-large eggs, room temperature

Preheat the oven to 350° F.
Resift the flour onto waxed paper; set aside.
In a small saucepan, place the butter and water.

Over high heat, bring the butter and water to a rolling boil. Remove from the heat. Add the almond extract; stir to blend. Add the flour all at once; using a small mixing spoon, stir vigorously until the mixture forms a soft ball.

Transfer the mixture to a medium mixing bowl. Add the eggs, one at a time, beating with an electric mixer on medium-high speed after each addition until well blended.

Remove the plastic wrap from the pastry. Spoon ½ of the topping mixture over each of the pastry strips. Using a small, narrow spatula, spread the topping as evenly and smoothly, and as close to the edges of the pastry, as possible. Bake for 50 to 55 minutes. The topping will rise and then fall during baking, like some cookies. When done, the topping will be crisp and browned.

Remove from the oven and place the cookie sheet on a wire rack. Let the baked strips stand 15 minutes to cool slightly before frosting.

FROSTING AND NUTS
½ recipe Powdered Sugar Frosting (page 580), substituting ½ teaspoon almond extract and ½ teaspoon clear vanilla for 1 teaspoon clear vanilla
⅓ cup finely chopped blanched almonds (run slivered blanched almonds through a nut chopper 3 times [see page 50])

Leave the baked strips on the cookie sheet. Divide the Powdered Sugar Frosting in half. Spoon ½ of the frosting over each baked strip and spread with a small, narrow spatula. Sprinkle ½ of the nuts over each frosted strip. Let the cookie sheet stand on the wire rack until the baked strips completely cool and the frosting sets.

Then, carefully run a large, thin spatula underneath the strips to loosen them from the cookie sheet. Using a sharp, thin-bladed knife, cut each strip in half lengthwise, and then into twelfths widthwise, thus cutting each strip into 24 bars. Arrange the bars in an airtight container.

MAKES 48

Drop Cookies

BUTTER BRICKLE COOKIES

1½ cups all-purpose flour
½ teaspoon baking soda
½ teaspoon salt
½ cup (¼ pound) butter, softened
¾ cup packed light brown sugar
1 extra-large egg
1 teaspoon pure vanilla extract
1 7.5-ounce package Bits 'O Brickle almond brickle baking chips
⅓ cup broken pecans

Preheat the oven to 350° F. Grease 2 or 3 cookie sheets (page 589); set aside.

Onto waxed paper sift together the flour, baking soda, and salt; set aside.

In a large mixing bowl, place the butter and brown sugar; using an electric mixer, cream well on medium-high speed. Add the egg and vanilla; beat on medium-high speed until smooth and creamy. Add the flour mixture; beat on low speed only until blended. Add the almond brickle baking chips and pecans; using a large mixing spoon, stir and fold in until evenly combined.

Drop the dough by rounded tablespoonsful, 2 inches apart, onto the prepared cookie sheets. Bake for 8 to 10 minutes, until lightly golden.

Using a thin spatula, place the baked cookies on waxed paper spread on the kitchen counter; let stand until completely cool.

Then, store the cookies in an airtight container.

MAKES ABOUT 42

ALMOND-BUTTER PUFFS

Food finery at its delicate best.

1¼ cups (½ pound plus 4 tablespoons)
   butter, softened
1½ cups powdered sugar
1 cup bread flour
¼ teaspoon salt
1 extra-large egg plus 1 extra-large egg
   yolk
2 cups bread flour
1 *tablespoon* pure vanilla extract
1 cup finely chopped, slivered blanched
   almonds (page 50)

Preheat the oven to 350° F. Oil lightly 2 or 3 cookie sheets (page 589); set aside.

In a large mixing bowl, place the butter and powdered sugar; using an electric mixer, cream well on medium-high speed. Add 1 cup of the flour and salt; beat on medium speed until blended. Add 1 egg plus 1 egg yolk and vanilla; beat well on medium speed. Add 2 cups flour and almonds; beat on low speed only until blended.

Drop the dough by rounded teaspoonsful, 1 inch apart, onto the prepared cookie sheets. Bake for 10 minutes, until faintly golden.

Using a thin spatula, place the baked cookies on waxed paper spread on the kitchen counter; let stand until completely cool.

Then, store the cookies in an airtight container.

MAKES 96

VARIATION: Shape the dough into ¾-inch-diameter balls and place, 3 inches apart, on lightly oiled cookie sheets. Using a table fork, press the top of each ball until the dough is about 1¼ inches in diameter. Lightly press a blanched almond sliver into the top of each cookie. Bake as above.

BUTTERSCOTCH OATMEAL COOKIES

Take your choice of either butterscotch or chocolate chips when you make these good, basic cookies.

1 cup all-purpose flour
½ teaspoon baking soda
½ cup butter or margarine, softened
⅓ cup granulated sugar
⅓ cup packed light brown sugar
2 extra-large eggs
½ teaspoon pure vanilla extract
1 cup quick-cooking rolled oats, uncooked
1 cup (6 ounces) butterscotch chips
½ cup broken English walnuts (optional)

Preheat the oven to 375° F. Grease lightly 2 or 3 cookie sheets (page 589); set aside.

Onto waxed paper, sift together the flour and baking soda; set aside.

In a large mixing bowl, place the butter, granulated sugar, and brown sugar; using an electric mixer; cream well on medium-high speed. Add the eggs, one at a time, beating well on medium-high speed after each addition. Add the vanilla; beat well on medium speed. Add the flour mixture; beat on low speed only until blended. Add the oats; beat on low speed only until combined. Add the butterscotch chips and walnuts (if included); using a large mixing spoon, stir and fold in until evenly combined.

Drop the dough by rounded tablespoonsful, 2 inches apart, onto the prepared cookie sheets. Bake for 7 minutes, until lightly golden.

Using a thin spatula, place the baked cookies on waxed paper spread on the kitchen counter; let stand until completely cool.

Then, store the cookies in an airtight container.

MAKES ABOUT 40

VARIATION: Chocolate chips may be substituted for the butterscotch chips.

CHOCOLATE CHIP COOKIES

2½ cups all-purpose flour
1 teaspoon baking soda
1 teaspoon salt
1 cup (½ pound) butter, softened
¾ cup granulated sugar
¾ cup packed light brown sugar
2 extra-large eggs
1¼ teaspoons pure vanilla extract
1 12-ounce package (2 cups) semisweet
  chocolate chips
1 cup broken pecans*

  *Broken black walnuts or coarsely chopped
  hazelnuts or macadamia nuts may be
  substituted.

Preheat the oven to 375° F.

Onto waxed paper, sift together the flour, baking soda, and salt; set aside.

In a large mixing bowl, place the butter, granulated sugar, and brown sugar; using an electric mixer, cream well on medium-high speed. Add the eggs, one at a time, beating well on medium-high speed after each addition. Add the vanilla; beat well on medium speed. Add the flour mixture in halves, beating on low speed after each addition only until blended. Add the chocolate chips and pecans; using a large mixing spoon, stir and fold in until evenly combined.

Drop the dough by rounded teaspoonsful, 2 inches apart, onto ungreased cookie sheets. Bake for 9 to 10 minutes, until lightly golden.

Using a thin spatula, place the baked cookies on waxed paper spread on the kitchen counter; let stand until completely cool.

Then, store the cookies in an airtight container.

MAKES ABOUT 84

M&M'S CHOCOLATE CHIP COOKIES: Follow the Chocolate Chip Cookies recipe, above, substituting 1 12-ounce package (1¾ cups) M&M's semisweet chocolate mini baking bits for the chocolate chips and eliminating the pecans.

QUICK-AS-A-WINK CHOCOLATE-COCONUT COOKIES

Simple, and simply delicious.

2 ounces (2 squares) unsweetened
  chocolate
1 14-ounce can (1¼ cups) sweetened
  condensed milk
1 7-ounce package (2⅔ cups) flaked
  coconut
⅓ cup chopped pecans

Preheat the oven to 350° F. Using Special Grease (page 56), grease 2 or 3 cookie sheets; set aside.

Place the chocolate in a tiny saucepan. Hold the tiny pan over (not touching) low simmering water in a small saucepan until the chocolate melts, stirring intermittently. Remove the tiny pan from the heat; set aside.

In a medium mixing bowl, place the condensed milk, coconut, pecans, and melted chocolate; stir until blended and evenly combined.

Drop the mixture by rounded teaspoonsful, 2 inches apart, onto the prepared cookie sheets. Bake for 12 minutes, until set.

Using a thin spatula, immediately place the baked cookies on waxed paper spread on the kitchen counter; let stand until completely cool.

Then, store the cookies in an airtight container.

MAKES ABOUT 48

COCONUT OATMEAL COOKIES

1½ cups all-purpose flour
½ teaspoon baking soda
½ cup (¼ pound) butter, softened
½ cup granulated sugar
½ cup packed light brown sugar
2 extra-large eggs
½ teaspoon pure vanilla extract
1 cup quick-cooking rolled oats, uncooked
¾ cup shredded coconut
½ cup chopped pecans

Preheat the oven to 350° F. Grease 2 or 3 cookie sheets (page 589); set aside.

Onto waxed paper, sift together the flour and baking soda; set aside.

In a large mixing bowl, place the butter, granulated sugar, and brown sugar; using an electric mixer, cream well on medium-high speed. Add the eggs, one at a time, beating well on medium-high speed after each addition. Add the vanilla; beat on medium-high speed until fluffy. Add the oats; beat on medium speed until combined. Add the flour mixture; beat on low speed only until blended. Add the coconut and pecans; using a large mixing spoon, stir and fold in until evenly distributed.

Drop the dough by rounded teaspoonsful, 2 inches apart, onto the prepared cookie sheets. Bake for 8 minutes, until lightly golden.

Using a thin spatula, place the baked cookies on waxed paper spread on the kitchen counter; let stand until completely cool.

Then, store the cookies in an airtight container.

MAKES ABOUT 60

EASTER EGG NESTS

Cute-looking and easy as pie to make, Easter Egg Nests are an ideal treat to make with children as assistant cooks.

1 cup (6 ounces) milk chocolate chips
1 cup (6 ounces) butterscotch chips
1 5-ounce can chow mein noodles
½ cup flaked coconut, tinted green (page 409)
About 10½ dozen small jelly beans in assorted colors

Line 2 cookie sheets with waxed paper; set aside.

In the top of a double boiler, place the chocolate chips and butterscotch chips. Place the top of the double boiler over (not touching) hot (not simmering) water in the bottom pan. Stir continuously to expedite the melting of the chips and to blend.

Remove the top of the double boiler from the bottom pan. Add the chow mein noodles to the melted chips; using a spoon, stir to combine, crushing the noodles into smaller pieces with the edge of the spoon as you mix.

Drop the mixture by rounded teaspoonsful onto the prepared cookie sheets, forming each cookie into a little nest with a slight indentation on the top. With your fingers, sprinkle a small amount of coconut over the center of each nest to simulate grass. Press 3 jelly beans of varied color into the coconut on each cookie to simulate eggs.

Place the cookie sheets of Easter Egg Nests in the refrigerator for a few minutes until set.

Then, store the cookies in an airtight container.

MAKES ABOUT 42

COCONUT MACAROONS

Often included on platters of gaily decorated Christmas cookies are Coconut Macaroons topped with ½ red candied cherry in keeping with the season.

2 tablespoons all-purpose flour
⅛ teaspoon salt
2 extra-large egg whites, room temperature
½ cup powdered sugar
1 teaspoon clear vanilla
7 ounces (2⅓ cups) shredded coconut

Preheat the oven to 300° F. Grease 2 or 3 cookie sheets (page 589); set aside.

In a small sauce dish, place the flour and salt; stir to combine; set aside.

Place the egg whites in a medium mixing bowl. Using an electric mixer, beat the egg whites on high speed until stiff peaks hold. While continuing to beat on high speed, slowly add the powdered sugar, then the flour mixture, and then the vanilla. Beat on high speed until well blended. Add the coconut; using a mixing spoon, fold in.

Drop the dough by rounded teaspoonsful, 2 inches apart, onto the prepared cookie sheets. Bake for 20 minutes. When done, the macaroons will be a light golden color.

Using a thin spatula, place the baked cookies on waxed paper spread on the kitchen counter; let stand until completely cool.

Store the cookies overnight in an airtight container before serving. Keep stored in an airtight container.

MAKES ABOUT 30

HOLIDAY DECORATION: Prior to baking, place ½ red candied cherry on the top of each mound of dough on the cookie sheet.

CORNFLAKES MACAROONS

Recipes for these supergood cookies appear fairly consistently in old cookbooks, and they pop up occasionally in current cookbooks. Cornflakes Macaroons will probably remain popular not only because they are great tasting, but also because their ingredients are consistent with healthful eating trends (no egg yolks and no added shortening).

2 extra-large egg whites, room temperature
1 cup sugar
½ teaspoon clear vanilla
2 cups cornflakes
½ cup broken pecans
1 cup shredded coconut

Preheat the oven to 325° F. Grease 2 or 3 cookie sheets (page 589); set aside.

Place the egg whites in a medium mixing bowl; using an electric mixer, beat the egg whites on high speed until soft peaks form. While continuing to beat on high speed, very gradually add the sugar and then the vanilla. Continue beating the egg white mixture on high speed until stiff, but still moist and glossy. Add the cornflakes, pecans, and coconut; using a large mixing spoon, fold in until evenly distributed.

Drop the dough by rounded teaspoonsful, 2 inches apart, onto the prepared cookie sheets. Bake for 15 minutes. When done, the cookies will not be brown.

Using a thin spatula, place the baked cookies on waxed paper spread on the kitchen counter; let stand until completely cool.

Then, store the cookies in an airtight container.

MAKES 48

BRAN FLAKES COOKIES

2 cups all-purpose flour
2 teaspoons baking powder
½ teaspoon baking soda
½ teaspoon salt
1 cup raisins
1 cup shredded coconut
1 cup vegetable shortening, softened
1 cup granulated sugar
1 cup packed light brown sugar
2 extra-large eggs
2 tablespoons whole milk
1 teaspoon pure vanilla extract
2 cups bran flakes

Preheat the oven to 350° F.

Onto waxed paper, sift together the flour, baking powder, soda, and salt; set aside. In a medium mixing bowl, place the raisins and coconut; stir to combine; cover and set aside.

In a large mixing bowl, place the vegetable shortening, granulated sugar, and brown sugar; using an electric mixer, cream well on medium-high speed. Add the eggs, one at a time, beating well on medium-high speed after each addition. Add the milk and vanilla; beat on medium-high speed until fluffy. Add the flour mixture; beat on low speed only until blended. Add the raisin mixture and bran flakes; using a large mixing spoon, stir and fold in until evenly distributed throughout the dough.

Drop the dough by rounded tablespoonsful, 2 inches apart, onto ungreased cookie sheets. Bake for 10 minutes. The cookies will fall when done; do not remove them from the oven too soon.

Using a thin spatula, place the baked cookies on waxed paper spread on the kitchen counter; let stand until completely cool.

Then, store the cookies in an airtight container.

MAKES 72

VARIATION: This recipe may be conveniently cut in half.

HONEY-GRANOLA COOKIES

1½ cups whole-wheat flour
1½ cups all-purpose flour
½ teaspoon baking powder
1 teaspoon baking soda
¾ teaspoon salt
2 teaspoons ground ginger
½ teaspoon ground nutmeg
1 extra-large egg
⅔ cup packed light brown sugar
⅔ cup honey
½ cup (¼ pound) margarine, softened
4 cups granola, homemade (page 84) or
   1 13-ounce commercial package
Whole, blanched almonds (optional)

Preheat the oven to 350° F. Using Special Grease (page 56), grease 2 or 3 cookie sheets; set aside.

Onto waxed paper, sift together the whole-wheat flour, all-purpose flour, baking powder, baking soda, salt, ginger, and nutmeg; set aside.

Place the egg in a large mixing bowl; using an electric mixer, beat the egg well on medium-high speed. Add the brown sugar and honey; beat well on medium-high speed. Add the margarine; continue beating on medium-high speed until well blended. Add the flour mixture in halves, beating on low speed after each addition only until blended. Add the granola; using a large mixing spoon, stir and fold in.

Drop the dough by heaping teaspoonsful, 2 inches apart, onto the prepared cookie sheets. If desired, place a whole, blanched almond in the center of each mound of cookie dough. Bake for 7 to 8 minutes, until golden.

Remove the cookies from the oven and let stand on the cookie sheets 1 minute. Then, using a thin spatula, place the cookies on waxed paper spread on the kitchen counter; let stand until completely cool.

Then, store the cookies in an airtight container.

MAKES ABOUT 96

OATMEAL-DATE COOKIES

2 cups all-purpose flour
1/2 teaspoon baking soda
1/4 teaspoon salt
1/2 teaspoon ground cloves
1/2 teaspoon ground cinnamon
1/4 teaspoon ground nutmeg
1 cup quick-cooking rolled oats, uncooked
1/2 cup (1/4 pound) butter or margarine, softened
1 cup packed light brown sugar
2 extra-large eggs
1 cup dates chopped very finely
1/2 cup homemade sour milk (page 58)

Preheat the oven to 375° F. Grease 2 or 3 cookie sheets (page 589); set aside.

Onto waxed paper, sift together the flour, baking soda, salt, cloves, cinnamon, and nutmeg. Place the flour mixture in a large mixing bowl. Add the oats; stir to combine; set aside.

In a large mixing bowl, place the butter and brown sugar; using an electric mixer, cream well on medium-high speed. Add the eggs, one at a time, beating well on medium-high speed after each addition. Add the dates; beat on medium speed only until combined. Add, alternately, the flour mixture in thirds, and the sour milk in halves, beating on low speed after each addition only until blended.

Drop the dough by rounded tablespoonsful, 2 inches apart, onto the prepared cookie sheets. Bake for 8 minutes, until lightly golden.

Using a thin spatula, place the baked cookies on waxed paper spread on the kitchen counter; let stand until completely cool.

Then, store the cookies in an airtight container.

MAKES ABOUT 60

OAT BRAN COOKIES

1 1/2 cups all-purpose flour
1/2 teaspoon baking soda
1/2 cup vegetable shortening, softened
1/2 cup granulated sugar
1/2 cup packed light brown sugar
2 extra-large eggs
1/2 teaspoon pure vanilla extract
1 cup oat bran
1/2 cup flaked coconut
1/2 cup broken pecans

Preheat the oven to 350° F.

Onto waxed paper, sift together the flour and baking soda; set aside.

In a medium mixing bowl, place the vegetable shortening, granulated sugar, and brown sugar; using an electric mixer, cream well on medium-high speed. Add the eggs, one at a time, beating well on medium-high speed after each addition. Add the vanilla; beat on medium-high speed until well blended. Add the oat bran; beat on medium speed until combined. Add the coconut and pecans; using a large mixing spoon, stir and fold in until evenly combined.

Drop the dough by rounded teaspoonfuls, 2 inches apart, onto ungreased cookie sheets. Bake for 8 minutes, until lightly golden.

Using a thin spatula, place the baked cookies on waxed paper spread on the kitchen counter; let stand until completely cool.

Then, store the cookies in an airtight container.

MAKES 60

MONSTER COOKIES

There's something to suit just about all cookie lovers in these behemoths, but there isn't any flour. Well, something had to give. Instructions for making these cookies in a more normal size are also given.

½ cup (¼ pound) butter or margarine, softened
1 cup granulated sugar
1 cup packed light brown sugar
3 extra-large eggs
2 teaspoons baking soda
1 tablespoon pure vanilla extract
1 12-ounce jar (1⅓ cups) creamy peanut butter
4½ cups quick-cooking rolled oats, uncooked
1 6-ounce package (1 cup) semisweet chocolate chips
1 8-ounce package peanut (or plain) M&M's candies

Preheat the oven to 325° F.

In a large mixing bowl, place the butter, granulated sugar, and brown sugar; using an electric mixer, cream well on medium-high speed. Add the eggs, one at a time, beating well on medium-high speed after each addition. Add the baking soda and vanilla; beat on medium-high speed until well blended. Add the peanut butter; beat on medium-high speed until blended. Add the oats; beat on medium-low speed until combined. Add the chocolate chips and M&M's; using a large mixing spoon, stir and fold in until evenly distributed.

Drop the dough by heaping tablespoonsful, 3 inches apart, onto ungreased cookie sheets. Bake for 10 to 12 minutes, until very lightly golden.

Remove the cookies from the oven and let stand on the cookie sheets until cooled slightly. Then, using a thin spatula, place the cookies on waxed paper spread on the kitchen counter; let stand until completely cool.

Then, store them in an airtight container.

MAKES ABOUT 36 MONSTER-SIZED COOKIES

VARIATION: For smaller cookies, drop the dough by heaping teaspoonsful, 2 inches apart, onto ungreased cookie sheets. Bake for 10 minutes at 325° F. Makes about 120 smaller-sized cookies.

SOUR CREAM DROP COOKIES

2¾ cups all-purpose flour
½ teaspoon baking powder
½ teaspoon baking soda
¼ teaspoon salt
½ cup (¼ pound) butter or vegetable shortening, softened
1½ cups sugar
2 extra-large eggs
1 teaspoon pure vanilla extract
1 cup homemade sour cream (page 58)

Onto waxed paper, sift together the flour, baking powder, baking soda, and salt; set aside.

In a large mixing bowl, place the butter and sugar; using an electric mixer, cream well on medium-high speed. Add the eggs, one at a time, beating well on medium-high speed after each addition. Add the vanilla; beat on medium-high speed until blended. Add, alternately, the flour mixture in thirds, and the sour cream in halves, beating on low speed after each addition only until blended. Cover the mixing bowl with aluminum foil and refrigerate the dough 1 hour.

Preheat the oven to 350° F. Grease well 2 or 3 cookie sheets (page 589); set aside.

Remove the dough from the refrigerator and drop it by rounded teaspoonsful, 2 inches apart, onto the prepared cookie sheets. Bake for 8 minutes, until lightly golden.

Using a thin spatula, place the baked cookies on waxed paper spread on the kitchen counter; let stand until completely cool.

Then, store the cookies in an airtight container.

MAKES ABOUT 156

FROSTED CHOCOLATE COOKIES

Ever popular and ever good, Frosted Chocolate Cookies are a staple in the world of Midwest cookies.

1½ cups all-purpose flour
1 teaspoon baking powder
½ teaspoon baking soda
¼ cup unsweetened cocoa powder
½ cup (¼ pound) butter, softened
1 cup packed light brown sugar
1 extra-large egg
½ teaspoon pure vanilla extract
½ cup homemade sour milk (page 58)
1 cup chopped pecans
1 recipe Chocolate Frosting (page 580)

Preheat the oven to 350°F. Grease lightly 2 or 3 cookie sheets (page 589); set aside.

Onto waxed paper, sift together the flour, baking powder, baking soda, and cocoa; set aside.

In a large mixing bowl, place the butter and brown sugar; using an electric mixer, cream well on medium-high speed. Add the egg and vanilla; beat on medium-high speed until fluffy. Add, alternately, the flour mixture in thirds, and the sour milk in halves, beating on low speed after each addition only until blended. Add the pecans; using a large mixing spoon, stir and fold in until evenly combined.

Drop the dough by rounded teaspoonsful, 2 inches apart, onto the prepared cookie sheets. Bake for 8 minutes, until set.

Using a thin spatula, place the baked cookies on waxed paper spread on the kitchen counter; let stand until completely cool.

Then, using a small, narrow, tapered spatula, frost the cookies with the Chocolate Frosting. Let the cookies stand until the frosting sets.

Store the cookies, single layer, separated by plastic wrap, in an airtight container.

MAKES 84

FROSTED ORANGE COOKIES

1¾ cups all-purpose flour
1 teaspoon baking powder
½ teaspoon baking soda
½ teaspoon salt
½ cup (¼ pound) butter, softened
¾ cup packed light brown sugar
1 extra-large egg
½ teaspoon orange extract
1 tablespoon plus 1 teaspoon very finely grated orange rind (page 47)
½ cup homemade sour milk (page 58)
1 recipe Orange Frosting (page 581)
Snipped orange gumdrops for decoration

Preheat the oven to 350°F. Oil lightly 2 or 3 cookie sheets (page 589); set aside.

Onto waxed paper, sift together the flour, baking powder, soda, and salt; set aside.

In a large mixing bowl, place the butter and brown sugar; using an electric mixer, cream well on medium-high speed. Add the egg; beat on medium-high speed until well blended. Add the orange extract and orange rind; beat on medium-high speed until blended and combined. Add, alternately, the flour mixture in thirds, and the sour milk in halves, beating on low speed after each addition only until blended.

Drop the dough by rounded teaspoonsful, 2 inches apart, onto the prepared cookie sheets. Bake for 8 to 9 minutes, until set.

Remove the cookies from the oven and let stand on the cookie sheets 1 minute. Then, using a thin spatula, place the cookies on wire cookie racks. Let the cookies stand until completely cool.

Then, using a small, narrow, tapered spatula, frost the cookies with the Orange Frosting. Decorate the top of each frosted cookie with a small, snipped piece of orange gumdrop. Let the cookies stand until the frosting sets.

Store the cookies, single layer, separated by plastic wrap, in an airtight container.

MAKES ABOUT 72

FROSTED MOLASSES COOKIES

Molasses is a product which results from the manufacture of cane and beet sugar. In the manufacture of cane sugar, the sugar-bearing juice is extracted from the cane by means of chopping and crushing or by diffusion, after which the extracted juice is clarified. The clarified sugarcane juice is then processed through a series of three boilings and evaporations which result in a mixture of crystallized raw sugar and a brown syrup which is molasses. The molasses is separated from the sugar crystals by means of centrifuging.

Molasses obtained after the first boiling contains a greater percentage of sugar and is lighter in color than molasses obtained after the second and third boilings. Molasses obtained from the first extraction is called light (or mild-flavored) molasses, and molasses obtained from the second extraction is called dark (or robust- or full-flavored) molasses. The very dark, heavy, and somewhat bitter syrup obtained after the third boiling is called blackstrap molasses. While blackstrap molasses is available on supermarket shelves for consumers who include it in their diets for its high iron content, it is used primarily in animal feed, for fermentation into alcohol, and for other commercial purposes. I recall that in the late 1940's molasses was mixed with a grain fed to our purebred Shorthorn cattle being fattened for show purposes as an inducement for them to eat abundantly. Molasses obtained from sugar beets is very low in sugar and generally is considered to be inedible.

Molasses was one of the provisions supplied to the Midwest frontier, sometimes arriving, with other foodstuffs, by steamboat up the Mississippi River during warm navigable months. Because sugar was in short supply, molasses was consistently used as a sweetener substitute. Molasses cookies were a pioneer food. Some of the very old recipes for molasses cookies call for them to be made with vinegar and require no shortening (vinegar molasses cookies). Other old molasses cookie recipes still in use today commonly call for lard as the shortening which helps to give the cookies that deep, rich, beloved flavor. This recipe is one of those old, incomparable ones handed down in my sister-in-law's family. The appeal of these cookies to modern palates has not diminished.

4½ cups all-purpose flour
2 teaspoons baking soda
1 teaspoon salt
1 teaspoon ground cinnamon
½ teaspoon ground nutmeg
½ teaspoon ground ginger
1 cup lard, softened
1½ cups packed light brown sugar
½ cup light (mild-flavored) molasses
3 extra-large eggs
1 teaspoon pure vanilla extract
½ cup homemade sour milk (page 58)
1 recipe Powdered Sugar Frosting (page 580)

Preheat the oven to 350° F. Grease 2 or 3 cookie sheets (page 589); set aside.

Onto waxed paper, sift together the flour, baking soda, salt, cinnamon, nutmeg, and ginger; set aside.

In a large mixing bowl, place the lard and brown sugar; using an electric mixer, cream well on medium-high speed. Add the molasses; beat on medium-high speed until blended. Add the eggs, one at a time, beating well on medium-high speed after each addition. Add the vanilla; beat on medium-high speed until blended. Add, alternately, the flour mixture in thirds, and the sour milk in halves, beating on low speed after each addition only until blended.

Drop the dough by rounded tablespoonsful, 2 inches apart, onto the prepared cookie sheets. Bake for 10 minutes, until lightly golden.

Using a thin spatula, place the baked cookies on waxed paper spread on the kitchen counter; let stand until completely cool.

Then, using a small, narrow, tapered spatula, frost the cookies with the Powdered Sugar Frosting. Let the cookies stand until the frosting sets.

Store the cookies, single layer, separated by plastic wrap, in an airtight container.

MAKES ABOUT 96

FRUITCAKE COOKIES

If you like really good fruitcake but don't have time to make it this holiday season, make these cookies instead. This big recipe yields about 13 dozen cookies—enough for gift giving as well as your own family's enjoyment. The recipe came from my grandmother's cookbook (your guarantee as to its excellence).

16 ounces diced candied mixed fruits
½ cup raisins
½ cup golden raisins
1 cup broken English walnuts
¼ cup all-purpose flour
3 cups all-purpose flour
1 tablespoon baking powder
¼ teaspoon salt
2 teaspoons ground cinnamon
½ teaspoon ground cloves
½ teaspoon ground nutmeg
1 cup (½ pound) butter, softened
2 cups sugar
2 extra-large eggs
¾ cup whole milk
4 ounces candied red cherries, quartered
   lengthwise, for decoration

Preheat the oven to 375° F. Grease 2 or 3 cookie sheets (page 589); set aside.

In a medium mixing bowl, place the candied mixed fruits, raisins, golden raisins, and walnuts; stir until evenly distributed. Add ¼ cup flour; toss to coat the fruits and nuts; set aside.

Onto waxed paper, sift together 3 cups flour, baking powder, salt, cinnamon, cloves, and nutmeg; set aside.

In a large mixing bowl, place the butter and sugar; using an electric mixer, cream well on medium-high speed. Add the eggs, one at a time, beating well on medium-high speed after each addition. Continue beating the mixture on medium-high speed until the mixture is light and fluffy. Add, alternately, the flour mixture in thirds, and the milk in halves, beating on low speed after each addition only until blended. Add the fruits and nuts mixture; using a large mixing spoon, stir and fold in until evenly distributed.

Drop the dough by rounded teaspoonsful, 2 inches apart, onto the prepared cookie sheets. Place a candied red cherry quarter in the center of each mound of cookie dough. Bake for 9 to 10 minutes, until lightly golden.

Using a thin spatula, place the baked cookies on waxed paper spread on the kitchen counter; let stand until completely cool.

Then, store the cookies in an airtight container.

MAKES ABOUT 156

HAYSTACKS

For those readers less familiar with farming, "hay" is a general term used to mean any number of dried herbaceous plant crops used for animal feel which supply both important nutrients and roughage. While alfalfa and red clover are the primary crops raised for hay in the Midwest, various grasses are used for hay in some sections of the Heartland.

These cookies are so named because they resemble stacks of dry hay. The marshmallows provide height and the coconut gives the appearance of stems protruding from the haystacks.

1 ounce (1 square) unsweetened chocolate
3 ounces cream cheese, softened
2 tablespoons half-and-half
1 teaspoon crème de cacao (cacao bean-
   and vanilla-flavored liqueur)
2 cups powdered sugar, sifted (page 57)
   (sift after measuring)
2 cups miniature marshmallows
1 cup flaked coconut

Line a cookie sheet with waxed paper; set aside.

Place the chocolate in a tiny saucepan. Hold the tiny pan over (not touching) low simmering water in a small saucepan until the chocolate melts, stirring intermittently. Remove the tiny pan from the heat; set aside.

(Recipe continues on next page)

Place the cream cheese in a medium mixing bowl. Using an electric mixer, beat the cream cheese on high speed only until smooth. Add the half-and-half; beat on medium-high speed until blended. Add the crème de cacao and melted chocolate; continue beating on medium-high speed until fluffy. Add the powdered sugar; beat on low speed to combine; then, beat on medium-high speed until completely blended and smooth. Add the marshmallows and coconut; using a small mixing spoon, stir and fold in until evenly distributed.

Drop the mixture by rounded teaspoonful onto the prepared cookie sheet. Refrigerate, uncovered, until the cookies are firm (about 3 hours).

Then, store the cookies, single layer, separated by plastic wrap, in an airtight container; keep refrigerated.

MAKES ABOUT 42

SUNFLOWER SEED COOKIES

While the use of hulled sunflower seeds as a cooking ingredient might seem contemporary to some of us, American Indians grew sunflowers for food long before the Europeans came to this land. The Indians dried sunflower seeds and then ground them, unshelled, into a meal. The common sunflower, Helianthus annuus, is native to North America, especially the western tier of Midwest states and the west-central section of the United States. In 1996, the top four sunflower-producing states, by rank, were North Dakota, South Dakota, Kansas, and Minnesota. (The sunflower is the official state flower of Kansas.) Sunflower-seed oil, pressed from the seeds and used in salad dressings and for cooking, is low in saturated fat and high in polyun-saturated fat (see page 795).

The appearance of sunflowers, with their yellow-petaled flower heads resembling sunbursts, is familiar to everyone. However, the huge size of the flower heads of cultivated sunflowers, which can be as much as one foot or more in diameter, is astonishing when you see these flowers for the first time. (The size of one I saw at our local farmers' market last Saturday amazed me.)

Hulled sunflower seeds are rich in nutrients and are usually available in the section of supermarkets where nuts are displayed. The recipe that follows makes sunflower seed cookies that are high in fiber and tops in taste. For a yeast bread containing sunflower seeds, see Honey-Seed Bread (page 421).

½ cup raw, hulled (unsalted) sunflower seeds
½ cup flaked coconut
1 cup Quaker MultiGrain cereal, uncooked (found at supermarket with oatmeal)
1 cup all-purpose flour
¼ teaspoon baking powder
½ teaspoon baking soda
½ cup (¼ pound) margarine, softened
½ cup granulated sugar
½ cup packed light brown sugar
1 extra-large egg
½ teaspoon pure vanilla extract
1 recipe Honey–Cream Cheese Frosting (page 583) (optional)

Preheat the oven to 350° F. Grease 2 or 3 cookie sheets (page 589); set aside.

In a medium mixing bowl, place the sunflower seeds, coconut, and MultiGrain cereal; stir to evenly combine; cover and set aside. Onto waxed paper, sift together the flour, baking powder, and baking soda; set aside.

In a large mixing bowl, place the margarine, granulated sugar, and brown sugar; using an electric mixer, cream well on medium-high speed. Add the egg and vanilla; beat on medium-high speed until light and fluffy. Add the flour mixture; beat on low speed only until blended. Add the sunflower seed mixture; using a large mixing spoon, stir until evenly combined and all dry ingredients are dampened.

Drop the dough by heaping teaspoonful, 2 inches apart, onto the prepared cookie sheets. Bake for 7 to 8 minutes, until lightly golden.

Using a thin spatula, place the baked cookies on waxed paper spread on the kitchen counter; let stand until completely cool.

Then, if desired, using a decorating bag fit with small round tip number 2 (page 383), pipe stripes (page 388) of Honey–Cream Cheese Frosting back and forth across the top of the cookies. Place the cookies, single layer, uncovered, in a container(s) with a lid(s). Refrigerate 2 hours, until the frosting sets; then, cover. For food safety, keep the cookies refrigerated due to the cream cheese in the frosting.

MAKES ABOUT 60

MACADAMIA NUT COOKIES

Although the tree Macadamia ternifolia was originally native to Australia, we associate macadamia nuts, the seeds of this tree, with Hawaii where they are one of our fiftieth state's largest crops. So what is a macadamia nut cookie recipe doing in a Midwest cookbook? Well, a lot of Midwesterners love macadamia nuts, as do I, and, more important, I like them in these thin, delicate cookies which I first made with macadamia nuts brought home from an Hawaiian vacation. If these justifications seem a bit weak, perhaps the inclusion of this recipe will become more understandable and acceptable after you are swept away by the exquisite taste of the cookies.

1⅓ cups all-purpose flour
1¼ cups (½ pound plus 4 tablespoons) butter, softened
1¼ cups powdered sugar
1 extra-large egg
1¾ teaspoons pure vanilla extract
1 7-ounce jar (1½ cups) macadamia nuts, chopped

Preheat the oven to 350° F. Grease lightly 2 or 3 cookies sheets (page 589); set aside.

Sift the floor onto waxed paper; set aside.

In a medium mixing bowl, place the butter and powdered sugar; using an electric mixer, cream well on medium-high speed. Add the egg and vanilla; beat on medium-high speed until well blended. Add the flour; beat on low speed only until blended. Add the nuts; using a medium mixing spoon, stir and fold in until evenly distributed.

Drop the dough by rounded teaspoonsful, 2 inches apart, onto the prepared cookie sheets. Bake for 10 to 12 minutes. Watch the cookies closely during baking. When done, the cookies should be golden brown around the edges. Be careful not to let these cookies get too brown, as it will ruin their delicate taste.

Using a thin spatula, place the baked cookies on waxed paper spread on the kitchen counter; let stand until completely cool.

Then, store the cookies in an airtight container.

MAKES ABOUT 48

HEALTH NUT COOKIES

These cookies contain all kinds of ingredients that are good for you.

2½ cups quick-cooking rolled oats, uncooked
1 cup broken pecans
½ cup golden raisins
1 cup whole-wheat flour
¾ teaspoon salt
1 teaspoon ground cinnamon
½ teaspoon ground nutmeg
2 extra-large eggs
¾ cup vegetable oil
1¼ cups honey
1 teaspoon pure vanilla extract
1½ cups untoasted (raw) wheat germ
½ cup nonfat dry milk
6½ dozen pecan halves
Honey-Cinnamon Glaze (recipe follows)

Preheat the oven to 325° F. Grease 2 or 3 cookie sheets (page 589); set aside.

In a medium mixing bowl, place the oats, pecans, and raisins; sir to combine; cover and set aside. Onto waxed paper, sift together the flour, salt, cinnamon, and nutmeg; set aside.

Place the eggs in a large mixing bowl. Using an electric mixer, beat the eggs well on medium-

(Recipe continues on next page)

high speed. Add the vegetable oil and honey; beat on medium-high speed until well blended. Add the vanilla; beat on medium-high speed until blended. Add the wheat germ; beat on low speed until blended. Add the flour mixture and dry milk; beat on low speed only until blended. Add the oats mixture; using a large mixing spoon, stir and fold in until evenly distributed. Cover the mixing bowl containing the cookie dough with plastic wrap; let stand 5 minutes to allow the dough to thicken.

Drop the dough by rounded teaspoonsful, 2 inches apart, onto the prepared cookie sheets. Place a pecan half in the center of each mound of cookie dough. Using a small, soft watercolor brush, brush a thin coat of the Honey-Cinnamon Glaze over each pecan half. Bake for 9 to 10 minutes, until golden.

Remove the cookies from the oven and let stand on the cookie sheets 2 minutes. Then, using a thin spatula, place the cookies on waxed paper spread on the kitchen counter; let stand until completely cool.

Store the cookies, single layer, separated by plastic wrap in an airtight container.

MAKES ABOUT 78

Honey-Cinnamon Glaze

1 tablespoon honey
Dash of ground cinnamon

In a tiny saucepan, place the honey and cinnamon; stir to combine. Over low heat, heat the mixture until thin, stirring intermittently.

MOTHER'S PINEAPPLE COOKIES

When we were growing up, the cookies Mother made the most often were these Pineapple Cookies, our very favorite. Mother always put any leftover frosting on Ritz crackers (an unlikely but swell-tasting, "down-home" combination) and topped them with half a pecan. Whenever I have extra Powdered Sugar Frosting, I make these homespun treats for my brother.

1 8¼-ounce can commercial crushed pineapple in heavy syrup
2 cups all-purpose flour
1 teaspoon baking powder
¼ teaspoon baking soda
¼ teaspoon salt
½ cup (¼ pound) butter, softened
½ cup granulated sugar
½ cup packed light brown sugar
1 extra-large egg
1 teaspoon pure vanilla extract
½ cup broken pecans
Frosting (recipe instructions, below)

Preheat the oven to 325° F. Grease lightly 2 or 3 cookie sheets (page 589); set aside.

Drain the pineapple in a sieve, reserving the juice for use in the frosting; set aside. Onto waxed paper, sift together the flour, baking powder, baking soda, and salt; set aside.

In a large mixing bowl, place the butter, granulated sugar, and brown sugar; using an electric mixer, cream well on medium-high speed. Add the egg and vanilla; beat on medium-high speed until thoroughly blended. Add the flour mixture; beat on low speed only until blended. The dough will be quite stiff. Add the drained pineapple and pecans; using a large mixing spoon, stir and fold in until evenly combined.

Drop the dough by rounded teaspoonsful, 2 inches apart, onto the prepared sheets. Bake for 12 to 14 minutes, until lightly golden brown.

Using a thin spatula, place the baked cookies on waxed paper spread on the kitchen counter; let stand until completely cool.

Then, using a small, narrow, tapered spatula, frost the cookies. Let stand until frosting sets.

Store the cookies, single layer, separated by plastic wrap, in an airtight container.

MAKES ABOUT 72

FROSTING: Frost the cookies with 1 recipe of Powdered Sugar Frosting (page 580), substituting ¼ cup reserved pineapple syrup for ¼ cup half-and-half or whole milk. If the reserved syrup measures less than ¼ cup, add water to make ¼ cup liquid.

MINCEMEAT COOKIES

There are additional delightful ways to savor mince-meat other than in a pie (albeit mincemeat pie devotees might ask, "Why look for any?"). For example, consider the possibility of savoring the special flavor of mincemeat over an extended period of time when you bake one recipe of these Mincemeat Cookies which yields about 7½ dozen. (A grand idea for serving a holiday crowd, too.) Designer Filled Cookies (page 640) present another option for using mincemeat in cookies. And for a different kind of mincemeat pie, see the recipe for Mincemeat–Rum Ice Cream Pie (page 671), a choice dessert.

2 cups cooked-down mincemeat,*
    homemade (page 726) or commercially
    canned
3¼ cups all-purpose flour
1 teaspoon baking soda
½ teaspoon salt
1 cup (¼ pound) butter, softened
1½ cups sugar
2 extra-large eggs
½ recipe Confectioners' Frosting
    (page 579) (optional)

  *Over low heat, simmer the mincemeat, uncovered, in a heavy-bottomed saucepan until little or no liquid remains. Stir often and be careful not to scorch the mincemeat.

Preheat the oven to 350° F. Using Special Grease (page 56), grease 2 or 3 cookie sheets; set aside.

Onto waxed paper, sift together the flour, baking soda, and salt; set aside.

In a large mixing bowl, place the butter and sugar; using an electric mixer, cream well on medium-high speed. Add the eggs, one at a time, beating well on medium-high speed after each addition. Add the flour mixture in halves, beating on low speed after each addition only until blended. Add the mincemeat; using a large mixing spoon, stir and fold in until marbled into the cookie dough.

Drop the dough by rounded teaspoonsful, 2 inches apart, onto the prepared cookie sheets.

Bake for 10 minutes, until lightly golden.

Using a thin spatula, place the baked cookies on waxed paper spread on the kitchen counter; let stand until completely cool.

Then, if desired, as soon as the cookies have completely cooled, use a decorating bag fit with small round tip number 3 (page 383) to pipe stripes (page 388) of Confectioners' Frosting back and forth across the top of the cookies. Let the cookies stand only until the frosting sets.

Then, immediately arrange the cookies, single layer, separated by plastic wrap, in an airtight container and refrigerate. If you choose not to pipe the cookies, store them in the refrigerator as soon as they completely cool after baking. Keep the cookies stored in the refrigerator because they contain meat.

MAKES ABOUT 90

NIGHTY NIGHTS

They bake overnight; plus, they're great for a bedtime treat. (It's also okay to have one for breakfast.)

1 cup (6 ounces) mint-flavored semisweet
    chocolate chips
1 cup chopped pecans
2 extra-large egg whites, room temperature
⅔ cup sugar
½ teaspoon clear vanilla

Preheat the oven to 350° F. Line 2 cookie sheets smoothly with aluminum foil; set aside.

In a small mixing bowl, place the chocolate chips and pecans; stir to combine; set aside.

Place the egg whites in a medium mixing bowl. Using an electric mixer, beat the egg whites on high speed until soft peaks hold. While continuing to beat on high speed, very gradually add the sugar and then the vanilla. Continue beating the egg white mixture on high speed until very stiff. Add the chocolate chip mixture; using a spoon, fold in until evenly distributed.

(Recipe continues on next page)

Drop the meringue mixture by heaping tea-spoonful, 2 inches apart, onto the prepared cookie sheets. Place the cookie sheets in the top half of the oven. Turn off the oven and leave the cookies overnight without opening the oven door until morning.

Store the cookies, single layer, separated by plastic wrap, in an airtight container.

MAKES 42

Molded Cookies

ARTIST'S PALETTE THUMBPRINTS

Thumbprint cookies derive their name from the fact that the baker's thumb becomes an implement to make a depression in the top of each unbaked cookie into which jam (or jelly) is placed after baking. This particular recipe is entitled "Artist's Palette Thumbprints" because I am suggesting that the indentations be filled with jams (or jellies) in a variety of colors to create an especially attractive and appealing array of cookies.

1½ cups all-purpose flour
½ teaspoon salt
½ cup plus 3 tablespoons butter, softened
½ cup sifted powdered sugar (page 57)
  (sift before measuring)
1 extra-large egg yolk
2 teaspoons pure vanilla extract
2 extra-large egg whites
1¾ cups chopped English walnuts
At least 4 kinds of jams in various colors,
  such as strawberry, peach, pineapple,
  plum, cherry, blueberry, and apricot

Onto waxed paper, sift together the flour and salt; set aside.

In a medium mixing bowl, place the butter and powdered sugar; using an electric mixer, beat on medium-high speed until blended and creamy. Add the egg yolk; beat well on medium-high speed. Add the vanilla; continue beating on

medium-high speed until blended. Add ½ of the flour mixture; beat on low speed only until blended. Add the remaining ½ of the flour mixture; beat on low speed only until the flour mixture is fully blended and the dough is smooth. Cover the mixing bowl with aluminum foil and refrigerate the dough 45 minutes, until cool enough to mold into balls easily. (If the dough becomes too stiff, let it stand, covered, at room temperature until it warms to the desired consistency.)

Meanwhile, place the egg whites in a small sauce dish; using a table fork, beat slightly; set aside. Distribute the walnuts over a piece of waxed paper; set aside.

Preheat the oven to 350° F. Line 2 or 3 cookie sheets with parchment baking paper. (If parchment baking paper is not available, the cookie sheets may be greased, page 589.) Set aside.

Using a 1-inch trigger scoop or melon baller, scoop portions of dough from the mixing bowl and roll in the palms of your hands to form 1-inch-diameter balls. Drop the balls of dough into the slightly beaten egg whites to coat; then, roll them in the nuts until they are fully and generously covered.

Place the nut-covered balls, 1½ inches apart, on the prepared cookie sheets. Press down on the top of each ball with your thumb, forming a deep cup in which jam will be placed *after* baking. The thumbprinting procedure will flatten the dough balls slightly. Bake for 15 minutes, until a very pale golden color.

Using a thin spatula, place the baked cookies on waxed paper spread on the kitchen counter; let stand until completely cool.

Then, fill the thumbprint cup in each cookie with about ⅛ teaspoon of one of the vari-colored jams. A tiny salt spoon or a demitasse spoon is excellent for use in filling the cups.

Store the cookies, single layer, separated by plastic wrap, in a loose container.

MAKES ABOUT 36

VARIATION: The thumbprint cups may be filled with jellies. Mint and cherry or strawberry jellies are attractive during the holiday season.

KRINGLA

These large Norwegian cookies shaped in the form of a figure eight, border on a sweet bread in consistency and taste. Though not common, Kringla may be glazed, as indicated in the recipe that follows. Some Norwegian people like to eat Kringla buttered.

3 cups all-purpose flour
1 tablespoon baking powder
1 teaspoon baking soda
½ teaspoon salt
½ cup (¼ pound) butter, softened
1 cup sugar
1 extra-large egg
1 teaspoon pure vanilla extract
1 cup buttermilk
1 recipe Glaze (page 585) (optional)

AFTERNOON OF THE FIRST DAY: Onto waxed paper, sift together the flour, baking powder, baking soda, and salt; set aside.

In a large mixing bowl, place the butter and sugar; using an electric mixer, cream well on medium-high speed. Add the egg and vanilla; beat on medium-high speed until well blended and fluffy. Add, alternately, the flour mixture in thirds, and the buttermilk in halves, beating on low speed after each addition only until blended. Using a rubber spatula, quickly turn the dough into a medium mixing bowl; cover tightly and refrigerate overnight.

THE NEXT DAY: Preheat the oven to 500° F.

Remove the dough from the refrigerator and divide it in half. On a floured pastry cloth (page 54), using floured hands, roll each half of the dough into a log about 12 inches long. Wrap one log in plastic wrap and refrigerate.

Using a sharp, floured knife, cut the remaining log into 20 equal pieces. On the floured pastry cloth, using floured hands, roll each piece of dough into a pencil-like stick 7 to 8 inches long. Carefully lift each dough stick to an ungreased cookie sheet and form it into a figure eight. To make a figure eight, lay the stick of dough on

the cookie sheet in the shape of the bottom loop (see illustration A).

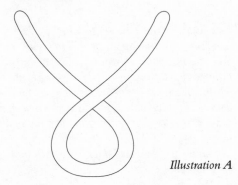

Illustration A

Bring the ends of the dough together to complete the figure eight. Lightly push the ends of the dough together; there is no need to pinch the dough and interfere with the uniformity of the shape (see illustration B).

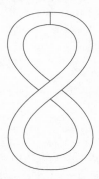

Illustration B

Bake the cookies for 5 minutes. The cookies will be pale.

Using a thin spatula, immediately place the baked Kringla on wire cookie racks; let stand until completely cool.

When cool, the Kringla may be glazed, if desired. Using a soft watercolor brush, apply the Glaze to the tops of the Kringla, following the figure eight; let stand on the wire racks until the glaze sets.

Store the Kringla, single layer, separated by plastic wrap, in an airtight container.

MAKES 40

DUTCH LETTERS
Banketstaven

In a litany of outstanding national foods, Dutch Letters (Banketstaven) are one of Holland's best-known and -loved culinary creations. The exquisite almond filling encased in flaky pastry is formed into long rolls which are shaped into letters of the alphabet before baking. In Holland, Dutch Letters traditionally are shaped into the first letter of the last name of the person to whom they will be given or the first letter of the last name of the baker. When they will not be given as gifts, Dutch Letters are usually made in the shape of the letter S.

2 cups (1 pound) butter
4 cups sifted all-purpose flour (sift before measuring)
1 cup refrigerated water
1 pound almond paste
2 extra-large eggs plus 1 extra-large egg yolk (reserve 1 extra-large egg white)
1 teaspoon pure vanilla extract
2 cups sugar
Crystal sugar* or granulated sugar for decoration

Crystal sugar has larger grains than either granulated sugar or sanding sugar (page 468). You may be able to secure crystal sugar from your baker, or it is available from Sweet Celebrations Inc. (see Product Sources, page 849).

AFTERNOON OF THE FIRST DAY: Remove the butter from the refrigerator and let stand 10 minutes before use in the recipe. (If the kitchen is especially warm, reduce the standing time to 5 minutes.)

Place the flour in a large mixing bowl. Using a knife, cut the butter into approximately tablespoon-sized pieces and drop into the bowl containing the flour. Using a pastry blender, cut the butter into the flour until the mixture is the texture of very coarse cornmeal interspersed with some pieces the size of small peas.

Tilt the mixing bowl and gently shake the flour mixture to one side of the bowl. Sprinkle about 2 tablespoons of the water over the mixture; using a table fork, lightly rake the moistened portion of the mixture to the other side of the bowl. Repeat the procedure until all the water has been added.

With floured hands, divide the pastry in half and quickly form each half into a ball. The pastry will be quite dry; do not be concerned if it does not hold together well in a ball. Wrap each half of the pastry in plastic wrap. Using your hand, slightly flatten each ball of pastry in the plastic wrap and then refrigerate overnight. Handle the pastry as little as possible.

EARLY THE NEXT DAY: Place the almond paste in a large mixing bowl. Using an electric mixer, beat the almond paste on high speed to smooth it as much as possible. Add 2 eggs plus 1 egg yolk, one at a time, beating well on medium-high speed after each addition. Add the vanilla; beat on medium-high speed until the mixture is smooth. Add 2 cups sugar; beat on medium-high speed until well blended. Cover the bowl with aluminum foil; refrigerate 2 to 3 hours until the almond paste mixture is well chilled.

Preheat the oven to 400° F. Grease 3 or more cookie sheets (page 589); set aside.

Using a sharp knife, cut the chilled almond paste mixture into 14 equal portions. On a buttered marble slab or countertop, using buttered hands, roll 7 of the almond paste portions into 13-inch-long rolls, each. Cover and refrigerate the remaining 7 portions.

Remove 1 ball of pastry from the refrigerator and remove the plastic wrap. Using a sharp knife, mark the pastry into 7 equal portions. Cut away, *in one piece,* 3 of the pastry portions. Wrap the remainder of the pastry in plastic wrap and set aside.

On a floured pastry cloth, using a stockinet-covered, then lightly floured rolling pin (page 54), roll the cutaway pastry into a 14 × 15-inch rectangle. Using a sharp, floured knife, cut the rolled pastry into three 5 × 14-inch strips. Place one of the almond paste rolls lengthwise down the center of each pastry strip.

Using a small, soft watercolor brush, brush a ¼-inch strip of water down one of the 14-inch sides of each rolled strip. Roll each strip of pastry lengthwise fairly tightly around the filling and toward the wet edge (making three 14-inch-long rolls). The wet edge will help seal the seam on each roll. Pinch the ends of the rolls to seal.

Arrange each roll, seam side down, in the shape of the letter S (or any desired letter), on a prepared cookie sheet. Repeat the procedure with the remaining almond paste rolls and pastry. (Press the last 2 portions of pastry together and roll into a 14 × 10-inch rectangle; cut into 2 pastry strips.) Let the filled cookie sheets stand.

Place the reserved egg white in a small mixing bowl. Using a handheld electric mixer, beat the egg white slightly on medium speed. Using the soft watercolor brush, brush the tops of the letters with beaten egg white. Then, sprinkle the letters generously with crystal (or granulated) sugar. Using a sharp fork, prick the tops of the letters every 2 inches. Bake for 18 to 20 minutes, until lightly golden.

Using a large, thin spatula, place the baked Dutch Letters on wire cookie racks; let stand until completely cool.

Store the Dutch Letters in a loose container.

To eat, use your fingers to break off desired portions of your served Dutch Letter and eat in the same manner as a cookie.

MAKES FOURTEEN 8-INCH-HIGH S LETTERS

GIFT IDEA: For a special gift, bake Dutch Letters in the initials of the favored person's name.

CHRISTMAS HOLLY WREATHS

Holidays are times for special, shared family activities. Children can participate in the fun and satisfaction of Christmastime baking by helping to make these pretty (and good-tasting, as well) holly wreaths. They're unbaked, and the procedures for making them present opportunities for children of various ages to assist.

3½ cups cornflakes
½ cup shredded coconut
½ cup (¼ pound) butter
30 large marshmallows
¼ teaspoon green liquid food coloring
Cinnamon Imperials candy (red hots)

In a large mixing bowl, place the cornflakes and coconut; using a large mixing spoon, stir until combined; set aside.

In the top of a double boiler, place the butter and marshmallows. Place the top of the double boiler over simmering water in the bottom pan. Stir the butter and marshmallows intermittently until melted and blended. Remove the double boiler from the heat, leaving the top of the double boiler in the bottom pan. Add the food coloring; stir vigorously until blended thoroughly.

Immediately pour the green mixture over the cornflakes mixture; using the large mixing spoon, toss until the cornflakes and coconut are completely coated with the green mixture.

Spoon heaping tablespoons of the mixture onto waxed paper spread on the kitchen counter. Butter your fingers and form wreaths about 2 inches in diameter. Lightly press 3 red hots, close together, into each wreath to simulate holly berries. Let the wreaths stand on the waxed paper 6 hours to partially dry.

Then, using a thin spatula, place the wreaths, single layer, in containers lined with waxed paper. Let the wreaths stand, uncovered, an additional 2 hours to continue drying. Then, cover the containers.

MAKES 20

PFEFFERNÜSSE
Peppernuts

These small, round, nut-shaped German Christmas cookies contain several spices including black pepper, the ingredient for which they are named. After baking, Pfeffernüsse are stored in an airtight container (preferably a tin) where they are left to season at least one week before they are served.

⅓ cup slivered blanched almonds
2 cups sifted all-purpose flour (sift before measuring)
1 teaspoon baking powder
¼ teaspoon salt
¼ teaspoon black pepper
1 teaspoon ground cinnamon
½ teaspoon ground nutmeg
¼ teaspoon ground cloves
Dash of ground mace
2 extra-large eggs
1 cup sugar
¼ cup (2 ounces) chopped candied citron
Brandy

Preheat the oven to 350° F. Grease 2 cookie sheets (page 589); set aside.

In a food processor, process the almonds *a few seconds* until ground. Be careful not to over-process, reducing the nuts to butter. Place the ground almonds in a small mixing bowl; set aside.

Onto waxed paper, sift together the flour, baking powder, salt, pepper, cinnamon, nutmeg, cloves, and mace. Place the flour mixture in a medium mixing bowl. Add the ground almonds; stir to combine; set aside.

Place the eggs in a medium mixing bowl. Using an electric mixer, beat the eggs on high speed until very thick (about 5 minutes). While continuing to beat on high speed, very gradually add the sugar. Add the flour mixture in thirds, beating on low speed after each addition only until blended. Add the citron; using a mixing spoon, stir and fold in until evenly combined.

Using a small melon baller, scoop small portions of dough from the mixing bowl and, with

damp hands, roll into small balls about ½ inch in diameter. Place the balls of dough, 1½ inches apart, on the prepared cookie sheets. Using an eye dropper, place 1 drop of brandy on the top of each ball. Bake for 12 to 13 minutes, until lightly browned.

Using a thin spatula, place the baked cookies on waxed paper spread on the kitchen counter; let stand until completely cool.

Store the cookies in an airtight container (such as a tin) for at least 1 week before serving.

MAKES ABOUT 84

VARIATION: If you prefer softer Pfeffernüsse, place a small slice of apple in the airtight container (tin) with the cookies. To prevent the apple slice from touching the cookies directly, place it on a tiny piece of plastic wrap. Replace the apple slice frequently.

RUM BALLS

½ cup powdered sugar
1½ cups rolled vanilla wafer crumbs (about 33 vanilla wafers)
8 ounces English walnuts, ground (page 50) (about 2 cups ground walnuts)
¼ cup Myers's (dark) rum
¼ cup honey

Place the powdered sugar in a sauce dish; set aside.

In a medium mixing bowl, place the vanilla wafer crumbs and walnuts; stir to combine. Add the rum and honey; stir to combine well.

Using a 1-inch trigger scoop or melon baller, scoop even portions of the mixture from the mixing bowl and, with damp hands, roll into balls 1 inch in diameter. Place the rolled balls on waxed paper spread on the kitchen counter. Then, roll the balls in the sauce dish of powdered sugar to coat.

Store the Rum Balls in an airtight container lined with waxed paper.

MAKES 60

LACE COOKIES

1 cup all-purpose flour
1 cup finely chopped pecans
½ teaspoon ground cinnamon (optional)
½ cup (¼ pound) butter
⅔ cup packed light brown sugar
½ cup light corn syrup
½ teaspoon pure vanilla extract

Have ready a clean piece of ⅝-inch-diameter wooden dowel cut to approximately 7½ inches in length.

Preheat the oven to 350° F. Using Special Grease (page 56), grease lightly 2 or 3 cookie sheets; set aside.

In a small mixing bowl, place the flour, pecans, and cinnamon (if desired); stir to combine; set aside.

In a small saucepan, melt the butter over low heat. Remove from the heat. Add the brown sugar and corn syrup; stir vigorously to blend. Over medium-high heat, bring the butter mixture to a boil, stirring constantly. Remove from the heat. Add the flour mixture; stir to blend and combine. Add the vanilla; stir well to blend.

Using a lightly greased measuring teaspoon to measure the batter and a lightly greased tableware teaspoon to push the batter off the measuring teaspoon, drop the batter for 5 or 6 cookies only, by even teaspoons, 3 inches apart, onto a prepared cookie sheet. Intermittently wash the teaspoons and regrease when the batter begins to stick to the spoons. Bake the cookies for 6 to 7 minutes, until lightly browned. The cookies will spread thinly and bubble during baking. While each batch of cookies is baking, cover the saucepan of remaining batter and place on top of the range (not over heat) to keep the batter warm and soft. If the batter becomes too stiff, heat slightly over medium heat, stirring constantly.

Remove the cookie sheet from the oven and place on a wooden board; let stand 1 minute. While the cookies are still warm and pliable, use a thin spatula to remove one cookie at a time from the cookie sheet and, using your hands, carefully roll it around the wooden dowel. Remove the dowel from the rolled cookie and place the cookie on waxed paper spread on the kitchen counter; let stand until cool. Bake only 5 to 6 cookies at a time and roll them quickly, as they cool rapidly and become impossible to roll without breaking.

When completely cool, store the cookies in an airtight container. Lace Cookies are better the day after baking because they become somewhat drier and more crispy.

MAKES ABOUT 72

VARIATION: Lace Cookies may be left unrolled, in which case, slightly less than 1 teaspoon of batter produces a smaller, more desirably sized flat cookie.

GRACE'S PEANUT CRISPIES

No bake; no fuss.

½ cup sugar
½ cup light corn syrup
½ cup chunky peanut butter
2 cups Rice Krispies cereal

In a small saucepan, place the sugar and syrup; stir to combine. Over low heat, stir the mixture constantly until the sugar dissolves. Remove from the heat. Add the peanut butter; stir to combine. Return to low heat and stir only until the peanut butter completely melts and blends; do not overcook. Remove from the heat. Add the cereal; stir until evenly combined.

Using a 1½-inch trigger scoop (see Note), quickly drop the mixture by even scoops onto waxed paper spread on the kitchen counter. Using your hands, immediately roll each portion into a ball and replace on the waxed paper; let stand until completely cool.

Then, store the cookies in an airtight container.

NOTE: A tablespoon may be substituted.

MAKES ABOUT 30

CRISPY COOKIES

2 cups all-purpose flour
½ teaspoon baking powder
1 teaspoon baking soda
½ teaspoon salt
½ cup vegetable shortening, softened
½ cup (¼ pound) butter or margarine, softened
1 cup granulated sugar
1 cup packed light brown sugar
2 extra-large eggs
2 cups quick-cooking rolled oats, uncooked
2 cups Rice Krispies cereal
1 cup shredded coconut

Preheat the oven to 375° F.

Onto waxed paper, sift together the flour, baking powder, baking soda, and salt; set aside.

In a large mixing bowl, place the vegetable shortening, butter, granulated sugar, and brown sugar; using an electric mixer, cream well on medium-high speed. Add the eggs, one at a time, beating well on medium-high speed after each addition. Add the flour mixture in halves, beating on low speed after each addition only until blended. Add the oats; beat on medium-low speed only until evenly combined.

Add the cereal and coconut; using a mixing spoon, work in until evenly distributed throughout the dough. The dough will be crumbly.

Using a small melon baller, scoop portions of dough from the mixing bowl and roll in the palms of your hands to form ¾-inch-diameter balls. Place the balls of dough, 1½ inches apart, on ungreased cookie sheets. Bake for 8 to 10 minutes, until lightly golden.

Using a thin spatula, place the baked cookies on waxed paper spread on the kitchen counter; let stand until completely cool.

Then, store the cookies in an airtight container.

MAKES ABOUT 108

PEANUT COOKIES

3 cups bread flour
¼ teaspoon baking soda
½ teaspoon salt
¾ cup lard or vegetable shortening, softened
2 cups sugar
¼ cup creamy peanut butter
3 extra-large eggs
1 teaspoon pure vanilla extract
1 cup unsalted peanuts without skins, chopped
¼ cup unsalted peanut halves without skins

Preheat the oven to 350° F.

Onto waxed paper, sift together the flour, baking soda, and salt; set aside.

In a large mixing bowl, place the lard, sugar, and peanut butter; using an electric mixer, beat on medium-high speed until light and fluffy. Add the eggs, one at a time, beating well on medium-high speed after each addition. Add the vanilla; beat on medium-high speed until blended. Add the flour mixture in halves, beating on low speed after each addition only until blended. Add the chopped peanuts; beat on medium speed only until evenly distributed.

Using a 1-inch trigger scoop or melon baller, scoop portions of dough from the mixing bowl and roll in the palms of your hands to form 1-inch-diameter balls. Place the balls of dough, 3 inches apart, on ungreased cookie sheets.

Using the bottom of a dampened, rigid spatula or drinking glass, flatten the dough balls to 1½ inches in diameter. Press a peanut half into the center of each unbaked cookie. Bake for 12 minutes, until lightly golden.

Using a thin spatula, place the baked cookies on waxed paper spread on the kitchen counter; let stand until completely cool.

Then, store the cookies in an airtight container.

MAKES 72

PEANUT BUTTER COOKIES

1 cup all-purpose flour
¾ teaspoon baking soda
¼ teaspoon salt
½ cup vegetable shortening
½ cup granulated sugar
½ cup packed light brown sugar
½ cup creamy peanut butter
1 extra-large egg
½ teaspoon pure vanilla extract

Preheat the oven to 375° F.

Onto waxed paper, sift together the flour, baking soda, and salt; set aside.

In a medium mixing bowl, place the vegetable shortening, granulated sugar, brown sugar, and peanut butter; using an electric mixer, cream well on medium-high speed. Add the egg and vanilla; beat on medium-high speed until light and fluffy. Add the flour mixture; beat on low speed only until blended.

Using a 1-inch trigger scoop or melon baller, scoop portions of dough from the mixing bowl and roll in the palms of your hands to form 1-inch-diameter balls. Place the balls of dough, 2 inches apart, on ungreased cookie sheets.

Using the tines of a table fork, flatten each ball of dough by pressing it twice, at right angles, to form a crisscross pattern (see illustration).

Bake for 8 to 10 minutes, until very lightly browned.

Using a thin spatula, place the baked cookies on waxed paper spread on the kitchen counter; let stand until completely cool.

Then, store the cookies in an airtight container.

MAKES ABOUT 54

CHOCOLATE PEANUT BUTTER BALLS

1 9-ounce package commercial chocolate wafers, rolled finely (2⅓ cups crumbs)
2½ cups powdered sugar, sifted (page 57) (sift after measuring)
1 cup (½ pound) butter
1 12-ounce jar (1⅓ cups) creamy peanut butter
3 11.5-ounce packages milk chocolate chips

Line 2 cookie sheets with waxed paper; set aside.

In a medium mixing bowl, place the chocolate wafer crumbs and powdered sugar; stir to combine; set aside.

In a medium saucepan, melt the butter over low heat. Add the peanut butter. Stir until the peanut butter melts and blends with the butter. Remove from the heat. Add the crumb mixture; stir until thoroughly combined. Cover the saucepan and refrigerate the mixture until cooled to room temperature (about 35 minutes).

Then, using a 1-inch trigger scoop or melon baller, scoop portions of the mixture from the saucepan and roll in the palms of your hands to form 1-inch-diameter balls. Place the balls of dough on the prepared cookie sheets; refrigerate, uncovered, for 30 minutes.

Then, place the chocolate chips in the top of a double boiler. Place the top of the double boiler over hot (not simmering) water in the bottom pan. Stir until the chocolate chips completely melt and the chocolate is smooth.

Remove the cookie sheets of rolled balls from the refrigerator. Using a candy-dipping fork or a table fork, dip the rolled balls in the chocolate, one at a time, to coat. Replace the coated balls on the waxed paper–lined cookie sheets. Leave the top of the double boiler over hot (not simmering) water in the bottom pan during the dipping process to retain the proper consistency of the chocolate.

Refrigerate the coated balls until the chocolate hardens.

MAKES ABOUT 108

SNICKERDOODLES

Snickerdoodles: a nonsense name for no-nonsense cookies with wide taste appeal. When you bake them, the surface—covered with a cinnamon-sugar mixture—cracks, giving Snickerdoodles a distinct identity. Research reveals that these cookies originated in New England in the 1800's, with nuts, raisins, and currants among the ingredients then.

2¾ cups all-purpose flour
1 teaspoon baking soda
½ teaspoon salt
2 teaspoons cream of tartar
2 tablespoons sugar
2 teaspoons ground cinnamon
½ cup (¼ pound) butter, softened
½ cup vegetable shortening, softened
1½ cups sugar
2 extra-large eggs

Preheat the oven to 400°F.

Onto waxed paper, sift together the flour, baking soda, salt, and cream of tartar; set aside. In a small sauce dish, place 2 tablespoons sugar and the cinnamon; stir well to combine; set aside.

In a large mixing bowl, place the butter, vegetable shortening, and 1½ cups sugar; using an electric mixer, cream well on medium-high speed. Add the eggs, one at a time, beating well on medium-high speed after each addition. Continue beating on medium-high speed until light and fluffy. Add the flour mixture in halves, beating on low speed after each addition only until blended.

Using a 1½-inch trigger scoop, measure level scoops of dough from the mixing bowl and roll in the palms of your hands to form balls (see Note). Place the balls of dough on waxed paper spread on the kitchen counter. Roll the balls in the cinnamon mixture to coat, and then place them, 2 inches apart, on ungreased cookie sheets (12 cookies to a 12 × 15½-inch cookie sheet). Bake for 9 minutes. The cookies will flatten during baking. The tops will have a cracked, cut glass appearance when baked.

Using a thin spatula, place the baked cookies on clean waxed paper spread on the kitchen counter; let stand until completely cool.

Then, store the cookies in an airtight container.

NOTE: If a 1½-inch trigger scoop is not available, shape tablespoonsful of dough into balls the size of table tennis balls.

MAKES ABOUT 48

WHOLE-WHEAT OATMEAL COOKIES

1¼ cups whole-wheat flour
½ teaspoon baking soda
½ cup (¼ pound) butter or margarine, softened
1 cup sugar
1 extra-large egg
½ teaspoon pure vanilla extract
½ cup quick-cooking rolled oats, uncooked
½ cup packed raisins
¾ cup broken English walnuts

Preheat the oven to 375°F.

Onto waxed paper, sift together flour and soda; set aside.

In a medium mixing bowl, place the butter and sugar; using an electric mixer, cream well on medium-high speed. Add the egg; beat on medium-high speed until blended. Add the vanilla; continue beating on medium-high speed until fluffy. Add the flour mixture; beat on low speed only until blended. Add the oats; beat on medium speed only until combined. Add the raisins and walnuts; using a mixing spoon, stir and fold in until evenly combined.

Using a 1-inch trigger scoop or melon baller, scoop portions of dough from the mixing bowl and roll in the palms of your hands to form 1-inch-diameter balls. Place the balls of dough, 2 inches apart, on ungreased cookie sheets. Using a small, rigid spatula, flatten the balls of dough to ¼-inch thickness. Bake for 8 to 10 minutes, until lightly golden.

Using a thin spatula, place the baked cookies on waxed paper spread on the kitchen counter; let stand until completely cool.

Then, store the cookies in an airtight container.

MAKES ABOUT 36

VARIATION: For 24 large cookies, increase the diameter of the dough balls to about 1¼ inches.

JERRY'S GINGERSNAPS

One of the ingredients called for in this recipe is unsulphured, light (or mild-flavored) molasses. Unsulphured molasses is molasses processed without the use of sulphur. For more information about molasses, see the headnote for Frosted Molasses Cookies (page 616).

2 cups all-purpose flour
2 teaspoons baking soda
¼ teaspoon salt
1 teaspoon ground cinnamon
½ teaspoon ground ginger
½ teaspoon ground cloves
¼ teaspoon ground allspice
1 cup sugar
¾ cup vegetable oil
1 extra-large egg
¼ cup unsulphured, light (mild-flavored) molasses
½ cup sugar

Preheat the oven to 375° F. Using Special Grease (page 56), grease 2 or 3 cookie sheets; set aside.

Onto waxed paper, sift together the flour, baking soda, salt, cinnamon, ginger, cloves, and allspice; set aside.

In a large mixing bowl, place 1 cup sugar and the vegetable oil; using an electric mixer, beat well on medium-high speed. Add the egg; beat on medium-high speed until blended. Add the molasses; beat on medium-high speed until completely blended. Add the flour mixture; beat on low speed only until blended; set aside.

Place ½ cup sugar in a small sauce dish; set aside.

Using a 1-inch trigger scoop or melon baller dipped into sugar, scoop even portions of dough from the mixing bowl and roll into 1-inch-diameter balls using lightly sugared hands. Roll the balls of dough in the sauce dish of sugar to coat, and then place them, 2 inches apart, on the prepared cookie sheets. Dip the trigger scoop or melon baller into sugar before scooping each portion of dough. Bake for 8 to 9 minutes, until set. The tops of the cookies will be cracked.

Remove the cookies from the oven and let stand on the cookie sheets 1 minute. Then, using a thin spatula, place the cookies on waxed paper spread on the kitchen counter; let stand until completely cool.

Then, store the cookies in an airtight container.

MAKES ABOUT 66

UNBAKED WHEAT GERM BALLS

A bounty of different-flavored, healthful wheat germ cookies may be made in a wink from the basic recipe that follows. Three flavor versions are given after the basic recipe, and creative cooks can come up with many more to suit their own taste fancies. It's easy—just follow the basic recipe, using 1 cup of dried or candied fruits and/or nuts plus complementary flavoring, and then roll the Wheat Germ Balls in a compatible topping.

Wheat germ is the small embryo within a kernel of wheat from which the grain sprouts. Untoasted (raw) wheat germ, as used in this recipe, is an extremely rich source of vitamins E and B_6. Untoasted wheat germ also contains large quantities of protein and important minerals and vitamins, and it is high in fiber. Wheat germ should be refrigerated after it is opened. A quart glass jar with a lid makes a good container for storing it. For another recipe using untoasted wheat germ, see Granola (page 84).

Follow the Basic Recipe to make the various-flavored Wheat Germ Balls given below.

BASIC RECIPE
2 cups untoasted (raw) wheat germ
Filling ingredients (from selected recipe, below)
⅓ cup whole milk
1¼ cups sugar
¼ cup plus 2 tablespoons (6 tablespoons) margarine
Flavoring ingredient (from selected recipe, below)
Topping ingredient (from selected recipe, below)

In a medium mixing bowl, place the wheat germ and filling ingredient(s); stir to combine; set aside.

In a small saucepan, place the milk and sugar; stir to combine. Add the margarine. Over medium-high heat, bring the milk mixture to a rolling boil, stirring constantly. Pour the milk mixture over the wheat germ mixture. Add the flavoring ingredient. Stir until the mixture is well combined.

Drop the mixture by tablespoonsful onto waxed paper spread on the kitchen counter; let stand until cool.

Then, in the palms of your hands, roll each mound of cooled dough into a ball about 1 inch in diameter and replace on the waxed paper.

Sprinkle the topping ingredient over a clean piece of waxed paper. Roll the balls of dough in the topping until well covered.

Store the wheat germ balls in an airtight container for at least 12 hours before serving.

MAKES ABOUT 24

Unbaked Wheat Germ Raisin Balls

FILLING
½ cup raisins
½ cup broken pecans
1 tablespoon unsweetened cocoa powder

FLAVORING
½ teaspoon pure vanilla extract

TOPPING
½ cup powdered sugar

Follow the Basic Recipe, above.

Unbaked Wheat Germ Apricot-Nut Balls

FILLING
1 6-ounce package (about 1 packed cup) dried apricots, diced (page 22) finely
½ teaspoon ground cinnamon
⅛ teaspoon ground nutmeg

FLAVORING
½ teaspoon pure vanilla extract

TOPPING
¾ cup finely chopped pecans

Follow the Basic Recipe, above.

Unbaked Wheat Germ
Pineapple-Coconut Balls

FILLING

8 ounces (1 cup) candied pineapple slices chopped finely

FLAVORING

2 teaspoons white rum *or* 1/2 teaspoon pure vanilla extract

TOPPING

1 cup shredded coconut

Follow the Basic Recipe, above.

Rolled Cookies

OLD-FASHIONED SUGAR COOKIES

3 cups sifted all-purpose flour (sift before measuring)
1/2 teaspoon baking soda
1/2 teaspoon salt
1 cup (1/2 pound) butter, softened
1 1/2 cups sugar
2 extra-large eggs
1 teaspoon pure vanilla extract
3 tablespoons homemade sour cream (page 58) (make 1/4 cup sour cream; use only 3 tablespoons)
Sugar for top of cookies

Onto waxed paper, sift together the flour, baking soda, and salt; set aside.

In a large mixing bowl, place the butter and sugar; using an electric mixer, cream well on medium-high speed. Add the eggs, one at a time, beating well on medium-high speed after each addition. Add the vanilla; beat on medium-high speed until light and fluffy. Add the sour cream; beat on medium speed until blended. Add the flour mixture in thirds, beating on low speed after each addition only until blended.

Divide the dough into thirds; wrap each third in plastic wrap and refrigerate at least 2 hours.

Preheat the oven to 400° F.

Remove 1 package of dough from the refrigerator. If the dough is too stiff to roll, let it stand, briefly, at room temperature in the plastic wrap until it is pliable. On a well-floured pastry cloth, using a stockinet-covered, then floured rolling pin (page 54), roll the dough to 3/16-inch thickness.

Using a 2-inch round cutter dipped in flour, cut out the cookies. After each cut, wipe the excess dough off the cutter and redip it in flour. Using a thin spatula, place the cutout cookies, 2 inches apart, on ungreased cookie sheets. Gather the remaining dough on the pastry cloth into a ball; rewrap it in the plastic wrap and refrigerate. Sprinkle each cutout cookie with sugar. Bake for 5 minutes, until the edge of the cookies is lightly golden.

Remove the cookies from the oven and let stand on the cookie sheets until cooled slightly. Then, using a thin spatula, place the cookies on waxed paper spread on the kitchen counter; let stand until completely cool.

Repeat the procedure with the remaining 2 packages of dough. Then, combine all the remaining dough from the 3 packages and continue making cookies until all the dough is used.

Store the cookies in an airtight container.

MAKES ABOUT 84

GINGERBREAD PEOPLE

2¾ cups sifted all-purpose flour (sift before measuring)
1 teaspoon baking soda
½ teaspoon salt
1 teaspoon ground ginger
1½ teaspoons ground cinnamon
½ cup (¼ pound) butter, softened
½ cup sugar
½ cup light (mild-flavored) molasses
½ cup buttermilk
Currants
½ recipe Confectioners' Frosting (page 579)

Onto waxed paper, sift together the flour, baking soda, salt, ginger, and cinnamon; set aside.

In a large mixing bowl, place the butter and sugar; using an electric mixer, cream well on medium-high speed. Add the molasses; beat well on medium-high speed. Add, alternately, the flour mixture in thirds, and the buttermilk in halves, beating on low speed after each addition only until blended.

Divide the dough in half; wrap each half in plastic wrap and refrigerate at least 2 hours.

Preheat the oven to 375° F. Grease 2 or 3 cookie sheets (page 589); set aside.

Remove 1 package of dough from the refrigerator. On a floured pastry cloth, using a stockinet-covered, then floured rolling pin (page 54), roll the dough to ¼-inch thickness.

Using a gingerbread person cookie cutter dipped in flour, cut out the cookies. After each cut, wipe the excess dough off the cutter and redip it in flour. Using a thin spatula, place the cutout cookies, 2 inches apart, on the prepared cookie sheets. Gather the remaining dough on the pastry cloth into a ball; rewrap it in the plastic wrap and refrigerate. Decorate part of the cookies with currants replicating eyes, noses, and buttons. Bake for 7 minutes, until the edges just begin to brown. Do not overbake.

Using a thin spatula, place the baked cookies on waxed paper spread on the kitchen counter; let stand until completely cool.

Repeat the procedure with the remaining ½ of the cookie dough. Then, combine all the remaining dough and continue making cookies until all the dough is used; refrigerate the dough intermittently if it becomes too soft.

When the cookies have completely cooled, decorate them imaginatively with the Confectioners' Frosting, using a decorating bag fit with small round tip number 2 (page 383). Some suggestions: pipe hair, eyes, noses, mouths, shirt collars and cuffs, neckties, belts and buckles, trouser cuffs, skirts with ruffled trim, and short-sleeved blouses; pipe names of family members and friends on Gingerbread People (page 388). Let the cookies stand until the frosting sets.

Store the cookies, single layer, separated by plastic wrap, in an airtight container.

MAKES ABOUT 36 5-INCH-TALL GINGERBREAD PEOPLE

CUTOUT COOKIES

Select cookie cutters in patterns appropriate for various holidays and occasions, and then have fun turning out festive, decorated cookies using this basic cutout cookie recipe. See To Decorate Cutout Cookies at the end of the recipe for general decorating instructions and suggestions. Let your imagination take it from there.

4 cups cake flour
1 teaspoon baking soda
¾ teaspoon salt
½ cup vegetable shortening, softened
½ cup (¼ pound) butter, softened
1 cup sugar
2 extra-large eggs
1 teaspoon pure vanilla extract
¼ cup whole milk

Onto waxed paper, sift together the flour, baking soda, and salt; set aside.

In a large mixing bowl, place the vegetable shortening, butter, and sugar; using an electric mixer, cream well on medium-high speed. Add the eggs, one at a time, beating well on medium-high speed after each addition. Add the vanilla; beat on medium-high speed until light and fluffy. Add, alternately, the flour mixture in thirds, and the milk in halves, beating on low speed after each addition only until blended.

Divide the dough into thirds; wrap each third in plastic wrap and refrigerate at least 2 hours.

Preheat the oven to 350° F. Oil lightly 2 or 3 cookie sheets; set aside.

Remove 1 package of dough from the refrigerator. On a well-floured pastry cloth, using a stockinet-covered, then floured rolling pin (page 54), roll the dough to ⅛-inch thickness.

Dip the cutting edge of the cookie cutter of choice in flour; cut out the cookies. After each cut, wipe the excess dough off the cutter and redip it in flour. Using a thin spatula, place the cutout cookies, 2 inches apart, on the prepared cookie sheets. Gather the remaining dough on the pastry cloth into a ball; rewrap it in the plastic wrap and refrigerate. Bake the cookies for 9 to 10 minutes, just until set. The bottoms will be pale or a very pale golden color. Do not overbake.

Using a thin spatula, place the baked cookies on waxed paper spread on the kitchen counter; let stand until completely cool.

Repeat the procedure with the remaining 2 packages of dough. Then, combine all the remaining dough from the 3 packages and continue making cookies until all the dough is used.

Store the cookies in an airtight container.

MAKES ABOUT 54 3-INCH CUTOUT COOKIES

TO DECORATE CUTOUT COOKIES

- Frost baked Cutout Cookies with Confectioners' Frosting (page 579) tinted in one or more colors of choice. Immediately after frosting the cookies, before the frosting dries, decorate them with colored sugar, nonpareils (page 24), cinnamon imperials (candy red hots), nuts, candied fruits, or other edible decorations.

- To decorate *unfrosted* Cutout Cookies, sprinkle or place colored sugar, nonpareils, nuts, etc. on the cookies before baking.

VALENTINE CUTOUT COOKIES

1 recipe Confectioners' Frosting (page 579)
Red and pink paste food coloring
1 recipe Cutout Cookies (page 634) made with a 3-inch, heart-shaped cookie cutter
½ recipe Cake Decorators' White Icing (page 576)

Tint ⅓ of the Confectioners' Frosting red and ⅓ of the frosting pink; leave the remaining ⅓ of the frosting untinted (white). Using the Confectioners' Frosting and a small, narrow, tapered spatula, frost ⅓ of the baked, heart-shaped Cutout Cookies with red frosting, ⅓ with pink frosting, and ⅓ with white frosting; let stand until the frosting sets.

Tint ⅓ of the Cake Decorators' White Icing red; leave the remaining ⅔ of the icing untinted (white). Fill one decorating bag with the red Cake Decorators' Icing and one decorating bag with the untinted Cake Decorators' White Icing. Using medium-small open-star tip number 16 (page 383), outline the frosting on the cookies with a shell border (page 389), piping a white border on the red- and pink-frosted cookies, and a red border on the white-frosted cookies. Let the cookies stand.

Using medium petal tip number 61 and a stick, pipe small white roses and red roses (page 393).

Place a rose in the center of each cookie, placing a white rose on red- and pink-frosted cookies, and a red rose on white- and pink-frosted cookies. (To attach the roses to the cookies, use small round tip number 3 to place a small dot of frosting in the center of each heart; then, position a rose on the dot of frosting on each heart to hold the rose in place. Pipe the dots 4 cookies at a time, and in the same color of frosting as the roses to be placed thereon.) Let the cookies stand until the frosting sets.

Then, store the cookies, single layer, in airtight containers.

MAKES ABOUT 54

SPRINGERLE

These beautiful, but very firm, traditional German Christmas cookies, imprinted with intricate Christmas designs and scenes, are often dunked in coffee when eaten. Sometimes they are allowed to become extremely dry and are drilled with tiny holes for hanging them on the Christmas tree.

3½ cups all-purpose flour
¼ teaspoon baking powder
⅛ teaspoon salt
4 extra-large eggs, room temperature
2 cups sugar
1 tablespoon finely grated lemon rind
    (page 47) (rind of about 3 lemons)
3 tablespoons anise seed
Additional sifted all-purpose flour
2 teaspoons anise seed (for storage
    container)

THE FIRST DAY: Onto waxed paper, sift together 3½ cups flour, baking powder, and salt; set aside.

Place the eggs in a large mixing bowl. Using an electric mixer, beat the eggs on high speed 8 minutes until thick. While continuing to beat on high speed, very gradually add the sugar (8 minutes additional beating time). Add the lemon rind; beat on high speed until evenly combined. Add the flour mixture in thirds, beating on low speed after each addition only until blended. The dough will be very thick and pasty. Cover the bowl and refrigerate the mixture 1 hour.

Grease lightly 3 cookie sheets. Sprinkle each greased cookie sheet evenly with 1 tablespoon anise seed; set aside.

On a lightly floured pastry cloth (page 54), knead the dough (page 23) about 5 minutes until pliable and smooth, kneading in additional sifted flour if necessary to make the dough stiff enough to hold the molded designs. Using a lightly floured rolling pin, roll the dough to ⅜-inch thickness. Sprinkle sifted flour lightly over the rolled dough. Using your fingers, spread the flour evenly and thinly over the surface of the

dough; let stand. Flour individual, wooden springerle molds; tap the molds to remove the excess flour. Press the molds very firmly into the rolled dough to imprint designs (see Note). Do not remove any excess flour from the tops of the cookies.

Using a sharp, thin-bladed knife dipped in flour, carefully cut out the cookies. Clean the knife intermittently when the dough begins to stick to it; then, redip it in flour. Using a thin spatula, place the cookies, 1 inch apart, on the prepared cookie sheets. Gather any remaining dough and knead briefly; reroll, impress designs, and cut. Repeat the procedure until all the dough is used. Let the unbaked cookies stand, *uncovered,* at room temperature, 24 hours to dry.

NOTE: A floured, carved Springerle rolling pin may also be used to imprint the cookies; however, the impressions made in the dough using the special rolling pin are usually not as precise as those achieved using individual molds. One of my prize culinary possessions is an antique German Springerle rolling pin, given to me by my dear German friend, Gertrud Acksen (mother of Siegfried Hoerner, one of those to whom this cookbook is dedicated). Gertrud also gave me several lovely, modern, individual Springerle molds which she purchased in Stuttgart.

24 HOURS LATER: The surface of the cookies should be dry and quite hard.

Preheat the oven to 300° F.

Using a soft, ½-inch watercolor brush, brush a small amount of water on the bottom of each cookie, taking extreme care not to get *any* water on the top of the cookies. Replace the cookies on the cookie sheets. Bake the cookies for 15 minutes, until a faint straw color. (The cookies will be nearly white.)

Using a thin spatula, place the baked cookies on wire cookie racks. Brush the cookies lightly with a dry, soft brush to remove any excess flour; let stand until completely cool.

Sprinkle 2 teaspoons anise seed over the bottom of an airtight container (such as a tin); store the cookies in the container. (The additional anise seed in the storage container will enhance the anise flavor of the cookies.) Allow Springerle to season at least 1 week before serving.

MAKES ABOUT 48 TO 60, DEPENDING UPON THE SIZE OF THE COOKIES

ZIMTSTERNE
Cinnamon Stars

A German Christmas cookie.

2 cups slivered blanched almonds
1 *tablespoon* ground cinnamon
1 teaspoon finely grated lemon rind
   (page 47) (rind of about 1 lemon)
⅓ cup egg whites (about 2 extra-large egg
   whites*), room temperature
Dash of salt
2 cups powdered sugar, sifted (page 57)
   (sift after measuring)
½ cup to 1 cup powdered sugar, sifted
   (sift after measuring)

*About 3 large egg whites.

In a food processor, process the almonds for *a few seconds* until ground. Be careful not to over-process, reducing the nuts to butter. Place the ground almonds in a medium mixing bowl. Add the cinnamon; stir to combine. Add the lemon rind; stir to combine. Cover the bowl and set aside.

In a medium mixing bowl, place the egg whites and salt; using an electric mixer, beat on high speed until soft peaks hold. While continuing to beat on high speed, very gradually add 2 cups powdered sugar; beat well on high speed.

Measure ½ cup of the egg white mixture and place in a small container; cover tightly and set aside. Add the almond mixture the to remaining egg white mixture; using a small mixing spoon, fold in until combined. Cover and let stand 30 minutes to allow time for the almonds to absorb some of the moisture.

Meanwhile, line 3 cookie sheets with the parchment baking paper; set aside. Dust well with powdered sugar a pastry cloth and stockinet–covered rolling pin (page 54).

Preheat the oven to 325° F.

Turn the almond mixture (dough) onto the pastry cloth. Dust your hands with powdered sugar and knead (page 23) just enough powdered sugar (about ½ cup to 1 cup) into the dough to make it stiff enough to roll and cut. Roll the dough to ¼-inch thickness. Avoid rolling the dough any thicker, as this may cause the cookies to lose their shape during baking.

Using a 2-inch star cutter dipped in powdered sugar, cut out the cookies. After each cut, wipe the excess dough off the cutter and redip in powdered sugar. Using a thin spatula, place the cutout cookies, 1 inch apart, on the prepared cookie sheets. Gather the remaining dough on the pastry cloth into a ball; reroll and cut out additional cookies. Repeat the procedure until all the dough is used. Cover the cutout cookies with plastic wrap after each cookie sheet is filled.

Using a small, narrow, tapered spatula, frost the cookies with a thin layer of the reserved egg white mixture. To frost each cookie, use the spatula to place a small amount of the egg white mixture in the center of the cookie. Using a circular motion with the spatula, spread the mixture to form a small circle. Then, pull the mixture toward the points of the star. Replace the frosted cookies on the lined cookie sheets. Bake for 12 to 15 minutes. When done, Zimtsterne should be just slightly brown on the outside and chewy on the inside.

Using a thin spatula, place the baked cookies on wire cookie racks; let stand until completely cool.

Then, store the cookies in an airtight container.

MAKES ABOUT 66

PINWHEEL COOKIES

Pinwheel cookies are made in one of two ways: (1) rolled-out dough is spread with a filling, after which the dough (with filling) is rolled and then sliced into cookies ready for baking; or (2) two or three layers of rolled-out dough, each in a different color and sometimes a different flavor, are stacked, after which they are rolled together and then sliced into cookies ready for baking. The pinwheel design of the cookies created by either of these techniques stays intact after baking.

The recipes that follow use the second technique for making three different styles of stacked-dough pinwheel cookies: (1) the primary recipe makes two-layer pinwheel cookies with color as the only variation between the layers; (2) the Chocolate Pinwheels recipe makes two-layer pinwheel cookies with one of the layers chocolate flavored (and chocolate colored); and (3) the Triple-Layer Pinwheels recipe makes attractive three-colored cookies, with the option of flavoring one of the layers with chocolate.

3 cups sifted all-purpose flour (sift before measuring)
½ teaspoon baking powder
¾ teaspoon salt
1 cup (½ pound) butter, softened
1 cup sugar
2 extra-large eggs
2 teaspoons pure vanilla extract
Pink paste food coloring*

*Any color of paste food coloring may be substituted.

AFTERNOON OF THE FIRST DAY: Onto waxed paper, sift together flour, baking powder, and salt; set aside.

In a large mixing bowl, place the butter and sugar; using an electric mixer, cream well on medium-high speed. Add the eggs, one at a time, beating well on medium-high speed after each addition. Add the vanilla; beat on medium-high speed until light and fluffy. Add the flour mixture in halves, beating on low speed after each addition only until blended.

Divide the dough in half in the mixing bowl.

Remove ½ of the dough from the mixing bowl and wrap it in plastic wrap; refrigerate. Using a toothpick, add a small amount of food coloring to the remaining ½ of the dough; using the electric mixer, beat on low speed only until evenly tinted. Wrap the tinted dough in plastic wrap; refrigerate. Refrigerate all the dough 1 hour.

Then, remove the package of untinted dough from the refrigerator. On well-floured waxed paper, using a stockinet-covered, then floured rolling pin (page 54), roll the dough into a 10 × 14-inch rectangle. If necessary, patch the dough during rolling to achieve an accurately sized rectangle. Slide the waxed paper with the rolled dough onto a cookie sheet; cover it with plastic wrap and refrigerate.

Repeat the rolling and refrigerating procedure using the tinted dough. Refrigerate all the rolled dough 45 minutes.

Then, remove the plastic wrap covering the dough on both cookie sheets. Quickly invert the tinted dough on top of the untinted dough; peel the waxed paper off the tinted dough. Using the rolling pin, very lightly roll the top of the layered dough to slightly seal the layers.

Using a sharp, thin-bladed knife dipped in flour, cut the rectangle of dough in half widthwise, dividing the layered dough into two 7 × 10-inch rectangles. Using floured hands, tightly roll each rectangle, jelly-roll fashion, from the 7-inch side of the rectangles. Lift the waxed paper under the dough to assist in rolling it forward. (Do not roll the waxed paper into the dough.) After rolling each rectangle of dough, carefully press the seam to seal.

Wrap each 7-inch-long roll tightly in plastic wrap. Very lightly roll each plastic-covered roll on the counter to achieve even circles of dough; refrigerate overnight.

THE NEXT DAY: Preheat the oven to 400° F.

On a floured board, remove the plastic wrap from the rolls of cookie dough. Using a sharp, thin-bladed knife dipped in flour, slice the cookies a scant ¼ inch thick. Intermittently wipe the knife and redip it in flour. Place the sliced cookies, 1½ inches apart, on ungreased cookie sheets. Bake for about 7 minutes. Do not allow the cookies to brown, as browning will detract from the colors of the cookies.

Using a thin spatula, place the baked cookies on waxed paper spread on the kitchen counter; let stand until completely cool.

Then, store the cookies in an airtight container.

MAKES ABOUT 66

CHOCOLATE PINWHEELS: Place 1 ounce (1 square) semisweet chocolate in a tiny saucepan. Hold the tiny pan over (not touching) low simmering water in a small saucepan until the chocolate melts, stirring intermittently. Remove the tiny pan from the heat; set aside. Follow the Pinwheels Cookies recipe, above, substituting the melted chocolate for the pink paste food coloring (add it to the second ½ of the dough).

TRIPLE-LAYER PINWHEELS: Follow the Pinwheel Cookies recipe, above, dividing the dough into thirds rather than halves. Tint 2 or 3 of the thirds of the dough. If one of the thirds is to be chocolate, use ½ ounce (½ square) semisweet chocolate and follow the procedure in the Chocolate Pinwheels recipe.

Roll each third of the dough into a 10 × 10-inch rectangle. Stack all 3 rectangles of the dough together. Do not cut the layered dough in half before rolling; in other words, make only one pinwheel roll of dough.

SCOTCH SHORTBREAD

Scotland has given us this wonderfully rich, buttery cookie which in that country was traditionally served on Christmas and New Year's Eve (there called Hogmanay). In American cooking nomenclature, Scotch Shortbread is definitely a cookie and does not remotely resemble bread, as its name implies. Shortbread is made with three ingredients: flour, sugar, and much butter (margarine won't do). Sometimes a scant amount of salt is added. I have chosen not to use salt but have taken the liberty of adding just a bit of baking powder which I think makes the crisp texture of these tender cookies even lighter and more delicate.

Traditionally, shortbread was made one of two ways: (1) the dough was cut into round cookies which were notched on the edges to look like sun rays, or (2) the dough was pressed into a large, round, engraved mold and after baking, the warm shortbread was cut into serving-sized wedges. Nowadays, Scotch Shortbread is made in all sorts of shapes, but I like making it in the shape of rectangular cookies, and adding a bit of tradition by imprinting a fluted design on the top of each cookie using the side of a fluted garnishing cutter.

2 cups sifted all-purpose flour (sift before measuring)
¼ teaspoon baking powder
1 cup (½ pound) butter, softened
½ cup powdered sugar

Onto waxed paper, sift together the flour and baking powder; set aside.

In a medium mixing bowl, place the butter and powdered sugar; using an electric mixer, beat on medium-high speed until *very* fluffy. Add the flour mixture; beat on low speed only until blended. Wrap the dough in plastic wrap and refrigerate about 2 hours.

Preheat the oven to 350° F.

Remove the dough from the refrigerator. If the dough is too stiff to roll, let it stand at room temperature in the plastic wrap for a few minutes. On a floured pastry cloth, using a stockinet-covered, then floured rolling pin (page 54), roll the dough to ⅜-inch thickness.

Using a ruler to measure, and a sharp, thin-bladed knife dipped in flour, cut the dough into precise 1¼ × 2-inch cookies. Using a small, thin spatula, carefully separate the cookies. Then, using the wide side of a floured, fluted garnishing cutter (see illustration, page 128), impress a wavy surface on the top of each cookie.

Using a thin spatula, place the cookies, 1½ inches apart, on ungreased cookie sheets. Gather the remaining dough into a ball, reroll, cut additional cookies, and impress the tops until all the dough is used. Bake the cookies for about 13 minutes. The cookies should be light in color.

(Recipe continues on next page)

Using a thin spatula, place the baked cookies on waxed paper spread on the kitchen counter. Handle carefully, as Scotch Shortbread breaks easily. Let them stand until completely cool.

Then, store the cookies in an airtight container.

MAKES ABOUT 24

DESIGNER FILLED COOKIES

These filled cookies are basically two cookies pressed together around the edge to contain a filling of conserve, mincemeat, or jam. The filling shows through a small round-, star-, or other-shaped opening cut out of the center of the top cookie.

4½ cups all-purpose flour
1½ teaspoons baking soda
½ teaspoon salt
1½ cups (¾ pound) butter, softened
2 cups sugar
4 extra-large eggs
2½ teaspoons pure vanilla extract
2 cups home-canned Rhubarb-Strawberry Conserve (page 761) or home-canned Brandied Mincemeat (page 726) or any home-canned or commercially canned conserve or jam of choice
¼ cup sugar for decoration

Onto waxed paper, sift together the flour, baking soda, and salt; set aside.

In a large mixing bowl, place the butter and 2 cups sugar; using an electric mixer, cream well on medium-high speed. Add the eggs, one at a time, beating well on medium-high speed after each addition. Add the vanilla; continue beating on medium-high speed until fluffy. Add the flour mixture in thirds, beating on low speed after each addition only until blended.

Divide the dough into fourths; wrap each fourth in plastic wrap and refrigerate at least 4 hours or overnight.

Preheat the oven to 375° F.

Remove 1 package of dough from the refrigerator. On a well-floured pastry cloth, using a stockinet-covered, then floured rolling pin (page 54), roll the dough to ⅛-inch thickness.

Using a 2¼-inch round cutter dipped in flour, cut out the cookie bottoms. After each cut, wipe the excess dough off the cutter and redip it in flour. Using a thin spatula, place the cutout cookie bottoms, 2 inches apart, on an ungreased cookie sheet. Gather the remaining dough on the pastry cloth into a ball; rewrap it in the plastic wrap and refrigerate.

Place ½ teaspoon conserve, mincemeat, or jam in the center of each cutout cookie bottom; set aside.

Remove another package of dough from the refrigerator and roll it to ⅛-inch thickness.

Using the 2¼-inch round cutter dipped in flour, cut out the cookie tops, leaving them on the pastry cloth. Then, using a floured ¾-inch round cutter (or any other small cutter, such as a scalloped or star-shaped cutter), make a cut in the center of each cutout cookie top. Using the spatula, place the cookie tops (minus the cutout centers) over the filled cookie bottoms. Using your fingers, lightly press the outside edge of the cookie tops to seal, maintaining the round shape of the cookies. Gather the remaining dough on the pastry cloth into a ball; rewrap it in the plastic wrap and refrigerate. Bake the cookies for 9 minutes. The edge of the cookies will be very lightly golden.

Using a thin spatula, place the baked cookies on waxed paper spread on the kitchen counter; let stand until completely cool.

Repeat the procedure with the remaining 2 packages of dough. Then, combine all the remaining dough and continue making cookies until all the dough is used.

Sprinkle a tiny amount of sugar around the top edge of the cool cookies, being careful not to sprinkle any sugar on the filling. Using a small, soft, watercolor brush, spread the sugar evenly around the top surface of each cookie.

Store the cookies in a loose container.

MAKES ABOUT 84

CHRISTMAS DESIGNER FILLED COOKIES: Follow the Designer Filled Cookies recipe, above, using a 2½-inch star cutter and a 1-inch round, tiny-scalloped cutter to cut the cookies. Fill the cookies with any red-colored jam or conserve.

CREAM-FILLED PASTRY FLUFFS

Tint the cream filling of these dainty sandwich cookies in a soft, pastel shade to match your tea table, or make them in a color and flavor to complement selected fruit or ice cream for a nice party dessert. See Variations at the end of the recipe for several color/flavor suggestions.

¾ cup (¼ pound plus 4 tablespoons) butter
2 cups all-purpose flour
1 teaspoon salt
½ cup plus 2 teaspoons half-and-half
3 tablespoons sugar
Cream Filling (recipe, below)

Preheat the oven to 375° F.

Remove the butter from the refrigerator and let stand 5 minutes before use in the recipe.

Onto waxed paper, sift together the flour and salt. Place the flour mixture in a large mixing bowl. Using a knife, cut the butter into approximately tablespoon-sized pieces and drop into the bowl containing the flour mixture. Using a pastry blender, cut the butter into the flour mixture until the mixture is the texture of very coarse cornmeal.

Tilt the mixing bowl and gently shake the flour mixture to one side of the bowl. Sprinkle 1 to 2 tablespoons of the half-and-half over the mixture; using a table fork, lightly rake the moistened portion of the mixture to the other side of the bowl. Repeat the procedure until all the half-and-half has been added.

With floured hands, gather the pastry into a ball and place it on a floured pastry cloth. Using a stockinet-covered, then lightly floured rolling pin (page 54), roll the pastry to ⅛-inch thickness.

Using a 2-inch round, tiny-scalloped cookie cutter dipped in flour, cut the cookies. Using a small, thin spatula, carefully place the cookies, 1 inch apart, on an ungreased cookie sheet. Gather the remaining pastry on the pastry cloth into a ball; reroll and cut additional cookies. Repeat the procedure until all the pastry is used.

Using a table fork, deeply prick each cookie 3 times in 3 neat, parallel rows to form a square design. Using your fingers, sprinkle the cookies lightly with sugar. Bake for 10 minutes. Remove the cookies from the oven before they brown.

Using a thin spatula, carefully place the cookies on wire cookie racks; let stand until completely cool.

Then, using a small, narrow, tapered spatula, spread a small amount of the Cream Filling on the non-sugar-glazed side of ½ of the cookies. Cover the filled cookies with the remaining ½ of the cookies, sugar-glazed side up, to make sandwiches. Let the cookies stand on the wire cookie racks until the filling sets.

Then, store the cookies in a loose container.

MAKES ABOUT 36

Cream Filling

1 cup powdered sugar, sifted (page 57) (sift after measuring)
1 tablespoon plus 1 teaspoon butter, melted
2 teaspoons half-and-half
½ teaspoon clear vanilla
12 drops peppermint extract
1 drop green liquid food coloring

In a small mixing bowl, place the powdered sugar, butter, half-and-half, vanilla, peppermint extract, and food coloring. Using an electric mixer, beat the mixture on medium-high speed only until blended and smooth.

VARIATIONS
- Substitute pink paste food coloring for the green liquid food coloring.

(Recipe continues on next page)

- To make Vanilla Cream Filling, increase the clear vanilla to ¾ teaspoon, and eliminate the peppermint extract and green liquid food coloring.

- To make Lemon Cream Filling, substitute lemon extract and yellow liquid food coloring for the peppermint extract and green liquid food coloring.

- To make Orange Cream Filling, substitute orange extract and orange paste food coloring for the peppermint extract and green liquid food coloring.

Refrigerator Cookies

TUTTI-FRUTTI ROLLS

This recipe combines candied fruits, marshmallows, and pecans in rich cookies which resemble stained-glass windows. Pass a small plate of these small, candylike tidbits for your wintertime dinner guests to nibble on while they sip coffee and chat at the end of the meal.

1⅓ cups finely rolled graham cracker crumbs (about 18 graham cracker squares), divided
¼ teaspoon ground cinnamon
4 ounces (½ cup) finely diced red candied cherries
2 ounces (¼ cup) finely diced green candied cherries
2 ounces (¼ cup) finely diced candied pineapple slices
½ cup quartered miniature marshmallows (to quarter, use kitchen scissors with wet blades)
¼ cup chopped pecans
¼ cup half-and-half
1 teaspoon pure vanilla extract

In a medium mixing bowl, place 1 cup graham cracker crumbs (set aside the remaining ⅓ cup crumbs) and cinnamon; stir to combine. Add the red candied cherries, green candied cherries, candied pineapple, marshmallows, and pecans; stir until the ingredients are evenly distributed; set aside.

In a small sauce dish, pour the half-and-half and vanilla; stir to blend. Add the half-and-half mixture to the crumb mixture; stir until well combined.

With damp hands, shape the mixture into 5 rolls, each about 5 inches long and 1¼ inches in diameter; set aside. Sprinkle the remaining ⅓ cup graham cracker crumbs over a piece of waxed paper. Roll the 5 rolls of cookie mixture in the crumbs until well covered. Wrap each roll in plastic wrap; refrigerate overnight.

Remove the rolls of cookie mixture from the refrigerator and unwrap. Using a sharp, thin-bladed knife, cut the rolls into ¼-inch slices (cookies).

Place the cookies, single layer separated by plastic wrap, in an airtight container. Store in the refrigerator.

MAKES ABOUT 96

OATMEAL REFRIGERATOR COOKIES

¾ cup all-purpose flour
½ teaspoon baking soda
½ teaspoon salt
½ cup (¼ pound) butter, softened
½ cup granulated sugar
½ cup packed light brown sugar
1 extra-large egg
½ teaspoon pure vanilla extract
1½ cups quick-cooking *or* old-fashioned rolled oats, uncooked
⅓ cup red maraschino cherries cut into eighths
¼ cup broken pecans

Onto waxed paper, sift together the flour, baking soda, and salt; set aside.

In a large mixing bowl, place the butter, granulated sugar, and brown sugar; using an electric mixer, cream well on medium-high speed. Add the egg and vanilla; beat on medium-high speed until well blended. Add the flour mixture; beat on low speed only until blended. Add the oatmeal, cherries, and pecans; using a large mixing spoon, stir and fold in until evenly combined.

Divide the dough in half. On a lightly floured pastry cloth (page 54), using floured hands, shape each half of the dough into a roll approximately 1¼ inches in diameter. Wrap each roll in plastic wrap. Refrigerate the rolls at least 2 hours. (The rolls may be refrigerated overnight.)

Preheat the oven to 350° F.

Remove the rolls of dough from the refrigerator and unwrap. Using a sharp, thin-bladed knife, cut the rolls into ¼-inch slices. Place the slices, 2 inches apart, on 3 ungreased cookie sheets. Bake for 10 minutes, until lightly golden.

Using a thin spatula, place the baked cookies on waxed paper spread on the kitchen counter; let stand until completely cool.

Then, store the cookies in an airtight container.

MAKES ABOUT 40

HOLIDAY VARIATION: For Christmas cookies, substitute ¼ cup red maraschino cherries and ¼ cup green maraschino cherries (cut into eighths) for ⅓ cup red maraschino cherries.

GUMDROP-OATMEAL COOKIES

Kids love them!

1 13-ounce package (2 cups) small gumdrops in assorted colors and flavors
1½ cups all-purpose flour
1 teaspoon baking soda
½ teaspoon salt
1 cup (½ pound) butter or margarine, softened
1 cup granulated sugar
1 cup packed light brown sugar
2 extra-large eggs
1 teaspoon pure vanilla extract
3 cups quick-cooking rolled oats, uncooked
½ cup broken pecans

THE FIRST DAY: Using kitchen scissors with wet blades, cut each gumdrop into 3 pieces; set aside. Onto waxed paper, sift together the flour, baking soda, and salt; set aside.

In a large mixing bowl, place the butter, granulated sugar, and brown sugar; using an electric mixer, cream well on medium-high speed. Add the eggs, one at a time, beating well on medium-high speed after each addition. Add the vanilla; continue beating on medium-high speed until fluffy. Add the flour mixture; beat on low speed only until blended. Add the oats; beat on medium speed only until combined. Add the gumdrops and pecans; using a large mixing spoon, stir and fold in until evenly distributed.

Divide the dough in half. On a lightly floured pastry cloth (page 54), using floured hands, shape each half of the dough into a roll approximately 14 inches long and 2¼ inches in diameter. Wrap each roll in plastic wrap. Refrigerate the rolls overnight.

THE NEXT DAY: Preheat the oven to 350° F.

Remove the rolls of dough from the refrigerator and unwrap. Using a sharp, thin-bladed knife, cut the rolls into ⅜-inch slices. Using your hands, reshape the circular form of the slices, if necessary. Place the slices, 2 inches apart, on ungreased cookie sheets. Bake for 12 minutes, until lightly golden.

Using a thin spatula, place the baked cookies on waxed paper spread on the kitchen counter; let stand until completely cool.

Then, store the cookies in an airtight container.

MAKES ABOUT 66

BUTTERSCOTCH ICEBOX COOKIES

These cookies are as Midwest as a courthouse in the center of a county seat town square.

2 cups all-purpose flour
½ teaspoon baking soda
½ teaspoon cream of tartar
½ cup (¼ pound) butter, softened
1 cup packed light brown sugar
1 extra-large egg
½ teaspoon pure vanilla extract
½ cup broken pecans

Onto waxed paper, sift together the flour, baking soda, and cream of tartar; set aside.

In a large mixing bowl, the place butter and brown sugar; using an electric mixer, cream well on medium-high speed. Add the egg and vanilla; continue beating on medium-high speed until fluffy. Add the flour mixture in halves, beating on low speed after each addition only until blended. Add the pecans; using a mixing spoon, stir and fold in until evenly distributed.

Divide the dough in half. On a lightly floured pastry cloth (page 54), using floured hands, shape each half of the dough into a roll approximately 10 inches long and 1¼ inches in diameter. Wrap each roll in plastic wrap. Refrigerate the rolls at least 2 hours.

Preheat the oven to 350°F.

Remove the rolls of dough from the refrigerator and unwrap. Using a sharp, thin-bladed knife, cut the rolls into ¼-inch slices. Place the slices, 2½-inches apart, on ungreased cookie sheets. Bake for 8 to 10 minutes. Watch closely; bake until golden, but not brown.

Using a thin spatula, place the baked cookies on waxed paper spread on the kitchen counter; let stand until completely cool.

Then, store the cookies in an airtight container.

MAKES ABOUT 72

Pressed Cookies

SPRITZ

Gaily decorated, Scandinavian Spritz cookies, pressed in many shapes, go hand in hand with Christmas. They are made by forcing the dough through a special cookie press. I suggest using a good-quality, manually operated cookie press rather than a battery-operated model which I have found difficult to control. Wilton Enterprises (see Product Sources, page 849) makes an excellent manually operated cookie press.

2¾ cups all-purpose flour
¼ teaspoon salt
1 cup (½ pound) butter, softened
⅔ cup sugar
1 extra-large egg
½ teaspoon pure vanilla extract
½ teaspoon almond extract
Red- and green-colored sugar, nonpareils (page 24), red and green candied cherries, whole almonds, and pecan halves for decoration
Liquid or paste food coloring (optional)

Preheat the oven to 400°F.

Onto waxed paper, sift together the flour and salt; set aside.

In a medium mixing bowl, place the butter and sugar; using an electric mixer, cream well on medium-high speed. Add the egg; beat on medium-high speed until well blended. Add the vanilla and almond extract; beat on medium-high speed until completely blended. Add the flour mixture in halves, beating on low speed after each addition only until blended.

Force the dough through a special cookie press for making spritz cookies onto ungreased cookie sheets, following the instructions which accompany the cookie press. Press the cookies 1 inch apart, using various disks of choice to make cookies of different shapes and designs.

If desired, part (or all) of the cookie dough may be tinted in a pale color (usually pale pink or pale green) before forcing it through the cookie press. To tint the dough, add a tiny amount of food coloring to the portion of dough to be tinted. Then, using the electric mixer, beat on low speed only until the dough is evenly colored.

Decorate the unbaked cookies attractively, using the suggested decorations in the ingredients list, above, or other decorative, edible items. If the dough is not moist enough to hold a particular decoration, use a small, soft, watercolor brush to brush a drop of water on the unbaked cookie where the decoration is to be placed.

After decorating the cookies, bake for 7 minutes. Watch the cookies closely and do not allow them to brown.

Using a thin spatula, place the baked cookies on waxed paper spread on the kitchen counter; let stand until completely cool.

Then, store the cookies in an airtight container.

MAKES ABOUT 90

Desserts and Ice Cream

If the horizon of Heartland dessert artisanship encompassed only pies, cakes, and cookies, it would be ample to warrant the glory and honor accorded. But in Middle America, the master craft of dessert making reaches into the stratosphere, where heavenly desserts—some lighter than clouds—abound.

Among the weightless gossamers are Snow Pudding (page 660) (a spoonful of faintly lemon-flavored fluff covered with a thin, Custard Sauce) and Maple Nut Mousse (page 665), for those who thought that chocolate mousse would go unchallenged eternally in St. Peter's dessert logbook.

My favorite among these billowy celestials is what our family affectionately calls Mrs. Dowell's Dessert (page 664), named after Belle Dowell, a dear old friend of my mother's from whom Mother acquired the recipe. If one were to comb the dictionary, the words to describe and adequately praise this exquisite chiffonlike dessert surely would still go wanting. All I can say is try it for the finale of your next dinner party. It likely will be as sensational as a solar eclipse!

And then there are the baking dishes filled with Midland desserts resplendent with fresh fruits in the iridescent hues of the rainbow: Apple Crisp (page 649), Cherry and Peach Cobblers (page 648), Rhubarb Rapture (page 654), and Apple Dumplings (page 650). These combination dough/batter and fruit dishes represent folk cooking at its best, and are usually considered seasonal desserts, prepared when the sun and warm rains have nurtured the fruits to their peak of perfection.

Later in the year, when carols waft the air, it is time to make English Plum Pudding (page 658), one of the all-time greats of desserts. Carefully lift the fancy fluted mold off the pudding (it has steamed for *six* hours), ignite the hot cognac you have poured over top, and usher it into the candlelit dining room on a silver tray. Most diners will agree, as they spoon fluffy Hard Sauce from the crystal bowl onto their warm servings, there can hardly be another choice more elegant.

Prepare to be moonstruck with Date Pudding with Amber Sauce (page 657), an old, old Midwest favorite which is baked, not steamed, but, like English Plum Pudding, is served warm. Similar to a triple-rich cake, especially with the died and gone to heaven Amber Sauce, it is neither difficult nor time-consuming to make. The recipe is from my grandmother's cookbook, and was awarded not only a blue ribbon, but also first place overall among twenty-nine classes in the Recipes of Yesteryear division at the 1989 Iowa State Fair.

In the same galaxy as Date Pudding with Amber Sauce is what I call Concerto for Dates and Nuts (page 666), a rich, wonderful dessert served with whipped cream. Also from the yellowed pages of Midwest cookery, this recipe came from Edith Shelley, a colleague who served it at a wedding shower given for me years ago. It still would be perfect to serve at a twenty-first-century party.

Faces will illuminate around your table like the northern lights when you serve either Creamy or Old-Fashioned (no eggs) Rice Pudding (pages 654, 655) at the conclusion of a family meal. Likewise, a custard-type dessert sure to be visited by smiles is Bread Pudding (page 660), made absolutely paradisal with a Lemon Sauce to which plumped raisins have been added.

Whether gobbled up as a dessert or a Sunday afternoon indulgence, the peerless quality of Midwest farm-style ice cream can only be described as divine. This velvety delicacy, alien to most commercial ice cream, is still made today, but made more easily with electric ice cream makers which, by and large, have supplanted the erstwhile hand-cranked models. Sentimentalists lament that some of the excitement and enchantment associated with an afternoon of ice cream making was lost with the hand cranking, when everyone took turns applying his/her elbow grease to the task.

The unique flavor of the ambrosial treat churning in those cold canisters derives from oodles of real cream, fresh eggs (now cooked in a custard for food safety), and delicious fresh fruit. Besides vanilla (page 669), strawberry (page 669), peach, raspberry, and blueberry are among the deluxe kinds reveled in on porches at the end of hot summer days. I am convinced that much of the finest, most gourmet-quality food is savored in simple, informal settings.

Included in this book are a number of shining stars in the Midland's Big Dipper of homemade sauces which transform vanilla ice cream into bona fide company fare (page 670). Ice cream pies are also a stellar dessert to serve at the end of a substantial party meal. Particularly if you make your own mincemeat, don't miss the opportunity to use it propitiously in Mincemeat–Rum Ice Cream Pie (page 671). Another good reason to invite ice cream pies to your luncheon or dinner party is that they are prepared in advance, eliminating the woe of party-day dessert making.

When you're pulling out all the stops in preparation for a full-scale dinner party, consider serving Pink Grapefruit Sorbet (page 672) between two of the courses (this minor course is called "intermezzo" [see page 23]). After you scoop small servings into stemmed sherbet glasses, decorate the sorbet with tiny suggestions of grapefruit zest—without doubt, a touch of ethereal class far surpassing commercially purchased sherbet in flavor and sophistication.

After sampling the lusciousness of Midwest desserts, I'm sure you will concur, no matter under which sign of the zodiac you were born: Heartland desserts are positively out of this world.

Desserts

CHERRY COBBLER

A cobbler is a thickened fruit mixture (like pie filling) spread in a baking dish with batter spooned over the top, all of which is baked until the shortcake-like topping is golden and has risen over the bubbly fruit. Cobblers are cut into individual servings and served warm, preferably before they cool from baking. While any number of fruits, such as apples, blueberries, and pears, may be used to make cobblers, cherry and peach cobblers are the most Midwest-typical.

¼ cup (4 tablespoons) butter
1 cup sifted all-purpose flour (sift before
    measuring)
1½ teaspoons baking powder
¼ teaspoon salt
2 tablespoons sugar
2 cups pitted, tart, fresh (or frozen and
    thawed) red cherries
¾ cup juice drained from cherries (and
    water) (see recipe procedures, below)
⅔ cup sugar
1 tablespoon plus 1 teaspoon quick-
    cooking tapioca
Dash of salt
1 tablespoon butter
1 extra-large egg
¼ cup whole milk

Remove ¼ cup butter from the refrigerator and let stand 10 minutes before use in the recipe.

Onto waxed paper, sift together the flour, baking powder, ¼ teaspoon salt, and 2 tablespoons sugar. Place the flour mixture in a large mixing bowl. Using a knife, cut the butter into approximately 8 pieces and drop into the bowl containing the flour mixture. Using a pastry blender, cut the butter into the flour mixture until the mixture is the texture of coarse crumbs. Cover the bowl and refrigerate.

Preheat the oven to 400° F.

Drain the cherries in a sieve, reserving the juice. Let the cherries stand. Add enough water to the natural cherry juice to make ¾ cup liquid. Pour the liquid into a medium saucepan. Add ⅔ cup sugar, tapioca, and a dash of salt; stir to combine. Over medium-high heat, bring the mixture to a boil, stirring constantly. Boil the mixture briskly 5 minutes, stirring almost constantly. Add the cherries. Return the mixture to a boil and boil an additional 5 minutes, continuing to stir. The mixture will be thickened and cooked. Remove from the heat. Add 1 tablespoon butter. Stir the cherry mixture until the butter melts; set aside.

Remove the flour mixture from the refrigerator. Using a tablespoon, make a well in the center of the flour mixture; set aside. Place the egg in a very small mixing bowl. Using an electric mixer, beat the egg slightly on medium speed. Add the milk; beat on medium speed only until blended. Pour the egg mixture, all at once, into the well in the flour mixture; using a small mixing spoon, stir and fold *only* until the flour mixture is moistened; set aside.

Pour the hot cherry mixture into an ungreased 6 × 10-inch baking dish; using a small, narrow spatula, spread evenly. Using a medium mixing spoon, drop 6 approximately equal spoonsful of the flour mixture, evenly spaced, over the cherry mixture. Do not spread or touch the flour mixture. It is not necessary to completely cover the fruit, as the flour mixture will spread during baking. Bake, uncovered, for 18 to 20 minutes. The topping will be golden.

Remove from the oven and place the baking dish on a wire rack.

Serve Cherry Cobbler warm (see Note). Cut the cobbler into 6 servings and serve on individual plates.

NOTE: Cobbler is at its best when served warm shortly after baking rather than rewarmed at a later time.

SERVES 6

SERVING SUGGESTION: Vanilla ice cream (home-made, page 669, or commercial) may be served as an accompaniment.

PEACH COBBLER

⅓ cup sugar
1 tablespoon plus 2 teaspoons cornstarch
¼ teaspoon ground nutmeg
½ cup water
3 cups peeled, halved, pitted, quartered, and sliced fresh peaches
1 tablespoon butter

Follow the Cherry Cobbler recipe, above, through refrigeration of the flour mixture.

Then, use the Peach Cobbler ingredients above, and place the sugar, cornstarch, and nut-meg in a medium saucepan; stir to combine. Add the water; stir to combine. Place the corn-starch mixture over medium heat; stir constantly until the sugar melts and the mixture is smooth. Add the peaches. Bring the mixture to a simmer and simmer until thickened, stirring constantly. Remove from the heat. Add the butter. Stir the peach mixture until the butter melts; set aside.

Remove the flour mixture from the refriger-ator and resume following the Cherry Cobbler recipe through stirring and folding the egg mix-ture into the flour mixture.

Continue following the Cherry Cobbler re-cipe through completion, substituting the peach mixture for the cherry mixture.

APPLE CRISP

When apple tree branches are so laden with juicy, ripe fruit they threaten to break under the burden, apple desserts are as plentiful as the golden autumn leaves swirling gently in the cool winds. Of course, Apple Pie (page 476) is a Midwest institution, but I dare say that nearly as many bubbling Apple Crisps fill the fall air with that captivating spicy-sweet fragrance. That's because Apple Crisp is so simple to make and the fla-vor so closely resembles Apple Pie. While Apple Pie reigns on a culinary throne, Apple Crisp is one of the handsome princes in the court.

½ cup (¼ pound) butter
½ cup granulated sugar
1 teaspoon ground cinnamon
¼ teaspoon ground nutmeg
5 cups pared, quartered, cored, and sliced apples* (about 4 large apples)
1 cup all-purpose flour
½ cup packed light brown sugar

*Golden Delicious apples are especially good for use in this recipe.

Remove the butter from the refrigerator; let stand.

Preheat the oven to 350° F. Butter a 6 × 10-inch baking dish; set aside.

In a small mixing bowl, place the granulated sugar, cinnamon, and nutmeg; stir to combine; set aside.

As the apples are prepared, place them in a large mixing bowl. Sprinkle the cinnamon-nutmeg mixture over the apples; toss to com-bine. Turn the apple mixture into the prepared baking dish; spread evenly; set aside.

In a medium mixing bowl, place the flour and brown sugar; stir to combine. Using a knife, cut the butter into approximately 8 pieces and drop into the bowl. Using a pastry blender, cut the butter into the flour mixture until it is the tex-ture of coarse crumbs. Spoon the mixture evenly over the apples; do not press the mixture into the apples and do not be concerned about the mixture mounding considerably above the sides of the baking dish. The dessert will bake down and will not bubble over in the oven. Bake, uncovered, for 40 minutes, until the apples are tender.

Serve warm or cool.

SERVES 8

SERVING SUGGESTIONS: Serve with Whipped Cream (page 373), vanilla ice cream (homemade, page 669, or commercial), or half-and-half.

VARIATION: Sprinkle ½ cup broken pecans, ½ cup plumped raisins (page 46), or ¼ cup of each over the apples prior to adding the flour mixture.

APPLE BROWN BETTY

Like Apple Crisp (page 649), Apple Brown Betty is baked in a baking dish. The principal difference between the two desserts is that a flour mixture is spooned over the top of Apple Crisp prior to baking, while a bread crumb mixture is layered with the spicy apple mixture in Apple Brown Betty. Brown Betty is an American dessert dating back to the nineteenth century. The origin of the name is unknown. While Brown Betty may be made with peaches, pears, apricots, and other fruits, Apple Brown Betty is the most popular and traditional way of making this great old dish.

½ cup sugar
½ teaspoon ground cinnamon
2 cups Fresh Bread Crumbs (page 48)
¼ cup (4 tablespoons) butter, melted
5 cups pared, quartered, cored, and sliced apples (about 4 large apples)
½ teaspoon finely grated lemon rind (page 47)
¼ cup water
1 tablespoon freshly squeezed, strained lemon juice

Preheat the oven to 375°F. Grease a 1½-quart round baking dish; set aside.

In a small mixing bowl, place the sugar and cinnamon; stir to combine; set aside. Place the bread crumbs in a medium mixing bowl. Drizzle the melted butter over the crumbs; toss lightly; set aside.

As the apples are prepared, place them in a large mixing bowl. Sprinkle the sugar mixture and lemon rind over the apples; toss to combine; set aside.

Distribute ⅓ of the bread crumb mixture evenly over the bottom of the prepared baking dish. Spread ½ of the apple mixture evenly over the bread crumb mixture. Cover the apple mixture with an additional ⅓ of the bread crumb mixture. Spread the remaining ½ of the apple mixture over the bread crumb mixture. Cover

the apple mixture with the remaining ⅓ of the bread crumb mixture; set aside.

Pour the water and lemon juice into a glass measuring cup with a pouring spout; stir to blend. Pour evenly over the layered mixture in the baking dish. Bake, covered, for 30 minutes. Uncover and bake for an additional 20 minutes, until the apples are tender.

SERVES 8

SERVING SUGGESTIONS
- Serve warm with a generous dollop of Whipped Cream (page 373) sprinkled sparingly with ground cinnamon for decoration.

- Place individual servings in large-sized sauce dishes or cereal bowls. Pass half-and-half in a medium-small pitcher at the table.

- Serve warm with warm Lemon Sauce (page 372).

APPLE DUMPLINGS

Whose heart is not warmed by the endearment "My sweet apple dumpling" from a loved one? The affectionate expression clearly derives from this dessert, which has been cherished through the years. In Horst Scharfenberg's cookbook The Cuisines of Germany, *there is an old recipe for apple dumplings, dated 1844, that calls for diced apples and grated white bread to be mixed with other ingredients and formed into balls (dumplings) which are then cooked in salted water. The dumplings are served with a wine sauce. But Apple Dumplings, as we know them, are whole, pared, and cored apples filled in the center with a spicy raisin mixture, and then wrapped in pastry and baked in a syrup that is often rose colored. They are usually served warm.*

What, exactly, are "dumplings"? Dumplings take many forms and are somewhat complex to define. See the definition on page 22 for various kinds of foods which may be categorized as dumplings.

2 cups water

1 cup sugar

¼ teaspoon ground cinnamon

¼ teaspoon ground nutmeg

3 tablespoons butter

3 drops red liquid food coloring (optional)

2 tablespoons sugar

⅛ teaspoon ground cinnamon

⅛ teaspoon ground nutmeg

¼ cup raisins, plumped (page 46) and drained well

¼ cup golden raisins, plumped (page 46) and drained well

2 tablespoons packed light brown sugar

8 cups cold water

1 tablespoon white vinegar

1 tablespoon salt

6 medium-sized (not too large) apples

2 cups all-purpose flour

1 teaspoon baking powder

1 teaspoon salt

⅔ cup refrigerated lard

½ cup whole milk

1 tablespoon plus 2 teaspoons butter

2 teaspoons sugar

In a medium saucepan, place 2 cups water, 1 cup sugar, ¼ teaspoon cinnamon, and ¼ teaspoon nutmeg; stir to combine. Over high heat, bring the sugar mixture to a boil, stirring constantly. Remove from the heat. Add 3 tablespoons butter and the food coloring; stir until the butter melts and the mixture blends. Cover the syrup mixture and set aside.

In a small sauce dish, place 2 tablespoons sugar, ⅛ teaspoon cinnamon, and ⅛ teaspoon nutmeg; stir to combine; set aside. In a small mixing bowl, place the raisins, golden raisins, and brown sugar; stir to combine; set aside.

In a small kettle or large mixing bowl, place 8 cups water, vinegar, and salt; stir until the salt dissolves; set aside.

Wash and pare the apples (leave the apples whole). As the apples are prepared, drop them into the vinegar solution to prevent discoloration. Then, using an apple corer, core the

apples and drop them back into the vinegar solution; set aside.

Preheat the oven to 375° F. Butter a 9 × 13-inch baking dish; set aside.

Onto waxed paper, sift together the flour, baking powder, and salt. Place the flour mixture in a large mixing bowl. Using a knife, cut the lard into approximately 12 pieces and drop about ⅔ of the pieces into the bowl. Using a pastry blender, cut the lard into the flour mixture until the mixture is the texture of cornmeal. Add the remaining ⅓ of the pieces of the lard; using the pastry blender, cut into the flour mixture until the size of small peas. Add the milk all at once; quickly stir only until the mixture is evenly moistened.

Using floured hands, gather the pastry into a ball and place it on a well-floured pastry cloth. Using a stockinet-covered, then floured rolling pin (page 54), roll the pastry into a rectangular shape, ⅛ inch thick. Using a ruler and a sharp, thin-bladed knife dipped in flour, cut the pastry into six 7-inch squares (it probably will be necessary to reroll the pastry scraps); set aside.

Drain the apples and rinse twice in clear water; drain well in a colander. Place the drained apples on 2 layers of paper towels and quickly dry them fairly well with additional paper towels.

Place 1 apple, stem side up, in the center of each pastry square. Loosely pack the raisin mixture into the core cavities of the apples, even with the top of the apples. Sprinkle 1 teaspoon of the cinnamon-nutmeg mixture over the top of each apple. Dot the top of the apples with the 1 tablespoon plus 2 teaspoons butter (slightly less than 1 teaspoon of butter per apple).

Bring the corners of the pastry together over the top of each apple; pinch together well to seal. Pinch the pastry edges together tightly to form pastry wings. Lightly fold the sealed wings against the side of each pastry-covered apple, folding each of the 4 wings in the same direction around the apple.

Place the dumplings, about 1 inch apart, in the prepared baking dish. Pour some of the syrup mixture over the dumplings and pour the

(Recipe continues on next page)

remainder in the baking dish around the dumplings. Sprinkle the 2 teaspoons sugar over the dumplings (about ⅓ teaspoon of sugar per dumpling). Bake, uncovered, for 35 minutes, until the pastry is golden and the apples are tender.

Remove from the oven and place the baking dish on a wire rack. Serve 1 Apple Dumpling per person. Best served warm.

SERVES 6

SERVING SUGGESTIONS

- Serve alone on dessert plates.

- Serve in bowls and pass half-and-half in a pitcher at the table.

- Serve a small dish of vanilla ice cream (home-made, page 669, or commercial) on the side.

BAKED APPLES

Baked Apples are similar to Apple Dumplings (page 650); however, Baked Apples are not wrapped in pastry and are only partially pared. The cores of these Baked Apples are filled with applejack-soaked currants, dates, and walnuts, and the apples are baked in a spice-flavored, buttery, maple syrup mixture—a perfect dessert for informal, company fare.

¼ cup currants, plumped (page 46) and drained well
¼ cup chopped dates, plumped (page 46) and drained well
2 tablespoons finely broken English walnuts
1 tablespoon packed light brown sugar
¼ cup applejack (page 19)
1 cup pure maple syrup
½ teaspoon ground cinnamon
¼ teaspoon ground nutmeg
2 tablespoons butter
8 cups cold water
1 tablespoon white vinegar
1 tablespoon salt
6 medium-sized red-skinned apples
1 tablespoon plus 2 teaspoons butter

2 cups (1 pint) half-and-half
½ recipe Whipped Cream (page 373)

In a small mixing bowl, place the currants, dates, walnuts, brown sugar, and applejack; stir to combine. Cover the bowl with plastic wrap; set aside.

In a small saucepan, place the maple syrup, cinnamon, and nutmeg; stir to combine. Over medium-high heat, bring the syrup mixture to a boil, stirring constantly. Remove from the heat. Add 2 tablespoons butter; stir until the butter melts. Cover the syrup mixture and set aside.

Preheat the oven to 350° F. Butter a 7 × 11-inch baking dish; set aside.

In a small kettle or large mixing bowl, place 8 cups water, vinegar, and salt; stir until the salt dissolves; set aside.

Wash the apples and leave them whole; do not pare. Using an apple corer, core the apples. As the apples are cored, drop them into the vinegar solution to prevent discoloration.

Then, starting at the stem end, pare approximately the top ¼ of each apple, leaving the skin on the lower ¾ of each apple. As the apples are pared, drop them back into the vinegar solution.

Drain the apples and rinse twice in clear water; drain well in a colander. Place the drained apples on 2 layers of paper towels and quickly dry them fairly well with additional paper towels.

Place the apples, stem side up, in the prepared baking dish. Pack the currant mixture into the core cavities of the apples. Strain the remaining currant mixture liquid in a small sieve. Pour the strained liquid into the packed core cavities and over the tops of the apples.

Spoon some of the syrup mixture over the apples and pour the remainder in the baking dish around the apples. Dot the top of the apples with the 1 tablespoon plus 2 teaspoons butter (slightly less than 1 teaspoon of butter per apple). Bake, uncovered, until fork-tender (about 30 to 40 minutes, depending upon the size and type of apples). Baste 2 or 3 times during baking.

Serve the Baked Apples warm in individual

bowls. Spoon some of the liquid in the baking dish over each apple. Pass a small pitcher of half-and-half and a bowl of Whipped Cream at the table; diners may prefer one or the other or both. Some prefer to eat Baked Apples plain.

SERVES 6

FRUIT COCKTAIL DESSERT

This is a perfect choice for a dessert party, such as a shower, when nothing else but coffee or tea will be served. It's rich and wonderful enough to carry the day. If guests ask you to share the recipe—and it's a sure bet they will—more than likely they will be surprised when you disclose that this delectable contains canned fruit cocktail.

1 17-ounce can commercial fruit cocktail in heavy syrup
¼ cup reserved fruit cocktail syrup
10 red maraschino cherries, cut in half lengthwise
¾ cup packed light brown sugar
¾ cup broken English walnuts
1 cup granulated sugar
1 cup all-purpose flour
1 teaspoon baking soda
¼ teaspoon salt
2 extra-large eggs
1 teaspoon pure vanilla extract
1 8¼-ounce can commercial crushed pineapple in heavy syrup
1 recipe Whipped Cream (page 373)
8 red maraschino cherries, cut in half, for decoration

Preheat the oven to 350° F. Grease and flour (page 589) a 9 × 13 × 2-inch baking pan; set aside.

Drain the fruit cocktail well in a sieve, reserving ¼ cup syrup. Set the reserved syrup aside. Add the 10 halved maraschino cherries to the fruit cocktail; set aside. In a small mixing bowl, place the brown sugar and walnuts; stir to combine; set aside.

Onto waxed paper, sift together the granulated sugar, flour, baking soda, and salt. Place the flour mixture in a large mixing bowl; stir briefly to completely combine. Using the spoon, make a well in the center of the flour mixture; set aside.

Place the eggs in a medium mixing bowl. Using an electric mixer, beat the eggs briefly on medium speed. Add the vanilla and ¼ cup reserved syrup; beat on medium speed to blend. Add the fruit cocktail (and cherries); using a large mixing spoon, stir to combine.

Pour the fruit cocktail mixture, all at once, into the well in the flour mixture; using the large mixing spoon, stir and fold only until the mixture blends and the fruit cocktail is evenly distributed.

Turn the mixture into the prepared baking pan; using a small, narrow spatula, spread evenly. Using a tablespoon, sprinkle the brown sugar mixture evenly over the top of the mixture in the baking pan. Bake for 30 minutes, until golden.

Remove from the oven and place the baking pan on a wire rack; let stand until the dessert completely cools. Then, cover the dessert tightly with aluminum foil or a baking-pan cover. Store at room temperature.

Shortly before serving, drain the pineapple in a small sieve. Using the back of a tablespoon, press and stir the pineapple until as much additional syrup as possible has been extracted. (Reserve the syrup for other uses.) Add the drained pineapple to the Whipped Cream; using a spoon, fold in until evenly combined.

To serve, cut the dessert into 15 servings and place the servings on individual plates. Spoon the whipped cream mixture over each serving. Decorate the whipped cream mixture on each serving with ½ maraschino cherry.

SERVES 15

RHUBARB RAPTURE

This rapturous dessert baked in a pan is composed of a fresh rhubarb mixture, with eggs and flour as thickeners, baked over a flaky, sweetened crust made with butter. Rhubarb has never been so lusciously ensconced! Go all the way and crown the top of each serving with a spoonful of whipped cream, or serve vanilla ice cream on the side.

¼ cup (4 tablespoons) butter
1 cup all-purpose flour
¼ cup plus 1 tablespoon powdered sugar
4 cups fresh rhubarb, cut diagonally into
    1½-inch lengths
1 cup all-purpose flour
2 cups granulated sugar
Dash of salt
3 extra-large eggs, beaten

Remove the butter from the refrigerator and let stand 10 minutes before use in the recipe.

Preheat the oven to 325° F.

Onto waxed paper, sift together 1 cup flour and the powdered sugar. Place the flour mixture in a large mixing bowl. Using a knife, cut the butter into approximately 8 pieces and drop into the bowl containing the flour. Using a pastry blender, cut the butter into the flour mixture until the mixture is the texture of coarse cornmeal interspersed with some pieces the size of small peas.

Turn the mixture into an ungreased 9 × 13 × 2-inch baking pan. Using the back of a tablespoon, pat the mixture firmly into the bottom of the pan. Bake for 10 minutes, or until golden brown.

Remove from the oven and place the baking pan on a wire rack; let stand until the baked crust completely cools.

Preheat the oven to 350° F.

Place the rhubarb in a large mixing bowl; set aside.

Carefully butter the sides of the baking pan *above* the cooled, baked crust; set aside.

In a medium mixing bowl, place 1 cup flour, granulated sugar, and salt; stir to combine. Add the eggs; stir only until combined. Pour the flour mixture over the rhubarb (with accumulated juice); stir lightly.

Using a large mixing spoon, spoon the rhubarb mixture evenly and carefully over the baked crust. Bake for 35 to 40 minutes. The top will be golden.

Remove from the oven and place the baking pan on the wire rack; let stand until the dessert completely cools.

To serve, cut the dessert into 15 servings and place on individual plates.

SERVES 12

SERVING SUGGESTIONS: Serve with vanilla ice cream (homemade, page 669, or commercial) or Whipped Cream (page 373).

CREAMY RICE PUDDING

1 cup whole milk
1 cup water
¾ cup raw long-grain rice (not instant)
1 tablespoon butter
¼ teaspoon salt
2 extra-large eggs
¾ cup whole milk
½ cup half-and-half
½ cup sugar
¼ teaspoon finely grated lemon rind
    (page 47)
1 teaspoon pure vanilla extract
½ cup raisins, plumped (page 46) and
    drained well
Ground cinnamon for garnish

Preheat the oven to 325° F. Butter a 1½-quart round or oval baking dish; set aside.

Into a medium saucepan, pour 1 cup milk and 1 cup water; stir to blend. Bring the mixture to a boil over medium heat. Add the rice, butter, and salt; stir to combine. Cover the saucepan and reduce the heat. Bring the rice mixture to a simmer, stirring occasionally. Simmer the rice mixture, covered, for 20 minutes, continuing to stir occasionally.

Remove the rice mixture from the heat; let stand, covered, until the liquid is completely absorbed (about 10 minutes).

Meanwhile, place the eggs in a medium mixing bowl. Using an electric mixer, beat the eggs slightly on medium speed. Add ¾ cup milk, half-and-half, sugar, lemon rind, and vanilla; stir to blend and combine. Add about 1 cup of the rice to the egg mixture; stir to combine. Add the remaining rice; stir to combine. Add the raisins; stir until evenly distributed.

Turn the mixture into the prepared baking dish. Carefully stir the mixture to assure that the rice and raisins are evenly distributed in the dish. Sprinkle the cinnamon lightly over the mixture. Place the baking dish in a 9 × 13 × 2-inch baking pan. Then, pour approximately 1¼ inches of very hot (not boiling) water into the pan around the baking dish. Bake, uncovered, for 45 to 50 minutes, or until a table knife inserted into the pudding near the center of the baking dish comes out clean.

Remove the baking dish from the baking pan and place on a wire rack.

Creamy Rice Pudding is best when served warm; however, it may also be served cold (store the pudding, covered, in the refrigerator).

SERVES 8

SERVING SUGGESTION: Whether served warm or cold, individual servings of pudding may be topped with Whipped Cream (page 373) and sprinkled sparingly with ground cinnamon.

VARIATION: Ground nutmeg may be substituted for ground cinnamon.

OLD-FASHIONED RICE PUDDING (NO EGGS)

½ cup raw long-grain rice (not instant)
4 cups (1 quart) whole milk
⅓ cup sugar
½ teaspoon salt
1 tablespoon butter
½ cup raisins, plumped (page 46) and drained well
¼ teaspoon ground cinnamon
1 teaspoon pure vanilla extract
Additional ground cinnamon for decoration

Preheat the oven to 300° F. Butter a 1½-quart round or oval baking dish; set aside.

In a medium mixing bowl, place the rice, milk, sugar, and salt; stir to combine. Add the butter in a single piece.

Pour the mixture into the prepared baking dish. Bake for 1 hour, stirring the mixture every 15 minutes.

Remove from the oven. Add the raisins and ¼ teaspoon cinnamon; stir to combine. Return to the oven. Bake for an additional 1 hour, stirring the mixture after 30 minutes.

Remove from the oven. Add the vanilla; stir to blend. Sprinkle the cinnamon over the top of the pudding to decorate.

Return the pudding to the oven; bake for an additional 30 minutes, undisturbed. Serve warm or cold.

SERVES 6

SERVING SUGGESTION: Whether served warm or cold, the pudding may be topped with a dollop of Whipped Cream (page 373).

TAPIOCA PUDDING

2 extra-large eggs, separated
⅓ cup quick-cooking tapioca
⅓ cup sugar
¼ teaspoon salt
4 cups (1 quart) whole milk
1½ teaspoons pure vanilla extract
2 tablespoons sugar

Place the egg yolks in the top of a double boiler. Using a handheld electric mixer, beat the egg yolks slightly on medium speed; set aside. In a small mixing bowl, place the tapioca, ⅓ cup sugar, and salt; stir to combine; set aside.

Pour the milk into a medium saucepan. Scald the milk (page 25). Add about ½ cup of the scalded milk to the egg yolks and quickly stir in. Add the tapioca mixture to the egg yolk mixture; stir to combine. Add the remaining scalded milk; stir to blend. Place the top of the double boiler over boiling water in the bottom pan. Cook the tapioca mixture until thick (about 10 minutes), stirring frequently.

Remove the top of the double boiler from the bottom pan and place it on a wire rack. Add the vanilla; stir until fully blended. Let the mixture stand until cooled slightly; then, refrigerate until cooled to room temperature, stirring occasionally.

Remove the tapioca mixture from the refrigerator; set aside. Place the egg whites in a medium mixing bowl. Using an electric mixer, beat the egg whites on high speed until soft peaks hold. While continuing to beat on high speed, very gradually add 2 tablespoons sugar and continue beating the egg white mixture until stiff, but still moist and glossy. Spoon the tapioca mixture over the egg white mixture; using a large mixing spoon, quickly fold in. Refrigerate, uncovered, until chilled. Then, cover and keep refrigerated.

SERVES 8

SERVING SUGGESTIONS
• Top individual servings with Whipped Cream (page 373). Place ½ red maraschino cherry atop the whipped cream on each serving.

• Top individual servings with sliced fresh peaches or other fruit and a dollop of Whipped Cream (page 373).

RED RASPBERRY TAPIOCA

1 cup fresh red raspberries
½ cup sugar
¼ cup quick-cooking tapioca
Dash of salt
1 tablespoon freshly squeezed, strained lemon juice
1 recipe Whipped Cream (page 373)
6 whole raspberries for decoration
6 small, fresh mint leaves for decoration

Place 1 cup raspberries in a flat-bottomed pan. Using a potato masher, crush the raspberries. Add the sugar; stir to combine. Let the raspberry mixture stand 1 hour.

Then, turn the raspberry mixture (including the liquid) into a sieve placed over a deep pan; drain well. Let the crushed raspberries stand in the sieve. Add enough water to the drained liquid to make 2 cups liquid. Pour the measured liquid into the top of a double boiler; set aside.

Press the crushed raspberries in the sieve through a food mill to remove the seeds; set aside the raspberry pulp (with the additional accumulated juice).

Add the tapioca and salt to the liquid in the top of the double boiler; stir to combine. Place the top of the double boiler over simmering water in the bottom pan. Cook the mixture until the tapioca is transparent (about 15 minutes), stirring constantly.

Remove the top of the double boiler from the bottom pan and place it on a wire rack. Add the raspberry pulp and lemon juice; stir to combine. Refrigerate the tapioca, uncovered, until chilled. Then, cover and keep refrigerated.

To serve, spoon the Red Raspberry Tapioca into footed goblets. Top with the Whipped

Cream. Decorate each serving with a whole raspberry and a small mint leaf. Place each goblet on a small (bread and butter–sized), doily-lined plate.

SERVES 6

DATE PUDDING WITH AMBER SAUCE

Awarded first place overall in the Recipes of Yesteryear division (29 classes) at the 1989 Iowa State Fair.

The food that comes to mind when most of us think of pudding is a thick, soft, creamy dessert made with eggs, milk, sugar, flavoring, and a thickener—most commonly flour, cornstarch, or tapioca. However, other foods are also designated as "pudding" in culinary nomenclature. One of the types of foods historically called pudding is a dense, rich, cakelike dessert that is either baked or steamed and often is served with a sauce; for example, this classic Date Pudding with Amber Sauce, which is baked, and traditional English Plum Pudding (page 658), which is steamed.

1 8-ounce package chopped dates (1 cup packed dates)
1 teaspoon baking soda
1 cup boiling water
1½ cups sifted cake flour (sift before measuring)
½ teaspoon salt
2 tablespoons butter, softened
1 cup sugar
1 extra-large egg
1 teaspoon pure vanilla extract
½ cup broken English walnuts
Amber Sauce (recipe follows)

Place the dates in a small saucepan. Sprinkle the baking soda over the dates. Add the boiling water; cover and let stand until cool.

Then, preheat the oven to 325° F. Using Special Grease (page 56), grease an 8 × 8 × 2-inch baking pan (see Note); set aside.

Onto waxed paper, sift together the flour and salt; set aside.

In a medium mixing bowl, place the butter and sugar; using an electric mixer, cream well on medium-high speed. Add the egg and vanilla; beat on medium-high speed until blended. Add, alternately, the flour mixture in thirds, and the date mixture (including the liquid) in halves, beating on low speed after each addition only until blended. Add the walnuts; using a medium mixing spoon, stir and fold in until evenly distributed.

Turn the batter into the prepared baking pan. Using a small, narrow spatula, lightly and quickly spread the batter evenly in the pan. Bake for 40 to 45 minutes, or until a wooden toothpick inserted into the center of the pudding comes out clean.

Remove the pudding from the oven and place on a wire rack.

Serve the Date Pudding warm, with warm Amber Sauce spooned over each serving. Cut the pudding into 9 servings.

NOTE: Although not as satisfactory, the pan may be greased and floured in substitution for using Special Grease.

SERVES 9

Amber Sauce

¼ cup (4 tablespoons) butter
1 cup packed light brown sugar
½ cup light corn syrup
½ cup half-and-half
1 teaspoon pure vanilla extract

In a small saucepan, melt the butter over low heat. Remove from the heat. Add the brown sugar and corn syrup; stir to combine. Add the half-and-half; stir well. Return to low heat. Cook slowly until the sugar dissolves and the sauce is thick, stirring constantly. Add the vanilla; stir to blend.

VARIATION: The Date Pudding and Amber Sauce recipes may be doubled. Bake the pudding in a 9 × 13 × 2-inch baking pan.

ENGLISH PLUM PUDDING

English Plum Pudding is a historical Christmas pudding steamed in a tall mold. (For more information about this type of pudding, see the headnote for Date Pudding with Amber Sauce, page 657.) Among the traditional ingredients in English Plum Pudding are raisins, currants, candied fruits, almonds, suet, bread crumbs, spices, and brandy. So why no plums in plum pudding? Research reveals that raisins used in desserts were called plums in the seventeenth century.

For the full beauty and grandeur of this aristocratic dessert, brandy is customarily poured over the top of it and ignited at the table before the pudding is sliced. Hard sauce traditionally is spooned over the individual servings—a snowy white foil for the dark pudding.

1½ cups raisins
1½ cups currants
1 cup cognac (page 21)
2 tablespoons diced candied citron
2 tablespoons diced candied orange peel
2 tablespoons diced candied lemon peel
1 cup chopped, slivered blanched almonds (page 50)
1½ cups fine, Fresh Bread Crumbs (page 48) (about 3 slices of bread)
1 cup (about ¼ pound) finely ground beef suet
1¾ cups unpared, quartered, cored, and medium-coarsely grated Golden Delicious apples (about 2 large apples)
1 cup all-purpose flour
½ cup sugar
½ teaspoon salt
1 teaspoon ground cinnamon
½ teaspoon ground allspice
½ teaspoon ground cloves
3 extra-large eggs
1 cup light (mild-flavored) molasses
1½ teaspoons very finely grated lemon rind (page 47) (rind of about 1 large lemon)
1 recipe Hard Sauce (recipe follows)

EVENING OF FIRST DAY: In a medium glass bowl, place the raisins and currants; stir to combine.

Add the cognac; stir until the fruits are coated. Cover the bowl tightly with plastic wrap; then, cover securely with aluminum foil. Let the mixture stand at room temperature.

THE NEXT DAY: Using vegetable shortening, grease well a 2-liter or 2-quart pudding steamer with cover (do not grease the cover); set aside.

Place a wire rack in the bottom of a large (such as 12-quart) kettle. On the wire rack, spread a 4-layer, damp piece of cheesecloth to prevent the pudding steamer from moving during the steaming process. Cover the kettle and set aside.

Turn the soaked raisins and currants, together with the cognac liquid, into a sieve placed over a deep pan. Using the back of a spoon, press the fruits against the sieve to extract as much liquid as possible. Let the fruits stand in the sieve to continue draining while preparing the other pudding ingredients.

In a large mixing bowl, place the citron, orange peel, lemon peel, and almonds; stir to combine. Cover the bowl with plastic wrap; set aside. In a medium mixing bowl, place the bread crumbs and suet; using your hands, rub the crumbs and suet together. Add the bread crumb mixture to the candied fruits mixture; stir to combine. Re-cover and set aside.

Prepare the apples; set aside. Transfer the raisins and currants from the sieve to a large mixing bowl; set aside. Reserve the cognac liquid.

Place the flour in a small mixing bowl. Sprinkle 2 tablespoons of the flour over the candied fruits–bread crumb mixture; stir to evenly coat; set aside. Sprinkle another 2 tablespoons of the flour over the raisin-currant mixture; stir to evenly coat; set aside. Onto waxed paper, sift together the remaining flour, sugar, salt, cinnamon, allspice, and cloves; set aside.

Place the eggs in an *extra-large* mixing bowl. Using an electric mixer, beat the eggs well on medium-high speed. Add the molasses, lemon rind, and reserved cognac liquid; beat on medium-high speed until completely blended. Add the flour mixture; beat on low speed only until blended. Add the apples; using a large mixing spoon, fold in until evenly combined. Add the candied fruits–bread crumb mixture and raisin-currant mixture; using the large mixing spoon, fold in and stir until evenly combined.

Spoon and gently press the batter into the prepared pudding steamer. The steamer should be about ¾ (or slightly more) full. Place the cover on the steamer and secure it closed. Place the steamer on the damp cheesecloth spread over the wire rack in the kettle. Pour boiling water into the kettle around the steamer until the surface of the water is approximately 2 inches below the top rim of the steamer. Cover the kettle.

Over high heat, bring the water in the kettle to a low simmer. Immediately reduce the heat to warm or low to maintain a low simmer. Steam the pudding for 6 hours. If necessary, add *boiling* water to the kettle once or twice to maintain the water depth. *Do not uncover the pudding steamer during the entire steaming period.*

At the end of the steaming period, remove the steamer from the kettle and place on a wire rack. Uncover the steamer; let stand 15 minutes.

Then, run a sharp, thin-bladed knife around the inside edge of the steamer and then around the center tube, running the knife only about ½ inch below the surface of the pudding. Quickly dip the steamer in and out of a kettle of cold water, being careful not to get any water on the pudding. Using a kitchen towel, quickly wipe the outside of the steamer to remove the excess water.

Place a silver or other attractive serving tray over the top of the steamer; invert and carefully lift the steamer off the pudding.

Using a sharp, thin-bladed knife dipped in hot water, slice the pudding like a cake and serve hot. (English Plum Pudding is very rich, so guard against cutting the servings too large.) Let the diners spoon a dollop of the Hard Sauce over their servings of pudding.

NOTE: English Plum Pudding is best when ripened 24 hours after steaming. This procedure achieves a better blend of the flavors. To ripen, proceed as follows:

Remove the steamer from the kettle after steaming and place on a wire rack. Uncover the steamer; let stand 2 hours. Re-cover and let stand until completely cool. Then, store the steamer containing the pudding on the wire rack in a cold place. (The pudding may be stored in the refrigerator.)

To reheat before serving, replace the covered steamer on the dampened piece of cheesecloth spread over the wire rack in the kettle. Carefully pour the boiling water into the kettle, following the same procedure as when previously steaming the pudding. Steam the pudding for 1 hour. Then, follow the recipe.

SERVES 16

Hard Sauce

½ cup (¼ pound) butter, softened
1 teaspoon pure vanilla extract
1 cup powdered sugar, sifted (page 57) (sift after measuring)

Place the butter in a medium-small mixing bowl. Using an electric mixer, beat the butter on medium-high speed until *very* fluffy. Add the vanilla; beat on medium-high speed until blended. While continuing to beat on medium-high speed, slowly add the powdered sugar, 1 heaping tablespoon at a time and continue beating the mixture until light and smooth.

Spoon the Hard Sauce into a small crystal or silver bowl. Serve soon after making; do not refrigerate.

TO FLAME THE PUDDING AT SERVING TIME: The English Plum Pudding may be flamed at serving time, if desired.

1 teaspoon butter
6 cubes sugar
¼ cup hot cognac

Unmold the pudding on a *hot* silver or oven-proof serving plate. Dot the top of the pudding with the butter. Place the sugar cubes equidistant from each other around the top of the pudding. Place the serving plate on a hot pad to

(Recipe continues on next page)

protect the serving table; lower the lights in the room. Pour the hot cognac evenly over the top of the pudding and ignite with a match. Immediately begin basting the pudding with the ignited cognac and lightly pressing the sugar cubes to prolong the flaming. When the flames stop, remove any remaining sugar cubes. Slice the pudding and serve.

SNOW PUDDING

Elegantly understated, Snow Pudding is an egg-white foam delicately flavored with lemon, with thin Custard Sauce gracefully spooned over the top like the winter sun over crystalline snow.

Note: This recipe contains uncooked egg whites (see page 262).

¼ cup cold water
2 teaspoons (1 envelope) unflavored gelatin
½ cup sugar
1 cup boiling water
3 tablespoons freshly squeezed, strained lemon juice
3 extra-large egg whites (reserve yolks for Custard Sauce)
¼ cup sugar
1 recipe Custard Sauce (page 372)

Place ¼ cup cold water in a small mixing bowl. Sprinkle the gelatin over the water; let stand 15 minutes.

Then, add ½ cup sugar and 1 cup boiling water to the gelatin mixture; stir until the sugar completely dissolves. Add the lemon juice; stir to blend. Refrigerate the gelatin mixture until it begins to set and is the consistency of unbeaten egg whites, stirring occasionally.

Then, remove the gelatin mixture from the refrigerator; set aside. Place the egg whites in a medium mixing bowl. Using an electric mixer, beat the egg whites on high speed until soft peaks hold. While continuing to beat on high speed, very gradually add ¼ cup sugar and continue beating the egg white mixture until stiff, but still moist and glossy.

Pour the gelatin mixture over the egg white mixture; using a large mixing spoon, fold in until nearly blended. Using the electric mixer, beat the mixture *briefly* on high speed to thoroughly blend.

Turn the mixture into a bowl; refrigerate until cold and set. Then, cover the bowl.

To serve, spoon the gelatin mixture (snow) into sherbet glasses; spoon Custard Sauce generously over the gelatin mixture. Place each glass on a small (bread and butter–sized), doily-lined plate.

SERVES 8

ALTERNATIVE SERVING PROCEDURE: To serve the Snow Pudding on a buffet or at the table, turn the gelatin mixture into a *very* lightly oiled 1-quart mold (see To Lightly Oil a Salad Mold, page 109) after blending. Unmold (page 109) on a flat, crystal plate. Serve the Custard Sauce alongside, in an attractive sauce dish with a ladle.

BREAD PUDDING WITH LEMON SAUCE

4 cups (1 quart) whole milk
2 cups Dried Bread Cubes (page 48) (cut good-quality, unsliced white bread into ⅝-inch-square cubes)
¾ cup sugar
½ teaspoon salt
1 tablespoon butter, melted
4 extra-large eggs
1 teaspoon pure vanilla extract
1 recipe Lemon Sauce with Raisins (page 372)

Preheat the oven to 350° F. Butter a 1½-quart round or oval baking dish; set aside.

Pour the milk into a medium saucepan. Scald the milk (page 25). Remove from the heat. Add the bread cubes; stir carefully, only until the bread cubes are coated with milk. Let the mixture stand 5 minutes.

Then, add the sugar, salt, and butter to the bread cube mixture; stir well; set aside.

Place the eggs in a small mixing bowl. Using an electric mixer, beat the eggs slightly on medium speed. Pour approximately ¼ cup liquid from the bread cube mixture over the eggs; stir quickly to blend. Then, add the egg mixture to the remaining bread cube mixture; stir to blend with the liquid in the bread cube mixture. Add the vanilla; stir to blend.

Pour the bread cube mixture into the prepared baking dish. Place the baking dish in a 9 × 13 × 2-inch baking pan. Then, pour very hot (not boiling) water into the pan to approximately ½ the height of the baking dish. Bake, uncovered, for 1 hour, or until a table knife inserted into the pudding near the center of the baking dish comes out clean.

Remove the baking dish from the baking pan and place on a wire rack. Let the pudding stand until cooled slightly; then, refrigerate. When the pudding is cold, cover; keep refrigerated.

Serve the Bread Pudding cold in individual sauce dishes. Spoon cold Lemon Sauce with Raisins over each serving.

SERVES 8

CHOCOLATE-CHERRY SOUFFLÉ

Concealed under this puffy chocolate soufflé you whisk from the oven to the table are cherry preserves. This is a sophisticated, seductive dessert to say the least. You will need a 1½-quart, straight-sided soufflé dish to make it. (For the definition of Soufflé, see page 26.)

½ cup cherry preserves, home canned
   (page 756) or commercially canned
3 tablespoons unsweetened cocoa powder
2 tablespoons powdered sugar
4 extra-large eggs, room temperature
1 teaspoon pure vanilla extract
1 recipe Custard Sauce (page 372)

Preheat the oven to 375° F. Butter a 7½ × 3-inch (1½-quart) ovenproof, round soufflé dish with straight sides. Using granulated sugar, sugar the inside of the dish as you would flour a baking pan (page 55).

Spread the cherry preserves evenly over the bottom of the prepared soufflé dish; set aside. In a small mixing bowl, place the cocoa and powdered sugar; stir to combine; set aside.

Separate the eggs, placing the egg yolks in a small mixing bowl and the egg whites in a large mixing bowl. Set the egg whites aside. Add the vanilla to the egg yolks; using an electric mixer, beat on medium speed only until smooth and blended; set aside. Using the electric mixer fit with clean, dry blades, beat the egg whites on high speed until soft peaks hold. While continuing to beat on high speed, very gradually add the cocoa mixture and continue beating the egg white mixture until stiff, but still moist and glossy. Add the egg yolk mixture; using a large mixing spoon, quickly and gently fold in.

Turn the mixture into the soufflé dish (over the cherry preserves). Using a small, narrow spatula, lightly and quickly spread the mixture evenly. Place the soufflé dish in the center of an oven rack on the lowest shelf level in the oven. Bake for 23 to 25 minutes, until the soufflé rises. Watch carefully, as both overbaking and underbaking can cause the soufflé to fall.

When done, remove the soufflé from the oven, and *quickly* cut into 4 servings using a sharp, thin-bladed knife. Using a small spatula, carefully remove the servings from the soufflé dish and place on individual plates. Spoon a small amount of the Custard Sauce over each serving and *serve immediately*. Time is of the essence when serving soufflés, as they begin to fall after only a few minutes out of the oven. The baking of soufflés must precisely coincide with the time they are to be served. Soufflés are customarily taken directly from the oven to the table where they are quickly displayed and then immediately cut, served, and consumed before time plays havoc with these evanescent delicacies.

SERVES 4

(Recipe continues on next page)

VARIATION: The Custard Sauce may be omitted, in which case the top of the soufflé should be sprinkled very lightly with powdered sugar before being presented at the table. To sprinkle the top of the soufflé, place 1 tablespoon powdered sugar in a very small hand strainer and shake it back and forth over the soufflé until the top is lightly decorated.

BAKED CUSTARD

3 extra-large eggs
¼ cup plus 1 tablespoon sugar
¼ teaspoon salt
¾ teaspoon pure vanilla extract
2 cups whole milk, scalded (page 25)
Ground nutmeg for garnish

Preheat the oven to 325° F.

Place the eggs in a medium mixing bowl. Using an electric mixer, beat the eggs slightly on medium speed. Add the sugar, salt, and vanilla. Using a large spoon, stir to combine. Slowly add the scalded milk, stirring constantly.

Ladle the mixture into five 6-ounce ovenproof glass custard cups. Sprinkle nutmeg lightly over the mixture in each custard cup.

Place the filled custard cups in a 9 × 13 × 2-inch baking pan. Then, pour very hot (not boiling) water into the pan to approximately ½ the height of the custard cups. Bake for 40 minutes, or until a table knife inserted into the custard halfway between the edge and the center of a custard cup comes out clean. The custard will continue cooking after removal from the oven, and the center of the custard will fully set. Avoid overbaking, causing the custard to become porous and watery.

Remove the custard cups from the baking pan and place on a wire cookie rack (see Note). Let the custard stand until cooled slightly; then, refrigerate. When the custard is cold, cover each custard cup with aluminum foil; keep refrigerated.

Serve Baked Custard cold, in the custard cups.

NOTE: The close-set wires of a cookie rack will keep the custard cups level while allowing for full air circulation.

SERVES 5

SERVING SUGGESTION: Each serving may be garnished with a small amount of Whipped Cream (page 373) at serving time. Spoon or pipe the Whipped Cream onto the center of each custard cup; if piped, use a decorating bag fit with large open-star tip number 6B (page 383).

CHEESECAKE

PASTRY
½ cup (¼ cup) butter
1 cup all-purpose flour
¼ cup sugar
½ teaspoon finely grated lemon rind (page 47)
1 extra-large egg yolk
¼ teaspoon pure vanilla extract

Remove the butter from the refrigerator and let stand 10 minutes before use in the recipe.

Preheat the oven to 400° F. Butter the bottom and side of a 9 × 3-inch springform pan; set aside.

In a large mixing bowl, place the flour, sugar, and lemon rind; stir to combine; set aside. In a small mixing bowl, place the egg yolk and vanilla; using a table fork, beat to blend; set aside. Using a knife, cut the butter into approximately 8 pieces and drop into the bowl containing the flour mixture. Using a pastry blender, cut the butter into the flour mixture until the mixture is the texture of coarse cornmeal interspersed with some pieces the size of small peas. Add the egg yolk mixture; using a table fork, quickly stir to combine.

With floured hands, gather ⅔ of the pastry into a ball and wrap in plastic wrap; refrigerate.

Remove the side of the prepared springform pan; set aside. Gather the remaining ⅓ of the pastry into a ball and place on a floured pastry cloth. Using a stockinet-covered, then floured rolling pin (page 54), roll the pastry to ⅛-inch thickness and into a circle slightly larger in diameter than the springform pan bottom. Place the buttered side of the springform pan bottom on the rolled pastry. Carefully invert the pastry cloth, pastry, and pan bottom; remove the pastry cloth. Run a sharp, thin-bladed knife dipped in flour around the edge of the springform pan bottom to remove the extra pastry. Gather the extra pastry into a ball; wrap in plastic wrap and refrigerate. Bake the bottom crust 4 to 5 minutes, or until light golden.

Remove from the oven and place the pan bottom (with crust) on a wire rack. Let stand until the crust completely cools.

Then, lock the side of the pan onto the pan bottom (leaving the crust on the pan bottom). Remove from the refrigerator the balls containing the remaining ⅔ of the pastry and the extra pastry; let stand at room temperature, in the plastic wrap, 10 minutes.

Unwrap the balls of pastry and press together to form one ball, handling the pastry minimally.

Roll the pastry (in a circle) to ⅛-inch thickness. Using the sharp, thin-bladed knife dipped in flour, cut the pastry into 2½-inch-wide strips. Cut and fit the pastry strips to cover the side of the pan, use your fingers to press the strips to the side of the pan. Patching may be necessary. Set aside while proceeding to make the Filling (recipe follows).

FILLING
36 ounces cream cheese, softened
1½ cups sugar
2 tablespoons plus 2 teaspoons all-purpose flour
1 teaspoon finely grated orange rind (page 47)
½ teaspoon finely grated lemon rind (page 47)
4 extra-large eggs plus 2 extra-large egg yolks
½ teaspoon pure vanilla extract
¼ cup whipping cream, unwhipped

Preheat the oven to 475° F.

In a large mixing bowl, place the cream cheese, sugar, flour, orange rind, and lemon rind; using an electric mixer, beat on high speed only until the cream cheese is *completely* smooth. Stop the electric mixer. Add the eggs, egg yolks, and vanilla; beat on medium speed only until blended. Add the cream; beat on medium speed only until blended. Do not overbeat the cream cheese mixture, which will incorporate too much air and cause the cheesecake to inflate, fall, and crack during baking.

Pour the cream cheese mixture into the pastry-lined pan. Bake for 10 minutes. Reduce the oven heat to 200° F. and bake for an additional 1 hour. To test for doneness, gently shake the cheesecake; the very center will jiggle slightly when done.

Remove the cheesecake from the oven and place on a wire rack; let stand to cool in the pan 30 minutes. Shortly before the 30-minute cooling period is over, prepare the Sour Cream Topping.

SOUR CREAM TOPPING
16 ounces commercial sour cream
¼ cup sugar
1 teaspoon clear vanilla

Preheat the oven to 475° F.

In a medium mixing bowl, place the sour cream, sugar, and vanilla; using a spoon, stir until well blended.

When the cheesecake has cooled 30 minutes, use a small, narrow spatula to spread the topping as evenly as possible over the top. Bake for 10 minutes. (The topping will completely set when the cheesecake is cold.)

Remove the cheesecake from the oven and place on a wire rack; let stand to cool in the pan 15 minutes. Then, carefully run a sharp, very thin-bladed knife around the inside edge of the pan to loosen the side of the cheesecake from the pan. Let the cheesecake stand in the pan on the wire rack to cool an additional 3 hours.

Then, carefully remove the side of the pan.

(Recipe continues on next page)

Leave the cheesecake on the pan bottom. Using kitchen scissors and your fingers, carefully remove any crust which may extend higher than the top surface of the cake. Place the cheesecake (on the pan bottom) in an airtight container and refrigerate 24 hours before serving. Keep stored in the refrigerator.

SERVES 16

OPTIONAL DECORATION: Thoroughly cold cheesecake may be decorated with tinted or untinted flowers, designs, and borders (page 388) made of cream cheese. Place 12 ounces of softened cream cheese in a medium-small mixing bowl. Using an electric mixer, beat the cream cheese on high speed only until fluffy. If desired, tint the beaten cream cheese, using paste food coloring. Place the cream cheese in a decorating bag(s) fit with an appropriate tip(s) and follow the same piping procedures employed when decorating cakes with piped icing (page 383).

MRS. DOWELL'S DESSERT

Of all desserts, this vanilla-flavored mousse, made with a scandalous amount of whipped cream and chilled between dustings of graham cracker crumbs, is one of my very favorites.

Note: This recipe contains uncooked egg whites (see page 262).

1¼ cups finely rolled graham cracker
    crumbs (about 16 graham cracker
    squares), divided
½ cup whole milk
2 teaspoons (1 envelope) unflavored gelatin
2 extra-large eggs, room temperature,
    separated
¾ cup sugar
¼ teaspoon salt
2 teaspoons pure vanilla extract
2 cups (1 pint) whipping cream, unwhipped
¼ cup sugar

Distribute ½ of the graham cracker crumbs evenly over the bottom of a 7 × 11 × 2-inch baking pan; set aside. Set aside the remaining ½ of the graham cracker crumbs. Pour the milk into a small sauce dish. Sprinkle the gelatin over the milk; let stand 15 minutes.

Meanwhile, place the egg yolks in the top of a double boiler. Using a handheld electric mixer, beat the egg yolks slightly on medium speed. Add ¾ cup sugar and the salt; beat on medium speed to combine. Add the gelatin mixture; stir to blend. Place the top of the double boiler over boiling water in the bottom pan. Cook the egg yolk mixture until thick (about 12 minutes), stirring constantly.

Remove the top of the double boiler from the bottom pan and place it on a wire rack. Add the vanilla; stir until blended. Refrigerate the egg yolk mixture until cooled to room temperature, stirring occasionally. Be careful not to let the mixture cool until set.

Meanwhile, pour the whipping cream into a medium mixing bowl. Using a standard-sized electric mixer, beat the cream on medium-high speed until it begins to stiffen. Reduce the mixer speed to medium-low and continue beating the cream until stiff, but still soft and fluffy; cover and refrigerate.

When the egg yolk mixture cools to room temperature, remove it from the refrigerator; set aside. Place the egg whites in a medium mixing bowl. Using the standard-sized electric mixer fit with clean, dry blades, beat the egg whites on high speed until soft peaks hold. While continuing to beat on high speed, very gradually add ¼ cup sugar and continue beating the egg white mixture until stiff, but still moist and glossy; set aside.

Remove the whipped cream from the refrigerator. Measure ½ cup whipped cream; cover and refrigerate for use as decoration.

Turn the remainder of the whipped cream into a large mixing bowl. Add the egg yolk mixture; using a large mixing spoon, fold together until combined and uniform in color. Add the egg white mixture; quickly and carefully fold in only until combined.

Using a large mixing spoon, spoon the mixture into the baking pan over the graham cracker crumbs; using a small, narrow spatula, lightly spread the mixture evenly. Using a teaspoon, sprinkle the remaining ½ of the graham cracker crumbs evenly over the mixture. Refrigerate the dessert, uncovered. As soon as the dessert is cold and set, cover with aluminum foil; keep refrigerated.

To serve, use a sharp, thin-bladed knife to cut the dessert into 12 servings. Using a decorating bag fit with medium open-star tip number 21 (page 383) and filled with the ½ cup reserved whipped cream, pipe a small rosette (page 390) atop each serving.

SERVES 12

OPTIONAL DECORATION: If a decorating bag and tip are not available, use a teaspoon to carefully place a small dollop of the reserved whipped cream atop and in the center of each serving.

MAPLE NUT MOUSSE

Note: This recipe contains uncooked egg whites (see page 262).

1 cup cold water
2 tablespoons (3 envelopes) unflavored gelatin
4 extra-large eggs, room temperature, separated
1½ cups (12 ounces) pure maple syrup
2 cups (1 pint) whipping cream
2 cups rolled vanilla wafer crumbs (about 44 vanilla wafers)
1½ cups chopped pecans
2 cups miniature marshmallows
½ cup quartered red maraschino cherries

Oil very lightly a 10-inch (12-cup) Bundt pan (see To Lightly Oil a Salad Mold, page 109); set aside.

Pour 1 cup cold water into a small sauce dish.

Sprinkle gelatin over the water; let stand 15 minutes.

Meanwhile, place the egg yolks in the top of a double boiler. Using a handheld electric mixer, beat the egg yolks slightly on medium speed. Add the syrup; beat on low speed only until blended. Place the top of the double boiler over boiling water in the bottom pan. Cook the syrup mixture until thick (about 18 minutes), beating twice during the cooking period with the electric mixer to retain complete smoothness, and otherwise stirring constantly. Add the gelatin mixture; stir well to blend.

Remove the top of the double boiler from the bottom pan and place it on a wire rack; let stand until the syrup mixture cools slightly. Then, refrigerate the syrup mixture *only* until cooled to room temperature, stirring intermittently. Do not allow the syrup mixture to cool until gelled.

Meanwhile, pour the whipping cream into a medium mixing bowl. Using a standard-sized electric mixer, beat the cream on medium-high speed until it begins to stiffen. Reduce the mixer speed to medium-low and continue beating the cream until stiff, but still soft and fluffy; cover and refrigerate.

When the syrup mixture cools to room temperature, remove it from the refrigerator; set aside. Place the egg whites in a large mixing bowl. Using the standard-sized electric mixer fit with clean, dry blades, beat the egg whites on high speed until stiff, but still moist and glossy. Add the syrup mixture, vanilla wafer crumbs, pecans, marshmallows, and cherries; using a large mixing spoon, gently fold in until evenly combined. Add the whipped cream; fold in.

Turn the mixture into the prepared Bundt pan; using a small, narrow spatula, smooth the surface. Refrigerate the mousse until cold and set. Keep refrigerated.

At serving time, unmold the mousse onto an attractive cake stand (see To Remove Salads from Large Molds, page 109). Slice and serve at the table.

SERVES 14

CONCERTO FOR DATES AND NUTS

Preparation time: Allegro
Consumption time: Presto

A richly orchestrated score which will receive a standing ovation.

¼ cup (4 tablespoons) butter
1 cup packed dark brown sugar
2 cups water
1 cup all-purpose flour
2 teaspoons baking powder
¼ teaspoon salt
1 cup sugar
½ cup whole milk
1 cup very coarsely cut, pitted dates (cut small dates into 3 pieces)
¾ cup broken English walnuts
1 recipe Whipped Cream (page 373)

Preheat the oven to 350° F. Using Special Grease (page 56), grease a 7 × 11-inch baking dish (see Note); set aside.

In a small saucepan, melt the butter over low heat. Remove from the heat. Add the brown sugar and water; stir to combine. Bring the mixture to a boil over medium-high heat, stirring constantly. Boil the mixture 1 minute, stirring continuously. Remove from the heat. Place the saucepan in a large bowl of cold water to cool the mixture; set aside.

Meanwhile, onto waxed paper, sift together the flour, baking powder, and salt. Place the flour mixture in a medium mixing bowl. Add the sugar; stir to combine. Using a tablespoon, make a well in the center of the flour mixture. Pour the milk, all at once, into the well in the flour mixture; using an electric mixer, beat on low speed only until blended. Add the dates and walnuts; using a mixing spoon, stir and fold in only until combined and evenly distributed; set aside.

Pour the brown sugar mixture into the prepared baking dish. Using the mixing spoon, spoon the date mixture over the brown sugar mixture. Using a small, narrow spatula, smooth the mixture some. Bake for 50 minutes. The top will be golden.

Remove from the oven and place the baking dish on a wire rack; let stand until the dessert completely cools. Then, cover the dessert with aluminum foil. Store at room temperature.

To serve, cut the dessert into 15 servings and spoon a generous dollop of the Whipped Cream on each serving.

NOTE: Although not as satisfactory, the pan may be greased and floured in substitution for using Special Grease.

SERVES 15

PISTACHIO ARABESQUE

This tantalizing dessert combines fresh, from-scratch ingredients with instant pudding and a small can of crushed pineapple. The pretty, pale-green mixture is chilled over a baked crust of shortbread crumbs, chopped pistachio nuts, and butter. But pistachios are not confined to the crust. These popular nuts also are used in the dessert filling and as the topping.

2 cups rolled shortbread cookie crumbs (use homemade Scotch Shortbread cookies, page 639, or about ¾ of a 10-ounce package of Lorna Doone Shortbread Cookies)
⅔ cup chopped, non–artificially colored pistachio nuts, divided
½ cup (¼ pound) butter, melted
8 ounces cream cheese, softened
1 14-ounce can (1¼ cups) sweetened condensed milk
¼ cup freshly squeezed, strained lime juice
1 3.4-ounce package instant pistachio-flavored pudding and pie filling
1 8-ounce can commercial crushed pineapple in unsweetened pineapple juice
1 cup (½ pint) whipping cream, unwhipped

Preheat the oven to 350° F. Butter well a 9 × 13-inch baking dish; set aside.

In a medium mixing bowl, place the cookie crumbs and 3 tablespoons of the pistachio nuts; stir to combine. Add the melted butter; stir until the crumbs and nuts are coated. Spoon the mixture into the prepared baking dish. Using the back of a tablespoon, press the mixture firmly and evenly over the bottom of the dish. Bake for 8 to 10 minutes, until lightly golden.

Remove from the oven and place the baking dish on a wire rack; let stand until the baked crust completely cools.

Then, place the cream cheese in a large mixing bowl. Using an electric mixer, beat the cream cheese on high speed until smooth and fluffy. Add the condensed milk and lime juice; beat on medium-high speed until blended. Add the pudding and pie filling; beat on medium-high speed until smooth; set aside.

Place 2 tablespoons of the remaining pistachio nuts in a small sauce dish; set aside for topping. Add the remaining pistachio and pineapple (undrained) to the cream cheese mixture; using a large mixing spoon, stir and fold in until evenly distributed; set aside.

Pour the whipping cream into a medium-small mixing bowl. Using the electric mixer fit with clean, dry blades, beat the cream on medium-high speed until it begins to stiffen. Reduce the mixer speed to medium-low and continue beating the cream until stiff, but still soft and fluffy. Add the whipped cream to the cream cheese mixture; using the large mixing spoon, fold in.

Spoon the mixture over the baked crust; using a long, narrow spatula, spread evenly. Sprinkle the reserved 2 tablespoons pistachio nuts evenly over the top. Refrigerate the dessert, uncovered; cover with aluminum foil when completely cold and set.

To serve, cut the dessert into 15 servings, using a sharp, thin-bladed knife dipped in moderately hot water and then dried. Redip the knife in the water and dry before making each cut.

SERVES 15

KAHLÚA ICEBOX DESSERT

When simplicity of preparation is the goal, new and experienced cooks alike will find this recipe appealing. Kahlúa and easy-to-make chocolate curls dress up this version of a time-honored dessert standby.

1 recipe Chocolate Decorator Whipped
   Cream (page 374)
¼ cup Kahlúa liqueur (page 23)
1 9-ounce package commercial, thin
   chocolate wafers
1 recipe Decorator Whipped Cream (plain)
   (page 374)
Narrow Chocolate Curls (page 407)

Make the Chocolate Decorator Whipped Cream and add the Kahlúa near the end of beating. Using a small, narrow spatula, frost the wafers on the flat side with the chocolate whipped cream mixture. Assemble the frosted wafers, sandwich style, in a long, continuous roll (about 14 inches long) on a serving plate; refrigerate while making the (plain) Decorator Whipped Cream.

Using a clean, small, narrow spatula, frost the outside of the roll, including the ends, with the (plain) Decorator Whipped Cream. Sprinkle some Narrow Chocolate Curls evenly over the top of the roll. Then, lightly press additional curls into the side and ends of roll. Refrigerate the finished dessert at least 4 hours before serving to allow sufficient time for the wafers to soften.

To serve, slice diagonally at a 45-degree angle into 8 servings.

SERVES 8

STRAWBERRIES, TRIPLE SEC, AND WHIPPED CREAM

Fresh strawberries, hulled (page 23) and cut
in half lengthwise
Triple Sec liqueur (page 26)
Whipped Cream (page 373)

Place individual servings of strawberries in crystal sherbet glasses. Pour about ½ ounce Triple Sec over each serving. Spoon a dollop of Whipped Cream over the strawberries in each serving. Place each sherbet glass on a small (bread and butter-sized), doily-lined plate.

VARIATION: Grand Marnier liqueur (page 23) may be substituted for the Triple Sec.

STRAWBERRY BAVARIAN CREAM

The fruit Bavarian creams in the recipes that follow are made with flavored gelatin, whipped cream, and fresh fruit. They're marvelous tasting and as easy to make as falling off a log. While this style of fruit Bavarian cream often is served for informal dining in the Midwest, more classical Bavarian cream consists of custard, gelatin, whipped cream, and flavoring, which may be pureed fruit.

1 3-ounce package wild strawberry–
flavored gelatin
1 cup boiling water
½ cup cold water
2½ cups hulled (page 23 and halved or
quartered(depending upon size),
lengthwise, fresh strawberries
1 recipe Whipped Cream (page 373)

Place the gelatin in a medium mixing bowl. Add 1 cup boiling water; stir until the gelatin completely dissolves. Add ½ cup cold water; stir to blend. Refrigerate the gelatin mixture until it begins to set and is the consistency of unbeaten egg whites.

Then, remove the gelatin mixture from the refrigerator. Add the strawberries and the Whipped Cream; using a medium mixing spoon, fold in, leaving a slight rippled effect.

Spoon the mixture into a glass serving bowl or into 8 individual, crystal sherbet glasses; refrigerate. When cold and set, cover the bowl or sherbet glasses with aluminum foil; keep refrigerated.

SERVES 8

OPTIONAL DECORATION: Decorate with the additional Whipped Cream and fresh strawberries, and small sprigs of fresh mint.

APRICOT BAVARIAN CREAM

1 3-ounce package apricot-flavored gelatin
2½ cups halved, pitted, and coarsely cut
fresh apricots

Follow the Strawberry Bavarian Cream recipe, above, substituting apricot-flavored gelatin and fresh apricots for the wild strawberry–flavored gelatin and fresh strawberries.

PEACH BAVARIAN CREAM

1 3-ounce package peach-flavored gelatin
2½ cups peeled, halved, pitted, quartered,
and sliced fresh peaches (if peaches are
large, split peach quarters in half
lengthwise before slicing)

Follow the Strawberry Bavarian Cream recipe, above, substituting the peach-flavored gelatin and fresh peaches for the wild strawberry––flavored gelatin and fresh strawberries.

Ice Cream

VANILLA ICE CREAM

1½ cups sugar
¼ cup plus 2 tablespoons all-purpose flour
⅛ teaspoon salt
¼ cup whole milk
2¾ cups whole milk
6 extra-large eggs, slightly beaten
2 tablespoons pure vanilla extract
4 cups (1 quart) whipping cream, unwhipped
4 cups (1 quart) half-and-half
About 2 cups whole milk
Crushed ice
Rock salt

Have ready a 6-quart electric ice cream freezer.

In the top of a double boiler, place the sugar, flour, and salt; stir to combine. Add ¼ cup milk; stir until smooth. Add 2¾ cups milk; stir to blend. Place the top of the double boiler over boiling water in the bottom pan. Cook the milk mixture until thick (about 10 minutes), constantly stirring with a spoon or beating with a handheld electric mixer on low speed. Add about ½ cup of the hot milk mixture to the eggs and quickly stir in. Then, add the egg mixture to the remaining milk mixture and stir vigorously to blend. Continue cooking the mixture 2 minutes, beating constantly with the electric mixer on low speed.

Remove the top of the double boiler from the bottom pan and place on a wire rack; let stand until the mixture cools to moderately warm.

Then, transfer the mixture to a large mixing bowl. Add the vanilla, whipping cream, and half-and-half; using the electric mixer; beat on low speed only until blended. Cover the bowl and refrigerate the ice cream mixture until cold.

Then, pour the ice cream mixture into the ice cream freezer can. Add milk (about 2 cups) to the full line. To make ice cream, use crushed ice and rock salt, and follow the freezer instructions.

NOTE: The ice cream mixture may be made and refrigerated 1 day in advance of making the ice cream.

STRAWBERRY ICE CREAM

6 cups hulled (page 23) fresh strawberries, divided
½ cup sugar

Place 3 cups of the strawberries in a flat-bottomed pan. Using a potato masher, mash the strawberries. Place the mashed strawberries in a medium mixing bowl; set aside. Cut the remaining strawberries in half or into quarters, lengthwise, depending upon the size of the berries. (If the strawberries are small, leave them whole.) Add the strawberries to the mashed berries. Add ½ cup sugar; stir to combine.

Follow the Vanilla Ice Cream recipe, above, adding the strawberry mixture to the ice cream mixture just before making the ice cream; stir until evenly distributed. (Less than 2 cups milk will be required to fill the ice cream freezer can to the full line.)

HOT FUDGE SUNDAE

Spoon Hot Fudge (page 371) over vanilla ice cream (homemade, left column, or commercial). Sprinkle with coarsely chopped cashews or pecans. Add a dollop of Whipped Cream (page 373) and top with 1 red maraschino cherry with stem.

HOT BUTTERSCOTCH SUNDAE: Follow the Hot Fudge Sundae recipe, above, substituting Hot Butterscotch Fudge (page 371) for Hot Fudge. Butter brickle or butter pecan ice cream may be substituted for the vanilla ice cream.

Sauces and Toppings for Ice Cream

BAKED NUTMEG BANANAS WITH ICE CREAM AND CARAMEL SAUCE

3 tablespoons butter
3 tablespoons packed light brown sugar
2 tablespoons freshly squeezed, strained lemon juice
1 tablespoon light corn syrup
¼ teaspoon ground nutmeg
3 firm, but ripe, bananas
¾ cup Caramel Sauce (page 370)
1 pint vanilla ice cream, homemade (page 669) or commercial

Preheat the oven to 325° F. Butter a 7 × 11-inch baking dish; set aside.

In a small saucepan, melt the butter over low heat. Remove from the heat. Add the brown sugar, lemon juice, syrup, and nutmeg; stir to combine. Bring the mixture to a boil over medium heat, stirring constantly. When the mixture reaches the boiling point, the sugar should be dissolved and all the ingredients completely blended. Remove the syrup mixture from the heat; set aside.

Peel the bananas; cut them in half widthwise. Then, cut each half in two lengthwise. Place the bananas, flat side down and single layer, in the prepared baking dish. Pour the hot syrup mixture over the bananas. Bake, uncovered, for 5 minutes.

Remove the baking dish from the oven. Using a small spatula, carefully turn the bananas over; baste with the syrup in the baking dish. Return to the oven and bake for an additional 5 minutes, until the bananas are just soft. Time the baking carefully, as overbaking will cause the bananas to become too soft and not hold their shape when removed from the baking dish.

Meanwhile, place the Caramel Sauce in a small saucepan. Over warm heat, warm the Caramel Sauce only until it is the consistency of a hot fudge. Remove from the heat.

When the baking time has elapsed, remove the baking dish of bananas from the oven; baste. Using a spatula, place 2 banana quarters, flat side up, on each of 6 medium dessert plates. Place the bananas to one side of each plate. Place a scoop of vanilla ice cream next to the bananas on each plate. (Do not place the ice cream on top of the bananas as the heat from the bananas will melt the ice cream too quickly.) Using a spoon, drizzle ribbons of the Caramel Sauce back and forth over both the bananas and ice cream. Serve immediately.

SERVES 6

PEANUT BUTTER BRICKLE ICE CREAM PIE

1 9-inch Unbaked Vanilla Wafer Crust pie shell (page 474)
1 quart butter brickle ice cream
1 cup (½ pint) whipping cream, unwhipped
½ teaspoon pure vanilla extract
½ cup chunky peanut butter, room temperature
2 tablespoons chopped, unsalted peanuts

Place the pie shell in the freezer until ready to fill. Let the ice cream stand at room temperature, in the container, *only* until slightly soft.

Meanwhile, pour the whipping cream into a medium-small mixing bowl. Using an electric mixer, beat the cream on medium-high speed until it begins to stiffen. Reduce the mixer speed to medium-low. Add the vanilla and continue beating the cream until stiff, but still soft and fluffy; cover and refrigerate.

In a large mixing bowl, place the softened ice cream and peanut butter; using the electric mixer, beat on medium speed only until combined, but not until the ice cream melts. Add the whipped cream; using a large mixing spoon, fold in.

Remove the pie shell from the freezer. Using the large mixing spoon, spoon the ice cream mixture into the pie shell; using a small, narrow spatula, spread evenly. Sprinkle the top of the pie filling with the chopped peanuts. Place the pie, uncovered, in the freezer. When firm, place the pie in a dome-topped, airtight container. Keep the pie in the freezer until ready to cut and serve (see To Cut and Serve Pies and Tarts, page 459, for procedure.)

SERVES 10

MINCEMEAT-RUM ICE CREAM PIE

1 9-inch Baked Nutmeg Graham Cracker Crust pie shell (page 472)
1 quart vanilla ice cream, homemade (page 669) or commercial
1 cup mincemeat, home canned (page 726) or commercially canned
½ teaspoon rum flavoring
Ground nutmeg for decoration
1 recipe Decorator Whipped Cream (page 374)

Place the cooled pie shell in the freezer until ready to fill. Let the ice cream stand at room temperature, in the container, *only* until slightly soft.

Meanwhile, in a small mixing bowl, place the mincemeat and rum flavoring; stir to blend; set aside.

Remove the softened ice cream from the container and place it in a large mixing bowl. Using an electric mixer, beat the ice cream on medium speed only until smooth, but not melted. Add the mincemeat mixture; using a large mixing spoon, stir to combine.

Remove the pie shell from the freezer. Using a large mixing spoon, spoon the ice cream mixture into the pie shell; using a small, narrow spatula, spread fairly evenly, mounding the mixture in the center of the pie. Sprinkle the nutmeg sparingly over the pie filling. Place the pie, uncovered, in the freezer; let stand until the filling hardens.

Then, using a decorating bag fit with large open-star tip number 6B (page 383), pipe a rope border (page 389) of Decorator Whipped Cream around the edge of the pie (not touching the crust), and a large rosette (page 390) in the center of the pie. Place the pie, uncovered, in the freezer. After the whipped cream garnish freezes, place the pie in a dome-topped, airtight container. Keep the pie in the freezer until ready to cut and serve (see To Cut and Serve Pies and Tarts, page 459, for procedure).

SERVES 10

PEPPERMINT STICK DESSERT

Here is a nice recipe which features peppermint stick ice cream in a sophisticated dessert. The refreshing flavor and coolness of the ice cream make it a welcome and appropriate finale to a heavy dinner. Over graham cracker crumbs, you freeze a layer of rich chocolate cream before spreading the softened ice cream generously over all. As the final touch, you garnish the top with Narrow Chocolate Curls. Allow at least 24 hours for this appealing concoction to freeze solidly before serving. Make-ahead desserts like this one go a long way toward relieving entertainment-day cooking fatigue.

¾ cup finely rolled graham cracker crumbs
   (about 10 graham cracker squares)
3 extra-large eggs
¼ cup whole milk
½ cup (¼ pound) butter
1 6-ounce package (1 cup) semisweet
   chocolate chips
2 cups powdered sugar
2 quarts peppermint stick ice cream
Narrow Chocolate Curls (page 407)

Spread the graham cracker crumbs evenly over the bottom of a 9 × 13 × 2-inch baking pan; set aside. In a small mixing bowl, place the eggs and milk; using a handheld electric mixer, beat on medium speed only until blended; set aside.

In the top of a double boiler, place the butter and chocolate chips. Place the top of the double boiler over simmering water in the bottom pan. Stir the butter and chocolate chips until melted and blended. Add about 2 tablespoons of the hot, chocolate mixture to the egg mixture and quickly stir in. Then, add the egg mixture to the remaining chocolate mixture and stir vigorously to blend. Cook the chocolate mixture 2 minutes over simmering water, beating constantly with the electric mixer on low speed.

Remove the top of the double boiler from the bottom pan. Add the powdered sugar; using the electric mixer, beat on low speed until blended.

Pour the chocolate mixture evenly over the graham cracker crumbs in the baking pan; using a small, narrow spatula, spread the mixture, being careful not to move the crumbs. Place the baking pan, uncovered, in the freezer; let stand until the chocolate mixture is firm.

Then, remove the ice cream from the freezer. Remove the ice cream from the container and place it in a large mixing bowl. Let stand until the ice cream is just soft enough to beat. (Do not allow the ice cream to melt.) Using a standard-sized electric mixer, beat the ice cream on medium speed until smooth.

Spoon the ice cream over the firm chocolate mixture; using a clean, small, narrow spatula, spread evenly. Sprinkle the Narrow Chocolate Curls over the top. Place the dessert in the freezer. When firm, cover tightly with aluminum foil. Let stand 24 hours to freeze solidly before serving.

To serve, use a sharp, thin-bladed knife to cut the dessert. Before making each cut, dip the knife blade into a glass of very hot water and then wipe the blade on a damp sponge to remove the excess water. (Serve frozen.)

MAKES 15 LARGE SERVINGS OR 30 SMALL SERVINGS

PINK GRAPEFRUIT SORBET

Note: This recipe contains an uncooked egg white (see page 262).

¼ cup sugar
2 cups water
1 cup freshly squeezed, strained, pink (or
   red) grapefruit juice
1 teaspoon finely grated grapefruit rind
   (page 47)
1 drop (no more) red liquid food coloring
1 extra-large egg white, room temperature
Grapefruit zest (page 46)

In a small saucepan, place the sugar and water; stir to combine. Over low heat, stir the mixture until the sugar completely dissolves. Remove from the heat and place the saucepan on a wire rack. Let stand until the syrup is cool.

Then, add the grapefruit juice and grapefruit rind; stir to blend and combine. Add the food coloring; stir until completely blended.

Pour the mixture into an 8 × 8 × 2-inch baking pan; place in the freezer for 2 hours.

Remove from the freezer and spoon the mixture into a blender beaker. Using the blender, puree the mixture until slushy. Transfer the mixture back to the baking pan and repeat the freezing and pureeing procedures.

Freeze the mixture a third time and, again, remove from the freezer after 2 hours; let stand. Place the egg white in a small mixing bowl. Using an electric mixer, beat the egg white on high speed until soft peaks hold. Place the beaten egg white in the blender beaker with the sorbet mixture for the final pureeing.

Pour the sorbet into a 6-inch-diameter × 2-inch-deep round cake pan. Cover the pan and freeze the sorbet until ready to serve.

Shortly before serving, remove the sorbet from the freezer and let stand to soften slightly. Decorate each serving with a tiny amount of grapefruit zest.

SERVING SUGGESTION: Nice to serve between dinner courses to cleanse the palate (intermezzo, page 23). As intermezzo, serve the sorbet in crystal sherbet glasses or saucer champagne glasses. Using a 1½-inch trigger scoop, place a small serving of sorbet in each glass and decorate the top of each serving very sparingly with grapefruit zest. Place the glasses of sorbet on small (bread and butter-sized), doily-lined plates. Provide small teaspoons for the diners.

Other Dessert Recipes

Candies

When I lived in New York City, opting for a candy splurge meant tripping to the Teuscher Chocolates store in Rockefeller Center for a small box of champagne truffles, or slipping into the candy room at Bloomingdale's to carefully select four Godiva chocolates—two for immediate eating (to counter shopping fatigue) and one for each of the succeeding two days.

Midwest homemade candy takes on much broader proportions. It peaks at Christmastime when a requisite batch of Fudge (page 685), the Heartland passion, follows on the heels of decorating the tree. Two additional holiday signature candies Divinity (page 678) and Peanut Brittle (page 681), can get you into the Christmas spirit as surely as Jingle Bells. In case you don't have the time or inclination to make these latter two confections, ask Santa. If you've been good, he'll probably arrange to have a friend drop by with a lush plateful for nibbling while you unwrap the presents.

Less frequently made are the exquisite, festive candies Penuche (page 686), Candied Orange Peel (page 685), and English-style toffee (see Chocolate-Almond Toffee, page 679), which can add an imaginative touch to the enticing holiday assortment on the end table.

A permissible overindulgence in this once-a-year candy regale will generally pacify one's sweet tooth until February, when Valentine's Day just wouldn't be Valentine's Day without candy. A box of homemade confections (preferably chocolates) tied with a flowing red ribbon will melt the heart of your love like Cupid's arrows.

Although plenty of candy making is carried on throughout the Midland, the total candy yield is outstripped by the profusion of pies, cakes, and cookies which materialize from the deft fingers of Midwest cooks. During those lapses between holidays, when nary a piece of homemade candy can be found in most candy dishes, a surprise plate of beautiful homemade confections passed at the end of a dinner party, after the coffee is poured, is always received with plaudits. (Make the pieces small so guests can sample each kind while chatting.)

When you're looking for an easy-to-make, informal candy to help cure the winter blahs, put Peanut Clusters (page 681) on your cooking agenda. Or, if your children or grandchildren think they don't like nuts, try Chocolate Cracker Snacks (page 691). Whichever of these ample recipes you make, put on your parka and boots and take a welcome dishful to your neighbor.

June wedding bells ring in intricately decorated wedding cakes usually flanked by doily-lined plates of tempting mints, the traditional nuptial candy throughout the Midwest and many other regions of the country as well. Customarily made in colors which match or complement the wedding color scheme, at elaborate weddings they are often individually decorated with tiny rosebuds or other flowers, rendering them almost too pretty to eat (see Cream Cheese Mints [page 683] and Pink Peppermints [page 684]).

In faithful adherence to the scrumptious Midwest candy calendar, candy makers turn out a litany of special goodies when fall rolls around. Halloween and Popcorn Balls (page 688) go hand in hand. Little ghosts and goblins give them a thumbs-up! For the older crowd, munching on a bowl of homemade Caramel Corn (page 690) while taking in a good rented movie seems to help soothe sore muscles from an afternoon of leaf raking.

Also autumn-like in character are homemade caramels, which bear little resemblance to the commercially purchased ones. I always thought I didn't care very much for caramels until I began to make them (see Pecan Caramels, page 674). Homemade caramels are creamy and have a wonderful buttery flavor, whereas I have found the commercial versions usually to be sticky-tough, with a rather ordinary, imitation-like flavor.

Candy making is fun. It is a specialty—a hobby—like cake decorating. It takes patience, attention to detail, and precision timing. The process of tempering, essential to achieving an unstreaked, glossy finish on chocolate, can be tedious. However, when meticulously carried out, tempering produces chocolate candy which is a source of great satisfaction to the diligent maker (see Tempering Chocolate, below).

Proper equipment is a must. A reliable candy thermometer, heavy pans of the proper size, and high-quality candy-dipping tools and molds are indispensable.

Candy is one of the little pluses in life. In one concentrated bite, it seems to represent everything that is desirable, opulent, and good.

SOURCES FOR CANDY-MAKING SUPPLIES

High-quality candy-making tools, molds, oil-based candy flavorings and colors, and other supplies are available from Wilton Enterprises and Sweet Celebrations Inc. (see Product Sources, page 849).

TEMPERING CHOCOLATE

PURPOSES FOR TEMPERING CHOCOLATE

There are three purposes for tempering chocolate:

- Preventing white streaks in the finished product.

- Achieving a shiny finish on the finished product.

- Achieving a firm set up of the chocolate.

WHAT IS TEMPERING?
Tempering chocolate is a three-step process:

- Melting the chocolate.
- Cooling the chocolate.
- Reheating the chocolate to the desired, usable temperature.

When chocolate is melted, the cocoa butter separates from the chocolate liquor (both are products of the cocoa bean). During the cooling process, the cocoa butter and liquor reblend. The reblended chocolate is then carefully increased in temperature to a usable consistency. Tempering requires some time and patience, but the results are worth the effort.

WHEN SHOULD CHOCOLATE BE TEMPERED?
Tempering is most often employed in making candy; for example, chocolate-dipped candies, chocolate-covered nuts, and molded chocolates. For the best results, chocolate used to make decorations for cakes, pies, and cookies should also be tempered.

TYPES OF CHOCOLATE WHICH ARE TEMPERED
In general, two types of chocolate are used in recipes which call for tempering:

- Real semisweet chocolate.
- Real milk chocolate.

Real white chocolate is a superior, ivory-colored product made with cocoa butter. It contains no chocolate liquor. White chocolate should be tempered when used in most candy making.

Confectioners' coating, also known as almond bark, candy coating, summer coating, and by various commercial names, contains little or no cocoa butter. It is made with a vegetable fat base. It need not be tempered; however, tempering results in a more shiny end product.

HOW TO TEMPER CHOCOLATE
1. Using a sharp knife, coarsely shave the chocolate. Place the shaved chocolate in the top of a double boiler and set aside. Pour water into the bottom pan of the double boiler to ½ inch from the bottom of the double boiler top when in place. Cover the bottom pan of the double boiler (without the double boiler top pan). Over medium heat, heat the water until hot (not simmering).

2. Remove the pan from the heat. Remove the cover and place the top of the double boiler over the hot water in the bottom pan. (The water should not be touching the bottom of the double boiler top.) Stir constantly until the chocolate just melts.

3. Replace the hot water in the bottom pan of the double boiler with cool (about 60° F.) water. Use a candy thermometer to assure the proper water temperature. Stir the melted chocolate until it cools to 85° F. Use the candy thermometer to determine the temperature. The chocolate will be very thick. If the water in the bottom pan of the double boiler becomes too warm during the cooling process due to the initial high temperature of the chocolate, thus making it difficult to reduce the chocolate temperature to 85° F., replace the warm water with fresh 60° F. water and continue stirring.

4. When the chocolate cools to 85° F., replace the water in the bottom pan of the double boiler with 90° F. water. Stir the chocolate constantly until it reaches suitable dipping temperature (about 88 to 90° F.). Keep the chocolate (in the double boiler top) over 90° F. water to maintain the dipping temperature. Stir the chocolate often during the dipping process to keep the cocoa butter properly blended. Replace the water if it becomes too cool, causing the chocolate to begin to thicken beyond a desirable dipping consistency. If the temperature of the chocolate is allowed to drop below 80° F., it will be necessary to retemper it.

5. Be careful not to get any water or moisture in the chocolate.

TO DIP CHOCOLATES

It is important to dip chocolates on a dry day in a cool (about 65° F.) kitchen. The candy centers should be 65 to 70° F. (room temperature) for dipping.

Drop one center at a time into 1 to 2 pounds of tempered chocolate (see Tempering Chocolate, page 671). (It is difficult to control the temperature of more than 2 pounds of dipping chocolate.) Lift the center out of the chocolate with a candy-dipping fork. Remove the excess chocolate by scraping the dipping fork on the edge of the pan (double boiler top). Place the dipped chocolate on waxed paper spread on the kitchen counter, and make an attractive swirl on top of the candy with the excess chocolate on the fork.

Allow the chocolates to stand until cool and set. Then, place them in an airtight container and store in a cool, dry place. Most chocolate-dipped candies may be stored for several weeks.

BOURBON BALLS

2½ cups (about 58) *finely rolled* vanilla
 wafers
2 tablespoons unsweetened cocoa powder
1 cup powdered sugar, sifted (page 57) (sift
 after measuring)
1 cup finely chopped English walnuts
2 tablespoons light corn syrup
⅓ cup bourbon
½ cup powdered sugar, sifted (sift after
 measuring)

In a large mixing bowl, place the vanilla wafer crumbs, cocoa, 1 cup powdered sugar, and the walnuts; stir to combine. Add the syrup and bourbon; stir until all particles are moistened.

Using a wet, 1-inch trigger scoop, scoop even portions of the mixture from the mixing bowl and, with damp hands, roll into balls. Place the shaped balls on a piece of waxed paper. Rinse the trigger scoop and your hands often in warm water.

Place ½ cup powdered sugar in a sauce dish. Roll each ball in the powdered sugar to coat.

Place the Bourbon Balls, single layer, on a clean piece of waxed paper in an airtight container; let stand to ripen 2 days.

If necessary, reroll the Bourbon Balls in additional sifted powdered sugar to coat before serving.

MAKES ABOUT 54

CARAMEL PUFF BALLS

You don't need to get out the candy thermometer and other specialized candy-making paraphernalia to prepare these puffy confections.

1 7.2-ounce box Rice Krispies cereal
½ cup (¼ pound) butter
1 14-ounce package commercial caramels
1 14-ounce can (1¼ cups) sweetened
 condensed milk
1 16-ounce package standard-sized
 marshmallows

Place 2 cups cereal in a medium mixing bowl; set aside. In a medium, heavy-bottomed saucepan, melt the butter over low heat. Add the caramels and condensed milk. Increase the heat to medium-low and stir constantly until the caramels melt and the mixture is creamy. Remove from the heat.

Butter your hands for easier handling. Using a small cooking fork, dip one marshmallow at a time in the caramel mixture and then roll it in the cereal until coated. Using a toothpick, push the coated marshmallows off the fork and onto waxed paper. Return the caramel mixture to low heat whenever it begins to thicken; stir until the creamy consistency is restored. Replenish the cereal in the bowl, 2 cups at a time, as needed.

Let the candy stand to dry about 1½ hours.

Then, store the candy, single layer, on clean waxed paper in airtight containers.

MAKES ABOUT 48

PECAN CARAMELS

1 cup (½ pound) butter
2 cups sugar
1¾ cups light corn syrup
1 cup (½ pint) whipping cream, unwhipped
1 cup (½ pint) half-and-half
1 cup broken pecans
1 teaspoon pure vanilla extract

Butter an 8 × 8 × 2-inch baking pan; set aside.

In a 3½-quart, heavy saucepan, melt 1 cup butter over low heat. Remove from the heat. Add the sugar, syrup, whipping cream, and half-and-half; stir to combine. Over medium–high heat, bring the mixture to a boil, stirring constantly. Reduce the heat to medium and attach a candy thermometer to the saucepan. Continue cooking the mixture at a moderate boil which covers the complete surface, *without stirring,* until the temperature reaches 236° F. (see Note).

Remove from the heat and detach the thermometer. Add the pecans and vanilla; stir until the pecans are evenly distributed.

Pour the mixture into the prepared baking pan. Place the baking pan on a wire rack. Let stand until the mixture completely cools.

Then, cover the baking pan with aluminum foil and refrigerate until the candy chills and sets.

Remove the candy from the refrigerator. Remove the aluminum foil and let stand at room temperature for a few minutes until the candy warms very slightly for easier cutting. Using a sharp, thin-bladed paring knife, cut the candy into 49 square pieces. If the uncut candy becomes too soft to cut sharp edges, refrigerate it for a few minutes.

Wrap each caramel neatly in a 3 × 5-inch piece of plastic wrap.

NOTE: This temperature is for use at sea-level locations. To adjust the temperature for preparation of this recipe at higher elevations, see Boiled Candies and Frostings, page 35.

MAKES 49

DIVINITY

Note: This recipe contains uncooked egg whites (see page 262).

2 extra-large egg whites, room temperature
2½ cups sugar
½ cup water
½ cup light corn syrup
¼ teaspoon salt
1 teaspoon pure vanilla extract
½ cup chopped pecans

Place the egg whites in a medium mixing bowl; set aside.

In a 3½-quart, heavy saucepan, place the sugar, water, syrup, and salt; stir to combine. Place the saucepan over medium heat. Stir the mixture constantly only until the sugar dissolves. Avoid splashing the mixture on the side of the saucepan to prevent the formation of crystals. Discontinue stirring after the sugar dissolves. Bring the mixture to a boil and attach a candy thermometer to the saucepan. Continue boiling the mixture over medium heat, *without stirring,* until the temperature reaches 250° F. (see Note) (about 15 minutes boiling time). During the boiling process, the syrup should bubble quite briskly over the entire surface. When the syrup temperature reaches 245° F. (see Note), use an electric mixer to beat the egg whites on high speed until stiff; set aside.

When the syrup temperature reaches 250° F. (see Note), remove from the heat and detach the thermometer. While beating with the electric mixer on high speed, pour the syrup in a tiny, steady stream into the beaten egg whites. This will take about 3½ to 4 minutes. While continuing to beat the mixture on high speed, add the vanilla. Continue beating on high speed until the mixture just *begins* to lose its gloss (about 4 to 5 minutes beating time after adding the vanilla). Test the candy by dropping a teaspoonful onto waxed paper. If the candy holds its form and does not flatten, it is ready. If the candy flattens, beat it another 20 to 30 seconds and test again.

When the candy is ready, add the pecans and fold in quickly, using a mixing spoon. Using a lightly buttered teaspoon, drop teaspoonsful of the candy onto waxed paper. Work quickly. If the candy becomes too stiff and chunky, add a *few drops* of hot water and, using the electric mixer, beat it until smooth.

Allow the candy to stand until it sets and loses its stickiness. Store in airtight containers.

Divinity should not be made when the weather or kitchen is humid.

NOTE: These temperatures are for use at sea-level locations. To adjust the temperatures for preparation of this recipe at higher elevations, see Boiled Candies and Frostings, page 35.

MAKES ABOUT 48

CHOCOLATE-ALMOND TOFFEE

Toffee is a hard but still crunchy candy made by boiling butter, sugar, and a bit of water to the hard-crack stage (295 to 310°F.). I boil this toffee to 300°F. The cooled and hardened candy is broken irregularly into serving-sized pieces. This recipe reflects one of the most popular ways of making toffee—with almonds and a layer of chocolate melted over the top.

1 cup unblanched, whole almonds
1½ cups (¾ pound) butter
1½ cups sugar
¼ cup water
¾ cup milk chocolate chips
½ cup sliced, unblanched almonds, ground finely (page 50)

Butter well a 9 × 13 × 2-inch baking pan; set aside. Butter the side of a 2½-quart heavy saucepan; set aside.

Scatter 1 cup whole almonds evenly over the bottom of the prepared baking pan. Place the baking pan on a wire rack; set aside.

Place 1½ cups butter in the prepared saucepan. Melt the butter over low heat. Remove from the heat. Add the sugar and water; stir to combine.

Over medium to medium-high heat, bring the mixture to a boil, stirring constantly. Attach a candy thermometer to the saucepan and continue boiling the mixture until the temperature reaches 300°F. (see Note) (about 12 to 15 minutes boiling time), stirring continuously.

Quickly pour the hot mixture over the almonds in the baking pan. Using the back of a spoon, spread the mixture evenly. Let the mixture stand 5 minutes, until the surface firms slightly.

Then, refrigerate the mixture, uncovered on a wire rack, for 30 minutes, until partially hardened.

Remove the candy mixture from the refrigerator; set aside. Place the chocolate chips in a very small saucepan. Hold the small saucepan over (not touching) hot water in a medium saucepan until the chocolate chips melt, stirring intermittently. Remove the small saucepan from the heat. Drizzle the melted chocolate back and forth over the candy mixture; using a small, narrow spatula, spread evenly. Refrigerate the candy a few minutes until the chocolate *begins* to harden.

Then, remove the candy from the refrigerator. Using a teaspoon, sprinkle the ground almonds evenly over the chocolate. Using the back of the teaspoon, *very lightly* press the ground almonds against the chocolate to facilitate adherence. Refrigerate, uncovered on the wire rack, for 2 hours, until the candy hardens.

Remove the candy from the refrigerator; let stand 10 minutes at room temperature.

Then, run a sharp, thin-bladed knife along the inside edges of the pan to loosen the sides of the candy from the pan. Using a spatula, lift the candy from the pan in one or more blocks. If the candy does not easily release from the pan, use the knife to cut out a small chunk of candy to facilitate running the spatula under the sheet of toffee. Place the sheet (or large chunks) of toffee on a piece of waxed paper. Using your hands, break the toffee into irregular, serving-sized pieces.

(Recipe continues on next page)

Store the toffee in an airtight container (such as a tin) lined with plastic wrap; keep refrigerated.

NOTE: This temperature is for use at sea-level locations. To adjust the temperature for preparation of this recipe at higher elevations, see Boiled Candies and Frostings, page 35.

MAKES ABOUT 2 POUNDS

CHOCOLATE-COVERED CHERRIES

Give yourself a midwinter lift by making beloved Chocolate-Covered Cherries for Valentine's Day or George Washington's birthday. One of the beauties of cooking is the satisfaction and feeling of personal worth derived from the creation of wonderful food. (And who can deny that we all can use a little praise from others now and then?)

Note: This recipe contains an uncooked egg white (see page 262).

2 cups sugar
½ cup plus 2 tablespoons water
2 tablespoons light corn syrup
1 extra-large egg white
5 drops cherry-flavored, oil-based candy flavoring
2 10-ounce jars small, red maraschino cherries, drained, rinsed, and thoroughly dried between several layers of paper towels
1 pound (16 squares) semisweet chocolate, tempered (page 675)

Butter lightly the side of a 3½-quart, heavy saucepan, starting from the top of the pan and buttering down the side about 3 inches only.

In the prepared saucepan, place the sugar, water, and syrup; stir to combine. Place the saucepan over medium-high heat. Stir the mixture only until the sugar melts; then, discontinue stirring, and cover the saucepan. Bring the mixture to a boil and boil 1 minute to allow time for any sugar which may have crystallized on the side of the pan to wash down. Uncover the saucepan and attach a candy thermometer. Continue cooking the mixture at a brisk boil, *without stirring,* until the temperature reaches 234° F. (see Note 1) (about 7 additional minutes).

Remove from the heat and detach the thermometer. Without stirring the mixture or scraping the side of the pan, pour the mixture onto a marble slab (see Note 2). Allow the mixture (fondant) to stand undisturbed until it cools to 110° F. (warm to the touch); the fondant will be translucent.

Then, place the egg white in a medium-small mixing bowl. Using an electric mixer, beat the egg white on high speed until stiff. Spoon the beaten egg white over the fondant on the marble slab. Using a small, narrow spatula, spread the egg white evenly over the fondant. (The egg white will cause the fondant to liquefy after the centers are dipped in chocolate.) Using a wide, firm spatula, work the fondant by scraping under the mixture from the outside edge to the center, and turning it over. Continue to work the fondant until it becomes white, opaque, and creamy in consistency (about 15 minutes). Then, take the fondant in your hands and knead it by folding it in half and pressing, until the fondant is completely smooth and free of lumps (about 5 minutes). During the kneading process, knead in 5 drops of cherry flavoring.

Shape the fondant into a ½-inch-diameter pencil. Cut the fondant pencil into ½-inch slices (or slices large enough to provide sufficient fondant to cover one cherry). With your hands, roll each slice of fondant around a maraschino cherry.

Then, dip the centers in the tempered chocolate following the procedures described in To Dip Chocolates (page 677). (Fondant made with egg white must be molded and dipped immediately after making.)

When cool, place the Chocolate-Covered Cherries in a covered container and refrigerate. These candies must be kept refrigerated because they contain uncooked egg white.

NOTE 1: This temperature is for use at sea-level locations. To adjust the temperature for preparation of this recipe at higher elevations, see Boiled Candies and Frostings, page 35.

NOTE 2: If a marble slab is not available, pour the mixture onto a laminated plastic counter or a platter which has been cooled with ice cubes and then thoroughly dried.

MAKES ABOUT 54

PEANUT BRITTLE

2 cups sugar
½ cup water
1 cup light corn syrup
12 ounces (2¼ cups) raw Spanish peanuts
1 tablespoon plus 1½ teaspoons butter
1½ teaspoons clear vanilla
2 teaspoons sifted baking soda

Butter the side of a 3½-quart, heavy saucepan; set aside. Butter lightly a 12 × 18 × 1-inch cookie pan; set aside.

In the prepared saucepan, place the sugar, water, and syrup; stir to combine. Over medium-high heat, bring the mixture to a boil, stirring constantly. Attach a candy thermometer to the saucepan. Continue cooking the mixture at a moderate boil which covers the complete surface, stirring occasionally, until the temperature reaches 230°F. (see Note). Add the peanuts; stir to combine. Continue cooking at a moderate boil, stirring almost constantly, until the temperature reaches 301°F. (see Note).

Remove from the heat and detach the thermometer. Quickly add the butter and vanilla. Sprinkle the baking soda over the mixture, stirring constantly. Stir quickly and well, until the baking soda completely blends and the mixture is no longer fluffy.

Then, immediately pour the mixture into the prepared cookie pan; using a spoon, spread very quickly. Place the cookie pan on a wire rack. Let stand until the Peanut Brittle completely cools.

Break the Peanut Brittle into pieces, using the handle of a heavy cooking utensil such as a large fork. Store the candy in an airtight container.

Peanut brittle must be made and stored in an environment with low humidity in order to achieve and maintain its dry, brittle composition.

NOTE: These temperatures are for use at sea-level locations. To adjust the temperatures for preparation of this recipe at higher elevations, see Boiled Candies and Frostings, page 35.

MAKES ABOUT 2 POUNDS

PEANUT CLUSTERS

Our family loves Peanut Clusters made from this recipe of my sister-in-law's. Dee uses one-half semisweet chocolate and one-half white confectioners' coating. Tempering the combination chocolate and confectioners' coating, properly hardens the clusters and makes them shiny.

12 ounces (12 squares) semisweet chocolate
12 ounces white confectioners' coating (almond bark), block style
2 12-ounce cans salted, whole peanuts without skins

Cover 2 cookie sheets with aluminum foil; smooth to remove any wrinkles; set aside.

Using a sharp knife, cut the chocolate and confectioners' coating into thin shavings and then chop. Place the chocolate and confectioners' coating in the top of a double boiler.

Temper the chocolate and confectioners' coating together, following the procedures described in How to Temper Chocolate (page 676). Bring the tempered mixture to 90°F. Then, add the peanuts and quickly stir to evenly distribute.

Drop the candy by rounded teaspoonful onto the prepared cookie sheets while leaving the top of the double boiler over the warm water in the bottom pan and stirring occasionally. Let the candy stand until completely cool and set.

Then, peel the Peanut Clusters off the aluminum foil and place in an airtight container.

MAKES ABOUT 84

PEANUT BARS

2½ tablespoons butter
1 10-ounce package (1⅔ cups) peanut
butter baking chips
1 14-ounce can (1¼ cups) sweetened
condensed milk
3 cups miniature marshmallows
2 12-ounce cans salted peanuts without
skins, divided

Butter a 9 × 13 × 2-inch baking pan; set aside.

In a medium saucepan, melt the butter over very low heat. Add the peanut butter chips; stir until melted. Remove from the heat and transfer the mixture to a medium mixing bowl. Add the condensed milk; using an electric mixer, beat on medium speed until blended. Add the marshmallows; using a spoon, stir to combine; set aside.

Place one 12-ounce can of peanuts in the prepared baking pan. Spread the peanuts evenly over the bottom of the pan.

Spread the marshmallow mixture evenly over the peanuts in the baking pan using 2 spoons (one to transport the marshmallow mixture and one to push the mixture into the baking pan). The marshmallow mixture will be heavy and difficult to handle. If it sticks to the spoons, first dip the spoons in water. Spread the remaining 12-ounce can of peanuts evenly over the marshmallow mixture. With your hands, press the candy firmly. Let the candy stand until completely set.

Then, using a sharp, thin-bladed knife, cut the candy into 54 approximately 1½-inch squares. Cover the baking pan with aluminum foil or a baking pan cover to store the bars.

MAKES 54

TURTLE BARS

Revel in this irresistible confection made similarly to traditional turtle candies, with pecans, chocolate, and caramel, but cut into bars. In a departure from usual candy-making techniques, this candy is baked. After you make these Turtle Bars the first time, I think you'll find yourself making them again and again.

1ST LAYER
2 cups all-purpose flour
1 cup packed light brown sugar
½ cup (¼ pound) butter, softened

2ND LAYER
1 cup coarsely broken pecans

3RD LAYER
½ cup (¼ pound) plus 3 tablespoons butter
½ cup packed light brown sugar

4TH LAYER
1 cup milk chocolate chips

DECORATION
48 pecan halves

Preheat the oven to 350°F.

In a large mixing bowl, place the flour and 1 cup brown sugar; stir to combine. Using a knife, cut ½ cup softened butter into approximately 8 pieces and drop into the bowl. Using a pastry blender, cut the butter into the flour mixture until the mixture is the texture of coarse crumbs.

Turn the mixture into an ungreased 9 × 13 × 2-inch baking pan. Using a tablespoon, spread the mixture evenly. Then, using the back of the tablespoon, pat the mixture firmly into the pan.

Sprinkle 1 cup broken pecans evenly over the mixture; set aside.

In a small saucepan, melt ½ cup plus 3 tablespoons butter over low heat. Add ½ cup brown sugar; stir to combine. Increase the heat to medium. Bring the mixture to a boil, stirring constantly. Boil the mixture 1 minute, stirring continuously.

Pour the mixture back and forth evenly over the crust and pecans in the baking pan. Use a small, narrow spatula to spread the mixture, if necessary. Bake for 18 minutes. The third layer of the bars still will be bubbling when the baking time elapses.

Remove from the oven and place the baking pan on a wire rack. Immediately sprinkle the chocolate chips evenly over the hot candy. When the chocolate chips have melted, use a clean, small, narrow spatula to spread the chocolate evenly. Let the candy stand 15 minutes.

Then, lightly press the pecan halves into the top of the uncut candy, situating them in what will be the center of each of the bars when cut.

When completely cool, use a sharp, thin-bladed knife to cut the candy into 48 bars. Cover the baking pan with aluminum foil or a baking pan cover to store the bars.

MAKES 48

CREAM CHEESE MINTS

Party-perfect molded Cream Cheese Mints in pure white or rainbow colors are a snap to make. Of course, if you decide to go all out and pipe little decorations on them, more skill and time will be entailed.

3 ounces cream cheese, softened
¼ teaspoon plus ⅛ teaspoon peppermint-flavored, oil-based candy flavoring
2¾ cups plus 2 tablespoons powdered sugar, sifted (page 57) (sift after measuring)
¼ cup granulated sugar

In a medium mixing bowl, place the cream cheese and peppermint flavoring; using an electric mixer, beat on high speed until smooth and blended. Add the powdered sugar; beat on low speed until combined. Then, beat on high speed only until blended.

Knead the mixture in your hands until smooth; set aside.

Place the granulated sugar in a small sauce dish. With your fingers, pinch off pieces of the candy mixture and roll into balls the size of mar-

bles. Roll the balls of candy mixture in the granulated sugar and press the balls into ungreased, clear plastic, mint candy molds. Using a small paring knife, remove any excess candy mixture above the surface level of the molds. Immediately unmold the mints onto a clean kitchen hand towel by inverting and flexing the molds. Hold the molds close to the hand towel to help prevent the mints from denting when they fall onto the towel.

Place the mints, single layer, in an airtight container; refrigerate (they must be kept refrigerated because they contain cream cheese).

MAKES ABOUT 72

OPTIONAL DECORATION
Paste food coloring in pale green, plus other pale colors of choice
¼ recipe Cake Decorators' White Icing, using ¼ teaspoon clear vanilla and no almond extract (page 576)

When the mints are cold, use paste food coloring to tint portions of the Cake Decorators' White Icing pale green and one or more other pale colors of choice for rosebuds. Using decorating bags filled with the tinted icings (page 383), pipe a tiny rosebud (page 394) with pale green leaves (page 391) on each mint. Use small petal tip number 101 to pipe the rosebuds and small leaf tip number 65 to pipe the leaves. Let the mints stand briefly until the decorations set. Then, replace the mints in the airtight container and refrigerate.

VARIATIONS
- Using oil-based candy flavoring, flavor the mints with other flavorings of choice.

- Using oil-based candy coloring, tint the mints in preferably pale (or other) colors of choice in keeping with the flavor of the mints. Add a few drops of coloring to the candy mixture after beating the mixture on low speed to combine the powdered sugar. Then, beat the candy mixture on high speed only until the powdered sugar and coloring are blended into the mixture.

PINK PEPPERMINTS

The finest mints are made with tempered confectioners' coating. While entitled Pink Peppermints, this recipe tells how to make these creamy-smooth mints in other colors and flavors. With a tiny rosebud meticulously piped on top, they're exquisite!

14 ounces white confectioners' coating
  (almond bark), block style or wafers
10 drops peppermint-flavored, oil-based
  candy flavoring
4 drops red, oil-based candy coloring

If using block-style confectioners' coating, shave it coarsely with a sharp knife. Temper the confectioners' coating, following the procedures described in How to Temper Chocolate (page 676), with the following exceptions:

- Add the flavoring and coloring immediately after the confectioners' coating melts (end of step 2, page 676); stir until blended.

- In step 4 (page 676), replace the water in the bottom pan of the double boiler with 100° F. (rather than 90° F.) water. Bring the temperature of the confectioners' coating to 98 to 100° F. (rather than 88 to 90° F.) and retain it at 98 to 100° F. while filling the molds.

Fill ungreased, clear plastic, mint candy molds with the confectioners' coating mixture using 2 teaspoons (one to transport the coating mixture and one to push the coating mixture into the molds). Be careful not to fill the molds too full, resulting in stands (excess candy on the bottom of the finished mints). Tap the bottom of the filled molds on the kitchen counter until air bubbles no longer surface on the candy. Refrigerate the filled molds until the candy is set, or place the filled molds in the freezer for just a few minutes until the candy is set.

When the candy is set, invert and flex the molds over a clean kitchen hand towel to remove the mints. Hold the molds close to the hand towel to help prevent the mints from denting when they fall onto the towel. Using a small, sharp, thin-bladed knife, carefully trim away any excess candy around the bottom of the mints (stands).

Place the Pink Peppermints, single layer, separated by waxed paper, in an airtight container. Store in a cool, dry place.

MAKES ABOUT 72

OPTIONAL DECORATION
**Paste food coloring in pale green, plus
  other pale colors of choice
¼ recipe Cake Decorators' White Icing,
  using ¼ teaspoon clear vanilla and no
  almond extract (page 576)**

Use paste food coloring to tint portions of the Cake Decorators' White Icing pale green and one or more other pale colors of choice for rosebuds. Using decorating bags filled with the tinted icings (page 383), pipe a tiny rosebud (page 394) with pale green leaves (page 391) on each mint. Use small petal tip number 101 to pipe the rosebuds and small leaf tip number 65 to pipe the leaves. Plain white rosebuds with pale green leaves are also effective on the pink mints. Let the mints stand until the decorations set. Then, place the mints, single layer, in airtight containers and store in a cool, dry place.

VARIATIONS
- Leave the mints untinted or, using oil-based candy coloring, tint the mints in other colors (preferably pale) of choice.

- Using oil-based candy flavoring, flavor the mints with other flavorings of choice such as crème de menthe, cinnamon, and amaretto. The flavoring and coloring of individual mints should be compatible.

CANDIED ORANGE PEEL

7 small navel oranges
4 cups granulated sugar
1 cup water
1 cup superfine sugar
6 ounces milk chocolate (bar or chips)

Wash the oranges well, removing any brand names or other marking stamped or taped on the skins. Using a small, sharp, thin-bladed knife, cut each orange lengthwise, only through the outer peel and white membrane, into fourths. (Cut 2 circles around each orange which transect both ends of the fruit.) With your fingers or the back of a spoon, detach each quarter of the peel (including the white membrane) from the pulp. (Reserve the pulp for other uses.)

Place the quarters of the peel in a large non-metallic bowl and cover with cold water. Place a nonmetallic plate directly on top of the peels. Weight the plate with a covered pint jar of water to hold the peels under the water. Cover the bowl with plastic wrap; let stand at cool room temperature about 18 hours.

Drain the peels in a colander. Place the peels in a large saucepan. Add water to cover the peels. Cover the saucepan. Over high heat, bring the peels to a boil. Immediately drain the peels in the colander. Repeat the boiling and draining process 2 more times to help remove the bitterness from the peels.

Then, using a small, sharp knife, cut the peels lengthwise into ¼-inch-wide strips; set aside.

In a clean, large, heavy saucepan, place 4 cups granulated sugar and 1 cup water; stir to combine. Over medium-low heat, bring the mixture to a boil, stirring constantly. Add the peels and continue cooking the mixture at a moderate boil which covers the complete surface. Reduce the heat to low as the mixture thickens. Cook the peels until translucent (about 30 minutes total cooking time), stirring occasionally.

Drain the peels in the colander and let stand until lukewarm and still sticky. Place 1 cup superfine sugar in a small mixing bowl. Roll each peel in the sugar and place on a wire cookie rack. Let the peels stand 2 to 3 hours until dry.

Then, if the chocolate is in bar form, use a sharp knife to chop it.

Place the chopped chocolate or chocolate chips in a very small saucepan. Hold the small saucepan over (not touching) hot in a medium saucepan until the chocolate melts, stirring intermittently. Remove the small saucepan from the heat.

Dip about ½ inch of one end of each peel into the chocolate to coat; place on waxed paper. Reheat the chocolate if it becomes too thick. Let the coated peels stand until the chocolate completely sets. Six ounces of chocolate will coat the ends of approximately ½ of the peels. Because some people prefer candied peel uncoated, serve both chocolate-coated and uncoated peel on the same candy plate.

Store the chocolate-coated peel and the uncoated peel in separate airtight containers.

MAKES 120 TO 144, DEPENDING UPON THE SIZE OF THE ORANGES

 CANDIED GRAPEFRUIT PEEL: Follow the Candied Orange Peel recipe, above, substituting 3 medium grapefruit for the oranges.

FUDGE

4 cups sugar
2 5-ounce cans (1¼ cups) evaporated milk
¾ cup (¼ pound plus 4 tablespoons) butter
1 12-ounce package (2 cups) semisweet chocolate chips
1 7-ounce jar marshmallow creme
1 teaspoon pure vanilla extract
1 cup broken pecans

Butter the side of a 3½ quart, heavy saucepan; set aside. Butter a 9 × 13 × 2-inch baking pan; set aside.

(Recipe continues on next page)

In the prepared saucepan, place the sugar and evaporated milk; stir to combine. Add the butter. Over *medium* heat (higher heat may cause the mixture to scorch), bring the mixture to a boil, stirring constantly. Attach a candy thermometer to the saucepan and continue boiling the mixture until the temperature reaches 236°F. (see Note) (about 8 minutes boiling time), stirring occasionally.

Remove from the heat and detach the thermometer. Add the chocolate chips, marshmallow creme, and vanilla. Using a handheld electric mixer, quickly beat the mixture on *low* speed until the chocolate chips melt and the mixture blends. Add the pecans; using a spoon, quickly stir to evenly distribute.

Pour the mixture into the prepared baking pan. Place the baking pan on a wire rack. Let stand until the Fudge completely cools.

Then, using a sharp, thin-bladed knife, cut the Fudge into 70 squares. Do not allow the Fudge to stand for an extended period of time before cutting as the drying of the candy (even if covered) may cause the surface to crack slightly when cut. Store the Fudge, single layer, in an airtight container.

NOTE: This temperature is for use at sea-level locations. To adjust the temperature for preparation of this recipe at higher elevations, see Boiled Candies and Frostings, page 35.

MAKES 70

HOLLY DECORATION
¼ recipe Cake Decorators' White Icing, using ¼ teaspoon clear vanilla and no almond extract (page 576)
Bright green and red paste food coloring

For the holidays, a sprig of holly may be piped on each piece of Fudge, using the Cake Decorators' White Icing tinted green and red with paste food coloring. Using a decorating bag fit with small leaf tip number 65 (page 383), pipe 2 green holly leaves (page 391) on a corner of each piece of candy. Then, using a decorating

bag fit with tiny round tip number 1, pipe 3 small red berries (see Dots, page 389) between the stem ends of the leaves.

PENUCHE

Penuche (pronounced puh-new'-chee) is a fudge made with brown sugar.

3 cups granulated sugar
2 cups packed light brown sugar
1⅓ cups half-and-half
¼ cup (4 tablespoons) butter, cut into 4 pieces
2 teaspoons pure vanilla extract
1½ cup broken pecans

Butter the side of a 3½-quart, heavy saucepan; set aside. Butter an 8×8×2-inch baking pan; set aside.

In the prepared saucepan, place the granulated sugar, brown sugar, and half-and-half; stir to combine. Over medium-high heat, bring the mixture to a boil, stirring constantly. Avoid splashing the mixture on the side of the saucepan to prevent the formation of crystals. Reduce the heat to medium and attach a candy thermometer to the saucepan. Continue cooking the mixture at a moderate boil which covers the complete surface, *without stirring,* until the temperature reaches 234°F. (see Note) (about 15 minutes boiling time).

Remove from the heat and place the saucepan on a wire rack. Do not detach the thermometer. Add the butter and vanilla, but *do not stir.* Let the mixture stand, *without stirring,* until cooled to 110°F.

Then, detach the thermometer and transfer the mixture to a medium mixing bowl. Using an electric mixer, beat the mixture on high speed until it just *begins* to lose its gloss (approximately 3 to 4 minutes). Quickly add the pecans; using a spoon, stir to evenly combine.

Turn the mixture into the prepared baking

pan; using a small, narrow spatula, spread evenly. Place the baking pan on the wire rack. Let stand until the Penuche cools slightly.

Then, while still warm, use a sharp, thin-bladed knife to score the Penuche into 64 squares. Replace the baking pan on the wire rack. Let stand until the Penuche completely cools.

When completely cool, cut the Penuche into squares along the scored lines. Store the Penuche, single layer, in an airtight container.

NOTE: This temperature is for use at sea-level locations. To adjust the temperature for preparation of this recipe at higher elevations, see Boiled Candies and Frostings, page 35.

MAKES 64

PEANUT BUTTER FUDGE

1 ½ cups granulated sugar
2 cups packed light brown sugar
¼ cup light corn syrup
1 cup (½ pint) whipping cream, unwhipped
½ cup chunky peanut butter
2 tablespoons butter, softened
1 teaspoon pure vanilla extract
¼ cup chopped, unsalted peanuts without skins

Butter the side of a 3½-quart, heavy saucepan; set aside. Butter an 8 × 8 × 2-inch baking pan; set aside.

In the prepared saucepan, place the granulated sugar, brown sugar, syrup, and whipping cream; stir to combine. Over medium-high heat, bring the mixture to a boil, stirring constantly. Attach a candy thermometer to the saucepan. Reduce the heat to medium-low and continue boiling the mixture, *without stirring,* until the temperature reaches 234° F. (see Note) (about 10 minutes total boiling time).

Remove from the heat and place the saucepan on a wire rack. Do not detach the thermome-

ter. Let the mixture stand, *without stirring,* until cooled to 110° F.

Then, detach the thermometer and transfer the mixture to a medium mixing bowl. Add the peanut butter, butter, and vanilla; using an electric mixer, beat on high speed until blended. Continue beating on high speed until the mixture becomes very thick, but is still glossy (about 4 minutes total beating time).

Quickly turn the mixture into the prepared baking pan and sprinkle evenly with the chopped peanuts. Place the baking pan on a wire rack. Let stand until the fudge completely cools.

Then, using a sharp, thin-bladed knife, cut the fudge into 36 squares. Store the fudge, single layer, in an airtight container.

NOTE: This temperature is for use at sea-level locations. To adjust the temperature for preparation of this recipe at higher elevations, see Boiled Candies and Frostings, page 35.

MAKES 36

VARIATION: For smooth fudge, substitute creamy peanut butter for chunky peanut butter and eliminate the chopped peanuts. After turning the mixture into the baking pan, let the fudge stand on a wire rack until cooled slightly. Then, while still warm, use a sharp, thin-bladed knife to score the fudge into 36 squares. If desired, place an unsalted peanut half in the center of each square. Replace the baking pan on the wire rack. Let stand until the fudge completely cools. When completely cool, cut the fudge into squares along the scored lines.

CHRISTMAS DECORATION: Whether chunky- or smooth-style Peanut Butter Fudge, decorate the center of each fudge square with ½ red candied cherry. (Use of chopped peanuts on chunky-style fudge is optional.)

SPICED PECANS

Use fresh, large, unbroken, and unnicked pecan halves when making these Spiced Pecans. Each year, I like to order lovely, orchard-fresh pecans right after they are harvested in Georgia in October. I store them in the freezer for use in making these sweetened nuts and pecan pies and for all my baking and cooking (see To Store Nuts, page 51). My source for pecans is Sunnyland Farms in Albany, Georgia (see Product Sources, page 849). They have a good catalog.

1 pound pecan halves
½ cup sugar
½ teaspoon ground cinnamon
¼ teaspoon ground nutmeg
¼ teaspoon plus ⅛ teaspoon salt
1 extra-large egg white
1 teaspoon water

Preheat the oven to 225°F. Butter a 10½ × 15½ × 1-inch cookie pan; set aside.

Sort the pecans, using only unbroken halves; set aside. In a small mixing bowl, place the sugar, cinnamon, nutmeg, and salt; stir to combine; set aside.

In a medium mixing bowl, place the egg white and water; using an electric mixer, beat on high speed until very frothy, but not stiff. Add the pecans; using a spoon, stir until completely coated. Add the cinnamon mixture; stir until thoroughly mixed.

Spread the pecans on the prepared cookie pan. Bake for 1 hour, using a large spatula to turn the pecans every 15 minutes.

Remove from the oven and turn the pecans once more. Place the cookie pan on a wire rack. Let the pecans stand until completely cool.

Then, store the Spiced Pecans in an airtight container.

MAKES 1 POUND

POPCORN BALLS

1 cup unpopped yellow popcorn (not microwave popcorn)
2 cups sugar
1 cup water
½ cup light corn syrup
¼ teaspoon salt
3 tablespoons butter, cut into 3 or more pieces
1 teaspoon pure vanilla extract
6 drops red liquid food coloring* (optional)

*Popcorn Balls may be tinted red, green, orange, or any desired color.

Butter the side of a 3½-quart, heavy saucepan; set aside.

Pop the corn in an electric corn popper; make no additions, such as salt or butter. Place the popped corn in a 12- to 16-quart kettle; set aside.

In the prepared saucepan, place the sugar, water, syrup, and salt; stir to combine. Place the saucepan over medium-high heat. Stir the mixture constantly until the sugar dissolves. Then, discontinue stirring. Bring the mixture to a boil and attach a candy thermometer to the saucepan. Continue boiling the mixture, *without stirring,* until the temperature reaches 260°F. (see Note) (about 15 minutes boiling time).

Remove from the heat and detach the thermometer. Add the butter, vanilla, and food coloring; stir briskly until the butter melts and the color is evenly blended.

Pour the mixture, in thirds, over the popcorn, carefully and quickly tossing with a large mixing spoon after each addition to coat the popcorn. Try to avoid breaking the popped kernels.

With buttered hands, shape large handsful of the popcorn into balls, pressing slightly until the balls hold their shape. Place the shaped balls on waxed paper. Keep your hands well buttered. Let the balls stand 2 hours, until dry.

Then, for gifts or an attractive presentation, wrap each Popcorn Ball in clear cellophane and tie with a narrow, red satin ribbon. Otherwise, wrap each ball snugly in clear plastic wrap.

NOTE: This temperature is for use at sea-level locations. To adjust the temperature for preparation of this recipe at higher elevations, see Boiled Candies and Frostings, page 35.

MAKES ABOUT 14

POPCORN CAKE

It's made in a tube pan in the shape of a big cake, but Popcorn Cake is made of popped corn, small gumdrops, and honey-roasted peanuts, all held together with a yummy syrup. Children and adult "kids" go for this conversation-piece candy, which you cut just like a cake.

⅔ **cup unpopped yellow popcorn (not microwave popcorn)**
1 **13-ounce package (2 cups) small gumdrops in assorted colors and flavors**
1 **12-ounce can honey roasted peanuts**
2 **cups sugar**
1 **cup water**
½ **cup light corn syrup**
¼ **teaspoon salt**
3 **tablespoons butter, cut into 3 or more pieces**
1 **teaspoon pure vanilla extract**

Butter the side of a 3½-quart, heavy saucepan; set aside. Butter well a 10 × 4-inch tube pan with a removable bottom; set aside.

Pop the corn in an electric corn popper; make no additions, such as salt or butter. Place the popped corn in a very large kettle or mixing bowl. Add the gumdrops and peanuts; using your hands, toss to combine evenly, being careful not to crush the popcorn; set aside.

In the prepared saucepan, place the sugar, water, syrup, and salt; stir to combine. Place the saucepan over medium-high heat. Stir the mixture constantly until the sugar dissolves. Then, discontinue stirring. Bring the mixture to a boil and attach a candy thermometer to the saucepan. Continue boiling the mixture, *without stirring,* until the temperature reaches 260° F. (see Note) (about 15 minutes boiling time).

Remove from the heat and detach the thermometer. Add the butter and vanilla; stir briskly until the butter melts and the vanilla blends.

Pour the syrup mixture, in halves, over the popcorn mixture, carefully and quickly tossing with a large mixing spoon after each addition to coat the popcorn mixture. Try to avoid breaking the popped kernels.

With buttered hands, lightly press large handsful of the popcorn mixture into the prepared tube pan. Place the tube pan on a wire rack. Let the cake stand 2 hours.

Then, run a sharp, thin-bladed knife around the inside edge and the center tube of the pan to loosen the cake. Lift the center tube section, with the cake, out of the pan. Then, run the knife around the bottom of the tube section under the cake. Invert the cake onto a 12-inch corrugated cardboard cake circle. Carefully lift the tube section off the cake. Store the cake in an airtight container.

At serving time, place the cake (on the cardboard cake circle) on a cake stand or serving tray and present the cake uncut. Using a sharp knife, cut pieces of the cake for diners, or let the diners cut their own.

NOTE: This temperature is for use at sea-level locations. To adjust the temperature for preparation of this recipe at higher elevations, see Boiled Candies and Frostings, page 35.

MAKES APPROXIMATELY 14 FULL SERVINGS

CARAMEL CORN

An old-time to current-age Midwest favorite, I remember eating lots of caramel corn at my grandparents' house when we were kids. No wonder caramel corn is a Midwest candy icon—about 90 percent of the popcorn grown in the United States comes from the Heartland. Indiana is the largest popcorn-producing state.

This recipe, made with peanuts, reminds me of Cracker Jack, that special caramel corn delight of tykes when we were growing up. Those boxes of Cracker Jack are still made, and there's still a prize in every box.

1¼ cups unpopped yellow popcorn (not microwave popcorn)
2¼ cups (12 ounces) salted Spanish peanuts (with skins)
1 cup (½ pound) butter
2 cups packed light brown sugar
½ cup light corn syrup
¾ teaspoon salt
½ teaspoon baking soda
1 teaspoon pure vanilla extract

Butter the side of a 3½-quart, heavy saucepan, starting from the top of the pan and buttering down the side about 3 inches only; set aside.

Pop the popcorn in a standard-sized electric corn popper; make no additions, such as salt or butter. Place the popped corn in a 12- to 16-quart kettle. Sprinkle the peanuts over the popcorn; set aside.

Preheat the oven to 250°F.

In the prepared saucepan, melt 1 cup butter over low heat. Remove from the heat. Add the brown sugar, syrup, and salt; stir to combine. Place the saucepan over medium heat. Stir the mixture constantly until the sugar dissolves. Attach a candy thermometer to the saucepan. Increase the heat to medium–high and bring the mixture to a boil, stirring constantly. Continue cooking the mixture at a brisk boil, stirring occasionally, until the temperature reaches 240°F. (see Note).

Remove from the heat and detach the thermometer. Add the baking soda and vanilla; stir to blend.

Pour ½ of the caramel mixture over the popcorn and peanuts; using a large mixing spoon, stir to coat. Using the mixing spoon, bring the uncoated popcorn and peanuts from the bottom of the kettle to the top. Add the remaining ½ of the caramel mixture and continue stirring until all the popcorn and peanuts are coated.

Spread the caramel corn equally and evenly in two 12 × 18 × 1-inch or two 10½ × 15½ × 1-inch cookie pans. Bake for 1 hour, stirring every 15 minutes. The caramel coating will be crisp.

Remove from the oven and place the cookie pans on wire racks. Let the Caramel Corn stand until completely cool. Then, store the Caramel Corn in an airtight container.

NOTE: This temperature is for use at sea-level locations. To adjust the temperature for preparation of this recipe at higher elevations, see Boiled Candies and Frostings, page 35.

MAKES ABOUT 7 QUARTS

SERVING SUGGESTION: Place Caramel Corn in individual, colorful paper or cellophane bags and serve for dessert at a tailgate lunch or a teenage buffet before a football game.

GIFT SUGGESTION: Place Caramel Corn in large, colorful tin containers with covers and give as holiday gifts.

CHOCOLATE CRACKER SNACKS

1 1-pound package Town House crackers, divided
1 12-ounce jar (about 1½ cups) chunky peanut butter
24 ounces white confectioners' coating (almond bark), block style
1 12-ounce package (2 cups) semisweet chocolate chips

Cover 2 cookie sheets with aluminum foil; smooth to remove any wrinkles; set aside.

Spread the peanut butter generously to cover one side of ½ of the crackers. Cover each spread cracker with a plain cracker to make sandwiches (use the remaining ½ of the crackers); set aside.

Using a sharp knife, shave the confectioners' coating coarsely and place it in the top of a double boiler. Add the chocolate chips.

Temper the confectioners' coating and chocolate chips together, following the procedures described in How to Temper Chocolate (page 676). Bring the tempered mixture to 90° F.

Using a candy-dipping fork or a table fork, dip the sandwiches, completely, in the tempered mixture and place them on the prepared cookie sheets. Let the dipped sandwiches stand until completely cool and set.

Then, peel the Chocolate Cracker Snacks off the aluminum foil and place, single layer, in an airtight container(s).

MAKES ABOUT 72

Beverages

I can hear it now: "Lemonade, made in the shade," voiced by my father with happy, anticipatory inflections as Mother began squeezing the lemons to make that old reliable thirst quencher on sweltering summer nights. Those were the days before air-conditioned homes and frozen lemonade, when many August evenings were spent on the outdoor porch —there to exploit any suggestion of breeze which might chance our way as we watched the motionless oak leaves on the mammoth trees.

But Corn Belt natives learn to take the hot nights in their stride, knowing this to be among the meteorological factors which make the Midwest one of the world's prime areas for growing corn. When you sit on farmhouse porches, you can clearly hear the cornstalks pop in nearby fields as they continue to grow in the heat of the night—music to farmers' ears.

The tartness of lemonade over ice cubes piled to the brim of your glass seemed to neutralize the sultriness of those evening hours better than anything else, and help put one in the frame of mind to sleep. You learned to lie very still under no covering, and let the loud, pulsating sound of the locusts lull you into slumber.

Lemonade (page 696) is still the old-fashioned summer favorite in the Midwest. State fairgrounds are studded with lemonade stands at fair time. It would be hard to imagine the fair without lemonade (see page 12 for more about this). In fact, I can't imagine a Heartland summer without lemonade. As I write these lines, it is early morning on July 10. My refrigerator is replete with a pitcher of fresh lemonade from which I will pour at least two glasses during the day for minibreaks on the porch. There stands a pitcher of limeade in the refrigerator also. If the writing goes well today, I just may reward myself with a small daiquiri before dinner.

Insofar as popular hot beverages go, Middle America is a coffee stronghold, perhaps because of the considerable Scandinavian and Germanic influences here. When you fill the creamer and sugar to accompany coffee served to guests, more times than not, neither is touched. Drinking coffee black is the predominate custom. In general, little espresso and cappuccino are drunk here although they are slowly half-inching upward in population awareness and consumption.

I wish Midwesterners would discover the joy of iced coffee. It would seem to be a beverage right down our alley, but it is virtually unavailable in coffee shops and restaurants unless a willing server makes it for you on the spot from hot coffee, or you order coffee and a glass filled with ice cubes and make it yourself. For my taste, canned iced coffee, introduced in recent years, bears little resemblance to plain, great, brewed coffee cooled quickly for later serving over ice.

Hot tea drinkers are definitely in the minority in most sections of the Heartland, but the abstainers make up for it in the summertime when iced tea becomes more the norm.

On the other side of the calendar, when the temperature outside has a minus sign in front of it, Cocoa (page 694) is a real comfort drink. Making it from scratch is simple and the result is delectable. Children are especially fond of it when miniature marshmallows float on top. Maybe they are even more crazy about the marshmallows than they are about the cocoa. When you're fixing my mug, top it with lots of whipped cream, please—enough so I can't see the cocoa underneath and will don a mustache with the first delicious sip.

Another remedy for blizzard blues is Hot Spiced Cider, made with or without applejack (page 699). It's a perfect "Let It Snow, Let It Snow, Let It Snow" romantic, fireside pleaser.

Across the plains, the holidays call for Eggnog (page 694), nowadays made with a cooked cus-tard base to avoid the consumption of raw eggs (see page 262 for more on the subject). Home-made eggnog is not difficult to make and is mar-velous to serve at an open house, flanked with fruitcake, pound cake, and holiday cookies and candies enticingly arranged on the table. Deco-rate the mantel with pine boughs and cones, giving the house that unmistakable holiday-time fragrance, and let the festivities begin!

We all associate particular foods or music with experiences we have had or persons we have known. In grade school, when often I would go to the house of my friend Sarah Smith (now Sarah Schierhorn) to play after school, Mrs. Smith would always serve us a grape juice treat (then made with canned grape juice), which I now call Grape Juice–Ginger Ale Refresher (page 696). I like to make it, not only because it conjures up pleasant childhood memories, but also because it appeals to people of all ages, can be made on the spur of the moment, and is sev-eral cuts above pop poured straight from the can. By the way, newcomers to the Midwest always comment on the fact that "pop" is the Midwest colloquialism for "soda."

PUNCH WITH REAL PUNCH

When people find out you are writing a cook-book, they often make helpful suggestions about items they would like to find in the book. One such request repeatedly made to me was to include good punch recipes.

Invariably, I find the punch served at wedding receptions and similar social gatherings to be overly sweet, boring, and blah. Such frequently encountered concoctions have given punch a bad name. Actually, punch can be a most de-lightful alcoholic or nonalcoholic drink appro-priate for serving on many occasions. One of my pet peeves is the gross skimping on liquor in supposedly alcoholic punches. A cupful of champagne in a huge punch bowl of fruit juice, champagne punch does not make. When serv-ing alcoholic punch, a bowl of nonalcoholic punch also should be available for guests who prefer it.

If you want to add punch to your brunch, I highly recommend Breakfast Punch (page 697) which emanates from Cedar Rapids, Iowa. For just the right group of close, fun-loving friends, this punch is bound to be a hit! Don't be surprised if it upstages the homemade cinnamon rolls and other goodies you have spent days preparing. If, after studying the recipe, you are fearful that Breakfast Punch may inflict a knock-out blow, decrease the vodka a little. Or, it is equally tasty without it at all.

I hope that the recipes in this chapter help fill the bill for readers searching for a variety of zippy punches. Most of them given here may be made with or without spirits. I know one thing —our family had fun testing them!

TO MAKE AN ICE RING

Many bowls of punch may be made especially glamorous and appealing by floating a beautifully arranged ice ring atop. Place your work of art in your bowl of irresistible punch just moments before the guests arrive.

To make a plain ice ring, fill an 8-inch ring mold with water, and freeze. To unmold, dip the mold briefly in warm water and invert.

To freeze decorative arrangements of strawberries, raspberries, grapes, or other edible foods in the ice ring, pour about ¼ inch cold water in the bottom of the mold, and freeze.

Arrange the fruit or other foods on top of the frozen water, placing the front of the fruit toward the bottom of the mold. Carefully pour about ⅛ inch additional cold water into the mold around the fruit. Guard against adding too much water, causing the fruit to float and the arrangement to be lost.

Place the mold in the freezer and let stand only until the fruit freezes in place. Then, add cold water to the top of the mold, and freeze.

Edible flowers (page 381) may be frozen in an ice ring, following the same procedures as for fruit.

COCOA

Swift and easy to make; warm and satisfying to drink.

3 tablespoons unsweetened cocoa powder
⅓ cup sugar
Dash of ground cinnamon
⅓ cup water
4 cups (1 quart) whole milk
¼ teaspoon pure vanilla extract
½ recipe Whipped Cream (page 373)
1 cup miniature marshmallows

In a medium saucepan, place the cocoa, sugar, and cinnamon; stir to combine. Add the water; stir to combine. Over medium heat, bring the mixture to a boil, stirring constantly. Add the milk; stir to blend. Increase the heat to medium-high and bring the mixture to just under boiling, stirring frequently.

Remove from the heat. Add the vanilla; stir to blend.

Pour the hot Cocoa into mugs. In two separate, small bowls with accompanying small serving spoons, serve the Whipped Cream and marshmallows for topping the Cocoa.

MAKES 4 SERVINGS

EGGNOG

The holidays hardly would seem complete without at least one cup of eggnog. Eggnogs have a long history, dating back to 1775 in America. "Nog" is an old English word for an ale; however, it is said that the English often made their eggnog with red wine. In America, this annual, festive indulgence is usually made with rum, brandy, or bourbon. Some recipes use both brandy and bourbon, but I prefer the smooth flavor of white rum blended with the eggs and whipped cream.

Although eggnog traditionally has been made with raw eggs, today's more informed food safety standards warn that it should be made either with a cooked cus-

tard base, as in this recipe, or with pasteurized eggs, as in commercial eggnog (see Egg Safety, page 262, for more on this subject).

6 extra-large eggs
1/2 cup sugar
Dash of salt
4 cups (1 quart) whole milk
1 teaspoon pure vanilla extract
2 cups (1 pint) whipping cream, unwhipped
1/4 cup powdered sugar
1 teaspoon pure vanilla extract
1 cup white rum (optional)
Ground nutmeg for garnish

Place the eggs in the top of a double boiler. Using a handheld electric mixer, beat the eggs slightly on medium speed. Add the sugar and salt; using a spoon, stir to combine; set aside.

Pour the milk into a medium saucepan. Over medium heat, heat the milk until hot, but do not scald. Remove from the heat. Gradually add the hot milk to the egg mixture, beating constantly with the electric mixer on medium speed. Place the top of the double boiler over (not touching) low simmering water in the bottom pan. Cook the mixture until it reaches 160° F. on a candy thermometer (about 8 minutes), stirring continuously. (When the mixture reaches 160° F., it will just coat the spoon.)

Remove the top of the double boiler from the bottom pan. Add 1 teaspoon vanilla; stir to blend. Cool the custard mixture quickly by placing the top of the double boiler in a large mixing bowl of ice water and stirring the mixture constantly for 10 minutes. Cover the top of the double boiler tightly with plastic wrap; then, cover securely with aluminum foil and refrigerate until the custard mixture is completely cold.

Near serving time, pour the whipping cream into a medium mixing bowl. Using a standard-sized electric mixer, beat the cream on medium-high speed until it begins to stiffen. Reduce the mixer speed to medium-low. Add the powdered sugar and 1 teaspoon vanilla; continue beating the cream until stiff, but still soft and fluffy. Cover the whipped cream and refrigerate.

Shortly before serving, pour the cold custard mixture into a large mixing bowl. Add the rum; stir to blend; set aside. Reserve 1 cup of the refrigerated whipped cream in a small bowl; cover and refrigerate. Add the remaining whipped cream to the custard mixture; using a large mixing spoon, stir and fold in, leaving small lumps of whipped cream in the Eggnog. To serve, ladle the Eggnog into punch cups, spoon a small dollop of the reserved whipped cream on top, and sprinkle with nutmeg.

To serve buffet style, pour the Eggnog into a punch bowl. Spoon the reserved whipped cream into a small, attractive silver or crystal bowl and supply a small silver spoon. Fill a clean, decorative salt shaker with nutmeg. Serve the Eggnog for the guests, or let the guests serve themselves.

MAKES ABOUT 2 QUARTS; 12 SERVINGS

EGGNOG COFFEE

6 cups hot, freshly brewed coffee, regular or decaffeinated
3/4 cup eggnog, homemade (page 694) or commercial
1/4 cup plus 2 tablespoons Myers's (dark) rum
1/2 recipe Whipped Cream (page 373)
Ground nutmeg for garnish

Pour the hot coffee into 6 mugs. To each mug of coffee, add 2 tablespoons eggnog and 1 tablespoon rum; stir to blend. Top with a dollop of the Whipped Cream. Sprinkle the nutmeg over the Whipped Cream.

MAKES 6 SERVINGS

LEMONADE

Lemonade is about as Midwest as it gets. See pages 692 and 12 for more about this cool drink's longtime role in coping with Midwest summer heat. When I was young, I remember my Aunt Tell making gallons of fresh lemonade which we would pour into quart canning jars over lots of ice and deliver to the several hired men cultivating corn on my Uncle Joe's large farm near Creston, Iowa. Aunt Tell would drive through the gates of the various fields, and I would run with the lemonade down the end rows of corn and wait at the particular rows where each worker was on his tractor cultivating. The men were all smiles when they spotted me waiting to hand them the cold, icy drink—a welcome relief in the blistering sun. Of course, that was in the days before air-conditioned tractor cabs, now fairly common, and modern herbicides which make cultivation of today's hybrid corn unnecessary for the most part. But Midwest summers are still scorchers, and we still love lemonade!

¾ cup freshly squeezed lemon juice (about 3 to 4 lemons)
½ cup sugar (superfine or granulated)
4 cups water
Sprigs of fresh mint for decoration (optional)

In a large pitcher, place the lemon juice, sugar, and water; stir until the sugar dissolves. Pour into tall glasses filled with ice cubes. Each glass may be decorated with a sprig of fresh mint.

MAKES 5 TO 6 SERVINGS

VARIATION: ½ cup freshly squeezed orange juice may be added to the mixture to produce a slightly less tart taste.

GRAPE JUICE–GINGER ALE REFRESHER

½ 12-ounce can (¾ cup) undiluted, frozen grape juice, thawed
¾ cup cold water
1 12-ounce can cold ginger ale

In a small pitcher, place the grape juice and water; stir to blend; set aside.

Fill 4 tall glasses nearly full of ice cubes. Into each glass, pour ¼ cup plus 2 tablespoons of the grape juice mixture (¼ of the grape juice mixture) and ¼ cup plus 2 tablespoons ginger ale (¼ of the ginger ale); stir briefly.

MAKES 4 SERVINGS

CHAMPAGNE PUNCH

If heretofore you have found most champagne punches to be disappointing, lacking in both "champagne" and "punch," a cup of this lively cheer should prove that champagne punch can live up to its name.

4 cups (1 quart) freshly squeezed, strained, cold orange juice
1 12-ounce can undiluted, frozen pineapple juice, thawed
1 cup cognac
½ cup Triple Sec liqueur (page 26)
1 1-liter bottle cold sparkling water
2 750-milliliter bottles cold champagne

Place a punch bowl in a larger bowl of small ice cubes or shaved ice. Pour some cold water over the ice cubes or shaved ice in the larger bowl. Into the punch bowl, pour the orange juice, pineapple juice, cognac, and Triple Sec liqueur; stir to blend.

Just before serving, add the sparkling water and champagne; stir, gently and briefly, to blend. Let the punch stand 1 or 2 minutes until the foam on top dissipates. Ladle into punch cups.

MAKES 3½ QUARTS; 20 SERVINGS

CRANBERRY-VODKA PUNCH

Cranberry-Vodka Punch is a gorgeous bright red color, particularly suitable for Christmas, Valentine's Day, or a patriotic occasion. If you serve it during the holiday season, freeze fresh cranberries in the ice ring you float atop the punch. (If the punch will be served over a rather long period of time, remove the ice ring before it melts to the point of releasing the cranberries into the punch. Raw cranberries are too tart to be enjoyed in the drink.)

8 cups (2 quarts) cold cranberry juice
1 12-ounce can undiluted, frozen pink
    lemonade, thawed
1 750-milliliter bottle vodka
1 2-liter bottle cold ginger ale
Ice ring (page 694)

Into a punch bowl, pour the cranberry juice and lemonade; stir to blend. Add the vodka; stir to blend. Add the ginger ale; stir until just blended. Unmold the ice ring and float it in the punch. Serve the punch immediately.

MAKES 5 QUARTS; 30 SERVINGS

DES MOINES CLUB PUNCH

1 12-ounce can undiluted, frozen orange
    juice, partially thawed
½ 6-ounce can (about ⅓ cup) undiluted,
    frozen lemonade, partially thawed
½ 6-ounce can (about ⅓ cup) undiluted,
    frozen limeade, partially thawed
½ cup grenadine (alcoholic or
    nonalcoholic)
1⅔ cups vodka (optional)
1 2-liter bottle plus 1 12-ounce can (about
    2½ quarts total) cold 7UP
Small ice cubes

Into a punch bowl, pour the orange juice, lemonade, limeade, grenadine, and vodka; stir until the juices completely thaw and all the ingredients blend. Add the 7UP and ice cubes; stir briefly to blend. Serve immediately.

MAKES 3½ QUARTS; 20 SERVINGS

BREAKFAST PUNCH

You will become known as a punch virtuoso when you serve this one at your next brunch or special breakfast.

¾ cup freshly squeezed, strained orange
    juice
¾ cup (6 ounces) undiluted, frozen
    pineapple juice, thawed
¾ cup water
1 medium-sized, ripe banana, peeled and
    cut into 1-inch chunks
1½ cups vodka

In a blender beaker, place the orange juice, pineapple juice, water, and banana chunks; process in the blender until the banana chunks blend with the juice. Add the vodka; process briefly until blended.

Pour the punch into a glass pitcher; cover with plastic wrap and refrigerate until ready to serve.

Then, stir the punch and place the pitcher in a wine cooler of ice to keep cold. To serve, pour the punch over ice cubes in 10-ounce rock glasses.

MAKES 8 SERVINGS

VARIATION: The amount of vodka may be reduced or it may be left out entirely; substitute additional water for the amount of vodka omitted.

ICEBERG PUNCH (ORANGE)

Little clumps of sherbet float like icebergs on top of this pretty, pale-colored punch. Each of the four versions of Iceberg Punch features a different sherbet, fruit juice, and optional liquor.

½ gallon orange sherbet
1½ cups freshly squeezed, strained orange juice
1 cup Grand Marnier liqueur (optional)
1 2-liter bottle cold sparkling water

Let the orange sherbet stand at room temperature, in the container, until softened (about 30 minutes).

Then, remove the softened sherbet from the container and place it in a large mixing bowl. Add the orange juice and Grand Marnier liqueur; stir to combine, leaving golf ball–sized chunks of sherbet.

Turn the mixture into a punch bowl. Add the ginger ale; stir briefly to blend. Serve immediately. Chunks of sherbet will float to the top of the punch, both in the punch bowl and in the punch cups when served, simulating icebergs.

MAKES 4 QUARTS; 24 SERVINGS

ICEBERG PUNCH (LEMON)

½ gallon lemon sherbet
1 6-ounce can (¾ cup) undiluted, frozen lemonade, thawed
2 6-ounce cans (1½ cups) cold water
1 cup vodka (optional)
1 2-liter bottle cold sparkling water

Follow the Iceberg Punch (Orange) recipe, above, substituting lemon sherbet for the orange sherbet, 6 ounces (¾ cup) frozen lemonade plus 12 ounces (1½ cups) water for the orange juice, and vodka for the Grand Marnier.

ICEBERG PUNCH (LIME)

½ gallon lime sherbet
1 6-ounce can (¾ cup) undiluted, frozen limeade, thawed
2 6-ounce cans (1½ cups) cold water
1 cup white rum (optional)
1 2-liter bottle cold sparkling water

Follow the Iceberg Punch (Orange) recipe, above, substituting lime sherbet for the orange sherbet, 6 ounces (¾ cup) frozen limeade plus 12 ounces (1½ cups) water for the orange juice, and white rum for the Grand Marnier.

ICEBERG PUNCH (RASPBERRY)

½ gallon raspberry sherbet
½ 12-ounce can (¾ cup) undiluted, frozen country raspberry juice, thawed
1 12-ounce can (1½ cups) cold water
1 cup Chambord raspberry liqueur (optional)
1 2-liter bottle cold sparkling water

Follow the Iceberg Punch (Orange) recipe, above, substituting raspberry sherbet for the orange sherbet, 6 ounces (¾ cup) frozen raspberry juice plus 12 ounces (1½ cups) water for the orange juice, and Chambord for the Grand Marnier.

SPRITZER PUNCH

A spritzer is a drink made of wine (usually white) and soda water. The added fruit juice makes this drink what I call Spritzer Punch.

1 750-milliliter bottle, cold German
  Riesling–Auslese (white) wine*
2 cups freshly squeezed, strained orange
  juice
1 12-ounce can undiluted, frozen white
  grape juice, thawed
1 1-liter bottle cold sparkling water
Small ice cubes

  *Auslese is a category of high-quality German
  wines which are made from fully ripened
  grapes. Wines that are labeled "Auslese" have
  a naturally high sugar content but contain no
  added sugar.*

Place a punch bowl in a larger, attractive bowl of crushed ice standing on a serving tray. Into the punch bowl, pour the wine, orange juice, and grape juice; stir to blend. Add the sparkling water; stir briefly to blend. Drop a small number of ice cubes into the punch. Serve immediately, ladling the punch into widemouthed (to facilitate serving) wine glasses or punch cups.

MAKES 2¾ QUARTS; 16 SERVINGS

HOT SPICED CIDER WITH APPLEJACK

2 2-inch pieces stick cinnamon
1 teaspoon whole allspice
10 whole cloves
8 cups (2 quarts) cider
¼ cup packed light brown sugar
¾ cup applejack (page 19) (optional)

Tie the stick cinnamon, allspice, and cloves in a damp cheesecloth bag (page 44); set aside. Pour the cider into a large saucepan or kettle. Add the brown sugar; stir to combine. Add the cheesecloth bag of spices. Over high heat, stir the mixture until the brown sugar dissolves. Cover and bring the mixture to a boil. Reduce the heat and simmer the mixture 15 minutes.

Remove from the heat. Remove and discard the cheesecloth bag of spices. Strain the hot cider through a piece of damp flannel secured, napped side up, in a sieve over a deep pan; let stand.

Clean the saucepan or kettle used to boil the cider to eliminate any remaining spice fragments. Pour the strained cider back into the saucepan or kettle. Add the applejack; stir to blend. Reheat, if necessary, but do not boil.

Ladle the spiced cider into mugs. Keep the remainder warm in the covered saucepan or kettle over very low heat.

MAKES 10 SERVINGS

TO SERVE IN A PUNCH BOWL: Pour the cider into a punch bowl which has been warmed with hot water. *Caution:* Do not pour hot water or hot cider into a cut glass or delicate crystal punch bowl (or any nonheatproof glass punch bowl). Float a few kumquats, each studded with 3 whole cloves, in the hot cider.

Canning

"Putting by" the bounty of their gargantuan gardens and fruit groves for the long winter months ahead was a summer and early fall priority for prairie frontier farmwives. Once a vital facet of subsistence, canning is now considered a hobby by most devotees who pursue it—and they number many in the Midwest.

Passionate canners describe their fast-growing hobby as "surefire euphoria!" Gloating over eight half-pints of gorgeous Strawberry Jam (page 750) cooling on the kitchen counter elicits one of the all-time highs in culinary adventure. "Why all the superlatives?" those who have yet to experience the exhilaration of lifting quart jars of Pears Amaretto (page 723) out of a boiling-water canner may ask. Read on.

Home-canned foods are sensational tasting, strikingly beautiful, and uniquely superior. It is virtually impossible to duplicate in commercially canned foods—regardless of how fancy they are hyped to be—the supreme flavor and quality of home-canned products. Volume canning simply does not permit the TLC possible with home canning, which starts with the fastidious hand selection of products ripened to the optimum point before processing. Foods often go from the garden to the jar in the same day.

Additives such as chemical preservatives and artificial flavorings are anathema to home canners. There is no need for artificial coloring, either. Mother Nature's own spectacular colors are vividly captured and retained in jars carefully stored in a dark, cool, dry, special storage place until called into service in the kitchen. (Of course, bright red and green coloring is traditionally added to a very few canned items such as maraschino cherries, Spiced Apple Rings [page 728], and Peppermint Pears [page 729].)

Besides the sheer natural beauty of home-canned food products, jars can be masterpieces of food arrangement—a true art form for those so inclined. From uniform peach halves overlapped symmetrically, to green beans, each precisely measured and standing vertically in the jar (sometimes alternating with wax beans), to mandarin orange segments suspended artistically in orange jelly—the sky's the limit when it comes to imaginative presentations worthy of exhibition.

While most of the time-honored canned items, such as Bread and Butter Pickles (page 766) and Raspberry Jam (page 751), are as popular with canners today as they were in the 1860's, the canning of designer products such as marinated mushrooms, pickled brussels sprouts, and kumquat marmalade, using produce now generally available in modern markets, is "in." Most state fair food competitions now include classes for canned foods which are trendy or reflect new eating patterns; for example, herb jelly, wine jelly, low-sugar jam, salsa, and barbecue sauce.

One of the greatest pluses about canning is the longevity of the end result—a triumph over the perennial bane of good cooks who see days of planning, marketing, and preparation perish before their eyes in one short hour at the Thanksgiving table. Two days of cold turkey sandwiches are the only concrete residual evidence of the whole undertaking. Canning allows repeat performances, over months, with not one iota of additional effort.

There are other benefits. No gift is more fashionable or appreciated by a host or hostess greeting you at the door than a jar of Blueberry Jam (page 748), Melon Ball Pickles (page 771), or some other delicacy you have painstakingly canned yourself. When the party giver spreads that luscious blueberry jam over toast the next morning, it is certain assurance that you will receive another invitation for dinner before long (most likely, when the blueberry jam is gone).

With a cache of canned delectables, the holi-day gift-giving dilemma is a thing of the past. Anyone would love to receive a beautiful jar of home-canned Plums in Port Wine (page 727) or Bell Pepper Relish (page 779), hand labeled and made "gifty" with a white doily draped over the lid and tied with a satin ribbon. And what could be nicer than taking a jar of Brandied Mincemeat (page 726) to a friend, neighbor, or business associate in time for use in a mincemeat pie for the holiday meal? Money can't buy such thoughtful gifts of self.

While the joy of giving away these gems in jars is enormously rewarding, the gratification derived from serving home-canned foods to your family can only be described as soul satisfying. Canning can be a binding family ritual passed down through the generations. Canning one or two traditional family favorites can help busy, working mothers fulfill their role as links in the perpetuation of long-standing, family food customs. Canning can also be a grand family project.

For four generations, Spiced Peaches (page 774), canned from an old family recipe, and at least three kinds of homemade jams and jellies, including Apple Butter (page 763), have graced our Christmas table. Other pickles and relishes, such as Corn Relish (page 777), Watermelon Rind Pickles (page 772), and Pickled Mixed Vegetables (page773), take their turn in rotation over the years.

When the snow flies, one of our family's prized dining pleasures is to open a jar of peaches for dessert. When spooned into the crystal sauce dishes, the aroma of green summer months permeates the room and prompts the conversation. We never seem to have too many shiny jars of peaches ready for opening on bitter-cold evenings when the crackling orange-yellow fire reflects against the frosted windows.

If you raise your own vegetables and fruits, the bliss is doubled. You're in for a real thrill when the tomatoes and basil used in Swiss Steak (page 160) you serve to friends in January were started indoors, from seeds, in April. Add to the praise from around the table the feeling of pioneer self-sufficiency gained from helping nature carry out its plan of seed to nourishment, and you have a memory not to be forgotten.

Canning commands dedication, time, and creativity, and it takes study, patience, and practice. But if you're looking for something challenging and really fun to add to your repertoire of life experiences and accomplishments, canning may be just your ticket. Canning is a special hobby of mine, and I rank it among my most satisfying endeavors.

If you want to jump in, the information, tips, and recipes in this chapter will get you started. But let me warn you: you may become wonderfully hooked!

Canning Techniques

When canning any food product, it is *critically* important to follow the most current guidelines for safe canning adopted by the U.S. Department of Agriculture. The recipes and instructions in *The Blue Ribbon Country Cookbook* conform to the latest published USDA guidelines as of the publication of this cookbook (see Sources Consulted, page 846).

The deadly *Clostridium botulinum* bacteria can survive and grow in jars of food which have not been properly processed. While this fact underscores the importance of judicious handling, the potential threat of food poisoning and botulism need not be a reason to avoid the considerable pleasure and benefits derived from home canning. Responsible, safe canning is reliably achieved by following the USDA guidelines and recommendations.

Many of the basic USDA-endorsed canning techniques are outlined in this section. For more detailed information on the endorsed principles and techniques of canning, as well as extended collections of tested recipes, it is highly recommended that persons who home-can secure one or both of the following publications:

Complete Guide to Home Canning. Agriculture. Information Bulletin No. 539. U.S. Department of Agriculture. Extension Service.

Available through your County Extension Service or by calling:

Superintendent of Documents
U.S. Government Printing Office
202-512-1800
Ask for GPO Stock No. 001-000-04521-1

To order by mail, write to:

Superintendent of Documents
U.S. Government Printing Office
P.O. Box 371954
Pittsburgh, Pennsylvania 15250-7954

Also may be accessed through the World Wide Web at: http://www.agen.ufl.edu/~foodsaf/canhome.html.

So Easy to Preserve, 3rd edition, Bulletin 989. The University of Georgia. Cooperative Extension Service. College of Agricultural and Environmental Sciences.

Available by writing to:

Agricultural Business Office
203 Conner Hall
University of Georgia
Athens, Georgia 30602-4356

In addition, the local Extension Service office serving your county may be contacted for expert information on canning. Some Extension Service offices operate a hotline to help answer canning questions.

FOOD PRODUCTS

Home-can only the highest-quality food products. Mediocre raw materials can only result in mediocre canned goods. Use very fresh, unblemished produce ripened to the optimum stage. Plan your canning calendar around the availability of fresh foods, preferably locally grown, at their peak of quality. Befriend a knowledgeable food market produce manager who will help obtain the products you want. The availability of superior food products dictates what foods you can and when you can them.

Many vegetables begin to lose their vitamins immediately after they are harvested. If harvested vegetables are not cooked or preserved, close to one half of their vitamins may be lost in only a few days.

Although one third to one half of vitamins A and C, thiamin, and riboflavin may be lost during the heating process in canning, the amounts of other vitamins in canned foods are only slightly lower than in fresh foods.

Given these facts, when top-quality vegetables are canned promptly after harvest, they can be more nutritious than fresh produce in supermarkets. Many good canners have their own well-tended gardens—the ideal source for fine, fresh produce.

CANNING EQUIPMENT

Before embarking on canning, it is necessary to acquire the proper equipment. The basic items required for canning most food products are enumerated in the Canning Equipment List on page 711. Of course, not all of the listed items are needed for canning every kind of food. Not shown on the list is specialized equipment, such as an apple parer and a cherry pitter, useful in the canning of specific food products.

Study the recipe you plan to use well in advance of canning to make certain the needed equipment is at hand. Good equipment is a must in order to can foods safely and proficiently.

TIME ALLOCATION

Canning demands major chunks of time. It cannot be hurried. Blanching, peeling, paring, chopping, grinding, straining, boiling, jar filling, and processing are among the tasks which can consume hours of uninterrupted time when canning large quantities of food. Canning is fun and one of the most rewarding culinary challenges when approached methodically and with a relaxed attitude. It is a food art jealous of time and patience.

RECIPES

Use tested recipes which comply with the USDA guidelines. Follow these recipes precisely. This chapter contains eighty-six recipes, all of which follow the USDA guidelines. In addition, the two publications recommended at the beginning of this section contain large collections of tested recipes which meet the USDA guidelines.

Measure or weigh ingredients accurately. Proportions of fresh foods to other ingredients not only will affect flavor, but also may affect safety.

Jellies, jams, conserves, and marmalades require a correct balance of fruit, sugar, pectin, and acid to achieve the desired jellying and texture. Therefore, do not reduce the amount of sugar called for in recipes for these items, as a runny product will be the consequence. Too little sugar also may allow the growth of yeasts and molds. If a low-sugar jellied product is desired, select a special recipe which meets this requirement. Recipes for low-sugar jellied products, as well as recipes utilizing liquid sweetener, are available. Some may be found in both of the recommended publications on page 702.

In recipe procedures for jellied products made with added pectin, the term "rolling boil" means a full, rapid boil that cannot be stirred down (see definition for Rolling Boil, page 25). To achieve a firm enough gel, it is important to bring mixtures with added pectin to a full rolling boil before commencing to count the specified boiling time—usually 1 minute. On the other hand, exceeding the specified time at which these mixtures remain at a rolling boil, even by a portion of a minute, may result in jellied products which are too stiff. Experience is the best teacher in these matters.

Be sure to check the expiration date on packages of fruit pectin. Unsatisfactory gelling may result from the use of old pectin.

Some recipes for jellied products call for the addition of butter or margarine to help control foaming during cooking. This is not recommended because butter or margarine may affect the flavor of stored jellied products. Skimming the foam off jellied product mixtures is not difficult; however, the procedure should be done expeditiously so the skimmed mixture can be poured into the jars before it begins to gel.

Do not double recipes for jellied products as a soft gel may result. Make one batch at a time.

For the reason of safety, it is important not to change the proportions of vinegar, water, and food in recipes for pickles and relishes. The acidity level of these canned products is critical to their safety as well as their flavor. Use commercially bottled vinegar of 5 percent acidity (50-grain acetic acid). Either cider or white vinegar may be used. Cider vinegar has good, mellow flavor; however, it may darken white or light-colored vegetables and fruits such as cauliflower, onions, and pears. White distilled vinegar is preferable for use in canning such foods. Do not use homemade vinegar or other vinegars of unknown acidity.

Use only canning or pickling salt in most pickle and relish products. Canning salt is a pure granulated salt. Other salts contain anticaking agents which may cause cloudy brine. Do not use flake salt (because it varies in density) or rock salt.

Do not alter the amount of salt called for in recipes for fermented sauerkraut and pickles. The type and amount of salt called for in approved recipes for these products are vital to their safety as well as their texture and flavor. The brine in these fermented products draws moisture and natural sugar from the vegetables. Lactic acid, which prevents their spoilage, is then produced.

While fresh-pack pickles and relishes are safely acidified with vinegar in tested recipes, reducing or eliminating the salt in these products may impair the quality of their texture and flavor. A few reduced-sodium pickle recipes are included in the two publications recommended at the beginning of this section.

JARS AND LIDS

Use only standard Mason-type jars made for home canning. They are available in 4-ounce, half-pint, 12-ounce, pint, 1½-pint, and quart sizes. Half-pint, pint, and quart jars are the most commonly used, and are the only three sizes of jars specified in this book's canning recipes. Although half-gallon Mason-type canning jars are available, they are recommended only for canning very acid juices. Food should be canned only in the size or sizes of jars prescribed in the recipe. The safe processing time for a particular food often differs with the size of jar. Jars used for canning should be completely free of cracks and chips.

Canning jars come with either regular (about 2⅜ inches) or widemouthed (about 3 inches) openings. Certain foods, such as larger solid foods, are more readily packed in widemouthed jars. Widemouthed jars with straight sides also lend themselves well to many artistic arrangements of canned foods.

The use of mayonnaise jars for canning is not recommended. Mayonnaise-type jars are tempered less than Mason-type jars, making them more subject to breakage. Mayonnaise jars especially should not be used for canning foods processed in a pressure canner due to the breakage hazard. In addition, mayonnaise jars have a more narrow sealing surface, making them more prone to sealing failures. Mason-type canning jars are not expensive. Given the time and effort involved in canning, it follows that only the best jars should be used.

Use standard two-piece, self-sealing metal lids which consist of a flat, metal lid containing sealing compound around the outer edge, and a metal band which screws onto the jar. The flat, metal lids should be used only *once;* however, the bands may be used repeatedly provided they are rust free. Lids may be purchased separately to pair with usable bands on hand. While new lids are generally good for five years from their manufacture date, it is a good practice to purchase only the quantity needed for a single year's canning.

The old-style, porcelain-lined, zinc lids used with rubber rings are no longer recommended because they often fail to seal. Likewise, bail-style jars with rubber rings are not safe for canning.

STERILIZING JARS AND PREPARING LIDS

As a first step, canning jars, new lids, and bands should be washed in hot, soapy water and rinsed thoroughly. Jars may be washed in a dishwasher. After rinsing new lids and new or used bands, place them, single layer, on a double layer of paper towels to dry.

While it is unnecessary to presterilize jars used to can foods processed 10 minutes or more in a boiling-water canner, or jars used to can foods processed in a pressure canner, I make a practice of doing so and call for the procedure in all the canning recipes in *The Blue Ribbon Country Cookbook*. Jars used to can foods processed less than 10 minutes, and jars used to can cucumber pickles processed by low-temperature pasteurization (see page 707 for explanation) *must be* presterilized.

To presterilize canning jars, place them, right side up, in the rack in a boiling-water canner. Fill the canner with hot (not boiling) water to cover the jars 1 inch. Cover the canner and place it over high heat. Bring the water to a boil and boil the jars for 10 minutes in locations with altitudes of less than 1,000 feet above sea level. In locations with altitudes of 1,000 feet or more, add 1 minute boiling time for each 1,000 feet above sea level. (See Boiling Point of Water at Various Altitudes, page 712, for information on how to find out the altitude of your location.)

When the proper boiling time for sterilization has elapsed, turn off the heat under the canner and leave the sterilized jars immersed in the water. Reheat the water to near boiling and remove the jars from the canner immediately or shortly before filling them with food. Use a jar lifter to remove the jars from the canner. Wear rubber gloves to avoid burns from the steam and hot water. Pour the hot water in the jars back into the canner. Place the jars, upside down, on a clean tea towel covering a very large wooden board or other work surface on which you will fill the jars. Turn each jar upright immediately before filling it.

Carefully follow the manufacturer's instructions to prepare the lids and bands for use. Some instructions call for boiling water to be poured over the lids and for the lids to be left in the hot water at least 3 minutes until used. Other instructions call for lids to be placed in water which is then brought to a simmer and removed from the heat. The lids are to be left in the hot water until used. Although not necessary, whatever treatment is instructed by the manufacturer for the lids, I simultaneously apply to the bands.

Use a 3-quart saucepan for treating the lids (and bands). A magnetic lid wand, specifically made for the purpose, may be used to handily lift lids and bands from the hot water. Tongs also work well.

FILLING THE JARS

HOT PACKING AND RAW PACKING

There are the two styles of packing foods into jars: hot packing and raw packing.

Hot packing means filling jars with hot foods which have been boiled 2 to 5 minutes or cooked for a longer period of time. Liquid used to cover solid foods in the jars is heated to boiling before being added.

Raw packing means filling jars with unheated, uncooked foods. As in hot packing, liquid used to cover raw-packed foods in the jars is heated to boiling before being added.

Hot packing is the preferred style for packing foods to be processed in a boiling-water canner. Raw packing is more suitable for vegetables to be processed in a pressure canner.

Many fresh foods contain from 10 percent to more than 30 percent air. The longevity of quality in canned foods is affected by the amount of air removed from the foods prior to sealing of the jars. Raw-packed fruits often float in the jars. The air trapped in and around foods which have been raw packed may cause discoloration and adversely affect the flavor of the foods within a short storage period.

Raw packing is appropriate and useful for canning foods which quickly lose their shape when heated in boiling liquid; for example, Grapes (page 718) and Kiwis (page 718). The recipes in this chapter for canning Blueberries (page 714) and Gooseberries (page 717) call for these fruits only to be blanched for a short time before being packed into the jars. Raw-packed fruits should be packed tightly because of shrinkage during processing. Raw-packed foods often require a longer processing time than the same foods hot packed.

It is often difficult to retain the shape of vine-ripened tomatoes in the jars when they are hot packed. If shape retention is desired, whole or halved tomatoes may be raw packed. The recipe for canning Tomatoes (page 736) includes procedures and processing times for both hot packing and raw packing.

Use the style(s) of pack specified in the recipe. Consult the two publications recommended at the beginning of this section, or call the local Extension Service office serving your county for information before raw packing a food when the recipe you have specifies only hot packing. It is necessary to find out whether or not the food can be safely raw packed and, if so, what the processing time should be.

PROCEDURES FOR FILLING JARS

Follow recipe instructions for filling jars, heeding the headspace requirements to the letter. Headspace is the unfilled space in a jar between the top of the food (or the liquid covering it) and the bottom of the lid. Use a ruler to assure proper measurement of headspace.

Headspace is required for the expansion of food during processing and for forming a vacuum in cooled jars. Air content of the food and processing temperature determine the amount of expansion. Air heated to high temperatures expands greatly; the higher the temperature, the greater the expansion. Too little headspace may cause food to boil out of the jar during processing, causing food on the lid compound to prevent sealing of the jar. Too much headspace may not allow the extra air in the top of the jar to be driven out during the time period specified for processing. This could prevent a good vacuum seal. In addition, air left in the jar may cause discoloration of the food.

Solid foods packed into jars should be surrounded and covered with liquid (syrup, juice, or water, depending upon the food product and recipe). Solid foods left uncovered by liquid at the top of the jar usually darken and develop an off flavor.

A widemouthed funnel, designed especially for home canning, makes efficient and tidy work of filling jars with liquids, sweet spreads, relishes, and small-sized solid foods such as corn, peas, and berries.

During the filling process, air is often trapped in jars, especially when solid foods are packed into jars and then are covered with a liquid. To remove air bubbles trapped in a filled jar, run a plastic knife or a narrow, rubber spatula into the jar between the food and the side of the jar. Turn the jar and carefully move the knife or spatula up and down, and against the food to release the air bubbles, allowing them to rise to the top of the jar and disperse.

After the release of air bubbles, often it is necessary to add a small amount of additional liquid or food to the jar to maintain the prescribed headspace (and to fully cover solid foods with liquid). Air generally is not trapped in jars filled with liquids alone; therefore, the procedure of removing air bubbles usually may be eliminated when canning these products. Recipes in *The Blue Ribbon Country Cookbook* indicate when air bubbles should be removed from filled jars.

Just before capping the jars, wipe the rim and the threads of each jar with a clean, damp sponge to assure that they are free from syrup or other food residue. To achieve a tight seal, jar rims must be perfectly clean. Rinse the sponge in clean, running water several times during the wiping procedure.

Remove one lid and band at a time from the hot water. Place the lid squarely on the jar rim and screw the band firmly onto the jar with your hand. Then, proceed to cap the next jar. Do not use a jar tightener to tighten the bands. Extreme overtightening prevents air from venting during processing and may cause the lids to buckle and the jars to break. However, bands not screwed tightly enough may allow liquid to escape from the jars during processing, resulting in sealing failures.

PROCESSING

Two methods of processing home-canned foods meet USDA guidelines: (1) the boiling-water bath method, and (2) the pressure canner method. The acidity of the food product to be canned determines which of the two methods is employed.

Acid foods are foods having a pH value of 4.6 or less (pH is a measure of acidity). Low-acid foods are foods having a pH value higher than 4.6.

Foods processed by the boiling-water bath method are processed in a boiling-water canner at boiling-water temperature (212° F. at sea level). While *Clostridium botulinum* bacterial cells are killed at boiling-water temperature, they can form spores that survive this temperature. Acid foods contain sufficient acidity to block the growth of botulinum spores. Therefore, acid foods are safely processed using the boiling-water bath method. The time required to process acid foods in boiling water ranges from 5 to 85 minutes.

Clostridium botulinum spores can be destroyed at a temperature of 240° F., or above, maintained for a specified length of time. This is achievable in a pressure canner operating at 10 to 15 pounds per square inch of pressure measured by gauge (PSIG). Low-acid foods must be processed at 240 to 250° F. using the pressure canner method. The time required to destroy bacteria in low-acid foods processed in a pressure canner at 240 to 250° F. ranges from

20 to 100 minutes, depending upon the kind of food, the size of jars, and the way the jars are packed.

The natural acidity in most fruits is high enough to safely can these foods at boiling-water temperature. The acid added to pickles and relishes also allows safe canning of these products at boiling-water temperature. In addition, sauerkraut, jellies, jams, preserves, conserves, marmalades, and fruit butters are safely processed at boiling-water temperature.

Foods falling into the low-acid category include all fresh vegetables (except tomatoes), and meats, poultry, fish, shellfish, wild game, and milk. These low-acid foods must be processed in a pressure canner.

While tomatoes and figs are considered to be acid foods, some of them have pH values slightly above 4.6. Therefore, if tomatoes and figs are processed using the boiling-water bath method, they must be further acidified with *bottled* lemon juice or citric acid to ensure a safe pH level. *Bottled* lemon juice must be used because the acidity is at a consistent level and is high enough to be safe. The recipes in this chapter for Tomatoes (page 736) and Tomato Juice (page 737) call for processing in a boiling-water canner and for the addition of 2 tablespoons of bottled lemon juice to each quart of these products (1 tablespoon to each pint) in accordance with the USDA guidelines. (If citric acid is used, add ½ teaspoon to each quart or ¼ teaspoon to each pint of these products. Food-grade citric acid is available at some supermarkets and at pharmacies. Do not substitute ascorbic acid for citric acid.)

Certain approved recipes for cucumber pickles permit processing in simmering water sustained at 180 to 185° F. for 30 minutes (see Bread and Butter Pickles, page 766, and Brined Dill Pickles, page 768). The advantage of this procedure, known as "low-temperature pasteurization," is that it results in crisper pickles. When canning by this procedure, it is very important to attach a candy thermometer to the canner and to continually monitor the temperature of the water. A temperature of 180° F. must be maintained for a full 30 minutes to avoid the possibility of spoilage. A temperature higher than 185° F. may cause the pickles to soften. This procedure should be used only when it is indicated in an approved recipe. Low-temperature pasteurization should never be used to process reduced-sodium pickles.

Open-kettle canning, a former canning method in which foods were heated and packed into hot jars which were then sealed and not further processed, is no longer accepted as safe. In open-kettle canning, bacteria, yeasts, and molds contaminating food in the jars are not destroyed by scientific processing, and lids are not reliably sealed. Botulism and spoilage are threats in food canned by the open-kettle method.

Steam canners are not recommended at this time because safe processing times for their use have not been adequately researched. Steam canners heat foods in a different way from boiling-water canners. Applying processing times used for boiling-water canning to steam canning may result in very underprocessed foods, risking the danger of food contamination and spoilage.

Canning by the inversion method, in which filled jars of jellies and jams are inverted for a few minutes and then turned upright, but are not processed in a boiling-water canner, *does not comply with current USDA guidelines,* even though you may find this canning method currently advocated by national companies or directed in some canning recipes.

Sealing with paraffin also is not an approved canning procedure because of potential mold contamination. Mycotoxins, which are known to cause cancer in animals, have been found in some jars of jelly having surface mold.

If you are new to canning, I suggest you begin by canning a plain fruit such as peaches or pears, which involves the boiling-water bath method of processing. Or, if you have a garden with an abundance of tomatoes, become a canning initiate by canning the oversupply (using the boiling-water bath method). Then, try a jam, such as strawberry, blueberry, or raspberry. Wait to can foods which require the use of a pressure canner until you gain more experience.

PROCEDURES FOR PROCESSING IN A BOILING-WATER CANNER

The water used to presterilize the jars in the boiling-water canner may be used to process the filled jars. After removing sterilized, empty jars from the canner (see Sterilizing Jars and Preparing Lids, page 705), it probably will be necessary to remove some of the water from the canner to accommodate the jars filled with food and ready for processing. Wearing rubber gloves, use a 4-cup glass measuring cup with a pouring spout to remove any necessary amounts of water from the canner.

Before loading jars in the canner, the water in the canner should be heated to about 180° F. for hot-packed foods and 140° F. for raw-packed foods. (A candy thermometer may be attached to the canner to gauge the water temperature. Detach and remove the thermometer before adding the jars of food.) Filled jars should not be plunged into boiling water due to the chance of breakage.

To load the canner with filled jars fit with lids, wear rubber gloves and use a jar lifter to place the jars in the rack resting on the bottom of the canner. Or, before loading the jars, the rack may be raised to a higher level in the canner by lifting the rack by its handles and hooking the handles over the rim of the canner. I prefer to leave the rack on the bottom of the canner during loading because the jars can be maintained in a more vertical position throughout the loading procedure. During the entire canning process and later, in storage of the canned foods, special care should be taken to keep the jars vertical in order to prevent food and liquid from splashing against the side of the jars in the headspace and against the bottom of the lids. (This is a criterion in the judging of canned foods in state fair competitions.)

If the jars are loaded into the rack in its raised position, or if the processed jars will be unloaded from the rack in its raised position, it is important to load the jars in a manner that keeps their weight evenly distributed around the rack. This will help prevent the rack from tilting when in the raised position due to a disproportionate amount of weight on one side, causing the jars to lean.

When all the jars to be processed are loaded into the rack and the rack is resting on the bottom of the canner, there should be at least 1 inch of water covering the tops of the jars. If necessary, add heated water. Cover the canner and turn the heat onto high under the canner. The canner should be no more than 4 inches greater in diameter than the burner or electric heating unit under it. Watch the canner closely. When the water reaches a rapid boil, begin counting the processing time, using a timer. Lower the heat to maintain a gentle, but steady, boil throughout the processing time.

Because the temperature at which water boils varies with altitude above sea level, it is necessary to know the altitude of the canning location to determine the length of processing time required for a particular food product. See Boiling Point of Water at Various Altitudes (page 712) for a more complete explanation and for suggested, reliable sources for finding out the altitude of your location. The recipes in this chapter for canned foods processed by the boiling-water bath method each contain a chart showing the proper processing time by altitude of canning location and by size of jars to be processed.

Processing times should be followed strictly. Underprocessing jeopardizes food safety. Overprocessing adversely affects the quality of the canned product and is unnecessary.

At the end of the processing time, turn off the heat under the canner. Before removing the jars from the canner, I usually carefully lift the rack to its raised position in order to pull the jars out of the boiling water moments after the processing time has elapsed. However, if preferred, the rack may be left on the bottom of the canner while the jars are removed.

Immediately lift the jars from the canner, using a jar lifter and wearing rubber gloves. Keeping the jars vertical, transporting them, one at a time, from the canner to a nearby dry, wooden board covered with a clean tea towel. Place the jars at least 1 inch apart. Do not retighten the bands, possibly causing the hot lid

gaskets to be cut through and the seals to fail. Do not touch or move the jars for at least 12 hours. To destroy microorganisms in foods processed in a boiling-water canner, processed jars must be cooled at room temperature. Processed jars should be placed in a location away from drafts. As the jars cool, you will hear snapping sounds as the lids seal.

After at least 12 hours, check the lid of each jar to make certain it has sealed. The lids of properly sealed jars are concave. To check a lid, press the middle of the lid with your finger. If the jar is properly sealed, the lid should not spring up when you release your finger.

A jar of food which did not seal may be reprocessed within 24 hours. To reprocess, remove the jar band and lid, and discard the lid. Check the jar sealing surface for any tiny nicks. If nicks are found, place the food in a different, sterilized jar. Place a new, properly prepared lid and a clean band on the jar and reprocess, using the same processing time as was used previously. Reprocessed food will be more soft and will be lower in nutritional value. A processed jar of food which did not seal also may be refrigerated and used within several days, or the food product may be frozen.

While keeping the jars vertical, transport them to a cool, dry, dark storage place such as a clean cabinet in a dry basement. The best storage temperature for canned foods is 50 to 70° F. The maximum safe storage temperature for canned foods is 95° F.

PROCEDURES FOR PROCESSING IN A PRESSURE CANNER

There are two acceptable types of pressure canners used for canning foods: dial-gauge canners and weighted-gauge canners. Carefully follow the manufacturer's instructions for operating whichever type of pressure canner you are using. Outmoded pressure canners and small pressure saucepans should not be used.

The altitude of the canning location is a factor in pressure canning as well as in boiling-water bath canning. Because temperatures are lower in pressure canners at higher altitudes, the pounds of pressure at which canned foods are processed vary with the altitude of the canning location. The type of pressure canner also affects the pounds of pressure required at various altitudes. In this chapter, each recipe for foods canned in a pressure canner contains a separate chart for each of the two types of pressure canners, showing the processing time and pounds of pressure required at various altitudes for designated sizes of jars. *Processing times and pressures should be followed strictly.*

Because air trapped in a pressure canner lowers the temperature reached at 5, 10, or 15 pounds of pressure, pressure canners should be vented 10 minutes before they are pressurized. After adding the recommended amount of hot water to the canner (follow the canner manufacturer's instructions), and after placing the filled jars on the rack in the canner and locking the lid, leave the vent open while the water in the canner comes to a boil over high heat. When steam from the boiling water begins to escape through the vent, set a timer for 10 minutes. After venting the pressure canner 10 minutes, close the vent or place the counterweight or weighted gauge over the vent to pressurize the canner.

Begin counting the processing time when the recommended pounds of pressure have been reached, as indicated by the dial gauge on a dial-gauge canner or by prescribed jiggling of the weight on a weighted-gauge canner. During the processing time, maintain the pressure as evenly as possible by finely regulating the heat under the canner. Fast and great fluctations of pressure may cause liquid to be lost from the jars. Do not lower the pressure in the canner by opening the vent.

When the processing time has elapsed, turn off the heat under the canner. If the heating unit under the canner is electric, move the canner off the heating surface. Let the pressure canner cool and depressurize naturally. Do not open the vent or remove the weight to hasten the reduction of pressure. Do not cool the canner with water. To destroy microorganisms in low-acid foods processed in a pressure canner, the pressure canner must be allowed to cool at room temperature until *completely* depressurized.

After the canner has completely depressurized, open the vent or remove the weight from the vent. After waiting 2 minutes, remove the lid, tilting the far side up to avoid being burned by escaping steam.

Remove the processed jars from the canner and let them stand at least 12 hours to cool, following the same procedures as for jars processed in a boiling-water canner (described in Procedures for Processing in a Boiling-Water Canner, page 708).

After letting processed jars cool at least 12 hours, check the lids for sealing and store the jars, following the same procedures as for jars processed in a boiling-water canner (described in Procedures for Processing in a Boiling-Water Canner, page 708).

The gauge on dial-gauge pressure canners should be checked for accuracy before use each year. Gauges may be checked at most local Extension Service offices. If a gauge is off by more than 1 pound at 5, 10, or 15 pounds of pressure, it should be replaced.

FINAL SAFETY ADVICE

Before opening a jar of canned food for consumption, recheck the lid to make sure it has remained concave and sealed. Do not use or even taste canned food from an unsealed jar or canned food that shows any sign of spoilage. If liquid spurts from a jar when it is opened, if you detect an unnatural odor, or if you notice any sign of mold on the surface of the food or on the bottom of the jar lid, dispose of the jar and food. Spoiled or suspect food and jars should be disposed of in a place where the food will not be consumed by humans or animals. Thoroughly scrub the counter or surface on which the jar was opened, the jar opener, your hands, and any clothing that may have come in contact with the food or container, using a solution of 1 part chlorine bleach to 5 parts water. Wet the surface with this solution and let it stand 5 minutes before rinsing. Place the sponge or cloth used for scrubbing in a plastic bag and dispose of it in the trash.

The warnings and precautionary USDA guidelines should not discourage interest in the enjoyable pursuit of canning. If the recommended guidelines are followed, canning and the sublime pleasure of eating exquisite canned foods can be enjoyed with safety.

CANNING EQUIPMENT LIST

7-quart boiling-water canner

12-quart dial-gauge or weighted-gauge pressure canner (for canning vegetables, meats, and other low-acid foods requiring pressure canning)

8-quart, heavy-bottomed, stainless steel kettle with cover (for canning most jellied products)

12-quart, heavy-bottomed, stainless steel kettle with cover (for general canning)

16-quart, heavy-bottomed stainless steel kettle (for canning large quantities and retaining prepared fruits in vinegar solution)

3-quart stainless steel saucepan with cover (for heating jar lids [and bands])

Large, medium, and small stainless steel saucepans with covers

5-gallon crock (for fermenting pickles and sauerkraut)

Crack-free, unchipped half-pint, pint, and quart Mason-type canning jars. Widemouthed jars are necessary when canning large-sized, solid foods

New, self-sealing jar lids (self-sealing lids may be used only once)

Clean, unrusted jar bands (bands may be reused if not corroded)

Blancher

Food mill

Food grinder

Large sieve

Small sieve

Colander

Jar lifter (for lifting jars in and out of the canner)

Magnetic lid wand or tongs (for lifting lids and bands out of hot water)

Widemouthed canning funnel (for filling jars)

1-cup glass measuring cup with pouring spout

2-cup glass measuring cup with pouring spout

4-cup glass measuring cup with pouring spout

Set of fractional measuring cups

Set of measuring spoons

Large stainless steel mixing spoon

Large stainless steel slotted spoon

Medium wooden mixing spoon with long handle (for stirring and handling fragile foods)

4 tableware stainless steel tablespoons (for skimming jellied products)

4 tableware stainless steel teaspoons (for skimming jellied products)

Sharp, thin-bladed paring knife

Sharp, thin-bladed slicing knife (the size of a steak knife)

Plastic knife or narrow, rubber spatula (for removing air bubbles from packed jars)

Potato masher (for crushing fruits used in some jellied products)

Vegetable parer

Vegetable brush

Candy thermometer

Kitchen scale

Timer

Untreated cheesecloth

Cotton flannel (for straining) (purchase from a fabric store)

Small wooden board (for cooling processed jars)

Large wooden board (for filling jars)

Clean tea towels

Small sponge (for wiping jar rims and threads)

Pot holders

Rubber gloves (to wear when stirring and handling hot foods and jars)

Blender (for preparing some products)

Food processor (not necessary, but convenient for preparing some products)

BOILING POINT OF WATER AT VARIOUS ALTITUDES

As altitude increases, atmospheric pressure decreases due to a thinner blanket of air. As the atmospheric pressure decreases, causing less weight of air on the surface of water, the boiling point of water also decreases. At sea level, water boils at 212° F. The following chart shows the boiling point of water at higher altitudes.

Altitude	Boiling Point of Water
Sea Level	212° F.
1,000 ft.	210° F.
2,000 ft.	208° F.
3,000 ft.	206° F.
4,000 ft.	204° F.
5,000 ft.	203° F.
6,000 ft.	201° F.
7,000 ft.	199° F.
8,000 ft.	197° F.

To find out the altitude of the location in which you live, call the local Extension Service office serving your county or your local district conservationist with the U.S. Department of Agriculture, Natural Resources Conservation Service.

Weather conditions also affect the boiling point of water, but to a far less extent than altitude. At a given altitude, high barometric pressure causes water to boil at a somewhat higher temperature and low barometric pressure causes water to boil at a somewhat lower temperature. Therefore, when recipes call for cooking jellies, jams, conserves, and marmalades to a specific number of degrees above the boiling point of water, it is a good idea to check the boiling point of water with a candy thermometer just before making these products.

Fruits

APPLES

16 cups cold water
2 tablespoons white vinegar
2 tablespoons salt
8 pounds apples which hold their shape when cooked, such as Golden Delicious or Jonathan
2½ cups sugar
10 cups water

In a 16-quart kettle, place 16 cups water, vinegar, and salt; stir until the salt dissolves; set aside.

Wash the apples. Pare (see Note), core, and cut the apples in half. After each step of preparing the apples, drop them into the vinegar solution to prevent discoloration. Let the apples stand.

In a 12-quart, heavy-bottomed, stainless steel kettle, place the sugar and 10 cups water; stir to combine. Over high heat, bring the sugar mixture to a boil, stirring until the sugar dissolves. Cover the kettle. Reduce the heat slightly and boil the sugar mixture (syrup) 5 minutes.

Meanwhile, secure a piece of damp cotton flannel, napped side up, in a sieve over a deep pan; set aside.

After the syrup has boiled 5 minutes, drain and rinse the apples twice, using fresh, cold water. Drain the apples well. Place the apples in the boiling syrup. Cover the kettle. Over high heat, return the syrup (with the apples) to a boil. Uncover the kettle. Reduce the heat and simmer the apples 7 minutes, stirring occasionally with a wooden mixing spoon.

Remove from the heat. Pack the hot apples (without syrup) into hot, sterilized, wide-mouthed, quart or pint jars, leaving ½-inch headspace; let stand.

Pour the hot syrup (from the kettle) over the

cotton flannel in the sieve to strain. Pour the strained syrup into a stainless steel saucepan. Over high heat, bring the syrup to a boil, stirring occasionally. Cover the apples in the jars with the hot syrup, maintaining ½-inch headspace.

Using a plastic knife or a narrow, rubber spatula, remove the air bubbles in the jars. Wipe the jar rims and threads. Place hot metal lids on the jars and screw the bands firmly.

Process in a boiling-water canner for the following time:

Processing Times

Altitude of Canning Location

Jar Size	0 to 1,000 ft.	1,001 to 3,000 ft.	3,001 to 6,000 ft.	Above 6,000 ft.
Pints and Quarts	20 min.	25 min.	30 min.	35 min.

Remove the jars from the canner and place on a dry, wooden board which has been covered with a tea towel. Let the jars stand, *undisturbed,* 12 hours to cool completely.

NOTE: An apple parer helps accomplish this task expeditiously and efficiently.

YIELDS ABOUT 4 QUARTS

APPLESAUCE

16 cups cold water
2 tablespoons white vinegar
2 tablespoons salt
15 pounds cooking apples
4 cups water
3½ cups sugar
2 tablespoons plus 1 teaspoon freshly squeezed, strained lemon juice
1 tablespoon plus ½ teaspoon ground cinnamon

In a 16-quart kettle, place 16 cups water, vinegar, and salt; stir until the salt dissolves; set aside.

Wash, pare (see Note), quarter, and core the apples. After each step of preparing the apples, drop them into the vinegar solution to prevent discoloration.

Drain and rinse the apples twice, using fresh, cold water. Drain the apples well. In a 12-quart, heavy-bottomed, stainless steel kettle, place the apples and 4 cups water. Cover the kettle. Over medium-high heat, bring the apples to a simmer. Reduce the heat and simmer the apples (covered) 15 to 20 minutes, or until tender, stirring occasionally.

Remove from the heat. Using a large, metal mixing spoon, stir the apples well. If the apples have not pureed during the cooking and stirring processes, press the apples (with all liquid) through a food mill.

Add the sugar, lemon juice, and cinnamon; stir until well combined. Over medium heat, heat the applesauce through, stirring constantly to prevent scorching.

Remove from the heat. Pour the hot applesauce into hot, sterilized pint or quart jars, leaving ½-inch headspace.

Using a plastic knife or a narrow, rubber spatula, remove the air bubbles in the jars. Wipe the jar rims and threads. Place hot metal lids on the jars and screw the bands firmly.

Process in a boiling-water canner for the following time:

Processing Times

Altitude of Canning Location

Jar Size	0 to 1,000 ft.	1,001 to 3,000 ft.	3,001 to 6,000 ft.	Above 6,000 ft.
Pints	15 min.	20 min.	20 min.	25 min.
Quarts	20 min.	25 min.	30 min.	35 min.

Remove the jars from the canner and place on a dry, wooden board which has been covered with a tea towel. Let the jars stand, *undisturbed,* 12 hours to cool completely.

NOTE: An apple parer helps accomplish this task expeditiously and efficiently.

YIELDS ABOUT 7 PINTS

BLUEBERRIES

1½ quarts blueberries*
½ cup sugar
2 cups water

*To maintain the shape of the blueberries, do
not blanch and place in jars more than
1½ quarts of berries at a time (see procedures,
below).*

Place the blueberries in a flat-bottomed pan.
Sort and stem the berries. Transfer the berries to
a colander. Run cold water over the blueberries
to wash; set aside.

In a small, stainless steel saucepan, place the
sugar and water; stir to combine. Over high
heat, bring the sugar mixture to a boil, stirring
until the sugar dissolves. Cover the saucepan.
Reduce the heat slightly and boil the sugar mixture (syrup) 5 minutes.

Meanwhile, carefully transfer the blueberries
to the basket of a blancher. Blanch the blueberries (page 44) 1½ minutes in fresh, boiling
water. Immediately drain the berries; set aside.

Pour ½ cup of the boiling syrup into each of
2 hot, sterilized, pint jars (or 1 quart jar). Add ½
of the blueberries to each pint jar, shaking the
jars intermittently as the blueberries are added
to achieve close packing without crushing the
berries. Leave ½-inch headspace.

Cover the blueberries in the jars with additional hot syrup, maintaining ½-inch headspace.

Using a plastic knife or a narrow, rubber spatula, remove the air bubbles in the jars. Wipe the
jar rims and threads. Place hot metal lids on the
jars and screw the bands firmly.

Process in a boiling-water canner for the following time:

Processing Times

Altitude of Canning Location

Jar Size	0 to 1,000 ft.	1,001 to 3,000 ft.	3,001 to 6,000 ft.	Above 6,000 ft.
Pints and Quarts	15 min.	20 min.	20 min.	25 min.

Remove the jars from the canner and place
on a dry, wooden board which has been covered
with a tea towel. Let the jars stand, *undisturbed,*
12 hours to cool completely.

YIELDS ABOUT 2 PINTS OR 1 QUART

SERVING SUGGESTIONS
• Use drained blueberries canned in either
syrup (as in the above recipe) or water (see
Variation, below), in muffins and pancakes
(see Blueberry Pancakes, page 455 [substitute
canned blueberries for fresh ones]).

• Spoon drained blueberries over vanilla ice
cream (homemade, page 669, or commercial).

VARIATION ~ **TO CAN BLUEBERRIES IN WATER:**
Follow the Blueberries recipe, substituting fresh,
boiling water for the boiling syrup.

WHITE CHERRIES

13 pounds Rainier (white) cherries
3 cups sugar
8 cups water

Wash the cherries; drain. Remove the stems.
Prick each cherry twice (on opposite sides) with
a large, sterilized needle or hat pin to prevent
bursting.

In a 12-quart, heavy-bottomed, stainless steel
kettle, place the sugar and water; stir to combine. Over high heat, bring the sugar mixture to
a boil, stirring until the sugar dissolves. Cover
the kettle. Reduce the heat slightly and boil the
sugar mixture (syrup) 5 minutes.

Then, place the cherries in the boiling syrup.
Cover the kettle. Over high heat, return the
syrup (with the cherries) to a boil. Uncover the
kettle. Reduce the heat and cook the cherries at
a low boil 4 minutes.

Remove from the heat. Pack the hot cherries
(without syrup) into hot, sterilized, quart or pint
jars, shaking the jars intermittently as the cherries are added to achieve close packing without
crushing the cherries. Leave ½-inch headspace.

Cover the cherries in the jars with the boiling syrup, maintaining ½-inch headspace. Using a teaspoon, skim any foam off the syrup at the top of the jars.

Using a plastic knife or a narrow, rubber spatula, remove the air bubbles in the jars. Wipe the jar rims and threads. Place hot metal lids on the jars and screw the bands firmly.

Process in a boiling-water canner for the following time:

Processing Times

| Jar Size | Altitude of Canning Location | | | |
	0 to 1,000 ft.	1,001 to 3,000 ft.	3,001 to 6,000 ft.	Above 6,000 ft.
Pints	15 min.	20 min.	20 min.	25 min.
Quarts	20 min.	25 min.	30 min.	35 min.

Remove the jars from the canner and place on a dry, wooden board which has been covered with a tea towel. Let the jars stand, *undisturbed,* 12 hours to cool completely.

YIELDS ABOUT 6 QUARTS

CHERRY SAUCE

6½ cups pitted, tart, red cherries (see
  recipe procedures, below)
5 cups sugar
1 1¾-ounce package powdered fruit pectin

Place the unpitted cherries in the sink filled with cold water. Sort and stem the cherries, discarding any that float. Drain the cherries in a colander. Pit the cherries (see Note).

Measure 6½ cups pitted cherries, including the juice, and place in an 8-quart, heavy-bottomed, stainless steel kettle; set aside. Place the sugar in a large mixing bowl; set aside.

Add the pectin to the cherries in the kettle; stir to combine. Over high heat, quickly bring the cherry mixture to a rolling boil, stirring constantly but carefully, to retain the wholeness of the cherries. Immediately add the sugar and

return the cherry mixture to a rolling boil over high heat, stirring continuously. Boil 1 minute (no longer; use a timer), stirring constantly. Immediately remove from the heat and skim the foam off the cherry mixture, using tableware tablespoons and teaspoons. Stir and skim the mixture an additional 20 minutes, until the syrup thickens sufficiently that the cherries will distribute evenly in the sauce and not float to the top of the jars.

Drain hot, sterilized, half-pint jars, upside down, on a clean tea towel.

Pour the Cherry Sauce into the drained jars, leaving ¼-inch headspace.

Wipe the jar rims and threads. Place hot metal lids on the jars and screw the bands firmly.

Process in a boiling-water canner for the following time:

Processing Times

| Jar Size | Altitude of Canning Location | | |
	0 to 1,000 ft.	1,001 to 6,000 ft.	Above 6,000 ft.
Half-pints	5 min.	10 min.	15 min.

Remove the jars from the canner and place on a dry, wooden board which has been covered with a tea towel. Let the jars stand, *undisturbed,* 12 hours to cool completely.

NOTE: The Westmark brand Kirschomat cherry pitter is an efficient tool to use for this task.

YIELDS ABOUT 6 HALF-PINTS

SERVING SUGGESTION: Serve as a topping over vanilla ice cream (homemade, page 669, or commercial).

CHERRY SAUCE WITH KIRSCHWASSER

1 half-pint canned Cherry Sauce
  (recipe, above)
3 tablespoons Kirschwasser (page 23)

At serving time, place the Cherry Sauce in a small mixing bowl. Add the Kirschwasser; stir to blend.

APRICOTS

16 cups cold water
2 tablespoons white vinegar
2 tablespoons salt
10 pounds apricots, divided
2½ cups sugar
5 cups water

In a 16-quart kettle, place 16 cups water, vinegar, and salt; stir until the salt dissolves; set aside.

Wash 2½ pounds of the apricots. Blanch the apricots (page 44) 30 seconds and immediately immerse them in cold water; drain. Peel, cut in half, and pit the apricots. As the apricots are prepared, drop them into the vinegar solution to prevent discoloration. Repeat the procedure 3 times to prepare the remaining apricots in 2½-pound batches. The apricots should be prepared in these small batches because they darken quickly in their skins after being blanched. Let the apricots stand.

In a 12-quart, heavy-bottomed, stainless steel kettle, place the sugar and 5 cups water; stir to combine. Over high heat, bring the sugar mixture to a boil, stirring until the sugar dissolves. Cover the kettle. Reduce the heat slightly and boil the sugar mixture (syrup) 5 minutes.

Meanwhile, secure a piece of damp cotton flannel, napped side up, in a sieve over a deep pan; set aside.

After the syrup has boiled 5 minutes, remove approximately ½ of the apricots from the vinegar solution. Rinse the apricots twice, using fresh, cold water. Drain the apricots well. Place ½ of the drained apricots in the boiling syrup. Over high heat, heat the apricots through only. Do not overcook.

Remove from the heat. Immediately pack the hot apricots (without syrup) into hot, sterilized, widemouthed pint or quart jars, leaving ½-inch headspace; let stand. Place the remaining ½ of the drained apricots in the boiling syrup and repeat the process.

Pour the hot syrup (from the kettle) over the cotton flannel in the sieve to strain. Pour the strained syrup into a stainless steel saucepan. Over high heat, bring the syrup to a boil, stirring occasionally. Cover the apricots in the jars with the hot syrup, maintaining ½-inch headspace.

Using a plastic knife or a narrow, rubber spatula, remove the air bubbles in the jars. Wipe the jar rims and threads. Place hot metal lids on the jars and screw the bands firmly. Let the jars of apricots stand.

Pour the remaining syrup back into the 12-quart kettle. Repeat the entire draining, rinsing, heating, and packing procedures, using the remaining ½ of the apricots. Cooked apricots tend to fray quite easily and quickly. Therefore, it is important to heat them and place them in the jars in small batches, as described above, in order to maintain their shape.

Process in a boiling-water canner for the following time:

Processing Times

Jar Size	Altitude of Canning Location			
	0 to 1,000 ft.	1,001 to 3,000 ft.	3,001 to 6,000 ft.	Above 6,000 ft.
Pints	20 min.	25 min.	30 min.	35 min.
Quarts	25 min.	30 min.	35 min.	40 min.

Remove the jars from the canner and place on a dry, wooden board which has been covered with a tea towel. Let the jars stand, *undisturbed,* 12 hours to cool completely.

YIELDS ABOUT 8 PINTS

VARIATION ~ **TO CAN UNPEELED APRICOTS:** Follow the Apricots recipe, above, eliminating the blanching and peeling procedures.

GOOSEBERRIES

2 quarts (about 2½ pounds) gooseberries
3 cups boiling water, divided

Wash the gooseberries and drain in a colander. Using a small, sharp paring knife, cut tiny portions off both ends of the gooseberries. Place the berries in a large mixing bowl.

Blanch ½ of the gooseberries (page 44) 20 seconds. Immediately drain the blanched gooseberries in a colander; set aside.

Pour ½ cup fresh, boiling water into 1 hot, sterilized pint or quart jar. Add the blanched gooseberries, shaking the jar intermittently as the gooseberries are added to achieve close packing without crushing the berries. Leave ½-inch headspace in the pint jar (if used); let stand.

Quickly blanch and drain the remaining ½ of the gooseberries. Repeat the procedure used for the first ½ of the berries, packing the gooseberries into 1 hot, sterilized, pint jar containing ½ cup boiling water or adding the gooseberries to the partially filled quart jar containing the first ½ of the berries (at this time, add no additional boiling water to the quart jar). Leave ½-inch headspace in both pint and quart jars.

Cover the gooseberries in the jars with additional fresh, boiling water, maintaining ½-inch headspace.

Using a plastic knife or a narrow, rubber spatula, remove the air bubbles in the jars. Wipe the jar rims and threads. Place hot metal lids on the jars and screw the bands firmly.

Process in a boiling-water canner for the following time:

Processing Times

Jar Size	Altitude of Canning Location		
	0 to 1,000 ft.	1,001 to 6,000 ft.	Above 6,000 ft.
Pints and Quarts	15 min.	20 min.	25 min.

Remove the jars from the canner and place on a dry, wooden board which has been covered with a tea towel. Let the jars stand, *undisturbed,* 12 hours to cool completely.

YIELDS ABOUT 2 PINTS OR 1 QUART

SERVING SUGGESTIONS

- Use in Gooseberry Pie (page 480) and Gooseberry-Date Pie (page 480).

- Use in Hot Curried Fruit (page 347).

- Use Gooseberries canned in syrup (see Variation, below) in Christmas Gooseberry Salad (page 114) and Mandarin Orange–Gooseberry Salad (page 114).

VARIATION ~ TO CAN GOOSEBERRIES IN SYRUP: In a saucepan, place 1 cup sugar and 4 cups water; stir to combine. Over high heat, bring the sugar mixture to a boil, stirring until the sugar dissolves. Cover the saucepan. Reduce the heat slightly and boil the sugar mixture (syrup) 5 minutes.

Follow the Gooseberries recipe, above, with the following exceptions: Blanch the gooseberries in the syrup. Using a slotted spoon, immediately remove the blanched gooseberries from the syrup and place in a colander over a mixing bowl. Add ½ cup of the boiling syrup, instead of water, to the jars prior to adding the berries. Cover the gooseberries in the jars with the boiling syrup instead of the water.

GRAPES

Sometimes it's fun to try your hand at canning an item not so often found in canners' larders, such as grapes.

6 pounds seedless white or red grapes
1 cup sugar
4 cups water

Wash the grapes and remove them from the stems; set aside.

In a medium-large, stainless steel saucepan, place the sugar and water; stir to combine. Over high heat, bring the sugar mixture to a boil, stirring until the sugar dissolves. Cover the saucepan. Reduce the heat slightly and boil the sugar mixture (syrup) 5 minutes.

Fill hot, sterilized, pint or quart jars with the raw grapes, leaving ½-inch headspace.

Cover the grapes in the jars with the hot syrup, maintaining ½-inch headspace.

Using a plastic knife or a narrow, rubber spatula, remove the air bubbles in the jars. Wipe the jar rims and threads. Place hot metal lids on the jars and screw the bands firmly.

Process in a boiling-water canner for the following time:

Processing Times

Jar Size	Altitude of Canning Location			
	0 to 1,000 ft.	1,001 to 3,000 ft.	3,001 to 6,000 ft.	Above 6,000 ft.
Pints	15 min.	20 min.	20 min.	25 min.
Quarts	20 min.	25 min.	30 min.	35 min.

Remove the jars from the canner and place on a dry, wooden board which has been covered with a tea towel. Let the jars stand, *undisturbed,* 12 hours to cool completely.

YIELDS ABOUT 6 PINTS

SERVING SUGGESTIONS

- Use in molded or mixed fruit salads.

- Combine with fresh and/or poached fruits in dessert fruit compotes (see Fresh Fruit Compote, page 436).

- Use in Hot Curried Fruit (page 437).

KIWIS

4 pounds kiwis (about 15 large kiwis)
1 cup sugar
4 cups water

Trim off both ends of the kiwis and carefully cut away the core at the stem end. Pare the kiwis and slice them widthwise ¼ inch thick; set aside.

In a medium-large, stainless steel saucepan, place the sugar and water; stir to combine. Over high heat, bring the sugar mixture to a boil, stirring until the sugar dissolves. Cover the saucepan. Reduce the heat slightly and boil the sugar mixture (syrup) 5 minutes.

Arrange the raw, sliced kiwis in hot, sterilized, widemouthed, pint jars, leaving ½-inch headspace.

Cover the sliced kiwis in the jars with the hot syrup, maintaining ½-inch headspace.

Using a plastic knife or a narrow, rubber spatula, remove the air bubbles in the jars. Wipe the jar rims and threads. Place hot metal lids on the jars and screw the bands firmly.

Process in a boiling-water canner for the following time:

Processing Times

Jar Size	Altitude of Canning Location			
	0 to 1,000 ft.	1,001 to 3,000 ft.	3,001 to 6,000 ft.	Above 6,000 ft.
Pints	15 min.	20 min.	20 min.	25 min.

Remove the jars from the canner and place on a dry, wooden board which has been covered with a tea towel. Let the jars stand, *undisturbed,* 12 hours to cool completely.

YIELDS ABOUT 4 PINTS

SERVING SUGGESTION: Use in fruit salads and compotes.

STRAWBERRIES

4 quarts firm strawberries, divided
2 cups sugar

THE FIRST DAY: Place 1 quart of the strawberries in a colander. Run cold water over the berries to wash. Using a strawberry huller, remove the green caps only; do not remove the center pith of the berries.

Place the prepared strawberries in a flat-bottomed pan. Using a potato masher, crush the berries. Press the crushed berries and juice through a food mill. Then, strain the pressed berries and juice through a sieve to remove the pulp. (Use a spoon to stir the pulp to expedite the juice draining through the sieve.) (Reserve the pulp for other uses such as ice cream topping.)

Measure 1 cup strained strawberry juice and pour it into a medium, stainless steel saucepan. Add the sugar; stir to combine. Over medium-high heat, bring the strawberry mixture to a boil, stirring constantly. Remove from the heat. Using tableware tablespoons and teaspoons, skim the foam off the strawberry mixture (syrup). Cover and let stand to cool.

Meanwhile, wash the remaining 3 quarts of the strawberries in the colander, one quart at a time to avoid bruising or crushing the berries. Remove the caps, leaving the center pith of the berries intact.

Place the strawberries in an 8-quart, heavy-bottomed, stainless steel kettle. Pour the cooled syrup over the berries. Over medium-high heat, bring the syrup (with the strawberries) to a boil.

Reduce the heat and cook the strawberries, uncovered, at a low boil, 4 minutes.

Remove from the heat. Cover the kettle and let the strawberries stand, in a cool place, overnight or at least 8 hours.

THE NEXT DAY: Secure a piece of damp cotton flannel, napped side up, in a sieve over a deep pan; set aside.

Over medium heat, gently bring the strawberries and syrup to a low boil; boil only 30 seconds.

Remove from the heat. Pack the hot strawberries (without syrup) into 2 hot, sterilized, pint jars (or 1 quart jar), shaking the jars intermittently as the strawberries are added to achieve close packing without crushing the berries. Leave ½-inch headspace. Let the strawberries stand.

Pour the hot syrup (from the kettle) over the cotton flannel in the sieve to strain. Pour the strained syrup into a stainless steel saucepan. Over high heat, bring the syrup to a boil, stirring occasionally. Cover the strawberries in the jars with the hot syrup, maintaining ½-inch headspace.

Using a plastic knife or a narrow, rubber spatula, remove the air bubbles in the jars. Wipe the jar rims and threads. Place hot metal lids on the jars and screw the bands firmly.

Process in a boiling-water canner for the following time:

Processing Times

Jar Size	Altitude of Canning Location		
	0 to 1,000 ft.	1,001 to 6,000 ft.	Above 6,000 ft.
Pints and Quarts	15 min.	20 min.	25 min.

Remove the jars from the canner and place on a dry, wooden board which has been covered with a tea towel. Let the jars stand, *undisturbed,* 12 hours to cool completely.

YIELDS ABOUT 2 PINTS OR 1 QUART

PEACHES

Peaches are one of the fruits most often home canned in the Midwest—because they're so good and are relished by virtually everyone, young and old.

32 cups (8 quarts) cold water
¼ cup white vinegar
¼ cup salt
15 pounds peaches*
2 cups sugar
8 cups water

  **Colorado, Michigan, Missouri, or Idaho peaches are preferable.*

In a 16-quart kettle, place 32 cups (8 quarts) water, vinegar, and salt; stir until the salt dissolves; set aside.

Wash the peaches. In batches, blanch the peaches (page 44) 1 minute and immediately immerse them in cold water; drain. Peel, cut in half, and pit the peaches. As the peaches are prepared, drop them into the vinegar solution to prevent discoloration. Let the peaches stand.

In a 12-quart, heavy-bottomed, stainless steel kettle, place the sugar and 8 cups water; stir to combine. Over high heat, bring the sugar mixture to a boil, stirring until the sugar dissolves. Cover the kettle. Reduce the heat slightly and boil the sugar mixture (syrup) 5 minutes.

After the syrup has boiled 5 minutes, remove approximately ⅓ of the peaches from the vinegar solution. Rinse the peaches twice, using fresh, cold water. Drain the peaches well. Place the drained peaches in the boiling syrup. Cover the kettle. Over high heat, bring the syrup (with the peaches) to a simmer. Uncover the kettle. Reduce the heat and simmer the peaches 6 minutes. Do not overcook.

Remove from the heat. Pack the hot peaches (without syrup) into hot, sterilized, wide-mouthed quart or pint jars, leaving ½-inch headspace; let stand.

Repeat the rinsing, draining, simmering, and packing procedures 2 additional times, using the remaining ⅔ of the peaches.

Secure a piece of damp cotton flannel, napped side up, in a sieve over a deep pan. Pour the hot syrup (from the kettle) over the cotton flannel in the sieve to strain. Pour the strained syrup into a stainless steel saucepan. Over high heat, bring the syrup to a boil, stirring occasionally. Cover the peaches in the jars with the hot syrup, maintaining ½-inch headspace.

Using a plastic knife or a narrow, rubber spatula, remove the air bubbles in the jars. Wipe the jar rims and threads. Place hot metal lids on the jars and screw the bands firmly.

Process in a boiling-water canner for the following time:

Processing Times

Jar Size	Altitude of Canning Location			
	0 to 1,000 ft.	1,001 to 3,000 ft.	3,001 to 6,000 ft.	Above 6,000 ft.
Pints	20 min.	25 min.	30 min.	35 min.
Quarts	25 min.	30 min.	35 min.	40 min.

Remove the jars from the canner and place on a dry, wooden board which has been covered with a tea towel. Let the jars stand, *undisturbed*, 12 hours to cool completely.

YIELDS ABOUT 7 QUARTS

FREEZER PEACHES

4 cups sugar
8 cups water
15 pounds peaches*
1 teaspoon powdered ascorbic acid**

 **The peaches should be fully ripened, but still firm and not mushy.*

***Available at pharmacies.*

THE FIRST DAY: In a 12-quart, heavy-bottomed, stainless steel kettle, place the sugar and water; stir to combine. Over high heat, bring the sugar mixture to a boil, stirring until the sugar dissolves. Cover the kettle. Reduce the heat slightly and boil the sugar mixture (syrup) 5 minutes.

Remove from the heat. Let the syrup stand, covered, until cooled to room temperature; then, refrigerate.

THE NEXT DAY: Wash the peaches in cold water; drain well and set aside.

Remove the syrup from the refrigerator. Add the ascorbic acid; stir until dissolved and blended; set aside.

Blanch the 4 peaches (page 44) 15 seconds only and immediately immerse them in very cold or iced water; drain well. (This short blanching process will make it easier to peel the peaches neatly; however, it is important not to overblanch, causing the peaches to lose their exterior firmness.) Let the peaches stand briefly.

Pour ½ cup of the cold syrup into each of 2 clean, cool (room temperature), widemouthed, pint canning jars; set aside.

Peel the blanched peaches. Cut the peaches in half, pit, and cut them into sections lengthwise. Work quickly in order to avoid discoloration of the fruit.

Pack the peaches into the 2 jars containing the syrup, leaving 1-inch headspace for expansion.

Cover the peaches in the jars with additional cold syrup, maintaining 1-inch headspace. Make sure that the peaches are covered with syrup. Place a piece of clean, crumpled waxed paper on top of the peaches in the jars to keep them immersed in the syrup.

Wipe the jar rims and threads. Place clean lids on the jars (leave the waxed paper in the jars) and screw the bands firmly.

Immediately place the jars in the freezer. The freezer temperature should be maintained at approximately −10° F. to assure that the temperature will not rise above 0° F. when unfrozen foods are added to the freezer.

Repeat the entire procedure with the remaining peaches, processing—from beginning to end —only 2 pints at a time.

To serve, thaw the peaches at room temperature.

YIELDS ABOUT 18 PINTS

VARIATION ~ **TO FREEZE PEACHES IN QUARTS:** Follow the Freezer Peaches recipe with the following exceptions: Pour 1 cup cold syrup into 1 quart jar before packing the peaches. Leave 1½-inch headspace. Process only 1 quart at a time.

YIELDS ABOUT 9 QUARTS

RHUBARB

4½ pounds rhubarb
1½ cups sugar

Wash the rhubarb and cut into 2-inch lengths. Measure 12 cups cut rhubarb and place in a heavy-bottomed, stainless steel kettle. Add the sugar; stir lightly. Cover the kettle. Let stand 4 hours to draw juice out of the rhubarb.

Then, over medium-high heat, bring the rhubarb mixture to a boil, stirring continuously. Boil the rhubarb *10 seconds only.*

Remove from the heat. Pack the hot rhubarb (without syrup) into hot, sterilized, pint or quart jars, leaving ½-inch headspace.

Cover the rhubarb in the jars with the hot syrup, maintaining ½-inch headspace.

Using a plastic knife or a narrow, rubber spatula, remove the air bubbles in the jars. Wipe the jar rims and threads. Place hot metal lids on the jars and screw the bands firmly.

Process in a boiling-water canner for the following time:

Processing Times

Jar Size	Altitude of Canning Location		
	0 to 1,000 ft.	1,001 to 6,000 ft.	Above 6,000 ft.
Pints and Quarts	15 min.	20 min.	25 min.

Remove the jars from the canner and place on a dry, wooden board which has been covered with a tea towel. Let the jars stand, *undisturbed,* 12 hours to cool completely.

YIELDS ABOUT 6 PINTS OR 3 QUARTS

MIXED FRUITS

16 cups cold water
2 tablespoons white vinegar
2 tablespoons salt
12 small Bartlett pears,* halved, cored, and
    pared
8 medium Golden Delicious apples,* pared,
    quartered, and cored
8 Colorado, Michigan, Missouri, or Idaho
    peaches, blanched (page 44), peeled,
    halved, and pitted
4 cups stemmed, seedless, whole white
    grapes
1½ cups sugar
4 cups water

*Approximately 3 pears, 2 apples, 2 peaches,
and 1 cup of grapes will be used in each quart
of mixed fruit.

In a large kettle, place 16 cups water, vinegar, and salt; stir until the salt dissolves. Pour the vinegar solution evenly into 3 large mixing bowls; set aside. (The vinegar solution will be used to prevent discoloration of the uncooked fruit.)

Prepare the fruit, as indicated above, dropping the pears, apples, and peaches separately into the 3 bowls of the vinegar solution as they are prepared; set aside.

In a 12-quart, heavy-bottomed, stainless steel kettle, place the sugar and 4 cups water; stir to combine. Over high heat, bring the sugar mixture to a boil, stirring until the sugar dissolves. Cover the kettle. Reduce the heat slightly and boil the sugar mixture (syrup) 5 minutes.

After the syrup has boiled 5 minutes, drain and rinse the pears twice, using fresh, cold water. Drain the pears well. Place the pears in the boiling syrup. Cover the kettle. Over high heat, bring the syrup (with the pears) to a simmer. Uncover the kettle. Reduce the heat and simmer the pears 4 minutes.

Remove from the heat. Using a slotted spoon,

remove the pears from the syrup and place in a clean mixing bowl; set aside.

Drain and rinse the apples twice, using fresh, cold water. Drain the apples well. Simmer the apples 5 minutes in the same syrup used for cooking the pears, following the same procedure.

Remove from the heat. Using the slotted spoon, remove the apples from the syrup and place in a separate, clean mixing bowl; set aside.

Drain and rinse the peaches twice, using fresh, cold water. Drain the peaches well. Place the peaches in the same boiling syrup used for cooking the pears and apples. Over high heat, heat the peaches through. Do not overcook.

Remove from the heat. Using the slotted spoon, remove the peaches from the syrup and place in a separate, clean mixing bowl; set aside.

Wash the grapes; do not cook or heat. Place the grapes in a separate mixing bowl; set aside.

Pack the fruit in layers by type of fruit, or pack the fruit mixed, into hot, sterilized, wide-mouthed, preferably quart jars (pint jars may be used), leaving ½-inch headspace; let stand.

Secure a piece of damp cotton flannel, napped side up, in a sieve over a deep pan. Pour the hot syrup (from the kettle) over the cotton flannel in the sieve to strain. Pour the strained syrup into a stainless steel saucepan. Over high heat, bring the syrup to a boil, stirring occasionally. Cover the fruit in the jars with the hot syrup, maintaining ½-inch headspace.

Using a plastic knife or a narrow, rubber spatula, remove the air bubbles in the jars. Wipe the jar rims and threads. Place hot metal lids on the jars and screw the bands firmly.

Process in a boiling-water canner for the following time:

Processing Times

Jar Size	Altitude of Canning Location			
	0 to 1,000 ft.	1,001 to 3,000 ft.	3,001 to 6,000 ft.	Above 6,000 ft.
Pints	20 min.	25 min.	30 min.	35 min.
Quarts	25 min.	30 min.	35 min.	40 min.

Remove the jars from the canner and place on a dry, wooden board which has been covered with a tea towel. Let the jars stand, *undisturbed,* 12 hours to cool completely.

YIELDS ABOUT 4 QUARTS

VARIATIONS: Other fruits of choice, such as plums and apricots, may be added or substituted.

PEARS AMARETTO

16 cups cold water
2 tablespoons white vinegar
2 tablespoons salt
7 pounds firm and not overripe Bartlett
   pears
⅓ cup blanched whole almonds
1½ cups sugar
3 cups water
½ cup Amaretto (page 19)

In a 16-quart kettle, place 16 cups water, vinegar, and salt; stir until the salt dissolves; set aside.

Wash, cut in half, core, and pare the pears. As the pears are prepared, drop them into the vinegar solution to prevent discoloration. Let the pears stand.

Fill a 12-quart, heavy-bottomed, stainless steel kettle about ⅓ full of fresh water. Cover the kettle. Over high heat, bring the water to a boil.

Meanwhile, drain and rinse the pears twice, using fresh, cold water. Drain the pears well. Place the pears, one layer at a time, in the boiling water in the kettle. Cover the kettle. Over high heat, bring the water (with the pears) to a simmer. Uncover the kettle. Reduce the heat and simmer the pears 3 minutes. Do not overcook.

Remove from the heat. Using a slotted spoon, immediately remove the pears from the water and place in a colander over a mixing bowl.

Pack the hot pears (without water) into hot, sterilized, widemouthed, quart or pint jars, sprinkling 2 tablespoons almonds evenly throughout each quart jar as it is packed (use 1 tablespoon almonds in pint jars). Leave ½-inch headspace. Let the pears stand.

In a large, stainless steel saucepan, place the sugar and 3 cups fresh water (not the same water used to cook the pears); stir to combine. Over high heat, bring the sugar mixture to a boil, stirring until the sugar dissolves. Cover the saucepan. Reduce the heat slightly and boil the sugar mixture (syrup) 5 minutes. Remove from the heat. Add the Amaretto; stir to blend.

Slightly spread the fingers of one of your hands and place them over the top of one of the filled jars. Invert the jar briefly over a bowl to drain away most of the liquid which has accumulated around the pears and almonds. Then, place the jar, right side up, on the work surface. Make certain that the pears settle back into the jar in order to retain ½-inch headspace. Repeat the procedure with the remaining 2 jars. (Draining the jars allows more of the Amaretto-flavored syrup to be added to the pears.)

Cover the pears in the jars with the hot syrup, maintaining ½-inch headspace.

Using a plastic knife or a narrow, rubber spatula, remove the air bubbles in the jars. Wipe the jar rims and threads. Place hot metal lids on the jars and screw the bands firmly.

Process in a boiling-water canner for the following time:

Processing Times

Jar Size	Altitude of Canning Location			
	0 to 1,000 ft.	1,001 to 3,000 ft.	3,001 to 6,000 ft.	Above 6,000 ft.
Pints	20 min.	25 min.	30 min.	35 min.
Quarts	25 min.	30 min.	35 min.	40 min.

Remove the jars from the canner and place on a dry, wooden board which has been covered with a tea towel. Let the jars stand, *undisturbed,* 12 hours to cool completely.

YIELDS ABOUT 3 QUARTS

PLAIN PEARS: Follow the Pears Amaretto recipe, above, omitting the Amaretto and almonds.

FRUIT COCKTAIL

16 cups cold water
2 tablespoons white vinegar
2 tablespoons salt
1½ cups sugar
4 cups water
2 pineapples
3½ pounds Bartlett pears
3½ pounds Colorado, Michigan, Missouri,
   or Idaho peaches
1½ pounds stemmed, seedless, whole white
   grapes
1 10-ounce jar red maraschino cherries

In a 16-quart kettle, place 16 cups water, vinegar, and salt; stir until the salt dissolves. Half-fill 2 large mixing bowls with the vinegar solution. Leave the remaining solution in the kettle; set aside. (The vinegar solution will be used to prevent discoloration of the uncooked fruit.)

In a 12-quart, heavy-bottomed, stainless steel kettle, place the sugar and 4 cups water; stir to combine. Over high heat, bring the sugar mixture to a boil, stirring until the sugar dissolves. Cover the kettle. Reduce the heat slightly and boil the sugar mixture (syrup) 5 minutes.

Meanwhile, secure a piece of damp cotton flannel, napped side up, in a sieve over a deep pan; set aside.

Pare and core the pineapples; cut into ½-inch cubes. Weigh 1¾ pounds cubed pineapple. Place the pineapple cubes in the boiling syrup. Cover the kettle. Over high heat, bring the syrup (with the pineapple cubes) to a simmer. Uncover the kettle. Reduce the heat and simmer the pineapple cubes 3 minutes.

Remove from the heat. Using a slotted spoon, remove the pineapple from syrup and place in a very large mixing bowl; set aside.

Pour the hot syrup (from the kettle) over the cotton flannel in the sieve to strain. Pour the strained syrup back into the kettle; set aside.

Wash, cut in half, core, and pare the pears. As the pears are prepared, drop them into the kettle containing the vinegar solution. Then, cut the prepared pears into ½-inch cubes. As the cubes are cut, drop them into one of the mixing bowls containing the vinegar solution. Drain and rinse the pear cubes twice, using fresh, cold water. Drain the pear cubes well. Over high heat, bring the syrup in the kettle to a boil and add the pear cubes. Simmer the pear cubes 2 minutes, following the same procedure as for the pineapple cubes.

Remove from the heat. Using the slotted spoon, remove the pear cubes from the syrup and place in the mixing bowl with the pineapple cubes; set aside.

Strain the syrup and pour it back into the kettle, following the previous procedure; set aside.

Wash the peaches. Blanch the peaches (page 44) 30 seconds and immediately immerse them in cold water; drain. Peel, quarter, and pit the peaches. Cut away the frayed flesh which surrounds the pits. As the peaches are prepared, drop them into the kettle containing the vinegar solution. Then, cut the prepared peaches into ½-inch cubes. As the cubes are cut, drop them into the remaining mixing bowl containing the vinegar solution. Drain and rinse the peach cubes twice, using fresh, cold water. Drain the peach cubes well. Over high heat, bring the syrup in the kettle to a boil and add the peach cubes. Simmer the peach cubes 2 minutes, following the same procedure as for the pineapple cubes.

Remove from the heat. Using the slotted spoon, remove the peach cubes from the syrup and place in the mixing bowl with the pineapple and pear cubes; set aside.

Strain the syrup, following the previous procedure. Pour the strained syrup into a stainless steel saucepan; set aside.

Wash the grapes. Add the uncooked grapes to the mixing bowl containing the cooked fruit; set aside.

Drain the maraschino cherries in a colander and rinse very well. Place the rinsed cherries between a double layer of paper towels to drain. Cut the cherries in half lengthwise; add to the mixing bowl containing the prepared fruit.

Using a large, wooden mixing spoon, *carefully* toss the fruit until evenly distributed, being cautious not to cut or crush the fruit.

Over high heat, bring the strained syrup to a boil. Pour ½ cup of the boiling syrup into each of 8 hot, sterilized, pint jars. Fill the jars with the fruit, leaving ½-inch headspace.

Cover the fruit in the jars with additional hot syrup, maintaining ½-inch headspace.

Using a plastic knife or a narrow, rubber spatula, remove the air bubbles in the jars. Wipe the jar rims and threads. Place hot metal lids on the jars and screw the bands firmly.

Process in a boiling-water canner for the following time:

Processing Times

Jar Size	Altitude of Canning Location			
	0 to 1,000 ft.	1,001 to 3,000 ft.	3,001 to 6,000 ft.	Above 6,000 ft.
Pints	20 min.	25 min.	30 min.	35 min.

Remove the jars from the canner and place on a dry, wooden board which has been covered with a tea towel. Let the jars stand, *undisturbed,* 12 hours to cool completely.

YIELDS ABOUT 8 PINTS

RASPBERRIES (RED OR BLACK)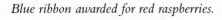

Blue ribbon awarded for red raspberries.

1½ quarts raspberries (red or black), divided
½ cup sugar
1 cup water

Place ½ of the raspberries (3 cups) in a colander. Run cold water over the berries to wash; set aside.

In a small, stainless steel saucepan, place the sugar and water; stir to combine. Over high heat, bring the sugar mixture to a boil, stirring until the sugar dissolves. Cover the saucepan.

Reduce the heat slightly and boil the sugar mixture (syrup) 5 minutes.

Then, carefully transfer the raspberries to the top of a blancher. Blanch the raspberries (page 44) *exactly 10 seconds* (no longer; see Note) in fresh, boiling water. Immediately drain the berries; set aside.

Pour ½ cup of the boiling syrup into 1 hot, sterilized, pint jar. Add the blanched raspberries, shaking the jar intermittently as the raspberries are added to achieve close packing without crushing the berries. Leave ½-inch headspace. Let the raspberries stand.

Repeat the procedure, using the remaining ½ of the raspberries.

Cover the raspberries in the jars with additional hot syrup, maintaining ½-inch headspace.

Using a plastic knife or a narrow, rubber spatula, remove the air bubbles in the jars. Wipe the jar rims and threads. Place hot metal lids on the jars and screw the bands firmly.

Process in a boiling-water canner for the following time:

Processing Times

Jar Size	Altitude of Canning Location		
	0 to 1,000 ft.	1,001 to 6,000 ft.	Above 6,000 ft.
Pints	15 min.	20 min.	25 min.

Remove the jars from the canner and place on a dry, wooden board which has been covered with a tea towel. Let the jars stand, *undisturbed,* 12 hours to cool completely.

NOTE: Raspberries are very soft and fragile. To maintain their wholeness, handle the berries very gently and take extreme caution not to blanch them longer than the specified 10 seconds. Due to their vulnerability to crushing, it is recommended that raspberries be canned only in pints, not quarts.

YIELDS ABOUT 2 PINTS

VARIATION ~ **TO CAN RASPBERRIES IN WATER:** Follow the Raspberries (Red or Black) recipe, substituting fresh, boiling water for the boiling syrup.

BRANDIED MINCEMEAT

4 pounds beef chuck neck meat cut into 3-inch cubes or chunks

8 cups water

1 15-ounce box (2½ cups) raisins

1 15-ounce box (2½ cups) golden raisins

2 10-ounce boxes (3½ cups) currants

4 ounces (½ cup) diced candied citron

4 ounces (½ cup) diced candied lemon peel

4 ounces (½ cup) diced candied orange peel

2¼ cups granulated sugar

2 cups packed light brown sugar

1 tablespoon plus 1 teaspoon ground cinnamon

2 teaspoons ground mace

1 teaspoon ground cloves

1 teaspoon ground nutmeg

1 tablespoon salt

1 pound suet

6 pounds Golden Delicious apples, pared,* quartered, and cored

2 cups reserved meat broth

¼ cup freshly squeezed, strained lemon juice

4 cups (1 quart) apple cider

1 cup good brandy

An apple parer helps accomplish this task expeditiously and efficiently.

In a large kettle, place the neck meat and water. Cover the kettle and bring the meat to a boil over high heat. Reduce the heat and simmer the meat about 2 hours, until tender.

Using a fork or slotted spoon, remove the meat from the kettle and place in a large bowl; cover and refrigerate until cold. Reserve the hot meat broth and strain it through a piece of damp cotton flannel secured, napped side up, in a sieve over a deep bowl. Cover the strained broth and refrigerate.

In a 12-quart, heavy-bottomed, stainless steel kettle, place the raisins, golden raisins, currants, citron, lemon peel, orange peel, granulated sugar, and brown sugar. Cover the kettle; set aside. In a small bowl, place the cinnamon, mace, cloves, nutmeg, and salt; stir to combine; cover and set aside.

Grind coarsely (page 49) the cold meat, suet, and apples; add to the ingredients in the kettle. Add the cinnamon mixture, 2 cups strained meat broth, lemon juice, and apple cider to the ingredients in the kettle. Stir all the ingredients to combine.

Cover the kettle. Over medium-high heat, bring the mixture to a simmer, stirring frequently. Reduce the heat to low. Uncover the kettle and simmer the mixture slowly for 1 hour, continuing to stir frequently.

Remove from the heat. Add the brandy; stir well.

Pack the hot mincemeat into hot, sterilized quart jars, leaving 1-inch headspace.

Using a plastic knife or a narrow, rubber spatula, remove the air bubbles in the jars. Wipe the jar rims and threads. Place hot metal lids on the jars and screw the bands firmly.

Process in a pressure canner for the following time and at the following pressure:

Processing Times and Pounds of Pressure

DIAL-GAUGE PRESSURE CANNER
Altitude of Canning Location

Jar Size	Processing Time	0 to 2,000 ft.	2,001 to 4,000 ft.	4,001 to 6,000 ft.	6,001 to 8,000 ft.
Quarts	90 min.	11 lbs.	12 lbs.	13 lbs.	14 lbs.

WEIGHTED-GAUGE PRESSURE CANNER
Altitude of Canning Location

Jar Size	Processing Time	0-1,000 ft.	Above 1,000 ft.
Quarts	90 min.	10 lbs.	15 lbs.

Remove the jars from the canner and place on a dry, wooden board which has been covered with a tea towel. Let the jars stand, *undisturbed,* 12 hours to cool completely.

YIELDS 7 QUARTS

FREEZER MINCEMEAT: Follow the Brandied Mincemeat recipe, above, through adding the brandy and stirring well. Then, cool the mincemeat quickly.

Pack the cooled mincemeat into clean, cool, widemouthed, quart canning jars, or rigid, plastic, quart freezer containers, leaving 1-inch headspace. Place the metal lids on the canning jars and screw the bands firmly, or place the lids on the plastic containers securely. Freeze immediately.

PLUMS IN PORT WINE

Awarded first place overall among all canned fruits (nineteen classes) at the 1990 Iowa State Fair.

8 pounds Italian prune plums
4 cups sugar
4 cups water
4 tablespoons coarsely shredded orange rind
2 3-inch pieces stick cinnamon
2⅔ cups good port wine

Wash the plums; drain. Prick each plum once with a large, sterilized needle or hat pin to prevent bursting. Pricking will not prevent the skins from cracking, but it will help prevent bursting.

In a 12-quart, heavy-bottomed, stainless steel kettle, place the sugar, water, orange rind, and stick cinnamon; stir to combine. Over high heat, bring the sugar mixture to a boil, stirring until the sugar dissolves. Cover the kettle. Reduce the heat slightly and boil the sugar mixture (syrup) 5 minutes.

Then, place the plums in the boiling syrup. Remove the kettle from the heat 3 minutes after adding the plums. Cover the kettle and let the plums stand 20 minutes.

Meanwhile, secure a piece of damp cotton flannel, napped side up, in a sieve over a deep pan; set aside.

Pack the plums (without syrup) into hot, sterilized, preferably widemouthed, quart or pint jars, leaving ½-inch headspace; let stand.

Pour the syrup (from the kettle) over the cotton flannel in the sieve to strain. Pour the strained syrup into a stainless steel saucepan. Over high heat, bring the syrup to a boil, stirring occasionally. Remove from the heat. Add the wine; stir to blend.

Cover the plums in the jars with the hot syrup, maintaining ½-inch headspace.

Using a plastic knife or a narrow, rubber spatula, remove the air bubbles in the jars. Wipe the jar rims and threads. Place hot metal lids on the jars and screw the bands firmly.

Process in a boiling-water canner for the following time:

Processing Times

Jar Size	Altitude of Canning Location			
	0 to 1,000 ft.	1,001 to 3,000 ft.	3,001 to 6,000 ft.	Above 6,000 ft.
Pints	20 min.	25 min.	30 min.	35 min.
Quarts	25 min.	30 min.	35 min.	40 min.

Remove the jars from the canner and place on a dry, wooden board which has been covered with a tea towel. Let the jars stand, *undisturbed,* 12 hours to cool completely.

YIELDS ABOUT 4 QUARTS

VARIATION: The plum skins may be peeled immediately following the 3 minutes of cooking. Eliminate letting the plums stand 20 minutes and proceed to pack the plums in the jars.

PLAIN PLUMS: Follow the Plums in Port Wine recipe, above, omitting the orange rind, cinnamon, and wine.

Spiced Fruits
(without Vinegar)

SPICED APPLE RINGS

16 cups cold water
2 tablespoons white vinegar
2 tablespoons salt
5 pounds bright red apples which hold
    their shape when cooked, such as
    Jonathan* (about 10 large apples)
6 cups sugar
8 cups water
4 3-inch pieces stick cinnamon
1 tablespoon red liquid food coloring

Select uniform apples with a diameter which will allow the stacked apple rings to fit nicely into the canning jars. Use widemouthed, pint canning jars with straight sides.

In a 16-quart kettle, place 16 cups water, vinegar, and salt; stir until the salt dissolves; set aside.

Wash the apples. Using an apple corer, core the apples; do not pare. As the apples are cored, drop them into the vinegar solution to prevent discoloration. Using a sharp, thin-bladed knife, slice the cored apples, evenly, ¼ inch thick. Be careful not to slice the apples too thinly. Reserve the end slices for other uses. Drop the apple slices back into the vinegar solution as each apple is sliced. Let the apple slices stand.

In a 12-quart, heavy-bottomed, stainless steel kettle, place the sugar, 8 cups water, stick cinnamon, and food coloring; stir to combine. Over high heat, bring the sugar mixture to a boil, stirring until the sugar dissolves. Cover the kettle. Reduce the heat slightly and boil the sugar mixture (syrup) 5 minutes. Remove from the heat.

Drain and rinse the apple rings twice, using fresh, cold water. Drain the apple rings well.

Place the apple rings in the hot syrup (removed from the heat). Cover the kettle and let the apple rings stand 10 minutes. This will help to firm the apples.

Then, over medium-high heat, bring the apple rings to a boil. Uncover the kettle. Reduce the heat and simmer the apple rings 10 minutes. Remove from the heat and let the apple rings stand in the syrup, uncovered, until cool. The apple rings will deepen in red color during the cooling period. A plate weighted with a small bowl of water may be carefully placed on top of the apple rings to keep them all fully submerged in the red syrup during the cooling period.

When the apple rings are cool, secure 4 layers of damp cheesecloth in a sieve over a deep pan; set aside.

Stack the apple rings (without syrup) in hot, sterilized, widemouthed, with straight sides pint jars, leaving ½-inch headspace; let stand.

Pour the syrup over the cheesecloth in the sieve to strain. Pour the strained syrup into a stainless steel saucepan. Over high heat, bring the syrup to a boil, stirring occasionally. Cover the apple rings in the jars with the hot syrup, maintaining ½-inch headspace.

Using a plastic knife or a narrow, rubber spatula, remove the air bubbles in the jars. Wipe the jar rims and threads. Place hot metal lids on the jars and screw the bands firmly.

Process in a boiling-water canner for the following time:

Processing Times

Jar Size	Altitude of Canning Location			
	0 to 1,000 ft.	1,001 to 3,000 ft.	3,001 to 6,000 ft.	Above 6,000 ft.
Pints and Quarts	20 min.	25 min.	30 min.	35 min.

Remove the jars from the canner and place on a dry, wooden board which has been covered with a tea towel. Let the jars stand, *undisturbed*, 12 hours to cool completely.

YIELDS ABOUT 4 TO 5 PINTS

NOTE: Do not attempt to double this recipe, as this will likely result in crushed and unevenly colored apple rings.

SERVING SUGGESTION: Especially nice with ham, fresh pork, and poultry.

PEPPERMINT PEARS

Pair bright-green Peppermint Pears with Christmas-red Spiced Apple Rings (page 728) on a divided serving dish and place it on the holiday dinner table near the turkey.

16 cups cold water
2 tablespoons white vinegar
2 tablespoons salt
7 pounds firm and not overripe Bartlett pears
4½ cups sugar
6 cups water
2 teaspoons peppermint extract
2 teaspoons green liquid food coloring
2¼ cups sugar
3 cups water
1 teaspoon peppermint extract
½ teaspoon green liquid food coloring

In a 16-quart kettle, place 16 cups water, vinegar, and salt; stir until the salt dissolves; set aside.

Wash, cut in half, core, and pare the pears. As the pears are prepared, drop them into the vinegar solution to prevent discoloration. Let the pears stand.

In a 12-quart, heavy-bottomed, stainless steel kettle, place 4½ cups sugar and 6 cups water; stir to combine. Over high heat, bring the sugar mixture to a boil, stirring until the sugar dissolves. Cover the kettle. Reduce the heat slightly and boil the sugar mixture (syrup) 5 minutes.

Remove the syrup from the heat. Add 2 teaspoons peppermint extract and 2 teaspoons food coloring; stir well to blend. Over medium-high heat, return the syrup to a boil.

Drain and rinse the pears twice, using fresh, cold water. Drain the pears well. Place the pears in the boiling syrup. Cover the kettle. Over high heat, bring the syrup (with the pears) to a simmer. Uncover the kettle. Reduce the heat and simmer the pears 3 minutes. Remove from the heat and let the pears stand in the syrup, uncovered, until cool.

When the pears are cool, make another batch of the syrup, using 2¼ cups sugar, 3 cups water, 1 teaspoon peppermint extract, and ½ teaspoon food coloring, and following the previous procedure; let stand.

Drain the pears and pack them into hot, sterilized, widemouthed, pint or quart jars, leaving ½-inch headspace.

Cover the pears in the jars with the second batch of hot syrup, maintaining ½-inch headspace. (The second batch of syrup contains proportionately less food coloring, making it more attractive in the jars.)

Using a plastic knife or a narrow, rubber spatula, remove the air bubbles in the jars. Wipe the jar rims and threads. Place hot metal lids on the jars and screw the bands firmly.

Process in a boiling-water canner for the following time:

Processing Times

Jar Size	Altitude of Canning Location			
	0 to 1,000 ft.	1,001 to 3,000 ft.	3,001 to 6,000 ft.	Above 6,000 ft.
Pints	20 min.	25 min.	30 min.	35 min.
Quarts	25 min.	30 min.	35 min.	40 min.

Remove the jars from the canner and place on a dry, wooden board which has been covered with a tea towel. Let the jars stand, *undisturbed,* 12 hours to cool completely.

YIELDS ABOUT 6 PINTS

SERVING SUGGESTION: Peppermint Pears complement the flavor of lamb, roast pork, and poultry.

Vegetables

ASPARAGUS SPEARS

6 pounds medium-diameter asparagus
spears

Use widemouthed, pint or quart canning jars
with straight sides. Measure the height of the
pint or quart canning jars to be used and deduct
1³⁄₁₆ inches (1 inch for headspace plus allowance
for liquid to cover the asparagus spears). This
measurement will be the exact length to cut the
asparagus spears. Measure 1 asparagus spear and
cut it at the stem end. Use this spear as a pattern
to cut the spears. Carefully place the cut spears
in a colander. Run cold water over the spears to
wash; let stand.

Secure a piece of damp cotton flannel, napped
side up, in a sieve over a deep pan; set aside.

Place the asparagus spears in the basket of a
blancher. Drop the basket into the blancher pan
containing boiling water over high heat. Cover
the blancher and return the water to boiling.
Reduce the heat and cook the asparagus spears
at a low boil 3½ minutes. Immediately remove
the blancher basket from the pan to drain the
asparagus; reserve the cooking liquid.

Pack the asparagus spears vertically (with the
tips up) and decoratively into hot, sterilized,
widemouthed, pint or quart jars with straight
sides; let stand.

Pour the hot cooking liquid over the cotton
flannel in the sieve to strain. Pour the strained
cooking liquid into a stainless steel saucepan.
Over high heat, bring the cooking liquid to a
boil. Cover the asparagus spears in the jars with
the hot cooking liquid, maintaining 1-inch
headspace.

Using a plastic knife or a narrow, rubber spat-

ula, remove the air bubbles in the jars. Wipe the
jar rims and threads. Place hot metal lids on the
jars and screw the bands firmly.

Process in a pressure canner for the following
time and at the following pressure:

Processing Times and Pounds of Pressure

DIAL-GAUGE PRESSURE CANNER

| Jar Size | Processing Time | Altitude of Canning Location | | | |
		0 to 2,000 ft.	2,001 to 4,000 ft.	4,001 to 6,000 ft.	6,001 to 8,000 ft.
Pints	30 min.	11 lbs.	12 lbs.	13 lbs.	14 lbs.
Quarts	40 min.	11 lbs.	12 lbs.	13 lbs.	14 lbs.

WEIGHTED-GAUGE PRESSURE CANNER

| Jar Size | Processing Time | Altitude of Canning Location | |
		0-1,000 ft.	Above 1,000 ft.
Pints	30 min.	10 lbs.	15 lbs.
Quarts	40 min.	10 lbs.	15 lbs.

Remove the jars from the canner and place
on a dry, wooden board which has been covered
with a tea towel. Let the jars stand, *undisturbed,*
12 hours to cool completely.

YIELDS ABOUT 6 PINTS OR 3 QUARTS

CUT ASPARAGUS: Follow the Asparagus Spears
recipe, above, with the following exceptions:
Cut the asparagus spears into 1½-inch lengths.
Pack the cut spears randomly into the jars, leaving 1 inch headspace.

CARROTS

7½ pounds carrots (without tops)

Wash the carrots. Cut off the ends, pare (page
45), and wash again. Slice the carrots widthwise
and/or lengthwise, or leave whole.

Place the carrots in a large, heavy-bottomed,
stainless steel kettle. Cover the carrots with boiling water. Cover the kettle. Over high heat,
bring the carrots to a boil. Reduce the heat and
simmer the carrots 5 minutes.

Remove from the heat. Pack the hot carrots (without cooking liquid) into hot, sterilized pint or quart jars, leaving 1-inch headspace.

Cover the carrots in the jars with the hot cooking liquid, maintaining 1-inch headspace.

Using a plastic knife or a narrow, rubber spatula, remove the air bubbles in the jars. Wipe the jar rims and threads. Place hot metal lids on the jars and screw the bands firmly.

Process in a pressure canner for the following time and at the following pressure:

Processing Times and Pounds of Pressure

DIAL-GAUGE PRESSURE CANNER

Jar Size	Processing Time	Altitude of Canning Location			
		0 to 2,000 ft.	2,001 to 4,000 ft.	4,001 to 6,000 ft.	6,001 to 8,000 ft.
Pints	25 min.	11 lbs.	12 lbs.	13 lbs.	14 lbs.
Quarts	30 min.	11 lbs.	12 lbs.	13 lbs.	14 lbs.

WEIGHTED-GAUGE PRESSURE CANNER

Jar Size	Processing Time	Altitude of Canning Location	
		0-1,000 ft.	Above 1,000 ft.
Pints	25 min.	10 lbs.	15 lbs.
Quarts	30 min.	10 lbs.	15 lbs.

Remove the jars from the canner and place on a dry, wooden board which has been covered with a tea towel. Let the jars stand, *undisturbed,* 12 hours to cool completely.

YIELDS ABOUT 6 PINTS OR 3 QUARTS

WHOLE-KERNEL CORN

22 pounds unshucked corn (about 34 medium ears)

Shuck the corn and carefully remove all the silk. Wash the corn; set aside.

Fill a 12-quart, heavy-bottomed, stainless steel kettle ½ to ⅔ full of water. Cover the kettle. Over high heat, bring the water to a rapid boil. Uncover the kettle.

In small batches, drop the ears of corn into the boiling water and boil 3 minutes. Immediately remove the ears from the water and place, single layer, on a folded tea towel spread on the kitchen counter or on a large wooden board. Bring the water to a rapid boil before boiling each batch of corn.

Using a medium, sharp knife, cut the kernels from the cobs at about ⅔ the depth of the kernels, leaving on the cobs any small, undeveloped kernels at the ends of the cobs. Do not scrape the cobs. Place the kernels in one or more large mixing bowls.

Fill hot, sterilized, pint or quart jars with the corn, leaving 1-inch headspace. Do not shake the jars to pack the corn or press the corn into the jars.

Cover the corn in the jars with fresh, boiling water, maintaining 1-inch headspace.

Using a plastic knife or a narrow, rubber spatula, remove the air bubbles in the jars. Wipe the jar rims and threads. Place hot metal lids on the jars and screw the bands firmly.

Process in a pressure canner for the following time and at the following pressure:

Processing Times and Pounds of Pressure

DIAL-GAUGE PRESSURE CANNER

Jar Size	Processing Time	Altitude of Canning Location			
		0 to 2,000 ft.	2,001 to 4,000 ft.	4,001 to 6,000 ft.	6,001 to 8,000 ft.
Pints	55 min.	11 lbs.	12 lbs.	13 lbs.	14 lbs.
Quarts	85 min.	11 lbs.	12 lbs.	13 lbs.	14 lbs.

WEIGHTED-GAUGE PRESSURE CANNER

Jar Size	Processing Time	Altitude of Canning Location	
		0-1,000 ft.	Above 1,000 ft.
Pints	55 min.	10 lbs.	15 lbs.
Quarts	85 min.	10 lbs.	15 lbs.

Remove the jars from the canner and place on a dry, wooden board which has been covered with a tea towel. Let the jars stand, *undisturbed,* 12 hours to cool completely.

YIELDS ABOUT 10 PINTS OR 5 QUARTS

CORN WITH RED PEPPERS AND BASIL

13 pounds unshucked corn (about
    20 medium ears)
¾ pound red bell peppers (about 2 large
    peppers)
1 tablespoon dried leaf basil

Shuck the corn and carefully remove all the silk. Wash the corn; set aside.

Fill a 12-quart, heavy-bottomed, stainless steel kettle ½ to ⅔ full of water. Cover the kettle. Over high heat, bring the water to a rapid boil. Uncover the kettle.

In small batches, drop the ears of corn into the boiling water and boil 3 minutes. Immediately remove the ears from the water and place, single layer, on a folded tea towel spread on the kitchen counter or on a large wooden board. Bring the water to a rapid boil before boiling each batch of corn.

Using a medium, sharp knife, cut the kernels from the cobs at about ⅔ the depth of the kernels, leaving on the cobs any small, undeveloped kernels at the ends of the cobs. Do not scrape the cobs. Place the kernels in one or more large mixing bowls; set aside.

Cut the red peppers lengthwise into 24 ¾ × 3-inch strips. Cut away any protruding flesh from the backs of the strips. Using a small, sharp knife, trim the ends of the strips to simulate ribbons (see illustration).

Carefully place the red pepper ribbons in a saucepan and cover with boiling water; let stand

3 minutes to soften the ribbons slightly. Remove the ribbons from the water and place them, flat and single layer, on paper towels; set aside.

Place about ½ inch of corn in the bottom of each of 6 hot, sterilized, widemouthed, preferably straight-sided, pint jars. Arrange 4 red pepper ribbons, shiny side out, decoratively around the inside of each jar against the side glass. Carefully fill the jars with corn, leaving 1-inch headspace. Then, sprinkle ½ teaspoon basil in each jar.

Cover the corn in the jars with fresh, boiling water, maintaining 1-inch headspace.

Using a plastic knife or a narrow, rubber spatula, remove the air bubbles in the jars. Wipe the jar rims and threads. Place hot metal lids on the jars and screw the bands firmly.

Process in a pressure canner for the following time and at the following pressure:

Processing Times and Pounds of Pressure

DIAL-GAUGE PRESSURE CANNER

Jar Size	Processing Time	Altitude of Canning Location			
		0 to 2,000 ft.	2,001 to 4,000 ft.	4,001 to 6,000 ft.	6,001 to 8,000 ft.
Pints	55 min.	11 lbs.	12 lbs.	13 lbs.	14 lbs.

WEIGHTED-GAUGE PRESSURE CANNER

Jar Size	Processing Time	Altitude of Canning Location	
		0-1,000 ft.	Above 1,000 ft.
Pints	55 min.	10 lbs.	15 lbs.

Remove the jars from the canner and place on a dry, wooden board which has been covered with a tea towel. Let the jars stand, *undisturbed,* 12 hours to cool completely.

YIELDS ABOUT 6 PINTS

CREAM-STYLE CORN

20 pounds unshucked corn (about 31 medium ears)

Shuck the corn and carefully remove all the silk. Wash the corn; set aside.

Fill a 12-quart, heavy-bottomed, stainless steel kettle ½ to ⅔ full of water. Cover the kettle. Over high heat, bring the water to a rapid boil. Uncover the kettle.

In small batches, drop the ears of corn into the boiling water and boil 3 minutes. Immediately remove the ears from the water and place, single layer, on a folded tea towel spread on the kitchen counter or on a large wooden board. Bring the water to a rapid boil before boiling each batch of corn.

Using a medium, sharp knife, cut the kernels from the cobs at about ½ the depth of the kernels, leaving on the cobs any small, undeveloped kernels at the ends of the cobs. Place the kernels in a large mixing bowl. Then, with the knife at a 90-degree angle to the cob, scrape the cobs using a downward motion. Add the scrapings to the bowl containing the kernels; stir to combine.

Fill hot, sterilized, pint (see Note) jars with the corn mixture, leaving 1-inch headspace. Do not shake the jars to the pack corn or press the corn into the jars.

Cover the corn mixture in the jars with fresh, boiling water, maintaining 1-inch headspace.

Using a plastic knife or a narrow, rubber spatula, remove the air bubbles in the jars. Wipe the jar rims and threads. Place hot metal lids on the jars and screw the bands firmly.

Process in a pressure canner for the following time and at the following pressure:

Processing Times and Pounds of Pressure

DIAL-GAUGE PRESSURE CANNER
Altitude of Canning Location

Jar Size	Processing Time	0 to 2,000 ft.	2,001 to 4,000 ft.	4,001 to 6,000 ft.	6,001 to 8,000 ft.
Pints	95 min.	11 lbs.	12 lbs.	13 lbs.	14 lbs.

WEIGHTED-GAUGE PRESSURE CANNER
Altitude of Canning Location

Jar Size	Processing Time	0-1,000 ft.	Above 1,000 ft.
Pints	95 min.	10 lbs.	15 lbs.

Remove the jars from the canner and place on a dry, wooden board which has been covered with a tea towel. Let the jars stand, *undisturbed*, 12 hours to cool completely.

NOTE: For processing safety, do not use quart jars because of the denseness of Cream–Style Corn.

YIELDS ABOUT 9 PINTS

GREEN AND WAX BEANS

This ribbon was awarded for a pint of green and wax beans packed vertically and alternately (see To Can Green and Wax Beans Vertically, below).

6 pounds green or wax beans*

*Green beans and wax beans may be canned separately or mixed.

Using a vegetable brush, wash the beans well. Cut off the ends; then cut into 1- to 2-inch lengths, depending upon your preference.

Place the beans in a large, heavy-bottomed, stainless steel kettle. Cover the beans with boiling water. Cover the kettle. Over high heat, bring the beans to a boil. Reduce the heat and cook the beans at a low boil for 5 minutes.

Remove from the heat. Pack the hot beans (without cooking liquid) loosely into hot, sterilized, pint or quart jars, leaving 1-inch headspace.

Cover the beans in the jars with the hot cooking liquid, maintaining 1-inch headspace.

Using a plastic knife or a narrow, rubber spatula, remove the air bubbles in the jars. Wipe the jar rims and threads. Place hot metal lids on the jars and screw the bands firmly.

Process in a pressure canner for the following time and at the following pressure:

(Recipe continues on next page)

DIAL-GAUGE PRESSURE CANNER
Altitude of Canning Location

Jar Size	Processing Time	0 to 2,000 ft.	2,001 to 4,000 ft.	4,001 to 6,000 ft.	6,001 to 8,000 ft.
Pints	20 min.	11 lbs.	12 lbs.	13 lbs.	14 lbs.
Quarts	25 min.	11 lbs.	12 lbs.	13 lbs.	14 lbs.

WEIGHTED-GAUGE PRESSURE CANNER
Altitude of Canning Location

Jar Size	Processing Time	0-1,000 ft.	Above 1,000 ft.
Pints	20 min.	10 lbs.	15 lbs.
Quarts	25 min.	10 lbs.	15 lbs.

Remove the jars from the canner and place on a dry, wooden board which has been covered with a tea towel. Let the jars stand, *undisturbed,* 12 hours to cool completely.

YIELDS ABOUT 6 PINTS OR 3 QUARTS

VARIATION ~ **TO CAN GREEN AND/OR WAX BEANS VERTICALLY:** After washing the beans, cut off the stem ends and trim the blossom ends, leaving about 1/8 inch of the "tails" intact; set aside.

Use widemouthed, pint canning jars with straight sides. Measure the height of the canning jars to be used and deduct 1 5/16 inches (1 inch for headspace plus allowance for liquid to cover the beans [and "tails"]). This measurement will be the exact length to cut the beans. Measure 1 bean and cut it at the stem end. Use this bean as a pattern to cut the beans.

Cook the cut beans, following the procedure in the Green and Wax Beans recipe. Pack the beans vertically (with the "tails" up) into hot, sterilized, widemouthed, pint jars with straight sides.

Cover the beans in the jars with the hot cooking liquid, maintaining 1-inch headspace.

Then, follow the Green and Wax Beans recipe to conclusion.

For a very showy jar, pack green and wax beans alternately around the inside of the jar against the side glass. Evenly mix the green and wax beans in the center of the jar.

YIELD ABOUT 6 PINTS

SAUERKRAUT

6 quarts distilled water
1/2 cup plus 1 tablespoon canning salt
25 pounds firm heads of fresh cabbage
1 cup canning salt (page 704), divided

Immediately prior to commencing preparation of the Sauerkraut, wash a 5-gallon crock in hot, soapy water. Rinse the crock well; then, scald with boiling water. Allow the crock to dry 2 or 3 minutes and then cover the top with plastic wrap. The least exposure of the inside of crock to air after scalding the better. Place the crock in a location at 70 to 75° F., where it will be packed with salted cabbage and stored during fermentation.

In an 8-quart, stainless steel kettle, place the distilled water and 1/2 cup plus 1 tablespoon canning salt (3 tablespoons canning salt to each 2 quarts distilled water); stir to combine. Cover the kettle. Over high heat, bring the mixture (brine) to a boil.

Remove from the heat. Uncover the kettle and let stand until the brine cools slightly. Then, cover the kettle and let stand at room temperature until the brine cools to 70 to 75° F. Or, refrigerate the brine until cooled to 70 to 75° F.; then, remove from the refrigerator.

Wash the cabbage heads under cold, running water; drain. Remove the outer leaves. Divide the cabbage into 5 approximately equal groups (about 5 pounds of cabbage per group). Prepare 1 group at a time, as follows:

Quarter and core the cabbage heads. Using a sharp knife, cut the cabbage, as uniformly as possible, into 1/8- to 3/16-inch-wide shreds. Place the shreds in a large kettle or plastic container. Sprinkle 3 tablespoons canning salt over the shreds; using a large mixing spoon or your hands, combine well; let stand.

Prepare and shred the second group of cabbage. Place the shreds in a second kettle or plastic container. Add the canning salt and combine, repeating the procedure as for the first cabbage group; let stand. Premixing the shredded cabbage and canning salt in a kettle or plastic container allows the cabbage to wilt slightly before placement in the crock, reducing breakage of the shreds when packed.

Place the first group of salted cabbage shreds in the crock. With your hands, press the cabbage shreds firmly into the bottom of the crock. Re-cover the crock with the plastic wrap.

Prepare, shred, salt, and combine the third group of cabbage, using the kettle or plastic container used for the first group; set aside. Pack the second cabbage group into the crock, repeating the procedure as for the first cabbage group.

Repeat the procedure until all 5 groups of cabbage have been packed into the crock. The rim of the crock must be at least 4 inches above the top of the cabbage shreds. If the liquid does not completely cover the cabbage when pressed down, add enough of the *cool* brine to cover.

Directly cover the packed cabbage with a clean, thin, white piece of cloth such as muslin, and tuck it down around the inside edge of the crock. Wash a dinner plate in soapy water (rewash the plate even if clean); rinse well. Dry the plate and allow it to cool briefly. Then, place the plate on top of the cloth. The plate should be only slightly smaller in diameter than the crock. Let stand.

Pour at least 1 gallon of *cool* brine into a 2-gallon, zipper-seal plastic bag; seal the bag securely. Place the filled and sealed bag in a second 2-gallon, zipper-seal plastic bag for extra protection; seal the second bag securely. Place the brine-filled bag on the plate in the crock as a weight to keep the cabbage covered with brine and to seal the fermenting cabbage from the outside air. The cabbage should be covered with 1 to 2 inches of brine. Make certain that the brine-filled bag rests firmly against the entire inside edge of the crock. Then, cover the top of the crock with a double thickness of a clean, unscented, heavy terry cloth towel.

Let the cabbage ferment, *undisturbed,* 4 weeks. The terry cloth towel may be lifted intermittently to inspect the crock; however, the brine-filled bag should not be touched, in order to maintain the airtightness of the fermenting cabbage. If the crock is kept at a temperature of 60 to 65° F., fermentation may take 5 to 6 weeks. The cabbage may not ferment if stored at a temperature below 60° F. At temperatures above 75° F., the sauerkraut may become soft. Normal fermentation is complete when the bubbling ceases.

To can fully fermented sauerkraut, place ½ of the sauerkraut and liquid in a 12-quart, heavy-bottomed, stainless steel kettle. Over medium-high heat, slowly bring the sauerkraut to a boil, stirring and turning the sauerkraut frequently. When the sauerkraut begins to boil, remove from the heat.

Pack the hot sauerkraut fairly tightly into hot, sterilized, quart or pint jars, leaving ½-inch headspace. Cover the sauerkraut in the jars with the hot sauerkraut liquid, maintaining ½-inch headspace.

Using a plastic knife or a narrow, rubber spatula, remove the air bubbles in the jars. Wipe the jar rims and threads. Place hot metal lids on the jars and screw the bands firmly.

Process in a boiling-water canner for the following time:

Processing Times

Jar Size	Altitude of Canning Location		
	0 to 1,000 ft.	1,001 to 6,000 ft.	Above 6,000 ft.
Pints	10 min.	15 min.	20 min.
Quarts	15 min.	20 min.	25 min.

Remove the jars from the canner and place on a dry, wooden board which has been covered with a tea towel.

Can the remaining ½ of the sauerkraut, repeating the procedure.

Let the jars stand, *undisturbed,* 12 hours to cool completely.

YIELDS ABOUT 14 QUARTS

NOTE: Fully fermented, uncanned sauerkraut may be kept tightly covered in the refrigerator for several months.

TOMATOES

Whole or Halved Tomatoes, Hot-Packed in Water

Caution: Because tomatoes are low in acid (see page 707), they must be canned carefully to insure safety from possible toxins. Add *bottled* lemon juice to the jars (see page 707), as specified in the recipe, to increase acidity. Follow processing times and procedures strictly. While tomatoes from dead or frost-killed vines may be eaten fresh or frozen, do not use them for canning, as they are especially low in acid.

3 gallons firm, vine-ripened tomatoes
½ cup plus 2 tablespoons *bottled* lemon juice, divided

Wash the tomatoes. In batches, blanch the tomatoes (page 44) 45 seconds and immediately immerse them in cold water; drain. Remove the stem ends (see Note) and peel the tomatoes. Carefully remove the tiny blossom ends. Leave the tomatoes whole or cut them in half, according to your preference.

Carefully place the tomatoes in a 16-quart, heavy-bottomed, stainless steel kettle. Cover the tomatoes with water. Cover the kettle. Over high heat, bring the tomatoes to a low boil. Reduce the heat and simmer the tomatoes gently for 3 minutes. Remove from the heat; uncover and let stand.

Pour 2 tablespoons *bottled* lemon juice into each hot, sterilized, widemouthed quart jar (or 1 tablespoon *bottled* lemon juice into each hot, sterilized, widemouthed, pint jar).

Pack the hot tomatoes into the jars, leaving ½-inch headspace.

Cover the tomatoes in the jars with the hot cooking liquid, maintaining ½-inch headspace.

Using a plastic knife or narrow, rubber spatula, remove the air bubbles in the jars. Wipe the jar rims and threads. Place hot metal lids on the jars and screw the bands firmly.

Process in a boiling-water canner for the following time:

Processing Times

Jar Size	Altitude of Canning Location			
	0 to 1,000 ft.	1,001 to 3,000 ft.	3,001 to 6,000 ft.	Above 6,000 ft.
Pints	40 min.	45 min.	50 min.	55 min.
Quarts	45 min.	50 min.	55 min.	60 min.

Remove the jars from the canner and place on a dry, wooden board which has been covered with a tea towel. Let the jars stand, *undisturbed,* 12 hours to cool completely.

NOTE: A tomato corer is a handy, inexpensive kitchen tool to use for this task.

YIELDS ABOUT 5 QUARTS

Whole or Halved Tomatoes,
Raw-Packed Without Added Liquid

3 gallons firm, vine-ripened tomatoes
½ cup plus 2 tablespoons *bottled* lemon juice, divided

Prepare the tomatoes, following the *first* paragraph in the hot-packed Tomatoes recipe, above; set aside.

Pour 2 tablespoons *bottled* lemon juice into each hot, sterilized, widemouthed, quart jar (or 1 tablespoon *bottled* lemon juice into each hot, sterilized, widemouthed, pint jar).

Pack the raw tomatoes *tightly* into the jars, leaving ½-inch headspace. Using a wooden spoon, press the tomatoes in the jars until the spaces between the tomatoes fill with juice. Leave ½-inch headspace. If necessary, add to the jars fresh, hot water or additional juice from other fresh tomatoes to maintain ½-inch headspace.

Using a plastic knife or a narrow, rubber spatula, remove the air bubbles in the jars. Wipe the jar rims and threads. Place hot metal lids on the jars and screw the bands firmly.

Process in a boiling-water canner for the following time:

Jar Size	Altitude of Canning Location			
	0 to 1,000 ft.	1,001 to 3,000 ft.	3,001 to 6,000 ft.	Above 6,000 ft.
Pints and Quarts	85 min.	90 min.	95 min.	100 min.

Remove the jars from the canner and place on a dry, wooden board which has been covered with a tea towel. Let the jars stand, *undisturbed,* 12 hours to cool completely.

NOTE: A tomato corer is a handy, inexpensive kitchen tool to use for this task.

YIELDS ABOUT 5 QUARTS

TOMATO JUICE

The added vegetable juices in this Tomato Juice give it a fantastic flavor. It's Tomato Juice Plus!

Caution: Because tomatoes are low in acid (see page 707), Tomato Juice must be canned carefully to insure safety from possible toxins. Add *bottled* lemon juice to the jars (see page 707), as specified in the recipe, to increase acidity. Follow processing times and procedures strictly. While tomatoes from dead or frost-killed vines may be eaten fresh or frozen, do not use them for canning, as they are especially low in acid.

14 pounds firm, vine-ripened tomatoes (16 cups juice; see recipe procedures, below)
3 tablespoons onion juice (see recipe procedures, below)
2 tablespoons green bell pepper juice (see recipe procedures, below)
2 tablespoons red bell pepper juice (see recipe procedures, below)
1½ teaspoons salt
1 tablespoon sugar
5 drops Tabasco pepper sauce
½ cup *bottled* lemon juice, divided

Wash the tomatoes. In batches, blanch the tomatoes (page 44) 1 minute and immediately immerse them in cold water; drain. Remove the stem ends (see Note), peel, remove the tiny blossom ends, quarter, and core the tomatoes (page 45).

In batches, process the tomatoes in a blender to make juice. Strain the juice through a sieve to remove the seeds. Measure 16 cups juice; set aside.

If you do not have onion, green pepper, and red pepper juices reserved from previously making Chili Sauce (page 783), Bell Pepper Relish (page 779), or Zucchini Relish (page 778), make onion, green pepper, and red pepper juices by chopping the vegetables, processing them separately in the blender, and then straining them separately in the sieve.

In an 8-quart, heavy-bottomed, stainless steel kettle, place the 16 cups (4 quarts) tomato juice, onion juice, green pepper juice, red pepper juice, salt, sugar, and pepper sauce. Cover the kettle. Over medium-high heat, bring the tomato juice mixture to a simmer. Uncover the kettle. Reduce the heat and simmer the tomato juice mixture 5 minutes. Remove from the heat. Skim the foam off the tomato juice mixture, using tableware tablespoons and teaspoons; let stand.

Pour 2 tablespoons *bottled* lemon juice into each hot, sterilized quart jar (or 1 tablespoon *bottled* lemon juice into each hot, sterilized pint jar).

Pour the hot Tomato Juice into the jars, leaving ½-inch headspace.

Wipe the jar rims and threads. Place hot metal lids on the jars and screw the bands firmly.

Process in a boiling-water canner for the following time:

Processing Times

Jar Size	Altitude of Canning Location			
	0 to 1,000 ft.	1,001 to 3,000 ft.	3,001 to 6,000 ft.	Above 6,000 ft.
Pints	35 min.	40 min.	45 min.	50 min.
Quarts	40 min.	45 min.	50 min.	55 min.

(Recipe continues on next page)

Remove the jars from the canner and place on a dry, wooden board which has been covered with a tea towel. Let the jars stand, *undisturbed,* 12 hours to cool completely.

NOTE: A tomato corer is a handy, inexpensive kitchen tool to use for this task.

YIELDS 4 QUARTS

Sweet Spreads

TYPES OF SWEET SPREADS

Sweet spreads are generally fruit products preserved by sugar. They are jellied (except butters) to varying degrees, and differ greatly in texture, flavor, and color, depending upon the fruit (or other product) and the way it is processed. There are six classifications of sweet spreads:

JELLY: A semisolid mixture generally made with fruit juice and sugar. Flavored liquids other than fruit juice are sometimes used. Jelly is beautiful in color, translucent, and tender enough to cut easily with a spoon, yet firm enough to hold its shape when turned from the container.

JAM: A thick spread made with crushed or chopped fruit cooked with sugar. Jam has the same brilliance and color as jelly, but is softer in texture.

PRESERVES: Small, whole fruit or uniformly sized, medium-large pieces of fruit in a clear, heavy, slightly jellied syrup. Preserves contain plump, tender fruit with natural color and flavor.

CONSERVES: Similar to jam, with the same consistency. Conserves generally—but not always—contain two or more fruits, one of which is usually a citrus fruit. They contain nuts and/or raisins and/or coconut. In their purest form, conserves contain both nuts and raisins. They are favored for meat and poultry accompaniments; however, they also may be used as spreads on bread products.

MARMALADE: Soft fruit jelly containing small pieces of fruit or peel evenly suspended in the translucent jelly. Marmalade often contains citrus fruit.

BUTTERS: Fruit pulp and sugar cooked to a rather thick consistency, but not jellied. Butters often contain spices.

Jellies

SHEETING IN JELLY MAKING

When making jellies *without added pectin,* a candy thermometer is the most reliable means of determining when the boiling jelly mixture reaches the jellying point and is done. The jellying point is reached when the jelly mixture reaches 8° F. above the boiling point of water (page 712).

Another way to determine when the jellying point has been reached is to test the jelly mixture for sheeting. To test for sheeting, dip a cool, metal tablespoon into the boiling jelly mixture and lift out a tablespoonful. Hold the spoon about 12 inches above the kettle (out of the steam) and pour the jelly mixture back into the kettle from the side of the spoon bowl. Before reaching the jellying point, the mixture first will drop off the spoon in syrupy drops. At the next stage before reaching the jellying point, two heavy drops of the jelly mixture will drop off the spoon. When the jellying point has been reached, the two drops of jelly mixture will flow together and break from the spoon in a single sheet (see illustrations, page 739).

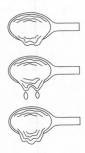

APPLE JELLY

5 pounds tart apples (7 cups juice; see
  recipe procedures, below)
5 cups water
9 cups sugar
1 1¾-ounce package powdered fruit pectin

Wash the apples; remove the stem and blossom
ends. Do not pare or core the apples. Cut the
apples into small pieces and place in an 8-quart,
heavy-bottomed, stainless steel kettle. Add the
water. Cover the kettle and bring the apples to
a boil over high heat. Reduce the heat and simmer the apples 10 minutes, stirring occasionally.

Remove from the heat. Using a potato
masher, crush the cooked apples in the kettle.
Cover the kettle. Simmer the apples an additional 5 minutes, or until the apples are soft, stirring occasionally.

Meanwhile, secure 4 layers of damp cheesecloth in a large sieve over a deep pan.

Pour the cooked apples and juice over the
cheesecloth in the sieve and let drain, undisturbed, at least 4 hours, until fully drained. Do
not stir or squeeze the apple mixture in the cheesecloth, as this may cause the jelly to be cloudy.
Squeezed juice must be re-strained.

Measure 7 cups strained apple juice and pour
into a clean, 8-quart, heavy-bottomed, stainless
steel kettle; set aside. Place the sugar in a large
mixing bowl; set aside.

Drain hot, sterilized, half-pint jars, upside
down, on a clean tea towel; let stand.

Add the pectin to the apple juice in the kettle; stir well to combine. Over high heat, bring
the apple juice mixture to a rolling boil, stirring
constantly. Immediately add the sugar and
return the apple juice mixture to a rolling boil
over high heat, stirring continuously. Boil the
mixture exactly 1 minute (use a timer), stirring
constantly. Immediately remove from the heat
and skim the foam off the jelly, using tableware
tablespoons and teaspoons.

Quickly pour the hot jelly into the drained
jars, leaving ¼-inch headspace.

Wipe the jar rims and threads. Place hot metal
lids on the jars and screw the bands firmly.

Process in a boiling-water canner for the following time:

Processing Times

Jar Size	Altitude of Canning Location		
	0 to 1,000 ft.	1,001 to 6,000 ft.	Above 6,000 ft.
Half-Pints	5 min.	10 min.	15 min.

Remove the jars from the canner and place
on a dry, wooden board which has been covered
with a tea towel. Let the jars stand, undisturbed,
12 hours to cool completely.

YIELDS ABOUT 10 HALF-PINTS

BLACKBERRY JELLY

3½ quarts blackberries (3½ cups juice; see
  recipe procedures, below)
5 cups sugar
1 1¾-ounce package powdered fruit pectin

Wash and sort the blackberries; drain in a colander. In a flat-bottomed pan, crush the berries, ⅓
at a time, using a potato masher.

Place the crushed berries, with the juice, in an
8-quart, heavy-bottomed, stainless steel kettle.
Over medium-high heat, bring the crushed
berries to a boil, stirring constantly. Reduce the

(Recipe continues on next page)

heat. Cover the kettle and simmer the berries 10 minutes, stirring occasionally.

Meanwhile, secure 4 layers of damp cheesecloth in a large sieve over a deep pan.

Pour the cooked blackberries and juice over the cheesecloth in the sieve and let drain, *undisturbed,* at least 5 hours, until fully drained. *Do not stir or squeeze the blackberry mixture in the cheesecloth,* as this may cause the jelly to be cloudy. Squeezed juice must be re-strained.

Measure 3½ cups strained blackberry juice (see Note) and pour into a clean, 8-quart, heavy-bottomed, stainless steel kettle; set aside. Place the sugar in a large mixing bowl; set aside.

Drain hot, sterilized half-pint jars, upside down, on a clean tea towel; let stand.

Add the pectin to the blackberry juice in the kettle; stir well to combine. Over high heat, bring the blackberry juice mixture to a rolling boil, stirring constantly. Immediately add the sugar and return the blackberry juice mixture to a rolling boil over high heat, stirring continuously. Boil the mixture exactly 1 minute (use a timer), stirring constantly. Immediately remove from the heat and skim the foam off the jelly, using tableware tablespoons and teaspoons.

Quickly pour the hot jelly into the drained jars, leaving ¼-inch headspace.

Wipe the jar rims and threads. Place hot metal lids on the jars and screw the bands firmly.

Process in a boiling-water canner for the following time:

Processing Times

Jar Size	Altitude of Canning Location		
	0 to 1,000 ft.	1,001 to 6,000 ft.	Above 6,000 ft.
Half-Pints	5 min.	10 min.	15 min.

Remove the jars from the canner and place on a dry, wooden board which has been covered with a tea towel. Let the jars stand, *undisturbed,* 12 hours to cool completely.

NOTE: If there is less than 3½ cups strained blackberry juice, squeeze the cheesecloth containing the blackberry mixture *over a separate pan or bowl* to extract additional juice. Then, strain the newly extracted juice, *undisturbed,* through 4 layers of damp cheesecloth or a piece of damp cotton flannel, napped side up, and add to the already extracted juice.

YIELDS ABOUT 5½ HALF-PINTS

CHERRY JELLY

12 cups pitted, tart, red cherries (3½ cups juice; see recipe procedures, below)
4½ cups sugar
1 1¾-ounce package powdered fruit pectin

THE FIRST DAY: Place unpitted cherries in the sink filled with cold water. Sort and stem the cherries, discarding any cherries that float. Drain the cherries in a colander. Pit the cherries (see Note 1).

Measure 12 cups pitted cherries, including the juice. In a food processor, chop approximately 2 cups of the pitted cherries at a time, using 3 quick on/off turns (see Note 2).

Place the chopped cherries, with the accumulated juice, in an 8-quart, heavy-bottomed, stainless steel kettle. Over high heat, bring the cherries to a boil, stirring constantly. Reduce the heat to low. Cover the kettle and simmer the cherries 10 minutes, stirring intermittently. Keep the heat low to help prevent the cherries from boiling over.

Meanwhile, secure 4 layers of damp cheesecloth in a large sieve over a deep pan.

Pour the cooked cherries and juice over the cheesecloth in the sieve and let drain, *undisturbed,* at least 5 hours, until fully drained. *Do not stir or squeeze the cherry mixture in the cheesecloth.*

Pour the strained cherry juice into a glass container; cover and refrigerate 24 hours.

NOTE 1: The Westmark brand Kirschomat cherry pitter is an efficient tool to use for this task.

NOTE 2: If a food processor is not available, hand-chop the cherries.

24 HOURS LATER: Ladle the cherry juice from the glass container into a mixing bowl without disturbing any white, cloudy sediment which may have settled on the bottom of the container; discard the sediment. Re-strain the cherry juice through a piece of damp cotton flannel secured, napped side up, in a large sieve over a deep pan. *Do not stir or squeeze the juice in the cotton flannel,* as this may cause the jelly to be cloudy. Squeezed juice must be re-strained.

Measure exactly 3½ cups re-strained juice and pour into a clean, 8-quart, heavy-bottomed, stainless steel kettle; set aside. Place the sugar in a medium mixing bowl; set aside.

Drain hot, sterilized, half-pint jars, upside down, on a clean tea towel; let stand.

Add the pectin to the cherry juice in the kettle; stir well to combine. Over high heat, bring the cherry juice mixture to a rolling boil, stirring constantly. Immediately add the sugar and return the cherry juice mixture to a rolling boil over high heat, stirring continuously. Boil the mixture exactly 1 minute (use a timer), stirring constantly. Immediately remove from the heat and skim the foam off the jelly, using tableware tablespoons and teaspoons.

Quickly pour the hot jelly into the drained jars, leaving ¼-inch headspace.

Wipe the jar rims and threads. Place hot metal lids on the jars and screw the bands firmly.

Process in a boiling-water canner for the following time:

Processing Times

Jar Size	Altitude of Canning Location		
	0 to 1,000 ft.	1,001 to 6,000 ft.	Above 6,000 ft.
Half-Pints	5 min.	10 min.	15 min.

Remove the jars from the canner and place on a dry, wooden board which has been covered with a tea towel. Let the jars stand, *undisturbed,* 12 hours to cool completely.

YIELDS ABOUT 5 HALF-PINTS

GRAPE JELLY

16 cups (about 5 pounds) Concord grapes (5 cups juice; see recipe procedures, below)
7 cups sugar
1 1¾-ounce package powdered fruit pectin

THE FIRST DAY: Wash the grapes well. Remove the grapes from the stems, discarding underripe and overripe grapes. Measure 16 cups grapes. In a flat-bottomed pan, crush the grapes, one layer at a time, using a potato masher.

Place the crushed grapes, with the juice, in an 8-quart, heavy-bottomed, stainless steel kettle. Over medium-high heat, bring the crushed grapes to a boil, stirring constantly. Reduce the heat. Cover the kettle and simmer the grapes 10 minutes, stirring occasionally.

Meanwhile, secure 4 layers of damp cheesecloth in a large sieve over a deep pan.

Pour the cooked grapes and juice over the cheesecloth in the sieve and let drain, *undisturbed,* at least 6 hours, until fully drained. *Do not stir or squeeze the grape mixture in the cheesecloth.*

Pour the strained juice into a glass container; cover and refrigerate 48 hours (see Note).

NOTE: The tartaric acid in grapes, from which cream of tartar is made, will frequently cause tartrate crystals to form in grape jelly. The purpose of refrigerating the grape juice for 48 hours is to allow time for the formation of any tartrate crystals in order that they can be removed before making the jelly (instructions for removal of any tartrate crystals from the grape juice are given later in the recipe procedures).

48 HOURS LATER: Ladle the grape juice from the glass container into a mixing bowl without disturbing any sediment (tartrate crystals) which may have settled on the bottom of the container; discard the sediment. Re-strain the grape juice through a piece of damp cotton flannel secured, napped side up, in a large sieve over a deep pan. *Do not stir or squeeze the juice in the cot-*

(Recipe continues on next page)

ton flannel, as this may cause the jelly to be cloudy. Squeezed juice must be re-strained.

Measure exactly 5 cups re-strained juice and pour into a clean, 8-quart, heavy-bottomed, stainless steel kettle; set aside. Place the sugar in a large mixing bowl; set aside.

Drain hot, sterilized, half-pint jars, upside down, on a clean tea towel; let stand.

Add the pectin to the grape juice in the kettle; stir well to combine. Over high heat, bring the grape juice mixture to a rolling boil, stirring constantly. Immediately add the sugar and return the grape juice mixture to a rolling boil over high heat, stirring continuously. Boil the mixture exactly 1 minute (use a timer), stirring constantly. Immediately remove from the heat and skim the foam off the jelly, using tableware tablespoons and teaspoons.

Quickly pour hot the jelly into the drained jars, leaving ¼-inch headspace.

Wipe the jar rims and threads. Place hot metal lids on the jars and screw the bands firmly.

Process in a boiling-water canner for the following time:

Processing Times

Jar Size	Altitude of Canning Location		
	0 to 1,000 ft.	1,001 to 6,000 ft.	Above 6,000 ft.
Half-Pints	5 min.	10 min.	15 min.

Remove the jars from the canner and place on a dry, wooden board which has been covered with a tea towel. Let the jars stand, *undisturbed,* 12 hours to cool completely.

YIELDS ABOUT 8 HALF-PINTS

MINT JELLY

Mint Jelly is often made using an apple jelly base, as in this recipe. The mint flavor is achieved by making an infusion (see the headnote for Basil Jelly, page 745) and then pressing the mint leaves in the infusion, together with the liquid, in a ricer to produce a more pronounced mint flavor. Because the mint leaves are pressed, the infusion becomes an extract, which is strained through a paper coffee filter before it is added to the apple juice. Green liquid food coloring is traditionally used in this jelly to give it that pretty, minty appearance.

1½ cups firmly packed, fresh mint leaves
1½ cups boiling water
5 pounds tart apples (6 cups plus 2 tablespoons juice; see recipe procedures, below)
5 cups water
9 cups sugar
½ teaspoon plus 3 drops green liquid food coloring
1 1¾-ounce package powdered fruit pectin

Place the mint leaves in a heatproof glass bowl. Pour 1½ cups boiling water over the leaves; cover and let stand 1 hour.

Then, press the leaves and liquid firmly in a potato ricer. Strain the mint liquid (extract) through a paper coffee filter. Measure ¾ cup plus 2 tablespoons mint extract; cover and refrigerate.

Wash the apples; remove the stem and blossom ends. Do not pare or core the apples. Cut the apples into small pieces and place in an 8-quart, heavy-bottomed, stainless steel kettle. Add 5 cups water. Cover the kettle and bring the apples to a boil over high heat. Reduce the heat and simmer the apples 10 minutes, stirring occasionally.

Remove from the heat. Using a potato masher, crush the cooked apples in the kettle. Cover the kettle. Simmer the apples an additional 5 minutes, or until the apples are soft, stirring occasionally.

Meanwhile, secure 4 layers of damp cheesecloth in a large sieve over a deep pan.

Pour the cooked apples and juice over the cheesecloth in the sieve and let drain, *undisturbed*, at least 4 hours, until fully drained. *Do not stir or squeeze the apple mixture in the cheesecloth,* as this may cause the jelly to be cloudy. Squeezed juice must be re-strained.

Measure 6 cups plus 2 tablespoons strained apple juice and pour into a clean, 8-quart, heavy-bottomed, stainless steel kettle; set aside. Place the sugar in a large mixing bowl; set aside.

Drain hot, sterilized, half-pint jars, upside down, on a clean tea towel; let stand.

Add the refrigerated mint extract and food coloring to the apple juice in the kettle; stir until evenly blended. Add the pectin; stir well to combine. Over high heat, bring the mint mixture to a rolling boil, stirring constantly. Immediately add the sugar and return the mint juice mixture to a rolling boil over high heat, stirring continuously. Boil the mixture exactly 1 minute (use a timer), stirring constantly. Immediately remove from the heat and skim the foam off the jelly, using tableware tablespoons and teaspoons.

Quickly pour the hot jelly into the drained jars, leaving ¼-inch headspace.

Wipe the jar rims and threads. Place hot metal lids on the jars and screw the bands firmly.

Process in a boiling-water canner for the following time:

Processing Times

Jar Size	Altitude of Canning Location		
	0 to 1,000 ft.	1,001 to 6,000 ft.	Above 6,000 ft.
Half-Pints	5 min.	10 min.	15 min.

Remove the jars from the canner and place on a dry, wooden board which has been covered with a tea towel. Let the jars stand, *undisturbed,* 12 hours to cool completely.

YIELDS ABOUT 10 HALF-PINTS

STRAWBERRY JELLY

3½ quarts strawberries (4 cups juice; see recipe procedures, below)
7½ cups sugar
2 3-ounce pouches liquid fruit pectin

Wash and sort the strawberries in batches. Hull the strawberries (page 23), using a strawberry huller. In a flat-bottomed pan, crush the strawberries, ⅓ at a time, using a potato masher.

Place the crushed berries, with the juice, in an 8-quart, heavy-bottomed, stainless steel kettle. Do not add water unless necessary to prevent scorching. This will depend upon how much natural juice is in the strawberries. If water must be added, add as little as possible. Over medium-high heat, bring the crushed berries to a boil, stirring constantly. Reduce the heat. Cover the kettle and simmer the berries 10 minutes, stirring occasionally.

Meanwhile, secure a piece of damp cotton flannel, napped side up, in a large sieve over a deep pan.

Pour the cooked strawberries and juice over the cotton flannel in the sieve and let drain, *undisturbed,* at least 4 hours, until fully drained. *Do not stir or squeeze the strawberry mixture in the cotton flannel,* as this may cause the jelly to be cloudy. Squeezed juice must be re-strained.

Measure 4 cups strained strawberry juice and pour into a clean, 8-quart, heavy-bottomed, stainless steel kettle. Add the sugar; stir to combine; set aside.

Drain hot, sterilized, half-pint jars, upside down, on a clean tea towel; let stand.

Over high heat, bring the strawberry juice mixture to a rolling boil, stirring constantly. Immediately add the pectin, stir to blend, and return the strawberry juice mixture to a rolling boil over high heat, stirring continuously. Boil the mixture exactly 1 minute (use a timer), stirring constantly. Immediately remove from the heat and skim the foam off the jelly, using tableware tablespoons and teaspoons.

(Recipe continues on next page)

Quickly pour the hot jelly into the drained jars, leaving ¼-inch headspace.

Wipe the jar rims and threads. Place hot metal lids on the jars and screw the bands firmly.

Process in a boiling-water canner for the following time:

Processing Times

Jar Size	Altitude of Canning Location		
	0 to 1,000 ft.	1,001 to 6,000 ft.	Above 6,000 ft.
Half-Pints	5 min.	10 min.	15 min.

Remove the jars from the canner and place on a dry, wooden board which has been covered with a tea towel. Let the jars stand, *undisturbed,* 12 hours to cool completely.

YIELDS ABOUT 7 HALF-PINTS

RED RASPBERRY JELLY

3½ quarts red raspberries (4 cups juice; see recipe procedures, below)
5½ cups sugar
1 1¾-ounce package powdered fruit pectin

In a colander, wash and sort the raspberries, one pint at a time. Place ½ of the raspberries in a flat-bottomed pan. Using a potato masher, crush the raspberries. Place the crushed berries, with the juice, in a mixing bowl; set aside. Crush the remaining ½ of the berries. Press all the crushed berries and juice through a food mill to remove many of the seeds; set aside.

Secure 4 layers of damp cheesecloth in a large sieve over a deep pan. Pour the pressed raspberry pulp over the cheesecloth in the sieve and let drain, *undisturbed,* at least 4 hours, until fully drained. *Do not stir or squeeze the raspberry pulp in the cheesecloth,* as this may cause the jelly to be cloudy. Squeezed juice must be re-strained.

Measure 4 cups strained raspberry juice and pour into an 8-quart, heavy-bottomed, stainless steel kettle; set aside. Place the sugar in a large mixing bowl; set aside.

Drain hot, sterilized, half-pint jars, upside down, on a clean tea towel; let stand.

Add the pectin to the raspberry juice in the kettle; stir well to combine. Over high heat, bring the raspberry juice mixture to a rolling boil, stirring constantly. Immediately add the sugar and return the raspberry juice mixture to a rolling boil over high heat, stirring continuously. Boil the mixture exactly 1 minute (use a timer), stirring constantly. Immediately remove from the heat and skim the foam off the jelly, using tableware tablespoons and teaspoons.

Quickly pour the hot jelly into the drained jars, leaving ¼-inch headspace.

Wipe the jar rims and threads. Place hot metal lids on the jars and screw the bands firmly.

Process in a boiling-water canner for the following time:

Processing Times

Jar Size	Altitude of Canning Location		
	0 to 1,000 ft.	1,001 to 6,000 ft.	Above 6,000 ft.
Half-Pints	5 min.	10 min.	15 min.

Remove the jars from the canner and place on a dry, wooden board which has been covered with a tea towel. Let the jars stand, *undisturbed,* 12 hours to cool completely.

YIELDS ABOUT 6 HALF-PINTS

WILD BLACK RASPBERRY JELLY

2 quarts wild black raspberries* (2 cups juice; see recipe procedures, below)
5 cups sugar
1 3-ounce pouch liquid fruit pectin

If wild black raspberries are not available, commercial black raspberries may be substituted.

Gather fully ripe raspberries. In a colander, wash and sort the raspberries carefully. Place the berries in a flat-bottomed pan. Using a potato masher, crush the berries.

Place the crushed berries, with the juice, in an 8-quart, heavy-bottomed, stainless steel kettle. Do not add water unless necessary to prevent scorching. This will depend upon how much natural juice is in the raspberries. If water must be added, add as little as possible. Over medium-high heat, bring the crushed berries to a boil, stirring constantly. Reduce the heat. Cover the kettle and simmer the berries 10 minutes, stirring occasionally.

Meanwhile, secure 4 layers of damp cheesecloth in a large sieve over a deep pan.

Pour the cooked raspberries and juice over the cheesecloth in the sieve and let drain, *undisturbed*, at least 4 hours, until fully drained. *Do not stir or squeeze the raspberry mixture in the cheesecloth*, as this may cause the jelly to be cloudy. Squeezed juice must be re-strained.

Measure 2 cups strained raspberry juice and pour into a clean, 8-quart, heavy-bottomed, stainless steel kettle. Add the sugar; stir to combine; set aside.

Drain hot, sterilized, half-pint jars, upside down, on a clean tea towel; let stand.

Over high heat, bring the raspberry juice mixture to a rolling boil, stirring constantly. Immediately add the pectin, stir to blend, and return the raspberry juice mixture to a rolling boil over high heat, stirring continuously. Boil the mixture exactly 1 minute (use a timer), stirring constantly. Immediately remove from the heat and skim the foam off the jelly, using tableware tablespoons and teaspoons.

Quickly pour the hot jelly into the drained jars, leaving ¼-inch headspace.

Wipe the jar rims and threads. Place hot metal lids on the jars and screw the bands firmly.

Process in a boiling-water canner for the following time:

Processing Times

Jar Size	Altitude of Canning Location		
	0 to 1,000 ft.	1,001 to 6,000 ft.	Above 6,000 ft.
Half-Pints	5 min.	10 min.	15 min.

Remove the jars from the canner and place on a dry, wooden board which has been covered with a tea towel. Let the jars stand, *undisturbed*, 12 hours to cool completely.

YIELDS ABOUT 4 HALF-PINTS

BASIL JELLY

The flavor of an herb usually is imparted in jelly by means of an infusion, as in this recipe. An infusion is a liquid, such as water, flavored by steeping in it a product such as an herb or tea. Infusions are easily made. When making an infusion for use in an herb jelly, it is highly important to use very fresh herbs, preferably straight from the garden, to achieve superior flavor.

1½ cups finely chopped, fresh basil leaves
3¼ cups water
A few drops green liquid food coloring
4 cups sugar
1 1¾-ounce package powdered fruit pectin

In a medium stainless steel saucepan, place the basil and water; stir to combine. Over high heat, bring the mixture to a boil. Remove from the heat; cover and let stand 1 hour.

Then, secure a piece of damp cotton flannel, napped side up, in a sieve over a deep pan. Pour the basil and liquid (infusion) over the cotton flannel in the sieve and let fully drain, *undisturbed*. *Do not stir or squeeze the infusion in the cotton flannel.* Squeezed infusion must be re-strained.

Measure 3 cups basil infusion and pour into an 8-quart, heavy-bottomed, stainless steel kettle. Add the food coloring; stir to blend; set aside.

(Recipe continues on next page)

Place the sugar in a medium mixing bowl; set aside.

Drain hot, sterilized, half-pint jars, upside down, on a clean tea towel; let stand.

Add the pectin to the basil infusion in the kettle; stir well to combine. Over high heat, bring the infusion mixture to a rolling boil, stirring constantly. Immediately add the sugar and return the basil infusion mixture to a rolling boil over high heat, stirring continuously. Boil the mixture exactly 1 minute (use a timer), stirring constantly. Immediately remove from the heat and skim the foam off the jelly, using tableware tablespoons and teaspoons.

Quickly pour the hot jelly into the drained jars, leaving ¼-inch headspace.

Wipe the jar rims and threads. Place hot metal lids on the jars and screw the bands firmly.

Process in a boiling-water canner for the following time:

Processing Times

Jar Size	Altitude of Canning Location		
	0 to 1,000 ft.	1,001 to 6,000 ft.	Above 6,000 ft.
Half-Pints	5 min.	10 min.	15 min.

Remove the jars from the canner and place on a dry, wooden board which has been covered with a tea towel. Let the jars stand, *undisturbed*, 12 hours to cool completely.

YIELDS ABOUT 4 HALF-PINTS

SERVING SUGGESTIONS

- Serve either as a garnish or as a sweet spread (with butter) for Dinner Rolls (page 423) with pork, veal, lamb, and wild game dinners (see Yellow Zucchini Rings Filled with Basil Jelly, page 406.

- Serve with toasted English muffins or toasted minibagels at an omelet or scrambled egg brunch.

BLUSH WINE JELLY

A beautiful, delicate, pale-pink color, this jelly is sublimely appropriate to pass in a crystal dish at a dinner party for guests to spread thinly on their hot, buttered dinner rolls. Wine jelly is quick and easy to make because wine is a ready-to-go ingredient, in contrast to the special processing of fruit required for fruit jelly.

½ cup freshly squeezed lemon juice
4½ cups sugar
1 750-milliliter bottle white zinfandel (blush) wine (about 3¼ cups)
1 1¾-ounce package powdered fruit pectin

Secure a small piece of damp cotton flannel, napped side up, in a small sieve over a bowl. Pour the lemon juice over the cotton flannel in the sieve and let drain. *Do not stir or squeeze the lemon juice in the cotton flannel,* as this may cause the jelly to be cloudy; set aside. Place the sugar in a medium mixing bowl; set aside.

Drain hot, sterilized half-pint jars, upside down, on a clean tea towel; set aside.

In an 8-quart, heavy-bottomed, stainless steel kettle, place the wine, lemon juice, and pectin; stir well to combine. Over high heat, bring the wine mixture to a rolling boil, stirring constantly. Immediately add the sugar and return the wine mixture to a rolling boil over high heat, stirring continuously. Boil the mixture exactly 1 minute (use a timer), stirring constantly. Immediately remove from the heat and skim the foam off the jelly, using tableware tablespoons and teaspoons.

Quickly pour the hot jelly into the drained jars, leaving ¼-inch headspace.

Wipe the jar rims and threads. Place hot metal lids on the jars and screw the bands firmly.

Process in a boiling-water canner for the following time:

Jar Size	Altitude of Canning Location		
	0 to 1,000 ft.	1,001 to 6,000 ft.	Above 6,000 ft.
Half-Pints	5 min.	10 min.	15 min.

Remove the jars from the canner and place on a dry, wooden board which has been covered with a tea towel. Let the jars stand, *undisturbed,* 12 hours to cool completely.

YIELDS ABOUT 5 HALF-PINTS

Jams

APRICOT JAM

8 cups cold water
1 tablespoon white vinegar
1 tablespoon salt
3½ pounds apricots (5 cups chopped apricots; see recipe procedures, below)
7 cups sugar
¼ cup freshly squeezed, strained lemon juice
1 1¾-ounce package powdered fruit pectin

In a 12-quart kettle, place the water, vinegar, and salt; stir until the salt dissolves; set aside.

Wash ½ of the apricots. Blanch the apricots (page 44) 30 seconds and immediately immerse them in cold water; drain. Peel, cut in half, and pit the apricots. As the apricots are prepared, drop them into the vinegar solution to prevent discoloration. Repeat the procedure to prepare the remaining ½ of the apricots. Prepare only ½ of the apricots at a time because apricots darken quickly in their skins after being blanched. Let the apricots stand.

Place the sugar in a large mixing bowl; set aside.

Drain and rinse the apricots twice, using fresh, cold water. Drain the apricots well. In a food processor, chop ¼ of the apricots at a time, using about 3 quick on/off turns (see Note). Pieces of apricot should remain—be careful not to puree the fruit by overprocessing. Place the chopped apricots, with the juice, in a mixing bowl.

Measure 5 cups chopped apricots, including the juice, and place in an 8-quart, heavy-bottomed, stainless steel kettle. Add the lemon juice; stir to blend; set aside.

Drain hot, sterilized, half-pint jars, upside down, on a clean tea towel; let stand.

Add the pectin to the apricot mixture in the kettle; stir well to combine. Over high heat, bring the apricot mixture to a rolling boil, stirring constantly. Immediately add the sugar and return the apricot mixture to a rolling boil over high heat, stirring continuously. Boil the mixture exactly 1 minute (use a timer), stirring constantly. Immediately remove from the heat and skim the foam off the jam, using tableware tablespoons and teaspoons.

Quickly pour the hot jam into the drained jars, leaving ¼-inch headspace.

Wipe the jar rims and threads. Place hot metal lids on the jars and screw the bands firmly.

Process in a boiling-water canner for the following time:

Jar Size	Altitude of Canning Location		
	0 to 1,000 ft.	1,001 to 6,000 ft.	Above 6,000 ft.
Half-Pints	5 min.	10 min.	15 min.

Remove the jars from the canner and place on a dry, wooden board which has been covered with a tea towel. Let the jars stand, *undisturbed,* 12 hours to cool completely.

NOTE: If a food processor is not available, hand-chop the apricots.

YIELDS ABOUT 7 HALF-PINTS

GRAPE JAM

9 cups stemmed Concord grapes (4 cups pressed grapes; see recipe procedures, below)
6 cups sugar
1 1¾-ounce package powdered fruit pectin

In small bunches, place the grapes in a colander and wash under cold, running water. Remove the grapes from the stems, selecting out only the fully ripe, unblemished fruit.

Measure 9 cups stemmed grapes. Place ½ of the grapes in a large, flat-bottomed pan. Using a potato masher, crush the grapes slightly. Place the crushed grapes, with the juice, in an 8-quart, heavy-bottomed, stainless steel kettle; set aside. Crush the remaining ½ of the grapes and add to the kettle.

Over medium-high heat, bring the crushed grapes to a simmer, stirring constantly. Reduce the heat. Cover the kettle and cook the grapes at a low simmer for 10 minutes, stirring frequently.

Remove from the heat. Press the cooked grapes and juice through a food mill to remove the seeds, pressing through as much of the skins as possible.

Measure 4 cups pressed grapes (including the juice) and place in a clean, 8-quart, heavy-bottomed, stainless steel kettle; set aside. Place the sugar in a large mixing bowl; set aside.

Drain hot, sterilized, half-pint jars, upside down, on a clean tea towel; let stand.

Add the pectin to the pressed grapes in the kettle; stir well to combine. Over high heat, bring the grape mixture to a rolling boil, stirring constantly. Immediately add the sugar and return the grape mixture to a rolling boil over high heat, stirring continuously. Boil the mixture exactly 1 minute (use a timer), stirring constantly. Immediately remove from the heat and skim the foam off the jam, using tableware tablespoons and teaspoons.

Quickly pour the hot jam into the drained jars, leaving ¼-inch headspace.

Wipe the jar rims and threads. Place hot metal lids on the jars and screw the bands firmly.

Process in a boiling-water canner for the following time:

Processing Times

Jar Size	Altitude of Canning Location		
	0 to 1,000 ft.	1,001 to 6,000 ft.	Above 6,000 ft.
Half-Pints	5 min.	10 min.	15 min.

Remove the jars from the canner and place on a dry, wooden board which has been covered with a tea towel. Let the jars stand, *undisturbed*, 12 hours to cool completely.

YIELDS ABOUT 6 HALF-PINTS

BLUEBERRY JAM

1½ quarts blueberries (4 cups crushed blueberries; see recipe procedures, below)
2 tablespoons freshly squeezed, strained lemon juice
4 cups sugar
1 1¾-ounce package powdered fruit pectin

Place the blueberries in a flat-bottomed pan. Sort and stem the berries. Transfer the berries to a colander. Run cold water over the blueberries to wash; set aside.

Wash and dry the flat-bottomed pan. In the flat-bottomed pan, crush the blueberries, ¼ at a time, using a potato masher. Crush the blueberries until opened, but not pureed. Place the crushed berries, with the juice, in a mixing bowl.

Measure 4 cups crushed blueberries, including the juice, and place in an 8-quart, heavy-bottomed, stainless steel kettle. Add the lemon juice; stir to blend; set aside. Place the sugar in a medium mixing bowl; set aside.

Drain hot, sterilized, half-pint jars, upside down, on a clean tea towel; let stand.

Add the pectin to the blueberry mixture in the kettle; stir well to combine. Over high heat, bring the blueberry mixture to a rolling boil, stirring constantly. Immediately add the sugar and return the blueberry mixture to a rolling boil over high heat, stirring continuously. Boil the mixture exactly 1 minute (use a timer), stirring constantly. Immediately remove from the heat and skim the foam off the jam, using tableware tablespoons and teaspoons.

Quickly pour the hot jam into the drained jars, leaving ¼-inch headspace.

Wipe the jar rims and threads. Place hot metal lids on the jars and screw the bands firmly.

Process in a boiling-water canner for the following time:

Processing Times

| Jar Size | Altitude of Canning Location | | |
	0 to 1,000 ft.	1,001 to 6,000 ft.	Above 6,000 ft.
Half-Pints	5 min.	10 min.	15 min.

Remove the jars from the canner and place on a dry, wooden board which has been covered with a tea towel. Let the jars stand, *undisturbed*, 12 hours to cool completely.

YIELDS ABOUT 6 HALF-PINTS

CHERRY JAM

Awarded first place overall among all jams (twenty classes) at the 1992 Iowa State Fair.

6 cups pitted, tart, red cherries (4 cups chopped cherries; see recipe procedures, below)
5 cups sugar
1 1¾-ounce package powdered fruit pectin

Place unpitted cherries in the sink filled with cold water. Sort and stem the cherries, discarding any cherries that float. Drain the cherries in a colander. Pit the cherries (see Note 1).

Measure 6 cups pitted cherries, including the juice. In a food processor, chop ¼ of the pitted cherries at a time, using 3 quick on/off turns (see Note 2). Place the chopped cherries, with the juice, in a mixing bowl.

Measure 4 cups chopped cherries, including the accumulated juice, and place in an 8-quart, heavy-bottomed, stainless steel kettle; set aside. Place the sugar in a large mixing bowl; set aside.

Add the pectin to the chopped cherries in the kettle; stir well to combine. Over high heat, bring the cherry mixture to a rolling boil, stirring constantly. Immediately add the sugar and return the cherry mixture to a rolling boil over high heat, stirring continuously. Boil the mixture exactly 2 minutes (use a timer), stirring constantly. Remove from the heat and skim the foam off the jam, using tableware tablespoons and teaspoons. Stir and skim the jam 10 additional minutes, or until the mixture thickens sufficiently that the cherry pieces will distribute evenly in the jam and not float to the top of the jars.

Drain hot, sterilized, half-pint jars, upside down, on a clean tea towel.

Pour the jam into the drained jars, leaving ¼-inch headspace.

Wipe the jar rims and threads. Place hot metal lids on the jars and screw the bands firmly.

Process in a boiling-water canner for the following time:

Processing Times

| Jar Size | Altitude of Canning Location | | |
	0 to 1,000 ft.	1,001 to 6,000 ft.	Above 6,000 ft.
Half-Pints	5 min.	10 min.	15 min.

Remove the jars from the canner and place on a dry, wooden board which has been covered with a tea towel. Let the jars stand, *undisturbed*, 12 hours to cool completely.

NOTE 1: The Westmark brand Kirschomat cherry pitter is an efficient tool to use for this task.

NOTE 2: If a food processor is not available, cut the pitted cherries into eighths.

YIELDS ABOUT 6 HALF-PINTS

PEACH JAM

8 cups cold water
1 tablespoon white vinegar
1 tablespoon salt
3 pounds peaches (4 cups chopped peaches; see recipe procedures, below)
5½ cups sugar
2 tablespoons freshly squeezed, strained lemon juice
1 1¾-ounce package powdered fruit pectin

In a 12-quart kettle, place the water, vinegar, and salt; stir until the salt dissolves; set aside.

Wash the peaches. Blanch the peaches (page 44) 45 seconds and immediately immerse them in cold water; drain. Peel, cut in half, and pit the peaches. If the peaches are large, cut each half in two. As the peaches are prepared, drop them into the vinegar solution to prevent discoloration. Let the peaches stand.

Place the sugar in a mixing large bowl; set aside.

Drain and rinse the peaches twice, using fresh, cold water. Drain the peaches well. In a food processor, chop ¼ of the peaches at a time, using 3 or 4 quick on/off turns (see Note). Pieces of peach should remain—be careful not to puree the fruit by overprocessing. Place the chopped peaches, with the juice, in a mixing bowl.

Measure 4 cups chopped peaches, including the juice, and place in an 8-quart, heavy-bottomed, stainless steel kettle. Add the lemon juice; stir to blend; set aside.

Add the pectin to the peach mixture in the kettle; stir well to combine. Over high heat, bring the peach mixture to a rolling boil, stirring constantly. Immediately add the sugar and return the peach mixture to a rolling boil over high heat, stirring continuously. Boil the mixture exactly 1 minute (use a timer), stirring constantly. Remove from the heat and skim the foam off the jam, using tableware tablespoons and teaspoons. Stir and skim the jam 3 additional minutes, until the jam thickens slightly. This procedure will help achieve even distribu-

tion of the fruit pieces in the jam, preventing the fruit pieces from floating to the top of the jars.

Drain hot, sterilized, half-pint jars, upside down, on a clean tea towel.

Pour the jam into the drained jars, leaving ¼-inch headspace. With the back of a teaspoon, push the fruit toward the bottom of each jar, making about 5 downward thrusts per jar, to further help distribute the pieces of fruit evenly.

Wipe the jar rims and threads. Place hot metal lids on the jars and screw the bands firmly.

Process in a boiling-water canner for the following time:

Processing Times

Jar Size	Altitude of Canning Location		
	0 to 1,000 ft.	1,001 to 6,000 ft.	Above 6,000 ft.
Half-Pints	5 min.	10 min.	15 min.

Remove the jars from the canner and place on a dry, wooden board which has been covered with a tea towel. Let the jars stand, *undisturbed,* 12 hours to cool completely.

NOTE: If a food processor is not available, hand-chop the peaches.

YIELDS ABOUT 6 HALF-PINTS

STRAWBERRY JAM

8 cups hulled strawberries (5 cups crushed strawberries; see recipe procedures, below)
7 cups sugar
1 1¾-ounce package powdered fruit pectin

Wash and sort the strawberries quickly in cold water; drain in a colander. Hull the strawberries (page 23), using a strawberry huller. In a flat-bottomed pan, crush the strawberries, ⅓ at a time, using a pastry blender (see illustration, page 464). Do not puree the strawberries; leave nice-sized pieces which will be attractive in the jam. Place the crushed strawberries, with the juice, in a mixing bowl.

Measure 5 cups crushed strawberries, including the juice, and place in an 8-quart, heavy-bottomed, stainless steel kettle. Place the sugar in a large mixing bowl; set aside.

Drain hot, sterilized, half-pint jars, upside down, on a clean tea towel; let stand.

Add the pectin to the crushed strawberries in the kettle; stir well to combine. Over high heat, bring the strawberry mixture to a rolling boil, stirring constantly. Immediately add the sugar and return the strawberry mixture to a rolling boil over high heat, stirring continuously. Boil the mixture exactly 1 minute (use a timer), stirring constantly. Immediately remove from the heat and skim the foam off the jam, using tableware tablespoons and teaspoons.

Quickly pour the hot jam into the drained jars, leaving 1/4-inch headspace.

Wipe the jar rims and threads. Place hot metal lids on the jars and screw the bands firmly.

Process in a boiling-water canner for the following time:

Processing Times

Jar Size	Altitude of Canning Location		
	0 to 1,000 ft.	1,001 to 6,000 ft.	Above 6,000 ft.
Half-Pints	5 min.	10 min.	15 min.

Remove the jars from the canner and place on a dry, wooden board which has been covered with a tea towel. Let the jars stand, *undisturbed,* 12 hours to cool completely.

YIELDS ABOUT 8 HALF-PINTS

RED RASPBERRY JAM

4 quarts red raspberries (5 cups strained pulp; see recipe procedures, below)
7 cups sugar
1 1 3/4-ounce package powdered fruit pectin

In a colander, wash and sort the raspberries, one pint at a time. Place 1/2 of the raspberries in a flat-bottomed pan. Using a potato masher, crush the raspberries. Place the crushed berries, with the juice, in a mixing bowl; set aside. Crush the remaining 1/2 of the berries. Press all the crushed berries and juice through a food mill to remove many of the seeds. Then, strain the raspberry pulp through a sieve to remove most of the remaining seeds.

Measure 5 cups strained raspberry pulp and pour into an 8-quart, heavy-bottomed, stainless steel kettle; set aside. Place the sugar in a large mixing bowl; set aside.

Drain hot, sterilized, half-pint jars, upside down, on a clean tea towel; let stand.

Add the pectin to the raspberry pulp in the kettle; stir well to combine. Over high heat, bring the raspberry mixture to a rolling boil, stirring constantly. Immediately add the sugar and return the raspberry mixture to a rolling boil over high heat, stirring continuously. Boil the mixture exactly 1 minute (use a timer), stirring constantly. Immediately remove from the heat and skim the foam off the jam, using tableware tablespoons and teaspoons.

Quickly pour the hot jam into the drained jars, leaving 1/4-inch headspace.

Wipe the jar rims and threads. Place hot metal lids on the jars and screw the bands firmly.

Process in a boiling-water canner for the following time:

Processing Times

Jar Size	Altitude of Canning Location		
	0 to 1,000 ft.	1,001 to 6,000 ft.	Above 6,000 ft.
Half-Pints	5 min.	10 min.	15 min.

Remove the jars from the canner and place on a dry, wooden board which has been covered with a tea towel. Let the jars stand, *undisturbed,* 12 hours to cool completely.

YIELDS ABOUT 8 HALF-PINTS

RED PLUM JAM

4 pounds tart, ripe but firm, red plums
(6 cups cooked plums; see recipe
procedures, below)
8 cups sugar
1 1¾-ounce package powdered fruit pectin

Wash, stem, quarter, and pit the plums. Do not
pare. If the plums are especially large, cut each
quarter in two.

In a food processor, chop the plums fairly
coarsely, in small batches, using about 5 quick
on/off turns (see Note).

Place the chopped plums, with the juice, in an
8-quart, heavy-bottomed, stainless steel kettle.
Over medium-high heat, bring the plums to a
boil, stirring constantly. Reduce the heat. Cover
the kettle and simmer the plums 5 minutes, stirring frequently.

Remove from the heat. Measure 6 cups
cooked plums, including the juice, and place in
a clean, 8-quart, heavy bottomed, stainless steel
kettle; set aside. Place the sugar in a large mixing bowl; set aside.

Add the pectin to the cooked plums in the
kettle; stir well to combine. Over high heat,
bring the plum mixture to a rolling boil, stirring
constantly. Immediately add the sugar and
return the plum mixture to a rolling boil over
high heat, stirring continuously. Boil the mixture exactly 1 minute (use a timer), stirring constantly. Remove from the heat and skim the
foam off the jam, using tableware tablespoons
and teaspoons. Stir and skim the jam 3 additional minutes, until the jam thickens slightly.
This procedure will help achieve even distribution of the fruit pieces in the jam, preventing the
fruit pieces from floating to the top of the jars.

Drain hot, sterilized, half-pint jars, upside
down, on a clean tea towel.

Pour the jam into the drained jars, leaving ¼-
inch headspace. With the back of a teaspoon,
push the fruit toward the bottom of each jar,
making about 3 downward thrusts per jar, to
further help distribute the pieces of fruit evenly.

Wipe the jar rims and threads. Place hot metal
lids on the jars and screw the bands firmly.

Process in a boiling-water canner for the following time:

Processing Times

Jar Size	Altitude of Canning Location		
	0 to 1,000 ft.	1,001 to 6,000 ft.	Above 6,000 ft.
Half-Pints	5 min.	10 min.	15 min.

Remove the jars from the canner and place
on a dry, wooden board which has been covered
with a tea towel. Let the jars stand, *undisturbed*,
12 hours to cool completely.

NOTE: If a food processor is not available, hand-
chop the plums.

YIELDS ABOUT 10 HALF-PINTS

SEEDLESS WILD BLACK RASPBERRY JAM

9 cups crushed, wild black raspberries* (see
recipe procedures, below)
6 cups sugar
1 1¾-ounce package powdered fruit pectin

*If wild raspberries are not available, commer-
cial black raspberries may be substituted.*

Gather fully ripe raspberries. In a colander, wash
and sort the raspberries carefully. In batches, place
the berries in a flat-bottomed pan and crush the
berries, using a potato masher. Place the crushed
berries, with the juice, in a mixing bowl.

Measure 9 cups crushed berries, including the
juice. Press the crushed berries and juice through
a food mill to remove many of the seeds. Then,
strain the raspberry pulp through a sieve to
remove most of the remaining seeds.

Pour the raspberry pulp into an 8-quart,
heavy-bottomed, stainless steel kettle; set aside.
Place the sugar in a large mixing bowl; set aside.

Drain hot, sterilized, half-pint jars, upside down, on a clean tea towel; let stand.

Add the pectin to the raspberry pulp in the kettle; stir well to combine. Over high heat, bring the raspberry mixture to a rolling boil, stirring constantly. Immediately add the sugar and return the raspberry mixture to a rolling boil over high heat, stirring continuously. Boil the mixture exactly 1 minute (use a timer), stirring constantly. Immediately remove from heat and skim the foam off the jam, using tableware tablespoons and teaspoons.

Quickly pour the hot jam into the drained jars, leaving ¼-inch headspace.

Wipe the jar rims and threads. Place hot metal lids on the jars and screw the bands firmly.

Process in a boiling-water canner for the following time:

Processing Times

Jar Size	Altitude of Canning Location		
	0 to 1,000 ft.	1,001 to 6,000 ft.	Above 6,000 ft.
Half-Pints	5 min.	10 min.	15 min.

Remove the jars from the canner and place on a dry, wooden board which has been covered with a tea towel. Let the jars stand, *undisturbed,* 12 hours to cool completely.

YIELDS ABOUT 6 TO 7 HALF-PINTS

PINEAPPLE JAM

2 pineapples (4½ cups chopped pineapple; see recipe procedures, below)
5½ cups sugar
1 1¾-ounce package powdered fruit pectin

Pare the pineapples, carefully removing all the eyes and brown parts. Cut the pineapples into 1-inch slices and core. Then, cut the slices into 1-inch chunks.

In a food processor, chop the pineapple chunks coarsely, in 1-cup batches, using about 3 quick on/off turns (see Note). Place the chopped pineapple, with the juice, in a mixing bowl.

Measure 4½ cups chopped pineapple, including the juice, and place in an 8-quart, heavy-bottomed, stainless steel kettle; set aside. Place the sugar in a large mixing bowl; set aside.

Add the pectin to the chopped pineapple in the kettle; stir well to combine. Over high heat, bring the pineapple mixture to a rolling boil, stirring constantly. Immediately add the sugar and return the pineapple mixture to a rolling boil over high heat, stirring continuously. Boil the mixture exactly 1 minute (use a timer), stirring constantly. Remove from the heat and skim the foam off the jam, using tableware tablespoons and teaspoons. Stir and skim the jam about 8 additional minutes, until the jam thickens slightly. This procedure will help achieve even distribution of the fruit pieces in the jam, preventing the fruit pieces from floating to the top of the jars.

Drain hot, sterilized, half-pint jars, upside down, on a clean tea towel.

Pour the jam into drained jars, leaving ¼-inch headspace. With the back of a teaspoon, push the fruit toward the bottom of each jar, making about 3 downward thrusts per jar, to further help distribute the pieces of fruit evenly.

Wipe the jar rims and threads. Place hot metal lids on the jars and screw the bands firmly.

Process in a boiling-water canner for the following time:

Processing Times

Jar Size	Altitude of Canning Location		
	0 to 1,000 ft.	1,001 to 6,000 ft.	Above 6,000 ft.
Half-Pints	5 min.	10 min.	15 min.

Remove the jars from the canner and place on a dry, wooden board which has been covered with a tea towel. Let the jars stand, *undisturbed,* 12 hours to cool completely.

NOTE: If a food processor is not available, hand-chop the pineapple.

YIELDS ABOUT 6 HALF-PINTS

TUTTI-FRUTTI JAM

Tutti-frutti is an Italian term meaning "all fruits." Originally, tutti-frutti was the name for a mixture of fresh fruits, sugar, and brandy usually made in a crock and allowed to ferment. Fresh fruits were added as they came into season, along with additional sugar and brandy. The brandied fruits were used as accompaniments to meats, or the mixture was served as a dessert or a sauce over ice cream, puddings, or other desserts. Now the term tutti-frutti is sometimes applied to ice cream, confections, desserts, or other sweet foods containing mixed, chopped, candied, or fresh fruits (see the cookie recipe for Tutti-Frutti Rolls, page 642).

In the recipes that follow, the only difference between Tutti-Frutti Jam and Tutti-Frutti Ice Cream Topping is the length of boiling time. Tutti-Frutti Ice Cream Topping is boiled for a shorter period, resulting in a less-jellied product (that is, a syrup rather than a jam).

1 large orange, peeled, diced ¼ inch square, and seeded (¾ cup diced orange)
1 8¼-ounce can commercial crushed pineapple in heavy syrup, well drained (⅔ cup drained pineapple)
¼ cup red maraschino cherries, diced into eighths
¼ cup freshly squeezed, strained lemon juice
5 cups sugar
8 cups cold water
1 tablespoon white vinegar
1 tablespoon salt
3 cups (about 2 pounds) fresh Bartlett pears diced ¼ inch square (see recipe procedures, below)
1 1¾-ounce package powdered fruit pectin

Prepare the diced orange, pineapple, maraschino cherries, and lemon juice; cover each separately and set aside. Place the sugar in a large mixing bowl; set aside.

In a 12-quart kettle, place the water, vinegar, and salt; stir until the salt dissolves; set aside.

Wash, cut in half, core, and pare the pears. As the pears are prepared, drop them into the vinegar solution to prevent discoloration.

Drain and rinse the pears twice, using fresh, cold water. Drain the pears well. Dice the pears. Measure 3 cups diced pears.

In an 8-quart, heavy-bottomed, stainless steel kettle, place the pears, diced orange, pineapple, cherries, and lemon juice; set aside, uncombined.

Drain hot, sterilized, half-pint jars, upside down, on a clean tea towel; let stand.

Add the pectin to the fruit in the kettle; stir to combine. Over high heat, bring the fruit mixture to a rolling boil, stirring constantly. Immediately add the sugar and return the fruit mixture to a rolling boil over high heat, stirring continuously. Boil the mixture exactly 1 minute (use a timer), stirring constantly. Remove from heat and skim the foam off the jam, using tableware tablespoons and teaspoons. Let the jam stand to cool *slightly* until sufficiently thick that the fruit will distribute evenly in the jars and not float to the top. Then, very briefly stir the jam to distribute the fruit evenly throughout the mixture.

Pour the jam into the drained jars, leaving ¼-inch headspace.

Wipe the jar rims and threads. Place hot metal lids on the jars and screw the bands firmly.

Process in a boiling-water canner for the following time:

Processing Times

Jar Size	Altitude of Canning Location		
	0 to 1,000 ft.	1,001 to 6,000 ft.	Above 6,000 ft.
Half-Pints	5 min.	10 min.	15 min.

Remove the jars from the canner and place on a dry, wooden board which has been covered with a tea towel. Let the jars stand, *undisturbed,* 12 hours to cool completely.

YIELDS ABOUT 6 HALF-PINTS

TUTTI-FRUTTI ICE CREAM TOPPING: Follow the Tutti-Frutti Jam recipe, above, with the following exception: After adding the sugar and returning the fruit mixture to a rolling boil, boil the mixture for only 30 seconds, rather than 1 minute.

SERVING SUGGESTION: Serve over vanilla ice cream (homemade, page 669, or commercial).

GOOSEBERRY JAM

Gooseberries are naturally very high in pectin; therefore, Gooseberry Jam should not be made with added pectin, but should be made by boiling it to the jellying point. Gooseberry Jam made with added pectin is nearly always too firm. (See the definition for pectin on page 24, and Sheeting in Jelly Making on page 738.)

5⅓ cups sugar
2 quarts (about 2½ pounds) gooseberries, divided

Place the sugar in an 8-quart, heavy-bottomed, stainless steel kettle; cover and set aside.

Wash 1 quart gooseberries and drain in a colander. Using a small, sharp paring knife, cut tiny portions off both ends of the berries. Place the berries in a medium mixing bowl; set aside. Wash, drain, and trim the remaining 1 quart berries; place in a separate, medium mixing bowl.

In a food processor, chop 1 quart of the gooseberries until medium-ground. Add the processed berries to the sugar in the kettle. Process the remaining 1 quart gooseberries in the food processor *just until the berries are crushed.* Add the crushed berries to the sugar mixture in the kettle. Stir the mixture well to combine.

Over medium-high heat, heat the gooseberry mixture until the sugar completely dissolves, stirring constantly. Attach a candy thermometer to the kettle. Increase the heat to high and bring the gooseberry mixture to a rolling boil, stirring constantly. Boil the mixture until the tempera-

ture reaches 8° F. above the boiling point of water (page 712) (about 10 minutes boiling time), stirring constantly.

Remove from the heat and detach the thermometer. Immediately skim the foam off the jam, using tableware tablespoons and teaspoons.

Quickly drain hot, sterilized, half-pint jars, upside down, on a clean tea towel.

Pour the hot jam into the drained jars, leaving ¼-inch headspace.

Wipe the jar rims and threads. Place hot metal lids on the jars and screw the bands firmly.

Process in a boiling-water canner for the following time:

Processing Times

Jar Size	Altitude of Canning Location		
	0 to 1,000 ft.	1,001 to 6,000 ft.	Above 6,000 ft.
Half-Pints	5 min.	10 min.	15 min.

Remove the jars from the canner and place on a dry, wooden board which has been covered with a tea towel. Let the jars stand, *undisturbed,* 12 hours to cool completely.

YIELDS ABOUT 5 HALF-PINTS

SERVING SUGGESTION: In addition to serving Gooseberry Jam in the traditional way on toast, breads, and rolls, use it in Candied Yams with Gooseberries (page 337).

LOUISE PIPER'S MULBERRY JAM

Red ribbon awarded to Louise Piper, 1992 Iowa State Fair.

Louise Piper is a great cook and big winner of blue ribbons at the Iowa State Fair and the Clay County (Iowa) Fair. For added flavor, Louise uses the unique ingredient Kool-Aid in her Mulberry Jam—and it results in a truly luscious sweet spread!

5 cups mulberries (3½ cups pulp; see recipe procedures, below)
¼ cup freshly squeezed, strained lemon juice
6 cups sugar
1 0.13-ounce package unsweetened raspberry Kool-Aid drink mix
1 1¾-ounce package powdered fruit pectin

In a colander, wash and sort the mulberries, ½ at a time. Place all the mulberries in a flat-bottomed pan. Using a potato masher, crush the mulberries. Press the crushed berries and juice through a food mill to remove the seeds.

Measure 3½ cups mulberry pulp and pour into an 8-quart, heavy-bottomed, stainless steel kettle. Add the lemon juice; stir to blend; set aside. Place the sugar in a large mixing bowl; set aside.

Drain hot, sterilized, half-pint jars, upside down, on a clean tea towel; let stand.

Add the Kool-Aid and pectin to the mulberry pulp in the kettle; stir well to combine. Over high heat, bring the mulberry mixture to a rolling boil, stirring constantly. Immediately add the sugar and return the mulberry mixture to a rolling boil over high heat, stirring continuously. Boil the mixture exactly 1 minute (use a timer), stirring constantly. Immediately remove from the heat and skim the foam off the jam, using tableware tablespoons and teaspoons.

Quickly pour the hot jam into the drained jars, leaving ¼-inch headspace.

Wipe the jar rims and threads. Place hot metal lids on the jars and screw the bands firmly.

Process in a boiling-water canner for the following time:

Processing Times

Jar Size	Altitude of Canning Location		
	0 to 1,000 ft.	1,001 to 6,000 ft.	Above 6,000 ft.
Half-Pints	5 min.	10 min.	15 min.

Remove the jars from the canner and place on a dry, wooden board which has been covered with a tea towel. Let the jars stand, *undisturbed,* 12 hours to cool completely.

YIELDS ABOUT 5 HALF-PINTS

Preserves

CHERRY PRESERVES

6 cups pitted, tart, red cherries (see recipe procedures, below)
5 cups sugar
⅓ cup light corn syrup

THE FIRST DAY: Place unpitted cherries in the sink filled with cold water. Sort and stem the cherries, discarding any cherries that float. Drain the cherries in a colander. Pit the cherries (see Note).

Measure 6 cups pitted cherries, including the juice, and place in an 8-quart, heavy-bottomed, stainless steel kettle. Add the sugar and corn syrup; using a wooden spoon, stir to combine, being careful not to break up the whole cherries. Over medium-high heat, bring the cherry mixture to a boil; boil rapidly for 15 minutes, stirring constantly and carefully with the wooden spoon.

Remove from the heat and skim the foam off the preserves, using tableware tablespoons and teaspoons.

Pour the hot preserves into a 12 × 18 × 1-inch cookie pan. Let the preserves stand, uncovered, in a cool place, 24 hours.

NOTE: The Westmark brand Kirschomat cherry pitter is an efficient tool to use for this task.

24 HOURS LATER: Place the cherry mixture in a clean, 8-quart, heavy-bottomed, stainless steel kettle. Over high heat, bring the cherry mixture to a boil; boil rapidly for 1 minute, stirring constantly with the wooden spoon. Immediately remove from the heat and skim the foam off the preserves, using tableware tablespoons and teaspoons. Stir and skim the preserves 10 additional minutes, or until the mixture thickens sufficiently that the cherries will distribute evenly in the preserves and not float to the top of the jars.

Drain hot, sterilized, half-pint jars, upside down, on a clean tea towel.

Pour the preserves into the drained jars, leaving ¼-inch headspace.

Wipe the jar rims and threads. Place hot metal lids on the jars and screw the bands firmly.

Process in a boiling-water canner for the following time:

Processing Times

Jar Size	Altitude of Canning Location		
	0 to 1,000 ft.	1,001 to 6,000 ft.	Above 6,000 ft.
Half-Pints	5 min.	10 min.	15 min.

Remove the jars from the canner and place on a dry, wooden board which has been covered with a tea towel. Let the jars stand, *undisturbed,* 12 hours to cool completely.

YIELDS ABOUT 5 HALF-PINTS

STRAWBERRY PRESERVES

Preserves are made with small, whole fruit or uniformly sized, medium-large pieces of fruit (see the description of preserves on page 738). The most elegant strawberry preserves are made with very small, whole strawberries, which are difficult to find nowadays. Commercial strawberries purchased at supermarkets and produce markets keep getting bigger and bigger (and, may I say, less and less endowed with that wonderful, old-fashioned strawberry flavor). For making these preserves (my Grandmother's recipe), I used to pick tiny, deep red, fabulously flavored strawberries in a U-Pick strawberry field in Dallas County. The proprietor kept about three long rows of these special strawberries principally for use in preserves. Unfortunately, the strawberry field is no longer there and I erred in not previously finding out what variety those little strawberries were. In time, I think I'll investigate that and start my own little patch of them.

2 quarts small, firm, uniformly sized strawberries
4 cups sugar
2 cups sugar
2 tablespoons freshly squeezed, strained lemon juice

THE FIRST DAY: Wash and sort the strawberries quickly in cold water; drain in a colander. Using a strawberry huller, remove the green caps only; do not remove the center pith of the berries; let stand.

Pour enough hot water into an 8-quart, heavy-bottomed, stainless steel kettle to cover the strawberries when added later. Cover the kettle. Over high heat, bring the water to a boil. Uncover the kettle. Add the strawberries and leave the strawberries in the kettle, uncovered, over high heat exactly 2 minutes (use a timer). Immediately remove from the heat and drain well.

Add 4 cups sugar to the strawberries in the kettle; using a wooden spoon, stir very briefly

(Recipe continues on next page)

and carefully to partially combine. Try to prevent crushing the berries. Over medium-high heat, heat the strawberry mixture until the sugar dissolves, stirring carefully with the wooden spoon. When the sugar dissolves, increase the heat to high. Bring the mixture to a rolling boil; boil exactly 2 minutes (use a timer), stirring only sufficiently to prevent scorching. Immediately remove from the heat.

After the bubbling stops, add 2 cups sugar and lemon juice; stir carefully. Over high heat, bring the mixture to a rolling boil; boil exactly 5 minutes (use a timer), stirring only minimally to help avoid breaking up the whole strawberries. Immediately remove from the heat and skim the foam off the preserves, using tableware tablespoons and teaspoons.

Pour the hot preserves into a 10½ × 15½ × 1-inch cookie pan. Let the preserves stand, uncovered, in a cool place, overnight or about 12 hours.

THE NEXT DAY: Drain hot, sterilized, half-pint jars, upside down, on a clean tea towel.

Pack the preserves into the drained jars, leaving ¼-inch headspace.

Wipe the jar rims and threads. Place hot metal lids on the jars and screw the bands firmly.

Process in a boiling-water canner for the following time:

Processing Times

Jar Size	0 to 1,000 ft.	1,001 to 6,000 ft.	Above 6,000 ft.
Half-Pints	5 min.	10 min.	15 min.

Remove the jars from the canner and place on a dry, wooden board which has been covered with a tea towel. Let the jars stand, *undisturbed,* 12 hours to cool completely.

YIELDS ABOUT 5 HALF-PINTS

Conserves

APRICOT-ALMOND CONSERVE

3 medium oranges
1 cup slivered, blanched almonds
16 cups cold water
2 tablespoons white vinegar
2 tablespoons salt
5 pounds apricots, divided
10 cups sugar
¼ cup Amaretto (page 19)

Wash the oranges. Cut off the ends and quarter the oranges lengthwise. Using a grapefruit knife, remove the pulp from each orange quarter by cutting next to the peel using a sawing motion. Set peels aside.

Trim away any white peel membrane remaining on the orange pulp. Cut the pulp into ½-inch cubes, removing and discarding any seeds. Place the orange cubes in a bowl; cover and set aside.

Cut the quarters of orange peel in half lengthwise. Using the grapefruit knife, cut away and discard as much of the white membrane as possible from the orange peels. Using a food grinder (page 49), finely grind the orange peels. Place the ground peel in a mixing bowl; cover and set aside.

Using the food grinder, coarsely grind the almonds. Place the ground almonds in a mixing bowl; cover and set aside.

In a 12-quart kettle, place the water, vinegar, and salt; stir until the salt dissolves; set aside.

Wash ½ of the apricots. Blanch the apricots (page 44) 30 seconds and immediately immerse them in cold water; drain. Peel, cut in half, and pit the apricots. As the apricots are prepared, drop them into the vinegar solution to prevent discoloration. Repeat the procedure to prepare the remaining ½ of the apricots. Prepare only

½ of the apricots at a time because apricots darken quickly in their skins after being blanched.

Drain and rinse all the apricots twice, using fresh, cold water. Drain the apricots well. Cut each apricot half into ninths.

In an 8-quart, heavy-bottomed, stainless steel kettle, place the apricots, orange cubes, orange peel, almonds, sugar, and Amaretto; stir to combine. Over medium-high heat, bring the apricot mixture to a boil, stirring constantly. Attach a candy thermometer to the kettle. Increase the heat to high; boil the apricot mixture until the temperature reaches 8° F. above the boiling point of water (page 712) (about 20 minutes boiling time), stirring constantly.

Remove from the heat and detach the thermometer. If any foam remains on the surface of the conserve, immediately skim it off, using tableware tablespoons and teaspoons.

Quickly drain hot, sterilized, half-pint jars, upside down, on a clean tea towel.

Pour the hot conserve into the drained jars, leaving ¼-inch headspace.

Wipe the jar rims and threads. Place hot metal lids on the jars and screw the bands firmly.

Process in a boiling-water canner for the following time:

Processing Times

Jar Size	Altitude of Canning Location		
	0 to 1,000 ft.	1,001 to 6,000 ft.	Above 6,000 ft.
Half-Pints	5 min.	10 min.	15 min.

Remove the jars from the canner and place on a dry, wooden board which has been covered with a tea towel. Let the jars stand, *undisturbed,* 12 hours to cool completely.

YIELDS ABOUT 12 HALF-PINTS

GOOSEBERRY CONSERVE

1½ quarts gooseberries, stem and blossom ends removed*
¾ cup finely diced (page 22), unpeeled orange (about 1 medium orange)
4 cups sugar
1 cup golden raisins

Use a small, sharp paring knife to cut tiny portions off both ends of the gooseberries.

In an 8-quart, heavy-bottomed, stainless steel kettle, place the berries, orange, sugar, and raisins; stir to combine. Over low heat, heat the mixture until the sugar completely dissolves, stirring constantly. Attach a candy thermometer to the kettle. Increase the heat to medium-high and bring the mixture to a rapid boil, stirring constantly. Boil the mixture until the temperature reaches 8° F. above the boiling point of water (page 712), stirring constantly.

Remove from the heat and detach the thermometer. If any foam remains on the surface of the conserve, immediately skim it off, using tableware tablespoons and teaspoons.

Quickly drain hot, sterilized, half-pint jars, upside down, on a clean tea towel.

Pour the hot conserve into the drained jars, leaving ¼-inch headspace.

Wipe the jar rims and threads. Place hot metal lids on the jars and screw the bands firmly.

Process in a boiling-water canner for the following time:

Processing Times

Jar Size	Altitude of Canning Location		
	0 to 1,000 ft.	1,001 to 6,000 ft.	Above 6,000 ft.
Half-Pints	5 min.	10 min.	15 min.

Remove the jars from the canner and place on a dry, wooden board which has been covered with a tea towel. Let the jars stand, *undisturbed,* 12 hours to cool completely.

YIELDS ABOUT 5 HALF-PINTS

GRAPE CONSERVE

5 pounds Concord grapes
8 cups sugar
1 9-ounce box (1½ cups) raisins
⅔ cup freshly squeezed, strained orange
   juice
1 cup chopped English walnuts

Wash the grapes. Remove the grapes from the stems, discarding any green or underripe fruit. Over a large, flat-bottomed pan, separate the grape pulp from the skins by squeezing each grape between your fingers, letting the pulp drop into the pan and placing the skins in an 8-quart, heavy-bottomed, stainless steel kettle. Set the kettle containing the skins aside.

Pour off ½ cup of the grape juice accumulated in the flat-bottomed pan and add to the skins in the kettle. If necessary, crush the pulp, using a potato masher, to extract additional juice to make ½ cup of grape juice. Cover the pan containing the pulp and set aside.

Over medium to medium-high heat, bring the skins and juice to a simmer, stirring constantly. Simmer the mixture 15 minutes, stirring nearly constantly. Remove from the heat and set aside.

Place the pulp, with the remaining accumulated juice, in a clean, heavy-bottomed, stainless steel kettle. Do not add water. Over medium to medium-high heat, bring the pulp to a boil, stirring constantly. Boil the pulp 3 minutes, stirring constantly.

Remove from the heat. Press the cooked pulp (including the juice) through a food mill to remove the seeds.

Measure 6 cups pressed pulp and place in the kettle containing the cooked skins. Add the sugar, raisins, and orange juice; stir to combine. Over low heat, heat the mixture until the sugar completely dissolves, stirring constantly. Attach a candy thermometer to the kettle. Increase the heat to medium-high and bring the mixture to a rapid boil, stirring constantly. Boil the mixture

until the temperature reaches 4° F. above the boiling point of water (page 712), stirring constantly. Add the walnuts and continue to boil the mixture until the temperature reaches 8° F. above the boiling point of water (about 15 minutes total boiling time), stirring constantly.

Remove from the heat and detach the thermometer. If any foam remains on the surface of the conserve, immediately skim it off, using tableware tablespoons and teaspoons.

Quickly drain hot, sterilized, half-pint jars, upside down, on a clean tea towel.

Pour the hot conserve into the drained jars, leaving ¼-inch headspace.

Wipe the jar rims and threads. Place hot metal lids on the jars and screw the bands firmly.

Process in a boiling-water canner for the following time:

Processing Times

Jar Size	Altitude of Canning Location		
	0 to 1,000 ft.	1,001 to 6,000 ft.	Above 6,000 ft.
Half-Pints	5 min.	10 min.	15 min.

Remove the jars from the canner and place on a dry, wooden board which has been covered with a tea towel. Let the jars stand, *undisturbed*, 12 hours to cool completely.

YIELDS ABOUT 7 HALF-PINTS

RHUBARB-STRAWBERRY CONSERVE

1 large orange
1 cup water
1 cup golden raisins
3 cups fresh rhubarb sliced ¼ inch thick
(see recipe procedures, below)
3 cups crushed strawberries (about
1½ quarts fresh strawberries) (see recipe
procedures, below)
5 cups sugar
½ cup chopped pecans

Using a sharp knife, dice (page 22) the entire orange (both the peel and pulp) very finely.

Place the diced orange in a small, stainless steel saucepan. Add 1 cup water. Cover the saucepan. Over medium heat, bring the mixture to a simmer. Uncover the saucepan and reduce the heat to medium-low. Simmer the mixture until the peel is softened (about 30 minutes).

Remove the orange mixture from the heat. Add the raisins; stir to combine; set aside.

If possible, select rhubarb stalks not exceeding ½ inch in width. If the stalks are wider, cut them in half lengthwise before slicing. Slice the rhubarb ¼ inch thick, measure 3 cups, and place in a medium mixing bowl; set aside.

Hull the strawberries (page 23), using a strawberry huller. Cut the hulled strawberries into quarters or halves, depending upon size, and place in a medium, stainless steel mixing bowl. Using a pastry blender (see illustration, page 464), crush the strawberries until the mixture is part juice and part strawberry flesh (do not puree).

Measure 3 cups crushed strawberries, including the juice, and place in an 8-quart, heavy-bottomed, stainless steel kettle. Add the orange-raisin mixture (including the liquid), rhubarb, and sugar; stir well to combine. Over low heat, heat the mixture until the sugar completely dissolves, stirring constantly. Attach a candy thermometer to the kettle. Increase the heat to medium-high and bring the mixture to a rapid boil, stirring constantly. Boil the mixture until the temperature reaches 4° F. above the boiling point of water (page 712), stirring constantly. Add the pecans and continue to boil the mixture until the temperature reaches 8° F. above the boiling point of water, stirring constantly.

Remove from the heat and detach the thermometer. If any foam remains on the surface of the conserve, immediately skim it off, using tableware tablespoons and teaspoons.

Quickly drain hot, sterilized, half-pint jars, upside down, on a clean tea towel.

Pour the hot conserve into the drained jars, leaving ¼-inch headspace.

Wipe the jar rims and threads. Place hot metal lids on the jars and screw the bands firmly.

Process in a boiling-water canner for the following time:

Processing Times

Jar Size	Altitude of Canning Location		
	0 to 1,000 ft.	1,001 to 6,000 ft.	Above 6,000 ft.
Half-Pints	5 min.	10 min.	15 min.

Remove the jars from the canner and place on a dry, wooden board which has been covered with a tea towel. Let the jars stand, *undisturbed,* 12 hours to cool completely.

YIELDS ABOUT 7 HALF-PINTS

Marmalades

ORANGE MARMALADE

5 or 6 large oranges
1 large lemon
6 cups water
About 5¾ to 6 cups sugar (see recipe
    procedures, below)

THE FIRST DAY: Wash the oranges. Cut off the ends and quarter the oranges lengthwise. Using a grapefruit knife, remove the pulp from each orange quarter by cutting next to the peel using a sawing motion. Set the pulp aside.

Using a small, sharp knife, cut each quarter of orange peel widthwise into ¹⁄₁₆-inch slices. Measure 4 cups sliced orange peel and place in an 8-quart, heavy-bottomed, stainless steel kettle; set aside.

Cut each quarter of orange pulp in half lengthwise. Cut each of the halves widthwise into ¼ inch slices, removing and discarding any seeds. Use all of the pulp, including the fruit meat and the membrane. Measure 3½ cups sliced orange pulp and add to the orange peel in the kettle; set aside.

Quarter the lemon lengthwise. Cut each quarter widthwise into ¹⁄₁₆-inch slices removing and discarding any seeds. Slice the peel and pulp together. Measure 1 cup lemon slices and add to the kettle containing the orange peel and pulp.

Add the water to the fruit in the kettle; stir to combine. Over high heat, bring the fruit mixture to a boil, uncovered, stirring intermittently. Reduce the heat and simmer the mixture (uncovered) 5 minutes, stirring occasionally.

Remove from the heat and cover the kettle. Let the fruit mixture stand 18 to 24 hours in a cool place.

18 TO 24 HOURS LATER: Over medium-high to high heat, bring the covered fruit mixture to a rapid boil, stirring intermittently. Rapidly boil the fruit mixture, covered, 1 hour, stirring occasionally.

Remove from the heat and measure the fruit mixture. Add the same amount of sugar as the measured fruit mixture. (For 1 cup of fruit mixture add 1 of cup sugar.) Stir the mixture to combine. Over low heat, heat the mixture until the sugar completely dissolves, stirring constantly. Attach a candy thermometer to the kettle. Increase the heat to medium-high and bring the mixture to a rapid boil, stirring constantly. Boil the mixture until the temperature reaches 8° F. above the boiling point of water (page 712), stirring frequently.

Remove from the heat and detach the thermometer. If any foam remains on the surface of the marmalade, immediately skim it off, using tableware tablespoons and teaspoons.

Quickly drain hot, sterilized, half-pint jars, upside down, on a clean tea towel.

Pour the hot marmalade into the drained jars, leaving ¼-inch headspace.

Wipe the jar rims and threads. Place hot metal lids on the jars and screw the bands firmly.

Process in a boiling-water canner for the following time:

Processing Times

Jar Size	Altitude of Canning Location		
	0 to 1,000 ft.	1,001 to 6,000 ft.	Above 6,000 ft.
Half-Pints	5 min.	10 min.	15 min.

Remove the jars from the canner and place on a dry, wooden board which has been covered with a tea towel. Let the jars stand, *undisturbed,* 12 hours to cool completely.

YIELDS ABOUT 6 HALF-PINTS

Butters

TO TEST FOR DONENESS OF BUTTERS

To determine when a butter has cooked down adequately and is thick enough to can, scoop a teaspoonful from the kettle and hold it away from the steam for 2 minutes. If properly done, the butter should remain mounded on the spoon.

Another test for doneness is to place a teaspoonful of the hot butter on a plate. If liquid does not run off around the edge of the butter, it is ready to be canned.

APPLE BUTTER

12 cups apple pulp (about 9 pounds apples) (see recipe procedures, below)
1½ cups water
6 cups sugar
2 teaspoons ground cinnamon
¾ teaspoon ground cloves
¾ teaspoon ground allspice

Wash, pare (see Note), quarter, and core the apples.

Place the apples in an 8-quart, heavy-bottomed, stainless steel kettle. Add the water. Over medium-high heat, bring the apples to a simmer, uncovered. Reduce the heat and simmer the apples (uncovered) until very tender (about 30 minutes, depending upon the apples), stirring frequently to prevent the apples from burning on the bottom of the kettle.

Remove from the heat. Press the cooked apples and liquid through a food mill.

Measure 12 cups apple pulp and place in a clean, 8-quart, heavy-bottomed, stainless steel kettle. Add the sugar, cinnamon, cloves, and allspice; stir to combine. Over medium heat, bring the mixture to a simmer, stirring constantly. Simmer the mixture gently for 10 to 15 minutes, or until it reaches the desired consistency (see To Test for Doneness of Butters, left column), stirring constantly to prevent scorching. Remove from the heat; let stand.

Drain hot, sterilized, pint or half-pint jars, upside down, on a clean tea towel.

Pour the hot Apple Butter into the drained jars, leaving ¼-inch headspace.

Wipe the jar rims and threads. Place hot metal lids on the jars and screw the bands firmly.

Process in a boiling-water canner for the following time:

Processing Times

Jar Size	Altitude of Canning Location		
	0 to 1,000 ft.	1,001 to 6,000 ft.	Above 6,000 ft.
Half-Pints	5 min.	10 min.	15 min.
Pints	10 min.	15 min.	20 min.

Remove the jars from the canner and place on a dry, wooden board which has been covered with a tea towel. Let the jars stand, *undisturbed*, 12 hours to cool completely.

NOTE: An apple parer helps accomplish this task expeditiously and efficiently.

YIELDS ABOUT 7 PINTS

APRICOT BUTTER

16 cups cold water
2 tablespoons white vinegar
2 tablespoons salt
6 cups apricot pulp (about 5½ pounds apricots) (see recipe procedures, below)
¼ cup water
3 cups sugar
2 tablespoons freshly squeezed, strained lemon juice
¼ teaspoon almond extract

In a 12-quart kettle, place 16 cups water, vinegar, and salt; stir until the salt dissolves; set aside.

Wash ½ of the apricots. Blanch the apricots (page 44) 30 seconds and immediately immerse them in cold water; drain. Peel, cut in half, and pit the apricots. As the apricots are prepared, drop them into the vinegar solution to prevent discoloration. Repeat the procedure to prepare the remaining ½ of the apricots. Prepare only ½ of the apricots at a time because apricots darken quickly in their skins after being blanched.

Drain and rinse the apricots twice, using fresh, cold water. Drain the apricots well. Place the apricots in an 8-quart, heavy-bottomed, stainless steel kettle. Add ¼ cup water. Over medium heat, bring the apricots to a simmer, stirring constantly. Simmer the apricots until soft, stirring constantly.

Remove from the heat. Press the cooked apricots and liquid through a food mill.

Measure 6 cups apricot pulp and place in a clean, 8-quart, heavy-bottomed, stainless steel kettle. Add the sugar; stir to combine. Over medium heat, bring the mixture to a simmer, stirring constantly. Simmer the mixture, uncovered, 30 minutes, or until it reaches the desired consistency (see To Test for Doneness of Butters, page 763), stirring frequently to prevent sticking.

Remove from the heat. Add the lemon juice and almond extract; stir well to blend; let stand.

Drain hot, sterilized pint or half-pint jars, upside down, on a clean tea towel.

Pour the hot Apricot Butter into the drained jars, leaving ¼-inch headspace.

Wipe the jar rims and threads. Place hot metal lids on the jars and screw the bands firmly.

Process in a boiling-water canner for the following time:

Processing Times

Jar Size	Altitude of Canning Location		
	0 to 1,000 ft.	1,001 to 6,000 ft.	Above 6,000 ft.
Half-Pints	5 min.	10 min.	15 min.
Pints	10 min.	15 min.	20 min.

Remove the jars from the canner and place on a dry, wooden board which has been covered with a tea towel. Let the jars stand, *undisturbed,* 12 hours to cool completely.

YIELDS ABOUT 3 PINTS

WILD PLUM BUTTER

4 cups wild plum pulp (see recipe procedures, below)
Water
3 cups sugar

Wash and sort the plums. Cut them in half and pit.

Place the plums in an 8-quart, heavy-bottomed, stainless steel kettle. Add a very small amount of water—only enough to prevent sticking. Over medium heat, bring the plums to a simmer, stirring constantly. Simmer the plums until soft, stirring constantly.

Remove from the heat. Press the cooked plums and liquid through a food mill.

Measure 4 cups plum pulp and place in a clean, 8-quart, heavy-bottomed, stainless steel kettle. Add the sugar (¾ cup sugar for each cup of pulp); stir to combine. Over medium heat, bring the mixture to a simmer, stirring constantly. Simmer the mixture until it reaches the desired consistency (see To Test for Doneness of

Butter, page 763), stirring constantly to prevent sticking. Remove from the heat; let stand.

Drain hot, sterilized half-pint or pint jars, upside down, on a clean tea towel.

Pour the hot Plum Butter into the drained jars, leaving ¼-inch headspace.

Wipe the jar rims and threads. Place hot metal lids on the jars and screw the bands firmly.

Process in a boiling-water canner for the following time:

Processing Times

Jar Size	Altitude of Canning Location		
	0 to 1,000 ft.	1,001 to 6,000 ft.	Above 6,000 ft.
Half-Pints	5 min.	10 min.	15 min.
Pints	10 min.	15 min.	20 min.

Remove the jars from the canner and place on a dry, wooden board which has been covered with a tea towel. Let the jars stand, *undisturbed,* 12 hours to cool completely.

YIELDS ABOUT 2 PINTS

PEAR BUTTER

This delicately flavored, softly textured butter is characterized by refinement.

16 cups cold water
2 tablespoons white vinegar
2 tablespoons salt
8 cups Bartlett pear pulp (about 7 pounds Bartlett pears) (see recipe procedures, below)
¼ cup water
4 cups sugar
⅓ cup freshly squeezed, strained orange juice
1¼ teaspoons finely grated orange rind (page 47)
1 teaspoon ground nutmeg

In a 12-quart kettle, place 16 cups water, vinegar, and salt; stir until the salt dissolves; set aside.

Wash, quarter, and core the pears (do not pare). As the pears are prepared, drop them into the vinegar solution to prevent discoloration.

Drain and rinse the pears twice, using fresh, cold water. Drain the pears well. Place the pears in an 8-quart, heavy-bottomed, stainless steel kettle. Add ¼ cup water. Over medium heat, bring the pears to a simmer, stirring constantly. Simmer the pears 10 minutes, or until soft, stirring constantly.

Remove from the heat. Press the cooked pears and liquid through a food mill.

Measure 8 cups pear pulp and place in a clean, 8-quart, heavy-bottomed, stainless steel kettle. Add the sugar, orange juice, orange rind, and nutmeg; stir to combine. Over medium heat, bring the mixture to a simmer, stirring constantly. Simmer the mixture, uncovered, 30 minutes, or until it reaches the desired consistency (see To Test for Doneness of Butter, page 763), stirring frequently to prevent sticking. Remove from the heat; let stand.

Drain hot, sterilized pint or half-pint jars, upside down, on a clean tea towel.

Pour the hot Pear Butter into the drained jars, leaving ¼-inch headspace.

Wipe the jar rims and threads. Place hot metal lids on the jars and screw the bands firmly.

Process in a boiling-water canner for the following time:

Processing Times

Jar Size	Altitude of Canning Location		
	0 to 1,000 ft.	1,001 to 6,000 ft.	Above 6,000 ft.
Half-Pints	5 min.	10 min.	15 min.
Pints	10 min.	15 min.	20 min.

Remove the jars from the canner and place on a dry, wooden board which has been covered with a tea towel. Let the jars stand, *undisturbed,* 12 hours to cool completely.

YIELDS ABOUT 4 PINTS

Pickles

See definition of Pickle, page 25.

BREAD AND BUTTER PICKLES

5 pounds pickling cucumbers 4 to 6 inches
   in length (about 1 gallon cucumbers)
1¼ pounds small, white onions, sliced
   ¹⁄₁₆ inch thick (about 8 small onions)
2½ cups green bell peppers cut lengthwise
   into fourths, then sliced widthwise ¹⁄₁₆
   inch thick (about 2 large peppers)
½ cup canning salt (page 704)
1 quart crushed ice
5 cups sugar
1½ teaspoons ground turmeric
½ teaspoon ground cloves
2 tablespoons mustard seed
1 teaspoon celery seed
5 cups cider vinegar (5 percent acidity)

Select fresh, crisp cucumbers. Wash the cucumbers; do not pare. Using a sharp, thin-bladed knife, slice the cucumbers widthwise ¹⁄₁₆ inch thick, *discarding the ends.*

Place the cucumber slices in a 12-quart, heavy-bottomed, stainless steel kettle. Add the onions, peppers, and canning salt; stir to combine.

Bury the ice throughout the mixture in the kettle. Place a dinner plate over the mixture in the kettle. Weight the plate with a water-filled, securely lidded quart jar. Cover the kettle and refrigerate 3 hours.

Meanwhile, in a large mixing bowl, place the sugar, turmeric, cloves, mustard seed, and celery seed; stir to combine. Add the vinegar; stir to combine; cover and set aside.

After 3 hours refrigeration, drain the pickle mixture thoroughly. Pour the vinegar mixture over the pickle mixture. Over medium-high heat, heat the mixture, uncovered, to scalding (page 25), but do not boil. Using a wooden spoon, paddle the mixture occasionally as it heats to scalding.

Remove from the heat. Pack the hot pickles (without liquid) into hot, sterilized, pint jars, leaving ½-inch headspace.

Cover the pickles in the jars with the hot pickle liquid, maintaining ½-inch headspace.

Using a plastic knife or a narrow, rubber spatula, remove the air bubbles in the jars. Wipe the jar rims and threads. Place hot metal lids on the jars and screw the bands firmly.

Process by low-temperature pasteurization (page 707), as follows: Place the filled jars in a boiling-water canner which is half full of 120° to 140° F. water. Add 120° to 140° F. water to a level 1 inch above the tops of the jars. Attach a candy thermometer to the canner. Cover the canner. Over medium to medium-high heat, heat the water in the canner to 180° to 185° F. and maintain that temperature range for 30 minutes, regulating the heat under the canner as required. Make certain that a water temperature of at least 180° F. is maintained for the full 30 minutes to avoid the possibility of spoilage. Temperatures above 185° F. may cause unnecessary softening of the pickles.

Remove the jars from the canner and place on a dry, wooden board which has been covered with a tea towel. Let the jars stand, *undisturbed,* 12 hours to cool completely.

YIELDS ABOUT 8 PINTS

DILLY BEANS

If spicy-hot food is your passion, you'll go for these Dilly Beans, spiked with plenty of cayenne pepper and flavored with fresh dill and garlic. Canned vertically, the uncut green beans are so attractive and appetizing looking, I serve them for an hors d'oeuvre right from the jar, letting nibblers pull out the beans with their fingers. (They always find this fun.) Dilly Beans also are a good picnic or tailgate lunch item because they're so easy to pack. Of course, they may be arranged on a dish and served on the table with just the right lunch or dinner.

4 pounds fresh green beans (see recipe
   procedures, below)
4 heads fresh dill
4 garlic cloves
1 teaspoon cayenne pepper, divided
2½ cups distilled water
2½ cups cider vinegar (5 percent acidity)
¼ cup canning salt (page 704)

Using a vegetable brush, wash the beans well. Cut the stem ends off the beans and trim the blossom ends, leaving about ⅛ inch of the "tails" intact; set aside.

Use widemouthed, pint canning jars with straight sides. Measure the height of the canning jars and deduct ¹³⁄₁₆ inch (½ inch for headspace plus allowance for liquid to cover the beans [and "tails"]). This measurement will be the exact length to cut the beans. Measure 1 bean and cut it at the stem end. Use this bean as a pattern to cut the beans.

Place the cut beans, carefully, in a medium, heavy-bottomed, stainless steel kettle. Cover the beans with boiling water. Cover the kettle. Over high heat, bring the beans to a boil. Reduce the heat and cook the beans at a low boil for 5 minutes.

Remove from the heat and drain immediately. Pack the beans vertically (with the "tails" up) into hot, sterilized, widemouthed, pint jars with straight sides. To each jar, add 1 dill head,

pushing the dill heads into the jars decoratively against the side glass, and maintaining ½-inch headspace. Then, to each jar, add 1 garlic clove. Sprinkle ¼ teaspoon cayenne pepper in each jar (see Note); set aside.

In a stainless steel saucepan, place the distilled water, vinegar, and canning salt; stir to combine. Over high heat, bring the vinegar mixture to a boil, stirring intermittently.

Cover the beans in the jars with the hot vinegar mixture, maintaining ½-inch headspace.

Using a plastic knife or a narrow, rubber spatula, remove the air bubbles in the jars. Wipe the the jar rims and threads. Place hot metal lids on the jars and screw the bands firmly.

Process in a boiling-water canner for the following time:

Processing Times

Jar Size	Altitude of Canning Location		
	0 to 1,000 ft.	1,001 to 6,000 ft.	Above 6,000 ft.
Pints	5 min.	10 min.	15 min.

Remove the jars from the canner and place on a dry, wooden board which has been covered with a tea towel. Let the jars stand, *undisturbed,* 12 hours to cool completely.

NOTE: For less hot Dilly Beans, sprinkle ⅛ teaspoon cayenne pepper in each jar.

YIELDS 4 PINTS

BRINED DILL PICKLES

20 pounds pickling cucumbers 3 to 5
   inches in length (about ½ bushel
   cucumbers)
¾ cup mixed pickling spice
10 heads fresh dill
10 quarts distilled water
2⅓ cups cider vinegar (5 percent acidity)
1¾ cups canning salt (page 704)
1 quart distilled water (to fill jar used as a
   weight)

Immediately prior to commencing preparation
of the pickles, wash a 5-gallon crock in hot,
soapy water. Rinse the crock well; then, scald
with boiling water. Allow the crock to dry 2 or
3 minutes and then cover the top with plastic
wrap. The least exposure of the inside of the
crock to air after scalding the better.

Place the crock in a place where a temperature of 70 to 75° F. can be maintained during
the fermentation period. While temperatures of
55 to 65° F. are acceptable, fermentation will
take longer (5 to 6 weeks). Temperatures above
80° F. will cause the pickles to become too soft.

Using a vegetable brush, scrub the cucumbers
thoroughly, making certain that all the soil particles have been removed from the ends of the
cucumbers. Cut a 1/16 inch slice off the blossom
end of the cucumbers and discard. It is important
that the blossom ends be fully removed because
the blossoms contain enzymes which can cause
the pickles to soften. Set the cucumbers aside.

Place ½ of the pickling spice and 5 heads of
dill in the bottom of the crock. Then, place the
cucumbers in the crock, filling the crock to
within 3 to 4 inches of the top. Place the remaining ½ of the pickling spice and 5 heads of
dill over the cucumbers. Re-cover the crock
with plastic wrap; let stand.

In a 16-quart, stainless steel kettle, place 10
quarts distilled water, vinegar, and canning salt;
stir until the salt dissolves and the mixture
(brine) is thoroughly blended. Pour the brine
over the cucumbers.

Select a dinner plate or glass pie plate slightly
smaller in diameter than the crock. Wash the
plate in soapy water (rewash the plate even if
clean); rinse well. Then, scald the plate, dry it,
and allow it to cool briefly. Place the plate over
the cucumbers in the crock. Weight the plate
with a washed, scalded, and securely lidded
quart jar filled with distilled water. The pickles
should be covered with 1 to 2 inches of brine.

Cover the top of the crock with a clean,
unscented, heavy terry cloth towel to help prevent contamination of the pickles. Tie the towel
with twine to secure it to the crock.

After a few days, scum will form on the surface of the brine. Using a scalded, stainless steel
spoon, remove the scum and mold every day, as
it will interfere with the desired fermentation
and cause the pickles to be soft. Do not stir the
pickles. Keep the pickles covered with the brine.
If necessary, add more brine, using the ingredient proportions in this recipe. Change the terry
cloth towel each week. *Caution:* If the pickles
become soft or slimy, or develop a disagreeable
odor, discard them.

In about 3 to 4 weeks, the pickles will be olive
green in color and should have achieved a desirable flavor.

Pack the pickles (without brine) into hot, sterilized, widemouthed, quart jars, leaving ½-inch
headspace. Add a whole or partial head of dill
from the crock to each jar pushing the dill heads
into the jars decoratively against the side glass,
and maintaining ½-inch headspace; let stand.

Pour the brine from the crock into a 16-
quart, stainless steel kettle. Over medium-high
heat, bring the brine to a boil. Reduce the heat
and simmer the brine 5 minutes. Strain the
brine through paper coffee filters to reduce
cloudiness.

Cover the pickles in the jars with the hot
brine, maintaining ½-inch headspace. The brine
will be cloudy due to yeast development during
fermentation; however, it will give an added flavor to the pickles. (If preferred, cover the pickles with hot, fresh brine, using 16 cups distilled
water, 4 cups cider vinegar [5 percent acidity],
and ½ cup canning salt.)

Using a plastic knife or a narrow, rubber spatula, remove the air bubbles in the jars. Wipe the jar rims and threads. Place hot metal lids on the jars and screw the bands firmly.

Process by low-temperature pasteurization (page 707), as follows: Place the filled jars in a boiling-water canner which is half full of 120 to 140° F. water. Add 120 to 140° F. water to a level 1 inch above the tops of the jars. Attach a candy thermometer to the canner. Cover the canner. Over medium to medium-high heat, heat the water in the canner to 180 to 185° F. and maintain that temperature range for 30 minutes, regulating the heat under the canner as required. Make certain that a water temperature of at least 180° F. is maintained for the full 30 minutes to avoid the possibility of spoilage. Temperatures above 185° F. may cause unnecessary softening of the pickles.

Remove the jars from the canner and place on a dry, wooden board which has been covered with a tea towel. Let the jars stand, *undisturbed, 12 hours* to cool completely.

YIELDS ABOUT 14 QUARTS, DEPENDING UPON THE SIZE OF THE PICKLES AND HOW THEY PACK IN THE JARS

EASY REFRIGERATOR SWEET DILL PICKLES

You don't have to be a master pickle maker to turn out these delicious sweet dills—nor do you need to can them. Start with a commercial jar of good dill pickles, then slice them and pour a spicy, vinegar/sugar syrup over them. After packing the pickles back into the jar, cover them with the syrup and place the jar in the refrigerator. In 10 days, you'll have some of the best-tasting pickles imaginable. Mother usually had a jar of these pickles in the refrigerator, ready for us to eat when we yearned for them. I think they're nearly unbeatable with a sandwich or a lunch of soup with cheese and ring bologna on crackers.

1 46-ounce jar unsliced, best-quality dill pickles (or 1 quart home-canned Brined Dill Pickles, page 768)
3 cups sugar
1 cup cider vinegar (5 percent acidity)
1 cup water
2 small stalks celery hearts with leaves (page 21)
3 tablespoons mixed pickling spice, tied in a cheesecloth bag (page 44)

Drain the pickles. Rinse in fresh, cold water and drain in a colander. Cut thin slices from the ends of the pickles and discard. Then, slice the pickles widthwise 5/16 inch thick and place in a large mixing bowl; set aside.

In a large, heavy-bottomed, stainless steel saucepan, place the sugar, vinegar, water, and celery; stir to combine. Over medium-high heat, bring the vinegar mixture to a boil, stirring constantly. Add the cheesecloth bag of pickling spice. Reduce the heat to medium and boil the mixture gently for 5 minutes.

Remove from the heat and immediately pour the vinegar mixture (including the cheesecloth bag) over the pickles; let stand until cool.

Pack the pickles back into the pickle jar, together with the celery, placing the cheesecloth bag midway in the jar. Cover the pickles in the jar with the vinegar mixture. Screw the lid on the jar.

Refrigerate the pickles and let stand in the refrigerator 10 days before serving. Remove the cheesecloth bag after 10 days standing in the refrigerator. The pickles will keep in the refrigerator for a long period of time.

YIELDS ONE 46-OUNCE JAR

PICKLED BEETS

5 pounds medium (about 1½ to 2 inches in diameter), trimmed, fresh beets (see recipe procedures, below)
2¼ cups sugar
3 cups cider vinegar (5 percent acidity)
1 cup distilled water
3 2-inch pieces stick cinnamon
1 teaspoon whole cloves
1 teaspoon whole allspice

Trim away a portion of the stems and roots of the beets, leaving 1 inch of the stems and 1 inch of the roots on the beets to prevent bleeding. Using a vegetable brush, scrub the trimmed beets well.

Place the beets in an 8-quart, heavy-bottomed, stainless steel kettle. Add fresh water to cover the beets. Cover the kettle. Over high heat, bring the beets to a boil. Reduce the heat and cook the beets at a low boil until just tender (about 25 minutes). *Drain the beets, discarding the cooking liquid.*

When the beets are cool enough to handle, trim off the ends and slip off the skins. Using the fluted arm of an egg slicer (see illustration), slice the beets ¼ inch thick; set aside.

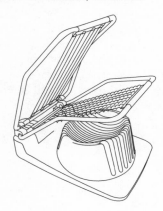

Egg Slicer

In a clean, 8-quart, heavy-bottomed, stainless steel kettle, place the sugar, vinegar, and distilled water; stir to combine. Add the stick cinnamon. Tie the cloves and allspice in a cheesecloth bag (page 44) and add to the vinegar mixture. Over medium-high heat, bring the vinegar mixture to a boil, stirring constantly. Add the beets. Return the mixture to a simmer. Reduce the heat and simmer the beets, uncovered, 5 minutes, stirring intermittently using a wooden spoon to help prevent cutting the beet slices.

Meanwhile, secure a piece of damp cotton flannel, napped side up, in a sieve over a deep pan; set aside.

Remove the beets from the heat. Remove and discard the stick cinnamon and cheesecloth bag. Pack the beets (without liquid) into hot, sterilized, pint jars, leaving ½-inch headspace; let stand.

Pour the hot beet liquid (from the kettle) over the cotton flannel in the sieve to strain. Pour the strained beet liquid into a stainless steel saucepan. Over high heat, bring the beet liquid to a boil. Cover the beets in the jars with the hot beet liquid, maintaining ½-inch headspace.

Using a plastic knife or a narrow, rubber spatula, remove the air bubbles in the jars. Wipe the jar rims and threads. Place hot metal lids on the jars and screw the bands firmly.

Process in a boiling-water canner for the following time:

Processing Times

Jar Size	Altitude of Canning Location			
	0 to 1,000 ft.	1,001 to 3,000 ft.	3,001 to 6,000 ft.	Above 6,000 ft.
Pints	30 min.	35 min.	40 min.	45 min.

Remove the jars from the canner and place on a dry, wooden board which has been covered with a tea towel. Let the jars stand, *undisturbed,* 12 hours to cool completely.

YIELDS ABOUT 5 PINTS

SERVING SUGGESTIONS
• Tasty with informal sandwich lunches.

- A good accompaniment for beef dishes such as Beef and Noodles (page 158), Chicken-Fried Steak (page 164), and Rib Roast (page 167).

- An excellent relish tray item.

VARIATION: Commercially canned, sliced beets may be substituted for fresh, cooked beets.

MELON BALL PICKLES

20 pounds slightly underripe cantaloupes
  (about 6 cantaloupes)
4 cups cider vinegar (5 percent acidity)
3½ cups distilled water
6 3-inch pieces stick cinnamon
1½ teaspoons ground mace
2 tablespoons whole allspice
1 tablespoon whole cloves
5 cups sugar

LATE IN THE DAY: Wash the cantaloupes. Cut the cantaloupes in half lengthwise and remove the seeds. Using a 1-inch melon baller, scoop whole melon balls. Measure 16 cups melon balls and place in a large mixing bowl; set aside.

In an 8-quart, heavy-bottomed, stainless steel kettle, place the vinegar, distilled water, stick cinnamon, and mace; stir to combine. Tie the allspice and cloves in a cheesecloth bag (page 44) and add to the vinegar mixture. Over medium-high heat, bring the vinegar mixture to a boil, stirring constantly. Reduce the heat and simmer the vinegar mixture, uncovered, 5 minutes.

Remove the vinegar mixture from the heat. Add the melon balls. Cover the kettle; let stand, in a cool place, overnight.

THE NEXT DAY: Remove the stick cinnamon and cheesecloth bag from the kettle, and reserve them. Using a slotted spoon, remove the melon balls from the vinegar mixture and place in a large mixing bowl; set aside.

Secure a piece of damp cotton flannel, napped side up, in a sieve over a deep pan. Pour the vinegar mixture over the cotton flannel in the sieve to strain.

Pour the strained vinegar mixture into a clean, 8-quart, heavy-bottomed, stainless steel kettle. Add the sugar; stir to combine. Over medium-high heat, bring the vinegar mixture to a boil, stirring until the sugar dissolves. Add the melon balls, reserved stick cinnamon, and reserved cheesecloth bag. Reduce the heat and simmer the mixture, uncovered, until the melon balls are semitranslucent (about 45 minutes), stirring intermittently.

Remove from the heat. Remove and discard the cheesecloth bag. Remove the stick cinnamon and reserve. Pack the melon balls (without syrup) into hot, sterilized, pint jars, leaving ½-inch headspace. Place 1 piece of the reserved stick cinnamon in each jar against the side glass; let stand.

Re-strain the syrup (from the kettle) through clean, damp cotton flannel in the sieve over a clean, deep pan. Pour the strained syrup into a stainless steel saucepan. Over high heat, bring the syrup to a boil, stirring occasionally. Cover the melon balls in the jars with the hot syrup, maintaining ½-inch headspace.

Using a plastic knife or a narrow, rubber spatula, remove the air bubbles in the jars. Wipe the jar rims and threads. Place hot metal lids on the jars and screw the bands firmly.

Process in a boiling-water canner for the following time:

Processing Times

Jar Size	Altitude of Canning Location		
	0 to 1,000 ft.	1,001 to 6,000 ft.	Above 6,000 ft.
Pints	10 min.	15 min.	20 min.

Remove the jars from the canner and place on a dry, wooden board which has been covered with a tea towel. Let the jars stand, *undisturbed,* 12 hours to cool completely.

YIELDS ABOUT 6 PINTS

(Recipe continues on next page)

- Melon Ball Pickles add a bit of zip and diversity to meals featuring more bland-tasting casseroles such as Macaroni and Cheese (page 285), Tuna-Noodle Casserole (page 297), and Ring Bologna Casserole (page 297).

- Place a small dish of Melon Ball Pickles on the lunch table when the fare is sandwiches and soup.

WATERMELON RIND PICKLES

Midwest Thanksgiving and Christmas dinners are cooking extravaganzas when a wide variety of pickles and relishes fill beautiful, family-heirloom, cut-glass and china serving dishes. So traditional and time-honored are Watermelon Rind Pickles, they often are among the glorious array blanketing the dining table.

1 25-pound watermelon
16 cups cold, distilled water
1 cup canning salt (page 704)
2 tablespoons whole cloves
2 tablespoons whole allspice
8 cups sugar
2⅓ cups white vinegar (5 percent acidity)
5 3-inch pieces stick cinnamon

EARLY THE FIRST DAY: Wash the watermelon. Cut the melon in half widthwise. Then, cut each half into quarters, making lengthwise cuts. Cut each eighth of the melon widthwise into 1-inch-wide slices.

Place each watermelon slice flat on a cutting board. Using a small, sharp paring knife, pare the rind, cutting away the green. Then, cut away the fruit meat, leaving no pink on the rind. (Reserve the fruit meat for other uses.) Cut each rind slice into 1-inch-square pieces. Measure 16 cups watermelon pieces; set aside.

In a 12-quart, stainless steel kettle, place the distilled water and canning salt; stir until the salt dissolves. Add the melon rind. Cover the kettle; let stand, in a cool place, 6 hours.

Then, drain and rinse the rind twice, using fresh, cold water. Drain the rind well. Place the rind in a clean, 12-quart, heavy-bottomed, stainless steel kettle. Add fresh water to cover the rind. Over high heat, bring the rind to a boil. Reduce the heat to medium-high. Cook the rind, uncovered, at a low boil, just until fork-tender (about 15 minutes), stirring intermittently.

Drain the rind in a colander; let stand. Tie the cloves and allspice in a cheesecloth bag (page 44); set aside.

In a clean, 12-quart, heavy-bottomed, stainless steel kettle, place the sugar and vinegar; stir to combine. Over medium-high heat, bring the vinegar mixture to a boil, stirring until the sugar dissolves. Add the cheesecloth bag and stick cinnamon. Reduce the heat to medium and boil the vinegar mixture (syrup), uncovered, 5 minutes, stirring occasionally.

Remove from the heat. Add the drained rind. Cover the kettle; let stand, in a cool place, overnight.

THE NEXT DAY: Over medium heat, bring the rind and syrup to a boil, stirring often. Cook the mixture, uncovered, at a low boil, until the rind is translucent (about 25 minutes), stirring intermittently.

Remove from the heat. Remove and discard the cheesecloth bag. Remove the stick cinnamon and reserve. Pack the rind (without syrup) into hot, sterilized, pint jars, leaving ½-inch headspace. Place 1 piece of the reserved stick cinnamon in each jar against the side glass; let stand.

Secure a piece of damp cotton flannel, napped side up, in a sieve over a deep pan. Pour the hot syrup (from the kettle) over the cotton flannel in the sieve to strain. Pour the strained syrup into a stainless steel saucepan. Over high heat, bring the syrup to a boil, stirring occasionally. Cover the rind in the jars with the hot syrup, maintaining ½-inch headspace.

Using a plastic knife or a narrow, rubber spatula, remove the air bubbles in the jars. Wipe the jar rims and threads. Place hot metal lids on the jars and screw the bands firmly.

Process in a boiling-water canner for the following time:

Processing Times

Jar Size	Altitude of Canning Location		
	0 to 1,000 ft.	1,001 to 6,000 ft.	Above 6,000 ft.
Pints	10 min.	15 min.	20 min.

Remove the jars from the canner and place on a dry, wooden board which has been covered with a tea towel. Let the jars stand, *undisturbed,* 12 hours to cool completely.

YIELDS ABOUT 5 PINTS

PICKLED MIXED VEGETABLES

1¼ pounds pickling cucumbers 3 to 4 inches in length, sliced ½ inch thick (cut off and discard both ends of cucumbers)
2 cups fluted carrot slices cut ½ inch thick (use a fluted garnishing cutter, page 128)
2 cups celery slices cut diagonally ½ inch thick
2 cups trimmed and peeled pearl onions (page 45)
20 strips red bell peppers cut ½ inch wide by 3 inches long (about 2 large peppers)
3 cups small cauliflower flowerets (about 1 small head cauliflower)
16 cups cold, distilled water
1 cup canning salt (page 704)
2 cups sugar
¼ cup mustard seed
2 tablespoons celery seed
6½ cups white vinegar (5 percent acidity)

THE FIRST DAY: In an 8-quart, stainless steel kettle, place the prepared cucumbers, carrots, celery, onions, peppers, and cauliflower; set aside.

In a large mixing bowl, place the distilled water and canning salt; stir until the salt dissolves. Then, pour the salt water over the vegetables in the kettle. Cover the kettle; let stand, in a cool place, 12 to 18 hours.

12 TO 18 HOURS LATER: Drain the vegetables thoroughly; set aside.

In a clean, 8-quart, heavy-bottomed, stainless steel kettle, place the sugar, mustard seed, celery seed, and vinegar; stir to combine. Over medium-high heat, bring the vinegar mixture to a boil, stirring constantly. Cover the kettle. Reduce the heat and boil the vinegar mixture 3 minutes. Add the vegetables. Cover the kettle and return the mixture to a simmer. Simmer the vegetables, covered, 5 minutes.

Remove from the heat. Decoratively arrange the vegetables (without liquid) in hot, sterilized, pint jars, leaving ½-inch headspace.

Cover the vegetables in the jars with the hot vinegar mixture, maintaining ½-inch headspace.

Using a plastic knife or a narrow, rubber spatula, remove the air bubbles in the jars. Wipe the jar rims and threads. Place hot metal lids on the jars and screw the bands firmly.

Process in a boiling-water canner for the following time:

Processing Times

Jar Size	Altitude of Canning Location		
	0 to 1,000 ft.	1,001 to 6,000 ft.	Above 6,000 ft.
Pints	15 min.	20 min.	25 min.

Remove the jars from the canner and place on a dry, wooden board which has been covered with a tea towel. Let the jars stand, *undisturbed,* 12 hours to cool completely.

YIELDS ABOUT 5 PINTS

SERVING SUGGESTIONS

• A lovely pickle accompaniment to pass at the table at meals featuring more plain-style entrées of beef, poultry, and fish.

• Nice for upscale picnics and tailgate lunches.

SPICED PEACHES

Spiced Peaches are one of the grand, venerated pickles outside the realm of cucumber pickles, and this old family recipe makes them exquisitely. These Spiced Peaches faithfully were served with family holiday turkey dinners when my mother was a child, and you can bank on them making their annual appearance at our family's festive table long after I've canned my last jar. They are nicest when canned and served whole, which generally necessitates your produce manager ordering a special lug of small-sized peaches for you. Although fairly large whole peaches will fit into wide-mouthed quart canning jars, sizable Spiced Peaches upset the visual and taste balance of individual plates of food, despite how delectable they are.

16 cups cold water
2 tablespoons white vinegar
2 tablespoons salt
8 pounds small peaches
9 cups sugar
1 quart white vinegar (5 percent acidity)
2 cups water
3 3-inch pieces stick cinnamon
1 tablespoon whole allspice
Whole cloves (3 for each peach)

In a 16-quart kettle, place 16 cups water, 2 tablespoons vinegar, and salt; stir until the salt dissolves; set aside.

Wash the peaches carefully. In batches, blanch the peaches (page 44) 1 minute and immediately immerse them in cold water; drain. Peel the peaches and leave them whole (unpitted) (or, if the peaches are too large, cut them in half and pit them). As the peaches are prepared, drop them into the vinegar solution to prevent discoloration. Let the peaches stand.

In a 12-quart, heavy-bottomed, stainless steel kettle, place the sugar, 1 quart vinegar, and 2 cups water; stir to combine. Over high heat, bring the vinegar mixture to a boil, stirring until the sugar dissolves. Cover the kettle. Reduce the heat slightly and boil the vinegar mixture (syrup) 1 minute. Add the stick cinnamon and allspice. Cover the kettle and boil the syrup 4 additional minutes.

Meanwhile, secure a piece of damp cotton flannel, napped side up, in a sieve over a deep pan; set aside.

Remove the syrup from the heat. Remove and discard the stick cinnamon. Pour the hot syrup over the cotton flannel in the sieve to strain. Pour the strained syrup back into the kettle. Over high heat, bring the syrup to a boil.

Meanwhile, drain and rinse the peaches twice, using fresh, cold water. Drain the peaches well. Place 3 whole cloves randomly in each peach. Gently place the peaches in the boiling syrup. Cover the kettle and return the syrup (with the peaches) to a simmer over high heat. Uncover the kettle. Reduce the heat and simmer the peaches until just tender (8 to 15 minutes, depending upon the size of the peaches). Do not overcook.

Remove from the heat. Do not remove the whole cloves from the peaches. Pack the peaches (without syrup) into hot, sterilized, wide-mouthed quart or pint jars, leaving ½-inch headspace; let stand.

Re-strain the syrup through clean, damp cotton flannel in the sieve. Pour the strained syrup into a stainless steel saucepan. Over high heat, bring the syrup to a boil, stirring occasionally. Cover the peaches in the jars with the hot syrup, maintaining ½-inch headspace.

Using a plastic knife or a narrow, rubber spatula, remove the air bubbles in the jars. Wipe the jar rims and threads. Place hot metal lids on the jars and screw the bands firmly.

Process in a boiling-water canner for the following time:

Processing Times

Jar Size	Altitude of Canning Location			
	0 to 1,000 ft.	1,001 to 3,000 ft.	3,001 to 6,000 ft.	Above 6,000 ft.
Pints	20 min.	25 min.	30 min.	35 min.
Quarts	25 min.	30 min.	35 min.	40 min.

Remove the jars from the canner and place on a dry, wooden board which has been covered with a tea towel. Let the jars stand, *undisturbed,* 12 hours to cool completely.

YIELDS ABOUT 4 QUARTS

SPICED SECKEL PEARS

So elegant are Spiced Seckel Pears, they should be reserved for special, more formal dining occasions when their delicacy is fully enjoyed and appreciated. They go especially well with veal and refined poultry dishes such as Roast Turkey Breast (page 214), Chicken Breasts Baked in Sherry Sauce (page 207), and Baked Cut-up Chicken (page 205). Seckel is a variety of petite, reddish brown pears, perfect for making spiced pears because of their small size and their firmness, which allows them to hold their shape exceptionally well after cooking. Spiced Seckel Pears are canned and served whole, with the stem left in. Put on your patience cap when you can them, because it will take ages to fastidiously pare these miniature-like fruits with your sharpest, thinnest paring knife.

2 tablespoons mixed pickling spice
2 2-inch pieces gingerroot, pared and cut in half lengthwise
2 teaspoons whole cloves
6 cups sugar
1 quart white vinegar (5 percent acidity)
5 cups water
16 cups cold water
2 tablespoons white vinegar
2 tablespoons salt
11 pounds barely ripe Seckel pears

THE FIRST DAY: Tie the pickling spice, gingerroot, and cloves in a cheesecloth bag (page 44); set aside.

In an 8-quart, heavy-bottomed, stainless steel kettle, place the sugar, 1 quart vinegar, and 5 cups water; stir to combine. Over medium heat, bring the sugar mixture to a boil, stirring until the sugar dissolves. Add the cheesecloth bag. Cover the kettle. Reduce the heat and boil the sugar mixture (syrup) at a low boil for 5 minutes.

Remove from the heat; let stand until the syrup is cooled slightly. Then, refrigerate the syrup in the covered kettle, leaving the cheesecloth bag in the syrup.

THE NEXT DAY: In a 16-quart kettle, place 16 cups water, 2 tablespoons vinegar, and salt; stir until the salt dissolves; set aside.

Remove the syrup from the refrigerator. Over medium-high heat, bring the syrup to a boil. Pour the hot syrup, including the cheesecloth bag, into a 12-quart, heavy-bottomed, stainless steel kettle; cover and set aside.

Wash the pears carefully; drain. Using a very sharp, pointed paring knife, thinly pare the pears, leaving the pears whole with the stem in. As the pears are prepared, drop them into the cool vinegar solution in the 16-quart kettle to prevent discoloration.

Remove approximately ⅓ of the pears from the vinegar solution. Rinse the pears twice, using fresh, cold water. Drain the pears well. Handle the pears carefully to avoid bruising or nicking. Place the drained pears, single layer, in the kettle containing the syrup (and cheesecloth bag). Cover the kettle. Over medium-high heat, bring the pears to a low boil. Reduce the heat and boil the pears gently for 10 to 15 minutes, just until they are tender, yet firm.

Remove from the heat. Using a slotted spoon, remove the pears from the syrup and place, no more than 2 layers deep, in a large, shallow dish (such as a baking dish); set aside, uncovered.

Repeat the draining, rinsing, and boiling procedures 2 additional times, using the remaining ⅔ of the pears.

Remove the cheesecloth bag from the kettle and discard. Secure a piece of damp cotton flannel, napped side up, in a sieve over a deep pan. Pour the hot syrup (from the kettle) over the cotton flannel in the sieve to strain; let stand. Rinse and dry the kettle. Pour the strained syrup back into the kettle; set aside.

Pack the pears, upright, into hot, sterilized, widemouthed, quart jars, leaving ½-inch headspace; let stand.

Over medium-high heat, bring the syrup to a

(Recipe continues on next page)

boil. Cover the pears in the jars with the hot syrup, maintaining ½-inch headspace.

Using a plastic knife or a narrow, rubber spatula, remove the air bubbles in the jars. Wipe the jar rims and threads. Place hot metal lids on the jars and screw the bands firmly.

Process in a boiling-water canner for the following time:

Processing Times

Jar Size	Altitude of Canning Location			
	0 to 1,000 ft.	1,001 to 3,000 ft.	3,001 to 6,000 ft.	Above 6,000 ft.
Quarts	25 min.	30 min.	35 min.	40 min.

Remove the jars from the canner and place on a dry, wooden board which has been covered with a tea towel. Let the jars stand, *undisturbed,* 12 hours to cool completely.

YIELDS ABOUT 5 QUARTS

Relishes

See the first definition of Relish, page 25.

PEACH CHUTNEY

Many kinds of chutney are made from a variety of fruits and combinations of fruits; most notably, apple, peach, pear, mango, apricot, cranberry, and apple-tomato (ripe or green). Emanating from India, chutney is used mainly as a condiment, but also, it is used as an ingredient in other dishes (see the definition of Chutney on page 21). For a guide to ways in which this unique-tasting relish may be used, see the Serving Suggestions at the end of this recipe.

5 cups cider vinegar (5 percent acidity)
1 pound light brown sugar
1 pound dark brown sugar
2 cups (10 ounces) crystallized ginger diced ³⁄₁₆ inch square
2 cups finely chopped onions (about 2 medium-large onions)
2 garlic cloves, pressed
3 tablespoons chili powder
¼ cup mustard seed
1 tablespoon plus 1 teaspoon canning salt (page 704)
16 cups cold water
2 tablespoons white vinegar
2 tablespoons table salt
16 cups peaches cut into approximately ½-inch cubes (about 8 pounds peaches) (see recipe procedures below)

In a 12-quart, heavy-bottomed, stainless steel kettle, place the cider vinegar, light brown sugar, dark brown sugar, ginger, onions, garlic, chili powder, mustard seed, and canning salt; stir to combine. Cover the kettle and set aside.

In a 16-quart kettle, place 16 cups water, white vinegar, and table salt; stir until the salt dissolves; set aside.

Wash the whole peaches. In batches, blanch the peaches (page 44) 1 minute and immediately immerse them in cold water; drain. Peel, cut in half, and pit the peaches. As the peaches are prepared, drop them into the white vinegar solution in the 16-quart kettle to prevent discoloration.

Drain and rinse the peaches twice, using fresh, cold water. Drain the peaches well. Cut the peaches into approximately ½-inch cubes.

Measure 16 cups cubed peaches and add to the brown sugar mixture in the 12-quart kettle; stir to combine. Over medium heat, bring the mixture to a simmer, stirring constantly until the brown sugar dissolves. Reduce the heat slightly and simmer the mixture, uncovered, at least 1 hour, or until the mixture is dark and reduced to the desired thickness. Stir the mixture frequently during the first stages of cooking and stir constantly as the mixture reduces and thickens to prevent sticking.

Remove from the heat. Pour the hot chutney into hot, sterilized, pint jars, leaving ½-inch headspace.

Using a plastic knife or a narrow, rubber spatula, remove the air bubbles in the jars. Wipe the jar rims and threads. Place hot metal lids on the jars and screw the bands firmly.

Process in a boiling-water canner for the following time:

Processing Times

Jar Size	Altitude of Canning Location		
	0 to 1,000 ft.	1,001 to 6,000 ft.	Above 6,000 ft.
Pints	10 min.	15 min.	20 min.

Remove the jars from the canner and place on a dry, wooden board which has been covered with a tea towel. Let the jars stand, *undisturbed,* 12 hours to cool completely.

YIELDS ABOUT 9 PINTS

SERVING SUGGESTIONS

- Serve as a condiment with curry dishes (see Shrimp Curry, page 266) and meats (see Hot Roast Pork Sandwiches with Chutney, page 353).

- Use as an ingredient in dips (see Chutney Dip, page 60).

- Use with cheeses (see Chutney Cheese Ball, page 72).

CORN RELISH

Corn Relish is a fundamental in Midwest cuisine. Served in a common pottery bowl, it adds pizzazz to a simple lunch; in an antique, hand-painted Haviland dish, it is at home on a beautifully appointed Thanksgiving dinner table. Homemade Heartland Corn Relish is usually made without flour thickening, which I definitely prefer. Commercially purchased corn relish is often gummy with thickener, which, to my palate, is ruinous to this delightful and refreshing relish.

10 cups fresh whole-kernel corn (about 17 medium ears or 11 pounds unshucked corn) (see recipe procedures, below)
2½ cups diced green bell peppers (about 3 large peppers) (see recipe procedures, below)
2½ cups diced red bell peppers (about 3 large peppers) (see recipe procedures, below)
2½ cups diced celery (see recipe procedures, below)
1¼ cups diced onions (about 1 extra-large onion) (see recipe procedures, below)
2 cups sugar
2 tablespoons plus 1½ teaspoons canning salt (page 704)
2½ teaspoons celery seed
5 cups cider vinegar (5 percent acidity)
2 tablespoons plus 1½ teaspoons dry mustard
1¼ teaspoons ground turmeric

Shuck the corn and carefully remove all the silk. Wash the corn; set aside.

Fill a 12-quart, heavy-bottomed, stainless steel kettle ½ to ⅔ full of water. Cover the kettle. Over high heat, bring the water to a rapid boil. Uncover the kettle.

In small batches, drop the ears of corn into the boiling water and boil exactly 5 minutes. Immediately remove the ears from the water and immerse briefly in cold water to stop the cooking. Place the ears, single layer, on a folded tea towel spread on the kitchen counter or on a large wooden board. Bring the water to a rapid boil before boiling each batch of corn.

Using a medium, sharp knife, cut the kernels from the cobs at about ⅔ the depth of the kernels, leaving on the cobs any small, undeveloped kernels at the ends of the cobs. Do not scrape the cobs. Measure 10 cups corn kernels and place in a mixing bowl; cover and set aside.

Dice the green peppers, red peppers, celery, and onions approximately ¼ inch square. Place each diced vegetable in a separate mixing bowl; set aside.

(Recipe continues on next page)

In an 8-quart, heavy-bottomed, stainless steel kettle, place the sugar, canning salt, and celery seed; stir to combine. Add the vinegar; stir well to combine. Add the green peppers, red peppers, celery, and onions; stir to combine. Over medium-high heat, bring the mixture to a simmer, stirring constantly. Reduce the heat and gently simmer the mixture, uncovered, 5 minutes, stirring occasionally.

Then, in a small mixing bowl, place the mustard, turmeric, and ½ cup of the simmered mixture from the kettle; stir well to combine. Add the mustard mixture to the hot mixture in the kettle; stir to combine. Gently simmer the mixture, uncovered, 5 additional minutes, stirring occasionally.

Remove from the heat. Pour the hot relish into hot, sterilized, pint jars, leaving ½-inch headspace.

Using a plastic knife or a narrow, rubber spatula, remove the air bubbles in the jars. Wipe the jar rims and threads. Place hot metal lids on the jars and screw the bands firmly.

Process in a boiling-water canner for the following time:

Processing Times

Jar Size	Altitude of Canning Location		
	0 to 1,000 ft.	1,001 to 6,000 ft.	Above 6,000 ft.
Pints	15 min.	20 min.	25 min.

Remove the jars from the canner and place on a dry, wooden board which has been covered with a tea towel. Let the jars stand, *undisturbed,* 12 hours to cool completely.

YIELDS ABOUT 9 PINTS

SERVING SUGGESTIONS
- A wonderful accompaniment for ham, fresh pork, beef, poultry, or fish.

- Serve at lunch with sandwiches and soup.

ZUCCHINI RELISH

6½ cups ground zucchini (about 3 pounds zucchini) (see recipe procedures, below)
3½ cups ground onions (about 5 medium onions) (see recipe procedures, below)
1½ cups ground green bell peppers (about 3 large peppers) (see recipe procedures, below)
1½ cups ground red bell peppers (about 3 large peppers) (see recipe procedures, below)
¼ cup plus 2 tablespoons canning salt (page 704)
Cold, distilled water
3 cups cider vinegar (5 percent acidity)
4 cups sugar
2 tablespoons celery seed
1 tablespoon mustard seed

Wash the zucchini. Cut off and discard the ends of the zucchini. Do not pare. Cut the zucchini into large pieces and grind coarsely (page 49). Drain the ground zucchini. Measure 6½ cups ground and drained zucchini; place in a large, stainless steel mixing bowl and set aside.

Cut off the ends and peel the onions. Cut the onions into large pieces and grind coarsely. Drain the ground onions, reserving the juice for use in making Tomato Juice (page 737). Measure 3½ cups ground and drained onions; place in a separate mixing bowl; set aside.

Wash the green peppers. Quarter the peppers lengthwise and cut away the seeds and white portions of the inner flesh. Cut the peppers into large pieces and grind coarsely. Drain the ground peppers, reserving the juice for use in making Tomato Juice. Measure 1½ cups ground and drained green peppers; place in a separate mixing bowl and set aside. Prepare the red peppers, following the same procedure as for the green peppers.

Redrain each of the vegetables. Add the onions, green peppers, and red peppers to the zucchini in the mixing bowl; stir until evenly distributed. Sprinkle the canning salt over the vegetables; stir to combine. Add distilled water to cover the vegetable mixture. Cover the mixing bowl with plastic wrap; let stand 2 hours at cool room temperature.

Then, drain ½ of the vegetables in a sieve, pressing the vegetables with the back of a spoon to remove as much liquid as possible. Place the drained vegetables in a large mixing bowl; set aside. Drain and press the remaining ½ of the vegetables; add to the mixing bowl of drained vegetables and set aside.

In an 8-quart, heavy-bottomed, stainless steel kettle, place the vinegar, sugar, celery seed, and mustard seed; stir to combine. Over high heat, bring the vinegar mixture to a boil, stirring constantly. Reduce the heat to medium-high. Add the vegetables. Bring the mixture to a simmer, stirring constantly. Simmer the mixture, uncovered, 10 minutes, stirring frequently. (Reduce the heat slightly, if necessary.)

Pour the hot relish into hot, sterilized, pint jars, leaving ½-inch headspace.

Using a plastic knife or a narrow, rubber spatula, remove the air bubbles in the jars. Wipe the jar rims and threads. Place hot metal lids on the jars and screw the bands firmly.

Process in a boiling-water canner for the following time:

Processing Times

| Jar Size | Altitude of Canning Location | | |
	0 to 1,000 ft.	1,001 to 6,000 ft.	Above 6,000 ft.
Pints	10 min.	15 min.	20 min.

Remove the jars from the canner and place on a dry, wooden board which has been covered with a tea towel. Let the jars stand, *undisturbed*, 12 hours to cool completely.

YIELDS ABOUT 5 PINTS

SERVING SUGGESTIONS
- Serve with hamburger and wiener sandwiches in the same way as you would serve sweet pickle relish.

- Serve in meat loaf, roast beef, and roast pork sandwiches.

- Serve as a relish with Broiled Ground Beef Patties (page 170) and Grilled Hamburger Steak (page 251).

BELL PEPPER RELISH

The recipe for this winsome-looking sweet relish, which contains equal amounts of green and red bell peppers as well as a generous quantity of onions, comes from my grandmother's cookbook. It is in her handwriting, so I don't know if it is an original recipe of hers or whether she acquired it from another source. She called it Sweet Pepper Hash. Not only is this relish superb-tasting, but also it's versatile, complementing numerous dishes (see the Serving Suggestions for a few of the many ways to use it).

4¼ pounds green bell peppers (about 12 large peppers)
4¼ pounds red bell peppers (about 12 large peppers)
1½ pounds onions (about 3 large onions)
2 cups sugar
2 tablespoons canning salt (page 704)
1 teaspoon ground cinnamon
3½ cups cider vinegar (5 percent acidity)

Wash the green and red peppers. Quarter the peppers lengthwise and cut away the seeds and white portions of the inner flesh. Cut the peppers into large pieces. Place the green and red peppers in separate mixing bowls; set aside.

Cut off the ends and peel the onions. Cut the onions into large pieces and place in a separate mixing bowl; set aside.

Coarsely grind (page 49), separately, the green peppers, red peppers, and onions, placing each of the ground vegetables in a separate mixing bowl. Drain the ground peppers and onions well, reserving the juice for use in making Tomato Juice (page 737).

In an 8-quart, heavy-bottomed, stainless steel kettle, place the ground peppers and onions. Cover the ground vegetables with boiling water;

(Recipe continues on next page)

let stand 10 minutes. Then, drain the vegetables well in a sieve. Return the vegetables to the kettle. Cover the vegetables, again, with boiling water. Over medium-high heat, bring the mixture to a boil.

Remove from the heat. Drain the vegetables well in the sieve. Return the vegetables to the kettle; set aside.

In a large mixing bowl, place the sugar, canning salt, and cinnamon; stir to combine. Add the vinegar; stir well to combine. Pour the vinegar mixture over the vegetables in the kettle; stir until the vegetables are evenly distributed. Over medium-high heat, bring the mixture to a simmer, stirring constantly. Reduce the heat and simmer the mixture, uncovered, 15 minutes, stirring occasionally.

Pour the hot relish into hot, sterilized, pint jars, leaving ½-inch headspace.

Using a plastic knife or a narrow, rubber spatula, remove the air bubbles in the jars. Wipe the jar rims and threads. Place hot metal lids on the jars and screw the bands firmly.

Process in a boiling-water canner for the following time:

Processing Times

Jar Size	Altitude of Canning Location		
	0 to 1,000 ft.	1,001 to 6,000 ft.	Above 6,000 ft.
Pints	10 min.	15 min.	20 min.

Remove the jars from the canner and place on a dry, wooden board which has been covered with a tea towel. Let the jars stand, *undisturbed,* 12 hours to cool completely.

YIELDS ABOUT 8 PINTS

SERVING SUGGESTIONS

• Serve as a condiment with hamburger and wiener sandwiches in the same way as you would serve sweet pickle relish.

• Pass Bell Pepper Relish at the table when serving Alice's Meat and Tater Pie (page 173), Broiled Ground Beef Patties (page 170), Grilled Hamburger Steak (page 251), and Hash (page 172).

PICCALLI

As savory as its name is catchy, Piccalli is made with green tomatoes, cabbage, green and red bell peppers, onions, vinegar, salt, and spices, and is sweetened slightly with brown sugar. Mind you, there is always some acceptable variance in ingredients among recipes of this kind. A favored relish with Midwest canners, Piccalli is one of those down-home yet ultra-gourmet delicacies.

5 cups chopped green tomatoes* (see recipe procedures, below)
7 cups finely shredded cabbage (if available, use a food processor fit with a shredding disk)
2¼ cups chopped onions (if available, use a food processor fit with a steel blade)
1⅔ cups green bell peppers uniformly hand-chopped into pieces approximately ¼ × ⅜ inch
1⅔ cups red red peppers uniformly hand-chopped into pieces approximately ¼ by ⅜ inch
½ cup canning salt (page 704)
3¾ cups cider vinegar (5 percent acidity)
2½ cups packed light brown sugar
2 tablespoons plus 1 teaspoon mixed pickling spice, tied in a cheesecloth bag (page 44)

Do not use tomatoes from dead or frost-killed vines.

AFTERNOON OF THE FIRST DAY: Wash the tomatoes. In batches, blanch the tomatoes (page 44) 2 minutes and immediately immerse them in cold water; drain. Remove the stem ends (see Note) and peel the tomatoes. Remove the tiny blossom ends. Cut the tomatoes lengthwise into quarters or sixths, depending upon their size. Remove and discard as many of the seeds and as much of the pouches containing them as possible (page 45) (they are more difficult to remove in green tomatoes). Cut away the cores (page 45).

Chop the tomatoes. (If available, use a food processor fit with a steel blade.)

Measure 5 cups chopped tomatoes and place in an 8-quart, stainless steel kettle. Add the cabbage, onions, green peppers, red peppers, and canning salt; stir to combine. Cover the kettle; let stand, at cool room temperature, overnight.

THE NEXT DAY: Place ⅓ of the prepared vegetables in the center of a clean, thin tea towel. Pull the corners of the tea towel tautly over the vegetables. With your hands, wring the tea towel of vegetables and press it on the bottom of a colander to remove as much liquid as possible. Place the drained vegetables in a large mixing bowl; cover and set aside. Repeat the procedure 2 more times to drain the remaining vegetables, adding them to the mixing bowl of drained vegetables.

In a clean, 8-quart, heavy-bottomed, stainless steel kettle, place the vinegar and brown sugar; stir to combine. Add the cheesecloth bag of pickling spice. Over medium-high heat, bring the vinegar mixture to a boil, stirring until the brown sugar dissolves. Reduce the heat to medium and boil the vinegar mixture (syrup) at a moderate rate, uncovered, 5 minutes, stirring frequently.

Remove from the heat. Add the vegetables; stir to combine. Over medium-high heat, bring the mixture to a boil, stirring constantly. Reduce the heat slightly and boil the mixture, uncovered, 2 minutes, stirring intermittently.

Remove from the heat. Remove and discard the cheesecloth bag. Pack the hot relish into hot, sterilized, pint jars, leaving ½-inch headspace. Pour the remaining syrup equally into the filled jars, maintaining ½-inch headspace.

Using a plastic knife or a narrow, rubber spatula, remove the air bubbles in the jars. Wipe the jar rims and threads. Place hot metal lids on the jars and screw the bands firmly.

Process in a boiling-water canner for the following time:

Processing Times

Jar Size	Altitude of Canning Location		
	0 to 1,000 ft.	1,001 to 6,000 ft.	Above 6,000 ft.
Pints	5 min.	10 min.	15 min.

Remove the jars from the canner and place on a dry, wooden board which has been covered with a tea towel. Let the jars stand, *undisturbed,* 12 hours to cool completely.

NOTE: A tomato corer is a handy, inexpensive kitchen tool to use for this task.

YIELDS ABOUT 4 PINTS

TOMATO CATSUP

When most of us hear the word "catsup" or "ketchup" (either spelling is correct), we think of tomato catsup, perhaps America's best-loved (and some might say "overused") condiment. But many kinds of catsup besides tomato catsup were made with regularity in earlier days. Mushroom, walnut (made with green English walnuts), and celery catsup, as well as many fruit catsups, such as grape, plum, apple, and cranberry, were among the most poular. In nineteenth-century Midwest state fair premium lists I have seen, tomato catsup and cucumber catsup appeared to be listed the most often for judging. Currently, there is a class for "Fruit Ketchup (plums, berries, etc.)" in the large Recipes of Yesteryear division at the Iowa State Fair. I wonder why the many intriguing catsups fell by the wayside? These interesting condiments would seem to be stylish enhancers for some of today's most popular foods like chicken breasts, broiled fish, and lean meats. Happily, some of these now-uncommon catsups sometimes turn up in gourmet stores for rediscovery.

Taking into account the broader horizon of catsup, it is defined, as follows: A thick sauce consisting of a pureed food (often including onions), vinegar, spices, salt, and usually sugar, used as a condiment especially with meats, fish, poultry, eggs, and certain vegetables. It also is used as an ingredient in cooking.

(Recipe continues on next page)

1½ cups cider vinegar (5 percent acidity)
2 3-inch pieces stick cinnamon
1 tablespoon celery seed
2 teaspoons whole cloves
1 teaspoon whole allspice
12 pounds tomatoes
1½ cups chopped onions
1 garlic clove, pressed
1 cup sugar
2 tablespoons salt
⅛ teaspoon cayenne pepper

THE FIRST DAY: In a small, stainless steel saucepan, place the vinegar, stick cinnamon, celery seed, cloves, and allspice. Cover the saucepan. Over high heat, bring the vinegar mixture to a boil. Remove from the heat and let stand at room temperature until incorporated into the recipe the next day. This allows time for the spices to steep in the vinegar and for the flavors to blend.

THE NEXT DAY: Wash the tomatoes. In batches, blanch the tomatoes (page 44) 45 seconds and immediately immerse them in cold water; drain. Remove the stem ends (see Note 1), peel, remove the tiny blossom ends, quarter, and seed and core the tomatoes (page 45). As the tomatoes are prepared, drop them into an 8-quart, heavy-bottomed, stainless steel kettle.

Using a potato masher, crush the tomatoes in the kettle; cover and set aside.

In a blender beaker, place the chopped onions; using the blender, puree. Add the pureed onions and pressed garlic to the crushed tomatoes in the kettle; stir to combine. Cover the kettle. Over medium-high heat, bring the tomato mixture to a simmer, stirring frequently to prevent the mixture from scorching on the bottom of the kettle. Uncover the kettle. Reduce the heat and simmer the tomato mixture 20 minutes, stirring frequently.

Press the tomato mixture through a food mill. Return the mixture to the kettle and cover. Over medium-high heat, bring the tomato mixture to a simmer, stirring frequently. Uncover the kettle. Reduce the heat and simmer the

tomato mixture until the volume is reduced by one-half (about 1 hour), stirring very frequently to prevent scorching. Remove from the heat and set aside.

Secure a piece of cotton flannel, napped side up, in a sieve over a deep pan; set aside.

Over high heat, bring the vinegar mixture to a boil. Remove from the heat. Remove and discard the stick cinnamon. Pour the vinegar mixture over the cotton flannel in the sieve to strain.

Add the strained vinegar mixture, sugar, salt, and cayenne pepper to the tomato mixture; stir to combine. Over medium-high heat, bring the tomato mixture to a simmer, stirring constantly. Reduce the heat and cook the mixture, uncovered, at a low simmer, until the catsup is reduced to the point that it will mound on a spoon without separation, stirring nearly constantly to prevent scorching.

Pour the hot catsup into hot, sterilized, pint jars, leaving ⅛-inch headspace. Wipe the jar rims and threads. Place hot metal lids on the jars and screw the bands firmly.

Process in a boiling-water canner for the following time:

Processing Times

Jar Size	Altitude of Canning Location		
	0 to 1,000 ft.	1,001 to 6,000 ft.	Above 6,000 ft.
Pints	15 min.	20 min.	25 min.

Remove the jars from the canner and place on a dry, wooden board which has been covered with a tea towel. Let the jars stand, *undisturbed*, 12 hours to cool completely.

NOTE 1: A tomato corer is a handy, inexpensive kitchen tool to use for this task.

NOTE 2: This recipe may be doubled.

YIELDS ABOUT 3 PINTS

VARIATION: To prepare hot catsup, increase the cayenne pepper to ¼ teaspoon.

CHILI SAUCE

One of the best, most typical of all Midwest homemade relishes is Chili Sauce. Like most other homemade relishes and pickled foods, commercial imitations do not hold a candle to the luscious, spicy culinary aristocrat created in the home kitchen. Although commercial chili sauce is a good product and I particularly like it for making Cocktail Sauce (page 361), it is quite different from homemade Chili Sauce which is more like a salsa in texture and flavor. Homemade Chili Sauce is used most often as a condiment (page 21), much in the same way and with the same foods as tomato catsup. It is excellent on meat loaf and ground beef.

16 cups tomato pulp (about 8 gallons tomatoes) (see recipe procedures, below)
2 cups ground green bell peppers (about 4 large peppers) (see recipe procedures, below)
⅔ cup ground red bell peppers (about 2 large peppers) (see recipe procedures, below)
4 cups ground onions (about 5 large onions) (see recipe procedures, below)
1 small, hot pepper
2 cups sugar
2 tablespoons canning salt (page 704)
½ teaspoon paprika
2½ cups cider vinegar (5 percent acidity)
3 4-inch pieces stick cinnamon
1 tablespoon plus 1 teaspoon whole cloves, tied in a cheesecloth bag (page 44)

Wash the tomatoes. In batches, blanch the tomatoes (page 44) 1 minute and immediately immerse them in cold water; drain. Remove the stem ends (see Note), peel, remove the tiny blossom ends, quarter, and seed and core the tomatoes (page 45). Pour off the surplus juice, reserving the juice for use in making Tomato Juice (page 737).

Using a blender, process the tomatoes, in batches, for 1 to 2 seconds to make pulp. Be careful not to overprocess the tomatoes and make juice.

Measure 16 cups tomato pulp and pour into an 8-quart, heavy-bottomed, stainless steel kettle; set aside.

Grind fairly coarsely (page 49) green peppers. Drain the ground green peppers, reserving the juice for use in making Tomato Juice (page 737). Measure 2 cups (ground and drained) green peppers; set aside.

Following the same procedure, grind, drain, and measure ⅔ cup ground red peppers and 4 cups ground onions, reserving the juice for use in making Tomato Juice, and setting aside each vegetable separately. Grind the hot pepper.

To the tomato pulp in the kettle, add the green peppers, red peppers, onions, hot pepper, sugar, canning salt, paprika, and vinegar; stir to combine. Over medium-high heat, bring the mixture to a simmer, stirring constantly. Reduce the heat and cook the mixture, uncovered, at a low simmer, for 30 minutes, stirring frequently. Add the stick cinnamon and cheesecloth bag of cloves. Continue simmering the mixture very slowly, uncovered, an additional 1½ hours, or until the mixture reaches the desired thickness, stirring frequently to prevent scorching.

Remove from the heat. Remove and discard the stick cinnamon and cheesecloth bag. Pour the hot Chili Sauce into hot, sterilized, pint jars, leaving ½-inch headspace. Wipe the jar rims and threads. Place hot metal lids on the jars and screw the bands firmly.

Process in a boiling water canner for the following time:

Processing Times

Jar Size	Altitude of Canning Location		
	0 to 1,000 ft.	1,001 to 6,000 ft.	Above 6,000 ft.
Pints	15 min.	20 min.	25 min.

Remove the jars from the canner and place on a dry, wooden board which has been covered with a tea towel. Let the jars stand, *undisturbed,* 12 hours to cool completely.

NOTE: A tomato corer is a handy, inexpensive kitchen tool to use for this task.

YIELDS ABOUT 8 PINTS

Nutrition

A Practical Approach to Nutrition
(or, You Can Be Trim and Eat the Good Stuff Too)

Y ou don't have to give up Butterscotch Pie and Chocolate Cake to be healthy and thin. You just have to moderate the *frequency* with which you eat them and the *quantity* you eat when you partake.

It's a shame to be denied some of the most delectable things in the world to eat merely because of not applying the discipline to control consumption of them. It is equally regrettable to throw in the towel and indulge in unconstrained eating habits that undermine our feeling of well-being, place us on the hazardous path to health problems, and play havoc with our appearance. It takes all the fun out of the self-indulgence.

Most healthy people can go through life enjoying the luxury of eating all the phenomenally delicious and tempting foods culinarians have to offer if an overall plan as well as common sense are applied throughout. North of the taste buds, there is another part of the human anatomy which must be engaged in order to implement and sustain proper eating habits—the brain, management headquarters for reasoning, decision making, and monitoring.

It's not that we're dealing with some yet uncharted field of study lacking in scientifically reliable conclusions. The bottom-line findings supported by scientific research and endorsed by the medical profession and nutritionists are fairly simple: (1) If we eat more calories than we use, we gain weight.[1] (2) No more than 30 percent of our daily calorie intake should be in fat and no more than one-third of that total fat intake should be in saturated fat.[2] (3) We should follow diets low in dietary cholesterol.[3]

A Mayo Clinic medical essay reports that "Ounce for ounce, fat provides more than twice as many calories as protein or carbohydrate (nine calories vs. four)."[4] Further, even when the number of calories is equal, a person consuming a diet high in fat tends to store more excess calories in body fat than a person consuming a lower-fat diet. According to the Mayo essay, "Less than 5 percent of all cases of obesity can be traced to a metabolic disorder or hormonal imbalances."[5]

Weight control and a balanced diet require adoption of a sustained, lifetime habit of proper eating. It does little good to go on a crash diet and then drift back into former bad habits which quickly return the body to the starting point. As intelligent as we are, we search desperately for magical solutions to our weight problems which circumvent what we perceive as our locked-in, unchangeable eating habits. Save the time, energy, and money—such solutions exist only in our fantasies.

The concept of food substitution is only a partial answer. We like to believe that we can retain our patterns of volume eating and over-consumption of the less healthy types of foods we have grown accustomed to while simultaneously losing weight and lowering our cholesterol, solely by substituting similar but more nutritionally acceptable foods for the culprits. That approach certainly has its merits and is vastly better than no planned effort at all; however, the substituted foods are often less satisfying because they are less tasty and, over time, we tend to creep back to the fond foods we were in the habit of eating. Plus, calories can add up surprisingly fast when eating high volumes even of many healthful foods.

The only lasting solution is to alter our habits. Rather than substituting two no-yolk eggs for two whole, real eggs, seven breakfasts a week, to lower cholesterol intake, the pattern needs changing. One whole, real egg with an English muffin two mornings a week and whole-grain cereal with fruit and skim milk the other five mornings is a habit-changing solution.

If your downfall is ice cream, rather than substituting lowfat frozen yogurt for the ice cream you have been in the habit of eating virtually every night for dessert, plan to have ice cream for dessert only once every week or two, and on those evenings, place only one moderately sized scoop in your dish rather than two giant ones, and spoon blueberries or strawberries over the top. You don't have to settle for frozen yogurt on those occasions. Revel in rich, incredible, real ice cream. Keep a colorful selection of lusciously juicy seasonal fruit on hand for refreshing desserts until it's time to break out the ice cream again. Why go through the rest of your life without ice cream?

In addition to the ice cream, every now and then fix a high-calorie, rich dessert made with butter, eggs, and all the ingredients which make it sumptuous. If it's brownies, eat one or two reasonably small bars frosted with plenty of sinfully rich chocolate frosting when they're fresh out of the pan. Set aside a couple of additional bars to savor the following day. If your family is small, give remaining brownies to friends and neighbors. If there are only two of you, for heaven's sake don't plan on eating brownies every day until they're gone. That would defeat your ability to eat them at all. Take your pick: a moderate quantity of the desserts you love best, or no rich desserts at all.

In general, many people need to cut down on the volume of food they eat. With machines doing much of the labor-intensive work nowadays, most Americans require less food and fewer calories than in previous decades to provide adequate energy and sustain healthy bodies.

How much food and how many calories are enough? That varies from person to person, depending upon age, gender, current weight, height, bone structure, level of physical activity, and other factors. As a general rule, reducing your daily calorie intake by 250 calories can help you lose about one-half pound per week (3,500 calories = 1 pound of fat).[6]

To methodically adopt an informed, pragmatic

nutrition plan, determine the number of daily calories you should be consuming in consultation with a medical doctor and/or a nutritionist. Then, plan *well-balanced* meals which do not exceed that daily calorie level. Become knowledgeable yourself about the nutritional values of foods and keep up to date on the United States government's latest recommendations for healthy eating. *Nutrition and Your Health: Dietary Guidelines for Americans* and *The Food Guide Pyramid* are basic reading. (See Dietary Guidelines for Americans, page 788, for excerpts and edited extractions from these United States government booklets, and for information about securing copies of these publications.)

With careful thought, place a planned portion of food on your plate and eat *no more*. It is not necessary to eat until you are full to eat properly. Sometimes, you could eat much more if you would let yourself. But don't. Working against you is the fact that it takes your brain approximately 20 minutes to receive the message that you are full.[7] When you know, based upon your professionally advised plan, that your body is getting the calories and nutrition it needs to sustain the life you lead, it is easier to stop eating. Don't let your mind dwell on more food you know you don't need. Instead, switch your thoughts to the table conversation or your work or recreation at hand. You will soon forget that you wanted more food.

Of course, a change in eating habits is a challenge for all of us. But the good news is that newly adopted, more healthful eating patterns become as habitual as the former, detrimental ones. And the fabulous benefits and satisfaction derived from the new habits reinforce continuation of them.

Eating three meals a day at approximately the same times and eating nothing, or very, very little, between those meals are vital conventions. Breakfast should not be something that happens only on the weekends. If it has not been a part of your normal routine, adding it to your schedule may require going to bed earlier and getting up earlier. Sleep time should not be reduced as you adopt a more healthful eating schedule.

If you get hungry in the middle of the afternoon, eating a celery or carrot stick, a small piece of fresh fruit, or a couple of whole-wheat crackers will help appease your appetite. Or, grab a piece of hard candy or a few cashews (single nuts, not handsful). Drinking a glass of water or lemonade often does the trick.

While drinking plenty of liquids is essential to a healthful diet plan (water is the best), the habit of either eating or drinking something all the time should be broken. Drinking pop (soda) all day long is symptomatic of this unhealthy eating syndrome.

Caffeine consumption should be kept minimal or, optimally, eliminated. Many healthy people drink a small amount of coffee or tea in the morning to get themselves going, and sometimes drink a pick-me-up cup of tea in the afternoon. Mixing a small amount of regular coffee with decaffeinated coffee can be a satisfying way to restricting your morning caffeine consumption. By all means, caffeine should not be routinely used to supplant sleep. This red-letter health mandate should be incorporated into any reasoned, healthy lifestyle.

Mealtimes should be highlights of the day and of life. Deliciously prepared and nicely served meals enjoyed with family and friends are a chunk of what life is all about. But eating needs to be kept in perspective. It should not be used as a psychological gratification in lieu of pursuing other worthwhile causes and efforts in life from which true, lasting satisfactions are earned and gained. Eating should not be a thoughtless, haphazard, undisciplined activity.

To achieve and maintain a healthy, supple, trim body, proper eating must be coupled with an established habit of exercise. Regular exercise, such as brisk walking or other aerobic exercise for a duration of 30 minutes several times a week, accomplishes much more than burning calories. The June, 1994 *Mayo Clinic Health Letter* includes the startling statement that "Regular exercise (about three to four times a week) reduces risk of death from all causes, including cardiovascular disease and cancer, by about 70 percent."[8] In addition to being beneficial to numerous heart functions, regular exercise increases levels of high-density lipoprotein (good) cholesterol and decreases levels of low-density and very low-density lipoprotein (bad) cholesterol and triglycerides, and can prevent or reduce high blood pressure.[9]

Stretching is a critical component of a well-designed exercise program. It helps achieve body flexibility and is an essential part of properly warming up the body before safely commencing most aerobic exercise. Our bodies are like jet airplanes. The pilot warms them up before taxiing down the runway for takeoff.

A conscientious program of exercise will improve your appearance by helping you increase muscle and lose fat. As we get older, the amount of muscle tends to decrease and body fat accounts for a greater percentage of our weight.[10] Not only does more muscle give us a firmer, better looking body, but also, muscle uses more calories than fat which assists us in the maintenance of proper weight.[11]

An exercise program should be launched under the guidance of a medical doctor. This is especially important if you plan to initiate a particularly vigorous type of exercise routine, or have existing health problems, or if exercise has not been a part of your life for many years.

It takes both proper eating and regular exercise built into your daily life to get the job done. We all probably have observed diligent, overweight sidewalk or mall walkers who, like clockwork, go through their paces every morning, and one year later appear not to have lost an ounce. While they have derived health benefits from the exercise, weightwise the only benefit they have realized from their steadfast exercising is an ability to overeat even more without putting on additional pounds. Depending upon the extent to which they are overweight and the general physical shape they are in, the months of sustained exercise could be harming their knees and backs by exacerbating the burden of too much weight on these body parts.

On the other side of the coin, dieting, without a concurrent exercise program, can reduce us to an acceptable weight level, but leave us saddled with flabby bodies. Of even greater consequence, the loss of weight alone may not mitigate existing health problems or help protect us against future health and life-threatening maladies.

When confronted with the need for weight loss and maintenance, we run scared at the forbidding thought of "forever." Most people are not willing to give up the foods they love forever, and they shouldn't have to. Heading into a diet to lose weight, most of us can do a pretty conscientious job of deprivation for a few weeks or months, but when our weight goal is close to attainment, we may revert to eating the foods of which we have been deprived, and all that was lost is soon gained back. Lifelong deprivation usually does not work. Adoption of new lifetime eating habits which include the rich foods most human beings love, but with *less frequency* and in *less quantity,* does work. That is a much more realistic, workable, and may I go so far as to say humane approach to good nutrition.

With such an approach, getting into shape can actually be fun—a challenge to be met and conquered just like all the other challenges we face every day. Achieving a healthy lifestyle can be enormously satisfying, and improve self-image and self-confidence. Being in control of oneself has euphoric fallout. In the morning, you catch a peek at your slim self in the mirror as you dress for the day. You think how wonderful it feels to have the vim to face the day with energy and enthusiasm, and not to be flirting with high blood pressure; high cholesterol; and knee, back, and leg problems due to improper eating, too much weight, and lack of exercise.

It takes stick-to-itiveness, but it's worth it. When you courteously listen to overweight friends and acquaintances carry on about their new diets as they self-righteously order greens without dressing for lunch, you are gracefully (f.) or dapperly (m.) seated across from them in your stylish suit which drapes handsomely over your trim body, and you proceed to order chocolate mousse for dessert—your splurge for the week, to be balanced with a carefully selected dinner that evening. If you happen to be a small person on a low-calorie diet, you may decide the serving is just too much, in which case you eat only half of it before asking the waiter to please remove the plate. You don't mind—you have learned that eating the remainder would have had diminishing taste returns. Moderation allows the pleasure of experiencing all good things.

Rose Lorenz Schwartz, my former dancing teacher who has been such an inspiration to me, and who is one of the people to whom this book is dedicated, remained slim and lithe, teaching dancing weekly to one thousand senior-citizen students in Sun City, Arizona, until just a few weeks before her recent death at age ninety-five. Perhaps you have read about her or have seen her featured on national television. Rose used to tell me: "When I am tempted to eat too much, I just remind myself that another bite is only a taste in my mouth for a few seconds and then it's gone. I have already had the pleasure of eating the food and benefiting from its nutritional value." I have been grateful for her words of wisdom. In a letter I received from her not too long ago, she said, "I attribute my health to my lifestyle, which is to eat right, get lots of rest, and EXERCISE." Simple, but such important advice.

[1]Mayo Foundation for Medical Education and Research, "Weight Control: What Works and Why," Mayo Clinic Health Letter, supplement: medical essay (June 1994): 2.

[2]U.S. Department of Agriculture and U.S. Department of Health and Human Services, Home and Garden Bulletin No. 232: Nutrition and Your Health: Dietary Guidelines for Americans, 4th ed. ([Washington, D.C.]: U.S. Department of Agriculture and U.S. Department of Health and Human Services, December 1995), 27–28.

[3]Ibid., 30.

[4]Mayo Foundation for Medical Education and Research, "Weight Control: What Works and Why," 3.

[5]Ibid., 3.

[6]Ibid., 5.

[7]Mayo Foundation for Medical Education and Research, "Health Tips: Curbing Your Appetite," Mayo Clinic Health Letter 12, no. 3 (March 1994): 5.

[8]Mayo Foundation for Medical Education and Research, "Exercise: Are the Risks Underplayed and the Benefits Overdone?," Mayo Clinic Health Letter 12, no. 6 (June 1994): 2.

[9]Ibid.

[10]Mayo Foundation for Medical Education and Research, "Weight Control: What Works and Why," 2–3.

[11]Ibid., 2, 5–6.

Dietary Guidelines for Americans

This section consists of excerpts and edited extractions from the following two booklets:

NUTRITION AND YOUR HEALTH: DIETARY GUIDELINES FOR AMERICANS (Home and Garden Bulletin No. 232), fourth edition, December 1995, published by the U.S. Department of Agriculture and the U.S. Department of Health and Human Services.

THE FOOD GUIDE PYRAMID (Home and Garden Bulletin No. 252), revised, October 1996, published by the U.S. Department of Agriculture, Center for Nutrition Policy and Promotion.

These booklets contain the United States government's latest recommendations to Americans for a healthful diet as of the dates of their publication.

For information about securing copies of these and other United States government publications on nutrition, write or call:

Consumer Information Center
Pueblo, Colorado 81009
Telephone 888-878-3256

The booklets may also be accessed through the CNPP (USDA's Center for Nutrition Policy and Promotion) Home Page (World Wide Web) at: http://www.usda.gov/fcs/cnpp.html

THE 7 DIETARY GUIDELINES FOR AMERICANS

The Dietary Guidelines for Americans provide advice for healthy Americans age 2 years and over about food choices that promote health and prevent disease. The seven dietary guidelines for Americans are:

- Eat a variety of foods.

- Balance the food you eat with physical activity—maintain or improve your weight.

- Choose a diet with plenty of grain products, vegetables, and fruits.

- Choose a diet low in fat, saturated fat, and cholesterol.

- Choose a diet moderate in sugars.

- Choose a diet moderate in salt and sodium.

- If you drink alcoholic beverages, do so in moderation.

Healthful diets enable people of all ages to work productively and feel their best. Food choices also can help to reduce the risk for chronic diseases, such as heart disease, certain cancers, diabetes, stroke, and osteoporosis, that are leading causes of death and disability among Americans. Good diets can reduce major risk factors for chronic diseases—factors such as obesity, high blood pressure, and high blood cholesterol.

Foods contain energy, nutrients, and other components that affect health. People require energy and certain other essential nutrients. These nutrients are essential because the body cannot make them and must obtain them from food. Essential nutrients include vitamins, minerals, certain amino acids, and certain fatty acids. Foods also contain other components such as fiber that are important for health. Although each of these food components has a specific function in the body, all of them together are required for overall health.

The carbohydrates, fats, and proteins in food supply energy, which is measured in calories. Carbohydrates and proteins provide about 4 calories per gram. Fat contributes more than twice as much—about 9 calories per gram. Alcohol, although not a nutrient, also supplies energy— about 7 calories per gram. While foods that are high in fat are also high in calories, many lowfat or nonfat foods also can be high in calories.

Physical activity fosters a healthful diet. Calorie needs vary by age and level of activity. Many older adults need less food, in part due to decreased activity compared with younger, more active individuals. Nearly all Americans need to be more active because a sedentary lifestyle is unhealthful. Increasing the calories spent in daily activities helps to maintain health and allows people to eat a nutritious and enjoyable diet.

The following calorie level suggestions for adults and teens are based on recommendations of the National Academy of Sciences and on calorie intakes reported by people in national food consumption surveys:

- 1,600 calories a day is about right for many sedentary women and some older adults.

- 2,200 calories a day is about right for most children, teenage girls, active women, and many sedentary men. Women who are pregnant or breastfeeding may need somewhat more.

- 2,800 calories a day is about right for teenage boys, many active men, and some very active women.

It is hard to know how much food children need to grow normally. If you are unsure, check with your doctor. Preschool children need the same variety of foods as older family members do, but may need less than 1,600 calories. For fewer calories, they can eat smaller servings. However, it is important that they have the equivalent of 2 cups of milk a day.

The Recommended Dietary Allowances represent the amounts of nutrients that are adequate to meet the needs of most healthy people. Although people with average nutrient requirements likely eat adequately at levels below the Recommended Dietary Allowances, diets that meet the Recommended Dietary Allowances are almost certain to ensure intake of enough essential nutrients by most healthy people. The Dietary Guidelines describe food choices that will help you meet these recommendations. Like the Recommended Daily Allowances, the Dietary Guidelines apply to diets consumed over several days and not to single meals or foods.

The Food Guide Pyramid (pictured on page 790) and the Nutrition Facts Label (sample shown on page 790) serve as educational tools to put the Dietary Guidelines into practice. The

Pyramid translates the Recommended Dietary Allowances and the Dietary Guidelines into the kinds and amounts of food to eat each day. The Nutrition Facts Label is designed to help you select foods for a diet that will meet the Dietary Guidelines. Most processed foods now include nutrition information. However, nutrition labels are not required for foods like coffee and tea (which contain no significant amounts of nutrients), certain ready-to-eat foods like unpackaged deli and bakery items, and restaurant food. Labels are also voluntary for many raw foods— your grocer may supply this information for the fish, meat, poultry, and raw fruits and vegetables that are consumed most frequently.

EAT A VARIETY OF FOODS. No single food can supply all nutrients in the amounts you need. To make sure you get all of the nutrients and other substances needed for health, choose the recommended number of daily servings from each of the five major food groups displayed in the Food Guide Pyramid. The Food Guide Pyramid illustrates the importance of balance among food groups in a daily eating pattern.

• Choose most of your foods from the grain products group (6 to 11 servings), the vegetable group (3 to 5 servings), and the fruit group (2 to 4 servings).

Food Guide Pyramid

Source: U.S. Department of Agriculture/U.S. Department of Health and Human Services

Sample Nutrition Facts Label
COOKIES

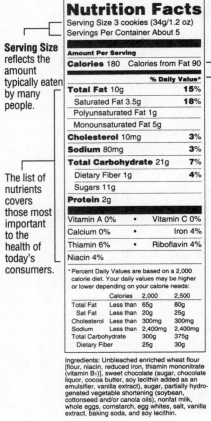

• Eat moderate amounts of foods from the milk group (2 to 3 servings) and the meat and beans group (2 to 3 servings).

• Choose sparingly foods that provide few nutrients and are high in fat and sugars.

A range of servings is given for each food group. The smaller number is for people who consume about 1,600 calories a day, such as many sedentary women. The larger number is for those who consume about 2,800 calories a day, such as active men.

What counts as a serving? The following are suggested serving sizes in the Food Guide Pyramid food groups:

Bread, Cereal, Rice, and Pasta Group

- 1 slice of bread
- 1 ounce of ready-to-eat cereal
- ½ cup of cooked cereal, rice, or pasta

Vegetable Group

- 1 cup of raw leafy vegetables
- ½ cup of other vegetables—cooked or chopped raw
- ¾ cup of vegetable juice

Fruit Group

- 1 medium apple, banana, orange
- ½ cup of chopped, cooked, or canned fruit
- ¾ cup of fruit juice

Milk, Yogurt, and Cheese Group

- 1 cup of milk or yogurt
- 1½ ounces of natural cheese
- 2 ounces of processed cheese

Meat, Poultry, Fish, Dry Beans, Eggs, and Nuts Group

- 2 to 3 ounces of cooked lean meat, poultry, or fish
- ½ cup of cooked dry beans or 1 egg counts as 1 ounce of lean meat. Two tablespoons of peanut butter or ⅓ cup of nuts counts as 1 ounce of meat.

Some foods fit into more than one group. Dry beans, peas, and lentils may be counted as servings in either the meat and beans group or the vegetable group. These "crossover" foods may be counted as servings from either one or the other group, but not from both.

Choosing a variety of foods within and across food groups improves dietary patterns because foods within the same group have different combinations of nutrients and other beneficial substances. People who do not need many calories or who must restrict their food intake need to choose nutrient-rich foods from the five major food groups with special care. They should obtain most of their calories from foods that contain a high proportion of essential nutrients and fiber.

Many women and adolescent girls need to eat more calcium-rich foods to get the calcium needed for healthy bones throughout life. By selecting lowfat or fat-free milk products and other lowfat calcium sources, they can obtain adequate calcium and keep fat intake from being too high.

Some good sources of calcium are:

- Most foods in the milk group*
  - ~ milk and dishes made with milk, such as puddings and soups made with milk
  - ~ cheeses, such as mozzarella, cheddar, Swiss, and Parmesan
  - ~ yogurt
- Canned fish with soft bones, such as sardines, anchovies, and salmon*
- Dark green leafy vegetables, such as kale, mustard greens, and turnip greens, and bok choy
- Tofu, if processed with calcium sulfate. Read the labels.
- Tortillas made from lime-processed corn. Read the labels.

Some foods in this group are high in fat, cholesterol, or both. Choose lower fat, lower cholesterol foods most often. Read the labels.

Young children, teenage girls, and women of childbearing age should also eat enough iron-rich foods, such as lean meats and whole-grain or enriched white bread, to keep the body's iron stores at adequate levels.

Some good sources of iron are:

- Meats—beef, pork, lamb, and liver and other organ meats*

- Poultry—chicken, duck, and turkey, especially dark meat; liver*

- Fish—shellfish, like clams, mussels, and oysters; sardines; anchovies; and other fish*

- Leafy greens of the cabbage family, such as broccoli, kale, turnip greens, and collards

- Legumes, such as lima beans and green peas; dry beans and peas, such as pinto beans, black-eyed peas, and canned baked beans

- Yeast-leavened whole-wheat bread and rolls

- Iron-enriched white bread, pasta, rice, and cereals. Read the labels.

Some foods in this group are high in fat, cholesterol, or both. Choose lean, lower fat, lower cholesterol foods most often. Read the labels.

Supplements of vitamins, minerals, or fiber also may help to meet special nutritional needs. However, supplements do not supply all of the nutrients and other substances present in foods that are important to health. Supplements of some nutrients taken regularly in large amounts are harmful. Daily vitamin and mineral supplements at or below the Recommended Dietary Allowances are considered safe, but usually are not needed by people who eat the variety of foods depicted in the Food Guide Pyramid.

Sometimes supplements are needed to meet specific nutrient requirements. For example, older people and others with little exposure to sunlight may need a vitamin D supplement. Women of childbearing age may reduce the risk of certain birth defects by consuming folate-rich foods or folic acid supplements. Iron supplements are recommended for pregnant women. However, because foods contain many nutrients and other substances that promote health, the use of supplements cannot substitute for proper food choices.

BALANCE THE FOOD YOU EAT WITH PHYSICAL ACTIVITY—MAINTAIN OR IMPROVE YOUR WEIGHT. Many Americans gain weight in adulthood, increasing their risk for high blood pressure, heart disease, stroke, diabetes, certain types of cancer, arthritis, breathing problems, and other illness. Therefore, most adults should not gain weight. If you are overweight and have one of these problems, you should try to lose weight, or at the very least, not gain weight. If you are uncertain about your risk of developing a problem associated with overweight, you should consult a health professional.

In order to stay at the same body weight, people must balance the amount of calories in the foods and drinks they consume with the amount of calories the body uses. Physical activity is an important way to use food energy. Most Americans spend much of their working day in activities that require little energy. In addition, many Americans of all ages now spend a lot of leisure time each day being inactive; for example, watching television or working at a computer. To burn calories, devote less time to sedentary activities like sitting. Spend more time in activities like walking to the store or around the block. Use stairs rather than elevators. Less sedentary activity and more vigorous activity may help you reduce body fat and disease risk. Try to do 30 minutes or more of moderate physical activity on most—preferably all—days of the week.

Even when people eat less high-fat food, they still can gain weight from eating too much of foods high in starch, sugars, or protein.

The pattern of eating may also be important. Snacks provide a large percentage of daily calories for many Americans. Unless nutritious snacks are part of the daily meal plan, snacking may lead to weight gain. A pattern of frequent binge-eating, with or without alternating periods of food restriction, may also contribute to weight problems.

Healthy weight *ranges* for adult men and women of all ages are shown in the graph on page 793.

The health risks due to excess weight appear to be the same for older as for younger adults.

Healthy Weight Ranges for Adults

ARE YOU OVERWEIGHT?

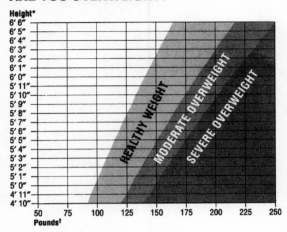

Height*
6' 6"
6' 5"
6' 4"
6' 3"
6' 2"
6' 1"
6' 0"
5' 11"
5' 10"
5' 9"
5' 8"
5' 7"
5' 6"
5' 5"
5' 4"
5' 3"
5' 2"
5' 1"
5' 0"
4' 11"
4' 10"

HEALTHY WEIGHT   MODERATE OVERWEIGHT   SEVERE OVERWEIGHT

50   75   100   125   150   175   200   225   250
Pounds†

* Without shoes.

† Without clothes. The higher weights apply to people with more muscle and bone, such as many men.

Source: Report of the Dietary Guidelines Advisory Committee on the Dietary Guidelines for Americans, 1995, pages 23-24.

Weight ranges are shown in the chart because people of the same height may have equal amounts of body fat but different amounts of muscle and bone. However, the ranges do not mean that it is healthy to gain weight, even within the same weight range. The higher weights in the healthy weight range apply to people with more muscle and bone.

Weights above the healthy weight range are less healthy for most people. The further you are above the healthy weight range for your height, the higher your weight-related risk. Weights slightly below the range may be healthy for some people but are sometimes the result of health problems, especially when weight loss is unintentional.

Research suggests that the location of body fat also is an important factor in health risks for adults. Excess fat in the abdomen (stomach area) is a greater health risk than excess fat in the hips and thighs. Extra fat in the abdomen is linked to high blood pressure, diabetes, early heart disease, and certain types of cancer. Smoking and too much alcohol increase abdominal fat and the risk for diseases related to obesity. Vigorous exercise helps to reduce abdominal fat and decrease the risk for these diseases. The easiest way to check your body fat distribution is to measure around your waistline with a tape measure and compare this with the measure around your hips or buttocks to see if your abdomen is larger. If you are in doubt, you may wish to seek advice from a health professional.

You do not need to lose weight if your weight is already within the healthy range in the graph, if you have gained less than 10 pounds since you reached your adult height, and if you are otherwise healthy. If you are overweight and have excess abdominal fat, a weight-related medical problem, or a family history of such problems, you need to lose weight. Healthy diets and exercise can help people maintain a healthy weight, and may also help them lose weight.

It is important to recognize that overweight is a chronic condition which can only be controlled with long-term changes. As people lose weight, the body becomes more efficient at using energy and the rate of weight loss may decrease. Increased physical activity will help you to continue losing weight and to avoid gaining it back.

Many people are not sure how much weight they should lose. Weight loss of only 5 to 10 percent of body weight may improve many of the problems associated with overweight, such as high blood pressure and diabetes. Even a smaller weight loss can make a difference. If you are trying to lose weight, do so slowly and steadily. A generally safe rate is ½ to 1 pound a week until you reach your goal.

Children need enough food for proper growth. To promote growth and development and prevent overweight, teach children to eat grain products; vegetables and fruits; lowfat milk products or other calcium-rich foods; beans, lean meat, poultry, fish, or other protein-rich foods; and to participate in vigorous activity. Limiting television time and encouraging children to play actively in a safe environment are helpful steps. Although limiting fat intake may help to prevent excess weight gain in children, fat should not be restricted for children younger than 2 years of age. Helping overweight children to achieve a healthy weight along with normal growth requires more caution. Modest reductions in dietary fat, such as the use of lowfat milk rather than whole milk, are not hazardous. However, major efforts to change a child's diet should be accomplished by monitoring of growth by a health professional at regular intervals.

CHOOSE A DIET WITH PLENTY OF GRAIN PRODUCTS, VEGETABLES, AND FRUITS. Grain products, vegetables, and fruits are key parts of a varied diet. They are emphasized in this guideline because they provide vitamins, minerals, complex carbohydrates (starch and dietary fiber), and other substances that are important for good health. They are also generally low in fat, depending on how they are prepared and what is added to them at the table. Most Americans of all ages eat fewer than the recommended number of servings of grain products, vegetables, and fruits, even though consumption of these foods is associated with a substantially lower risk for many chronic diseases, including certain types of cancer.

Most of the calories in your diet should come from grain products, vegetables, and fruits. These include grain products high in complex carbohydrates—breads, cereals, pasta, rice—found at the base of the Food Guide Pyramid, as well as vegetables such as potatoes and corn. Dry beans (like pinto, navy, kidney, and black beans) are included in the meat and beans group of the Pyramid, but they can count as servings of vegetables instead of meat alternatives.

Fiber is found only in plant foods like whole-grain breads and cereals, beans and peas, other vegetables, and fruits. Because there are different types of fiber in foods, choose a variety of foods daily. Eating a variety of fiber-containing plant foods is important for proper bowel function, can reduce symptoms of chronic constipation, diverticular disease, and hemorrhoids, and may lower the risk for heart disease and some cancers. However, some of the health benefits asso-ciated with a high-fiber diet may come from other components present in these foods, not just from fiber itself. For this reason, fiber is best obtained from foods rather than supplements.

Fruits and vegetables are excellent sources of vitamin C, vitamin B_6, carotenoids, including those which form vitamin A, and folate. The antioxidant nutrients found in plant foods (e.g., vitamin C, carotenoids, vitamin E, and certain minerals) are presently of great interest to scientists and the public because of their potentially beneficial role in reducing the risk for cancer and certain other chronic diseases. Scientists are also trying to determine if other substances in plant foods protect against cancer.

Some good sources of carotenoids are:

• Dark green leafy vegetables, such as spinach, collards, kale, mustard greens, and turnip greens; broccoli; carrots; pumpkin and calabaza; red peppers; sweet potatoes; and tomatoes

• Fruits like mangoes, papayas, and cantaloupes

Folate, also called folic acid, is a B vitamin that, among its many functions, reduces the risk of a serious type of birth defect.

Some good sources of folate are:

• Dry beans (like red beans, navy beans, and soybeans), lentils, chickpeas, cow peas, and peanuts

• Many vegetables, especially leafy greens (spinach, cabbage, Brussels sprouts, romaine, and loose-leaf lettuce), peas, okra, sweet corn, beets, and broccoli

• Fruits, such as blackberries, boysenberries, kiwis, oranges, plantains, strawberries, orange juice, and pineapple juice

Minerals, such as potassium, found in a wide variety of vegetables and fruits, and calcium, found in certain vegetables (see page 791), may help reduce the risk for high blood pressure.

Some good sources of potassium are:

• Vegetables and fruits in general, especially

~ potatoes and sweet potatoes

~ spinach, Swiss chard, broccoli, winter squashes, and parsnips

~ dates, bananas, cantaloupes, mangoes, plaintains, dried apricots, raisins, prunes, orange juice, and grapefruit juice

~ dry beans, peas, and lentils

• Milk and yogurt—they have less sodium than cheese; cheese has much less potassium and usually has added salt.

CHOOSE A DIET LOW IN FAT, SATURATED FAT, AND CHOLESTEROL. Some dietary fat is needed for good health. Fats supply energy and essential fatty acids and promote absorption of the fat-soluble vitamins A, D, E, and K.

Most people are aware that high levels of saturated fat and cholesterol in the diet are linked to increased blood cholesterol levels and a greater risk for heart disease. More Americans are now eating less fat, saturated fat, and cholesterol-rich foods than in the recent past, and fewer people are dying from the most common form of heart disease. Still, many people continue to eat high-fat diets, the number of overweight people has increased, and the risk of heart disease and certain cancers (also linked to fat intake) remains high. This guideline emphasizes the continued importance of choosing a diet with less total fat, saturated fat, and cholesterol.

Choose a diet that provides no more than 30 percent of total calories from fat. For example, at 2,000 calories per day, the suggested upper limit of calories from fat is about 600 calories. Divide the suggested upper limit of calories from fat per day by 9 to get the suggested upper limit of grams of fat per day (each gram of fat has 9 calories) (600 calories from fat ÷ 9 = about 65 grams of fat).

Fats contain both saturated and unsaturated (monounsaturated and polyunsaturated) fatty acids. Saturated fat raises blood cholesterol more than other forms of fat. Reducing saturated fat to less than 10 percent of total calories (one-third of the suggested upper limit of calories from all forms of fat) will help you lower your blood cholesterol level. The fats from meats, milk, and milk products are the main sources of saturated fats in most diets. Many bakery products are also sources of saturated fats. Vegetable oils supply smaller amounts of saturated fat.

Olive and canola oils are particularly high in monounsaturated fats; most other vegetable oils, nuts, and high-fat fish are good sources of polyunsaturated fats. Both kinds of unsaturated fats reduce blood cholesterol when they replace saturated fats in the diet.

Partially hydrogenated vegetable oils, such as those used in many margarines and shortenings, contain a form of unsaturated fat known as trans-fatty acids that may raise blood cholesterol levels, although not as much as saturated fat.

The fats in most fish are low in saturated fatty acids and contain a certain type of polyunsaturated fatty acid (omega-3) that is under study because of a possible association with a decreased risk for heart disease in certain people.

The body makes the cholesterol it requires. In addition, cholesterol is obtained from food. Dietary cholesterol comes from animal sources such as egg yolks, meats (especially organ meats, such as liver), poultry, fish, and higher-fat milk products. Many of these foods are also high in saturated fats. Choosing foods with less cholesterol and saturated fat will help lower your blood cholesterol levels. On 2,000-calorie and 2,500-calorie diets, the Nutrition Facts Label lists the Daily Value for cholesterol as 300 milligrams.

Advice given in this section does not apply to infants and toddlers below the age of 2 years. After that age, children should gradually adopt a diet that, by about 5 years of age, contains no more than 30 percent of calories from fat. As they begin to consume fewer calories from fat, children should replace these calories by eating more grain products, fruits, vegetables, and low-fat milk products or other calcium-rich foods, and beans, lean meat, poultry, fish, or other protein-rich foods.

GRAMS OF FAT IN SELECTED FOODS

From Each of the Six Food Groups in the Food Guide Pyramid

Food and Portion	Grams of Fat
BREAD, CEREAL, RICE, AND PASTA GROUP	
Bread, 1 slice	1
Hamburger roll, bagel, English muffin	2
Tortilla, 1	3
Rice, pasta, cooked, ½ cup	Trace
Plain crackers, small, 3–4	3
Breakfast cereal, 1 ounce	*
Pancakes, 4-inch diameter, 2	3
Croissant, 1 large (2 ounces)	12
Doughnut, 1 medium (2 ounces)	11
Danish, 1 medium (2 ounces)	13
Cake, frosted, 1/16 average	13
Cookies, 2 medium	4
Pie, fruit, 2-crust, ⅙ 8-inch pie	19
VEGETABLE GROUP	
Vegetables, cooked, ½ cup	Trace
Vegetables, leafy, raw, 1 cup	Trace
Vegetables, nonleafy, raw, chopped, ½ cup	Trace
Potatoes, scalloped, ½ cup	4
Potato salad, ½ cup	8
French fries, 10	8
FRUIT GROUP	
Whole fruit: medium apple, orange, banana	Trace
Fruit, raw or canned, ½ cup	Trace
Fruit juice, unsweetened, ¾ cup	Trace
Avocado, ¼ whole	9

Food and Portion	Grams of Fat
MILK, YOGURT, AND CHEESE GROUP	
Skim milk, 1 cup	Trace
Nonfat yogurt, plain, 8 ounces	Trace
Lowfat milk, 2%, 1 cup	5
Whole milk, 1 cup	8
Chocolate milk, 2%, 1 cup	5
Lowfat yogurt, plain, 8 ounces	4
Lowfat yogurt, fruit, 8 ounces	3
Natural cheddar cheese, 1½ ounces	14
Process cheese, 2 ounces	18
Mozzarella, part skim, 1½ ounces	7
Ricotta, part skim, ½ cup	10
Cottage cheese, 4% fat, ½ cup	5
Ice cream, ½ cup	7
Ice milk, ½ cup	3
Frozen yogurt, ½ cup	2
MEAT, POULTRY, FISH, DRY BEANS, EGGS, AND NUTS GROUP	
Lean meat, poultry, fish, cooked, 3 ounces	6
Ground beef, lean, cooked, 3 ounces	16
Chicken, with skin, fried, 3 ounces	13
Bologna, 2 slices	16
Egg, 1	5
Dry beans and peas, cooked, ½ cup	Trace
Peanut butter, 2 tablespoons	16
Nuts, ⅓ cup	22

Food and Portion	Grams of Fat
FATS, OILS, AND SWEETS	
Butter, margarine, 1 teaspoon	4
Mayonnaise, 1 tablespoon	11
Salad dressing, 1 tablespoon	7
Reduced-calorie salad dressing, 1 tablespoon	*
Sour cream, 2 tablespoons	6
Cream cheese, 1 ounce	10
Sugar, jam, jelly, 1 teaspoon	0
Cola, 12 fluid ounces	0
Fruit drink, ade, 12 fluid ounces	0
Chocolate bar, 1 ounce	9
Sherbet, ½ cup	2
Fruit sorbet, ½ cup	0
Gelatin dessert, ½ cup	0

Check product label.

Use the Nutrition Facts Label to find out the number of grams of total fat and saturated fat in specific food products.

CHOOSE A DIET MODERATE IN SUGARS. Sugars are carbohydrates. Dietary carbohydrates also include the complex carbohydrates starch and fiber. During digestion, all carbohydrates except fiber break down into sugars. Sugars and starches occur naturally in many foods that also supply other nutrients. Examples of these foods include milk, fruits, some vegetables, breads, cereals, and grains. Sugars are often added to foods during processing and preparation or when they are eaten. The body cannot tell the difference between naturally occurring and added sugars because they are identical chemically.

Scientific evidence indicates that diets high in sugars do not cause hyperactivity or diabetes.

The most common type of diabetes occurs in overweight adults. Avoiding sugars alone will not correct overweight. To lose weight, reduce the total amount of calories from the food you eat and increase your level of physical activity.

If you wish to maintain your weight when you eat less fat, replace the lost calories from fat with equal calories from fruits, vegetables, and grain products, found in the lower half of the Food Guide Pyramid.

Some foods that contain a lot of sugars supply calories but few or no nutrients. These foods are located at the top of the Pyramid. For very active people with high-calorie needs, sugars can be an additional source of energy. However, because maintaining a nutritious diet and a healthy weight is very important, sugars should be used in moderation by most healthy people and sparingly by people with low-calorie needs. This guideline cautions about eating sugars in large amounts and about frequent snacks of food and beverages containing sugars that supply unnecessary calories and few nutrients.

Sugar substitutes, such as sorbitol, saccharin, and aspartame, are ingredients in many foods. Most sugar substitutes do not provide significant calories and, therefore, may be useful in the diets of people concerned about calorie intake. However, foods containing sugar substitutes may not always be lower in calories than similar products that contain sugars. Unless you reduce the total calories you eat, the use of sugar substitutes will not cause you to lose weight.

To avoid getting too many calories from sugars, try to limit your added sugars to 6 teaspoons a day if you eat about 1,600 calories, 12 teaspoons at 2,200 calories, or 18 teaspoons at 2,800 calories. These amounts are intended to be averages over time. The patterns are illustrations of healthful proportions in the diet, not rigid prescriptions.

ADDED SUGARS IN SELECTED FOODS

Food and Portion	Teaspoons of Added Sugar
BREAD, CEREAL, RICE, AND PASTA GROUP	
Bread, 1 slice	0
Muffin, 1 medium	1
Cookies, 2 medium	1
Danish pastry, 1 medium	1
Doughnut, 1 medium	2
Ready-to-eat cereal, sweetened, 1 ounce	*
Pound cake, no-fat, 1 ounce	2
Angel food cake, 1/12 tube cake	5
Cake, frosted, 1/16 average	6
Pie, fruit, 2-crust, 1/6 8-inch pie	6
FRUIT GROUP	
Fruit, canned in juice, 1/2 cup	0
Fruit, canned in light syrup, 1/2 cup	2
Fruit, canned in heavy syrup, 1/2 cup	4

Check product label.

Note: 1 teaspoon of sugar = 4 grams.

Food and Portion	Teaspoons of Added Sugar
MILK, YOGURT, AND CHEESE GROUP	
Milk, plain, 1 cup	0
Chocolate milk, 2%, 1 cup	3
Lowfat yogurt, plain, 8 ounces	0
Lowfat yogurt, flavored, 8 ounces	5
Lowfat yogurt, fruit, 8 ounces	7
Ice cream, ice milk, or frozen yogurt, 1/2 cup	3
Chocolate shake, 10 fluid ounces	9
OTHER	
Sugar, jam, jelly, 1 teaspoon	1
Syrup or honey, 1 tablespoon	3
Chocolate bar, 1 ounce	3
Fruit sorbet, 1/2 cup	3
Gelatin dessert, 1/2 cup	4
Sherbet, 1/2 cup	5
Cola, 12 fluid ounces	9
Fruit drink, 12 fluid ounces	12

CHOOSE A DIET MODERATE IN SALT AND SODIUM. Sodium and sodium chloride (commonly known as salt) occur naturally in foods, usually in small amounts. Salt and other sodium-containing ingredients are often used in food processing. Some people add salt and salty sauces to their food at the table, but most dietary sodium or salt comes from foods to which salt has already been added during processing or preparation. Although many people add salt to enhance the taste of foods, their preference for doing so may weaken with eating less salt.

In the body, sodium plays an essential role in the regulation of fluids and blood pressure. Many studies in diverse populations have shown that a high sodium intake is associated with higher blood pressure. Most evidence suggests that many people at risk for high blood pressure reduce their chances of developing this condition by consuming less salt or sodium. Some questions remain, partly because other factors may interact with sodium to affect blood pressure.

Following other guidelines in the Dietary Guidelines for Americans may also help prevent high blood pressure. An important example is the guideline on weight and physical activity. The role of body weight in blood pressure control is well documented. Blood pressure increases with weight and decreases when weight is reduced. The guideline to consume a diet with plenty of fruits and vegetables is relevant because fruits and vegetables are naturally lower in sodium and fat and may help with weight reduction and control. Consuming more fruits and vegetables also increases potassium intake (see page 795), which may help to reduce blood pressure. Increased physical activity helps lower blood pressure and control weight. Alcohol consumption has also been associated with high blood pressure.

Another reason to reduce salt intake is the fact that high salt intake may increase the amount of calcium excreted in the urine and, therefore, increase the body's need for calcium.

Sodium has an important role in the body. However, most Americans consume more sodium than is needed. The Nutrition Facts Label lists the Daily Value for sodium as 2,400 milligrams for 2,000-calorie and 2,500-calorie diets. One level teaspoon of salt provides approximately 2,000 milligrams of sodium.

There is no way at present to tell who might develop high blood pressure from eating too much sodium. However, consuming less salt or sodium is not harmful and can be recommended for the healthy, normal adult.

IF YOU DRINK ALCOHOLIC BEVERAGES, DO SO IN MODERATION. Alcoholic beverages supply calories but few or no nutrients. The alcohol in these beverages has effects that are harmful when consumed in excess. These effects of alcohol may alter judgment and can lead to dependency and a great many other serious health problems. Alcoholic beverages have been used to enhance the enjoyment of meals by many societies throughout human history. If adults choose to drink alcoholic beverages, they should consume them only in moderation.

Moderation is defined as no more than one drink per day for women and no more than two drinks per day for men.

Count as a drink:

- 12 ounces of regular beer (150 calories)
- 5 ounces of wine (100 calories)
- 1.5 ounces of 80-proof distilled spirits (100 calories)

Current evidence suggests that moderate drinking is associated with a lower risk for coronary heart disease in some individuals. However, higher levels of alcohol intake raise the risk for high blood pressure, stroke, heart disease, certain cancers, accidents, violence, suicides, birth defects, and overall mortality. Too much alcohol may cause cirrhosis of the liver, inflammation of the pancreas, and damage to the brain and heart. Heavy drinkers are at risk of malnutrition because alcohol contains calories that may substitute for those in more nutritious foods.

CALORIE TABLE

A calorie is a measure of energy. Science defines a calorie as the amount of energy required to raise the temperature of 1 gram of water by 1 degree Celsius.

In the following table, calorie values are rounded to the nearest 5 calories.

Food and Portion	Calories
BREADS, CEREALS, AND OTHER GRAIN PRODUCTS	
Breads	
Bagel, plain, 3-inch diameter, 1	165
Cracked wheat, 18-slices-per-pound loaf, 1 slice	65
French, 18-slices-per-pound loaf, 1 slice	70
Italian, 18-slices-per-pound loaf, 1 slice	70
Pita, 5¼-inch diameter, 1	
white	125
whole wheat	115
Pumpernickel, 18-slices-per-pound loaf, 1 slice	60
Raisin, 18-slices-per-pound loaf, 1 slice	70
Rye, 18-slices-per-pound loaf, 1 slice	65
Vienna, 18-slices-per-pound loaf, 1 slice	70
White	
regular slice, 18-slices-per-pound loaf, 1 slice	65
thin-slice, 22-slices-per-pound loaf, 1 slice	55
Whole wheat, 18-slices-per-pound loaf, 1 slice	60
Rolls	
Croissant, 4½ × 4 × 1¾ inches, plain, 1	230
Dinner, 2½-inch diameter, 1	85
Frankfurter or hamburger, 1	130
Hard, medium, 1	155
Submarine, medium, ½	145

Food and Portion	Calories
Quick Breads, Biscuits, Muffins, and Breakfast Pastries	
Baking powder biscuit, 2-inch diameter, 1	
from home recipe	115
from mix	105
from refrigerated dough	55
Banana bread, ½-inch slice of 5 × 9-inch loaf, 1	150
Coffeecake	
crumb-type, piece 2⅝ × 2 inches, 1	100
yeast-type, piece ⅛ of 8-inch diameter, 1	130
Corn bread, piece 2½ × 2½ × 1½ inches, 1	160
Danish pastry, plain, 5-inch diameter, 1	395
Doughnuts	
cake-type, plain, 3¼-inch diameter, 1	165
yeast-leavened, glazed, 3¾-inch diameter, 1	245
English muffin, plain, 1	130
Muffin, 2⅝-inch diameter, 1	
blueberry or corn	165
bran	125
Pancake, plain, 5-inch diameter, 1	90
Toaster pastry, 4¼ × 3 × ⅜ inches, 1	210
Waffle	
from mix, 7-inch diameter (about 2¾ ounces), 1	205
from frozen (about 1½ ounces), 1 square	100
Breakfast Cereals	
All-Bran, 1 ounce (about ½ cup)	70
Bran flakes (40% bran), 1 ounce (about ⅔ cup)	90
Cheerios, 1 ounce (about 1 cup)	110
Cornflakes, 1 ounce (about 1 cup)	110
Corn (hominy) grits	
regular or quick, cooked, ¾ cup	110
instant, plain, prepared, 1 packet	80
Corn Pops, 1 ounce (about 1 cup)	105

Food and Portion	Calories
Cream of Wheat	
regular or quick, cooked, ¾ cup	100
instant, cooked, ¾ cup	130
Mix 'n Eat, plain, prepared, 1 packet	100
Frosted Flakes, 1 ounce (about ¾ cup)	110
Frosted Mini-Wheats, 1 ounce (about ½ cup)	100
Grape-Nut Flakes, 1 ounce (about ¾ cup)	100
Honey Smacks, 1 ounce (about ¾ cup)	105
Nature Valley Granola, 1 ounce (about ¼ cup)	130
Oatmeal or rolled oats	
regular, quick, or instant, cooked, ¾ cup	110
instant, prepared, 1 packet	
plain	105
flavored	150
Raisin bran, 1 ounce (about ½ cup)	85
Rice Chex, 1 ounce (about ¾ cup)	110
Rice Krispies, 1 ounce (about 1 cup)	110
Shredded wheat, plain	
spoon size, 1 ounce (about ½ cup)	100
large biscuit (about ¾ ounce), 1	85
Special K, 1 ounce (about 1¼ cups)	110
Total, 1 ounce (about ¾ cup)	100
Wheaties, 1 ounce (about 1 cup)	100

Pasta and Rice

(For pasta and rice mixtures, see Mixed Dishes, page 807.)

Food and Portion	Calories
Macaroni, cooked, plain, ½ cup	75
Noodles, cooked, plain, ½ cup	100
Rice, cooked, plain, ½ cup	
brown	115
instant	90
white, long grain	105
Spaghetti, cooked, plain, ½ cup	75

Crackers

Food and Portion	Calories
Cheese, plain, 1-inch square, 10	50
Graham, plain, 2½-inch square, 2	55
Matzo, 6-inch square, 1	120
Oyster, 10	45
Rye wafers, whole grain, 1⅞ × 3½ inches, 2	50
Saltines, 1⅞-inch square, 2	25
Sandwich-type, peanut butter or cheese filled, 2	80
Snack-type, round, about 2-inch diameter, 2	30
Whole wheat, 1⅞ × 1⅝ inches, 2	30

FRUITS

Fruits

(Calories in cooked and canned fruit include both fruit and liquid.)

Food and Portion	Calories
Apples, raw, medium, 1	80
Applesauce, canned, ½ cup	
unsweetened	50
sweetened	95
Apricots	
raw (about 12 per pound), 3	50
canned, halves, ½ cup	
in juice	60
in heavy syrup	105
dried halves, cooked, unsweetened, ½ cup	105
Avocados	
California varieties, 8 ounces each, ½	140
Florida varieties, 16 ounces each, ½	245
Bananas, medium, 1	105
Blueberries, ½ cup	
raw	40
frozen	
unsweetened	40
sweetened	95
Cantaloupe, raw	
medium melon, ¼	60
cubed, ½ cup	25
Cherries, ½ cup	
raw	
sour	40
sweet	50
canned, sweet	
in juice	70
in heavy syrup	105
Cranberry sauce, ¼ cup	105
Dates, dried, pitted, whole, 5	115

Food and Portion	Calories
Fruit cocktail, canned, ½ cup	
in juice	55
in heavy syrup	90
Grapefruit	
raw, white, pink, or red	
medium, ½	40
sections, ½ cup	35
canned, ½ cup	
in juice	45
in light syrup	75
Grapes, raw, adherent skin (Thompson, Red Flame, Tokay, and Emperor), ½ cup	55
Honeydew melon, raw	
6- to 7-inch melon, ⅛	55
cubed, ½ cup	30
Kiwis, raw, medium, 1	45
Nectarines, raw, medium, 1	65
Oranges, raw, medium, 1	60
Peaches	
raw	
whole, medium, 1	40
sliced, ½ cup	35
canned, ½ cup	
in juice	55
in light syrup	70
in heavy syrup	95
dried halves, cooked, unsweetened, ½ cup	100
frozen, sliced, sweetened, ½ cup	120
Pears	
raw, medium, 1	100
canned, ½ cup	
in juice	60
in heavy syrup	100
Pineapple	
raw, diced, ½ cup	40
canned	
crushed, tidbits, or chunks, ½ cup	
in juice	75
in heavy syrup	100
slices, 2	
in juice	55
in heavy syrup	75
Plantains, sliced, cooked, ½ cup	110

Food and Portion	Calories
Plums	
raw, medium, 1	35
canned, ½ cup	
in juice	75
in heavy syrup	115
Prunes	
dried, cooked, unpitted, ½ cup	
unsweetened	130
sweetened	150
dried, uncooked, 5	85
Raisins, 1 snack pack, ½ ounce (1½ tablespoons)	40
Raspberries, ½ cup	
raw	30
frozen, sweetened	130
Rhubarb, cooked, sweetened, ½ cup	140
Strawberries, ½ cup	
raw, sliced	25
frozen, sweetened, sliced	110
Tangerines, raw, medium, 1	35
Watermelon, raw	
wedge or slice (about 1¼-pound piece), 1	90
diced, ½ cup	25

Fruit Juices

(A 6-fluid-ounce serving is ¾ cup.)

Food and Portion	Calories
Apple juice or cider, canned or bottled, 6 fluid ounces	85
Apricot nectar, canned, 6 fluid ounces	105
Cranberry juice cocktail, bottled, sweetened, 6 fluid ounces	110
Grape, 6 fluid ounces	
canned or bottled	115
frozen concentrate, sweetened, reconstituted	95
Grapefruit, 6 fluid ounces	
fresh	70
canned	
unsweetened	70
sweetened	85
frozen concentrate, unsweetened, reconstituted	75
Lemon, fresh, canned, or bottled, 1 tablespoon	5

Food and Portion	Calories	Food and Portion	Calories
Lime, fresh, canned, or bottled, 1 tablespoon	5	Cauliflower, flowerets	
		raw, 4	10
Orange, unsweetened, 6 fluid ounces		cooked, ½ cup	20
fresh or frozen concentrate, reconstituted	85	Celery	
canned	80	raw, stalk 7½ × 1¼ inches, 1	5
Pineapple, canned, unsweetened,		cooked, diced, ½ cup	10
6 fluid ounces	105	Chives, chopped, raw, 1 tablespoon	Trace
Prune, canned or bottled, 6 fluid ounces	135	Collards, chopped, cooked, ½ cup	10

VEGETABLES

Vegetables
(Calories are for cooked vegetables prepared from raw, canned, or frozen.)

Food and Portion	Calories	Food and Portion	Calories
Alfalfa sprouts, raw, ½ cup	5	Corn, cooked	
		on cob, 5-inch ear, 1	80
Artichoke, globe or French, cooked,		kernels, ½ cup	90
1 medium	55	cream-style, ½ cup	90
Asparagus, cooked		Cucumbers, raw, 6 to 8 slices	10
cuts and tips, ½ cup	20	Eggplant, cubed, cooked, ½ cup	15
medium spears, 4	15	Endive, pieces for salad, raw, 1 cup	5
Beans, cooked, ½ cup		Kale, chopped, cooked, ½ cup	20
lima (baby or Fordhook)	110	Lettuce, raw	
snap (green or yellow)	25	head (iceberg)	
Bean sprouts, mung, ½ cup		pieces for salad, 1 cup	5
raw	15	wedge, ⅙ of 6-inch head	10
cooked	30	loose-leaf, pieces for salad, 1 cup	5
Beets, diced or sliced, cooked, ½ cup	25	Mushrooms	
Beet greens, chopped, cooked, ½ cup	20	raw	
Broccoli		1 medium	5
raw, flowerets, 3	10	pieces, ½ cup	10
cooked		cooked, pieces, ½ cup	20
chopped, ½ cup	25	Mustard greens, chopped, cooked, ½ cup	10
5-inch spears, 3	30	Okra	
Brussels sprouts, cooked		3-inch pods, fried, 8	115
medium sprouts, 4	35	cooked, sliced, ½ cup	30
½ cup	30	Onions	
Cabbage, ½ cup		raw, chopped, 2 tablespoons	
raw		young green	5
plain, shredded, or sliced	10	mature	5
coleslaw	70	cooked, mature, whole or sliced, ½ cup	30
cooked, shredded	15	Onion rings, breaded, frozen, prepared,	
Carrots		2- to 3-inch-diameter rings, 2	80
raw		Peas, green, cooked, ½ cup	65
7½ × 1⅛ inches, 1	30	Peppers, sweet, green or red	
shredded, ½ cup	25	raw	
cooked, sliced, ½ cup	35	chopped, ½ cup	20
		ring, 3-inch diameter, ¼ inch	
		thick, 1	Trace
		cooked, medium, 1	20

Food and Portion	Calories
Potatoes	
au gratin, home-prepared, ½ cup	175
baked, 4¾ × 2⅓ inches, flesh and skin, 1	220
boiled without skin	
2½-inch diameter, 1	105
diced or sliced, ½ cup	67
French-fried (from frozen), 2- to 3½-inch strips, 10	
fried	160
oven-heated	110
hashed brown (from frozen), ½ cup	155
mashed, ½ cup	
from home recipe	
milk added	80
milk and fat added	115
from dehydrated flakes, milk and fat added	110
puffs, oven-heated, 10	175
salad, home-prepared, ½ cup	130
scalloped, home-prepared, ½ cup	120
Pumpkin, canned, ½ cup	30
Radishes, raw, medium, 4	5
Sauerkraut, heated, ½ cup	15
Spinach	
raw, pieces for salad, 1 cup	5
cooked, chopped, ½ cup	20
Squash, ½ cup	
summer, sliced	
raw	10
cooked	20
winter	
baked, cubed	40
boiled, mashed	45
Sweet potatoes	
baked, 5 × 2 inches, peeled, 1	115
candied, piece 2½ × 2 inches, 1	145
canned, vacuum or syrup pack, ½ cup	
pieces	90
mashed	115
Tomatoes	
raw, medium, 1	25
cooked, ½ cup	25
Tomato sauce, ½ cup	35
Turnips, cubed, ½ cup	
raw	20
cooked	15
Turnip greens, chopped, cooked, ½ cup	15

Food and Portion	Calories
Vegetable Juices	
(A 6-fluid-ounce serving is ¾ cup.)	
Tomato juice, 6 fluid ounces	30
Vegetable juice cocktail, 6 fluid ounces	35
MEAT, POULTRY, FISH, AND ALTERNATES	
(Serving sizes are cooked, edible part.)	
Beef	
Corned beef, canned, 3 ounces (2 slices 4½ × 2½ × ¼ inches)	210
Ground beef, broiled, 3 ounces	
regular	245
lean	230
extra lean	215
Oven-cooked roast, 3 ounces (2 slices 4½ × 2½ × ¼ inches)	
relatively fat cuts, such as rib	
lean and fat	225
lean only	165
relatively lean cuts, such as eye of round	
lean and fat	195
lean only	140
Pot roast, braised or simmered, 3 ounces (2 slices 4½ × 2½ × ¼ inches)	
relatively fat cuts, such as chuck blade	
lean and fat	330
lean only	235
relatively lean cuts, such as bottom round	
lean and fat	225
lean only	190
Steak, top sirloin, broiled, 3 ounces	
lean only	160
Veal	
Veal cutlet, broiled or braised, 3 ounces (1 piece 4½ × 2½ × ½ inches)	185
Pork	
Cured	
Ham, canned, heated, lean and fat, 3 ounces (2 slices 4½ × 2½ × ¼ inches)	160
Ham, roasted, 3 ounces (2 slices 4½ × 2½ × ¼ inches)	
lean and fat	205
lean only	135

Food and Portion	Calories
Pork (cont.)	
Fresh	
Tenderloin, lean only, roasted, 3 ounces	140
Top loin chop, boneless, lean only, broiled, 3 ounces	175
Shoulder (picnic), braised, 3 ounces (2 slices 4½ × 2½ × ¼ inches)	
lean and fat	280
lean only	210
Lamb	
Ground lamb, broiled, 3 ounces	305
Leg, roasted, 3 ounces (2 slices 4½ × 2½ × ¼ inches)	
lean and fat	235
lean only	160
Shoulder chop, broiled, 3 ounces of meat	
lean and fat (from about a 5-ounce chop, as purchased)	285
lean only (from about a 7-ounce chop, as purchased)	175
Sausage and Luncheon Meats	
Bacon, cooked, medium slices, 3	110
Bologna, 2 ounces (2 slices 4½ × ⅛ inches)	
beef and pork	180
chicken or turkey	115
Braunschweiger, 2 ounces (2 slices 2½ × ⅜ inches)	205
Canadian bacon, cooked, 2 slices (2 ounces uncooked)	85
Chicken roll, light meat, 2 ounces (2 slices 4½ × ⅛ inches)	90
Frankfurter, heated, 1 (10 per pound unheated)	
beef and pork	150
chicken or turkey	110
Ham, chopped, 2 ounces (2 slices 4 × 4 inches)	140
Ham, boiled, 2 ounces (2 slices 6¼ × 4 inches)	
regular	90
extra lean	75
Pork sausage	
bulk, cooked, 1 patty (about 2 ounces uncooked)	100
link, cooked, 2 links 4 × ⅞ inches (2 ounces uncooked)	95

Food and Portion	Calories
Salami, 2 ounces (2 slices 4½ × ⅛ inches)	140
Vienna sausage, canned, sausages 2 × ⅞ inches, 3 (about 1¾ ounces)	135
Organ Meats	
Beef liver, fried, 3 ounces (1 piece 6½ × 2⅜ × ⅜ inches)	185
Chicken liver, cooked	
1 liver	45
3 ounces (about 4 livers)	195
Poultry	
Chicken	
fried	
breast half, 1 medium	
meat only	160
flour-coated, meat and skin	215
batter-dipped or breaded, meat and skin	365
drumstick, 1 medium	
meat only	80
flour-coated, meat and skin	120
batter-dipped or breaded, meat and skin	195
thigh, 1 medium	
meat only	110
flour-coated, meat and skin	160
batter-dipped or breaded, meat and skin	235
roasted	
breast half, 1 medium	
meat only	140
meat and skin	190
drumstick, 1 medium	
meat only	75
meat and skin	110
Turkey, roasted, 3 ounces (3 slices 3 × 2 × ¼ inches)	
light meat only	135
light meat and skin	165
dark meat only	160
dark meat and skin	185
Fish and Shellfish	
Clams, canned, drained, 3 ounces (about 5 to 9 medium)	80
Crabmeat, canned or cooked, 3 ounces (about ⅔ cup)	85
Cod, breaded, fried, 3 ounces	180
Fish, battered, fried, 3 ounces	185

Food and Portion	Calories	Food and Portion	Calories
Fish sticks, frozen, reheated, 3	175	**NUTS AND SEEDS**	
Flounder, baked or broiled, 3 ounces	115	Almonds, 1 ounce (about 22)	165
Haddock, baked or broiled, 3 ounces	110	Cashews, dry-roasted or oil-roasted, 1 ounce (about 18)	160
Ocean perch, breaded, fried, 3 ounces	190	Coconut, dried, sweetened, flaked, 2 tablespoons	45
Oysters, breaded, fried, large, 3	155	Mixed nuts, with peanuts, 1 ounce (about 20 assorted)	
Salmon, 3 ounces		dry-roasted	165
baked or broiled, red (piece 3 × 1¾ × 1 inches)	145	oil-roasted	175
canned, drained (about ½ cup)	125	Peanuts, dry-roasted or oil-roasted, 1 ounce (about 28 whole)	165
Sardines, Atlantic, canned in oil, drained, 3 ounces (about 7 medium)	175	Peanut butter, 2 tablespoons	190
Shrimp, 3 ounces		Pecans, 1 ounce (about 20 halves)	185
canned (about 27 medium)	100	Pistachio nuts, dry-roasted, 1 ounce (about 47)	170
French-fried, 5 large or 8 medium	210	Sesame seeds, 1 tablespoon	50
Tuna, chunk light, drained, 3 ounces (about ½ cup)		Sunflower seeds, roasted, hulled, 2 tablespoons	105
canned in oil	170	Walnuts	
canned in water	110	black, chopped, 1 ounce (about ¼ cup)	170
		English, 1 ounce (about 14 halves)	180
EGGS		**MILK, YOGURT, AND CHEESE**	
Deviled, 1 large	125	**Fluid Milk**	
Fried, 1 large	95	Buttermilk, 1 cup	100
Hard or soft cooked, 1 large	80	Lowfat, no milk solids added, 1 cup	
Omelet, plain, 1 large egg, milk and fat added	105	1% fat	105
		2% fat	120
Poached, 1 large	80	Skim, no milk solids added, 1 cup	85
Scrambled in fat, 1 large, milk added	105	Whole, 1 cup	150
DRY BEANS AND PEAS		**Canned Milk**	
(For bean mixtures, see Mixed Dishes, page 807.)		Condensed, sweetened, undiluted, ½ cup	490
Baked beans, canned, ½ cup		Evaporated, undiluted, ½ cup	
with pork and tomato sauce	155	whole	170
with pork and sweet sauce	140	skim	100
Black-eyed peas, cooked, drained, ½ cup	95	**Milk Beverages**	
Chickpeas (garbanzos), cooked, drained, ½ cup	150	Chocolate milk, 1 cup	
		2% fat	180
Lima, cooked, drained, ½ cup	105	whole	210
Pinto, cooked, drained, ½ cup	95	Eggnog, plain, commercial, 1 cup	345
Red kidney, canned with liquid, ½ cup	110		
White navy (pea), Great Northern, cooked, drained, ½ cup	120		

Food and Portion	Calories
Malted milk, prepared from powder with whole milk, 1 cup	
natural	210
chocolate-flavored	200
Thick shake, commercially prepared, 10 fluid ounces	
chocolate	360
vanilla	355

Yogurt

Food and Portion	Calories
Made from lowfat milk, with added nonfat milk solids	
8-ounce container	
plain	145
flavored	195
fruit varieties	230
6-ounce container	
flavored	145
fruit varieties	175
Made from skim milk, with added nonfat milk solids, plain, 8-ounce container	125
Made from whole milk	
8-ounce container	
plain	140
flavored	230
fruit varieties	270
6-ounce container	
flavored	170
fruit varieties	200

Cheese

Food and Portion	Calories
American	
process	
1-ounce slice	105
1-inch cube	65
shredded, ½ cup (2 ounces)	210
process cheese food	
1-ounce slice	90
1-inch cube	55
1 tablespoon	50
process cheese spread, 1 tablespoon	45
Blue, crumbled, ¼ cup	120
Brick	
1-ounce slice	105
1-inch cube	65
Cheddar	
1 ounce	115
1-inch cube	70
shredded, ½ cup (2 ounces)	225

Food and Portion	Calories
Colby	
1-ounce slice	110
1-inch cube	70
Cottage cheese, ½ cup	
creamed (4% fat)	110
lowfat (2% fat)	100
dry curd (less than ½% fat)	60
Cream cheese	
1 ounce	100
1-inch cube	55
1 tablespoon	50
Edam or Gouda	
1 ounce	100
1-inch cube	60
Feta, crumbled, ¼ cup	90
Mozzarella, made with whole milk or part-skim milk (low moisture)	
1 ounce	80
1-inch cube	50
shredded, ½ cup (2 ounces)	160
Muenster	
1 ounce	105
1-inch cube	65
Parmesan, grated, 1 tablespoon	25
Provolone	
1-ounce slice	100
1-inch cube	60
Swiss, natural	
1-ounce slice	105
1-inch cube	55
shredded, ½ cup (2 ounces)	210
Swiss, process	
1-ounce slice	95
1-inch cube	60
shredded, ½ cup (2 ounces)	185

MIXED DISHES AND FAST FOOD ENTRÉES

Mixed Dishes

Food and Portion	Calories
Bean salad, sweet-sour dressing, ½ cup	70
Beef and vegetable stew, 1 cup	175
Chili with beans, 1 cup	305
Egg roll, with meat, 1	120
Fried rice, with meat, 1 cup	290

Food and Portion	Calories
Lasagna, piece 2½ × 4 inches, ⅙ of 8-inch square	330
Macaroni and cheese, 1 cup	515
Potpie, frozen, baked, 8 ounces beef	540
chicken	495
Quiche Lorraine, ⅛ of 8-inch quiche	470
Spaghetti in tomato sauce with cheese, 1 cup	155
Spaghetti with meat sauce or meat balls and tomato sauce, 1 cup	310

FAST FOOD ENTRÉES

Food and Portion	Calories
Breakfast sandwich (egg, cheese, Canadian bacon, English muffin), 1	385
Cheeseburger, with catsup, mustard, lettuce, tomatoes, pickles, and/or onions 2-ounce patty (before cooking)	360
4-ounce patty (before cooking)	565
Chicken, fried (see Poultry, page 805)	
Enchilada, with beef and cheese, 1	325
Fish sandwich, with 1¾-ounce fried fish fillet, tartar sauce, and cheese	525
Hamburger sandwich, with catsup, mustard, lettuce, tomatoes, pickles, and/or onions 2-ounce patty (before cooking)	280
4-ounce patty (before cooking)	510
double meat patty	540
Pizza, ⅛ of 15-inch-diameter pizza cheese	255
pepperoni	325
Roast beef sandwich, 2½ ounces meat, without condiments	345
Taco, meat, 1 small	370
large	570

SOUPS

Canned Soups

(Canned, condensed, prepared with equal volume of water unless otherwise stated.)

Food and Portion	Calories
Bean with bacon, 1 cup	170
Beef bouillon, broth, or consommé, 1 cup	15
Beef noodle, 1 cup	85

Food and Portion	Calories
Chicken broth, 1 cup	40
Chicken noodle, 1 cup	75
Chicken rice, 1 cup	60
Clam chowder, 1 cup Manhattan-style	80
New England-style prepared with water	95
prepared with skim milk	130
prepared with whole milk	165
Cream of broccoli, 1 cup	235
Cream of chicken, 1 cup prepared with water	115
prepared with skim milk	160
prepared with whole milk	190
Cream of mushroom, 1 cup prepared with water	130
prepared with skim milk	170
prepared with whole milk	205
Minestrone, 1 cup	80
Pea, 1 cup green	165
split, with ham	195
Tomato, 1 cup prepared with water	85
prepared with skim milk	130
prepared with whole milk	160
Vegetable, 1 cup with beef, chicken, or turkey	80
vegetarian	70

Dehydrated Soups

(One packet, prepared with 6 fluid ounces of water.)

Food and Portion	Calories
Chicken noodle	35
Onion	25
Tomato vegetable	55

DESSERTS, SNACK FOODS, AND CANDIES

Cakes

Food and Portion	Calories
Angel food cake, without frosting, 1/16 of 10-inch tube cake	145
Boston cream pie, 1/12 of 8-inch round cake	225
Carrot cake, with cream cheese frosting, 1/16 of tube cake	340

Food and Portion	Calories
Cheesecake, 1/12 of 9-inch round cake	405
Devil's food or chocolate cake, with chocolate frosting, 1/16 of 8- or 9-inch round, 2-layer cake	285
Fruitcake, dark, 1/32 of 7-inch round cake	165
Gingerbread, 1/9 of 8-inch square cake	240
Pound cake, without frosting, 1/16 of loaf 5 × 9 × 3 inches	220
Cupcakes, with frosting, 2¾-inch diameter	
chocolate	155
not chocolate	170
Sponge cake, without frosting, 1/16 of 10-inch tube cake	145
Yellow cake	
without frosting, 1/16 of Bundt or tube cake	190
with chocolate frosting, 1/16 of 8- or 9-inch round, 2-layer cake	290

Cookies

Food and Portion	Calories
Brownie, with nuts, 2-inch square, 1	
without frosting	130
with frosting	175
Chocolate chip cookie, 2-inch diameter, 1	50
Fig bar, 1½-inch square, 1	55
Oatmeal cookie, with raisins, 2⅝-inch diameter, 1	60
Peanut butter cookie, 2⅝-inch diameter, 1	80
Sandwich cookie, chocolate or vanilla, 1½-inch diameter, 1	55
Shortbread cookie, 2-inch diameter, 1	75
Sugar cookie, 2½-inch diameter, 1	70
Vanilla wafer, 1¾-inch diameter, 1	20

Pies

Food and Portion	Calories
One-crust pies, 1/8 of 9-inch pie	
Chocolate cream	405
Custard	285
Lemon meringue	340
Pecan	485
Pumpkin	330
Strawberry	385

Food and Portion	Calories
Two-crust pies, 1/8 of 9-inch pie	
Apple	455
Blueberry	410
Cherry or peach	405
Fried pies	
Apple	310
Cherry	285

Milk-Based Desserts

Food and Portion	Calories
Custard, baked, ½ cup	130
Ice cream, ½ cup	
regular (about 10% fat)	135
rich (about 16% fat)	175
Ice milk, ½ cup	
hardened	95
soft serve	115
Puddings, ½ cup *(Prepared from mix with whole milk; puddings prepared with skim milk are about 30 calories less per ½-cup serving.)*	
chocolate	
instant	160
regular	160
chocolate mousse	190
rice	160
tapioca	130
vanilla	
instant	150
regular	140
Sherbet, ½ cup	135
Yogurt, frozen, ½ cup	105

Other Desserts

Food and Portion	Calories
Fruit juice bars, frozen, 2½ fluid ounces	70
Gelatin dessert, prepared, plain, ½ cup	70
Popsicle, 3-fluid-ounce size	70

Snack Foods

Food and Portion	Calories
Cheese curls or puffs	
10 pieces	85
1-ounce package	160
Corn chips	
10 chips	95
1-ounce package	150
Crackers (see Crackers, page 801)	

Food and Portion	Calories
Nuts (see Nuts and Seeds, page 806)	
Popcorn, 1 cup	
air-popped	30
popped in vegetable oil	65
Pork rinds, deep-fried, 1 ounce (about 1 cup)	150
Potato chips, regular	
10 chips	105
1-ounce package	145
Pretzels	
Dutch, twisted, 2¾ × 2⅝ inches, 1	60
Soft, twisted, 1	190
Stick, 2½ inches long, 10	20
Thin, twisted, 3¼ × 2¼ × ¼ inches, 5	115

Candies

Food and Portion	Calories
Caramels, 1 ounce (about 3 pieces)	
chocolate	85
plain	110
Tootsie Roll, 1¼-ounce roll	140
Chocolate, sweetened	
candy-coated, 10 pieces	
plain	35
with peanut butter	35
with nuts	100
milk (about 1½-ounce bar)	
plain	245
with almonds	235
with rice cereal	215
with peanuts (1¾-ounce bar)	280
semisweet chips, ¼ cup	215
Fondant, 10 pieces	
uncoated	
candy corn	35
mints, pastel (about ⅝-inch square)	75
chocolate-coated	
miniature mints	95
Fruit leather, 1 ounce	80
Fudge, vanilla or chocolate, 1 ounce	
plain	110
with nuts	120
Granola bar (about 1½ ounces), 1	
oats, raisins, coconut	195
oats, peanuts, wheat germ	205
Gumdrops, 1 ounce (about 8 pieces)	95
Hard candy, 1 ounce (about 5 pieces or 2 lollipops)	105

Food and Portion	Calories
Jelly beans, 1 ounce (10 pieces about ¾ × ½ inch)	95
Licorice	
bite-sized, ¼ cup	170
stick, 6½ inches long, 1	40
shoestring, 43 inches long, 1	70
Marshmallows, 1 ounce (about 1⅛-inch diameter), about 4	90

BEVERAGES
(See also the Milk, Vegetable, and Fruit sections.)

Fruit Drinks

Food and Portion	Calories
Fruit-flavored drink, prepared from powder, 8 fluid ounces	
presweetened	
regular	120
low calorie	5
sugar added	90
Fruit drinks, canned, 8 fluid ounces	
fruit punch	115
grape or orange	125
Lemonade or limeade, frozen concentrate, sweetened, reconstituted, 8 fl. ounces	100

Carbonated Beverages

Food and Portion	Calories
Club soda, 12-ounce can	0
Cola-type, 12-ounce can	
regular	150
diet	5
Fruit-flavored, 12-ounce can	
regular	150
diet	0
Ginger ale, 12-ounce can	
regular	125
diet	0
Root beer, 12-ounce can	
regular	150
diet	0

Coffee and Tea

Food and Portion	Calories
Coffee and tea, brewed or instant, unsweetened, 6-fluid-ounce cup	Trace
Tea, instant, presweetened mix, 8 fluid ounces	
regular	25
low calorie	5

Food and Portion	Calories
Alcoholic Beverages	
Beer, 12-ounce can or bottle	
regular	150
light	100
Gin, rum, vodka, scotch, or bourbon, 1½-fluid-ounce jigger	105
Wines	
table, red or white, 5-fluid-ounce glass	100
dessert, 3½-fluid-ounce glass	155
coolers, 8-fluid-ounce glass	120

SUGARS, SYRUPS, JAMS, AND JELLIES	
Chocolate syrup, 1 tablespoon	
thin-type	40
fudge-type	70
Honey, 1 tablespoon	65
Jams and preserves, 1 tablespoon	55
Jellies, 1 tablespoon	50
Sugar, granulated or brown, 1 tablespoon	50
Table syrup, 1 tablespoon	55

FATS, OILS, AND CREAMS	
Fats and Oils	
Butter or stick margarine	
1 teaspoon or 1 pat	35
1 tablespoon	100
Margarine, soft, 1 teaspoon	
regular	35
diet	15
Table spread, 1 teaspoon	25
Oil, 1 tablespoon	120
Salad dressings, commercial, 1 tablespoon	
regular	
blue or Roquefort cheese	75
buttermilk	55
creamy-type	70
French	65
Italian	70
mayonnaise	100
mayonnaise-type	55
Russian	75
Thousand Island	60
low calorie	
French	20
Italian	15
mayonnaise or mayonnaise-type	35
Thousand Island	25

Food and Portion	Calories
Cream	
Half-and-half (milk and cream), 1 tablespoon	20
Light, coffee or table, 1 tablespoon	30
Sour, 1 tablespoon	30
Whipped, pressurized, 2 tablespoons	20
Whipping, heavy	
unwhipped, 1 tablespoon	50
whipped, 2 tablespoons	50

Imitation Cream Products	
(Made with vegetable fat.)	
Creamers	
liquid, 1 tablespoon	20
powdered, 1 teaspoon	10
Sour dressing (nonbutterfat sour cream), 1 tablespoon	25
Whipped dessert topping, 2 tablespoons	
frozen	30
powdered, made with whole milk	20
pressurized	25

CONDIMENTS	
Barbecue sauce, 1 tablespoon	10
Catsup, 1 tablespoon	20
Gravy, 2 tablespoons	
meat or poultry	20
mushroom	10
Horseradish, 1 tablespoon	5
Mustard, prepared, yellow, 1 teaspoon	5
Olives, canned	
green, stuffed or with pits, 4 small or 3 large	15
ripe, Mission, pitted, 3 medium or 2 extra large	15
Pickles	
dill, 3¾ inches long, 1	5
sweet gherkin, about 2½ inches long, 1	20
Relish, sweet, finely chopped, 1 tablespoon	20
Soy sauce, 1 tablespoon	10
Steak sauce, 1 tablespoon	10
Tartar sauce, 1 tablespoon	7

Menu Planning

The Importance of Menu Planning

Menu planning not only is essential for successful entertaining, but also is fundamental to healthful and gratifying everyday dining. Menu planning should be adopted as a pleasant, habitual priority no matter how busy life may be. In fact, it may be said that the busier one is, the more important menu planning becomes—to help assure good nutrition for the energy and feeling of well-being needed to meet the challenges and rigors of an active life, and to orchestrate satisfying mealtimes which help placate stress and bring busy families together.

Weekly Household Menu Planning

Household menu planning is best done on a weekly basis for several reasons:

GOOD NUTRITION

The Dietary Guidelines for Americans—the United States government's seven recommendations to Americans for a healthful diet—apply to diets consumed over several days and not to single meals or foods (pages 788–799). The first Dietary Guideline is "Eat a Variety of Foods." Foods contain combinations of nutrients and other healthful substances. No single food can supply all nutrients in the needed amounts. Pre-arranging menus one week at a time affords a better opportunity to consciously include a greater variety of healthful foods in diets.

The Food Guide Pyramid (page 790) is a useful tool which translates the Dietary Guidelines into recommended daily servings of particular food groups. Nutrition Facts Labels (page 790), now found on most packaged foods, also help menu planners to select foods which ensure enough essential nutrients, and to know the calorie, fat, cholesterol, and sodium content of foods.

Planning weekly menus based upon the Dietary Guidelines for Americans, with the assistance of the Food Guide Pyramid and Nutrition Facts Labels, will promote good health, and help to reduce the risk for chronic diseases such as heart disease, certain cancers, diabetes, stroke, and osteoporosis, which are leading causes of death and disability among Americans (see page 789).

SAVINGS OF TIME AND MONEY

A weekly menu from which a shopping list of needed foods is made, allows for one major marketing trip a week, possibly augmented by a brief midweek stop at the supermarket. Not only does weekly grocery shopping save a significant amount of time, but also it eliminates the taxing frustration and hassle caused by the daily quandary over what to have for dinner. When fatigued, it is easy to throw in the towel and opt to eat out, or, if you live in a city or suburb, order in—both of which can develop into expensive and possibly less nutritious habits.

Seven-day meal planning also contributes to time and money frugality by enabling good use of leftovers in timesaving ways.

MEAL APPEAL

Advance meal planning generally results in more interesting, good-looking plates of food due to prethought to considerations such as food color and decoration (see Menu Planning Considerations, below).

Menu-Planning Considerations

There are a number of things to consider when planning menus, whether for everyday meals or for entertaining:

SEASON OF THE YEAR

Menus should be planned around the availability of foods at their peak quality. Although more and more produce items are becoming available year-round, shipped from many points on the globe, most produce is at its best when grown closer to home and consumed during the height of its particular growing season; for example, winter grapefruit, summer tomatoes, fall pears, and spring asparagus.

Midwesterners are enamored of the four distinct seasons which characterize the climate in this region. Weather variety is a welcome spice of life, they contend. Writing the menus for this chapter made me more acutely aware of the extent to which Heartlanders associate particular foods and menus with each of the four seasons. In tune with nature, our taste buds seem to house food calendars which prompt yearnings for cantaloupe in the summer and apples in the fall.

The mercurial outdoor temperature in the Midwest—part and parcel of the changeable seasons—is a persuasive governor of our eating patterns. When it's below zero, hot, robust stews and heavy meat dishes are needed to ward off the cold. Scorching summers beg for lighter fare and, as a partial throwback to the days before air-conditioning, foods which can be prepared without turning on the oven.

WHAT GOES WITH WHAT

Flavor, texture, and balance are central considerations in determining what foods go well together.

FLAVOR. A recipe should be reviewed for spices, herbs, sweetness, tartness, saltiness, and secondary ingredients before deciding its menu teammates. To illustrate, Chicken and Noodles delicately flavored with sautéed mushrooms and chicken broth (see recipe, page 210) requires fairly bland accompaniments if the delicacy of this dish is not to be drowned in overriding flavors. Mashed Potatoes and Baking Powder Biscuits are the subtly flavored, traditional Midwest complements to this favorite poultry fare. I chose to include both on the family dinner menu in this chapter (page 835).

Deciding to go ahead and reflect a personal but somewhat unconventional dining fondness, I suggested that in addition to butter, Apply Jelly be served with the biscuits. Jelly was selected over jam because it is lighter in texture, making it less predominate. Apple Jelly was chosen because its flavor is among the least pronounced of all jellies, and because its color is similar to that of the biscuits and main dish, making it less distractive. (I didn't want to draw undue attention to what other diners might judge an unorthodox food on a table with Chicken and Noodles.) This mental exercise in menu planning is related here to illustrate the various types of flavor and concomitant considerations encountered in the organization of menus.

TEXTURE. Variation in food textures makes a meal more interesting and palatable. For the Chicken and Noodles menu discussed above, Green Beans and a salad of Sliced Oranges on Leaf Lettuce with Poppy Seed Dressing were selected as complementary items to provide a diversity of textures without hampering the overall mood of the dinner. The Green Beans also function to give the entrée plate more eye appeal by supplying a color that contrasts with the other food on the plate.

BALANCE. While a nutritionally balanced meal might arguably require inclusion of a protein, carbohydrate, vegetable, and fruit, it is not a necessity that an item from each of the five main food groups in the Food Guide Pyramid be included in every single meal (see Good Nutrition, page 812). Sound nutrition does require that each meal reflect a balance of foods from several of the food groups, and that the day's and week's menus encompass the balance of foods set forth in the Dietary Guidelines for Americans as translated on the Food Guide Pyramid. Nutritionally balanced meals are also more pleasing to eat because of their diversity.

Balance also applies to the heaviness and intensity of menu components. A light salad luncheon entrée could appropriately be followed by a rich dessert. Lightish ambrosia might be a welcome finale to a hearty meal of pot roast, potatoes, and gravy. When assessing the balance of a proposed meal, the entire menu must be considered. When a meal is served in courses, the taste and texture of one course should comfortably lead to the next course.

Whether served in courses or at one time, all items on a menu, considered together, should add up to a satisfying, well-balanced whole.

Of course, it goes without saying that calories are always a key consideration that hope will not vanish (see pages 800–810). While I am totally committed to weight control and proper nutrition, I am also a strong advocate of pies, cakes, and cookies supremely made with butter, eggs, whole milk, and other wonderful ingredients, but consumed in reasonably small quantities and at wide intervals. (As the Food Guide Pyramid schools: "Fats, Oils, & Sweets: USE SPARINGLY.")

When it comes to menu planning, I am a firm believer that family holiday meals and occasions when friends are entertained, are special, festive times of celebration, friendship, and love, when a guiltless jumping of the calorie track is not only permissible, but desirable. That's part of what it's all about! Over the course of the holidays, two slices of Pumpkin Pie, Mashed Potatoes with plenty of Turkey Gravy, and a few pieces of to-die-for Fudge will not shipwreck the weight and health of most people who day in and day out vigilantly monitor their nutrition and calorie consumption. The nutrition- and calorie-abiding should not be compelled to sacrifice on special dining occasions because of the 365-day-a-year undisciplined eaters at the table. "Harsh," you say? Perhaps, but I prefer to call it "looking reality squarely in the eye."

APPEARANCE

The appearance of a plate or table of food is a potent element of its palatability. Planning and arranging a plate of food is like painting a picture. The colors should be compatible and help to convey the tone of the meal. On a hot summer day, pale hues can elicit a feeling of coolness and calm. Monochromatic plates of food generally should be avoided.

When planning a menu, visualize how the foods will look on the plate. Select foods of various shapes which will arrange attractively. For example, try to avoid choosing foods which are all round in shape. A plate of all round-shaped foods could prove artistically and palatably monotonous.

If arranging plates of food in the kitchen before bringing them to the table, give thought to how you place the foods on the plate. When steak or other meat requiring cutting is on the menu, place it on the right side of the plate so the diner can cut it conveniently. Then, place the plate in front of the diner in that position. If you are aware of left-handed guests, reverse the arrangement of foods on their plates.

When possible, include decoration as the final touch—even if it's just a sprig of watercress or parsley (see pages 379–409).

TIME AVAILABILITY

Selection of menu items must be realistically weighed against the time available to prepare and serve them.

For people working outside of the home, preparation of more time-consuming dishes on the weekends, with planning for use of leftovers in snappy-to-prepare menu items the first day or two of the week, helps alleviate some of the after-work time crunch.

More formal entertaining and entertaining large groups in all manner of style present special time problems. A written schedule for marketing, advance preparation of foods, table setting, final food preparation, serving, and cleanup during and after the event are necessary in order to conduct smooth, relaxed parties. This kind of detailed forethought assures that the menu is doable with the available time and help.

At formal dinner parties, it is virtually imperative that competent help be engaged to carry out final preparation of food courses and to serve them. When one course is cleared from the table, the next one should be ready for service within a short period of time. Party-time assistance allows the host/hostess to remain at the table with the guests for the majority of the meal—a more gracious way to preside over formal dinners.

In most modern households, the menu planning, food preparation, and serving of everyday meals and meals served at informal parties are carried out entirely by household members. Pleasurable family dining and entertaining are the reward for organized menu planning and food preparation.

Suggested Menus

The menus that follow run the gamut from formal dinner parties to casual picnics. They may be simplified by eliminating or substituting dishes, or made more elaborate by adding or replacing menu items. The menus may be prepared as presented or used as guidelines and imagination generators for the creation of your own special party fare and family meals.

NOTE: When not otherwise specified in the menus, it is presumed that milk will be served with meals to children and to adults who wish it, and that coffee (preferably decaffeinated) or tea will be served to adults with or after dessert.

Although dessert sweets appear in many of the family menus, they are included for the purpose of suggesting menu items which might be selected at times when it is decided that a dessert sweet will be served. In menu planning, the consumption of sweets should be paced (see Balance, page 814).

Menus for Entertaining

HOLIDAYS

Christmastime Buffet Brunch

Breakfast Punch
Guest choice, with or without spirits (page 697)

(Serve informally before the buffet.)

MAIN BUFFET

Fresh Fruit Compote (page 346); omit citrus fruits)
Eggsotic Eggs (page 268)
Tiny Sausage Patties (page 189)

Miniature Cranberry-Orange Muffins (page 445)
Pat Berry's Julekake (sliced) (page 422)
Ribbed Butter Balls (page 396)

SIDE BUFFET

Platters of Christmas Cookies and Candies:
Lebkuchen (page 600)
Charlotte's Butter Rum Cheese Bars (page 601)
Spritz (page 644)
Decorated Cutout Cookies (page 634)
Fudge with Holly Decoration (page 685)
Divinity (page 678)   Peanut Brittle (page 681)

Coffee—guest choice, regular or decaffeinated
Hot Tea

(If you have an overabundance of cookies and candies, arrange a small, decorative plateful or boxful tied in a red, satin ribbon for each guest to take home. Keep the surprise packages of goodies out of the guests' view until they begin to leave.)

Holiday Open House

Egg Nog
Guest choice, with or without spirits (page 694)

(Other alcoholic and nonalcoholic drinks may be made available for guests who prefer them.)

MAIN BUFFET

Swedish Meatballs (page 78)
Sausage Puffs (page 76)
Shrimp with Louis Dressing Dip (page 62)

Christmas Cheese Ball (page 70)
Decorated Deviled Eggs (page 267)
Red and Green Vegetable Tray (page 69)

SIDE BUFFET

Traditional Holiday Fruitcake (page 564)
Rum Balls (page 626)
Christmas Holly Wreaths (page 625)

(For greater elegance, pass the Sausage Puffs and Decorated Deviled Eggs on trays to the guests. For a less elaborate open house, serve only the sweet foods, in which case two or more items, such as Pound Cake, page 552, Coconut Macaroons with Holiday Decoration, page 611, and Chocolate-Almond Toffee, page 679, could be added to the menu.)

FORMAL DINNER PARTIES

Hors d'Oeuvres:
Tartlets with Crabmeat Filling (page 70)
Bok Choy Stuffed with Red Caviar (page 66)
Deviled Eggs with Dillweed and Caper Decoration
(page 267)
Pigs in a Blanket (Saucijzebroodjes) (page 76)

Cocktails

....

Scalloped Lobster (page 81)
Elegant Crackers (page 449)

Wine: Chardonnay

....

Sophisticated Salad (page 125)
Toasted Sesame Bread (page 428)

....

Veal Tenderloin Roulades with Wild Rice
(page 180)
Peas with Mushrooms and Shallots (page 327)
Garnish: Tomato Rose (page 405) on a
Bed of Coriander

Petite Cloverleaf Rolls (page 424)

Butter Roses (page 394)

Blush Wine Jelly (page 746)

Wine: Cabernet Sauvignon

....

Champagne

Apricot Chiffon Pie with Sugared Violets
(page 499)

....

Coffee

Lace Cookies (page 627)

Tutti-Frutti Rolls (page 642)

Rum Balls (page 626)

....

Cognac

◆

Hors d'Oeuvres:
Cucumber Wheels (page 67)
Tray Decoration: Cucumber Rose (page 399)
Spinach Bars (page 79)
Triple-Layer Caviar Spread (page 66)
Cherry Tomatoes Stuffed with Curried
Chicken Salad (page 68)

Champagne Cocktails

....

Consommé Madrilène (page 91)
Cheese Straws (page 450)

Wine: Sauvignon Blanc

....

Salad: Shrimp, Avocado, and Melon
on Belgian Endive
Sherried Dressing with Fennel and Thyme
(page 149)
Deluxe Sesame Seed Crackers (page 449)

....

Roast Beef Tenderloin with Mushroom Sauce
(page 162)
Wild Rice with Bacon and Onions (page 277)
Tomato Baskets of Vegetables (page 340)
Toasted Parmesan Bread (page 429; omit parsley
and use small-diameter bread)

Wine: Cabernet Sauvignon

....

Lemon Chiffon Pie (page 504)

Coffee

....

Chocolate-Covered Cherries (page 680)
Penuche (page 686)
Candied Orange Peel (page 685)

MODERATELY ELABORATE DINNER PARTIES

Winter

Hors d'Oeuvre:
Artichoke Dip (page 73)   Assorted Crackers

All-Yellow Vegetable Salad (page 125)
Deluxe Crackers (page 449)

Loin of Pork with Brandied Apples (page 186)
Natural Juice
Boiled, Unpared, Small Potatoes (page 328)
Lightly Tossed in Melted Butter
Snow Peas (page 327)

Whole-Wheat Orange Bread (page 440)
Butter Curls (page 395)

Whipped Cream Cake
with Crème de Menthe Frosting (page 539)

Coffee

◆

Hors d'Oeuvres:
Blue Cheese–Whiskey Spread (page 64)
Water Chestnut Roll-ups (page 78)

Beet and Watercress Salad (page 126)
Elegant Crackers (page 449)

Spareribs and Sauerkraut with Potatoes (page 187)
Mixed Peas and Carrots
(see page 302 for preparation of carrots)

Toasted Herb Bread (page 428)

Grapefruit and Orange Tart (page 514)

Coffee

◆

GERMAN FARE

Hors d'Oeuvres:
Braunschweiger Spread (page 65)
Pumpernickel Cocktail Bread
Swiss and Smoked Cheeses   Assorted Crackers

Wine: German Riesling–Kabinett from the
Reingau or Mosel-Saar-Ruwer Region

Beer

Sauerbraten with Potato Dumplings (page 169)
Red Cabbage with Red Wine (page 311)
Cucumber Salad (page 131)

Honey-Seed Bread (page 421)
Fluted Butter Wedges (page 395)

Black Forest Cherry Torte
(Schwarzwälder Kirschtorte) (page 570)

Coffee with Brandy and Whipped Cream

Spring

Hors d'Oeuvre:
Crabmeat Supreme with Sautéed Toast Points
(page 74)

Hearts of Palm–Persimmon Salad (page 123)
Elegant Crackers (page 449)

Roast Leg of Lamb with Mint Jelly Glaze
(page 196)
Roast Lamb Gravy (page 377)

Oven-Browned Potatoes (page 334)

Mixed Carrots, Peas, and Cauliflower (see page 302
for preparation of carrots and cauliflower)

Peppermint Pears (page 729)

Cloverleaf Rolls (page 424)

Butter Curls (page 395)

....

Jerri Goreham's Chocolate-Nut Bundt Cake
(page 548)

Vanilla Ice Cream (page 669) with a Piped Rosette
of Chocolate Decorator Whipped Cream
(page 374)

Coffee

◆

Shrimp Mousse with Dill
Served as an Hors d'Oeuvre (page 80)

....

Fantasia Salad: (page 132)
Deluxe Sesame Seed Crackers (page 449)

....

Veal Piccata with Thyme (page 182)
New Potatoes with Parsley (page 331)
Vegetable Bundles (page 324)

Butterhorn Rolls (page 424)

Butter Roses (page 394)

....

Butterscotch Pie (page 489)

Coffee

◆

....

Hors d'Oeuvre:
Symphony Spread (page 65)

Fresh Asparagus Salad (page 131)
Sautéed Toast Points (page 430)

....

Perch Fillets with Hazelnuts and White Wine
(page 221)

Rice in Ring Mold (page 273; omit pine nuts)
filled with Peas, Mushrooms, and Shallots
(page 327)

Carrots Cosmopolitan (page 312)
Baking Dish Decoration: Carrot Bow (page 398)
with Leek Ribbons (page 401)

Parker House Rolls (page 424)

Ribbed Butter Balls (page 396)

Pear Butter (page 765)

....

Rhubarb Custard Pie (page 497)

Coffee

Summer

Hors d'Oeuvres:
Kale Dip (page 61)
Deviled Ham Delectables (page 74)

....

Grilled Tenderloin Fillets (page 250)
Onion Butter Stars (page 369)
Twice-Baked Potatoes (page 329)
Baked Tomato Halves Parmesan (page 404)
Field of Dreams Salad (page 127; omit tomatoes)
Toasted Bacon Bread (page 427)

....

Mrs. Dowell's Dessert (page 664)

Coffee

◆

Hors d'Oeuvres:
Stuffed Fennel Sticks (page 69)
Cherry Tomatoes Stuffed with Curried Chicken
Salad (page 68)

....

Grilled Lobster Tails
Basted with Tarragon Butter Sauce (page 258)
Clarified Butter (page 370)
Rice Pilaf (page 274)
Mixed Miniature Vegetables (page 302)
Cucumber-Dill Ring (page 135)
Made in Individual Salad Molds

Hard Rolls   Butter Curls (page 395)

....

Concerto for Dates and Nuts (page 666)

Coffee

◆

Hors d'Oeuvre:
Raw Vegetable Platter with Dip (page 61)

....

Sherried Beef Broth (page 88)
Rice Crackers (page 450)

....

Nasturtium Salad (page 132)
Sautéed Toast Points (page 430)

....

Poached Salmon Steaks (page 225)
Hollandaise Sauce (page 367)
New Potatoes (see New Potatoes with Parsley, page
331; omit lemon juice and parsley)
Baked Cucumbers (page 317)
Plate Decoration: Bell Pepper Leaves and Flower
Petals in Assorted Colors (page 402)

....

Strawberry Tart (page 513)

Coffee

Fall

Hors d'Oeuvre:
Hot Bourbon-Cheese Dip (page 72)

....

Cream of Broccoli Soup (page 92)
Cheese Straws (page 450)

....

Tossed Salad: Bibb Lettuce, Arugula, Hearts of
Palm, and Chopped Eggs
Lemon Pepper Dressing (page 148)

....

Wild Pheasant with Port Wine Sauce (page 238)
Wild Rice Cooked in Chicken Broth (page 276)
Patty Davis's Scalloped Corn (page 316)
Apple-Lingonberry Garnish (page 397)
Whole-Wheat Prune Bread (page 440)
Ribbed Butter Balls (page 396)

....

Mincemeat–Rum Ice Cream Pie (page 671)

Coffee

◆

Hors d'Oeuvre:
Shrimp-Cheese Log (page 71)

....

Hickory-Smoked Ham Mousse (page 82)
Sautéed Toast Points (page 430)

....

Fresh Pear Salad with Ginger Dressing (page 111)

Siegfried's Flank Steak Roulade with Potatoes
(page 162)

Green Beans with Marjoram (page 306)

Petite Baking Powder Biscuits (page 446)

Butter Pats

Cherry Cheese Pie (page 509)

Coffee

◆

SPAGHETTI DINNER

Hors d'Oeuvres:

Summer Sausage–Horseradish Dip (page 62)

Pizza Mushrooms (page 77)

Antipasto Platter:

Sliced Hard Salami

Sliced Provolone Cheese

Ripe Greek Olives

Fennel and Tomatoes Braised in Wine (page 319;
fully reduce or drain; serve room temperature)

Deviled Eggs with Caper Decoration (page 267)

Marinated Artichoke Hearts (use Basic Vinaigrette
Dressing, page 152, for marinade)

Pickled Beets (page 770)

Pickled Mixed Vegetables (page 773)

Sardines

Italian Bread (sliced ½ inch thick)

Fluted Butter Wedges (page 395)

Wine: Chianti Classico Riserva

Grace's Spaghetti and Meatballs (page 288)

Tossed Salad: Boston Lettuce, Romaine, Shredded
Carrots, and Chopped Celery
Italian Salad Dressing (page 148)

Garlic Bread (page 368)

Fresh Pears Stuffed with Rum–Flavored Ricotta
Cheese (page 345)

Biscotti

Wine: Dolcetto

Espresso

◆

BUFFET DINNER

Hors d'Oeuvres:

Shrimp (page 62)   Cocktail Sauce (page 361)

Mini Bagels with Smoked Salmon (page 69)

(Serve informally before the buffet.)

MAIN BUFFET

Traditional Baked Ham (page 192)

Cinnamon Yam Balls (page 336)

Buffet Vegetables (page 323)

Tossed Salad: Bok Choy, Bibb Lettuce, Watercress,
and Belgian Endive with Pine Nuts
Basic Vinaigrette Dressing (page 152)

Mini-Sized Cornmeal Muffins (page 443)

Butter Pats

SIDE BUFFET

Joy McFarland's Mile-High Torte (page 568)

Coffee

Pink and White Peppermints Respectively
Decorated with Pink and Yellow Rosebuds
(page 684)

*(Pass on a doily-lined silver or crystal plate a short time
after dessert.)*

INFORMAL DINNERS

Winter

CHILI DINNER

Hors d'Oeuvre:
Guacamole (page 62)

....

Dee's Chili (page 97)
Seven-Layer Salad (page 140)

Hot, Buttered Italian Bread

....

Lemon-Filled Sponge Cake (page 557)

Coffee

◆

Hors d'Oeuvre:
Assorted Cheeses and Crackers

....

Ham Loaf with Horseradish Sauce (page 193)
Scalloped Potatoes (page 330)
Dinner Brussels Sprouts (page 309)
Zippy Vegetable Salad Mold (page 137;
omit green bell peppers)

Whole-Wheat Dinner Rolls
Butter Pats

....

Crème de Menthe Bars (page 601)
Vanilla Fudge Swirl Ice Cream

Coffee

◆

Hors d'Oeuvre:
Chutney Cheese Ball (page 72)   Crackers

◆

Iowa Pork Chops (page 185)
Rhubarb-Strawberry Conserve (page 761)
Broccoli-Rice Casserole (page 273)
Apricot Salad (page 116)
Toasted Parmesan-Parsley Bread (page 429)

....

Graham Cracker Fudge Pie (page 487)

Coffee

Spring

Hors d'Oeuvres:
Edam Cheese   Cheddar Crackers
Smoked Almonds

....

Vegetable Salad: Red Cherry Tomatoes, Sliced
Green Zucchini, Diagonally Sliced Carrots,
Sliced Celery, Yellow Bell Pepper Strips, Peas, and
Sliced Mushrooms on Leaf Lettuce
Mustard Dressing (page 149)

....

Beef Brisket (page 166)
Steamed, Unpared, Small, Yukon Gold Potatoes
(page 328) Lightly Tossed in Melted Butter
Fresh Green Beans (page 305)

Toasted Herb Bread with Parsley and Thyme
(page 428)

....

Fresh Strawberries and Blueberries with Triple Sec
Scotch Shortbread (page 639)

Coffee

◆

Hors d'Oeuvre:
Dried Beef and Green Pepper Spread (page 66)

Lasagna (page 290)
Lettuce Salad: Romaine, Boston Lettuce, Arugula, and Radicchio
Basic Vinaigrette Dressing (page 152)
Relish Tray: Carrot Curls (page 398), Celery Brushes (page 399), Grooved Cucumber Slices (page 399), and Ripe Greek Olives
Toasted Parmesan-Parsley Bread (page 429)

German Chocolate Cake (3 Layer) (page 531)
Coffee

◆

Hors d'Oeuvres:
Dill Pickle Roll-ups (page 70)
Beer Nuts (page 83)

Fish Chowder (page 96)   Oyster Crackers
Tossed Salad: Red-tip Leaf Lettuce, Chinese Cabbage, Kidney Beans (canned, drained, and rinsed), Sliced Yellow Zucchini, Fresh Green Beans (cooked; page 305), Sliced Celery, and Red Tomatoes (blanched, page 44; peeled; quartered; seeded and cored, page 45; and cut into chunks)
French Dressing (page 148)
Deviled Eggs Decorated with a Tiny Black Olive Strip and Parsley Leaves (page 267)

Strawberry "Shortcake" (with Angel Food Cake) (page 555)
Coffee

Summer

BARBECUED RIBS
ON THE PATIO OR IN THE BACKYARD

Hors d'Oeuvres:
Raw Vegetable Platter with Vegetable Dip (page 61)
Oyster Cracker Snacks (page 83)

Gary's Hickory-Smoked Pork Ribs (page 252)
Calico Beans (page 278)
Coleslaw (page 133)
Corn Bread (page 441)
Butter Pats

Frosted Brownies (page 602)
Hot and Iced Coffee   Hot and Iced Tea

◆

FISH FRY
COOK AND SERVE OUTDOORS OR INDOORS

Taco Spread (page 63)   Tortilla Chips

Panfried Walleye Fillets (page 224)
Lemon Wedges   Tartar Sauce (page 361)
American Fries (page 330)
Green Beans with Bacon and Onions (page 305)
Toasted Herb Bread (page 428; omit chives)

Peach Pie (page 481)
Hot and Iced Coffee   Hot and Iced Tea

◆

CORN FEED
ON THE PORCH, DECK, OR PATIO

Hors d'Oeuvres:

Bourbon Bangers (page 79)

Dilly Beans (page 767)

....

Just-Picked and Shucked Corn on the Cob
(page 315)
Melted Butter
Potato Salad (page 133)
Onions in Foil (page 260)
Homegrown, Vine-Ripened, Sliced Tomatoes

....

Homemade Strawberry Ice Cream (page 669)

....

Peanut Clusters (page 681)

Hot and Iced Coffee   Hot and Iced Tea

Fall

Hors d'Oeuvres:

Blue Cheese Spread (page 64)

Asparagus Rolls (page 73)

....

Brandied Pork Stew with Thyme Dumplings
(page 98)
Citrus Fruit Three-Layer Party Salad (page 115)

Wine: Beaujolais-Villages (before November 15);
Beaujolais Nouveau (after November 15)

....

Harvest Moon Cake (page 534)
Cinnamon Ice Cream

Coffee

◆

Hors d'Oeuvre:
ABC Dip (page 62)

....

Wild Goose Pâté (page 242)
Pumpernickel Bread
Cornichon Pickle Fans (page 402)

....

Wild Rice Soup (page 95)
Fruit Salad: Orange and Grapefruit Sections
(page 47) on Leaf Lettuce
Poppy Seed Dressing (page 150)
Decoration: Maraschino Cherry Half

Soy Whole-Wheat Muffins (page 444)

Butter Pats

....

Butter Pecan Ice Cream
with Hot Maple Brandy Sauce (page 371)
Dream Bars (page 598)

Coffee

◆

Hors d'Oeuvres:
Gouda in Puff Pastry (page 75)
Unsalted Cashews

....

Vegetable Collage with Chèvre (page 128)

....

Rosemary Chicken Breasts
with Red Raspberry Sauce (page 208)
Baked Rice (page 275)
Asparagus Spears Amandine (page 303)

Butterhorn Rolls (page 424)

Butter Pats

....

Gingerbread (page 544)
Whipped Cream (page 373)

Coffee

◆

Hors d'Oeuvre:
Asparagus Rolls (page 73)

....

Tossed Salad: Bibb Lettuce, Belgian Endive, and
Watercress
Basic Vinaigrette Dressing (page 152)
Rice Crackers (page 450)

....

Alice's Meat and Tater Pie (page 173)
Glazed Carrots (page 313)

....

Apple Dumplings (page 650)   Half-and-Half

Coffee

Hurry-Up Informal Dinner

Hors d'Oeuvre:
Last-Minute Cheese Spread (page 64)   Crackers

....

Boston Lettuce, Hearts of Palm, and Mushroom
Salad (page 123)

Warm Dinner Rolls
Butter Pats

....

Dinner-in-a-Hurry Casserole (page 296)
Asparagus Spears (page 303)
Sliced Tomatoes (in season) or Corn Relish
(home canned, page 777, or commercially canned)

....

Vanilla Ice Cream
with Fresh Red Raspberries and Blueberries
Cookies

Coffee

LUNCHEONS

Winter

Aperitif: Red Dubonnet
(on the rocks with lemon twist, optional)

....

Chicken Breasts Stuffed with Spinach and
Mushrooms (page 205)
Rice in Ring Mold (page 273)
Peach and Cottage Cheese Salad (page 111)
Janet Stern's Mandel (Almond) Bread (page 438)
Butter Roses (page 394)

....

Maple Nut Mousse (page 665)

Coffee   Tea

Spring

BUFFET STYLE

Aperitif: Dry Sack Sherry

....

Hot Chicken Salad (page 141)
Fresh Fruit Compote (page 346)
Petite Caramel Rolls (Sticky Rolls)
(page 427; without pecans)
Ribbed Butter Balls (page 396)

....

French Silk Pie (page 492)

Coffee   Tea

Summer

Aperitif: German Riesling-Spätlese Wine

. . . .

Tuna–Almond Luncheon Salad (page 143)
Cooked, Cold Asparagus Spears (page 303)
and Uncut Green Beans (page 305)
Dill Sauce (page 363)

Small Butterhorn Rolls
(page 424; serve barely warm)
Butter Curls (page 395)

. . . .

Glazed Fresh Blueberry Pie (page 478)

Hot and Iced Coffee   Hot and Iced Tea

Fall

BRIDGE LUNCHEON

Aperitif: Kir (3 ounces light, dry white wine
and ¾ ounce crème de cassis, page 21)

. . . .

Lobster Salad (page 146) with Garnish

Thinly Sliced Toasted Herb Bread
(page 428; without chives)

. . . .

Lady Baltimore Cake (page 537)

Coffee   Tea

. . . .

At the Bridge Tables:
Spiced Pecans (page 688)
Cream Cheese Mints (page 683)

EUROPEAN-STYLE LUNCH IN THE PARK OR GARDEN

French or Italian Bread

Semisoft to Hard Cheeses for Slicing
(such as Gruyère, Groviera, Italian-made Fontina,
American Swiss, Provolone, Port-Salut, Brick, and
European-made Muenster)

Marinated Dried Italian Olives (page 399)
(optional)

Full-Bodied Red Wine*
(such as Barolo [Italian], Barbaresco [Italian], a
strong Bordeaux, and Cabernet Sauvignon)

. . . .

Fresh Fruits: Grapes, Apples, and Strawberries

Amaretti and/or Italian Rum Cake (optional)

*Although I prefer red wine on these outings, white wines,
such as Chardonnay, Chablis, and Semisweet Vouvray
(French), also complement the fare.*

AFTERNOON TEA OR RECEPTION

BUFFET STYLE

Tea Sandwiches:

Pared and Thinly Sliced Seedless Cucumbers and
Watercress with Dilled Soft-Style Cream Cheese
(between thin slices of White Bread, page 419)

Thinly Sliced Radishes and Soft-Style Cream
Cheese (between thin slices of Limpa
[Swedish Rye Bread], page 420)

Open-Faced Chicken Salad
(follow recipe, page 68; omit Cherry Tomatoes and
Curry Powder; include decoration)
(on thin slices of Whole-Wheat Bread, page 419)

Open-Faced Crabmeat Salad
(follow recipe, page 70; omit Tartlet Shells;
include decoration) (on thin slices of
White Bread, page 419)

Thinly Sliced Lemon Bread (page 435) and Butter
(close-faced)

....

Petits Fours
Cream-Filled Pastry Fluffs (page 641)

Pink Peppermints (in colors to match table decor;
decorated with piped rosebuds, page 684)

Spiced Pecans (page 688)

Tea   Coffee

SUNDAY BRUNCH

BUFFET STYLE

Champagne

Bloody Marys

Orange Blossoms
(freshly squeezed, strained orange juice and gin)

MAIN BUFFET

Arranged Fresh Fruit Platter:

Strawberries, Mangoes, Pineapple, Kiwis, Seedless
Red and White Grapes, Cantaloupe,
and Honeydew Melon

Chicken à la King (page 209)
over Puff Pastry Shells (Patty Shells) (page 470)

Brunch Eggs (page 265)

Bedeviled Bacon (page 191)

Marie Dalbey's Sour Cream Coffee Cake
(page 452)

Small Cinnamon Rolls (page 426)

Cranberry Nut Bread (page 434)

Fluted Butter Wedges (page 395)

SIDE BUFFET

Marble Cake (page 550)

Cornflakes Macaroons (page 607)

Coffee

COCKTAIL PARTY

Cocktails

Wines: Guest Choice of American Chardonnay (or
French Meursault), German Riesling–Kabinett, and
French Tavel (a rosé)

SERVE ON ONE OR MORE TABLES

Shrimp (a generous amount on ice)
with Dips (page 62)
Cocktail Sauce (page 361)

Hot Swiss Cheese Sauce (page 368)

Winglets Oriental (page 79)

Petite Potatoes (page 68)

Arranged Mixed Platter: Cucumber and Cheese
Canapés (page 67), Tartlets with Crabmeat Filling
(page 70), and Deviled Eggs (each decorated with a
tiny sprig of fresh dillweed and 3 capers) (page 267)

PASS ON TRAYS

Deviled Ham Delectables (page 74)

Sausage Puffs (page 76)

AFTER-THE-THEATER SUPPER

BUFFET STYLE

Champagne

....

Chicken Divan (page 206)

Orange Baskets Filled with Mixed Fresh Fruits
(page 401)

Small Cloverleaf Rolls (page 424)

Butter Roses (page 394)

....

Colette Wortman's Danish Puff (page 606)

Artist's Palette Thumbprints (page 622)

Coffee (regular and decaffeinated)

FALL FOOTBALL TAILGATE LUNCH

Beverages of Choice
(alcoholic and/or nonalcoholic)

....

Cold,* Sliced, Glazed Ham Loaf (page 194)
Carnival Salad (page 138)
Deviled Eggs (page 267)
Brown Bread (page 442) and Orange Butter (page 369) Sandwiches (cut in half)

....

Saint and Sinner Crunchies (page 606)
Snickerdoodles (page 630)

Coffee

....

Munchies (page 83) in Individual, Small
Zipper-Seal Plastic Bags
(to take to the game)

*If served within 2 hours after baking, the Ham Loaf
may be served warm.*

TEENAGE PREGAME DINNER

Hors d'Oeuvre:

Taco Spread (page 63)

Soft Drinks

....

Sloppy Joes (page 354)
Scalloped Corn (page 315)
Apple Salad (page 110)
Fat-Free (Skim) and Whole Milk
Soft Drinks

....

Milky Way Cake (page 551)
Vanilla Ice Cream (page 669)

Menus For Family Meals

HOLIDAYS

Thanksgiving Dinner

Roast Stuffed Turkey (page 212)
Sage Dressing (page 215)
Mashed Potatoes (page 332)
Turkey Gravy (page 378)
Candied Yams (page 337)
Vegetable Medley (page 308)
Spiced Peaches (page 774)
Watermelon Rind Pickles (page 772)
Cranberry-Orange Salad (page 117)
Cloverleaf Rolls (page 424)
Ribbed Butter Balls (page 396)
Wild Plum Butter (page 764)
Blackberry Jelly (page 739)

....

Pumpkin Pie (page 496)

Apple Pie (page 476) with Vanilla Ice Cream
(page 669)

Coffee   Milk

◆

Cup of Corn Chowder (page 96)

....

Roast Turkey Breast (page 214)
Yams Grand Marnier with Cranberries and
Kumquats (page 337)
Creamed Brussels Sprouts with Chestnuts
(page 309)
Relish Tray: Celery Brushes (page 339), Carrot

Curls (page 398), and Radish Roses (page 404)

Butterhorn Rolls (page 424)

Fluted Butter Wedges (page 395)

....

Vanilla Ice Cream (page 669) Sprinkled with
Ground Nutmeg

Pumpkin Bars with Cashew Frosting (page 592)

Coffee   Milk

◆

Roast Stuffed Turkey (page 212)
Oyster Dressing (page 215)

Mashed Potatoes (page 332)
Turkey Gravy (page 378)

Green Bean Casserole (page 305)

Carrots Cosmopolitan (page 312)

Jellied Cranberry Sauce (page 364)
Melon Ball Pickles (page 771)   Piccalli (page 780)

Pineapple–Cream Cheese Salad (page 120)

Pumpkin Bread (page 437)

Butter Pats

....

Cran-Apple Pie (page 476)
with Vanilla Ice Cream (page 669)

Coffee   Milk

Christmas Eve Dinner

Oyster Stew (page 103)   Oyster Crackers

Fluffy Egg Confetti Salad (page 136)

Arranged Platter: Lightly Marinated Fresh Green
Beans, Asparagus, and Red Cocktail Tomatoes; and
Olives (see Rhapsody Salad, page 129, for prepara-
tion of green beans and asparagus; use White Wine
Vinaigrette Dressing, page 153, for marinade)

....

Yule Log (page 560)

Coffee   Milk

Late Christmas Eve Snack

Egg Nog Coffee (page 695)

Zimtsterne (Cinnamon Stars) (page 637)

◆

Gouda in Puff Pastry (page 75)

Arranged Platter: Whole Strawberries and
Small Bunches of Green Grapes

Wine: Sauvignon Blanc or Beaujolais

Christmas Morning Breakfast

Broiled Grapefruit (page 347)

....

Brunch Eggs (page 265)

Bedeviled Bacon (page 191)

Cinnamon Rolls (page 426)

Lingonberry–Oat Bran Muffins (page 445)

Fluted Butter Wedges (page 395)

Coffee   Milk

(Continue serving coffee around the Christmas tree.)

Christmas Dinner

Roast Stuffed Turkey (page 212)
Chestnut Dressing (page 215)
Turkey Gravy (page 378)
Duchess Potatoes (page 333)
Scalloped Oysters (page 228)
Glazed Carrots with Kumquats (page 313)
Corn Relish (page 777)
Pickled Mixed Vegetables (page 773)
Christmas Gooseberry Salad (page 114)

Parker House Rolls (page 424)
Butter Pats
Apple Butter (page 763)   Cherry Jelly (page 740)

Melinda's Pumpkin Chiffon Pie (page 503)
Brandied Mincemeat Pie (page 486)

Coffee   Milk

◆

Wild Turkey Breast over Rice
with Spiced Grape Sauce (page 243)
Asparagus Spears Amandine (page 303)
Corn Pudding (page 316)
Strawberry-Avocado Holiday Salad (page 113)

Mincemeat Bread
with Ribbed Orange Butter Balls (page 436)

Eggnog Chiffon Pie (page 502)

Coffee   Milk

◆

Baked Goose with Apricot-Cognac Dressing
(page 241)
Corn-Oyster Casserole (page 317)
Braised Celery (page 314)
Spiced Seckel Pears (page 775)
Frosty Christmas Salad (page 112)

Cloverleaf Rolls (page 424)
Butter Curls (page 395)
Louise Piper's Mulberry Jam (page 756)

English Plum Pudding (page 658)
Coffee   Milk

Easter Breakfast

Freshly Squeezed Orange Juice
Cubed Mangoes and Blueberries

Scrambled Eggs with Fresh Savory (page 266)
Plate Garnish: Strawberry Fans (page 404)

Hot Cross Buns (page 424)
Butter Pats

Coffee   Milk

Easter Dinner

Ham Baked in Sherry Sauce (page 191)
Mashed Potatoes in a Casserole (page 333)
Asparagus Spears (page 303)
Baked Fruit (page 348)
Perfection Salad (page 136)

Butterhorn Rolls (page 424)
Ribbed Butter Balls (page 396)
Strawberry Jelly (page 743)

Butter Pecan Ice Cream with Rum Sauce
(page 373)
Easter Egg Nests (page 610)

Coffee   Tea   Milk

◆

Bibb Lettuce, Watercress, and Artichoke Hearts
Salad (page 122)
Deluxe Crackers (page 449)

....

Crown Roast of Pork Filled with Fresh Mixed
Vegetables Rosemary (page 183)
Oven-Browned Potatoes (page 334)
Platter Decoration: Tomato Roses (page 405)

Scalloped Apples (page 345)

Whole-Wheat Rolls

Butter Pats

....

Peppermint Stick Dessert (page 672)

Coffee   Tea   Milk

Fourth of July

AT HOME OR ON A PICNIC

Lemonade (page 696)

Beer

Peanuts in the Shell

....

Fried Chicken (page 211)

Potato Salad (page 133)

Baked Beans (page 277)

Marinated Cucumbers and Onions (page 130)

Decoration: Green Onion Flowers in Red, White,
and Blue (page 400)

Brown Bread (page 442) and Butter Sandwiches
(cut in half)

....

Lattice-Top Cherry Pie (page 479)

LATER WHILE YOU WATCH THE FIREWORKS

M&M's Chocolate Chip Cookies (page 609)

Coffee   Iced Tea   Lemonade

FAMILY BIRTHDAY DINNER

Zucchini and Green Bean Salad (page 131)

....

Rib Roast (Standing or Rolled)
with Natural Juices (au jus) (page 167)
Garnish: Freshly Shredded Horseradish (page 46)
Baked Potatoes (page 328)   Butter Pats
Popovers (page 454)
Lightly Glazed Miniature Carrots (page 313)

....

Birthday Cake of Choice: 3-Layer White Cake
(page 525), White and Chocolate 2-Layer Cake
(page 527), Yellow Cake (page 532), Chocolate
Cake (page 529), or Other Layer Cake
Ice Cream: Vanilla (page 669) or Other Ice Cream
of Choice Compatible with the Selected Cake

Coffee   Milk

SUNDAY DINNER

Scalloped Chicken (page 210)

Creamed New Potatoes and Peas
with Snipped Chives (page 331)

Spiced Apple Rings (page 728)

Ginger Ale Fruit Salad (page 121)

Butterhorn Rolls (page 424)

Butter Pats

....

Cherry Pie (page 479)

Coffee   Milk

PICNICS

Lemonade (page 696)

Oyster Cracker Snacks (page 83)

....

Wieners Grilled at the Picnic   Wiener Buns
Bell Pepper Relish (page 779)
Macaroni Salad (page 139)
Three-Bean Salad (page 132)

....

Aunt Tell's Devil's Food Cake (page 548)

◆

Beer

Soft Drinks

Beer Nuts (page 83)

....

Beef Salad Sandwiches (page 351)
Baked Beans (page 277)
Colorful Marinated Vegetables
with Sweet Basil Dressing (page 127)
Deviled Eggs (page 267)

....

Trail Mix Bars (page 598)

◆

BREAKFAST COOKOUT IN THE WOODS

Grapefruit Juice
Tomato Juice (page 737)

....

Ham Steak (page 193; omit glazed pineapple)
Fried Eggs (page 266)
American Fries (page 330)

Cinnamon-Sugar and Vanilla-Frosted Cake
Doughnuts (pages 453 and 454)

Butter (optional)

Coffee   Milk

EVERYDAY MEALS

Weekday Breakfasts

Large Glass Freshly Squeezed Orange Juice
Grapefruit Half

....

100% Whole-Wheat Shredded Squares with Sliced
Bananas and Strawberries
Fat-Free (Skim) Milk

100% Whole-Wheat Toast
Butter
Apricot Jam (page 747)

Coffee   Fat-Free (Skim) Milk

◆

Tomato Juice (page 737)
Cantaloupe Wedge

....

Poached Egg

Toasted English Muffin

Butter

Wild Black Raspberry Jelly (page 744)

Coffee   Milk

Weekend Breakfasts

Large Glass Freshly Squeezed Orange Juice
Honeydew Melon Wedge   Lime Wedge
Decoration: Sprig of Fresh Mint

....

Soft-Cooked Eggs (page 264)

Sausage Links

Dutch Apple Bread (page 434)

Butter

Coffee   Milk

◆

Mixed, Freshly Squeezed Orange and
Grapefruit Juice

Fresh Strawberries and Blackberries

French Toast (page 429)

Butter   Hot, Pure Maple Syrup

Canadian Bacon

Coffee   Milk

◆

Pineapple Juice

Orange and Grapefruit Sections (page 47)

Broiled Top Loin Steaks (1 inch thick) (page 166)

Fried Eggs (page 266)

American Fries (page 330)

Oat Bran Muffins (page 444)

Butter

Coffee   Milk

Packed Lunches

Egg Salad Sandwich (page 352)

Boston Lettuce   Cracked-Wheat Bread

Carrot and Celery Sticks

Easy Refrigerator Sweet Dill Pickles (page 769)

Apple

Frosted Chocolate Cookie (page 615)

Milk   Coffee   Tea

◆

Cold Meat Loaf Sandwich (page 171)

Tomato Catsup (page 781)   Leaf Lettuce

White Bread (page 419)

Green and Yellow Bell Pepper Strips

Ripe Olives

Fresh Apricot and/or Plum

Unsalted Mixed Nuts

Milk   Coffee   Tea

◆

Peanut Butter

Low-Sodium Whole-Wheat Wafers

Pineapple Coleslaw (page 133)

Carrot Sticks

Tangerine

Sunflower Seed Cookie (page 618)

Milk   Coffee   Tea

Weekend Lunches

Cream of Tomato Soup (page 92)

Open-Faced Grilled Cheese Sandwiches
(page 354)

Celery Sticks

Bread and Butter Pickles (page 766)

Fresh Pears

Milk   Coffee   Tea

◆

Kidney Bean Salad (page 132)
Colby Cheese   Crackers
Sliced Tomatoes

....

White Grapes
Whole-Wheat Oatmeal Cookies (page 630)

Milk   Coffee   Tea

◆

S U M M E R

Mesquite-Grilled Chicken Breast Sandwiches
(page 254)
Sourdough Buns
Copper Pennies (page 126)

....

Sliced, Fresh Peaches
Monster Cookies (page 614)

Milk   Iced Coffee   Iced Tea

Weekday Dinners

W I N T E R

Sorority House Salad (page 125; omit celery)

....

Farm-Style Beef Stew (page 100)

100% Whole-Wheat Muffins (page 443)
Butter

....

Canned Peaches (page 720)
Butterscotch Icebox Cookies (page 644)

Coffee   Tea   Milk

◆

Spanish Rice (page 275)
Tossed Salad: Romaine, Sliced Seedless Cucumbers,
Sliced Celery, Shredded Carrots, and Alfalfa Sprouts
Italian Salad Dressing (page 148)

Garlic Bread (page 368)

....

Ambrosia (page 344)

Coffee   Tea   Milk

◆

Ring Bologna Casserole (page 297)
Broccoli-Cauliflower Salad (page 126)

Whole-Wheat Bread (page 419)
Butter

....

Sour Cream Spice Cake (page 545)

Coffee   Tea   Milk

◆

Tossed Salad: Red-tip Boston Lettuce,
Yellow Bell Peppers, Radishes, Celery, and
Red Cherry Tomatoes
Mustard Dressing (page 149)

....

Bean Soup (page 89)

Corn Bread (page 441)
Butter
Cherry Jelly (page 740)

....

Fresh Pineapple and Strawberries

Coffee   Tea   Milk

◆

S P R I N G

Colorful Marinated Vegetables
with Sweet Basil Dressing (page 127)

Salmon Loaf (page 224)   Lemon Wedges
New Potatoes with Parsley (page 331)
Creamed Peas (page 327)

....

Rhubarb Rapture (page 654)
with Whipped Cream (page 373)

Coffee   Tea   Milk

◆

Dutch Lettuce Salad (page 123)

....

Mother's Meat Loaf (page 171)
Allegro Scalloped Potatoes (page 330)
Steamed Broccoli (page 302)

....

Fresh Fruit Compote
(page 346; select 3 or more fruits)

Coffee   Hot and Iced Tea   Milk

◆

Chicken and Noodles (page 210)
Mashed Potatoes (page 332)
Baking Powder Biscuits (page 446)
Butter
Apple Jelly (page 739)
Green Beans (page 305)
Salad: Sliced Oranges on Leaf Lettuce
Poppy Seed Dressing (page 150)
Decoration: Red Maraschino Cherry Half

....

Baked Custard (page 662)

Coffee   Hot and Iced Tea   Milk

◆

Brie
Small, Plain Water Crackers

Spinach Salad (page 137)
Toasted Sesame Bread (page 428)

....

Bread Pudding with Lemon Sauce (page 660)

Coffee   Hot and Iced Tea   Milk

◆

S U M M E R

Grilled Hamburger Steak (page 251)
Chili Sauce (page 783)
Twice-Baked Potatoes (page 329)
Pea Salad (page 130)
Toasted Parmesan–Parsley Bread (page 429)

....

Watermelon

Iced Coffee   Iced Tea   Milk

◆

Warm Chicken–Vegetable Salad with
Pistachio Nuts and Raspberry Vinaigrette
Dressing (page 142)

American Indian Fry Bread (page 442)
Honey
Butter   Red Raspberry Jam (page 751)

....

Strawberry Bavarian Cream (page 668)

Iced Coffee   Iced Tea   Milk

◆

Sliced Tomatoes and Lettuce Salad (page 122)

....

Pork Chop Dinner in Foil (page 299)

....

Cherry Cobbler (page 648)

Iced Coffee   Iced Tea   Milk

Orange Roughy Parmesan (page 258)

Baked Rice (page 275)

Steamed Green and Yellow Zucchini (page 302)

Tossed Salad: Leaf Lettuce, Garbanzo Beans,
Red and Orange Bell Peppers, and Parsley
Basil Vinaigrette Dressing (page 153)

....

Old-Fashioned Peach Shortcake (page 448)

Iced Coffee   Iced Tea   Milk

◆

FALL

Baked Cut-Up Chicken (page 205)

Baked Acorn Squash (page 339)

Sugar Snap Peas (page 327)

Coleslaw (page 133)

Zucchini Bread (page 439)

Butter

....

Canned Plums (page 727)

Coffee   Tea   Milk

◆

Garden Salad (page 128)

....

Hamburger Stuff (page 171)
Tomato Catsup (page 781)

Whole-Kernel Corn (page 731)

Whole-Wheat Bread (page 419)

Butter

....

Apple Crisp (page 649)

Coffee   Tea   Milk

◆

Waffles (page 456)
Butter   Hot, Pure Maple Syrup
Fried Eggs (page 266)
Sausage Patties (page 189)

....

Fresh Fruit Compote (page 346)

Coffee   Tea   Milk

◆

Stewed Rutabagas with Root Vegetables (page 338)

Wedge of Iceberg Lettuce
Thousand Island Dressing (page 147)

Limpa (Swedish Rye Bread) (page 420)

Butter

....

Cubed Papaya(s) with a Bit of Cranberry Juice

Coffee   Tea   Milk

Weekend Dinners

Caesar Salad (page 122)

....

Pot Roast with Vegetables (page 168)
Pot Roast Gravy (page 376)

Toasted Herb Bread with Finely Snipped,
Fresh Parsley and Rosemary Leaves
(page 428; omit chives)

....

Small Hot Fudge Sundae (page 669)

Coffee   Tea   Milk

◆

Martha Cotter's Seven-Layer Dinner (page 298)
Twenty-four Hour Salad (page 112)

Banana Cream Pie (page 491)

Coffee   Tea   Milk

◆

Hors d'Oeuvres:
Swiss and Blue Cheeses
Pickled Herring
Assorted Crackers

Vegetable Soup (page 93)
Mandarin Orange Salad (page 116)

Black Walnut Bars (page 597)

Coffee   Tea   Milk

◆

SUMMER

Rotisserie Chicken with Orange-Ginger Glaze
(page 256)
Allegro Scalloped Potatoes (page 330)
Corn on the Cob (page 315)
Melted Butter
Cucumber Salad (page 131)

Fresh Mixed Fruits: Strawberries, Raspberries, and
Blueberries
Chocolate Chip Cookies (page 609)

Iced Coffee   Iced Tea   Milk

Permissions and Courtesies

Adaptation of the Mary Florence Ponder story from the Iowa State Fair cookbook *Winners Every One!,* copyright © 1986 by the Iowa State Fair. By permission of the publisher.

Picture of the Illinois State Fair logo. By permission of the Illinois State Fair.

Picture of the Indiana State Fair logo. By permission of the Indiana State Fair.

Picture of the Iowa State Fair logo. By permission of the Iowa State Fair.

Picture of the Kansas State Fair logo. By permission of the Kansas State Fair.

Picture of the Michigan State Fair logo. By permission of the Michigan State Fair.

Picture of the Minnesota State Fair logo. By permission of the Minnesota State Fair.

Picture of the Missouri State Fair logo. By permission of the Missouri State Fair.

Picture of the Nebraska State Fair logo. By permission of the Nebraska State Fair.

Picture of the North Dakota State Fair logo. By permission of the North Dakota State Fair.

Picture of the South Dakota State Fair logo. By permission of the South Dakota State Fair.

Picture of the Wisconsin State Fair logo. By permission of the Wisconsin State Fair.

Edited extractions from *Publication N-2857: What's in a Recipe?,* prepared by Phyllis Olson and Diane Nelson. Published March 1986 by Iowa State University, Cooperative Extension Service. By permission of the publisher.

Information and extractions from *Pamphlet 41: High Altitude Food Preparation,* prepared by Pat Kendall. Revised. Published January 1995 by Colorado State University Cooperative Extension. By permission of the publisher.

Information and extractions from *Bulletin 497A: High Altitude Baking* by Pat Kendall and Willene Dilsaver. Revised. Published April 1992 by Colorado State University Cooperative Extension. By permission of the publisher.

Pictures of retail cuts of beef, veal, pork, and lamb, copyright © 1986 by the National Live Stock and Meat Board. Reprinted by permission of the National Cattlemen's Beef Association and the National Pork Producers Council.

Grilled Iowa Pork Chops recipe and adaptation of Mushroom-Stuffed Pork Burgers recipe. Courtesy of the Iowa Pork Producers Association.

Grant Wood, *Dinner for Threshers,* 1934. The Fine Arts Museums of San Francisco, Gift of Mr. and Mrs. John D. Rockefeller III, 1979.7.105. Photograph of picture published by permission of The Fine Arts Museums of San Francisco.

Mississippi Flyway and Central Flyway maps. Courtesy of the U.S. Department of the Interior, Fish and Wildlife Service.

Excerpt from "On Eating and Drinking" from *The Prophet* by Kahlil Gibran, copyright 1923 by Kahlil Gibran, and renewed 1951 by Administrators C.T.A. of Kahlil Gibran Estate, and Mary G. Gibran. By permission of Alfred A. Knopf, Inc.

Map: Pheasant Distribution and Abundance as Hens Per Square Mile for North America in Spring 1986, from "Distribution and Abundance of the Ring-Necked Pheasant in North America" by Robert B. Dahlgren, in *Pheasants: Symptoms of Wildlife Problems on Agricultural Land: Proceedings of a Symposium Held at the 49th Midwest Fish and Wildlife Conference in Milwaukee, Wisconsin, December 8, 1987,* edited by Diana L. Hallet, William R. Edwards, and George V. Burger. Bloomington, Ind.: The Northcentral Section of The Wildlife Society, 1988, 34. By permission of The Northcentral Section of The Wildlife Society.

Picture of pasta types, from *A Passion for Pasta!,* copyright © 1995 by Borden, Inc. By permission of the publisher.

Sources Consulted

VOLUME AND WEIGHT MEASURES

U.S. Department of Commerce. National Institute of Standards and Technology. *NIST Handbook 44: Specifications, Tolerances, and Other Technical Requirements for Weighing and Measuring Devices.* 1994 ed. Edited by Henry V. Oppermann and Tina G. Butcher. Washington, D.C., October 1993.

INTRODUCTION

The Midwest's Blue Ribbon Bounty

Iowa State Fair. *Winners Every One!* Des Moines, 1986.

Breadbasket of the Nation

Daugherty, Arthur, Agricultural Economist, U.S. Department of Agriculture, Economic Research Service, Washington, D.C. Telephone interviews by author, 29 April 1992 and 1 May 1992.

Holden, Howard R., Deputy State Statistician, U.S. Department of Agriculture, National Agricultural Statistics Service, Iowa Agricultural Statistics Service. Telephone interview by author, 3 October 1997.

Kreidberg, Marjorie. *Food on the Frontier.* St. Paul: Minnesota Historical Society Press, 1975.

McKenna, James L., U.S. Department of Agriculture, Rural Electrification Administration, Washington, D.C. Telephone interview by author, 27 April 1992.

The New Encyclopaedia Britannica, 15th ed. S.v. "Middle West," and "United States of America, Middle West."

U.S. Department of Agriculture. Economic Research Service. *Foreign Agricultural Trade of the United States* (January–February–March 1997), coordinated by Joel L. Green. Washington, D.C., n.d. Table 7, 12–23.

U.S. Department of Agriculture. Economic Research Service. Tables entitled "All commodities: States' rankings for cash receipts, 1996," "Corn: States' rankings for cash receipts, 1996," "Soybeans: States' rankings for cash receipts, 1996," "Hogs: States' rankings for cash receipts, 1996," "Feed crops: States' rankings for cash receipts, 1996," "Oil crops: States' rankings for cash receipts, 1996," and "Wheat: States' rankings for cash receipts, 1996," by Roger P. Strickland and Cheryl J. Steele. Internet Web Site (www.econ.ag.gov), Farm Business Economics Briefing Room. Washington, D.C., 30 September 1997.

Heartland State Fairs

Bliss, Ralph K. *History of Cooperative Agriculture and Home Economics Extension in Iowa—The First Fifty Years.* Ames: Iowa State University of Science and Technology, 1960.

Encyclopedia Americana, 1988 ed., vol XIV, 318–19.

Gobeli, Virginia C., National 4-H Program Leader, U.S. Department of Agriculture; Cooperative State Research, Education, and Extension Service; Families, 4-H, and Nutrition, Washington, D.C. Written communication to author, 16 December 1997.

Iowa Department of Agriculture. "Educational Value of Fairs," *Greater Iowa,* vol. II, no. 3 (15 June 1910): 3. Des Moines.

Iowa Department of Agriculture. *Greater Iowa,* vol. VIII, no. 9 (September 1916). Des Moines.

Iowa Department of Agriculture. "The Uses of State Fairs," *Greater Iowa,* vol. II, no. 4 (1 July 1910): 2. Des Moines.

Iowa Department of Agriculture. "Wireless Messages at Fair," *Greater Iowa,* vol. I, no. 5 (14 August 1909): 1. Des Moines.

Iowa Department of Agriculture. "Wright Bros.' Birdmen Are Coming," *Greater Iowa,* vol. III, no. 3 (7 July 1911): 1. Des Moines.

Iowa State Fair. "Early Years," *Iowa State Fair Historical Highlights.* Des Moines, n.d.

Iowa State Fair. "National Survey of State Fair Food Departments." Des Moines, 1993.

Michigan State Fair Office, Detroit. Telephone interview by author, 9 March 1993.

Miller, Lewis, Executive Vice President, International Association of Fairs and Expositions, Springfield, Missouri. Telephone interview by author, 8 October 1992.

National 4-H Council. *National 4-H Council: Youth in 4-H [1996].* Chevy Chase, Md., n.d.

North Dakota State Fair Office, Minot. Telephone interview by author, 9 October 1992.

Office of the *Federal Register.* National Archives and Records Administration. *The United States Government Manual,* 1990–91. Washington, D.C., 1 July 1990.

Ohio State Fair Office, Columbus. Telephone interview by author, 8 March 1993.

Schramm, Henry W. *Empire Showcase: A History of the New York State Fair.* Utica: North Country Books, 1985.

Schwager, Marty, Consumer Education Director, Iowa Pork Producers Association, Des Moines. Telephone interview by author, 17 February 1996.

Schwieder, Dorothy. *75 Years of Service: Cooperative Extension in Iowa.* Ames, Iowa: Iowa State University Press, 1993.

South Dakota State Fair Office, Huron. Telephone interview by author, 9 October 1992.

Stephenson, Dave, Columbus, Ohio. Telephone interviews by author, 8 March 1993 and 13 January 1994.

CHAPTER INTRODUCTIONS

Hors d'Oeuvres, First-Course Appetizers, and Snacks

U.S. Department of Agricultural. Agricultural Statistics Service. Agriculture Statistics Board. *Dairy Products, 1996 Summary.* Washington, D.C., May 1997, 30.

Soups and Stews

Kreidberg, Marjorie. *Food on the Frontier.* St. Paul: Minnesota Historical Society Press, 1975.

1993 Mobil Road Atlas—Trip Planning Guide. New York: H. M. Gousha, 1993.

Meats

U.S. Department of Agriculture. Economic Research Service. Tables entitled "Cattle and calves: States' rankings for cash receipts, 1996," "Meat animals: States' rankings for cash receipts, 1996," and "Hogs: States' rankings for cash receipts, 1996," by Roger P. Strickland and Cheryl J. Steele. Internet Web Site (www.econ.ag.gov), Farm Business Economics Briefing Room. Washington, D.C., 30 September 1997.

U.S. Department of Agriculture. Human Nutrition Information Service. Consumer Nutrition Division. *Nationwide Food Consumption Survey 1977–78, Report No. H-7: Food Consumption: Households in the Northeast, Seasons and Year 1977 –78.* Washington, D.C.: Government Printing Office, August 1983.

U.S. Department of Agriculture. Human Nutrition Information Service, Consumer Nutrition Division. *Nationwide Food Consumption Survey 1977– 78, Report No. H-8: Food Consumption: Households in the North Central Region, Seasons and Year 1977– 78.* Washington, D.C.: Government Printing Office, August 1983.

U.S. Department of Agriculture. Human Nutrition Information Service. Consumer Nutrition Division. *Nationwide Food Consumption Survey 1977– 78, Report No. H-9: Food Consumption: Households in the South, Seasons and Year 1977–78.* Washington, D.C.: Government Printing Office, August 1983.

U.S. Department of Agriculture. Human Nutrition Information Service. Consumer Nutrition Division. *Nationwide Food Consumption Survey 1977–78, Report No. H-10: Food Consumption: Households in the West, Seasons and Year 1977–78.* Washington, D.C.: Government Printing Office, August 1983.

Poultry and Stuffings (Dressings)

Wood, Grant. *Dinner for Threshers.* Oil on hardboard. 1934. The Fine Arts Museums of San Francisco, San Francisco.

Fish and Shellfish

Conover, Marion, Chief of Fisheries, Iowa Department of Natural Resources, Des Moines. Telephone interview by author, 17 June 1994.

Wild Game

Canfield, Dave. "1997 Bowhunter Deer Forecast." *Bowhunter: Big Game Special 1997* 26, no. 7 (September 1997).

Dahlgren, Robert B. "Distribution and Abundance of the Ring-Necked Pheasant in North America": Map: Pheasant Distribution and Abundance As Hens Per Square Mile for North America in Spring 1986. In *PHEASANTS: Symptoms of Wildlife Problems on Agricultural Land: Proceedings of a Symposium Held at the 49th Midwest Fish and Wildlife Conference in Milwaukee, Wisconsin, December 8, 1987,* edited by Diana L. Hallet, William R. Edwards, and George V. Burger. Bloomington, Ind.: The Northcentral Section of The Wildlife Society, 1988, 34.

Encyclopaedia Britannica, 1967 ed. S.v. "Turkey," by Stanley J. Marsden.

Gesner, George, ed. *Anthology of American Poetry.* New York: Avenel Books, 1983.

Gibran, Kahlil. *The Prophet.* New York: Alfred A. Knopf, Inc., September 1923.

Little, Terry, Wildlife Research Supervisor, Iowa Department of Natural Resources, Fish and Wildlife Division, Des Moines, Iowa. Telephone interview by author, 5 February 1998.

U.S. Department of Commerce. Bureau of the Census. Population Estimates Program. *Report No. PPL-68. Estimates of the Population of States by Age Groups and Sex: 1990 and 1996.* Washington, D.C., 21 April 1997.

U.S. Department of the Interior. Fish and Wildlife Service. *Central Flyway.* Graphic. Washington, D.C., n.d.

U.S. Department of the Interior. Fish and Wildlife Service. *Mississippi Flyway.* Graphic. Washington, D.C., n.d.

U.S. Department of Interior, Fish and Wildlife Service, and U.S. Department of Commerce, Bureau of the Census. *1996 National Survey of Fishing, Hunting, and Wildlife-Associated Recreation.* Washington, D.C., November 1997, 102.

Outdoor Cooking

U.S. Department of Health and Human Services. National Institutes of Health. National Heart, Lung, and Blood Institute. National Cholesterol Education Program. *NIH Publication No. 93-3095: Second Report of the Expert Panel on Detection, Evaluation, and Treatment of High Blood Cholesterol in Adults (Adult Treatment Panel II).* Bethesda, Md., September 1993.

Eggs

Saunders, Richard [Benjamin Franklin]. *Poor Richard: The Almanacks for the Years, 1733–1758.* New York: Paddington Press; reprint, Bonanza Books, 1979.

U.S. Department of Health and Human Services. National Institutes of Health. National Heart, Lung, and Blood Institute. National Cholesterol Education Program. *NIH Publication No. 93-3095: Second Report of the Expert Panel on Detection, Evaluation, and Treatment of High Blood Cholesterol in Adults (Adult Treatment Panel II).* Bethesda, Md., September 1993.

Rice and Beans

Anderson, Beth. *Wild Rice for All Seasons Cookbook.* Minneapolis: Beth Anderson Associates, 1984.

Kreidberg, Marjorie. *Food on the Frontier.* St. Paul: Minnesota Historical Society Press, 1975.

The New Encyclopaedia Britannica, 15th ed. S.v. "Wild Rice."

U.S. Department of Agriculture. Economic Research Service. Tables entitled "Potatoes: States' rankings for cash receipts, 1996" and "Rice: States' rankings for cash receipts, 1996," by Roger P. Strickland and Cheryl J. Steele. Internet Web Site (www.econ.ag.gov), Farm Business Economics Briefing Room. Washington, D.C., 30 September 1997.

U.S. Department of Agriculture, Human Nutrition Information Service. *Agriculture Handbook Number 8-11: Composition of Foods: Vegetables and Vegetable Products,* rev., by Nutrition Monitoring Division. Principal investigators: David B. Hatowitz and Ruth H. Matthews. Washington, D.C.: Government Printing Office, August 1984.

U.S. Department of Agriculture. Human Nutrition Information Service. *Agriculture Handbook Number 8-20: Composition of Foods: Cereal Grains and Pasta,* rev., and Supplement, by Nutrition Monitoring Division. Principal investigators: Dennis L. Drake, Susan E. Gebhardt, and Ruth H. Matthews. Washington, D.C.: Government Printing Office, October 1989 and 1991 Supplement.

Pasta

Borden, Inc. *A Passion for Pasta!* Photograph. Columbus, Ohio: Borden, Inc. 1995.

Bugialli, Guiliano. *Bugialli on Pasta.* New York: Simon and Schuster, 1988.

Bugialli, Guiliano. *The Fine Art of Italian Cooking.* New York: Times Books, 1989.

Charley, Helen. *Food Science.* 2d ed. New York: Macmillan Publishing Co., 1982.

Herbst, Sharon Tyler. *Food Lover's Companion.* Hauppauge, N.Y.: Barron's, 1990.

The American Home Economics Association. *Handbook of Food Preparation.* 8th ed. Alexandria, Va., 1980.

The New Encyclopaedia Brittanica, 15th ed. S.v. "Food Processing: Other Cereal and Starch Products, Alimentary pastes," and "pasta."

U.S. Department of Agriculture. Human Nutrition Information Service. *Agriculture Handbook Number 8-20: Composition of Foods: Cereal Grains and Pasta,* rev., and Supplement, by Nutrition Moni-

toring Division. Principal investigators: Dennis L. Drake, Susan E. Gebhardt, and Ruth H. Matthews. Washington, D.C.: Government Printing Office, October 1989 and 1991 Supplement.

Fruits

Elias, Thomas S., and Peter A. Dykeman. *Edible Wild Plants: A North American Field Guide.* New York: Sterling Publishing Co., 1990.

U.S. Department of Agriculture. Economic Research Service. Tables entitled "Fruits and nuts: States' rankings for cash receipts, 1996" and "Apples: States' rankings for cash receipts, 1996," by Roger P. Strickland and Cheryl J. Steele. Internet Web Site (www.econ.ag.gov), Farm Business Economics Briefing Room. Washington, D.C., 30 September 1997.

Widrlechner, Mark, Horticulturist, Plant Introduction Station, Iowa State University, Ames. Telephone interview by author, 15 June 1994.

Young, Kay. *Wild Seasons: Gathering and Cooking Wild Plants of the Great Plains.* Lincoln: University of Nebraska Press, 1993.

Sandwiches

U.S. Department of Agriculture. Human Nutrition Information Service. Consumer Nutrition Division. *Nationwide Food Consumption Survey 1977–78, Report No. H-7: Food Consumption: Households in the Northeast, Seasons and Year 1977–78.* Washington, D.C.: Government Printing Office, August 1983.

U.S. Department of Agriculture. Human Nutrition Information Service. Consumer Nutrition Division. *Nationwide Food Consumption Survey 1977–78, Report No. H-8: Food Consumption: Households in the North Central Region, Seasons and Year 1977–78.* Washington, D.C.: Government Printing Office, August 1983.

U.S. Department of Agriculture. Human Nutrition Information Service. Consumer Nutrition Division. *Nationwide Food Consumption Survey 1977–78, Report No. H-9: Food Consumption: Households in the South, Seasons and Year 1977–78.* Washington, D.C.: Government Printing Office, August 1983.

U.S. Department of Agriculture. Human Nutrition Information Service. Consumer Nutrition Division. *Nationwide Food Consumption Survey 1977–78, Report No. H-10: Food Consumption: Households in the West, Seasons and Year 1977–78.* Washington, D.C.: Government Printing Office, August 1983.

Garnishes and Decorations
James, William. *William James: Writings 1878–1899. Is Life Worth Living?* New York: The Library of America, 1992.

Breads and Rolls
Encyclopaedia Brittanica, 1967 ed. S.v. "Bread."

The New Encyclopaedia Brittanica, 15th ed. S.v. "bread."

SPECIAL SECTIONS

Food Safety
American Egg Board. *Eggcyclopedia.* 3d ed., rev. Park Ridge, Ill., April 1994.

American Egg Board. *Salmonella & Egg Safety.* Park Ridge, Ill., May 1995.

American Egg Board. *The Egg Handling & Care Guide.* rev. Park Ridge, Ill., September 1994.

Carr, Tom. "Trichinosis: Risk and Prevention," *Facts from the Meat Board: Meat Science: Series FS/MS 004.* Chicago: National Live Stock and Meat Board, Meat Science Department, 1992.

Gentsch, Cynthia C., and Susan Templin Conley. "From USDA's Meat and Poultry Hotline: A Barbeque Handbook." *Food News for Consumers* (Summer 1991); reprint, Washington, D.C.: U.S. Department of Agriculture, Food Safety and Inspection Service, n.d.

National Pork Producers Council. Pork Information Bureau. *National Survey Confirms Millions of Consumers Are Cooking Pork Wrong.* Des Moines, January 1992.

National Pork Producers Council. Pork Information Bureau. *Pork Industry to Mom: Teach Your Children Medium—Not Well.* Minneapolis, January 1992.

Parmley, Mary Ann. "Researching Microwave Safety." *Food News for Consumers* (Summer 1990); reprint, Washington, D.C.: U.S. Department of Agriculture. Food Safety and Inspection Service, n.d.

Parmley, Mary Ann, and Diane VanLonkhuyzen. "The Whys Behind USDA's Food Safety Rules," *Food News for Consumers* (Spring 1991); reprint, Washington, D.C.: U.S. Department of Agriculture, Food Safety and Inspection Service, n.d.

Templin, Susan, CiCi Williamson, and Marilyn Johnston. "How to Microwave Safely." *Food News for Consumers* (Spring 1990); reprint, Washington, D.C.: U.S. Department of Agriculture, Food Safety and Inspection Service, n.d.

U.S. Department of Agriculture. Agriculture Marketing Service. *Home and Garden Bulletin Number 263: How to Buy Poultry.* Washington, D.C., July 1995.

U.S. Department of Agriculture. Agriculture Marketing Service. *Home and Garden Bulletin Number 264: How to Buy Eggs.* Washington, D.C., July 1995.

U.S. Department of Agriculture. Food and Drug Administration. *Consumer Bulletin AMS-602: Handling Eggs Safely at Home.* rev. Washington, D.C., January 1992.

U.S. Department of Agriculture. Food Safety and Inspection Service. Cooperative State Research, Education and Extension Service. *Take the Guesswork Out of Roasting a Turkey.* Washington, D.C., n.d.

U.S. Department of Agriculture. Food Safety and Inspection Service. "Focus On: Egg Products." *Food Safety Focus: From USDA's Meat and Poultry Hotline.* Washington, D.C., n.d.

U.S. Department of Agriculture. Food Safety and Inspection Service. Food Safety & Consumer Education Office. "Turkey Basics: Safe Defrosting." *Consumer Information from USDA.* Washington, D.C., November 1996.

U.S. Department of Agriculture. Food Safety and Inspection Service. Food Safety & Consumer Education Office. "Turkey Basics: Stuffing." *Consumer Information from USDA.* Washington, D.C., November 1996.

U.S. Department of Agriculture. Food Safety and Inspection Service. "From USDA's Meat and Poultry Hotline: Pack-Up-And-Go with Summer Foods." *Food News for Consumers* (Summer 1991); reprint, Washington, D.C., n.d.

U.S. Department of Agriculture. Food Safety and Inspection Service. *Home and Garden Bulletin No. 248: A Quick Consumer Guide to Safe Food Handling.* Washington, D.C., August 1995.

U.S. Department of Agriculture. Food Safety and Inspection Service. "Safe Food to Go—For Lunches and Picnics." *Food News for Consumers* (Summer 1988); condensed reprint, Washington, D.C., May 1988.

Williamson, CiCi. "Why the Experts Say Cook It." *Food News for Consumers* (Spring 1991); reprint, Washington, D.C.: U.S. Department of Agriculture Food Safety and Inspection Service, n.d.

The Functions of Ingredients in Batters and Doughs

Iowa State University. Cooperative Extension Service. *Publication N-2857: What's in a Recipe?,* prepared by Phyllis Olson and Diane Nelson. Ames, March 1986.

McComber, Diane, Associate Professor of Food Science and Human Nutrition, Iowa State University, Ames. Consultation and correspondence with author, June 1994.

To Cook and Bake at High Altitudes

Charley, Helen. *Food Science.* 2d ed. New York: Macmillan Publishing Co., 1982.

Colorado State University Cooperation Extension. *Pamphlet 41: High Altitude Food Preparation,* rev., prepared by Pat Kendall. Fort Collins, January 1995.

Johnson, Jeff, Coordination Meteorologist, U.S. Department of Commerce, National Oceanic and Atmospheric Administration, Johnston, Iowa. Telephone interview by author, 11 January 1997.

Kendall, Pat, Professor and Extension Food and Nutrition Specialist, Colorado State University, Fort Collins. Telephone interview by author, 9 January 1997 and correspondence with author, January 1997.

Kendall, Pat, and Willene Dilsaver. *Bulletin 497A: High Altitude Baking.* rev. Fort Collins: Colorado State University Cooperative Extension, April 1992.

Kendrick, Ruth A., and Pauline H. Atkinson. *Candymaking.* Los Angeles: HPBooks, 1987.

The American Home Economics Association. *Handbook of Food Preparation.* 8th ed. Alexandria, Va., 1980.

To Use Herbs

Hollis, Sarah. *The Country Diary Herbal.* New York: Henry Holt and Co., 1990.

Kowalchik, Claire, and William H. Hylton, eds. *Rodale's Illustrated Encyclopedia of Herbs.* Emmaus, Pa.: Rodale Press, 1987.

Tone Bros., Inc. *Spice Advice Chart.* Des Moines, 1989.

Today's Leaner Meats

National Live Stock and Meat Board and National Pork Board. *Possibilities with Pork.* Chicago, 1991.

National Live Stock and Meat Board in cooperation with the American Heart Association. *Meat Nutrient Facts.* Chicago, 1995.

Savell, J. W., H. R. Cross, D. S. Hale, and Lisa Beasley. *National Beef Market Basket Survey: Final Report to the National Cattlemen's Foundation, Inc.* n.p.: Texas A&M University, Department of Animal Science, Meats & Muscle Biology Section, June 1988.

U.S. Department of Agriculture. Human Nutrition Information Service. *Agriculture Handbook Number 8-10: Composition of Foods: Pork Products,* rev., by Nutrition Minitoring Division. Principal investigator: Barbara A. Anderson. Assisted by: Lynn E. Dickey and I. Margaret Hoke. Washington, D.C.: Government Printing Office, December 1992.

U.S. Department of Agriculture. Human Nutrition Information Service. *Agriculture Handbook Number 8-13: Composition of Foods: Beef Products,* rev., by Nutrition Monitoring Division. Principal investigators: Barbara A. Anderson and I. Margaret Hoke. Washington, D.C.: Government Printing Office, May 1990.

U.S. Department of Agriculture. Science and Education Administration. *Agriculture Handbook Number 8-5: Composition of Foods: Poultry Products,* rev., by Consumer and Food Economics Institute. Principal investigator: Linda P. Posati. Washington, D.C.: Government Printing Office, August 1979.

Edible Flowers

Creasy, Rosalind. *Cooking from the Garden.* San Francisco: Sierra Club Books, 1988.

Duke, James A., Economic Botanist, U.S. Department of Agriculture, Agricultural Research Service, Beltsville, Maryland (retired). Writings on the subject of edible flowers and correspondence with author 1995 and 1996.

Elias, Thomas S., and Peter A. Dykeman. *Edible Wild Plants: A North American Field Guide.* New York: Sterling Publishing Co., 1990.

Holis, Sarah. *The Country Diary Herbal.* New York: Henry Holt and Co., 1990.

Kowalchik, Claire, and William H. Hylton, eds. *Rodale's Illustrated Encyclopedia of Herbs.* Emmaus, Pa.: Rodale Press, 1987.

Young, Kay. *Wild Seasons: Gathering and Cooking Wild Plants of the Great Plains.* Lincoln: University of Nebraska Press, 1993.

Using a Decorating Bag to Pipe Garnishes and Decorations

Wilton Enterprises, Inc. *The Wilton Method: Basic Cake Decorating Course.* Woodridge, Ill., 1987.

Wilton Enterprises, Inc. *The Wilton Method: Basic Cake Decorating Course 2.* Woodridge, Ill., 1987.

Wilton Enterprises. *Wilton Cake Decorating: 1998 Wilton Yearbook.* Woodridge, Ill., 1997.

Baking Yeast Breads and Rolls

Berry, Pat. Urbandale, Iowa. Consultation with author, 1995 and 1996.

Better Homes and Gardens. *Homemade Bread Cook Book.* Des Moines: Meredith Corp., 1973.

Better Homes and Gardens. *Old-Fashioned Home Baking.* Des Moines: Meredith Corp., 1990.

Charley, Helen. *Food Science.* 2d ed. New York: Macmillan Publishing Co., 1982.

Farm Journal Food Editors. *Homemade Bread.* Edited by Nell B. Nichols. Garden City, N.Y.: Doubleday and Co., 1969.

McComber, Diane, Associate Professor of Food Science and Human Nutrition, Iowa State University, Ames. Consultation and correspondence with author, 1995 and 1996.

Secrets for Making Successful Pastry Piecrust

McComber, Diane, Associate Professor of Food Science and Human Nutrition, Iowa State University, Ames. Consultation and correspondence with author, December 1993 and January 1994.

Canning

Ball Corporation. *Ball Blue Book: The Guide to Home Canning and Freezing,* ed. 31. Muncie, Ind., 1987.

Ball Corporation. *Ball Blue Book: The Guide to Home Canning and Freezing,* ed. 32. Muncie, Ind., 1987.

Iowa State University. Cooperative Extension Service. *Pm-1368: Preserve It Right: Making Pickled Products.* Ames, July 1989.

Kerr Glass Manufacturing Corp. *Kerr Home Canning & Freezing Book.* Los Angeles, 1989.

Kraft General Foods, Inc. *Sure-Jell Fruit Pectin Leaflets.* White Plains, N.Y., n.d.

Nichols, Nell B., and Kathryn Larson, eds. *Farm Journal's Freezing & Canning Cookbook.* Garden City, N.Y.: Doubleday and Co., 1978.

The University of Georgia. Cooperative Extension Service. College of Agricultural and Environmental Sciences. *Bulletin 989: So Easy to Preserve,* 3d ed., by Susan Reynolds and Paulette Williams. Revised by Judy Harrison. Athens, 1993.

U.S. Department of Agriculture. Extension Service. *Agriculture Information Bulletin No. 539: Complete Guide to Home Canning.* Washington, D.C.: Government Printing Office, May 1989.

Nutrition

Mayo Foundation for Medical Education and Research. "Exercise: Are the Risks Underplayed and the Benefits Overdone?," *Mayo Clinic Health Letter* 12, no. 6 (June 1994).

Mayo Foundation for Medical Education and Research. "Health Tips: Curbing Your Appetite," *Mayo Clinic Health Letter* 12, no. 3 (March 1994).

Mayo Foundation for Medical Education and Research. "Weight Control: What Works and Why," *Mayo Clinic Health Letter,* supplement: medical essay (June 1994).

U.S. Department of Agriculture. Center for Nutrition Policy and Promotion. *Home and Garden Bulletin No. 252: The Food Guide Pyramid.* rev. Washington, D.C.: Government Printing Office, October 1996.

U.S. Department of Agriculture. Human Nutrition Information Service. *Agriculture Information Bulletin 364: Calories & Weight: The USDA Pocket Guide.* Washington, D.C.: Government Printing Office, March 1990.

U.S. Department of Agriculture and U.S. Department of Health and Human Services. *Home and Garden Bulletin No. 232: Nutrition and Your Health: Dietary Guidelines for Americans.* 4th ed. Washington, D.C.: Government Printing Office, December 1995.

Menu Planning

U.S. Department of Agriculture. Center for Nutrition Policy and Promotion. *Home and Garden Bulletin No. 252: The Food Guide Pyramid.* rev. Washington, D.C.: Government Printing Office, October 1996.

U.S. Department of Agriculture and U.S. Department of Health and Human Services. *Home and Garden Bulletin No. 232: Nutrition and Your Health: Dietary Guidelines for Americans.* 4th ed. Washington, D.C.: Government Printing Office, December 1995.

GENERAL

All Saints Parish. *All Saints 1914–1989: Celebrating 75 Years of Faith* [cookbook]. Des Moines, 1990.

American Egg Board. *Encyclopedia.* 3rd ed., rev. Park Ridge, Ill., April 1994.

Anderson, Beth. *Wild Rice for All Seasons Cookbook.* Minneapolis: Beth Anderson Associates, 1984.

Anderson, Kenneth N., and Lois E. Anderson. *The International Dictionary of Food & Nutrition.* New York: John Wiley & Sons, Inc., 1993.

Atwood, Mary S. *A Taste of India.* Boston: Houghton Mifflin Co., 1969.

Austin, Elizabeth S., and Oliver L. Austin, Jr. *The Random House Book of Birds.* New York: Random House, 1970.

Baker, Mina, and Betty J. Bergman, eds. *Pella Collectors Cook Book,* 8th ed. Pella, Iowa: Central College Auxiliary, 1982.

Beard, James. *James Beard's American Cookery.* Boston: Little, Brown and Co., 1972.

Better Homes and Gardens. *All-Time Favorite Vegetable Recipes.* Des Moines: Meredith Corp., 1977.

Better Home and Gardens. *Candy.* Des Moines: Meredith Corp., 1984.

Better Homes and Gardens. *Cookies for Christmas.* Des Moines: Meredith Corp., 1985.

Better Homes and Gardens. *Old-Fashioned Home Baking.* Des Moines: Meredith Corp., 1990.

Better Homes and Gardens. *Pies and Cakes.* New York: Meredith Press, 1996.

Better Homes and Gardens Creative Ideas. *Holiday Cooking.* (1986.)

Better Homes and Gardens Creative Ideas. *Holiday Desserts.* (1988.)

Better Homes and Gardens Editors. *Salad Book.* Des Moines: Meredith Publishing Co., 1958.

Biller, Rudolf. *Garnishing and Decoration.* n.p.: Virtue & Co., n.d.

Birkby, Evelyn, ed. *KMA Festival Cookie Book.* Shenandoah, Iowa: KMA Radio, 1983.

Brand, Mildred. *Ideals Candy Cookbook*. n.p.: Ideals, 1979.

Brennan, Georgeanne, Isaac Cronin, and Charlotte Glenn. *The New American Vegetable Cookbook: The Definitive Guide to America's Exotic & Traditional Vegetables*. Berkeley, Calif.: Aris Books, 1985.

Brethren Publishing House. *Granddaughter's Inglenook Cookbook*. Elgin, Ill., 1942.

Brown & Bigelow. *A Merry Christmas at Your House*. St. Paul, Minn., 1956.

Brown & Bigelow. *Game & Fish: Their Preparation and Special Cooking*. St. Paul, Minn., 1960.

Budgen, June. *The Book of Garnishes*. Tucson: HPBooks, 1986.

Charley, Helen. *Food Science*. 2d ed. New York: Macmillan Publishing Co., 1982.

Claiborne, Craig, ed. *The New York Times Cook Book*. New York: Harper and Row, 1961.

Collier's Encyclopedia, 1993 ed. S.v. "George Washington," by Esmond Wright.

Committee from St. Cecilia's Church and St. Michael's Church. *Hastings Catholic Community Cookbook*. Hastings, Nebr.: Vaughan's Printers, n.d.

Crowley, Jerry. *The Fine Art of Garnishing*. Baltimore: Lieba Inc., 1978.

Culinary Arts Institute. *The German & Viennese Cookbook*. Chicago, 1956.

Culinary Arts Institute. *The Gourmet Foods Cookbook*. Chicago, 1955.

Cunningham, Marion. *The Fannie Farmer Cookbook*. 13th ed. New York: Alfred A. Knopf, 1990.

Dinsmore, James J. *A Country So Full of Game: The Story of Wildlife in Iowa*. Iowa City: University of Iowa Press, 1994.

Elias, Thomas S., and Peter A. Dykeman. *Edible Wild Plants: A North American Field Guide*. New York: Sterling Publishing Co., 1990.

Encyclopaedia Brittanica, 1967 ed. S.v. "Brazil Nuts," "Bun," and "Corn," by Paul C. Mangelsdorf.

Farm Journal Food Editors. *America's Best Vegetable Recipes: 666 Ways to Make Vegetables Irresistible.*

Edited by Nell B. Nichols. Garden City. N.Y.: Doubleday and Co., 1970.

Farm Journal Food Editors. *Great Home Cooking in America: Heirloom Recipes Treasures for Generations*. Garden City, N.Y.: Doubleday and Co., 1976.

Farm Journal Food Editors. *Homemade Bread*. Edited by Nell B. Nichols. Garden City, N.Y.: Doubleday and Co., 1969.

Farm Journal Food Editors. *Homemade Cookies*. Edited by Nell B. Nichols. Garden City, N.Y.: Doubleday and Co., 1971.

General Mills, Inc. *Betty Crocker's Christmas Cookbook*. New York: Golden Press, 1983.

Gerhard, Frank. *Kulinarische Streifzüge durch Schwaben*. Künzelsau, Germany: Sigloch Edition, 1979.

Gifts O' the Wild. *Original Minnesota Ojibway (Chippewa) Indian Recipes*. Guthrie, Minn., 1983.

Herbst, Sharon Tyler. *Food Lover's Companion*. Hauppauge, N.Y.: Barron's, 1990.

Hodgson Mill, Inc. *Recipes for Unprocessed Wheat Bran and Untoasted Wheat Germ*. Effingham, Ill., n.d.

Huck, Virginia, and Ann H. Anderson, eds. *100 Years of Good Cooking*. St. Paul: The Minnesota Historical Society, 1958.

Iowa Department of Agriculture & Land Stewardship in Cooperation with Iowa Honey Producers Association. *Honey Recipe Book*. Des Moines, 1971.

Iowa Pork Producers Association. *Ground Pork Instead*. Des Moines, n.d.

Iowa Pork Producers Association. *Iowa Pork Tent Recipes: Iowa Chops*. Des Moines, 1984.

Iowa State Fair. *Fun Fest Favorites: Recipes from the Iowa State Fair*. Des Moines, 1990.

Iowa State Fair. *Prize Winning Recipes: From the Iowa State Fair!* 2d ed. Des Moines, n.d.

Iowa State Fair. *Recipes to Savor: Iowa State Fair Cookbook*. Des Moines, 1988.

Iowa State Fair. *The Only Cookbook of Its Kind: Recipes from the Iowa State Fair*. Des Moines, 1993.

Iowa State Fair. *Winners Every One!* [cookbook]. Des Moines, 1986.

Kappa Alpha Theta Alumnae of Des Moines. *Noel Nibbles.* Des Moines, 1973.

Kendrick, Ruth A., and Pauline H. Atkinson. *Candymaking.* Los Angeles: HPBooks, 1987.

Kreidberg, Marjorie. *Food on the Frontier.* St. Paul: Minnesota Historical Society Press, 1975.

Larousse, David Paul. *Edible Art: Forty-Eight Garnishes for the Professional.* New York: Van Nostrand Reinhold, 1987.

Mariani, John F. *The Dictionary of American Food and Drink.* New Haven: Ricknor & Fields, 1983.

Marsh, Dorothy B., ed. *Good Housekeeping Cook Book.* New York: Rinehart & Co., 1955.

Meredith Corporation. *Better Homes and Gardens Meat Cook Book.* Des Moines: Meredith Press, 1969.

Meredith Corporation. *Better Homes and Gardens New Cook Book.* 10th ring-bound ed. Des Moines: Meredith Corp., 1989.

Meredith Publishing Company. *Better Homes and Gardens New Cook Book.* Des Moines: Meredith Publishing Co., 1953.

Michigan United Conservation Clubs. *Wildlife Chef.* 2d ed., rev. and enl. Lansing, 1981.

National Live Stock and Meat Board. *Beef: Retail Cuts: Where They Come From; How to Cook Them.* Photograph. Chicago, 1986.

National Live Stock and Meat Board. *Lamb: Retail Cuts: Where They Come From; How to Cook Them.* Photograph. Chicago, 1986.

National Live Stock and Meat Board. *Pork: Retail Cuts: Where They Come From; How to Cook Them.* Photograph. Chicago, 1986.

National Live Stock and Meat Board. *Veal: Retail Cuts: Where They Come From; How to Cook Them.* Photograph. Chicago, 1986.

Nichols, Nell B., ed. *Farm Journal's Complete Pie Cookbook.* Garden City, N.Y.: Doubleday and Co., 1965.

Peace Lutheran Church. *The Lord's Harvest.* Hastings, Nebr.: Fundcraft Publishing, 1978.

Peck, Paula. *The Art of Fine Baking.* New York: Barnes & Noble Books, 1993.

Polushkin, Maria. *The Dumpling Cookbook.* New York: Workman Publishing Company, Inc., 1997.

Pullen, Pauline Evans. *The Missouri Sampler: A Collection of Favorite Recipes from All Counties.* Springfield: Pauline E. Pullen, 1987.

Robbins, Chandler S., Bertel Bruun, and Herbert S. Zim. *A Guide to Field Identification: Birds of North America.* New York: Golden Press, 1966.

Roemig, Sue, ed. *German Recipes: Old World Specialties from the Amana Colonies.* Iowa City: Penfield Press, 1985.

Rombauer, Irma S., and Marion Rombauer Becker. *Joy of Cooking.* New York: Bobbs–Merrill, 1975.

Rubash, Joyce. *Master Dictionary of Food and Wine.* New York: Van Nostrand Reinhold, 1990.

Scharfenberg, Horst. *The Cuisines of Germany: Regional Specialties and Traditional Home Cooking.* New York: Poseidon Press, 1989.

Schik, Susan, ed. *Schik Family Recipe Book.* Hastings, Nebr.: Tom Schik, n.d.

Schneider, Elizabeth. *Uncommon Fruits & Vegetables: A Commonsense Guide.* New York: Harper and Row, 1986.

Small, Marvin. *The World's Best Recipes.* n.p.: Hawthorn Books, 1955; reprint, New York: Pocket Books, Cardinal ed. 1957.

Stephenson's Apple Farm Restaurant. *Stephenson's Old Apple Farm Receipts.* Kansas City, Mo., 1967.

Sully Christian School Circle. [Cookbook]. Iowa Falls: General Publishing and Binding, 1970.

The American Home Economics Association. *Handbook of Food Preparation.* 8th ed. Alexandria, Va., 1980.

The Chapel by the Sea, United Presbyterian Church. *Women's Association Cook Book II.* Fort Myers Beach, Fla., 1979.

The New Encyclopaedia Brittanica, 15th ed. S.v. "Food Processing: Sugar" by Margaret A. Clarke and "Molasses."

The Popcorn Institute. *Popcorn Production Study 1995*. Chicago: The Popcorn Institute, 18 January 1996.

Time Incorporated. *Picture Cook Book*. New York, 1958.

"Two Good Layer Cakes," *Woman's Day* (February 1940): 36.

Van Klompenburg, Carol. *Delightfully Dutch: Recipes and Traditions*. Iowa City: Penfield Press, 1984.

Van Klompenburg, Carol, comp. *Dutch Treats: Recipes, Folklore, Proverbs*. Iowa City: Penfield Press, 1987.

What Cheer Methodist Church, Mary Circle. *Methodist Church Cook Book*. What Cheer, Iowa, 1964.

Williams, Sallie Y. *The Art of Presenting Food*. New York: Hearst Books, 1982.

Women of Plymouth Church, eds. *'76 Cook Book*. Des Moines: Plymouth Congregational United Church of Christ, 1976.

Ying, Mildred, ed. *The New Good Housekeeping Cookbook*. New York: Hearst Books, 1986.

Product Sources

Sunnyland Farms, Inc.
Jane and Harry Willson
Willson Road at Pecan City
P.O. Box 8200
Albany, Georgia 31706-8200
800-999-2488

Sweet Celebrations Inc.
P.O. Box 39426
Edina, Minnesota 55439-0426
800-328-6722

Wilton Enterprises
2240 West 75th Street
Woodridge, Illinois 60517-0750
630-963-7100

Acknowledgments

O ur world is interdependent—humankind's works result from collaboration. Personal creative products are an amalgamation of the maker's family, childhood, teachers, friends, advisers, and life experiences, interfused with his/her own efforts and unique, individual spirit.

While *The Blue Ribbon Country Cookbook* carries my name as "author," "catalyst" would be a more appropriate designation. Those to whom this cookbook is dedicated have influenced my life in special ways which led to and made possible the writing of the book. Immense credit is due many other people, organizations, and agencies who shared their knowledge, talents, and time to culminate in this volume. My thank you to those recognized below for their gracious help and meaningful contributions.

A book is written to share with others. That requires its publication. Someone must sell it and someone must buy it. My deepest gratitude to Angela Miller and Coleen O'Shea, my agents, whose undaunted belief in the book and considerable business acumen led to sale of the manuscript. And my profound appreciation to Katie Workman, my editor at Clarkson Potter, for her insightful grasp of the purpose and need for this lengthy cookbook, and for her steadfast patience and enthusiasm while I readied the manuscript for delivery. I am most thankful for the alignment of the book with such a fine editor and prestigious publishing house.

Thanks also to all those at Clarkson Potter and Crown who have made this book possible, including Mark McCauslin, Julie Baker, Erica Youngren, Wendy Schuman, Joan Denman, Tony Davis, Pat Stenbeck, Diane Dugal, and Merri Ann Morrel. And thanks to food stylist Kevin Crafts, photographer Tom Eckerle, and designer Maggie Hinders for their work on the jacket.

My wonderful New York friends, Tom Wells and Lee Tannen, were instrumental at every step of the way in bringing this book to reality—as sounding boards, door openers, and staunch supporters. In near mystifying ways, they were the links in the chain of people who played key roles in bringing the book into being. For example, it was at a dinner party given by Tom and Lee that I met Cici Winant, who arranged my introduction to Angela Miller.

Nine years ago, before deciding to write the book, Alix Nelson encouraged me to pursue the idea, and helped me organize an initial proposal to test the waters of interest. Many thanks to Alix. It never would have happened without her.

Throughout the initial stages of the book's creation, Al Lowman's professional expertise and belief in the project kept the book on track. The book's state fair–blue ribbon central theme was Al's idea, and it was only because of his insistence, that the narrative about the Midwest state fairs, way of life, and cooking style was incorporated into the book. I am forever grateful to him.

Many thanks to the Midwest state fairs which provided their logos for inclusion in the collage on page 9, and assisted with the book in many other ways. In particular, I am grateful to the Iowa State Fair for their help and support. Kathie Swift, Marketing Director, graciously made the historical archives of the fair available to me for research, and advised me on several aspects of the copy; and

Arlette Hollister, Superintendent of the Food Department, has been a most supportive colleague.

Candace Manroe, gifted writer, edited the Introduction to the book, and coached me on the conversion of my technical writing style into a more relaxed, storybook form for the narrative sections of the book. I learned much from Candace. Trying to emulate her masterful way with words is indeed humbling and will always keep me reaching.

Sharon Soder's clear and accurate illustrations greatly assist in making certain recipe procedures more understandable. How lucky to have this talented artist's skillful pictures punctuate the recipes and decorate the chapter headlines!

I am immeasurably grateful for the significant contributions of Diane McComber, Associate Professor of Food Science and Human Nutrition at Iowa State University, who meticulously critiqued several of the book's technical sections. A more intellectually astute contributor and willing friend one could not find.

Pat Kendall, Professor and Extension Food and Nutrition Specialist, Colorado State University, and national expert on high-altitude cooking and baking, helped me immensely on this technical subject. I am extremely appreciative of her kind assistance.

I was especially privileged to have Dr. James A. Duke, noted authority on edible flowers, serve as consultant for the section on the subject which appears in the Garnishes and Decorations chapter. A special thank you is extended to Dr. Duke for so generously and thoroughly critiquing the edible flowers section twice, and for sending me copies of many papers he has authored on the subject as well as other resource information from his personal files—all rendered while under heavy demand for his valuable time and expertise.

Bread and roll artisan Pat Berry served worthily as consultant on yeast-bread and -roll recipes. Her blue ribbon recipe for Julekake (Norwegian Christmas Bread) can be found on page 422.

Two other consummate culinarians, Joy McFarland and Louise Piper, whose names will go down in the Iowa State Fair annals as leading blue ribbon winners, have each graciously shared a winning recipe for inclusion in this book (see Joy McFarland's Mile-High Torte, page 568, and Louise Piper's Mulberry Jam, page 756).

My neighbor, Grace Montognese, could serve as the ultimate role model for Midwestern-style neighborliness. From three wonderful Italian dishes reflecting her Old World heritage, to favorite cookie recipes, to loaning boxes full of great cookbooks from her incredible collection, Grace's giving and sharing materialized within these pages in notable ways.

While out in the kitchen concocting and testing, the computer world sailed by me. Deb Mahon, computer genius, stepped in to save the day. With unbelievable expertise, she put the entire cookbook (most of which I had handwritten) into her computer and then, with the patience of Job, entered all of my editing changes. With more time on the horizon, I plan to move the IBM Selectric to the side and, with Deb's help, tackle computer-speak.

Many thanks to David Belin, attorney, and Sharon Willmore, CPA, for their counsel and assistance relative to the business aspects of the book.

In an era when the topic of wasteful government spending stokes many heated discussions, research for the book proved a vivid reminder that many tax dollars support unheralded, often forgotten, government programs fundamental to our nation's commerce, economy, health, education, culture, and general standard of living. I wish to sing the praises of the United States Department of Agriculture and its cadre of unsung, well-degreed professionals who are responsible for the research, statistics, and information dissemination pertaining to nutrition, food safety, agricultural commodities, and many other areas serving the public interest. My numerous calls for information and assistance were consistently met with sincere interest, warm courtesy, efficiency, and help beyond the call of duty.

I experienced similar cooperation and willingness on the part of personnel at the United States Department of Health and Human Services, the United States Department of Commerce, the United States Department of the Interior, and the General Services Administration, as well as many state agencies, and private corporations and organizations.

Particular words of gratitude go to Wilton Enterprises for the pictures and instructions for piping garnishes and decorations; to the National Cattlemen's Beef Association and the National Pork Producers Council for the pictures of beef, veal, pork, and lamb retail cuts; and to Creamette Pasta for the picture showing various types of pasta. These useful additions to *The Blue Ribbon Country Cookbook* are sure to be consulted often by readers.

My sincere thanks to the following agencies, corporations, and organizations, and named personnel therein, who will find the fruits of their assistance and efforts on the pages of this book:

Alltrista Consumer Products Company

American Lamb Council: Priscilla Root

Borden Foods Corporation: Becky S. Honigford, Administrative Secretary, Product Publicity

Borden, Inc.: North American Pasta and Sauce—Lynn Anderson, Manager of Corporate Communications; North American Pasta Products—Jeanne W. Fox, Manager of Media Communications

Cooks' Ware: Nancy and Dick Sanders, Owners

Dahl's Food Marts: Ed Beltrame, Don Bennett, Don Hart, John Hawxby, Wally Hawxby, Jim Hubbartt, Denny Johnson, Cliff Nelson, Don Relph, Charles Thyberg

Des Moines Club: Kevin Robinson, General Manager

Des Moines Public Library

Hershey Foods Corporation: Cheryl A. Reitz, Senior Consumer Food Publicist

Hodgson Mill, Inc.: Kristin Dougherty, Hope R. Yingst

International Association of Fairs and Expositions: Lewis Miller, Executive Vice President

International Dairy Foods Association: Linda A. Leger, Assistant Director

Iowa Association of Electric Cooperatives: Jody Garlock, Managing Editor

Iowa Department of Natural Resources: Marion Conover, Chief of Fisheries; Terry Little, Wildlife Research Supervisor; Jan Myers; Irene Ray; Terry Z. Riley, Ph.D., Upland Wildlife Research Biologist

Iowa Pork Producers Association: Joyce Hoppes, Consumer Information Director; Jeff Schnell, Public Policy Director; Marty Schwager, Consumer Education Director

Iowa State Fair: Arlette Hollister, Superintendent, Food Department; Kathie Swift, Marketing Director

Illinois State Fair: Janet Mathis, Deputy Superintendent; Suzanne Moss, Manager, Promotional Events

Indiana State Fair: William H. Stinson, Executive Director; Cynthia C. Hoye, Marketing Director

Kansas State Fair: Robert A. Gottschalk, General Mgr.; Joan R. Brown, Operations Manager

Michigan State Fair: John C. Hertel, General Manger; Alice Diefenthaler, Community Arts Coordinator; Joan Schwedt

Minnesota State Fair: Susan Ritt, Marketing Director

Missouri State Fair: Gary D. Slater, Director; Wendy Baker, Public Information Specialist; Heather Willard, Marketing/Publicity

Nebraska State Fair: John Skold, General Manager

New York State Fair

North Dakota State Fair: Leslie S. Herslip, Marketing Director; Renae Korslien

Ohio State Fair

South Dakota State Fair: Milo Rypkema, Commission Chairman; Christine Duxbury, Sr. Secretary; Holly Hornung

Wisconsin State Fair: Julie Carlson, Director of Public Relations

Iowa State University: Cooperative Extension Service—Dr. William Edwards; Susan B. Klein, Nutrition and Health Field Specialist; Diane Nelson, Extension Communication Systems; Plant Introduction Station—Mark Widrlechner, Ph.D., Horticulturist

Italian Importing Co.: Mary and John Sitroneto, Owners

Knapp Properties Inc.: R. Stephen Vilmain, President, Restaurant Division; Jody Valentine

Kraft General Foods, Inc.

Libbey Glass Inc.: Lucille Lee

Mayo Clinic Health Letter: Christopher Frye, Managing Editor; Marie Cranor, Secretary

National Cattlemen's Beef Association: Marietta J. Buyck, Director of Producer Education; Terence R. Dockerty, Ph.D., Director of Research Information; Kim First, Director of Customer Service; Jim Gibb, Ph.D., Vice President, Center for Quality; H. Kenneth Johnson, Executive Director, Value Based Meat Systems; James O. Reagan, Ph.D., Executive Director, Science and Technology

National Corn Growers Association: KayAnn Miller, Manager, Public Relations

National 4-H Council: Rachel Nastor, Marketing Assistant

National Pork Producers Council: Robin Kline, M.S., R.D., Director of Consumer Affairs

National Rifle Association of America: Billy R. Templeton, Wildlife Management Specialist

Nebraska Soybean Board: Phyllis Staats, Consumer Information Specialist

Pennsylvania State University: Thomas S. Dimick, Research Support Staff, Food Science Department

Plymouth Congregational United Church of Christ: Nancy Wallace, President, Women's Fellowship

Random House, Inc.: Patricia Flynn, Director, Copyright & Permissions

Red Star Yeast & Products

State Library of Iowa: Beth Henning, Coordinator, State Data Center

Sweet Celebrations Inc.: Christine Dalquist

The Fine Arts Museums of San Francisco: Mary Haas

The Northcentral Section of The Wildlife Society: Gary E. Potts, President; David J. Case, Past President

The Popcorn Institute: Kristin Stromberg, Marketing Coordinator

The Quaker Oats Company: Susan Regal

The University of Georgia: Cooperative Extension Service—Elizabeth L. Andress, Extension Leader for Food, Nutrition, and Health

The Windrow Restaurant: Janet and Bill Hayes, Owners; Kelly Bellcock, Chef

Tone Brothers, Inc.: Diane M. Ward, Certified Home Economist

United States Department of Agriculture:

Agricultural Research Service: Bernadette McAuliffe, Writer; Judy Ducellier, Plant Germplasm Program Assistant; Mary Y. Hama, Economist

Center for Nutrition Policy and Promotion: John S. Webster, Director, Public Information; Jackie Haven, Nutritionist

Cooperative State Research, Education, and Extension Service: Virginia C. Gobeli, Ed.D., National 4-H Program Leader, Families, 4-H, and Nutrition; Jan Singleton, Ph.D., R.D. National Program Leader, Food Science and Nutrition

Economic Research Service: Arthur Daugherty, Agricultural Economist; Mark J. Gehlhar Ph.D., Economist; Stephen A. MacDonald, Agricultural Economist; Judy Putnam, Economist; Roger P. Strickland, Head, Farm Sector Income Accounts

Food Safety and Inspection Service: Susan Templin Conley, Director, Food Safety Education and Communications Staff; Charles R. Edwards, Director, Labeling, Product and Technology Standards Division; Diane VanLonkhuyzen, Supervisor, Meat and Poultry Hotline; Meat and Poultry Hotline Technical Information Specialists

Foreign Agricultural Service: Joel L. Greene, Agricultural Economist

National Agricultural Statistics Service: Doyle R. Fuchs, Deputy State Statistician, Texas Agricultural Statistics Service; Howard R. Holden, Deputy State Statistician, Iowa Agricultural Statistics Service; Muriel Laliberte, Secretary, Livestock and Economics Branch

Rural Electrification Administration: James L. McKenna

United States Department of Commerce:

    National Institute of Standards and Technology: Joan Koenig, Weights and Measures Coordinator

    National Oceanic and Atmospheric Administration: Jeff Johnson, Warning Coordination Meteorologist, Johnston, Iowa

    United States Bureau of the Census: Nancy White, Program Assistant

United States Department of Health and Human Services:

    Food and Drug Administration: Tina Gilliam, Printing Specialist

    National Institutes of Health: National Heart, Lung, and Blood Institute

United States Department of the Interior:

    Fish and Wildlife Service: Janet L. Miller, Editor, Office of Public Affairs; Robert B. Dahlgren, Ph.D., Biologist, Retired

General Services Administration:

    Consumer Information Center: Carole Collins, Senior Media Specialist

Van Nostrand Reinhold Company Inc.: Carl Maddalone, Permission Manager

West Des Moines Public Library

Whitetails Unlimited, Inc.: Peter Gerl, Executive Director

Wilton Enterprises: Zella Junkin, Manager, Consumer Affairs

People often ask, "Where did you get the recipes for the book?" Many were handed down in our immediate family, others are the result of research, some are original dishes, and a good number of recipes and ideas came from friends, family members, and acquaintances whose names appear in the list that follows. Some of the persons are deceased, and I am happy that *The Blue Ribbon Country Cookbook* can help serve as a vehicle for the perpetuation and recognition of their contributions to the Midwest cooking tradition. In addition, several of the people listed assisted with the book in ways other than via recipes. My appreciation is extended to each and every one of you for your important contributions:

Julie A. Abbott, M.D., M.P.H., Gertrud Acksen, Kelly Adams, Susan Albaugh, Tommy Allen, Barbara Amend, Nancy Amend

Florence Barns, Chris Bening, Mary Berndt, Alice Bernstein, Teri Bognanno, Joanne Brown, Mary and Dave Brown, Mary Burgess, Marlene Bushman

Martha Cotter, Pauline Crenshaw

Marie Dalbey, Peg Danielson, Patty Davis, Dorothy Davison, Kay DeWitt, Elizabeth and George Dinsdale, Belle Dowell

Janet and Charles Fillman, Floy Flanders

Jean Yvonne Galloway, Denise Goode, Ada Goreham, Anna Goreham, Jerri Goreham, Nancy and Dick Goreham, Tiss Goreham, Ethel Graaff, Werner Greiner, Kathy Griffin

Brent Halling, Scott Halling, Gayle Hamilton, Ruth Henss, Josephine Herndon, Hank Higdon, Joy Holmquist

Margaret Johnson, Teri Johnson, Marj Jordan

Jim Kascoutas, Bill Keefer, Sylvia Keefer, Karen King

Jane LaMair, Mary Ann Lane, David Paul Larousse, Shirley and Lou Lauro, Ken Lepley, Isabel Levin, Irene and George Loder

Carol Mapes, Alpha Markell, Dorothy Martin, Judy Merrill, Barbara Millington

Meredith Noble, Dianna Nolin

Dan Perkins, Rose Lee Pomerantz, Jerome J. Pratt

Mina Baker Roelofs, Ellen Roupe, Don Roush, Jesse Roush

Bernice Safris, Opal Sallow, Donna Sandin, Jacalyn See, M.S., R.D., Ernie Seneca, Edith Shelley, Shirlie and Keith Simmer, Christie Smith, Dora Smith, Jeannie Snyder, Bret Staples, Nina Staples, Dave Stephenson, Janet Stern, June Street

Sharon Teale, Barbara Tellein, Ellen Thomas

Laura Van Sant, Melinda von Reis

Charlotte Watkins, Susan and Chuck Weiss, Paula Wilcher, Connie Wilson, Linda Wilson, Colette Wortman, Fauntell Wray, Lynne Wright, Gene Zefron

Index

METRIC CONVERSION TABLES

To Convert (U.S.)	To (Metric)	Multiply By[1]
Teaspoons	Milliliters	4.9289
Tablespoons	Milliliters	14.787
Fluid Ounces	Milliliters	29.5735
Cups (Liquid)	Milliliters	236.5882
Fluid Ounces	Liters	0.0296
Pints (Dry)	Liters	0.5506
Pints (Liquid)	Liters	0.4732
Quarts (Dry)	Liters	1.1012
Quarts (Liquid)	Liters	0.9464
Gallons (Dry)	Liters	4.4048
Gallons (Liquid)	Liters	3.7854
Pecks (Dry)	Liters	8.8098
Bushels (Dry) (Struck[2])	Liters	35.2391
Ounces (Avoirdupois)	Grams	28.3495
Pounds (Avoirdupois)	Grams	453.5924
Ounces (Avoirdupois)	Kilograms	0.0283
Pounds (Avoirdupois)	Kilograms	0.4536

To Convert (Metric)	To (U.S.)	Multiply By[1]
Milliliters	Teaspoons	0.2029
Milliliters	Tablespoons	0.0676
Milliliters	Fluid Ounces	0.0338
Milliliters	Cups (Liquid)	0.0042
Liters	Fluid Ounces	33.8140
Liters	Pints (Dry)	1.8162
Liters	Pints (Liquid)	2.1134
Liters	Quarts (Dry)	0.9081
Liters	Quarts (Liquid)	1.0567
Liters	Gallons (Dry)	0.2270
Liters	Gallons (Liquid)	0.2642
Liters	Pecks (Dry)	0.1135
Liters	Bushels (Dry) (Struck[2])	0.0284
Grams	Ounces (Avoirdupois)	0.0353
Grams	Pounds (Avoirdupois)	0.0022
Kilograms	Ounces (Avoirdupois)	35.274
Kilograms	Pounds (Avoirdupois)	2.2046

To Convert (Metric)	To (Metric)	Multiply By[1]
Milliliters	Liters	0.001
Liters	Milliliters	1000.0
Grams	Kilograms	0.001
Kilograms	Grams	1000.0

[1]Approximate factors.
[2]Struck measure. A **heaped** bushel is equal to 1¼ **struck** bushels.

See Volume and Weight Measures, page 886.

VOLUME AND WEIGHT MEASURES

VOLUME MEASURES

U.S. Customary Measures				Metric Measures[1]
Dash[2]	=	Less than 1/8 tsp		
1/4 tsp	=	15 drops	.04 fl oz	1.23 mL
1/2 tsp	=	30 drops	.08 fl oz	2.46 mL
3/4 tsp	=	45 drops	.13 fl oz	3.70 mL
1 tsp	=	60 drops	1/6 fl oz	4.929 mL
1/4 Tbsp	=	3/4 tsp	.13 fl oz	3.70 mL
1/3 Tbsp	=	1 tsp	1/6 fl oz	4.929 mL
3/8 Tbsp	=	1 1/8 tsp	.19 fl oz	5.55 mL
1/2 Tbsp	=	1 1/2 tsp	1/4 fl oz	7.39 mL
5/8 Tbsp	=	1 7/8 tsp (1 3/4 tsp+ 1/8 tsp)	.31 fl oz	9.24 mL
2/3 Tbsp	=	2 tsp	1/3 fl oz	9.86 mL
3/4 Tbsp	=	2 1/4 tsp	.37 fl oz	11.09 mL
7/8 Tbsp	=	2 1/2 tsp	.44 fl oz	12.94 mL
1 Tbsp	=	3 tsp	1/2 fl oz	14.787 mL
1/8 cup	=	2 Tbsp	1 fl oz	29.574 mL
1/4 cup	=	4 Tbsp	2 fl oz	59.15 mL
1/3 cup	=	5 1/3 Tbsp (5 Tbsp + 1 tsp)	2 2/3 fl oz	78.85 mL
3/8 cup	=	6 Tbsp	3 fl oz	88.72 mL
1/2 cup	=	8 Tbsp	4 fl oz	118.29 mL
5/8 cup	=	10 Tbsp	5 fl oz	147.87 mL
2/3 cup	=	10 2/3 Tbsp (10 Tbsp + 2 tsp)	5 1/3 fl oz	157.71 mL
3/4 cup	=	12 Tbsp	6 fl oz	177.44 mL
7/8 cup	=	14 Tbsp	7 fl oz	207.01 mL
1 cup (liq)	=	16 Tbsp	8 fl oz	236.582 mL
1/2 pt (dry)	=	1 cup		275.31 mL
1/2 pt (liq)	=	1 cup (liq)	8 fl oz	236.589 mL
1 pt (dry)	=	2 cups		550.610 mL
1 pt (liq)	=	2 cups (liq)	16 fl oz	473.177 mL
1 qt (dry)	=	2 pt (dry) or 4 cups (dry)		1.101 L
1 qt (liq)	=	2 pt (liq) or 4 cups (liq)	32 fl oz	0.946 L
1 gal (dry)	=	4 qt or 8 pt		4.405 L
1 gal (liq)	=	4 qt (liq) or 8 pt (liq)	128 fl oz	3.785 L
1 peck (dry)	=	2 gal (dry) or 8 qt (dry)		8.810 L
1 bu (dry) (struck[3])	=	4 pecks (dry) or 8 gal (dry)		35.239 L

[1]Approximate measures.
[2]Not a standard volume measure.
[3]Struck measure. A **heaped** bushel is equal to 1 1/4 **struck** bushels.

See page 885 for Metric Conversion Tables.

WEIGHT MEASURES

U.S. Ounces and Pounds (Avoirdupois Weight)			Metric Measures[1]
1/4 oz	=		7.087 g
1/2 oz	=		14.175 g
3/4 oz	=		21.262 g
1 oz	=		28.350 g
16 oz	=	1 lb	453.592 g
1 lb	=		0.4536 kg
2 lbs	=		0.9072 kg

[1]Approximate measures.

METRIC CONVERSIONS

Metric Measures		U.S. Measures[1]
1 milliliter	=	0.203 tsp
		0.0676 Tbsp
		0.0338 fl oz
		0.0042 cups
		0.0021 pt (liq)
		0.0011 qt (liq)
		0.00026 gal (liq)
1 liter	=	33.8140 fl oz
		4.2268 cups
		1.8162 pt (dry)
		2.1134 pt (liq)
		0.9081 qt (dry)
		1.0567 qt (liq)
		0.2270 gal (dry)
		0.2642 gal (liq)
		0.1135 peck (dry)
		0.0284 bu (dry)
1 gram	=	0.0353 oz (avdp)
1 kilogram	=	2.2046 lb (avdp)

[1]Approximate measures.

ABBREVIATIONS[1]

Avoirdupois	avdp	Milliliter	mL
Bushel	bu	Ounce	oz
Fluid Ounce	fl oz	Peck	pk
Gallon	gal	Pint	pt
Gram	g	Pound	lb
Kilogram	kg	Quart	qt
Liquid	liq	Tablespoon	Tbsp
Liter	L	Teaspoon	tsp

[1]These abbreviations are used for both singular and plural items.